Sourcebook of Equal Educational Opportunity

Reference books published by
Marquis Academic Media

Annual Register of Grant Support
Consumer Protection Directory
Directory of Publishing Opportunities
Directory of Registered Lobbyists and Lobbyist Legislation
Environmental Protection Directory
NASA Factbook
NIH Factbook
NSF Factbook
Sourcebook of Equal Educational Opportunity
Standard Education Almanac
Standard Medical Almanac
Yearbook of Adult and Continuing Education
Yearbook of Higher Education
Yearbook of Special Education
Worldwide Directory of Computer Companies
Worldwide Directory of Federal Libraries

Sourcebook of Equal Educational Opportunity®

Second edition

Marquis Academic Media
Marquis Who's Who, Inc.
200 East Ohio Street
Chicago, Illinois 60611

Library of Congress Card Number 77-75482
International Standard Book Number 0-8379-2902-4

Distributed in the United Kingdom by
George Prior Associated Publishers
Rugby Chambers, 2 Rugby Street
London WC1N 3QU

Manufactured in the United States of America.

Contents

Preface

The second edition of *Sourcebook of Equal Educational Opportunity*, formerly entitled *Yearbook of Equal Educational Opportunity*, is designed to present a comprehensive picture of the current status of equal opportunity in education. It contains statistical and narrative data gathered from a variety of government and private sources tracing from historical roots the struggle for equal access and quality education. A credit line appended to each excerpt identifies the original source of the selection.

Although the universe of groups which could be incorporated in such a sourcebook might exceed the six chosen for inclusion, in order to adequately cover each one, selection has been limited to those which represent substantial numbers of persons and/or have secured the special attention of federal and state programs to obtain equal access to educational opportunities.

This volume consists of seven sections and two indexes, subject and geographic. "Part One: General" is composed of three subsections: Population Characteristics provides an overview of the composition, distribution, and growth rate of the total U.S. population and statistics on income, employment and education; Melting Pot vs. Cultural Pluralism focuses on the trend in education toward cultural diversity and ethnic identity giving recognition to the heterogeneous composition of the population; Sexism and Racism explores the subtle prejudices of racial and sexual stereotypes which have been purveyed, often unconsciously, in textbooks and curricula.

"Part Two: American Indian/Native Alaskan"

begins with a look at the historical roots of Indian education and seeks to give a definition of its purpose and objectives for the future. Information is also included on the current social and economic status of the American Indian and progress that has been made toward self-determination via governance and administration of instructional programs with an emphasis on the cultural worth and richness of Indian heritage and Amerindian languages. Statistics are included on the number of Bureau of Indian Affairs schools in operation, the number of students enrolled, facilities available, and Indian tribes participating.

"Part Three: Asian American/Pacific Islander" presents demographic factors on Chinese, Philippino, Hawaiian, Korean, Japanese, American Samoan and Guamanian Americans. Special emphasis is given to the large number of new immigrants of Indochinese descent who have entered the United States in the past few years. Information on the bilingual/bicultural programs created to meet the special needs of both Cambodian and Vietnamese students are included as well as a listing of the National Indochinese Clearinghouse Bilingual Resource Centers and a directory of Asian American bilingual projects throughout the country.

"Part Four: Black" traces school desegregation from the 1954 Supreme Court decision in Brown v. Board of Education to the present and includes a U.S. Commission on Civil Rights analysis of the progress of integration in selected school districts throughout the country and suggestions for future planning. Statistics on the enrollment of Black students and racial composition of elementary and secondary teaching staffs accompany an assessment of the use of standardized achievement tests and the scoring of Black students.

"Part Five: Disadvantaged/White Ethnic" reviews opportunity programs for the disadvantaged in higher education including compensatory education, special admission policies for minorities and disadvantaged, and precollege preparatory programs. Also presented is an attempt at defining and assessing ethnic studies programs and a look at migrant education and the impact of the Elementary and Secondary Education Act as amended to include migrant children.

"Part Six: Hispanic" presents selected social, economic and demographic characteristics of persons of Mexican, Puerto Rican, Cuban, Central or South American, and other Spanish origins. The current status of education for Mexican American children, largely in the Southwest, is assessed as is the role of parent, teacher, and school administrator in obtaining quality education for language-minority children. A detailed portrait of Puerto Rican students—both mainland U.S. residents and those living in Puerto Rico—is also provided, as is an article on "pocho Spanish" and a look at the effectiveness of bilingual programs. A listing of national Spanish-speaking organizations completes the section.

"Part Seven: Women" begins with a statistical composite of the female population with emphasis on educational attainment, employment, and income. An attempt is made to understand the role of women in society—who they are, why they work, and how much progress has been made toward equal opportunity. A look at sex-role stereotyping and the socialization process from preprimary through graduate and professional training, as well as an appraisal of the role of the media in reinforcing these stereotypes, are included. Suggestions are made on how to identify and combat sexism in educational materials and guidelines are provided for filing sex discrimination complaints. Lists of women's studies programs, organizations focusing on women-related information and services, and non-sexist publishers conclude the section.

So that each edition of *Sourcebook of Equal Educational Opportunity* will be of maximum benefit to users, Marquis Academic Media, a division of Marquis Who's Who, Inc., welcomes reactions to the content and organization of the book.

Part one:
Equal educational opportunity
(general)

Population characteristics

POPULATION PROFILE OF THE UNITED STATES: 1975

POPULATION GROWTH

The rate of population growth in the United States was slightly higher in 1975 than in 1974 but considerably lower than in 1970. By January 1976, the total population reached 214.5 million, representing an increase of four-fifths of 1 percent over the 213 million a year earlier. The corresponding increase in 1974 was three-fourths of 1 percent.

In 1975, as in 1974, the birth rate was 14.9 per 1,000 population. However, the more refined total fertility rate declined from 1,857 children per 1,000 women in 1974 to 1,800 in 1975, with both rates implying less than two children per woman if the present level continues. About 2.1 children per woman are required for population replacement in the absence of population growth through net immigration.

By far the strongest preference among wives under 25 years of age is for a two-child family. Married women of this age range reported in 1975 that they expect an average of 2.2 children in their lifetime. Those 35 to 39 years old, who have already had nearly all the children they expect to have, reported that they believe they will have 3.1 children.

SOCIAL CHARACTERISTICS

The net effect of the declining child population and the continuing increase in the elderly population is that the dependency ratio has dropped from 78 to 71 between 1970 and 1975. This measure is the ratio of the population under 18 and 65 and over per 100 population 18 to 64 years old.

In 1975, the number of divorces exceeded 1 million for the first time in U.S. history, whereas the number of marriages dropped to the lowest level since 1969. Divorces increased 6 percent between 1974 and 1975, while marriages decreased 4 percent. Young adults continued to increase their tendency to postpone marriage. Forty percent of the women 20 to 24 years of age and 60 percent of the men of this age in 1975 had never married.

The number of households with a female head increased by 30 percent between 1970 and 1975. During this period the number of persons under 35 who maintained a household entirely alone doubled; it rose from about 1-1/2 million to about 3 million.

College enrollment continued to grow most rapidly among persons in their late twenties and early thirties, among women, and among blacks. It reached 10.9 million in the fall of 1975 including 1.2 million who were 35 years old and over. About one-fourth of the persons 25 to 34 years of age—as compared with 9 percent of those 65 and over—had completed 4 or more years of college.

POPULATION DISTRIBUTION

Contrary to historic trends, metropolitan areas as a whole are no longer gaining population through migration from nonmetropolitan areas in the United States. Only 2 of the 8 largest metropolitan areas (Washington, D.C. and San Francisco-Oakland-San Jose) grew by as much as 3 percent between 1970 and 1974. The rate of decline in the farm population has diminished from 4.8 percent per year in the 1960's to 1.8 percent in the 1970's.

More blacks are moving to the South, and fewer blacks are leaving the South. Changes in the population of Florida account for one-quarter of the South's population growth since 1970 and one-half of its net inmigration. The Mountain States have been growing fastest since 1970 (16 percent), and next were the South Atlantic States, (10 percent).

EMPLOYMENT AND INCOME

Over 92 million persons were in the civilian labor force in 1975. This number was about 10 million above the 1970 level and 23 million above the 1960 level. Since 1960, about 14 million women and 9 million men have been added to the labor force (net). The unemployment rate rose sharply between the first half of 1974 and the second quarter of 1975 and then declined slightly during the last half of 1975.

Recent sharp decreases in employment have occurred among those in the manufacturing and construction industries. Two million fewer were employed in these industries in 1975 than in 1974. Unemployment rates were also highest among workers in these industries and among those in entertainment and recreation services. By contrast, employment in the mining industry rose by 12 percent.

Changes in the occupation distribution show a net loss of 1.4 million male blue-collar workers between 1974 and 1975. Two other occupation groups showed substantial gains; professional workers were up 410,000, and service workers (except private household) by 340,000. The increase among professional workers was much larger for women than for men.

Median family income in 1974 was $12,840. On a constant dollar basis, this was 4 percent below the 1973 level. The median income in 1974 was $13,360 for white families, $7,810 for black families, and $9,560 for families of Spanish origin. Among persons who received income in 1974, the median income for men was $8,380, and that for women was $3,080.

Average (mean) income per family member is a measure that tends to adjust for differences between groups with respect to family size. It varied widely in 1974 between white husband-wife families and black husband-wife families—$4,624 versus $2,955. Average income per member of families with a female head was $2,994 for white persons and $1,492 for black persons.

The number of poor persons in the United States declined by about 15 million during the 1960's, but the number in 1974 (24.3 million) was not significantly different from that in 1969. About 16.3 million white persons, 7.5 million black persons, and 2.6 million persons of Spanish origin (mostly white) were below the poverty level in 1974. These numbers represented 12 percent of all persons, 9 percent of white persons, 31 percent of black persons, and 23 percent of persons of Spanish origin.

ETHNIC GROUPS

The black population numbered approximately 23.8 million in March 1975 and comprised 11 percent of the total U.S. population. Three-fourths of the black population lived in metropolitan areas and three-fifths in central cities within these areas. Among black persons 20 to 24 years of age, 27 percent had completed at least 1 year of college. A majority of black families (61 percent) had a husband and wife present; 35 percent had a woman as the head.

The 11.2 million persons of Spanish origin in 1975 constituted 5 percent of the population in the United States. Of this total, 6.7 million were of Mexican origin, 1.7 million of Puerto Rican origin, 700,000 of Cuban origin, 700,000 of Central or South American origin, and 1.4 million of other Spanish origin.

Persons of Spanish origin in the United States include a heavy concentration (44 percent) of children under 18 years of age, largely because of their relatively high birth rate. By contrast, they include only 4 percent at ages 65 and over, as compared with 10 percent for the total United States population. Four of every 5 persons of Spanish origin lived in metropolitan areas. Twenty-two percent of those 20 to 24 years old had completed at least 1 year of college; this is one-half the 43 percent for all persons of that age in the United States.

COLLEGE ENROLLMENT OF THE POPULATION 16 YEARS OLD AND OVER BY AGE: OCTOBER 1975, OCTOBER 1972, AND OCTOBER 1970
(Numbers in thousands. Civilian noninstitutional population)

Age	Number enrolled			Percent change in number enrolled	
	1975	1972	1970	1972-1975	1970-1975
Total enrolled in college 16 to 34 years old	9,697	8,313	7,413	16.6	30.8
16 and 17 years old[1]	293	295	260	-0.7	12.7
18 and 19 years old	2,943	2,680	2,594	9.8	13.5
20 and 21 years old	2,313	2,116	1,857	9.3	24.6
22 to 24 years old	1,679	1,461	1,354	14.9	24.0
25 to 29 years old	1,616	1,229	939	31.5	72.1
30 to 34 years old	853	531	410	60.6	108.0
35 years and over	1,183	783	(NA)	51.1	(NA)

NA Not available.
[1]Includes the small number of those 14 and 15 years old enrolled in college.
Source: U.S. Bureau of the Census, Current Population Reports, Series P-20, No. 260 and No. 222, and unpublished data.

ESTIMATES OF THE POPULATION OF THE UNITED STATES, AND ANNUAL INCREASE, BY TYPE OF POPULATION: JANUARY 1, 1970 TO JANUARY 1, 1976

(Numbers in thousands)

Year	Total population including Armed Forces overseas	Resident population	Civilian population
POPULATION			
(January 1)			
1976....................................	214,529	214,047	212,390
1975....................................	212,796	212,302	210,602
1974....................................	211,205	210,691	208,950
1973....................................	209,711	209,136	207,306
1972....................................	208,088	207,396	205,496
1971....................................	206,076	205,156	203,109
1970....................................	203,849	202,717	200,466
POPULATION INCREASE			
1975....................................	1,733	1,745	1,788
1974....................................	1,591	1,611	1,652
1973....................................	1,494	1,554	1,644
1972....................................	1,623	1,741	1,810
1971....................................	2,012	2,240	2,386
1970....................................	2,227	2,440	2,644
PERCENT INCREASE			
1975....................................	0.81	0.82	0.85
1974....................................	0.75	0.76	0.79
1973....................................	0.71	0.74	0.79
1972....................................	0.78	0.84	0.88
1971....................................	0.98	1.09	1.17
1970....................................	1.09	1.20	1.32

Source: Data consistent with Current Population Reports, Series P-25, No. 621.

PERCENT OF THE POPULATION 3 TO 34 YEARS OLD ENROLLED IN SCHOOL AND IN COLLEGE BY AGE: OCTOBER 1975 AND OCTOBER 1970

(Civilian noninstitutional population)

Age	1975		1970	
	Male	Female	Male	Female
PERCENT ENROLLED IN SCHOOL				
Total, 3 to 34 years old............	56.0	51.5	59.7	53.2
3 and 4 years old..........................	30.6	32.4	21.2	19.8
5 and 6 years old..........................	94.3	95.2	88.9	90.2
7 to 13 years old..........................	99.0	99.6	99.0	99.4
14 and 15 years old........................	98.4	98.0	98.2	98.0
16 and 17 years old........................	90.7	87.2	91.3	88.6
18 and 19 years old........................	49.9	44.2	54.4	41.6
20 and 21 years old........................	35.3	27.4	42.7	23.6
22 to 24 years old.........................	20.0	12.6	21.2	9.4
25 to 29 years old.........................	13.1	7.2	11.9	4.3
30 to 34 years old.........................	7.7	5.6	5.3	3.1
PERCENT ENROLLED IN COLLEGE				
Total, 16 to 34 years old............	16.9	13.0	16.9	10.5
16 and 17 years old........................	2.9	4.0	3.4	3.4
18 and 19 years old........................	36.7	36.7	40.2	34.6
20 and 21 years old........................	34.0	26.6	40.9	22.3
22 to 24 years old.........................	19.7	12.0	20.6	8.9
25 to 29 years old.........................	12.7	6.9	10.6	3.7
30 to 34 years old.........................	7.5	5.0	4.8	2.6

Source: U.S. Bureau of the Census, Current Population Reports, Series P-20, No. 222, and unpublished data.

SCHOOL ENROLLMENT OF THE POPULATION 3 TO 34 YEARS OLD BY LEVEL OF SCHOOL AND RACE: OCTOBER 1975 AND OCTOBER 1970

(Numbers in thousands. Civilian noninstitutional population)

Level of school and race	1975	1970	Percent change, 1970 to 1975
ALL RACES			
Total, 3 to 34 years old enrolled in school[1].............................	60,971	60,357	1.0
Nursery school.............................	1,749	1,096	59.6
Kindergarten.................................	3,381	3,183	6.2
Elementary school..........................	30,462	33,950	-10.3
High school.................................	15,683	14,715	6.6
College.....................................	9,697	7,413	30.8
Male..................................	5,342	4,401	21.4
Female.................................	4,355	3,013	44.5
WHITE			
Total enrolled, 3 to 34 years old....	51,435	51,719	-0.5
Nursery school.............................	1,432	893	60.4
Kindergarten.................................	2,838	2,706	4.9
Elementary school..........................	25,425	28,638	-11.2
High school.................................	13,224	12,723	3.9
College.....................................	8,516	6,759	26.0
Male..................................	4,774	4,065	17.4
Female.................................	3,743	2,693	39.0
BLACK			
Total enrolled, 3 to 34 years old....	8,387	7,829	7.1
Nursery school.............................	275	178	54.5
Kindergarten.................................	461	426	8.2
Elementary school..........................	4,507	4,868	-7.4
High school.................................	2,197	1,834	19.8
College.....................................	948	522	81.6
Male..................................	442	253	74.7
Female.................................	506	269	88.1

[1] In addition 1,183 persons 35 years old and over were enrolled in college, including 569 males and 614 females.

Source: U.S. Bureau of the Census, Current Population Reports, Series P-20, No. 222, and unpublished data.

HOUSEHOLDS BY TYPE AND SIZE: 1975, 1970, AND 1960

(Numbers in thousands)

Subject	1975		1970		1960		Percent increase	
	Number	Percent	Number	Percent	Number	Percent	1970 to 1975	1960 to 1970
Total households.............	71,120	100.0	63,401	100.0	52,799	100.0	12.2	20.1
Primary families............	55,563	78.1	51,456	81.2	44,905	85.0	8.0	14.6
Husband-wife.....................	46,951	66.0	44,728	70.5	39,254	74.3	5.0	13.9
Other male head..................	1,485	2.1	1,228	1.9	1,228	2.3	20.9	-
Female head.....................	7,127	10.0	5,500	8.7	4,422	8.4	29.6	24.4
Primary individuals.........	15,557	21.9	11,945	18.8	7,895	15.0	30.2	51.3
Living alone[1]....................	13,939	19.6	10,851	17.1	6,917	13.1	28.5	56.9
With nonrelative(s) present........	1,618	2.3	1,094	1.7	978	1.9	47.9	11.9
Male........................	5,912	8.3	4,063	6.4	2,716	5.1	45.5	49.6
Under 35 years...................	2,420	3.4	1,093	1.7	442	0.8	121.4	147.3
Living alone[1]....................	1,710	2.4	809	1.3	(NA)	(NA)	111.4	(NA)
With nonrelative(s) present......	710	1.0	284	0.4	(NA)	(NA)	150.0	(NA)
35 to 64 years...................	2,142	3.0	1,732	2.7	1,315	2.5	23.7	31.7
65 years and over.................	1,346	1.9	1,238	2.0	960	1.8	8.7	29.0
Female.......................	9,645	13.6	7,882	12.4	5,179	9.8	22.4	52.2
Under 35 years...................	1,547	2.2	857	1.4	401	0.8	80.5	113.7
Living alone[1]....................	1,237	1.7	640	1.0	(NA)	(NA)	93.3	(NA)
With nonrelative(s) present......	310	0.4	217	0.3	(NA)	(NA)	42.9	(NA)
35 to 64 years...................	3,218	4.5	2,969	4.7	2,399	4.5	8.4	23.8
65 years and over.................	4,884	6.9	4,057	6.4	2,378	4.5	20.4	70.6
Average size of household.........	2.94	(X)	3.14	(X)	3.33	(X)	(X)	(X)
Members under 18 years...........	0.93	(X)	1.09	(X)	1.21	(X)	(X)	(X)
Members 18 years and over........	2.01	(X)	2.05	(X)	2.12	(X)	(X)	(X)

- Represents zero.
X Not applicable.
NA Not available.
[1]One-person household.

Source: U.S. Bureau of the Census, Current Population Survey, Series P-20, Nos. 287, 279, 170, and 106, and unpublished data.

POPULATION 25 YEARS OLD AND OVER WHO HAVE COMPLETED AT LEAST FOUR YEARS OF HIGH SCHOOL, AND PERSONS WHO HAVE COMPLETED AT LEAST FOUR YEARS OF COLLEGE, BY AGE:

MARCH 1975 AND MARCH 1970

Age	1975		1970	
	High school, 4 years or more	College, 4 years or more	High school, 4 years or more	College, 4 years or more
NUMBER OF GRADUATES				
Total, 25 years and over.....	73,114	16,244	60,378	12,063
25 to 34 years.....................	24,390	6,443	18,364	3,926
35 to 44 years.....................	16,162	3,644	14,806	2,958
45 to 54 years.....................	15,027	2,862	13,563	2,336
55 to 64 years.....................	10,097	1,692	8,066	1,594
65 years and over.................	7,438	1,603	5,579	1,249
PERCENT OF POPULATION				
Total, 25 years and over.....	62.5	13.9	55.2	11.0
25 to 34 years.....................	81.1	21.4	73.9	15.8
35 to 44 years.....................	71.5	16.1	64.3	12.8
45 to 54 years.....................	63.7	12.1	58.2	10.0
55 to 64 years.....................	51.8	8.7	43.8	8.7
65 years and over.................	35.2	7.6	28.3	6.3

Source: U.S. Bureau of the Census, Current Population Reports, Series P-20, No. 279, and unpublished data.

ESTIMATES OF THE POPULATION OF STATES: JULY 1, 1974 AND 1975

(Population in thousands. Resident population includes estimated Armed Forces personnel residing in each State)

Region, division, and State	Resident population					Civilian population				
	July 1, 1975[1] (provisional)	July 1, 1974[1]	April 1, 1970[2] (census)	Change, 1970 to 1975		July 1, 1975 (provisional)	July 1, 1974	April 1, 1970[2]	Change, 1970 to 1975	
				Number	Percent				Number	Percent
United States................	213,121	211,381	203,304	9,817	4.8	211,445	209,676	201,133	10,313	5.1
REGIONS:										
Northeast....................	49,461	49,413	49,061	401	0.8	49,350	49,293	48,857	492	1.0
North Central...............	57,669	57,558	56,593	1,076	1.9	57,505	57,387	56,382	1,123	2.0
South.......................	68,113	67,149	62,812	5,301	8.4	67,258	66,284	61,734	5,523	8.9
West........................	37,878	37,262	34,838	3,039	8.7	37,333	36,711	34,159	3,174	9.3
NORTHEAST:										
New England.................	12,198	12,148	11,847	351	3.0	12,150	12,099	11,750	400	3.4
Middle Atlantic.............	37,263	37,264	37,213	50	0.1	37,199	37,194	37,107	92	0.2
NORTH CENTRAL:										
East North Central..........	40,979	40,902	40,266	713	1.8	40,901	40,821	40,165	736	1.8
West North Central..........	16,690	16,657	16,328	362	2.2	16,604	16,566	16,217	387	2.4
SOUTH:										
South Atlantic..............	33,715	33,208	30,679	3,036	9.9	33,191	32,681	29,995	3,195	10.7
East South Central..........	13,544	13,412	12,808	736	5.7	13,440	13,305	12,678	762	6.0
West South Central..........	20,855	20,529	19,325	1,530	7.9	20,627	20,299	19,061	1,566	8.2
WEST:										
Mountain....................	9,644	9,440	8,290	1,354	16.3	9,527	9,324	8,167	1,361	16.7
Pacific.....................	28,234	27,821	26,549	1,686	6.3	27,806	27,387	25,992	1,813	7.0
NEW ENGLAND:										
Maine.......................	1,059	1,049	994	66	6.6	1,049	1,040	982	67	6.8
New Hampshire...............	818	808	738	80	10.9	813	804	734	80	10.9
Vermont.....................	471	468	445	26	5.9	471	468	445	26	5.9
Massachusetts...............	5,828	5,799	5,689	138	2.4	5,814	5,784	5,658	155	2.7
Rhode Island................	927	938	950	-23	-2.4	923	931	915	8	0.9
Connecticut.................	3,095	3,086	3,032	63	2.1	3,081	3,072	3,016	64	2.1
MIDDLE ATLANTIC:										
New York....................	18,120	18,101	18,242	-121	-0.7	18,094	18,074	18,210	-116	-0.6
New Jersey..................	7,316	7,322	7,171	145	2.0	7,289	7,291	7,112	177	2.5
Pennsylvania................	11,827	11,841	11,801	26	0.2	11,816	11,829	11,785	31	0.3
EAST NORTH CENTRAL:										
Ohio........................	10,759	10,745	10,657	102	1.0	10,744	10,731	10,638	106	1.0
Indiana.....................	5,311	5,313	5,196	116	2.2	5,302	5,302	5,188	114	2.2
Illinois....................	11,145	11,160	11,113	32	0.3	11,107	11,121	11,057	50	0.5
Michigan....................	9,157	9,117	8,882	275	3.1	9,143	9,103	8,866	276	3.1
Wisconsin...................	4,607	4,566	4,418	189	4.3	4,605	4,564	4,416	189	4.3
WEST NORTH CENTRAL:										
Minnesota...................	3,926	3,905	3,806	120	3.1	3,923	3,902	3,801	122	3.2
Iowa........................	2,870	2,857	2,825	45	1.6	2,869	2,856	2,825	45	1.6
Missouri....................	4,763	4,772	4,678	85	1.8	4,738	4,744	4,639	98	2.1
North Dakota................	635	636	618	17	2.7	622	623	606	16	2.7
South Dakota................	683	681	666	17	2.6	677	675	661	16	2.5
Nebraska....................	1,546	1,541	1,485	61	4.1	1,535	1,529	1,473	61	4.2
Kansas......................	2,267	2,266	2,249	18	0.8	2,240	2,237	2,212	28	1.3
SOUTH ATLANTIC:										
Delaware....................	579	577	548	31	5.7	574	572	542	32	5.9
Maryland....................	4,098	4,089	3,924	174	4.4	4,051	4,038	3,850	200	5.2
District of Columbia........	716	721	757	-40	-5.4	708	713	746	-37	-5.0
Virginia....................	4,967	4,910	4,651	315	6.8	4,816	4,762	4,458	358	8.0
West Virginia...............	1,803	1,784	1,744	59	3.4	1,802	1,784	1,744	58	3.4
North Carolina..............	5,451	5,375	5,084	367	7.2	5,349	5,276	4,960	389	7.8
South Carolina..............	2,818	2,775	2,591	227	8.8	2,748	2,704	2,513	235	9.4
Georgia.....................	4,926	4,877	4,588	338	7.4	4,877	4,829	4,497	380	8.5
Florida.....................	8,357	8,099	6,791	1,565	23.0	8,265	8,004	6,685	1,580	23.6
EAST SOUTH CENTRAL:										
Kentucky....................	3,396	3,354	3,221	175	5.4	3,361	3,317	3,172	189	6.0
Tennessee...................	4,188	4,149	3,926	262	6.7	4,166	4,127	3,900	266	6.8
Alabama.....................	3,614	3,575	3,444	170	4.9	3,590	3,550	3,410	180	5.3
Mississippi.................	2,346	2,334	2,217	129	5.8	2,323	2,311	2,196	127	5.8
WEST SOUTH CENTRAL:										
Arkansas....................	2,116	2,068	1,923	192	10.0	2,106	2,058	1,915	192	10.0
Louisiana...................	3,791	3,762	3,642	148	4.1	3,753	3,730	3,600	152	4.2
Oklahoma....................	2,712	2,681	2,559	152	6.0	2,684	2,653	2,522	163	6.5
Texas.......................	12,237	12,017	11,199	1,037	9.3	12,083	11,858	11,025	1,059	9.6
MOUNTAIN:										
Montana.....................	748	737	694	53	7.7	742	731	688	53	7.7
Idaho.......................	820	796	713	107	14.9	814	790	708	106	14.9
Wyoming.....................	374	362	332	42	12.5	370	358	329	41	12.5
Colorado....................	2,534	2,515	2,210	324	14.7	2,488	2,468	2,159	329	15.2
New Mexico..................	1,147	1,119	1,017	130	12.7	1,131	1,104	1,000	131	13.1
Arizona.....................	2,224	2,160	1,775	448	25.3	2,197	2,133	1,747	450	25.8
Utah........................	1,206	1,179	1,059	147	13.8	1,202	1,174	1,056	146	13.9
Nevada......................	592	574	489	103	21.1	584	566	479	104	21.8
PACIFIC:										
Washington..................	3,544	3,494	3,413	131	3.8	3,491	3,444	3,342	149	4.5
Oregon......................	2,288	2,255	2,092	197	9.4	2,286	2,253	2,088	198	9.5
California..................	21,185	20,876	19,971	1,214	6.1	20,896	20,579	19,577	1,319	6.7
Alaska......................	352	341	303	49	16.3	326	315	270	56	20.8
Hawaii......................	865	854	770	95	12.3	806	797	715	91	12.8

[1]The resident population estimates for July 1, 1974 and July 1, 1975 differ slightly from that published in Series P-25 ,No. 608 because of updated military statistics. The civilian estimates are consistent with that report.

[2]Includes officially recognized changes to census counts through September 1975. The "official" 1970 census counts used in apportionment are shown in 1970 Census of the Population, Volume I, Characteristics of the Population, Part A, Number of Inhabitants, p. VIII.

Source: U. S. Bureau of the Census, Current Population Reports, Series P-25, No. 615.

POPULATION OF THE UNITED STATES, BY METROPOLITAN—NONMETROPOLITAN RESIDENCE AND RACE: 1975 AND 1970

(Numbers in thousands. Minus sign (-) before a figure denotes decrease)

Residence and race	1975[1]	1970[2]	Change, 1970 to 1975	Percent change		Average annual percent change[3]	
				1970 to 1975	1960 to 1970[4]	1970 to 1975	1960 to 1970[4]
Total...................	208,683	199,819	8,864	4.4	13.3	0.9	1.3
Metropolitan areas[5].............	141,993	137,058	4,935	3.6	16.6	0.7	1.5
In central cities[6]...........	60,902	62,876	-1,974	-3.1	6.5	-0.6	0.6
Outside central cities.......	81,091	74,182	6,909	9.3	26.7	1.8	2.4
Nonmetropolitan areas..........	66,690	62,761	3,929	6.3	6.8	1.2	0.7
White....................	181,636	175,276	6,360	3.6	11.9	0.7	1.1
Metropolitan areas[5].............	121,277	118,938	2,339	2.0	14.0	0.4	1.3
In central cities[6]...........	45,559	48,909	-3,350	-6.8	0.1	-1.4	-
Outside central cities.......	75,718	70,029	5,689	8.1	26.1	1.6	2.3
Nonmetropolitan areas..........	60,359	56,338	4,021	7.1	7.8	1.4	0.8
Black and other races......	27,047	24,543	2,504	10.2	24.3	1.9	2.2
Metropolitan areas[5].............	20,716	18,120	2,596	14.3	36.9	2.7	3.1
In central cities[6]...........	15,343	13,967	1,376	9.9	36.5	1.9	3.1
Outside central cities.......	5,373	4,153	1,220	29.4	38.1	5.2	3.2
Nonmetropolitan areas..........	6,331	6,423	-92	-1.4	-1.6	-0.3	-0.2

- Represents zero.
[1]April-centered annual averages from the Current Population Survey.
[2]For comparability with data from the Current Population Survey, figures from the 1970 census have been adjusted to exclude inmates of institutions and members of the Armed Forces living in barracks and similar types of quarters.
[3]Based on the method of exponential change.
[4]Based on total 1970 and 1960 census populations, including the categories not covered in the Current Population Survey.
[5]Population of the 243 SMSA's as defined in 1970 census publications.
[6]1975 data for the central cities refer to their January 1, 1970, boundaries and exclude areas annexed since 1970.

Source: U.S. Bureau of the Census, 1970 Census of Population, Vol. I, U.S. Summary, tables 38 and 48, and State parts, tables 24 and 27; PHC(2), U.S. Summary, table 1, and State parts, tables 1 and 4; 1960 Census of Population, Vol. I, State parts, tables 20-22, 27, and 28; and unpublished data.

SELECTED CHARACTERISTICS BY RACE AND SPANISH ORIGIN: 1975

Selected characteristics	Total	White	Black	Spanish origin[1]
AGE				
Total population.....................	209,572	182,500	23,785	11,202
Percent............................	100.0	100.0	100.0	100.0
Under 18 years.........................	31.7	30.5	40.0	44.3
18 to 64 years.........................	58.3	58.9	52.7	52.1
65 years and over.....................	10.1	10.5	7.2	3.6
Median age.............................	28.7	29.5	23.0	20.7
TYPE OF RESIDENCE				
United States......................	209,572	182,500	23,785	[2]10,795
Percent............................	100.0	100.0	100.0	100.0
Metropolitan areas.....................	68.0	66.8	75.2	81.4
Central cities.........................	29.2	25.2	58.1	49.2
Suburbs................................	38.8	41.6	17.1	32.1
Nonmetropolitan areas..................	32.0	33.2	24.8	18.6
EDUCATION				
Total, 25 years and over.............	116,897	104,065	11,096	4,762

See footnotes at end of table.

SELECTED CHARACTERISTICS BY RACE AND SPANISH ORIGIN: 1975—Continued

Selected characteristics	Total	White	Black	Spanish origin[1]
Percent:				
High school graduates....................	62.5	64.5	42.5	37.9
Completed some college.................	26.3	27.2	15.5	15.0
Total, 20 to 24 years................	18,360	15,883	2,162	99.2
Percent:				
High school graduates....................	84.2	86.0	71.7	59.4
Completed some college.................	41.0	42.7	26.7	21.6
TYPE OF FAMILY				
All families.........................	55,712	49,451	5,498	2,477
Percent.........................	100.0	100.0	100.0	100.0
Husband-wife families....................	84.3	86.9	60.9	77.6
Other male head.........................	2.7	2.6	3.9	3.7
Female head.............................	13.0	10.5	35.3	18.8
SIZE OF FAMILY				
Percent.............................	100.0	100.0	100.0	100.0
2 persons...............................	37.4	38.5	29.4	23.2
3 persons...............................	21.8	21.6	22.7	22.5
4 persons...............................	19.7	19.9	17.8	20.5
5 persons or more......................	21.1	20.0	30.1	33.8
LABOR FORCE STATUS				
Persons, 16 years and over...........	151,268	133,501	15,541	[3]6,724
In civilian labor force....................	92,613	82,084	9,123	4,024
Percent in civilian labor force.........	61.2	61.5	58.7	59.8
Percent unemployed.....................	8.5	7.8	14.7	12.7
EMPLOYMENT				
Total employed, 16 years and over....	84,783	75,713	7,782	[3]3,510
Percent.............................	100.0	100.0	100.0	100.0
White-collar workers.......................	49.8	51.7	30.8	33.0
Blue-collar workers........................	33.0	32.4	39.3	46.7
Service workers...........................	13.7	12.3	27.3	16.8
Farm workers.............................	3.5	3.6	2.7	3.5
INCOME IN 1974				
Median income of persons with income:				
Male, 14 years and over.................	$8,379	$8,794	$5,370	$6,507
Female, 14 years and over...............	$3,079	$3,133	$2,806	$3,072
Number below low-income level..............	24,260	16,290	7,467	2,601
Percent below low-income level.............	11.6	8.9	31.4	23.2
Total families......................	55,712	49,451	5,498	2,477
Percent.........................	100.0	100.0	100.0	100.0
Under $5,000...........................	13.0	11.1	31.5	21.6
$5,000 to $9,999........................	22.6	21.9	30.0	31.1
$10,000 to $14,999......................	24.3	25.1	19.1	24.3
$15,000 and over.......................	39.8	42.1	19.4	23.1
Median family income......................	$12,836	$13,356	$7,808	$9,559

[1]Persons of Spanish origin may be of any race.
[2]Data for Spanish origin persons by type of residence are based on the March 1974 Current Population Survey.
[3]Unadjusted data for the month of March 1975.

Source: U.S. Bureau of the Census, Current Population Reports, Series P-20, Nos. 283, 287, and 290; Series P-23, Nos. 54 and 55; Series P-60, No. 99; and unpublished tabulations of the March 1975 Current Population Survey.

INCOME IN 1974 OF PERSONS AND FAMILIES, AND POVERTY STATUS IN 1974 OF PERSONS, BY RACE AND SPANISH ORIGIN

(Persons and families as of March 1975)

Selected characteristics	Total	White	Black	Spanish origin[1]
MEDIAN INCOME OF PERSONS 14 YEARS OLD AND OVER WITH INCOME				
All Persons				
Male..	$8,379	$8,794	$5,370	$6,507
Female..	$3,079	$3,114	$2,806	$3,072
Year-Round Full-Time Workers				
Male..	$12,152	$12,434	$8,705	$9,007
Female..	$6,957	$7,021	$6,371	$5,957
FAMILIES				
Number.........................thousands..	55,712	49,451	5,498	2,477
Percent.............................	100.0	100.0	100.0	100.0
Under $5,000.............................	13.1	11.1	31.5	21.5
$5,000 to $9,999.........................	22.7	21.9	30.0	31.2
$10,000 to $14,999.......................	24.3	25.1	19.1	24.3
$15,000 and over.........................	39.8	42.1	19.4	23.1
Median income.............................	$12,836	$13,356	$7,808	$9,559
POVERTY STATUS OF PERSONS				
Number Below Poverty Level				
Total.............................	24,260	16,290	7,467	2,601
In families.............................	19,440	12,517	6,506	2,394
With a male head.........................	10,877	8,238	2,320	1,473
With a female head.......................	8,563	4,279	4,186	921
Unrelated individuals.......................	4,820	3,773	961	207
Male...	1,607	1,200	351	107
Female.......................................	3,212	2,573	611	100
Percent Below Poverty Level				
Total.............................	11.6	8.9	31.4	23.2
In families.............................	10.2	7.5	30.3	22.6
With a male head.........................	6.5	5.5	16.6	16.6
With a female head.......................	36.8	27.6	55.9	53.2
Unrelated individuals.......................	25.5	23.2	41.0	33.7
Male...	20.4	18.3	29.9	29.0
Female.......................................	29.3	26.5	51.9	40.7

[1]Persons of Spanish origin may be of any race.

Source: U.S. Bureau of the Census, Current Population Reports, Series P-60, No. 99.

POPULATION OF SPANISH ORIGIN BY SEX AND TYPE OF SPANISH ORIGIN: MARCH 1975

(Numbers in thousands. Civilian noninstitutional population)

Type of origin	Total		Male		Female	
	Number	Percent	Number	Percent	Number	Percent
Persons of Spanish origin....	11,202	100.0	5,498	100.0	5,705	100.0
Mexican..............................	6,690	59.7	3,346	60.9	3,344	58.6
Puerto Rican........................	1,671	14.9	765	13.9	906	15.9
Cuban...............................	743	6.6	369	6.7	374	6.6
Central or South American..........	671	6.0	325	5.9	346	6.1
Other Spanish.......................	1,428	12.7	693	12.6	735	12.9

Source: U.S. Bureau of the Census, Current Population Reports, Series P-20, No. 290.

U.S. Bureau of the Census, Current Population Reports, Series P-20, No. 292. "Population Profile of the United States: 1975." U.S. Government Printing Office, Washington, D.C. 1976.

SCHOOL ENROLLMENT—SOCIAL AND ECONOMIC CHARACTERISTICS OF STUDENTS
OCTOBER 1975 (Advance report)

INTRODUCTION

The total number of persons 3 to 34 years old enrolled in school in the fall of 1975 was 61 million students, 1 percent higher than in 1974. The net gain in the school population between 1974 and 1975 reflects a large increase in the college population, moderate increases in secondary schools and nursery schools,[1] no significant change in kindergartens, and declines in elementary school enrollment paralleling to a large extent shifts in the age structure of the population. Elementary enrollment declined by 680,000, or 2 percent, because the number of births in the United States declined in the early 1960's and has been reducing the number of children of school age since 1970.

Elementary and Preliminary Enrollment. There is some evidence that enrollment in nursery schools increased between 1974 and 1975 even though the number of 3- and 4-year old children decreased by 4 percent. The increase in enrollment among these preschool children during the past year occurred only in public nursery schools; enrollment in private nursery schools was about the same. In 1975 a larger proportion of nursery school students were enrolled in public schools than in 1974—one-third of nursery school students were enrolled in public schools in 1975 compared with about one-fourth in 1974. The enrollment rate of 3- and 4-year old children has been increasing steadily over the past 10 years; 32 percent of 3- and 4-year olds were enrolled in 1975 compared with 21 percent in 1970 and 11 percent in 1965 (table 2). This increased participation apparently has occurred because nursery schools are becoming more accessible to parents, and because parents are willing to enroll preschool children in formal educational programs.

The number of pupils in public elementary schools (kindergarten through 8th grade) was at about the same level in the fall of 1975 as in 1965 (about 30.0 million); but the enrollment in private elementary schools declined by about 30 percent during that period. The number of pupils enrolled in private elementary schools has remained at about 3.8 million since 1973. That level is down from the 5.5 million enrolled in private schools in 1965 and 4.5 million in 1970.

The decline in total elementary school enrollment (including kindergarten) during the past 10 years was partially offset by an increase in the participation of 5- and 6-year old children in kindergartens. The number of students in kindergartens increased between 1965 and 1975 while the number of students in the first

through eighth grades declined. The increased enrollment ratios of children at preschool ages may create new opportunities for teachers in a period when elementary schools have declining enrollment.

College Enrollment. The number of persons enrolled in college was 10.9 million persons in 1975, including 1.2 million persons 35 years old and over. This was a 10-percent increase since 1974 and one of the largest numerical 1-year increases in enrollment during the past 10 years (table 1). The gain in college enrollment from 1974 to 1975 was due to a very large increase among full-time students, reversing the trends toward a greater proportion of part-time students observed between 1970 and 1974.[2] The increase between 1974 and 1975 occurred primarily among younger students who were enrolled in the first or second year of college (table 3).

Although the number of persons of college age continued to increase during the 1970's, a lower proportion of persons 18 and 19 years old (the usual ages of first entering college) have been enrolled in school than in the late 1960's (table 2).[3] For example, enrollment rates for civilian men 18 and 19 years old declined from 60 percent in 1968 to 46 percent in 1974. However, in 1975, when the unemployment rate for teenagers was the highest for several years,[4] the enrollment rates for men increased to 50 percent (table 2). Among women, the change between 1974 and 1975 in the proportion of those 18 and 19 years old enrolled in school was also significant. If enrollment rates for persons 16 to 34 years old had remained at the same level as in 1974, about 9.1 million persons 16 to 34 years old would have been in college in 1975 instead of the 9.7 million actually enrolled at those ages. Thus, changes in enrollment rates by age accounted for about 70 percent of the increase in college enrollment from 1974 to 1975.

There were nearly 1 million Black college students in 1975 (under age 35), an increase of 16 percent in 1 year (table 1). Black persons now account for 10 percent of all college students compared with about 7 percent in 1970 and 5 percent in 1965. Currently,

---

[1] The net gain for secondary enrollment is significantly different at the 68 percent level of confidence while the net gain for nursery school enrollment is significantly different at the 95 percent level of confidence.

[2] The proportion of part-time students enrolled in college in 1974 and 1975 was significantly different at the 86 percent level of confidence.

[3] See **Current Population Reports**, Series P-20, No. 260, p. 2, for a discussion of the effects of the Armed Forces population on college enrollment rates from 1963 to 1972.

[4] **Employment and Earnings: November 1975.** U.S. Department of Labor, Bureau of Labor Statistics, Volume 22, No. 5, chart 9.

Blacks represent 12 percent of all persons of college age (18 to 24 years old). College enrollment rates for Blacks are still slightly lower than for Whites in part because a lower proportion of Blacks 18 to 21 years old have graduated from high school and thus are not eligible for college enrollment. For example, 27 percent of Blacks 18 to 21 years old were not in school and had not graduated from high school compared with 15 percent for Whites. The college enrollment rate among high school graduates 18 to 21 years old was about the same for Blacks as for Whites—41 percent and 43 percent, respectively.

In the 5 years since 1970, college enrollment increased by 31 percent, due particularly to an increase in the number of women students (table 1). The number of women enrolled in college increased by 45 percent compared with 21 percent for men during this period.

[5] C. Arnold Anderson, Mary Jane Bowman, and Vincent Tinto. **Where Colleges Are and Who Attends.** (New York: McGraw-Hill Book Company), 1972.

*This material has not been excerpted in its entirety.

However, men still have higher enrollment rates than women in every relevant age group.

Another factor which accounts for the increased number of students in the past 5 years has been the growth of community, or two-year colleges which are less expensive and nearer to population centers than other institutions.[5] About one-half of the increase in undergraduates during the past 5 years occurred in two-year colleges. In this period, two-year college enrollment increased by about 50 percent while undergraduate enrollment in other colleges increased by 21 percent (table 5). Junior colleges attract persons who are older than other undergraduates and who are more likely to be enrolled part time. About one-half of undergraduates 25 to 34 years old were in junior colleges in 1975 compared with 38 percent in 1970, an increase of 166 percent in the number of 25-to 34-year-old undergraduates in two-year colleges in the 5-year period. Thus, the observed enrollment increases among persons over age 25 during the 1970's have occurred largely, but not exclusively, in two-year colleges.

College Enrollment of the Population 16 Years Old and Over, by Age: October 1970, 1974, and 1975

College enrollment (in thousands)

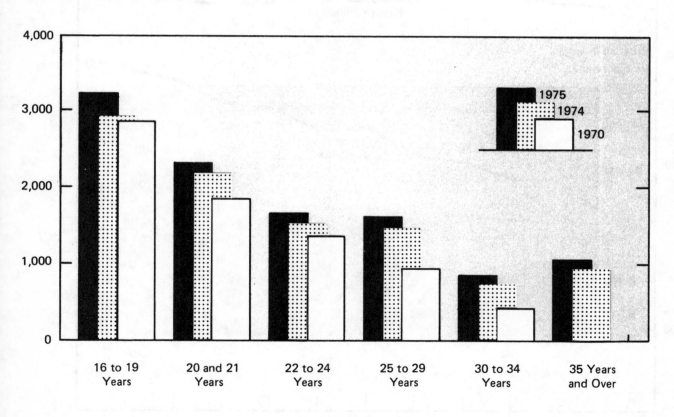

Age

School Enrollment of the Population 3 to 34 Years Old by Level:
October 1965 to October 1975

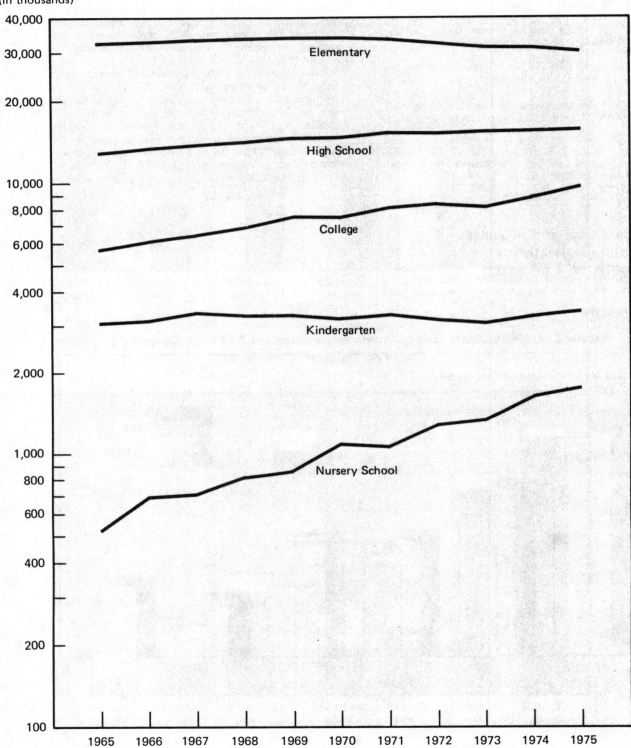

Enrolled in School
(in thousands)

SCHOOL ENROLLMENT OF THE POPULATION 3 TO 34 YEARS OLD, BY LEVEL AND CONTROL OF SCHOOL AND RACE: OCTOBER 1965 TO OCTOBER 1975

(Numbers in thousands. Civilian noninstitutional population)

Level and control of school	1975	1974	1973	1972	1971	1970	1969	1968	1967	1966	1965
ALL RACES											
Total enrolled..........	60,969	60,259	59,392	60,142	61,106	60,357	59,913	58,791	57,656	56,167	54,701
Nursery school.................	1,748	1,607	1,324	1,283	1,066	1,096	860	816	713	688	520
Public......................	574	423	400	402	317	333	245	262	230	215	127
Private.....................	1,174	1,184	924	881	749	763	615	554	484	473	393
Kindergarten.................	3,393	3,252	3,074	3,135	3,263	3,183	3,276	3,268	3,312	3,115	3,057
Public......................	2,851	2,726	2,582	2,636	2,689	2,647	2,682	2,709	2,678	2,527	2,439
Private.....................	542	526	493	499	574	536	594	559	635	588	618
Elementary school.............	30,446	31,126	31,469	32,242	33,507	33,950	33,788	33,761	33,440	32,916	32,474
Public......................	27,166	27,956	28,201	28,693	29,829	30,001	29,825	29,527	28,877	28,208	27,596
Private.....................	3,279	3,169	3,268	3,549	3,678	3,949	3,964	4,234	4,562	4,706	4,878
High school.................	15,683	15,447	15,347	15,169	15,183	14,715	14,553	14,145	13,790	13,364	12,975
Public......................	14,503	14,275	14,162	14,015	14,057	13,545	13,400	12,793	12,498	11,985	11,517
Private.....................	1,180	1,172	1,184	1,155	1,126	1,170	1,153	1,352	1,292	1,377	1,457
College.....................	9,697	8,827	8,179	8,313	8,087	7,413	7,435	6,801	6,401	6,085	5,675
Public......................	7,704	6,905	6,224	6,337	6,271	5,699	5,439	4,948	4,540	4,178	3,840
Private.....................	1,994	1,922	1,955	1,976	1,816	1,714	1,995	1,854	1,861	1,908	1,835
Full time[1].....................	7,098	6,345	6,083	6,309	6,199	5,763	5,810	5,357	4,976	4,847	4,414
Percent....................	73.3	71.9	74.4	75.9	76.7	77.7	78.1	78.8	77.7	79.7	77.8
Part time[1].....................	2,592	2,476	2,090	1,999	1,883	1,650	1,625	1,444	1,425	1,238	1,261
WHITE											
Total enrolled..........	51,430	50,992	50,617	51,314	52,081	51,719	51,465	50,608	49,721	48,620	47,451
Nursery school.................	1,432	1,340	1,087	1,079	888	893	676	664	564	564	451
Public......................	392	293	242	285	225	198	136	163	134	127	93
Private.....................	1,040	1,048	845	794	664	695	539	501	429	437	358
Kindergarten.................	2,845	2,745	2,584	2,633	2,735	2,706	2,803	2,775	2,840	2,693	2,648
Public......................	2,363	2,268	2,139	2,185	2,207	2,233	2,289	2,272	2,254	2,163	2,086
Private.....................	483	477	445	448	527	473	515	504	587	530	562
Elementary school.............	25,412	26,051	26,531	27,185	28,187	28,638	28,572	28,634	28,415	28,012	27,679
Public......................	22,351	23,063	23,506	23,869	24,720	24,923	24,803	24,580	24,044	23,469	22,976
Private.....................	3,059	2,990	3,025	3,316	3,466	3,715	3,768	4,054	4,371	4,542	4,703
High school.................	13,224	13,073	13,091	12,959	12,998	12,723	12,588	12,280	11,997	11,643	11,356
Public......................	12,112	11,966	11,967	11,876	11,937	11,599	11,502	11,007	10,769	10,312	9,961
Private.....................	1,112	1,107	1,124	1,083	1,061	1,124	1,085	1,272	1,228	1,329	1,395
College.....................	8,516	7,781	7,324	7,458	7,273	6,759	6,827	6,255	5,905	5,708	5,317
Public......................	6,724	6,049	5,550	5,644	5,624	5,168	4,967	4,501	4,155	3,914	3,568
Private.....................	1,792	1,732	1,773	1,814	1,650	1,591	1,860	1,753	1,750	1,795	1,749
Full time[1].....................	6,180	5,571	5,402	5,674	5,555	5,221	5,307	4,919	4,604	4,556	4,111
Percent....................	72.6	71.6	73.8	76.1	76.4	77.2	77.7	78.7	78.0	79.8	77.3
BLACK											
Total enrolled..........	8,400	8,215	7,834	7,959	8,178	7,829	7,680	7,448	7,196	[2]7,547	[2]7,252
Nursery school.................	276	227	210	185	151	178	170	132	140	125	72
Public......................	171	121	146	113	90	129	102	89	92	88	37
Private.....................	105	106	64	72	61	49	68	43	47	37	35
Kindergarten.................	468	463	423	448	464	426	425	448	418	420	407
Public......................	426	416	391	402	422	374	361	397	375	364	353
Private.....................	42	47	32	46	42	53	64	51	44	56	54
Elementary school.............	4,509	4,585	4,473	4,573	4,877	4,868	4,785	4,716	4,618	4,904	4,796
Public......................	4,344	4,455	4,277	4,382	4,712	4,668	4,633	4,569	4,444	4,739	4,620
Private.....................	165	131	196	191	165	200	151	146	173	165	176
High school.................	2,199	2,125	2,044	2,025	2,006	1,834	1,808	1,718	1,651	1,721	1,619
Public......................	2,140	2,072	1,988	1,971	1,951	1,794	1,751	1,656	1,605	1,673	1,556
Private.....................	59	54	56	54	55	41	57	62	46	48	62
College.....................	948	814	684	727	680	522	492	434	370	282	274
Public......................	782	659	537	582	532	422	372	359	280	(NA)	(NA)
Private.....................	166	155	147	145	148	100	120	75	90	(NA)	(NA)
Full time[1].....................	740	588	536	525	534	427	401	338	271	210	218
Percent....................	78.2	72.4	78.3	72.3	78.5	81.8	81.5	77.9	73.2	74.5	79.6

NA Not available.

[1] Includes only persons 16 to 34 years old.

[2] Enrollment figures in nursery school, kindergarten, elementary school, and high school, are for Black and other races. College enrollment figures refer to Black only.

ENROLLMENT STATUS OF THE POPULATION 3 TO 34 YEARS OLD, BY AGE, SEX, RACE, SPANISH ORIGIN, AND SELECTED EDUCATIONAL CHARACTERISTICS: OCTOBER 1975

(Numbers in thousands. Civilian noninstitutional population)

Age, sex, race, and Spanish origin	Population	Enrolled in school						Not enrolled in school					
		Total		Below college level[1]		In college		Total		High school graduate		Not high school graduate	
		Number	Percent	Number	Percent	Number	Percent	Number	Percent	Number	Percent	Number	Percent
ALL RACES													
Total, 3 to 34 years	113,445	60,969	53.7	51,272	45.2	9,697	8.5	52,476	46.3	36,994	32.6	15,481	13.6
3 and 4 years	6,676	2,101	31.5	2,101	31.5	-	-	4,574	68.5	-	-	4,574	68.5
5 and 6 years	6,956	6,590	94.7	6,590	94.7	-	-	365	5.3	-	-	365	5.3
7 to 9 years	10,354	10,287	99.3	10,287	99.3	-	-	67	0.7	-	-	67	0.7
10 to 13 years	15,936	15,817	99.3	15,817	99.3	-	-	119	0.7	-	-	119	0.7
14 and 15 years	8,453	8,300	98.2	8,293	98.1	7	0.1	153	1.8	3	-	149	1.8
16 and 17 years	8,313	7,398	89.0	7,112	85.6	286	3.4	915	11.0	201	2.4	715	8.6
18 and 19 years	8,024	3,765	46.9	822	10.2	2,943	36.7	4,259	53.1	2,973	37.0	1,286	16.0
20 and 21 years	7,669	2,393	31.2	80	1.0	2,313	30.2	5,276	68.8	4,005	52.2	1,271	16.6
22 to 24 years	10,694	1,728	16.2	49	0.5	1,679	15.7	8,966	83.8	7,413	69.3	1,553	14.5
25 to 29 years	16,652	1,679	10.1	63	0.4	1,616	9.7	14,973	89.9	12,401	74.5	2,572	15.4
30 to 34 years	13,718	910	6.6	57	0.4	853	6.2	12,808	93.4	9,998	72.9	2,810	20.5
Male, 3 to 34 years	56,289	31,555	56.1	26,212	46.6	5,342	9.5	24,734	43.9	17,321	30.8	7,414	13.2
3 and 4 years	3,409	1,052	30.9	1,052	30.9	-	-	2,357	69.1	-	-	2,357	69.1
5 and 6 years	3,546	3,346	94.4	3,346	94.4	-	-	200	5.6	-	-	200	5.6
7 to 9 years	5,277	5,236	99.2	5,236	99.2	-	-	41	0.8	-	-	41	0.8
10 to 13 years	8,119	8,031	98.9	8,031	98.9	-	-	88	1.1	-	-	88	1.1
14 and 15 years	4,300	4,231	98.4	4,224	98.3	6	0.1	69	1.6	2	-	67	1.6
16 and 17 years	4,201	3,811	90.7	3,689	87.8	122	2.9	390	9.3	71	1.7	319	7.6
18 and 19 years	3,891	1,940	49.9	514	13.2	1,426	36.7	1,951	50.1	1,348	34.6	603	15.5
20 and 21 years	3,693	1,304	35.3	48	1.3	1,256	34.0	2,389	64.7	1,783	48.3	606	16.4
22 to 24 years	5,140	1,030	20.0	19	0.4	1,011	19.7	4,110	80.0	3,390	66.0	719	14.0
25 to 29 years	8,075	1,061	13.1	35	0.4	1,025	12.7	7,014	86.9	5,855	72.5	1,160	14.4
30 to 34 years	6,639	512	7.7	17	0.2	496	7.5	6,127	92.3	4,872	73.4	1,254	18.9
Female, 3 to 34 years	57,156	29,414	51.5	25,059	43.8	4,355	7.6	27,741	48.5	19,673	34.4	8,068	14.1
3 and 4 years	3,267	1,049	32.1	1,049	32.1	-	-	2,218	67.9	-	-	2,218	67.9
5 and 6 years	3,410	3,244	95.1	3,244	95.1	-	-	166	4.9	-	-	166	4.9
7 to 9 years	5,078	5,051	99.5	5,051	99.5	-	-	27	0.5	-	-	27	0.5
10 to 13 years	7,817	7,786	99.6	7,786	99.6	-	-	31	0.4	-	-	31	0.4
14 and 15 years	4,153	4,070	98.0	4,068	98.0	1	-	83	2.0	1	-	82	2.0
16 and 17 years	4,112	3,587	87.2	3,423	83.3	163	4.0	525	12.8	129	3.1	396	9.6
18 and 19 years	4,133	1,825	44.2	309	7.5	1,517	36.7	2,308	55.8	1,625	39.3	683	16.5
20 and 21 years	3,976	1,089	27.4	32	0.8	1,058	26.6	2,887	72.6	2,222	55.9	664	16.7
22 to 24 years	5,554	697	12.6	29	0.5	668	12.0	4,857	87.4	4,023	72.4	834	15.0
25 to 29 years	8,577	618	7.2	28	0.3	590	6.9	7,959	92.8	6,546	76.3	1,412	16.5
30 to 34 years	7,079	398	5.6	40	0.6	357	5.0	6,681	94.4	5,126	72.4	1,555	22.0
WHITE													
Total, 3 to 34 years	96,815	51,430	53.1	42,913	44.3	8,516	8.8	45,385	46.9	32,985	34.1	12,401	12.8
3 and 4 years	5,518	1,697	30.8	1,697	30.8	-	-	3,821	69.2	-	-	3,821	69.2
5 and 6 years	5,795	5,494	94.8	5,494	94.8	-	-	301	5.2	-	-	301	5.2
7 to 9 years	8,654	8,600	99.4	8,600	99.4	-	-	54	0.6	-	-	54	0.6
10 to 13 years	13,387	13,292	99.3	13,292	99.3	-	-	95	0.7	-	-	95	0.7
14 and 15 years	7,145	7,023	98.3	7,020	98.3	3	-	122	1.7	3	-	118	1.7
16 and 17 years	7,043	6,289	89.3	6,040	85.8	249	3.5	754	10.7	159	2.3	594	8.4
18 and 19 years	6,855	3,185	46.5	573	8.4	2,613	38.1	3,670	53.5	2,665	38.9	1,005	14.7
20 and 21 years	6,593	2,097	31.8	54	0.8	2,042	31.0	4,496	68.2	3,521	53.4	975	14.8
22 to 24 years	9,255	1,506	16.3	44	0.5	1,461	15.8	7,749	83.7	6,581	71.1	1,169	12.6
25 to 29 years	14,578	1,459	10.0	48	0.3	1,410	9.7	13,119	90.0	11,080	76.0	2,039	14.0
30 to 34 years	11,993	788	6.6	51	0.4	737	6.1	11,205	93.4	8,975	74.8	2,229	18.6
Male, 3 to 34 years	48,347	26,785	55.4	22,011	45.5	4,774	9.9	21,563	44.6	15,563	32.2	6,000	12.4
3 and 4 years	2,825	871	30.8	871	30.8	-	-	1,954	69.2	-	-	1,954	69.2
5 and 6 years	2,963	2,796	94.4	2,796	94.4	-	-	167	5.6	-	-	167	5.6
7 to 9 years	4,423	4,388	99.2	4,388	99.2	-	-	35	0.8	-	-	35	0.8
10 to 13 years	6,838	6,767	99.0	6,767	99.0	-	-	71	1.0	-	-	71	1.0
14 and 15 years	3,645	3,590	98.5	3,587	98.4	3	0.1	55	1.5	2	0.1	53	1.4
16 and 17 years	3,569	3,249	91.0	3,141	88.0	108	3.0	320	9.0	58	1.6	262	7.3
18 and 19 years	3,343	1,657	49.6	374	11.2	1,283	38.4	1,686	50.4	1,228	36.7	458	13.7
20 and 21 years	3,202	1,164	36.3	30	0.9	1,134	35.4	2,038	63.7	1,573	49.1	465	14.5
22 to 24 years	4,505	926	20.5	16	0.4	909	20.2	3,579	79.5	3,012	66.9	567	12.6
25 to 29 years	7,159	936	13.1	26	0.4	911	12.7	6,223	86.9	5,277	73.7	946	13.2
30 to 34 years	5,875	440	7.5	14	0.2	426	7.3	5,435	92.5	4,412	75.1	1,022	17.4
Female, 3 to 34 years	48,468	24,645	50.8	20,902	43.1	3,743	7.7	23,823	49.2	17,422	35.9	6,401	13.2
3 and 4 years	2,693	826	30.7	826	30.7	-	-	1,867	69.3	-	-	1,867	69.3
5 and 6 years	2,831	2,697	95.3	2,697	95.3	-	-	134	4.7	-	-	134	4.7
7 to 9 years	4,231	4,211	99.5	4,211	99.5	-	-	19	0.5	-	-	19	0.5
10 to 13 years	6,549	6,525	99.6	6,525	99.6	-	-	23	0.4	-	-	23	0.4
14 and 15 years	3,500	3,433	98.1	3,433	98.1	-	-	67	1.9	1	-	66	1.9
16 and 17 years	3,474	3,040	87.5	2,899	83.4	141	4.1	434	12.5	101	2.9	333	9.6
18 and 19 years	3,512	1,529	43.5	198	5.6	1,330	37.9	1,983	56.5	1,436	40.9	547	15.6
20 and 21 years	3,391	933	27.5	24	0.7	908	26.8	2,458	72.5	1,948	57.5	510	15.0
22 to 24 years	4,750	580	12.2	28	0.6	552	11.6	4,170	87.8	3,569	75.1	601	12.7
25 to 29 years	7,419	522	7.0	23	0.3	500	6.7	6,897	93.0	5,803	78.2	1,094	14.7
30 to 34 years	6,118	348	5.7	37	0.6	311	5.1	5,770	94.3	4,563	74.6	1,207	19.7

See footnotes at end of table.

ENROLLMENT STATUS OF THE POPULATION 3 TO 34 YEARS OLD, BY AGE, SEX, RACE, SPANISH ORIGIN, AND SELECTED EDUCATIONAL CHARACTERISTICS: OCTOBER 1975—
Continued

(Numbers in thousands. Civilian noninstitutional population)

Age, sex, race, and Spanish origin	Population	Enrolled in school						Not enrolled in school					
		Total		Below college level[1]		In college		Total		High school graduate		Not high school graduate	
		Number	Percent	Number	Percent	Number	Percent	Number	Percent	Number	Percent	Number	Percent
BLACK													
Total, 3 to 34 years...........	14,543	8,400	57.8	7,452	51.2	948	6.5	6,144	42.2	3,350	23.0	2,793	19.2
3 and 4 years...................	1,007	344	34.2	344	34.2	-	-	663	65.8	-	-	663	65.8
5 and 6 years...................	1,029	972	94.4	972	94.4	-	-	57	5.6	-	-	57	5.6
7 to 9 years....................	1,505	1,494	99.3	1,494	99.3	-	-	11	0.7	-	-	11	0.7
10 to 13 years..................	2,286	2,265	99.1	2,265	99.1	-	-	21	0.9	-	-	21	0.9
14 and 15 years.................	1,182	1,151	97.4	1,150	97.3	1	0.1	31	2.6	-	-	31	2.6
16 and 17 years.................	1,137	987	86.9	954	83.9	33	2.9	149	13.1	33	2.9	116	10.2
18 and 19 years.................	1,030	485	47.1	225	21.8	260	25.3	544	52.9	283	27.5	262	25.4
20 and 21 years.................	967	262	27.1	25	2.6	237	24.5	704	72.9	427	44.1	278	28.7
22 to 24 years..................	1,216	173	14.2	4	0.4	168	13.8	1,043	85.8	706	58.0	337	27.8
25 to 29 years..................	1,728	163	9.4	12	0.7	151	8.7	1,565	90.6	1,083	62.7	482	27.9
30 to 34 years..................	1,458	103	7.1	6	0.4	97	6.7	1,355	92.9	819	56.2	536	36.8
Male, 3 to 34 years.............	6,946	4,199	60.5	3,757	54.1	442	6.4	2,747	39.5	1,473	21.2	1,274	18.3
3 and 4 years...................	505	157	31.1	157	31.1	-	-	348	68.9	-	-	348	68.9
5 and 6 years...................	519	492	94.9	492	94.9	-	-	27	5.1	-	-	27	5.1
7 to 9 years....................	754	750	99.4	750	99.4	-	-	4	0.6	-	-	4	0.6
10 to 13 years..................	1,147	1,134	98.9	1,134	98.9	-	-	13	1.1	-	-	13	1.1
14 and 15 years.................	603	588	97.6	588	97.6	-	-	15	2.4	-	-	15	2.4
16 and 17 years.................	555	490	88.2	475	85.6	14	2.6	66	11.8	12	2.1	54	9.7
18 and 19 years.................	476	238	49.9	127	26.7	111	23.2	238	50.1	106	22.3	132	27.7
20 and 21 years.................	435	125	28.7	18	4.2	107	24.5	310	71.3	177	40.8	132	30.4
22 to 24 years..................	540	79	14.7	3	0.6	76	14.1	460	85.3	320	59.3	140	25.9
25 to 29 years..................	773	91	11.8	10	1.2	82	10.6	682	88.2	485	62.7	197	25.5
30 to 34 years..................	640	55	8.6	2	0.3	53	8.3	585	91.4	373	58.3	212	33.1
Female, 3 to 34 years..........	7,597	4,200	55.3	3,695	48.6	506	6.7	3,397	44.7	1,877	24.7	1,520	20.0
3 and 4 years...................	502	187	37.3	187	37.3	-	-	315	62.7	-	-	315	62.7
5 and 6 years...................	510	479	94.0	479	94.0	-	-	31	6.0	-	-	31	6.0
7 to 9 years....................	751	744	99.2	744	99.2	-	-	6	0.8	-	-	6	0.8
10 to 13 years..................	1,139	1,131	99.3	1,131	99.3	-	-	8	0.7	-	-	8	0.7
14 and 15 years.................	579	562	97.2	561	96.9	1	0.2	16	2.8	-	-	16	2.8
16 and 17 years.................	582	498	85.6	479	82.4	19	3.2	84	14.4	22	3.8	62	10.7
18 and 19 years.................	553	247	44.7	98	17.6	150	27.0	306	55.3	176	31.9	130	23.4
20 and 21 years.................	532	137	25.8	7	1.3	130	24.5	395	74.2	249	46.8	146	27.3
22 to 24 years..................	676	93	13.8	1	0.2	92	13.6	583	86.2	385	57.0	197	29.2
25 to 29 years..................	955	72	7.5	3	0.3	69	7.2	884	92.5	598	62.6	285	29.9
30 to 34 years..................	818	48	5.9	4	0.4	44	5.4	770	94.1	446	54.5	324	39.6
SPANISH ORIGIN													
Total, 3 to 34 years...........	6,825	3,741	54.8	3,330	48.8	411	6.0	3,084	45.2	1,345	19.7	1,738	25.5
3 and 4 years...................	441	120	27.3	120	27.3	-	-	320	72.7	-	-	320	72.7
5 and 6 years...................	507	467	92.1	467	92.1	-	-	40	7.9	-	-	40	7.9
7 to 9 years....................	689	686	99.6	686	99.6	-	-	3	0.4	-	-	3	0.4
10 to 13 years..................	1,040	1,032	99.2	1,032	99.2	-	-	8	0.8	-	-	8	0.8
14 and 15 years.................	490	469	95.6	469	95.6	-	-	21	4.4	2	0.4	20	4.0
16 and 17 years.................	515	444	86.2	430	83.6	13	2.6	71	13.8	3	0.6	68	13.2
18 and 19 years.................	489	215	44.0	97	19.9	118	24.1	274	56.0	127	25.9	147	30.1
20 and 21 years.................	410	113	27.5	11	2.8	101	24.7	297	72.5	168	40.9	130	31.6
22 to 24 years..................	547	77	14.1	2	0.3	76	13.8	470	85.9	242	44.2	228	41.7
25 to 29 years..................	894	74	8.3	6	0.7	68	7.6	820	91.7	437	48.8	383	42.9
30 to 34 years..................	803	44	5.5	10	1.2	35	4.3	758	94.5	367	45.8	391	48.7
Male, 3 to 34 years.............	3,345	1,944	58.1	1,725	51.6	219	6.5	1,402	41.9	612	18.3	790	23.6
3 and 4 years...................	230	61	26.7	61	26.7	-	-	169	73.3	-	-	169	73.3
5 and 6 years...................	247	221	89.7	221	89.7	-	-	25	10.3	-	-	25	10.3
7 to 9 years....................	370	369	99.6	369	99.6	-	-	1	0.4	-	-	1	0.4
10 to 13 years..................	530	524	98.8	524	98.8	-	-	6	1.2	-	-	6	1.2
14 and 15 years.................	249	243	97.4	243	97.4	-	-	7	2.6	2	0.7	5	1.9
16 and 17 years.................	262	232	88.3	229	87.2	3	1.2	31	11.7	2	0.6	29	11.1
18 and 19 years.................	229	119	51.9	65	28.5	53	23.4	110	48.1	50	21.8	60	26.3
20 and 21 years.................	187	58	31.3	7	3.6	52	27.7	128	68.7	72	38.5	56	30.2
22 to 24 years..................	262	42	15.9	2	0.6	40	15.3	221	84.1	116	44.1	105	40.0
25 to 29 years..................	406	48	11.9	3	0.8	45	11.1	357	88.1	193	47.5	165	40.6
30 to 34 years..................	373	27	7.2	2	0.4	25	6.7	346	92.8	178	47.8	168	45.0
Female, 3 to 34 years..........	3,479	1,797	51.7	1,605	46.1	192	5.5	1,682	48.3	733	21.1	949	27.3
3 and 4 years...................	210	59	27.9	59	27.9	-	-	152	72.1	-	-	152	72.1
5 and 6 years...................	260	245	94.4	245	94.4	-	-	14	5.6	-	-	14	5.6
7 to 9 years....................	319	317	99.5	317	99.5	-	-	2	0.5	-	-	2	0.5
10 to 13 years..................	510	508	99.7	508	99.7	-	-	2	0.3	-	-	2	0.3
14 and 15 years.................	241	226	93.8	226	93.8	-	-	15	6.2	-	-	15	6.2
16 and 17 years.................	253	212	84.0	202	79.9	10	4.1	40	16.0	1	0.5	39	15.5
18 and 19 years.................	261	97	37.1	32	12.3	65	24.8	164	62.9	77	29.5	87	33.5
20 and 21 years.................	223	54	24.3	5	2.1	49	22.2	169	75.7	96	43.0	73	32.7
22 to 24 years..................	285	36	12.5	-	-	36	12.5	249	87.5	126	44.3	123	43.2
25 to 29 years..................	488	26	5.3	3	0.7	23	4.6	463	94.7	244	49.9	219	44.8
30 to 34 years..................	430	18	4.1	8	1.9	10	2.2	412	95.9	189	44.0	223	51.9

- Represents zero.
[1] Includes nursery school, kindergarten, and grades 1 to 12.

Note: Persons of Spanish origin may be of any race.

Undergraduate College Enrollment by Age and Full-Time Status for Four-Year and Two-Year Colleges: October 1975

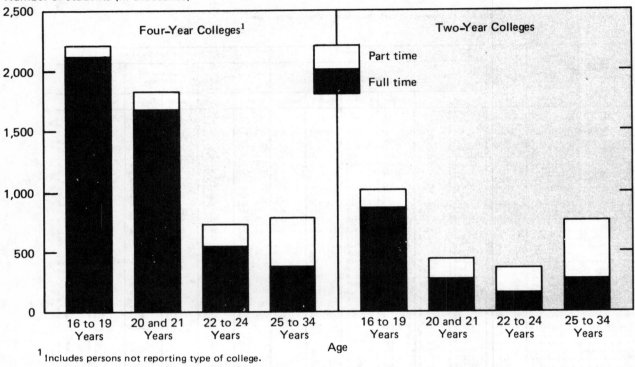

Number of students (in thousands)

1 Includes persons not reporting type of college.

U.S. Bureau of the Census, Current Population Reports, Series P-20, No. 294. "Population Characteristics: School Enrollment — Social and Economic Characteristics of Students, October 1975" (advance report). U.S. Government Printing Office, Washington, D.C. June 1976.

COLLEGE PLANS OF HIGH SCHOOL SENIORS: OCTOBER 1975

Overview. This report presents statistics on the post-high school educational plans of seniors enrolled in high school in October 1975. Information is presented on college and vocational school plans of seniors by such characteristics as their sex, race, metropolitan-nonmetropolitan residence, region of residence, family income, and the educational attainment and occupation of their family head. The data are based on responses of high school seniors to the Current Population Survey conducted in October 1975 by the Bureau of the Census. These same data have been collected on an annual basis since 1972. Similar data were also collected in the October 1965 and October 1959 Current Population Surveys.

Post-high school plans of seniors. A higher proportion of 1976 high school graduates will be attending college in the fall of 1976 than have the graduates in the past 2 years, if the plans of these students in October of their senior year are fulfilled (table A). Forty-nine percent of the 3.3 million seniors who reported their intentions expressed definite plans to attend college, compared with 44 percent in 1974 and 43 percent in 1973 (a figure not statistically different from the 1974 figure). An additional 25 percent of the 1975 seniors indicated that they "may" attend college upon completion of their high school education.

Although about one-fourth of seniors in 1975 did not plan to attend a regular college or university, a large portion of this group (about 38 percent) did plan to attend a post-secondary business, technical, trade or similar type of vocational school. This group represented approximately 1 of every 10 high school seniors in 1975.[1]

Differences by sex and race of seniors. There is some evidence that a somewhat higher proportion of females than males had definite plans to attend college in 1975 (51 percent and 47 percent, respectively) as was the case in 1974. However, the proportion of men who indicated that they "may" attend college was slightly larger than that for women, so that the proportion of seniors who were at least considering college attendance was the same for men and women (table A). A somewhat higher proportion of men than women with definite college plans wished to attend a four-year college only, while the proportion of women who planned to attend only a two-year college exceeded that for men.

---

[1] Since postsecondary vocational school plans were only asked of students who indicated that they did not plan to attend a regular college, this figure may represent an underestimate of student interest in vocational school attendance.

Table A. Plans to Attend College of High School Seniors 14 to 34 Years Old, by Sex: 1972 to 1975

(Excluding seniors not reporting)

Sex of student and year	Number reporting college plans (thousands)	Percent of those reporting who--			
		Plan to attend college	May attend college	Do not plan to attend college	
				Total	Plan or may attend vocational school
BOTH SEXES					
1975	3,306	48.9	25.1	26.0	9.8
1974	3,406	43.6	26.9	29.5	10.3
1973	3,346	42.9	28.4	28.7	10.9
1972	3,242	46.2	27.1	26.6	12.0
MALE					
1975	1,686	46.6	27.5	25.9	9.5
1974	1,650	40.9	28.5	30.7	11.2
1973	1,710	43.5	28.6	28.0	9.6
1972	1,670	46.1	29.8	24.0	10.2
FEMALE					
1975	1,620	51.4	22.6	26.0	10.1
1974	1,755	46.2	25.4	28.4	9.6
1973	1,637	42.3	28.2	29.4	12.2
1972	1,573	46.3	24.3	29.2	13.8

A smaller proportion of Black than White high school seniors had definite plans to attend college (40 percent compared with 49 percent, table B). However, the larger proportion of Black than White students who indicated they "may" attend college raised the proportion of Black students who were at least considering college to about three out of four, a figure not different from that for Whites.

About 48 percent of seniors of Spanish origin indicated definite plans to attend college and an additional 37 percent reported they may do so. Because of sampling variability, these figures should not necessarily be interpreted as different from those for either White or Black students, even though they may appear to be.

Differences by type of residence and region of seniors. The college expectations of high school seniors living outside metropolitan areas in 1975 were lower than those of students living within such areas (table C). About 52 percent of metropolitan seniors had definite plans to attend college, compared with about 42 percent of their nonmetropolitan peers. However, a higher proportion of nonmetropolitan seniors (15 percent) were considering attendance at a post-secondary vocational school than were their metropolitan

counterparts (8 percent). Within metropolitan areas, there was no difference in the proportion of seniors with definite college plans between residents of central cities and suburban areas.

A higher proportion of students in the West had definite plans to attend college (59 percent) than in any of the other regions. Also, a higher proportion (50 percent) of seniors in Western States who planned on attending college expected to attend both (or had not decided between attending) a two-year and four-year college than in the other regions combined (27 percent); this fact in part reflects the large two-year college system in the State of California.

Differences by control of high school. Students enrolled in private schools were more likely to plan enrollment in college than students in public high schools. About two-thirds (68 percent) of the 260,000 high school seniors enrolled in private high schools who reported their intentions expressed definite plans to attend college in the future, compared with about 47 percent of students enrolled in public high schools (table C). In addition, of those students who expected to attend college, about 78 percent of those who attended private high schools compared with 51 percent of their counterparts at public schools wished to attend a four-

Table B. Plans to Attend College of High School Seniors 14 to 34 Years Old, by Race and Spanish Origin: 1972 to 1975

(Excluding seniors not reporting)

Race of student and year	Number reporting college plans (thousands)	Percent of those reporting who--			
		Plan to attend college	May attend college	Do not plan to attend college	
				Total	Plan or may attend vocational school
WHITE					
1975................................	2,780	49.4	23.8	26.7	9.7
1974................................	2,927	44.6	26.2	29.2	9.7
1973................................	2,858	43.2	27.6	29.3	11.2
1972................................	2,785	46.4	26.4	27.1	12.0
BLACK					
1975................................	462	40.5	34.6	24.7	11.3
1974................................	422	36.0	31.8	32.2	14.5
1973................................	451	38.6	34.1	27.5	10.0
1972................................	413	44.6	33.4	22.5	11.4
SPANISH ORIGIN[1]					
1975................................	180	47.8	36.7	15.6	2.2
1974................................	219	47.9	29.7	22.4	2.3
1973................................	(NA)	(NA)	(NA)	(NA)	(NA)
1972................................	140	49.3	27.9	22.9	10.0

NA Not available.
[1]Persons of Spanish origin may be of any race.

year college only. Only 12 percent of private high school seniors were not considering the possibility of college attendance in the future, compared with 27 percent of students at public schools.

Differences by family income. The tendency for family income (for the most part parental) to play a strong role in determining the college plans of high school seniors continued to persist in 1975: As family (parental) income increased, so did the proportion of seniors with definite plans to attend college. For example, about 81 percent of students in families with income over $25,000 had definite plans to attend college whereas only 39 percent of students in families with income under $10,000 had such plans. Because of this differential, students from families with income over $25,000 represented about one out of five students with definite college plans, while for high school seniors as a whole, they represented only about one of every eight students. The vast majority (71 percent) of the seniors from a high-family-income background who planned to attend college intended to enroll in a four-year college only, whereas about 60 percent of students with definite plans and family income below $10,000 were considering enrollment in a two-year college. Also, about 15 percent of students with income under $10,000 were considering attending a postsecondary vocational school compared with students from families with high income (5 percent).

Differences associated with educational attainment of family head. College aspirations of high school seniors in 1975 were positively associated with the educational attainment of the heads of their respective families (table E). Seventy-eight percent of students who were members of families in which the head was a college graduate, for example, had definite college plans, whereas only 45 percent of students whose family head had completed 4 years of high school but no college, and 32 percent of those in families whose head had not completed any years of high school, had like plans.

However, plans to attend college were reported by many students whose family head had only a moderate to small amount of formal education. Over half (55 percent) of the seniors who definitely planned to enroll in a college or university were members of families in which the head had never attended college, and 23 percent were members of families in which the head had not graduated from high school.

College plans and college attendance. At this time it is not possible to ascertain whether the 1975 high school seniors' aspirations regarding college attendance will be fulfilled. The Census Bureau has, however, collected longitudinal data relating to college plans and actual college attendance of two previous groups of high school students, namely those who

Table C. Plans to Attend College of High School Seniors 14 to 34 Years Old, by Type of Residence, Region, and Control of School: October 1975

(Excluding seniors not reporting)

Type of residence, region, and control of school	Number reporting college plans (thousands)	Percent of those reporting who--			
		Plan to attend college	May attend college	Do not plan to attend college	
				Total	Plan or may attend vocational school
TYPE OF RESIDENCE					
Metropolitan....................	2,322	51.8	25.9	22.4	7.6
In central cities..............	939	52.2	28.5	19.3	7.5
Outside central cities.........	1,383	51.5	24.1	24.4	7.7
Nonmetropolitan.................	984	42.3	23.2	34.6	14.9
REGION					
Northeast.......................	754	45.9	26.3	27.7	8.5
North Central..................	987	42.9	25.9	31.2	11.9
South..........................	945	50.9	23.6	25.4	11.4
West...........................	621	59.1	24.5	16.4	5.5
CONTROL OF SCHOOL					
Public high school.............	3,044	47.3	25.5	27.2	10.2
Private high school............	262	67.6	19.8	12.2	5.3

Table D. Percent Distribution of Plans to Attend College by Family Income in Preceding 12 Months for High School Seniors in Primary Families: October 1975

(Excluding seniors not reporting)

Family income	Total reporting on college plans	Plan to attend college	May attend college	Do not plan to attend college	
				Total	Plan or may attend vocational school
PERCENT DISTRIBUTION BY FAMILY INCOME					
Total.....................	100.0	49.9	25.0	25.1	9.6
Under $10,000....................	100.0	38.6	27.5	33.9	14.6
$10,000 to $14,999...............	100.0	43.1	27.7	29.2	11.1
$15,000 to $24,999...............	100.0	56.3	23.9	19.8	5.8
$25,000 and over.................	100.0	81.2	11.3	7.9	4.5
Not reported.....................	100.0	39.2	32.0	28.9	9.6
PERCENT DISTRIBUTION BY COLLEGE PLANS					
Total, with income reported	100.0	100.0	100.0	100.0	100.0
Under $10,000....................	28.8	21.8	32.7	39.5	43.8
$10,000 to $14,999...............	26.7	22.6	30.5	31.5	30.8
$15,000 to $24,999...............	31.1	34.4	30.7	24.9	18.8
$25,000 and over.................	13.3	21.1	6.2	4.2	6.2

Table E. Percent Distribution of Plans to Attend College of High School Seniors 14 to 34 Years Old in Primary Families, by Years of School Completed by the Family Head: October 1975

(Excluding seniors not reporting)

Years of school completed by family head	Total reporting on college plans	Plan to attend college	May attend college	Do not plan to attend college	
				Total	Plan or may attend vocational school
PERCENT DISTRIBUTION BY YEARS OF SCHOOL COMPLETED					
Total.....................	100.0	49.9	25.0	25.1	9.6
Elementary: 0 to 8 years........	100.0	31.6	28.9	39.7	15.3
High school: 1 to 3 years........	100.0	36.9	29.7	33.3	12.0
4 years.............	100.0	45.3	27.5	27.3	10.6
College: 1 to 3 years........	100.0	61.8	21.7	16.8	6.8
4 years or more.....	100.0	77.5	15.2	7.2	2.6
PERCENT DISTRIBUTION BY COLLEGE PLANS					
Total.....................	100.0	100.0	100.0	100.0	100.0
Elementary: 0 to 8 years........	14.9	9.5	17.3	23.7	23.8
High school: 1 to 3 years........	18.5	13.7	22.0	24.6	23.2
4 years.............	35.4	31.7	38.4	38.0	38.7
College: 1 to 3 years........	12.0	15.0	10.5	8.1	8.6
4 years or more.....	19.2	30.2	11.8	5.6	5.3

were seniors in October 1965 and in October 1959.[2] Data from these studies indicate that 68 percent of the high school seniors in 1959 who planned to attend college did so in 1960, a figure not statistically different from that for the 1965 seniors who planned to attend and had done so by February 1967 (70 percent).[3] These data do not necessarily suggest that some of these students were overly optimistic about attending college. Some for instance, may plan to defer college entrance for a year or longer after graduation from high school. For example, by 1971, 77 percent of the 1965 seniors with college plans had attended college.[4]

Although some students in both previous studies indicated that they would not attend college, a small but significant proportion of these seniors in both 1960 and 1965 had actually attended college in the year following graduation. Of all the high school seniors in 1959 who graduated, 42 percent were attending college in 1960. For the high school seniors of 1965, 47 percent had attended college by February 1967. More recent data from the National Longitudinal Study of the High School Class of 1972, an ongoing survey sponsored by the National Center for Educational Statistics, show that 64 percent of the high school seniors interviewed in the spring of 1972 had actually attended some kind of post-secondary school or college by October 1973 (1½ years after graduation from high school), and about 50 percent were currently taking courses at a college or postsecondary vocational school.[5] When originally interviewed as high school seniors, 59 percent indicated they were planning on attending a college or vocational school in the year following their graduation.

---

[2] See the reports "Factors Related to High School Graduation and College Attendance: 1967," Current Population Reports, Series P-20, No. 185; "Factors Related to College Attendance of Farm and Nonfarm High School Graduates: 1960," Farm Population, Series Census—ERS (P-27), No. 32; and "Educational Status, College Plans, and Occupational Status of Farm and Nonfarm Youths: October 1959," Farm Population, Series Census—ERS (P-27), No. 30.

[3] Even though the figures appear similar, the data for high school seniors in 1965 and 1959 are not strictly comparable due to the nature of the question. See discussion on page 5 of "College Plans of High School Seniors: October 1972," Current Population Reports, Series P-20, No. 252.

[4] A. J. Jaffe and Walter Adams, 1971-72 Progress Report and Findings: Follow-up of Cross-section of 1965-66 High School Seniors and Related Materials, Bureau of Applied Social Research, Columbia University, July 1972, page 30.

[5] See National Center for Educational Statistics, "National Longitudinal Study of the High School Class of 1972: Comparative Profiles One and One-Half Years After Graduation," N.C.E.S. 76-220, and "National Longitudinal Study of the High School Class of 1972: Tabular Summary of Student Questionnaire Data," N.C.E.S. publication No. 74-227a and b.

RELATED REPORTS

Data on college plans of high school seniors for October 1974, 1973 and 1972 were published in **Current Population Reports,** Series P-20, Nos. 284, 270, and 252, respectively.

Statistics on school enrollment for October 1975 were presented in **Current Population Reports,** Series P-20, No. 294. Statistics on school enrollment for years prior to 1975 have been published annually in the P-20 Series of **Current Population Reports.**

Data on characteristics of high school seniors by graduation status and high school graduates by college attendance status are presented in "Factors Related to High School Graduation and College Attendance: 1967," **Current Population Reports,** Series P-20, No. 185. Data on college plans and college attendance of high school graduates are also presented in "Factors Related to College Attendance of Farm and Nonfarm High School Graduates: 1960," **Farm Population,** Series Census-ERS (P-27), No. 32; and "Educational Status, College Plans, and Occupational Status of Farm and Nonfarm Youths: October 1959," **Farm Population,** Series Census-ERS (P-27), No. 30. Statistics on college attendance and related factors, including type of college, living arrangements, marital status, field of specialization, and college rank, can be found in "Characteristics of Students and Their Colleges: October 1966," **Current Population Reports,** Series P-20, No. 183.

1960 and 1970 census data. Statistics on school enrollment for cities, standard metropolitan statistical areas, States, regions, and the United States appear in reports of the decennial censuses. Detailed statistics for 1970 on school enrollment by age and socioeconomic characteristics for regions and the United States are included in Subject Reports of the 1970 census, especially in PC(2)-5A, **School Enrollment.**

Figures on school enrollment from the October Current Population Surveys differ from decennial census data for reasons in addition to the difference in the dates. In the first place, the survey data exclude the institutional population and members of the Armed Forces. These two groups were included in the census. Second, there were differences in field work. The small group of Current Population Survey enumerators were more experienced and had more intensive training and supervision than the large number of temporary census enumerators and may have more often obtained more accurate answers from respondents. Third, the census was taken in April and relates to enrollment since February 1, whereas the surveys were taken in October and relate to enrollment in the current term. This difference in months of the year affects not only the extent of school enrollment (through "drop-outs" during the school year, etc.) but also the level of school in which persons of a given age are enrolled.

Table 1. PLANS TO ATTEND COLLEGE OF HIGH SCHOOL SENIORS 14 TO 34 YEARS OLD, BY SELECTED CHARACTERISTICS: OCTOBER 1975

(Numbers in thousands. Civilian noninstitutional population)

Selected characteristic	All high school seniors	Plan to attend college				May attend college				Do not plan to attend college				School plans not reported
		Total	Two-year college only	Four-year college only	Two-year and four-year college	Total	Two-year college only	Four-year college only	Two-year and four-year college	Total	Plan to attend vocational school	May attend vocational school	No vocational school plans	
Age and Sex														
Total......................	3,431	1,617	-223	871	523	830	253	60	516	860	190	133	537	125
14 to 16 years....................	389	217	33	133	51	71	18	1	51	88	26	10	52	14
17 years.......................	2,310	1,174	153	661	361	566	160	49	357	518	119	77	322	53
18 to 34 years.................	731	225	37	78	111	193	75	10	108	254	46	46	163	59
Male.......................	1,746	785	70	457	259	463	134	32	297	437	98	62	278	60
14 to 16 years..................	164	89	10	58	21	29	6	1	22	43	14	3	27	3
17 years.......................	1,132	567	40	351	176	303	83	25	196	238	58	34	146	24
18 to 34 years.................	450	129	20	48	62	131	46	6	79	156	26	25	105	33
Female.....................	1,685	832	153	414	264	366	119	28	219	422	92	71	259	65
14 to 16 years..................	225	129	23	75	30	41	12	-	29	44	12	7	25	11
17 years.......................	1,178	607	113	309	184	263	77	24	161	280	61	43	176	29
18 to 34 years.................	281	96	17	30	49	62	29	4	29	98	19	21	58	25
Sex of Household Head														
Male head.....................	2,818	1,350	179	747	424	673	205	42	426	691	137	109	445	104
Male student..................	1,440	659	62	391	206	386	118	20	248	348	69	50	229	47
Female student................	1,379	691	117	356	218	287	87	21	178	343	68	59	217	58
Female head...................	613	268	44	125	99	157	48	19	90	168	53	24	91	20
Male student..................	307	127	7	66	53	77	17	12	49	89	28	12	49	14
Female student................	306	141	37	58	46	79	31	7	41	79	24	12	43	7
Race and Spanish Origin														
White														
Both sexes...................	2,886	1,374	183	774	418	663	226	44	393	742	162	107	474	106
Male..........................	1,455	677	57	406	213	361	118	22	221	366	80	50	237	50
Female........................	1,431	697	125	367	205	302	108	22	172	376	82	57	237	56
Black														
Both sexes...................	480	187	31	81	75	160	27	16	118	114	26	26	62	18
Male..........................	245	70	8	36	26	97	16	10	71	67	15	12	40	10
Female........................	236	118	23	45	49	63	11	6	46	47	11	13	22	8
Spanish Origin[1]														
Both sexes...................	186	86	14	28	44	66	21	2	44	28	-	4	24	6
Male..........................	105	43	6	10	26	45	18	-	27	13	-	1	11	5
Female........................	82	43	8	18	18	22	3	2	17	15	-	3	12	1
Control of High School														
Public........................	3,160	1,440	207	733	499	777	245	53	479	827	181	128	519	116
Private.......................	271	177	15	138	24	52	8	8	37	32	9	5	18	9
Other Relative in Household Attending College														
Other relative in household attending college..............	561	388	43	232	113	108	23	4	81	46	7	6	32	18
No other relative in household attending college..............	2,870	1,229	179	639	410	722	230	56	436	814	183	126	504	106
Type of Residence														
Metropolitan......................	2,415	1,202	166	662	374	601	187	46	369	519	99	77	343	93
In central city...............	977	490	59	269	162	268	74	21	173	181	34	36	111	38
Outside central city..........	1,438	712	107	393	212	333	112	26	195	338	65	41	232	55
Nonmetropolitan...................	1,016	416	57	209	149	228	66	14	148	340	91	56	193	32
Region														
Northeast.....................	786	346	50	210	86	198	61	16	121	209	33	31	145	32
North Central.................	1,022	423	49	277	97	256	76	22	158	308	68	49	191	35
South.........................	972	481	60	263	158	223	66	17	140	240	74	34	133	27
West..........................	651	367	64	122	182	152	49	5	98	102	16	18	68	30

See footnotes at end of table.

Table 1. PLANS TO ATTEND COLLEGE OF HIGH SCHOOL SENIORS 14 TO 34 YEARS OLD, BY SELECTED CHARACTERISTICS: OCTOBER 1975—Continued

(Numbers in thousands. Civilian noninstitutional population)

Selected characteristic	All high school seniors	Plan to attend college				May attend college				Do not plan to attend college				School plans not reported
		Total	Two-year college only	Four-year college only	Two-year and four-year college	Total	Two-year college only	Four-year college only	Two-year and four-year college	Total	Plan to attend vocational school	May attend vocational school	No vocational school plans	
PERCENT DISTRIBUTION														
Age and Sex														
Total.......................	100.0	47.1	6.5	25.4	15.2	24.2	7.4	1.8	15.1	25.1	5.5	3.9	15.6	3.6
14 to 16 years...................	100.0	55.9	8.6	34.1	13.2	18.1	4.6	0.3	13.2	22.6	6.7	2.6	13.3	3.5
17 years........................	100.0	50.8	6.6	28.6	15.6	24.5	6.9	2.1	15.5	22.4	5.1	3.3	13.9	2.3
18 to 34 years..................	100.0	30.8	5.0	10.6	15.2	26.4	10.3	1.4	14.7	34.8	6.2	6.3	22.3	8.0
Male...........................	100.0	45.0	4.0	26.2	14.8	26.5	7.7	1.8	17.0	25.0	5.6	3.6	15.9	3.4
14 to 16 years...................	100.0	54.1	6.0	35.3	12.8	17.8	3.7	0.8	13.3	26.4	8.3	1.7	16.5	1.8
17 years........................	100.0	50.1	3.5	31.0	15.6	26.8	7.3	2.2	17.3	21.0	5.1	3.0	12.9	2.1
18 to 34 years..................	100.0	28.8	4.5	10.6	13.7	29.1	10.2	1.3	17.6	34.7	5.8	5.6	23.3	7.4
Female.........................	100.0	49.4	9.1	24.6	15.7	21.7	7.0	1.7	13.0	25.1	5.5	4.2	15.4	3.8
14 to 16 years...................	100.0	57.2	10.4	33.2	13.5	18.4	5.4	-	13.1	19.7	5.5	3.2	10.9	4.7
17 years........................	100.0	51.5	9.6	26.3	15.7	22.3	6.6	2.0	13.7	23.7	5.1	3.6	15.0	2.4
18 to 34 years..................	100.0	34.0	5.9	10.7	17.4	22.1	10.4	1.6	10.1	34.9	6.9	7.3	20.7	9.0
Sex of Household Head														
Male head......................	100.0	47.9	6.4	26.5	15.0	23.9	7.3	1.5	15.1	24.5	4.9	3.9	15.8	3.7
Male student....................	100.0	45.8	4.3	27.2	14.3	26.8	8.2	1.4	17.2	24.2	4.8	3.5	15.9	3.2
Female student..................	100.0	50.1	8.5	25.8	15.8	20.8	6.3	1.6	12.9	24.9	4.9	4.3	15.7	4.2
Female head....................	100.0	43.7	7.1	20.3	16.2	25.6	7.8	3.0	14.7	27.4	8.6	3.9	14.9	3.3
Male student....................	100.0	41.3	2.3	21.5	17.4	25.2	5.4	3.8	16.0	29.1	9.3	3.9	15.9	4.4
Female student..................	100.0	46.1	11.9	19.1	15.0	26.0	10.2	2.3	13.5	25.8	8.0	3.9	13.9	2.2
Race and Spanish Origin														
White														
Both sexes..................	100.0	47.6	6.3	26.8	14.5	23.0	7.8	1.5	13.6	25.7	5.6	3.7	16.4	3.7
Male...........................	100.0	46.6	3.9	27.9	14.7	24.8	8.1	1.5	15.2	25.2	5.5	3.4	16.3	3.4
Female.........................	100.0	48.7	8.8	25.7	14.3	21.1	7.5	1.6	12.0	26.3	5.7	4.0	16.6	3.9
Black														
Both sexes..................	100.0	39.0	6.5	16.9	15.6	33.4	5.6	3.3	24.5	23.7	5.4	5.4	12.9	3.8
Male...........................	100.0	28.5	3.2	14.7	10.6	39.7	6.6	4.0	29.1	27.6	6.2	5.1	16.3	4.1
Female.........................	100.0	49.9	9.9	19.3	20.8	26.8	4.6	2.5	19.7	19.7	4.6	5.7	9.4	3.5
Spanish Origin[1]														
Both sexes..................	100.0	46.0	7.4	14.8	23.8	35.7	11.2	0.9	23.6	15.0	-	2.2	12.7	3.4
Male...........................	100.0	40.7	6.0	9.6	25.2	42.7	16.9	-	25.7	12.0	-	1.2	10.8	4.6
Female.........................	100.0	52.8	9.2	21.6	21.9	26.6	3.8	2.0	20.8	18.8	-	3.6	15.1	1.8
Control of High School														
Public..........................	100.0	45.6	6.6	23.2	15.8	24.6	7.8	1.7	15.2	26.2	5.7	4.0	16.4	3.7
Private.........................	100.0	65.4	5.7	51.0	8.7	19.3	2.9	2.8	13.7	11.9	3.8	1.9	6.6	3.3
Other Relative in Household Attending College														
Other relative in household attending college...........	100.0	69.3	7.7	41.4	20.2	19.3	4.1	0.8	14.4	8.2	1.3	1.1	5.8	3.2
No other relative in household attending college...............	100.0	42.8	6.3	22.3	14.3	25.1	8.0	1.9	15.2	28.3	6.4	4.4	17.6	3.7
Type of Residence														
Metropolitan....................	100.0	49.8	6.9	27.4	15.5	24.9	7.7	1.9	15.3	21.5	4.1	3.2	14.2	3.8
In central city................	100.0	50.1	6.0	27.5	16.5	27.5	7.6	2.1	17.7	18.6	3.5	3.6	11.4	3.9
Outside central city...........	100.0	49.5	7.4	27.4	14.8	23.2	7.8	1.8	13.6	23.5	4.5	2.9	16.1	3.8
Nonmetropolitan.................	100.0	40.9	5.6	20.6	14.7	22.5	6.5	1.4	14.6	33.5	9.0	5.5	19.0	3.1
Region														
Northeast.......................	100.0	44.0	6.4	26.7	10.9	25.3	7.8	2.0	15.4	26.6	4.1	4.0	18.5	4.1
North Central...................	100.0	41.4	4.8	27.1	9.5	25.1	7.4	2.2	15.5	30.1	6.6	4.8	18.6	3.5
South...........................	100.0	49.5	6.2	27.1	16.2	23.0	6.8	1.8	14.4	24.7	7.6	3.5	13.7	2.8
West............................	100.0	56.4	9.8	18.7	27.9	23.3	7.6	0.7	15.0	15.7	2.5	2.8	10.4	4.6

- Represents zero or rounds to zero.
[1] Persons of Spanish origin may be of any race.

Table 2. PLANS TO ATTEND COLLEGE OF HIGH SCHOOL SENIORS 14 TO 34 YEARS OLD IN PRIMARY FAMILIES, BY SEX OF STUDENT AND FAMILY INCOME IN PRECEDING 12 MONTHS: OCTOBER 1975

(Numbers in thousands. Civilian noninstitutional population)

Sex of student and family income	All high school seniors	Plan to attend college				May attend college				Do not plan to attend college				School plans not reported
		Total	Two-year college only	Four-year college only	Two-year and four-year college	Total	Two-year college only	Four-year college only	Two-year and four-year college	Total	Plan to attend vocational school	May attend vocational school	No vocational school plans	
Both sexes	3,276	1,580	213	859	507	791	230	58	502	796	179	125	492	110
Under $5,000	285	102	13	38	51	82	26	6	50	92	32	7	53	9
$5,000 to $7,499	265	82	11	35	36	74	16	3	55	104	24	27	53	5
$7,500 to $9,999	302	136	26	54	56	72	25	4	43	85	19	12	54	9
$10,000 to $14,999	793	331	67	144	119	213	65	18	130	224	37	48	139	25
$15,000 to $24,999	911	504	59	296	149	214	69	20	125	177	32	20	125	16
$25,000 and over	390	310	21	221	68	43	10	2	31	30	12	5	13	8
Not reported	330	114	16	70	28	93	20	6	67	84	22	6	56	39
Male	1,694	770	68	451	251	449	128	32	289	422	91	61	271	52
Under $5,000	172	56	5	23	28	54	16	3	35	56	20	3	33	6
$5,000 to $7,499	143	50	3	19	28	40	10	1	29	49	10	10	29	3
$7,500 to $9,999	136	54	8	20	26	41	12	-	29	38	7	6	25	3
$10,000 to $14,999	377	138	18	65	55	115	32	10	73	115	22	20	73	9
$15,000 to $24,999	487	253	22	160	71	121	38	18	66	103	16	12	75	9
$25,000 and over	186	145	6	110	29	21	5	-	16	16	6	3	6	5
Not reported	192	74	5	55	14	56	14	-	42	45	10	6	29	17
Female	1,583	809	145	408	256	342	102	27	213	373	88	64	221	58
Under $5,000	113	46	8	15	23	28	10	3	15	36	11	4	20	3
$5,000 to $7,499	122	32	7	16	9	34	6	1	26	55	14	17	24	2
$7,500 to $9,999	166	82	18	34	30	30	12	4	14	47	12	6	29	6
$10,000 to $14,999	415	192	49	79	64	98	33	8	57	109	15	28	66	16
$15,000 to $24,999	425	251	37	137	78	93	31	3	59	74	16	8	50	6
$25,000 and over	204	165	15	112	38	22	5	2	16	14	6	2	6	3
Not reported	138	41	12	15	14	37	5	6	26	39	12	-	27	21
PERCENT DISTRIBUTION														
Both sexes	100.0	48.2	6.5	26.2	15.5	24.1	7.0	1.8	15.3	24.3	5.5	3.8	15.0	3.4
Under $5,000	100.0	35.8	4.5	13.4	17.9	28.8	9.2	2.0	17.5	32.3	11.1	2.6	18.6	3.1
$5,000 to $7,499	100.0	30.9	4.0	13.2	13.7	27.8	6.0	1.0	20.8	39.3	9.2	10.2	19.9	1.9
$7,500 to $9,999	100.0	45.2	8.7	17.8	18.6	23.7	8.1	1.3	14.3	28.1	6.4	3.8	17.8	3.1
$10,000 to $14,999	100.0	41.7	8.5	18.2	15.1	26.9	8.2	2.3	16.4	28.2	4.7	6.0	17.5	3.2
$15,000 to $24,999	100.0	55.3	6.5	32.5	16.3	23.5	7.6	2.2	13.7	19.4	3.5	2.2	13.7	1.7
$25,000 and over	100.0	79.5	5.4	56.8	17.4	10.9	2.5	0.4	8.1	7.6	3.2	1.2	3.2	1.9
Not reported	100.0	34.6	4.9	21.3	8.4	28.2	5.9	1.8	20.5	25.4	6.6	1.8	16.9	11.7
Male	100.0	45.5	4.0	26.6	14.8	26.5	7.6	1.9	17.1	24.9	5.4	3.6	16.0	3.1
Under $5,000	100.0	32.4	3.0	13.3	16.1	31.5	9.3	1.7	20.5	32.6	11.8	1.7	19.1	3.4
$5,000 to $7,499	100.0	35.0	2.4	13.3	19.3	28.2	7.0	1.0	20.2	34.6	7.1	7.2	20.2	2.2
$7,500 to $9,999	100.0	39.8	6.1	14.4	19.3	30.2	9.0	-	21.2	27.8	5.4	4.1	18.3	2.1
$10,000 to $14,999	100.0	36.6	4.8	17.2	14.6	30.5	8.5	2.7	19.3	30.4	5.8	5.3	19.3	2.4
$15,000 to $24,999	100.0	52.0	4.6	32.8	14.7	24.9	7.8	3.6	13.5	21.2	3.2	2.5	15.5	1.9
$25,000 and over	100.0	77.9	3.2	58.9	15.8	11.1	2.6	-	8.5	8.6	3.3	1.8	3.5	2.4
Not reported	100.0	38.3	2.4	28.6	7.2	29.3	7.5	-	21.8	23.4	5.0	3.2	15.2	9.1
Female	100.0	51.1	9.2	25.8	16.2	21.6	6.5	1.7	13.5	23.6	5.5	4.1	14.0	3.7
Under $5,000	100.0	41.0	6.7	13.6	20.7	24.6	9.1	2.5	13.0	31.7	10.0	3.9	17.7	2.7
$5,000 to $7,499	100.0	26.2	6.0	13.1	7.1	27.4	4.8	1.0	21.5	44.9	11.7	13.7	19.6	1.5
$7,500 to $9,999	100.0	49.5	10.9	20.6	18.1	18.3	7.4	2.3	8.6	28.3	7.2	3.6	17.4	3.8
$10,000 to $14,999	100.0	46.3	11.7	19.1	15.5	23.6	7.9	2.0	13.8	26.3	3.7	6.7	15.9	3.9
$15,000 to $24,999	100.0	59.1	8.6	32.2	18.3	22.0	7.4	0.7	13.9	17.4	3.9	1.8	11.7	1.5
$25,000 and over	100.0	81.0	7.3	54.9	18.8	10.8	2.4	0.7	7.7	6.7	3.0	0.8	3.0	1.5
Not reported	100.0	29.6	8.5	11.1	10.1	26.7	3.7	4.4	18.6	28.2	8.9	-	19.3	15.4

- Represents zero or rounds to zero.

Table 3. PLANS TO ATTEND COLLEGE OF HIGH SCHOOL SENIORS 14 TO 34 YEARS OLD IN PRIMARY FAMILIES, BY YEARS OF SCHOOL COMPLETED BY THE FAMILY HEAD: OCTOBER 1975

(Numbers in thousands. Civilian noninstitutional population. Excludes students in families whose head is a member of the Armed Forces, and students who are family heads or married, spouse present)

Years of school completed by family head	All high school seniors	Plan to attend college				May attend college				Do not plan to attend college				School plans not reported
		Total	Two-year college only	Four-year college only	Two-year and four-year college	Total	Two-year college only	Four-year college only	Two-year and four-year college	Total	Plan to attend voca-tional school	May attend voca-tional school	No voca-tional school plans	
ALL STUDENTS														
Total............	3,258	1,572	213	852	507	787	230	58	498	789	179	123	487	110
Elementary: 0 to 4 years........	59	25	3	5	18	17	3	-	14	10	1	3	6	7
5 to 7 years........	190	50	11	22	16	61	14	6	41	77	19	12	46	3
8 years.............	237	74	15	12	48	58	18	4	36	100	21	16	62	5
High school: 1 to 3 years........	603	215	50	89	77	173	42	11	119	194	38	32	124	21
4 years.............	1,153	498	88	249	161	302	92	23	187	300	72	45	183	53
College: 1 to 3 years........	390	236	27	129	79	83	35	5	43	64	14	12	38	8
4 years or more......	626	474	20	345	108	93	26	10	56	44	13	3	29	14
Percent Distribution														
Total............	100.0	48.3	6.5	26.1	15.6	24.1	7.1	1.8	15.3	24.2	5.5	3.8	15.0	3.4
Elementary: 0 to 4 years........	(B)	(B)	(B)	(B)	(B)	(B)	(B)	(B)	(B)	(B)	(B)	(B)	(B)	(B)
5 to 7 years........	100.0	26.0	5.7	11.7	8.7	32.2	7.4	3.2	21.7	40.2	9.7	6.3	24.1	1.5
8 years.............	100.0	31.4	6.1	4.9	20.3	24.3	7.4	1.6	15.3	42.2	8.9	6.9	26.4	2.1
High school: 1 to 3 years........	100.0	35.7	8.2	14.8	12.7	28.6	7.0	1.8	19.8	32.2	6.4	5.3	20.5	3.4
4 years.............	100.0	43.2	7.6	21.6	14.0	26.2	8.0	2.0	16.2	26.0	6.3	3.9	15.8	4.6
College: 1 to 3 years........	100.0	60.4	7.0	33.1	20.3	21.2	8.9	1.2	11.1	16.4	3.6	3.9	9.7	2.0
4 years or more......	100.0	75.7	3.2	55.2	17.3	14.9	4.2	1.7	9.0	7.1	2.0	0.4	4.6	2.3
MALE STUDENTS														
Total............	1,684	764	68	445	251	449	128	32	289	419	91	61	267	52
Elementary: 0 to 4 years........	38	18	3	-	15	15	2	-	13	4	1	1	1	2
5 to 7 years........	109	23	4	10	9	38	9	2	28	46	14	6	26	1
8 years.............	127	38	5	7	26	29	6	4	19	58	12	8	39	2
High school: 1 to 3 years........	320	113	22	42	49	105	27	7	71	90	15	12	62	13
4 years.............	549	210	21	124	66	158	45	9	103	153	29	28	96	28
College: 1 to 3 years........	203	111	5	66	41	51	23	5	24	37	10	3	24	3
4 years or more......	338	251	9	196	46	53	16	6	32	31	9	3	19	3
Percent Distribution														
Total............	100.0	45.4	4.0	26.4	14.9	26.7	7.6	1.9	17.2	24.9	5.4	3.6	15.9	3.1
Elementary: 0 to 4 years........	(B)	(B)	(B)	(B)	(B)	(B)	(B)	(B)	(B)	(B)	(B)	(B)	(B)	(B)
5 to 7 years........	100.0	21.4	4.0	9.5	7.9	35.0	8.0	1.4	25.6	42.3	13.2	5.3	23.9	1.3
8 years.............	100.0	29.9	3.6	5.9	20.4	23.0	4.8	3.0	15.1	45.9	9.6	6.0	30.3	1.2
High school: 1 to 3 years........	100.0	35.2	6.8	13.1	15.3	32.7	8.5	2.2	22.0	28.0	4.8	3.7	19.5	4.1
4 years.............	100.0	38.3	3.8	22.5	12.0	28.7	8.3	1.6	18.8	27.9	5.3	5.2	17.5	5.0
College: 1 to 3 years........	100.0	55.0	2.3	32.4	20.3	25.2	11.3	2.2	11.7	18.2	4.7	1.4	12.0	1.6
4 years or more......	100.0	74.2	2.6	58.0	13.6	15.7	4.6	1.7	9.4	9.2	2.8	0.8	5.6	0.9
FEMALE STUDENTS														
Total............	1,574	808	145	407	256	338	102	27	209	370	88	63	220	58
Elementary: 0 to 4 years........	21	8	-	5	3	3	1	-	1	6	-	1	4	5
5 to 7 years........	81	26	6	12	8	23	5	5	13	31	4	6	20	1
8 years.............	109	36	10	4	22	28	11	-	17	41	9	9	24	3
High school: 1 to 3 years........	282	103	28	47	28	68	15	4	49	105	23	20	61	8
4 years.............	605	288	67	126	95	144	47	14	84	147	44	17	87	25
College: 1 to 3 years........	187	124	23	64	38	31	12	-	20	27	4	9	13	4
4 years or more......	288	223	11	149	62	40	11	4	25	13	3	-	10	11
Percent Distribution														
Total............	100.0	51.3	9.2	25.9	16.3	21.5	6.5	1.7	13.3	23.5	5.6	4.0	14.0	3.7
Elementary: 0 to 4 years........	(B)	(B)	(B)	(B)	(B)	(B)	(B)	(B)	(B)	(B)	(B)	(B)	(B)	(B)
5 to 7 years........	100.0	32.2	7.9	14.7	9.6	28.5	6.5	5.5	16.4	37.4	5.1	7.8	24.5	1.8
8 years.............	100.0	33.1	9.1	3.9	20.1	25.9	10.4	-	15.5	37.8	8.1	8.0	21.7	3.2
High school: 1 to 3 years........	100.0	36.3	9.8	16.7	9.8	24.0	5.2	1.4	17.3	37.0	8.2	7.1	21.7	2.7
4 years.............	100.0	47.6	11.1	20.8	15.8	23.9	7.8	2.2	13.9	24.3	7.2	2.8	14.4	4.1
College: 1 to 3 years........	100.0	66.4	12.0	34.0	20.3	16.7	6.3	-	10.5	14.5	2.4	4.9	7.2	2.4
4 years or more......	100.0	77.5	3.9	51.9	21.7	13.9	3.8	1.5	8.6	4.6	1.2	-	3.5	4.0

- Represents zero or rounds to zero.
B Base less than 75,000.

Table 4. PLANS TO ATTEND COLLEGE OF HIGH SCHOOL SENIORS 14 TO 34 YEARS OLD IN PRIMARY FAMILIES, BY MAJOR OCCUPATION GROUP OF FAMILY HEAD: OCTOBER 1975

(Numbers in thousands. Civilian noninstitutional population. Excludes students in families whose head is a member of the Armed Forces, and students who are family heads or married, spouse present)

Major occupation group of family head	All high school seniors	Plan to attend college				May attend college				Do not plan to attend college				
		Total	Two-year college only	Four-year college only	Two-year and Four-year college	Total	Two-year college only	Four-year college only	Two-year and four-year college	Total	Plan to attend vocational school	May attend vocational school	No vocational school plans	School plans not reported
Total...........................	3,258	1,572	213	852	507	787	230	58	498	789	179	123	487	110
In civilian labor force................	2,886	1,434	192	799	443	677	203	48	427	688	149	111	428	88
Employed...........................	2,784	1,394	185	775	434	647	199	47	401	656	143	109	404	86
Professional, tech., & kind. wkrs..	428	299	17	203	78	78	27	6	45	40	14	6	20	11
Managers and admin., exc. farm.....	485	325	36	205	84	84	21	9	54	65	18	8	40	11
Clerical and kindred workers.......	210	105	9	57	39	53	13	8	31	48	13	12	23	4
Sales workers.....................	184	100	10	61	29	38	15	1	22	37	7	10	20	8
Craft and kindred workers..........	571	223	43	105	76	156	60	9	87	167	27	23	117	25
Operatives, except transport.......	264	104	31	41	32	66	17	3	46	83	15	14	54	11
Transport equipment operatives.....	158	62	11	23	28	34	9	1	23	61	9	14	38	-
Farmers and farm managers..........	107	49	6	28	15	18	3	1	13	41	16	2	23	-
Farm laborers and supervisors......	29	10	-	4	5	11	3	-	8	9	1	-	7	-
Laborers, except farm..............	123	29	6	14	9	50	13	3	34	39	4	10	24	5
Service workers, exc. private hshld	219	87	16	32	39	57	14	5	38	64	17	11	36	11
Private household workers..........	7	1	-	1	-	3	3	-	-	2	1	-	1	-
Unemployed........................	102	40	7	24	9	30	3	2	25	31	5	2	24	1
Not in labor force....................	372	138	21	53	65	109	28	10	72	101	30	12	59	23
PERCENT DISTRIBUTION														
Total...........................	100.0	48.3	6.5	26.2	15.6	24.2	7.1	1.8	15.3	24.2	5.5	3.8	14.9	3.4
In civilian labor force................	100.0	49.7	6.7	27.7	15.3	23.5	7.0	1.7	14.8	23.8	5.2	3.8	14.8	3.0
Employed...........................	100.0	50.1	6.6	27.8	15.6	23.2	7.1	1.7	14.4	23.6	5.1	3.9	14.5	3.1
Professional, tech., & kind. wkrs..	100.0	69.9	4.0	47.4	18.2	18.2	6.3	1.4	10.5	9.3	3.3	1.4	4.7	2.6
Managers and admin., exc. farm.....	100.0	67.0	7.4	42.3	17.3	17.3	4.3	1.9	11.1	13.4	3.7	1.6	8.2	2.3
Clerical and kindred workers.......	100.0	50.0	4.3	27.1	18.6	25.2	6.2	3.8	14.8	22.9	6.2	5.7	11.0	1.9
Sales workers.....................	100.0	54.3	5.4	33.2	15.8	20.7	8.2	0.5	12.0	20.1	3.8	5.4	10.9	4.3
Craft and kindred workers..........	100.0	39.1	7.5	18.4	13.3	27.3	10.5	1.6	15.2	29.2	4.7	4.0	20.5	4.4
Operatives, except transport.......	100.0	39.4	11.7	15.5	12.1	25.0	6.4	1.1	17.4	31.4	5.7	5.3	20.5	4.2
Transport equipment operatives.....	100.0	39.2	7.0	14.6	17.7	21.5	5.7	0.6	14.6	38.6	5.7	8.9	24.1	-
Farmers and farm managers..........	100.0	45.8	5.6	26.2	14.0	16.8	2.8	0.9	12.1	38.3	15.0	1.9	21.5	-
Farm laborers and supervisors......	(B)	(B)	(B)	(B)	(B)	(B)	(B)	(B)	(B)	(B)	(B)	(B)	(B)	(B)
Laborers, except farm..............	100.0	23.6	4.9	11.4	7.3	40.7	10.6	2.4	27.6	31.7	3.3	8.1	19.5	4.1
Service workers, exc. private hshld	100.0	39.7	7.3	14.6	17.8	26.0	6.4	2.3	17.4	29.2	7.8	5.0	16.4	5.0
Private household workers..........	(B)	(B)	(B)	(B)	(B)	(B)	(B)	(B)	(B)	(B)	(B)	(B)	(B)	(B)
Unemployed........................	100.0	39.2	6.9	23.5	8.8	29.4	2.9	2.0	24.5	30.4	4.9	2.0	23.5	1.0
Not in labor force....................	100.0	37.1	5.6	14.2	17.5	29.3	7.5	2.7	19.4	27.2	8.1	3.2	15.9	6.2

- Represents zero or rounds to zero.
B Base less than 75,000.

U.S. Bureau of the Census, Current Population Reports, Series P-20, No. 299. "College Plans of High School Seniors: October 1975." U.S. Government Printing Office, Washington, D.C. 1976.

Melting pot vs. cultural pluralism

Educating for a "New Pluralism"

In 1909, an educator wrote that a major task of education in American cities was to "break up these (immigrant) groups or settlements, to assimilate and amalgamate these people as part of our American race, and to implant in their children, so far as can be done, the Anglo-Saxon conception of righteousness, law and order, and popular government. . ."

Sixty years later, the Congress of the United States passed the Ethnic Heritage Studies Act, giving official "recognition (to) the heterogeneous composition of the Nation and the fact that in a multiethnic society a greater understanding of the contributions of one's own heritage and those of one's fellow citizens can contribute to a more harmonious, patriotic and committed populace. . ."

What brought about this ideological switch? Does the change in talk about American society reflect reality or just rhetoric? Do we really mean that the "melting pot" concept has been replaced, or have we just exchanged the slogan of "cultural pluralism" for earlier images without changing the reality? How are these ideas reflected in our schools, in what our children learn?

This report examines these and related questions. It looks at theory and practice; at past, present, and future; and it attempts to offer practical responses to the multiethnic reality of American life. It focuses on schools as instruments for making American pluralism work.

RENEWED INTEREST IN ETHNICITY

During the first quarter of this century, there was considerable interest in ethnic groups. After all, America had absorbed an incredibly large number of immigrants, and the task of molding these disparate groups into one nation was a difficult one. Many studies were done and many organizations formed to help ethnic groups in their transition to American-ness. On the surface they seemed successful: people did learn English, become citizens, and adopt "the Anglo-Saxon conception of righteousness."

The world wars and the Depression that separated them, the economic boom following World War II, and the suburbanization stage of metropolitan development in the '50s all contributed to a greater emphasis on the forces that unified people with a lesser emphasis on ethnic differences and distinctiveness. "Intergroup relations" concentrated on Blacks as the largest left-out group and emphasized legal desegregation, first of the Armed Forces, then of public schools, public accommodations, employment, and housing. The central intergroup issue was prejudice, and theorists concentrated on understanding those individual attitudes that resulted in discriminatory behavior.

But toward the late 1960s, two things happened that forced us to look at ourselves again as a multiethnic, not merely a Black-white, society. Even as the Kerner Commission reported in 1968 that "we are moving toward two societies, one Black, one white," it was becoming clear that among both white and non-white Americans, there was still considerable diversity. And while that report spoke eloquently and with necessary urgency about the needs of Blacks, it masked the degree to which there were still important unmet needs among segments of the white population as well. Social and economic needs and unresolved problems of ethnic group identity began to surface among Jews, Italians, Poles, Greeks, and other groups.

The first important influence on this new consciousness and expression was economics. In 1967, real purchasing power for blue collar workers declined, and the onward-and-upward success stories for the children and grandchildren of earlier immigrants seemed to be coming to an end. It no longer looked like the children could automatically go to college, with costs constantly rising. Nor did it seem that passing down an apprentice-ship in the union to one's son was a sure thing. The home that was finally purchased might become subject to real estate speculation and could lose in value, wiping out all the years of saving for it. Suddenly the American dream did not look as close to coming true as it once did.

At the same time that the economic squeeze began, another force sparked what might be called an "identity squeeze." The Black movement, focus of considerable public attention—if not adequate programmatic response—appeared to switch from a central integrationist thrust to one based on Black identity. This approach, combining power and culture, is still generating controversy, but it did gain legitimacy among some leaders of American opinion. A "my own group first" strategy looked like one which had the potential to pay off.

From the viewpoint of white ethnic groups, these changes in economics and identity expression, coming together as they did, might have communicated this message: "Here we were, taught by our parents and schools that in America everyone could make it, if we would only become real Americans and drop those elements that made us different. But now we see we are *not* making it, and the people who look like they are making progress seem to be doing it by emphasizing their identity, not by denying it. Maybe that's the way we should go, too."

This response has been described as reactive, as "me too," and as essentially opportunistic and false. For some, it may have been. But for many, especially the new generation of ethnic leaders, it was a real response. It was in part a sense that the requirement for success in America seemed to be an estrangement from family and history; that for all its rhetoric about pluralism, America didn't mean for ethnicity to go beyond the boundaries of food, a few statues or parades honoring heroes, or colorful costumes and dances.

For many individuals from ethnic communities, this new feeling about the importance of ethnic background took the form of questions rather than certainties. What does my history mean to me? How tied do I want to be to my family and neighborhood? How much do I know about where my grandparents and parents came from, or why, or what they went through? What does it mean to "be American"—is that some standardized image, and who set it up? How much am I, or have I become, just "white"? And—probably most important—what do I want to be? How do I arrive at a blending of my personal individuality, my family and cultural roots, and my American-ness?

One of the first places looked to for help in sorting out some of these problems was the school. The Black complaint against invisibility in curriculum was echoed first by Spanish-language groups, American Indians, and Asian-Americans. Then the protest was picked up by white ethnic groups, who realized that their parents and grandparents had been relegated to "huddled masses" and "wretched refuse from teeming shores" in the gospel of American history. Everyone now wanted to be included.

For schools, this naturally created great difficulty. When would there be time to teach anything else in American history if all these demands were met? Whose version of ethnic groups' stories would be told? What should happen in homogeneous ethnic classrooms, in mixed settings, or where students did not consider themselves ethnic? What did teachers have to work with in the way of material, and what training should they have in dealing with ethnicity?

Other social forces complicated things even more. Non-English speaking groups were discovered to suffer tremendous harm by the absence of sound bilingual programs. Women complained about educational materials and practices that perpetuated sex-typing and discrimination. Labor union leaders demanded more attention to working class history, as they felt that part of their younger members' rebellion grew from ignorance of labor's past struggles.[1]

For schools, there is a growing recognition that these forces— multiethnicity, feminism, and working class awareness—cannot be wished away. There is also an understanding that they can be educationally constructive if handled well, or fragmenting and narrowing if dealt with badly. A search is beginning for ways of responding to these complicated educational issues to help students learn to live in a genuinely pluralistic society.

ETHNIC IDENTITY—WHAT IS IT?

"Identity" is a word that has come to be used very loosely, usually paired with such other terms as "crisis" or "quest." "I am going through an identity crisis" is, in some college dormitories, as common a statement as "I think I'm getting the flu." But what the word means, or how schools can help a child to understand or define it, is far more difficult to pin down. We have a feeling about individual identity, that, like love, we will know it when we are face to face with it.

In a similar way, the word "ethnic" is much used and less clear. Some use it as a substitute for "Black" or "nonwhite"; others associate it with descendants of European immigrants. Time after time, people drawn together to discuss ethnic concerns raise questions of definition even though "we all know who and what we're talking about."

Ethnicity

Ethnicity is a concept that is extremely difficult to deal with because it has both conscious and unconscious elements. On the unconscious, descriptive level, ethnicity refers to a commonness of traits related to heredity and cultural influences. These traits may be physical, especially where the ethnic group has married within itself for a long time; they may be behavioral, such as gestures or other forms of "body language"; they may be emotional, such as reactions to pain; or they may be cultural, related to values such as the importance of family or education. In all of these cases, we need to add that ethnic background leads only to a *tendency* toward having any particular trait, a likelihood that is greater in one ethnic group than another, and not to a reliable prediction about any one individual.

Ethnicity is most often related to nationality and cultural background, including people bound together by "real or imagined common origin," as Andrew Greeley says. David Danzig's theories began to point to the inseparable influences of religion and national origin, and he preferred the term "religio-ethnic" as more accurate. And Milton Gordon coined the word "ethclass" to take into account the close correlation of ethnicity and economic background.[2]

Otto Feinstein's experiences with ethnic communities and curriculum led him to this definition of "ethnicity":

> *Ethnicity means peoplehood, a sense of commonality or community derived from networks of family relations which have over a number of generations been the carriers of common experiences. Ethnicity, in short, means the culture of people and is thus critical for values, attitudes, perceptions, needs, mode of expression, behavior and identity.*

Of course ethnic background is not the only influence on an individual's traits and behavior, and we do not know all we need to know about the precise nature of its impact. But we do know that ethnic background does distinguish between people at the values and behavioral level whether or not they themselves identify consciously with that background.[3] In other words, one does not have to "feel ethnic" in order to have one's actions and ideas influenced by that ethnicity.

Identity

Like ethnicity, identity has both conscious and unconscious elements. Some theories about the formation of identity say we are born with our essential personality directions; others say almost everything is learned from how important people in our lives react to us. In between is considerable variation of opinion around just what shapes identity and in what way. And the role of group influences on that identity—ethnic group, economic group, social group, or regional background—seems to be one of the least understood elements.

If we look at two of the important theorists of identity, we receive hints as to its dynamics: Erik Erikson, whose interest is in individual development; and Kurt Lewin, from social psychology. Erikson, looking back on his work in this field, says that the more he writes about identity, "the more the word becomes a term for something as unfathomable as it is all-pervasive."[4]. He quotes Freud as referring to "obscure emotional forces, which were the more powerful the less they could be expressed in words," when Freud talked about the influence of his own Jewish background. What Freud was sensing, in Erikson's view, was "a deep communality known only to those who shared in it, and only expressible in words more mythical than conceptual."

The language sounds more like mystery and poetry than science, and indeed, we know how uncooperative human beings are about fitting themselves into tight neat compartments of someone's theory. But Erikson does not leave his analysis at the level of intuition; he suggests just how important group background factors are in the total scheme of personal identity.

When he first used the term identity, Erikson says, he was referring to "a sense of personal sameness and historical continuity." In fact, he continues:

> . . . *We cannot separate personal growth and communal change, nor can we separate the identity crisis in individual life and contemporary crises in historical development because the two help to define each other. . .*

Social psychology offers more help in how to look at group identity, especially if we look back at the significant work of Kurt Lewin. Introducing a collection of Lewin's work, Gordon Allport summarizes the unifying theme: "The group to which an individual belongs is the ground for his perceptions, his feelings, and his actions."[5]

Lewin does not go deeply into the actual mechanism through which a group influences those who are born into it.[6] But from his years of working with individuals and groups, he is emphatically certain of the importance of groups in people's lives, and how many groups every individual is a part of.

> . . . *Every individual belongs to many overlapping groups: to his family, his friends, his professional or business group, and so on. He can be loyal to all of them without being thrown into a constant state of uncertainty.*

> *Not the* belonging to many groups *is the cause of the difficulty, but an* uncertainty *of belongingness.*

As Kurt Lewin looks at it, it is crucial that a person feel at home with his group affiliations; that he not, especially if he is a member of a minority ethnic group, undergo the experience of group self hatred. For people in many groups, avoiding this pitfall is difficult, since the institutions of the larger society (schools very definitely included) often act to discourage identification with ethnic background.[7] Not knowing which signals to follow, those of the "mainstream" society or those more "obscure emotional forces" of his own, the person can easily become confused and end up as what Lewin originally called a "marginal" person, feeling at home in neither setting rather than feeling comfortable in both.

> *Those marginal men and women* (Lewin says) *are in somewhat the same position as an adolescent who is no longer a child and certainly does not want to be a child any longer, but who knows at the same time that he is really not accepted as a grown-up. This uncertainty about the ground on which he stands and the group to which he belongs often makes the adolescent loud, restless, at once timid and aggressive, over-sensitive and tending to go to extremes, over-critical of others and himself.*

This analogy between someone with a marginal ethnic identity and an adolescent can be extended if we again look to Erik Erikson. He says all adolescents have certain problems to solve before their personalities become truly integrated and whole, and one of the main problems is the achievement of close relationships with others. It is not at all easy, Erikson says, for the adolescent to risk the still-fragile self that is in the making by offering it to others in relationships. Until a person is sure enough about that identity—sure of "the ground on which he stands"—he or she will remain confused and unable to deal with others.

Many ethnic groups, white and non-white, are in different stages of questioning their own identities. Jews debate the "who is a Jew" issue, Chicanos discuss the difference between identifying as "Chicano" or "Mexican-American," Poles still consider name changes, and many other examples exist of such uncertainty. One result of the confusion is, as Lewin and Erikson predicted, aggressiveness about themselves and great uncertainties in relationships with others.

Perhaps, according to this model, it is important for those committed to improved intergroup relations to be concerned with more than racism and other prejudices. There is a need to respond more creatively to the question of "who am I?" It is difficult to demand an understanding of other groups' needs and perceptions without some understanding of "my own."

Many of us, even when we come to understand the slippery concept of "ethnic identity," fear that a focus on differences will backfire, will produce fragmentation rather than better intergroup feeling. If we go along with the Lewin-Erikson analysis, we see that it is the avoidance of differences, pretending they do not exist, that generates confusion and conflict. If we can help children learn that "different" does not need to imply "better" or "worse"—admittedly, an extremely difficult task to accomplish—then the schools will be helping to create a new and vital American pluralism.

In his book *Dominated Man*, Albert Memmi sees the avoidance of difference as common to the racist and what he calls the "sentimental anti-racist." The racist assigns value judgments to real or overblown group differences, and of course values his own group more highly. In Memmi's view, "We must come around to recognizing certain differences among human beings and to showing that these differences are neither harmful nor scandalous."[8]

Pluralism and differences are sometimes seen as obstacles to national or even global unity. "We are all human beings," some insist and, "that should be our only allegiance." Even Erikson, though recognizing the fundamental impact of ethnic communal forces, puts ethnicity in the category of a "pseudospecies" which prevents the development of "an all-inclusive human identity." But in another place he also says, "I would characterize as too wide the identity of a 'human being'. . ."

It should not be necessary to choose between a narrow allegiance only to one's own group and an overly diffuse "human" identity which does not meet the need for a "ground on which to stand." It should be possible to develop a balance of identities. Every individual must have the right (legal, of course, but also in terms of freedom from pressure) to choose his or her life directions without ethnic background as a limiting factor. But a parallel right to be strongly attached to one's ethnic group should also exist, without the negative characterization our society puts on such attachment through use of such value-laden words as "parochial" or "narrow." And finally, along with those two rights, there must be an obligation on the part of people from all ethnic groups to work toward national unity in which all groups can participate. In short, we need to create a new ethic for America, a *pluralistic ethic* which balances the needs of the individual, the group, and the total society.

SCHOOLS AND CULTURAL VARIATION

Only part of the schools' role in bringing about a new pluralism will be accomplished by the curriculum. Other aspects will be more related to the school's values, the subtle messages and signals it gives to different groups, and the way it creates a "fit," a synchronization, between the school culture and the various cultures children bring into the school.

Achievement and Learning

Looking at the history of ethnic groups' relationships to the public schools, some historians are beginning to find that the great myth of schools serving as "engines of upward mobility" has not been equally true for all ethnic groups. From studies of achievement in the early part of the century and a few studies of ethnic mobility, it looks like an ethnic group "made it" into the middle class and *then* saw its children do well.[9]

Even today, there are differences among white ethnic groups as to how frequently the young people go to college. Sometimes these differences are equally related to the group's still being lower middle or working class. But how many schools that have noncollege-bound students mixed in among the total student body make these students feel that they are as important and as valued as those off to campus life after high school graduation?

Usually quite the opposite is true—students in vocational tracks or who are just lower achievers are more often relegated to a category known as "greasers." For them, schools are not pluralistic settings, in which their different achievement or career objective—or even they themselves—are equally valued. Many students from working class ethnic backgrounds who do go to college go with the feeling that they do not belong there. As one teacher put it, "They feel they are not worth educating."[10]

So being of working class origins often adds another kind of personal marginality, another dimension of group self-hatred, which often comes on top of the student's uncertainty about his ethnic background. And if the student is a girl, she has that sex-related dimension of identity to deal with as well, giving schools an extremely difficult but therefore more essential job to do in helping toward meaningful personal development.

What we know from research about differential ethnic achievement is still mostly speculation. One study suggests that some ethnic groups' backgrounds lead to a predisposition toward certain forms of learning over others. At the same socio-economic level, for instance, Jewish and Black children did better on measures of verbal skill and Chinese on tests of space conceptualization.[11] This is not to say, as we have already pointed out, that any one individual child should ever automatically be assumed to have certain skills; only that on the average he or she may be more likely to be stronger in one area or another.

Just as important as not using such data (if they are eventually supported by more research) to pigeonhole any particular child is what we need to learn from these studies about our standards of achievement. Are they pluralistic enough so that we can evaluate a student strong in space concepts as equal to one who excels in verbal skills? Or have we set up something of a hierarchy of skills and overloaded our judgments to favor one kind of learning (favoring particular ethnic groups) over others? And if this is the case, are schools subtly communicating to different ethnic children a sense of their place in the hierarchy?[12]

We do not know precisely how valid the few studies of group learning patterns are, and we know even less about the reasons behind those differences. One factor that is speculated about is the child's self-esteem, or his or her sense of security about identity. Most of the studies in this area pick up from the pioneering work of Kenneth Clark in the mid-Sixties, but they principally focus on Black-white differences in self-esteem, not on the relationship between a secure identity and school performance or learning. One research project that did include a measure of school achievement found that among the white students low achievement and low self-esteem went together but the researchers did not ask which came first.[13] They assumed that self-esteem was lowered by low performance; but might it not be the other way around? There is probably much information in studies of Head Start experiences, and it is hoped that similar work will be done in a number of ethnic communities and schools.

Behavior Styles

Schools can communicate to a child his or her worthwhileness in many ways and through many symbols. Some are obvious—

celebrations, food, posters, art work—but other "school symbolism" is less clear and perhaps even less available to conscious awareness.

The anthropological work of Fred Erickson contains fascinating clues as to how schools, as institutions of authority, can undermine self-concepts or promote them, through communications styles. His observations come from the perspective of Edward T. Hall[14] which includes such abstract terms as "kinesics" and more well-known ones such as "body language." Through watching the smallest units of behavior—walking, gestures, distancing or crowding close to others—Erickson concludes that ethnic background has a relationship to verbal and non-verbal communication styles. How much eye contact one needs to know another is listening, how often the other needs to say "uh huh" or "really?" to let us know he is still with the conversation, whether one looks an authority figure in the eye while being criticized, what kinds of gestures are appropriate, how much to touch another person—these seemingly automatic and often unconscious elements of communication, which according to Erickson vary with ethnic background, can make that communication suceed or fail. Would-be communicators, such as teachers and children, can be either "synchronized" with each other or "out of phase" and talking past each other.

Many of the specific culture-based characteristics are not yet uncovered by Erickson and others in this new field. But having questions to ask and a framework in which to observe, gives us a chance to redefine some of the possible inter-ethnic problems in a school. What might be expressed as behavior issues, prejudice, inattentiveness and unresponsiveness may, in reality, consist more of a conflict in communications styles, an unsynchronized pattern between two people. For instance, teachers from Northern European ethnic backgrounds may be uneasy when children from other backgrounds cluster very close together. "It always gives me the feeling they're about to start trouble," said one teacher. But for the children, this closeness may well be their own cultural pattern and if they are forced to sit quietly at tables a "safe" distance apart, their ability to learn may be impaired. These cultural influences, says Erickson, persist over many generations, after conscious ethnicity disappears.

The implications of this work, which needs further development, are that schools may need to tolerate many different behavior standards rather than insisting on just one. Communicating to children that their own patterns are acceptable, and at the same time maintaining basic ground rules that everyone can agree on no matter what their cultural background—that is the essential nature of a pluralistic system, and such a school setting would be a living example of a pluralistic society.

The schools' role in bringing about a "new pluralism" includes many noncurricular aspects. First, the need for effective ethnic role models represented by a diverse teaching and administrative staff should be recognized. Educators must be tolerant of the stormy emotional nature of group identity and allow for a commitment to choice of identities and group loyalties, which may well shift with events and pressures and needs. Allowance must be made not only for differences among and between ethnic groups, but also differences in career and educational objectives and achievement that may be related to social class and sex as well as to ethnic background. Educators must recognize the subtle signals that a school may inadvertently be giving to different groups through inadequate understanding of hidden aspects of difference and do something about this problem.

THE CURRICULUM AS PROMOTER OF PLURALISM

There are, of course, curriculum decisions that directly affect ethnic awareness, knowledge and identity. In the next section of this collection. Philip Rosen elaborates a number of possible approaches to this curriculum area, based on examples of work under way throughout the country. He looks at programs that relate to multiethnicity as well as to single group ethnic identity, and his findings and suggestions emphasize a concern for the neglected area of white ethnic studies. The most important aspect of his paper is the variety of ways school leadership can look at what is generally called "ethnic studies."

Rosen's teaching experience in an ethnically mixed Philadelphia school has led him to pay particular attention to teaching strategies that go beyond an emphasis on ethnic heroes (even though such an emphasis may be one important element in a program). In stressing broader approaches, he is heeding warnings of Erik Erikson, who says:

> Identity . . . contains a complementarity of past and future both in the individual and in society: it links the actuality of a living past with that of a promising future. Any romanticizing of the past or any salesmanship in the creation of future "postures" will not fill the bill.

According to Rosen's framework, there are numerous questions to ask when we look at ethnic studies programs: What content is covered, both in terms of groups studied and approach used? Are courses separate or incorporated into existing curricula? Are they mini-courses or do they run throughout a semester or year? What is the balance of cognitive and affective, emotion-based learning?

In looking at groups covered by ethnic studies courses now being taught, Rosen finds most are mono-cultural, or single-group. Some take what he calls a "human relations," or anti-prejudice, approach. Others subsume ethnic studies under what really are bilingual programs, which may or may not include a bicultural component. And a few take the approach Rosen favors of cross-cultural, multiethnic content, that includes teaching concepts basic to an understanding of pluralism as well as conveying comparative data about various groups.

Different disciplines can be brought to bear on any one of these approaches. History is most commonly used, but there are also programs incorporating a psychological dimension, some that emphasize socio-economic and socio-political factors (usually including a study of group conflicts), and some that emphasize the strictly cultural level of ethnicity in the narrow meaning of the term (i.e., costumes, foods, music, art, etc.). Many courses consist of a combination of disciplines, especially those that are multiethnic.

Rosen discusses the advantages and disadvantages of structuring ethnic curriculum as a separate course, whether of long or short duration, as against a more integrative, incorporative strategy of curriculum building. The latter type of program might make ethnicity more "normal," less in the realm of the exotic, and could contribute toward adding substance and depth to existing courses even when few ethnic children are in the classroom. And this can be quite important in helping prepare all of our young people to live in a more honestly pluralistic America.

The degree to which ethnic studies courses contain cognitive material, whether in the traditional didactic teaching method or the newer inquiry-based methods, and how much they are oriented toward the affective, more emotion-related elements is the last dimension Rosen describes. He feels that affective considerations are quite important, and indeed if we look back to the discussion of Erikson and Lewin, we can see just how important they become. Such approaches do not have to replace content, but they can make content all the more exciting and meaningful to the child.

Rosen's discussion of these ideas is intended to help schools clarify their thinking around ethnic studies and group identity curriculum design, so that new programs do not become mere responses to political pressures, educational trends, or the availability of federal funds. For, as a recent statement by the American Association of Colleges for Teacher Education recognized, education for pluralism can strengthen the entire system. In part, their statement says:

> Multicultural education rejects the view that schools should seek to melt away cultural differences or the view that schools should merely tolerate cultural pluralism. . . . Cultural pluralism is a concept that aims toward a heightened sense of being and wholeness of the entire society based on the unique strengths of each of its parts. . . . To accept cultural pluralism is to recognize that no group lives in a vacuum—that each group exists as part of an interrelated whole. . . . Schools and colleges must assure that their total educational process and educational content reflect a commitment to cultural pluralism. [15]

The stated commitment of the teachers' colleges is heartening, since, as Philip Rosen concludes in his paper, teachers are often inadequately prepared to deal with ethnic issues in curricular and noncurricular aspects of school life. But at least, as Rosen's listing of programs and resources indicates, each teacher and each school system does not have to start from the very beginning.

THE NEED FOR MORE RESOURCES: STATE PROGRAMS

Much new work in the field of group identity studies has been stimulated by the discussion and the passage of the Ethnic Heritage Studies Act of 1972. The enthusiasm and the scope of applicants for the first round of appropriations showed how ridiculously underfinanced the original Congressional appropriation of $2.5 million was. Nevertheless the passage of the Act catalyzed a great deal of new thinking and program planning. It would be a lost opportunity if this planning were allowed to stop just because the small first-year federal appropriation could not meet the scope of requests. Other resources must be found.

In our final section, we look at state Legislatures as potential sources of additional leadership and money in this area. We find that many states have statutes and policy statements that use language suggesting a multiethnic approach to pluralism, but that much of the implementation is limited to meeting (however inadequately) the complaints of the more vocal minorities. In two cases, Hawaii and California, the resolutions are inclusive enough to incorporate attention to working class concerns, trade unions, and women's activities along with a mandate for multiethnic education.

Most educational legislation stems from the state level, either in the form of required course content or allowable subject matter. Some states require teacher training in multiethnicity, some set standards for classroom materials, and others list those groups within the state whose histories are to be included in curricula. But only as educators and ethnic leaders have begun to press for specific state-level approaches to ethnic studies have bills been introduced to establish specific departments and/or allocate funds for program development.

There are many models for state activity in the group identity field, and the final section of this report concludes with a checklist of possibilities. The question of state support for ethnic studies programs, especially if they are conceived as broadly as the Hawaii and California laws, has potential as an excellent coalition issue. White and non-white ethnic groups, educators, intergroup relations organizations, parents, researchers, union leaders, feminists, community resource institutions like museums and historical societies, even mental health professionals concerned over the enhancement of identity—all these groups can unite around a constructive role by state leadership in this area.

CONCLUSION

In the mid-Sixties, the American Jewish Committee published "The Shortchanged Children of Suburbia," a report on suburban schools' failure (or inability) to teach children about "human differences." Based on a research project by Dr. Alice Miel, then at Columbia Teachers College, "Shortchanged Children" concluded that America's youngsters were being taught a homogenized, artificial view of American life and American groups. One standard of behavior—"whether a person is clean and nice"—predominated, and even elementary information about Blacks was absent from the curriculum and the children's consciousness.

Since then, there have been significant changes and solid progress in some school systems. The currents of the late 1960s left few school systems untouched; new textbooks and supplementary materials have been published; new courses have been added to teachers' training. But how much these new approaches, designed to remedy Black and other non-white minorities' invisibility or distortion, "took" with the students—that is difficult to say. For many whites, especially those only a generation or two removed from a Southern or Eastern European background, the result of these programs was a question—"What about me?"

Ethnic, really multiethnic, ferment is now accepted as part of the 1970s social climate. Our cliches have changed; few people extol the melting pot terminology any more, even though many undoubtedly still wish it had worked. But now the difficult task is just beginning, especially in the schools. How do we go from a society where differences were ignored or even denied, to a nation aware of its diversity and its problems but not paralyzed by the complexity of either? How do we teach that "different" need not mean "better" or "worse?" How, in teaching, do we help define the nature of today's and tomorrow's new pluralism?

Footnotes

Educating for a "New Pluralism"

1. For a detailed look at one group affected by a combination of these forces, working class ethnic women, see Nancy Seifer, *Absent From the Majority: Working Class Women in America* (New York: National Project on Ethnic America, 1973).

2. See Andrew Greeley, *Why Can't They Be Like Us?* (New York: Institute of Human Relations Press, American Jewish Committee, 1969); Milton Gordon, *Ethnicity in American Life* (New York: Oxford University Press, 1964); and David Danzig, "The Social Framework of Ethnic Conflict in America," in Murray Friedman, ed., *Overcoming Middle Class Rage* (Philadelphia: Westminster Press, 1971).

3. Some examples of this ethnic influence are contained in Irving Levine and Judith Herman, "The Life of White Ethnics," *Dissent* (Winter 1972).

4. This and subsequent quotations are from Erik Erikson, *Identity: Youth and Crisis* (New York: W.W. Norton, 1968).

5. Kurt Lewin, *Resolving Social Conflicts* (New York: Harper and Row, 1948).

6. For a more detailed look at the psychological theories involving socialization and the relationship among ethnic group, family and individual development, see Joseph Giordano. *Ethnicity and Mental Health* (New York: National Project on Ethnic America, 1973).

7. See Philip Perlmutter, "Ethnic Education: Can It be Relevant," reprinted by the Institute on Pluralism and Group Identity from *Massachusetts Teacher.* This article contains brief historical examples of how educators have explicitly rejected affiliation with ethnicity. Additional historical examples can be found in two recent books: Stanley Feldstein and Lawrence Costello, ed., *The Ordeal of Assimilation* (New York: Doubleday Anchor, 1974); and Joseph Ryan, ed., *White Ethnics: Their Life in Working Class America* (Englewood Cliffs, N.J.: Prentice-Hall Spectrum Books, Fall 1974).

8. Albert Memmi, *Dominated Man* (New York: Orion Press, 1968).

9. See Colin Greer, *The Great School Legend* (New York: Viking Press, 1972); and David K. Cohen, "Immigrants in Schools," *Review of Educational Research.* Vol. 40 (February, 1970).

10. For an excellent description of teaching such students, see Leonard Kriegel, "When Blue Collar Students Go to College," *Saturday Review* (July 22, 1972), from his book *Working Through* (New York: Saturday Review Press, 1972).

11. Gerald Lesser and Susan S. Stodolsky, "Learning Patterns in the Disadvantaged." *Harvard Educational Review.* Vol. 37 (Fall, 1967).

12. For observations from a primarily Polish school setting, see Howard F. Stein, "Confirmation of the White Ethnic Stereotype," *School Review.* Vol. 82 (May, 1974).

13. Morris Rosenberg and Roberta G. Simmons, *Black and White Self-Esteem: The Urban School Child* (Washington, D.C.: American Sociological Association—Rose Monograph Series, 1971). This report also summarizes other self-esteem studies of the 1960s.

14. See Edward T. Hall, *The Silent Language* (New York: Fawcett, 1969); and *The Hidden Dimension* (New York: Doubleday, 1969).

15. The full statement is published in the *Bulletin* of the American Association of Colleges of Teacher Education (Washington, D.C., November, 1972).

The Schools and Group Identity. "Educating for a New Pluralism" by Judith Herman, Institute on Pluralism and Group Identity — American Jewish Committee, New York, NY. October 1974.

Problems and Promises of Urban Public Schools

by Frank Brown

The struggle for survival in the United States has always been difficult for the poor and even more difficult for minorities. In this country, each participant in the game of life is supposed to be guaranteed an equal chance to play the game. This guarantee came via federal, state and, finally, local legislation. However, if one views the whole sphere of human activities, education has the clearest legislated mandate. Each citizen has a right to a free public education. Federal, state and local laws are less clear on other areas of human life, such as economics and social welfare. Evidence also suggests that minorities have not been given an equal chance to maximize educational opportunities in this country.

It is clear that through legislative Acts and judicial interpretation of those Acts quality education is viewed as a right and a necessity for life in a modern society. Public schools are institutions mandated by law with the responsibility of providing American youth with equal and quality education.[1]

Urban public schools offer several benefits to the public education system. First, these schools include a wide diversity of racial, ethnic, and socio-economic classes that reflect the total society. This diversity offers urban schools an opportunity to teach students to respect people of different races, cultures and economic classes. Second, with the large proportion of children of the poor that are concentrated in urban schools, these institutions present an excellent opportunity to concentrate resources and trained manpower on special problems that might be associated with children from poor families.[2] Third, urban schools represent an opportunity to tap a huge pool of underdeveloped human resources. Fourth, urban schools are of critical importance to minorities, especially Black and Puerto Rican Americans, because of the huge concentration of Blacks and Puerto Ricans in urban centers. The implication is clear—if the quality of urban schools are good, then most minorities will receive a good education.

Finally, urban schools may serve as a major economic source for minorities and the poor. In many communities, the local school budget represents the single largest budget in the community. The budget is more important when one considers the fact that approximately 90.0 per cent of the budget is distributed as salary.

---

[1]*Brown vs Board of Education of Topeka*, 347 US 483 (1954); and *Serrano v. Priest*, 96 California Rptr. 601 (1971).

[2]Even though it is implied through Title I of ESEA and many articles on the "disadvantaged" that children of the poor need special resources in order to catch up to the children of the well-to-do, it must be stated that educational disadvantages may be a poor school rather than a poor home life.

In short, several important ways in which the schools may serve the community are: (1) to teach basic skills to children; (2) to provide the proper socialization for students via appropriate curriculum and role models (the presence of professionals who are from minority groups); and, (3) to provide a viable source of employment and income for the community.[3] There are several aspects of school life and politics of which the minority community ought to be aware. These include racial integration, equalization of school finance, employment of minority teachers and administrators, the training of school personnel, the politics of education, school employee organizations, educational research and evaluation, Title I of ESEA, and community control.[4] The reader must keep in mind that the issue is quality education and the above items, such as racial integration and community control, are merely means toward that end. Evidence of action taken by local, state, and the Federal Government suggests that very little may be expected from those units to improve urban education on their own accord. Legislative bodies, whether local, state, or federal, have not moved to improve education except where forced to do so by court mandates and community pressure. Even when faced with court mandates, legislative bodies have devised countless schemes to circumvent these mandates. In other words, favorable remedies by local school boards, state legislatures, and the Federal Government are not expected for some time. The major legal responsibility, however, rests with the state legislature, not with local school boards or the Federal Government.

RACIAL INTEGRATION

The 1954 decision of the U.S. Supreme Court in the case of *Brown* vs *Board of Education of Topeka, Kansas*, terminated one hundred years of efforts by Black Americans to achieve quality education for their children. Despite the shortcoming of the Court's decree—failure to order schools to integrate immediately and set guidelines for racial integration—the decision was of monumental importance, first, in breaking down the wall of physical and psychological isolation between the races that produced among Blacks a feeling of inferiority and dispair; second, in opening the doors for the elimination of racial barriers in other areas of public life; and, third, in producing among Blacks a hope for a new way of life in the United States. The results of implementing the 1954 Supreme Court decision indicates that racially integrated schools may not represent quality education unless safeguards are defined and imposed. Blacks in integrated schools may actually receive education that is inferior to that provided in a segregated school.

Regarding the proposition that racially integrated schools may

---

[3]The term "community" as used here refers to minority individuals rather than to physical space.
[4]These issues will not be treated in great detail here. Readers who desire more detail information are encouraged to review textbooks available on the various topics, such as: M. Fantini (ed.), *Community Control and the Urban Schools* (New York: Praeger Publishers, 1970); and H. Levin, *Community Control of Schools* (New York: Brookings Institution, 1970).

not represent quality education, one has only to look at the attributes of schools that offer quality education, as defined by the American standard. Good schools are those that enroll students who score high on standardized reading and mathematics tests. Generally, good schools are well-financed and enroll students from a mixture of different social classes. Little or no improvement is expected in the quality of education for minority students who are integrated into a poorly financed school system that includes white students from poor families. Again, it must be emphasized that safeguards for minorities in integrated schools must be defined and implemented in order for integrated schools to offer opportunities for a quality education to minorities. Let us assume that the proposition that calls for well-financed schools and a mixture of different social classes have been met. School officials in integrated schools may use numerous schemes such as "tracking," special classes and programs to produce a school-within-a-school environment that is inferior to a segregated school. This conclusion also assumes that two-way busing may be necessary to achieve racial integration.

Finally, I am suggesting that, given safeguards, an integrated education is superior to a segregated one, based on the notions that racial isolation is not good for whites and minorities and that policy-makers, who are white, will make more resources available to schools that house their children. This brings us to the issue of school finance.

SCHOOL FINANCE

A major attribute of good schools is that of being well-financed.[5] Poor schools are generally poorly financed.[6] Further, urban public schools spend less money on schools than suburban schools. Beginning with the California Court Case, Serrano *vs* California, individuals concerned about equal educational opportunity are moving through the Courts to get more money for urban schools. Currently, several states have court cases pending regarding the equalization of school financing within the individual states. This process appears to be the most promising chance of improving the quality of urban education within the next decade. However, minorities must provide evidence that counters the argument that money does not make a difference.[7] It is difficult to rationalize such a conclusion since children from middle-class and wealthy families never have attended poorly financed schools in the United States and probably never will. Therefore, we never will know how wealthy children will perform in a poorly financed school. What about children of the poor attending well-financed schools? Again, there is little evidence that children of the poor

[5]*Fleischmann Commission*, (Volume 1; New York: Viking Press, 1973.)
[6]*Ibid.*
[7]J. Coleman, *Equality of Educational Opportunity* (Washington, D.C., U.S. Government Printing Ofrice, 1966); C. Jencks, *Inequality* (New York: Basic Books, 1972); Mosteller and Moynihan, *On Equality of Educational Opportunity* (New York: Vintage Books, 1972).

ever attended adequately financed schools. There is little or no evidence that urban youngsters attend adequately financed schools. Therefore, it seems impossible for researchers to draw the conclusion that there would be a difference in education in Harlem (New York) schools, where $1200 per pupil is spent annually, if $2800 were spent, as is the case with some suburban New York City schools. It is a "Catch 22" type question to which we will never know the answer unless the expenditures for the two schools are equalized. If money does not make a difference, give the children of Harlem $2800, and those of suburbia, $1200; then, return twelve years later and we may have an answer to the question, "does money make a difference?" Like racially integrated schools, safeguards must be made to insure that children of the poor who do attend wealthy schools are *not* placed in a "poor school within a school." Many researchers seem to assume that all pupils within a school (the poor, the minorities, and the wealthy) are treated equally—a mistake that renders many of their conclusions invalid and useless.

MINORITY TEACHERS AND ADMINISTRATORS

As stated earlier, schools should serve as a socializing agent through proper role models, and as an economic base. The employment of minority teachers and administrators may serve to do both. However, the employment of minority school personnel has slowed down in recent years. Several events have encouraged this trend. First, the integration of schools in the South has resulted in the reduction of Black teachers and administrators. Many whites feel that if they must accept integration, at least they can opt for white teachers. Unfortunately, many Blacks feel that white teachers are better than Black teachers. However, Black teachers in segregated schools produced the major portion of today's Black professionals.[8]

In the past, Black teacher candidates had only to deal with state legislative bodies which enacted laws that made it impossible to qualify for teaching positions. For example, in some states, college applicants were generally required to have completed extensive units in a foreign language in high school in order to gain admission. If Black applicants were lucky enough to finish college, the state required that they passed a culturally biased examination. If applicants passed the written portion of the examination, few made it past the oral portion of the exam.[9] Today, in many school districts, minorities find that their admission to the teaching profession and the regulation of their behaviors within the profession are guided by teacher-union and board of education negotiated contracts. In most cases, both employee organization and board of

[8]H.M. Bond, *Black American Scholars*, (Detroit: Balamp Publishing, 1972); and F. Brown, "Education and the Black Community: Some New Perspectives," *The Educational Forum*, November, 1973.

[9]For information on changes to tests, see: *Alternatives to Written Test; Judicial Mandates for Affirmative Action*, published by National Civil Service League, Washington, D.C.

education are white dominated, and may have interests that are in conflict with the interest of minority teachers and children.

Given an integrated system, minority teachers must feel free to seek employment in a wide variety of settings—integrated and segregated, urban and non-urban.

TRAINING URBAN SCHOOL TEACHERS AND ADMINISTRATORS

Teacher training institutions must do a better job of training teachers to function in urban schools. The most important aspects of that training should be to teach potential teachers to believe: (1) that minority youngsters are capable of a high level of cognitive development; (2) that minority students (and their parents) are interested in their education; (3) that good teaching can make a difference in the academic achievement of minority students; (4) to recognize racist traits that may be reflected in their teaching, i.e., "busy work," paternalistic behavior toward minority students, and lack of respect for minority culture and folkways; and most important, (5) to quit when one feels that he cannot relate to minority students. The above concerns apply equally to minority and non -minority teachers and administrators.

POLITICS OF EDUCATION

Nothing is more political than education. It is through education that individuals are screened to share in the wealth of this nation.[10] Education also means protecting the jobs of white professionals; the redistribution of tax dollars; giving poor children the same opportunities for life chances as the wealthy; setting the tone for determination of what is good, what is beauty, and valuable in this country; and a redistribution of economic and political power. The quality of elementary and secondary education also determines who gets an opportunity to share in society's acceptable form of welfare, such as government supported institutions of higher education, travel on tax supported airlines, and recreation at tax supported country clubs.[11]

Whether minorities realize it or not, when they seek quality education they are asking for social, psychological, and economic equality as well, and such demands are wholly political. The politics of education are intense at all levels of government—local, state, and national. Politics is the art of allocating resources; and, in today's world, education serves the function of sorting individuals into two camps, "the haves and the have nots." Unfortunately, too many minorities are sorted into the "have nots" category. Even though education is not the only route out of this category, it appears, at least for minorities, the most viable and promising way out.

---

[10]Jencks, op. cit; and P. Taubman and T. Wales, *Higher Education and Earnings: College as an Investment and a Screening Device* (New York: McGraw-Hill, 1974).

[11]Tax dollars for the poor are referred to as welfare, while tax dollars for the wealthy are called subsidy.

EDUCATIONAL EMPLOYEE ORGANIZATIONS

Teacher unions are late arrivals on the educational scene but they have emerged as one of the most powerful policy-making bodies in the history of employee organizations. Since teacher unions get their power from the state legislature, one may assume that they express the philosophy of the state on urban education. Otherwise, the states would curtail the powers of teacher unions to negotiate with boards of education. (States may or may not pass legislation regulating teacher unions.) Finally, teacher unions, whether minority or white control, are mainly concerned about the welfare of their membership. Therefore, the community must assume the major responsibility for the education of their children.

COMMUNITY CONTROL

Community control of public elementary and secondary schools is a political question. Because public education is a state function, not local or federal, the reader will need answers to several important questions in order to bring clarity to the community control issue. Will a white controlled state legislature turn over hugh urban school budgets to minotiry communities? Will state legislatures permit minority professionals to control the curriculum in urban schools and the teaching process? Will state legislatures adequately fund community controlled schools? Will state laws permit local communities to set personnel qualification standards and the passage of laws needed to deal adequately with teacher unions and other employee organizations? Community control, as viewed here, may involve racially integrated or segregated communities.

It must be remembered that community control, like integration, and other organizational remedies, are only means to an end. Politically, is community control a viable alternative? Politically, maybe; educationally, yes. White controlled state legislatures are not likely to react positively to the questions raised above. Can a city with a minority voting majority order community control for its schools. No. Schools are entities of the state. Local municipal officials have little or no control. For example, Black majority cities such as Newark, New Jersey, and Gary, Indiana (and both mayors are Black) have no real power over the public schools in those cities. In other words, if the residents of Newark desired community control (small local units), they would have to get permission from the governor and the state legislature. Black Mayor Kenneth Gibson would have little say in the matter. His authority to appoint school board members is delegated by the state and, as such, may be taken away by the state. Further, suburban legislators have moved into the urban school picture to protect teachers (suburban residents) and other professionals from local control. In New York State, when New York City and Buffalo enacted statutes requiring teachers to reside within those cities, the state passed a law prohibiting such local statutes. The future for effective community control is, indeed, bleak.

TITLE I

In 1965, Congress passed the Elementary and Secondary Education Act (ESEA) designed to give added help to poor and economically disadvantaged school children, generally referred to as compensatory education. That portion of ESEA that dealt with compensatory education was designated Title I. By passage of ESEA, Congress admitted that not all children in this country received quality education.

Title I of ESEA must be viewed from a relative perspective. That is, the education for the disadvantaged must be compared to relevant others, within the cities and in suburbia. Also, Title I must be viewed from a short term *and* a long term perspective.

Is Title I compensatory? No. Maybe a scenario will aid in explaining the non-compensatory nature of Title I. Let us assume that within Urban City U.S.A. there are many disadvantaged children and close by in Suburbia City U.S.A. reside many emotionally advantaged school age children. There are three groups or classes of school children: middle-class suburban, middle-class urban, and children of the urban poor. In terms of disadvantages, there are only two groups: the middle class (suburban and urban) and the poor. In other words, the middle class, regardless of geographical location, receives a high quality and high cost education, while the poor receives a low quality and low cost education. The Fleischmann Commission's study of education in New York City concluded that New York operated two sets of schools, one for the well-to-do and one for the poor.[12] In relative dollar amounts, the disadvantaged is still disadvantaged. ESEA requires that Title I schools receive from local districts no less than the "average" for non-Title I schools in the district. "Average" as used here does not refer to the mean cost, but to a compatibility average computed by the U.S. Office of Education. Therefore, theoretically, Title I schools should receive average (mean) district funding plus Title I funds. For example, a Title I school may receive $600 per pupil from local funds and $200 from Title I, making the total per pupil expenditure $800. This is the general public view of Title I, which is incorrect. The law states that Title I schools must be compatible with the average non-Title I school. Compatibility is defined in such a way that it eliminates cost of teacher experience from the formula. Therefore, it is possible for Title I schools to be judged compatible with non-Title I schools while receiving less than average (mean) funding ($600) from the local district. With this formula, a ghetto school with all inexperienced teachers where the cost per pupil is $400 may be judged compatible to a wealthy neighborhood school with all experienced teachers at a cost of $2,000 per pupil. This compatibility law is perhaps the most subtle form of racism ever en-

[12]*Fleischmann Commission*, (Vol. 2; New York: Viking Press, 1973).

acted by Congress.[13] Urban schools still spend more money for the education of the wealthy population.

From a short range perspective, Title I may be considered a success in getting a few dollars to depressed schools (not districts) and providing jobs for community people. From a long range perspective, it must be considered a failure; it never was allowed to work, nor was it compensatory. It retarded the drive for racially integrated schools; equity in school financing; and provided researchers with an inadequate data base which resulted in conclusions that Blacks are intellectually inferior, and that neither money nor schooling makes a difference in school success. We have allowed urban schools to fall victim to the Title I syndrome that provides for special teaching programs for the poor. The long term success or failure of Title I has nothing to do with whether or not these programs resulted in increased educational benefits for the poor.[14] Only the most naive viewer would expect significant educational gains from Title I programs. More than likely, Title I funds legitimized low expenditures for Title I schools.

EDUCATIONAL RESEARCH AND EVALUATION

Educational research and evaluation cannot be separated from school policies, school programs, educational finance, or school politics. When financially depressed urban schools sought more state and federal aid, policy makers used the findings of researchers to deprive them such aid. Researchers argued that, educationally, money does not make a difference in the ability of schools to deliver quality education. Yet, the poor remain in low cost schools and the middle class in high cost ones. When the poor demanded a better education and an accountability scheme to insure quality education, researchers argued that the lack of quality education was due to the intellectual inferiority of the poor.[15] Again, policy makers used these agruments to withdraw support of school accountability legislation. The above examples are given to remind the reader that educational research and evaluation is sometimes objective, sometimes subjective, sometimes rational, sometimes irrational, and often times political and racist.

SUMMARY

Urban schools are in need of drastic improvement. Yet, solutions to the problem cannot be long range. Unlike other areas of human life, elementary and secondary education once denied is

---

[13]Letter from U.S. Commissioner of Education indicated that teacher experience is not related to student achievement. (But good schools have more experienced teachers than poor ones.)

[14]A.H. Passow, *Compensatory Instructional Intervention*, in F.N. Kerlinger, *Review of Research in Education 2*, (Itasca: Illinois, F.E. Peacock Publishers, 1974).

[15]A. Jensen, "How Much Can We Boost IQ and Scholastic Achievement?" *Harvard Educational Review*, XXXIX (Winter, 1969), 1-123.

rarely recaptured.[16] While possession of a quality education is not a must for every individual to lead a happy and productive life, collectively, a group cannot afford not to fight for the best education possible. However, if we are permitted to refer to the average individual, a poor education is a road to hard times. The quality of one's education may determine his life earnings, his type of employment, his life style, his choice of a mate, his neighborhoood, his life span, his health and the destiny of his off-springs. In other words, education is fast becoming society's major sorting institution. By controlling one's level of education, society can regulate the allocation of life rewards. Even though race is a big factor in the United States, and there are always exceptions to the rule, education is the only factor over which individuals and their communities may exercise some control.

---

[16]F. Brown, *op. cit.*

"Problems and Promises of Urban Public Schools" by Frank Brown. The Journal of Negro Education. Vol. XLIV, Summer 1975, No. 3. p. 247-56.

I.Q. tests and minority children

Traditional tests of intelligence are inappropriate for minority children, particularly children of non-English speaking backgrounds. Such diverse groups as the National Education Association, popular press, courts, civil rights organizations, state and federal agencies and school psychologists have all pointed to the failure of the test publishing industry to fully consider the cultural and linguistic differences of minority children when constructing, publishing and selling tests.

Publishers have responded to this criticism by:

1. translating existing intelligence tests for non-English speaking children;
2. adjusting norms for ethnic sub-groups;
3. attempting to construct culture-free tests.

There are distinct problems with each of these approaches. In addition, there are problems concerning the basic validity and utility of information produced by IQ tests. A discussion of the inadequacy of the response of test publishers and a presentation of several other issues follows.

Translations

Translating existing intelligence tests for non-English speaking children often creates more problems than it solves. Regional differences within a language make it almost impossible to use a single translation. Thus, while the word "toston" refers to a half dollar for a Chicano child, for a Puerto Rican it refers to a squashed section of fried banana. Mono-lingual translations are also inappropriate because the language familiar to non-English speaking children is often a combination of two languages as in the case of "poncho" or "tex-mex". Furthermore, many non-English speaking children have never learned to read in their spoken language. One finds many examples of tests written in Spanish being given to Chicano children who may <u>speak</u> Spanish but have had no prior instruction in <u>reading</u> Spanish.

Another problem in translating tests is that the direct translation of a word or phrase in one language may result in a word which is not used with the same frequency or have the same potency in the second language. For example, the word <u>pet</u> is a common word in English. Its Spanish equivalent, <u>animal domestico</u>, is almost never used. Also, translating a word from one language to another can vastly alter its meaning, like the wide variety of seemingly harmless English words. which translate into Spanish swear words or "palabras verdes". Thus, translating a large egg into a "huevon" may satisfy grammatical requirements and seem harmless to a translator, but it has a more earthy connotation for Chicanos and Puerto Ricans.

Ethnic Norms

The second major response of the testing industry to criticism has been to establish or propose re-establishment of regional and ethnic norms; in other words, to "compensate" minority children for their "deprived backgrounds". Not only will such a practice lead to lower expectations for minorities (which, in turn, lowers children's aspirations to succeed), it is as shortsighted as awarding Chicano children extra points because "they speak a little Spanish." Ethnic norms take no account of the complex reasons why minority children on average score lower than Anglos on IQ, and they are potentially dangerous because they provide a basis for invidious comparisons between different racial groups. The tendency is to assume that lower scores are ultimately indicative of lower potential, thereby contributing to the self-fulfilling prophecy of lower expectations for minorities as well as reinforcing the genetic inferiority argument advanced by Jensen (1971) and others.

Furthermore, if test publishers and users are willing to consider the establishment of ethnic norms, similar arguments could be made for the establishment of norms based on sex differences as well. Considering sex and ethnicity would require an almost infinite set of different norm tables in order to account for all of the different ethnic subgroups in the United States. From the practical point alone this leads to an absurdity. Finally, the establishment of ethnic norms assumes that the groups are ethnically homogeneous with little or no cross-over or intermarriage. One might wonder what publishers would propose to do with a set of male/female twins who had a Mexican father and a Hungarian mother?

Culture-Free Tests

Another way in which the testing industry has responded to criticism of conventional IQ tests has been to create "culture-free" tests. Such tests are difficult, if not impossible, to construct. In tests of mental ability an attempt is made to determine the ability of a child to manipulate certain elements of a problem into a predetermined solution. But if all or some of the elements are not equally familiar to the child, the test is unfairly biased. The

influence of culture on conventional IQ test items is subtle in some cases, blatant in others. But the fact remains that in a large number of traditional IQ tests, the items are measuring something other than that for which they were designed. Items particularly influenced by cultural factors fall into the following general classifications:

Socialization. Items of this type are couched in such a way as to actually be measures of the child's family value system. The referent system is, of course, the dominant Anglo-American middle-class. The confounding effects of this problem are particularly evident in the "Comprehension" scale of the Weschler Intelligence Scale for Children (WISC) where children were asked such questions as:
"What is the thing to do if you lose your friend's balls? or "What is the thing to do if a fellow much smaller than yourself starts a fight?"
Allowing for the stilted manner in which the questions are phrased and assuming that the child knows all of the vocabulary, it still seems perfectly obvious that this type of question has little or nothing to do with a child's ability to process, manipulate and/or code information; the answers depend almost exclusively on whether a child has been socialized under the particular ethical system implied by the question.

Productivity or Level of Aspiration. Many tests confound what they hope to measure with a measure of productivity or level of aspiration. For example, in a large number of tests the child who produces the largest number of responses is rewarded while the child who stops responding after only a few attempts is punished by receiving a lower score. Thus, in the Draw-A-Man test the child who produces the more elaborate figure stands the better chance of receiving the higher score, the assumption being that all subjects will produce as many responses as they are able--that they all have the same level of aspiration.

Timed tests and "endurance" tests also fall prey to a confusion between the measurements of ability and the measurement of aspiration. In timed tests, which constitute the majority of published group tests, the children are asked to work quickly, quietly and efficiently without regard for the child who is simply not in a hurry and not particularly motivated to be so. The endurance test, for the purpose of boosting statistical reliability, requires that the child answer a large number of questions which vary little in content. This problem is particularly evident in group tests such as the Lorge-Thorndike and the California Test Bureau series. Similar to the "endurance" test is the test where items are sequenced in order of increasing difficulty. This design feature characterizes most of the standardized tests. In this situation the child is forced--by design--to encounter increasing levels of failure and frustration. In the case of the child who starts out fearfully, as do most minority children, the first indication of failure or difficulty is enough to discourage him or her from continuing and one finds the child "staring blankly off into space".

Experience or Specific Learning. In tests which require answers of fact, there is an implicit assumption that all the children taking the test will have had an even chance, more or less, of having been exposed to the facts being tested. The spuriousness of this assumption is witnessed by any number of examples where children are asked questions of vocabulary. In such instances, it is impossible to determine whether a minority child has missed a test item because he lacks the capacity to understand a given word or because he simply has never been exposed to the word. Nitroglycerin (in the WISC), fire hydrant (in the Betty Caldwell Preschool Inventory and Peabody Picture Vocabulary Test) or crevice (in the Otis-Lennon) are terms unlikely to be heard or used in the home of the average low SES or minority child.

The WISC, perhaps the most widely-used individually-administered intelligence test in the world, is replete with examples of the importance of specific experience on test results. Take the WISC "General Information" item, "In what kind of store do we buy sugar?" If a child lives on an Indian reservation, he might buy his sugar in a drug store or at a trading post. A Chicano child might reply to that question, "at the Chinitos", a small variety shop owned by a Chinese family. Yet these are not acceptable responses for credit in the WISC. Consider another WISC item, "Where is Chile?" What if a child eats chile, as a Chicano child might. Or consider the item, "What is the thing to do if you lose one of your friend's balls?" The acceptable WISC responses are "Give him one of mine. . . try to get it back or replace it. . .or try to find it." A probable reaction of a Barrio or inner city child (depending on the size of the other child) would be avoidance, to escape the child's anger. That is not to say that these kinds of experience-based items are only found in the WISC scale. They are examples of these kinds of biases found in almost all tests of intelligence.

The Validity and Utility of the IQ Score

The basic justification behind the use of the IQ score is that it statistically predicts to mental retardation and low achievement. In fact, the IQ test is the sine quo non for screening children suspected of mental retardation. Mercer (1971) found that of those persons who would have been labelled as mentally retarded if their classification depended solely on test scores, a full 84% had completed 8 grades or more in school, 83% had held a job, 80% were financially independent or a housewife, and almost 100% were able to do their own shopping and to travel alone. In other words, it is probable that even at the task for which experts agree the IQ test is best suited--screening for mental retardation--the IQ measure has a dubious real life validity.

The IQ test is also considered by many educators and politicians to be a useful instrument for teachers--for discovering unnoticed learning problems or intellectual strengths, for example. Indeed, many states mandate that districts administer IQ tests several times in a child's succession through the school system. But does the result really help the teacher? Let us take a typical example. A teacher suspects a child of having a severe learning disability. She asks the school or district psychologist to test the child. The psychologist gives the child the WISC in which he scores, let us say, an IQ of 87. This psychologist happens to be extremely conscientious, so he devotes the next few days to writing up an extensive report of his impressions of the child's performance and potential. The child comes from a poor background, the psychologist writes. He has many sibs and is low in the hierarchy with regard to getting attention. After much reviewing the child's school file and his own notes, the psychologist writes a report and hands it to the teacher. The teacher responds in surprise, "But I knew all that. What I want to know is what to do; how can I teach this child." Thus, in most cases neither the psychologist nor the teacher are any wiser despite considerable time and expense administering and evaluating the IQ test. In this situation the psychologist often finds him or herself in the middle of the delicate quasi political-social balance between the classroom teacher, the principal, the district administration, the child and his family.

While few psychologists would agree with the notion that educational decisions affecting the life of the child should be made exclusively on the basis of a single full scale IQ score, the fact nevertheless remains that these decisions are made by educators who, through personal fiat supported by state mandate, ignore both the individual subscale profiles as well as psychologists' admonitions, simply for the sake of practical expediency. The results is, of course, a form of default institutional racism.

Informational Needs Within the Educational System and the IQ Tests

Much of the controversy surrounding IQ tests and minority children focuses on whether the IQ model is a valid one. A more practical, and less abstract issue which needs to be answered concerns the general utility of the information produced by the test, i.e., what can one do with the information provided by such a test? In order to answer this question we must consider who is asking the question and for what purpose. It should be apparent that there are qualitative differences concerning the type of information needed within the educational system. These differences depend on the source of the need. To a large extent, much of the confusion surrounding the issue of whether to test stems from a failure to consider these differences. A consideration of the qualitative difference between these different needs will hopefully lend some clarity to the general controversy as well as serve to introduce a procedure that attempts to meet some of the specific needs of each.

There are three general levels of organization within the educational system that require information traditionally obtained through IQ testing. These three may be described as (1) the funding level which involves educational agencies supra-ordinate to the local school districts; (2) the local level which consists of both district personnel and building-principals and finally; (3) the classroom teacher, paraprofessional and parent. Whether or not the IQ score information can serve any ultimate useful function will depend on the particular and peculiar needs of each of these three groups. It is unfortunate that historically all three attempt to use the IQ score for radically different and often conflicting purposes.

Consider first the supra-ordinate funding agencies such as state and federal departments of education. For purposes of determining the allocation of funds, these agencies require information concerning educational and program needs at the school district level. While one source of information they generally use are IQ measures, one wonders whether the information produced by IQ tests

adds anything of value to needs assessment. More appropriate "needs assessment" procedures, it would seem, would be restricted to the assessment of whether specific educational programs in areas of reading, arithmetic or the like are needed rather than attempting to infer specific need from omnibus assessments based on so poorly understood a concept as IQ.

The supra-ordinate agencies have a second related informational need. In contrast to needs assessments which very often can be conducted through examinations of school attendance records, age-grade placement patterns and achievement data in the broad sense, funding agencies need to know about the effectiveness of particular programs.

Due to "accountability" and "evaluation/audit" requirements, the agencies chiefly responsible for the allocation of funds have mandated that testing be conducted at the child level as a means of collecting information which can be used to evaluate educational programs. In actuality, program evaluations can be made through a variety of means or procedures, none of which necessarily has anything to do with IQ or summary-score types of measures discussed above. For example, a reasonable assessment of program effectiveness can be made through the collection of nominal data at various levels of school and community organizations. Thus, administrators, teachers, parents and children can be interviewed as to their perceptions of the effectiveness of the different processes of the program. On the other hand, more product-oriented assessments, at the child level, can be made according to the specific educational objective of the program. The reporting of these latter data can be made on the basis of group change scores, without reference to individual scores, eliminating the potential dangers inherent in individual scores. Finally, all of the various data can be integrated to produce a report which describes the program and weights the relative importance of each aspect of the program in recommending changes in various parts of the total operation.

It is interesting to note that there is a paradoxical element in using IQ scores to evaluate program-related change. The paradox stems from the fact that the IQ model is based on the notion that intelligence is static and hence not subject to change. What this means is that educators have been using IQ scores to evaluate change which can not occur according to the IQ model. The IQ model, which negates time or age through the division of mental age by chronological age, is by definition a static model and, therefore, inappropriate for measuring program-related change which must take place over time.

At the local level, school district personnel need information as to the needs of children and the effectiveness of individual programs in the same way as do the supra-ordinate agencies. However, needs assessments are usually conducted at the state level and school officers more often than not use the state-provided information as a statement of need, preferring not to conduct detailed expensive in-house initiated research.

Ideally, the evaluation of individual programs should center around the collection of data which follows directly from the particular program objectives and activities. However, it is often the case that instruments of evaluation have very little to do with actual programs. Rather than program-specific measures, very often IQ or nationally normed achievement tests are used. Since IQ and other such scores provide precious little in the way of information about the effectiveness of individual programs and program components, there results great confusion in interpreting program evaluations. For example, in comparison with an appropriate "control group" suppose that children who participated in a special program on arithmetic computation had received higher scores on a group IQ score than they had the year before. With this type of evaluation officials would be hard put to say exactly which aspects of the program had led to the improved IQ scores since the connection between the two remains either ill-defined or nonexistent. However, in contrast, a test (administered before and after a specific program) which sampled from each of the different aspects of the program would provide specific information on which aspects of the program led to improved scores and which did not. In other words using IQ scores to evaluate programs not specifically designed for the purpose of elevating IQ scores is a little like using a thermometer to record height changes in a given period of time.

Unfortunately, the last to be considered in the educational heirarchy is the classroom teacher and what she needs in order to assist the learner. What can the teacher do with an IQ score? The limited utility of the IQ or for that matter any other summary score whether it be reading level according to grade equivalent score, grade point average, percentile rank or the like has already been discussed. Perhaps the fact that to a large extent the tests do not provide the teacher with much usable information is historically related to that fact that psychological tests were initially developed for purposes not functionally related to the present daily needs of the classroom teacher. It is also of some interest to note that even to the present day it is not the classroom teachers who either design the format of the information produced by the testing or, select the specific test or tests which are to be used.

There is still another way in which the use of IQ scores in the classroom might be questioned. Given it is possible to avoid the problems associated with adopting tests which employ the IQ model there is a final question at the teacher-level concerning the ultimate functional use of the IQ score. If it is given that the IQ score is an accurate index of the children in a classroom, then what? What a teacher is asked to do is to discriminate between scores in designing curriculum for each and every child on the basis of information which she can not discriminate. What would a teacher do differently for a child with an IQ of 92 that she would or would not do for a child with an IQ of 100? One might agree that these two scores are functionally equivalent because they are both within the normal range (i.e., within one standard deviation of the mean). However, what about the case of a child who has an IQ score of 84 which is approximately a standard deviation below the mean and in some states considered as possibly falling into "EMR", "retarded" or "slow learner" categories? In the one case where the comparison is made between 92 and 100 there would be no difference in educational recommendation, however, in the other case where scores of 92 and 84 are compared, very different educational recommendations would be made. In both cases there is the same absolute difference in scores.

The point is that we have been basing educational decisions on IQ tests which often produce questionable results. In many cases, the same criticisms apply to achievement tests which provide collapsed scores. Functionally, what programmatic difference can the teacher infer from scores provided in grade equivalent terms. What are the different educational decisions to be drawn from reading grade equivalency scores of 3.2 versus 3.6 and 3.6 versus 4.0? In the case of both the IQ score and the collapsed achievement score, the teacher, who is ultimately the person held "accountable", is simply not being provided with enough information upon which to base sound daily educational decisions, the teacher is thus by default forced to make arbitrary decisions which in most cases can not be defended. The fact that the tests have "predictive validity" in that they forecast failure on the part of Spanish-speaking or other minorities and success for the majority only speaks to the inappropriateness of the curriculum and to the failure of the American educational system to provide education for many of its children.

PAPI: A Piagetian-Based Alternative

In the following, a computer-based model will be described which was designed with many of the above concerns in mind. This model has been successfully tested in a variety of ways in three Southwestern and two Western states. The discussion provided below will outline the elements of the model. More substantive discussion concerning the psychometric features of the measures the model employs are subjects of several other articles currently in the journals or being prepared for publication.

The program Assessment Pupil Instruction (PAPI) system uses a number of Piagetian-based measures to generate two basic types of information by means of a centralized computer data-processing program.

The first type of information provided by the PAPI system is statistical in nature and is meant for program evaluation at the funding, administrative and district levels. The second type of information is oriented towards the needs of the teacher and consists of recommended activities specifically designed for each child in the classroom.

In its present form, PAPI uses four Piagetian-based measures developed jointly and individually by Pascual-Leone and DeAvila. Two types of measures are used. The first is used as a base measure of achievement where information is collected which follows from classroom activity. The second type of measure attempts to provide an index of the child's current level of development and involves three different tests.

In the following section, each of the four tests in the battery is described. The first to be described is the measure employed as the basic achievement index. The following three are used to provide an index of level of development. The description of the tests is followed by a more detailed detailed description of the PAPI system.

1. Cartoon Conservation Scales (CCS)

Several measures of Piaget's conservation tasks are assessed by means of a cartoon format developed by De Avila, Struthers and Randall (1969). In Avila's procedure, three horizontal cartoons are presented in which two children are discussing the task. In the first frame an equality is established between two objects according to the dimension being tapped (i.e., number, length, substance, etc.). In the second frame an identity transformation is depicted and in the third frame the question of equality is asked. On the right side of the panel three possible answers are presented in a vertical order. The three alternatives which show the characters responding to the question are randomly ordered as to correctness in order to avoid position effects. Similarly, within a scale wording is altered from panel to panel in order to avoid the possible effects of acquiescence. Background on the conservation scales and an illustration of the dialogue from each scale are presented below.

Struthers and De Avila (1967) and De Avila et al (1969) and others have validated the CCS procedure in a variety of ways. In one study De Avila, et al (1969) tested thirty male and female first grade subjects using both group and individual clinical methods. Statistically significant correlations were obtained across the two methods of assessment (r = 0.663). The scales also possessed a high degree of internal consistency as shown by an examination of factor analytic structure and reliability indices.

In its current form the CCS consists of thirty cartoon panels; six examples of five tasks. The panels are presented to the subjects and the story line is read and elaborated upon in order to facilitate understanding of the question. The subjects task is to mark the one (alternative) "that makes the story true."

2. Water Level Task (WLT)
The conservation of the horizontality of water described by Piaget and Inhelder (1948), and used by Smedslund (1963), Dodwell (1963), Rebelsky (1964), Beilin, Kagan and Rabinowitz (1966) and Pascual-Leone (in press). This task involves the subject being able to break perceptual set to recognize that no matter what angle a bottle placed on a flat horizontal surface is viewed from, the water level will always be parallel to the horizontal surface. A more complete description of the relative parameters of this type of task can be found in the semantic-pragmatic analysis of Pascual-Leone (in press).
A special version of Pascual-Leone's group tests developed by Pascual-Leone and De Avila is used. Subjects are presented with individual booklets which contain five horizontal or vertical two-dimensional bottles, eight two-dimensional-tilted bottles and four three-dimensional bottles, two of which are also tilted. The subject is asked to draw a line where the top of the water would be if the bottle were half full and then to place an "X" in the part that contained the water.

3. Figural Intersections Test (FIT)
The figural intersection test is a group administered paper-administered paper-and-pencil test in which subjects are required to place a dot in the intersection space of a varying number of geometrical figures. It was developed by Pascual-Leone and constitutes a

figural analogue to Piaget's work on intersection of classes. In a series of unpublished studies, Pascual-Leone has shown the test to have a high degree of internal consistency (split-half reliability = .89) as well as being significantly related to tests of similar logical structure (Pascual-Leone and Smith, 1968). For example, it has shown a high correlation with the WLT described above. Combined with the WLT, and ST described below, in the present context, it is taken as an index of developmental level. This relationship has been previously found in a series of unpublished studies by Pascual-Leone and Parkinson at York University, and De Avila (1971).

4. Serial Task (ST)
The serial task (De Avila, (1971) is a short term memory task which is individually administered in two phases. First, subjects are pre-exposed to the stimulus materials used in a second testing phase. In the pre-exposure or pre-training phase, each subject is shown a series of 10 different 35mm color slide transparencies of pictures depicting a donkey, house, airplane, etc. Subjects sit facing a screen situated on a wall six feet away. The 10 illustrations are presented by means of a Kodak 650 carousel slide projector. To introduce the task, each subject is shown each figure and asked to give its name and color (i.e., "a yellow hat"). Following this initial introductory phase and after the subject is able to correctly identify each figure ten times when presented in rapid random succession, the testing phase takes place.

The test phase is conducted in a "free recall" manner where, without any prior knowledge of the length of a list, the subject is asked to reproduce the list ignoring the order in which the individual items are presented. Subjects are shown a series of individually presented figures terminated by a blank slide, and asked to tell the experimenter what they have seen. The exposure time for each individual slide is .750 msec. There is no requirement that the sequence of the presentation be maintained, or that the subject respond within a specified period of time, or produce a predetermined number of responses. The child is simply asked to reproduce what he has seen using whatever labels are convenient.

There are seven sets of figures presented to each subject. These seven sets vary as to the number of stimuli within a series. The number of figures presented within a series, as well as the individual figures, are randomly varied. Finally, each illustration is presented no more than once within a series.

The PAPI system uses these four measures to produce several types of information each of which has a particular function. First, psychometric information on each test is produced as a means of assuring that the tests used in any given case have satisfactory levels of reliability and validity. This information is of primary importance to the researcher or program evaluator as a check against various types of problems associated with test administration, sampling procedures and so on. The second type of information produced by the PAPI system can be described as developmental-normative. These data provide normative information regarding the current developmental levels of the entire sample. Moreover, these data can also be stored to serve as base-line data which can be compared across temporal (as in a pre-post design) or situational/program dimensions. In summary, these two types of information, the psychometric and the normative/developmental data, are geared to the needs of program evaluation and needs assessment at the administrative levels.

The third type of information generated by the PAPI system consists of lists of recommended classroom activities for each child tested. These activities are geared to providing children with experience in specific educational activities thought to be important in the overall educational/program objectives.

In generating the suggested classroom activities for each child, four factors are taken into account:

1) The child's achievement level with respect to the concepts measured by the CCS.
2) The child's developmental level as measured by the WLT, FIT and ST tests.
3) The achievement level of the child's referent group with respect to the concepts measured by the CCS.
4) The developmental level of the child's referent group as measured by the WLT, FIT and ST tests.

An example of one computer printout which lists specific classroom activities is provided below. Using the four factors listed above, the following example would indicate that:

1. The child's overall developmental test profile is similar to children of the referent group who have already acquired the concept.

2. The child does not understand the concept.

It is then inferred that a specific set of activities are developmentally/educationally appropriate with respect to the concept of number as tested by the CCS. For example, this conjunction of conditions would lead to the following set of recommended classroom activities:

Concept of Number

This child does not have a concept of number, however, he is ready to learn. Train him by going through this sequence, using concrete actual objects only.

A. Sorting and classifying objects by
   1. Color
   2. Texture
   3. Size
   4. Weight
   5. Number
   6. Whatever other attributes you can think of

B. Counting Activities, such that the child learns...
   1. Sequence, numbers increase by one each time
   2. Invariance
      A. Pattern, 5 objects bunched and 5 objects in a row are both 5
      B. Objects, 5 elephants and 5 flies are both 5
   3. Symbols, learn the arbitrary names of the numerals

C. Concept and language of equalities and inequalities
   1. . which has more, is bigger, is longer, etc.
   2. . which has less, is smaller, is shorter, etc.
   3. . which has just as much, is just as big, is just as long, etc.

The above is an example of what is sent directly to the teacher. It can also be sent to the home so that the parents are made fully aware of what the teacher is trying to accomplish with the child.

In this way, possibly with some guidance from the teacher, the parent can participate in the child's education while supporting the teacher.

It should be noted that the PAPI system is designed so that a child's peer or referent group can be designed according to any number of nominal descriptors such as grade, sex or ethnic group. Thus far, only chronological age has been used because of the importance of the age variable in Piaget's theory. It should also be noted that, in the present description of PAPI system, the CCS is treated as an achievement test rather than as a test of development as it was originally designed. Actually, any test of achievement can be used within the system as long as it is linguistically and culturally appropriate and is constructed in such as way that it can be used to generate suggested activities.

In summary, the PAPI system can be used with any child to produce educational program data, or data for program evaluation. The purpose of the present discussion has not been to suggest that the system is in any way a complete educational package. Further development is needed in creating test procedures and in training educators, on how to use this type of system. But given the problems associated with testing, the PAPI system suggests one approach to the issue which speaks to the different needs of people within the educational community.

Summary

The major thesis has been that test publishers and the users of standardized IQ and summary-score achievement tests have failed to consider the problems associated with testing the minority child. And since the results of these tests are used to determine the educational and, by extension, the economic and social future of school-age children, it behooves test publishers and the educational community to take a harder look at the minority child's cultural background. It is the authors' opinion that consideration of these issues leads to the conclusion that the problem of testing cannot be solved by attempts to recreate standardized tests for minority children which are based on old conceptions of intelligence and educational achievement. It is concluded that what is required is a radical change in the whole approach to testing and the generation of entirely different models of education and of testing. There is growing support for this conclusion (for example see McClelland, 1973). The PAPI system is just one step in an attempt to move in a new direction.

References

Beilin, H., Kagan, J. and Rabinowitz, R. Effects of verbal and perceptual training on water level representation. Child Development, 1966, 37, 317-328.

De Avila, E. A. The use of artificial language in the study of processing capacity, immediate memory and Piaget's cognitive development variable. Unpublished doctoral research, York University, 1971.

De Avila, E. A., Struthers, J. A. and Randall, D. L. A group measure of the Piagetian concepts of conservation and egocentricity. Canadian Journal of Behavioural Science, 1969, 1(4), 263-272.

Dodwell, P. C. Children's understanding of number and related concepts. Canadian Journal of Psychology, 1960, 14, 191-205.

Jensen, A. R. Do schools cheat minority children? Educational Research, 1971, 14, 3-28.

McClelland, D. Testing for competence rather than for "intelligence". American Psychologist, 1973, 28, 1-14.

Mercer, J. The meaning of mental retardation. In Richard Koch and James Dobson (Eds.), The mentally retarded child and his family: A multidisciplinary handbook. New York: Brunner/Mazel, Inc., 1971.

Pascual-Leone, J. and Smith, J. The encoding and decoding of symbols of children. A new experimental paradigm and a neo-Piagetian model. Journal of Experimental Child Psychology, 1968, 8, 328-355.

Piaget, J. and Inhelder, B. La representation de l'espace chez l'enfant. Paris: P.U.F., 1948. English translation: The Child's Conception of Space. London: Routledge and Kegan Paul, 1956.

Rebelsky, F. Adult perception of the horizontal. Perceptual and Motor Skills, 1964, 19, 371-374.

Smedslund, J. The effect of observation on children's representation of the spatial orientation of a water surface. Journal of Genetic Psychology, 1963, 102, 195-201

Struthers, J. and De Avila, E. A. Development of a group measure to assess the extent of pre-logical and pre-causal thinking in primary school age children. Paper presented to National Science Teacher's Association Convention, Detroit, 1967.

I.Q. Tests and Minority Children. Developed by Multilingual Assessment Program, Stockton, CA. Published by the Dissemination and Assessment Center for Bilingual Education, Austin, TX. Reprinted August 1976.

The Ups and Downs of Minority Enrollment

by Curt Koehler

The last five years have seen the nation's colleges and universities enroll more blacks, chicanos and native Americans than ever before.

While statisticians agree that numerical and probably even percentage increases in minority enrollment are evident, they disagree over the exact percentages of this enrollment and point out that minority groups are still widely underrepresented in higher education.

More importantly, recent troubling reports on enrollments and finances reveal that both current and future gains are endangered:

--According to a survey of 360 institutions by the American Council on Education (ACE) the nationwide proportion of 1973 minority freshman declined for the first time in over a decade.

--After stating that the major mission of American higher education is equal access for all, the National Commission on the Financing of Postsecondary Education said that this mission has not been accomplished and probably cannot be accomplished under current financing arrangements.

--"Without dramatically increased (minority) college enrollment and completion rates," predicted the College Entrance Examination Board, "There is little prospect that minority groups will make significant gains toward equity, either in terms of income level or participation in the professional, technical and managerial segments of our society."

--A survey by the New York Times found that "the early results of minority recruitment programs have brought stark evidence of a high dropout rate and a disproportionate level of failures by minority graduates of professional examinations."

The ACE report said the proportion of minority students to students at all institutions dropped from 14.8% for the class of '76 to 13% for the class of '77. Most of the reduction was accounted for by black enrollment which declined from 8.7% for the class of '76 to 7.8% for the class of '77.

(As a caveat, it should be noted that analysists of minority enrollment percentages must proceed cautiously because of different reporting procedures employed, differing definitions of minorities, and different classifications of institutions under study. For example,

for 1970 the ACE reported minority enrollment at 11.3%, the US Office of Civil Rights at 10.5%, and an independent researcher, Fred Crossland, at eight percent. Also, in schools with a small total enrollment an increase or decrease of a dozen students can seemingly indicate significant changes of policy.)

What's the Problem?

Standard explanations for problems with minority enrollment include claims of limitations on the numbers of minority students qualified for traditional academic programs, increasingly competitive recruiting for those who are qualified, plus spiraling costs for higher education which hit students from low income families first and hardest.

Some critics, however, equate the end of the widely publicized and frequently violent demonstrations for minority rights in the late '60's with current enrollment problems.

Discussing the decline of black enrollment at Harvard, University of Massachusetts professor William L. Strickland said, "The increase in black admissions at Harvard in the 1960's demonstrated that the myth of academic qualifications was actually a political question. Their decline demonstrates that politics have changed."

Black enrollment in Harvard Graduate School dropped from five percent in 1970 to two percent in 1973. Black admission to Harvard College fell 17.5% from 1972 to 1973, followed by a 11% increase for 1974.

As causes for the decline the Harvard Crimson cited the death of Harvard's minority recruiter and "clerical racism," the bureaucratic problems of locating, admitting, and retaining minority students.

"It is precisely the racism of 'clerical inefficiency' that is the hardest to pin down and the hardest to combat," said the Crimson. "There is no recognizable ill-will, nor is there any overt discrimination that can be attacked. But the end result is always the same: a repressed minority continues to be repressed."

Many schools have targeted eventual minority enrollment to equal the minority representation in the population as a whole. Most have failed to meet even their short term goals.

In 1972 the interim chancellor of the University of Wisconsin at Eau Claire said black enrollment there should increase by 25-50% during the 1973-74 academic years. It remained constant.

In 1970 the University of Michigan set a target of 10% black enrollment by 1973. The actual enrollment was 7.3%.

Ohio State, with a current minority enrollment of 5-6%, "would like to see" minority representation "somewhat at the same level" as the 11-12% representation state-wide.

Some schools, nonetheless, reported significant progress in increasing and maintaining minority enrollments in a 1972 National Association of State Universities and Land Grant Colleges survey of member institutions.

Schools that reported enrolling blacks in a proportion equal to or greater than the proportion of black's in the state's population included the City College of New York (CCNY) (42,565), Wayne State University (6,548), Temple University (4,346) and Rutgers University (4,330).

Investigation indicates most successful minority enrollment programs have been based on a combination of substantial recruitment plus retention efforts.

A survey conducted by the Educational Testing Service (ETS) of the nation's graduate schools identified characteristics of successful programs as: active recruiting, coordination, admissions, and student services above the departmental level; institution and department cooperation in recruitment; clear definitions of the types of students sought; and special admissions arrangements for students with marginal credentials.

Graduate schools at Massachusetts Institute of Technology (MIT), Yale, and Princeton all had either full time recruiters or a long range minority program, and all reported high stable levels of minority enrollment.

In general, the ETS survey found that the more successful graduate schools emphasized remedial programs after provisional acceptance, instead of lowered admissions standards for special groups.

One student at Rutgers cited the educational counseling and tutorial services provided by the school's Educational Opportunity Program as being particularly effective in retaining minority students. The University currently has 5600 minority students who make up 15% of the entire student body.

The Money Crunch

Even as more and more schools commit themselves to significant minority enrollment, however, rising tuitions and related costs plus inflation pose new problems.

Federal financial assistance to higher education has supported the rise in tuitions by rechannelling money that was formerly given directly to institutions into individual student grant and loan programs. Under recent programs, low income students would be expected to finance their educations with a combination of Basic Opportunity Grants, available in amounts up to $1400 per year (though expected to average $475 next year) and Guaranteed Student Loans.

Larry Friendman, President of the National Student Association, termed this financing package "utter garbage" and said the amounts available were an "insult" when compared with the composite costs of tuition, room and board, books and related expenses. Friedman further said banks are especially unwilling to loan money as hoped for in the financing program to "women, ethnic minorities, and the poor who need them the most."

Consequently, the outlook for low-income minority students is especially bleak.

One administrator at Ohio State said he thought the funding priority for his school's minority recruitment program was low because the program was "perceived as all black... It would not surprise me (that) if a majority of the students in our program were not black our level of priority would be higher," he said.

Another administrator, however, denied that race made any difference and said that income was the deciding factor. "Traditionally the poor have never been significantly looked after by society," he said.

Concurrent with recent tuition increases, the ACE report found that the percentage of 1973 freshmen reporting that their parents earn $20,000 or more per year was 27.4, up more than seven percent from 1972 and more than 15% from 1966. In the $6000 or less bracket were 11% of the 1973 freshmen compared to 14% in 1972 and almost 20% in 1966.

The increase in students with higher parental income reinforced the trend found by the survey every year since it began in 1966.

Academic Standards

Some of the loudest and most bitter clashes arising out of the trend toward increasing minority enrollments have been over the issue of "academic standards."

"'Academic excellence,'" said one student at American University, "has been the classic code for administrators to curtail minority recruitment programs."

At City College of New York (CCNY),

where open admissions regulations have guaranteed a place for every high school graduate in the city, polarization over standards has been particularly intense.

"Honest debate on open admissions has ended here," said one student. "Anyone opposed to it is labeled a bigot even though more whites have benefitted from open admissions than blacks or Puerto Ricans."

Affirmative action programs, and their implicit connection with "quotas," have also drawn their share of criticisms.

The Supreme Court recently declined to render a judgement on a case involving a white student who claimed he was denied admission to the University of Washington law school in order to allow the school to admit less traditionally qualified minority students. The case drew widely varied opinions from schools, labor unions, and ethnic groups as illustrated by the 26 friend of the court briefs filed.

Similar affirmative action programs are in operation in undergraduate, graduate, and professional schools across the country.

"Black students with potential are accepted," said an admissions officer at Rutgers medical school. "The government encourages their acceptance. This means that white premedical students suffer the consequences."

The New York Times reported that certain early minority recruitment efforts for law schools were "disasterous." Of 14 minority students admitted to the UCLA law school in 1967, only two eventually passed the bar examination. In the class of 1971, 12 out of 39 went on to pass the examination while for the class of 1973 so far nine out of an admitted class of 64 have passed.

A black psychiatrist at Case Western Reserve University Hospital severely criticized such programs, saying schools were not taking care to search out and admit the best students available.

"I wouldn't hit a dog with some of the minority students I've seen," he told the Times, "and I have an idea that you honkies are taking in these dummies so that eight years from now you'll be able to turn around and say, 'Look how bad they all turned out!'"

Yet "quotas" of some sort do seem to be an accepted part of admission procedures, at least for the time being.

"If you left the admissions procedures totally to the majority-controlled universities, do you actually think they would go out of their way to embrace minority students?" asked the Daily Tar Heel, the campus paper at the University of North Carolina.

The Past and Future

In all, given the distant and recent history of minority enrollment, controversy, bitterness, and some violence seem sure to mark the forseeable future for this aspect of American higher education. The problem is by no means solved.

For some critics, recent trends and events as outlined in this article indicate but one more stage in the furtherence of racist policies of entrenchment designed to restrict access to this nation's colleges and universities. They charge that the fundamental problems of racism and classism are yet to be dealt with, and they frankly question whether the higher education establishment really intends to allow and support equal access for all.

For others, however, these events are but scattered setbacks as desired goals are fitted to everday realities, and they see the general acceptance of the trend towards minority enrollment as a just and natural part of society. Based upon the current commitment to and consciousness surrounding minority enrollment they contend that time alone--time spent working out the logistical and human dimensions of the problem--is now the commodity most needed to deepen and enlarge the significance of increasing minority enrollment.

Alan Pifer, president of the Carnegie Corporation, said the extention of higher education to more and more minorities in general and blacks in particular has already begun to provide significant leadership for both minority and majority communities. "There is no reason to suppose that substance rather than show in the national integration of the American leadership class will not grow," said Pifer.

"It is surprising," Pifer continued, "how little is known about the ways minority and majority communities can live together harmoniously and with respect for the autonomy of each other's cultures... The search for this knowledge will, I believe, be one of our major preoccupations for the balance of this century, with respect to blacks and other minorities as well."

"The Ups and Downs of Minority Enrollment." By Curt Koehler, College Press Service Third World Students. Edited by Tony Hewitt and Charles Mullings of the National Third World Student Coalition and Chip Berlet, United States National Student Association. Published by USNSA, Washington, D.C. August 1974.

Minority Group Participation in Graduate Education

Summary, Conclusions, and Recommendations

This nation has made a commitment to ensure equality of opportunity for all persons. In graduate education that promise has not yet been realized for minority men and women. Inequalities in the participation of blacks, Chicanos, Puerto Ricans, and American Indians in advanced study are clear. While minority men and women comprise more than 16 percent of the total population, they represent less than 6 percent of all students enrolled in master's and doctorate programs in U.S. colleges and universities. Minority persons born in this country earned less than 5 percent of the doctorates awarded in 1973–74. We believe this situation is inconsistent with the societal goal of equal opportunity and that positive action is required to improve the participation of minority persons in graduate study.

Graduate and professional education provide a major avenue for entrance into leadership and professional positions in this society. As scientists, professionals, and members of higher education faculties, minority men and women can bring a wealth of intellectual talent and skills for the benefit of all persons. As role models for future generations, they become change agents for society and for the socioeconomic mobility of their own groups. As minorities are enabled to participate more fully in the political, social, and economic institutions of this country, the very fact of their participation will contribute to a more just and humane society by signifying the diminution of past inequities. We affirm our belief that:

Increased minority participation in graduate education is an important national goal to be realized for the social, economic, intellectual, and cultural well-being of all persons. It is for the collective benefit of society that the representation of minority group persons among those earning advanced degrees be increased.

Individual equity is a fundamental concern. Distinctions that confer opportunity and status according to race, religion, sex, or national origin must be removed so that minority persons may be afforded a full opportunity to pursue graduate study according to individual motivation and intellectual potential.

The establishment of goals toward which to strive and by which to measure progress in realizing equal opportunity in graduate education is essential. The Carnegie Commission on Higher Education has stated that:

> The transcendent goal is that inequality in one generation should not, inevitably, be a legacy of succeeding generations. Each young person should have a full chance to demonstrate his intellectual ability and respond to his motivations to excel in constructive endeavor. From a national point of view, we cannot afford the domestic brain drain of able young persons who, through no fault of their own, are handicapped in making valuable contributions to the life of society.[1]

We concur. The long-range goal should be elimination of barriers that determine the extent of an individual's participation in higher education

---

[1] Carnegie Commission on Higher Education, *A Chance to Learn: An Action Agenda for Equal Opportunity in Higher Education* (New York: McGraw-Hill, 1970), p. 3.

according to racial or ethnic identity. Minority men and women should participate in all levels of education in numbers roughly approximating their population proportion. We recognize, however, that cultural traditions specific to certain minority groups may influence the feasibility of attaining this goal. Therefore, while affirming its desirability and utility in assessing progress, a degree of tentativeness is necessary in stating this goal. We propose a series of measures to be used as indices of progress in moving toward equality of educational opportunity:

- Enrollment in graduate education proportional to the share of baccalaureates received by minority men and women.
- Parity in award of Ph.D.'s to minority persons proportional to baccalaureates awarded.
- Enrollment in graduate education approximating the distribution of minority individuals in the pertinent age cohort of the U.S. population.
- Parity in award of Ph.D.'s to minority persons approximating their distribution in the pertinent age cohort of the total population.

Some may interpret goals premised on a parity concept to mandate equality of educational outcome. We do not find *approximate* equality to be an unreasonable objective—for persons of equivalent intellectual potential, motivation, and aspiration. We do reject prediction of educational achievement based on racial or ethnic identity (as well as economic status and sex). This is clearly unacceptable.

Others may worry that the issue of equal participation may be carried to an extreme. Precise arithmetic distribution of persons by age, race, income level, ethnic identity, and sex in every discipline specialty, type of school, and degree level is both impractical and unnecessary. Distinctions must be made among differences that are acceptable or a matter of choice and those that are unjust. We also do not intend to imply quotas wherein it might be inferred that certain groups are overrepresented and thereby should be denied further educational opportunity. Common sense and reasonable judgments must prevail.

Attention to broad numerical targets should not be allowed to detract from the more fundamental goal of setting into motion a self-sustaining process wherein minority participation is the accepted norm rather than the result of special effort. As such, our proposed set of actions should be viewed as serving in the role of a catalyst. Their very success should obviate the need for their existence. While a broad range of activities will be required in the coming years to assist minority students, the long-run outcome should be creation of an educational environment conducive to minority student access and achievement.

The existence of barriers specific to minority students in graduate education is reflected by the low levels of participation. Present disparities are striking. Minorities (excluding Orientals) comprise only 6–7 percent of total graduate enrollments and less than 5 percent of doctorates awarded to native-born U.S. citizens. In 1973–74, the proportion of (U.S. native-born) doctorates awarded to blacks was 3.5 percent, while Puerto Ricans earned 0.2 percent and Chicanos and other Spanish Americans received 0.6 percent. Persons identified as American Indians comprised 0.5 percent of total doctorates. Minority women, as is true of nonminority women, are also underrepresented in doctorate study. For every Ph.D. degree awarded to a minority woman, four were conferred on minority men.

The patterns of minority enrollments among disciplines differ from those of nonminority students. In 1973–74, black, Hispanic, and American Indian persons received 2.6 percent of natural science doctorates awarded to native-born U.S. citizens yet comprised almost 5 percent of doctorates in all disciplines. The apparent "overconcentration" of minority students in the field of education is often considered problematic. In 1973–74, 59 percent of the black Ph.D.'s earned degrees in education, compared with 25 percent of all students. Yet blacks received only 8 percent of all doctorates conferred in education. While a 100 percent increase in the number of minority doctorates in education is needed to bring minority participation to the level attained by nonminority persons, a sixfold increase over current levels would be required in the natural science fields. This problem should not be viewed as one of overrepresentation in certain disciplines, but rather as one of varying degrees of inadequate participation in all fields. A more balanced distribution among disciplines compatible with realistic career opportunities should be encouraged.

There is a pronounced shift among disciplines as black students move to higher levels of education, with many who received baccalaureates in science fields switching to other disciplines for graduate work. For example, 52 percent of the 1973–74 black Ph.D.'s who had majored in the life sciences in college continued in that field for doctoral study, while 80 percent of white Ph.D.'s with undergraduate training in the life sciences earned a Ph.D. in the same field. Education is the preferred choice of those black students who change disciplines. While only one-third of the 1973–74 black doctorates had earned a bachelor's degree in education, 59 percent received education doctorates. This pattern of field-switching is greatly accentuated for black students relative to majority students. These data suggest that efforts to encourage a broader distribution of black students among fields of study may also be effective through altering the causes for these shifts at the graduate level.

While expansion of the numbers of minority persons entering and completing graduate study is a high priority, the quality of the student's educational experience is an overriding concern. Since the quality of graduate programs varies among institutions, as do curricular offerings and emphases, the choice of institution attended by a student is key. There is no significant difference in the proportions of minority and nonminority students enrolled in public *vis-à-vis* private Ph.D.-granting institutions, although minorities are less likely to have earned a doctorate from one of the major research universities. In 1973–74, 24 graduate schools conferred 50 percent of the doctorates earned by blacks. About one-fifth of black graduate students attend predominantly black institutions, most of which do not offer doctoral study.

While the last decade has witnessed a rapid growth in minority participation in higher education, current evidence concerning the continuation of these increases is equivocal. Data reported by the U.S. Bureau of the Census show a steady convergence in the proportions of white and black high school graduates entering college and increases in the total number of blacks enrolled in college. However, the figures for blacks are characterized by large year-to-year fluctuations, and many have questioned the reliability of these data for pinpointing annual enrollment levels. Moreover, other evidence indicates the persistence of black/white disparities in college entrance and overall college participation; in 1974, 22 percent of blacks between the ages of 18 and 21 years were enrolled in college compared with 32 percent of whites in the corresponding age group.

The availability of minority persons with bachelor's degrees is critical to the outcome of efforts to enroll minority students in graduate education. In 1973–74, black, Hispanic, and American Indian persons earned about 7 percent of all bachelor's degrees. Blacks received 5.3 percent of total baccalaureates, a lower figure than some observers had previously estimated. Since most black students attend nonminority colleges and universities, it has been assumed that this distribution would also be reflected in degree attainment. However, black colleges graduated almost one-half of all black baccalaureates. These data indicate the need to examine the influence of different types of institutions on the educational achievement of black students.

The past few years have witnessed sharp increases in doctoral attainment by blacks. Minority persons (including Asians) comprised 3.3 percent of the doctorates conferred by the major research universities during the period 1969–72 but accounted for 5.8 percent in the following 3 years. The percentage of total doctorates awarded to U.S. native-born blacks rose from 2.8 percent in 1972–73 to 3.5 percent the following year, although comparable figures for Hispanics and American Indians showed little change.

Under the assumption that increases in graduate enrollments should precede changes in doctoral attainment, it is useful to contrast graduate enrollments in Ph.D.-granting institutions with the number of doctorates conferred the same year. Comparison of 1973 figures reveals that black enrollment proportions exceed degree achievement, whereas Hispanic and American Indian proportions are about equal. From this, some expansion in the number of black doctorates in the next few years might be predicted, but no increase could be forecast for Spanish-surnamed or American Indian Ph.D.'s.

Asian participation follows a different pattern. Persons of Asian origin comprise about 1 percent of total graduate enrollments but receive more than 4 percent of the doctorates. Their apparent "overrepresentation" in doctoral attainment may stem from a choice of doctoral in preference to master's study or greater persistence in degree achievement.

Minority persons are typically older than nonminorities upon completion of their doctoral work. This fact has stimulated speculation that the recent expansion in graduate minority enrollments may be attributed, in part, to a one-time phenomenon. The opening up of opportunities for minorities in graduate education has encouraged many older individuals to return to school for advanced study. Certainly, various federal and private programs in the 1960's and early 1970's focused on assisting black college faculty to upgrade their academic credentials. Hence, once the initial influx of students from this source has ceased, the growth in Ph.D. attainment may level off. Following this line of reasoning, recent trends may be inappropriate predictors of the long-run outlook.

An informal survey of 66 graduate institutions on recent changes in first-year minority graduate enrollments suggests a shift in the distribution of minority students among graduate schools. While data limitations necessarily preclude extrapolation to national trends, certain patterns emerged. Institutions that had recently implemented special efforts to encourage minority participation, as well as schools located in the South, reported increases in first-year minority enrollments from 1973 to 1974. Several other schools noted a stabilization or decline in minority participation. Lack of financial assistance and preference for professional study were two factors among those cited to explain this development. The availability of qualified applicants did not appear to be a major factor, since more than one-half of the graduate schools indicated that the academic qualifications of the minority applicants had improved, while only one institution indicated a contrary experience. For various reasons, it appears that the process has not been set into motion wherein increased minority participation is the rule at all institutions.

An understanding of the population distribution of minority persons is essential to assessment of minority participation. Blacks, Hispanics, and American Indians presently comprise 16 percent of the U.S. population, but this proportion is rising, reflecting their higher birth rates. Minority persons will represent an increasing share of the total college-age population in the future; in 1990, minority persons 20–24 years old will constitute more than 22 percent of all persons in that age-group.

Access, choice, and achievement are the most widely accepted measures of educational participation. Unfortunately, available data by which to assess these measures are, at best, incomplete and often no more than gross estimates. Definitional problems in identification of minority groups—categories that are ambiguous or overlapping—often confuse collection and interpretation of data. For this reason:

We endorse the aims of the Federal Interagency Committee on Education and the U.S. Office of Management and Budget in coordinating development of common definitions for racial and ethnic groups for use by federal agencies in the collection and reporting of data. We further recommend that nongovernmental organizations and institutions use common definitions whenever such use is compatible with their individual purposes in collecting data on race and ethnicity.

Careful specification of citizenship status is required for accurate assessment of the status of the principal minority groups. The educational backgrounds of noncitizens often differ from those of the resident U.S. population; the effect of merging data on citizens and noncitizens may obscure the educational characteristics of U.S. minority persons. In 1973–74, minority men and women, including noncitizens, received 12 percent of the Ph.D.'s conferred by the nation's universities, but only 6 percent were conferred to U.S. citizen minorities. Orientals obtained 60 percent of all doctorates awarded to minority persons, but only 6 percent of Oriental Ph.D.'s were born in the United States. We believe that:

While provision of opportunity in graduate study for foreign citizens is a worthwhile goal, it should not be confused with equal educational opportunity for U.S. citizens. We recommend that citizenship status be specified in the collection and reporting of data pertaining to the educational status of minority persons, whenever pertinent and feasible to do so

Accurate data for use in monitoring minority group participation in higher education in the coming years is needed. Information about the availability of minority persons holding higher education degrees is essential to formulation of affirmative action plans required by the federal government. Present data-collection activities are fragmented, lack comparability, are often inaccurate, and are neither sufficiently sensitive nor comprehensive to meet these needs. Moreover, the multiplicity and duplication of sporadic sample surveys impose an enormous administrative burden on institutions providing such information. There is a need to consolidate, improve, and expedite the collection, analysis, and dissemination of racial and ethnic data in order to provide a regular assessment of minority access and achievement in higher education.

We recommend that the Secretary of the Department of Health, Education, and Welfare direct the National Center for Educational Statistics

(NCES) *with the cooperation and support of the Office for Civil Rights* (OCR) *to collect, on an annual basis, enrollment figures and degrees conferred to individuals by race and ethnic identity in higher education institutions. These data would be collectible under the legal obligation of the Civil Rights Act of 1964 and made available to* OCR *for this purpose.*

To many, attainment of a bachelor's degree signifies that, at last, socio-economic, educational, and cultural disparities among persons of various income, racial, and ethnic backgrounds have been overcome. We believe, however, that many minority men and women still face special handicaps that disadvantage them relative to nonminority students. All students may be affected by individual circumstances, such as financial constraints, family obligations, and poor undergraduate preparation that prevent graduate school attendance, but for minorities such handicaps are more frequent and mutually reinforcing.

Minority students typically experience difficulty in financing under-graduate study. They must rely more on scholarship, work–study, and loan programs in contrast to nonminority students, who receive greater family support. Whereas in 1974–75 black and Hispanic college-bound high school seniors estimated that their parents would contribute about $200 toward college expenses, the median figure for whites was over $1,100. That same year minority students comprised one-third of the persons assisted through the major U.S. Office of Education aid programs. Upon graduation from college, immediate employment opportunities may appear more rewarding than advanced study in view of the prospect of further financial difficulties, the academic risk of graduate study (about one-half of all doctoral candidates fail to complete the Ph.D. degree), and labor market uncertainties.

Award of a bachelor's degree clearly does not certify equality of educational background. Some institutions provide better academic preparation for graduate study than others, since colleges differ as to curricular emphases, degree requirements, and standards for evaluating achievement. Further, the type of institution attended may influence a student's interest in postgraduate training. Current evidence suggests that the distribution of minority students among institutions differs from that of nonminority students. For example, blacks are more likely to attend 2-year and less-prestigious 4-year colleges. In 1973–74, slightly less than one-half of the bachelor's degrees earned by blacks were conferred by the predominately black schools.

Apart from differences among institutions, the quality of undergraduate education also varies *within* individual institutions. In some instances, minority students may be counseled into a form of "tracking" that is inappropriate training for graduate study. Others have entered special programs designed to remedy secondary education deficiencies, but such programs may not provide the intensive preparation necessary for advanced study. As a consequence, many talented students have uneven academic backgrounds that may lower performance in graduate study. Therefore:

We urge undergraduate institutions to sustain, and strengthen where necessary, their commitment to the education of minority students— whether admitted through "open admissions" processes, or enrolled in Educational Opportunity Programs or regular academic programs—to ensure that such students obtain an education comparable in quality to that of all students in the institution. Any compromise in standards for evaluation of academic performance and curricula does a disservice both to the student and society.

Other access problems exist. Minority student admissions has been the subject of extensive debate. The basic dilemma is how to identify those students with strong academic promise despite uneven records of achievement. Many minority students are "late bloomers," having entered college with a poor high school background, and do not realize their academic potential until late in their undergraduate careers. The widespread (and controversial) use of standardized tests presents another hurdle, since minority students typically receive lower test scores relative to other students. Apart from questions concerning their differential impact on minorities, there is broad agreement that tests are only modest predictors of Ph.D. attainment for all students. Attrition in graduate school is high and influenced by a host of other factors that are not measured by tests, such as motivation, persistence, and compatibility with departmental expectations and resources.

Advanced study in the scientific disciplines presents added barriers. The problem of "automatic tracking" is primary. For certain fields of study—for example, chemistry, physics, and engineering—extensive preparatory coursework is required. The long time period needed to obtain these prerequisites almost precludes advanced study if a student does not decide to study a scientific discipline in high school. Low academic self-confidence, combined with intimidating impressions of the rigors of scientific study, the scarcity of minority scientists and engineers to serve as visible success models, and the lack of cultural support for pursuit of scientific careers, may further discourage minority students.

In addition to barriers to access, other factors affect performance during graduate study. Attitudes are an elusive yet significant influence on the quality of the educational experience. Minority students may perceive insensitivity or indifference on the part of the faculty, while faculty may be uncomfortable or naive in responding to minority styles and aims. The unfamiliarity of many graduate schools with the education of minority students may reinforce the unease of students, while intentional or unintentional biases can demoralize the student. The lengthy "apprenticeship" relation in doctoral study may be perceived as constraining for the minority person for whom newly realized social and individual autonomy may be an important consideration. Moreover, the research interests of the minority student may be grounded in a strong ethnic consciousness and thus differ from the academic and professional concerns of departmental faculty.

Although the educational aspirations of minority students are as high as or higher than those of white students, minorities are less likely to receive the thoughtful advice and guidance necessary to realize those aspirations. This circumstance underscores the importance of diversifying the ethnic and racial composition of college and university faculty to provide appropriate role models for minority youth and to reassure potential applicants that an institution is receptive to minority students.

Efforts to increase access are constrained by high attrition in elementary, secondary, and undergraduate education. If educational progress is viewed as successive levels of a pyramid, it is clear that minorities cluster at the bottom but are scarce at the apex—graduate and professional education. The success of efforts at the graduate level is related to development of an adequate pool of minority baccalaureates qualified to proceed to advanced study. In 1973, 85 percent of white persons 20 or 21 years of age had completed high school, compared with 68 percent of black and 58 percent of Hispanic persons in that age group. However, despite the failures of successive levels of the educational pyramid, we suggest that substantial gains in minority participation can be achieved now by focusing on the existing pool of high school seniors and students already enrolled in college. Mounting evidence indicates that minority students experience much higher attrition during college relative to the overall student body. Efforts to improve college entrance and retention rates could significantly augment the pool of minority candidates for graduate study.

The present is not the best of all possible worlds for higher education, especially when compared with the expansionary decade of the 1960's. Efforts to promote minority participation in graduate education are both helped and hindered by recent developments.

Financial difficulties are obvious. Federal support of graduate students has plummeted. Institutions faced with the prospect of declining enrollments in the coming decade, a leveling off of research support, and uncertainties in state appropriations feel hard-pressed to maintain current expenditure levels. Special efforts for minority graduate students compete directly with other program priorities for a shrinking pool of resources. The sudden, strong emergence of the women's movement has caused many to express concern that minority interests are being overshadowed. Although the problems and situation of minorities and women differ in many respects, attention to the needs of these groups is often merged, and they are frequently forced to compete for public visibility, resources, and employment opportunities.

The development of nontraditional and more flexible programs to meet the needs of new groups of students in innovative learning environments offers expanded opportunities for minorities. Moreover, as the forecast declines in higher educational enrollments are realized, universities may be encouraged to look beyond their traditional recruitment areas for a broader range of student interests, backgrounds, and educational objectives.

The pessimistic outlook for the academic labor market and uncertainties in the nonacademic sector have caused many to question the wisdom of encouraging minority students to pursue doctoral study. In our view, employment uncertainties should not serve as a rationale for limiting efforts to increase minority participation. However, careful counseling to inform potential students of realistic career opportunities—all students, not only minorities—must be given the highest priority. Moreover, the labor market experience of minorities may differ from that of nonminorities in two respects. First, employment openings for minority graduates in certain disciplines, especially those with a professional orientation, may arise from manpower needs related to the minority community. The field of education is one example; the demand for minority educators with advanced degrees is stimulated, in part, by bilingual–bicultural programs mandated by the federal government. Second, other disciplines, such as economics, psychology, and the health sciences, may have applications specific to minority concerns. The impact of affirmative action regulations on employment prospects for minorities is widely contested. While affirmative action efforts will definitely expand the representation of minority persons in the pool of candidates considered for employment, we are uncertain as to the effect of ethnic or racial status in selection of the individual to be hired in a position requiring an advanced degree.

While most agree about the desirability of increasing minority participation, considerable controversy exists about the legality of various programs designed to achieve this goal. The immediate debate centers on issues raised in the well-known *DeFunis* v. *Odegaard* case, in which an applicant to the University of Washington law school claimed that he was denied admission while less-qualified minority persons were given preference by virtue of their minority status.

Since the U.S. Supreme Court did not rule on the merits of this case, the fundamental legal questions remain unresolved. The basic precepts of the "equal protection" clause of the Fourteenth Amendment presume the unconstitutionality of racial classifications, although the courts have ruled that race-conscious policies may be permitted to overcome prior discrimination. The key question, crystallized by the *DeFunis* case, and for which there is no clear judicial guidance, is when and for what purpose may use of a race-conscious policy be allowed? This issue concerns not only admission decisions but also a wide range of programs that are "targeted" to minorities, such as financial aid, summer institutes, and supportive services.

While many agencies and institutions have implemented minority programs, others have been reluctant to do so for fear of legal complications. Although similar cases are likely to be presented to the U.S. Supreme Court in the near future, it is uncertain if and when the Court will choose to rule on the substantive issues. In the meantime, questions about the constitutionality of a broad spectrum of "targeted" activities remain unanswered. As long as such legal uncertainties exist, initiation of special programs for minority students will continue to be inhibited; but, on the other hand, sincere, thoughtful efforts need not be precluded.

Few minority men and women are members of the academic faculties of colleges and universities; in 1975 blacks represented only 2 percent of the faculties at major research universities. Expansion of career opportunities for minority persons in higher education institutions is a desirable social and educational goal; moreover, current civil rights legislation and regulations have strong implications for the academic employment of minority doctorates. Executive Order 11246 requires colleges and universities holding federal contracts to take affirmative action to ensure that institutions do not discriminate in their employment practices on the basis of race, color, religion, sex, or national origin. But the requirements of the Executive Order are premised on a static concept; the employment targets for minority faculty are derived from the available supply of qualified candidates.

We concur in the objectives of affirmative action in the employment of minority faculty in colleges and universities as required under Executive Order 11246. We emphasize, however, that affirmative action as specified by the federal government will result in increased minority participation on faculties of colleges and universities only if there is an increase in the pool of qualified minority candidates.

The federal government and graduate institutions have a joint responsibility. Neither sector should condition its efforts upon the other. If persons of minority background are to join the faculties of colleges and universities, graduate schools must expand opportunities for minorities to enter and complete graduate study. The federal government, through its obligations to ensure the civil rights of all persons (affirmative action being but one example), must support efforts to promote minority participation in graduate study.

Effective commitment to expanding opportunities for minority graduate students requires that such commitment be a publicly articulated institutional and departmental priority. Only through active support from the central campus administration, the graduate school, and faculty can equal opportunity objectives be achieved. In the absence of a strong commitment and extensive faculty involvement, it is unlikely that other activities and attitudes will be influenced in ways that create an institutional environment supportive of minority student achievement. We believe that:

Graduate institutions have the primary responsibility for encouraging and assisting minority students in attaining a high-quality graduate education. Initiative must derive from the institutions themselves, since they have the fundamental responsibility for selecting those who will receive the benefits of advanced education and enabling those persons to realize their educational goals. While government and other organizations must provide assistance, such support should be viewed as a complement, not a substitute, to existing institutional activities.

Opinions about the appropriate focus of programmatic efforts are sharply divided. Some hold that such programs should be limited to students believed to have strong academic potential but who, for a variety of reasons, are not competitive with respect to traditional admissions criteria or, if admitted, might be high-risk students without special assistance. This approach assumes that not all minority students require, and thus should not receive, financial or academic support. Others believe that attention should be directed to those students with demonstrated outstanding academic ability, with the goal being to ensure their representation among those qualified to enter top-level academic and professional positions. This debate is reflected in the diversity of recruitment, admissions, supportive service, and financial aid activities implemented by institutions.

The feasibility of recruiting graduate trainees is dependent on the adequacy of the pool of students qualified for graduate study. Although a major responsibility must rest at the elementary and secondary levels, substantial gains in the number of eligible candidates can be realized through efforts directed toward minority students already enrolled in undergraduate study. Therefore, we stress that:

Faculty and staff must be active in identifying, motivating, and improving the academic preparation of talented minority students early in their undergraduate careers. For advanced study in some disciplines, such as the natural and quantitative social sciences, this developmental approach is essential. Science internships, undergraduate honors programs, and summer research institutes are possible program models.

Fundamental to any recruitment procedure is the need to identify prospective students, motivate such students to apply to graduate school, and inform them of the basic admissions requirements and the programs available at the institution. A less obvious, but equally important, purpose is to help applicants in evaluating their qualifications and goals in relation to the expectations and resources of individual departments. While most schools and departments engage in the identification, motivation, and information functions, efforts in the second area are less satisfactory and should be improved.

The propriety of giving special attention to minority applicants in the admissions process is widely debated. Some institutions advocate strict nondiscrimination policies, while others pursue affirmative practices. In general, modification of procedures for minority applicants takes the form of permitting flexibility in the interpretation of certain criteria supplemented by information from other sources, such as personal interviews and recommendations. The aim is to liberalize requirements that appear to be inadequate indicators of intellectual ability to enable a broader, often more intensive, examination of academic potential. In most instances, these procedures would be desirable for evaluation of all applicants (minority and nonminority), although they may be more time-consuming and costly.

Ideally, admissions decisions represent the middle link of a coordinated continuum from recruitment, admissions, financial support, and supportive services. If a student is well-acquainted with the resources and requirements for graduate study, and if the department is cognizant of the student's academic background and objectives, then the admissions decision is simplified. A department can decide whether it has the capability to assist a student in strengthening his or her academic background if needed. Clearly, the "sink-or-swim" attitude resulting from a guesswork admissions mode is costly both to the student and school in the event a student fails.

Many students, both minority and nonminority, benefit from some form of supportive services. It has been a long-standing practice to provide assistance to students with uneven academic preparation. For example, graduate students often enroll in undergraduate courses, special mathematics courses are offered for students with nonscience college backgrounds, and a 2-year M.B.A. program may offer 1 year of basic work in the field without academic credit. What is generally unacceptable are separate courses geared at a slower-than-normal pace or enrollment in major courses with the expectation that the student will need extensive tutoring or other help. Most graduate schools offer supportive services to minority students similar to those afforded to all students, although they may be provided to the former to a greater extent. For minority students, the availability of counselors to acquaint them with academic resources, advise on realistic career opportunities, aid in social adjustments, and bolster academic self-confidence is essential. Assistance to improve the basic writing and quantitative skills of minority students is another frequently cited need.

The inadequacy of financial aid funds for minority students is a pressing institutional concern. Many believe that lack of financial support is the foremost obstacle to increased minority participation. The level of funding allocated to graduate minority student aid varies greatly among institutions—from zero to over $3 million per year. In general, funds come from university operating budgets, although special state appropriations and federal, foundation, and private funds have played a significant role.

Philosophies and attitudes toward "targeting" funds solely for minorities are mixed. Consideration of financial need in the award of aid to minority students is more common than for other students. Minority students tend to be supported with special monies rather than by regular departmental funds, and a central problem is how to motivate departments to commit a proportionate share of their resources—research and teaching assistantships and stipends—to minority students. Mechanisms for financial support that designate minorities as a "second class" or a "free good" and special programs without faculty involvement tend to isolate students and, in the long run, are unsuccessful.

The paradox of successful recruitment activities, financial assistance, and programs of supportive services for minorities is that their very success should lead to their self-extinction. However, we are not aware of any institution that has reached the point where minorities are routinely integrated into the mainstream of institutional and departmental activities.

Four recommendations are offered:

1. RELATION OF SELECTION PROCESS TO STUDENT ACHIEVEMENT

Prior to admission, graduate departments and faculty should thoroughly inform prospective students of the available opportunities and expectations of individual departments and the institution in order to ensure a successful match between student interests and educational goals and those of the department. Once a student has been admitted, we believe that the graduate department has a clear obligation to assist that student, in whatever ways necessary and appropriate, to achieve his educational objectives and perform at a level consistent with individual potential and the academic expectations of the department.

2. ASSESSMENT OF ACADEMIC PERFORMANCE

Diversity and flexibility in the selection and evaluation of student applicants are desirable features of the graduate admissions process. However, we also wish to emphasize our belief in the importance of maintaining the highest standards for evaluation of educational achievement and the award of graduate degrees. We firmly oppose any compromise in the standards for academic performance in graduate education.

3. INTEGRATION OF THE STUDENT INTO THE MAINSTREAM OF TEACHING AND RESEARCH ACTIVITIES

Programs that isolate or tend to denote the minority student as "second class" should be avoided. The aim of all institutional efforts must be to bring minority students into the mainstream of teaching, research, and other departmental and institutional activities. Special emphasis should be placed on development of financial support mechanisms that encourage individual departments to "invest" in a commitment to assisting the student to achieve his or her educational goals. Faculty should be encouraged to involve minority students as research and teaching assistants in individual departments.

4. EVALUATION OF MINORITY STUDENT ACCESS AND ACHIEVEMENT

Graduate departments and faculty should monitor the effectiveness of their efforts to promote minority participation in advanced study. Such evaluation should include both academic achievement and the broader experiences of minority students, since failure to complete graduate study may result from intangible factors in the teaching environment and social relationships with other students and faculty that influence academic success.

Since the Higher Education Act of 1965, the federal government has shown a consistent, although uneven, commitment to equalizing opportunity in elementary, secondary, and baccalaureate education. However, this commitment has, at best, had limited impact at the graduate level.

We believe there is a clear federal responsibility to support efforts directed toward improving the participation of minority persons in graduate education. Present support of research and advanced training should be extended to recognize the importance of involving minority persons. The talents of minority men and women as scholars, professionals, scientists, and teachers constitute a valuable national resource. Individual equity is another concern. Distinctions that confer status and opportunity on the basis of race or ethnic identity must be removed. The federal government, through its authority and resources, is best able to redress social inequities. Executive Order 11246, calling for affirmative action in higher education employment, and various directives stemming from the Civil Rights Act of 1964 exemplify the federal government's broad obligation to foster social justice. Yet requirements for affirmative action cannot be achieved without concurrent efforts to increase the number of minority persons with advanced degrees. A strong federal role is critical to attainment of these objectives.

We urge the executive and congressional branches to express a resolution for federal support of and increased concern for minority participation in graduate education. Strong national leadership is essential to achievement of equal opportunity goals in graduate education.

Responsible federal policy must recognize the pluralistic nature of barriers constraining minority participation. While one course of action must be directed toward assisting individual minority students, another concern is creation of an institutional environment that is supportive of minority student achievement. For these reasons, we believe the federal government should channel support to minority students through institutions with the capability and commitment to sustain effective programmatic efforts.

The U.S. Office of Education should implement a program of competitive institutional grants for the purpose of supporting efforts to increase minority participation in graduate education. Funds should be provided for a broad range of activities, including student aid, tuition, supportive services, and administrative costs. Selection of grant recipients should be based on evaluation of institutional commitment and program effectiveness.

The approach embodied in current federal training grant programs is suggested as an appropriate model for implementation of this proposal. Institutional initiative and flexibility as to program scope, emphasis, and organization should be encouraged. Accordingly, funds should be available for a variety of purposes—tuition, student stipends, additional support personnel, special summer programs, and research and evaluation directly related to program effectiveness. An 8 percent administrative allowance should be provided.[2] The federal role should complement, not supplant, institutional efforts; therefore, provision for maintenance of effort should be a condition of the award. Initial grants should cover a 3- to 5-year period, with renewal contingent upon demonstration of program success as measured by student achievement.

An annual appropriation of $50 million would permit support of a total of 6,500 students or about 1,500–2,500 new entrants each year, depending on the number of years students are supported through the program. This figure represents less than 1 percent of total graduate enrollments in U.S. colleges and universities.

The following distribution of funds is suggested as appropriate for implementation of a balanced program of activities, although considerable variation in individual grants should be permitted:

1. Student assistance and tuition   65-70 percent
2. Special new programs and supportive services   25-30 percent
3. Research and evaluation   5 percent

Student assistance should be awarded on the basis of academic merit and financial need. Financial support available through this program

---

[2] Alternatively, if an institution with ongoing activities only requires funds for student assistance in order to expand minority participation, a cost-of-education allowance of $4,500 per additional full-time student might be allocated. In its report *Federal Policy Alternatives toward Graduate Education*, NBGE urged that cost-of-education allowances accompanying federal fellowships be increased to $4,500 to reflect in part the rapid cost increases of the past decade.

should be closely linked with existing institutional mechanisms for student aid, such as departmental fellowships and research and teaching assistantships.

Examples of special, new programs that might be funded through an institutional grant include:

1. Activities designed to identify, motivate, and prepare talented undergraduate students for advanced study;
2. cooperative recruitment, admissions, and financial aid programs involving departments in a specific field of study administered by several graduate institutions; and
3. summer institutes to strengthen preparation for graduate work.

Funds should be available to support research pertinent to minority student achievement. In addition, mechanisms for evaluation by individual institutions of their activities should be required.

Legislative authority for implementation of this program is provided under Title IX of the Higher Education Act of 1965, as amended in 1972. Part A presently authorizes grants to institutions for "(1) faculty improvement; (2) the expansion of graduate and professional programs of study; (3) the acquisition of appropriate institutional equipment and materials; (4) cooperative arrangements among graduate and professional schools; and (5) the strengthening of graduate and professional school administration." Research pertinent to the improvement of graduate programs is also allowed. Authorization for fellowships is specified under Part B of Title IX and stresses "the need to prepare a larger number of teachers and other academic leaders from minority groups." Part C provides public service graduate or professional fellowships, and Part D authorizes fellowships for "persons of ability from disadvantaged backgrounds as determined by the Commissioner, undertaking graduate or professional study." Technical amendment of this legislation would permit implementation of our program as proposed.

The mission-oriented federal agencies have implemented a variety of programs designed to involve more minorities in education and research pertinent to the individual programmatic missions of these agencies. Most agency efforts target funds to minority institutions through programs such as training grants or activities to strengthen the research capabilities of faculties and departments. Only a few target money directly to minority students because of concern about the political and legal implications of doing so.

Programs that assist minority colleges are effective yet necessarily limited in scope. While they may have a significant impact on the undergraduate education of minority students, at the graduate level minority institutions comprise only a small share of total graduate enrollments. Moreover, most minority graduate schools do not possess the capabilities for scientific research comparable to those of the leading research universities in this country, and few offer doctoral work. Consequently, most agency programs have only a minimal impact on minority participation in doctoral-level education and research activities. It is unfortunate that legal uncertainties, compounded by the absence of clear national leadership on these issues, both limit the scope and inhibit the potential for expansion of the efforts of federal agencies—and will continue to do so in the foreseeable future.

We believe it fundamental to the national interest to encourage the development and involvement of underutilized minority talent in scientific and research activities. Accomplishment of these goals requires that attention be directed to three broad areas:

1. Early identification, motivation, and preparation of talented undergraduate students for graduate study in science;
2. increased opportunities for advanced (primarily doctoral) training of minority persons leading to careers in science and research; and
3. strengthening the academic credentials and research capabilities of minority scientists and faculty.

Initiative and diversity of approaches in resolving these underlying problems should be encouraged. We urge that a variety of programs such as those described in this report be sustained insofar as their effectiveness is demonstrated and the need for these activities remains. There are, however, striking omissions in the array of programmatic efforts sponsored by the mission-oriented agencies.

First and foremost is the lack of activities directed toward increasing the involvement of minority students in scientific research and training in Ph.D.-granting institutions. We believe that this area deserves the highest priority. Second, greater efforts to prepare and assist talented undergraduates in nonminority institutions for advanced study are essential in view of the extensive curricular prerequisites for graduate work in science.

A number of alternatives are proposed for consideration:

1. As one means of encouraging graduate faculty to identify and involve talented minority graduate students in research projects in universities (primarily at the doctoral level), the federal mission agencies should provide unrestricted supplemental funds to graduate institutions, earmarked to reimburse principal investigators who employ minority students on research grants. Funds would be allocated as a share of the normal stipend paid to minority students for their services, thus partially reimbursing the project for costs of employing these students. This activity would complement the institutional grants program previously recommended since all institutions and departments would be eligible to receive such reimbursements, given the voluntary, decentralized nature of the program. Combined funding from several agencies at a level of $5 million per year would permit support of 2,000 students with an average reimbursement of $2,500.

2. Cooperative programs between undergraduate and graduate institutions would facilitate a developmental approach in motivating, preparing, and assisting undergraduate minority students to enter and successfully complete advanced study in the scientific disciplines. Mechanisms to gain exposure to and experience in research projects prior to entry in graduate school might be one component of this kind of effort.

3. Early identification of undergraduates who show extraordinary promise in science and engineering, complemented by undergraduate honors or research assistant opportunities, offers another means of increasing the pool of minority students who are interested in, qualified for, and aware of opportunities for graduate study in science and engineering.

4. The consortium model exemplified by existing efforts in the fields of law and business administration may be effectively used for the scientific disciplines. Through this approach, graduate departments in a single discipline or a group of related disciplines may consolidate their identification, recruitment, financial assistance, and supportive service activities. Resources and expertise would be pooled for the benefit of all participating

institutions and departments, and the importance of faculty involvement emphasized. Joint summer institutes, research internship experiences, and exchange of undergraduate students among institutions for graduate study are possible features of this activity.

5. Alteration of the tendency for many minorities with undergraduate training in the natural sciences to shift into other fields for doctoral study would sharply expand the supply of new candidates for graduate study in the scientific disciplines. Programs to strengthen and update the scientific background of minority persons—many of whom may have completed their bachelor's degrees some year previously—who wish to undertake graduate work would address this problem.

Professional associations have initiated various activities designed to increase minority participation in the professions and in graduate education. Most disciplinary societies have established *ad hoc* committees and surveyed minority representation in graduate study, and a few have implemented small fellowship programs. In general, however, these special activities have been constrained by their *ad hoc,* temporary nature. Programs have been peripheral to the mainstream of association concerns. Consequently, as other program priorities emerge and financial constraints become more severe, these special programs often disappear for lack of support.

We urge professional associations to draw upon the prestige and talents of members and to assign a high priority to promoting increased opportunities for minority men and women in graduate study and in the professions. Associations should facilitate communication and serve in a coordinating role among departments and among faculty to:

1. Disseminate and publicize successful program models designed to promote minority group participation;

2. encourage leadership and commitment from members with the highest standing in the discipline in addressing these concerns;

3. encourage and facilitate cooperation among institutions and departments to implement special programs; and

4. continue to monitor and evaluate the status of minority persons in the discipline.

A variety of activities should be implemented with the encouragement and involvement of professional societies, including short-term summer workshops to strengthen student preparation in specific subject areas prerequisite to work in the major disciplines, i.e., quantitative skills for advanced study in the social sciences, cooperation among institutions and departments for the recruitment and financial support of minority students, and association-sponsored fellowship programs.

A recent report on the state role in graduate education and research declared that:

While graduate education with its attendant research, including masters' and doctoral programs, is clearly a national resource, it is also a regional, state, and local resource. Primary responsibility for providing educational opportunity constitutionally and historically rests with the states.[3]

[3] Education Commission of the States, *The States and Graduate Education*, Report No. 59 (Denver, Colorado: Education Commission of the States, February 1975), p. 1.

The necessity of a state role in facilitating minority student access and achievement in graduate education is dictated by two broad considerations. First, the specific emphasis and form of advanced training are a function of employment and research needs as well as traditional patterns of support for graduate education within individual states. State and regional manpower requirements also derive, in part, from the skills and training necessary to address concerns pertinent to the resident minority communities. Second, the history, size, composition, education, and socioeconomic circumstance of the minority population vary among states and affect participation throughout higher education.

Although equal educational opportunity is a widely accepted goal in postsecondary education, the basic philosophies and programmatic efforts adopted by states are diverse. While direct state programs to assist economically and educationally disadvantaged students are widespread at the undergraduate level, only a few states award aid to graduate students on the basis of financial need. We are not aware of any statewide programs to assist graduate students considered to have educational deficiencies.

State higher education programs that use racial or ethnic criteria in determining eligibility are rare; however, state scholarships for persons of American Indian heritage and grants for black college faculty pursuing terminal degrees are notable examples. Although not restricted to minority individuals, programs to train personnel to implement federal and state bilingual–bicultural requirements benefit the minority population. Several states have undertaken or coordinated surveys of ethnic and racial enrollments in higher education, and many have initiated detailed examination of minority participation in institutions and programs.

There is an important distinction between institutional activities that are supported by state funds and programs and those that are administered on a direct, statewide basis. We believe the former strategy is preferable in view of the decentralized nature of graduate education and research and the importance of involving minority graduate students in the mainstream of departmental research and teaching activities.

The states have both an obligation and special capabilities to address issues of minority access and achievement in graduate education. Insofar as master plans have been developed in individual states, such plans should specify a concern about equality of educational opportunity in graduate education. States should encourage and respond to institutional initiatives in development of efforts directed to this end. We recommend that states provide support to institutions for:

1. Financial assistance for disadvantaged graduate students to advance the participation of minority persons;

2. provision of supportive services within institutions; and

3. development of cooperative programs between undergraduate and graduate institutions to identify, encourage, and strengthen the academic preparation of talented minority undergraduates for entry to graduate study.

Private, nonprofit foundations have demonstrated strong commitment to advancement of equal opportunity objectives. They have supported programs to provide financial assistance to minority students, to strengthen minority institutions, to develop leadership capabilities in the minority community, to undertake relevant research, and to improve the academic preparation of minority students. Foundations have contributed support for innovative programs, provided "seed money" for promising new efforts, and assisted other activities that might not have otherwise been initiated because of the reluctance or inability of institutions and government to act. While minorities have realized significant gains over the past decade, unresolved problems remain. Unfortunately, total foundation support directed to promotion of minority participation in education is projected to decline in the coming years.

We urge foundations to initiate, develop, and sustain commitment to and selective support of programs to improve minority participation in graduate education as an important complement to federal, institutional, and other activities.

Through their involvement in activities to advance the cause of minority education, foundations have developed a high level of expertise and insight as to effective and ineffective ways to address these issues. Yet other organizations involved in minority concerns, institutions, government, and individuals do not normally receive the benefits of the knowledge developed from the experience of foundations. Systematic dissemination of both informal and formal evaluation of significant programs has in general not occurred.

We recommend that foundations consider various means of sharing the insights gained through their specific experiences in minority concerns. Two possibilities are suggested:

1. Periodic conferences sponsored either singly or jointly by foundations with relevant activities to exchange information about particular subject areas, with the aim of identifying effective program approaches. The proceedings of such conferences should be published and broadly disseminated.

2. Systematic codification and dissemination of knowledge derived from their activities in order to provide information about productive program efforts. The availability of such information would be useful to other institutions and individuals who are interested and involved in these concerns.

Minority men and women are severely underrepresented in managerial and professional positions in business and industrial firms. The importance of bringing more minority persons into these positions in the private sector is underscored by federal efforts to ensure equal employment opportunities for them. Business and industry have a fundamental interest in and responsibility for increasing the supply of highly educated minority persons. We suggest two strategies for the private sector to contribute to increased minority participation in graduate education.

Provision of financial support to graduate institutions or a consortium of graduate departments that normally provide personnel with advanced degrees to particular business or industrial firms. One example of productive cooperation between graduate departments and the private sector is the graduate business school consortia which seek to increase the number of minority persons with M.B.A. degrees. Various business firms contribute funds for recruitment, stipends, and other activities.

Identification, encouragement, and financial assistance for promising minority employees to undertake advanced study that will enable them to move into high level positions. This strategy has particular significance in view of the economic forces tending to encourage minority baccalaureates to accept immediate employment upon graduation. Promising minority students may be diverted from graduate study although their long-run career goals may be best served by undertaking advanced study.

For almost a half century a number of black institutions have offered programs of graduate study. Presently, 28 schools award the master's degree, including four that confer the doctorate. About one-fifth of all black students pursuing advanced study nationwide attend a predominately black institution. These schools have, moreover, experienced vigorous enrollment growth. In 1967 the black graduate schools enrolled 8,500 students, but 6 years later attendance had risen to almost 20,000.

In view of the significance of these schools, the National Board on Graduate Education concluded that a report on minority group participation in graduate education must give high priority to discussion of the black graduate schools. Several questions emerged for consideration. First, what is the role and mission of the black graduate institutions in light of the rapidly changing context of higher education? Second, what is the current status of the black graduate schools as indicated from a profile of basic data on enrollments, degrees, faculty, and program offerings? With respect to the problems facing these schools, are there distinctions between the problems that are endemic to all sectors of higher education and those that are unique to the black institutions? And finally, what are the needs and priorities of these schools for coming years? A thoughtful discussion of these issues is presented in the Supplement to this report, entitled "Mission, Status, Problems, and Priorities of the Black Graduate Schools," prepared by the Conference of Deans of Black Graduate Schools.

"Summary, Conclusions, and Recommendations," Minority Group Participation in Graduate Education. Number 5, June 1976. National Board on Graduate Education, National Research Council, Washington, D.C.

Bilingual Bilcultural Education: Its Status and Future in the United States

Bilingual instruction, a recent inauguration in the United States, resulted from a public concern for the academic, social, and economic difficulties experienced by non-English and partial bilingual speakers in the American community. These problems have been repeatedly documented in published governmental statistics on educational employment and income trends related to ethnic background, and many educators believe today that they may be solved through bilingual education.

The advent of this educational innovation has given rise to a host of technical concepts, and experiences which are often misused or misunderstood. They include such terms as:

•**Bilingual—bicultural education:** Instruction in two languages and cultures. English as a second language in the American context, and the native language and culture of the learners.

•**Bilingual Program:** A program of instruction given in two languages—English and the native idiom of the students.

•**Bilingual Individual:** An individual who speaks two languages, though not necessarily with equal proficiency.

•**Bilingualism:** The ability to function in two languages, though not necessarily with equal proficiency.

•**Biculturalism:** The ability to function in two cultures, though not necessarily with equal proficiency.

•**Balanced bilingualism—biculturalism:** The ability to function equally effectively in two languages and cultures.

In its ideal form, the overall purpose of bilingual-bicultural education is to produce balanced bilingualism and biculturalism within the learners. In this country, its intention is to equalize learning opportunities for non-English and partial bilingual speakers within this framework. The objective of this educational innovation is to enable children to:

1. Achieve fluency and literacy in both languages.

2. Function effectively in the American and native cultures.

3. Progress in academic subjects at the same rate as other children.

4. Develop a positive self-concept and pride in their dual linguistic and cultural heritages.

Parents are expected to participate in the planning, development, and evaluation of bilingual instruction. In this manner, schools establish a close relationship with the target community, resulting in a mutual recognition of cultural pluralism—a concept consistent with the democratic principle of choice, central to the American way of life.

There are two major ways of implementing bilingual instruction in the public schools: as a self-sustained, continuous program (true bilingual education), or as a temporary measure to ease the transfer of "bilingual" speakers into the regular school curriculum (transitional bilingual education).

The latter approach prevails in the United States, as a result of pragmatic considerations, such as local policy, community wishes, scheduling problems, and the like.

Among the most common categories of staff utilization are:

•**one class taught by one teacher:** a balanced bilingual-bicultural individual.

•**two classes taught by a team of two teachers:** an English as a Second Language specialist, and a native language specialist.

•**one class taught by one teacher and a part-time specialist:** A native language teacher and a "visiting" English as a Second Language specialist.

These staff members usually decide in which language each subject matter is to be taught. In Language Arts, of course, listening, speaking, reading, and writing are taught separately in each language. The amount of time devoted to each language during the day varies from one program to the next, and so does the format of instruction.

In respect to the latter, three of the most common instructional combinations may be noted;

1. Separate lessons, with different contents, taught in each language.

2. The same lesson, taught in each language, at different time of the day.

3. The same lesson, taught in both languages concurrently, with brief thought units in each language on an alternating basis. As a rule, the contents of bilingual instruction match those of regular classes, with appropriate modifications in the selection and organization of curriculum items, as required by the use of two languages.

ESL (English as a Second Language) instruction plays a major role in bilingual education but only as one of its components and not a replacement. It is a highly specialized subject matter which must be taught by a trained teacher in order to be successful. Its goal is "total communication" in English, command of oral and written skills, (requiring a near-native), as well as nonverbal auxiliary skills (thought, action and reaction patterns, gestures, and vocal markers).

However, language cannot be taught in a vacuum. Bilingual education, therefore, includes a "history and culture" component intended to prevent the alienation of the learners from the mainstream of American life, by teaching them how to function effectively in two cultural situations, and by fostering within them a positive self-concept associated with their ethnic heritage.

In the implementation of bilingual instruction, the ideal bilingual teacher is an individual who possesses balanced knowledges and skills in two languages and cultural contexts (American and native), and who has completed a bilingual—bicultural training program leading to certification. Unfortunately, such highly qualified instructors are not always readily available, and bilingual positions are often filled by individuals who are dominant in one or the other language or by untrained bilinguals who hold some sort of certification. Results of such indiscriminate hirings practices are usually disastrous.

Staffing difficulties are also intensified by problems associated with the selection and use of bilingual materials at all educational levels (pre-kindergarten-adult): first, the scarcity and poor quality of parallel bilingual materials available on the market; and second, the obvious inadequacy of monolingual texts. Such restrictions place responsibility for material adaptation and development squarely upon the teachers' shoulders, thus adding an unwelcome burden to their daily assignment.

The evaluation of learning achievement also presents bilingual educators with some unsolved questions. In the first place, bilingual programs are, by nature, oriented toward both humanistic and behavioristic objectives. Thus, certain types of bilingual bicultural behaviors lend themselves readily to objective measurement (pronunciation accuracy, vocabulary and grammatical knowledge, fluency of bilingual-bicultural response, use of gestures, language dominance, cultural knowledge, and the like): but others, which are equally important as the former (changes in attitude, perceptions, self-concepts, or understandings) can only be evaluated inadequately through inferences and personal judgement.

In addition, most existing standardized bilingual tests include items which are either linguistically inaccurate, or culturally irrelevant, and, thus, produce distortions in the students' scores. Consequently, in light of the inadequacy of measuring devices, the assessment of bilingual learning may be said to reflect rarely the true achievements of the students.

All in all the complexities and variations found in bilingual education have created considerable confusion in the public mind so far. For the sake of an accurate record, the following points should be noted:
•Bilingual learning is **NOT** an unAmerican activity, but an alternative to educational failure for children with limited English knowledge.

•A bilingual program is **NOT** a watered down curriculum in which to "unload" non-English and partial bilingual speakers, but a regular course of study in two languages.

•A bilingual program is **NOT** a program strictly designed for Spanish speakers: it serves any language group.

•A bilingual program is **NOT** an ESL program: it includes ESL as well as native language instruction.

•In a bilingual program the ESL component is **NOT** synonymous with "remedial English" or "remedial reading."

•In a bilingual program the "history and culture" component is **NOT** an expression of minority group militancy, but a recognition of cultural pluralism.

Several other factors have also contributed to the confusion by undermining unconsciously the very foundation of bilingual education. They are:
•The middle-class orientation of school personnel who expect non-English and partial bilingual learners to measure up to culturally irrelevant standards.

•The alienation of bilingual parents and students from school values, which leads them to suspect educational policies, including those related to bilingual education.

•The preconceived and erroneous notions of most American teachers and bilingual students about each other's motives and expectations, (stereotypes).

•The negative feelings associated by most people with foreign accents and "foreign" ways.

•The hidden resentment of second and third generation immigrants whose parents never had bilingual instruction.

•The association of bilingual learning with "poverty" programs, rather than with "enrichment" programs, and with compensatory education rather than with "quality" education, as a result of federal funding.

•The suspicion that bilingual education is a hidden form of segregation.

•The accusations of "preferential" hiring practices (i.e., restricted to minority personnel) aimed against certain school boards by teachers and other individuals.

Under the circumstances, if any conclusion may be drawn at the present time concerning the future of bilingual education in the United States, it is essentially that its potential has not yet been achieved. However, there is no foreseeable reason why the promise of equal learning opportunity underlying the philosophy of this educational innovation cannot be fulfilled within this decade, through the united efforts of dedicated teachers, administrators, and community leaders. Unless the schools succeed in offering viable alternatives to present standards of academic excellence, which will be relevant to their multi-ethnic population, the reality of cultural pluralism in this "nation of immigrants" remains questionable, for it is only through mutual understanding—linguistic and other—that the true spirit of American democracy will be freed from the shackles of prejudice, discrimination, and wasted manpower. And the first step toward the actualization of this ideal will be taken, when bilingual instruction is awarded its rightful status in the public schools, as a legitimate and desirable form of education for all children in the United States.

"Bilingual, Bicultural Education: Its Status and Future in the United States" by Eliane C. Condon. NJEA Review, December, 1974. New Jersey Education Association, Trenton, NJ.

Second annual report, National Advisory Council on Bilingual Education

1.0 Introduction

The National Advisory Council on Bilingual Education respectfully submits its Second Annual Report to the Congress and the President on the condition of bilingual education in the nation. This Report has been compiled from the Council's review of the available information and literature acquired from Federal and State agencies, project personnel, professional and academic associations; from site visits to bilingual projects made by individual Council members; and from testimony presented before the Council at public hearings held in several regions of the country. The report summarizes the current state of bilingual education efforts and makes constructive recommendations for the fulfillment of the Congressional mandate, "to establish equal education opportunity for all children".

The National Advisory Council on Bilingual Education was created by Section 732(a) of the Elementary and Secondary Education Act of 1965, as amended in 1974 (ESEA Title VII). The 1974 Amendments established the Council, described its composition, and set forth its functions. The Council is composed of fifteen members who are appointed by the Secretary of Health, Education and Welfare. Eight members must have experience dealing with the educational problems of children with limited English-speaking ability, one must represent boards of education operating bilingual education programs, three must have experience in training teachers for bilingual education, two must have general experience in elementary and secondary education, and two must have classroom experience in bi-

lingual teaching. Finally, the members generally should be representative of the population of limited English-speaking persons and of the geographic areas in which they reside.1/

The Council is mandated to advise the Commissioner of Education on policy matters arising under ESEA Title VII, and under other programs for persons of limited English-speaking ability. In particular, the Council is directed to submit a report to the Congress and the President each year not later than November 1 "on the condition of bilingual education in the nation" and on the administration of Title VII and other bilingual education programs.

The contents of the Annual Report are set forth in Section 731(c). The report is to include:

(1) An assessment of the educational needs of persons of limited English-speaking ability and the extent to which those needs are being met by current federal, state, and local efforts;

(2) A report on and evaluation of Title VII activities in the previous year, and an assessment of their contribution to the policy of the Act, as set forth in Section 702(a);

(3) A statement of the activities planned for the succeding period and their estimated cost;

(4) An estimate of the number of teachers and other personnel needed to carry out

---

1/ Appendix A contains a list of current council members and their professional affiliations, and a copy of the Council's charter.

programs of bilingual education and a description of the activities underway to prepare such needed personnel;

(5) A description of the personnel, their functions, and the information available at the regional offices of the Department of Health, Education and Welfare relating to bilingual programs.

To accurately assess the success and potential of bilingual education, and to advise the Commissioner of Education, the Council for the first time, in 1975-1976 held a series of three public hearings throughout the nation. These hearings were conducted in Philadelphia, Pennsylvania on October 16-17, 1975; Albuquerque, New Mexico on January 21-22, 1976; and Portland, Oregon on April 22-23, 1976. In all cases participants were widely solicited to attend and to give the Council the benefit of their observations.

The Council wishes to take this occasion to formally thank those who participated at the public hearings, and to assure them that their oral comments and written statements were carefully considered and incorporated into the Second Annual Report, both as factual data and as recommendations. A complete digest of the hearings, subcategorized by major issues raised at the hearings, is included as Appendix B of this report.

1.1 Structure of Report

This report presents, in addition to other relevant information, the information required by the legislation in a format designed to offer a clear and comprehensive picture of the state of the art of bilingual education. An analysis and assessment of six major topic areas, testimony given at the Council's public hearings, and information gathered by individual council members through site visits form the basis for the Advisory Council's recommendations. The six major topic areas are: 1.0 History, growth and future potential of the bilingual/multicultural approach; 2.0 the needs of the bilingual population; 3.0 administration, operation, and activities of the Office of Bilingual Education; 4.0 the administration and coordination of federal level programs; 5.0 state and local developments furthering the growth of bilingual education; and 6.0 research and development efforts providing theoretical and evaluative rationales for bilingual education.

Under each of these six topic areas, recommendations offered by the Council are detailed and the major issues and recommendations raised at the hearings are discussed; these are followed by a summary of available data, overviews of applicable studies which have been completed, descriptions of programs in progress, and/or a review of work-in-progress for the fiscal year 1977 Report of the Commissioner of Education. In this manner, it is hoped that the reader will be apprised not only of the Advisory Council's recommendations regarding the issues, but also of the efforts presently being undertaken, and the local level response to those activities. Preceding the body of the report is an overview of Council recommendations.

1.2 Overview of National Advisory Council Recommendations

The National Advisory Council on Bilingual Education, as advisors to the Commissioner of Education, the Congress, and the President, offers recommendations designed to encourage the continued development and expansion of bilingual/multicultural education throughout the nation.

Essentially, the Council's recommendations address the following major issues: the future of the bilingual/multicultural approach; needs assessment of the bilingual population; research and development relevant to bilingual/multicultural education; and the administration, operation, and activities of the Office of Education/Office of Bilingual Education.

Each recommendation is included and discussed in detail in the chapter to which it pertains.

1.3 Overview of Public Hearings Testimony

The National Advisory Council's Public Hearings on bilingual education elicited testimony from witnesses representing state and federal bilingual projects, parent advisory groups, various language groups, school systems, and academic experts. Detailed evidence concerning the problems encountered by language minority groups in obtaining assistance, as well as concrete examples of successful ongoing programs, were presented. Suggestions for the improvement of federal administration of bilingual education programs were expressed.

The suggestions of the witnesses at the public hearings were related to the following areas of concern: the growth and future potential of the bilingual/multicultural approach; the needs of the bilingual population; the administration and coordination of federal level programs; the administration, operation and activities of the Office of Education/Office of Bilingual Education; state and local developments in the field of bilingual education;

and research and development activities in the area of bilingual/multicultural education.

Issues, opinions and recommendations raised at the public hearings are detailed in each chapter, as they correspond to the topic areas. A complete digest of the testimony is included in Appendix B of this report.

2.0 History, Growth, and Future Potential of the Bilingual/Multicultural Approach

The Council's recommendations and the issues raised at the public hearings reflect an expanded concept of the role of bilingual education in American society. Increasingly, emphasis is placed upon the ability of bilingual education to foster the nation's perception of its own culturally pluralistic nature. Rather than viewing bilingual education as a remedial program designed to correct the linguistic handicaps of a portion of the population, both the Council and the witnesses at the public hearings stressed the need to capitalize on the cultural richness inherent in diversity.

2.1 National Advisory Council Recommendations

In reference to this issue, the National Advisory Council makes the following recommendations to Congress and the President.

. A national awareness of bilingual/multicultural education as an asset should be further encouraged. A first step would be the creation of a 1977 White House Conference on Bilingual/Multicultural Education to reflect the commitment of the Executive Branch of the Federal Government. The Council requests that the President initiate this program of national awareness as a positive example to the people of this country of the benefits of a bilingual/multicultural education system.

. The Council further recommends that the Legislative Branch redefine and amend Title VII to reflect the pluralistic, social and economic values which are representative of the Nation. and are inherent achievements of quality bilingual/multicultural education.

This legislation should include:

a. That maintenance model bilingual programs be established to serve as national examples;

b. That bilingual education be taken out of compensatory education to reflect national commitment and to remove the stigma associated with remedial programs; and

c. That "limited English-speaking ability" be redefined legislatively to include those children who suffer language interference resulting from second language (other than English) influence. This is directed to remedy the situation of students who have a minimal command of two languages and are limited speakers of both, but who do not qualify for bilingual education under current legislation.

2.2 Public Hearings Testimony

The testimony given at the public hearings reflects the same positive impetus. Witnesses generally suggested that:

. The bilingual/multicultural approach must be stressed within the bilingual education programs, and communicated to the general public. Maintenance model bilingual programs were widely supported, in that they fully recognize a child's ethnic self-worth, rather than viewing linguistic and cultural differences as mere tools for learning another culture, or problems to be remedied. It was recommended that English-speaking student involvement be supported and encouraged at the federal level, and that recognition of cultural pluralism should be a prime goal of bilingual education. Funds should be directly earmarked for parent/community involvement in Title VII programs. Although parent/community involvement is encouraged under Title VII, many witnesses felt that it should be more stringently required. It was suggested that an involved community is the most important single factor in bringing about the eventual shift of responsibility from federal to state and local education agencies. Witnesses also reasoned that for several language groups, the community is an essential resource in the development of relevant educational programs, and that increased involvement fosters mutual understanding between program and parent.

To appreciate the significance of these recommendations and suggestions, it is necessary to examine the current definition and rationale for bilingual education, its historical roots, and the judicial and legislative decisions which have influenced the direction of bilingual education.

2.3 Historical Roots of Bilingual Education

The roots of bilingual education in this country can be traced from the very birth of the nation;

however, its use as a viable instructional method has fluctuated as a result of historical influences. Prior to the 20th Century, bilingual education was used by many groups in the United States to provide quality education: several of the original colonies offered instruction in German and English; the Cherokee nation provided bilingual education throughout the 1800's; and the New Mexico Territory School Law of 1884 allowed each school district to decide whether instruction would be in Spanish, English, or both.

The United States' growth toward world power status in the last century has had great impact, first negative then positive, on the bilingual education field. The growth of a major power requires consolidation and a national self-perception of homogeneity and shared purpose, rather than diversity; thus the "melting pot" theory, manifest destiny, and the nationalistic fervor of World War I precluded recognition of cultural pluralism. The further expansion of the international influence and contacts of the United States during and after World War II stimulated interest in linguistic abilities. Familiarity with other languages and cultures came to be valued for its military, diplomatic, and commercial utility, and to be appreciated as the American G.I.s' and businessmen were exposed to the knowledge and experience of older European and Asian societies.

Following World War II2/, four significant developments positively influenced the growth of bilingual education:
1. The English as a Second Language Approach (ESL), de-

rived from Army language school methods (stressing oral language development as a prerequisite to literacy in a second language), was adopted by many educators to meet the needs of persons of limited English speaking ability.
2. The orbiting of Sputnik by the Soviet Union, perceived as a threat to the United States' International primacy, forced the nation to reconsider its educational priorities. The National Defense Education Act (NDEA) recognized the significance of math, science, and language training.
3. The influx of educationally motivated Cuban refugees into the Miami area in the early sixties caused a massive and ultimately successful demand for bilingual education. This program was an excellent example of the success possible through a combination of federal funding and the target group's involvement in providing direction and resources to the program.
4. Other educators, following the lead of the Miami Cubans, worked in their own districts and institutions to provide field-level support for bilingual education. This led to Congressional hearings which resulted in the passage of the Bilingual Education Act.

The Bilingual Education Act of 1968, as amended by the Elementary and Secondary Education Amendments of 1974, in concert with the Civil Rights Act of 1964, provided the legislative basis for bilingual education. Additionally, these two laws represent the development and definition of two federal roles in bilingual education:

2/ According to DHEW/Office of Bilingual Education's "Rationale for Bilingual Education."

(1) the civil rights compliance/enforcement activity, and (2) the capacity building role.3/ These two roles have been further clarified and defined through subsequent administrative and judicial pronouncements.

2.4 ESEA Title VII - Developmental Overview

With the enactment of the Bilingual Education Act of 1968, as part of P.L. 90-247, Congress declared it the policy of the United States to fund local education agencies to explore novel educational approaches to meet the needs of children of limited English-speaking ability. Funds were authorized for the development and operation of these programs in school systems with a high concentration of such children from low income families, and for personnel training purposes. As can be seen from the chart in Chapter 4, $117.9 million was spent between 1969 and 1973 under this Act, which became Title VII of the Elementary and Secondary Education Act; 88 percent of that amount was devoted to classroom projects, while 12 percent went for various special projects such as curriculum and dissemination centers.

The Office of Education established a Division of Bilingual Education to administer this Act. The preliminary programs funded under the '68 Act revealed a greater need for bilingual education than anticipated; a stronger federal effort in assisting state and local education agencies was indicated.

_____

3/ As defined by the Under Secretary of the Department of Health, Education and Welfare, December 2, 1974 Memorandum pursuant to testimony before the General Subcommittee on Education and Labor.

Thus, the 1974 Bilingual Education Act, enacted as part of the Elementary and Secondary Education Amendments of 1974, P.L. 93-380, announced a broader national policy on bilingual education. The 1974 Act states that special educational provision must be made for persons of limited English-speaking ability, because there are significant numbers of such children with unique educational needs which can best be met by bilingual/bicultural educational methods and techniques. The law declares it to be U.S. policy to: (a) encourage bilingual education methods and techniques and (b) fund state and local agencies to develop and carry out such programs at the elementary and secondary level.

The 1974 Act broadened and clarified the federal role in bilingual education. The law authorizes discretionary grants to LEA's or to institutions of higher education applying jointly with LEA's for the development and operation of bilingual programs. These programs are sponsored in order to assist states and LEA's in meeting the educational needs of the target population and to demonstrate successful techniques by sponsoring programs eventually leading to the identification and dissemination of models of effective projects. In support of a capacity building role if the Federal Government, the law authorizes financial assistance: (1) to institutions for the purpose of training teachers and other program personnel; (2) to individuals who are studying to train teachers of bilingual education; (3) to develop and disseminate curricula and teaching materials; and (4) to foster innovation and reform of graduate education in the field.

These additional responsibilities are reflected in the law's establishment of a separate Office of Bilingual Education within the Office of Education. Of equal importance, to more nearly match the program's scope to its promise, 1974 marked a sharp increase in appropriations for Title VII. From the $33.2 million obligated in fiscal '73, funding increased to $67.2 million in '74, and $84.8 million in '75, the first effective year of the new Act, and to $97.8 million in '76. With its new legislative mandate and a stronger dollar commitment from the Congress, the Office of Bilingual Education, while continuing its funding of classroom projects, has embarked on a capacity building effort to provide the specialized research and development, information referral, and technical consultant services needed to support effective local projects. The National Network for Bilingual Education, now composed of 19 centers throughout the nation, was established. Materials development, resource training, and assessment and dissemination centers were funded to service and coordinate local efforts.

Similarly, to coordinate and focus future project efforts, the 1974 Act directed the National Institute of Education and the Office of Education to jointly undertake a program of research directed toward developing methods of measuring the success of individual projects, approaches, and the program as a whole. Consonant with the demonstration orientation of the program, the 1974 legislation reshapes the federal program to provide more comprehensive theoretical and evaluation underpinnings for bilingual education.

2.5 Civil Rights Compliance/ Enforcement Activities

Litigation arising under Title VI of the 1964 Civil Rights Act, which bans discrimination in the operation of any federally assisted program stimulated the growth of bilingual education. Title VI of the Civil Rights Act states that participation in or receipt of the benefits of federally sponsored programs may not be restricted upon the basis of race, color or national origin. In Lau v. Nichols, 414 U.S. 563 (1974), the Supreme Court held that the failure of the San Francisco school system to provide English-language or other adequate instruction to 1800 Chinese American students who did not speak English denied them meaningful participation in the school program, and thus violated Title VI. The landmark decision for bilingual education directed the district to remedy the situation, although no specific remedy was mandated. In Serna v. Portales Municipal Schools, 499 F.2d 1149 (10th Cir. 1974), under facts similar to those in Lau, but with Spanish-speaking plaintiffs, the circuit court affirmed a district court order requiring the establishment of a bilingual/bicultural education program to remedy the consequences of past discrimination. The school system was ordered to offer courses in English as a second language, and to teach other courses in Spanish.

In Lau, the Supreme Court relied upon the interpretive guidelines published by the Office of Civil Rights four years earlier in 1970. At that time, a memorandum was issued to school districts "with more than five percent national origin-minority group children." This memo directed that, to be in compliance with Title VI of the 1964 Civil Rights Act, a district must:

1. Affirmatively act to remedy English language disabilities of minority children which exclude them from "ef-

- fective participation" in school.
2. Avoid assignment criteria which are based upon English language skills.
3. Adapt ability grouping systems to meet the language skill needs of minority children as soon as possible; and
4. Adequately notify minority parents of activities normally called to the attention of other parents, if necessary by messages in their native language.

In 1975, the "five percent memo" was clarified and elaborated upon in the Office of Civil Rights' "Task Force Findings Specifying Remedies Available for Eliminating Past Educational Practices Ruled Unlawful under Lau v. Nichols." The Task Force Findings set forth the elements to be included in a remedial plan to be submitted by school districts which are found by OCR to be in non-compliance with Title VI. Such a plan should describe:

1. The method by which the district intends to identify the primary language(s) of its students;
2. The measures to be used in identifying each student's educational needs, and the appropriate program to meet those needs;
3. Its plans for implementing the educational programs indicated by the results of step two, such as bilingual/bicultural, transitional, or high intensive language training programs, for appropriate skill combinations and grade levels;
4. Show that its required and elective course offering are not designed to have a discriminatory effect, e.g., by having the effect of unjustifiably channelling language

minorities into certain courses;
5. Describe the district's plan to secure a sufficient number of qualified teachers linguistically and culturally familiar with the background of the target students to staff its instructional program, if necessary by training paraprofessionals.
6. Give assurances that implementation of the above steps will not create racially or ethnically identifiable schools or classes;
7. Describe its plans to effectively notify parents of affected children of activities which are called to the attention of other parents, in the appropriate language, and inform them also of relevant aspects of programs designed for their children; and
8. Describe the evaluation design(s) to be used to evaluate the educational success of the program, both in the process and as an end result.

The Task Force Findings clarified the previous Office of Civil Rights memo's phrase, "School Districts With More than Five Percent National Origin-Minority Group Children." This phrasing left some uncertainty as to whether the five percent figure should be calculated by separate nationalities or languages, or cumulatively. Moreover, no definition was provided for the term "national origin-minority group children." The Task Force Findings adopt the term "student(s) whose primary or home language is other than English," a classification somewhat more easily determinable than that used earlier. Furthermore, the Task Force Findings declare that, while school systems retain an obligation to satisfy the educational needs of any student of non-English home language, due to staff limitations, the Office of Civil Rights will require Lau compliance plans only from those districts with twenty or more students of the same non-English home language.

The Office of Civil Rights has increased its Title VI school system compliance activities in recent years. For example, in 1973-74, 72 school districts, four percent of those with five percent or more linguistic minority children enrolled, were subjected to a compliance investigation. In 1975-76, over 300 districts were so investigated. Enforcement proceedings to terminate federal financing to non-complying systems have been successfully prosecuted.

Thus, the obligation to meet the needs of limited English speaking students has been established by the Supreme Court, and the circumstances under which it applies have been prescribed by the Office of Civil Rights.

2.6 Definition and Rationale for Bilingual Education

Definitions: The 1974 Bilingual Education Act defines a program of bilingual education as:

"A program of instruction, designed for children of limited English-speaking ability in elementary or secondary schools, in which, with respect to the years of study to which such program is applicable -- there is instruction given in, and study of, English and, to the extent necessary to allow a child to progress effectively through the educational system, the native language of the children of limited English-speaking ability, and such instruction is given with appre-

ciation for the cultural heritage of such children, and, with respect to elementary school instruction, such instruction shall, to the extent necessary, be in all courses or subjects of study which will allow a child to progress effectively through the educational system."

The philosophy of the Office of Bilingual Education regarding instructional approach expresses the practical implications of this definition:

"The bilingual education technique makes use of two languages, English, and the one the child uses at home. This approach does not simply involve translation, but rather uses the languages interchangeably, one at a time, often at a different time of the day. The student drills in listening, speaking, reading, writing, and other academic skills, and learns the history and culture associated with both languages, acquiring the skills and knowledge necessary to academic development and progress, regardless of language. This does not suggest that it is to be considered as a compensatory effort. It does suggest, however, that instruction in English as a second language is a necessary part of instruction but is not sufficient to establish an educational program. A bilingual education program recognizes the need to develop and maintain native language and cultural skills, it values language as a transmittal of culture. Thus, it is believed, the child progresses at the same pace as English-speaking children but without the devaluation of his/her culture and self-concept, developing both linguistically and cognitively."

Rationale: A number of theories on the educational advantages of utilizing a bilingual/multicultural approach have been proposed. Basically, according to these theories, a child from a non-English dominant background learn better in a bilingual/multicultural setting because of the positive effect this environment has on the cognitive and/or affective domain.

Theories which stress the affective domain generally point out that use of the native language and culture of the student as instructional modes formally supports and validates the child's own cultural traditions and values. This formal recognition of the child's self-worth gives the child self-esteem and confidence. The child will generally be more motivated to learn because he/she will approach school with confidence in his/her abilities to face demanding tasks, rather than with fear and anxiety, which inhibit intellectual growth.[4]

The cognitive approach stresses the necessity of utilizing the native language and culture as tools for skills acquisition. The Commissioner's Report to Congress discusses the pedagogical rationale for bilingual education. It notes that many informed educators believe that a child learns to read more rapidly in a second language if he/she is first taught to read in the dominant language; and that the child achieves a greater general knowledge of other subject matter in the school language if first taught these subjects in the native language. The

rationales for this opinion range from the axiomatically simple to complex linguistic, cognitive, and psychological theories of learning. Simply, children progress more effectively through school if they are familiar with the medium of instruction. A more complex linguistic argument posits that language is part of a total conceptual framework for viewing the world; and that learning a new language entails learning a new conceptualizing construct. This imposes a nearly impossible double task on the non-English dominant child attempting to learn basic skills.

A number of psychologists and educational theorists believe that children learn basic skills in a certain unchangeable order, and that each successive skill is based upon preceding skills. For example, the skill of reading must be preceded by the skills of good visual and aural discrimination, a wide range of vocabulary, knowledge of sentence structure and exposure to the language. Non-English dominant children may have these skills relative to their own language and culture in which the child is most advanced, rather than "handicapping" the child by attempting to teach the skill in a language for which he/she has no tools.

There are numerous additional theories and rationales for bilingual education, and it is not within the scope of this report to discuss them. It is sufficient to note the trends of thought which have influenced legislative and judicial approaches to the issue. The 1974 Act mandates additional research in the field of bilingual education, which will produce more objective data and theoretical bases for bilingual education. Completed and ongoing studies in this area, which will be presented in full in the 1977 Commissioner's

---

[4] For a more complete discussion of these concepts, see A Better Chance to Learn: Bilingual/Bicultural Education, U.S. Commission on Civil Rights, Clearinghouse Publication 51, May 1975.

Report, will be discussed in Chapter 7.

3.0 Needs of the Bilingual Population

The National Advisory Council is required by Congress to report on activities to assess the educational needs of persons of limited English-speaking ability. This chapter provides data which is currently available concerning this mandate; it summarizes surveys which are in progress to be available for the 1977 Commissioner's report; and it indicates, through Council recommendations and hearings testimony, the perceived needs of the bilingual population. The major areas of interest are: the determination of the number of limited English-speaking persons, manpower needs, and materials needs.

The results of the studies and surveys described in this chapter will provide statistical data concerning the needs of the bilingual population. To appreciate the actual situation which these figures represent, the testimony at the public hearings (Appendix B) would be considered. The Advisory Council offers a number of recommendations designed to address these needs. Witnesses at the public hearings also expressed suggestions related to the needs of the bilingual population.

3.1 National Advisory Council Recommendations

The National Advisory Council presents the following recommendations to the Office of Bilingual Education regarding the needs of the bilingual population:

. The Council recommends that the Office of Bilingual Education set the following as an important funding area:

bilingual/multicultural training for educational counselors and special educators to provide a more complete program for students participating in bilingual/multicultural programs. The Council recommends that the Office of Bilingual Education place greater emphasis in its capacity building mode to include the following:
(a) the preparation of bilingual teachers and paraprofessionals,
(b) materials development and dissemination, and
(c) development of adequate testing methods and instruments for children of limited English-speaking ability.

3.2 Public Hearings Testimony

Witnesses at the public hearings described extensive needs.

Although practitioners from different regions placed varying emphases upon these needs, the following opinions were generally shared:

. More programs should be implemented for the training of bilingual teachers and paraprofessionals, both in-service and pre-service. Witnesses of every language group concurred that the shortage of properly trained teachers is a serious problem, and additional efforts should be undertaken to solve it.
. The development and dissemination of materials should be expanded. Teachers of all language groups need adequate curriculum and materials. Secondary level vocational and career education materials for children who enter the system at a secondary

level, and virtually all types of materials for Native American and Asian American children at all levels, are in immediate demand, according to testimony.

Adequate testing methods for non-English dominant children should be developed. Although it was noted that some work is occurring in this area, more tests are needed in order to validate bilingual programs and to aid in the placement of children. There is a particular demand for acultural intelligence and skills tests, diagnostic and prescriptive tests for the non-English dominant, and tests to measure bilinguality.

3.3 Estimated Number of Persons of Limited English-Speaking Ability

The Commissioner of Education is charged, by Section 731(c)(1)(A) of the Bilingual Education Act, as amended by P.L. 93-380, with the responsibility of reporting to Congress, on or before July 1, 1977, the results of a survey of the number of persons of limited English-speaking ability in the nation and the extent to which their educational needs are being met by current program efforts. In addition, he is to generate a five year plan to begin on that date, together with cost estimates, for extending bilingual education to all phases of the limited English-speaking population, including necessary personnel training. Section 501(b)(4) of P.L. 93-380 directs the National Center for Educational Statistics to conduct a survey of the number of limited English-speaking children and adults. NCES, in cooperation with the Office of Education, has undertaken The Bilin-

gual Supplement to the Spring 1976 Survey of Income and Education in order to fulfill this mandate. Preliminary to this, NCES has recently completed a Survey of Languages supplement to the July 1975 Current Population Survey. Results of this study will be reported herein. In addition, to fulfill the other mandates of the legislation concerning resources necessary to fulfill the educational needs of persons of limited English-speaking ability, the Office of Education has requested NCES to undertake two surveys regarding state and local education agencies' efforts to satisfy the needs of the target population. The Survey of State Education Agencies and the SIE Pupil Survey will be discussed in Chapter 6; the other surveys will be discussed here as they relate to the issues.5/

Results from the Survey of Languages, conducted in July 1975 as a supplement to the Current Population Survey, provide estimates of the numbers of persons of limited English-speaking ability in the nation. In order to accurately assess the meaning of these figures, it is necessary to review the method by which they were reached.

The Current Population Survey is conducted monthly by the Census Bureau on behalf of the Bureau of Labor Statistics, and seeks to generate national estimates of labor force characteristics. Approximately 42,000 households, selected by stratified sample, are polled in person by trained inter-

---

5/ For a more detailed discussion of methodology and/or results of the surveys covered in this section, see The Commissioner's Report on the Condition of Bilingual Education in the Nation, 1976.

viewers. The Survey of Languages consisted of a series of questions concerning language use which were appended to the regular Current Population Survey inquiries concerning labor force status of household members. Specifically, these questions related to the primary and secondary languages spoken in the household, the birthplace and usual language of each member of the household.

The Survey of Languages served two purposes: first, it piloted sampling and questioning techniques to be further refined and utilized in the larger Bilingual Supplement to the Survey of Income and Education. Second, it produced the first "hard" data concerning the number of limited English-speaking persons and their distribution by age, geography and language. While these data are necessarily preliminary and subject to substantial revision upon the completion of the Bilingual Supplement, they at least provide a sense for the magnitude of the population to be served.

In the Bilingual Education Act, Congress identified three classes of persons who may be of limited English-speaking ability: (1) those not born in the United States; (2) those whose native language is other than English; and (3) those "from environments where a language other than English is dominant." The number of persons possessing one or more of these characteristics constitutes the outer boundary of the target population; while all those contained within the three categories do not necessarily "have difficulty speaking and understanding instruction in the English language," the problems of those who do not fall within one of the three groups are not addressed by bilingual education. While the first two clauses of the Congressional definition are objectively

stated and easily determinable, the third, rhose "from environments where a language other than English is dominant," is subject to several definitions. The approach taken by the Survey was that the household was the best indicator of the environment.

Two estimates of the target population may be gleaned from the results of this survey.6/ A high estimate includes all the persons who fall into the following categories:

1. Persons who usually speak a language other than English 7,255,000

2. Persons (other than the above) who live in households where the usual household language is not English 1,287,000

3. Persons (other than the above) who live in households where the usual household language is English but another language is spoken 15,836,000

4. Additional foreign-born persons 3,311,000

5. All others for which non-English is the usual household language, the individual language, or who are foreign-born 231,000

6/ Figures from the Commissioner's Report on the Condition of Bilingual Education in the Nation, 1976.

6. Persons for whom the usual household and individual language was not reported, but who live in a household where a non-English language is spoken and who are native-born   735,000

   28,655,000

While these figures almost certainly include all persons of limited English-speaking ability, it is likely that they also contain a significant number of persons with no English impairment.

A low estimate includes the following categories:

1. Persons who usually speak a language other than English   7,255,000

2. Persons (other than the above) who live in households where the usual language is not English   1,287,000

3. Foreign-born persons not included above   6,424,000

4. All others for which non-English is the usual household language, the individual language or who are foreign-born   231,000

   15,197,000

Note that the most significant difference between the two figures is the inclusion in the first, and exclusion from the second, of individuals living in households where the "usual" language is English, but another language is spoken. While this estimate may therefore exclude some persons of limited English-speaking ability, the Commissioner's Report chooses the low figure as the basis for current approximation, as it seems to correspond more closely to the Congress's definition.

The total figures of the two charts distribute by age group as follows:

Age	Broad Definition	Narrow Definition
4 - 5	978,000	481,000
6 - 18	7,172,000	3,118,000
19 and over	20,506,000	11,597,000
	28,656,000	15,196,000

From these figures, it may be concluded for current purposes that the boundaries of the target population -- those limited English speaks of preschool, elementary and secondary age -- range between a broad figure of 8.15 million to a narrow figure of 3.6 million.

Responses concerning the language(s) spoken in the household provide rough figures for the distribution of the target population across linguistic groups. Without detailing the distribution across age brackets and languages, it suffices to observe that, relying upon the "narrow estimate", Spanish is the overwhelming language within all ages. Persons of Spanish household backgrounds constituted 49 percent of the narrow estimate group and 69 percent of those of school age within that group.

The Bilingual Supplement to the Spring 1976 Survey of Income and Education will supply the bulk of the data on needs assessment required by Congress in the Bilingual Education Act. It was administered in Spring of 1976 as an addition to the Survey of Income and Education, an annual poll of over 190,000 households mandated by Section 822(a) of P.L. 93-380. The bulk of the Survey of Income and Education sought information concerning numbers and characteristics of children in poverty. To those questions, two additions were made. The first contained the inquiries in the 1975 Survey of Languages Supplement to the Current Population Survey, further refined on the basis of that pilot survey. Second, the MELP, or Measure of English Language Proficiency, developed by the Center for Applied Linguistics under contract with NCES, tested respondents who, because of previous answers, were thought to be of potentially limited English-speaking ability. The resultant data will, for the first time, provide reliable estimates of the numbers of persons actually of limited English-speaking ability, rather than those who merely fall into the initial Congressional qualifications. Data from the Bilingual Supplement, which has not yet been fully processed and made available at this writing, will provide state by state distributions of numbers of limited English-speaking children, ages 4 to 13, arrayed by age group and linguistic background.

To ensure maximum usefulness of the Bilingual Supplement to the Survey of Income and Education, NCES has undertaken coordination efforts on two fronts. In the development stage, questions, format and sampling technique were coordinated throughout the HEW Bilingual Education Coordination Council and the OE task force, chaired by a representative of the Office of Planning, Budgeting and Evaluation, responsible for the Commissioner's 1977 Report. To provide each state education agency with a working knowledge of the design, content and potential of the SIE and its supplements, NCES offered a two-day seminar for SEA personnel. With this technical assistance, the states will be prepared to understand and utilize the data as they appear, beginning in March of 1977, and will know the inferences which may properly be drawn from, and the limitations of, that data.

The National Center for Educational Statistics plans to continue its supportive research in bilingual education. Currently under consideration is a study to determine the degree of overlap among a number of legislatively defined child target groups (including the poor, migrant, dropouts, limited English speakers, the handicapped, etc.). The data produced by such a study, if undertaken, would support further coordination efforts by identifying promising areas of cooperation of those target groups with the largest overlap among programs.

3.4 Manpower Needs

The Commissioner's Report on the Condition of Bilingual Education estimates that 129,000 teachers are required to fulfill the needs of the bilingual target population. The Commissioner's Report bases this estimate upon the 3.6 million children who are narrowly defined by the 1975 Survey of Languages Supplement to the Current Population Survey (discussed above), as being in need of bilingual education; and on statistics of average teacher/pupil ratios, average English dominant/non-English dominant ratios in bilingual classrooms, and average numbers of bilingual teachers currently engaged in secondary schools. The Commissioner's Report cautions that this figure is imprecise, both because it is based upon a preliminary estimate of the target population, and because no reliable count of teachers currently employed is available. Thus, the 129,000 figure broadly estimates total teachers needed, not reduced by teachers already in bilingual classrooms or persons training for bilingual/bicultural certification. The greatest proportion of teachers are needed in elementary classrooms -- 108,852; the largest single language group is Spanish -- 78,283. Smaller but significant numbers of teachers are needed for Asian American and other Indo-European languages (including, in order of size, Italian, German, Filipino, Chinese, French, Korean, Greek, Portuguese, and Japanese). Significantly, the Commissioner's Report estimates the 24,979 teachers are needed for language groups under the category "Other," suggesting that, for at least the 34 language groups funded under Title VII and not listed above, bilingual teachers are needed. The ten major language groups mentioned, according to the Commissioner's Report, "are of sufficiently large numbers as to merit special programs designed to prepare bilingual education teachers."

To obtain the more precise definition of manpower needs and available human resources needed for the 1977 Commissioner's Report to Congress, NCES, in coordination with the Office of Education, has undertaken two surveys. One, the Institutions of Higher Education Survey, will provide estimates of the number of teachers and other educational personnel currently in training for bilingual education positions. The other, the Survey of Teachers' Language Skills, will estimate the number of classroom teachers currently in bilingual assignments and the number of certified teachers with second lan-

guage fluency, and thus the potential to teach in bilingual classrooms. This data, combined with the results of the Bilingual Supplement to the Spring 1976 Survey of Income and Education, will provide a better estimate of the teacher shortage and the costs of alleviating the shortage.

3.5 Needs for Instructional Materials

While no comprehensive bibliography of bilingual instructional materials is yet available, most sources agree that more and better texts and curriculum materials, in a wider range of languages, subjects and grade levels, are needed. While the problem has eased somewhat in recent years for Spanish-targeted projects, an acute shortage of materials for the other, smaller linguistic groups continues. For these non-Hispanic tongues, the problem is twofold: first, the potential market for materials is too small to persuade commercial publishers to make the substantial investment of development; second, where appropriate materials exist, perhaps because of government funding, interested persons may not be able to learn of them or obtain them, because of inadequate coordination of available information.

To generate the needed information concerning available and soon to be available materials, and to aid intelligent allocation of development resources, two studies have been undertaken. The first, recently completed by the Educational Products Information Exchange Institute under contract with NIE, will provide a "Buyer's Guide," with description and analysis, of bilingual educational materials available in five languages. Complementing this effort, the Office of Education in July of 1976, contracted for a Study of the State of Bilingual Materials Development, to include a compendium of materials available and under development in twelve languages. In addition, this study will identify gaps in the present inventory of materials and critically assess current methods of field testing and disseminating materials. The results of this study will be reported to Congress in the 1977 Commissioner's Report.

Additionally, nine Materials Development Centers, most of them less than two years old, are developing products for a broad assortment of target languages and subjects (see Table 1). As the National Network of which these Materials Development Centers are a part established itself (See Chapter 4) more systematically developed and reliable materials will be produced through the process of field testing, evaluation, production and dissemination. In

1976, seven million dollars was spent under Title VII to support these Materials Development Centers alone, in addition to the necessary corollary functions of Dissemination and Assessment Centers and Resource/Training Centers, which orient users in available resources and their proper use.

Efforts are underway to establish a National Clearinghouse of Bilingual Education. The Bilingual Education Act of 1974, directed OE and NIE to jointly establish such a Clearinghouse to collect, analyze and disseminate information about bilingual education and related programs. When established, the Clearinghouse will alleviate the current situation of some projects operating without adequate instructional materials which do exist, because they lack information regarding materials availability.

Table 1
Materials Development Centers 1975-76
Completed & In-Progress Materials

Site	Language	Materials Available	Status	Dissemination Status
1-Arizona Materials Development Center	Spanish	2 teacher training manuals	Completed	unpublished
		1 booklet - "Developing & Learning Through Motor Coordination"	Completed	DACBE available
		Teacher Training K - 3		
		1 - Reading in Spanish	1-pilot testing	unpublished
		2 - Self Concept	2-pilot testing	
		3 - Language Arts	3-writing	
		4 - Instruction	4-writing	
		5 - Math in Spanish	5-planning	
		6 - Science in Spanish	6-planning	
		7 - Social Studies in Spanish	7-planning	
		8 - Paraprofessional	8-planning	
		9 - Parent	9-planning	
		10 - Philosophy in Bilingual Education	10-writing	
2-California Polytechnic, Pomona, California	Spanish	1 - 2 teacher's manuals		
		a) Language Development in a Bilingual Setting	written 5/76	unpublished
		b) Curriculum Development in a Bilingual Setting	pilot 6/76	
		2 - Designs for Social Studies Curriculum 7 - 12	pilot	
		3 - Science Curriculum Grade 9	pilot 9/76	unpublished

Site	Language	Materials Available	Status	Dissemination Status
3-Spanish Curricula Development Center Miami, Florida	Spanish	1 - Interdisciplinary Education Kits: Language Arts, Social Studies, Science/Math, Fine Arts, Spanish as a Second Language, Criterion Reference Tests; Grades 1 - 3	Revision in Progress	Available through DACBE - 1976
		Same subjects Grade 4 Grade 5 Grade 6	Pilot Writing Planning	Completed 77 - 79 Completed 78 - 80 Completed 79 - 81
4-Asian American Bilingual Center Berkeley, Cal.	Chinese	Integrated Curriculum: Reading/Language Arts, Math, Social Studies, Science & Fine Arts Gr. pk - 1	1-Writing & Pilot 7/76	Completed 1979
		Gr. 2 - 3	Design	Completed 1979
	Filipino	Gr. k - 1	Writing & Pilot	Completed 1979
	Japanese Korean	Gr. 2 - 3	Design	Completed 1979
	Samoan	Gr. pk - 3	Design 3/76	Completed 1980
5-National Materials Development Center for French and Portuguese	French	1 - Gr. k-6 Adaptation of existing materials French Language, French Reading, Social Studies, Math, Science, Arts	Planning	1 - Gr. k-1, available 1977 Gr. 2, available 1978 Gr. 3-4, available 1979 Gr. 5-6, available 1980
		2 - Readers, 3 - 6 3 - Development of new Materials: 1) Social Studies 7 - 12	Pilot 6/76 Pilot 1 & 2, 6/76	2 - Gr. 3, available 1977 Gr. 4, available 1978 Gr. 5, available 1979 Gr. 6, available 1980
		2) French Language, Arts & Literature, 8 - 12 3) Vocational Materials, 7 - 12		3 - available yearly from 1976-1982
		4 - Teacher Training 1-Bibliographics 2-Resource Guides 3-Courses and Workshop Guides	Pilot 6/76 Pilot 6/76 Planning	Available 9/76 Available 9/76
		a) Social Studies b) Cross-cultural Ed. c) Diagnosis of Student Needs		a) Available 1977 b) Available 1977 c) Available 1977
		d) Culture of Francophone		d) Available 1978
		e) Career Awareness f) North American-French Language		e) Available 1978 f) Available 1979
		g) North American-French Literature		g) Available 1979
		h) Community Awareness i) Vocational Education		h) Available 1980 i) Available 1980
	Portuguese	Grades 3 - 6 1) Readers	Pilot 6/76	1) Grade 3 6/76 through Grade 6, 1980
		2) Portuguese Language 3) Social Studies 4) Portuguese as a Second Language	Pilot 6/76 Planning Pilot 6/76	2,3,4) Grade 3 - 1977 Grade 4 - 1978 Grade 5 - 1979 Grade 6 - 1980
		Grades 7 - 12 Portuguese Language & Literature	Planning	Grade 7 - 1977 Grade 8 - 1977 Grade 9 - 1978 Grade 10 - 1978 Grade 11 - 1979 Grade 12 - 1980

Site	Language	Materials Available	Status	Dissemination Status
6-Native American Materials Development Center	Navajo + four Native American languages by 1981	Reading, Math, Science 4 - 6 in Navajo	Planning	Limited products will be available by April, 1976. They will not be tested by then.
7-Bilingual Materials Development Center* Fort Worth, Texas	Spanish	Math, Science, Communication skills-Spanish & English, Fine Arts, Social Studies; Gr. 6-9	Planning & Writing	Grade 6 - 1979 Grade 7 - 1981 Grade 8 - 1980 Grade 9 - 1982 6/76
*(subcontracted to Lafayette, La.)	French	Social Science, Language Arts, Holidays - Grade 6	Planning & Writing	
8-Northeast Center for Curriculum Development New York, N.Y.	Spanish	Language Arts, Social Studies, Art, Literature, Career Education, Grades 6-9	Grade 6-Writing Grade 7 - 9, Planning	Grade 6 - 1977 Grade 7 - 1978 Grade 8 - 1979 Grade 9 - 1979
	Italian	Language Arts, Social Studies, Science, Fine Arts, Math, CRT, Grade k - 3	Grade k - 1, Writing Grade 2 - 3, Planning	k - 1977 1 - 1978 2 - 1979 3 - 1979
	Greek	Language Arts, Social Studies, Fine Arts, Science, Math, CRT, Grade k - 3	Grade k - 1, Writting Grade 2 - 3, Planning	k - 1977 1 - 1978 2 - 1979 3 - 1979
9-Midwest Materials Development Center	Spanish	Social Studies, Language Arts, Folklore, Grades 3 - 6	Grade 3 - Adapting existing materials Gr. 4 - Writing Gr. 5 - Planning	3 - 1977 4-5 - 1978

* This material has not been excerpted in its entirety.

Second Annual Report, National Advisory Council on Bilingual Education, 1976. Published by the National Institute of Education, Office of Bilingual Education, Washington, D.C. in conjunction with Research Associates, Washington, D.C. November 1976.

NATIONAL NETWORK FOR BILINGUAL EDUCATION

The NATIONAL NETWORK FOR BILINGUAL EDUCATION was created to facilitate the delivery of services to programs of bilingual education. The major role of the Centers is to coordinate planning, communications. and assistance for LEA's (Local Education Agencies), IHE's (Institutions of Higher Education), and SEA's (State Education Agencies).

RESOURCE CENTERS (7) provide direct services on effective practices and procedures to LEA's and IHE's, train classroom personnel in the use of bilingual instructional materials, and field test materials from the development centers.

MATERIALS DEVELOPMENT CENTERS (9) develop instructional, teacher training, and testing materials in the languages and at the grade levels of the bilingual target groups being served.

DISSEMINATION AND ASSESSMENT CENTERS (2) evaluate, publish, and disseminate the materials developed. In addition, they provide informational services to LEA's, IHE's, SEA's, and the other Network Centers.

RESOURCE CENTERS

BABEL/CIMA Resource Center
Berkeley Unified School District
2168 Shattuck Avenue, Second Floor
Berkeley, California 94704
(415) 644-6154
Contact: Dr. Roberto Cruz or
          Celia Z. La Forge

Service region: Chinese, Pilipino, Spanish, and Native
                  American projects in Northern California,
                  Idaho, Montana, Washington, Wyoming; also
                  Alaska and the Trust Territories

Bilingual Resource Center
Institute for Cultural Pluralism
San Diego State University
5544 1/2 Hardy Avenue
San Diego, California 92182
(714) 286-5193, 6606, or 6608
Contact: Dr. M. Reyes Mazón or
          Rafael Fernández

Service region: Portuguese, Pilipino, and Spanish pro-
                  jects in Southern California, Southern
                  Arizona, South Texas, Southern Nevada,
                  and Hawaii

Midwest Resource Center
Northwest Educational Cooperative
500 South Dwyer Avenue
Arlington Heights, Illinois 60005
(312) 253-5713
Contact: María Medina Swanson

Service region: Illinois, Indiana, Iowa, Kansas,
                  Michigan, Minnesota, Missouri, Nebraska,
                  North Dakota, Ohio, South Dakota, and
                  Wisconsin

Bilingual Multicultural Resource Center
University of Southwestern Louisiana
P. O. Box 3388 USL
Lafayette, Louisiana 70501
(318) 233-3850
Contact: Dr. Robert Fontenot

Service region: Alabama, Arkansas, Florida, Georgia,
                 Kentucky, Louisiana, Mississippi, North
                 Carolina, South Carolina, Tennessee,
                 Oklahoma, and the New England franco-
                 phone area

Bilingual Education Resource Center
University of New Mexico
College of Education
Albuquerque, New Mexico 87131
(505) 277-3551
Contact: José A. Gandert, Jr.

Service region: Native American bilingual education pro-
                 grams in New Mexico, Utah, Colorado,
                 Northern Arizona, and North Texas

Regional Cross-Cultural Training and Resource Center
New York City Board of Education
110 Livingston Street, Room 224
Brooklyn, New York 11201
(212) 858-5505, 5506, 5507, or 5508
Contact: Carmen L. Velkas

Service region: New York, New Jersey, Delaware, Maryland,
                 Pennsylvania, West Virgina, Virginia, and
                 Puerto Rico

Multilingual Multicultural Resource and Training Center
Providence School Department
Fox Point School, Box 434
455 Wickenden Street
Providence, Rhode Island 02903
(401) 331-3627
Contact: Adeline Becker

Service region: Connecticut, Maine, Massachusetts, New
                 Hampshire, Rhode Island, and Vermont:
                 Portuguese programs

MATERIALS DEVELOPMENT CENTERS

Santa Cruz Bilingual Materials Development Center
University of Arizona at Tucson
Box 601 College of Education
1201 E. Speedway
Tucson, Arizona 85721
(602) 884-1618, 1461, or 3724
Contact: Dr. Elizabeth Antley

Responsibility: Teacher training materials - transport-
                    able packets
                 Grades K-3
                 Spanish

Asian American Bilingual Center
Berkeley Unified School District
2168 Shattuck Avenue, Third Floor
Berkeley, California 94704
(415) 848-3199
Contact: Linda Wing

Responsibilities: Social studies, language arts, math,
                        science, and fine arts
                      Grades PK-3
                      Cantonese (Chinese), Pilipino, Korean,
                        Japanese, Lauwan
                      Needs assessment
                      Grades PK-3
                      Samoan

Multilingual Multicultural Materials Development Center
California State Polytechnic University
Office of Teacher Preparation
3801 W. Temple Avenue
Pomona, California 91768
(714) 598-4984
Contact: Roberto Ortiz

Responsibilities: Social studies - films and filmstrips
                      Grades 7,8,9
                      Spanish
                      Teacher's manuals
                      Grades K-12
                      Spanish
                      Language assessment instruments - to
                        determine level of teacher's
                        proficiency
                      Grades K-12
                      Spanish

Spanish Curricula Development Center
Dade County Public Schools
7100 N.W. Seventeenth Avenue
Miami, Florida 33147
(305) 696-1484
Contact: Ralph F. Robinett

Responsibilities: Language arts, social studies, fine
                        arts, Spanish as a second language,
                        science, math - (teacher guides include
                        Puerto Rican, Mexican American,
                        Cuban, and multiethnic editions)
                      Grades 1-3 completed
                      Grade 4 in progress
                      Grades 5-6 projected
                      Spanish
                      Health (multiethnic teacher guides
                        only)
                      Grades 4-6
                      Spanish

Eastern Tri-Center Plan for Bilingual Multicultural
   Education
New Hampshire College and University Council
168 South River Road
Manchester, New Hampshire   03102
(603) 668-7209 or 7198
Contact: Robert Parris

Responsibilities: Subject areas as needed
                      Grades K-6 to be reviewed
                      Grades K-12 and Adult
                      French, Acadian French, Canadian
                        French, Haitian French, Portuguese

Native American Materials Development Center
Ramah Navajo School Board, Inc.
Box 248
Ramah, New Mexico 87321
(505) 783-5801
Contact: Gloria Emerson

Responsibilities: Subject areas as needed
                     Grades K-3
                     Native American languages

Northeast Center for Curriculum Development
New York C.S.D. #7
I.S. 184 - Complex 419 (District 7)
778 Forest Avenue
Bronx, New York 10456
(212) 993-2182, 2183, or 2184
Contact: Aurea E. Rodríguez

Responsibilities: Social studies, language arts, fine
                        arts
                     Grades 1-9
                     Spanish

                     Research
                     Grades K-6
                     Greek, Italian, Haitian

Bilingual Materials Development Center
Ft. Worth Independent School District
6000 Camp Bowie Boulevard, Suite 390
Ft. Worth, Texas 76116
(817) 731-0736
Contact: Carlos E. Pérez

Responsibilities: Fine arts, Spanish as a second
                        language, language arts, social
                        studies, science, math
                     Grades 6-9
                     Spanish

                     English as a second language
                     Grades 7-8
                     Spanish

                     Social studies, language arts
                     Grade 6
                     French: Subcontracted to
                              Acadiana Bilingual Bicultural
                                 Education Project
                              Youngsville, Louisiana 70592
                              (318) 856-5073
                              Contact: Kathleen Price

Midwest Materials Development Center
Milwaukee Board of School Directors
5225 West Vliet Street or
P. O. Drawer 10K
Milwaukee, Wisconsin 53201
(414) 671-5420
Contact: Francisco Urbina

Responsibilities: Language arts, fine arts, social
                        studies - cultural aspects emphasized
                     Grade 3 to be revised
                     Grades 4-6
                     Spanish

DISSEMINATION AND ASSESSMENT CENTERS

Assessment and Dissemination Center at Fall River
Fall River Public Schools
385 High Street
Fall River, Massachusetts 02720
(617) 678-1425
Contact: John Correiro

Processes materials produced by:

      Asian American Bilingual Center   Asian languages
      Berkeley, California

      Eastern Tri-Center Plan for   French, Portuguese
        Bilingual Multicultural
        Education
      Manchester, New Hampshire

      Northeast Center for Curriculum   Greek, Italian,
        Development   Spanish
      Bronx, New York

      Midwest Materials Development   Spanish
        Center
      Milwaukee, Wisconsin

Dissemination and Assessment Center for Bilingual Education

Dissemination: Education Service Center, Region XIII
               6504 Tracor Lane
               Austin, Texas 78721
               (512) 926-6129 or 8080
               Contact: Juan D. Solís or
                        Ernest Pérez

Assessment: University of Texas at San Antonio
               Hemisfair Plaza, Building 204
               San Antonio, Texas 78285
               (512) 222-9151
               Contact: Juan D. Solís or
                        Ernesto Bernal

Processes materials produced by:·

      Santa Cruz Bilingual Materials   Spanish
        Development Center
      Tucson, Arizona

      Cal-Poly Bilingual Materials Deve- Spanish
        lopment Center
      Pomona, California

      Spanish Curricula Development Center Spanish
      Miami, Florida

      Native American Materials   Native American
        Development Center   languages
      Ramah, New Mexico

      Bilingual Materials Development   Spanish,
        Center   French
      Ft. Worth, Texas

Directory of Title VII ESEA Bilingual Education Programs: 1975-76. Dissemination and Assessment Center for Bilingual Education. Austin, TX. January 1976.

Sexism and racism

Racism in the English Language

Language and Culture

An integral part of any culture is its language. Language not only develops in conjunction with a society's historical, economic and political evolution, but also reflects that society's attitudes and thinking. Language not only *expresses* ideas and concepts but actually *shapes* thought.[1] If one accepts that our dominant white culture is racist, then one would expect our language—an indispensable transmitter of culture—to be racist as well. Whites, as the dominant group, are not subjected to the same abusive characterization by our language that people of color receive. Aspects of racism in the English language that will be discussed in this essay include terminology, symbolism, politics, ethnocentrism, and context.

Before beginning our analysis of racism in language we would like to quote part of a TV film review which shows the connection between language and culture.[2]

Depending on one's culture, one interacts with time in a very distinct fashion. One example which gives some cross-cultural insights into the concept of time is language. In Spanish, a watch is said to "walk." In English, the watch "runs." In German, the watch "functions." And in French, the watch "marches." In the Indian culture of the Southwest, people do not refer to time in this way. The value of the watch is displaced with the value of "what time it's getting to be." Viewing these five cultural perspectives of time, one can see some definite emphasis and values that each culture places on time. For example, a cultural perspective may provide a clue to why the negative stereotype of the slow and lazy Mexican who lives in the "Land of Manana" exists in the Anglo value system, where time "flies," the watch "runs" and "time is money."

A Short Play on "Black" and "White" Words

Some may blackly (angrily) accuse him of trying to blacken (defame) the English language, to give it a black eye (a mark of shame) by writing such black words (hostile). They may denigrate (to cast aspersions; to darken) him by accusing him of being blackhearted (malevolent), of having a black outlook (pessimistic, dismal) on life, of being a blackguard (scoundrel)—which would certainly be a black mark (detrimental fact) against him. Some may black-brow (scowl at) him and hope that a black cat crosses in front of him because of this black deed. He may become a black sheep (one who causes shame or embarrassment because of deviation from the accepted standards), who will be blackballed (ostracized) by being placed on a blacklist (list of undesirables) in an attempt to blackmail (to force or coerce into a particular action) him to retract his words. But attempts to blackjack (to compel by threat) him will have a Chinaman's chance of success, for he is not a yellow-bellied Indian-giver of words, who will whitewash (cover up or gloss over vices or crimes) a black lie (harmful, inexcusable). He challenges the purity and innocence (white) of the English language. He doesn't see thing in black and white (entirely bad or entirely good) terms, for he is a white man (marked by upright firmness) if there ever was one. However, it would be a black day when he would not "call a spade a spade," even though some will suggest a white man calling the English language racist is like the pot calling the kettle black. While many may be niggardly (grudging, scanty) in their support, others will be honest and decent—and to them he says, that's very white of you (honest, decent).

The preceding is of course a white lie (not intended to cause harm), meant only to illustrate some examples of racist terminology in the English language.

Obvious Bigotry

Perhaps the most obvious aspect of racism in language would be terms like "nigger," "spook," "chink," "spick," etc. While these may be facing increasing social disdain, they certainly are not dead. Large numbers of white Americans continue to utilize these terms. "Chink," "gook," and "slant-eyes" were in common usage among U.S. troops in Vietnam. An NBC nightly news broadcast, in February 1972, reported that the basketball team in Pekin, Illinois, was called the "Pekin Chinks" and noted that even though this had been protested by Chinese Americans, the term continued to be used because it was easy, and meant no harm. Spiro Agnew's widely reported "fat Jap" remark and the "little Jap" comment of lawyer John Wilson, during the Watergate hearings, are surface indicators of a deep-rooted Archie Bunkerism.

Many white people continue to refer to Black people as "colored," as for instance in a July 30, 1975 *Boston Globe* article on a racist attack by whites on a group of Black people using a public beach in Boston. One white person was quoted as follows:

> We've always welcomed good colored people to South Boston but we will not tolerate radical blacks or Communists. . . . Good colored people are welcome in South Boston, black militants are not.

Many white people may still be unaware of the disdain many African Americans have for the term "colored," but it often appears that whether used intentionally or unintentionally, "colored" people are "good'" and "know their place," while "Black" people are perceived as "uppity" and "threatening" to many whites. Similarly, the term "boy" to refer to African American men is now acknowledged to be a demeaning term, though still in common use. Other terms such as "the pot calling the kettle black" and "calling a spade a spade" have negative racial connotations but are still frequently used, as for example when President Ford was quoted in February 1976 saying that even though Daniel Moynihan had left the U.N., the U.S. would continue "calling a spade a spade."

Color Symbolism

The symbolism of white as positive and black as negative is pervasive in our culture, with the black / white words used in the beginning of this essay only one of many aspects. "Good guys" wear white hats and ride white horses, "bad guys" wear black hats and ride black horses. Angels are white, and devils are black. The definition of *black* includes "without any moral light or goodness, evil, wicked, indicating disgrace, sinful," while that of *white* includes "morally pure, spotless, innocent, free from evil intent."

A children's TV cartoon program, *Captain Scarlet*, is about an organization called Spectrum, whose purpose is to save the world from an evil extra-terrestrial force called the Mysterons. Everyone in Spectrum has a color name—Captain Scarlet, Captain Blue, etc. The one Spectrum agent who has been mysteriously taken over by the Mysterons and works to advance their evil aims is Captain Black. The person who heads Spectrum, the good organization out to defend the world, is Colonel White.

Three of the dictionary definitions of white are "fairness of complexion, purity, innocence." These definitions affect the standards of beauty in our culture, in which whiteness represents the norm. "Blondes have more fun" and "Wouldn't you really rather be a blonde" are sexist in their attitudes toward women generally, but are racist white standards when applied to third world women. A 1971 *Mademoiselle* advertisement pictured a curly-headed, ivory-skinned woman over the caption, "When you go blonde go all the way," and asked: "Isn't this how, in the back of your mind, you always wanted to look? All wide-eyed and silky blonde down to there, and innocent?" Whatever the advertising people meant by this particular woman's innocence, one must remember that "innocent" is one of the definitions of the word white. This standard of beauty when preached to all women is racist. The statement "Isn't this how, in the back of your mind, you always wanted to look?" either ignores third world women or assumes they long to be white.

Time magazine in its coverage of the Wimbledon tennis competition between the black Australian Evonne Goolagong and the white American Chris Evert described Ms. Goolagong as "the dusky daughter of an Australian sheepshearer," while Ms. Evert was "a fair young girl from the middle-class groves of Florida." *Dusky* is a synonym ogf "black" and is defined as "having dark skin; of a dark color; gloomy; dark; swarthy." Its antonyms are "fair" and "blonde." *Fair* is defined in part as "free from blemish, imperfection, or anything that impairs the appearance, quality, or character; pleasing in appearance, attractive; clean; pretty; comely." By defining Evonne Goolagong as "dusky," *Time* technically defined her as the opposite of "pleasing in appearance; attractive; clean; pretty; comely."

The studies of Kenneth B. Clark, Mary Ellen Goodman, Judith Porter and others indicate that this pervasive "rightness of whiteness" in U.S. culture affects children before the age of four, providing white youngsters with a false sense of superiority and encouraging self-hatred among third world youngsters.

Ethnocentrism or From a White Perspective

Some words and phrases that are commonly used represent particular perspectives and frames of reference, and these often distort the understanding of the reader or listener. David R. Burgest[3] has written about the effect of using the terms "slave" or "master." He argues that the psychological impact of the statement referring to "the master raped his slave" is different from the impact of the same statement substituting the words: "the white captor raped an African woman held in captivity."

> Implicit in the English usage of the "master-slave" concept is ownership of the "slave" by the "master," therefore, the "master" is merely abusing his property (slave). In reality, the captives (slave) were African individuals with human worth, right and dignity and the term "slave" denounces that human quality thereby making the mass rape of African women by white captors more acceptable in the minds of people and setting a mental frame of reference for legitimizing the atrocities perpetuated against African people.

The term slave connotes a less than human quality and turns the captive person into a thing. For example two, McGraw-Hill Far Eastern Publishers textbooks (1970) stated, "At first it was the slaves who worked the cane and they got only food for it. Now men work cane and get money." Next time you write about slavery or read about it, try transposing all "slaves" into "African people held in captivity," "Black people forced to work for no pay" or "African people stolen from their families and societies." While it is more cumbersome, such phrasing conveys a different meaning.

Passive Tense

Another means by which language shapes our perspective has been noted by Thomas Greenfield,[4] who writes that the achievements of Black people—and

Black people themselves—have been hidden in

the linguistic ghetto of the passive voice, the subordinate clause, and the 'understood' subject. The seemingly innocuous distinction (between active/passive voice) holds enormous implications for writers and speakers. When it is effectively applied, the rhetorical impact of the passive voice— the art of making the creator or instigator of action totally disappear from a reader's perception—can be devastating.

For instance, some history texts will discuss how European immigrants came to the United States seeking a better life and expanded opportunities, but will note that "slaves *were brought* to America." Not only does this omit the destruction of African societies and families, but it ignores the role of northern merchants and southern slaveholders in the profitable trade in human beings. Other books will state that "the continental railroad *was built,*" conveniently omitting information about the Chinese laborers who built it or the oppression they suffered.

Another example. While touring Monticello, Greenfield noted·that the tour guide

made all the black people at Monticello "disappear" through her use of the passive voice. While speaking of the architectural achievements of Jefferson in the active voice, she unfailingly shifted to passive when speaking of the work performed by Negro slaves and skilled servants.

Noting a type of door that after 166 years continued to operate without need for repair, Greenfield remarks that the design aspect of the door was much simpler than the actual skill and work involved in building and installing it. Yet his guide stated: "Mr. Jefferson designed these doors . . ." while "the doors **were installed** in 1809." The workers who installed those doors were African people whom Jefferson held in bondage. The guide's use of the passive tense enabled her to dismiss the reality of Jefferson's slaveholding. It also meant that she did not have to make any mention of the skills of those people held in bondage.

Politics and Terminology

"Culturally deprived," "economically disadvantaged" and "underdeveloped" are other terms which mislead and distort our awareness of reality. The application of the term "culturally deprived" to third world children in this society reflects a value judgment. It assumes that the dominant whites are cultured and all others without culture. In fact, third world chidren generally are bicultural, and many are bilingual, having grown up in their own culture as well as absorbing the dominant culture. In many ways, they are equipped with skills and experiences which white youth have been deprived of, since most white youth develop in a monocultural, monolingual environment. Burgest[5] suggests that the term "culturally deprived" be replaced by "culturally dispossessed," and that the term "economically disadvantaged" be replaced by "economically exploited." Both these terms present a perspective and implication that provide an entirely different frame of reference as to the reality of the third world experience in U.S. society.

Similarly, many nations of the third world are described as "underdeveloped." These less wealthy nations are generally those that suffered under colonialism and neo-colonialism. The "developed" nations are those that exploited their resources and wealth. Therefore, rather than referring to these countries as "underdeveloped," a more appropriate and meaningful designation might be "over exploited." Again, transpose this term next time you read about "underdeveloped nations" and note the different meaning that results.

Terms such as "culturally deprived," "economically disadvantaged" and "underdeveloped" place the responsibility for their own conditions on those being so described. This is known as "Blaming the Victim."[6] It places responsibility for poverty on the victims of poverty. It removes the blame from those in power who benefit from, and continue to permit, poverty.

Still another example involves the use of "non-white," "minority" or "third world." While people of color are a minority in the U.S., they are part of the vast majority of the world's population, in which white people are a distinct minority. Thus, by utilizing the term minority to describe people of color in the U.S., we can lose sight of the global majority / minority reality—a fact of some importance in the increasing and interconnected struggles of people of color inside and outside the U.S.

To describe people of color as "non-white" is to use whiteness as the standard and norm against which to measure all others. Use of the term third world to describe all people of color overcomes the inherent bias of "minority" and "non-white." Moreover, it connects the struggles of third world people in the U.S. with the freedom struggles around the globe.

The term third world gained increasing usage after the 1955 Bandung Conference of "non-aligned" nations, which represented a third force outside of the two world superpowers. The "first world" represents the United States, Western Europe and their sphere of influence. The "second world" represents the Soviet Union and its sphere. The "third world" represents, for the most part, nations that were, or are, controlled by the "first world" or West. For the most part, these are nations of Africa, Asia and Latin America.

"Loaded" Words and Native Americans

Many words lead to a demeaning characterization of groups of people. For instance, Columbus, it is said, "discovered" America. The word discover is defined as "to gain sight or knowledge of something previously unseen or unknown; to discover may be to find some existent thing that was previously unknown." Thus, a continent inhabited by millions of human beings cannot be "discovered." For history books to continue this usage represents a Eurocentric (white European) perspective on world history and ignores the existence of, and the perspective of, Native Americans. "Discovery," as used in the Euro-American context, implies the right to take what one finds, ignoring the rights of those who already inhabit or own the "discovered" thing.

Eurocentrism is also apparent in the usage of "victory" and "massacre" to describe the battles between Native Americans and whites. Victory is defined in the dictionary as "a success or triumph over an enemy in battle or war; the decisive defeat of an opponent." Conquest denotes the "taking over of control by the victor, and the obedience of the conquered." Massacre is defined as "the unnecessary, indiscriminate killing of a number of human beings, as in barbarous warfare or persecution, or for revenge or plunder." Defend is described as "to ward off attack from; guard against assault or injury; to strive to keep safe by resisting attack."

Eurocentrism turns these definitions around to serve the purpose of distorting history and justifying Euro-American conquest of the Native American homelands. Euro-Americans are not described in history books as invading Native American lands, but rather as defending their homes against "Indian" attacks. Since European communities were constantly encroaching on land already occupied, then a more honest interpretation would state that it was the Native Americans who were "warding off," "guarding" and "defending" their homelands.

Native American victories are invariably defined as "massacres," while the indiscriminate killing, extermination and plunder of Native American nations by Euro-Americans is defined as "victory." Distortion of history by the choice of "loaded" words used to describe historical events is a common racist practice. Native Americans are further characterized by the further mis-use of language. Rather than portraying Native Americans as human beings in highly defined and complex societies, cultures and civilizations, history books use such adjectives as "savages," "beasts," "primitive," and "backward."

Another term that has questionable connotations is tribe. The Oxford English Dictionary defines this noun as "a race of people; now applied especially to a primary aggregate of people in a primitive or barbarous condition, under a headman or chief." Morton Fried,[7] discussing "The Myth of Tribe," states that the word "did not become a general term of reference to American Indian society until the nineteenth century. Previously, the words commonly used for Indian populations were 'nation' and 'people.'" Since "tribe" has assumed a connotation of primitiveness or backwardness, it is suggested that the use of "nation" or "people" replace the term whenever possible in referring to Native American peoples.

The term tribe invokes even more negative implications when used in reference to African peoples. As Evelyn Jones Rich[8] has noted, the term is "almost always used to refer to Third World People and it implies a stage of development which is, in short, a put-down."

"Loaded" Words and Africans

Conflicts among diverse peoples within African nations are often referred to as "tribal warfare," while conflicts among the diverse peoples within European countries are never described in such terms. If the rivalries between the Ibo and the Hausa and Yoruba in Nigeria are described as "tribal," why not the rivalries between Serbs and Slavs in Yugoslavia, or Scots and English in Great Britain, Protestants and Catholics in Ireland, or the Basques and the Southern Spaniards in Spain? Conflicts among African peoples in a particular nation have religious, cultural, economic and/or political roots. If we can analyze the roots of conflicts among European peoples in terms other than "tribal warfare," certainly we can do the same with African peoples, including correct reference to the ethnic groups or nations involved. For example, the terms "Kaffirs," "Hottentot" or "Bushmen" are names imposed by white Europeans. The correct names are always those by which a people refer to themselves. (In these instances Xhosa, Khoi-Khoin and San are correct.[9])

The generalized application of "tribal" in reference to Africans—as well as the failure to acknowledge the religious, cultural and social diversity of African peoples—is a decidedly racist dynamic. It is part of the process whereby Euro-Americans justify, or avoid confronting their oppression of third world peoples. Africa has been particularly insulted by this dynamic, as witness the pervasive "darkest Africa" image. This image, widespread in Western culture, evokes an Africa covered by jungles and inhabited by "uncivilized," "cannibalistic," "pagan," "savage" peoples. This "darkest Africa" image avoids the geographical reality. Less than 20 per cent of the African continent is wooded savanna, for example. The image also ignores the history of African cultures and civilizations. Ample evidence suggests this distortion of reality was developed as a convenient rationale for the European and American slave trade. The Western powers, rather than exploiting, were civilizing and christianizing "uncivilized" and "pagan savages" (so the rationalization went). This dynamic also served to justify Western colonialism. From Tarzan movies to racist children's books like *Doctor Dolittle* and *Charlie and the Chocolate Factory*, the image of "savage" Africa and the myth of "the white man's burden" has been perpetuated in Western culture.

A 1972 *Time* magazine editorial lamenting the demise of *Life* magazine, stated that the "lavishness" of *Life's* enterprises included "organizing safaris into darkest Africa." The same year, the *New York Times'* C.L. Sulzberger wrote that Africa has "a history as dark as the skins of many of its people." Terms such as "darkest Africa," "primitive," "tribe" ("tribal") or "jungle," in reference to Africa, perpetuate myths and are especially inexcusable in such large circulation publications.

Ethnocentrism is similarly reflected in the term "pagan" to describe traditional religions. A February 1973 *Time* magazine article on Uganda stated, "Moslems account for only 500,000 of Uganda's 10 million people. Of the remainder, 5,000,000 are Christians and the rest pagan." *Pagan* is defined as "Heathen, a follower of a polytheistic religion; one that has little or no religion and that is marked by a frank delight in and uninhibited seeking after sensual pleasures and material goods." *Heathen* is defined as "Unenlightened; an unconverted member of a people or nation that does not acknowledge the God of the Bible. A person whose culture or enlightenment is of an inferior grade, especially an irreligious person." Now, the people of Uganda, like almost all Africans, have serious religious beliefs and practices. As used by Westerners, "pagan" connotes something wild, primitive and inferior—another term to watch out for.

The variety of traditional structures that African people live in are their "houses," not "huts." A hut is "an often small and temporary dwelling of simple construction." And to describe Africans as "natives" (noun) is derogatory terminology—as in, "the natives are restless." The dictionary definition of *native* includes: "one of a people inhabiting a territorial area at the time of its discovery or becoming familiar to a foreigner; one belonging to a people having a less complex civilization." Therefore, use of "native," like use of "pagan" often implies a value judgment of white superiority.

Qualifying Adjectives

Words that would normally have positive connotations can have entirely different meanings when used in a racial context. For example, C. L. Sulzberger, the columnist of the *New York Times*, wrote in January 1975, about conversations he had with two people in Namibia. One was the white South African administrator of the country and the other, a member of SWAPO, the Namibian liberation movement. The first is described as "Dirk Mudge, who as senior elected member of the administration is a kind of acting Prime Minister. . . ." But the second person is introduced as Daniel Tijongarero, an intelligent Herero tribesman who is a member of SWAPO. . . ." What need was there for Sulzberger to state that Daniel Tijongarero is "intelligent"? Why not also state that Dick Mudge was "intelligent"—or do assume he wasn't?

A similar example form a 1968 *New York Times* article reporting on an address by Lyndon Johnson stated, "The President spoke to the well-dressed Negro officials and their wives." In what similar circumstances can one imagine a reporter finding it necessary to note that an audience of white government officials was "well-dressed"?

Still another word often used in a racist context is "qualified." In the 1960's white Americans often questioned whether Black people were "qualified" to hold public office, a question that was never raised (until too late) about white officials like Wallace, Maddox, Nixon, Agnew, Mitchell, et al. The question of qualifications has been raised even more frequently in recent years as white people question whether Black people are "qualified" to be hired for positions in industry and educational institutions. "We're looking for a qualified Black" has been heard again and again as institutions are confronted with affirmative action goals.

A few final observations. The sports pages of newspapers and magazines call third world athletes by their first names much more frequently than white athletes. And many newspaper editorials are written in a "we"—"they" form. For example: "We try to give our Negro citizens the things they ask for," said Mayor Lee. Think about the assumptions implicit in the words "we," "our" and "they."

Wrap-Up

A *Saturday Review* editorial[10] on "The Environment of Language" stated that language

> . . . has as much to do with the philosophical and political conditioning of a society as geography or climate. . . . people in Western cultures do not realize the extent to which their racial attitudes have been conditioned since early childhood by the power of words to ennoble or condemn, augment or detract, glorify or demean. Negative language infects the subconscious of most Western people from the time they first learn to speak. Prejudice is not merely imparted or superimposed. It is metabolized in the bloodstream of society. What is needed is not so much a change in language as an awareness of the power of words to condition attitudes. If we can at least recognize the underpinnings of prejudice, we may be in a position to deal with the effects.

To recognize the racism in language is an important first step. Consciousness of the influence of language on our perceptions can help to negate much of that influence. But it is not enough to simply become aware of the affects of racism in conditioning attitudes. While we may not be able to change the language, we can definitely change our usage of the language. We can avoid using words that degrade people. We can make a conscious effort to use terminology that reflects a progressive perspective, as opposed to a distorting perspective. It is important for educators to provide students with opportunities to explore racism in language and to increase their awareness of it, as well as learning terminology that is positive and does not perpetuate negative human values.

Footnotes

1. Simon Podair, "How Bigotry Builds Through Language," *Negro Digest,* March '67

2. Jose Armas, "Antonio and the Mayor; A Cultural Review of the Film," *The Journal of Ethnic Studies,* Fall, '75

3. David R. Burgest, "The Racist Use of the English Language," *Black Scholar,* Sept. '73

4. Thomas Greenfield, "Race and Passive Voice at Monticello," *Crisis,* April '75

5. David R. Burgest, "Racism in Everyday Speech and Social Work Jargon," *Social Work,* July '73

6. William Ryan, *Blaming the Victim,* Pantheon Books, '71

7. Morton Fried, "The Myth of Tribe," *Natural History,* April '75

8. Evelyn Jones Rich, "Mind Your Language," *Africa Report,* Sept. / Oct. '74

9. Steve Wolf, "Catalogers in Revolt Against LC's Racist, Sexist Headings," *Bulletin of Interracial Books for Children,* Vol. 6, Nos. 3&4, '75

10. "The Environment of Language," *Saturday Review,* April 8, '67

Also see:

Roger Bastide, "Color, Racism and Christianity," *Daedalus,* Spring '67

Kenneth J. Gergen, "The Significance of Skin Color in Human Relations," *Daedalus,* Spring '67

Lloyd Yabura, "Towards a Language of Humanism," *Rhythm,* Summer '71

UNESCO, "Recommendations Concerning Terminology in Education on Race Questions," June '68

Racism in the English Language. By Robert B. Moore, Ed.D. Published by The Racism and Sexism Resource Center for Educators, c/o The Council on Interracial Books for Children, 1841 Broadway, New York, NY 10023. 1976.

"Fact Sheets on Institutional Racism"

WEALTH

Economist Henry S. Terrell finds that Blacks own 1.2% of business equity, 1.2% of farm equity and 0.1% of stock equity in U.S.A.

NEW YORK TIMES, 1974

STOCK EXCHANGE

Out of 650 membership seats on the American Stock Exchange, only one belongs to a Black firm. The same firm has a seat on the 1,366-seat New York Stock Exchange, and an integrated firm has purchased a seat for its Puerto Rican business partner. All other seats are white owned.

Public Information offices of American Stock Exchange and New York Stock Exchange, July/75

BUSINESS

In the 1,000 largest corporations, Blacks are 72 of 14,000 members of the Boards of Directors.

BLACK ENTERPRISE, June/73

Gross receipts of Black-owned business represented only 0.3% of gross business receipts, and other minorities had 0.4% of the total.

Minority-owned businesses are likely to be small operations. Only 2% are corporations. Over 3/4 of Black-owned, and 2/3 of other minority-owned, firms had *no* paid employees.

U.S. Bureau of the Census, July/72

Blacks received 6.5% of total U.S. income in 1970, but less than 1% of all investment and property incomes.

EBONY, Oct/72

Of the $8.5 billion spent annually by the nation's school systems to acquire the buildings, books, pencils and paper consumed in the process of educating more than 50 million children, only a microscopic percentage will go to Black firms.

BLACK ENTERPRISE, Sept/72

In 1969, there were 1,099 minority-owned printing and publishing establishments, just under 3% of the total. About half of these firms have Black ownership. Employment within these firms amounted to less than 1% of total industry employment, and business receipts amounted to less than 0.5% of industry receipts.

U.S. Bureau of the Census, July/72

BANKS

Of about 14,000 banks in U.S., there are 37 Black controlled banks and 44 Black controlled savings and loan associations. Minority banks had less than 1% of nation's bank assets, yet accounted for over 33% of loans to minorities.

BLACK ENTERPRISE, June/73

Assets of 37 Black controlled banks are $600 million. White controlled banks have $700 billion in assets.

JET, 9/6/73

At the end of 1970, the total assets of the top ten Black National Bankers Association member banks were less than the assets of the 300th largest white bank in the U.S.

RACE RELATIONS REPORTER, 1/3/72

In 1970, non-white minorities accounted for 2.7% of bank officials and managers.

ECONOMIC PRIORITIES REPORT, Sept-Oct/72

"In positions above office and clerical level, minority women consistently fare the worst—in no case do more than 3% of these employees attain either professional and technical, or official manager status. In contrast, over half of all white men are employed at these levels, and bank employees in general average 10% professional and technical, and 15% officials and managers."

ECONOMIC PRIORITIES REPORT, Sept-Oct/72

UNION CONTROL

Only 2 of the 35 members of the AFL-CIO Executive Council are Black.
BUSINESS WEEK, 5/18/74

In large unions employing more than 100 people each, the professional officials and office managers who set policy and exercise control were:

	in 1970:	in 1971:
White	89.1%	89.3%
Black	7.6%	7.5%
Spanish-surnamed	2.8%	2.6%
Oriental	.3%	.45%
American Indian	.2%	.15%

But, just as in most American businesses, their categories of semi- and unskilled factory-type duties as operators and laborers, had:

	in 1970:	in 1971:
White	30.45%	37.65%
Black	30.45%	29.6%
Spanish-surnamed	39.1%	32.75%
Oriental	none	none
American Indian	none	none

Equal Employment Opportunities Commission, 1972

UNION MEMBERSHIP

In 1972 minorities were 15.6% of all union members. They represented a higher proportional rate of membership in the work force than whites, but were *under*-represented in policy making positions.

In large unions employing more than 100 people each, the total white collar officials in 1973 were 85.7% white and the blue collar workers were 57% minorities.

Equal Employment Opportunities Commission, 1974

BUILDING TRADES

THE TOP

THE BOTTOM

In 1972	% Total Minorities	% Black	% Spanish Surnamed	% Asian Americans	% Native Americans
Plumbers & Pipefitters	4.4	1.5	2.1	0.1	0.7
Sheetmetal	7	1.1	5.3	0.1	0.5
Electrical	7.5	2.6	4.0	0.3	0.6
Operating Engineers	6.2	3.9	1.2	0.1	1.0
Laborers	43.4	29.1	12.9	.3	1.1

Minorities still appear to be locked out of the higher paying jobs.

NATIONAL CORPORATIONS

1974 nation-wide summary of 35,796 companies:

	Office Managers	Sales Workers	Laborers	Service Workers
All Minorities	5.1%	9.2%	31 %	31.3%
Blacks	2.9	5.5	20.3	23.5
Spanish-speaking	1.5	2.7	9.6	6.4

Equal Employment Opportunities Commission, 1974

MISCELLANEOUS

In 54 major symphony orchestras surveyed, about 1% of the 4,690 musicians were minorities.
Symphony of the New World, Sept/74

Of more than 37,000 well-paid airplane pilots, less than 100 are Black.
BLACK ENTERPRISE, April/74

Of 3,960 advertising employees in Chicago, 6.8% are minorities and only 5% within that group are in upper-level positions.
JET, April/75

MEDIAN INCOME

The Income Gap Per Cent of Black to White	Median Income (Blacks)	Median Income (Whites)
1964 50%	$3,724	$6,858
1965 50%	3,886	7,251
1966 58%	4,507	7,792
1967 59%	4,875	8,234
1968 60%	5,360	8,937
1969 61%	5,999	9,794
1970 61%	6,279	10,236
1971 60%	6,440	10,672
1972 59%	6,864	11,549
1973 58%	7,269	12,595
1974 58%	7,800	13,400

Bureau of the Census, July/75

INCOME AND EDUCATION

Black men with high school diplomas earn less than whites with an 8th grade education.
U.S. Census, 1970

Black men with college diplomas earn less than white men with high school diplomas.
EBONY, Dec/72

LOW AND HIGH

	BLACK	WHITE
Over $10,000 year	24.7%	49.8%
Over $12,000 year	17.4	36.4
Over $25,000 year	1.3	5.0

55.3% of Blacks earn under $7,000 per year.

N.Y. TIMES, 1/7/73

POVERTY

In 1973 the poverty level was $4,540 for a family of four. 31% of all Blacks lived below this level and 8% of all whites, 50% of Black aged and 27% white aged.
U.S. Bureau of the Census, 1974

UNEMPLOYMENT

	1974 2nd Quarter	1975 2nd Quarter
White	4.6%	8.0%
All other	9.1	14.3
Black	9.7	15.1
Spanish surnamed	7.7	12.9
White veterans 20-34 years	5.0	9.7
Black veterans 20-34 years	10.5	15.4

Discouraged workers who "give up the search for work" are "not counted as unemployed." The discouraged workers total was at a record high of 1.2 million in the second quarter of 1975. Blacks were 27.8% of this group.
U.S. Bureau of Labor Statistics, 7/3/75

TEENAGERS

Unemployment of Black teenagers is 40.2%.
U.S. Labor Dept., N.Y. TIMES, 5/21/75

About 1/4 of all Black teenagers seeking jobs in any year since 1957 have been unable to find them. Those who have found jobs earn a median income of just over $600 a year.
N.Y. TIMES, 7/1/75

Projections based on census reports show that during the 1970's the number of Black teenagers will increase by 24% and the number of Blacks aged 20 to 24 will increase by 36%—a rate of increase 5x greater than of young whites.
Civil Rights Digest, Summer/74

PROFESSIONAL AND TECHNICAL OCCUPATIONS OF BLACK WORKERS—1970

	Number of Blacks 616,300	*Black Percentage In Profession* 5.4%
Accountants	16,200	2.3
Actors	600	6.7
Architects	1,300	2.3
Athletes	2,300	4.4
Authors	400	1.6
Chemists	3,800	3.5
Clergy	13,500	6.1
Dentists	2,400	2.6
Designers	1,900	1.8
Draftsworkers	7,600	2.6
Editors and Reporters	3,300	2.2
Engineers	14,300	1.2
Lawyers and Judges	3,700	1.3
Librarians	7,900	6.5
Nurses, Registered	65,200	7.8
Personnel and Labor Relations Workers	14,900	5.1
Pharmacists	2,800	2.5
Photographers	1,900	3.0
Physicians	6,000	2.1
Public Relations and Publicity Writers	2,300	3.2
Social and Recreation Workers	41,100	15.3
Social Scientists	3,500	3.1
Teachers, Elementary	134,600	9.4
Teachers, High School	65,500	6.6
Teachers, University	16,300	3.3
Technicians, Medical and Dental	24,400	9.0

U.S. Department of Commerce

LOW AND HIGH INCOME

In 1973—Blacks as percentage of all employed:

Professional and technical	5.8%	Household workers	37.6%
Managers and proprietors	3.2%	Craft workers	6.3%
Sales	3.1%	Service workers	16.6%

Civil Rights Commission, July 1975

In 1970, of employed Native American males: 70% were blue collar or service workers, 9% were white collar workers.

Bureau of the Census, June/1973

Occupational Distribution of Employees in the Utilities Industry by Race—1970

	Black	Spanish-Surname
Officials & Managers	1.2%	3.8%
Professionals	1.3	3.8
Technicians	2.3	6.2
Sales	0.5	0.8
Office & Clerical	25.5	27.5
Blue Collar	57.4	54.4
Service	11.8	3.9

Equal Employment Opportunities Commission/1971

SCHOOL BOARDS

In 1973 non-whites were about 1.5% of all elected school board members. Non-white students were almost 22% of all students.

National Education Association, 1974

In 1974 in the 11 southern states 325 out of 17,500 school board members were Black.

Voter Education Project, 1974

PROFESSIONAL STAFFS AND SCHOOL BOARDS

Based on 1970 Census

City	% Minority Students	% Minority Teachers	Race of Superintendent	School Board White	School Board Other
Atlanta	82.5%	59.6%	Black	4	5
Berkeley	74	31.7	Black	3	3
Boston	38	6	white	5	0
Chicago	69.3	36.4	white	7	4
Dayton	45	31.7	white	6	1
Detroit	71.5	42.4	white	4	9
El Paso	64	23.7	white	5	2
Harrisburg	65.4	22	Black	9	0
Los Angeles	50.9	22.3	white	6	1
Minneapolis	12.7	5.8	white	7	1
Newark	88	36.7	Black	4	5
New Orleans	77.2	56.8	white	4	1
New York	63	8.5	white	180	99
Oakland	71.9	29.1	white	5	2
Philadelphia	65.9	32.2	white	6	3
Phoenix	25.7	14.7	white	5	0
San Antonio	80	27.5	white	3	4
Trenton	79	29.3	white	6	3
Wilmington	88	57.9	Black	3	4

MINORITIES IN POLICY-MAKING POSITIONS IN PUBLIC EDUCATION, Nov/74

In Denver, Chicanos are 25% of students, but 2.3% of teachers.
600 of Colorado's 27,000 public school teachers are Chicanos.

N.Y. TIMES, 7/2/75

In 1972-73, out of 199 Bureau of Indian Affairs schools, only 13 were operated by the Indian communities they serve.

U.S. Dept of Interior, 1973

In 5 southwestern states, Mexican Americans constitute:

17% of all pupils	28.2% of all custodians
3% of all principals	5.6% of all students entering college
4% of all teachers	

U.S. Commission on Civil Rights, April/1971

Ratio of PRINCIPALS TO STUDENTS—New York City for 1972-73

Black Principals to Black Students	1: 2,992
Spanish-Surnamed Principals to Spanish-Surnamed students	1:15,169
White Principals to white students	1: 509

Ratio of TEACHERS TO STUDENTS—New York City for 1972-73

Black teachers to Black students	1: 84
Spanish-surnamed Principals to Spanish-surnamed students	1:262
White teachers to white students	1: 8

Metropolitan Applied Research Council, Jan/1974

For students with behavioral problems, San Francisco has introduced a Guidance Service Center. 101 students attend the center. 96 are Black. The staff is all white.

RACE RELATIONS REPORTER, May/73

COLLEGE FACULTY

In 1969, whites made up 96.3% of all 4-year and 2-year college faculties; Blacks were 2.2%, and other minorities, 1.6%.

Statistical Abstract of the U.S., 1972

N.Y. STATE

Of 9,400 faculty members at the State University of New York, only 32 were Puerto Ricans, and of 3,056 in the school's administration, only a handful were Puerto Ricans.

N.Y. TIMES, 2/15/72

SOUTHWEST

There are 20 white students to every white faculty member. For Mexican Americans, the student-to-faculty ratio is 100 to one. 6,000 more Chicano faculty members would have to be hired to attain the same ratio enjoyed by whites.

N.Y. TIMES, 9/24/72

N.Y. CITY

At Bronx Community College, 8 1/2% of the instructional personnel are non-white, while 61% of the custodians are non-white. At Brooklyn College, 7% of the instructional staff are non-white, while 63% of the custodians are non-white.

N.Y. AMSTERDAM NEWS, 3/25/72

MINORITY PROFILE

NATIONALLY 1974

WHO GRADUATES HIGH SCHOOL?
65% of Blacks are high school graduates;
90% of whites are graduates;
27% of Chicanos graduate;
26% of Puerto Ricans graduate from high school

NATIONALLY 1972

WHO GOES TO SEGREGATED SCHOOLS?
45% of Black students are still in schools over 80% Black.
11% of Black students are still in 100% segregated schools.

NATIONALLY 1970

WHO DROPS OUT OF HIGH SCHOOL?
22% of Blacks are dropouts at 16 years of age;
12% of whites are dropouts at the same age.
item: In the Boston public schools, 90% of Puerto Rican junior high school students drop out. In New York City, Puerto Ricans have the highest dropout rate of all groups. Chicanos drop out at a rate 3 times that of Anglos. Half of all Indian youths never get beyond 8th grade.

National Education Association, 1974

11 southern states 1973

WHO GETS EXPELLED OR SUSPENDED?
Almost 1/3 of all enrolled pupils are Black, but
2-1/2 times as many Black pupils are suspended as are white pupils;
2-1/2 to 3 times as many Black pupils are expelled as are white pupils.

Southern Regional Council, 1974

SUSPENSIONS

City	% Minority Students	% Minority Suspensions
New York	64.4%	85.9%
Houston	56.4	71
Cleveland	59.9	70.8
Memphis	58	70.2
Dallas	49.4	68.5

At secondary school level, nation-wide, white suspensions are 4.1%, Black 12.8%, Puerto Rican 9.4% and Chicano 7.1%.

CHILDREN OUT OF SCHOOL IN AMERICA, 1974

A HEW survey of 2,908 school systems which enrolled 95% of all public school minority students found: 6% of Black students were suspended at least once, compared to 5% of the total minorities, and only 3% of the whites. Black students are 27% of all students in the poll, but 42% of all suspensions and 37% of all expulsions.

JET, 3/27/75

PUERTO RICANS

86% of the Puerto Rican students in New York City are below normal reading levels.

In New York City, where Puerto Ricans number about 1/4 of all pupils, only 4,418 of 105,000 non-English-speaking students of Spanish background had any kind of bilingual instruction in the last year of school. A fivefold increase in bilingual classroom teachers, from about 800 at present to 4,200 is needed to give these students help.

The Puerto Rican children in New York City's schools have the system's worst dropout rate—57%, compared with 46% for Blacks and 29% for others.
N.Y. TIMES, 5/7/72

In Boston, studies show between 31% and 42% of Puerto Rican children are out of school.
RACE RELATIONS REPORTER, May/73

In Newark, N.J., the high school dropout rate for Puerto Ricans is 42%.
N.Y. TIMES, Sept/74

MEXICAN AMERICANS

While nearly 86% of Anglo students are still in school by the 12th grade, the number of Mexican Americans has dropped to 60.3% and the number of Blacks to 66.8%.

51% of Mexican Americans and 56% of Black pupils in the 4th grade are reading below grade level, compared with 26% of Anglo students. By the 8th grade, it is 64% for Mexican Americans and 58% for Blacks. By the 12th grade, despite the fact that many of the poorest achievers have left school, 63% of the Mexican Americans and 70% of the Blacks are below grade level; for whites, the number is 34%.
U.S. Commission on Civil Rights, Oct/71

While an estimated 4,000 persons in the southwest identify Spanish as their mother tongue, only 25% of the elementary and 11% of the secondary schools send notices in Spanish to Spanish-speaking parents.

While 47% of all Mexican American first-graders in the southwest don't speak English as well as the average first-grader, many educators forbid the use of the child's native language for his instruction. Students have reported being hit, slapped and beaten in the face for speaking Spanish in their schools.

91.7% of the elementary schools in the southwest, and 98.5% of its secondary schools, do not use Spanish as well as English in conducting PTA meetings.

Although 17% of the student population in the southwest is Mexican American, only 6.5% of the schools offer bilingual programs and only 2.7% of the pupils are enrolled in these classes. Arizona, Colorado and New Mexico have less than 1% of their pupils enrolled in such classes.
U.S. Commission on Civil Rights, May/72

The dropout rate for Mexican Americans in the Southwest is 40%, compared to 10% for whites.
N.Y. TIMES, 7/2/75

INDIANS

For Indian students, dropout rates are twice the national average.
Achievement levels are far below those of whites. 18% of the students in federal Indian schools go to college and only 3% graduate, whereas 50% of the nation's high school graduates attend college and 32% graduate.
MILWAUKEE JOURNAL, 3/4/73

BLACKS

In San Francisco, Blacks in 6th grade are over 2-½ years behind the district norm. Reading scores in Boston's Black schools were the poorest.
RACE RELATIONS REPORTER, May/73

EMR CLASSES

In 505 school districts in Alabama, Georgia, South Carolina, Mississippi and Arkansas, which had classes for those labelled EMR (educable mentally retarded), over 80% of students were Black, though less than 40% of total district enrollment was Black. (This type of ratio is common throughout the country. . . . Foundation for Change)
CHILDREN OUT OF SCHOOL IN AMERICA, 1974

COLLEGE

In 1973—Blacks enrolled in colleges and universities *decreased* from 8.7 to 7.8% of first year students. Total minorities dropped from 14.8 to 13% in that class.

In 1973—Students from families with incomes less than $6000 were down to 11.1% of first year class. In 1972 they were 14.1%. Students from families with incomes over $30,000 were 11.2% of first year class. In 1972 they were 9.1%.

American Council on Education, 1974

90% of Native American college students drop out of school.

Integrated Educ., RACE & SCHOOLS, May-June/72

In 1974 for ages 18-28 years—enrolled in college: (full & part-time) 18% of Blacks compared to 25% of whites.

Census Bureau, July/1975

At the graduate level, minorities constitute 7.3% of students.

Health, Education and Welfare, Oct/1971

The Dept. of Justice charged that Mississippi's 25 state colleges and universities are illegally segregated.

N.Y. TIMES, 1/21/75

LAW SCHOOLS

At 17 major Southern law schools, there were less than 200 Black first year students in 1972. The minority dropout rate from law schools is twice that of whites.

Law Students' Civil Rights Research Council, 1972

In 1973, only 7% of law students were non-white.

GUILD PRACTITIONER, Spring/74

ENGINEERS

There is only one Black student to approximately 140 white students in the senior classes of the predominantly-white engineering colleges of the United States.

Integrated Educ., RACE & SCHOOLS, Oct/70

ARCHITECTS

From 1 to 2% of all architects belong to minority groups. The percentage of those being trained stands at about 4%.

N.Y. AMSTERDAM NEWS, 12/31/72

MEDICAL

First-year enrollments in medical schools for 1972-73 were:

Black American	957 or	7.1% of total enrollment
American Indian	34	.3%
Mexican American	137	1.0%
Puerto Rican (Mainland)	44	.3%
Asian American	231	2.7%

Association of American Medical Colleges, 1973

TEACHERS

A National Education Association survey found that more than 30,000 teaching jobs for Blacks had been eliminated in 17 Southern and border states through desegregation and discrimination since 1954.

EBONY, Jan/73

EDUCATION BUDGETS

In the central cities of 37 metropolitan areas in 1970, 36% of total local expenditures went to education. In suburbs, it was 56%.

U.S. Commission on Civil Rights, May/73

Fact Sheets on Institutional Racism. Compiled and published by The Racism and Sexism Center for Educators, c/o The Council on Interracial Books for Children, 1841 Broadway, New York, NY 10023. August 1975.

"Fact Sheets on Institutional Sexism"

DEFINITION OF SEXISM

SEXISM IS: Any attitude, action or institutional structure which subordinates a person or group because of their sex.

—OR—

Any assignment of roles in society on the basis of sex.

—OR—

Exploitation of females, individually or as a group, by males.

SEXISM CAN BE: Individual, cultural or institutional

—AND—

Intentional or unintentional.

EXAMPLES OF SEXISM

INDIVIDUAL SEXISM:
"After you, M'am."
"That's a woman driver for you."
"Billy, please carry the movie projector. Sally, you wash the backboard."

CULTURAL SEXISM:
"Our textbook is, MEN WHO MADE AMERICA GREAT."
"Do you want the baby blanket in pink or blue?"
"The erector set is for John and the Barbie doll for Jill."

INSTITUTIONAL SEXISM:
"We're not sexist, we just hire and promote the most experienced people."
Presidents of industry, boards of directors, universities, medical associations and of the U.S.A. have been, and still are 99-9/10ths male (and white).
Women earn 57% of what men earn for similar work.

RANDOM THOUGHTS ON SEXISM AND RACISM

WHITE WOMEN ARE: Opressed (by males) but they are also oppressors (or Third World women and men).

POOR WHITE WOMEN ARE: Doubly oppressed (because of their sex and because of their class).

THIRD WORLD WOMEN ARE: Doubly oppressed (by racism and by sexism).

POOR THIRD WORLD WOMEN ARE: Triply oppressed (by race, sex and class) and . . . A *very* large proportion of Third World women are poor . . .

SEXISM— LIKE RACISM— IS PROFITABLE
Racism maintains a ready pool of cheap, underpaid labor which is profitable in our economic system. This pool of cheap labor is utilized as potential competition to white labor, and keeps white wages lower than the would otherwise be.

Sexism may be basic to the survival of our present economic system because it provides both cheap and unpaid labor. Women do the same work as men do for about 43% less money. And millions of women also do unpaid household work which would be worth about $9,000 per woman per year if it were paid for. This free labor maintains the present labor force, creates the next generation's labor force and cares for the old, worn out labor force—all without cost to the employers.

ECONOMY

EMPLOYMENT

36 million women are in the U.S. civilian labor force. They represent 39.5% of all the labor force.

ABOUT WOMEN WHO WORK 1 9 7 5

Almost 3/5 are married, living with their husbands, and helping to support their families. More than 1/5 are single. Nearly 1/5 are widowed, divorced or separated.

13.6 million working women had children under 18 years.
5.1 million working women had children under 6 years.

Half of the married women whose husbands earn between $7,000 and $9,999 are working.

Minority women represent 45.2% of the minority work force. About one out of eight women in the labor force is of a minority race (higher than their percentage in the general population).

Nationally, women earn 57% of what men earn.
                    U.S. Dept. of Labor

WHAT WOMEN EARN 1 9 7 4

Median Earnings of Year-round Full-time Workers

Women	Men	Women's Earnings As Percent of Men's
$6,772	$11,835	57.2%

Of the 34.6 million women in the work force, 2/3 perform low-paid clerical service or factory jobs.
                    U.S. Dept. of Labor

1 9 7 3

	Female	Male
Median Wage for Managers and Administrators	$7,024	$13,386
Median Wage for Clericals	6,054	9,716
Median Wage for Salespeople	4,445	11,610
Earning more than $15,000	1.1%	13.5%
Earning less than $7,000	74%	30%

Corporate Information Center "Brief"

1 9 7 2

Median Incomes of Full-Time Women Workers By Occupation

Major Occupation Group	Median Income	Percent of Men's Income
Professional and technical workers	$8,796	68%
Nonfarm managers and administrators	7,306	53%
Clerical workers	6,039	63%
Sales workers	4,575	40%
Operatives, including transportation	5,021	58%
Service workers (except private household)	4,606	59%
Private household	2,365	*
Nonfarm laborers	4,755	63%

*Percent not shown where median income of men is based on fewer than 75,000 individuals.   *U.S. Dept. of Labor, Women's Bureau*

1 9 7 3

Comparative Income for Similar Work

Occupation	Median Wage Women	Men	Women's Income As Percent of Men's
Managers, Administrators	$7,998	$14,737	54.3%
Sales workers	4,674	12,031	38.8
Clerical workers	6,458	10,619	60.8
Nonfarm laborers	5,286	8,037	65.8

U.S. Labor Bureau

EFFECT OF RACISM ON INCOME 1 9 7 3

Median Earnings of Year-round Full-time Workers

All Women	Minority Women	Men
$6,335	$5,772	$11,186

U.S. Dept. of Labor

1 9 7 2

Comparative Median Income

	Women	Men
Spanish speaking	$2,647	$5,786
Black	5,147	7,301
White	5,998	10,593

U.S. Dept. of Commerce

EFFECT OF RACISM ON OCCUPATION

1 9 7 4

Black women represent about 12% of *all* women in the U.S.A.

Profession	% BLACK Women Among ALL WOMEN in Profession
Building Cleaners	33.4%
Cleaners and Servants	61.4
Clothing Pressers	40.6
Farm Laborers	17.4
File Clerks	21.0
Laundry and Dry Cleaning Operators	31.8
Managers and Administrators	4.2
Non-Farm Laborers	24.0
Postal Clerks	21.8
Practical Nurses	23.8
Private Household Workers	38.6
Teachers' Aides	22.8
Textile Operators	21.7
White Collar Workers	7.1

Note: These statistics are for "Black and other races," but do *not* include Hispanic Americans. They represent about 90% Black women.

U.S. Dept. of Labor

EFFECT OF RACISM ON OCCUPATION 1 9 6 0- 1 9 7 0

[Percent distribution]

Occupational group	All workers 1960	All workers 1970	Puerto Ricans [1] 1960	Puerto Ricans [1] 1970	Blacks [2] 1960	Blacks [2] 1970
BOTH SEXES						
Total	100.0	100.0	100.0	100.0	100.0	100.0
White-collar workers	51.7	57.9	18.7	33.4	29.2	43.1
Professional and technical	12.0	15.7	2.4	4.8	6.8	9.9
Managers, officials, and proprietors	9.4	7.8	2.8	3.6	3.4	3.1
Clerical workers	22.8	27.1	10.6	20.2	16.2	26.7
Salesworkers	7.5	7.3	2.9	4.8	2.8	3.4
Blue-collar workers	35.2	28.5	65.1	48.1	40.8	32.9
Craftsworkers and supervisors	11.1	10.2	8.0	11.3	7.0	9.0
All others [3]	24.1	18.3	57.1	36.8	33.8	23.9
Service workers	13.0	13.6	16.1	18.5	29.9	24.0
Private household	2.1	1.3	.3	.3	9.8	4.5
Other service workers	10.9	12.3	15.8	18.2	20.1	19.5
MEN						
Total	100.0	100.0	100.0	100.0	100.0	100.0
White-collar workers	45.9	49.2	18.2	27.2	27.0	33.3
Professional and technical	11.8	15.4	2.2	4.0	5.2	7.9
Managers, officials, and proprietors	12.4	10.6	3.7	4.5	5.0	4.3
Clerical workers	13.4	14.8	9.2	13.7	14.1	17.2
Salesworkers	8.3	8.4	3.1	5.0	2.7	3.9

Occupational group	All workers 1960	All workers 1970	Puerto Ricans [1] 1960	Puerto Ricans [1] 1970	Blacks [2] 1960	Blacks [2] 1970
MEN—Continued						
Blue-collar workers	42.4	37.7	61.3	51.6	50.9	47.5
Craftsworkers and supervisors	16.6	16.2	11.2	15.5	11.6	15.3
All others [3]	25.8	21.5	50.1	36.1	39.3	32.2
Service workers	11.7	13.1	20.6	21.2	22.0	19.2
Private household	.2	.1	.1	.1	.9	.3
Other service workers	11.5	13.0	20.5	21.1	21.1	18.9
WOMEN						
Total	100.0	100.0	100.0	100.0	100.0	100.0
White-collar workers	62.2	70.9	19.9	46.5	32.0	54.7
Professional and technical	12.3	16.3	2.9	6.5	8.8	12.2
Managers, officials, and proprietors	4.1	3.8	1.1	1.7	1.4	1.8
Clerical workers	39.6	45.1	13.4	34.0	18.9	37.8
Salesworkers	6.2	5.7	2.5	4.3	2.9	2.9
Blue-collar workers	22.5	15.1	72.4	40.6	27.9	15.7
Craftsworkers and supervisors	1.4	1.4	1.9	2.4	1.2	1.5
All others [3]	21.2	13.7	70.5	38.2	26.7	14.2
Service workers	15.3	14.0	7.7	12.9	40.0	29.6
Private household	5.5	2.9	.8	.8	21.2	9.4
Other service workers	9.8	11.1	6.9	12.1	18.8	20.2

[1] Data for Puerto Ricans are for the New York area (New York City, Nassau-Suffolk, Westchester and Rockland Counties). In 1970, 96 percent of the Puerto Ricans in this area lived in the city itself.

[2] Data for 1960 are for black and other races. In 1960, blacks constituted 95.3 percent of the category.

[3] Includes operatives, laborers, and farmworkers. Farm managers and laborers constituted less than 1 percent of the total in both 1960 and 1970.

NOTE: Data for 1960 are for employed persons age 14 and over; 1970 data are for employed persons age 16 and over. The effect of excluding 14- and 15-year-olds in 1970 is minimal, since they were only 0.4 percent of all employed persons. Figures for individual items may not add to totals because of rounding.

U.S. Dept. of Labor

EDUCATION AND ITS EFFECT ON INCOME 1974

Years of School Completed	Median Income Women	Men	Women's Median Income as Percent of Men's
Elementary School	$5,135	$9,406	54.6%
High School	6,623	12,017	55.1
College	9,057	15,503	58.4
Doctorate	16,400	18,700	87.7
Doctorate + 22 years experience	21,800	27,100	80.4

OR—put another way—a male high school graduate earns more than a female college graduate.

Educational Testing Service, 1975

UNION MEMBERSHIP AND CONTROL 1973

Amalgamated Clothing Workers Union: 75% female membership—2 women on governing board of 23

Int'l Ladies Garment Workers Union and Communications Workers of America: Majority of members are women; *no* women sit on national governing boards

New York School of Industrial and Labor Relations

Unions have organized less than 25% of the workers in 5 of the 9 industries in which women constitute more than 40% of total employment (textiles, finance, service, state and local governments)

U.S. Dept. of Labor

1972

46 of thousands of union leadership posts are held by women.

National Project of Ethnic America, A.J.C.

1974

Of the 185 U.S. trade unions, 6 have women in the top elective posts.

AFL-CIO   25% of the members are women
4.7% of key leadership positions are held by women

Monthly Labor Review Oct/74

WHERE WOMEN ARE EMPLOYED 1973

Women Continue to Find Jobs More Easily in Some Industries Than in Others

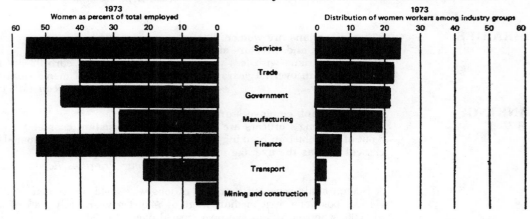

U.S. Dept. of Labor

ECONOMY

UNEMPLOYMENT 1974

Unemployment rates are generally higher for women than men. Young women of minority races have the highest unemployment rates:

Unemployed as Percent of Civilian Labor Force, 1974

	Women White	Other	Men White	Other
16 to 19 years	14.5%	34.6%	13.6%	31.6%
20 to 24 years	8.2	18.0	7.8	15.4
25 and over	4.3	6.3	2.8	5.1

1 9 7 5

Unemployment rates for people 20 years and over

White	6.5% males	6.8% females
Other	12.1%	12.1%

WHAT IS WOMEN'S WORK

1 9 7 4

Profession	% Women In Profession	Profession	% Women In Profession
Assemblers	50.1%	Receptionists	97.4%
Bank Tellers	91.5	Sales Clerks	69.4
Bank Officials	21.4	Sales Representa-	
Clerical Workers	77.6	tives (Wholesale)	4.8
Craft Workers	4.5	Secretaries	99.2
Engineers	1.3	Sewer Workers	95.8
Insurance Agents	13.3	Social Workers	61.3
Lawyers	7.0	Teachers (Pre-school)	97.9
Librarians	81.7	(Elementary School)	84.3
Nurses (Practical)	86.8	(Secondary School)	48.3
Nurses (Registered)	98.0	(College, Univ.)	30.9
Physicians	9.0	School Administrators	27.8
Private Household		Telephone Operators	93.8
Workers	97.8		

Approximately equal proportions of women and men are professional or technical workers, but women are heavily concentrated in the lower paying teaching and nursing fields, while more men are found in such higher paying professions as law, medicine and engineering.

U.S. Dept. of Labor

MEDICINE

% Women in Medical Professions

7.6% of doctors	7.0% of obstetricians
1.0% of surgeons	5.0% of internists
20.0% of pediatricians	98.0% of registered nurses
13.0% of psychiatrists	86.8% of practical nurses

U.S. Dept. of Labor

LIBRARIES

82% of librarians are women, but . . .
19% of deans and directors of library schools are women.
Women librarians with less than 5 years of experience earn 92% of men's salaries. Women librarians with over 20 years of experience earn 70% of men's salaries.

Association of American Colleges and Universities

BANKING
1 9 7 0

61% of all bank employees are women.
10% of banking's officers are women (usually assistant cashiers).
9 out of 10 women in banking are employed in clerical jobs (compared to 4 out of 10 women in clerical jobs as the average for all industries).

Economic Priorities Report, Sept.Oct/72

A Boston study revealed that 58% of jobs were held by women. 86.2% of these women held clerical positions at a median wage of $4,584 a year. Only 2.4% of the women earned over $10,000, whereas 51% of the men earned over $10,000.

INSURANCE

Women pay more than men for the same health insurance, despite Labor Dept. statistics which show that both men and women lost an average of 5.1 days of work because of illness.

	5 year	1 year
Accident & Sickness Plan costs for Men	$496.70	$320
Women	762.80	496

Organization for Women Office Workers, Sept/74

SECURITIES
1 9 7 4

89.4% of clerical staffs are female.
7.7% of top positions are held by women.

Organization for Women Office Workers, Sept/74

RETAIL TRADE

80% of sales people are women.
85% of clerical positions are held by women.

Intergrated Education Sept.Oct/75

ENGINEERING 1 9 7 1

Of 100,000 engineers in the U.S., 0.5% were women.

Engineering Foundation Conference, 1971

LAW ENFORCEMENT 1 9 7 4

No women have ever been employed as State Troopers by the Indiana State Police Department of 937 Troopers.

One woman police officer in Oakland Police Department of 708 officers.

74 of 8,245 police officers in Philadelphia are women (0.9%). Of the 19 job classifications for officers, only 4 are open for women.

1 of 360 Des Moines police officers is a woman.

No women in Ames (Iowa) Police Department of 27 officers.
No women in Newton (Iowa) Police Department of 25 officers.

19 women in New Orleans Police Department of 1,139 (1.7%).
22 women in Portland Police Bureau of 730 officers (3%).
10 women in Honolulu Police Department of 1,461 officers (0.7%).

American Civil Liberties Union, Sept/75

1 9 7 3

2% of all police officers are female.

International Association of Chiefs of Police

0.3% of state police officers are female.

Race Relations Information Center

35,796 NATIONAL COMPANIES 1 9 7 4

		Office Mgrs.	Professionals	Office Workers & Clerks	Service Jobs
White	Men	82.9%	67.5%	17.6%	32.0%
	Women	12.0	25.3	68.9	36.7
Minority	Men	4.0	4.3	2.9	16.1
	Women	1.1	2.9	10.6	15.2

U.S. Equal Economic Opportunity Report

WOMEN AS PERCENT OF EMPLOYED WORKERS

1 9 7 4

Occupational Participation Rates:

Women as a Percent of the Total Employed Workers

Occupational Group			
Total employed	38.9	Professional:	
Professional:	40.5	Drafting technicians	7.7
Accountants	23.7	Designers	24.0
Lawyers & judges	7.0	Editors & reporters	43.6
Librarians	81.7	Painters & sculptors	41.6
Chemists	14.0	Public relations	28.8
Personnel & labor rel.	34.9		
Pharmacists	16.5	Clerical workers:	77.6
Physicians (including		Bank tellers	91.5
osteopaths)	9.8	Bookkeepers	89.2
Registered nurses	98.0	Cashiers	87.7
Psychologists	41.4	Collectors, bill &	
Social workers	61.3	account	46.0
Teachers, college &		Dispatchers, vehicle	24.2
university	30.9	Insurance adjusters	45.6
Elem. School teachers	84.8	Mail carriers	7.5

Occupational Group

Messengers	23.7	Operatives:	31.1
Payroll timekeepers	77.4	Checkers, inspectors	50.6
Postal clerks	28.0	Gas station attendants	5.3
Secretaries	99.2	Graders and sorters	75.0
Shipping & receiving clerks	15.9	Packers and wrappers, except meat	63.1
Storekeepers & stock clerks	25.2	Photo process workers	47.0
Telephone operators	93.8	Weavers	59.5
Ticket & station agents	38.0	Welders	5.0
Typists	96.2	Busdrivers	37.4
Office machine operators	71.3	Delivery workers	4.4
		Taxicab drivers	11.5
Laborers, except farm:	8.1		
		Farmers and farm managers	6.0
Managers:	18.5	Farmer owner tenants	6.0
Purchasing agents	17.9		
		Farm laborers & super-visors:	27.4
Salesworkers:	41.8	Farm laborers (wage workers)	14.6
Hucksters & peddlers	75.1	Farm laborers (unpaid family)	63.6
Insurance agents	13.3		
News vendors	25.3		
Real estate agents	38.3	Service workers except private household:	58.7
		Bartenders	32.6
Craft workers:	4.5	Cooks	58.8
Bakers	41.1	Food Counter workers	85.2
Compositors and typesetters	19.9	Waiters	91.8
Decorators & window dressers	62.4	Attendants, recreation	35.9
		Hairdressers	92.4
Painters, construc-tion & maintenance	2.6	Guards & watchers	6.1
		Nursing aides	86.9

U.S. Dept. of Labor

TRUCK DRIVERS

Truck Drivers (U.S. Census Bureau)	Men	Women
1960	1,549,713	7,724
1970	1,359,505	20,120

New York Times, Jan. '72

EDUCATION

VOCATIONAL TRAINING

1970

Vocational Training of Persons 18 Years Old and Over

	Total	Business of Office Work	Nursing Or Other Health Field	Engineering Or Science Technician
Male	63,277,575	2,279,950	408,629	1,897,434
Female	70,035,905	6,205,489	2,692,442	104,660
White				
Male	56,528,005	2,137,471	363,842	1,788,766
Female	62,148,588	5,786,458	2,359,956	94,163
Black				
Male	5,957,663	112,717	36,019	77,543
Female	7,072,461	350,424	293,707	7,827
Persons of Spanish Origin or Descent				
Male	2,431,496	78,786	16,248	48,669
Female	2,634,841	187,357	70,854	4,196

U.S. Dept. of Labor

WHO STARTS
COLLEGE

Percent Women of First Year Law Students: 23.7%
Percent Women of First Year Med Students: 22.2%

1 9 7 4

In the fall of 1974, the percentage of women in the opening enrollment of full-time students in public institutions of higher education were:

Universities	Four-Year Institutions	Two-Year Institutions
40.9%	46.5%	41.3%

Citizens Advisory Council on the Status of Women

WHO IS IN
COLLEGE
1 9 7 3

Males (18 to 24)		Females (18 to 24)	
Black	White	Black	White
19%	29%	14%	21%

WHO
COMPLETES
COLLEGE
1 9 7 3

Percent of population over 14 years of age:

2.7% Spanish speaking women   6.1% White women
3.3% Black women   7.7% White men

SPECIAL
COLLEGE
ENROLLMENTS
1971-1972

	Men	Women
Dentistry	4,932	160
Medicine	11,229	1,696
Optometry	768	26
Osteopathy	655	31
Veterinary	1,278	228
Law	29,262	3,875

COLLEGE
DEGREES
1971-1972

	Men	Women
B.A.s	497,200	386,300
M.A.s	148,100	101,980
Ph.D.s	28,060	5,270
Dentistry	3,820	40
Medicine	8,420	830
Law	20,260	1,500

U.S. Dept. of Labor

ELEMENTARY
EDUCATION

Administrators were	27.8% female
Secondary teachers were	48.3% female
Elementary teachers were	84.3% female
Pre-school teachers were	97.9% female

In all recent years, male administrators and male teachers averaged higher incomes than females.

JOB SLOTS
AND PAY
1970-1971

Women were:

     67% of all public school teachers
     21% of all elementary school principals
      3% of all high school principals
     26% of all school administrators
less than 1% of all superintendents
less than 5% of the chief state school officials

The average wage for men was $9,854.
The average wage for women was $8,953.

Resource Center for Sex Roles in Education

SCHOOLBOARDS

Women constitute less than 13% of officeholders.

Women's National Education Fund

COLLEGES AND
UNIVERSITIES
1971-1972

Deans of Men earned $14,421.
Deans of Women earned $12,848.

1974

Percent of Women Among Full-Time Faculty

Professors	10.3%
Associate Professors	16.9%
Assistant Professors	27.1%
Instructors	40.6%

National Center for Educational Statistics

FACULTY SALARY 1974-1975

Number and Average Salary of Full-Time Instructional Faculty on 9-10 Month Contracts in Institutions of Higher Education, by Level of Institution, Rank, and Sex: 50 States and District of Columbia

RANK AND SEX	TOTAL		UNIVERSITIES		OTHER 4-YEAR		2-YEAR	
	NO. OF FACULTY	AVERAGE SALARY	NO. OF FACULTY	AVERAGE SALARY	NO. OF FACULTY	AVERAGE SALARY	NO. OF FACULTY	AVERAGE SALARY
TOTAL.	252,404	$15,269	90,213	$16,704	108,592	$14,342	53,599	$14,736
MEN.	190,708	15,926	73,488	17,421	81,492	14,876	35,728	15,244
WOMEN.	61,696	13,243	16,725	13,552	27,100	12,736	17,871	13,724
PROFESSORS	52,510	20,653	26,125	22,514	23,225	18,875	3,160	18,343
MEN.	47,087	20,909	24,473	22,674	20,239	19,041	2,375	18,649
WOMEN.	5,423	18,433	1,652	20,145	2,986	17,753	785	17,417
ASSOCIATE PROFESSORS	58,323	15,920	24,717	16,623	28,926	15,214	4,680	16,569
MEN.	48,456	16,069	21,422	16,746	23,517	15,372	3,517	16,614
WOMEN.	9,867	15,185	3,295	15,820	5,409	14,529	1,163	16,435
ASSISTANT PROFESSORS	76,108	13,104	28,864	13,582	40,054	12,658	7,170	13,713
MEN.	55,486	13,276	21,958	13,769	28,804	12,825	4,701	13,813
WOMEN.	20,622	12,642	6,906	12,989	11,247	12,237	2,469	13,522
INSTRUCTORS.	50,280	12,825	8,580	10,737	14,130	10,404	27,570	14,716
MEN.	29,838	13,520	4,410	10,976	7,481	10,624	17,947	15,354
WOMEN.	20,442	11,812	4,170	10,486	6,649	10,157	9,623	13,529
LECTURERS.	2,398	11,980	1,564	12,343	650	11,455	184	10,749
MEN.	1,444	12,713	998	12,919	359	12,375	87	11,753
WOMEN.	954	10,869	566	11,327	291	10,320	97	9,847
UNDESIGNATED RANK. .	12,805	13,308	363	12,337	1,607	10,936	10,835	13,693
MEN.	8,417	13,738	227	13,463	1,089	11,170	7,101	14,142
WOMEN.	4,388	12,483	136	10,457	518	10,445	3,734	12,841

National Center for Education Statistics

LOSING GROUND 1975

Women on faculties of colleges and universities lost ground compared to 1974. They held less positions, increased their salaries less than males (5.8% to 6.3%) and remained at lower wage scales.

New York Times, Feb. 9, '76

Ph.D.'s AND JOBS 1975

Of almost 207,500 science and engineering PhD's in the U.S. labor force, 93.4% are white and 92.1% are male.

Women earned 32% of the master's degrees and 10% of the doctorates in math in 1973, but only 6.7% of full time math scientists at 20 leading universities were women. In biology, women earned 30% of master's and 21.5% of doctorates in 1973, but only 12% of employed PhD's were women.

Scientific Manpower Commission, 1976

In social sciences the unemployment rate for women was 4 times higher than for men with similar training. Women PhD's were unemployed between 2 and 4 times as often as men PhDs.

Scientific Manpower Commission, '76

The freshperson class contained 16.9 percent of women who planned "traditionally masculine" careers, the highest such figure in ten years. 16.6 percent of women planned to seek a doctorate or similar advanced degree, also the highest number in many years.

New York Times, Jan. 11, '76

NEW MEXICO

There are 85 male and no female school superintendents in New Mexico.
There are 160 male secondary principals and 4 female.
Ten times as many men as women are school personnel directors.

NEW YORK CITY

The number of women elementary and secondary principals declined by more than 50% in seventeen years.

Integrated Education, Jan./Feb. '76

SPORTS

BOYS vs. GIRLS

New Jersey is the only state that has ruled that Little League cannot discriminate on the basis of sex.

A survey of 50 school districts in 17 counties showed that the average sports department had 2 times as many activities for boys as for girls.

Women's Equity Action League

At major state universities, 1300 times more was spent for men's sports than women's. In one case, 9/10 of 1% of a $2 million athletic budget was spent on women's sports facilities. In another case, $2,600,000 was spent on men's facilities and nothing on women.

Project on the Status and Education of Women, 1974

United Way Unified Charity gives boys' organizations $4 for every $1 that goes to girls' organizations.

New York Times, 12/3/75

Fact Sheets on Institutional Sexism. The Racism/Sexism Resource Center, c/o The Council on Interracial Books for Children, 1841 Broadway, New York, NY 10023. March 1976.

Part two:
American Indian/Native Alaskan

American Indian/Native Alaskan

INDIAN EDUCATION: WHERE AND WHITHER?

By WILLIAM G. DEMMERT, JR.

The logical place to begin discussing Indian education is with its definition. And here the first problem is encountered. A definition depends on one's perspective—that is, whether the concepts used are those of the Indian community or the non-Indian community.

Historically the Indian or "inside" definition embraced nothing more than a core curriculum consisting of three subjects: survival, religion, and how to act. These were inseparable. The non-Indian or "outside" definition depends upon the historical period studied and has fluctuated between extinction or surrender of cultural identity and self-determination.

In the late 1960s and early 1970s, much data were collected on educational achievement among Indians. It was discovered that the average educational level for all Indians was 8.4 years; that from grades 8 through 12 the dropout rate was estimated variously to be from 39 to 48 percent; that Indian students scored significantly lower in measures of achievement at every grade than the average white pupil. Especially alarming was the finding that the lag was greater at grade 12 than grade one, indicating that the longer the Indian student stayed in school, the further behind he or she fell. There are statistics that show 25 percent of all Indian children who start school are unable to speak English. They underscore the Indian's vital need for bilingual education. In 1970 a survey showed 36 percent of Indian parents had not continued their education beyond grade school. As an expected consequence,

parental participation in their children's educational process was minimal: In 40 percent of the cases surveyed, parents never bothered to consult teachers with respect to their youngster's academic progress, and nearly 70 percent of the parents had made no contact with teachers regarding their child's classroom behavior.

These academic problems are in a sense part of the debris from the collision between the pastoral world of the Indian and the "bigger, more complex, and faster" juggernaut world of the white man. The impact, while hardly noticed by whites, was shattering to the Indian. From his crumpled and torn remnant he looked out upon a puzzling new kind of life with patterns more diverse than those of all the Indian nations that formerly had covered the continent.

And what was in it for the Indian? Rural isolation, urban assimilation, termination of tribal governments, stereotypes invented by whites, cultural shock, to mention some of the aspects of the "new life," all of them contributing factors to the later learning problems of Indians and the reason Indian children have their own brand of educational needs. When the Indian's longing to retain an Indian identity is added to this confused mix, the result is an education problem so complex as to require hard and continued analysis to figure out what is meant by "meeting the special educational needs" of Indian students. The educational systems that serve Indian children—the public schools, the BIA schools, and some alternative schools—are just beginning to recognize this fact and to become sensitive to these needs and to attempt dealing with them effectively.

To place the problem of Indian education in a workable historic perspective, it may be well to start with the first major study on problems of educating Indian students, a report published in 1928 by Lewis Meriam. Among its major findings, the Meriam Report noted that: (1) Indians were excluded from management of their own affairs; (2) Indians were receiving poor quality of services (especially health and education) from public officials who were supposed to be serving the Indian's needs; and (3) Indians were under an imposed educational system of another culture.

The official Government attitude for educating the Indian up to the time of the Meriam Report was to remove the child as far as possible from his home environment. However, the study pointed to the evils of a regimented boarding school life working against the kind of initiative and independence that was once a vital part of the Native American's way of life. It called upon the Federal Government to help the Indian retain or, in some cases, redevelop his original initiative and spirit.

The importance of holding on to parts of one's culture was recognized in the Meriam Report. In this respect, the report helped bring the Federal Government around to reevaluating and questioning its underlying principles and eventually to recognizing the need for a change in point of view. This conclusion slowed the process of Indian education as it was then practiced, a process that had alienated a people and caused their withdrawal of support and trust. Thus, the Meriam Report was instrumental in reversing official philosophy for dealing with the Indians and in bringing Indians a brighter outlook.

Although the findings of the Meriam Report remain as valid as when the report was first published, the change it suggested is only now becoming evident through the current movement by Indians to operate and run once again their own educational systems. There is the beginning of an Indian renaissance that must succeed if Indians are to direct their own destiny and to participate in directing the future of this country, as its original inhabitants have the right to do.

Some 40 years after the publication of the Meriam Report, two major studies on Indian education were conducted: One by the Senate Committee on Indian Education resulted in a seven-volume report summarized under the title *Indian Education: A National Tragedy—A National Challenge;* the other, conducted under the direction of Robert J. Havighurst and funded by a National Study of American Indian Grant, was the largest of its kind ever undertaken, involving more Indians and a greater geographical spread than any other study to date. These two reports clearly emphasize the need for major change of direction in Indian education, both public and Federal. Their recommendations support the Indian demand for control and call for Federal funding of basic and adult education, as well as construction of appropriate facilities.

From these past studies it is apparent that the educational needs of the Indian community are varied, not well documented, but informally known to the Indian. Many of the original issues—the lack of control by Indians of their own schools, poor quality of services, irrelevant education content, inadequate funding—have been partially resolved or are improving. Further assessments of needs must ask some specific questions:

□ What is the proper Federal role in Indian education?

□ What is the State responsibility toward federally recognized tribes?

□ What are the postsecondary needs of Indian students and what would it cost to satisfy those needs?

□ What will the movement toward tribally controlled schools mean in terms of Federal resources for both construction and programs?

□ What are the early childhood educational needs of the Indian community?

□ What level of funding is needed to ensure academic success among Indian students?

The list is long and the questions are just a few of the more important ones.

It's not, however, as if the questions have sprung suddenly from limbo and the solutions must be worked out from scratch. A number of facts are already known that signal some of the more pressing needs. For example, at least 40,000 Indian students are interested in pursuing an academic degree; this past year only about 17,000 received financial aid from special programs for Indian students. And again, of the teachers working with Indian students, less than 0.1 percent are Indians, clearly indicating a need for Indian teachers if Indian self-determination (this means Indians running programs, controlling services, and participating in Federal decisions that affect them as Indians) is to become a reality. A majority of the public schools that Indians attend are in low economic base areas and consequently the important community-based early childhood programs look to for support.

The Education Amendments of 1974 added two sections to Part B: One provides authority to make grants for special educational programs for teachers of Indian children; the other provides authority to award fellowships for Indian students in graduate and professional programs leading toward a professional or graduate degree in engineering, medicine, law, business, forestry, and other specializations.

Part C was written to help Indian tribes, organizations, institutions, and State and local agencies plan, demonstrate, and operate programs for improving employment and educational opportunities for adult Indians. It concentrates on teaching to achieve literacy, increasing the number of General Equivalency Diploma graduates, and providing wider opportunity for job training. It also deals with curriculums that promote a sense of self-pride based on Indian history and culture, and stresses those most needed by Indian communities—legal education, consumer education, vocational counseling, and community education.

Part D gives the Act itself additional strength to implement its provisions. It provides for the establishment of the Office of Indian Education, within the Office of Education, to administer the project authorities of the Act under the direction of a Deputy Commissioner of Indian Education. The National Advisory Council on Indian Education was also established under Part D to provide policy direction and guidance. The law stipulates that the Council be composed of 15 persons who are Indians or Alaskan natives appointed by the President from nominations submitted by Indian tribes and organizations.

Through its service, demonstration, and training activities under the Indian Education Act, the Office of Education is assisting the educational system of the United States by strengthening the system's capacity to provide an equal education for Indian students. The Federal assistance provided under the Act is supplementary to funds intended to benefit Native Americans in other Office of Education programs administered under Impact Aid, Title I of the Elementary and Secondary Education Act, and the Handicapped Education legislation. All this is in addition to education programs administered by other Federal agencies such as the Bureau of Indian Affairs.

Nonetheless, this piece of legislation is having a major effect on Indian Education:

For the first time parents of Indian children have a strong voice in helping decide the content of programs in which their children participate. It is laying a base for a change of attitude in public schools with respect to such special Indian concerns as curriculum, teaching methods, testing, and future direction. The 1972 Act has created a minor revolution in Indian education and stimulated new direction, thought, and leaders. In short, it has done for Indian education what the Elementary and Secondary Education Act of 1965 has done for the general student population in the United States.

This has been the Federal role in contemporary times. It has caused change for the better in relatively short time. Although the United States Constitution has not provided for a Federal role in local education, it would appear to be a legitimate role, and one that may be reaching a pinnacle. It seems that State education agencies and local education agencies sometimes feel their roles are threatened by some of the new trends introduced by the Federal Government. However, as the local and State leaders become more experienced in working with the Federal Government, they will begin to assume a leading role in initiating new educational trends. This movement may take a few more years to develop and materialize, but there is every promise that it will happen. When it does, it will be easier to make change. And that is good. It means our educators are learning their business politically as well as educationally. It means change will come about more smoothly. It means our schools will be more flexible. And it means that as a Nation we are becoming more comfortable with diversity.

U.S. Office of Education. American Education, "Indian Education: Where and Whither?" By William G. Demmert, Jr. U.S. Department of Health, Education, and Welfare, Washington, D.C. August/September 1976.

Education of Indian Children in 1975

Indian children attend public, Federal, Private and mission schools. In fiscal year 1975 there were 190,226 Indian students, age 5 to 18 years, inclusive, enrolled in these schools in the United States.

Education of Indian children residing in the States of California, Idaho, Michigan, Minnesota, Nebraska, Oregon, Texas, Washington and Wisconsin is the responsibility of the state concerned.

In 1975 more than half (63.7 percent) of all Indian children of school age (5 - 18) attended public schools. Of those enrolled in school, 69.9 percent attended public schools, 24.6 percent attended Federal schools, and 5.5 percent attended mission and other schools.

For more than three centuries Indian education in the United States was largely under the direction of missionaries. As early as 1568 the Jesuit Fathers organized a school at Havana, Cuba, for Indian children from Florida. This was the first school attended by Indian children from Florida. This was the first school attended by Indian children who lived within the United States.

Many of the treaties between the United States and Indian tribes provided for the establishment of schools for Indian children. Congress has also provided schools for Indian children where other educational facilities were not available. In 1842, there were 37 Indian schools in operation and by 1881 the number had increased to 106. In 1975 the Bureau of Indian Affairs operated 193 schools with an enrollment of 46,880 Indian children, and 19 dormitories for 2,926 children attending public schools.

The primary objective of Federal schools operated for Indian children living on Indian-owned or restricted trust lands is to prepare them for successful living. In Federal schools children develop basic academic skills, acquire an understanding of the social and economic world which surrounds them, learn improved standards of living, follow practices which assure optimum health, acquire the necessary vocational training to qualify for gainful employment, and obtain sufficient education to enter special schools, and institutions of higher learning. The system of schools provided by the Federal Government for Indian children meets program standards required by the States in which they operate.

A full 4-year high school course was offered at 25 schools. 7 other schools offered high school training at less than the 4 year course.

Indian children are entitled to the same opportunities for public school education as are provided for other citizens living within a State. It is encouraging to note that the States have assumed responsibility for the education of 132,876 (63.7 percent) school-age Indian children in the States where the Bureau of Indian Affairs has direct educational responsibility. Over one-third are educated at no cost to the Bureau of Indian Affairs. In some States, however, tax-exempt, Indian-owned lands and large numbers of Indian children within a school district may create financial burdens for which local funds are inadequate. As early as 1890, contracts providing for financial assistance to schools attended by Indian children were negotiated with individual districts. It was recognized then, as today, that Indian children become better adjusted to living with all people in a community when they associate with other children in public schools. The Johnson-O'Malley Act, which became law in 1934, authorized the Secretary of the Interior to enter into contracts with States for the education of Indians and to permit the use of Federal school buildings and equipment by local school authorities. Consequently, some States with large Indian populations now have no Federal schools within their boundaries.

Under the terms of Public Law 874, 81st Cong. (64 Stat. 1100), as amended August 13, 1958, administered by the Department of Health, Education, and Welfare, a new Federal aid resource was made available to eligible school districts educating Indian children. This aid is available to meed partial costs of normal school operation. Additional supplemental aid for the education of Indian children under the Johnson-O'Malley program is limited to districts that do not qualify under the Public Law 874 program and to districts meeting educational problems under extraordinary circumstances, including special services and special programs designed to facilitate the education of Indian children.

In fiscal year 1975, the Bureau of Indian Affairs entered into contracts with 9 States, 71 school districts in other States, and with 34 tribal groups in accordance with approved plans which specify conditions under which financial aid es extended. In addition to these, aid was provided through contracts for the education in public schools of 1,488 out-of-district Indian children living in dormitories operated by the Bureau of Indian Affairs in 7 towns adjacent to the Navajo Reservation, and in Albuquerque, New Mexico.

In summary, then, the Bureau of Indian Affairs had direct responsibility for the 49,806 children enrolled in Federal schools and housed in Federal dormitories, and partial financial responsibility for approximately two-thirds of those enrolled in public schools.

Statistics concerning Indian Education are published annually by the Bureau of Indian Affairs and are available upon request.

Congressional appropriations to the Bureau of Indian Affairs are limited to the education of children of one-fourth or more degree of Indian blood and native children in Alaska, except for the Cherokee Agency where children of less than one-quarter degree of Indian blood enrolled in the tribe may attend Federal schools. Native children in Alaska are Indian, Eskimo, and Aleut. The 16 tables below relate to Indians and native children, as defined above, and to their schools.

Table 1 shows the enumeration of all Indian children from 5 to 18 years, inclusive, and those over 18 who are enrolled in school by area, agency, and school status.

For Indian children who are enrolled in public schools and are no longer a Federal education responsibility, the Bureau must rely on the public school systems to provide census information. Indian mobility accounts for the children, 5 to 18 years inclusive, who are shown under the caption "Information Not Available."

Five-year-olds have been included with the school-age population since fiscal year 1969 when kindergarten classes were added in some schools operated by the Bureau of Indian Affairs.

It should be noted that children over 18 are not included in the enumeration of school-age population. Table 1 is based on the annual school census of Indian children 5 to 18 years old, while Tables 3 through 10 are derived from annual attendance reports of individual schools operated by the Bureau of Indian Affairs and cover all students enrolled regardless of their ages.

Table 2 indicates numbers of schools by area. Table 3 indicates enrollment and average daily attendance in Federal schools by type of school and area. Average daily attendance for all schools was 75.4 percent in 1975 as compared to 80.1 percent in 1974.

In fiscal year 1975, the Bureau of Indian Affairs operated kindergarten classes in 101 schools (35 borading schools and 66 day schools) with an enrollment of 2,485 children. All kindergarten pupils attend school on a day basis. The kindergarten enrollment represented 5.3 percent of the total enrollment.

Tables 4, 5, and 6 list individual schools and dormitories operated by the Bureau of Indian Affairs, mailing address, enrollment, average daily attendance, and grades taught.

The Albuquerque Dormitory is operated in conjunction with the Albuquerque Indian School but is shown with peripheral dormitories because these dormitory students attend public schools under conditions identical to other peripheral dormitories.

Table 7 indicates grade level. In 1975 enrollment in kindergarten and first four grades decreased 3,472 pupils to 17,187 as compared to the previous year's 20,659. This group represented 44.1 percent of the entire student body. An enrollment of 2,445 ungraded elementary students account for 5.2 percent of the total enrollment.

In line with the Bureau's policy of encouraging public school enrollment of Indian children, many students transfer to public schools when they reach the sixth grade and have acquired some facility in the use of the English language. This is a factor in the seemingly low numbers of graduates of Federal high schools. In fiscal year 1975, 1,511 high school students graduated, a decrease of 55 students from 1974.

Table 8 indicates the number of high school graduates, number of 8th grade completions, and number of Post High completions or placements.

Table 9 indicates students according to their degree of Indian blood. Full bloods comprise 76.5 percent of the total and only 6.6 percent are less than one-half Indian blood.

Table 10 shows tribal designation of students in Federal schools. One hundred and forty-one specific tribes or tribal groups and Aleuts, Eskimos, and the various tribes of Indians in Alaska were represented in 1975.

Ninety-five tribes had fewer than 39 members each and these are grouped together as "All Other Tribes." Aleuts, Eskimos, Navajos, Sioux, Chippewas, and Pueblos (including Hopi, shown separately) are the most numerous and together comprise 77.5 percent of the total enrollment.

Table 11 indicates the completed school construction, both new and replacement, during fiscal year 1975.

In fiscal year 1975, the Bureau of Indian Affairs participated for the eighth year in the Elementary and Secondary Education Act. Table 12 indicates the extent of the activities carried out under Titles I, II, III, and VII of the program. Also Title III of the National Defense Education Act.

Table 13 indicates the number of undergraduate and graduate students who received scholarship grants in fiscal year 1975, also the number of students earning degrees.

Table 14 shows the number of students enrolled in schools by States, receiving assistance through contracts funded under the Johnson-O'Malley Act which became law in 1934.

Table 15 shows the number of Indian pupils enrolled in schools being operated under contract to Indian groups.

Table 16 indicates the activities being conducted and the number of participants in the Adult Education program.

1/ In addition dormitory facilities are provided 2,926 children who attend public schools.

2/ Includes 2,926 children who live in Federal dormitories and attend public schools.

3/ Children recorded at their own agency but who reside off the reservation.

4/ Estimated by Anadarko Area Office.

5/ Estimated by Juneau Area Office.

6/ Estimated by Muskogee Area Office.

7/ Navajos under jurisdiction of Zuni Agency included with Navajos of New Mexico.

Table 1. Annual School Census Report of Indian Children
Fiscal Year 1975

Area Agency	Total 5-18 Enumerated	Federal Schools 1/ 5-18	Over 18	Public Schools 2/ 5-18	Over 18	Other Schools 5-18	Over 18	TOTAL 5-18	Over 18	Not in School 5-18 only	Unknown 3/ 5-18 only
GRAND TOTAL	208,607	46,748	1,642	132,876	2,603	10,602	13,043	190,226	17,288	11,240	7,141
ABERDEEN	22,474	10,016	206	8,895	364	2,272	2,348	21,183	2,918	554	737
Cheyenne River	2,540	1,750	37	446	21	104	187	2,300	245	221	19
Crow Creek	733	372	5	29	0	330	59	731	64	2	0
Flandreau	154	3	0	146	14	3	0	152	14	2	0
Fort Berthold	1,620	618	0	890	0	41	252	1,549	252	12	59
Fort Totten	937	600	0	280	0	46	63	926	63	911	0
Lower Brule	271	229	5	7	0	8	2	244	7	20	7
Pine Ridge	4,737	3,031	39	842	11	676	446	4,549	496	0	188

Table 1 ---continued---

		TOTAL IN SCHOOL									
Area Agency	Total 5-18 Enumerated	Federal Schools 1/ 5-18	Over 18	Public Schools 2/ 5-18	Over 18	Other Schools 5-18	Over 18	TOTAL 5-18	Over 18	Not in School 5-18 only	Unknown 3/ 5-18 only
Rosebud	2,567	52	0	1,974	270	429	323	2,455	593	112	0
Sisseton	1,282	53	6	1,167	0	11	145	1,231	151	51	0
Standing Rock	1,887	903	12	864	8	107	193	1,874	213	13	0
Turtle Mountain	4,373	2,330	102	1,075	40	394	449	3,799	591	110	464
Winnebago	936	47	0	889	0	0	229	936	229	0	0
Yankton	437	28	0	286	0	123	0	437	0	0	0
ALBUQUERQUE	13,756	2,368	27	9,511	122	1,031	788	12,910	937	533	313
Jicarilla	864	72	0	721	8	64	62	857	70	7	0
Mescalero	829	34	0	654	10	61	71	749	81	39	41
Northern Pueblos	1,628	576	12	938	66	48	153	1,562	231	17	49
Southern Pueblos	7,147	1,513	15	4,855	18	362	385	6,730	418	194	223
Southern Ute	284	3	0	259	0	7	47	269	47	15	0
Ute Mountain	553	79	0	415	0	22	13	516	13	37	0
Zuni	2,451	91	0	1,669	20	467	57	2,227	77	224	0
ANADARKO	11,504	980	34	10,018	486	103	1,436	11,101	1,956	369	34
Anadarko	3,494	374	0	2,798	0	66	1,150	3,238	1,150	256	0
Concho 4/	1,500	113	32	1,240	24	35	167	1,388	223	112	0
Horton	1,298	8	0	1,262	115	0	0	1,270	115	0	28
Pawnee	935	60	2	866	13	2	8	928	23	1	6
Shawnee	4,277	425	0	3,852	334	0	111	4,277	445	0	0
BILLINGS	12,649	988	102	9,051	151	1,571	1,541	11,610	1,794	684	355
Blackfeet	2,763	232	23	2,376	103	38	251	2,646	377	110	7
Crow	2,040	63	17	1,290	16	487	337	1,840	370	91	109
Flathead	1,296	22	14	1,153	13	20	115	1,195	142	101	0
Fort Peck	2,053	84	0	1,642	0	102	290	1,828	290	102	123
Fort Belknap	1,065	59	24	714	0	29	163	802	187	147	116
Northern Cheyenne	1,329	451	6	373	1	504	170	1,328	177	1	0
Rocky Boy's	546	10	0	472	18	0	101	482	119	64	0
Wind River	1,557	67	18	1,031	0	391	114	1,489	132	68	0
EASTERN	3,904	2,748	97	964	4	45	169	3,757	270	126	21
Cherokee	2,009	1,361	51	583	0	2	70	1,946	121	63	0
Choctaw	1,542	1,307	35	170	2	2	69	1,479	106	42	21
Seminole	353	80	11	211	2	41	30	332	43	21	0
JUNEAU 5/	22,796	4,904	205	16,868	133	661	108	22,433	446	363	0
Juneau	22,796	4,904	205	16,868	133	661	108	22,433	446	363	0
MINNEAPOLIS	8,566	162	1	4,583	350	165	0	4,910	351	20	3,636
Great Lakes	717	0	0	717	28	0	0	717	28	0	0
Minnesota	6,351	32	0	2,752	0	0	0	2,784	0	0	3,567
Red Lake	1,273	78	0	943	278	163	0	1,184	278	20	69
Sac & Fox	225	52	1	171	44	2	0	225	45	0	0
MUSKOGEE 6/	21,042	723	129	19,904	0	0	2,966	20,627	3,095	0	415
Five Civilized Tribes & Osage	21,042	723	129	19,904	0	0	2,966	20,627	3,095	0	415
NAVAJO	58,696	18,356	557	28,561	727	3,068	1,535	49,985	2,819	7,532	1,179
Arizona	31,754	11,784	332	12,480	355	2,020	1,054	26,284	1,741	4,880	590
New Mexico 7/	24,731	5,908	203	14,842	327	953	412	21,703	942	2,458	570
Utah	2,211	664	22	1,239	45	95	69	1,998	136	194	19
PHOENIX	22,267	5,215	242	14,366	120	1,438	1,176	21,019	1,538	805	443
Colorado River	1,647	77	17	1,257	0	0	75	1,334	92	0	313
Fort Apache	3,330	762	32	1,996	19	348	129	3,106	180	204	20
Hopi	2,185	1,501	1	597	32	87	253	2,185	286	0	0
Nevada	2,714	267	87	2,221	0	22	162	2,510	249	113	91
Papago	3,368	987	12	2,033	15	188	107	3,208	134	150	10
Pima	3,857	695	43	2,861	37	228	167	3,784	247	73	0
Salt River	1,203	419	8	668	3	24	39	1,111	50	83	9
San Carlos	2,373	260	14	1,566	6	474	165	2,300	185	73	0
Truxton Canyon	1,153	220	21	818	4	36	51	1,074	76	79	0
Uintah & Ouray	437	27	7	349	4	31	28	407	39	30	0
PORTLAND	10,953	288	42	10,155	146	248	976	10,691	1,164	254	8
Colville	1,794	59	7	1,576	96	159	75	1,794	178	0	0
Fort Hall	1,051	41	15	867	0	8	52	916	67	135	0
Northern Idaho	1,026	7	1	981	31	17	95	1,005	127	21	0
Spokane	606	33	0	527	0	15	46	575	46	23	8
Umatilla	356	20	4	336	0	0	63	356	67	0	0
Warm Springs	1,030	3	3	966	3	3	80	1,002	86	28	0
West Washington	2,867	49	1	2,818	0	0	414	2,867	415	0	0
Yakima	2,223	46	11	2,084	16	46	151	2,176	178	47	0

Table 2. Number of Schools Operated by the Bureau of Indian Affairs by Type
Fiscal Year 1975

Area	Grand Total	Boarding Total	Day Total	Day Regular	Trailer
GRAND TOTAL	193 1/	77	116	115	1
Aberdeen	29	6	23	23	
Albuquerque	14	3	11	11	
Anadarko	5	5			
Cherokee 2/	1		1	1	
Choctaw 2/	7	3	4	4	
Juneau	54	2	52	52	
Muskogee	2	2			
Navajo	59	49	10	9	1
Phoenix	20	6	14	14	
Portland	1	1			
Seminole 2/	1		1	1	

1/ The Bureau of Indian Affairs also operated 19 dormitories for children attending public schools.
2/ Under jurisdiction of Eastern Area Office headquartered in Washington, D.C.

Table 3. Enrollment and Average Daily Attendance (all ages) by
Types of Schools Operated by the Bureau of Indian Affairs
Fiscal Year 1975

Area	Grand Total Enrollment	Grand Total A.D.A.	Boarding Enrollment	Boarding A.D.A.	Day Enrollment	Day A.D.A.
GRAND TOTAL	46,880 1/	35,357.7	30,886	22,320.3	15,994	13,037.4
Aberdeen	8,282	5,989.5	3,121	2,357.1	5,161	3,632.4
Albuquerque	3,552	1,865.8 3/	1,700	219.8 3/	1,852	1,646.0
Anadarko	2,470	884.2 4/	2,470	884.2 4/	-	-
Cherokee 2/	1,266	1,076.1	-	-	1,266	1,076.1
Choctaw 2/	1,322	1,113.7	1,034	855.7	288	258.0
Juneau	4,987	4,301.1	641	492.4	4,346	3,808.7
Muskogee	538	358.0	538	358.0	-	-
Navajo	18,911	15,344.2	17,753	14,351.6	1,158	992.6
Phoenix	5,032	4,076.0	3,141	2,478.8	1,891	1,598.1
Portland	488	322.7	488	322.7	-	-
Seminole 2/	32	25.5	-	-	32	25.5

1/ Federal facilities were provided for a total of 49,806 children, 2,926 of whom lived in Federal dormitories
    and attended public schools.
2/ Under jurisdiction of Eastern Area Office headquartered in Washington, D.C.
3/ Does not include ADA's for IAIA and SIPI.
4/ Does not include ADA's for Haskell Indian Jr. College.

Table 4. Boarding Schools Operated by the Bureau of Indian Affairs
Fiscal Year 1975

Area/State/School	Post Office Address	Zip Code	Enrollment			Average Daily Attendance			Grades
			Total	Boarding	Day	Total	Boarding	Day	
GRAND TOTAL			30,886	25,838	5,048	21,464.4	18,088.1	3,376.5	
ABERDEEN			3,121	1,516	1,605	2,357.1	1,051.3	1,305.8	
North Dakota			584	342	242	482.0	244.5	237.5	
Standing Rock	Fort Yates, N.D.	58538	324	82	242	284.5	47.0	237.5	K-12
Wahpeton	Wahpeton, N.D.	58075	260	260		197.5	197.5		1-8
SOUTH DAKOTA			2,537	1,174	1,363	1,875.1	806.8	1,068.3	
Cheyenne-Eagle Butte	Eagle Butte, S.D.	57627	860	198	662	685.5	161.6	523.9	K-12
Flandreau	Flandreau, S.D.	57028	755	755		490.6	490.6		9-12
Oglala Community	Pine Ridge, S.D.	57770	818	117	701	632.3	87.9	544.4	1-12
Pierre	Pierre, S.D.	57501	104	104		66.7	66.7		S
ALBUQUERQUE			1,700	1,700		219.8 1/	219.8		
New Mexico			1,700	1,700		219.8	219.8		
Albuquerque	Albuquerque, N.M.	87100	320	320		219.8	219.8		7-12
Institute of American Indian Arts	Santa Fe, N.M.	87501	257	257					
Southwestern Indian Polytechnic Inst.	Albuquerque, N.M.	87114	1,123	1,123					
ANADARKO			2,470	2,470		884.2 1/	884.2		
Kansas			1,108	1,108					
Haskell Indian Junior College	Lawrence, Kansas	66044	1,108	1,108					
OKLAHOMA			1,362	1,362		884.2	884.2		
New Concho	Concho, Okla.	73022	354	354		207.2	207.2		6-8-S
Chilocco	Chilocco, Okla.	74635	360	360		258.2	258.2		9-12-S
Fort Sill	Lawton, Okla.	73501	330	330		201.0	201.0		9-12
Riverside	Anadarko, Okla.	73005	318	318		217.8	217.8		9-12
EASTERN			1,034	180	854	855.7	148.6	707.1	
Mississippi			1,034	180	854	855.7	148.6	707.1	
Bogue Chitto	Rt.2, Phila., Ms.	39350	183	12	171	154.8	14.7	140.1	K-7
Conehatta	Conehatta, Miss.	39057	181	15	166	160.8	13.7	147.1	K-8
Choctaw Central	Philadelphia, Ms.	39050	670	153	517	540.1	120.2	419.9	K-12
JUNEAU			641	641		492.4	492.4		
Alaska			641	641		492.4	492.4		
Mt. Edgecumbe	Mt. Edgecumbe, Ak.	99835	538	538		402.9	402.9		9-12
Wrangell Institute	Wrangell, Alaska	00029	103	103		89.5	89.5		S
MUSKOGEE			538	538		358.0	358.0		
Oklahoma			538	538		358.0	358.0		
Seneca	Wyandotte, Okla.	74370	188	188		135.4	135.4		1-8-S
Sequoyah	Tahlequah, Okla.	74464	350	350		222.6	222.6		9-12
NAVAJO			17,753	15,488	2,265	14,351.6	12,574.2	1,777.4	
Arizona			10,736	9,114	1,622	9,021.2	7,704.2	1,317.0	
Chinle	Chinle, Ariz.	86503	740	740		586.6	586.6		1-7-S
Crystal	Navajo, N.M.	87328	125	107	18	114.4	99.1	15.3	K-5-S
Dennehotso	Kayenta, Ariz.	86033	247	187	60	202.9	155.9	47.0	K-5-S
Dilcon	Winslow, Ariz.	86047	754	419	335	682.8	379.3	303.5	K-8-S
Greasewood	Ganado, Ariz.	86505	535	361	174	452.7	311.9	140.8	K-8-S
Hunter's Point	St. Michaels, Az.	86511	175	175		145.7	145.7		1-5-S
Kaibeto, Lower	Tonalea, Ariz.	86044	165	112	53	131.8	89.7	42.1	K-1-S
Kaibeto, Upper	Tonalea, Ariz.	86044	441	405	36	374.2	346.7	27.5	2-8
Kayenta	Kayenta, Ariz.	86033	582	582		582.7	582.7		1-8-S
Kinlichee	Ganado, Ariz.	86505	225	208	17	179.5	164.6	14.9	K-8-S
Leupp	Winslow, Ariz.	86047	505	474	31	472.4	444.0	28.4	K-8-S
Low Mountain	Chinle, Ariz.	86503	172	44	128	138.4	35.7	102.7	K-3-S
Lukachukai	Lukachukai, Ariz.	86507	411	190	221	302.1	147.1	155.0	K-6-S
Many Farms Elem.	Chinle, Ariz.	86503	405	405		311.3	311.3		7-8
Many Farms High	Chinle, Ariz.	86503	853	853		628.5	628.5		9-12
Tuba City High	Tuba City, Ariz.	86045	343	343		229.3	229.3		9-11
Nazlini	Ganado, Ariz.	86505	148	120	28	138.5	105.4	22.1	K-5-S
Pine Springs	Houck, Ariz.	86505	81	61	20	64.0	53.1	10.9	K-3
Pinon	Pinon, Ariz.	86510	326	201	125	260.1	163.5	96.6	K-3-S
Rocky Ridge	Tuba City, Ariz.	86045	159	72	87	151.1	67.1	84.0	K-3-S
Seba Dalkai	Winslow, Ariz.	86047	112	87	25	97.3	77.8	19.5	K-3-S
Shonto	Shonto, Ariz.	86044	1,024	887	137	891.7	781.3	110.4	K-8-S
Teecnospos	Teecnospos, Ariz.	86514	464	412	52	384.9	341.2	43.7	K-8
Toyei	Ganado, Ariz.	86505	591	554	37	456.2	433.5	22.7	K-8-S
Tuba City Elem.	Tuba City, Ariz.	86045	951	951		875.6	875.6		1-8-S
Wide Ruins	Chambers, Ariz.	86502	202	164	38	177.5	147.6	29.9	K-5-S

1/ ADA's are not applicable for post-high students at IAIA, SIPI, & Haskell Indian Jr. College.

Table 4 ---continued---

Area/State/School	Post Office Address	Zip Code	Enrollment			Average Daily Attendance			Grades
			Total	Boarding	Day	Total	Boarding	Day	
Phoenix			3,141	2,817	324	2,478.8	2,185.5	293.3	
Arizona			1,851	1,527	324	1,481.5	1,188.2	293.3	
Keams Canyon	Keams Canyon, Ariz.	86304	279	221	58	267.3	214.4	52.9	1-8-S
Phoenix Indian	Phoenix, Ariz.	85011	878	878		641.9	641.9		7-12
Santa Rosa	Sells, Ariz.	85634	444	178	266	388.1	147.7	240.4	K-8
Theodore Roosevelt	Ft. Apache, Ariz.	85926	250	250		184.2	184.2		2-8
Nevada			505	505		374.1	374.1		
Stewart	Stewart, Nev.	89437	505	505		374.1	374.1		9-12
California			785	785		623.2	623.2		
Sherman Indian High	Riverside, Calif.	92503	785	785		623.2	623.2		9-12
Portland			488	488		322.7	322.7		
Oregon			488	488		322.7	322.7		
Chemawa	Chemawa, Oregon	97306	488	488		322.7	322.7		9-12
New Mexico			5,647	5,028	619	4,505.9	4,061.9	444.0	
Baca	Prewitt, N.Mex.	87045	37	37		30.7	30.7		1-S
Canoncita	Laguna, N.Mex.	87026	143	53	90	117.0	46.8	70.2	K-4-S
Chi Chil Tah	Gallup, N.Mex.	87301	132	88	44	125.4	83.6	41.8	K-3-S
Crownpoint	Crownpoint, N.Mex.	87313	568	568		412.8	412.8		1-8-S
Dlo'ay Azhi	Thoreau, N.Mex.	87323	119	119		93.7	93.7		1-5-S
Dzilth-Na-O-Dilth-hle	Bloomfield, N.Mex.	87413	373	251	122	305.7	213.5	92.2	K-8
Lake Valley	Crownpoint, N.Mex.	87313	119	89	30	103.3	78.7	24.6	K-3-S
Mariano Lake	Gallup, N.Mex.	87301	84	55	29	65.2	42.9	22.3	K-3-S
Nenahnezad	Fruitland, N.Mex.	87416	347	306	41	283.9	269.5	19.8	K-7
Pueblo Pintado	Cuba, N.Mex.	87013	166	117	49	144.7	105.1	39.6	K-4-S
Sanostee	Shiprock, N.Mex.	87420	441	337	104	331.7	273.5	58.2	K-8-S
Shiprock	Shiprock, N.Mex.	87420	395	395		271.9	271.9		7-9
Standing Rock	Crownpoint, N.Mex.	87313	28	28		27.6	27.6		1-2-S
Toadlena	Toadlena, N.Mex.	87324	226	204	22	211.6	192.3	19.3	K-8
Tohatchi	Tohatchi, N.Mex.	87325	318	318		273.9	273.9		1-8-S
Torreon	Cuba, N.Mex.	87013	64	49	15	54.3	44.0	10.3	1-2-S
Whitehorse Lake	Cuba, N.Mex.	87013	35	21	14	27.3	17.4	9.9	K-2-S
Wingate Elem.	Ft. Wingate, N.Mex.	87316	741	741		565.3	565.3		1-8-S
Wingate High	Ft. Wingate, N.Mex.	87316	856	797	59	642.4	606.6	35.8	9-12
Utah			1,370	1,346	24	824.5	808.1	16.4	
Aneth	Aneth, Utah	84510	284	261	23	192.5	177.1	15.4	K-6-S
Intermountain	Brigham City, Utah	84302	1,057	1,057		606.4	606.4		9-12
Navajo Mountain	Tuba City, Ariz.	86504	29	28	1	25.6	24.6	1.0	1-S

Table 5. Day Schools Operated by the Bureau of Indian Affairs Fiscal Year 1975

Area Agency and State School	Post Office Address	Zip Code	(All Ages) Enrollment	A.D.A.	Grades
	GRAND TOTAL		15,994	13,037.4	
ABERDEEN			5,161	3,632.4	
Cheyenne River, S. Dakota			371	304.3	
Bridger	Howes, S. Dak.	57748	38	27.5	1-7
Cherry Creek	Cherry Creek, S. Dak.	57622	146	115.8	K-9
Promise	Mobridge, S. Dak.	57601	21	18.1	1-6
Red Scaffold	Faith, S. Dak.	57626	55	47.1	1-8
Swiftbird	Gettysburg, S. Dak.	57442	42	32.3	1-6
White Horse	White Horse, S. Dak.	57661	69	63.5	1-8
Fort Berthold, N. Dakota			265	235.7	
Twin Buttes	Halliday, N. Dak.	58636	72	63.8	K-8
White Shield	Roseglen, N. Dak.	58775	193	171.9	K-12
Fort Totten, N. Dakota			202	160.9	
Fort Totten	Fort Totten, N. Dak.	58335	202	160.9	K-6
Pierre, S. Dakota			456	382.4	
Fort Thompson Community	Fort Thompson, S. Dak.	57339	254	205.8	K-6-S
Lower Brule	Lower Brule, S. Dak.	57548	202	176.6	K-12
Pine Ridge, S. Dakota			1,814	1,326.4	
American Horse	Allen, S. Dak.	57714	169	139.9	K-8
Crazy Horse	Wanblee, S. Dak.	57577	326	239.4	K-12
Little Wound	Kyle, S. Dak.	57752	516	372.3	K-12

Table 5 ---continued---

Area Agency and State School	Post Office Address	Zip Code	(All Ages)		Grades
			Enrollment	A.D.A.	
Loneman	Oglala, S. Dak.	57764	358	273.6	K-8
Manderson	Manderson, S. Dak.	57756	266	163.0	K-8
Porcupine	Porcupine, S. Dak.	57772	179	138.2	K-8
Sisseton, S. Dakota			34	25.0	
Big Coulee	Peever, S. Dak.	57257	27	18.9	K
Enemy Swim	Waumbay, S. Dak.	57273	7	6.1	4
Standing Rock, N. Dakota			194	156.2	
Bullhead	Bullhead, S. Dak.	57621	90	72.8	K-8
Little Eagle	Little Eagle, S. Dak.	57639	104	83.4	1-8
Turtle Mountain, N. Dakota			1,825	1,041.5	
Dunseith	Dunseith, N. Dak.	58329	105	83.7	K-5-S
Turtle Mountain Community	Belcourt, N. Dak.	58316	1,720	957.8	K-12-S
ALBUQUERQUE			1,852	1,646.0	
Northern Pueblos, N. Mexico			455	406.6	
San Ildefonso	Santa Fe, N. Mex.	87501	24	21.0	1-6
San Juan	San Juan, N. Mex.	87566	98	89.1	K-6
Santa Clara	Espanola, N. Mex.	87532	119	106.1	K-6
Taos Pueblo	Taos, N. Mex.	87571	194	172.4	K-2-S
Tesuque	Santa Fe, N. Mex.	87501	20	18.0	1-5
Southern Pueblos, N. Mexico			1,397	1,239.4	
Isleta Elementary	Isleta, N. Mex.	87022	275	236.3	K-8
Jemez	Jemez Pueblos, N. Mex.	87024	130	119.9	K-S
Laguna	Laguna, N. Mex.	87026	430	373.4	K-8
San Felipe	Algodones, N. Mex.	87001	257	232.1	K-7
Sky City Community	San Fidel, N. Mex.	87049	236	216.5	K-5
Zia	San Ysidro, N. Mex.	87053	69	61.2	K-7
EASTERN			1,586	1,359.6	
Cherokee, N. Carolina			1,266	1,076.1	
Cherokee Central	Cherokee, N.C.	28719	1,266	1,076.1	K-12-S
Choctaw, Mississippi			288	258.0	
Chitimacha	Jeanerette, La.	70544	58	54.8	K-8
Red Water	Carthage, Miss.	39051	102	96.0	K-7
Standing Pine	Rt.2, Walnut Grove, Miss.	39189	63	56.0	K-6
Tucker	Philadelphia, Miss.	39350	65	51.2	K-5
Seminole, Florida			32	25.5	
Ahfachkee	Bx.40, Clewiston, Fla.	33440	32	25.5	K-6
JUNEAU			4,346	3,808.7	
Alaska			4,346	3,808.7	
Akiachak	Akiachak, Alaska	99551	104	93.7	K-8
Akiak	Akiak, Alaska	99552	2	1.7	8
Alakanuk	Alakanuk, Alaska	99554	162	147.2	1-8
Barter Island	Barter Island, Alaska	99747	34	27.4	1-8
Beaver	Beaver, Alaska	99724	21	18.1	3-8-S
Brevig Mission	Brevig Mission, Alaska	99563	41	39.1	1-8
Chevak	Chevak, Alaska	99561	130	121.4	1-8
Chifornak	Chifornak, Alaska	99561	51	147.8	1-8
Diomede	Diomede, Alaska	99762	42	33.2	1-8
Eek	Eek, Alaska	99578	52	50.4	1-8
Elim	Elim, Alaska	99739	43	38.0	1-8
Emmonak	Emmonak, Alaska	99581	184	171.4	K-8
Gambell	Gambell, Alaska	99742	99	83.0	1-8
Golovin	Golovin, Alaska	99762	27	23.1	1-8
Goodnews Bay	Goodnews Bay, Alaska	99589	67	62.6	1-8
Grayling	Grayling, Alaska	99590	44	39.3	1-8
Hooper Bay	Hooper Bay, Alaska	99604	200	179.9	K-8
Kalskag	Kalskag, Alaska	99607	38	33.0	1-8
Kasigluk	Kasigluk, Alaska	99609	76	72.9	1-8
Kiana	Kiana, Alaska	99749	91	80.1	K-8
Kipnuk	Kipnuk, Alaska	99614	113	104.9	K-8
Klukwan	Klukwan, Alaska	99831	9	8.1	1-6
Kotlik	Kotlik, Alaska	99620	101	95.2	K-8

Table 5 ---continued---

Area Agency and State School	Post Office Address	Zip Code	(All Ages) Enrollment	A.D.A.	Grades
Kotzebue	Kotzebue, Alaska	99752	677	516.9	K-12-S
Kwethluk	Kwethluk, Alaska	99621	127	118.1	K-8
Kwigillingok	Kwigillingok, Alaska	99622	57	53.2	1-8
Lower Kalskag	Lower Kalskag, Alaska	99626	48	44.9	1-7
Mekoryuk	Mekoryuk, Alaska	99630	58	53.9	1-8
Mountain Village	Mountain Village, Alaska	99632	164	149.3	K-8
Napakiak	Napakiak, Alaska	99634	76	67.5	1-8
Napaskiak	Napaskiak, Alaska	99635	68	37.6	1-8
Newtok	Newtok, Alaska	99636	43	33.5	1-8
Nightmute	Toksook Bay, Alaska	99637	40	37.3	1-8
Nunapitchuk	Nunapitchuk, Alaska	99641	93	69.7	1-9
Oscarville	Napaskiak, Alaska	99635	8	7.4	1-7
Pilot Station	Pilot Station, Alaska	99650	84	70.8	1-8
Quinhagak	Quinhagak, Alaska	99655	94	88.5	1-8
St. Michael	St. Michael, Alaska	99659	45	38.7	1-8
Savoonga	Savoonga, Alaska	99769	125	124.8	K-9
Scammon Bay	Scammon Bay, Alaska	99662	54	49.3	1-8
Shageluk	Shageluk, Alaska	99665	38	33.8	1-8
Shaktoolik	Shatoolik, Alaska	99771	28	27.0	1-8
Sheldon Point	Sheldon Point, Alaska	99666	37	29.2	1-8
Stebbins	Stebbins, Alaska	99671	66	62.9	1-8
Tanunak	Tanunak, Alaska	99681	91	84.3	K-8-S
Tetlin	Tetlin, Alaska	99779	28	25.1	1-8
Toksook Bay	Toksook Bay, Alaska	99637	93	86.7	1-8-S
Tuluksak	Tuluksak, Alaska	99679	56	48.4	1-8
Tuntutuliak	Tuntutuliak, Alaska	99680	68	63.1	1-8
Unalaklette	Unulakleet, Alaska	99684	127	107.3	K-8
Venetie	Venetie, Alaska	99781	27	17.7	1-7
Wainwright	Wainwright, Alaska	99782	95	90.3	1-8
NAVAJO			1,158	992.6	
Regular Day Schools			1,085	932.0	
Arizona			636	559.7	
New Cottonwood	Chinle, Arizona	86503	304	264.7	K-6
Red Lake	Tonalea, Arizona	86044	202	174.1	K-5-S
Chilchinbeto	Kayenta, Arizona	86033	130	120.9	K-3-S
New Mexico			449	372.3	
Alamo	Magdalena, N. Mex.	87825	60	48.4	K-1
Beclabito	Shiprock, N. Mexico	87420	51	45.4	K-5
Bread Springs	Gallup, N. Mexico	87301	76	68.6	K-3-S
Cove	Shiprock, N. Mexico	87420	123	94.7	K-7
Jones Ranch	Gallup, N. Mexico	87301	50	43.3	K-4-S
Red Rock	Shiprock, N. Mexico	87420	89	71.9	K-6
Trailer School			73	60.6	
Ojo Encino	Cuba, N. Mexico	87103	73	60.6	K-3-S
PHOENIX			1,891	1,598.1	
Truxton Canyon, Arizona			37	33.0	
Supai	Supai, Arizona	86435	37	33.0	1-5
Fort Apache, Arizona			396	325.7	
Cibecue	Cibecue, Arizona	85901	290	225.1	K-8
John F. Kennedy	White River, Arizona	85941	106	100.6	K-6
Hopi, Arizona			767	676.2	
Hopi	Oraibi, Arizona	86039	180	147.2	K-8
Hotevilla	Hotevilla, Arizona	86030	116	107.3	K-7
Moencopi	Tuba City, Arizona	86045	61	54.4	K-5
Polacca	Polacca, Arizona	86042	163	144.1	K-6
Second Mesa	Second Mesa, Arizona	86043	247	223.2	K-6
Papago, Arizona			156	119.4	
Kerwo	Box 8, Ajo, Arizona	85321	58	47.9	K-4
Santa Rosa Ranch	Sells, Arizona	85634	18	16.9	K-5
Vaya Chin	Sells, Arizona	85634	80	54.6	K-4
Pima, Arizona			297	251.8	
Casa Blanca	Bapchule, Arizona	85221	138	119.4	K-4
Gila Crossing	Laveen, Arizona	85339	159	132.4	K-5
Salt River, Arizona			238	192.0	
Salt River	Scottsdale, Arizona	85256	238	192.0	K-6

Table 6. Dormitories Operated by the Bureau of Indian Affairs for Children Attending Public Schools
Fiscal Year 1975

TYPE OF DORMITORY Area/Dormitory	Post Office Address	Zip Code	(all ages) Enrollment	A.D.A.	Grades
GRAND TOTAL			2,926	2,187.5	
RESERVATION DORMITORIES			1,438	959.4	
ABERDEEN			301	164.1	
Rosebud	Mission, S. Dakota	57555	301	164.1	K-12-S
ALBUQUERQUE			344	259.9	
Ignacio	Ignacio, Colorado	81137	160	123.3	3-12
Jicarilla	Dulce, New Mexico	87528	70	52.0	K-12-S
Ramah	Ramah, New Mexico	87321	114	84.6	K-12
ANADARKO			11	7.9	
Fort Sill	Lawton, Oklahoma	73501	11	7.9	9-12
BILLINGS			163	94.2	
Blackfeet	Browning, Montana	59417	163	94.2	1-10-S
MUSKOGEE			509	353.6	
Carter Seminary	Ardmore, Oklahoma	73401	136	102.4	1-12
Eufaula	Eufaula, Oklahoma	74432	161	90.0	K-12-S
Jones Academy	Hartshorne, Oklahoma	74547	212	161.2	1-12
NAVAJO			110	79.7	
Huerfano	Bloomfield, N. Mexico	87413	110	79.7	1-6-S
PERIPHERAL DORMITORIES			1,488	1,228.1	
ALBUQUERQUE			140	109.9	
Albuquerque	Albuquerque, N. Mexico	87100	140	109.0	5-12
NAVAJO			1,348	1,118.2	
Aztec	Aztec, N. Mexico	87410	153	117.1	9-12
Flagstaff	Flagstaff, N. Mexico	86001	191	165.6	8-12
Holbrook	Holbrook, Arizona	86025	317	282.5	6-12
Magdalena	Magdalena, New Mexico	87825	193	166.6	K-12-S
Richfield	Richfield, Utah	84701	134	95.2	8-12
Snowflake	Snowflake, Arizona	85937	122	107.8	9-12
Wingate	Ft. Wingate, N. Mexico	87316	20	11.4	11-12
Winslow	Winslow, Arizona	86047	218	172.0	3-12

Table 7. Enrollment by Grade in Schools Operated by the Bureau of Indian Affairs
Fiscal Year 1975

Grade	1/ GRAND TOTAL	Aberdeen	Albuquerque	Anadarko	Cherokee 2/	Choctaw 2/	Juneau	Muskogee	Navajo	Phoenix	Portland	Seminole 2/
GRAND TOTAL	46,880	8,282	3,552	2,470	1,266	1,322	4,987	538	18,911	5,032	488	32
Kindergarten	2,485	502	307	–	121	90	162	–	978	320	–	5
First	3,566	675	149	–	69	90	520	7	1,689	361	–	6
Second	3,724	587	258	–	89	111	528	12	1,816	317	–	6
Third	3,748	592	216	–	107	99	538	20	1,863	307	–	6
Fourth	3,664	520	228	–	156	135	503	18	1,794	309	–	1
Fifth	3,650	545	246	–	83	134	512	28	1,769	328	–	5
Sixth	3,373	684	149	54	87	124	474	29	1,503	266	–	3
Seventh	3,541	671	78	66	115	173	453	40	1,575	370	–	–
Eighth	3,272	699	153	92	111	116	438	34	1,258	371	–	–
Ungraded Elem.	2,445	504	126	142	5	–	160	–	1,489	19	–	–
Subtotal Elem.	33,468	5,979	1,910	354	943	1,072	4,288	188	15,734	2,968		32
Ninth	3,446	813	76	324	104	96	206	97	1,059	571	100	–
Tenth	2,996	621	83	265	94	65	206	102	864	568	128	–
Eleventh	2,528	480	104	241	64	53	159	83	693	505	146	–
Twelfth	2,045	389	95	173	61	36	128	68	561	420	114	–
Ungraded Sec.	5	–	–	5	–	–	–	–	–	–	–	–
Subtotal Sec.	11,020	2,303	358	1,008	323	250	699	350	3,177	2,064	488	–
Subtotal Elem. & Secondary	44,488	8,282	2,268	1,362	1,266	1,322	4,987	538	18,911	5,032	488	32
Post High	2,392	–	1,284	1,108	–	–	–	–	–	–	–	–

1/ Exclusive of enrollment 2,926 children living in Federal dormitories and attending public schools.
2/ Under jurisdiction of Eastern Area Office headquartered in Washington, D.C.

Table 8. Completions and Number of Graduates of Schools Operated by the Bureau of Indian Affairs
Fiscal Year 1975

Area	High School Graduates	8th Grade Completions	Post Graduates Completions or Placements
GRAND TOTAL	1,511	2,584	287
Aberdeen	331	583	
Albuquerque	70	43	85
Anadarko	138	34	202
Cherokee 1/	53	91	
Choctaw 1/	39	117	
Juneau	101	375	
Muskogee	47	24	
Navajo	356	1,040	
Phoenix	300	277	
Portland	76	-	
Seminole 1/	-	-	

1/ Under jurisdiction of Eastern Area Office headquartered in Washington, D.C.

Table 9. Enrollment by Degree of Indian Blood in Schools Operated by the Bureau of Indian Affairs
Fiscal Year 1975

Area		Full Blood No.	%	Three-Fourths No.	%	One-half No.	%	Less than One-half No.	%
GRAND TOTAL	46,880 1/	35,843	76.5	3,231	6.9	4,684	10.0	3,122	6.6
Aberdeen	8,282	2,433	29.4	1,529	18.5	2,650	32.0	1,670	20.1
Albuquerque	3,552	2,896	81.5	167	4.7	381	10.7	108	3.1
Anadarko	2,470	1,285	52.0	373	15.1	493	20.0	319	12.9
Cherokee 2/	1,266	135	10.7	352	27.8	238	18.8	541	42.7
Choctaw 2/	1,322	1,268	95.9	8	.6	44	3.3	2	.2
Juneau	4,987	4,230	84.8	357	7.2	265	5.2	135	2.8
Muskogee	538	110	20.4	138	25.7	136	25.3	154	28.6
Navajo	18,911	18,626	98.5	79	.4	138	.7	68	.4
Phoenix	5,032	4,636	92.1	128	2.6	228	4.5	40	.8
Portland	488	198	40.6	100	20.5	106	21.7	84	17.2
Seminole 2/	32	26	81.3			5	15.6	1	3.1

1/ Exclusive of enrollment of 2,926 children living in Federal dormitories and attending public schools.

2/ Under jurisdiction of Eastern Area Office headquartered in Washington, D.C.

Table 10. Enrollment by Tribe in Schools Operated by the Bureau of Indian Affairs
Fiscal Year 1975

	GRAND TOTAL	Aberdeen	Albuquerque	Anadarko	Cherokee 1/	Choctaw 1/	Juneau	Muskogee	Navajo	Phoenix	Portland	Seminole 1/
GRAND TOTAL	46,880 2/	8,282	3,552	2,470	1,266	1,322	4,987	538	18,911	5,032	488	32
Aleuts, Eskimos & Indians	5,160 3/	2	37	13			4,985		1	1	121	
Apache	1,054	1	144	59					66	844		
Araphoe	186	37	35	79					33	1	1	
Assiniboine	69	34	8	11					7	7	2	
Blackfeet	141	77	8	35		2			6		13	
Caddo	68		1	62				5				
Cherokee	1,581		19	67	1,256	2		232	4	1		
Cheyenne	249	2	51	187				3	4		2	
Chippewa	2,338	2,228	40	51					11	3	5	
Chitimacha	66					66						
Choctaw	1,400	1	3	98		1,245		51		2		
Colville	148		13	34			1		13		87	
Comanche	147		18	129								
Creek	261	1	11	112	2	2		129		2	2	
Crow	166	46	33	52					26	9		
Havasupai	92		1							91		
Hopi	1,231		34	20		1			6	1,169	1	
Hualapai	83		6	7						70		
Kickapoo	52	2	1	48				1				
Kiowa	300	4	18	272				6				
Menominee	52	51	1									
Mission	64		1						51	12		
Mohave	43	2	6	5						30		
Navajo	19,192	3	486	153				1	18,347	202		
Omaha	99	46	15	35					3			
Oneida	61	48	8	2					3			
Ottawa	57	3		4					50			
Paiute	130		15	7	1			1	20	84	2	
Papago	1,040		15	40					3	982		
Pawnee	94	1	11	63				13	4	2		
Pima	1,240		57	23				1	17	1,142		
Ponca	120		10	102				8				
Potawatomi	71	2	4	58				3			4	
Pueblo	2,248		2,119	68					6	54	1	
Sac & Fox	70	4	7	57				2				
Seminole	135		2	52		3		36	10			32
Seneca	42	2	8	19				11			2	
Shoshone	223	26	24	35					87	38	13	
Sioux	5,568	5,263	121	144		1	1		23	12	3	
3 Affiliated Tribes 4/	382	338	23	15					3	1	2	
Ute	186		20	19	5				100	41	1	
Washoe	58	21	3	2					17	35	1	
Winnebago	58		16	15				1	1	4		
Yakima	96		7	21	2				4		62	
All other tribes 4/	759	37	92	195				34	45	193	163	

1/ Under jurisdiction of Eastern Area Office headquartered in Washington, D.C.
2/ Exclusive of 2,926 children living in Federal dormitories and attending public schools.
3/ Alaska natives
4/ Includes Arikara, Gros Ventre and Mandan Tribes of the Fort Berthold Reservation.
5/ Includes 94 tribes represented by 1 to 38 members.

Table 11. School Construction Summary
Fiscal Year 1975

Area	Name of School	Quarters	Space in Classrooms		
			New	Replace	Total
ABERDEEN	Fort Totten Kindergarten	1	20	–	20
	Loneman	1	20	–	20
	Mandaree	1	20	–	20
	White Shield	1	20	–	20
	Turtle Mt. Elementary		360	410	770
	Cheyenne Eagle Butte K-12		114	1,497	1,611

Table 11. School Construction Summary Fiscal Year 1975 (continued)

ALBUQUERQUE	Santa Clara	1	20	-	20
JUNEAU	Akiachak Kindergarten	1	20	-	20
	Savoonga Kindergarten	1	20		20
	Toksook Bay Kindergarten	1	20		20
NAVAJO	Gray Hill Boarding High School		1,000		1,000
	Gray Hill Dormitory (600 spaces)				
PHOENIX	Sherman School Symnasium				
	Phoenix School Gymnasium				
	Hopi Kindergarten	1	20		20
	Polacca Kindergarten	2	40		40
	Gila Crossing Kindergarten	1	20		20

Table 12. Participation in Programs Authorized by Public Law 89-10, as amended
Fiscal Year 1975

TITLE I

Summary of Title I Projects by Areas

Area	Number
ABERDEEN	37
ALBUQUERQUE	15
ANADARKO	5
BILLINGS	3
JUNEAU	15
MUSKOGEE	3
NAVAJO	62
PHOENIX	26
PORTLAND	2
CENTRAL	1
EASTERN	12
TOTAL	181

The above figures include summer school projects, Area technical
assistance projects, and peripheral dormitories, in addition to
regular Title I projects funded within each area.

TITLE I

Major Academic Priorities and Target Children Served

Area	Academic Priorities	No. of Target Children
ABERDEEN	Academic, General	5,322
ALBUQUERQUE	English, Reading	1,293
ANADARKO	Special Education, Reading	607
BILLINGS	Remedial-General Academic	272
JUNEAU	General Academic, Special Ed.	3,040
MUSKOGEE	General Academic	402
NAVAJO	General Academic, Special Ed.	16,515
PHOENIX	General Academic, Special Ed.	4,117
PORTLAND	Reading, Math	1,200
EASTERN	General Academic	954
	TOTAL	33,722

TITLE II

Assistance to Library and Media

In fiscal year 1975 there were 41 projects for 91 schools with an enrollment of 12,725
children that received services from Title II. Sixty-six percent of the total funds
available was spent on printed materials and thirty-four percent was spent on non-printed
materials. Sixty-one schools were in the kindergarten to 8 group; seven were kindergarten
to 12 and twenty-three were schools in the 7-12 group.

Table 12. Participation in Programs Authorized by Public Law 89-10, as amended
Fiscal Year 1975, cont'd.

ESEA TITLE III
SUPPLEMENTARY EDUCATIONAL CENTERS AND SERVICES

Area	Project Title and Location	Target Enrollment	Year of Operation
ABERDEEN	Pilot Diagnostic Prescriptive Teaching Flandreau Indian School Flandreau, South Dakota	31	Third
	Woonspe Waste Anami-Sioux Cultural Studies Little Eagle and Bullhead Day Schools c/o Standing Rock Agency Fort Yates, North Dakota	100	First
	Guidance Utilizing Individual Dev. Pine Ridge Agency Pine Ridge, South Dakota	325	Second
	Personal Development & Family Living Turtle Mountain Community H.S. Belcourt, North Dakota	449	First
	Guidance and Counseling Twin Buttes School Halliday, North Dakota	30	First
ALBUQUERQUE	Plant Science through Hydroponics Ramah Navajo High School Ramah, New Mexico	421	Second
JUNEAU	Community Child Development Akiachak Day School Akiachak, Alaska	20	Third
MUSKOGEE	Language Arts Improvement via Typing Laboratory Seneca Indian School Wyandotte, Oklahoma	192	Second
PHOENIX	Hopi Handicapped Project Hopi Agency Keams Canyon, Arizona	18	Second

TITLE VI -- PART B

Area	No. of Projects	No. Children Served
Aberdeen	2	398
Albuquerque	6	131
Navajo	3	34
Phoenix	2	140
Portland	2	31
Juneau	5	114
Muskogee	1	35
Eastern	2	413
Central	1	-

TITLE VII - BILINGUAL EDUCATION

Area	Description of Project	Language
Aberdeen	Bilingual teaching at Loneman School, Pine Ridge, South Dakota	Lakota
Albuquerque	Bilingual teaching at Sky City Day School, San Fidel, New Mexico Tewa English Language Project Santa Fe, New Mexico	Pueblo

Table 12. Participation in Programs Authorized by Public Law 89,10, as amended
Fiscal Year 1975, cont'd.

Area	Description of Project	Language
Eastern	Bilingual Education for Choctaws of Mississippi, Philadelphia, Miss.	Choctaw
	Bilingual teaching at Ahfachkee Day School, Florida	Seminole
Juneau	Yup'ik Teacher Training Demonstration Project, Bethel	Native Alaskan
Navajo	Bilingual teaching at Cottonwood Day School, Chinle, Arizona	Navajo
	Lake Valley Bilingual Program Crownpoint, New Mexico	
Phoenix	Bilingual teaching at Kerwo Day School, Sells, Arizona	Papago

N.D.E.A. Title III – STRENGTHENING CURRICULA WITH MATERIALS AND EQUIPMENT

Area	Project Title, Location	Target Group	Year of Operation
Albuquerque	Language Project San Juan, New Mexico	99	1
	Anatomy, et. al. IAIA, Santa Fe, New Mexico	60	1
	Music Laguna, New Mexico	55	1
Navajo	Exploratory Method of Instruction Shiprock, New Mexico	350	1
	Science Resource for Grades 6, 7, & 8 Greasewood, New Mexico	80	1
	Chuska Science Project Tohatchi, New Mexico	123	1
Phoenix	Science Project Keams Canyon, Arizona	229	1

Table 13. Bureau of Indian Affairs Higher Education Program
Fiscal Year 1975

Area	Total Number Students	Number Under-Graduates	Number Graduates Students	Under-Graduate Earning Degree	Graduates Earning Degree

GRAND TOTALS

ABERDEEN
ALBUQUERQUE
ANADARKO
BILLINGS
EASTERN
JUNEAU
MINNEAPOLIS   (Data Not Complete at Time of Printing)
MUSKOGEE
NAVAJO
PHOENIX
PORTLAND
SACRAMENTO
SPECIAL PROGRAMS

Table 14. Number of Students enrolled in Public Schools in
States receiving Assistance through Johnson'O'Malley funding

Area/State	Number of Students Enrolled	Area/State	Number of Students Enrolled
ABERDEEN	7,791	NAVAJO	31,825
Nebraska	865	New Mexico	16,582
North Dakota	2,143	Arizona	13,815
South Dakota	4,783	Utah	1,428
ALBUQUERQUE	7,348	PHOENIX	9,254
Colorado	897	Arizona	6,024
New Mexico	6,451	Nevada	2,710
		Utah	520
ANADARKO	4,277		
Kansas	220	PORTLAND	8,656
Oklahoma (Western)	4,057	Idaho	1,648
		Oregon	1,025
BILLINGS	7,867	Washington	5,983
Montana	6,869		
Wyoming	998	SACRAMENTO	2,450
		California	2,450
JUNEAU	14,879		
Alaska	14,879	EASTERN	2,745
		Florida	245
MINNEAPOLIS	7,611	Mississippi	100
Minnesota	3,467	New York	2,400
Wisconsin	3,202		
Iowa	231		
Michigan	711	GRAND TOTAL	115,225
MUSKOGEE	10,522		
Oklahoma (Eastern)	10,522		

Table 15. Enrollments in Schools Contracted to Indian Groups for Operation, Fiscal Year 1975

Area/School	P.O. Address & Zip Code		TOTAL	Enrollment Boarding	Day	Grades Taught
	GRAND TOTAL		2,799	881	1,918	
	Total		1,334	524	810	
Aberdeen						
Crow Creek	Ft. Thompson, S. Dak.	57339	232	115	117	7-12
Mandaree	New Town, N. Dak.	58763	207		207	K-12
St. Michael's	St. Michael, N. Dak.	58335	147		147	K-6
Theodore Jamerson	Bismarck, N. Dak.	58501	93		93	1-8
St. Francis	St. Francis, S. Dak.	57572	409	409		1-12
Ojibwa	Belcourte, N. Dak.	58316	246		246	K-8
Albuquerque	TOTAL		164		164	
Ramah Navajo	Ramah, N. Mexico	87321	164		164	7-12
Anadarko	Total		54		54	
Hammon	Hammon, Oklahoma	73650	54		54	K-12
Billings	Total		467	69	398	
Busby	Busby, Montana	59016	364	69	295	K-12
Wyoming	Ethete, Wyoming	82520	103		103	9-12
Eastern	Total		47		47	
Miccosukee	Homestead, Fla.	33030	47		47	S
Navajo	Total		703	288	415	
Borrego Pass	Crownpoint, N. Mex.	87045	121		121	K-5
Rock Point	Chinle, Arizona	86503	315	156	159	K-6-S
Rough Rock	Chinle, Arizona	86503	267	132	135	K-12-S
Phoenix	Total		30		30	
Blackwater	Sacaton, Arizona	85247	30		30	K-1

Statistics Concerning Indian Education, Fiscal Year 1975. Bureau of Indian Affairs, U.S. Office of Indian Education Programs, Washington, D.C. 1976.

Through Education: Self Determination

Most Indian children in the United States are born to poverty and its potentially destructive effects on their lives. Consider the Indian boy or girl in 1974:

Their family averages about $2,000 annual income, nearly five times less than the average American family.

Their parents will probably die twenty years sooner than those of other children. They are eight times more susceptible to fatal accidents, homicides, and destructive diseases.

Their chances for survival until age one are three times less favorable than for the white infant. Chances for their survival until adolescence or young adulthood are four times less favorable than for other children.

By general population standards, the educational attainment of their parents also is low. Some Indian children's academic and career success may be affected adversely by a lack of English in the home, as well. Whatever the ultimate causes may be demonstrated to be, Indian boys and girls typically do not compare favorably with other children on standardized tests of verbal ability, one index of probable success in school. They compare quite favorably, however, with other children on tests not involving verbal ability. Accordingly, their record of progress in school may be low by conventional standards, although not always lower than those of other minority children.

Most Indian children are enrolled in some kind of formal schooling. The principal aim of their formal education is to assimilate them into the larger social and economic systems of the nation, so that they may be personally and socially productive. The aims of Indian culture are not always continuous with those of the schools, however. In seeking to assimilate the children into the economics of the larger society, the nation may be depriving them of their own cultural heritage as Indians. This may happen as an unintended result of conventional schooling, despite the wish of many Indian parents and community leaders that their children should retain, even emphasize, their Indian-ness while acquiring the skills needed to achieve a modicum of economic independence. The lack of harmony between the two cultures may have an adverse effect on young Indians' school achievement, as well.

The special needs of Indian children are not always understood by the public school districts that serve the off-reservation Indian family. Most Indian pupils are taught as though they were part of a large, undifferentiated minority; yet, the Indian community itself is characterized by great diversity, both in language and values. For example, there are over 300 Indian languages. In only 45 of these, however, are there as many as 1,000 speakers. Moreover, there are few English cognates in Indian languages. The Indian child who acquires his first language from non-English speaking parents will have to acquire English almost entirely as a foreign language. For the English speaking Indian child, his own native language may have to be acquired, as well, if he is to achieve full development as an Indian.

Indian pupils also tend to be lumped unthinkingly with other minorities in the public schools. Too often they are classified and treated solely as "underachievers," "dropouts" or "chronic absentees." With rare exceptions, little regard is given to their unique need to be considered as Indians. Left unassisted, they tend to lose ground in the public schools, academically and culturally, with each succeeding year they remain in school. Conventional school programs themselves tend to add to the Indian pupil's personal and academic problems. This seems to occur, even though the particular school, viewed on other criteria, may number among the nation's finest.

Unfortunately, this situation is not self-correcting. The very factors needed to alter these conditions are missing. For example:

(1) The governance and administration of schools and school districts that enroll significant numbers of Indian pupils remain principally non-Indian. Parents of Indian pupils and representatives of Indian communities generally remain uninvolved in decisions affecting the schooling of their children, even though parental involvement has been established to be a vital force for the improvement of learning among other minority pupils.

(2) School programs in which Indian pupils are enrolled continue to be geared to the needs and requirements of majority pupils. Their teachers largely are non-Indian. They are tested and graded against standards based on white populations. Indian pupils tend not to be motivated to learn by such tests and marks. At worst, some are disabled by them.

(3) The nation's teacher training programs remain largely unchanged by the need to prepare Indian teachers to work with Indian pupils in the public schools. Even in those states with the heaviest concentrations of Indian population, the percent of Indian teachers in the schools falls below the percent of Indians in the total population.

(4) Special leadership training programs for potential Indian leaders in education have been developed in a few prestigious institutions. However, the established Indian school administrator often is unaffected by those programs. Most Indian administrators are untrained or underprepared for the tasks they carry out.

(5) Instructional programs for Indian pupils enrolled in the public schools lack an identifiable research base. Accordingly, most schools resort to remediation and other standard approaches long associated with education

of disadvantaged pupils when confronting the learning problems of Indian pupils. Moreoever, the nation's universities have not been charged seriously to develop needed research. Neither have they sought to prepare Indian researchers for this task.

(6) Local school districts are not prepared to make the extra expenditure that may be required to support those special programs for Indian pupils that are presumed to be effective. Earlier federal programs have not proved to be especially productive in this regard, even though such programs as ESEA Title I have provided some support for the general population of "disadvantaged" pupils, Indian children included.

(7) Given the great diversity within the Indian community itself, there seems to be no overwhelming consensus among Indian adults as to the specific content and emphasis in public schooling that would be most desirable and effective for their children. A much needed vocational education, for example, sometimes is seen by Indian parents to be an inferior offering, hence rejected as inappropriate for their children.

In recent years, the level of awareness among educators of the special condition of the Indian pupils has increased. In part, this has resulted from an out-migration of Indian families from the compounds and reservations, and from the rural areas to the central cities. The vast majority of Indian pupils now are reported to attend school off the traditional reservation. At least ten Indian pupils now are reported to be enrolled in 2500 local school districts. Such dispersion has always been the case with the majority of Eastern Native Americans. It is becoming increasingly so for the Western Indian populations, as well.

In 1973, the Office of Education projected enrollments of Indian pupils from various survey data. It estimated that 326,354 Indian children and youth presently are of school age. Of these, 12,000 were considered to be not in school. An additional 29,138 were estimated to be enrolled in school districts, each of whose aggregate enrollment of Indian pupils was fewer than ten. About 48,000 pupils were reported to be enrolled in schools on reservations operated by the Bureau of Indian Affairs (BIA). About 9,000 pupils were estimated to be enrolled in private or mission schools. Over 225,000 pupils were estimated to be enrolled in 2,565 different local school districts.

The dispersion of Indian populations among diverse local school jurisdictions may have broadened public concern for the education of Indian children. It also makes it extremely difficult to mount and sustain the kind of special programs for Indian pupils that seem needed today on a national scale. Earlier federal efforts to assist local school districts to serve Indian pupils have not always achieved their desired results. This was especially indicated in the case of P.L. 874 funds,

the identity of which ended at the school district level rather than the individual Indian pupil to be benefited. More recently, ESEA Title I funds have been available to those local school districts with a heavy concentration of low-income families. Although these funds were expected to be targeted in attendance areas with high incidence of low-income families, only one-third of the eligible disadvantaged Indian children in the Title I population actually were reported to have participated in Title I supported programs overall. Moreover, the level of support available to local education agencies for these special services was minimal.

The introduction of a special funding program for Indian pupils through the Indian Education Act of 1972 offered a potentially attractive incentive for local education agencies to develop needed new programs and services specifically for their Indian pupils. Hampered by the fact that the aid came too late in 1973 for many districts to apply, only limited progress can be reported at this date. Moreover, only ten percent of the funds authorized for the program actually was appropriated for distribution to the districts that did apply. Nonetheless, 135,297 Indian pupils were enrolled in some way in special programs developed under the Indian Education Act of 1972. Parents and community leaders in 435 local school jurisdictions also were involved in forming local project plans, marking a potentially major breakthrough in this area of concern.

It is evidently too early to tell how much good was accomplished in the field by the Indian Education Act in FY 1974. What is clear is this: the needs that were identified earlier have been validated by the participating local school districts in their applications for assistance under the Act. Moreover, the local districts evidently sought to design special program objectives and activities that were in line with the most immediate and compelling of those needs, with major exceptions. The level of funding available in the first year was insufficient to enable the local districts to bring their current instructional practices up to the state of the art. Nonetheless, a serious beginning was made in the 435 local districts.

A number of correlary needs also were identified by the districts. At least three major initiatives seem warranted thereby. They are:

(1) Emphasize the development of correlary services needed to reinforce the regular classroom instruction of Indian pupils. These include:

★ New materials and methods for fostering language development

★ New methods for promoting a healthy self-image among Indian children and youth

★ Career counseling for Indian students

★ New techniques for involving Indian parents and community representatives in decisions affecting the education of Indian pupils and in the actual education of young children, as well.

(2) Concentrate in developing appropriate inservice training programs for established teachers of Indian pupils, and in forming new preparation programs for Indian men and women who might be persuaded to enter teaching.

(3) Consider certain administrative changes in current approaches to the special education of Indian pupils. These include:

★ Concentrate available funds on those programs that demonstrably work with Indian pupils, particularly in the areas of reading, language development, and career education.

★ Target program efforts to promote a measurable result with the limited number of pupils that might be served from available funds.

★ Extend services to pre-school children for desired long-range effects, particularly in bicultural language development.

★ Extend special services to out-of-school youth for potentially valuable short-range effects, particularly in career development.

★ Earmark an appropriate portion of available R & D funds to train Indian researchers to develop and explore new models for the education of Indian families.

★ Encourage local school jurisdictions to form interdistrict programs to reach the 29,138 pupils not now touched in any way by the Indian Education Act.

In the report that follows, special attention is given to an analysis of the 435 funded projects. A number of basic questions are addressed therein, including:

To what extent did IEA funds reach the pupils for whom intended?

To what extent were available dollars translated into potentially useful programs and services, as anticipated by the Act?

To what extent were such programs and services related to demonstrable needs of Indian pupils and the public school districts that seek to address those needs?

How adequate were the program proposals themselves? To what extent were applications under the Act denied for cause?

What areas of need appear to be untouched by current program proposals?

What administrative action would seem to increase the effectiveness of programs for Indian pupils?

THE INDIAN EDUCATION ACT OF 1972

Report of Progress for the First Year of the Program

The Indian Education Act of 1972 (IEA) was enacted June 23, 1972, as Title IV, Public Law 92-318, Educational Amendments of 1972. The Act has as its principal policy objective ". . .to provide financial assistance to local educational agencies to develop and carry out elementary and secondary school programs specially designed to meet (the special educational needs of Indian students in the United States)." To local school districts that qualify, grants may be made up to one-half their average annual expenditure per pupil.

Similar amendments to other educational legislation also were made at the same time in order to provide special funding for teacher training, innovative projects, and adult education. Provisions for an Office of Indian Education also were authorized and a national advisory committee on Indian education was created, as well.

IEA an Extension of Earlier Aid

These enactments are logical extensions of earlier congressional efforts to improve the quality of public education for Indian pupils. As early as 1934, federal funds were made available through provisions of the Johnson O'Malley Act for scholarships and related expenditures on behalf of Indian students. In 1952, P.L. 874 and 815 were established. These funds were available to compensate local school districts whose tax resources were limited by the presence of non-taxable federal properties or operations on or near the school districts. In 1971, $30,000,000 was granted to local districts from these three funding sources. It is not clear, however, that the funds actually were employed by the districts to mount special programs for Indian pupils. Indeed, the districts were not required to do so. Funds simply were paid into their general operating accounts and employed to support the districts' general education programs.

Under provisions of Title I of the Elementary and Secondary Education Act of 1965, federal funds also were provided those local school districts that reported a high concentration of low-income families in residence. These funds were made available to the districts so that they might offer special programs for all classes of "disadvantaged pupils" in attendance, disadvantaged Indian pupils included. Although 70% of all Indian pupils residing in public school districts were reported in 1970 to be "disadvantaged," under provisions of the Act, only one-fourth actually were enrolled in special Title I programs. Moreover, the average expenditure per pupil for such programs was too low to make an appreciable difference in pupil achievement feasible, in most cases.

IEA Provides Special Aid

The Indian Education Act of 1972 clearly focuses P.L. 874 and other federal funding programs on the special education of Indian pupils. Whereas earlier enactments permitted local school districts to develop special programs for Indian pupils if they chose to do so, the Indian Education Act clearly specifies that such programs will be developed, if federal funds are to be made available for that purpose.

The Act has five basic provisions. They are:

Part A: Amends P.L. 874 to permit grants to be made to local education agencies for the purpose of developing special educational programs to meet the special education needs of Indian pupils in elementary and secondary schools.

Part B: Amends Title VIII of the Elementary and Secondary Education Act of 1965 to support planning, pilot, and demonstration projects for improving educational opportunities for Indian children, including the training of teachers of Indian pupils and the dissemination of information concerning exemplary educational practices.

Part C: Amends Title III of the Elementary and Secondary Education Amendments of 1966 to provide grants to state and local educational agencies, and to Indian tribes, institutions, and organizations, to improve educational opportunities for adult Indians.

Part D: Establishes in the U. S. Office of Education an Office of Indian Education under a Deputy Commission of Indian Education. Part D also provides for a new national advisory committee of Indians to be appointed by the President to advise on all matters concerning Indian education.

Part E: Amends Title V of the Higher Education Act of 1965 to dedicate five percent of appropriated funds to the preparation of teachers for Indian children, with preference granted the preparation of Indian teachers. Also amends ESEA to permit the U. S. Commissioner to designate certain schools on or near reservations to be classified as "local education agencies" for purposes of the Act.

Eligible Districts

The substantive legislation was enacted in June, 1972, and the appropriation bill was signed on October 31, 1972. Applications from local education agencies had to be submitted on or before June 30, 1973, about one month before funds were released. An estimated 2,565 local school districts were identified by the 1973 Census of Indians to be eligible under provisions of the Act. That is, these were the districts that enrolled no fewer than ten Indian pupils; or, if fewer than ten were enrolled in a district, the actual Indian enrollment constituted one-half or more of the district's total enrollment.

The target population of the legislation included an estimated 269,354 elementary and secondary school age Indian children and youth. This represents approximately 82% of the 326,354 Indians estimated in the 1973 census to be of school age. Of the larger number, 48,000 were believed to attend schools operated by the Bureau of Indian Affairs (hence, not a target of this legislation) and another 9,000 in private or mission schools.

Of the 269,354 potential target pupils, 29,138 were estimated to be enrolled in districts not now eligible for assistance under the Act by reason of the fact that their aggregate enrollment of Indian pupils was less than ten. Another 12,000 children and youth were estimated to be not in school.

The 2,565 eligible districts themselves represent about 71% of all school districts currently operating in the United States. They are located in the 49 continental states and the District of Columbia. Their aggregate enrollment in 1973 was estimated to be 21,416,607, about 1.6% or 228,216 of which were Indian pupils.

About 70% of the pupils reside in eight states, however. These are: Alaska, Arizona, California, Montana, New Mexico, North Carolina, Oklahoma, and Washington. Five states and the District of Columbia each enroll fewer than 100 Indian pupils. The majority of states enroll fewer than 1,000 pupils. Nonetheless, it is clear that the population of Indian pupils truly is nationwide, and fairly widely dispersed through the general population. The data for each state is presented in Table 1.

Special Needs of Indian Pupils

Indian children consistently perform as well as comparable Anglo children on non-verbal tests of ability, according to Havighurst and others.[1] Nonetheless, they consistently underachieve in reading and mathematics, and on standardized tests based on measures of verbal ability, when compared to national norms.[2]

Two major factors are associated with this:

(1) Just as children from other minority groups, Indian pupils come from homes characterized by poverty[3] and limited education of parents.[4] About half are brought up in a non-English speaking environment;[5]

(2) Many Indian children are reared in a traditional culture that well may be out of harmony with the

Table 1   Distribution of Indian Pupils by State

	No. of Eligible Districts	Fall 1972 Total Enrollment	Fall 1972 Indian Enrollment
Alabama	2	42,020	81
Alaska	29	81,623	15,888
Arizona	136	428,601	26,798
Arkansas	10	90,049	519
California	481	4,195,544	15,417
Colorado	32	441,018	2,309
Connecticut	17	192,779	303
Delaware	2	14,496	55
D. C.	1	140,000	18
Florida	33	1,072,902	2,390
Georgia	14	386,937	408
Idaho	14	33,107	1,856
Illinois	25	842,649	2,204
Indiana	21	407,258	853
Iowa	10	154,694	664
Kansas	26	233,126	1,400
Kentucky	5	175,202	113
Louisiana	4	253,757	234
Maine	8	38,222	239
Maryland	10	779,591	1,660
Massachusetts	10	199,042	278
Michigan	133	1,101,539	4,554
Minnesota	96	519,299	9,660
Mississippi	5	53,050	68
Missouri	48	335,750	934
Montana	78	106,808	10,795
Nebraska	26	145,043	1,826
Nevada	15	131,107	2,728
New Hampshire	2	23,234	23
New Jersey	12	141,728	290
New Mexico	32	224,445	21,883
New York	71	1,700,124	5,692
North Carolina	47	571,576	14,312
North Dakota	33	66,919	3,187
Ohio	33	768,199	1,017
Oklahoma	543	596,170	40,260
Oregon	46	308,279	2,367
Pennsylvania	12	99,495	199
Rhode Island	12	81,479	158
South Carolina	11	200,756	395
South Dakota	56	97,665	7,956
Tennessee	7	301,096	193
Texas	58	1,365,000	2,502
Utah	30	300,029	4,447
Vermont	2	22	22
Virginia	22	576,491	937
Washington	160	700,345	12,635
West Virginia	8	134,636	172
Wisconsin	94	538,203	6,098
Wyoming	10	15,523	1,219
	2,565	21,416,607	228,216

principal objectives of the public schools, namely: to assimilate the Indian pupil into the main stream of values of the Anglo society.

The former has been identified clearly as a non-school factor that adversely affects pupil achievement.[6] The latter also may account for poor achievement and high dropout rate.[7] The Indian pupil could be led to withdraw from the school culture and, in his indifference to or lack of acceptance of conventional values, drop out of school in substantially greater numbers than other pupils.[8]

Havighurst also reported that community leaders in his study believed that the public schools should pursue a "man of two cultures" approach in educating Indian children and youth.[9] They contend that for a part of his education, the Indian child should be prepared to make his way in the larger society and economy along with all other children and youth, regardless of ethnic differences. For another significant part, however, leaders felt that the Indian child should learn about his own culture. That the two objectives might be in conflict was recognized. Indeed, if the school is successful in the one, it may be unable to be so with respect to the other. Havighurst's study suggests that Indian pupils, in general, have the emotional strength to handle such conflict when fairly presented, however.[10]

Without special attention, it seems clear that Indian children and youth have a limited future.[11] Their median family income in 1972 was the nation's lowest. [12] Unemployment exceeded the national average by ten times.[13] While the birth rate among Indian families was twice the national average,[14] infant mortality was thrice the national average.[15] For every major disease except cancer, heart or vascular disease, the death rate among Indian adults exceeded national averages by two or more times.[16] As late as 1967, the median age at death for the Indian adult was 50.[17] By contrast, the average Anglo lives to age 70.

The educational future of Indian children is equally constricted. Although an estimated 90% of Indian children of school age attend school,[18] only 50% complete 12th grade.[19] About 18,000 Indians reach age 18 each year.[20] Only 17% enter college, as compared to 38% of the general 18-year old population.[21] Of those who enter college, only 4% are expected to graduate.[22] In 1970, the National Center for Educational Statistics estimated that there were only 29,269 full-time Indian students in college and 1,608 in graduate school.

The public schools that serve Indian students confront certain realities about their pupils that must be addressed. These may be summarized as follows:

★ Indian pupils are not materially different from other pupils in their basic academic abilities; however, they evidence the same characteristics as other children of poverty, namely: substantial underachievement at verbal and verbal-dependent tasks, absenteeism, and early dropout. Teaching methods to cope with these conditions are known but not widely practiced.

★ Indian pupils may be caught up in rival and, perhaps, irreconcilable value systems that make the task of school adjustment far more difficult for the Indian than majority pupil.

★ There is a broad consensus among Indian parents and leaders that their children should be prepared to take a role in the dominant society. There also is an insistent demand that their children be taught about their own culture as well, a task most schools simply are not competent to perform.

★ There is no broad consensus, however, in support of specific content of curriculum that is appropriate for Indian children. The background of Indian children itself is so diverse that the notion of a standard Indian curriculum itself would seem to be inappropriate.

★ There is no organized body of research, other than Havighurst and related studies, on which curriculums for Indian children readily can be built.

★ Indian teachers are in short supply. So few Indian youth complete college that it will be necessary for many years to employ and train Anglo teachers to work with Indian children. Whereas Anglo teachers may be adequate to teach Indian pupils to read and figure, they may not be the best choice for schooling Indian children about their own culture.

School Districts That Serve Indian Pupils

The 2,565 American public school districts that enroll Indian pupils themselves have special problems. For example, fewer than one percent of their enrolled Indian pupils receive instruction from Indian teachers.[23] Teacher-parent interaction is limited in these schools, providing little basis for building understanding about home or school.[24] Teachers themselves are pessimistic about the educational future of their Indian pupils.[25] Curriculums in these schools are essentially uniform. Few seem responsive to the Indian pupils' special need for different language and cultural materials.

However, most schools are concerned about their ability to teach Indian pupils in the basic curriculum. Ninety-two percent identified a need to provide special instruction in mathematics and reading.[26] Half were seeking assistance in offering English as a second language.[27] Every district surveyed in 1970 was concerned with dropout prevention, and felt that their programs were inadequate in this regard.[28] About one-third indicated a need for special programs for neglected and delinquent Indian children and youth.[29] About one-fourth

indicated a need for special programs for emotionally and/or mentally disturbed pupils.[30]

The several districts also seemed unequal in their financial ability to provide special programs for Indian pupils. The median expenditure per pupil in average daily attendance in the districts in 1973 was $810. The range of expenditures, however, varied from a low of $578 to a high of $1,549. Clearly, in 1973, place of pupil residence made a difference of as much as $1,000 per pupil in the dollars available to support his basic education.[31] The place of the pupil's residence in 1973 loomed as the major school factor in determining the quality of his education. For the favored district, provision of special services for Indian pupils would seem to be feasible. However, the very lowest expenditure districts may have a difficult time in mounting substantive special programs for their Indian pupils until their regular programs for all pupils are adequate by national standards.[32]

Potential Impact of the Indian Education Act in 1973

Eleven million dollars were available for funding local school district projects in 1973 under provisions of Part A of the Indian Education Act. An additional five million were available for Part B, permitting grants to be made to 51 agencies, ranging from $2,460 to $300,000. One-half million was available to support ten adult education projects under Part C.

Who Received the Funds?

Of the 2,565 local educational agencies that were eligible to receive grants under Part A of the legislation, 547 applied and 435 grants actually were made in 1973. A greater number of districts might well have applied for grants. However, the applicant districts had only about one month from the time of notification until the end of the fiscal year to apply. Nonetheless, the grants to the 435 districts had the potential to reach 135,297 Indian pupils, representing 59% of all enrolled Indian pupils in the 2,565 eligible districts. The median expenditure per pupil supported by IEA grants was about 10% of the districts' average annual regular per pupil expenditure, or $81. These data are presented in Table 2.

Not reached, of course, in 1973, were 122,057 Indian pupils, 92,919 of whom were enrolled in eligible districts not seeking or not receiving a grant, and 29,138 pupils in districts with fewer than ten Indian pupils in enrollment. The program was unable to reach approximately 12,000 Indian youth believed not to be enrolled in school.

Entitlement and Funding

Applicant districts received less funds than entitled in 1973. If all eligible districts had applied for and received

Table 2

Distribution of IEA Funds in 1973 by State

State	No. of Districts which Applied	No. of Unfunded Districts	No. of Funded Districts	Latest Indian Enrolment in Funded Districts	Expenditures per Pupil in ADA	1973 Re-allocation Amount	1973 Expenditure per Indian Pupil
Alabama	0	0	0		$ 587		
Alaska	17	8	9	10,757	1,472	$1,532,982	$143
Arizona	31	7	24	19,292	771	1,440,024	75
Arkansas	0	0	0		578		
California	26	9	17	1,273	874	107,705	85
Colorado	7	3	4	594	828	47,616	80
Connecticut	1	0	1	32	1,030	3,191	100
Delaware	0	0	0		1,022		
D. C.	0	0	0		1,174		
Florida	4	2	2	190	807	14,844	78
Georgia	0	0	0		690		
Idaho	8	4	4	583	629	35,502	61
Illinois	1	0	1	150	1,026	14,900	99
Indiana	0	0	0		801		
Iowa	2	1	1	219	892	18,912	86
Kansas	6	4	2	174	808	13,611	78
Kentucky	0	0	0		657		
Louisiana	1	0	1	85	768	6,320	74
Maine	6	4	2	148	739	10,589	72
Maryland	1	0	1	527	1,017	51,888	98
Massachusetts	0	0	0		917		
Michigan	21	8	13	1,179	998	113,915	97
Minnesota	22	4	18	6,710	1,031	669,760	100
Mississippi	0	0	0		581		
Missouri	2	2	0		752		
Montana	31	3	28	6,039	822	480,590	80
Nebraska	8	4	4	233	833	18,791	81
Nevada	5	4	1	202	799	15,626	77
New Hampshire	0	0	0		789		
New Jersey	0	0	0		1,166		
New Mexico	15	2	13	19,642	732	1,391,986	71
New York	10	0	10	2,202	1,549	330,223	150
North Carolina	18	1	17	12,871	668	832,390	65
North Dakota	15	2	13	2,845	$719	$ 198,038	$ 70
Ohio	2	0	2	381	787	29,029	76
Oklahoma	181	16	165	25,826	660	1,650,210	64
Oregon	5	3	2	808	979	76,583	95
Pennsylvania	0	0	0		939		
Rhode Island	1	1	0		982		
South Carolina	0	0	0		638		
South Dakota	21	4	17	6,579	760	484,074	74
Tennessee	0	0	0		603		
Texas	0	0	0		691		
Utah	6	0	6	2,358	680	155,235	66
Vermont	0	0	0		828		
Virginia	0	0	0		776		
Washington	43	14	29	7,907	914	699,675	88
West Virginia			1	22	708	1,508	69
Wisconsin	23	1	22	4,495	969	421,688	94
Wyoming	6	1	5	974	901	84,961	87
	547	112	435	135,297	$ 810 (median)	$10,952,366	$81 (median)

the maximum allowable amount of Part A funds, their annual entitlement would have been about $200 millions (i.e. about one-half their average expenditure per pupil times the number of Indian pupils in enrollment). For the 435 funded districts, their maximum entitlement in 1973 was $113 millions. Only $11.5 millions were allocated, however. Accordingly, individual district entitlements among the 435 funded districts were ratably reduced to approximately 10% of their maximum entitlement, therefore.

Level of Special Support

The median level of suport from IEA grants for the special education of Indian pupils in 1973 was about $81. The range of support around the mid-point varied in accordance with each participant district's average annual per pupil expenditure for all enrolled pupils. This varied from $150 per Indian pupil in New York to as little as $61 per Indian pupil in Idaho. When the IEA funds were added to the district's base per pupil expenditure from all other sources, the range of total support per Indian pupil varied from $1,650 per Indian pupil in New York to about $670 per Indian pupil in Idaho. Certain lower expenditure states (e.g. Alabama and Mississippi) did not submit an application. The vast majority of funded districts expended less than $110 in differential expenditure to support its special programs for Indian pupils in 1973. These values also are recorded in Table 2.

Size of Grant

About half of the 435 grants were under $10,000. Three-fourths fell under $20,000. About 15% fell between $20,000 and $50,000, and 11% exceeded $50,000. There was an obvious relationship between the size of the grant and the number of Indian pupils potentially to be served in the funded district. Districts with greater numbers of Indian pupils received larger grants. These distributions are reproduced in Table 3.

Numbers of Indian Pupils Served

The most typical project grant had the potential to serve about one or two hundred Indian pupils. About 25 grants served 1000 or more pupils, whereas 183 grants served fewer than 100 Indian pupils. These data are reproduced in Table 4.

Denial of Applications

A number of applications were denied for cause. Criteria for grant approval were given in the legislation itself and served as the principal basis for grant awards. Of 105 cases analyzed, as many as 86 were denied in part for failure to provide required information of parent and/or community participation in project development. In 34 instances, provisions for project evaluation were inadequate and in ten cases fiscal control was lacking.

In Table 5, a ranking of reasons for project denial or reduction is presented. More than one reason may have been given for any one project, hence the total number of reasons cited may exceed the number of projects. The principal reasons are instructive, however. Most projects that were denied funding were denied because of the failure of the applying districts to involve Indian parents and community representatives in shaping the districts' proposals.

TABLE 3

Relation between Size of Grant and Number of Indians with the Recipient LEA

Size of Grant	Number of Indians in LEA's								Total LEA's
	1–25	25–49	50–99	100–199	200–499	500–999	1000–4999	5000–9999	
Under $1,000	15								15
$1,000–$4,999	31	55	38						124
$5,000–$9,999		1	40	42	1				84
$10,000–$19,999			3	55	38		2		98
$20,000–$49,999				1	50	11	1		63
$50,000–$99,999					1	22	5		28
$100,000–$199,999						3	10		13
$200,000–$499,999							4	1	5
$500,000–$1,000,000								2	2
Total LEA's	46	56	81	98	90	36	22	3	432
Per Cent	10.6	13.0	18.8	22.7	20.8	8.3	5.1	0.7	100.0

Table 4

Number of Indian Pupils Served by 432 Funded Projects

No. of Indian Pupils in LEA's	No. of LEA's	Percent	Cummulative Percent
Under 25	46	10.6	10.6
25 - 49	56	13.0	23.6
50 - 99	81	18.8	42.4
100 - 199	98	22.7	65.1
200 - 499	90	20.8	85.9
500 - 999	36	8.3	94.2
1000 - 4999	22	5.1	98.3
5000 - 9999	3	0.7	100.0
TOTAL	432	100.0	100.0

Table 5

Frequent Reasons for Denial or Reduction
of Part A Proposals
(105 cases)

Count	Reason for Denial or Reduction
86	Parent committee information vague or now shown
62	No stated community involvement
34	Evaluation provisions vague or lacking
30	File incomplete
30	Narrative vague
19	Program not geared to special Indian needs
10	No provisions for fiscal control
9	Budget not specified or feasible

*Impact and Effectiveness
of the Funding Program*

Insufficient time has elapsed between the funding of proposals and this report to assess the impact of the funding program on the needs of Indian students and the schools that serve them. Studies of the impact and effectiveness of funded proposals are in process and will constitute the basis for subsequent reports.

It was possible, however, to ascertain the extent to which funded projects were consistent with known needs of students and their schools. Moreover, it was possible to estimate the extent to which project objectives were directed toward the most compelling of those needs and the extent to which project budgets were consistent with those objectives.

In general, these observations seem warranted:

(1) The needs identified by the funded districts coincided with those, described earlier in this paper, toward which the legislation was directed.

(2) Applicants under Part A and Part B, as well, largely designed their projects to address the most immediate and compelling of these needs.

(3) Proposed expenditures, with some exceptions, were consistent with those objectives.

Projects also appeared to be focused on the most pressing pupil and school needs, although they appeared to be rather imprecisely focused within the schools themselves. In many instances, the entire Indian pupil population in the district was considered to be the target population for the project. Yet, most projects were funded at a level (between $10 and $20 thousands) where more narrow focusing and targeting might have been expected for best results.

Most projects met minimum expectations with respect to the involvement of Indian parents and community members. For many of the projects, new Indian parent advisory committees had been formed to assist in project development. Many projects also proposed also to employ Indians as consultants, or para-professionals in the classroom, and to emphasize home contacts on the part of school faculties.

Given the short amount of time in which applicants had to develop their proposals, it would appear that the program was reasonably well begun. At minimum, the requirements and expectations of the Act in largest part were met. Time is needed for the schools and school districts to place their projects fully into operation and for the effects on Indian pupils and communities, if any, to develop.

These observations are described in greater detail as follows:

Validation of Needs

Applicant districts were expected to identify and document the basic needs to which their project proposals were directed. Each applicant provided a narrative statement concerning the needs of Indian students within the district and the district's requirements for addressing those needs. Only about 30% of the project applicants provided documentary evidence of those needs, however. The other 70% of the districts may encounter problems later in validating evidence of project effectiveness.

The several narrative statements were examined. No precise classification and cataloguing of needs was feasible. However, it was possible to count the number of times one or another stated need was identified by the districts. Given the limitations of the methodology, these "counts" were used to estimate the priority among needs identified by the districts.

In general, districts provided evidence in their narrative statements of two broad classes of needs in the districts: those pertaining to the Indian pupils themselves and those pertaining to the schools that serve them.

Indian Students' Personal Needs

Districts identified several areas of concern with respect to Indian pupils. Chief among these were the needs of Indian pupils for assistance in the areas of social adjustment and formation of adequate self-concepts. These are reported in Table 6.

Table 6

Personal or Social Needs of Indian Pupils	Number of Districts Citing Need
Conduct Problems	21
Social Adjustment	155
Delinquency	6
Alcohol/Drug Abuse	9
Suicide	1
Self Concept	219
Peer Acceptance	33
Not Stated	152
Physical Fitness	1
Parent Involvement	1
Isolation	0

Districts also identified certain academic deficiencies among their Indian pupils that required treatment. Largely, these referred to their consistently low performance on standardized tests and in academic subjects, and their high rate of absenteeism and school dropout. These data are presented in Table 7.

Table 7

Needs of Academic Achievement	No. of Districts Citing Need
Dropout rate	138
Absenteeism	98
Low grades on academic subjects	136
Low scores on standardized tests	100
Not stated	150
Low motivation	2
No jobs	1
Poor community	1

Contrary to other known evidence, applicant districts did not identify pupil health as a major concern in developing their projects. This might reflect a certain unawareness of health problems among school authorities. It could mean also that they directed their concern toward certain classes of "educational" problems without seeking to describe other important problem areas in the school district. Thirty-six applicants, however, cited health needs in the district. These are presented in Table 8.

Table 8

Pupil Health Needs	No. of Districts Citing Need
High mortality rate	1
Child diseases	3
No prevention care	20
Diet deficiencies	8
Not stated	399
No doctor	1
No hospital	1
No clothes	2
No dollars for Care	1
No Psychologist	1
General health problems	4

About ten percent of the districts also evidenced concern about the basic economic plight of Indian students. They referred to high unemployment among Indians in the district and to their generally low income. It was not clear, however, whether the districts were describing the economic condition of Indian parents, or were referring to a lack of vocational training and guidance for Indian pupils.

Areas of Need in Schools That Enroll Indian Pupils

Certain curriculum deficiencies were consistently noted by districts. Most of these centered on the "cultural" content of curriculum, indicating some continuing concern, even conflict, about the appropriateness of standard school curricula for Indian pupils. Evidence of concern with technical and vocational training opportunities in the school also were noted, as was a concern for the curriculums in reading, language development, and mathematics. These data are described in Table 10.

Table 9

Economic Needs of Indian Families	No. of Districts Citing Need
Unemployment	48
Low income	48
Illiteracy	12
Not stated	349

Table 10

Areas of Needed Curriculum Improvement	No. of Districts Citing Need
Cultural	223
Technical	72
Text books	26
Language arts	15
Not stated	107
Reading	18
Indian History	7
Recreation program	4
Physical education	10
Art	9
Remedial reading	23
Remedial language	1
Library	2
Driver education	1
Drafting	1
Auto mechanic	1
Arts and crafts	7
Remedial mathematics	15
Mathematics	8
Forestry/Logging	1
Vocational training	18
Agriculture	1
Music	9
Special education	4
Health	2
Science	2
Speech	3
Indian culture	4
Indian language	1
Shop	1

The schools seemed equally concerned with inadequacies in their teaching. Deficiencies in teaching methods and/or techniques were identified by the majority of applicant districts as a major problem to be addressed in these districts. This observation is consistent with earlier studies. It also follows from the districts' evident concern with the low achievement of their Indian pupils, and the possible negative effects of inappropriate teaching methods on achievement. Results are reported in Table 11.

Table 11

Area of Needed Methodological Improvement	No. of Districts Citing Need
Test Methods	17
Teaching Methods	248
Teaching Techniques	77
Not stated	138

A majority of districts also indicated their concern about their instructional staffs. About one-third of the districts indicated that they were understaffed. About the same number were concerned that their teachers lacked adequate information about Indians. Only 18 districts indicated that their teachers lacked appropriate training. Only three districts felt that they needed Indian teachers to work with their pupils. These data are presented in Table 12.

Table 12

Areas of Needed Staff Improvement	No. of Districts Citing Need
Lack of training	18
Lack of Indian information	124
Poor attitude toward Indians	17
Understaffed	142
Not stated	185
No Indian teacher	3

Nearly one-half of the districts noted major inadequacies in their correlary service programs, especially the areas of student counseling and community/parent relationships. The concern for counseling appears to be consistent with the districts' earlier expressed concerns about their Indian pupils' problems of social adjustment and in forming adequate self-concepts. Other correlary service needs also were identified in some districts, recreation and transportation services chief among them. These data are represented in Table 13.

Table 13

Areas of Needed Improvement in Special Services	No. of Districts Citing Need
Testing	30
Counseling	204
Community/Parent relations	116
Transportation	49
Auditorium	4
Broadcast facilities	7
Recreation	38
School readiness	21
Not stated	154
Physical fitness	1
Tutoring	6
Library materials	1
Reading specialist	1
Work-Study	1
Skills training	1
Language specialist	0
Adult education	0

About one-fourth of the districts cited major inadequacies in their instructional materials and supplies for use with Indian pupils. This appeared to be consistent with the districts' earlier expressed concern for more cultural relevance in curriculum. About one-fifth of the districts cited major needs for instructional equipment, as well. Only 24 districts identified a need for new facilities in working with Indian pupils. See Table 14.

Table 14

Major School Needs	No. of Districts Citing Need
Buildings	24
Equipment	85
Materials and Supplies	119
Not stated	276

It seems clear that the applicant districts themselves tend to identify the same type and intensity of needs and requirements as were made by other data sources. In general, they are concerned about the personal and social as well as academic needs of their Indian pupils. They seem less concerned about their student's basic health and economic needs, however. Most districts are concerned about the lack of cultural relevance of their curricula for Indian pupils and the lack of appropriate information concerning Indians on the part of their teachers. They cite a similar need for new materials

and supplies, as well. The districts seem equally concerned by their lack of appropriate counseling services. A small group of districts also seems concerned by deficiencies in their relationships with Indian parent and community groups. Curiously, however, few districts indicated their concern with the basic preparation of their teachers or with the lack of Indian teachers among their faculties. Most cited a lack of sufficient staff to offer special services for Indian pupils.

Project Objectives

Applicants also identified specific objectives for their proposed projects. Ostensibly, project objectives should be responsive to educational needs of the Indian children to be served and the schools that purport to serve them. In general, it was found that project objectives correspond with those needs.

Highest priority among project objectives was given to counseling and related social development services. The objectives for such service programs corresponded almost exactly to pupil needs, as cited earlier by the majority of districts. See Table 15.

Table 15

Counseling and Social Development Objectives	No. of Districts Citing Objective
Self Care	146
Diet/Health	26
Peer Relations	50
Family Relations	39
Self Image	235
Not Stated	145
Academic Problems	1

Most districts reflected their concern that Indian pupils receive assistance in forming an adequate self-image. Most also saw this as a major objective for their counseling programs. For many, it might well be considered to be a major objective of instructional programs, as well. Certainly, better and richer information about Native Americans could become a part of standard curriculum. The ill-informed and patronizing treatment of Indians in standard school texts is widely documented, for example. Priorities for curriculum objectives are presented in Table 16.

The most salient curriculum objective was reading, followed by "social adjustment," an objective that overlaps the counseling objectives cited above. Performing arts and local Indian studies strengthen the self-image and social development themes already cited by the districts. They appear to be consistent, therefore, not only in relating their major counseling and curriculum objectives to expressed needs. They appear also to be consistent in relating both counseling and curriculum objectives to the same pupil needs.

The districts placed high priority on the design of new curriculum and in the development of new cultural materials. Although these tasks are not mutually exclusive, the districts' evident concern for new curriculum content and materials clearly is reflected in these curriculum development objectives. Data are cited in Table 17.

Table 16

Curriculum Objectives	No. of Districts Citing Objective
Language Development	95
Communications Skills	71
Bilingual Education	36
Reading	138
Mathematics	85
Science	22
Social Studies/History	39
Literary Arts	11
Graphic Arts	40
Performing Arts	111
Indian Studies-Local	107
Indian Studies-National	26
N/A	20
Health	17
Social Adjustment	130
Career Education	91
Recreation/Physical Education	36
Not Stated	46
Music	2
Parent-Child Communication	1
Basic Skills	3
Indian Crafts	1

Table 17

Curriculum Development Objectives	No. of Districts Citing Objectives
Design curriculum	132
Develop cultural materials	165
Develop objectives	51
Locate materials	56
Create materials	32
Evaluate materials	11
Implementation	117
Not stated	71
N/A	27

Low priority was assigned to developing health services for Indian pupils in the schools. Although this was consistent with the districts' own expressed needs in this area, the extent of school related health services proposed falls well below needs cited from other sources. Table 18 contains relevant data.

Table 18

Proposed Health Program Objectives Health Program Development	No. of Districts Citing Objectives
Nursing Service	14
Physical Examinations	6
Speech Defects	4
Hearing Defects	5
Vision Defects	3
Nutrition	5
Hygiene	3
Shots and Inoculations	0
Not stated	401

There was a remarkable consistency in the way in which most districts proposed to meet their staffing requirements in their Indian Education projects. Most districts proposed to enlarge their regular teaching staff. About one-fourth proposed to add para-professionals to work with Indian students and about one-fifth proposed to retain Indian consultants to work with staff and students. Only 72 districts proposed to require their staff to obtain additional training. About one-fourth of the districts proposed to extend their contact with parents and Indian families, however. Staffing objectives are cited in Table 19.

Table 19

Staffing Objectives for Funded IEA Programs

Teaching Staff	No. of Districts Citing Objectives
Be enlarged	283
Receive training	72
Develop curriculum	56
Indian consultant	97
Para-professional	108
Contact with home	115
Not stated	69

Although the themes for staffing cited above appear to fit the schools' objectives in counseling, it is not clear that they are consonant with their academic objectives, as well. Moreover, the districts posed limited objectives for staff development. Only 75 districts proposed to provide in-service training for faculties; 312 districts simply planned to add new staff. In view of stated needs of teachers for more adequate information concerning Indians and Indian life, and the equally evident need for improved teaching methods and techniques in working with Indian pupils, heavy reliance on new staff acquisition as an improvement strategy may prove to be optimistic. The omission of training for present and potential future staff may prove to be serious. The inclusion of Indian consultants and paraprofessional assistants in the classroom would seem to be an appropriate step, however.

Districts were not clear in the kinds of instructional materials they proposed to use in the several projects. Although a serious need was identified for instructional materials, particularly in the areas of language development and Indian culture, the objectives proposed by most districts did not coincide precisely with those needs. Indeed, 200 districts proposed to use already prepared materials (even though these were deemed to be inadequate for their programs). About 100 districts proposed to develop their own new materials or employ specialists to do so, however. Highly specialized components, such as placement tests and lesson plans, were mentioned only in a few cases.

Information from the districts concerning their plans for instruction largely was unstated, or ambiguous when stated. The predominant mode of instruction proposed was some form of tutorial or individualized instruction, based on pupil interest or academic concern. A few districts proposed to use guest speakers, field trips, group projects, others an extensive use of media.

Table 20

Modes of Planned Instruction	No. of Districts Citing Mode
Standard	46
Guest speaker	38
Individualized-academic	145
Individualized-interest	76
Group project	34
Audio-visual development	57
Tutorial	94
Created material	38
Field trips	59
Not stated	122
Library	1
On-the-job training	3

About 10% of the districts proposed simply to extend their standard teaching methods more intensively to Indian pupils. These data are summarized in Table 20.

The districts were equally unclear in the extent to which special instructional activities for Indian children might be offered. In 67 districts, such instruction was planned on a daily basis. In 21, on a weekly basis. However, 282 districts failed to state what pattern of instruction would be used.

Dollars and Objectives

Project budgets for all grants, including parts A, B, and C, in general, were consistent with project objectives and program needs and requirements. About 61% of all projected expenditures were allocated to personnel salaries and benefits. Other direct costs were estimated to be about 37%, with two percent allocated to indirect costs. These budget allocations seem to be in line with established patterns of educational expenditures. They also reflect the fact that education is a labor intensive industry, hence the fairly high proportion of total expenditure allocated to salaries and benefits for personnel.

In order to describe the relationships between budget and program objectives and budget and program needs and requirements, two indexes were designed: the first to describe the program assigned to each category of need and objectives, and the second to describe the extent of proposed budget priority assigned to each need and major objective.

Program and budget priorities for each major area of needs are reproduced in Table 21.

The "program count index" is the simple ratio of program counts for each category of need or objective, divided by the total number of proposals. Hence, a program count index of .3578 may be interpreted to mean that program priority was assigned a particular need or objective approximately 35 times in each 100 proposals.

The budget index is less directly interpreted, thanks to the fact that there is no way directly of estimating the proportion of a proposal's budget that is to be allocated by the school district to any one of the proposal's stated needs or objectives. Instead, the total budgets of all proposals that included a given need or objective were summed. This sum was then divided by the total budget for all proposals. The resulting index provided a rough approximation of the extent of concentration of funds in those proposals that address each category of needs and objectives. An index of .4953 then would be interpreted to mean that 49 of each 100 dollars of proposed expenditures were assigned or attributed to a specific need or objective. The same dollars might be allocated concurrently to different objectives, however.

Although the budget index was larger than the program count in almost every instance, the differences have no significance in the analysis. The two indices co-vary in the same way, hence perform satisfactorily for the level of analysis and interpretation employed.

From Table 21 in which priority indices are related to different categories of program needs and require-ments, highest program priorities were assigned to five classes of needs, namely:

★ Improvement of student self-concept
★ Reducation in rates of absenteeism and drop-out
★ Improvement of student's academic and test performance
★ Extension and improvement of counseling services
★ Enrichment of the cultural content of curriculum

Table 21

Program and Budget Priorities
for Pupil and School Needs

Program Needs	Program Count	Budget Index
1. PUPILS' PERSONAL-SOCIAL NEEDS		
Social Adjustment	.3578	.4953
Self Concept	.5046	.6980
Drop-out Rate/Absenteeism	.5413	.5457
Low Grades/Low Scores	.5390	.6750
Health	.0803	.1244 ·
Economic	.1950	.3343
2. SCHOOL NEEDS		
Curriculum Needs:		
Cultural	.5138	.6749
Technical	.1651	.1637
Language	.0367	.0196
Reading	.0963	.0887
Indian Culture	.0275	.0204
Vocational courses	.0115	.0208
Mathematics	.0528	.0644
Staff Needs:		
Poor attitude toward Indians, or lack of Indian information	.3211	.5146
Understaffed	.3280	.3878
Needs for Special Services:		
Testing	.0688	.1373
Counseling	.4656	.6202
Community-Parent relations	.2661	.4396
Transportation	.1124	.4396
Needs for Facilities:		
Building	.0550	.0567
Equipment	.1950	.3273
Materials and supplies	.2729	.3874

Program and budget priorities for each major program objective are cited in Table 22.

It seems clear that these areas also were among the higher budget priorities as well. Budget priorities near or in excess of .5000 also were observed for projects that emphasized social adjustment activities (.4953) and for projects that sought to correct teachers' lack of information concerning Indians (.5146). By and large, from Table 21, it seems clear that there was a major relationship between needs and program and budget priorities, with the exceptions noted.

Budget support for major program objectives also seemed consistent with needs. Highest program priorities were assigned to two major program objectives, namely: improving counseling services for individual pupils (.5390) and enlarging professional staff (.6491). Budget priority was assigned these objectives. However, budget priority also was assigned to two lower priority program objectives, namely: improving language and communications skills programs (.5051) and programs of the literary and performing arts (.5610).

Focusing and Targeting Funds

All the dimensions for proper and effective targeting appeared to be present in the administration of the several projects. It is too early for definitive evidence of successful targeting to have developed, however. Subsequent reports will examine these activities in detail.

Program funds were targeted to those eligible districts most in need of assistance. Only 18% of the eligible districts received grants in 1973. These districts included 59% of the Indian pupils known to be enrolled in public school, however.

Program funds largely were focused on the immediate and compelling personal needs of pupils, and on the evident needs of the schools that enroll Indian pupils. Exceptions were noted, to be sure. Within school districts, the extent to which program and program funds were concentrated is not clear. On-site examination will be needed to gather evidence in this regard. Most proposals

Table 22

Program and Budget Priorities
for IEA Project Objectives

PROGRAM OBJECTIVES	Program Count	Budget Index
BUILDING	.0780	.0955
EQUIPMENT	.0376	.4606
HEALTH	.0734	.1510
STAFF		
Be enlarged	.6491	.7682
Receive training	.1651	.2669
Develop curriculum	.1284	.1757
Indian consultant	.2225	.2776
Para-professionals	.2477	.3841
Contact with home	.2638	.4304
CURRICULUM		
Language development and communication skills	.3807	.5051
Reading	.3188	.4124
Mathematics	.1950	.2094
Literary, Graphic and Performing Arts	.3716	.5610
Indian Studies	.3028	.3307
COUNSELING AND SOCIAL		
Self Care	.3349	.2959
Peer and Family Relations	.2041	.4285
Self Image	.5390	.6307

lacked an appropriate specificity in planning. This suggests that the districts might spread their limited project funds over the total Indian pupil population within the district, or a substantial portion thereof. For example, no specification of grade level was given in 175 proposals. Ostensibly, the program was to be extended to all Indian children in all grades. The most frequent grade range mentioned was Kindergarten through 12th Grade, normally the full range of grades within the district.

Either the districts plan to offer a broad band of materials and services for their district, or the kind of generic services that do not need to be modified or adapted to the various grades within the district. This is a common approach to be sure. In ESEA Title I programs, for example, the tendency early in the program was to reach as many eligible children as possible, even though funds available would be spread to the point of ineffectiveness. Accordingly, any tendency in IEA projects to spread project benefits widely should be watched carefully.

A second major situation also should be monitored carefully. It was observed earlier that two-thirds of the Indian pupils in public schools attended school in districts that expended less than $810 per pupil, the median per pupil expenditure for all eligible districts in 1973. Many of these districts were deficient in their basic educational services for all pupils, since variation in expenditure among districts is not caused solely by differences in costs for comparable public services. It is not known that these lower expenditure districts can or will provide needed differential services and programs for Indian children in the face of larger, more fundamental needs for all pupils in the district.

A similar situation was encountered in 1968 in the early days of the administration of ESEA Title I. Many Title I programs for disadvantaged pupils in relatively poor districts became used with the same effect as general aid. The situation warrants careful and extended study to determine if differential program effects can be achieved with Indian pupils with special categorical assistance (e.g., ESEA I or IEA IV) before the local district has attained at least the national average in its provisions for basic programs and services.

Parent Involvement and Evaluation

The sponsoring legislation mandated that Indian parents and community representatives play an important part in designing and developing special programs for their Indian children. Although 105 districts failed to state whether a parent committee had been formed for this purpose, 273 districts reported that such a committee was newly formed. Fifty-four other districts continued to use an existing committee in modified or intact form.

The extent to which Indians were involved in planning

was reported to be high in 165 projects and moderate in 136. The remaining districts reported low or token participation. These data suggest that parental involvement may not be taken for granted. Careful encouragement may be essential for the future of the program.

Indian involvement in project planning, of course, is a key to later project evaluation. Much of the cultural content of the projects can only be validated by Indian parents and community members, for example:

Applicants under IEA Part A were required to provide effective procedures for an annual evaluation of local projects. Good evaluation requires that project objectives be framed in specific if not measurable terms. In three-fourths of the funded projects, applicants identified program objectives. In only 119 cases, however, were objectives phrased in specific performance terms. In the remaining 316 districts, an evaluation may be difficult or impossible to achieve.

Four basic themes were identified by the districts as a basis for evaluation. Some districts sought more than one major project outcome, hence indicated more than one evaluative criteria. The themes and number of district responses for each are:

Table 23

Evaluation Criteria	Number of Districts Emphasizing This Criteria
Education Change	304
Staff Change	27
Personal/Social Growth of Pupils	284
Effective Parent/Community Relations	107
Not Stated	35

Many proposals failed to specify the means to be employed in conducting the terminal project evaluation. The legislation requires that educational achievement be included as one basis for evaluation. In so doing, however, districts might give attention to the development of criterion-referenced instruments specifically geared to measure educational growth in specific Indian subgroups. The routine use of standardized tests for this purpose should be questioned, both on cultural as well as technical grounds.

Unmet Needs

The districts' heavy emphasis on "self-concept" development among Indian pupils warrants careful study. It is not clear that great numbers of Indian boys and girls have developed inadequate self-concepts, even though public school teachers believe this to be true. In order to clear the air of unwarranted sentimentality in this regard, special studies by competent researchers should be initiated, perhaps utilizing Part B funds.

The districts' concern for new teaching methods and techniques also warrants study and development. A major study to determine which, if any, methods best work with different kinds of Indian children would seem to be a worthwhile investment under IEA. Results of such research should be introduced into new programs for the retraining of teachers of Indian pupils now in service and into new programs for the preparation of Indian teachers.

The districts' concern for new cultural materials should not be left solely to the districts themselves to resolve. An organized effort with Indian directors and teachers of Indian-controlled schools also might produce useful material for public and other private schools as well.

There is a continuing need for more valid and reliable data concerning Indian pupils and the schools that teach them. Existing data are inadequate for planning and evaluation responsibilities in all jurisdictions of government: local, State, or Federal. At minimum, an information system should be developed and introduced that permits local, State, and Federal program administrators to trace the end point of program expenditure to the pupil and to relate dollar investments for Indian education to the impact and effectiveness of specific programs with those pupils.

There is a need also to involve members of the Indian communities systematically in decisions affecting the public education of their children. It should not be assumed that Indian pupils will respond to routine remediation programs. Nor should it be assumed that the token involvement of Indian parents in project development—such as experienced in some projects in 1973— will influence basic education policies and programs affecting their children.

Moreover, local districts are not uniform in their ability to design and develop special programs for Indian pupils. Admittedly a by-product of deadlines not of the districts' own choosing, many proposals lacked the integrity of design needed to guarantee a reasonable impact on their pupils, staffs, curricula, and community. It is clear also that districts need to invest much more heavily in the design of evaluation formats and instrumentation if they are to learn significantly from the projects they carry out.

Possible Administrative Actions

Consistent with the observations above, several administrative actions might be justified in 1974. Among these are:

1. The Federal office well might provide—or assist in providing through appropriate State or independent agencies—technical assistance to those local districts that are concerned with the development and evaluation of special programs for Indian pupils.

2. Grants also could be made to encourage research in three key areas, namely:

   (a) Financing and targeting special programs for Indian children;

   (b) Developing new teaching methods and techniques for Anglo teachers to employ in teaching Indian pupils their basic skills, and for Indian teachers to employ in teaching Indian pupils about their cultural heritage; and

   (c) Developing instructional materials appropriate to the new teaching methods.

3. A major new thrust could be undertaken to recruit, prepare, and place Indian teachers to teach in the public schools not solely to improve instruction for Indian children but to enrich the cultural experience for all enrolled children.

4. Consideration should be given to extend the potential benefits of the Act more broadly to Indian children and youth not now reached, while seeking to target current levels of support effectively on those numbers of pupils who are served. Specifically, consideration should be given to a downward extension of program support to include preschool children, particularly those who later might otherwise require special language training. Thought also should be given to special incentives to the number of districts with fewer than 10 Indian pupils in enrollment. Such districts need to be encouraged to form interdistrict programs, whenever appropriate, to reach the 29,138 pupils not now touched by the Indian Education Act. Similar program extensions to reach the 12,000 out-of-school youth also need consideration.

REFERENCES

The 31 source citations in the section entitled "Special Needs of Indian Pupils" refer to two major documents, namely:

The Indian Education Act of 1972, A Brief History, Analysis, Issue and Outlook (Washington, D. C.: CPI Associates, Inc., 1973), 101 pp.

To Live on This Earth, Robert J. Havighurst and Estelle Fuchs (Synopsis prepared by William J. Benham, Acting Director, Office of Indian Education Programs, Bureau of Indian Affairs).

1. *The Indian Education Act of 1972*, p. 72.
2. p. 67
3. p. 69
4. p. 69
5. p. 76
6. p. 76
7. p. 77
8. p. 77
9. p. 78
10. p. 78
11. p. 70
12. p. 69
13. p. 69
14. p. 46
15. p. 47
16. p. 48
17. p. 49
18. p. 63
19. p. 64
20. p. 64
21. p. 64
22. p. 65
23. p. 71
24. p. 70
25. p. 70
26. p. 70
27. p. 70
28. p. 63
29. p. 64
30. p. 64
31. Such discrepancies reflect real program differences since the cost of comparable public services varies by less than one-half among the districts.
32. Two-thirds of the Indian pupils live in districts that expend less than $810 per pupil in 1972-73.

Through Education: Self Determination. National Advisory Council on Indian Education, Washington, D.C. March 1975.

Teaching North American Indian Languages

Within the last few years, interest in the study and teaching of North American Indian languages has developed at a rapid pace. This interest has been accompanied by an increase in the number of college courses in these languages, by publications and conferences, and by a new and widespread emphasis on Indian bilingual education. The extent of this upsurge can be illustrated by one example: the majority of Amerindian language college courses designed either to teach the language itself, or to help native speakers acquire skills of literacy and analysis, have been instituted since 1970. Fifty-seven percent of the courses offered in 1973 had been in existence for at most one year, and 80 percent had originated after 1970.

This increase is indeed remarkable. But it is equally remarkable that so many institutions have been able to secure the help of trained linguists to implement their new programs. One wonders how this need for linguists could be met so rapidly. The answer to this question can be found in a brief review of the history of American Indian linguistics. Such a review shows the importance of the study of Amerindian languages, particularly during the last hundred years, in the training of the linguists who are working with present-day programs.

Historical Perspective

During the first centuries of European colonization in the Americas, the principal interest in the Amerindian languages was utilitarian. Some studied a language because they wished to convert the Indians to Christianity, others because they wanted to carry on trade with them. From these studies there emerged the first publications concerned with American Indian languages. Among the earliest of these were a translation of the Bible into Massachusetts by John Eliot in 1664 (the first Bible published in what would later become the United States), and a grammar of Narragansett by Roger Williams, published at about the same time.

In addition to the missionaries and traders there were individuals--among them Thomas Jefferson--who were interested in the languages themselves and often collected and compared word lists. By the beginning of the nineteenth century this interest was especially motivated by the desire to discover the origin of these languages and their speakers. Those who insisted on a literal interpretation of the Bible tried to prove Indian kinship with the Hebrews. But as the century progressed, a growing number, who were students of the developing science of ethnology, considered the Indians to be of Asian ancestry. Also during this period, attention came to be focused on the variety of Amerindian languages and the number of different families that might exist, and as a result, the principal students of these languages were concerned more with classification than with the in-depth study of any particular language.

The publication in 1890 of John Wesley Powell's classification of language families north of Mexico marked the end of what has been called the "first period of linguistic research in America"--a period in which most of the work was done by persons who were not primarily linguists.

The second period of research was distinguished by the development of scientific methods for analyzing grammatical and phonological data. By the early 1900s Franz Boas had become the leader in the collection of detailed grammatical data and was applying what was then known about phonetic and morphological analysis. By 1886 he was studying the Indians of British Columbia, particularly the Kwakiutl, and recording the languages of the area. In the years that followed, he continued to study the languages of many other North American Indian groups. He collected and analyzed masses of texts and tales, and thus became the first of many anthropological linguists who, in order to better understand the various cultures, studied native American languages. Boas' greatest contribution to linguistic study was the development of the detailed analytical study of a language. In his famous Introduction to the Handbook of American Indian Languages (1911), Boas explained the basic linguistic characteristics of languages, using illustrations from Amerindian languages, and presented evidence which refuted the nineteenth-century idea that all American Indian languages have a similar structure.

One of Boas' most famous students was Edward Sapir, who refined the analytical techniques. Like Boas, Sapir was an anthropologist who considered the study of language important to the understanding of a culture; unlike Boas, however, he had had formal linguistic training, including the study of Indo-European comparative linguistics. Sapir was the first American linguist to systematically apply the comparative method to American Indian languages. He showed that regular sound correspondences could be drawn between certain of these languages and that, as a result, proto-forms (that is, the forms of a parent language) could be reconstructed. From these studies he was able to propose genetic relationships which created new groups (Algonquian-Ritwan and Na-Dene) and augmented some that were already established (Hokan and Uto-Aztecan). These new groupings enabled him to reduce Powell's fifty-eight separate families to twenty-two. Later, in his article "Central and North American Languages," written for the Encyclopedia Britannica (1929), he proposed a further classification of Amerindian languages into six superstocks, although he said they were "far from demonstrable" at that time. Although there has been some revision of these six, Sapir's contribution to the historical picture of American Indian languages marked an important step in language classification. In addition to his contribution to Amerindian comparative linguistics and to descriptive techniques, Sapir, through the work of his students, exerted a far-reaching influence on the study of native American languages throughout North America.

A contemporary of Sapir's, Leonard Bloomfield, also made significant contributions to the study of Amerindian comparative linguistics. Like Sapir, he had been trained in Indo-European comparative linguistics. He became a specialist in the Algonquian languages and through the use of comparative techniques was able to set up a parent language, which he called Proto-Central-Algonquian. This was an important step in American Indian historical linguistics, for it laid the foundation for later studies that extended the knowledge of language relationships.

Descriptive techniques developed during the first half of the twentieth century, particularly by Sapir and his students, made possible much more accurate recording of the phonology and morphology of

languages than could be done by those gathering data during earlier
periods. The improved techniques in phonology have been especially
helpful in developing usable orthographies for literacy programs at
all educational levels.

However, during this early period, problems of syntax were not
handled as explicitly as has been possible in recent years. The development of generative transformational grammar, based on the theory
which Noam Chomsky first set forth in <u>Syntactic Structures</u> (1957) and
refined in <u>Aspects of the Theory of Syntax</u> (1965), has helped to
clarify syntactic and semantic problems and has brought more attention
to the study of syntax. Most Amerindian linguists are now using the
techniques of transformational grammar. Chomsky's <u>Aspects</u>, which
stresses the importance of the underlying syntactic structure rather
than the surface form, has placed renewed reliance on the intuition
of the native speaker. It has focused attention on the need for
linguistically trained native speakers as language analysts and teachers. As a result, academic programs are gradually being developed
for native speakers.

Current Developments

The current interest in Amerindian languages is an important
consequence of a growing belief in cultural pluralism--the recognition of the right of each group to preserve its own cultural identity.
Pluralism is now superseding the long-accepted "melting pot" theory--
the idea that all diverse cultural groups should be assimilated into
a homogeneous society. With this new emphasis on cultural identity
has come a realization of the importance of a native language. As a
result, each American Indian group wants to preserve its language, if
it is viable. If the language is dying, the group often wants to
revitalize it in some way. The accelerating interest in these languages has led not only to a rapid increase in the number of courses
and other types of programs in universities and colleges, but also to
the development of Indian bilingual education programs in many elementary and secondary schools.

University and College Programs

The many courses which have been recently instituted in colleges
and universities are especially important to the development of Amerindian linguistics. Most of these new courses are of a practical nature,
many of them stressing language learning for both native and non-native
Americans. Others are designed to teach skills of literacy and language
analysis, principally to native speakers. However, the traditional academic courses dealing with these languages have also increased in number,
and larger enrollments are reported. The traditional courses include
general surveys of North American Indian languages, and linguistic
field methods and language analysis classes for the training of professional linguists.

Although institutions in many parts of the United States and
Canada have introduced both the practical and academic types of
courses in recent years, the interest has been particularly great in
those areas near concentrations of Indian populations. One such

area includes the north central states from the Dakotas through Minnesota and Wisconsin. Colleges and junior colleges throughout the state of Minnesota, for instance, are initiating language programs in Ojibwa and Dakota, and there is some attempt to introduce these courses into primary and secondary schools both on and off reservations. Local Indian organizations also sponsor language classes.

The increase in practical courses has been particularly noticeable in small colleges located near Indian groups. Such institutions rarely had any such courses prior to 1968. These courses sometimes develop from the efforts of an Indian group to preserve its language. For example, a class in Shoshoni at the Elko Community College, Elko, Nevada, was instituted in this way. Initially, a small Shoshoni tribal group on the Duck Valley Reservation near Owyhee, Nevada, requested help from the University of Utah in developing language-learning and literacy courses. In a summer experiment, classes were taught with the help of a native speaker using linguist-developed materials. This experiment led to the course now taught at Elko Community College.

Native speakers have been involved in the development of courses at many other institutions. For example, a course in Puget Sound Salish at the University of Washington represents an attempt to resolve the dialect differences of several small groups (Skagit, Snohomish, Snoqualmie, Duwamish, Puyallup, and Nisqually) so that a strong language program can be established.

Some of the more populous Indian groups are developing their own junior colleges with native language courses as part of the culturally oriented curriculum. Among these colleges are the Lakota Higher Education Center, Pine Ridge, South Dakota; Sinte Gleska, Rosebud, South Dakota; and the Navajo Community College, Many Farms, Arizona.

There is also a growing trend toward the acceptance of a native American language to fulfill the foreign or second language requirement of some departments. For example, Eastern Montana College at Billings accepts a knowledge of Cree, Crow, or Northern Cheyenne; the University of Washington at Seattle, Puget Salish; the University of Utah, Navajo; and the University of Minnesota, Ojibwa or Dakota.

The work on Amerindian languages at colleges often includes projects which cover a wider sphere than course offerings. For example, the Wisconsin Native American Languages Project at the University of Wisconsin at Milwaukee, funded by a grant promoted by the Great Lakes Intertribal Council, Inc., includes the languages of the Ojibwa, Potawatomi, Menominee, and Oneida. It is designed to involve native speakers in linguistic study which will train them to prepare instructional and reference materials and to teach their language.

Another project covering a wide sphere of activity is located at D-Q University, Davis, California. The university was established in 1970 and is devoted to the interests of American Indian and Chicano students. A National Center of Native American Language Education is being set up within the university, with plans for language study and development of teaching materials. In addition, an extensive survey of the present state of Amerindian languages is projected, including a

study of dialect differences within individual languages and a survey
of the present ages of speakers.

Another research project, the British Columbia Indian Language Project, is being carried on by British Columbia Indians with the assistance
of Randy Bouchard, a linguist. Although aimed at the preservation of
all British Columbia native languages, the project has concentrated so
far on Salish languages, with some work on Haida. Plans include the
preservation of oral materials through the use of tapes and the development of language-teaching materials for the schools.

There is evidence of a growing interest in American Indian languages which is wider in scope than that encompassed by specific courses
and research projects. For example, Charlton Laird has included several
chapters in these languages in his recent book Language in America (1970).
Most books written previously about the development of language in this
country ignored the languages of cultural minorities and dealt almost
solely with American English. Even high school materials are beginning
to reflect this new trend: Scholastic Magazine has recently prepared
a wall map for high schools showing both cultural and linguistic historical areas of North American Indians.

Bilingual Education

Another important consequence of the new emphasis on cultural pluralism has been the development of Indian bilingual education in elementary and secondary schools. Under the "melting pot" theory, every
effort was made not only to establish English as the dominant language
of a child of a minority culture but to eradicate his native language.
However, under bilingual education there is a place for more than one
language in the classroom, and instruction in two languages if the child
needs it.

History. The great majority of Amerindian bilingual projects have
been initiated since Elementary and Secondary Education Act (ESEA)
Title VII funds became available in 1968. But attempts at bilingual
education for Indians in the United States are much older. In the
late 1930s the Bureau of Indian Affairs established a program on the
Navajo reservation to promote first-language literacy. Motivation for
this program arose from the fact that almost nine out of ten Navajo
adults did not speak English, and their children were not adapting to
an English language curriculum. The U.S. government needed to
communicate with Navajos on such problems as overgrazing, water development, sanitation, and disease control. Bilingual education was viewed
as a method that would help, and a program was begun for teaching both
reading and writing in Navajo. Some adults were trained to serve as
interpreters on technical matters. At the same time, bilingual reading
materials were prepared for the Hopi, Tewa, and Sioux. However, Indian
parents were not enthusiastic about the programs, nor was Congress
willing to renew the appropriation during World War II; hence, all these
programs were abandoned before they could be firmly and permanently
established in the curriculum.

Shortly after World War II, the Bureau of Indian Affairs instituted
a five-year plan for use with Navajos who were 12 to 16 years old and

who had previously had little or no schooling. Navajo was used successfully as one of the languages of instruction to help these students become prepared for vocational training and complete their schooling in
English. However, this project was looked upon as a "crash program"
designed to accelerate the education of a particular group, and after
the five years had come to an end, use of the native language in the
classroom was abandoned.

These early experiments with bilingual education are examples of
the original intent of the program--to use the native language to
achieve mastery of the English language and adaptation to "American"
culture. During the late 1960s, however, the growing emphasis on
cultural pluralism focused the attention of Indian leaders on bilingual
education as a means of preserving native languages. Robert E. Lewis,
governor of the Pueblo of Zuni, emphasized this in his keynote address
to the first National Indian Bilingual Education Conference, April 1973,
when he said that preserving the language comes first in bilingual
education, for it helps preserve the culture. Bilingual education, which
includes both reading and writing in the home language, is needed to
overcome the feeling of shame which the Indian has often felt about using
his language.

The first experiments in Indian bilingual education in the 1960s
were initiated in schools on the Navajo reservation in Arizona--at Fort
Defiance, in 1965; at the Rough Rock Demonstration School, Chinle, in
1966; and in 1968 at the Rock Point Boarding School, Chinle, and the
Kayenta Public School. Two planning conferences conducted by the
Center for Applied Linguistics in 1968 and 1969 led to the development
of the first Navajo bilingual/bicultural kindergarten programs--at
Sanostee, Toadlena, Lower Greasewood, and Cottonwood.

Current Projects. The granting of federal funds under Tital VII of
the ESEA gave the impetus that was really needed for widespread development of bilingual education projects. In 1969, the first Indian bilingual
education programs so funded were initiated at Tahlequah, Oklahoma, using
the Cherokee language; at Grants, New Mexico, using Keresan (Laguna); in
some San Juan County, Utah, schools, using Navajo; and in a Ukiah, California, school, using Pomo. During the next three years, 18 more programs
were established under Title VII, involving the following 12 languages:
Choctaw, Cree, Crow, Yuk Eskimo, Keresan (Acoma), Mikasuki, Northern
Cheyenne, Passamaquoddy, Seminole, Lakota, Ute, and Zuni. Fifteen additional programs are now in operation or under consideration. These involve some languages or dialects not previously represented: Apache,
Inupiat Eskimo, Menominee, Papago, Eskimo (St. Lawrence Island Yupik),
Tewa, Keresan (Zia), and some northern Athapaskan languages.

In addition to projects funded by Title VII, bilingual education
is carried on as part of the regular programs in some schools, such
as the Jemez and San Felipe Day Schools in New Mexico. In Alaska, a
new law requires that a bilingual education program be conducted in all
villages with at least 15 fluent speakers attending school, and the
Alaska State-Operated School System is sponsoring several bilingual
education projects, including programs in Inupiat and Yupik Eskimo,
Tlingit, Haida, and certain Athapaskan languages, principally Kutchin,
upper Kuskokwim, and Central Koyukon. Participation is optional for
non-natives.

The rapid growth of Indian bilingual education and the need to exchange ideas and discuss common problems led to the first National Indian Bilingual Education Conference* (NIBEC), held in April 1973 at Albuquerque, with the Language Development Branch of the Bureau of Indian Affairs acting as coordinator. A second conference was held in May 1974 in Billings, Montana, and a third in Calgary, Alberta, in April 1975. Persons working with both U.S. and Canadian Indian bilingual education projects attended these conferences.

Bilingual education has stimulated a community interest in the schools, replacing the indifference or actual hostility which often existed previously. In areas populated by homogeneous Amerindian groups, native Americans are seeking control of school policies. Community-controlled schools can be found, for instance, on the Rocky Boy reservation (Cree) in Montana and on the Navajo reservation. Among the Navajo schools are the Rough Rock Demonstration School, devoted in part to the training of native teachers for bilingual teaching and producing classroom materials; the Rock Point Community School, which also produces materials; Ramah Navajo High School; and the Borrego Pass School. Many native teachers are responding to this growing community interest. For example, Navajo teachers now have their own organization-- Diné Bi'olta' Association--which holds workshops to train teachers and also prepares some classroom materials in Navajo.

This new interest in Amerindian bilingual education exists in several countries besides the United States. In Peru, for example, a recent law stipulates that Quechua and Aymara Indian students be taught first in their native language before they are trained in Spanish. Projects for training native speakers as classroom aides in the lower grades are under way in Mexico and Guatemala. In the province of Quebec, Canada, a project for "Amerindianization of the Schools" is now in operation, directed by Raymond Gagné, Minister of Indian Affairs. Plans call for the linguistic and pedagogical training of native speakers as classroom teachers so that the native language and culture can be integrated into the curriculum wherever there are Amerindian children. If the Amerindian language is predominant in the homes, it will be the basic language of the school, and English and/or French will be taught as second languages. However, among Indian groups where English or French has become the home language, the native American tongue will be taught as a second language. Similar plans are being developed in other parts of Canada.

Materials Production. The first step in any bilingual program is the selection of an orthography which will facilitate learning and will also be acceptable to the native community. If the language has never been written, there are fewer problems with community acceptance. But if a system has been introduced previously, conflicts sometimes arise because of competing systems. One such problem has arisen with the Cherokee and Cree syllabaries, where tradition is so strong that older speakers, even some who are not literate, consider their own syllabary a part of their culture. The primary disadvantage of using a syllabary is that the child must learn two entirely different writing systems--the Roman letters so that he can function adequately in a predominantly

*Now Native American Bilingual Education Conference

English-speaking society (or French, in some parts of Canada) and the native syllabary so that he can become literate in his own language. Since linguists have demonstrated that with some small changes the Roman alphabet can be adapted to all American Indian languages, many bilingual education teachers feel it is advantageous to use this alphabet for the native language.

However, in those cases where tradition has made a syllabary an important part of the culture, literacy materials are being prepared in that orthography. Changes in the order of syllabary characters may be made to facilitate learning. For example, in the Cherokee Primer (developed in 1965 by Professor Willard Walker, a linguist working with a tribal literacy project) the traditional order of the syllabary characters was altered to permit the introduction of high-frequency syllables first, thus enabling the student to begin reading before he had mastered the whole system. In past years the Cree syllabary has been adapted to various Cree and Ojibwa dialects, to Chipewyan and Slave (both northern Athapaskan), and to Eastern Eskimo. It is now being used for literacy materials in those languages. It seems especially well suited to Eskimo and is extensively used for Eastern Eskimo, although the Roman alphabet is used for orthographies by some Eastern Eskimos. At the University of Alaska an 18-letter alphabet has been developed for Yupik (Western) Eskimo.

Another orthographical problem encountered with some languages is the extent to which diacritics need to be used with the Roman alphabet. At a conference convened in 1969 in Albuquerque by the Center for Applied Linguistics for the Bureau of Indian Affairs, a Navajo orthography was recommended for BIA-sponsored publications for use in its school system. The Rock Point School is experimenting with simplification of a highly complex Navajo orthography by eliminating certain diacritics. To determine the extent to which these diacritics can be eliminated without impeding reading ability, teachers present material written in both the complex and the simplified forms.

In the production of materials for teaching native languages, many questions must be considered, such as the kinds of subject matter which are best suited for classroom materials at various levels; the dialect differences that must be recognized; special speech forms of a particular language--male and female, adult and infant--that must be considered; and changes in the language that are taking place, including borrowings. Adequate answers can come only after extensive investigation of the language as it is presently spoken. One group carrying on such an investigation is the Navajo Reading Study, which is based at the University

of New Mexico and produces materials for Indian bilingual education. From the studies it has made of the speech of children entering school, it has obtained information concerning vocabulary levels, use of borrowed terms, and English-speaking ability.

At present, most of the reading materials in native American languages are primers and readers for the first and second grades. Reading materials for older students and for adults who have become literate are almost non-existent. Some teachers of older children are using materials produced by the students themselves. For example, experience stories written in conjunction with a language lesson have served on later occasions as classroom reading material. Students sometimes produce a community news sheet in the native language (at Ramah Navajo High School, for example) or make word lists of items important to their culture. Some tribal headquarters, such as the Cherokee at Tahlequah, Oklahoma, and the Micmac at Fredericton, New Brunswick, are publishing newspapers in the native language, thus encouraging literacy among adults.

Multimedia resources are being used for some native language materials. For example, the San Juan County, Utah, bilingual project has produced 32 multimedia Navajo language materials, including sound film strips of coyote tales, animated films based on those tales, a film on Navajo numbers, Navajo alphabet flash cards, and other items.

In the preparation of bilingual education materials, the choice of the language in which the child should be taught to read must be considered carefully. Evidence from psychological studies has favored initial learning in the child's home language. There is reason to believe that in teaching reading in a second language, the association of the written symbols with sounds of the language is more easily and efficiently taught if the child has already made the association through learning to read his own language.

Reactions to Bilingual Programs. Although most Amerindian groups have welcomed the inclusion of their native language in the school curriculum, there has been resistance from some members who have grown up believing that the English language, and consequently English-speaking teachers, are superior. Some participants in NIBEC I asserted that while the Indian community accepted native aides in a classroom, they often objected to a native teacher's handling the classroom alone. Another objection to bilingual education has been that it might hinder Amerindian young people from being successful if they should leave the reservation or the native village. In 1970, Yuk Eskimos objected to use of the native language in the classroom because they felt that English is the road to success. They had to be convinced that their language would be used only in the lower grades to help children learn English more readily. After the project had been initiated, they were delighted to see that children not only learned English more easily, but did better work in all subjects and enjoyed school more. Similar success with other bilingual education projects is overcoming objections to the use of the native language in the classroom. But acceptance of native teachers with full responsibility for the class is not so easily accomplished. Participants at NIBEC I felt that this acceptance will depend in part on the training these teachers receive and their ability to prove their efficiency. There is a great need for pedagogical training, to enable native American speakers to be certified for classroom teaching, and for linguistic training, to enable them to function well in a bilingual education program and to develop or adapt language materials as needed.

Linguistic Training for Native Speakers

The skills of native speakers trained in linguistics are needed in all types of American Indian language programs--language analysis, materials production, college courses, and bilingual education programs. In most practical college courses stressing language learning, one or more native speakers assist a professional linguist. But the many demands made upon professional linguists to prepare materials and teach several courses limit the number of language classes which can be conducted in this way. If these classes are to increase significantly, native speakers with a knowledge of linguistics will be needed to conduct many of them. Some institutions, such as the University of Manitoba, have been unable to institute projected language teaching courses because of the lack of funds for preparing native speakers to serve as teachers. A similar need exists in bilingual education projects. These programs cannot be firmly established until many native speakers have the training necessary to teach their language and assume full classroom responsibility.

For the development of all types of Amerindian language activities there is a great need to establish training programs and to interest gifted native speakers in the study of their language. Some steps have been taken in the past to involve American Indians in the study of linguistics and the teaching of their language. Occasionally native speakers have been trained as linguists. Juan Dolores (Papago), William Jones (Algonquian), and Edward Dozier (Tewa) are a few of those who have published their studies.

Occasionally non-Indian linguists have collaborated with native speakers in study and publication. The teamwork of linguist Robert Young and William Morgan, Sr., a native speaker of Navajo, is an early example. Together they produced linguistic studies and teaching materials, some of which are now being used in schools on the Navajo reservation.

There are at least two recent publications produced through this type of collaboration. One is a new textbook, Seneca Today, by the linguist Ruth Dudley and Ester Blueye, a native speaker of Seneca (to appear). It is used at the State University of New York at Buffalo. The other is An Introduction to the Luiseño Language by Villiana Hyde (1971). This book presents a series of carefully prepared lessons written by Mrs. Hyde and graduate students in linguistics at the University of California at San Diego under the direction of Professor Margaret Langdon. Unlike most linguistic descriptions of a language, which are intended for linguists, this book is designed as a text which can be used by native speakers to understand their language and to learn to read it. The book can also be used by non-native speakers who wish to learn Luiseño.

Another example of the collaboration of a native speaker with a professional linguist has been that of Albert Alvarez, a native speaker of Papago, and Professor Kenneth Hale. They have published some linguistic materials for the use of native Papago speakers. (See the Selected Bibliography for Aztec-Tanoan, Appendix B, Part 2.) However, Professor Hale's objective was broader than the production of linguistic materials. He wanted to train Alvarez in the skills of language analysis so that Alvarez himself could produce materials. Professor Hale has described this work in his essay, "A New Perspective on American Indian Linguistics." The Appendix which concludes the essay contains some of Alvarez's linguistic description of Papago. In the essay, Professor Hale makes this statement:

The point of view which will be central in this paper is that the future of American Indian linguistics (i.e., the extent to which it will advance significantly) will depend critically on how successful an effort there is to engage American Indians in the active study of their own languages--not as informants as in the past, but as linguists, philologists, lexicographers, creative writers, and the like.

If native American speakers are to engage in the study of their language as professionals, extensive linguistic training programs will be needed. Professor Hale proposed a plan for such training in The Indian Historian (Summer 1969, pp. 15-18, 28). Since that time he has conducted a tutorial project in linguistics for gifted native American speakers as part of the graduate program at the Massachusetts Institute of Technology. After an initial intensive study of general linguistics, particularly phonology and syntax, the student is led to apply the principles he has learned to an analysis of his native language. Most of the tutorial guidance is supplied by a linguist who has some knowledge of that language. Because of the expense involved with this type of program, only a few native Americans can be admitted each year. In 1973-74 there were three students--two Navajo and one Hopi. One of the Navajos, Paul Platero, is a Ph.D. candidate. He has conducted summer language workshops in the Navajo community and has also visited many Navajo schools encouraging language scholarship. He recently started a journal, Diné Bizaad Náníl'įįh (Navajo Language Review) dedicated to language studies, both theoretical and practical, with special emphasis on linguistics, child language, and bilingual education. The Review is now published approximately four times a year by the Center for Applied Linguistics, with Platero as editor, for the Navajo Linguistic Society.

Several publications designed for the linguistic training of Navajo speakers have been produced in connection with the MIT program. They appear officially in the "Bibliography of Navajo Reading Materials," BIA Curriculum Bulletin #13. It is the hope of those working with the program at MIT that a special Master's degree program directed more specifically toward the language-scholarship needs of the American Indian communities can be developed in the future.

The great demand for native speakers with the linguistic and pedagogical training that will enable them to become certified teachers in bilingual classrooms will require many college programs. At least two institutions in Canada have recently established training programs. The University of Quebec at Chicoutimi is initiating a teacher training program for native Americans which will lead to the following: (1) Elementary Teaching Certificate; (2) Bachelor of Elementary Education; and (3) Certificate in Linguistic Technology. This program is part of the project for the "Amerindianization of the Schools" initiated in 1973 by the Department of Indian Affairs of the Province of Quebec. The second Canadian program, which leads to a diploma in Native American Languages, but not to certification, was begun in September 1974 at the University of Victoria, Victoria, British Columbia. This program is intended to guide native speakers in the study of their language so that they can prepare teaching materials, and to train native personnel to teach their language in British Columbia schools. A few universities and colleges

in the United States have established programs for training native American teachers, among them the University of Alaska and the University of
New Mexico.

Many more such programs will be needed if bilingual classrooms
are to be adequately staffed. In the meantime, emergency measures
are being taken to provide personnel. Native speakers serve as classroom aides in most bilingual education classrooms. In California, two
native speakers of Hupa were certified under the "eminent persons" regulations of the California Teacher Accreditation Code in order to enable
them to teach their language at the Hupa Valley Unified School in Humboldt County in Northern California.

Conferences and Publications

In addition to the numerous study and teaching programs dealing
with Amerindian languages, there have been an increasing number of conferences, many of them held annually, such as the International Conference
on Salish Languages, the Algonquian Conference, the Uto-Aztecan Conference,
and the Conference on Hokan Languages. Some conferences have been regional
in scope, rather than oriented toward a language group, such as the Workshop on Research Problems in Southwest Areal Linguistics held in 1972 and
1973. The first Inter-American Conference on Bilingual Education,
organized by the Center for Applied Linguistics and the Council on
Anthropology and Education, was held in Mexico City in November 1974.
Many of the papers presented at the Conference dealt with Indian
education in the Americas. The Center also held a conference in Eugene,
Oregon, in August 1973, on priorities for research, training native
Americans in linguistics, and developing necessary pedagogical materials.
(See Appendix E for the recommendations of the conference.)

A number of informal periodicals have appeared in recent years, some
of them, such as the Algonquian Linguistics Newsletter, closely associated
with the conference for the language group. Others are published by individual American Indian communities, such as Agenutemagen (News in Micmac)
and the Cherokee Nation News, which prints some material in the Cherokee

syllabary. Two newsletters with useful general information about American
Indian languages are Language in American Indian Education, which was
published by the Bureau of Indian Affairs from 1970 to 1972 (William R.
Slager, ed.), and the Newsletter of the Conference on American Indian
Languages Clearinghouse, (James L. Fidelholtz, ed.). (For more detailed
information about periodicals, see Appendix B, Part 1.)

The Linguistic Reporter, published by the Center for Applied Linguistics, contains news of educational projects, conferences, and publications relating to American Indian linguistics. It includes a section
devoted to bilingual/bicultural education.

A publication which will serve as a valuable reference work in the
future is now being prepared under the sponsorship of the Smithsonian
Center for the Study of Man. It is the new edition of the Bureau of
American Ethnology Handbook of North American Indians, intended to replace the two volumes of the BAE #30, published in 1907 and 1910.

William C. Sturtevant is general editor of this encyclopedic work. One volume will be devoted to a variety of topics related to American Indian languages, including sketches of about fourteen languages, each representing a different family or an isolate.

Looking Ahead

The accelerating interest in American Indian languages which has received its impetus from the new emphasis on cultural pluralism has brought a marked increase in college courses, bilingual education programs, and publications and conferences dealing with these languages. If these programs are to become permanently established, the great need for native speakers with the training necessary to carry them forward must be met.

A Survey of the Current Study and Teaching of North American Indian Languages in the United States and Canada. Jeanette P. Martin, University of Utah, ERIC Clearinghouse on Languages and Linguistics/Center for Applied Linguistics, Arlington, VA. May 1975. p. 1-13.

HEW News

November 8, 1976

American Indian children and adults will receive broader educational opportunities as a result of nearly $22.6 million in grants awarded by HEW's Office of Education.

A total of 219 grants have been made to Indian tribes, institutions, and organizations, and to institutions of higher education to help meet the special educational needs of Indians and to provide for the training of Indian educational personnel. They follow more than 1,000 awards totaling over $31.8 million made to public elementary and secondary schools earlier this year.

Grants were made under the Indian controlled schools program, special programs for Indian children and adults, and the educational personnel training program, all authorized under the Indian Education Act of 1972.

Of those announced today, 132 grants totaling $15,389,098 were awarded for activities such as bilingual and bicultural education, curriculum development, language development, reading, tutoring, and counseling. The largest grant in this category--$475,000-- will enable the Lac Courte Oreille Chippewa Tribe in Stone Lake, WI, to offer native language, crafts, and folklore along with the more standard school curriculum. The smallest grant of $20,075, will help the Quileute Tribe in Washington to revive its native language on the reservation and publish a Quileute dictionary as well as other classroom materials.

Indian-controlled schools on, or near, reservations in 13 States have been awarded $3,181,818 for 26 new programs to make school life more rewarding for their students. At the St. Stephens School in Wyoming, for example, the children will have 15 members of the Arapahoe and Shoshone tribes working with teachers to make their native languages, crafts, and history part of daily classroom activities. The Navajo Tribe will use the money at their Rough Rock Demonstration School in Arizona to hire tribal consultants and create bilingual and bicultural courses that can be used by schools on other Indian reservations.

Some $4 million also has been allocated to meet the educational needs of adult Indians. Sixty-one awards have been made in 27 States. The largest-- $158,787--will continue to fund a program begun last year by the United Indians of All Tribes Foundation in Seattle. It includes employment of Native American consultants for the development of bilingual and bicultural courses. Also emphasized is education to help Indians adjust to living in cities rather than on reservations and the development of material for remedial teaching to enable students to earn a General Equivalency Diploma (GED). The smallest grant-- $15,000 --to the Yerington Paiute Tribe, in Yerington, NV, is also scheduled for training leading to the GED for students who were unable to finish high school.

Some $152 million has been expended in 3,946 grants for the improvement of Indian education since the Act was passed in 1972.

"HEW News." Office of Education, U.S. Department of Health, Education, and Welfare, Washington, D.C. November 8, 1976.

Part three:
Asian American/Pacific Islander

Asian American/Pacific Islander

Asian Americans and Pacific Peoples—Demographic Factors

In 1970 the official population count of the United States was 203,211,926.[16] This total included 2,089,932 individuals identified as being Americans of Chinese, Pilipino, Hawaiian, Korean, and Japanese descent and those Americans categorized by the Census Bureau under "Other."[17] The "Other" category included Guamanian, Samoan, Malayan, Polynesian, Thai, etc. Although census statistics are available for the population on Guam and American Samoa, there are no census figures available for the number of Guamanians and Samoans who reside in the United States. Community representatives estimate that there are about 36,000 Guamanians and Samoans in the country.[18]

Immigration Trends

Prior to 1965, immigration quotas for Eastern Hemisphere countries prevented large-scale immigration to the United States. The national origins quota system assigned the largest number of admissions to those groups who were racially and ethnically close to the majority population in the country. Thus, the lion's share of the allocations were to Western Hemisphere countries.

Reform legislation in 1965 eliminated discriminatory quota provisions and opened up Asian immigration to the United States.

16. U.S., Department of Commerce, Bureau of the Census, Census of Population: 1970. Vol. I Characteristics of the Population, Part A Number of Inhabitants, Section 1 United States, Alabama-Mississippi (Issued May 1972), p. 1-41.

17. The Census Bureau provides complete count data for Japanese, Chinese, and Pilipinos. Data for Koreans, Hawaiians, and "others" are derived from 20-percent and 15-percent sample data of the population. For more information on racial group data collected by the Census Bureau, see Appendix B in Vol. I Characteristics of the Population, Part 1 United States Summary, section 2.

18. Estimates from representatives of Guamanian and Samoan communities in Southern California. Other community members suggest that the figure is closer to 50,000.

Eastern Hemisphere countries are now limited to 20,000 visas annually per country. The increasing numbers of immigrants from Asia and the Pacific to the United States are indicated in Table I.

TABLE I

Immigrants Born in Specified Countries and Areas--1972

Country of Birth	1965	1972	Percent Change
China & Taiwan	4,057	17,339	+ 327.4%
Japan	3,180	4,757	+ 49.6%
Korea	2,165	18,876	+ 771.9%
Philippines	3,130	29,376	+ 838.5%
Western Samoa		199	Unknown

Source: U.S., Department of Justice, Immigration and Naturalization Service, 1972 Annual Report.

These figures indicate a substantial and rapid increase in the number of immigrants from Asian and Pacific countries. The average percentage change for Asian countries was +485.3 percent, for all Oceania[19] +117.3 percent. In comparison, the percentage change for all immigrants from Northern and Western Europe for the same period, was down by more than two-thirds.[20]

The Immigration and Nationality Act of October 3, 1965, established three major categories of immigrants: the immediate relatives of United States citizens, natives of Eastern Hemisphere countries and their dependencies, and "special" immigrants, comprised primarily of natives of independent countries in the Western Hemisphere.[21]

It also established four preferences for specified relatives of United States citizens and resident aliens, including unmarried adult sons and daughters; spouses and unmarried sons and daughters of aliens lawfully admitted for permanent residence; married sons and daughters of United States citizens; and brothers and sisters of United States citizens. The Immigration and Nationality Act, as amended, also offered two preference classifications, preference clauses three and six, based on occupational qualifications, including professionals, skilled, and unskilled.

Many foreign relatives of American citizens of Asian and Pacific Island descent took advantage of the immigration policy changes to be

---

19. The term Oceania refers to islands in the Pacific.

20. U.S., Department of Justice, Immigration and Naturalization Service, 1972 Annual Report, p. 4. (Hereinafter cited as INS, 1972 Annual Report.)

21. 8 U.S.C. §1101 et seq. (1970) (corresponds to The Act of October 3, 1965, Pub. L. 89-236 §1-6, 8-15, 17-19, 24, 79 Stat. 911-920, 922.)

reunited with their families. A significant number of professionals from Korea and the Philippines were among those to immigrate to the United States under preference three.

Immigration continues to play a large role in the growth of Asian American and Pacific Peoples communities in the United States. The West Coast attracted more than 30 percent of the Chinese, Korean, and Pilipino immigrants who entered the United States in 1972; the majority of these immigrants settled in California. For example, 18,517 immigrants from Taiwan, Korea, and the Philippines were identified in California as of June 30, 1972; whereas for the same group and period, only 10,051 were reported in New York.[22] A possible explanation for this West Coast settlement is that San Francisco and Los Angeles are major ports of entry. The large concentrations of non-English-speaking Asian Americans and Pacific Peoples in these urban centers are particularly attractive to immigrants. For these immigrants, the cultural, linguistic, and dietary familiarities ease the transition into American society.

Urban and Rural Settlement Patterns

In 1970, 1,229,515 of the Asian American and Pacific Peoples in the United States lived in urban areas, while 127,123 lived in rural areas.[23] (See Table II)

TABLE II

Urban and Rural Settlement Figures for Asian Americans and Pacific Peoples in the United States: 1970

	Total	Urban	Rural Farm And Nonfarm
Chinese	431,583	417,032	14,551
Filipino	336,731	288,287	48,444
Hawaiian	99,958[1]		
Japanese	588,324	524,196	64,128
Korean	69,510[1]		

1. United States excluding Alaska

Statistics regarding the urban and rural residence of Guamanians, Samoans, Hawaiians, and Koreans are unavailable for the mainland.

22. INS figures are for immigrants admitted by specified countries of birth and city for the year ending June 30, 1972. Data are lacking for Guamanians, Japanese, and Samoans.

23. Bureau of the Census, Census of Population: 1970, Subject Reports, Final Report PC(2)-1G Japanese, Chinese, and Filipinos in the United States. (Hereinafter cited as PC(2)-1G Japanese, Chinese, and Filipinos in the United States.) Tabular and text data on the Japanese, Chinese, Pilipino, Korean, and Hawaiian population in this report are based upon sample data collected by the Census Bureau as presented in the subject report. Unless otherwise specified, data for Asian Americans and Pacific Peoples are derived from the subject report.

As reported by the Census Bureau, the majority of Asian Americans and Pacific Peoples are located on the West Coast: California (549,307); Oregon (12,453); and Washington (41,052).[24] About 60 percent of the total Asian Americans and Pacific Peoples in the United States reside on the West Coast. (See Table III) Official statistics regarding the Guamanians and Samoans are lacking.

TABLE III

Total Asian American and Pacific Peoples Population
Of the West Coast - 1970

	California	Oregon	Washington
Chinese	170,419	4,774	9,376
Filipino	135,248	1,466	11,488
Hawaiian	14,454		
Japanese	213,277	6,213	20,188
Korean	15,909		

The Population in California

About 90 percent (502,270) of the 549,307 Asian Americans and Pacific Peoples living in California reside in urban areas, with about 10 percent or 25,485 residing in rural farm and nonfarm areas.[25] (See Table IV)

TABLE IV

Comparison of Urban and Rural Population of
Asian Americans and Pacific Peoples in California - 1970

	Urban	Rural
Chinese	167,773	2,646
Filipino	125,960	9,288
Hawaiian		
Japanese	199,726	13,551
Korean	8,811[1]	

1. Figures are incomplete for Koreans, with only the Los Angeles-Long Beach Standard Metropolitan Statistical Area (SMSA) identified. Standard metropolitan statistical areas (SMSA's) are defined by the Office of Management and Budget as a county or group of contiguous counties which contains at least one city of 50,000 inhabitants or twin cities with a combined population of at least 50,000.

The approximate locations of the metropolitan areas housing significant populations of Asian Americans and Pacific Peoples in California are shown in figure 1.

24. PC(2)-1G, Japanese, Chinese, and Filipinos in the United States. Figure includes Japanese, Chinese, Filipino, Hawaiian, and Korean only.

25. Figures exclude Samoans and Guamanians.

FIGURE 1

Los Angeles County, which includes the State's largest city, Los Angeles, had 238,223 Asian Americans and Pacific Peoples in 1970. This figure accounted for 3.5 percent of the county's 7,032,075 people.[26] Japanese Americans represented the highest Asian subgroup with 1.5 percent of the county total.

San Francisco County[27] had 108,410 Asian Americans and Pacific Peoples, which was 15.2 percent of the total population.[28] Chinese Americans represented the largest subgroup in San Francisco--8.2 percent of all Asian Americans and Pacific Peoples residing in the county. The city of San Francisco has the second largest concentration of these groups in the State. (See Table V).

TABLE V

Asian Americans and Pacific Peoples in
California's Largest Metropolitan Centers--1970

	Los Angeles[1]	San Francisco[2]	San Diego[4]	Sacramento
Chinese	40,798	58,696	4,500 [b]	8,199
Filipino	33,459	24,694	9,431	
Hawaiian	4,634			
Hawaiian, South Asian and Other		12,099	1,000 [b]	
Japanese	104,078	11,705	7,621 [a]	6,980
Korean	8,650	10,000[3]	1,000	
Other Asian	46,604			

1. Los Angeles County Census.
2. Chinatown Census.
3. Estimate supplied by Korean Consulate, San Francisco 1973.
4. PC(2)-IG Japanese, Chinese, and Filipinos in the Unites States; (a) standard metropolitan statistical area only; (b) United Pan Asian Community estimates.

---

26. Los Angeles County Population by Race: 1970 Census. Report based on 1970 census data filed with the California State Advisory Committee by Mayor Thomas Bradley, October 1973. (Hereinafter cited as Los Angeles County Census.)

27. The city of San Francisco is coextensive (has the same boundaries) with the county.

28. San Francisco Department of City Planning, Chinatown, 1970 Census: Population and Housing Summary & Analysis. (August 1972.) (Hereinafter cited as Chinatown Census.)

A significant number of Asian Americans and Pacific Peoples reside in Orange County (10,716);[29] Sacramento County (22,415);[30] and San Diego County (17,052).[31] Scattered settlements or pockets of the diverse ethnic Asians and Pacific Peoples can also be found throughout the State.

The Effects of Inaccurate, Hidden, or Unavailable Data

Testimony at both open meetings suggested that data on Asian Americans and Pacific Peoples were rarely collected accurately or consistently by Federal, State, and local agencies. Witnesses pointed out many discrepancies in population estimates generated by inaccurate collection systems. Sid Gloria of San Francisco's Pilipino community noted:

> Our precise numbers [nationally] are obscured by bureaucratic decisions to include him [the Pilipino] as Oriental, non-white, or others.... Estimates...vary from 450,000 to half a million....Available information is sketchy and somewhat dated.

Sister Bernadette Giles, a member of the San Francisco Human Rights Commission, testified that:

> The 1970 Census showed...55,000 Chinese in San Francisco....[The] Department of Public Health reported...61,000 Chinese....Many community groups feel the actual number is higher. Language barriers and culture patterns inhibit many Chinese from participating in census counts.

Faye Munoz of the Guamanian Association of Long Beach noted:

> Rough estimates indicate 30,000 to 45,000 Guamanians in the State of California and the West Coast...and 50,000 to 75,000 Hawaiians. The numbers of Guamanians, American Samoans, and Hawaiians cannot be accurately made because of free traffic flow between the islands and the...mainland...no census data or records are kept.

Ruby Whang, vice chairperson of the Korean American Association of Northern California, stated:

---

29. Figures for Japanese only.

30. Sacramento Standard Metropolitan Statistical Area figure for Japanese and Chinese only.

31. Figures for Japanese and Pilipinos only from 1970 census. Unified Pan Asian Community estimates a total of 54,000 for all Asian Americans and Pacific Peoples in San Diego.

> ...authorities are especially hard on Koreans
> because records are kept according to nation-
> alities, and Koreans fall under 'others'.

Community representatives alleged that the use of the category "other" effectively discounts their existence as individual communities and handicaps their attempts to justify proposals for community programming and funding. Kathy Fong, executive director, Chinese for Affirmative Action, testified:

> It is almost impossible to draw an accurate
> profile of the Chinese in the San Francisco
> area since the data compiled by EEOC [Equal
> Employment Opportunity Commission], HRD
> [California Department of Human Resources
> Development, recently renamed Employment
> Development Department], Department of Labor,
> and the Bureau of the Census do not breakdown
> specific labor force information on the
> Chinese.

In their attempts to obtain funding for a Mental Health Center, Bay Area Pilipinos were requested by the Alameda County Board of Commissioners to provide statistics. Cora Santa Ana, manpower planner for the Alameda County Manpower Area Planning Council, said:

> This was an entirely unjust thing....I could
> not provide statistics...[since the data] is
> not available [and] very few agencies keep
> them....What data is available is largely
> inadequate.

Statistical data can be utilized to document community needs and expenditures of monies for numerous community-based programs. This data can also be used to demonstrate discriminatory practices.[32] Cora Santa Ana asserted that the lack of data "seriously impairs our ability to document discrimination, not just in employment, but in education, health, and housing...."

When asked to provide comprehensive manpower service planning for Pilipinos in Alameda County, Ms. Santa Ana turned to the Summary Manpower Indicators. She noted:

> There was nothing in [here] on us Pilipinos....
> The categories listed...white, black, other
> races, Spanish American.

She also pointed out that in the March 1973 Manpower Report of the President to Congress:

---

32. The U.S. Commission on Civil Rights report, To Know or Not to Know (February 1973), reports the findings of a Commission study to determine the most effective way to collect and use racial and ethnic data. The report notes that "collection and analysis of these data are the most effective and desirable means of measuring Federal program impact upon minority beneficiaries and for assuring that equal opportunity policies are working effectively." (p. 3).

[There is] nothing in [it] on us [Pilipinos].
Even at the highest level of government, there
is no recognition of our needs, no recognition
of our problems.

Kerry Doi, employed with the Services for Asian Youth, noted
that in a Greater Los Angeles Community Action Agency report:

The ethnic breakdown is white, Spanish American,
and black. Notice no breakdown on Asians.

The absence of statistically valid data may effectively hamper
community programming and makes it difficult to determine if discrim-
ination does in fact exist in local, State, and Federal programs.
It also prevents the employment force from being properly identified.
Grace Blaszkowski, Asian American Affairs Office, San Diego County
Human Relations Commission, asserted:

Perhaps no other group of people have suffered
so deeply from a failure by the Federal Government to maintain an accurate reporting system
as the Asian Americans.

The failure by private and governmental agencies to collect
complete data and the inadequacy of available data prevent
Asian Americans and Pacific Peoples from full participation in all
aspects of community programming and development. In effect, no
data means invisibility.

COMMUNITIES' PERCEPTIONS OF ISSUES AND CONCERNS

Asian Americans and Pacific Peoples have often been grouped as
Orientals and Islanders. Although they have similar traditions, each
community is unique. "Americanization," however, has eroded many
traditional concepts and values. The concept of filial obedience and
the highly ordered system of kinship relations are important to the
economic and social well-being of a Chinese family in an agrarian
society, but in American (and Western) society these values often conflict with ideas of egalitarianism and individualism. Often certain
customs and mores are misunderstood or unaccepted by the majority
society. In the Samoan culture, an individual may use his father's,
mother's, or relative's name on different occasions. In American
Samoa, the different names are used with pride. But in the United
States, this is viewed as an alias rather than a legitimate social
custom. When the majority society deny the cultural and linguistic
differences among these people, Asian Americans and Pacific Peoples
become victims of mistaken identity.

While there are varying opinions about the structure of American
pluralism--witness the controversy surrounding bilingual/bicultural
education--community leaders pointed out that the cultural and
linguistic differences among their peoples contribute to the richness
of American society.

Reverend Young Pin Lim told the Advisory Committee in San Francisco:

> I think of America as a great orchestra. An orchestra consists of many kinds of musical instruments....Each instrument keeps its own individuality...it contributes its best to the harmony of the orchestra. A trombone is always a trombone, but when it tries to be a clarinet, it will make the harmony of the orchestra disastrous.
>
> The great American society consists of many races, as an orchestra, and the individual race can contribute its best to the society by perfecting its individuality. That means each race understands its own heritage, but is flexible to adapt itself to the environment.

CHINESE AMERICANS

The Chinese in California are mainly urban dwellers. According to 1970 census figures they reside primarily in the San Francisco (58,696), Los Angeles (40,798), and Sacramento (10,457) SMSA's. The United Pan Asian Community estimates 4,500 Chinese Americans in San Diego. Chinese Americans represent 8.2 percent of the San Francisco County population and 0.6 percent of the Los Angeles County population.

Prior to 1965, the areas referred to as Chinatown in San Francisco and Los Angeles had developed into communities with the majority population native-born. With the increase in the number of immigrants since 1965, these areas now have largely foreign-born residents.

The majority of these immigrants cannot speak English fluently and lack occupational skills. Testimony at both open meetings suggested that the lack of language proficiency in English posed some serious socioeconomic problems. Community members alleged that these problems remain unresolved because of neglect by local, State, and Federal agencies.

Chinatowns in urban areas perpetrate their status as tourist attractions in order to survive. The employment offered by tourist-related industries, such as restaurants and gift shops, is menial, usually requiring long hours and offering low pay. These Chinatowns must also house the increasing local populations. The results have been severe overcrowding, high rents, underemployment, and unemployment.

During Commission staff investigation, more than 80 Chinese Americans from San Francisco, Los Angeles, and San Diego were interviewed. Twenty-six Chinese Americans appeared before the Advisory Committee and discussed their community concerns in education, bilingual services, housing, social services for the elderly, employment, and immigration. Although there have been more than 19 youth-gang-related killings in San Francisco's Chinatown betweeen 1971 and 1974, the community was reluctant to talk about this issue. Many community members viewed the problem as an outward manifestation of the frustration felt by Chinatown's youth. This frustration, they noted, was connected to the community's concerns voiced at the Advisory Committee's open meeting and the failure of appropriate agencies to provide resources to deal with these issues.

Representatives of the San Francisco and Los Angeles Chinese American communities perceived education as an issue of major concern.[33]

Education

Chinese witnesses felt that all levels of education--preschool through higher education--were at issue. Lucinda Lee Katz, director of the Chinatown Community Children's Center, San Francisco, testified about the need for child care and preschool facilities. According to Ms. Katz, established centers have waiting lists of more than 500 children. Parents are being told that their children will have to wait at least 2 years before receiving services. She noted:

> In the San Francisco Chinatown area, there
> are 3,600 children under age six. There are
> five day care centers serving 230 children
> and five preschool or Head Start centers
> serving 250 children. The 480 children or
> 13 percent being served, by no means meets
> the needs of our community.

Georgiana Lee, a recent Chinese immigrant now living in Los Angeles, echoed Ms. Katz' concern:

> I always want to put my children in day care
> children's center so that I can find a job to
> help support the family....I tried to place
> my children into Castelar's Children Center,
> but I find out that there are 180 to 200
> children that are on the waiting list....I
> feel that Chinatown is in desperate need of
> a child care center....That is not only my
> need, it's also the need of my friends, [my]
> neighbors, and my relatives.

Chinese immigrant mothers and teachers testifying at the open meeting in Los Angeles told the Advisory Committee of the alienation and isolation felt by many immigrant Chinese children in the public

33. At the beginning of the 1972-73 academic year, the San Francisco community had been divided on the issue of busing to achieve integration in the city's schools. Opponents of the plan established Chinese Freedom Schools and boycotted buses. By June 1973, the issue had subsided and community spokespersons noted that enrollment in the Freedom schools had dropped by approximately half.

schools. May Chen, a teacher and member of the National Advisory Committee on Bilingual-Bicultural Education to the Department of Health, Education, and Welfare, said:

> School textbooks and curriculum in the past
> and present show not only a tendency to ignore
> or overlook the Chinese American, but actually,
> in many ways, serve to downgrade, distort, and
> humiliate us. For example, consider this
> remark from a current State-adopted social
> studies text: 'Immigration laws change often.
> In 1882, not only were Chinese excluded but
> also criminals, paupers, and the insane.' Are
> we to be classed with the outcasts of American
> society?

She told the Advisory Committee that many Chinese Americans would prefer bilingual educational opportunity rather than the more prevalent English as a second language (ESL) classes offered by many school districts. She said:

> Aside from schools which have received Federal
> support for bilingual programs, many school
> administrators appear to adopt a policy which
> in effect opposes bilingual opportunities for
> Chinese-speaking students. A statement from
> one school teacher manual says, 'Since our
> main objective is to help the students develop
> the ability to function in English, ESL [English
> as a Second Language] teachers have to be aware
> of the native languages of their students and
> their cultures. But the courses must be con-
> ducted in English; the native languages of the
> pupils don't have to be used at all.'[34]

Angelina Yu, a recent immigrant, told the Advisory Committee of her concerns for her children's education:

> At Castelar Elementary School, around 56 percent
> of the students speak a primary language other
> than English. State achievement tests given to

---

34. This statement is from a school in the Los Angeles District, but Western Regional Office staff have identified similar types of state-ments from other school districts. In San Francisco, the Neighborhood Legal Assistance Foundation filed a class action suit in December 1973 against the officials of the San Francisco Unified School District. The suit charged the school system with failure to provide adequate instruction to approximately 1,800 students of Chinese ancestry who did not speak English and were thus denied a meaningful opportunity to participate in the public educational programs. After appeal to the Supreme Court, the district case was decided in favor of the complain-ants, (Lau v. Nichols, 414 U.S. 563 (1974) The school district is now required to come up with plan to educate those students whose only language is Chinese.

all of the children reflect the students' language handicap.

Peter Woo, who taught English as a second language (ESL) in Los Angeles' Chinatown for 2 1/2 years, described his perception of ESL programs for Chinese:

The existing ESL program is heavily academic in its substance; it's not geared for students who have to worry how to make both ends meet daily. It is a program...to prepare those who are going to complete their high school diploma or college.

Language difficulties also affect Chinese Americans in higher education. According to Terry Lee, a former counselor for the Equal Opportunities Program at San Francisco University:

There seems to be a widely held notion that Asian Americans don't have any problems. This fallacy is especially prevalent in higher education. I have worked with Chinese students from low-income families with non-English speaking parents. They have poor grades, especially in English and the social sciences. Since Chinese is their primary language, they have difficulties in their classes.

The Chinese American communities in San Francisco, Los Angeles, and San Diego felt that the most glaring evidence of neglect for Asian Americans was the lack of Asian Americans in school administrative positions throughout the State. In the San Diego Unified School District, for example, there was only one Asian American administrator out of a total administrative force of 407 in December 1973. According to the San Diego City School ethnic survey, there were 4,450 Asian American students (classified as Orientals and other nonwhites) at that time. The Asian American students comprised 3.6 percent of the total enrollment of 124,534.[35]

Roger Tom, a teacher at a predominantly Chinese American public school in San Francisco, told the Advisory Committee:

In 1972, 14.9 percent of the district's students were Chinese....Chinese Americans constituted 5.4 percent of the teaching staff, 3.9 percent of the field administrative staff, and only 1.4 percent of the central office administrative staff.

Community witnesses noted that it was important for Asian American children to observe that their own racial and ethnic group was adequately represented among school employees. Witnesses

35. Tetsuyo Kashima, Asian Crisis in the San Diego Unified School District (San Diego 1973). A report adapted from a paper presented to an education workshop of the Japanese American Citizens League Conference, San Diego, May 22, 1970.

charged that numerous school districts in the State failed to provide this educational opportunity to their children.

Employment

In San Francisco, a panel of community witnesses alleged that employment discrimination against the Chinese was based on a number of factors. One factor, stereotyping, whether positive or negative, worked to the disadvantage of the Chinese American.

Kathy Fong, executive director, Chinese for Affirmative Action, told the Advisory Committee of this concern:

> While some ethnic groups are negatively stereotyped as lazy, shiftless, or trouble-makers, the Chinese are commonly stereotyped in positive stereotypes of the super-worker. The super stereotype, as well as the negative stereotype of the Chinese, are tremendous detriments to decent and fair employment. The notion that all Chinese are hard working, conscientious, and willing to work overtime, is frequently abused by employers who want to get coolie labor.
>
> Employers of Chinese describe their employees as quiet and uncomplaining and express the sentiment that if a minority person must be hired at all, let it be the least trouble-some. Out of fear of losing their job, a fear based upon past historical discrimination and threats of deportation, many Chinese hesitate to report their grievances of lower salaries, longer hours, and similar unequal treatment.

Ms. Fong felt that some Chinese were denied jobs because of their accent, but she questioned how the standards for acceptable English were determined, "since European accents, such as French or British, are considered romantic or sophisticated." She pointed out that many Chinese were often denied promotions on the basis of "unacceptable English."

The difficulty of drawing an accurate employment profile of the Chinese in the San Francisco area was another factor. According to 1970 census figures, the total population in the San Francisco-Oakland SMSA was 2,987,859. This figure includes 116,315 individuals of Chinese, Japanese, and Pilipino descent; 91,338 were 25 years old and over. The 1970 Equal Employment Opportunity Commission employment profile which covered the SMSA showed that in the 15 largest industrial categories, the total employment was 540,988, including 25,935 Asian Americans. The profile did not include a significant percentage of Asian Americans in employable age groups, nor did it provide a break down of specific labor force information for Asian Americans. Kathy Fong noted that there was also no break down of specific labor force information on Chinese by either the Department of Labor or the Human Resources Development (HRD, recently renamed Employment Development Department). Without an accurate employment profile, unemployment problems and employment discrimination would continue, she said.

The issue of underemployment of Chinese American workers was another community concern. Ms. Fong stated:

> A glaring example of underemployment can be
> seen by comparing the high educational
> attainment level of Asians with their number
> in managerial and supervisorial occupations
> in industry and government.

Census data show that in 1970 the median school years completed by those 25 years and older in the San Francisco-Oakland SMSA were: black, 11.7; Chinese Americans, 12.0; Japanese Americans, 12.7; Pilipinos, 12.4; Spanish-surnamed, 11.3; and white, 12.4. Yet, of the 25,935 Asian Americans employed, only 1,044 or 4 percent held white-collar official and managerial positions. In contrast, 52,101 or 9.6 percent of the total number of employees (540,988) covered by the EEOC profile were in such positions.

"The existence of a Chinese subeconomy," Ms. Fong stated, "helps absorb some of the Chinese who are rejected for employment in San Francisco." If these substandard jobs were not included, she said, the 1973 unemployment rate of 4.9 percent for Chinese Americans would jump to 6.1 percent.

The Advisory Committee also heard testimony from Joyce Law, coordinator of the Chinatown Community Services Center, which provides counseling and referral services to immigrants and other members of the Los Angeles Chinese community. Ms. Law specifically deplored the minimal manpower training programs and bilingual employment resources for Chinese Americans. She said:

> HRD [recently renamed Employment Development
> Department] has been able to serve only the
> English-speaking Chinese people. In other
> words, they put the burden on Chinese Ameri-
> cans that they have to learn English first
> before they can be served by HRD [EDD].
> I recently asked a representative of HRD [EDD]
> how many slots of Manpower Development and
> Training Act, ESL, were available for Chinese.
> His answer was 14...slots available for 1,000
> Chinese families with four or more persons
> per family.

GUAMANIAN AMERICANS

On August 1, 1950, a law popularly known as the Organic Act of Guam[44] was enacted by Congress conferring American citizenship

---

44. Organic Act of Guam, ch. 512, 64 Stat. 384 (codified in scattered sections of 8, 48 U.S.C.).

upon the inhabitants of the territory of Guam. This legislation
and its subsequent amendments, which extended constitutional
guarantees, ostensibly grants the same rights to the citizens of
Guam as enjoyed by all other Americans, except that Guamanians
cannot vote in national elections while residing in Guam. They
may do so if they live in the United States. This restriction is
based on the fact that Guam is a territory, and exercise of the
franchise requires that a citizen qualify under the laws of a particular State. Since Guam is not a State, a Guamanian living
there at the time of a national election cannot vote.

According to INS figures, 11,930 Guamanians immigrated to the
Unites States between 1963 and 1972. Community representatives
asserted, however, that there were approximately 30,000 to 45,000
Guamanians residing in California alone. Precise data were difficult
to obtain.[45] Staff investigators identified concentrations of
Guamanians in the cities of Carson, Long Beach, San Pedro, Santa Ana,
and Wilmington.

The Advisory Committee and Commission staff met with more than
35 members of the Guamanian community. The community voiced concerns
over inadequate educational programs, the relatively low number of
Guamanian professionals within the communities, the menial job
options, and neglect and indifference on the part of Federal agencies
responsible for administering the trust territories. Here the
Advisory Committee will present community perceptions of prejudice
against Guamanians in two area: employment and education.

Employment

Data on the employment status of Guamanians are difficult to
obtain. Guamanian Americans are not tabulated separately in
government planning programs; statistics from private industry are
unavailable. Thus, the employment problems go unrecognized, at the
very least, by many Federal, State, and local agencies.

Employment concerns of the community focused on the lack of
job counseling and the related menial, low paying jobs obtained by
Guamanians. Faye Munoz, a member of the Guamanian Association of
Long Beach, stated that Guamanians can only get low status
employment:

> [There are]...hundreds of men from the islands
> who...were recruited into the U.S. Navy, [and]
> locked into classifications which limit growth
> and promotion.

Upon retirement from the Navy, she added, Guamanians had not
developed skills for the existing job market.

---

45. Immigration and Naturalization Service notes that between 1820-
1972, 23,442 Pacific Island peoples from U.S. administered areas
(Guam, American Samoa, and other Pacific territories) immigrated to
the mainland; from 1934-1951, this number included the Philippines.

Education

Witnesses at the open meetings noted that the educational system accommodated Guamanians rather than educated them, as evidenced by the lack of Guamanian professionals. Ms. Munoz felt that teachers and peers humiliated Guamanian children because of their physical characteristics, dress, mannerisms, and language. The results are that children become discouraged and apathetic toward education, she said. Ms. Munoz added that without adequate education, Guamanians cannot fully participate in mainland society.

JAPANESE AMERICANS

There is no record of immigration from Japan until 1861. During the period 1891 through 1930 a total of 273,038 immigrants arrived. This figure accounted for more than two-thirds of the total Japanese immigration for the period 1820 through 1972.[46]

Mainly an urban dwelling people, Japanese Americans reside in Los Angeles County (104,078), San Francisco County (11,705), Orange County (10,716), San Diego County (7,621), and Sacramento County (6,980).[47] There are fewer numbers of Japanese Americans scattered throughout California's other counties. Japanese Americans accounted for 1.5 percent of the Los Angeles County population; 1.9 percent of Los Angeles City population, and 1.6 percent of San Francisco City population.

The Advisory Committee and Commission staff interviewed 46 Japanese Americans in Los Angeles and 32 in San Francisco. In addition, group meetings were held with more than 270 Japanese Americans.

Japanese American spokespersons alleged discrimination against their communities in education, employment, social services, and in programs for the elderly.

Community members pointed out that in the area of education, Japanese Americans face a steady rise in the school dropout rate among their youth. They pointed out that educators ignored Asian American participation in American history and that Japanese American history was excluded from textbooks. Community members asserted that Federal and State agencies provided inadequate services to their community, pointing out the lack of bilingual services and the employment and underemployment problems of foreign-trained professionls. They also believed that redevelopment plans for areas predominantly Japanese American discriminated against the elderly and small shopkeepers.

Employment

Employment concerns of the community focused not on unemployment, but on underemployment and minimal upward mobility. While

---

46. Based on data in the INS, 1972 Annual Report, the total figure for this period, ending June 30, 1972, was 375,070.

47. PC(2)-1G, Japanese, Chinese, and Filipinos in the United States.

the unemployment rate of Japanese Americans in 1970 was 3.6 percent--low in comparison with other minority groups--many Japanese Americans are at the lower levels of big business and civil service employment.

Edison Uno, an instructor in Asian American Studies at San Francisco State University, told the Advisory Committee:

> By comparison with other minorities, it may be true that Japanese Americans have gained a degree of parity at the entry level of employment. However, this does not mean that we have had an equal employment opportunity in all areas of employment, especially in blue-collar jobs, management and executive positions, union and skilled crafts, political appointments, and public media.

Employment opportunities in the skilled trades was another concern. Mark Masaoka, an apprentice plumber in Los Angeles, told the Advisory Committee of his concerns about construction jobs for Japanese Americans. He said:

> Through the Little Tokyo Redevelopment Project...there will be some 50 million dollars of construction in our community....We rightfully claim our share of the jobs. But I am wary and concerned, and, I add, suspicious, that as far as opening up employment opportunities, our people are going to be left holding a bag of horse manure. Because even though Little Tokyo is 70 percent Asian, you and I know that there are not automatically going to be 70 percent Asians on the job site.

Education

Community representatives pointed out that in the area of education Japanese Americans were faced with a steady rise in the school dropout rate among their youth. They also pointed out the few numbers of Asian American graduate students in relation to their undergraduate enrollment and the scarcity of Asian American staff at all levels of education. They complained that educators are insensitive to Asian American students by failing to consider Asian Americans in developing curricula and by ignoring their role in American history.

The problems and perceptions of Japanese Americans exist and persist in contrast to 1970 census data on educational attainment. Census figures show that 77.1 percent and 76.8 percent of all Japanese Americans 25 years and over in the San Francisco-Oakland and Los Angeles-Long Beach SMSAs, respectively, had completed high school and that the median school years completed in both SMSAs was 12.7.[50]

Paul Takagi, an associate professor of criminology at the University of California at Berkeley, told the Advisory Committee that he felt Asian Americans were considered competent but not qualified for special programs available for other minority students in institutions of higher learning. Dr. Takagi supported this claim with racial and ethnic statistics of faculty and students at the University of California at Berkeley showing that Asian Americans were not represented in graduate and professional schools in proportion to their undergraduate enrollment. Nor were they proportionally represented on most department faculties.[51]

Other witnesses expressed concern over the statewide lack of Asian American administrators at local levels of education. Tetsuyo Kashima, a teacher in the San Diego Unified School District, told the Advisory Committee of the educational deficiences he perceived within the San Diego Unified School District. He stated that there was only one Asian American administrator among 407 to oversee 4,450 Asian American (classified as orientals and other nonwhite) students. Mr. Kashima felt such data indicated that Asian Americans were relatively forgotten within school systems.

Immigration and Bilingual Services

Community testimony suggested that bilingual services for Asian Americans should be provided by the Immigration and Naturalization Service. Steve Nakasone, a second-year law student at Loyola School of Law and a counselor at One-Stop Immigration Center, and Hanaye Gimi, a 77-year-old grandmother, told the Advisory Committee about the concerns among Japanese immigrants. Mr. Nakasone alleged that:

> First, the immigration law itself is unduly
> harsh and acts in a discriminating manner
> towards Japanese. Second, the immigration
> department in its administration of the law
> acts arbitrarily in denying aliens benefits
> to which they are legally entitled. Third,
> the immigration department does not effec-
> tively communicate with alien Americans and
> often treats them as though they were not
> human beings.

Mr. Nakasone alleged that the Immigration and Naturalization

50. PC(2)-1G, Japanese, Chinese, and Filipinos in the United States.

51. Data submitted by the University of California at Berkeley at the open meeting in San Francisco were the same as that submitted by Dr. Takagi, but in a different form. This data showed: 2,224 or 12.8 percent Asian American undergraduates and 421 or 5.1 percent Asian American graduate students; 313 or 5.9 percent Asian American academic employees and 368 or 7.0 percent Asian American career staff. Letter to California Advisory Committee dated June 21, 1973, from Chancellor Albert H. Bowker, University of California at Berkeley, on file in the Western Regional Office.

Service (INS) was given wide discretion in applying the law and that such discretion was sometimes abused.

Mrs. Gimi told the Advisory Committee, through a translator, of her personal experience with the Los Angeles INS office. Mrs. Gimi immigrated to the United States in 1918. As a permanent resident, she received old age security benefits. Recently, her social worker insisted that she would need to get a green card to continue her benefits. Because Mrs. Gimi had lost her green card when she and her family were relocated to a concentration camp, she requested that INS issue her a new one. According to Mrs. Gimi, INS denied her request because it could not verify her entry. When she sent INS a copy of her passport proving her legal entry, she was told that she would have to apply for a new green card at a cost of $35. Mrs. Gimi said:

> This makes me very mad. I have worked hard
> and contributed my fair share to this country.
> At the age of 77, I have earned by benefits
> and I have a right to keep them. This is
> unfair to me. I have paid my dues to my
> country. I am entitled to the benefits I am
> now receiving. Why must I pay for the mis-
> takes of the immigration department?

KOREAN AMERICANS

Since 1969, immigration from Korea has increased significantly. Immigration and Naturalization Service figures show that in 1969, 12,478 Korean immigrants entered the United States; in 1972, the number was 23,473.

The Advisory Committee and Commission staff interviewed 33 Korean Americans in Los Angeles and 27 in San Francisco. In addition, more than 100 Korean Americans met with members of the Advisory Committee and Commission staff in group meetings during the investigation. Testimony from Korean Americans throughout the State was strikingly similar. The Advisory Committee found a common thread of concern over State licensing of foreign-educated professionals, immigration, employment, and education.

Community members told the Advisory Committee that Korean American professionals trained in Korea had extensive problems in obtaining State licenses; that social services had not provided for the needs of Korean American immigrants whose knowledge of and facility in English was limited; and that the public school system had not responded with pro- gramming for the increasing enrollment of Korean American students.

Foreign-Educated Professionals

At the Los Angeles open meeting, the Korean American panel on problems faced by foreign-educated professionals received much community support. Advisory Committee chairperson Herman Sillas noted, for the record, a Korean delegation of approximately 200 persons carrying 15 to

20 poster placards in the hearing room. They were protesting indifference on the part of the State in licensing foreign-educated professionals.

While California does permit foreign-educated doctors, dentists, and practical nurses to apply for licensure, foreign-educated pharmacists have been severely restricted from taking the examination administered by the State Board of Pharmacy. Kong Mook Lee, a Korean-educated pharmacist and vice president of the Korean Pharmacist Association of California, estimates that there are at least 300 experienced pharmacists in Southern California born and educated in Korea, who cannot practice their profession. He noted that the Immigration and Naturalization Service gives high priority preferences to Koreans with pharmaceutical training, with the implication that persons of their educational training and experience would be welcome additions to the United States. Yet when these practicing pharmacists come to California, they are denied the opportunity even to take the examinations. The majority of the Korean-educated pharmacists have neither the time nor the money to go back to school. To survive and support families, these professionals must take unskilled jobs often paying low wages, he said. Mr. Lee added:

> We never expected to lose our profession at
> the same time as we immigrated to this
> beautiful and wealthy country. Today, most
> of us find ourselves in a job which is incon-
> sistent with our qualifications and experience.
> We are suffering from starvation wages.

Yung Gill Kook, vice president of the Korean American Political Association of Southern California, told Commission staff:

> The Korean American community in Los Angeles
> would benefit not just from their services.
> If they are allowed to work with dignity in
> the profession of their training--instead of
> as restaurant busboys or gardeners' assis-
> tants--and to earn standard wages for their
> work, they would be in a position to give our
> community additional strength and leadership.
> This is important to all of us.

Foreign-educated pharmacists seeking licensure in California are predominantly from Asian countries. Out of 220 written requests for licensure information received by the Board of Pharmacy as of January 1974, 16 were from graduates of schools in Korea and 132 from the Philippines. A candidate for the licensure examination, however, must have graduated from a school on the board's accredited list. No foreign school has ever been included on the list.[52] Even though the State law was amended in March 1972 to allow foreign-trained pharmacists upon certification by the Board of Pharmacy to take the examination, none have been permitted by the board to do so.[53]

---

52. West's Ann. Cal. Bus. and Prof. Code §4085 (West's Supp. 1974).

53. West's Ann. Cal. Bus. and Prof. Code §4089.5 (West's Supp. 1974), amending West's Ann. Cal. Bus. and Prof. Code §4089 (1955).

Other States, including New York, permit foreign-trained pharmacists to be licensed if they meet certain educational and experience requirements and pass the State licensure examination. Foreign-educated professionals in California would have to repeat their education in an accredited school or seek work in another field.

Hakto Pak, medical doctor, spoke on behalf of 30 Korean-educated physicians who had immigrated to the United States and were facing severe problems in obtaining licenses to practice medicine. Dr. Pak described the average Korean immigrant physician as being over 40 years of age and having had a least 10 years practical experience. As in the pharmacists' situation, the Korean physicians were forced to find jobs as clerks and technicians to support their families. Such employment left little time to prepare for licensure examinations.

Another witness, Dr. Chin Choi, told the Advisory Committee that he had served the Korean Field Army as chief surgeon and was decorated in 1952 with a bronze star by President Harry Truman for his services to the U.S. Army. Later Dr. Choi was promoted to the rank of full colonel. He returned to school at Kyoto University in Japan where he received a doctorate in biological medicine. Dr. Choi immigrated to the United States in September 1972 and has received only excuses as to why he cannot practice medicine in California, he claimed.

Punja Yhu, a registered nurse, spoke on behalf of 600 Korean-educated nurses now residing in the Los Angeles area. She said that these nurses had the equivalent education and training of registered nurses in this country. Of the 600 nurses in the area, she said, only 200 had been able to obtain State licensure as registered nurses. Ms. Yhu pointed out that foreign-trained nurses have language and monetary difficulties in preparing for the licensure examinations. She asserted that foreign-trained nurses were exploited by hospitals and medical clinics who employ them as nurses' aides at $1.85 an hour and have them perform tasks usually assigned to registered nurses.

Employment

The problem of English language proficiency has hampered Korean Americans in their search for employment. Underemployment of Korean American professionals was another critical complaint.

In Los Angeles Sama Rhee and Henry Yum told the Advisory Committee about the language problems facing the Korean community and the effect on employment opportunities. Mr. Rhee said:

> The Korean population in Los Angeles County
> is about 50,000....Eighty to 85 percent of them
> are newcomers from Korea, with about the same
> percentages being unable to speak English.

Mr. Yum, who handles approximately 1,500 Korean employment referrals for the State's Employment Development Department in Los Angeles, told the Advisory Committee of the problems his Korean clients face when they apply for jobs:

Due to the lack of conversational English, the
average Korean, regardless of his educational
background and experience, must accept minimal
type jobs such as janitors, warehousemen,
nurses' aides. The irony of this that a recent
survey revealed that 70 percent of the Korean
immigrants are professionals.

Dora Kim, a manpower service representative for the Employment
Development Department in San Francisco, told the Advisory Committee
that she was the only bilingual Korean worker in that agency. She
said that her work with non-English-speaking Koreans was a full-time
job and still the need was unmet. Ms. Kim claimed that because
Koreans had an English language handicap, many professionals such
as pharmacists, accountants, nurses, etc., were forced to take low-
paying, low-skilled jobs.

Education

The educational needs of a growing Korean American student
enrollment are many. Witnesses felt that English as a second
language programs should be developed; that bilingual programs
should be instituted, and bilingual staff hired; and that curricula
should reflect the needs of Korean American students.

Reverend Young Pin Lim told the Advisory Committee of the
educational concerns of the Korean American community in San Francisco.
He stated that since public agencies had not provided day care facilities and schools with Korean-speaking staff, the Korean community had
formed its own school. The main purpose of the school was to teach
English and provide citizenship training. He noted, however, that
this community-supported school had created a heavy financial burden
on its supporters.

Lenore Blank, a community representative, focused her testimony
on the need for bilingual, bicultural education for Korean students
in the San Francisco Unified School District. Ms. Blank estimated
that there were approximately 1,000 Korean students in that district,
but only one Korean teacher out of 2,300.

PILIPINO AMERICANS

The first major immigration of Pilipinos followed the Spanish-
American War when Spain ceded the Philippines, along with Puerto Rico
and Guam, to the United States. Male Pilipinos were recruited to work
the sugar plantations in Hawaii and the farmlands of the San Joaquin
and Imperial Valleys in California. These migratory farm laborers
established the Pilipino settlements or "Manila Towns" in Seattle,
Portland, San Francisco, Stockton, Delano, Los Angeles, and elsewhere
in the farmlands along the West Coast.[54]

54. For a discussion of historical and contemporary issues related
to the Pilipino experience, see Royal F. Morales, Makibaka: The
Pilipino American Struggle (Los Angeles: Mountainview Publishers,1974).

The Tydings-McDuffie Act of 1934 established a Philippine Commonwealth and provided for independence in 1946.[55] The United States immigration laws were applied, and the annual Pilipino quota was limited to 50.

Following the end of World War II, on July 4, 1946, the Philippines became a sovereign independent state. Concurrently, the annual immigration quota for the Philippines was raised to 100. Many of the Philippine Scouts who had fought alongside American troops migrated to the United States and later sent for their families. As an inducement to Pilipino migration, the Philippines Trade Act of 1946 granted nonquota immigrant status to Philippine citizens who had resided in the United States for a continuous period of 3 years prior to November 30, 1941.[56] The nonquota status was also granted to their spouses and unmarried children under 18 years of age.

The Immigration Act of 1965 produced an increase in immigration of relatives of Pilipino Americans and encouraged members of the professions to migrate to this country. During the period 1966 through 1972, 143,483 Pilipinos immigrated to the United States. The 1970 Census indicated that there were 336,823 Pilipinos in the United States. Between the 1960 and 1970 census, the population growth of Pilipinos had increased 95 percent.

Based upon 1972 INS figures, Pilipino immigration is the largest from all Asian countries and Pacific Islands. The general trend of population increase is likely to continue. In Los Angeles County, Pilipinos are 0.5 percent (33,459) of the county population. In San Francisco, Pilipinos account for 3.5 percent (25,694) of the county population. California has 135,248 Pilipino residents or 40 percent of the total number of Pilipino Americans in the United States.

The Advisory Committee and staff interviewed 27 Pilipinos in San Francisco and Alameda Counties, 22 Pilipinos in Los Angeles, and 10 in San Diego. From these interviews, a myriad of concerns emerged. Immigrant professionals found that their certifications were not recognized in the United States and that in some cases they were not even permitted to take State professional licensing examinations to prove their capabilities. Pilipino senior citizens, retired from low-paying jobs as farm laborers or domestics receive small or no pensions and social security benefits. Racist legislation in California prohibited Pilipinos from marrying white women in the past.[57] Because of this legislation and a scarcity of Pilipino women in this country 50 years ago, many elderly Pilipino men now live alone.

---

55. 22 U.S.C. §1394 (1970) (corresponds to the Act of Mar. 24, 1934, ch. 84, 48 Stat. 456.)

56. Philippines Trade Act of 1946, ch. 244 §231, 60 Stat. 141 (1946).

57. West's Ann. Cal. Civil Code §60 (1933). For historical analysis on Pilipino immigration and American discriminatory policies, see for example C.M. Goethe, "Filipino Immigration Viewed as a Peril," in Current History, 34:354-355, June 1931, and Bruno Lasker, Filipino Immigration to the Continental United States and Hawaii (Chicago: Univ. of Chicago Press, 1931).

Unemployment and underemployment were also perceived as critical issues. And Pilipino youth echoed the concerns of other Asian Americans and Pacific Peoples regarding the lack of sensitivity toward their culture in school curricula. Pilipino community members expressed concern over the growing school dropout rates of Pilipino youth.

Foreign-Educated Professionals

Immigrants who came to the United States under Preference Three of the Immigration and Nationality Act of 1965 found that their certifications were not recognized here. Even though some had 10 or more years experience, they have had to study for State dental and medical board examinations or complete teacher credential programs before they could practice. They have had to work as technicians and aides until they could pass the examinations.

In Los Angeles, Jenny Batongmalaque, a medical doctor, and Leon Barinaga, an attorney, described the problems a Pilipino-trained professional has had in obtaining a license to practice in California. She said:

> In Los Angeles, there are several hundred [Pilipino] unlicensed physicians working in jobs that are totally unrelated to their knowledge and expertise. Some are even jobless. They have no opportunity to review or to attend review classes. They cannot afford to pay the tuition and they have no time because they have to earn a living to feed themselves and their families.

Dr. Batongmalaque recommended to the Advisory Committee that assistance be given to unlicensed foreign medical graduates.

Mr. Barinaga commented:

> When most of the professionals apply for visas, they are granted visas under the preference for professionals. We are accepted as professionals as defined by the Immigration and Naturalization Service and the Department of Labor. However, when we come here, we're not allowed to practice that profession under which we were granted the visa...because of the State's strict licensing procedures. That's an inconsistency....

Dr. Amancio G. Ergina, executive secretary of the Filipino American Council of San Francisco, shared similar information with the Advisory Committee on the situation for professionals in San Francisco:

> We are faced with some 800 teachers without work, some 250 accountants looking for employ-

ment, 150 dentists working as clerks, waiters and busboys. We have hundreds of pharmacists, hundreds of optometrists working as clerks; doctors of medicine as medical technicians; and, in fact, we know three doctors who are working as babysitters.

Pilipinos from San Diego voiced similar complaints of underemployment and underutilization of professionals.

Senior Citizens and Youth

The problems of the senior citizens and youth in Pilipino communities were quite similar. Both groups expressed concerns over bilingual needs, social services, financial support, and employment. Pilipino youth were particularly concerned about the neglect of their culture in the educational system and the insensitivity of educators to their needs as students.

In Los Angeles, Milagros de la Cruz, former president of the Los Angeles Harbor Area Filipino American Community, Inc, talked about the social service concerns facing elderly Pilipinos in the harbor area:

> Today, many pioneers [from the Philippines] remain here as senior citizens with social problems and needs. There is a need for bilingual Pilipino staff in the DPSS [Department of Public Social Services] to serve these needy non-English or limited English-speaking Pilipinos. This need for bilingual staff is also true for the Department of Human Resources Development [EDD].

Al Santos, vice president of Filipino Senior Citizens in the Temple area, told the Advisory Committee of the frustrations facing 4,000 to 5,000 Pilipino elderly living in central Los Angeles. He said:

> The needy elderly Pilipino Americans are suffering from unprecedented problems that are devastating the lives of these aged people. The Pilipino American elderly are confronted with cultural barriers that exclude them from receiving their rightful benefits.

He traced the history of the Pilipino pioneers in Los Angeles and pointed out that Pilipinos were exploited as cheap farm labor with no provisions for retirement benefits, health care, or social security benefits. They receive few if any of these benefits today.

Members of Pilipino youth panels discussed their concerns before the Advisory Committee. At both open meetings, they alleged that the school system discouraged their participation by ignoring Pilipino history and culture and by failing to provide remedial classes for those with language problems. Mario Hidalgo, a student at the Mission High School in San Francisco, stated that newly arrived Pilipino youth have two handicaps in the United States. Since they begin school in the Philippines 2 years later than in the United States, Pilipino youth are at least 2 years behind their American counterparts. And while they are taught the basic English language in Pilipine schools, they speak English differently. Mr. Hidalgo said:

> Because we speak English differently, the teachers have this stereotype that we are dumb. Because of this, we are put in classes for slower students.

Mr. Hidalgo noted that the insensitivity of school teachers to their language problems has discouraged Pilipino youths and contributed to the rising school dropout rate among Pilipino youth.

Peter Almazol, an advisor to the Pilipino Youth Club in San Francisco, asserted that the lack of bicultural programs in the school system contributed to a "negative self-image" among Pilipino youth. He said that many Pilipino youth drop out of school because they cannot identify with the majority teachers in their schools. He added that more Pilipino youths have come into conflict with law enforcement agencies and that Pilipino organizations cannot get funding to help their own people.

Ethnic Identity and Exclusion in Employment and Social Services

Tony Grafilo, executive director, Pilipino Organizing Committee, summarized the concerns and problems of approximately 24,000 Pilipinos in San Francisco:

> The testimony you are seeking is out there ...in the faces of the Pilipinos living on these streets and alleys. The conditions speak louder than words. The eyes of my brothers and sisters reveal oppression.

Another witness, Dr. Amancio Ergina, executive secretary of the Filipino American Council of San Francisco, described misconceptions outsiders have of Pilipinos:

> I wonder if any of the members of the Committee knows what a Pilipino is? The fact is that when he looks for a job, he is mistaken for a Japanese or a Chinese because his skin is too brown to be either white or black. When he is introduced to someone, he is mistaken for a Latino because his name is a Spanish surname. When he looks for an apartment for rent, he is mistaken for a black. This mistaken identity has been carried on by the establishment and in every sector of our community, private and government.

Sid Gloria, a spokesperson for the Pilipino American community in San Francisco, echoed Dr. Ergina's frustration at government misidentification of Pilipinos:[58]

> Today, the record of the Pilipino experience
> would suggest that we are still 'guests' of
> the United States. Our precise numbers are
> obscured by bureaucratic decisions to include
> us as Oriental, nonwhite, or others. Conse-
> quently, the Pilipino is often not recognized
> as a specific group with specific problems.
> Moreover, Pilipinos cannot qualify for many
> governmental programs because there are no
> data to support their claims.

Cora Santa Ana of Oakland summarized three ways she felt exclusion affected the Pilipino community: 1) the negligible impact of revenue sharing in the Pilipino community; 2) the insensitivity and lack of responsiveness on the part of public and private agencies resulting in underutilization of services; and 3) the lack of data or inadequacy of data which is provided by these agencies.

Underemployment and unemployment were the major concerns of many Pilipino community people. Peope Balista and Roy Balista, both of San Diego, asserted that there was both subtle and overt discrimi- nation against Pilipino Americans in all areas of employment. Their major complaint was that almost all government agency affirmative action plans omitted Pilipino Americans from their goals and timetables.

Tony Grafilo alleged that State and Federal agencies were insensitive to the needs of Pilipinos. He said:

> HRD [EDD] has not been sensitive to the
> unemployment, underemployment problems of
> Pilipinos in San Francisco. They don't
> even have a reporting system that properly
> identifies how many Pilipinos were placed
> through their efforts.

Grace Blaszkowski of the Asian American Affairs Office, San Diego County Human Relations Commission, stated that 80 percent of the Pilipino labor force in San Diego were employed by the U.S. Navy. The major con- cern of these Pilipinos was the lack of Pilipino officers despite the fact that Pilipinos were the second largest minority group in the Navy nationwide, Ms. Blaszkowski said. She added:

> Pilipinos are only recruited as stewards,

---

58. The Immigration and Naturalization Service has placed Pilipino immigrants under varying countries or regions: prior to 1934, the Pilippines are recorded under separate tables as insular travel; from 1934-1951, the Philippines are included under Pacific Islands; and beginning with the year 1952, the Philippines are included under Asia. See footnote 16 in the 1973 annual report of the INS.

which is a classic example of discrimination
against an ethnic minority.

Sid Valledor, director of Project Hanapin, in San Francisco, a
research demonstration project for Pilipinos funded in part by DHEW,
alleged that Pilipino Americans were excluded from policymaking
boards and commissions of San Francisco. He noted:

> Of the dozens of policy-planning boards,
> commissions...whose memberships are in the
> hundreds and who are either elected by the
> people or appointed by elected officials,
> and whose decisions on public policies and
> public money determine the destiny of our
> city and the welfare and circumstances of
> all of its citizens--there is only one,
> single, solitary Pilipino on such boards.

> Institutional racism is best reflected in
> the employment of Pilipinos by the city and
> county of San Francisco. It is pathetic that
> less than 2 percent are Pilipinos, and there
> are none in supervisory [positions] outside
> of the Board of Education. The Housing
> Authority Commission employs 59.1 percent
> minorities. Out of this, there is only one
> Pilipino employed, representing less than
> half [of one] percent. The San Francisco
> Redevelopment Agency employs 54.5 percent
> minorities, but has only 11 Pilipinos
> employed, which is 3.5 percent of the total
> work force.

SAMOAN AMERICANS

American Samoa is a United States possession in the Pacific.[59]
Samoans of American Samoa are classified as American nationals.
According to the Immigration and Nationality Act of June 27, 1952,
a "national" is a citizen of the United States or "a person who,
though not a citizen of the United States, owes permanent allegiance
to the United States."[60] As nationals, American Samoans enjoy
diplomatic protection and have a right of free entry to the United
States, but have no political rights.

It is difficult to obtain data concerning the number of Samoan
Americans residing in the United States. INS figures indicate that

---

59. The archipelago is divided administratively into two parts. American Samoa is comprised of six islands and is a dependency of the United
States. Western Samoa, which consists of nine islands, is a self-
governing nation that until 1962 was a United Nations trust territory
administered by New Zealand.

60. 8 U.S.C. §1101 et. seq. (1970) (corresponds to The Act of June 27,
1952, ch. 477, 66 Stat. 163).

97,973 non-immigrants (aliens admitted for temporary periods) were admitted from Pacific Islands under American administration between 1963 and 1972, but there is no specific breakdown of Samoan Americans in this number. The Census Bureau does not specify the number of Samoan Americans in the United States but includes Samoans under "all other races." Community members, however, estimate that there are between 45,000 and 48,000 Samoan Americans on the West Coast.

The military has been the major source of outside contact for Samoans in the Pacific. Many of the older males enlisted in the American Armed Forces and settled in California following World War II. Their families joined them later. Even today, community spokespersons noted, Samoan people send their sons and daughters to serve in different branches of the United States Military.

California's Samoan Americans are concentrated in communities adjoining military establishments, such as the South Bay area of Los Angeles, Long Beach, San Diego, and San Francisco. Nonmilitary Samoan Americans, as well as present and retired military personnel, have gravitated toward these Samoan cultural enclaves.

At the time of the open meetings, the Samoan American community in California was a relatively new community. Its concerns were similar to those expressed by other Pacific Peoples. The Advisory Committee and Commission staff interviewed 29 Samoan Americans in Los Angeles and 21 in San Francisco. Commission staff also attended a total of 10 community meetings where more than 160 Samoan Americans from throughout the State discussed their concerns. Frustration and alienation of Samoan Americans were quite evident at these meetings.

Social Services

Samoan Americans have many problems, community representatives said, because of insensitivity by government officials to Samoan culture and the need for bilingual workers in outreach positions.

Palafu Tili, a community representative, told the Advisory Committee about problems and frustrations of Samoan families who utilize public social services. Mr. Tili asserted that the Los Angeles County Department of Public Social Services in Los Angele (DPSS) was unwilling or unable to help Samoan clients. Mr. Tili cited the following case:

> On November 12, 1973, a Samoan mother walked
> into the Carson Community Center with six
> welfare checks uncashed. Why? Because the
> name on the check did not match the name of
> the mother's identification card. It was a
> typing error in the spelling of the name.
> But...to worsen the situation, the spelling
> error changed the name into a [swear] word
> in the Samoan Language. The mother had
> made several trips for 6 months in hopes of
> correcting this error so that she could cash
> her welfare checks. However, because the

social worker she met with did not speak
Samoan, and she spoke little English, the
error had gone uncorrected.

The elderly experience problems through no fault of their own,
according to Mr. Tili. He said that the Samoan Government did not
keep birth and death certificates prior to 1900. The DPSS held up
processing of claims where this lack of proof [of birth or death]
existed, he said. The only official document carried by most
Samoans coming to the United States has been an affidavit with the
seal of the Samoan Government or the seal of the church. The DPSS
has questioned the legality of such documents. Mr. Tili commented:

We are tired of investigations that include
suspicious statements by the investigators
that make us feel like criminals. We are
not seeking help to make us rich; we are
seeking help because we are poor and hungry.
Many of our elders are too old to work and
cannot speak English well. Please do something before our situation gets worse.

On January 1, 1974, the Social Security Administration, by an
act of Congress, took over many of the adult services handled by
State and local social service agencies.[61] In Los Angeles, the
social service agency was the Los Angeles County Department of Public
Social Services (DPSS). Members of the Samoan community told the
Advisory Committee that they feared this transfer of services from the
DPSS to the Social Security Administration would not resolve any of
their problems. Amani Magalei of the Oriental Service Center in Los
Angeles said:

For years DPSS, in its efforts to study and
understand the numerous problems related to
our Samoan clients, has not been able to
come up with a definite solution to cope with
our situation. The complexity of these
related problems is the result of poor communications due to language barriers and a
severe lack of understanding of our cultural
background. And most of all, [it] is the
absence of Samoan bilingual workers in the
DPSS who speak and understand both our
language and other culture....The Social
Security Administration offices...have no
Samoan staff and the misunderstandings will
occur again.

At the time this report was being prepared, the fears and
warnings of the Samoan community became a reality. Community
spokespersons notified Commission staff that the computers have

61. Social Security Amendments of 1972, Pub. L. 92-603, 86 Stat. 1329
(1972); 42 U.S.C. §401 et. seq. (Supp. 1974) amending 42 U.S.C. 401
et. seq. (1970).

incorrectly spelled many Samoan names on their social security checks. Community spokespersons said that their people were not able to cash their checks and that there was no attempt by Social Security Administration staff to explain and correct these errors for the non-English-speaking Asian Americans and Pacific Peoples.

Community witnesses felt that employment counseling and training programs for Samoan Americans were also badly needed. Loe Teo a member of the Samoan American Council of Southern California, talked about employment discrimination facing Samoan Americans. Mr. Teo explained that the major industry in Samoa is farming. Therefore, Samoans coming to the United States generally do not have any training or experience in industrial and other urban occupations available in Los Angeles. This lack of experience has led many to accept menial, low paying positions, he said.

Immigration

The community pointed out the need for Samoan bilingual workers at the INS and at ports of arrival. The Samoan community also questioned the denial of citizenship rights to trust territory residents of American Samoa, and cited this denial as an example of discrimination against them.

In Los Angeles, Lauvale Tialavea Morris, president of the Samoan American Council of Southern California, told the Advisory Committee about the services that the INS provided Samoan people. Mr. Morris said:

> Our Number One problem is petitions for travel visas. For example, in order for us to file a petition for student [visa]...or a permanent visa, we have to apply to the Office of the American Ambassador in Wellington, New Zealand. This means that often times our brothers and sisters from Western Samoa have to ask and sometimes beg the American Ambassador to share the yearly quota assigned to New Zealand with the people of Western Samoa.

Samoan Americans felt the issue of immigration could be easily helped by granting full citizenship rights to residents of American Samoa.

Youth

The testimony on Samoan youth problems focused on the inability of public schools to provide for the special needs of these students. Non-English-speaking Samoan students often receive academic instruction in a language they do not understand, witnesses said. Samoan American parents told of their confusion about the administrative structure of the public schools and the procedures to seek assistance. The families said that there were few Samoan American staff in educational institutions to aid them.

In Los Angeles, the Advisory Committee heard testimony from a Samoan youth panel. Mabel Tufele asserted that the Los Angeles Unified School District has been unable to provide for the special educational needs of the Samoan American student. Because of this, she claimed, the Samoan American student had the lowest level of achievement in education of any group. She stated:

> Samoan children in particular are being deprived of their right to an education by a system which was designed by and for middle-class whites. This system lacks the flexibility to adjust to groups which are alien because of economic conditions, language, color, cultural heritage, and outlook.

The community recommended that bilingual instruction and programming be implemented for their children.

RECOMMENDATIONS

Since Report I is a background report, the recommendations are general in nature.

Clearly, many Asian Americans and Pacific Peoples are invisible to the governmental agencies which are responsible for providing public services. Discrimination against Asian Americans and Pacific Peoples is as much the result of omission as commission. Until recently, many Asian Americans and Pacific Peoples were identified by some Federal agencies as members of the majority (white) population. The Equal Employment Opportunity Commission and the Office of Federal Contract Compliance, U.S. Department of Labor, have major responsibilities for monitoring and enforcing equal employment opportunity in both public and private business. Chinese, Japanese, and Pilipino employees, are identified on these agencies' compliance forms as minority groups to consider in affirmative action activities.

However, other Asian Americans and Pacific Peoples are not so identified; in some cases, they are designated as "white."[62] Guamanian and Samoan Americans face additional problems. First, their national origins are incorrectly identified, and second, they must convince government agencies of their minority status. Community spokespersons perceived that they were neglected by social service agencies and that their needs were overlooked. It is apparent that when people are not counted, they are not served.

---

62. Telephone conversation with Mr. Herbert Hammerman, Chief, Employment Survey, Office of Research, Equal Employment Opportunity Commission, Washington, D.C., Jan. 30, 1974. On file in the Western Regional Office, U.S. Commission on Civil Rights, are copies of Equal Employment Opportunity Commission reporting forms. Office of Federal Contract Compliance follows Equal Employment Opportunity Commission guidelines on racial/ethnic data collection.

Recommendations:

  1. <u>The California Advisory Committee recommends</u>
<u>that the U.S. Bureau of the Census immediately</u>
<u>take steps to conduct a special census of all</u>
<u>Asian Americans and Pacific Peoples.</u>

  Present methods to collect racial and ethnic data undercount
or omit specific Asian Americans and Pacific Peoples. The Advisory
Committee recommends that the Census Bureau reassess its data
collection methods on Asian Americans and Pacific Peoples and that
an Asian American Advisory Board be utilized to insure the effectiveness of the special census.

  2. <u>The Advisory Committee recommends that all</u>
<u>Federal agencies which develop and fund programs</u>
<u>in the social service areas immediately take</u>
<u>steps to develop adequate and accurate data</u>
<u>which measures the specific needs of all Asian</u>
<u>American and Pacific Peoples communities.</u>

  This recommendation is particularly directed towards Federal
agencies in Federal Region IX (Arizona, California, Guam, Hawaii,
and Nevada) which contains more than 50 percent of the total Asian
American and Pacific Peoples population. Similar undertakings by
Federal agencies in other Federal regions--particularly those which
cover New York, Alaska, Oregon, and Washington State--would ensure
an adequate and accurate count of Asian Americans and Pacific Peoples
nationwide.

  3. <u>The Advisory Committee recommends that all</u>
<u>California agencies with social service respon-</u>
<u>sibilities immediately reassess community needs</u>
<u>and determine the extent of underutilization</u>
<u>and underrepresentation of Asian Americans and</u>
<u>Pacific Peoples in their programs.</u>

  This assessment is essential in view of the large numbers of
Asian Americans and Pacific Peoples who are eligible but not receiving
social services from the State or are unfamiliar with social service
programs in their areas.

  4. <u>The Advisory Committee recommends that</u>
<u>all public social service agencies provide</u>
<u>bilingual Asian American and Pacific Peoples</u>
<u>outreach employees, as well as printed</u>
<u>material in Asian and Pacific languages.</u>

  In view of the increased migration from Asia and the Pacific in
recent years, the need for bilingual staff and materials is critical.
Bilingual staff and materials would assist Asian Americans and Pacific
Peoples in areas such as employment, housing, and education, and
enable the social service agencies to provide public services for
those in need.

Asian Americans and Pacific Peoples: A Case of Mistaken Identity. A Report of the California Advisory Committee to the United States Commission on Civil Rights, Washington, D.C. November 8, 1976.

Japanese, Chinese, and Filipinos in the United States

Japanese Population by Sex and Urban and Rural Residence: 1970

[Data based on 20-percent sample, see text. For meaning of symbols, see text]

United States Regions Divisions States	Total			Urban			Rural nonfarm			Rural farm		
	Total	Male	Female	Total	Male	Female	Total	Male	Female	Total	Male	Female
United States	588 324	271 453	316 871	524 196	241 434	282 762	50 561	23 052	27 509	13 567	6 967	6 600
REGIONS												
Northeast	39 125	17 221	21 904	35 215	15 734	19 481	3 716	1 383	2 333	194	104	90
North Central	42 670	18 082	24 588	38 410	16 630	21 780	3 266	899	2 367	994	553	441
South	28 504	9 809	18 695	24 460	8 588	15 872	3 712	1 091	2 621	332	130	202
West	478 025	226 341	251 684	426 111	200 482	225 629	39 867	19 679	20 188	12 047	6 180	5 867
NORTHEAST												
New England	7 570	3 082	4 488	6 472	2 620	3 852	1 086	456	630	12	6	6
Middle Atlantic	31 555	14 139	17 416	28 743	13 114	15 629	2 630	927	1 703	182	98	84
NORTH CENTRAL												
East North Central	33 554	14 543	19 011	30 833	13 721	17 112	2 284	582	1 702	437	240	197
West North Central	9 116	3 539	5 577	7 577	2 909	4 668	982	317	665	557	313	244
SOUTH												
South Atlantic	16 412	5 517	10 895	13 976	4 844	9 132	2 288	622	1 666	148	51	97
East South Central	3 198	1 161	2 037	2 485	927	1 558	676	222	454	37	12	25
West South Central	8 894	3 131	5 763	7 999	2 817	5 182	748	247	501	147	67	80
WEST												
Mountain	20 318	9 330	10 988	16 482	7 466	9 016	2 027	912	1 115	1 809	952	857
Pacific	457 707	217 011	240 696	409 629	193 016	216 613	37 840	18 767	19 073	10 238	5 228	5 010
NEW ENGLAND												
Maine	215	98	117	165	68	97	50	30	20	–	–	–
New Hampshire	252	84	168	131	30	101	121	54	67	–	–	–
Vermont	73	27	46	9	5	4	64	22	42	–	–	–
Massachusetts	4 715	1 919	2 796	4 313	1 753	2 560	402	166	236	–	–	–
Rhode Island	744	260	484	632	201	431	112	59	53	–	–	–
Connecticut	1 571	694	877	1 222	563	659	337	125	212	12	6	6
MIDDLE ATLANTIC												
New York	19 794	9 439	10 355	18 954	9 171	9 783	794	250	544	46	18	28
New Jersey	6 344	2 582	3 762	5 371	2 221	3 150	946	344	602	27	17	10
Pennsylvania	5 417	2 118	3 299	4 418	1 722	2 696	890	333	557	109	63	46
EAST NORTH CENTRAL												
Ohio	5 896	2 105	3 791	5 370	1 960	3 410	480	125	355	46	20	26
Indiana	2 100	806	1 294	1 626	668	958	392	108	284	82	30	52
Illinois	17 645	8 371	9 274	17 041	8 172	8 869	527	140	387	77	59	18
Michigan	5 464	2 263	3 201	4 722	2 011	2 711	602	156	446	140	96	44
Wisconsin	2 449	998	1 451	2 074	910	1 164	283	53	230	92	35	57
WEST NORTH CENTRAL												
Minnesota	2 693	1 180	1 513	2 430	1 076	1 354	199	84	115	64	20	44
Iowa	773	324	449	569	239	330	156	54	102	48	31	17
Missouri	2 320	784	1 536	2 101	756	1 345	190	24	166	29	4	25
North Dakota	312	127	185	228	82	146	53	18	35	31	27	4
South Dakota	199	82	117	137	44	93	15	11	4	47	27	20
Nebraska	1 253	547	706	875	332	543	76	25	51	302	190	112
Kansas	1 566	495	1 071	1 237	380	857	293	101	192	36	14	22
SOUTH ATLANTIC												
Delaware	432	168	264	293	126	167	135	42	93	4	–	4
Maryland	3 637	1 321	2 316	3 253	1 182	2 071	352	122	230	32	17	15
District of Columbia	716	290	426	716	290	426	–	–	–	–	–	–
Virginia	3 296	1 073	2 223	2 866	931	1 935	375	132	243	55	10	45
West Virginia	266	80	186	143	68	75	123	12	111	–	–	–
North Carolina	2 088	642	1 446	1 494	517	977	561	105	456	33	20	13
South Carolina	675	219	456	487	152	335	188	67	121	–	–	–
Georgia	1 334	493	841	1 181	458	723	149	35	114	4	–	4
Florida	3 968	1 231	2 737	3 543	1 120	2 423	405	107	298	20	4	16
EAST SOUTH CENTRAL												
Kentucky	920	340	580	660	243	417	243	92	151	17	5	12
Tennessee	857	275	582	733	236	497	118	39	79	6	–	6
Alabama	1 043	386	657	850	327	523	179	52	127	14	7	7
Mississippi	378	160	218	242	121	121	136	39	97	–	–	–
WEST SOUTH CENTRAL												
Arkansas	588	252	336	443	177	266	131	65	66	14	10	4
Louisiana	876	282	594	748	258	490	113	24	89	15	–	15
Oklahoma	1 214	319	895	1 038	278	760	140	31	109	36	10	26
Texas	6 216	2 278	3 938	5 770	2 104	3 666	364	127	237	82	47	35
MOUNTAIN												
Montana	613	262	351	451	192	259	117	49	68	45	21	24
Idaho	2 012	1 009	1 003	940	483	457	374	182	192	698	344	354
Wyoming	457	189	268	311	131	180	76	25	51	70	33	37
Colorado	7 861	3 642	4 219	6 641	3 017	3 624	620	288	332	600	337	263
New Mexico	937	377	560	845	322	523	74	44	30	18	11	7
Arizona	2 530	1 025	1 505	2 204	886	1 318	238	95	143	88	44	44
Utah	4 862	2 368	2 494	4 159	2 016	2 143	434	206	228	269	146	123
Nevada	1 046	458	588	931	419	512	94	23	71	21	16	5
PACIFIC												
Washington	20 188	8 973	11 215	18 277	8 097	10 180	1 483	656	827	428	220	208
Oregon	6 213	2 752	3 461	4 857	2 160	2 697	580	195	385	776	397	379
California	213 277	100 204	113 073	199 726	93 403	106 323	7 485	3 754	3 731	6 066	3 047	3 019
Alaska	854	336	518	558	201	357	291	130	161	5	5	–
Hawaii	217 175	104 746	112 429	186 211	89 155	97 056	28 001	14 032	13 969	2 963	1 559	1 404

Social Characteristics of the Japanese Population by Urban and Rural Residence: 1970

[Data based on sample, see text. For minimum base for derived figures (percent, median, etc.) and meaning of symbols, see text]

United States Regions States With 10,000 or More Japanese Population	United States				Northeast			
	Total	Urban	Rural nonfarm	Rural farm	Total	Urban	Rural nonfarm	Rural farm
RELATIONSHIP TO HEAD OF HOUSEHOLD								
Total population	588 324	524 196	50 561	13 567	39 125	35 215	3 716	194
Under 18 years old	170 036	151 121	14 574	4 341	9 027	8 082	904	41
Living with both parents	151 855	135 271	12 527	4 057	8 013	7 251	721	41
Percent of all under 18 years	89.3	89.5	86.0	93.5	88.8	89.7	79.8	...
Head of household	168 576	151 554	13 521	3 501	13 153	12 290	808	55
Head of family	133 927	119 234	11 396	3 297	8 657	7 972	636	49
Female head	13 827	12 437	1 248	142	881	815	66	–
Primary individual	34 649	32 320	2 125	204	4 496	4 318	172	6
Female primary individual	17 904	16 603	1 183	118	2 296	2 199	97	–
Wife of head	151 651	134 077	14 432	3 142	11 704	10 145	1 495	64
Other relative of head	241 563	214 587	20 288	6 688	11 578	10 352	1 151	75
Nonrelative of head	12 836	12 028	628	180	1 678	1 589	89	–
In group quarters	13 698	11 950	1 692	56	1 012	839	173	–
Inmate of institution	2 289	1 483	806	–	98	50	48	–
Other	11 409	10 467	886	56	914	789	125	–
FAMILIES BY PRESENCE OF CHILDREN								
Total families	133 927	119 234	11 396	3 297	8 657	7 972	636	49
With own children under 18 years	78 634	70 850	6 039	1 745	4 558	4 225	311	22
With own children under 6 years	32 997	30 274	2 292	431	2 712	2 562	145	5
Husband–wife families	114 611	101 984	9 657	2 970	7 505	6 903	553	49
With own children under 18 years	69 614	62 817	5 126	1 671	4 008	3 730	256	22
With own children under 6 years	30 557	28 129	2 003	425	2 574	2 453	116	5
Families with female head	13 827	12 437	1 248	142	881	815	66	–
With own children under 18 years	7 749	6 921	778	50	500	450	50	–
With own children under 6 years	2 136	1 868	262	6	126	97	29	–
CHILDREN EVER BORN								
Women ever married, 15 to 24 years old	9 858	9 000	777	81	633	559	74	–
Children per 1,000 women ever married	759	737	997	...	596	569	...	–
Women ever married, 25 to 34 years old	38 726	35 459	2 916	351	3 860	3 481	366	13
Children per 1,000 women ever married	1 656	1 633	1 873	2 097	1 392	1 372	1 571	...
Women ever married, 35 to 44 years old	63 175	56 033	6 122	1 020	4 957	4 231	720	6
Children per 1,000 women ever married	2 301	2 264	2 520	3 045	2 043	1 975	2 428	...
PLACE OF BIRTH								
Total population	586 675	523 485	49 979	13 211	39 035	35 210	3 625	200
Foreign born	122 500	109 659	10 792	2 049	19 134	17 700	1 408	26
Native	464 175	413 826	39 187	11 162	19 901	17 510	2 217	174
Born in State of residence	342 925	302 064	31 492	9 369	9 873	8 564	1 216	93
Born in different State	83 228	77 673	4 274	1 281	6 294	5 524	709	61
Northeast	4 363	4 032	304	27	1 423	1 250	166	7
North Central	9 359	8 683	574	102	603	560	43	–
South	6 143	5 525	492	126	483	409	74	–
West	63 363	59 433	2 904	1 026	3 785	3 305	426	54
Born abroad, at sea, etc	14 938	13 799	989	150	1 160	1 032	122	6
State of birth not reported	23 084	20 290	2 432	362	2 574	2 390	170	14
SCHOOL ENROLLMENT								
Total enrolled, 3 to 34 years old	172 711	155 592	12 860	4 259	7 887	7 008	847	32
Nursery school	5 765	5 403	317	45	552	514	38	–
Public	1 624	1 472	128	24	84	73	11	–
Kindergarten	8 462	7 644	655	163	520	481	39	–
Public	7 518	6 756	609	153	473	441	32	–
Elementary (1 to 8 years)	78 028	69 720	6 308	2 000	3 543	3 025	494	24
Public	72 939	64 836	6 125	1 978	3 290	2 792	480	18
High school (1 to 4 years)	42 127	36 696	3 946	1 485	1 399	1 221	170	8
Public	39 750	34 445	3 829	1 476	1 249	1 077	164	8
College	38 329	36 129	1 634	566	1 873	1 767	106	–
Percent enrolled, 3 to 34 years old	58.8	58.3	59.6	74.2	42.8	41.9	51.6	...
3 and 4 years old	31.4	32.2	25.7	12.4	35.4	36.0	...	...
5 and 6 years old	86.5	86.9	82.6	82.2	77.7	76.6	86.0	...
7 to 13 years old	97.5	97.6	97.1	98.1	96.7	96.5	97.7	...
14 to 17 years old: Male	96.3	96.7	93.4	95.3	92.1	90.8	...	–
Female	96.2	96.3	95.2	98.1	93.4	93.1	95.2	–
18 to 24 years old: Male	55.6	56.6	40.7	61.1	48.4	49.2	40.3	...
Female	48.4	49.0	33.8	63.1	31.3	32.7	19.0	–
25 to 34 years old	9.8	10.1	6.5	5.2	10.0	10.0	9.3	–
YEARS OF SCHOOL COMPLETED								
Total, 25 years old and over	353 707	313 611	31 986	8 110	27 090	24 426	2 521	143
No school years completed	6 465	5 136	1 098	231	374	346	28	–
Elementary: 1 to 4 years	8 361	6 718	1 361	282	496	450	43	3
5 to 7 years	22 340	18 351	3 205	784	1 702	1 537	165	–
8 years	29 970	24 225	4 658	1 087	2 156	1 775	330	51
High school: 1 to 3 years	43 301	37 557	4 760	984	3 601	3 156	424	21
4 years	138 946	123 879	11 421	3 646	7 654	6 674	912	68
College: 1 to 3 years	48 001	44 322	2 952	727	3 131	2 894	237	–
4 years or more	56 323	53 423	2 531	369	7 976	7 594	382	–
Median school years completed	12.5	12.5	12.1	12.2	12.7	12.7	12.3	11.5
Percent high school graduates	68.8	70.7	52.8	58.5	69.3	70.3	60.7	47.6

Social Characteristics of the Japanese Population by Urban and Rural Residence: 1970—Continued

[Data based on sample, see text. For minimum base for derived figures (percent, median, etc.) and meaning of symbols, see text]

United States Regions States With 10,000 or More Japanese Population	North Central				South			
	Total	Urban	Rural nonfarm	Rural farm	Total	Urban	Rural nonfarm	Rural farm
RELATIONSHIP TO HEAD OF HOUSEHOLD								
Total population	**42 670**	**38 410**	**3 266**	**994**	**28 504**	**24 460**	**3 712**	**332**
Under 18 years old	11 156	10 086	792	278	6 027	5 125	830	72
Living with both parents	9 774	8 916	613	245	4 798	4 119	623	56
Percent of all under 18 years	87.6	88.4	77.4	88.1	79.6	80.4	75.1	...
Head of household	11 940	11 062	653	225	7 379	6 480	817	82
Head of family	8 632	7 928	504	200	5 034	4 395	566	73
Female head	1 055	863	172	20	1 300	1 093	196	11
Primary individual	3 308	3 134	149	25	2 345	2 085	251	9
Female primary individual	1 800	1 685	104	11	1 456	1 307	140	9
Wife of head	13 163	11 506	1 424	233	11 453	9 581	1 754	118
Other relative of head	14 736	13 306	1 021	409	7 403	6 323	955	125
Nonrelative of head	1 323	1 152	44	127	698	611	80	7
In group quarters	1 508	1 384	124	–	1 571	1 465	106	–
Inmate of institution	118	84	34	–	82	48	34	–
Other	1 390	1 300	90	–	1 489	1 417	72	–
FAMILIES BY PRESENCE OF CHILDREN								
Total families	**8 632**	**7 928**	**504**	**200**	**5 034**	**4 395**	**566**	**73**
With own children under 18 years	4 847	4 423	311	113	3 018	2 655	337	26
With own children under 6 years	2 220	2 076	119	25	1 432	1 249	172	11
Husband-wife families	**7 209**	**6 747**	**319**	**143**	**3 609**	**3 177**	**370**	**62**
With own children under 18 years	4 125	3 857	170	98	1 938	1 737	175	26
With own children under 6 years	2 010	1 922	63	25	1 088	973	104	11
Families with female head	**1 055**	**863**	**172**	**20**	**1 300**	**1 093**	**196**	**11**
With own children under 18 years	598	461	133	4	1 029	867	162	–
With own children under 6 years	167	114	53	–	319	251	68	–
CHILDREN EVER BORN								
Women ever married, 15 to 24 years old	812	697	115	–	796	659	132	5
Children per 1,000 women ever married	825	805	948	–	726	634	1 212	–
Women ever married, 25 to 34 years old	3 290	2 935	314	41	3 249	2 770	443	36
Children per 1,000 women ever married	1 640	1 610	1 869	...	1 671	1 636	1 797	...
Women ever married, 35 to 44 years old	6 116	5 095	910	111	6 923	5 752	1 126	45
Children per 1,000 women ever married	2 294	2 225	2 491	3 838	2 164	2 165	2 131	...
PLACE OF BIRTH								
Total population	**42 492**	**38 420**	**3 055**	**1 017**	**28 350**	**24 395**	**3 644**	**311**
Foreign born	13 467	12 066	1 155	246	12 783	10 931	1 803	49
Native	29 025	26 354	1 900	771	15 567	13 464	1 841	262
Born in State of residence	13 895	12 508	856	531	4 798	3 806	859	133
Born in different State	11 997	11 167	668	162	7 406	6 715	597	94
Northeast	519	495	18	6	886	836	36	14
North Central	1 497	1 265	157	75	758	670	75	13
South	979	851	95	33	1 522	1 278	198	46
West	9 002	8 556	398	48	4 240	3 931	288	21
Born abroad, at sea, etc	1 128	946	175	7	1 948	1 652	261	35
State of birth not reported	2 005	1 733	201	71	1 415	1 291	124	–
SCHOOL ENROLLMENT								
Total enrolled, 3 to 34 years old	**11 389**	**10 342**	**808**	**239**	**5 695**	**4 929**	**667**	**99**
Nursery school	297	277	20	–	151	145	6	–
Public	94	74	20	–	16	10	6	–
Kindergarten	524	444	72	8	328	296	32	–
Public	481	401	72	8	216	192	24	–
Elementary (1 to 8 years)	5 093	4 596	348	149	2 876	2 407	432	37
Public	4 657	4 179	329	149	2 726	2 301	388	37
High school (1 to 4 years)	2 542	2 269	219	54	1 057	901	106	50
Public	2 386	2 113	219	54	989	839	100	50
College	2 933	2 756	149	28	1 283	1 180	91	12
Percent enrolled, 3 to 34 years old	**56.9**	**57.4**	**54.2**	**48.1**	**43.5**	**43.4**	**43.1**	**59.6**
3 and 4 years old	22.6	22.9	...	–	26.8	30.3	...	...
5 and 6 years old	81.3	81.0	...	...	75.5	77.5	64.5	...
7 to 13 years old	98.3	98.5	97.5	96.1	95.7	95.2	98.3	...
14 to 17 years old: Male	96.0	96.0	...	...	90.5	89.7	92.4	...
Female	95.5	96.2	92.6	...	93.9	94.1	...	...
18 to 24 years old: Male	57.7	60.5	54.9	12.5	37.3	36.9	36.4	...
Female	45.2	46.7	26.4	...	32.7	34.3	16.6	...
25 to 34 years old	12.4	12.7	10.6	–	8.0	8.2	6.7	...
YEARS OF SCHOOL COMPLETED								
Total, 25 years old and over	**26 780**	**24 066**	**2 145**	**569**	**19 329**	**16 478**	**2 630**	**221**
No school years completed	148	132	13	3	165	139	18	8
Elementary: 1 to 4 years	433	382	47	4	427	349	72	6
5 to 7 years	1 151	1 003	113	35	1 227	985	230	12
8 years	2 188	1 877	202	109	1 383	1 128	240	15
High school: 1 to 3 years	3 621	3 107	452	62	3 318	2 746	495	77
4 years	9 925	8 735	920	270	7 307	6 211	1 018	78
College: 1 to 3 years	3 674	3 402	225	47	2 246	1 911	324	11
4 years or more	5 640	5 428	173	39	3 256	3 009	233	14
Median school years completed	12.6	12.6	12.3	12.3	12.4	12.5	12.3	11.7
Percent high school graduates	71.8	73.0	61.4	62.6	66.3	67.6	59.9	46.6

Social Characteristics of the Japanese Population by Urban and Rural Residence: 1970—Continued

[Data based on sample, see text. For minimum base for derived figures (percent, median, etc.) and meaning of symbols, see text]

United States Regions States With 10,000 or More Japanese Population	West				California			Hawaii		
	Total	Urban	Rural nonfarm	Rural farm	Total	Urban	Rural	Total	Urban	Rural
RELATIONSHIP TO HEAD OF HOUSEHOLD										
Total population	478 025	426 111	39 867	12 047	213 277	199 726	13 551	217 175	186 211	30 964
Under 18 years old	143 826	127 828	12 048	3 950	63 334	59 369	3 965	67 084	57 665	9 419
Living with both parents	129 270	114 985	10 570	3 715	57 546	54 002	3 544	60 150	51 691	8 459
Percent of all under 18 years	89.9	90.0	87.7	94.1	90.9	91.0	89.4	89.7	89.6	89.8
Head of household	136 104	121 722	11 243	3 139	63 504	59 860	3 644	59 335	50 445	8 890
Head of family	111 604	98 939	9 690	2 975	49 251	46 070	3 181	52 165	44 238	7 927
Female head	10 591	9 666	814	111	4 882	4 674	208	4 426	3 845	581
Primary individual	24 500	22 783	1 553	164	14 253	13 790	463	7 170	6 207	963
Female primary individual	12 352	11 412	842	98	7 023	6 757	266	3 741	3 213	528
Wife of head	115 331	102 845	9 759	2 727	53 742	50 441	3 301	48 766	41 614	7 152
Other relative of head	207 846	184 606	17 161	6 079	87 070	81 224	5 846	102 954	88 784	14 170
Nonrelative of head	9 137	8 676	415	46	4 972	4 827	145	2 975	2 803	172
In group quarters	9 607	8 262	1 289	56	3 989	3 374	615	3 145	2 565	580
Inmate of institution	1 991	1 301	690	–	579	482	97	1 138	601	537
Other	7 616	6 961	599	56	3 410	2 892	518	2 007	1 964	43
FAMILIES BY PRESENCE OF CHILDREN										
Total families	111 604	98 939	9 690	2 975	49 251	46 070	3 181	52 165	44 238	7 927
With own children under 18 years	66 211	59 547	5 080	1 584	30 066	28 298	1 768	30 066	26 160	3 906
With own children under 6 years	26 633	24 387	1 856	390	12 729	12 154	575	11 790	10 413	1 377
Husband–wife families	96 288	85 157	8 415	2 716	42 439	39 644	2 795	45 337	38 374	6 963
With own children under 18 years	59 543	53 493	4 525	1 525	26 835	25 240	1 595	27 536	23 954	3 582
With own children under 6 years	24 885	22 781	1 720	384	11 745	11 234	511	11 251	9 924	1 327
Families with female head	10 591	9 666	814	111	4 882	4 674	208	4 426	3 845	581
With own children under 18 years	5 622	5 143	433	46	2 835	2 703	132	1 954	1 703	251
With own children under 6 years	1 524	1 406	112	6	884	831	53	421	384	37
CHILDREN EVER BORN										
Women ever married, 15 to 24 years old	7 617	7 085	456	76	3 168	3 052	116	3 425	3 140	285
Children per 1,000 women ever married	769	754	980	...	633	621	940	911	897	1 070
Women ever married, 25 to 34 years old	28 327	26 273	1 793	261	14 692	14 219	473	10 795	9 616	1 179
Children per 1,000 women ever married	1 691	1 670	1 954	2 031	1 573	1 568	1 732	1 850	1 817	2 120
Women ever married, 35 to 44 years old	45 179	40 955	3 366	858	22 567	21 270	1 297	16 786	14 731	2 055
Children per 1,000 women ever married	2 352	2 312	2 677	2 946	2 195	2 181	2 417	2 584	2 530	2 968
PLACE OF BIRTH										
Total population	476 798	425 460	39 655	11 683	212 121	198 770	13 351	217 669	186 802	30 867
Foreign born	77 116	68 962	6 426	1 728	44 683	41 962	2 721	20 821	16 923	3 898
Native	399 682	356 498	33 229	9 955	167 438	156 808	10 630	196 848	169 879	26 969
Born in State of residence	314 359	277 186	28 561	8 612	113 199	104 454	8 745	180 641	155 713	24 928
Born in different State	57 531	54 267	2 300	964	41 687	40 484	1 203	4 087	3 782	305
Northeast	1 535	1 451	84	–	1 187	1 115	72	173	168	5
North Central	6 501	6 188	299	14	4 323	4 239	84	800	720	80
South	3 159	2 987	125	47	2 076	1 981	95	651	614	37
West	46 336	43 641	1 792	903	34 101	33 149	952	2 463	2 280	183
Born abroad, at sea, etc	10 702	10 169	431	102	6 435	6 227	208	2 660	2 535	125
State of birth not reported	17 090	14 876	1 937	277	6 117	5 643	474	9 460	7 849	1 611
SCHOOL ENROLLMENT										
Total enrolled, 3 to 34 years old	147 740	133 313	10 538	3 889	67 052	62 966	4 086	65 590	57 569	8 021
Nursery school	4 765	4 467	253	45	2 040	1 996	44	2 380	2 173	207
Public	1 430	1 315	91	24	784	760	24	546	476	70
Kindergarten	7 090	6 423	512	155	3 368	3 199	169	3 224	2 802	422
Public	6 348	5 722	481	145	3 064	2 895	169	2 880	2 488	392
Elementary (1 to 8 years)	66 516	59 692	5 034	1 790	29 397	27 736	1 661	30 772	26 814	3 958
Public	62 266	55 564	4 928	1 774	27 713	26 059	1 654	28 366	24 505	3 861
High school (1 to 4 years)	37 129	32 305	3 451	1 373	15 485	14 200	1 285	18 133	15 340	2 793
Public	35 126	30 416	3 346	1 364	14 983	13 705	1 278	16 690	13 998	2 692
College	32 240	30 426	1 288	526	16 762	15 835	927	11 081	10 440	641
Percent enrolled, 3 to 34 years old	60.9	60.4	62.3	77.4	60.8	60.3	70.5	60.3	60.0	63.1
3 and 4 years old	31.9	32.6	27.0	14.9	29.2	30.0	11.2	34.8	35.7	28.5
5 and 6 years old	88.1	88.6	83.5	83.2	87.5	87.5	88.5	90.8	91.4	87.1
7 to 13 years old	97.6	97.6	96.9	98.2	98.0	98.1	96.5	97.1	97.2	97.1
14 to 17 years old: Male	96.7	97.2	92.8	95.7	97.5	98.0	92.5	95.8	96.3	93.3
Female	96.5	96.5	95.5	98.7	97.6	97.6	96.3	95.8	95.6	96.7
18 to 24 years old: Male	57.0	57.9	40.1	70.6	64.4	64.5	62.9	46.7	48.1	34.0
Female	50.4	50.8	38.5	63.9	53.4	52.7	68.2	45.9	47.1	31.0
25 to 34 years old	9.7	10.0	5.6	5.8	12.2	12.2	11.9	5.9	6.3	3.1
YEARS OF SCHOOL COMPLETED										
Total, 25 years old and over	280 508	248 641	24 690	7 177	126 373	118 209	8 164	126 586	107 044	19 542
No school years completed	5 778	4 519	1 039	220	2 317	2 126	191	3 023	2 026	997
Elementary: 1 to 4 years	7 005	5 537	1 199	269	1 530	1 360	170	5 131	3 877	1 254
5 to 7 years	18 260	14 826	2 697	737	5 351	4 827	524	11 787	9 059	2 728
8 years	24 243	19 445	3 886	912	7 865	6 985	880	14 427	10 865	3 562
High school: 1 to 3 years	32 761	28 548	3 389	824	13 582	12 599	983	15 941	13 178	2 763
4 years	114 060	102 259	8 571	3 230	50 885	47 168	3 717	50 979	44 954	6 025
College: 1 to 3 years	38 950	36 115	2 166	669	23 548	22 464	1 084	11 591	10 400	1 191
4 years or more	39 451	37 392	1 743	316	21 295	20 680	615	13 707	12 685	1 022
Median school years completed	12.5	12.5	12.0	12.2	12.6	12.7	12.4	12.3	12.3	10.3
Percent high school graduates	68.6	70.7	50.5	58.7	75.8	76.4	66.3	60.3	63.6	42.2

Social Characteristics of the Japanese Population by Urban and Rural Residence: 1970—Continued

[Data based on sample, see text. For minimum base for derived figures (percent, median, etc.) and meaning of symbols, see text]

United States Regions States With 10,000 or More Japanese Population	Illinois			New York			Washington		
	Total	Urban	Rural	Total	Urban	Rural	Total	Urban	Rural
RELATIONSHIP TO HEAD OF HOUSEHOLD									
Total population	**17 645**	**17 041**	**604**	**19 794**	**18 954**	**840**	**20 188**	**18 277**	**1 911**
Under 18 years old	4 890	4 717	173	4 667	4 545	122	5 793	5 045	748
Living with both parents	4 510	4 355	155	4 270	4 184	86	5 102	4 470	632
Percent of all under 18 years	92.2	92.3	89.6	91.5	92.1	70.5	88.1	88.6	84.5
Head of household	5 395	5 302	93	7 222	7 070	152	5 754	5 318	436
Head of family	3 989	3 901	88	4 690	4 581	109	4 429	4 069	360
Female head	351	334	17	358	338	20	554	515	39
Primary individual	1 406	1 401	5	2 532	2 489	43	1 325	1 249	76
Female primary individual	593	593	–	1 137	1 126	11	730	699	31
Wife of head	4 781	4 512	269	5 373	4 956	417	5 423	4 881	542
Other relative of head	6 545	6 342	203	5 751	5 575	176	7 712	6 882	830
Nonrelative of head	445	414	31	1 067	1 021	46	414	336	78
In group quarters	479	471	8	381	332	49	885	860	25
Inmate of institution	30	30	–	50	40	10	113	100	13
Other	449	441	8	331	292	39	772	760	12
FAMILIES BY PRESENCE OF CHILDREN									
Total families	**3 989**	**3 901**	**88**	**4 690**	**4 581**	**109**	**4 429**	**4 069**	**360**
With own children under 18 years	2 321	2 276	45	2 615	2 562	53	2 608	2 373	235
With own children under 6 years	978	954	24	1 695	1 666	29	909	832	77
Husband–wife families	**3 467**	**3 396**	**71**	**4 163**	**4 080**	**83**	**3 684**	**3 380**	**304**
With own children under 18 years	2 111	2 076	35	2 415	2 376	39	2 213	2 020	193
With own children under 6 years	921	897	24	1 661	1 641	20	808	743	65
Families with female head	**351**	**334**	**17**	**358**	**338**	**20**	**554**	**515**	**39**
With own children under 18 years	159	149	10	169	155	14	369	339	30
With own children under 6 years	38	38	–	22	13	9	101	89	12
CHILDREN EVER BORN									
Women ever married, 15 to 24 years old	315	283	32	251	236	15	398	371	27
Children per 1,000 women ever married	756	707	...	478	445	...	636	633	...
Women ever married, 25 to 34 years old	1 079	1 036	43	2 121	2 010	111	1 154	1 015	139
Children per 1,000 women ever married	1 577	1 569	...	1 292	1 279	1 532	1 784	1 757	1 986
Women ever married, 35 to 44 years old	1 991	1 808	183	2 012	1 816	196	2 434	2 203	231
Children per 1,000 women ever married	2 093	2 046	2 563	1 876	1 782	2 745	2 234	2 210	2 463
PLACE OF BIRTH									
Total population	**17 463**	**16 930**	**533**	**19 805**	**19 042**	**763**	**20 244**	**18 400**	**1 844**
Foreign born	4 856	4 638	218	11 254	10 897	357	5 338	4 887	451
Native	12 607	12 292	315	8 551	8 145	406	14 906	13 513	1 393
Born in State of residence	5 931	5 730	201	4 185	3 969	216	9 662	8 762	900
Born in different State	5 603	5 527	76	2 556	2 454	102	3 849	3 436	413
Northeast	50	50	–	348	322	26	49	42	7
North Central	363	346	17	219	197	22	469	427	42
South	240	240	–	205	191	14	157	130	27
West	4 950	4 891	59	1 784	1 744	40	3 174	2 837	337
Born abroad, at sea, etc	304	288	16	495	461	34	810	761	49
State of birth not reported	769	747	22	1 315	1 261	54	585	554	31
SCHOOL ENROLLMENT									
Total enrolled, 3 to 34 years old	**4 878**	**4 757**	**121**	**3 843**	**3 741**	**102**	**6 513**	**5 876**	**637**
Nursery school	114	100	14	330	330	–	205	177	28
Public	54	40	14	53	53	–	66	58	8
Kindergarten	266	249	17	302	289	13	246	212	34
Public	237	220	17	275	262	13	231	197	34
Elementary (1 to 8 years)	2 207	2 152	55	1 576	1 546	30	2 893	2 509	384
Public	1 983	1 936	47	1 480	1 450	30	2 786	2 420	366
High school (1 to 4 years)	1 157	1 130	27	638	621	17	1 543	1 386	157
Public	1 060	1 033	27	525	508	17	1 505	1 354	151
College	1 134	1 126	8	997	955	42	1 626	1 592	34
Percent enrolled, 3 to 34 years old	**59.3**	**59.7**	**49.3**	**38.1**	**38.0**	**40.2**	**64.9**	**64.7**	**66.6**
3 and 4 years old	25.7	23.8	...	41.5	42.0	–	36.9	37.0	...
5 and 6 years old	84.6	84.5	...	78.5	77.8	...	79.0	82.0	...
7 to 13 years old	98.5	98.5	...	94.8	94.7	...	97.9	97.5	100.0
14 to 17 years old: Male	94.9	95.7	...	89.7	89.1	...	97.9	97.6	...
Female	96.1	96.0	...	93.1	94.5	...	95.1	94.4	...
18 to 24 years old: Male	57.9	58.6	...	46.7	46.2	...	62.9	65.1	...
Female	37.8	39.4	–	33.1	32.5	...	55.2	56.7	...
25 to 34 years old	11.5	11.6	...	8.0	7.9	10.4	13.0	13.6	6.6
YEARS OF SCHOOL COMPLETED									
Total, 25 years old and over	**10 887**	**10 512**	**375**	**13 707**	**13 061**	**646**	**11 807**	**10 793**	**1 014**
No school years completed	58	55	3	204	198	6	152	148	4
Elementary: 1 to 4 years	185	164	21	195	183	12	103	101	2
5 to 7 years	313	300	13	717	704	13	488	447	41
8 years	717	669	48	850	756	94	901	820	81
High school: 1 to 3 years	1 175	1 127	48	1 415	1 273	142	1 317	1 203	114
4 years	4 250	4 090	160	3 633	3 430	203	5 217	4 745	472
College: 1 to 3 years	1 801	1 748	53	1 783	1 719	64	1 527	1 378	149
4 years or more	2 388	2 359	29	4 910	4 798	112	2 102	1 951	151
Median school years completed	12.7	12.7	12.3	13.0	13.0	12.3	12.6	12.6	12.6
Percent high school graduates	77.5	78.0	64.5	75.3	76.2	58.7	74.9	74.8	76.1

Age, Marital Status, Education, and Industry of the Japanese Population for Selected Standard Metropolitan Statistical Areas and Cities: 1970

[Data based on 20-percent sample, see text. For meaning of symbols, see text]

Standard Metropolitan Statistical Areas With 5,000 or More Japanese Population Cities With 5,000 or More Japanese Population	Standard metropolitan statistical areas									
	Anaheim— Santa Ana— Garden Grove, Calif.	Chicago, Ill.	Denver, Colo.	Fresno, Calif.	Honolulu, Hawaii	Los Angeles— Long Beach, Calif.	New York, N.Y.	Sacramento, Calif.	San Diego, Calif.	San Francisco— Oakland, Calif.
AGE										
Male, all ages	4 952	7 680	2 650	2 920	80 760	50 856	8 187	5 621	2 849	15 158
Under 5 years	500	503	165	146	5 816	3 709	936	300	232	1 098
5 to 9 years	701	784	219	253	7 237	4 630	633	466	365	1 145
10 to 14 years	576	629	332	376	8 145	4 916	311	524	354	1 348
15 to 19 years	444	694	289	342	7 761	4 369	301	692	282	1 414
20 to 24 years	316	553	134	226	6 647	3 894	390	426	336	1 294
25 to 29 years	219	472	136	112	5 958	3 931	886	309	144	1 211
30 to 34 years	383	351	136	81	4 659	3 603	1 195	273	119	966
35 to 39 years	452	530	163	127	5 087	3 761	983	330	189	1 085
40 to 44 years	396	669	218	192	6 137	4 474	609	434	218	1 274
45 to 49 years	372	851	305	219	6 547	4 295	456	529	153	1 319
50 to 54 years	244	573	191	315	5 666	3 185	295	477	172	1 066
55 to 59 years	107	416	109	133	3 678	1 786	247	231	54	487
60 to 64 years	36	172	40	92	2 318	1 067	228	106	70	278
65 to 69 years	88	149	68	108	1 868	1 069	220	206	31	404
70 to 74 years	53	103	78	66	1 325	802	212	109	33	290
75 years and over	65	231	67	132	1 911	1 365	285	209	97	479
Female, all ages	5 764	8 052	2 985	2 720	88 265	54 138	8 443	6 337	4 772	18 429
Under 5 years	462	447	181	107	5 853	3 616	879	298	197	1 084
5 to 9 years	585	553	180	201	7 116	4 355	473	558	397	1 193
10 to 14 years	578	687	311	260	8 046	4 604	346	600	350	1 250
15 to 19 years	360	616	279	196	8 230	4 495	264	539	251	1 251
20 to 24 years	344	521	225	279	7 862	4 399	495	434	274	1 556
25 to 29 years	431	461	180	100	5 996	4 239	1 095	352	330	1 515
30 to 34 years	597	540	198	195	5 094	4 041	1 026	393	589	1 482
35 to 39 years	737	753	272	213	6 538	4 792	918	601	990	1 853
40 to 44 years	762	905	322	218	7 995	5 185	725	701	610	2 379
45 to 49 years	346	896	318	329	7 399	4 723	457	590	331	1 603
50 to 54 years	162	482	168	171	5 763	2 866	402	424	103	934
55 to 59 years	70	323	71	91	3 479	1 566	245	182	67	600
60 to 64 years	51	188	28	32	2 381	1 065	218	116	59	365
65 to 69 years	67	171	78	104	2 156	1 341	264	161	59	425
70 to 74 years	80	269	86	89	1 744	1 228	264	142	76	422
75 years and over	132	240	88	135	2 613	1 623	372	246	89	517
MARITAL STATUS										
Male, 14 years old and over	3 306	5 898	2 016	2 241	61 370	38 689	6 366	4 447	1 977	11 821
Single	1 066	2 095	629	844	21 327	13 864	1 909	1 668	861	4 419
Married, wife present	2 050	3 353	1 181	1 243	36 266	22 368	3 729	2 552	1 001	6 586
With spouse of same race	1 799	2 818	966	1 169	33 500	20 654	3 145	2 321	838	5 817
Separated	36	45	15	7	208	275	88	14	12	88
Other married, wife absent	47	77	53	50	1 166	607	407	40	62	299
Widowed	36	184	85	69	1 329	692	162	106	26	227
Divorced	71	144	53	28	1 074	883	71	67	15	202
Female, 14 years old and over	4 281	6 533	2 365	2 201	68 928	42 475	6 779	5 011	3 925	15 134
Single	782	1 531	539	618	19 527	11 090	1 419	1 164	516	4 000
Married, husband present	2 995	4 116	1 467	1 238	39 638	24 987	4 299	3 065	2 767	8 900
With spouse of same race	1 808	2 829	944	1 133	33 520	20 539	3 117	2 367	823	5 822
Separated	28	61	47	24	415	429	113	36	54	197
Other married, husband absent	154	75	27	21	1 593	564	133	115	286	296
Widowed	263	546	235	266	5 839	3 706	632	518	197	1 238
Divorced	59	204	50	34	1 916	1 699	183	113	105	503
YEARS OF SCHOOL COMPLETED										
Male, 25 to 34 years old	602	823	272	193	10 617	7 534	2 081	582	263	2 177
Elementary: Less than 5 years	4	11	3	9	67	67	28	–	14	19
5 to 7 years	9	4	–	–	51	4	7	–	–	10
8 years	–	17	–	–	110	66	47	6	–	10
High school: 1 to 3 years	15	62	28	–	410	446	149	14	32	92
4 years	138	139	82	18	5 444	1 695	320	109	16	357
College: 1 to 3 years	174	169	42	87	2 026	2 655	187	237	77	613
4 years or more	262	421	117	79	2 509	2 601	1 343	216	124	1 076
Female, 25 to 34 years old	1 028	1 001	378	295	11 090	8 280	2 121	745	919	2 997
Elementary: Less than 5 years	4	14	5	6	67	82	13	5	5	28
5 to 7 years	23	10	12	4	110	49	23	6	15	19
8 years	10	26	14	10	73	56	30	5	25	51
High school: 1 to 3 years	99	103	62	–	611	487	77	55	247	246
4 years	373	360	163	79	5 451	3 237	801	244	398	947
College: 1 to 3 years	267	203	62	106	2 266	2 379	429	250	152	857
4 years or more	252	285	60	90	2 512	1 990	748	180	77	849
INDUSTRY										
Total employed, 16 years old and over	4 352	7 591	2 567	2 332	83 002	50 307	7 295	5 285	2 394	16 012
Agriculture, forestry, and fisheries	714	60	92	731	1 686	4 950	77	719	510	1 276
Construction	53	102	41	60	8 574	1 031	67	180	47	288
Manufacturing: Durable goods	1 217	1 313	233	37	2 623	6 300	568	110	246	781
Nondurable goods	106	847	111	134	6 234	3 937	684	151	208	695
Transportation, communication, and other public utilities	90	333	167	57	5 849	2 562	613	109	81	1 185
Wholesale and retail trade	851	1 921	799	524	20 680	12 528	2 376	1 003	490	3 346
Personal services	148	371	149	130	5 090	2 551	297	387	116	1 892
Professional and related services	662	1 540	500	396	14 849	8 432	1 302	857	455	3 487
Other industries	511	1 104	475	263	17 417	8 016	1 311	1 769	241	3 062

Age, Marital Status, Education, and Industry of the Japanese Population for Selected Standard Metropolitan Statistical Areas and Cities: 1970—Continued

[Data based on 20-percent sample, see text. For meaning of symbols, see text]

Standard Metropolitan Statistical Areas With 5,000 or More Japanese Population / Cities With 5,000 or More Japanese Population	SMSA's — Con.		Cities							
	San Jose, Calif.	Seattle–Everett, Wash.	Chicago, Ill.	Honolulu, Hawaii	Los Angeles, Calif.	New York, N.Y.	Sacramento, Calif.	San Francisco, Calif.	San Jose, Calif.	Seattle, Wash.
AGE										
Male, all ages	**7 783**	**6 549**	**5 623**	**52 163**	**27 272**	**6 617**	**3 342**	**5 597**	**3 376**	**4 905**
Under 5 years	598	416	358	3 497	1 822	768	146	435	342	256
5 to 9 years	730	605	553	3 887	1 952	410	318	360	378	350
10 to 14 years	818	595	410	4 581	2 287	181	307	400	356	406
15 to 19 years	760	682	468	5 035	2 190	204	361	406	266	550
20 to 24 years	623	568	397	4 906	2 377	336	241	490	255	489
25 to 29 years	672	455	405	4 444	2 398	821	180	481	292	335
30 to 34 years	601	291	240	2 858	1 964	1 012	165	397	322	205
35 to 39 years	542	400	400	2 964	2 023	801	188	419	242	275
40 to 44 years	618	437	478	3 750	2 321	466	317	467	298	290
45 to 49 years	551	752	580	4 338	2 339	336	321	604	193	607
50 to 54 years	484	364	440	3 916	1 780	240	272	314	126	277
55 to 59 years	201	238	352	2 636	1 010	199	154	186	59	172
60 to 64 years	145	143	125	1 721	658	210	50	146	44	122
65 to 69 years	163	182	130	1 342	737	188	125	151	76	178
70 to 74 years	115	107	85	1 038	552	201	77	125	46	107
75 years and over	162	314	202	1 250	862	244	120	216	81	286
Female, all ages	**8 394**	**7 530**	**5 549**	**57 124**	**28 213**	**6 687**	**3 638**	**6 913**	**3 711**	**5 536**
Under 5 years	615	398	288	3 622	1 799	741	182	349	309	197
5 to 9 years	685	587	380	3 758	1 920	331	349	407	379	381
10 to 14 years	847	608	541	4 627	2 119	253	333	424	334	459
15 to 19 years	645	628	397	5 498	2 271	160	265	337	205	523
20 to 24 years	578	565	348	5 943	2 709	449	235	654	325	454
25 to 29 years	793	474	303	4 155	2 302	955	205	669	408	340
30 to 34 years	627	489	293	2 822	1 958	821	224	565	318	269
35 to 39 years	929	635	400	3 664	2 213	705	307	707	410	401
40 to 44 years	759	840	547	5 012	2 617	540	383	858	299	620
45 to 49 years	556	728	680	5 042	2 492	342	390	684	205	561
50 to 54 years	439	401	420	4 048	1 665	321	263	334	139	317
55 to 59 years	174	211	251	2 618	948	182	128	267	59	185
60 to 64 years	182	149	134	1 727	674	175	34	136	69	129
65 to 69 years	152	179	143	1 568	808	238	98	165	63	154
70 to 74 years	213	271	224	1 274	756	191	96	174	91	248
75 years and over	200	367	200	1 746	962	283	146	183	98	298
MARITAL STATUS										
Male, 14 years old and over	**5 799**	**5 025**	**4 386**	**41 230**	**21 759**	**5 299**	**2 635**	**4 472**	**2 367**	**3 958**
Single	2 182	1 746	1 561	14 870	8 460	1 611	928	1 771	881	1 468
Married, wife present	3 369	2 952	2 441	23 514	11 619	3 013	1 568	2 326	1 397	2 189
With spouse of same race	2 992	2 665	2 072	21 915	10 731	2 548	1 448	2 095	1 250	2 073
Separated	15	30	40	177	197	84	14	47	10	30
Other married, wife absent	60	86	62	871	397	382	12	136	26	81
Widowed	113	93	160	920	453	142	67	102	28	85
Divorced	60	118	122	878	633	67	46	90	25	105
Female, 14 years old and over	**6 373**	**6 042**	**4 493**	**46 080**	**22 770**	**5 396**	**2 827**	**5 826**	**2 740**	**4 575**
Single	1 510	1 482	1 165	13 854	6 561	1 172	642	1 778	656	1 245
Married, husband present	4 021	3 591	2 622	25 209	12 384	3 336	1 714	3 069	1 728	2 565
With spouse of same race	3 004	2 630	2 084	22 048	10 681	2 530	1 488	2 106	1 245	2 040
Separated	57	43	42	287	264	108	21	100	6	30
Other married, husband absent	85	76	37	1 006	284	104	42	98	33	58
Widowed	589	671	473	4 189	2 239	497	321	526	265	538
Divorced	111	179	154	1 535	1 038	179	87	255	52	139
YEARS OF SCHOOL COMPLETED										
Male, 25 to 34 years old	**1 273**	**746**	**645**	**7 302**	**4 362**	**1 833**	**345**	**878**	**614**	**540**
Elementary: Less than 5 years	–	–	5	52	42	28	–	10	–	–
5 to 7 years	–	–	4	30	4	7	–	–	–	–
8 years	–	5	6	98	42	35	6	–	–	5
High school: 1 to 3 years	23	35	45	286	235	130	14	53	12	35
4 years	268	171	99	3 560	999	292	81	124	129	121
College: 1 to 3 years	351	165	150	1 463	1 570	171	155	250	193	109
4 years or more	631	370	336	1 813	1 470	1 170	89	441	280	270
Female, 25 to 34 years old	**1 420**	**963**	**596**	**6 977**	**4 260**	**1 776**	**429**	**1 234**	**726**	**609**
Elementary: Less than 5 years	9	9	6	44	53	9	5	10	–	–
5 to 7 years	14	16	–	74	38	17	6	–	5	6
8 years	10	5	15	44	33	25	–	10	10	5
High school: 1 to 3 years	57	92	49	375	258	63	17	81	19	49
4 years	385	311	200	3 343	1 643	680	152	398	177	176
College: 1 to 3 years	459	235	127	1 510	1 354	361	159	380	241	140
4 years or more	486	295	199	1 587	881	621	90	355	274	233
INDUSTRY										
Total employed, 16 years old and over	**7 358**	**6 531**	**5 604**	**56 751**	**28 236**	**6 008**	**3 310**	**6 550**	**3 070**	**5 084**
Agriculture, forestry, and fisheries	1 010	394	25	648	2 888	35	285	58	242	222
Construction	141	120	76	5 557	522	50	127	142	65	96
Manufacturing: Durable goods	1 648	833	936	1 526	3 176	365	62	222	721	543
Nondurable goods	249	479	553	4 303	2 355	600	95	295	79	409
Transportation, communication, and other public utilities	223	277	251	3 978	1 429	541	80	598	90	229
Wholesale and retail trade	1 149	1 576	1 490	14 676	7 057	2 025	660	1 572	603	1 269
Personal services	651	566	293	3 988	1 600	242	274	954	260	497
Professional and related services	1 475	1 283	1 112	10 269	4 499	1 014	453	1 268	645	1 009
Other industries	812	1 003	868	11 806	4 710	1 136	1 274	1 441	365	810

Chinese Population by Sex and Urban and Rural Residence: 1970

[Data based on 20-percent sample, see text. For meaning of symbols, see text]

United States Regions Divisions States	Total			Urban			Rural nonfarm			Rural farm		
	Total	Male	Female	Total	Male	Female	Total	Male	Female	Total	Male	Female
United States	431 583	226 733	204 850	417 032	219 258	197 774	13 671	7 013	6 658	880	462	418
REGIONS												
Northeast	115 089	61 899	53 190	111 337	60 009	51 328	3 663	1 846	1 817	89	44	45
North Central	37 811	20 559	17 252	36 554	19 885	16 669	1 159	609	550	98	65	33
South	32 462	16 929	15 533	30 032	15 746	14 286	2 425	1 178	1 247	5	5	–
West	246 221	127 346	118 875	239 109	123 618	115 491	6 424	3 380	3 044	688	348	340
NORTHEAST												
New England	17 334	9 363	7 971	16 238	8 815	7 423	1 096	548	548	–	–	–
Middle Atlantic	97 755	52 536	45 219	95 099	51 194	43 905	2 567	1 298	1 269	89	44	45
NORTH CENTRAL												
East North Central	30 388	16 377	14 011	29 492	15 884	13 608	811	434	377	85	59	26
West North Central	7 423	4 182	3 241	7 062	4 001	3 061	348	175	173	13	6	7
SOUTH												
South Atlantic	17 803	9 084	8 719	16 479	8 448	8 031	1 324	636	688	–	–	–
East South Central	3 636	1 978	1 658	3 220	1 799	1 421	416	179	237	–	–	–
West South Central	11 023	5 867	5 156	10 333	5 499	4 834	685	363	322	5	5	–
WEST												
Mountain	8 886	4 943	3 943	8 435	4 669	3 766	404	262	142	47	12	35
Pacific	237 335	122 403	114 932	230 674	118 949	111 725	6 020	3 118	2 902	641	336	305
NEW ENGLAND												
Maine	89	51	38	65	35	30	24	16	8	–	–	–
New Hampshire	268	129	139	156	77	79	112	52	60	–	–	–
Vermont	203	91	112	117	50	67	86	41	45	–	–	–
Massachusetts	14 018	7 593	6 425	13 401	7 285	6 116	617	308	309	–	–	–
Rhode Island	1 023	557	466	1 013	552	461	10	5	5	–	–	–
Connecticut	1 733	942	791	1 486	816	670	247	126	121	–	–	–
MIDDLE ATLANTIC												
New York	81 903	44 158	37 745	80 574	43 457	37 117	1 310	696	614	19	5	14
New Jersey	8 755	4 620	4 135	7 952	4 232	3 720	733	349	384	70	39	31
Pennsylvania	7 097	3 758	3 339	6 573	3 505	3 068	524	253	271	–	–	–
EAST NORTH CENTRAL												
Ohio	5 263	2 864	2 399	5 123	2 797	2 326	123	50	73	17	17	–
Indiana	1 926	969	957	1 777	894	883	145	71	74	4	4	–
Illinois	14 077	7 601	6 476	13 953	7 511	6 442	119	85	34	5	5	–
Michigan	6 611	3 521	3 090	6 223	3 294	2 929	356	210	146	32	17	15
Wisconsin	2 511	1 422	1 089	2 416	1 388	1 028	68	18	50	27	16	11
WEST NORTH CENTRAL												
Minnesota	1 992	1 118	874	1 937	1 078	859	55	40	15	–	–	–
Iowa	957	536	421	923	523	400	34	13	21	–	–	–
Missouri	2 460	1 331	1 129	2 379	1 311	1 068	81	20	61	–	–	–
North Dakota	78	27	51	45	16	29	27	5	22	6	6	–
South Dakota	285	171	114	267	153	114	18	18	–	–	–	–
Nebraska	534	340	194	525	331	194	9	9	–	–	–	–
Kansas	1 117	659	458	986	589	397	124	70	54	7	–	7
SOUTH ATLANTIC												
Delaware	508	253	255	479	240	239	29	13	16	–	–	–
Maryland	5 961	2 852	3 109	5 610	2 689	2 921	351	163	188	–	–	–
District of Columbia	2 767	1 457	1 310	2 767	1 457	1 310	–	–	–	–	–	–
Virginia	2 407	1 217	1 190	2 272	1 142	1 130	135	75	60	–	–	–
West Virginia	266	136	130	175	103	72	91	33	58	–	–	–
North Carolina	1 134	591	543	911	505	406	223	86	137	–	–	–
South Carolina	393	249	144	322	206	116	71	43	28	–	–	–
Georgia	1 327	689	638	1 175	632	543	152	57	95	–	–	–
Florida	3 040	1 640	1 400	2 768	1 474	1 294	272	166	106	–	–	–
EAST SOUTH CENTRAL												
Kentucky	565	318	247	514	305	209	51	13	38	–	–	–
Tennessee	1 429	817	612	1 366	771	595	63	46	17	–	–	–
Alabama	467	237	230	453	237	216	14	–	14	–	–	–
Mississippi	1 175	606	569	887	486	401	288	120	168	–	–	–
WEST SOUTH CENTRAL												
Arkansas	904	453	451	639	334	305	265	119	146	–	–	–
Louisiana	1 161	685	476	1 032	596	436	129	89	40	–	–	–
Oklahoma	875	458	417	850	448	402	25	10	15	–	–	–
Texas	8 083	4 271	3 812	7 812	4 121	3 691	266	145	121	5	5	–
MOUNTAIN												
Montana	264	163	101	264	163	101	–	–	–	–	–	–
Idaho	574	326	248	471	283	188	56	31	25	47	12	35
Wyoming	104	62	42	89	52	37	15	10	5	–	–	–
Colorado	1 605	877	728	1 595	872	723	10	5	5	–	–	–
New Mexico	459	298	161	417	267	150	42	31	11	–	–	–
Arizona	3 739	1 944	1 795	3 577	1 842	1 735	162	102	60	–	–	–
Utah	1 175	703	472	1 144	684	460	31	19	12	–	–	–
Nevada	966	570	396	878	506	372	88	64	24	–	–	–
PACIFIC												
Washington	9 376	4 957	4 419	9 059	4 797	4 262	301	150	151	16	10	6
Oregon	4 774	2 624	2 150	4 571	2 509	2 062	164	95	69	39	20	19
California	170 419	88 286	82 133	167 773	86 810	80 963	2 302	1 289	1 013	344	187	157
Alaska	183	124	59	137	91	46	46	33	13	–	–	–
Hawaii	52 583	26 412	26 171	49 134	24 742	24 392	3 207	1 551	1 656	242	119	123

Social Characteristics of the Chinese Population by Urban and Rural Residence: 1970

[Data based on sample, see text. For minimum base for derived figures (percent, median, etc.) and meaning of symbols, see text]

United States Regions States With 10,000 or More Chinese Population	United States				Northeast			
	Total	Urban	Rural nonfarm	Rural farm	Total	Urban	Rural nonfarm	Rural farm
RELATIONSHIP TO HEAD OF HOUSEHOLD								
Total population	431 583	417 032	13 671	880	115 089	111 337	3 663	89
Under 18 years old	138 613	133 389	4 871	353	36 090	34 694	1 366	30
Living with both parents	124 838	120 523	3 978	337	32 865	31 636	1 199	30
Percent of all under 18 years	90.1	90.4	81.7	95.5	91.1	91.2	87.8	...
Head of household	121 404	117 867	3 333	204	33 343	32 342	982	19
Head of family	94 931	91 908	2 844	179	25 852	24 961	872	19
Female head	6 345	6 212	125	8	1 282	1 248	34	–
Primary individual	26 473	25 959	489	25	7 491	7 381	110	–
Female primary individual	8 182	8 011	154	17	1 935	1 913	22	–
Wife of head	82 334	79 506	2 688	140	22 362	21 577	769	16
Other relative of head	196 586	190 158	5 938	490	51 580	49 925	1 601	54
Nonrelative of head	14 811	14 405	360	46	4 298	4 187	111	–
In group quarters	16 448	15 096	1 352	–	3 506	3 306	200	–
Inmate of institution	1 787	1 280	507	–	389	302	87	–
Other	14 661	13 816	845	–	3 117	3 004	113	–
FAMILIES BY PRESENCE OF CHILDREN								
Total families	94 931	91 908	2 844	179	25 852	24 961	872	19
With own children under 18 years	59 862	57 853	1 891	118	16 280	15 659	602	19
With own children under 6 years	29 172	28 035	1 095	42	8 186	7 807	375	4
Husband–wife families	84 284	81 555	2 576	153	23 331	22 507	805	19
With own children under 18 years	55 528	53 700	1 714	114	15 282	14 709	554	19
With own children under 6 years	27 985	26 894	1 049	42	7 880	7 501	375	4
Families with female head	6 345	6 212	125	8	1 282	1 248	34	–
With own children under 18 years	3 080	2 962	114	4	646	612	34	–
With own children under 6 years	792	763	29	–	169	169	–	–
CHILDREN EVER BORN								
Women ever married, 15 to 24 years old	8 099	7 727	372	–	2 268	2 167	101	–
Children per 1,000 women ever married	786	787	766	–	878	893	554	–
Women ever married, 25 to 34 years old	27 692	26 446	1 205	41	7 759	7 350	405	4
Children per 1,000 women ever married	1 778	1 778	1 754	...	1 751	1 767	1 447	...
Women ever married, 35 to 44 years old	26 711	25 919	730	62	6 918	6 703	207	8
Children per 1,000 women ever married	3 005	2 999	3 199	...	2 955	2 958	2 855	...
PLACE OF BIRTH								
Total population	433 469	418 624	13 975	870	116 519	112 626	3 774	119
Foreign born	204 232	199 355	4 726	151	70 629	68 723	1 878	28
Native	229 237	219 269	9 249	719	45 890	43 903	1 896	91
Born in State of residence	166 768	159 915	6 277	576	30 690	29 637	993	60
Born in different State	31 631	29 711	1 874	46	6 674	6 019	631	24
Northeast	7 189	6 764	401	24	3 178	2 896	258	24
North Central	4 803	4 443	355	5	812	696	116	–
South	5 388	5 075	313	–	913	829	84	–
West	14 251	13 429	805	17	1 771	1 598	173	–
Born abroad, at sea, etc	12 166	11 786	360	20	2 743	2 663	80	–
State of birth not reported	18 672	17 857	738	77	5 783	5 584	192	7
SCHOOL ENROLLMENT								
Total enrolled, 3 to 34 years old	158 616	153 728	4 579	309	38 746	37 511	1 179	56
Nursery school	3 775	3 623	152	–	877	831	46	–
Public	1 275	1 259	16	–	304	293	11	–
Kindergarten	7 315	7 051	257	7	1 996	1 897	99	–
Public	6 375	6 184	184	7	1 754	1 678	76	–
Elementary (1 to 8 years)	63 541	61 442	1 933	166	16 423	15 882	516	25
Public	57 236	55 253	1 832	151	14 740	14 240	484	16
High school (1 to 4 years)	32 729	31 560	1 088	81	8 570	8 328	234	8
Public	29 651	28 604	966	81	7 724	7 502	214	8
College	51 256	50 052	1 149	55	10 880	10 573	284	23
Percent enrolled, 3 to 34 years old	62.2	62.5	55.0	66.5	58.2	58.4	52.1	...
3 and 4 years old	23.9	24.0	23.6	–	23.0	22.9	25.1	...
5 and 6 years old	84.2	84.6	75.2	...	84.2	84.5	78.4	...
7 to 13 years old	96.4	96.4	97.1	85.0	95.8	95.6	100.0	...
14 to 17 years old: Male	95.3	95.5	88.7	...	95.4	95.3	95.9	...
Female	95.2	95.3	94.1	...	94.7	94.6	...	...
18 to 24 years old: Male	70.8	71.1	62.0	...	66.5	66.5	66.5	...
Female	58.2	58.5	48.1	...	52.5	52.7	46.0	...
25 to 34 years old	18.3	18.5	11.1	...	13.8	13.9	10.6	...
YEARS OF SCHOOL COMPLETED								
Total, 25 years old and over	227 165	219 785	6 893	487	62 607	60 637	1 929	41
No school years completed	25 205	24 773	380	52	8 662	8 537	125	–
Elementary: 1 to 4 years	11 522	11 192	292	38	3 813	3 772	41	–
5 to 7 years	24 296	23 675	572	49	9 007	8 887	110	10
8 years	12 780	12 311	438	31	4 178	4 091	77	10
High school: 1 to 3 years	22 121	21 322	736	63	6 397	6 315	78	4
4 years	48 071	46 424	1 509	138	10 596	10 345	243	8
College: 1 to 3 years	24 929	24 138	743	48	4 474	4 278	196	–
4 years or more	58 241	55 950	2 223	68	15 480	14 412	1 059	9
Median school years completed	12.4	12.4	12.7	12.1	11.6	11.4	16.4	...
Percent high school graduates	57.8	57.6	64.9	52.2	48.8	47.9	77.7	...

Social Characteristics of the Chinese Population by Urban and Rural Residence: 1970—Continued

[Data based on sample, see text. For minimum base for derived figures (percent, median, etc.) and meaning of symbols, see text]

United States Regions States With 10,000 or More Chinese Population	North Central				South			
	Total	Urban	Rural nonfarm	Rural farm	Total	Urban	Rural nonfarm	Rural farm
RELATIONSHIP TO HEAD OF HOUSEHOLD								
Total population	37 811	36 554	1 159	98	32 462	30 032	2 425	5
Under 18 years old	11 455	11 017	393	45	10 207	9 338	869	–
Living with both parents	10 393	10 027	321	45	9 145	8 412	733	–
Percent of all under 18 years	90.7	91.0	81.7	...	89.6	90.1	84.3	–
Head of household	10 453	10 171	269	13	8 502	7 943	559	–
Head of family	7 742	7 506	223	13	6 670	6 201	469	–
Female head	260	260	–	–	300	290	10	–
Primary individual	2 711	2 665	46	–	1 832	1 742	90	–
Female primary individual	663	654	9	–	524	487	37	–
Wife of head	7 101	6 827	267	7	6 208	5 753	455	–
Other relative of head	14 942	14 462	418	62	13 594	12 453	1 136	5
Nonrelative of head	1 878	1 820	42	16	1 642	1 581	61	–
In group quarters	3 437	3 274	163	–	2 516	2 302	214	–
Inmate of institution	141	116	25	–	109	69	40	–
Other	3 296	3 158	138	–	2 407	2 233	174	–
FAMILIES BY PRESENCE OF CHILDREN								
Total families	7 742	7 506	223	13	6 670	6 201	469	–
With own children under 18 years	5 103	4 944	146	13	4 464	4 092	372	–
With own children under 6 years	2 975	2 864	106	5	2 541	2 313	228	–
Husband–wife families	7 231	7 006	212	13	6 120	5 681	439	–
With own children under 18 years	4 897	4 738	146	13	4 169	3 817	352	–
With own children under 6 years	2 874	2 763	106	5	2 420	2 203	217	–
Families with female head	260	260	–	–	300	290	10	–
With own children under 18 years	132	132	–	–	186	178	8	–
With own children under 6 years	53	53	–	–	95	90	5	–
CHILDREN EVER BORN								
Women ever married, 15 to 24 years old	873	828	45	–	776	717	59	–
Children per 1,000 women ever married	698	705	...	–	693	658	...	–
Women ever married, 25 to 34 years old	3 192	3 053	132	7	2 767	2 525	242	–
Children per 1,000 women ever married	1 491	1 443	2 311	...	1 547	1 550	1 517	–
Women ever married, 35 to 44 years old	1 931	1 880	51	–	1 865	1 746	119	–
Children per 1,000 women ever married	3 006	3 026	...	–	2 985	2 967	3 252	–
PLACE OF BIRTH								
Total population	37 791	36 537	1 176	78	32 710	29 983	2 719	8
Foreign born	21 803	21 248	555	–	17 345	16 347	998	–
Native	15 988	15 289	621	78	15 365	13 636	1 721	8
Born in State of residence	9 324	8 964	321	39	7 770	6 869	901	–
Born in different State	3 895	3 679	205	11	4 964	4 443	521	–
Northeast	864	843	21	–	1 150	1 053	97	–
North Central	1 052	983	69	–	640	520	120	–
South	546	536	10	–	1 692	1 519	173	–
West	1 433	1 317	105	11	1 482	1 351	131	–
Born abroad, at sea, etc	907	890	17	–	811	737	74	–
State of birth not reported	1 862	1 756	78	28	1 820	1 587	225	8
SCHOOL ENROLLMENT								
Total enrolled, 3 to 34 years old	15 812	15 429	353	30	11 984	11 071	913	–
Nursery school	481	476	5	–	281	246	35	–
Public	100	100	–	–	32	32	–	–
Kindergarten	783	775	8	–	452	382	70	–
Public	703	695	8	–	285	265	20	–
Elementary (1 to 8 years)	4 904	4 779	117	8	4 348	3 948	400	–
Public	4 239	4 120	111	8	3 940	3 568	372	–
High school (1 to 4 years)	2 257	2 164	71	22	1 926	1 757	169	–
Public	2 012	1 926	64	22	1 644	1 501	143	–
College	7 387	7 235	152	–	4 977	4 738	239	–
Percent enrolled, 3 to 34 years old	63.3	63.9	48.2	...	58.9	59.1	55.9	–
3 and 4 years old	29.5	30.8	...	...	20.6	19.5	28.5	–
5 and 6 years old	84.5	85.5	...	...	74.9	75.5	...	–
7 to 13 years old	98.1	98.1	95.7	...	95.5	95.5	95.1	–
14 to 17 years old: Male	96.4	96.7	...	...	92.9	93.1	...	–
Female	95.9	95.7	...	...	93.4	92.8	...	–
18 to 24 years old: Male	78.8	79.1	68.9	–	71.4	71.3	72.8	–
Female	64.0	64.4	...	–	63.1	63.1	63.4	–
25 to 34 years old	32.7	33.4	14.1	–	25.1	25.8	15.7	–
YEARS OF SCHOOL COMPLETED								
Total, 25 years old and over	19 489	18 870	566	53	16 905	15 692	1 208	5
No school years completed	1 155	1 151	4	–	1 074	1 013	61	–
Elementary: 1 to 4 years	548	536	–	12	730	683	47	–
5 to 7 years	1 672	1 643	29	–	1 471	1 306	165	–
8 years	1 148	1 128	20	–	673	592	81	–
High school: 1 to 3 years	1 701	1 600	72	29	1 713	1 533	175	5
4 years	2 613	2 520	81	12	2 651	2 426	225	–
College: 1 to 3 years	1 764	1 722	42	–	1 624	1 535	89	–
4 years or more	8 888	8 570	318	–	6 969	6 604	365	–
Median school years completed	14.5	14.5	16.4	...	13.3	13.6	12.3	...
Percent high school graduates	68.1	67.9	77.9	...	66.5	67.3	56.2	–

Social Characteristics of the Chinese Population by Urban and Rural Residence: 1970 — Continued

[Data based on sample, see text. For minimum base for derived figures (percent, median, etc.) and meaning of symbols, see text]

United States Regions States With 10,000 or More Chinese Population	West Total	West Urban	West Rural nonfarm	West Rural farm	California Total	California Urban	California Rural	Hawaii Total	Hawaii Urban	Hawaii Rural
RELATIONSHIP TO HEAD OF HOUSEHOLD										
Total population	246 221	239 109	6 424	688	170 419	167 773	2 646	52 583	49 134	3 449
Under 18 years old	80 861	78 340	2 243	278	54 853	54 035	818	18 382	17 063	1 319
Living with both parents	72 435	70 448	1 725	262	49 639	49 006	633	16 062	15 036	1 026
Percent of all under 18 years	89.6	89.9	76.9	94.2	90.5	90.7	77.4	87.4	88.1	77.8
Head of household	69 106	67 411	1 523	172	48 753	48 136	617	14 029	13 195	834
Head of family	54 667	53 240	1 280	147	37 437	36 903	534	12 304	11 602	702
Female head	4 503	4 414	81	8	2 937	2 916	21	1 170	1 121	49
Primary individual	14 439	14 171	243	25	11 316	11 233	83	1 725	1 593	132
Female primary individual	5 060	4 957	86	17	3 890	3 869	21	801	719	82
Wife of head	46 663	45 349	1 197	117	32 447	32 009	438	10 182	9 490	692
Other relative of head	116 470	113 318	2 783	369	79 379	78 370	1 009	26 915	25 211	1 704
Nonrelative of head	6 993	6 817	146	30	5 334	5 237	97	734	675	59
In group quarters	6 989	6 214	775	–	4 506	4 021	485	723	563	160
Inmate of institution	1 148	793	355	–	662	480	182	312	174	138
Other	5 841	5 421	420	–	3 844	3 541	303	411	389	22
FAMILIES BY PRESENCE OF CHILDREN										
Total families	54 667	53 240	1 280	147	37 437	36 903	534	12 304	11 602	702
With own children under 18 years	34 015	33 158	771	86	23 496	23 177	319	7 343	6 922	421
With own children under 6 years	15 470	15 051	386	33	10 763	10 624	139	3 071	2 856	215
Husband–wife families	47 602	46 361	1 120	121	32 884	32 413	471	10 428	9 825	603
With own children under 18 years	31 180	30 436	662	82	21 620	21 345	275	6 688	6 327	361
With own children under 6 years	14 811	14 427	351	33	10 373	10 239	134	2 885	2 695	190
Families with female head	4 503	4 414	81	8	2 937	2 916	21	1 170	1 121	49
With own children under 18 years	2 116	2 040	72	4	1 453	1 435	18	457	408	49
With own children under 6 years	475	451	24	–	277	277	–	141	122	19
CHILDREN EVER BORN										
Women ever married, 15 to 24 years old	4 182	4 015	167	–	2 897	2 828	69	895	829	66
Children per 1,000 women ever married	771	769	826	...	762	762	...	806	813	...
Women ever married, 25 to 34 years old	13 974	13 518	426	30	9 953	9 813	140	2 499	2 274	225
Children per 1,000 women ever married	1 905	1 901	2 009	...	1 815	1 825	1 079	2 351	2 313	2 738
Women ever married, 35 to 44 years old	15 997	15 590	353	54	11 499	11 320	179	3 165	2 968	197
Children per 1,000 women ever married	3 029	3 017	3 513	...	2 966	2 967	2 916	3 206	3 149	4 056
PLACE OF BIRTH										
Total population	246 449	239 478	6 306	665	170 374	167 916	2 458	52 375	48 875	3 500
Foreign born	94 455	93 037	1 295	123	77 711	76 988	723	5 809	5 480	329
Native	151 994	146 441	5 011	542	92 663	90 928	1 735	46 566	43 395	3 171
Born in State of residence	118 984	114 445	4 062	477	69 630	68 324	1 306	41 550	38 641	2 909
Born in different State	16 098	15 570	517	11	11 692	11 454	238	1 386	1 316	70
Northeast	1 997	1 972	25	–	1 578	1 564	14	221	217	4
North Central	2 299	2 244	50	5	1 730	1 697	33	262	254	8
South	2 237	2 191	46	–	1 837	1 798	39	148	148	–
West	9 565	9 163	396	6	6 547	6 395	152	755	697	58
Born abroad, at sea, etc	7 705	7 496	189	20	5 591	5 478	113	1 170	1 122	48
State of birth not reported	9 207	8 930	243	34	5 750	5 672	78	2 460	2 316	144
SCHOOL ENROLLMENT										
Total enrolled, 3 to 34 years old	92 074	89 717	2 134	223	65 509	64 512	997	16 922	15 926	996
Nursery school	2 136	2 070	66	–	1 502	1 473	29	491	454	37
Public	839	834	5	–	686	686	–	102	97	5
Kindergarten	4 084	3 997	80	7	2 799	2 760	39	914	866	48
Public	3 633	3 546	80	7	2 634	2 595	39	676	628	48
Elementary (1 to 8 years)	37 866	36 833	900	133	25 776	25 511	265	8 388	7 861	527
Public	34 317	33 325	865	127	24 103	23 838	265	6 625	6 133	492
High school (1 to 4 years)	19 976	19 311	614	51	13 694	13 446	248	4 495	4 141	354
Public	18 271	17 675	545	51	13 196	12 954	242	3 321	3 024	297
College	28 012	27 506	474	32	21 738	21 322	416	2 634	2 604	30
Percent enrolled, 3 to 34 years old	64.3	64.5	57.7	66.5	65.0	65.0	64.7	61.6	62.1	54.8
3 and 4 years old	24.0	24.1	23.8	–	24.1	24.0	...	27.1	27.5	22.2
5 and 6 years old	85.4	85.6	78.3	...	85.6	85.7	...	85.6	86.2	75.8
7 to 13 years old	96.6	96.7	96.6	82.4	96.6	96.7	90.0	96.3	96.4	95.8
14 to 17 years old: Male	95.4	95.7	86.1	...	95.9	96.2	80.7	93.7	94.2	87.4
Female	95.6	95.7	92.0	...	95.7	95.7	93.3	95.0	95.4	90.5
18 to 24 years old: Male	71.1	71.5	55.9	...	75.6	75.5	79.3	45.5	46.8	25.6
Female	59.0	59.5	42.4	–	61.7	61.7	62.0	43.9	45.3	22.6
25 to 34 years old	15.6	15.8	8.0	...	16.3	16.2	20.4	7.5	8.0	1.2
YEARS OF SCHOOL COMPLETED										
Total, 25 years old and over	128 164	124 586	3 190	388	88 307	87 008	1 299	28 310	26 538	1 772
No school years completed	14 314	14 072	190	52	11 972	11 830	142	1 183	1 103	80
Elementary: 1 to 4 years	6 431	6 201	204	26	4 533	4 446	87	1 429	1 332	97
5 to 7 years	12 146	11 839	268	39	8 884	8 831	53	2 109	1 926	183
8 years	6 781	6 500	260	21	4 218	4 154	64	1 807	1 639	168
High school: 1 to 3 years	12 310	11 874	411	25	8 004	7 865	139	3 066	2 786	280
4 years	32 211	31 133	960	118	19 210	18 882	328	10 666	10 052	614
College: 1 to 3 years	17 067	16 603	416	48	12 759	12 584	175	2 948	2 729	219
4 years or more	26 904	26 364	481	59	18 727	18 416	311	5 102	4 971	131
Median school years completed	12.4	12.4	12.3	12.3	12.3	12.3	12.5	12.4	12.4	12.1
Percent high school graduates	59.4	59.5	58.2	58.0	57.4	57.3	62.7	66.1	66.9	54.4

Social Characteristics of the Chinese Population by Urban and Rural Residence: 1970—Continued

[Data based on sample, see text. For minimum base for derived figures (percent, median, etc.) and meaning of symbols, see text]

United States Regions States With 10,000 or More Chinese Population	Illinois			Massachusetts			New York		
	Total	Urban	Rural	Total	Urban	Rural	Total	Urban	Rural
RELATIONSHIP TO HEAD OF HOUSEHOLD									
Total population	**14 077**	**13 953**	**124**	**14 018**	**13 401**	**617**	**81 903**	**80 574**	**1 329**
Under 18 years old	4 498	4 471	27	4 526	4 224	302	25 443	24 962	481
Living with both parents	4 097	4 078	19	4 151	3 849	302	23 184	22 785	399
Percent of all under 18 years	91.1	91.2	...	91.7	91.1	100.0	91.1	91.3	83.0
Head of household	3 881	3 848	33	3 737	3 596	141	24 091	23 731	360
Head of family	2 920	2 902	18	2 920	2 786	134	18 546	18 266	280
Female head	109	109	–	187	187	–	905	899	6
Primary individual	961	946	15	817	810	7	5 545	5 465	80
Female primary individual	213	213	–	183	176	7	1 457	1 447	10
Wife of head	2 694	2 676	18	2 503	2 390	113	15 956	15 724	232
Other relative of head	6 133	6 104	29	6 418	6 082	336	37 126	36 589	537
Nonrelative of head	414	403	11	555	542	13	3 018	2 957	61
In group quarters	955	922	33	805	791	14	1 712	1 573	139
Inmate of institution	69	59	10	52	42	10	265	214	51
Other	886	863	23	753	749	4	1 447	1 359	88
FAMILIES BY PRESENCE OF CHILDREN									
Total families	**2 920**	**2 902**	**18**	**2 920**	**2 786**	**134**	**18 546**	**18 266**	**280**
With own children under 18 years	1 941	1 931	10	1 977	1 864	113	11 512	11 305	207
With own children under 6 years	1 051	1 051	–	1 068	970	98	5 515	5 380	135
Husband—wife families	**2 705**	**2 687**	**18**	**2 625**	**2 491**	**134**	**16 671**	**16 418**	**253**
With own children under 18 years	1 874	1 864	10	1 827	1 714	113	10 849	10 654	195
With own children under 6 years	1 021	1 021	–	1 001	903	98	5 358	5 223	135
Families with female head	**109**	**109**	**–**	**187**	**187**	**–**	**905**	**899**	**6**
With own children under 18 years	39	39	–	104	104	–	415	409	6
With own children under 6 years	14	14	–	33	33	–	85	85	–
CHILDREN EVER BORN									
Women ever married, 15 to 24 years old	294	291	3	280	261	19	1 612	1 592	20
Children per 1,000 women ever married	731	739	–	946	977	...	922	925	...
Women ever married, 25 to 34 years old	1 102	1 096	6	963	922	41	5 146	4 990	156
Children per 1,000 women ever married	1 652	1 651	...	1 746	1 733	...	1 833	1 843	1 519
Women ever married, 35 to 44 years old	856	851	5	671	638	33	5 106	5 053	53
Children per 1,000 women ever married	3 114	3 115	...	3 250	3 266	...	2 955	2 955	...
PLACE OF BIRTH									
Total population	**13 912**	**13 765**	**147**	**14 127**	**13 347**	**780**	**83 181**	**81 882**	**1 299**
Foreign born	7 946	7 879	67	7 089	6 801	288	53 595	52 871	724
Native	5 966	5 886	80	7 038	6 546	492	29 586	29 011	575
Born in State of residence	3 777	3 748	29	4 565	4 255	310	21 757	21 417	340
Born in different State	1 079	1 050	29	1 065	933	132	2 631	2 504	127
Northeast	209	209	–	469	422	47	826	802	24
North Central	243	229	14	121	101	20	332	305	27
South	171	171	–	151	133	18	539	498	41
West	456	441	15	324	277	47	934	899	35
Born abroad, at sea, etc	311	304	7	358	348	10	1 830	1 801	29
State of birth not reported	799	784	15	1 050	1 010	40	3 368	3 289	79
SCHOOL ENROLLMENT									
Total enrolled, 3 to 34 years old	**5 415**	**5 375**	**40**	**5 265**	**5 033**	**232**	**27 175**	**26 740**	**435**
Nursery school	150	150	–	127	108	19	478	462	16
Public	45	45	–	43	32	11	239	239	–
Kindergarten	322	322	–	359	314	45	1 312	1 299	13
Public	269	269	–	306	273	33	1 175	1 169	6
Elementary (1 to 8 years)	1 902	1 882	20	1 978	1 863	115	11 938	11 794	144
Public	1 508	1 488	20	1 876	1 761	115	10 701	10 563	138
High school (1 to 4 years)	972	965	7	1 079	1 042	37	6 327	6 252	75
Public	817	810	7	1 016	979	37	5 743	5 668	75
College	2 069	2 056	13	1 722	1 706	16	7 120	6 933	187
Percent enrolled, 3 to 34 years old	**61.6**	**61.6**	**...**	**60.7**	**60.8**	**56.6**	**58.2**	**58.4**	**50.6**
3 and 4 years old	29.1	29.1	–	30.8	30.2	...	21.1	20.8	27.3
5 and 6 years old	89.5	89.5	–	87.8	87.8	...	83.6	84.2	...
7 to 13 years old	98.0	98.0	...	98.3	98.2	...	95.1	95.1	100.0
14 to 17 years old: Male	95.0	94.9	...	97.9	97.8	...	95.3	95.3	...
Female	94.7	94.7	–	96.7	96.7	–	93.9	93.8	...
18 to 24 years old: Male	73.0	72.9	...	68.2	68.0	...	65.1	65.1	...
Female	61.0	61.3	...	56.7	57.6	...	51.1	50.7	...
25 to 34 years old	24.6	24.8	–	18.3	19.0	–	11.9	11.8	14.8
YEARS OF SCHOOL COMPLETED									
Total, 25 years old and over	**7 337**	**7 258**	**79**	**7 084**	**6 803**	**281**	**44 993**	**44 325**	**668**
No school years completed	543	543	–	714	714	–	7 125	7 078	47
Elementary: 1 to 4 years	244	239	5	414	414	–	3 037	3 020	17
5 to 7 years	819	803	16	1 035	1 031	4	7 001	6 951	50
8 years	621	621	–	534	524	10	3 096	3 071	25
High school: 1 to 3 years	767	757	10	716	708	8	4 889	4 870	19
4 years	1 199	1 199	–	1 304	1 241	63	7 721	7 690	31
College: 1 to 3 years	663	658	5	465	436	29	3 121	3 043	78
4 years or more	2 481	2 438	43	1 902	1 735	167	9 003	8 602	401
Median school years completed	12.6	12.6	...	12.1	12.0	16.6	10.4	10.3	16.7
Percent high school graduates	59.2	59.2	...	51.8	50.2	92.2	44.1	43.6	76.3

Age, Marital Status, Education, and Industry of the Chinese Population for Selected Standard Metropolitan Statistical Areas and Cities: 1970

[Data based on 20-percent sample, see text. For meaning of symbols, see text]

Standard Metropolitan Statistical Areas With 5,000 or More Chinese Population Cities With 5,000 or More Chinese Population	Standard metropolitan statistical areas									
	Boston, Mass.	Chicago, Ill.	Honolulu, Hawaii	Los Angeles– Long Beach, Calif.	New York N.Y.	Sacra- mento, Calif.	San Francisco– Oakland, Calif.	San Jose, Calif.	Seattle– Everett, Wash.	Washing- ton, D.C.– Md.–Va.
AGE										
Male, all ages	6 585	6 449	24 533	21 840	41 486	5 307	45 393	4 182	4 030	3 910
Under 5 years	536	604	1 915	2 012	3 114	344	3 202	368	284	316
5 to 9 years	552	552	2 501	1 971	3 437	587	4 012	426	420	413
10 to 14 years	602	502	2 630	2 093	3 756	555	4 364	398	377	265
15 to 19 years	697	607	2 485	2 039	4 115	743	4 948	342	423	342
20 to 24 years	762	593	1 883	2 191	3 388	501	4 364	630	391	240
25 to 29 years	567	542	1 411	1 628	2 164	211	2 354	319	271	278
30 to 34 years	534	655	1 211	1 997	3 158	312	2 854	438	347	301
35 to 39 years	433	493	1 529	1 922	2 991	414	3 112	380	276	342
40 to 44 years	352	412	1 667	1 440	2 718	325	3 050	283	234	261
45 to 49 years	376	430	1 798	1 442	2 679	375	3 219	231	211	336
50 to 54 years	272	285	1 530	866	2 407	223	2 156	118	185	193
55 to 59 years	248	213	1 238	670	2 236	218	2 133	114	170	178
60 to 64 years	222	163	789	595	1 765	136	1 945	65	150	163
65 to 69 years	172	129	799	403	1 566	118	1 478	40	124	106
70 to 74 years	122	110	713	289	971	129	1 110	–	71	97
75 years and over	138	159	434	282	1 021	116	1 092	30	96	79
Female, all ages	5 572	5 546	24 364	19 660	35 613	5 150	43 009	3 837	3 671	3 948
Under 5 years	506	518	1 736	1 612	2 988	426	2 988	414	342	366
5 to 9 years	548	547	2 295	1 914	3 275	490	3 737	457	404	448
10 to 14 years	553	502	2 753	1 844	3 336	549	4 093	315	406	357
15 to 19 years	636	597	2 346	1 888	3 478	713	4 743	331	383	284
20 to 24 years	653	617	2 136	2 352	3 801	569	4 771	540	367	374
25 to 29 years	493	526	1 304	1 774	2 681	294	2 389	450	318	411
30 to 34 years	420	478	1 355	1 767	2 761	298	2 958	344	309	438
35 to 39 years	329	417	1 437	1 512	2 598	368	2 945	260	196	226
40 to 44 years	322	368	1 771	1 381	2 597	405	3 574	173	221	265
45 to 49 years	329	241	1 777	949	1 955	312	2 319	198	187	236
50 to 54 years	209	193	1 588	646	1 620	161	2 036	120	123	144
55 to 59 years	185	160	1 122	623	1 526	145	1 942	68	124	106
60 to 64 years	117	117	810	479	1 115	130	1 506	56	96	89
65 to 69 years	122	114	828	437	787	149	1 341	39	69	82
70 to 74 years	56	37	611	214	491	70	830	24	47	36
75 years and over	94	114	495	268	604	71	837	48	79	86
MARITAL STATUS										
Male, 14 years old and over	5 057	4 887	18 100	16 112	31 921	3 951	34 670	3 067	3 025	2 971
Single	2 195	1 969	6 462	6 524	11 143	1 630	13 420	1 283	1 178	1 106
Married, wife present	2 350	2 485	10 283	8 343	16 356	2 038	17 791	1 647	1 516	1 566
With spouse of same race	2 144	2 240	7 325	7 289	15 232	1 859	16 783	1 439	1 355	1 346
Separated	36	54	76	128	421	18	240	15	50	43
Other married, wife absent	330	201	426	523	2 335	131	1 494	61	187	150
Widowed	120	136	423	292	1 395	84	1 199	21	57	71
Divorced	26	42	430	302	271	50	526	40	37	35
Female, 14 years old and over	4 073	4 070	18 151	14 689	26 651	3 788	32 991	2 716	2 587	2 852
Single	1 371	1 268	5 281	4 728	7 753	1 327	10 535	829	759	889
Married, husband present	2 250	2 437	10 034	8 124	15 640	2 020	17 646	1 628	1 511	1 623
With spouse of same race	2 093	2 204	7 273	7 160	15 158	1 883	16 663	1 418	1 354	1 357
Separated	31	17	154	128	222	19	255	18	18	29
Other married, husband absent	117	75	448	403	766	75	649	65	74	101
Widowed	286	248	1 788	1 019	1 977	284	3 262	131	184	160
Divorced	18	25	446	287	293	63	644	45	41	50
YEARS OF SCHOOL COMPLETED										
Male, 25 to 34 years old	1 101	1 197	2 622	3 625	5 322	523	5 208	757	618	579
Elementary: Less than 5 years	76	20	73	75	293	28	122	–	5	16
5 to 7 years	44	35	19	80	450	37	147	5	–	4
8 years	40	43	24	34	175	15	72	–	12	–
High school: 1 to 3 years	135	146	113	242	690	39	392	37	63	26
4 years	189	169	1 135	527	1 217	104	1 325	73	156	35
College: 1 to 3 years	113	163	469	749	665	113	1 369	123	109	115
4 years or more	504	621	789	1 918	1 832	187	1 781	519	273	383
Female, 25 to 34 years old	913	1 004	2 659	3 541	5 442	592	5 347	794	627	849
Elementary: Less than 5 years	58	55	83	154	536	66	381	5	42	27
5 to 7 years	77	78	56	136	566	35	409	11	32	50
8 years	37	58	28	98	294	26	170	–	46	–
High school: 1 to 3 years	81	108	192	235	691	51	453	30	45	61
4 years	189	195	1 207	776	1 401	151	1 510	115	144	197
College: 1 to 3 years	122	122	463	996	748	115	1 197	181	134	130
4 years or more	349	388	630	1 146	1 206	148	1 227	452	184	384
INDUSTRY										
Total employed, 16 years old and over	5 391	5 305	21 538	18 315	33 400	3 911	38 727	3 346	3 122	3 358
Agriculture, forestry, and fisheries	13	14	222	72	17	98	218	301	13	18
Construction	66	53	1 082	459	343	103	977	32	19	62
Manufacturing: Durable goods	321	564	955	1 995	1 285	76	1 619	895	376	60
Nondurable goods	812	546	1 293	1 977	6 660	223	4 935	94	379	72
Transportation, communication, and other public utilities	89	135	1 824	711	1 430	86	2 236	126	114	71
Wholesale and retail trade	1 954	1 822	5 126	5 943	11 540	1 577	12 443	697	1 259	904
Personal services	404	437	1 147	913	3 901	186	2 754	62	132	308
Professional and related services	1 230	1 225	4 064	3 501	4 403	736	5 990	827	527	976
Other industries	502	509	5 825	2 744	3 821	826	7 555	312	303	887

Age, Marital Status, Education, and Industry of the Chinese Population for Selected Standard Metropolitan Statistical Areas and Cities: 1970—Continued

[Data based on 20-percent sample, see text. For meaning of symbols, see text]

Standard Metropolitan Statistical Areas With 5,000 or More Chinese Population / Cities With 5,000 or More Chinese Population	Boston, Mass.	Chicago, Ill.	Honolulu, Hawaii	Los Angeles, Calif.	New York, N.Y.	Oakland, Calif.	Sacramento, Calif.	San Francisco, Calif.	Seattle, Wash.
AGE									
Male, all ages	**3 978**	**4 827**	**18 210**	**14 438**	**37 881**	**6 147**	**4 107**	**30 327**	**3 473**
Under 5 years	341	408	1 211	1 183	2 833	436	271	2 041	220
5 to 9 years	328	359	1 511	1 149	3 022	539	458	2 524	328
10 to 14 years	338	395	1 916	1 324	3 352	552	433	2 929	357
15 to 19 years	332	435	1 833	1 525	3 654	792	553	3 282	380
20 to 24 years	441	498	1 478	1 398	3 188	557	337	2 655	349
25 to 29 years	313	421	1 138	1 069	2 015	273	137	1 522	234
30 to 34 years	273	506	833	1 256	2 937	354	240	1 795	274
35 to 39 years	261	344	1 045	1 166	2 750	454	334	1 951	214
40 to 44 years	219	284	1 207	941	2 430	398	255	2 001	197
45 to 49 years	245	315	1 336	1 011	2 398	440	319	2 220	183
50 to 54 years	194	203	1 255	611	2 152	326	164	1 478	156
55 to 59 years	193	170	1 006	507	2 116	338	154	1 513	161
60 to 64 years	175	139	676	492	1 667	232	131	1 504	140
65 to 69 years	121	112	725	339	1 471	184	108	1 190	113
70 to 74 years	88	101	657	231	911	135	107	877	71
75 years and over	116	137	383	236	985	137	106	845	96
Female, all ages	**3 185**	**4 049**	**18 307**	**12 841**	**32 301**	**5 829**	**4 092**	**28 752**	**3 057**
Under 5 years	295	358	1 159	909	2 692	419	346	1 816	267
5 to 9 years	266	345	1 587	1 117	2 909	450	353	2 404	298
10 to 14 years	272	390	1 945	1 214	2 945	505	454	2 813	329
15 to 19 years	406	446	1 748	1 261	3 096	654	531	3 267	349
20 to 24 years	362	507	1 699	1 621	3 550	702	445	3 054	326
25 to 29 years	255	366	947	1 092	2 431	387	199	1 344	253
30 to 34 years	175	335	901	1 009	2 509	359	242	1 931	218
35 to 39 years	205	279	961	943	2 337	299	289	1 979	148
40 to 44 years	203	292	1 316	981	2 316	447	341	2 463	187
45 to 49 years	182	174	1 480	644	1 761	357	254	1 588	172
50 to 54 years	149	127	1 301	465	1 481	289	127	1 384	106
55 to 59 years	134	121	890	492	1 440	343	117	1 381	124
60 to 64 years	89	103	674	379	1 084	168	123	1 142	91
65 to 69 years	90	89	733	343	743	197	137	993	63
70 to 74 years	45	33	526	165	461	109	70	621	47
75 years and over	57	84	440	206	546	144	64	572	79
MARITAL STATUS									
Male, 14 years old and over	**3 046**	**3 737**	**14 045**	**11 019**	**29 351**	**4 726**	**3 047**	**23 420**	**2 639**
Single	1 244	1 570	5 137	4 654	10 239	1 878	1 168	8 898	1 076
Married, wife present	1 401	1 818	7 748	5 400	14 895	2 583	1 648	11 741	1 265
With spouse of same race	1 303	1 671	6 000	4 788	13 947	2 478	1 539	11 269	1 165
Separated	32	38	65	107	373	20	18	179	40
Other married, wife absent	255	158	349	433	2 256	109	96	1 271	175
Widowed	102	115	362	206	1 340	62	78	1 018	53
Divorced	12	38	384	219	248	74	39	313	30
Female, 14 years old and over	**2 406**	**3 013**	**13 966**	**9 865**	**24 317**	**4 619**	**3 025**	**22 250**	**2 216**
Single	823	951	4 108	3 271	6 994	1 456	986	7 125	683
Married, husband present	1 268	1 765	7 558	5 202	14 305	2 538	1 656	11 622	1 233
With spouse of same race	1 254	1 639	5 975	4 703	13 886	2 427	1 573	11 223	1 156
Separated	14	11	137	91	204	71	14	139	14
Other married, husband absent	73	59	322	304	665	67	55	465	64
Widowed	216	202	1 512	792	1 896	387	259	2 462	184
Divorced	12	25	329	205	253	100	55	437	38
YEARS OF SCHOOL COMPLETED									
Male, 25 to 34 years old	**586**	**927**	**1 971**	**2 325**	**4 952**	**627**	**377**	**3 317**	**508**
Elementary: Less than 5 years	61	20	56	50	288	21	18	88	5
5 to 7 years	34	35	19	73	437	7	37	134	—
8 years	23	37	14	28	175	—	11	59	12
High school: 1 to 3 years	105	116	91	149	673	62	34	279	63
4 years	133	150	805	357	1 147	151	104	975	137
College: 1 to 3 years	83	116	339	485	624	168	99	847	85
4 years or more	147	453	647	1 183	1 608	218	74	935	206
Female, 25 to 34 years old	**430**	**701**	**1 848**	**2 101**	**4 940**	**746**	**441**	**3 275**	**471**
Elementary: Less than 5 years	53	49	67	113	514	62	50	299	42
5 to 7 years	67	63	51	123	548	46	27	323	27
8 years	20	40	23	57	275	36	22	120	36
High school: 1 to 3 years	52	84	112	158	651	80	46	311	33
4 years	96	154	759	416	1 253	196	129	873	121
College: 1 to 3 years	36	85	334	571	658	184	100	724	79
4 years or more	106	226	502	663	1 041	142	67	625	133
INDUSTRY									
Total employed, 16 years old and over	**3 313**	**3 982**	**16 571**	**12 454**	**30 715**	**5 331**	**3 190**	**26 127**	**2 709**
Agriculture, forestry, and fisheries	13	—	132	61	13	18	62	123	8
Construction	40	43	734	242	304	101	74	653	12
Manufacturing: Durable goods	79	402	710	1 125	1 010	275	30	856	241
Nondurable goods	619	391	1 060	1 656	6 442	549	215	3 859	368
Transportation, communication, and other public utilities	42	119	1 278	435	1 339	168	72	1 685	97
Wholesale and retail trade	1 490	1 439	4 025	4 307	10 843	2 016	1 377	8 547	1 178
Personal services	261	368	947	707	3 595	341	163	2 063	111
Professional and related services	492	859	3 277	2 102	3 754	898	455	3 165	424
Other industries	277	361	4 408	1 819	3 415	965	742	5 176	270

Age of the Filipino Population by Sex and Urban and Rural Residence: 1970

[Data based on 20-percent sample, see text. For minimum base for derived figures (percent, median, etc.) and meaning of symbols, see text]

United States Regions States With 10,000 or More Filipino Population	Total			Urban			Rural nonfarm			Rural farm		
	Total	Male	Female	Total	Male	Female	Total	Male	Female	Total	Male	Female
UNITED STATES												
All ages	336 731	183 175	153 556	288 287	153 966	134 321	44 526	26 191	18 335	3 918	3 018	900
Under 1 year	8 337	4 537	3 800	7 342	3 990	3 352	969	535	434	26	12	14
1 year	7 932	3 954	3 978	7 047	3 527	3 520	855	418	437	30	9	21
2 years	7 361	3 879	3 482	6 359	3 343	3 016	981	532	449	21	4	17
3 years	7 320	3 867	3 453	6 377	3 406	2 971	920	441	479	23	20	3
4 years	7 774	4 161	3 613	6 849	3 580	3 269	876	536	340	49	45	4
5 years	7 485	3 705	3 780	6 439	3 242	3 197	1 005	443	562	41	20	21
6 years	7 739	3 932	3 807	6 712	3 419	3 293	1 017	503	514	10	10	–
7 years	7 090	3 544	3 546	6 005	3 018	2 987	1 021	484	537	64	42	22
8 years	6 673	3 568	3 105	5 728	3 049	2 679	912	510	402	33	9	24
9 years	6 466	3 428	3 038	5 418	2 868	2 550	974	542	432	74	18	56
10 years	7 125	3 780	3 345	5 989	3 179	2 810	1 071	576	495	65	25	40
11 years	6 030	3 111	2 919	5 023	2 608	2 415	977	487	490	30	16	14
12 years	6 011	3 214	2 797	5 042	2 716	2 326	908	464	444	61	34	27
13 years	5 695	3 006	2 689	4 774	2 541	2 233	866	435	431	55	30	25
14 years	5 755	2 934	2 821	4 747	2 367	2 380	930	524	406	78	43	35
15 years	5 458	2 799	2 659	4 508	2 294	2 214	904	474	430	46	31	15
16 years	5 167	2 729	2 438	4 265	2 288	1 977	844	406	438	58	35	23
17 years	5 084	2 529	2 555	4 135	2 040	2 095	860	436	424	89	53	36
18 years	4 721	2 362	2 359	4 038	1 977	2 061	633	352	281	50	33	17
19 years	4 574	2 350	2 224	3 848	1 966	1 882	672	359	313	54	25	29
20 years	4 987	2 448	2 539	4 447	2 206	2 241	500	213	287	40	29	11
21 years and over	201 947	113 338	88 609	173 195	94 342	78 853	25 831	16 521	9 310	2 921	2 475	446
Under 5 years	38 724	20 398	18 326	33 974	17 846	16 128	4 601	2 462	2 139	149	90	59
5 to 9 years	35 453	18 177	17 276	30 302	15 596	14 706	4 929	2 482	2 447	222	99	123
10 to 14 years	30 616	16 045	14 571	25 575	13 411	12 164	4 752	2 486	2 266	289	148	141
15 to 19 years	25 004	12 769	12 235	20 794	10 565	10 229	3 913	2 027	1 886	297	177	120
20 to 24 years	30 262	14 054	16 208	26 794	12 212	14 582	3 287	1 715	1 572	181	127	54
25 to 29 years	34 504	15 179	19 325	31 185	13 550	17 635	3 134	1 478	1 656	185	151	34
30 to 34 years	29 180	13 824	15 356	26 460	12 442	14 018	2 608	1 297	1 311	112	85	27
35 to 39 years	22 293	11 133	11 160	19 899	10 057	9 842	2 227	967	1 260	167	109	58
40 to 44 years	18 424	8 901	9 523	15 951	7 595	8 356	2 275	1 202	1 073	198	104	94
45 to 49 years	12 871	6 278	6 593	10 785	5 044	5 741	1 865	1 056	809	221	178	43
50 to 54 years	8 228	4 392	3 836	6 676	3 355	3 321	1 374	898	476	178	139	39
55 to 59 years	13 867	10 857	3 010	10 892	8 385	2 507	2 558	2 074	484	417	398	19
60 to 64 years	16 056	13 816	2 240	12 445	10 504	1 941	3 046	2 771	275	565	541	24
65 to 69 years	11 100	9 211	1 889	8 474	7 039	1 435	2 127	1 692	435	499	480	19
70 to 74 years	5 733	4 924	809	4 456	3 767	689	1 133	1 028	105	144	129	15
75 to 79 years	2 602	2 078	524	2 111	1 644	467	417	376	41	74	58	16
80 to 84 years	883	636	247	702	510	192	176	126	50	5	–	5
85 years and over	931	503	428	812	444	368	104	54	50	15	5	10
Under 18 years	120 502	62 677	57 825	102 759	53 475	49 284	16 890	8 746	8 144	853	456	397
18 years and over	216 229	120 498	95 731	185 528	100 491	85 037	27 636	17 445	10 191	3 065	2 562	503
62 years and over	30 440	25 246	5 194	23 624	19 370	4 254	5 725	4 866	859	1 091	1 010	81
65 years and over	21 249	17 352	3 897	16 555	13 404	3 151	3 957	3 276	681	737	672	65
Median age	26.2	28.3	24.5	26.1	27.7	24.8	26.2	31.7	21.5	48.6	56.3	20.6
REGIONS												
Northeast												
All ages	30 231	14 476	15 755	28 178	13 254	14 924	2 042	1 222	820	11	–	11
Under 1 year	983	555	428	934	532	402	49	23	26	–	–	–
1 year	832	477	355	785	449	336	47	28	19	–	–	–
2 years	683	413	270	657	387	270	26	26	–	–	–	–
3 years	569	279	290	536	268	268	33	11	22	–	–	–
4 years	637	337	300	584	302	282	53	35	18	–	–	–
5 years	594	347	247	530	311	219	64	36	28	–	–	–
6 years	528	246	282	488	222	266	40	24	16	–	–	–
7 years	399	180	219	341	141	200	58	39	19	–	–	–
8 years	426	217	209	392	194	198	34	23	11	–	–	–
9 years	375	208	167	324	177	147	51	31	20	–	–	–
10 years	334	207	127	298	183	115	36	24	12	–	–	–
11 years	240	121	119	207	110	97	33	11	22	–	–	–
12 years	273	174	99	250	162	88	23	12	11	–	–	–
13 years	277	124	153	240	110	130	37	14	23	–	–	–
14 years	246	120	126	231	113	118	15	7	8	–	–	–
15 years	234	95	139	207	88	119	27	7	20	–	–	–
16 years	254	102	152	235	94	141	19	8	11	–	–	–
17 years	180	47	133	168	43	125	12	4	8	–	–	–
18 years	290	95	195	276	95	181	14	–	14	–	–	–
19 years	289	123	166	271	109	162	18	14	4	–	–	–
20 years	384	127	257	350	110	240	34	17	17	–	–	–
21 years and over	21 204	9 882	11 322	19 874	9 054	10 820	1 319	828	491	11	–	11

Age of the Filipino Population by Sex and Urban and Rural Residence: 1970—Continued

[Data based on 20-percent sample, see text. For minimum base for derived figures (percent, median, etc.) and meaning of symbols, see text]

United States Regions States With 10,000 or More Filipino Population	Total			Urban			Rural nonfarm			Rural farm		
	Total	Male	Female	Total	Male	Female	Total	Male	Female	Total	Male	Female
REGIONS — Continued												
Northeast — Continued												
Under 5 years	3 704	2 061	1 643	3 496	1 938	1 558	208	123	85	–	–	–
5 to 9 years	2 322	1 198	1 124	2 075	1 045	1 030	247	153	94	–	–	–
10 to 14 years	1 370	746	624	1 226	678	548	144	68	76	–	–	–
15 to 19 years	1 247	462	785	1 157	429	728	90	33	57	–	–	–
20 to 24 years	3 633	1 185	2 448	3 290	974	2 316	343	211	132	–	–	–
25 to 29 years	5 623	2 133	3 490	5 397	1 991	3 406	226	142	84	–	–	–
30 to 34 years	3 874	1 880	1 994	3 667	1 737	1 930	207	143	64	–	–	–
35 to 39 years	2 467	1 266	1 201	2 259	1 148	1 111	208	118	90	–	–	–
40 to 44 years	1 573	787	786	1 414	700	714	159	87	72	–	–	–
45 to 49 years	834	325	509	774	306	468	54	19	35	6	–	6
50 to 54 years	542	208	334	518	194	324	24	14	10	–	–	–
55 to 59 years	669	450	219	621	406	215	48	44	4	–	–	–
60 to 64 years	805	602	203	762	564	198	43	38	5	–	–	–
65 to 69 years	647	516	131	647	516	131	–	–	–	–	–	–
70 to 74 years	489	422	67	476	413	63	13	9	4	–	–	–
75 to 79 years	191	147	44	166	127	39	20	20	–	5	–	5
80 to 84 years	102	48	54	102	48	54	–	–	–	–	–	–
85 years and over	139	40	99	131	40	91	8	–	8	–	–	–
Under 18 years	8 064	4 249	3 815	7 407	3 886	3 521	657	363	294	–	–	–
18 years and over	22 167	10 227	11 940	20 771	9 368	11 403	1 385	859	526	11	–	11
62 years and over	2 062	1 549	513	1 983	1 487	496	74	62	12	5	–	5
65 years and over	1 568	1 173	395	1 522	1 144	378	41	29	12	5	–	5
Median age	27.5	28.7	26.8	27.6	28.9	26.9	24.9	25.8	24.0	...		...
North Central												
All ages	**27 283**	**12 514**	**14 769**	**25 709**	**11 809**	**13 900**	**1 435**	**647**	**788**	**139**	**58**	**81**
Under 1 year	880	442	438	826	416	410	54	26	28	–	–	–
1 year	727	325	402	713	320	393	14	5	9	–	–	–
2 years	773	391	382	757	380	377	16	11	5	–	–	–
3 years	729	421	308	685	392	293	44	29	15	–	–	–
4 years	656	349	307	608	317	291	48	32	16	–	–	–
5 years	616	263	353	576	245	331	40	18	22	–	–	–
6 years	526	263	263	472	228	244	54	35	19	–	–	–
7 years	488	250	238	455	241	214	33	9	24	–	–	–
8 years	449	243	206	402	211	191	47	32	15	–	–	–
9 years	371	178	193	339	167	172	27	11	16	5	–	5
10 years	460	234	226	409	203	206	45	31	14	6	–	6
11 years	352	186	166	314	166	148	33	20	13	5	–	5
12 years	296	180	116	281	175	106	10	–	10	5	5	–
13 years	250	111	139	232	103	129	12	8	4	6	–	6
14 years	195	131	64	195	131	64	–	–	–	–	–	–
15 years	206	93	113	193	84	109	8	4	4	5	5	–
16 years	208	78	130	199	74	125	9	4	5	–	–	–
17 years	170	100	70	139	83	56	22	13	9	9	4	5
18 years	261	113	148	241	108	133	20	5	15	–	–	–
19 years	259	135	124	225	111	114	34	24	10	–	–	–
20 years	329	129	200	317	129	188	5	–	5	7	–	7
21 years and over	18 082	7 899	10 183	17 131	7 525	9 606	860	330	530	91	44	47
Under 5 years	3 765	1 928	1 837	3 589	1 825	1 764	176	103	73	–	–	–
5 to 9 years	2 450	1 197	1 253	2 244	1 092	1 152	201	105	96	5	–	5
10 to 14 years	1 553	842	711	1 431	778	653	100	59	41	22	5	17
15 to 19 years	1 104	519	585	997	460	537	93	50	43	14	9	5
20 to 24 years	2 891	765	2 126	2 745	738	2 007	128	16	112	18	11	7
25 to 29 years	4 422	1 476	2 946	4 254	1 461	2 793	164	11	153	4	4	–
30 to 34 years	3 457	1 469	1 988	3 318	1 406	1 912	127	57	70	12	6	6
35 to 39 years	2 252	1 154	1 098	2 098	1 061	1 037	139	81	58	15	12	3
40 to 44 years	1 509	705	804	1 392	654	738	106	51	55	11	–	11
45 to 49 years	875	336	539	784	298	486	91	38	53	–	–	–
50 to 54 years	491	187	304	458	174	284	20	9	11	13	4	9
55 to 59 years	596	416	180	581	406	175	15	10	5	–	–	–
60 to 64 years	784	620	164	745	589	156	29	24	5	10	7	3
65 to 69 years	611	518	93	578	495	83	28	23	5	5	–	5
70 to 74 years	229	203	26	219	193	26	10	10	–	–	–	–
75 to 79 years	141	103	38	141	103	38	–	–	–	–	–	–
80 to 84 years	72	40	32	64	40	24	8	–	8	–	–	–
85 years and over	81	36	45	71	36	35	–	–	–	10	–	10
Under 18 years	8 352	4 238	4 114	7 795	3 936	3 859	516	288	228	41	14	27
18 years and over	18 931	8 276	10 655	17 914	7 873	10 041	919	359	560	98	44	54
62 years and over	1 567	1 261	306	1 492	1 219	273	60	42	18	15	–	15
65 years and over	1 134	900	234	1 073	867	206	46	33	13	15	–	15
Median age	27.1	28.4	26.5	27.2	28.5	26.5	25.6	21.9	25.9	32.7	...	...

Age of the Filipino Population by Sex and Urban and Rural Residence: 1970—Continued

[Data based on 20-percent sample, see text. For minimum base for derived figures (percent, median, etc.) and meaning of symbols, see text]

United States Regions States With 10,000 or More Filipino Population	Total			Urban			Rural nonfarm			Rural farm		
	Total	Male	Female	Total	Male	Female	Total	Male	Female	Total	Male	Female

REGIONS — Continued

South

	Total	Male	Female	Total	Male	Female	Total	Male	Female	Total	Male	Female
All ages	29 250	16 421	12 829	27 014	15 161	11 853	2 124	1 218	906	112	42	70
Under 1 year	892	435	457	842	422	420	50	13	37	–	–	–
1 year	806	451	355	771	427	344	29	24	5	6	–	6
2 years	857	413	444	816	404	412	41	9	32	–	–	–
3 years	711	344	367	641	315	326	66	25	41	4	4	–
4 years	867	473	394	824	445	379	37	22	15	6	6	–
5 years	709	366	343	666	352	314	38	14	24	5	–	5
6 years	625	362	263	591	341	250	34	21	13	–	–	–
7 years	553	297	256	507	281	226	42	16	26	4	–	4
8 years	549	328	221	526	313	213	23	15	8	–	–	–
9 years	434	235	199	411	232	179	18	3	15	5	–	5
10 years	513	238	275	477	208	269	36	30	6	–	–	–
11 years	352	195	157	342	190	152	10	5	5	–	–	–
12 years	349	190	159	329	182	147	20	8	12	–	–	–
13 years	280	147	133	272	139	133	8	8	–	–	–	–
14 years	275	139	136	265	136	129	10	3	7	–	–	–
15 years	241	134	107	235	128	107	6	6	–	–	–	–
16 years	225	136	89	193	118	75	32	18	14	–	–	–
17 years	206	99	107	194	94	100	12	5	7	–	–	–
18 years	308	207	101	293	192	101	15	15	–	–	–	–
19 years	362	221	141	326	195	131	36	26	10	–	–	–
20 years	528	344	184	452	296	156	76	48	28	–	–	–
21 years and over	18 608	10 667	7 941	17 041	9 751	7 290	1 485	884	601	82	32	50
Under 5 years	4 133	2 116	2 017	3 894	2 013	1 881	223	93	130	16	10	6
5 to 9 years	2 870	1 588	1 282	2 701	1 519	1 182	155	69	86	14	–	14
10 to 14 years	1 769	909	860	1 685	855	830	84	54	30	–	–	–
15 to 19 years	1 342	797	545	1 241	727	514	101	70	31	–	–	–
20 to 24 years	3 762	2 424	1 338	3 345	2 126	1 219	411	298	113	6	–	6
25 to 29 years	4 450	2 282	2 168	4 115	2 105	2 010	335	177	158	–	–	–
30 to 34 years	3 540	1 896	1 644	3 297	1 760	1 537	243	136	107	–	–	–
35 to 39 years	2 387	1 390	997	2 252	1 312	940	128	71	57	7	7	–
40 to 44 years	1 597	816	781	1 409	736	673	165	80	85	23	–	23
45 to 49 years	727	376	351	674	352	322	53	24	29	–	–	–
50 to 54 years	468	204	264	426	192	234	31	12	19	11	–	11
55 to 59 years	519	346	173	487	326	161	32	20	12	–	–	–
60 to 64 years	580	442	138	510	382	128	64	54	10	6	6	–
65 to 69 years	482	386	96	434	362	72	32	14	18	16	10	6
70 to 74 years	349	281	68	304	245	59	41	36	5	4	–	4
75 to 79 years	106	64	42	93	55	38	9	5	4	4	4	–
80 to 84 years	69	46	23	59	41	18	10	5	5	–	–	–
85 years and over	100	58	42	88	53	35	7	–	7	5	5	–
Under 18 years	9 444	4 982	4 462	8 902	4 727	4 175	512	245	267	30	10	20
18 years and over	19 806	11 439	8 367	18 112	10 434	7 678	1 612	973	639	82	32	50
62 years and over	1 414	1 068	346	1 248	961	287	137	88	49	29	19	10
65 years and over	1 106	835	271	978	756	222	99	60	39	29	19	10
Median age	25.8	25.8	25.9	25.8	25.8	25.7	26.3	25.7	27.0	42.8	...	...

West

	Total	Male	Female	Total	Male	Female	Total	Male	Female	Total	Male	Female
All ages	249 967	139 764	110 203	207 386	113 742	93 644	38 925	23 104	15 821	3 656	2 918	738
Under 1 year	5 582	3 105	2 477	4 740	2 620	2 120	816	473	343	26	12	14
1 year	5 567	2 701	2 866	4 778	2 331	2 447	765	361	404	24	9	15
2 years	5 048	2 662	2 386	4 129	2 172	1 957	898	486	412	21	4	17
3 years	5 311	2 823	2 488	4 515	2 431	2 084	777	376	401	19	16	3
4 years	5 614	3 002	2 612	4 833	2 516	2 317	738	447	291	43	39	4
5 years	5 566	2 729	2 837	4 667	2 334	2 333	863	375	488	36	20	16
6 years	6 060	3 061	2 999	5 161	2 628	2 533	889	423	466	10	10	–
7 years	5 650	2 817	2 833	4 702	2 355	2 347	888	420	468	60	42	18
8 years	5 249	2 780	2 469	4 408	2 331	2 077	808	440	368	33	9	24
9 years	5 286	2 807	2 479	4 344	2 292	2 052	878	497	381	64	18	46
10 years	5 818	3 101	2 717	4 805	2 585	2 220	954	491	463	59	25	34
11 years	5 086	2 609	2 477	4 160	2 142	2 018	901	451	450	25	16	9
12 years	5 093	2 670	2 423	4 182	2 197	1 985	855	444	411	56	29	27
13 years	4 888	2 624	2 264	4 030	2 189	1 841	809	405	404	49	30	19
14 years	5 039	2 544	2 495	4 056	1 987	2 069	905	514	391	78	43	35
15 years	4 777	2 477	2 300	3 873	1 994	1 879	863	457	406	41	26	15
16 years	4 480	2 413	2 067	3 638	2 002	1 636	784	376	408	58	35	23
17 years	4 528	2 283	2 245	3 634	1 820	1 814	814	414	400	80	49	31
18 years	3 862	1 947	1 915	3 228	1 582	1 646	584	332	252	50	33	17
19 years	3 664	1 871	1 793	3 026	1 551	1 475	584	295	289	54	25	29
20 years	3 746	1 848	1 898	3 328	1 671	1 657	385	148	237	33	29	4
21 years and over	144 053	84 890	59 163	119 149	68 012	51 137	22 167	14 479	7 688	2 737	2 399	338

Age of the Filipino Population by Sex and Urban and Rural Residence: 1970—Continued

[Data based on 20-percent sample, see text. For minimum base for derived figures (percent, median, etc.) and meaning of symbols, see text]

United States Regions States With 10,000 or More Filipino Population	Total			Urban			Rural nonfarm			Rural farm		
	Total	Male	Female	Total	Male	Female	Total	Male	Female	Total	Male	Female
REGIONS — Continued												
West — Continued												
Under 5 years	27 122	14 293	12 829	22 995	12 070	10 925	3 994	2 143	1 851	133	80	53
5 to 9 years	27 811	14 194	13 617	23 282	11 940	11 342	4 326	2 155	2 171	203	99	104
10 to 14 years	25 924	13 548	12 376	21 233	11 100	10 133	4 424	2 305	2 119	267	143	124
15 to 19 years	21 311	10 991	10 320	17 399	8 949	8 450	3 629	1 874	1 755	283	168	115
20 to 24 years	19 976	9 680	10 296	17 414	8 374	9 040	2 405	1 190	1 215	157	116	41
25 to 29 years	20 009	9 288	10 721	17 419	7 993	9 426	2 409	1 148	1 261	181	147	34
30 to 34 years	18 309	8 579	9 730	16 178	7 539	8 639	2 031	961	1 070	100	79	21
35 to 39 years	15 187	7 323	7 864	13 290	6 536	6 754	1 752	697	1 055	145	90	55
40 to 44 years	13 745	6 593	7 152	11 736	5 505	6 231	1 845	984	861	164	104	60
45 to 49 years	10 435	5 241	5 194	8 553	4 088	4 465	1 667	975	692	215	178	37
50 to 54 years	6 727	3 793	2 934	5 274	2 795	2 479	1 299	863	436	154	135	19
55 to 59 years	12 083	9 645	2 438	9 203	7 247	1 956	2 463	2 000	463	417	398	19
60 to 64 years	13 887	12 152	1 735	10 428	8 969	1 459	2 910	2 655	255	549	528	21
65 to 69 years	9 360	7 791	1 569	6 815	5 666	1 149	2 067	1 655	412	478	470	8
70 to 74 years	4 666	4 018	648	3 457	2 916	541	1 069	973	96	140	129	11
75 to 79 years	2 164	1 764	400	1 711	1 359	352	388	351	37	65	54	11
80 to 84 years	640	502	138	477	381	96	158	121	37	5	–	5
85 years and over	611	369	242	522	315	207	89	54	35	–	–	–
Under 18 years	94 642	49 208	45 434	78 655	40 926	37 729	15 205	7 850	7 355	782	432	350
18 years and over	155 325	90 556	64 769	128 731	72 816	55 915	23 720	15 254	8 466	2 874	2 486	388
62 years and over	25 397	21 368	4 029	18 901	15 703	3 198	5 454	4 674	780	1 042	991	51
65 years and over	17 441	14 444	2 997	12 982	10 637	2 345	3 771	3 154	617	688	653	35
Median age	25.7	28.9	22.9	25.4	27.8	23.3	26.4	33.8	20.1	49.5	56.5	19.1
STATES												
California												
All ages	135 248	74 798	60 450	125 960	68 198	57 762	6 948	4 549	2 399	2 340	2 051	289
Under 1 year	2 854	1 582	1 272	2 757	1 506	1 251	97	76	21	–	–	–
1 year	2 881	1 460	1 421	2 738	1 396	1 342	133	59	74	10	5	5
2 years	2 647	1 402	1 245	2 477	1 330	1 147	168	72	96	2	–	2
3 years	2 692	1 445	1 247	2 628	1 408	1 220	55	31	24	9	6	3
4 years	2 924	1 473	1 451	2 837	1 421	1 416	83	52	31	4	–	4
5 years	3 054	1 554	1 500	2 900	1 479	1 421	135	66	69	19	9	10
6 years	3 101	1 555	1 546	2 988	1 511	1 477	108	39	69	5	5	–
7 years	2 750	1 388	1 362	2 640	1 316	1 324	100	67	33	10	5	5
8 years	2 729	1 434	1 295	2 604	1 376	1 228	113	58	55	12	–	12
9 years	2 692	1 402	1 290	2 548	1 327	1 221	119	62	57	25	13	12
10 years	2 963	1 646	1 317	2 810	1 579	1 231	126	57	69	27	10	17
11 years	2 512	1 280	1 232	2 376	1 211	1 165	127	63	64	9	6	3
12 years	2 529	1 316	1 213	2 374	1 225	1 149	135	71	64	20	20	–
13 years	2 473	1 353	1 120	2 312	1 270	1 042	151	79	72	10	4	6
14 years	2 370	1 138	1 232	2 209	1 055	1 154	130	78	52	31	5	26
15 years	2 239	1 165	1 074	2 101	1 073	1 028	127	81	46	11	11	–
16 years	2 278	1 226	1 052	2 131	1 168	963	126	53	73	21	5	16
17 years	2 339	1 106	1 233	2 135	993	1 142	166	88	78	38	25	13
18 years	1 875	968	907	1 749	885	864	100	62	38	26	21	5
19 years	2 084	1 085	999	1 897	989	908	151	85	66	36	11	25
20 years	2 253	1 181	1 072	2 117	1 108	1 009	108	49	59	28	24	4
21 years and over	81 009	46 639	34 370	74 632	41 572	33 060	4 390	3 201	1 189	1 987	1 866	121
Under 5 years	13 998	7 362	6 636	13 437	7 061	6 376	536	290	246	25	11	14
5 to 9 years	14 326	7 333	6 993	13 680	7 009	6 671	575	292	283	71	32	39
10 to 14 years	12 847	6 733	6 114	12 081	6 340	5 741	669	348	321	97	45	52
15 to 19 years	10 815	5 550	5 265	10 013	5 108	4 905	670	369	301	132	73	59
20 to 24 years	11 739	5 805	5 934	11 072	5 399	5 673	570	321	249	97	85	12
25 to 29 years	11 866	5 309	6 557	11 335	5 016	6 319	385	170	215	146	123	23
30 to 34 years	10 958	5 074	5 884	10 626	4 881	5 745	257	118	139	75	75	–
35 to 39 years	9 097	4 379	4 718	8 687	4 197	4 490	336	118	218	74	64	10
40 to 44 years	7 765	3 660	4 105	7 390	3 441	3 949	251	126	125	124	93	31
45 to 49 years	5 322	2 454	2 868	4 975	2 211	2 764	171	91	80	176	152	24
50 to 54 years	3 534	1 825	1 709	3 217	1 553	1 664	203	158	45	114	114	–
55 to 59 years	5 909	4 557	1 352	5 110	3 823	1 287	501	442	59	298	292	6
60 to 64 years	7 625	6 679	946	6 393	5 492	901	807	766	41	425	421	4
65 to 69 years	5 214	4 507	707	4 286	3 641	645	565	507	58	363	359	4
70 to 74 years	2 594	2 321	273	2 175	1 912	263	335	325	10	84	84	–
75 to 79 years	1 106	880	226	984	778	206	83	74	9	39	28	11
80 to 84 years	235	188	47	208	161	47	27	27	–	–	–	–
85 years and over	298	182	116	291	175	116	7	7	–	–	–	–
Under 18 years	48 027	24 925	23 102	45 565	23 644	21 921	2 199	1 152	1 047	263	129	134
18 years and over	87 221	49 873	37 348	80 395	44 554	35 841	4 749	3 397	1 352	2 077	1 922	155
62 years and over	13 882	11 973	1 909	11 634	9 838	1 796	1 496	1 402	94	752	733	19
65 years and over	9 447	8 078	1 369	7 944	6 667	1 277	1 017	940	77	486	471	15
Median age	26.6	29.3	24.4	26.2	28.2	24.6	31.3	51.0	20.8	55.7	57.7	19.2

Age of the Filipino Population by Sex and Urban and Rural Residence: 1970—Continued

[Data based on 20-percent sample, see text. For minimum base for derived figures (percent, median, etc.) and meaning of symbols, see text]

United States Regions States With 10,000 or More Filipino Population	Total			Urban			Rural nonfarm			Rural farm		
	Total	Male	Female	Total	Male	Female	Total	Male	Female	Total	Male	Female
STATES — Continued												
Hawaii												
All ages	95 680	54 206	41 474	65 191	36 474	28 717	29 652	17 205	12 447	837	527	310
Under 1 year	2 293	1 295	998	1 614	913	701	664	376	288	15	6	9
1 year	2 240	1 026	1 214	1 644	743	901	586	279	307	10	4	6
2 years	2 065	1 069	996	1 397	694	703	660	375	285	8	—	8
3 years	2 236	1 177	1 059	1 547	841	706	683	330	353	6	6	—
4 years	2 356	1 346	1 010	1 698	932	766	629	385	244	29	29	—
5 years	2 136	965	1 171	1 445	666	779	680	288	392	11	11	—
6 years	2 566	1 286	1 280	1 834	932	902	727	349	378	5	5	—
7 years	2 473	1 199	1 274	1 699	843	856	752	347	405	22	9	13
8 years	2 062	1 082	980	1 409	725	684	642	353	289	11	4	7
9 years	2 182	1 158	1 024	1 457	760	697	692	393	299	33	5	28
10 years	2 451	1 266	1 185	1 625	833	792	799	423	376	27	10	17
11 years	2 272	1 173	1 099	1 529	801	728	727	362	365	16	10	6
12 years	2 156	1 144	1 012	1 452	794	658	686	350	336	18	—	18
13 years	1 986	1 063	923	1 387	739	648	574	306	268	25	18	7
14 years	2 393	1 249	1 144	1 612	802	810	743	415	328	38	32	6
15 years	2 180	1 132	1 048	1 486	793	693	680	332	348	14	7	7
16 years	1 864	1 026	838	1 230	704	526	603	298	305	31	24	7
17 years	1 846	994	852	1 217	684	533	617	310	307	12	—	12
18 years	1 674	808	866	1 211	561	650	445	241	204	18	6	12
19 years	1 241	584	657	864	410	454	359	160	199	18	14	4
20 years	1 124	481	643	890	401	489	229	75	154	5	5	—
21 years and over	51 884	31 683	20 201	34 944	20 903	14 041	16 475	10 458	6 017	465	322	143
Under 5 years	11 190	5 913	5 277	7 900	4 123	3 777	3 222	1 745	1 477	68	45	23
5 to 9 years	11 419	5 690	5 729	7 844	3 926	3 918	3 493	1 730	1 763	82	34	48
10 to 14 years	11 258	5 895	5 363	7 605	3 969	3 636	3 529	1 856	1 673	124	70	54
15 to 19 years	8 805	4 544	4 261	6 008	3 152	2 856	2 704	1 341	1 363	93	51	42
20 to 24 years	6 288	2 983	3 305	4 673	2 238	2 435	1 584	719	865	31	26	5
25 to 29 years	6 606	3 266	3 340	4 707	2 355	2 352	1 869	892	977	30	19	11
30 to 34 years	5 980	2 900	3 080	4 352	2 142	2 210	1 608	754	854	20	4	16
35 to 39 years	4 925	2 392	2 533	3 601	1 835	1 766	1 278	531	747	46	26	20
40 to 44 years	5 166	2 604	2 562	3 626	1 750	1 876	1 510	843	667	30	11	19
45 to 49 years	4 556	2 595	1 961	3 076	1 707	1 369	1 454	875	579	26	13	13
50 to 54 years	2 703	1 647	1 056	1 654	985	669	1 009	641	368	40	21	19
55 to 59 years	5 289	4 356	933	3 380	2 848	532	1 852	1 464	388	57	44	13
60 to 64 years	4 885	4 240	645	2 908	2 478	430	1 926	1 723	203	51	39	12
65 to 69 years	3 398	2 602	796	1 880	1 429	451	1 430	1 089	341	88	84	4
70 to 74 years	1 715	1 392	323	976	750	226	702	616	86	37	26	11
75 to 79 years	935	789	146	635	513	122	286	262	24	14	14	—
80 to 84 years	318	248	70	204	171	33	114	77	37	—	—	—
85 years and over	244	150	94	162	103	59	82	47	35	—	—	—
Under 18 years	39 757	20 650	19 107	27 282	14 199	13 083	12 144	6 271	5 873	331	180	151
18 years and over	55 923	33 556	22 367	37 909	22 275	15 634	17 508	10 934	6 574	506	347	159
62 years and over	9 332	7 489	1 843	5 442	4 290	1 152	3 718	3 054	664	172	145	27
65 years and over	6 610	5 181	1 429	3 857	2 966	891	2 614	2 091	523	139	124	15
Median age	24.1	28.2	20.2	23.5	26.8	20.4	25.8	32.1	19.7	28.4	37.8	18.3
Illinois												
All ages	12 355	5 549	6 806	12 201	5 491	6 710	136	51	85	18	7	11
Under 1 year	403	253	150	394	248	146	9	5	4	—	—	—
1 year	319	145	174	313	145	168	6	—	6	—	—	—
2 years	329	144	185	329	144	185	—	—	—	—	—	—
3 years	271	172	99	266	172	94	5	—	5	—	—	—
4 years	268	152	116	264	148	116	4	4	—	—	—	—
5 years	305	151	154	305	151	154	—	—	—	—	—	—
6 years	178	85	93	171	78	93	7	7	—	—	—	—
7 years	183	83	100	178	78	100	5	5	—	—	—	—
8 years	104	51	53	104	51	53	—	—	—	—	—	—
9 years	154	75	79	154	75	79	—	—	—	—	—	—
10 years	160	87	73	160	87	73	—	—	—	—	—	—
11 years	130	73	57	130	73	57	—	—	—	—	—	—
12 years	77	55	22	77	55	22	—	—	—	—	—	—
13 years	104	43	61	104	43	61	—	—	—	—	—	—
14 years	103	61	42	103	61	42	—	—	—	—	—	—
15 years	42	11	31	42	11	31	—	—	—	—	—	—
16 years	65	27	38	65	27	38	—	—	—	—	—	—
17 years	68	30	38	68	30	38	—	—	—	—	—	—
18 years	119	53	66	119	53	66	—	—	—	—	—	—
19 years	91	55	36	91	55	36	—	—	—	—	—	—
20 years	124	63	61	124	63	61	—	—	—	—	—	—
21 years and over	8 758	3 680	5 078	8 640	3 643	4 997	100	30	70	18	7	11

Age of the Filipino Population by Sex and Urban and Rural Residence: 1970—Continued

[Data based on 20-percent sample, see text. For minimum base for derived figures (percent, median, etc.) and meaning of symbols, see text]

United States Regions States With 10,000 or More Filipino Population	Total			Urban			Rural nonfarm			Rural farm		
	Total	Male	Female	Total	Male	Female	Total	Male	Female	Total	Male	Female
STATES — Continued												
Illinois — Continued												
Under 5 years	1 590	866	724	1 566	857	709	24	9	15	–	–	–
5 to 9 years	924	445	479	912	433	479	12	12	–	–	–	–
10 to 14 years	574	319	255	574	319	255	–	–	–	–	–	–
15 to 19 years	385	176	209	385	176	209	–	–	–	–	–	–
20 to 24 years	1 435	329	1 106	1 408	329	1 079	27	–	27	–	–	–
25 to 29 years	2 356	769	1 587	2 323	769	1 554	33	–	33	–	–	–
30 to 34 years	1 667	714	953	1 667	714	953	–	–	–	–	–	–
35 to 39 years	1 019	521	498	1 016	521	495	–	–	–	3	–	3
40 to 44 years	633	269	364	618	259	359	15	10	5	–	–	–
45 to 49 years	339	121	218	328	110	218	11	11	–	–	–	–
50 to 54 years	185	46	139	181	46	135	–	–	–	4	–	4
55 to 59 years	329	237	92	325	233	92	4	4	–	–	–	–
60 to 64 years	430	326	104	423	319	104	–	–	–	7	7	–
65 to 69 years	286	259	27	276	254	22	10	5	5	–	–	–
70 to 74 years	115	106	9	115	106	9	–	–	–	–	–	–
75 to 79 years	21	17	4	21	17	4	–	–	–	–	–	–
80 to 84 years	20	10	10	20	10	10	–	–	–	–	–	–
85 years and over	47	19	28	43	19	24	–	–	–	4	–	4
Under 18 years	3 263	1 698	1 565	3 227	1 677	1 550	36	21	15	–	–	–
18 years and over	9 092	3 851	5 241	8 974	3 814	5 160	100	30	70	18	7	11
62 years and over	745	610	135	731	605	126	10	5	5	4	–	4
65 years and over	489	411	78	475	406	69	10	5	5	4	–	4
Median age	27.7	29.2	27.0	27.7	29.1	27.0	25.8	...	...	...	...	...
New York												
All ages	14 045	6 557	7 488	13 648	6 382	7 266	392	175	217	5	–	5
Under 1 year	429	264	165	413	259	154	16	5	11	–	–	–
1 year	321	192	129	311	182	129	10	10	–	–	–	–
2 years	338	207	131	327	196	131	11	11	–	–	–	–
3 years	212	102	110	208	102	106	4	–	4	–	–	–
4 years	299	146	153	283	135	148	16	11	5	–	–	–
5 years	226	126	100	214	126	88	12	–	12	–	–	–
6 years	221	122	99	213	119	94	8	3	5	–	–	–
7 years	170	71	99	165	66	99	5	5	–	–	–	–
8 years	134	60	74	131	60	71	3	–	3	–	–	–
9 years	153	75	78	139	70	69	14	5	9	–	–	–
10 years	165	112	53	161	108	53	4	4	–	–	–	–
11 years	127	52	75	118	52	66	9	–	9	–	–	–
12 years	109	76	33	96	68	28	13	8	5	–	–	–
13 years	99	45	54	99	45	54	–	–	–	–	–	–
14 years	128	74	54	124	74	50	4	–	4	–	–	–
15 years	92	48	44	88	48	40	4	–	4	–	–	–
16 years	111	43	68	108	43	65	3	–	3	–	–	–
17 years	83	21	62	79	21	58	4	–	4	–	–	–
18 years	160	44	116	151	44	107	9	–	9	–	–	–
19 years	117	34	83	113	34	79	4	–	4	–	–	–
20 years	160	56	104	153	49	104	7	7	–	–	–	–
21 years and over	10 191	4 587	5 604	9 954	4 481	5 473	232	106	126	5	–	5
Under 5 years	1 599	911	688	1 542	874	668	57	37	20	–	–	–
5 to 9 years	904	454	450	862	441	421	42	13	29	–	–	–
10 to 14 years	628	359	269	598	347	251	30	12	18	–	–	–
15 to 19 years	563	190	373	539	190	349	24	–	24	–	–	–
20 to 24 years	1 498	432	1 066	1 445	414	1 031	53	18	35	–	–	–
25 to 29 years	2 702	980	1 722	2 664	969	1 695	38	11	27	–	–	–
30 to 34 years	1 913	845	1 068	1 859	812	1 047	54	33	21	–	–	–
35 to 39 years	1 134	536	598	1 102	523	579	32	13	19	–	–	–
40 to 44 years	626	283	343	608	269	339	18	14	4	–	–	–
45 to 49 years	399	126	273	389	126	263	10	–	10	–	–	–
50 to 54 years	286	123	163	271	118	153	15	5	10	–	–	–
55 to 59 years	417	281	136	412	276	136	5	5	–	–	–	–
60 to 64 years	472	380	92	458	366	92	14	14	–	–	–	–
65 to 69 years	376	291	85	376	291	85	–	–	–	–	–	–
70 to 74 years	296	244	52	296	244	52	–	–	–	–	–	–
75 to 79 years	102	76	26	97	76	21	–	–	–	5	–	5
80 to 84 years	60	20	40	60	20	40	–	–	–	–	–	–
85 years and over	70	26	44	70	26	44	–	–	–	–	–	–
Under 18 years	3 417	1 836	1 581	3 277	1 774	1 503	140	62	78	–	–	–
18 years and over	10 628	4 721	5 907	10 371	4 608	5 763	252	113	139	5	–	5
62 years and over	1 190	882	308	1 176	873	303	9	9	–	5	–	5
65 years and over	904	657	247	899	657	242	–	–	–	5	–	5
Median age	28.4	29.8	27.6	28.4	29.8	27.7	24.3	28.4	23.5	...	–	...

Age of the Filipino Population by Sex and Urban and Rural Residence: 1970—Continued

[Data based on 20-percent sample, see text. For minimum base for derived figures (percent, median, etc.) and meaning of symbols, see text]

United States Regions States With 10,000 or More Filipino Population	Total			Urban			Rural nonfarm			Rural farm		
	Total	Male	Female	Total	Male	Female	Total	Male	Female	Total	Male	Female
STATES — Continued												
Washington												
All ages	11 488	6 743	4 745	9 984	5 782	4 202	1 115	681	434	389	280	109
Under 1 year	290	149	141	258	143	115	21	–	21	11	6	5
1 year	239	124	115	214	109	105	25	15	10	–	–	–
2 years	198	125	73	157	103	54	30	18	12	11	4	7
3 years	246	151	95	231	136	95	11	11	–	4	4	–
4 years	192	122	70	169	102	67	13	10	3	10	10	–
5 years	203	103	100	170	93	77	27	10	17	6	–	6
6 years	236	143	93	214	121	93	22	22	–	–	–	–
7 years	287	183	104	247	149	98	12	6	6	28	28	–
8 years	283	159	124	245	138	107	28	16	12	10	5	5
9 years	276	177	99	229	149	80	41	28	13	6	–	6
10 years	236	96	140	220	86	134	11	5	6	5	5	–
11 years	166	92	74	145	71	74	21	21	–	–	–	–
12 years	258	116	142	231	98	133	13	9	4	14	9	5
13 years	274	148	126	189	120	69	71	20	51	14	8	6
14 years	162	97	65	141	81	60	15	10	5	6	6	–
15 years	214	102	112	157	61	96	45	33	12	12	8	4
16 years	205	90	115	166	75	91	39	15	24	–	–	–
17 years	197	125	72	172	106	66	–	–	–	25	19	6
18 years	163	91	72	143	75	68	14	10	4	6	6	–
19 years	203	141	62	143	96	47	60	45	15	–	–	–
20 years	174	88	86	161	79	82	13	9	4	–	–	–
21 years and over	6 786	4 121	2 665	5 982	3 591	2 391	583	368	215	221	162	59
Under 5 years	1 165	671	494	1 029	593	436	100	54	46	36	24	12
5 to 9 years	1 285	765	520	1 105	650	455	130	82	48	50	33	17
10 to 14 years	1 096	549	547	926	456	470	131	65	66	39	28	11
15 to 19 years	982	549	433	781	413	368	158	103	55	43	33	10
20 to 24 years	1 054	483	571	927	420	507	103	58	45	24	5	19
25 to 29 years	899	422	477	837	396	441	57	21	36	5	5	–
30 to 34 years	776	326	450	715	295	420	56	31	25	5	–	5
35 to 39 years	715	368	347	631	340	291	64	28	36	20	–	20
40 to 44 years	449	191	258	402	185	217	37	6	31	10	–	10
45 to 49 years	368	125	243	340	112	228	20	5	15	8	8	–
50 to 54 years	279	188	91	243	165	78	36	23	13	–	–	–
55 to 59 years	650	538	112	548	441	107	65	60	5	37	37	–
60 to 64 years	902	821	81	754	684	70	84	78	6	64	59	5
65 to 69 years	520	467	53	448	402	46	45	38	7	27	27	–
70 to 74 years	206	171	35	186	151	35	8	8	–	12	12	–
75 to 79 years	58	49	9	34	25	9	15	15	–	9	9	–
80 to 84 years	36	29	7	30	23	7	6	6	–	–	–	–
85 years and over	48	31	17	48	31	17	–	–	–	–	–	–
Under 18 years	4 162	2 302	1 860	3 555	1 941	1 614	445	249	196	162	112	50
18 years and over	7 326	4 441	2 885	6 429	3 841	2 588	670	432	238	227	168	59
62 years and over	1 372	1 207	165	1 153	995	158	125	118	7	94	94	–
65 years and over	868	747	121	746	632	114	74	67	7	48	48	–
Median age	25.9	29.2	23.4	26.3	29.5	23.7	22.4	23.3	20.5	27.5	55.5	21.9

Social Characteristics of the Filipino Population by Urban and Rural Residence: 1970

[Data based on sample, see text. For minimum base for derived figures (percent, median, etc.) and meaning of symbols, see text]

United States Regions States With 10,000 or More Filipino Population	United States				Northeast			
	Total	Urban	Rural nonfarm	Rural farm	Total	Urban	Rural nonfarm	Rural farm
RELATIONSHIP TO HEAD OF HOUSEHOLD								
Total population	336 731	288 287	44 526	3 918	30 231	28 178	2 042	11
Under 18 years old	120 502	102 759	16 890	853	8 064	7 407	657	–
Living with both parents	100 421	85 575	14 147	699	6 993	6 394	599	–
Percent of all under 18 years	83.3	83.3	83.8	81.9	86.7	86.3	91.2	–
Head of household	90 292	77 638	11 912	742	9 159	8 770	384	5
Head of family	71 326	61 734	9 100	492	6 666	6 328	338	–
Female head	6 119	5 716	374	29	681	666	15	–
Primary individual	18 966	15 904	2 812	250	2 493	2 442	46	5
Female primary individual	5 698	5 404	249	45	1 480	1 460	15	5
Wife of head	55 932	48 565	7 084	283	5 241	4 861	374	6
Other relative of head	156 600	133 669	21 757	1 174	10 742	9 960	782	–
Nonrelative of head	14 400	12 790	1 466	144	2 448	2 403	45	–
In group quarters	19 507	15 625	2 307	1 575	2 641	2 184	457	–
Inmate of institution	1 457	959	498	–	93	88	5	–
Other	18 050	14 666	1 809	1 575	2 548	2 096	452	–

Social Characteristics of the Filipino Population by Urban and Rural Residence: 1970—Continued

[Data based on sample, see text. For minimum base for derived figures (percent, median, etc.) and meaning of symbols, see text]

United States Regions States With 10,000 or More Filipino Population	United States				Northeast			
	Total	Urban	Rural nonfarm	Rural farm	Total	Urban	Rural nonfarm	Rural farm
RELATIONSHIP TO HEAD OF HOUSEHOLD								
FAMILIES BY PRESENCE OF CHILDREN								
Total families	71 326	61 734	9 100	492	6 666	6 328	338	—
With own children under 18 years	48 187	41 919	5 977	291	4 169	3 908	261	—
With own children under 6 years	28 791	25 489	3 202	100	3 066	2 897	169	—
Husband—wife families	61 375	52 947	8 012	416	5 739	5 416	323	—
With own children under 18 years	42 512	36 829	5 430	253	3 751	3 501	250	—
With own children under 6 years	25 996	22 915	2 991	90	2 858	2 694	164	—
Families with female head	6 119	5 716	374	29	681	666	15	—
With own children under 18 years	4 210	3 919	278	13	328	317	11	—
With own children under 6 years	2 393	2 253	133	7	168	163	5	—
CHILDREN EVER BORN								
Women ever married, 15 to 24 years old	9 522	8 256	1 232	34	946	844	102	—
Children per 1,000 women ever married	1 086	1 048	1 324	...	837	788	1 245	—
Women ever married, 25 to 34 years old	26 936	24 179	2 709	48	3 259	3 126	133	—
Children per 1,000 women ever married	2 018	1 964	2 488	...	1 470	1 455	1 827	—
Women ever married, 35 to 44 years old	18 590	16 172	2 270	148	1 513	1 365	148	—
Children per 1,000 women ever married	3 300	3 263	3 537	3 716	2 670	2 612	3 203	—
PLACE OF BIRTH								
Total population	336 823	287 855	45 166	3 802	30 492	28 456	2 029	7
Foreign born	178 970	156 861	19 711	2 398	20 257	19 023	1 234	—
Native	157 853	130 994	25 455	1 404	10 235	9 433	795	7
Born in State of residence	110 294	88 121	21 180	993	5 350	4 940	403	7
Born in different State	24 118	22 278	1 770	70	2 255	2 016	239	—
Northeast	2 761	2 549	212	—	780	661	119	—
North Central	2 440	2 196	236	8	246	237	9	—
South	4 984	4 605	372	7	554	506	48	—
West	13 933	12 928	950	55	675	612	63	—
Born abroad, at sea, etc	8 430	7 604	740	86	687	637	50	—
State of birth not reported	15 011	12 991	1 765	255	1 943	1 840	103	—
SCHOOL ENROLLMENT								
Total enrolled, 3 to 34 years old	93 596	79 600	13 247	749	5 965	5 454	511	—
Nursery school	2 406	2 135	259	12	272	244	28	—
Public	901	746	143	12	87	87	—	—
Kindergarten	6 785	5 694	1 056	35	494	453	41	—
Public	5 962	4 928	999	35	360	319	41	—
Elementary (1 to 8 years)	51 763	43 457	7 929	377	2 674	2 385	289	—
Public	45 511	37 455	7 679	377	1 834	1 555	279	—
High school (1 to 4 years)	19 904	16 429	3 205	270	844	779	65	—
Public	17 827	14 482	3 112	233	669	611	58	—
College	12 738	11 885	798	55	1 681	1 593	88	—
Percent enrolled, 3 to 34 years old	46.0	45.0	52.7	56.2	30.3	29.6	39.3	—
3 and 4 years old	14.5	14.4	14.0	...	19.0	19.1	...	—
5 and 6 years old	81.1	80.8	83.5	...	80.5	80.5	80.8	—
7 to 13 years old	96.1	96.2	95.7	96.1	96.9	96.9	96.3	—
14 to 17 years old: Male	92.9	92.9	92.8	90.1	98.4	98.2	...	—
Female	92.6	92.3	93.2	100.0	82.5	80.9	...	—
18 to 24 years old: Male	27.5	28.6	21.1	17.8	26.4	30.0	8.0	—
Female	23.2	23.5	19.6	42.0	17.4	17.9	9.3	—
25 to 34 years old	6.9	7.1	4.6	1.7	8.2	7.9	14.3	—
YEARS OF SCHOOL COMPLETED								
Total, 25 years old and over	176 672	150 848	23 044	2 780	17 955	16 934	1 010	11
No school years completed	9 862	5 826	3 415	621	323	323	—	—
Elementary: 1 to 4 years	16 819	11 735	4 510	574	584	549	35	—
5 to 7 years	20 657	16 503	3 584	570	1 298	1 192	106	—
8 years	8 966	7 329	1 455	182	731	685	41	5
High school: 1 to 3 years	23 702	20 604	2 738	360	1 968	1 813	155	—
4 years	35 087	30 771	4 054	262	2 345	2 160	185	—
College: 1 to 3 years	21 828	20 130	1 574	124	2 059	1 911	142	6
4 years or more	39 751	37 950	1 714	87	8 647	8 301	346	—
Median school years completed	12.2	12.4	8.0	6.0	15.5	15.7	12.9	...
Percent high school graduates	54.7	58.9	31.9	17.0	72.7	73.1	66.6	...

Social Characteristics of the Filipino Population by Urban and Rural Residence: 1970—Continued

[Data based on sample, see text. For minimum base for derived figures (percent, median, etc.) and meaning of symbols, see text]

United States Regions States With 10,000 or More Filipino Population	North Central				South			
	Total	Urban	Rural nonfarm	Rural farm	Total	Urban	Rural nonfarm	Rural farm
RELATIONSHIP TO HEAD OF HOUSEHOLD								
Total population	27 283	25 709	1 435	139	29 250	27 014	2 124	112
Under 18 years old	8 352	7 795	516	41	9 444	8 902	512	30
Living with both parents	7 328	6 952	356	20	7 618	7 193	400	25
Percent of all under 18 years	87.7	89.2	69.0	...	80.7	80.8	78.1	...
Head of household	7 778	7 421	321	36	7 505	6 969	496	40
Head of family	5 907	5 607	277	23	6 391	5 946	420	25
Female head	559	525	34	–	731	682	37	12
Primary individual	1 871	1 814	44	13	1 114	1 023	76	15
Female primary individual	958	931	14	13	598	544	39	15
Wife of head	5 332	4 923	390	19	5 300	4 824	459	17
Other relative of head	10 690	9 994	616	80	11 189	10 518	620	51
Nonrelative of head	2 034	1 986	44	4	871	811	56	4
In group quarters	1 449	1 385	64	–	4 385	3 892	493	–
Inmate of institution	44	34	10	–	121	87	34	–
Other	1 405	1 351	54	–	4 264	3 805	459	–
FAMILIES BY PRESENCE OF CHILDREN								
Total families	5 907	5 607	277	23	6 391	5 946	420	25
With own children under 18 years	3 814	3 587	217	10	4 628	4 293	316	19
With own children under 6 years	2 693	2 569	124	–	3 346	3 142	191	13
Husband—wife families	5 108	4 856	235	17	5 485	5 089	383	13
With own children under 18 years	3 475	3 293	178	4	3 973	3 678	282	13
With own children under 6 years	2 508	2 395	113	–	2 877	2 687	177	13
Families with female head	559	525	34	–	731	682	37	12
With own children under 18 years	251	220	31	–	583	543	34	6
With own children under 6 years	155	144	11	–	442	428	14	–
CHILDREN EVER BORN								
Women ever married, 15 to 24 years old	876	772	97	7	937	821	116	–
Children per 1,000 women ever married	992	988	...	...	1 003	963	1 284	–
Women ever married, 25 to 34 years old	3 052	2 843	203	6	3 341	3 087	254	–
Children per 1,000 women ever married	1 709	1 698	1 892	...	1 852	1 847	1 906	–
Women ever married, 35 to 44 years old	1 448	1 321	113	14	1 606	1 447	136	23
Children per 1,000 women ever married	3 039	3 025	3 142	...	3 141	3 142	2 926	...
PLACE OF BIRTH								
Total population	27 080	25 417	1 540	123	28 891	26 617	2 196	78
Foreign born	18 434	17 491	897	46	17 882	16 599	1 264	19
Native	8 646	7 926	643	77	11 009	10 018	932	59
Born in State of residence	4 649	4 319	275	55	4 119	3 710	383	26
Born in different State	1 926	1 709	217	–	4 125	3 854	263	8
Northeast	181	175	6	–	690	642	48	–
North Central	547	477	70	–	310	249	53	8
South	441	432	9	–	1 249	1 156	93	–
West	757	625	132	–	1 876	1 807	69	–
Born abroad, at sea, etc	765	653	105	7	1 220	1 109	111	–
State of birth not reported	1 306	1 245	46	15	1 545	1 345	175	25
SCHOOL ENROLLMENT								
Total enrolled, 3 to 34 years old	5 811	5 412	375	24	6 095	5 714	375	6
Nursery school	306	296	10	–	205	181	24	–
Public	59	59	–	–	35	35	–	–
Kindergarten	474	429	45	–	520	486	34	–
Public	417	379	38	–	229	215	14	–
Elementary (1 to 8 years)	2 862	2 629	221	12	3 470	3 257	207	6
Public	1 835	1 658	165	12	2 922	2 709	207	6
High school (1 to 4 years)	751	660	79	12	892	826	66	–
Public	495	424	64	7	763	697	66	–
College	1 418	1 398	20	–	1 008	964	44	–
Percent enrolled, 3 to 34 years old	33.8	33.3	40.3	...	31.1	31.7	22.8	...
3 and 4 years old	15.5	15.9	...	–	12.0	11.5	19.4	–
5 and 6 years old	80.2	81.8	...	–	70.2	70.1	...	...
7 to 13 years old	95.2	95.1	94.7	...	95.0	94.9	97.5	...
14 to 17 years old: Male	88.8	90.3	...	...	90.6	91.6	...	...
Female	97.3	97.2	...	...	94.8	94.4	...	...
18 to 24 years old: Male	30.2	29.3	...	–	11.6	12.5	5.3	–
Female	17.7	17.8	16.8	–	21.1	21.8	14.6	–
25 to 34 years old	9.0	9.1	6.2	–	5.8	6.0	2.8	–
YEARS OF SCHOOL COMPLETED								
Total, 25 years old and over	15 520	14 703	737	80	15 374	14 148	1 150	76
No school years completed	158	144	9	5	275	254	21	–
Elementary: 1 to 4 years	323	281	42	–	573	479	77	17
5 to 7 years	745	699	33	13	1 274	1 123	143	8
8 years	453	386	54	13	508	446	46	16
High school: 1 to 3 years	1 159	1 055	93	11	2 369	2 174	186	9
4 years	1 843	1 687	145	11	3 332	3 068	256	8
College: 1 to 3 years	2 039	1 952	83	4	2 537	2 407	130	–
4 years or more	8 800	8 499	278	23	4 506	4 197	291	18
Median school years completed	16.5	16.5	12.9	...	12.8	12.8	12.4	...
Percent high school graduates	81.7	82.6	68.7	...	67.5	68.4	58.9	...

Social Characteristics of the Filipino Population by Urban and Rural Residence: 1970—Continued

[Data based on sample, see text. For minimum base for derived figures (percent, median, etc.) and meaning of symbols, see text]

United States Regions States With 10,000 or More Filipino Population	West				California			Hawaii		
	Total	Urban	Rural nonfarm	Rural farm	Total	Urban	Rural	Total	Urban	Rural
RELATIONSHIP TO HEAD OF HOUSEHOLD										
Total population	249 967	207 386	38 925	3 656	135 248	125 960	9 288	95 680	65 191	30 489
Under 18 years old	94 642	78 655	15 205	782	48 027	45 565	2 462	39 757	27 282	12 475
Living with both parents	78 482	65 036	12 792	654	39 878	37 878	2 000	33 007	22 373	10 634
Percent of all under 18 years	82.9	82.7	84.1	83.6	83.0	83.1	81.2	83.0	82.0	85.2
Head of household	65 850	54 478	10 711	661	37 073	34 570	2 503	23 381	15 330	8 051
Head of family	52 362	43 853	8 065	444	29 347	27 606	1 741	18 942	12 805	6 137
Female head	4 148	3 843	288	17	2 632	2 572	60	1 213	1 017	196
Primary individual	13 488	10 625	2 646	217	7 726	6 964	762	4 439	2 525	1 914
Female primary individual	2 662	2 469	181	12	1 968	1 885	83	484	374	110
Wife of head	40 059	33 957	5 861	241	22 688	21 721	967	14 113	9 444	4 669
Other relative of head	123 979	103 197	19 739	1 043	62 763	59 541	3 222	52 539	36 226	16 313
Nonrelative of head	9 047	7 590	1 321	136	5 274	4 876	398	3 113	2 115	998
In group quarters	11 032	8 164	1 293	1 575	7 450	5 252	2 198	2 534	2 076	458
Inmate of institution	1 199	750	449	–	526	348	178	528	306	222
Other	9 833	7 414	844	1 575	6 924	4 904	2 020	2 006	1 770	236
FAMILIES BY PRESENCE OF CHILDREN										
Total families	52 362	43 853	8 065	444	29 347	27 606	1 741	18 942	12 805	6 137
With own children under 18 years	35 576	30 131	5 183	262	19 774	18 728	1 046	13 123	9 130	3 993
With own children under 6 years	19 686	16 881	2 718	87	11 035	10 518	517	7 091	5 021	2 070
Husband-wife families	45 043	37 586	7 071	386	25 243	23 727	1 516	16 330	10 907	5 423
With own children under 18 years	31 313	26 357	4 720	236	17 291	16 351	940	11 714	8 027	3 687
With own children under 6 years	17 753	15 139	2 537	77	9 855	9 371	484	6 489	4 558	1 931
Families with female head	4 148	3 843	288	17	2 632	2 572	60	1 213	1 017	196
With own children under 18 years	3 048	2 839	202	7	1 929	1 879	50	881	758	123
With own children under 6 years	1 628	1 518	103	7	1 057	1 037	20	456	379	77
CHILDREN EVER BORN										
Women ever married, 15 to 24 years old	6 763	5 819	917	27	3 684	3 472	212	2 334	1 713	621
Children per 1,000 women ever married	1 145	1 106	1 370	...	1 039	1 026	1 250	1 371	1 335	1 470
Women ever married, 25 to 34 years old	17 284	15 123	2 119	42	10 101	9 769	332	5 787	4 099	1 688
Children per 1,000 women ever married	2 209	2 144	2 656	...	1 964	1 965	1 940	2 634	2 563	2 809
Women ever married, 35 to 44 years old	14 023	12 039	1 873	111	8 049	7 665	384	4 937	3 525	1 412
Children per 1,000 women ever married	3 414	3 378	3 632	3 613	3 147	3 149	3 115	3 935	3 922	3 970
PLACE OF BIRTH										
Total population	250 360	207 365	39 401	3 594	135 641	126 203	9 438	95 354	64 515	30 839
Foreign born	122 397	103 748	16 316	2 333	79 058	73 456	5 602	33 623	21 864	11 759
Native	127 963	103 617	23 085	1 261	56 583	52 747	3 836	61 731	42 651	19 080
Born in State of residence	96 176	75 152	20 119	905	36 976	34 199	2 777	54 120	36 670	17 450
Born in different State	15 812	14 699	1 051	62	11 115	10 591	524	1 755	1 551	204
Northeast	1 110	1 071	39	–	734	707	27	174	168	6
North Central	1 337	1 233	104	–	961	902	59	175	137	38
South	2 740	2 511	222	7	1 950	1 843	107	425	360	65
West	10 625	9 884	686	55	7 470	7 139	331	981	886	95
Born abroad, at sea, etc	5 758	5 205	474	79	3 470	3 358	112	1 583	1 275	308
State of birth not reported	10 217	8 561	1 441	215	5 022	4 599	423	4 273	3 155	1 118
SCHOOL ENROLLMENT										
Total enrolled, 3 to 34 years old	75 725	63 020	11 986	719	39 365	37 349	2 016	30 524	20 660	9 864
Nursery school	1 623	1 414	197	12	843	816	27	662	493	169
Public	720	565	143	12	404	377	27	258	143	115
Kindergarten	5 297	4 326	936	35	2 796	2 632	164	2 173	1 418	755
Public	4 956	4 015	906	35	2 657	2 493	164	2 009	1 284	725
Elementary (1 to 8 years)	42 757	35 186	7 212	359	21 266	20 228	1 038	18 402	12 319	6 083
Public	38 920	31 533	7 028	359	19 058	18 031	1 027	17 124	11 205	5 919
High school (1 to 4 years)	17 417	14 164	2 995	258	8 501	7 977	524	7 519	5 026	2 493
Public	15 900	12 750	2 924	226	7 590	7 076	514	7 097	4 697	2 400
College	8 631	7 930	646	55	5 959	5 696	263	1 768	1 404	364
Percent enrolled, 3 to 34 years old	51.6	50.8	56.2	56.9	49.7	49.5	52.1	54.5	53.3	57.4
3 and 4 years old	14.2	14.1	13.8	...	13.5	13.5	13.9	15.4	16.0	14.1
5 and 6 years old	82.6	82.1	85.4	...	80.9	80.9	80.9	85.7	85.3	86.6
7 to 13 years old	96.2	96.3	95.7	95.7	96.3	96.2	98.2	96.0	96.3	95.2
14 to 17 years old: Male	92.9	92.9	93.1	92.8	95.0	95.4	90.5	91.2	90.0	93.8
Female	92.9	92.8	92.8	100.0	92.9	93.5	84.9	93.2	92.2	95.2
18 to 24 years old: Male	30.8	31.9	24.8	19.0	33.2	34.2	20.0	24.8	24.7	25.0
Female	25.5	26.0	21.1	...	26.6	26.7	24.6	23.5	23.7	23.0
25 to 34 years old	6.4	6.8	3.8	1.8	7.8	7.9	4.6	3.3	3.4	3.1
YEARS OF SCHOOL COMPLETED										
Total, 25 years old and over	127 823	105 063	20 147	2 613	71 523	65 677	5 846	46 720	31 161	15 559
No school years completed	9 106	5 105	3 385	616	2 970	2 030	940	5 781	2 786	2 995
Elementary: 1 to 4 years	15 339	10 426	4 356	557	5 979	4 738	1 241	8 649	5 098	3 551
5 to 7 years	17 340	13 489	3 302	549	9 016	7 847	1 169	7 022	4 625	2 397
8 years	7 274	5 812	1 314	148	3 838	3 425	413	2 798	1 846	952
High school: 1 to 3 years	18 206	15 562	2 304	340	10 286	9 568	718	6 411	4 678	1 733
4 years	27 567	23 856	3 468	243	14 776	14 070	706	10 636	7 879	2 757
College: 1 to 3 years	15 193	13 860	1 219	114	10 953	10 526	427	3 139	2 355	784
4 years or more	17 798	16 953	799	46	13 705	13 473	232	2 284	1 894	390
Median school years completed	11.4	12.1	7.1	5.7	12.2	12.4	6.9	8.7	9.8	6.5
Percent high school graduates	47.4	52.0	27.2	15.4	55.1	58.0	23.3	34.4	38.9	25.3

Social Characteristics of the Filipino Population by Urban and Rural Residence: 1970—Continued

[Data based on sample, see text. For minimum base for derived figures (percent, median, etc.) and meaning of symbols, see text]

United States Regions States With 10,000 or More Filipino Population	Illinois			New York			Washington		
	Total	Urban	Rural	Total	Urban	Rural	Total	Urban	Rural
RELATIONSHIP TO HEAD OF HOUSEHOLD									
Total population	**12 355**	**12 201**	**154**	**14 045**	**13 648**	**397**	**11 488**	**9 984**	**1 504**
Under 18 years old	3 263	3 227	36	3 417	3 277	140	4 162	3 555	607
Living with both parents	2 885	2 849	36	2 988	2 848	140	3 405	2 933	472
Percent of all under 18 years	88.4	88.3	...	87.4	86.9	100.0	81.8	82.5	77.8
Head of household	3 725	3 684	41	4 693	4 616	77	3 421	2 943	478
Head of family	2 760	2 732	28	3 211	3 139	72	2 544	2 167	377
Female head	282	282	–	360	360	–	157	127	30
Primary individual	965	952	13	1 482	1 477	5	877	776	101
Female primary individual	511	503	8	913	908	5	100	100	–
Wife of head	2 331	2 263	68	2 367	2 256	111	1 899	1 685	214
Other relative of head	4 496	4 455	41	4 858	4 702	156	5 237	4 513	724
Nonrelative of head	1 189	1 189	–	1 453	1 443	10	358	336	22
In group quarters	614	610	4	674	631	43	573	507	66
Inmate of institution	4	–	4	65	60	5	96	59	37
Other	610	610	–	609	571	38	477	448	29
FAMILIES BY PRESENCE OF CHILDREN									
Total families	**2 760**	**2 732**	**28**	**3 211**	**3 139**	**72**	**2 544**	**2 167**	**377**
With own children under 18 years	1 594	1 578	16	1 752	1 701	51	1 672	1 422	250
With own children under 6 years	1 138	1 138	–	1 261	1 219	42	985	860	125
Husband–wife families	**2 348**	**2 320**	**28**	**2 693**	**2 621**	**72**	**2 207**	**1 908**	**299**
With own children under 18 years	1 470	1 454	16	1 596	1 545	51	1 459	1 265	194
With own children under 6 years	1 065	1 065	–	1 204	1 162	42	904	793	111
Families with female head	**282**	**282**	**–**	**360**	**360**	**–**	**157**	**127**	**30**
With own children under 18 years	97	97	–	110	110	–	119	99	20
With own children under 6 years	59	59	–	41	41	–	62	54	8
CHILDREN EVER BORN									
Women ever married, 15 to 24 years old	344	317	27	412	382	30	377	322	55
Children per 1,000 women ever married	965	950	...	799	738	...	952	863	...
Women ever married, 25 to 34 years old	1 427	1 394	33	1 405	1 362	43	806	744	62
Children per 1,000 women ever married	1 558	1 555	...	1 389	1 385	...	2 140	2 065	...
Women ever married, 35 to 44 years old	592	584	8	661	638	23	578	481	97
Children per 1,000 women ever married	2 787	2 812	...	2 425	2 384	...	3 080	3 252	...
PLACE OF BIRTH									
Total population	**12 308**	**12 147**	**161**	**13 557**	**13 229**	**328**	**11 594**	**10 166**	**1 428**
Foreign born	9 133	9 049	84	9 391	9 212	179	6 201	5 557	644
Native	3 175	3 098	77	4 166	4 017	149	5 393	4 609	784
Born in State of residence	1 982	1 942	40	2 522	2 391	131	3 210	2 659	551
Born in different State	500	494	6	554	554	–	1 328	1 171	157
Northeast	58	58	–	159	159	–	50	50	–
North Central	105	105	–	69	69	–	108	108	–
South	163	163	–	216	216	–	130	111	19
West	174	168	6	110	110	–	1 040	902	138
Born abroad, at sea, etc	187	168	19	263	256	7	318	263	55
State of birth not reported	506	494	12	827	816	11	537	516	21
SCHOOL ENROLLMENT									
Total enrolled, 3 to 34 years old	**2 155**	**2 155**	**–**	**2 369**	**2 242**	**127**	**3 541**	**3 038**	**503**
Nursery school	100	100	–	89	67	22	99	86	13
Public	21	21	–	18	18	–	53	40	13
Kindergarten	194	194	–	198	192	6	190	160	30
Public	158	158	–	172	166	6	172	142	30
Elementary (1 to 8 years)	959	959	–	951	932	19	1 844	1 581	263
Public	566	566	–	616	597	19	1 600	1 337	263
High school (1 to 4 years)	280	280	–	345	340	5	887	744	143
Public	164	164	–	256	251	5	734	591	143
College	622	622	–	786	711	75	521	467	54
Percent enrolled, 3 to 34 years old	**27.1**	**27.3**	**...**	**29.8**	**28.8**	**62.5**	**53.5**	**51.6**	**66.6**
3 and 4 years old	15.8	16.0	...	16.6	15.1	...	14.4	11.3	...
5 and 6 years old	76.6	77.1	...	86.4	85.7	...	77.7	78.4	...
7 to 13 years old	91.7	92.2	–	96.0	95.8	...	97.5	97.4	98.2
14 to 17 years old: Male	84.5	84.5	–	100.0	100.0	–	91.8	89.5	...
Female	96.6	96.6	–	82.0	80.8	...	92.6	91.4	...
18 to 24 years old: Male	25.9	25.9	–	38.8	36.6	...	42.1	41.3	46.0
Female	16.7	17.1	–	17.9	17.8	...	28.9	30.5	...
25 to 34 years old	6.8	6.9	–	8.9	8.2	...	8.0	7.4	15.4
YEARS OF SCHOOL COMPLETED									
Total, 25 years old and over	**7 447**	**7 356**	**91**	**8 853**	**8 662**	**191**	**5 906**	**5 216**	**690**
No school years completed	65	65	–	188	188	–	243	200	43
Elementary: 1 to 4 years	104	95	9	329	329	–	395	350	45
5 to 7 years	287	283	4	642	620	22	843	655	188
8 years	213	200	13	363	348	15	432	382	50
High school: 1 to 3 years	572	565	7	830	813	17	1 017	884	133
4 years	809	790	19	933	923	10	1 225	1 124	101
College: 1 to 3 years	1 150	1 128	22	926	909	17	704	646	58
4 years or more	4 247	4 230	17	4 642	4 532	110	1 047	975	72
Median school years completed	16.5	16.5	...	16.2	16.2	16.5	12.0	12.1	9.4
Percent high school graduates	83.3	83.6	...	73.4	73.5	71.7	50.4	52.6	33.5

Age, Marital Status, Education, and Industry of the Filipino Population for Selected Standard Metropolitan Statistical Areas and Cities: 1970

[Data based on 20-percent sample, see text. For meaning of symbols, see text]

Standard Metropolitan Statistical Areas With 5,000 or More Filipino Population / Cities With 5,000 or More Filipino Population	Standard metropolitan statistical areas									
	Chicago, Ill.	Honolulu, Hawaii	Los Angeles–Long Beach, Calif.	New York, N.Y.	Norfolk–Portsmouth, Va.	Salinas–Monterey, Calif.	San Diego, Calif.	San Francisco–Oakland, Calif.	San Jose, Calif.	Seattle–Everett, Wash.
AGE										
Male, all ages	5 194	37 275	16 779	5 873	3 588	3 584	8 440	23 243	3 691	4 518
Under 5 years	804	4 322	1 734	823	518	401	1 113	2 291	355	472
5 to 9 years	413	4 159	1 598	375	316	375	1 119	2 346	340	459
10 to 14 years	299	4 068	1 258	327	77	369	764	2 252	370	359
15 to 19 years	149	3 116	1 063	167	117	353	524	1 875	381	284
20 to 24 years	309	2 303	1 255	373	762	346	931	1 786	322	287
25 to 29 years	715	2 407	1 629	859	716	156	770	1 686	279	278
30 to 34 years	692	2 203	1 571	748	464	158	776	1 620	227	230
35 to 39 years	488	1 857	1 274	492	337	126	780	1 282	174	240
40 to 44 years	245	1 794	994	240	139	57	509	1 245	176	122
45 to 49 years	110	1 773	562	106	54	79	331	831	109	88
50 to 54 years	41	1 009	245	118	5	175	46	757	76	98
55 to 59 years	218	2 873	820	253	4	280	175	1 259	250	416
60 to 64 years	315	2 547	1 247	352	20	343	212	1 898	286	622
65 to 69 years	259	1 446	935	277	32	193	176	1 147	195	372
70 to 74 years	101	696	404	244	19	120	156	640	90	115
75 years and over	36	702	190	119	8	53	58	328	61	76
Female, all ages	6 374	29 378	15 239	6 582	1 861	2 563	6 629	21 083	3 077	3 150
Under 5 years	668	3 823	1 626	588	474	204	1 068	2 081	331	320
5 to 9 years	442	4 145	1 531	364	257	272	1 033	2 271	353	310
10 to 14 years	245	3 653	1 300	224	149	346	622	2 133	366	340
15 to 19 years	183	2 911	1 036	307	37	294	516	1 863	269	304
20 to 24 years	1 014	2 430	1 567	911	107	287	313	2 224	391	395
25 to 29 years	1 503	2 410	2 146	1 561	313	188	768	2 070	298	334
30 to 34 years	943	2 272	1 873	961	242	193	746	1 863	258	293
35 to 39 years	456	1 777	1 195	546	177	149	691	1 704	228	206
40 to 44 years	328	1 933	1 039	307	61	175	414	1 370	229	179
45 to 49 years	213	1 417	605	225	10	203	196	1 130	145	165
50 to 54 years	119	703	391	147	7	107	79	741	49	62
55 to 59 years	92	601	346	126	21	46	55	628	24	91
60 to 64 years	99	440	248	87	–	31	62	432	47	64
65 to 69 years	22	464	134	75	–	35	40	312	66	38
70 to 74 years	9	208	85	48	6	11	8	128	8	20
75 years and over	38	191	117	105	–	22	18	133	15	29
MARITAL STATUS										
Male, 14 years old and over	3 739	25 546	12 361	4 422	2 688	2 493	5 565	16 779	2 672	3 305
Single	1 014	9 079	3 744	1 356	1 145	889	1 846	5 404	988	1 078
Married, wife present	2 277	12 209	6 635	2 413	823	1 228	2 485	8 526	1 324	1 580
With spouse of same race	1 657	8 786	4 485	1 518	518	762	1 768	6 790	886	971
Separated	78	247	242	101	11	35	19	392	36	79
Other married, wife absent	238	2 351	1 114	300	672	172	1 054	1 633	191	198
Widowed	63	914	207	128	15	76	53	334	49	108
Divorced	69	746	419	124	22	93	108	490	84	262
Female, 14 years old and over	5 061	18 530	10 999	5 445	1 014	1 803	4 042	15 027	2 107	2 232
Single	2 438	5 134	3 508	2 682	113	525	830	4 700	607	673
Married, husband present	2 186	10 821	6 043	2 004	699	944	2 517	8 180	1 301	1 299
With spouse of same race	1 667	8 764	4 454	1 522	543	749	1 759	6 769	915	954
Separated	53	189	183	152	12	33	32	188	19	31
Other married, husband absent	229	1 165	550	238	182	138	469	981	85	81
Widowed	118	671	447	311	14	112	114	655	48	98
Divorced	37	550	268	58	6	51	80	323	47	50
YEARS OF SCHOOL COMPLETED										
Male, 25 to 34 years old	1 407	4 610	3 200	1 607	1 180	314	1 546	3 306	506	508
Elementary: Less than 5 years	10	131	58	31	56	5	60	51	–	12
5 to 7 years	19	189	35	17	33	4	17	50	12	–
8 years	–	143	19	16	–	16	6	34	5	4
High school: 1 to 3 years	54	812	406	128	339	67	578	438	44	56
4 years	118	2 184	823	121	343	84	343	969	136	139
College: 1 to 3 years	274	779	789	195	330	102	437	835	138	84
4 years or more	932	372	1 070	1 099	79	36	105	929	171	213
Female, 25 to 34 years old	2 446	4 682	4 019	2 522	555	381	1 514	3 933	556	627
Elementary: Less than 5 years	30	251	48	69	–	10	58	100	4	–
5 to 7 years	38	411	112	37	22	21	153	174	24	20
8 years	26	99	84	31	–	10	62	74	11	10
High school: 1 to 3 years	154	763	350	142	86	80	246	463	45	90
4 years	206	1 827	713	193	85	90	322	871	196	129
College: 1 to 3 years	247	712	654	270	97	95	282	816	109	114
4 years or more	1 745	619	2 058	1 780	265	75	391	1 435	167	264
INDUSTRY										
Total employed, 16 years old and over	6 839	24 966	14 556	6 881	527	2 381	2 814	18 377	2 802	3 064
Agriculture, forestry, and fisheries	17	1 593	220	12	16	595	69	346	216	121
Construction	78	3 190	240	104	9	12	54	311	64	40
Manufacturing: Durable goods	541	1 422	2 282	262	34	85	310	1 374	867	597
Nondurable goods	552	2 375	1 118	556	–	266	184	941	108	249
Transportation, communication, and other public utilities	149	1 881	635	341	26	43	51	1 762	95	231
Wholesale and retail trade	863	4 938	2 769	720	98	473	487	2 806	391	650
Personal services	227	2 378	514	251	18	174	298	1 515	112	209
Professional and related services	3 632	2 740	3 854	3 176	270	378	791	3 944	551	617
Other industries	780	4 449	2 924	1 459	56	355	570	5 378	398	350

Age, Marital Status, Education, and Industry of the Filipino Population for Selected Standard Metropolitan Statistical Areas and Cities: 1970—Continued

[Data based on 20-percent sample, see text. For meaning of symbols, see text]

Standard Metropolitan Statistical Areas With 5,000 or More Filipino Population / Cities With 5,000 or More Filipino Population	SMSA's—Con.		Cities						
	Stockton, Calif.	Washington, D.C.–Md.–Va.	Chicago, Ill.	Honolulu, Hawaii	Los Angeles, Calif.	New York, N.Y.	San Diego, Calif.	San Francisco, Calif.	Seattle, Wash.
AGE									
Male, all ages	**4 775**	**2 247**	**4 155**	**16 575**	**9 928**	**5 277**	**5 245**	**13 425**	**3 575**
Under 5 years	316	200	639	1 831	1 099	718	736	1 226	352
5 to 9 years	225	230	290	1 602	813	298	794	1 236	297
10 to 14 years	420	162	187	1 510	550	283	469	1 187	268
15 to 19 years	310	113	114	1 235	550	148	335	1 056	211
20 to 24 years	276	186	259	1 098	719	364	512	1 006	230
25 to 29 years	150	235	648	1 131	1 006	828	444	951	238
30 to 34 years	124	185	532	912	1 072	698	478	953	164
35 to 39 years	98	222	390	703	728	458	438	778	170
40 to 44 years	168	133	188	826	567	166	270	715	88
45 to 49 years	146	83	81	782	292	76	234	483	73
50 to 54 years	102	37	41	497	132	103	24	479	93
55 to 59 years	481	128	181	652	516	217	110	749	330
60 to 64 years	764	107	257	1 286	829	310	120	1 176	551
65 to 69 years	622	125	220	748	601	265	143	759	332
70 to 74 years	329	64	92	394	298	230	110	461	111
75 years and over	244	37	36	368	156	115	28	210	67
Female, all ages	**2 203**	**2 350**	**5 273**	**12 498**	**8 697**	**5 969**	**4 186**	**12 141**	**2 500**
Under 5 years	274	279	558	1 633	892	523	737	1 085	225
5 to 9 years	308	189	344	1 557	738	310	606	1 143	238
10 to 14 years	272	194	185	1 339	622	179	364	1 138	268
15 to 19 years	285	78	160	1 116	520	257	351	1 139	237
20 to 24 years	219	247	843	1 187	1 055	834	165	1 322	331
25 to 29 years	218	374	1 335	1 079	1 368	1 497	474	1 170	258
30 to 34 years	119	322	772	1 089	1 126	894	519	1 141	242
35 to 39 years	113	206	353	756	646	497	447	1 024	148
40 to 44 years	122	178	254	904	590	269	203	758	148
45 to 49 years	137	99	165	695	343	187	152	671	141
50 to 54 years	40	54	73	369	213	124	59	516	57
55 to 59 years	51	33	86	217	221	123	43	357	86
60 to 64 years	16	55	99	166	163	73	37	334	49
65 to 69 years	20	23	17	229	84	71	21	191	27
70 to 74 years	4	11	5	58	34	48	8	81	20
75 years and over	5	8	24	104	82	83	–	71	25
MARITAL STATUS									
Male, 14 years old and over	**3 889**	**1 680**	**3 084**	**11 983**	**7 542**	**4 039**	**3 299**	**9 992**	**2 715**
Single	1 807	468	862	4 532	2 329	1 272	1 031	3 230	924
Married, wife present	1 125	989	1 845	5 166	3 984	2 157	1 593	4 862	1 219
With spouse of same race	661	636	1 412	3 679	2 813	1 402	1 158	4 109	820
Separated	102	33	73	150	156	97	13	218	74
Other married, wife absent	396	90	186	1 274	677	273	559	1 164	187
Widowed	217	45	63	444	145	119	33	204	95
Divorced	242	55	55	417	251	121	70	314	216
Female, 14 years old and over	**1 414**	**1 713**	**4 213**	**8 222**	**6 573**	**4 991**	**2 546**	**9 000**	**1 816**
Single	434	568	2 157	2 214	2 340	2 517	523	3 067	596
Married, husband present	807	893	1 703	4 600	3 424	1 793	1 594	4 552	1 017
With spouse of same race	639	619	1 426	3 707	2 793	1 412	1 151	4 041	806
Separated	33	56	53	120	80	143	23	127	25
Other married, husband absent	75	121	190	594	322	213	287	686	58
Widowed	40	56	73	366	211	280	70	379	81
Divorced	25	19	37	328	196	45	49	189	39
YEARS OF SCHOOL COMPLETED									
Male, 25 to 34 years old	**274**	**420**	**1 180**	**2 043**	**2 078**	**1 526**	**922**	**1 904**	**402**
Elementary: Less than 5 years	18	4	10	84	39	31	35	26	12
5 to 7 years	14	11	11	81	19	17	7	33	–
8 years	6	–	–	62	19	16	–	23	–
High school: 1 to 3 years	63	26	43	344	211	117	298	231	39
4 years	84	78	103	854	485	121	221	518	115
College: 1 to 3 years	65	85	234	376	504	190	294	451	64
4 years or more	24	216	779	242	801	1 034	67	622	172
Female, 25 to 34 years old	**337**	**696**	**2 107**	**2 168**	**2 494**	**2 391**	**993**	**2 311**	**500**
Elementary: Less than 5 years	13	10	17	133	33	69	35	39	–
5 to 7 years	28	32	29	190	53	32	108	88	10
8 years	17	6	20	59	24	31	30	32	–
High school: 1 to 3 years	65	45	115	288	144	137	171	265	75
4 years	63	86	187	822	378	173	190	466	97
College: 1 to 3 years	77	95	194	335	373	234	203	494	94
4 years or more	74	422	1 545	341	1 489	1 715	256	927	224
INDUSTRY									
Total employed, 16 years old and over	**2 968**	**2 109**	**5 862**	**12 142**	**9 301**	**6 330**	**1 830**	**11 234**	**2 521**
Agriculture, forestry, and fisheries	1 727	23	17	138	91	8	27	45	61
Construction	35	61	56	1 734	145	90	38	194	30
Manufacturing: Durable goods	61	67	439	601	1 142	223	219	500	437
Nondurable goods	101	69	454	944	675	509	108	522	221
Transportation, communication, and other public utilities	44	116	129	1 053	394	313	28	1 270	166
Wholesale and retail trade	273	205	774	2 580	1 738	661	292	1 744	536
Personal services	73	220	201	1 626	358	233	195	1 014	193
Professional and related services	274	680	3 077	1 570	2 482	2 916	530	2 334	563
Other industries	380	668	715	1 896	2 276	1 377	393	3 611	314

Social Characteristics of the Hawaiian Population by Urban and Rural Residence: 1970

[Data based on sample, see text. For minimum base for derived figures (percent, median, etc.) and meaning of symbols, see text]

United States States With 10,000 or More Hawaiian Population Standard Metropolitan Statistical Areas With 5,000 or More Hawaiian Population	United States (excluding Alaska)	States		Honolulu, Hawaii, SMSA
		California	Hawaii	
RELATIONSHIP TO HEAD OF HOUSEHOLD				
Total population	**99 958**	**14 454**	**72 395**	**55 175**
Under 18 years old	41 743	5 076	32 603	25 036
Living with both parents	31 604	3 889	24 814	18 953
Percent of all under 18 years	75.7	76.6	76.1	75.7
Head of household	23 200	4 308	15 949	12 099
Head of family	18 941	3 235	13 583	10 339
Female head	2 519	358	1 897	1 480
Primary individual	4 259	1 073	2 366	1 760
Female primary individual	1 897	436	1 038	809
Wife of head	17 616	2 704	12 273	8 968
Other relative of head	52 671	5 966	41 527	31 865
Nonrelative of head	3 100	739	1 410	1 173
In group quarters	3 371	737	1 236	1 070
Inmate of institution	954	139	672	556
Other	2 417	598	564	514
FAMILIES BY PRESENCE OF CHILDREN				
Total families	**18 941**	**3 235**	**13 583**	**10 339**
With own children under 18 years	13 047	2 190	9 365	7 191
With own children under 6 years	7 469	1 458	5 034	3 804
Husband—wife families	**15 382**	**2 763**	**10 872**	**8 284**
With own children under 18 years	10 956	1 859	7 841	6 016
With own children under 6 years	6 602	1 303	4 456	3 358
Families with female head	**2 519**	**358**	**1 897**	**1 480**
With own children under 18 years	1 692	293	1 205	949
With own children under 6 years	728	145	475	379
CHILDREN EVER BORN				
Women ever married, 15 to 24 years old	3 517	583	2 205	1 706
Children per 1,000 women ever married	1 334	1 063	1 476	1 416
Women ever married, 25 to 34 years old	6 987	1 211	4 635	3 454
Children per 1,000 women ever married	3 063	2 528	3 379	3 309
Women ever married, 35 to 44 years old	5 449	861	3 769	2 854
Children per 1,000 women ever married	4 181	3 386	4 506	4 409
PLACE OF BIRTH				
Total population	**98 836**	**14 416**	**71 274**	**54 309**
Foreign born	590	159	204	114
Native	98 246	14 257	71 070	54 195
Born in State of residence	70 913	3 480	64 606	48 918
Born in different State	18 595	9 352	1 517	1 325
Northeast	447	71	187	159
North Central	635	128	209	178
South	1 142	301	286	283
West	16 371	8 852	835	705
Born abroad, at sea, etc	954	334	367	318
State of birth not reported	7 784	1 091	4 580	3 634
SCHOOL ENROLLMENT				
Total enrolled, 3 to 34 years old	**33 024**	**4 394**	**24 671**	**19 068**
Nursery school	993	106	791	619
Public	430	47	341	248
Kindergarten	2 272	313	1 769	1 331
Public	2 053	293	1 595	1 184
Elementary (1 to 8 years)	18 957	2 407	14 602	11 373
Public	17 014	2 206	13 033	9 957
High school (1 to 4 years)	7 972	835	6 384	4 817
Public	6 898	775	5 458	4 020
College	2 830	733	1 125	928
Percent enrolled, 3 to 34 years old	**52.1**	**45.0**	**55.1**	**55.3**
3 and 4 years old	23.5	20.6	24.2	23.6
5 and 6 years old	84.3	84.3	86.4	87.8
7 to 13 years old	96.7	98.0	96.4	96.5
14 to 17 years old: Male	91.3	96.6	90.7	90.3
Female	91.3	84.8	91.6	90.6
18 to 24 years old: Male	24.0	26.6	21.7	21.6
Female	23.1	23.4	20.5	20.5
25 to 34 years old	4.9	8.5	2.9	3.3
YEARS OF SCHOOL COMPLETED				
Total, 25 years old and over	**44 707**	**6 798**	**31 767**	**23 836**
No school years completed	475	49	356	249
Elementary: 1 to 4 years	1 858	158	1 456	845
5 to 7 years	4 405	427	3 407	2 333
8 years	4 431	411	3 506	2 426
High school: 1 to 3 years	9 748	1 327	7 260	5 597
4 years	17 041	2 812	12 118	9 435
College: 1 to 3 years	4 231	1 122	2 318	1 812
4 years or more	2 518	492	1 346	1 139
Median school years completed	12.1	12.4	12.0	12.0
Percent high school graduates	53.2	65.1	49.7	52.0

Social Characteristics of the Korean Population by Urban and Rural Residence: 1970

[Data based on sample, see text. For minimum base for derived figures (percent, median, etc.) and meaning of symbols, see text]

United States
States With 10,000 or More
  Korean Population
Standard Metropolitan Statistical
  Areas With 5,000 or More
  Korean Population

	United States (excluding Alaska)	California	Standard metropolitan statistical areas		
			Honolulu, Hawaii	Los Angeles—Long Beach, Calif.	New York, N.Y.
RELATIONSHIP TO HEAD OF HOUSEHOLD					
Total population	69 510	15 909	8 914	8 811	4 925
Under 18 years old	24 316	5 318	3 328	2 816	1 568
Living with both parents	20 477	4 281	2 664	2 257	1 376
Percent of all under 18 years	84.2	80.5	80.0	80.1	87.8
Head of household	15 738	4 163	2 419	2 665	1 459
Head of family	12 112	3 098	2 031	1 997	1 063
Female head	1 779	519	371	250	55
Primary individual	3 626	1 065	388	668	396
Female primary individual	1 752	479	258	294	188
Wife of head	18 481	4 049	1 625	2 073	1 140
Other relative of head	30 241	6 813	4 492	3 671	1 958
Nonrelative of head	2 861	512	188	216	285
In group quarters	2 189	372	190	186	83
Inmate of institution	298	73	118	37	12
Other	1 891	299	72	149	71
FAMILIES BY PRESENCE OF CHILDREN					
Total families	12 112	3 098	2 031	1 997	1 063
With own children under 18 years	8 507	2 043	1 364	1 251	708
With own children under 6 years	5 748	1 314	584	838	579
Husband—wife families	9 956	2 449	1 586	1 649	957
With own children under 18 years	7 044	1 675	1 089	1 083	657
With own children under 6 years	5 011	1 162	492	770	560
Families with female head	1 779	519	371	250	55
With own children under 18 years	1 320	326	252	142	32
With own children under 6 years	681	131	92	53	14
CHILDREN EVER BORN					
Women ever married, 15 to 24 years old	3 142	568	200	257	148
Children per 1,000 women ever married	842	956	955	751	750
Women ever married, 25 to 34 years old	11 441	2 235	565	1 226	757
Children per 1,000 women ever married	1 403	1 329	1 747	1 221	1 210
Women ever married, 35 to 44 years old	5 389	1 360	685	603	320
Children per 1,000 women ever married	2 287	2 371	2 769	2 347	2 122
PLACE OF BIRTH					
Total population	70 598	16 684	8 938	9 395	4 685
Foreign born	38 145	9 560	1 881	5 782	2 937
Native	32 453	7 124	7 057	3 613	1 748
Born in State of residence	15 316	3 370	6 075	2 019	708
Born in different State	5 555	1 775	288	786	256
Northeast	824	60	31	16	44
North Central	1 144	269	50	155	48
South	954	131	35	38	55
West	2 633	1 315	172	577	109
Born abroad, at sea, etc	5 111	1 011	210	347	234
State of birth not reported	6 471	968	484	461	550
SCHOOL ENROLLMENT					
Total enrolled, 3 to 34 years old	21 374	5 133	3 017	2 817	1 201
Nursery school	753	141	116	89	86
Public	130	38	29	33	—
Kindergarten	1 350	242	200	105	98
Public	1 171	230	172	100	66
Elementary (1 to 8 years)	10 722	2 326	1 605	1 125	435
Public	9 717	2 163	1 386	1 029	367
High school (1 to 4 years)	3 506	1 044	694	614	237
Public	3 225	996	634	572	167
College	5 043	1 380	402	884	345
Percent enrolled, 3 to 34 years old	44.9	46.8	62.4	45.1	36.2
3 and 4 years old	22.3	25.2	35.7	34.0	30.0
5 and 6 years old	77.6	75.5	89.7	78.3	84.6
7 to 13 years old	96.8	95.8	99.0	92.8	98.8
14 to 17 years old: Male	93.1	92.4	90.8	91.8	. . .
Female	93.1	92.5	92.6	91.0	91.2
18 to 24 years old: Male	50.7	40.8	39.6	36.0	44.8
Female	25.5	36.8	37.1	45.9	29.6
25 to 34 years old	14.4	16.7	10.1	17.9	10.6
YEARS OF SCHOOL COMPLETED					
Total, 25 years old and over	37 706	8 896	4 596	5 109	2 964
No school years completed	1 071	255	202	172	41
Elementary: 1 to 4 years	1 063	192	158	90	49
5 to 7 years	3 020	445	251	204	217
8 years	2 089	336	262	132	91
High school: 1 to 3 years	3 655	642	617	258	162
4 years	8 541	2 211	1 872	1 168	407
College: 1 to 3 years	4 598	1 774	553	1 207	360
4 years or more	13 669	3 041	681	1 878	1 637
Median school years completed	12.9	13.6	12.4	14.3	16.4
Percent high school graduates	71.1	79.0	67.6	83.2	81.1

Japanese, Chinese, and Filipinos in the United States. 1970 Census of Population Subject Reports, U.S. Department of Commerce, Bureau of the Census, Washington, D.C. July 1975.

Meeting the English language needs of Indochinese students

Schools receiving Vietnamese and other Indochinese refugees as students will have teaching the English language as a high priority to insure that the students can participate in the activities of the school and community as rapidly as possible. At the same time, teachers and administrators must be concerned with monitoring students' cognitive development and providing for their effective needs. The following is intended to assist school administrators in their initial planning for meeting these needs.

1. Can the school expect Indochinese children to adjust to the school without special provision?

Recent court decisions, notably Lau vs. Nichols, have been clear in stating that when a student's language and cultural differences make it impossible for him to profit by instruction, the school has the responsibility to provide for his special instructional needs. The Center for Applied Linguistics, the U.S. Civil Rights Commission, and the Office of Civil Rights have recommended that the best way to meet these needs is through a program of bilingual/bicultural education. The goal of the school should be to make Vietnamese students, as well as all other students, feel comfortable and successful at school, to become part of the school community.

What education has learned in recent years about teaching students who come from language and cultural groups very different from the school is that the most efficient way of assimilating them includes considering and making special provision for these differ-ences. To ignore the unique qualities a child brings to school is essentially the same thing as ignoring the child. The educational goal of academic adjustment cannot be achieved without special attention to the needs and unique characteristics of this new group -- the Vietnamese.

The answer to the question is: Vietnamese students will succeed in adjusting to the school when the school makes such success possible.

2. How much English can we expect Vietnamese students to know when they come to the school?

Information from all four resettlement camps indicates that school-age students at all levels vary widely in their ability to use English. All school children in Vietnam were required to study either French or English as a foreign language. Proficiency levels at the camps indicated, however, that the majority of refugees spoke English at the beginner or early intermediate levels. For older students who had received several years of training in English the ability to read and write was greater than the ability to speak. Schools preparing to receive Vietnamese students should plan to test each student's ability to use the English language. A publication of the Indochinese Clearinghouse entitled Testing English Language Proficiency should provide help in language testing. The type of program planned by the school should be consistent with the finding of this testing program.

It should be noted that: too many variables were present in the resettlement camp programs for school administrators to be able to assume that since Vietnamese students studied some English there, they would be able to fit in comfortably in an English-speaking classroom. English-language ability will vary from student to student. At best the amount of English taught in the camps has been small. There is much for the school to do.

3. What models exist for organizing instruction in English for speakers of another language?

One thing is certain: the student who has limited or no command of the English language is in need of directed, structured instruction in English. No school should assume that a non-English speaking Vietnamese child can be placed in a regular English-speaking class and can just "pick up" English on his own. Although individual learning will vary, the school can well assume that the ease and speed with which Vietnamese students learn English will depend largely on the effort the school expends in providing for their language needs. Some patterns of instruction to be considered are:

a. A bilingual/bicultural program (BBE) is the optimum type in which staff members are able to offer instruction to students both in English and in Vietnamese. In such programs teachers extend a child's ability to use Vietnamese while developing his ability to function in English. Such programs should be considered in districts receiving large enough numbers of refugees to make it economically feasible. (After the current school year, this will, in fact, be required by Office of Civil Rights guidelines for compliance with the Lau decision.) A commitment to a full bilingual program will require the employing

of bilingual personnel, acquisition of instructional materials in Vietnamese, and extensive in-service education. Sound bilingual programs are planned and operated to reflect the wishes of the community and the parents of students involved.

b. A support bilingual education program will employ some of the better practices of bilingual education, particularly assessing and building upon what the child already knows, developing a rich understanding of his culture and language, actively transferring skills and concepts already developed in the Vietnamese school system to those used in this country's schools, using material in the child's native language wherever possible and using key bilingual staff members to assure that the child continues his cognitive development while he is learning the English language. A support bilingual program will require the employing of some bilingual staff members (principally aides) and the acquisition of available materials about Vietnamese culture, history, and lifestyle (preferably in the Vietnamese language).

c. A structured developmental English program may be conducted independently or, preferably, in conjunction with a full bilingual or support bilingual program. Developmental English instruction involves the application of second-language teaching techniques to control material derived from the regular curriculum, and conducted within the regular classroom on an individualized basis. Such instruction emphasizes learning language for use in the communication of information, and relates reinforcement activities to communicational goals. Games, peer tutoring, etc., are used as much as possible.

The optimum program would provide that each student be given special developmental English instruction by a qualified teacher who coordinates such instruction with the student's other school work.

The school should give a significant number of the teaching staff some intensive in-service training in methods of developmental English instruction and individualized instruction so that these can be incorporated into the regular instruction of the classroom. A person trained in ESL methods may work in close conjunction with regular classroom teacher, but unless the ESL specialist is experienced in regular classroom teaching, such a person should not work alone with students.

d. A "pull-out" ESL program (English as a Second Language) is not recommended by the Center for Applied Linguistics, particularly at the elementary level (new OCR guidelines for Lau compliance prohibit it at the lower elementary level). It may, however, be necessary and even desirable at the upper secondary level, so long as it is closely coordinated with content instruction in the rest of the curriculum and does not lead to segregation of the students within the school.

In pull-out situations, teachers should closely coordinate English instruction with the rest of the curriculum. The goal of ESL instruction should be to assist the student to move into the regular school program as fully and as rapidly as possible.

Well-designed bilingual and ESL programs are compatible programs. The effective bi-

lingual program provides for the teaching of a second language along with the extension of the child's first language. Both ESL specialists and classroom teachers who teach English in bilingual education programs should have special expertise if they are to be effective. The bilingual teacher must be able to communicate with the child in his own language and to develop his full range of skills in that language. In addition, the teacher must understand, respect, and teach the native culture of the student. This includes significant modification in the curriculum to fit different cognitive styles, and close attention to the choice of appropriate materials.

The effective ESL program should employ the practices of bilingual education which will consider the language and culture of the student, carefully building second language instruction on the system of language the child has already acquired. Although an ESL program can be conducted by a teacher who is not able to speak fluently the child's first language, the ESL teacher must know a good bit about the student's language in order to plan instruction, and the more the teacher can know, the better. Unfortunately, many people trained in ESL are familiar only with teaching foreign students at the college level, or with teaching in another country, and are not sufficiently familiar with the needs of the American classroom to be useful except as an aide, or in a team-teaching situation.

The National Institute of Education is producing descriptions of the Vietnamese language to help teachers. Titles of forthcoming bulletins on the subject are: Teaching English Pronunciation to Vietnamese; Teaching English Suffixes to Vietnamese; A Brief Look at the Vietnamese Language: Sounds & Spelling; A Brief Look at the Vietnamese Language: The Structure of Sentences.

4. How much time should be budgeted for the teaching of English?

With all the demands on the Vietnamese student's time during the school day, the teacher will have to set aside time for special instruction in English. Just how much time is required will depend on the rest of the school schedule, the language ability of the child, and the type of program decided on by the school. Certain guidelines might be helpful:

. The student will need some directed instruction every day if possible. Furthermore, several shorter sessions are better than one long one.

. The decision about what the student can afford to miss in order to receive adequate English instruction will partially depend upon the priorities of instruction the school has set and partially upon the needs of the child. If a student cannot understand enough English to follow a lesson, say in arithmetic, it would be best if he could be given the essentials of the lesson in his own language (or French, if he knows that), and spend the remaining time in individualized practice learning the key vocabulary and phrases needed to follow the instruction in English.

. In a school where several classroom teachers are partially or well-trained in ESL instruction, that work can be coordinated with regular classwork and the student misses very little. In pull-out ESL programs, particularly those not well coordinated with the rest of the instructional program, the student is likely to miss a great deal.

. Learning English as a second language takes considerable time, and the older the student, the more time it is likely to take. The school should not be unrealistic about expecting students to learn the language in a matter of a few weeks. Programs conducted by skilled teachers will naturally teach more language in a shorter time, but individual students will vary in the time needed to develop certain fluency levels.

5. What pitfalls should a school avoid in attempting to meet the English needs of Indochinese students?

. Avoid the assumption that all children should be able to learn English all by themselves by just sitting in an English-speaking classroom. Though some students, particularly younger ones, seem to have great facility for learning a second language, it cannot be assumed that all children do.

• Do not assume that any teacher, regardless of training, can be successful in teaching English as a second language. Such instruction requires skill, understanding, and knowledge. Conversely, do not assume that anyone, just because they speak Vietnamese or Cambodian, can teach in those languages.

• Avoid the mistake, common in most ESL programs and materials of emphasizing pronunciation in early stages of instruction. Learning key vocabulary and building fluency in basic communication patterns should be the first goal. Pronunciation should be secondary. For many students, listening practice should be given high priority.

• Do not assume that difficulties in pronouncing English sounds represent a pathological condition. Americans trying to pronounce Vietnamese would have many more problems.

• Avoid the assumption that "All children are basically alike". Southeast Asian cultures are radically different from American culture at often very deep levels, which are difficult to recognize. Teachers must be aware of differences and modify their teaching strategies and procedures as well as their attitudes and expectations accordingly.

• Do not assume that the purchase of instructional materials will be sufficient. Most ESL materials have been produced for older students, and even the majority of

these are out-dated in terms of current language learning theory. In any event, any materials purchased will have to be adapted for the specific language and cultural background of the students. Priority should be given to providing training and specialist assistance for teachers, and wherever possible, to recruiting and providing classroom aides from the student's native language group.

6. Where can a school turn for help in teaching English to Vietnamese students?

• The National Indochinese Clearinghouse of the Center for Applied Linguistics can provide publications which can be helpful. A listing of available materials appears periodically in the NIC Alert Bulletins. The NIC can also recommend consultants or organizations which can provide technical assistance to schools on a contractual basis.

• Teachers of English to Speakers of Other Languages (TESOL), a professional organization for specialists and persons with responsibility for ESL programs, provides information through its journals and other publications. In many areas TESOL members are making their services available to schools receiving Vietnamese students. Information about available consultants and a list of TESOL state affiliates can be secured from the National Indochinese Clearinghouse.

• Universities with ESL teacher-training programs can be

sources of information and consultative help. A listing of these is available from the TESOL office, School of Languages and Linguistics, Georgetown University, Washington, D.C., 20057. A wealth of literature on English as a second language, both resource and instructional material, is presently available and should be studied by school personnel planning programs for the Vietnamese.

REFERENCES

Bibliography

1. DeCamp, Jennifer. ERIC Materials Relating to Vietnamese. and English. Arlington, Va.: ERIC Clearinghouse on Language and Linguistics, 1975.

A 30-item bibliography of relevant books and articles available through the ERIC system.

2. Robson, Barbara and Kent Sutherland. A Selected Annotated Bibliography for Teaching English to Speakers of Vietnamese. Arlington, Va.: Center for Applied Linguistics, 1975.

A 300-item bibliography covering basic texts, audiovisual aids, literacy materials, testing materials, cross-cultural references, etc., for both children and adults.

Language Teaching Methodology

1. Finocchiaro, Mary. English as a Second Language: From Theory to Practice. New York: Regents, 1974. $3.25.

Newly revised practical guide to curriculum planning, lesson planning, adaptation of materials and language testing. Discusses specific techniques for teaching pronunciation, grammar, reading and writing. Appendix contains useful definitions, an extensive bibliography.

2. Rivers, Wilga M. Speaking in Many Tongues: Essays in Foreign-Language Teaching. Rowley, Mass.: Newbury House, 1972. $5.50. Paperback.

Collection of 11 articles written between 1968 and 1972, on various aspects of foreign-language teaching. Indexed by subject for easy reference. Good, practical articles useful to the language teacher whatever his background.

3. Stevick, Earl W. Helping People Learn English. New York: Abingdon Press, 1957.

This is a small down-to-earth, sane, sensible book which is expressly designed to acquaint the non-experienced native speaker of English with the ins and outs of teaching English as a second language. It gives general guidelines on teaching pronunciation, and an easy-to-understand introduction to the mechanics of pronunciation. The sections on teaching grammar are equally good.

4. Saville-Troike, Muriel. Foundations for Teaching English as a Second Language. Englewood Cliffs, N.J.: Prentice-Hall, in press. $6.95. Paperback.

Brand-new (not available until January) discussion of the linguistic, psychological and cultural aspects of teaching English as a foreign language. Of special use to the teacher with no special training in ESL are chapters on survival skills for teachers and students, the role of ESL in bilingual education, strategies for instruction, and preparation for teaching.

Bilingual/Bicultural Education

1. Abrahams, Roger D. and Rudolph C. Troike, eds. Language and Cultural Diversity in American Education. Englewood Cliffs, N.J.: Prentice-Hall, 1972.

This anthology of essays contains among its sections: The Problem, which is concerned with the teaching of linguistically and culturally different students; Cultures in Education, emphasizing the importance of the educator in helping children of all backgrounds through a better understanding of those various cultures; Language, which presents basic information concerning language, acquisition, grammar, competence and performance, dialects, and the history of the English language; Sociolinguistics, dealing with the role of language in social interaction and with the effects of bilingualism and multilingualism.

2. Mackey, William Francis. Bilingual Education in a Binational School. Rowley, Mass.: Newbury House, 1972.

A case study of the JFK School in Berlin. Of special interest is the author's often-quoted "Typology of Bilingual Education".

3. Saville, Muriel and Rudolph C. Troike. A Handbook of Bilingual Education. Washington, D.C.: TESOL, 1971.

Addressed to teachers and administrators, this handbook is a practical guide for those working in bilingual programs. The authors review the history and

fundamental considerations of bilingual education and consider the linguistic, psychological, sociocultural, and pedagogical problems involved. Each section contains a good bibliography.

4. Ulibarri, Horacio. "Bilingualism." In Emma Marie Birkmaier, ed., Britannica Review of Foreign Language Education, Vol. I. Chicago: Encyclopaedia Britannica, 1968. 229-258.

The author discusses the nature of bilingualism, the interrelationships between bilingualism and biculturalism, the problems faced by educators in handling the situation, and the implications for teachers. The relationship of bilingualism to acculturation and biculturism is noted, as are studies concerning these areas and others, including testing and social class stratification.

National Indochinese Clearinghouse 1975-1976

Soon after the Indochinese refugees started to arrive in the U.S., the Center for Applied Linguistics was funded by the U.S. Office of Education, Department of Health, Education and Welfare, to establish and operate a National Indochinese Clearinghouse. The main focus of the Clearinghouse was to be the collection, analysis and dissemination of materials to meet the pressing educational needs of teachers of refugees and the refugees themselves. These included an understanding of the Vietnamese and Cambodian educational systems; grade placement; language testing; English as a second language (ESL) techniques, methods and materials; bilingual education possibilities; textbooks written in Vietnamese and Cambodian; cross-cultural consideration; etc. As we began to collect and analyze materials, it became apparent that another step would have to be added to our work process: that of adaptation. The majority of material we handled was not in a form readily useable by the classroom teacher, so the adaptation (or assimilation) process was added before information and materials were disseminated.

Our basic field of concentration during the 1975-76 school year was the general K-12 classroom teacher. The Refugee Education Guides we developed, the information in our *Alert Bulletins*, etc. was aimed at classroom teachers, administrators, speech or reading or DP teachers, who were unfamiliar with the needs of the non-English or limited-English speaking child, and found themselves faced with educating one or more refugee children. While much of the information which appeared in our General Information Series was useful to the ESL professional, or the adult education teacher, or the bilingual education teacher, our basic aim was to help non-professional language teachers and administrators across the country (and there were thousands) deal effectively with the language and culture needs of Indochinese refugee children.

In staffing the Clearinghouse we were aware of the "mix" needed to fulfill our goals: linguists, ESL specialists, southeast Asian scholars, cross-cultural specialists, elementary and secondary school teachers. We were also aware that the "mix" had to take into account national background as well as professional expertise, and the staff included Americans, Vietnamese and Cambodians.

An early staff decision was to allow those we were working for and with to have direct and immediate access to the Clearinghouse, so a toll-free telephone "hot-line" was installed. As soon as the line was in working order, the telephones started to ring, and there was rarely a chance to catch one's breath for the first

four months. But we found out what school teachers and administrators and state and local education agency personnel needed, and we tried to couple their needs with our estimation of information they should have, both in our telephone answers and our subsequent Refugee Education Guides.

The hot-line was our contact point for quickly assisting educators. We followed this with three other contact points: 1) a series of Indochinese Refugee Education Guides; 2) periodic *Refugee Alert Bulletins*; 3) *Personnel Resources Directories for the Education of Indochinese Refugees*. (See Appendix A for a full listing.) In this way we were better able to give the teacher sustained help throughout the school year.

The following "box-score" might aid in gauging the magnitude of the staff's work. During the first nine months of operation (August 1975 - April 1976) the Clearinghouse compiled the following statistics:

Hotline calls—approximately 15,000 calls
Mailing list compiled—approximately 10,000 names
Information/material collected and analyzed—approximately 1,200 volumes
Refugee Education Guides/Alert Bulletins/Personnel Resources Directories prepared—47
Refugee Education Guides/Alert Bulletins/Personnel Resources Directories distributed—approximately 70,000 copies
Workshop/Conference participation—32

Our research and products were closely tied with technical assistance to local education agencies being offered by five of the ESEA Title VIII Bilingual Resource Centers: 1) the Regional Cross-Cultural Training and Resource Center in New York City; 2) the Bilingual Education Service Center in Arlington Heights, Illinois; 3) the National Bilingual Resource Center in Lafayette, La.; 4) the Institute for Cultural Pluralism in San Diego, Calif.; 5) the Bay Area Bilingual Education League in Berkeley, Calif. We also worked closely with the Office of Education's Indochinese Refugee Task Force, various state education agencies, and the academically based Southeast Asian studies departments and research centers across the country.

There were some general principles which guided our mode of operation at the Clearinghouse from the beginning. We tried to produce quality work, linguistically or cross-culturally correct, without being overly academic or pedantic. We tried to provide educators and volunteers with enough easily readable information to help them in their specific teaching tasks, but we also tried to guide them to further, more complex studies in the references which appeared at the end of almost every Refugee Education Guide. We tried to be eminently practical—helping the inexperienced teacher along what we believed to be the easiest, least frustrating, and most result-oriented route—even though that route may not have been the most fashionable in professional circles. And finally, we tried to maintain for ourselves, for the teachers and volunteers we worked with, and for the refugee students, a sense of humor and a sense of compassion in trying and often emotionally charged situations.

In setting the general pattern for the Clearinghouse and its products, we think we have demonstrated how linguistic and cross-cultural scholars can respond to practical educational and social needs in an emergency situation. If a similar emergency does arise (and we all hope that it never does), we think the American educational community is now in a better position to respond than it was in June of 1975.

A BRIEF SKETCH OF THE REFUGEE CHILD IN THE U.S.

Introduction

When the Vietnamese and Cambodian refugees arrived in the U.S. a year and a half ago, in May 1975, nearly 50,000 of them were under 17 years of age. This massive influx of Indochinese children into the U.S. school system caused great concern among those teachers who had to teach them and among those education officials who had to provide for their educational needs. The primary focus of this concern was centered on the basic question of how best to help these children continue their cognitive education in a totally different school environment.

Based on information collected by the National Indochinese Clearinghouse over the past 18 months, it is now safe to say that, thanks to the efforts of U.S. education officials and also to the traditionally positive attitude of parents regarding education, all the school-age refugee children—with very few and isolated exceptions—have been going to school, and for the most part, placed at a grade level generally commensurate with their abilities.

This is no small achievement when we remember that last September, when the Vietnamese and Cambodian children shyly walked into their unfamiliar American classrooms all over the nation, not a single one of their teachers had ever set eyes on a real-life Indochinese child, and the teachers' unfamiliarity with their previous schooling as well as their cultural background was matched only by the children's bewilderment at the strange environment of their American schools.

One year and a half after the children's admission to American schools, the reports received on the children's progress are now generally encouraging, although some problems remain. The Vietnamese chidren are reported to be doing very well in mathematics and science but still need a lot of help in mastering the English language. They are said to relate well with their American peers, but still show signs of being inhibited in their relations with their teachers and other elders.

These observations and others like them that have been reported to us have served as the basis for some tentative conclusions about the Vietnamese refugee child in the U.S. These tentative conclusions, which we report in this section, can be of some use in the teacher's attempt to gain some insights into that refugee child in her class. For, that little Indochinese child playing tag during recess with his American classmates—with his unzipped jacket open to the unfamiliar cold—is in many ways different from the American child he is pursuing in the school yard. It is well to let this picture sink into our minds because, in itself, it is symbolic of another, more difficult pursuit on the part of the refugee child in the U.S.: catching up with his American peer, not just in a game of tag, but in real life.

The profile of the refugee child offered here is an aggregate picture based on reports from teachers, direct observations, and conversations with parents as well as with the children themselves. The experiences are mainly those of Vietnamese children and parents, and the teachers of these children. Not that we have overlooked the Cambodian, Laotian and Black Tai child. It is just that the overwhelming majority of Indochinese refugees in this country are Vietnamese, and therefore, the reports we received reflect their experiences more than those of other Indochinese refugees. We can say, however, that the experiences of the Cambodian, Laotian and Black Tai child have been amazingly similar to that of the Vietnamese child, and that the aggregate profile we draw certainly includes them.

The War Experience

A former American reporter in Vietnam, talking about a little Vietnamese war orphan he adopted and brought back to the U.S. once said that when the nine-year old fellow wasn't a boy, he was a little old man. The reporter was referring, of course, to all the experiences which, as a child born in war, growing up in war and witnessing the brutal scenes of war, the boy had gone through. Although in the case of this orphan the experiential makeup seemed to be extreme, it is fair to say that compared to an American child, the Indochinese refugee child is, in many ways, a life-wise little individual. His experiences with physical dangers, death, deprivations, insecurity as well as with adult behaviors—

made more admirable or more reprehensible under unusual conditions of crisis—are a matter of record. Most refugee children have seen, directly or indirectly, war and its effects on society and people. Whether these experiences and the hazardous and trauma-filled exit from their native land have affected them in any significant way, it is difficult to say. We are aware of no systematic effort to examine this problem. Thus, with the children "getting along very nicely", it is well for a teacher to keep this particular aspect of their emotional makeup in mind, just in case expert psychological help is needed.

English Language Problems

Section III of this Manual will deal with the language problems of refugee children and techniques for teaching English. In general, three factors have influenced English language learning over the past year: age of the student, motivation of the student, and the type of English language instruction received. The younger the child, the easier it was to learn English. The most difficult situation was that of the high student, given little direct help with language learning, and expected to keep up with his American peers. Hopefully this was not a common situation, but we do know that it did occur.

English language learning still remains as a major need for the current year. Even though the majority of refugee students did get some instruction and can now follow classwork to some degree, full participation in the entire curriculum will depend on how well the student can handle English. Continued special instruction is called for.

Parental Pressure

Compared to an American child, the Vietnamese child is under more intense pressure from his parents to study. Products of a culture which places a high value on "book learning", Vietnamese refugee parents have been reported not just to encourage their children to study but in many cases, with characteristic authoritarian display, to force children to study and to do well in school.

This traditional parental concern over study and learning can sometimes be seen to involve a rather restricted definition of what learning is. A Vietnamese parent in Virginia once reportedly withdrew his son from the high school track team because he felt the son had no business associating himself with the track team while his time could be better spent alone at a desk at home "learning" more English. Learning English was thus seen to involve a book and a desk and not communication with other people.

This concern can, in some cases, translate into an over-solicitous attitude on the part of the parents regarding help in homework. In one case reported to us, a child's homework was almost always perfect. The teacher therefore had an erroneous idea of the progress of the child, which led her to give the child less attention than he needed and deserved. Getting less attention from the teacher, the child had to rely even more on the parents at home: a vicious cycle unwittingly entered into by some Vietnamese parents (and, of course, by any other overeager parents anywhere).

A Minimized Play Cycle

An American educator in Vietnam with a good knowledge of Vietnamese home-life once observed that in the eat-sleep-work-play routine of a child's life "the Vietnamese child seems to have a shorter play-cycle than his American counterpart." It is not unusual, he said, to find a Vietnamese high school student spending the entire weekend at his study desk at home furiously studying and "learning", to the intense pride of his parents. Play was not insisted on for the Vietnamese child, nor was it elevated to the level of a counterpart and necessary complement of work, as it is in the U.S. The saying about all work and no play was not valid for the Vietnamese child, and play was seen only as a reward bestowed for good work. While the refugee child has changed somewhat during the last year, he and his parents still have a hard time putting school athletic activities into proper perspective.

Respect For Age

According to a study on the problems of aging conducted by a team of experts from the University of Maryland, American children have less and less contacts with old people and thus grow more and more unfamiliar with people of old age. The Vietnamese child, who very often lives close to or with grandparents under the same roof, can be said to have more experience in this regard. His behavior toward the aged as well as toward his elders is usually one of respect and obedience which is inculcated early in the confines of the family. This is often seen in the manners which he is taught to use when dealing with his elders; manner which, to an American, seem to be formal and "exceedingly polite". Early in the 1975 school year, many Vietnamese children were reported to come to their teachers, when summoned, with their arms folded across their chests in a posture of respect. They were reported to bow their heads when passing their teachers in the hall and were observed to hand finished work to the teachers with both hands, eyes cast slightly downward. After a year and a half in a culture which is impatient with formality and cumbersome etiquette, these children are now reported to have largely abandoned these practices, probably having found out they could get by without them.

Caught Between Two Forces

The seemingly simple fact of cultural adjustment mentioned above helps to focus our attention, however, on an important cross-cultural problem for the Vietnamese child in America. While he is freed from the observance of these Vietnamese forms of politeness *at school*, he is still bound to them *at home* where these forms are insisted upon by the parents. What this amounts to, is the necessity on the part of the child to "switch cultures", so to speak, displaying one set of manners at school and another set of manners at home. This ability to switch two cultures on or off as the situation requires is the essence of cross-cultural adjustment. And upon this ability depends much of his success in being accepted by both forces: his family on one hand, and the new society in which he now lives on the other. It is an acquired ability which, even for an adult, requires a keen sense of observation and a conscious effort. Many Vietnamese children are reportedly still not very successful in acquiring it. This, in a real sense, is what is behind those complints voiced by the Vietnamese parents we talked to, who confided in us that somehow their children brought home "some pretty bad manners from school". The parents were appalled at the directness and the diminished deference which the children now display at home.

This problem also helps to reinforce a key point being made by educators involved in bilingual-bicultural education. The typical American school environment is not always, for all children, an extension of the home. The refugee child is the subject of a tug-of-war between two forces, with the school representing the new and dominant culture in which he now lives, and the family embodying the old culture from which he was uprooted.

The Passive Learning Style

American educators familiar with Vietnamese education often point out that the Vietnamese child tends to learn things the "passive way" rather than the "active way" which American children are encouraged to adopt. The child is said to learn by listening, watching and imitating rather than by actively doing things and discovering things for himself. Still other experts point out that this essentially non-dynamic aproach to learning has deep roots in the Vietnamese culture. Although this question cannot be delved into here, it is necessary to keep this in mind when a Vietnamese child still displays reluctance or even discomfort at the way a certain subject matter is handled at school. His poor work, if it comes to that, might not be simple laziness, but rather might be a manifestation of his uneasiness with his new approach to learning. It will probably take some time for a refugee child to get accustomed to learning via the discovery process. It might be noted here that when this active, dynamic approach to learning is extended from the not-so-large confines of a classroom to cover the child's life outside of the school as well (after-school jobs, extra-curricular activities, etc.), an added burden is put on the child, and adjustment problems become more pronounced.

"They're very reluctant to ask questions"

This was what a teacher in Pennsylvania once said about the two Vietnamese girls in her social studies class. It was difficult in this case to tell how much of the girls' reticence was due to the lack of adequate English proficiency and how much as due to a 'cultural factor'. But most observers of Vietnamese children's behavior—Vietnamese as well as non-Vietnamese—agree that a Vietnamese child tends to place the teacher on a high level of respect and is less inclined to be "familiar" with the teachers than his American counterpart. It is pointed out that the Vietnamese teachers themselves, who usually prefer a formal and serious atmosphere in the classroom and who are great disciplinarians, tend to maintain a certain distance between themselves and the pupils. Vietnamese educators are quick to point out that it is not the case that a Vietnamese child cannot express himself in class; but rather that self-expression on the part of the children is practiced under such tight control that, to an American teacher, the Vietnamese classroom would seem inhibitive.

There is evidence that this control was what initially the Vietnamese refugee children expected from their new teachers in America. The two girls mentioned above, seeing for the first time the lively atmosphere in their American classmates lacked respect for the teacher and that the teacher was "too easy on the students". Present reports indicate that after a year there is less reluctance to participate in class discussion, and that there is a better understanding of the nature of the American classroom, but the majority of refugee children are still far from outgoing.

There is, however, another dimension to this question. After spending years under more rigid control, the Vietnamese child is reported to be a little confused by the new freedom he finds in the American classroom. Without much experience in exercising this freedom, he is often reported not to know where the limit of this freedom is, which makes him susceptible to becoming an actual disciplinary problem. Documented cases of this kind have come to our attention, and will probably continue to occur during the current school year.

Agility, Manual Dexterity and a Genius at Improvisations

An Indochinese child is usually of slighter build than

an American child of the same age. This slight build combines with a quick reflex to make him excel in games where agility, not muscular strength, is called for. He is usully superb at ping-pong and soccer, but is a poor acquisition for other rougher games.

His manual dexterity has been praised time and again by American teachers, and his handwriting has often been called good or superior. Living all his life in a culture where children's toys are scarce, most of his toys are usually simple and are often invented and made by the child himself from discarded things around the house, a little-noticed fact which may have contributed to the formation of a characteristic trait which his elders are said to be remarkable for: the Vietnamese genius at improvisations. It has been reported that many very young Vietnamese children quickly become bored with American toys, and look for sticks, blocks, clothespins, etc. in their classrooms with which to improvise.

The Vietnamese child, even the older child, is also reported to be afraid of the dark, and more often than not, believes in ghosts. A teacher may have to be a little more solicitous of the child on gloomy, wintery days.

The brief sketch presented above comprises only a few of a multitude of pieces that make up the interesting puzzle which is the Indochinese refugee child. Next to his parents and others in his family, the teacher will probably be the outsider who will get to know him best. As for his oft-mentioned adjustment problems, it is useful to recall here what six Vietnamese refugee children in a small Maryland town unanimously told one of our staff researchers. Asked whether they would like to go back to Vietnam if there was a chance to do so, all of them replied ''No'', but they also added that they would like for all of their relatives to come over here to live with them instead. Two Vietnamese parents, who witnessed this little fun-poll, grimaced upon hearing the children's negative answer, thus confirming for us something we had often heard before, namely a deep attachment on the part of the Vietnamese adults for their native land. For the children, this is clearly something they don't seem to be too concerned about.

WHAT DOES IT MEAN TO LEARN A SECOND LANGUAGE?

In learning to speak English (his second, or maybe third language), the refugee child has to master four different aspects of the language. First, he must learn to understand spoken English, and to pronounce it in such a way that he is readily understood by native English speakers. He must also learn how to combine words into sentences which express what he wants to say. In addition, he must learn vocabulary in English suitable for his work in the classroom and his social life outside it. And finally, he must learn the correct style of English—whether formal, informal, colloquial, etc.—to use in the various social situations he finds himself in. These four aspects of language—pronunciation, sentence structures, vocabulary, and styles—will be learned in different ways and at different rates by the refugee child, depending on his age, his motivation, and the amount of special attention his language problems get.

There is a correlation between the age of a child and his ability to learn a language. The very young child—between the ages of one and four or five—can learn a language simply by hearing it spoken around him. As the child grows older, he gradually loses this ability, so that by the time he is in high school he and his teachers have to make a directed effort if he is to learn more than isolated words and phrases.

This six- or seven-year-old, for example, will quickly pick up vocabulary, pronunciation and the simpler structures of conversational English; in a very short time he will sound pretty much like his American classmates. (He will probably, however, need help learning the more complex structures which occur in written English; otherwise, he will have trouble later on in understanding his textbooks and writing in more formal English.) In contrast, the older child—say, the thirteen- or fourteen-year-old—will pick up understandable pronunciation, but he will speak with an accent. And, unless he is given special help, he will have a great deal of trouble with English sentence structures.

Naturally, the interaction between age and language learning is mitigated by several other factors. The most important of these is motivation: the child who for one reason or another is highly motivated to learn a language will overcome all kinds of obstacles, and seem to pick it up almost overnight; conversely, the child who doesn't want to learn a language simply won't, even in an optimum language-learning situation. Motivation comes in all sizes and shapes, of course, but in general the greatest source for the refugee child will be his peers: he will want to learn English so he can interact with them. This is one of the reasons why it is so important to place the refugee child with other children his age: if he is with children much younger than he, he will not identify with them, and therefore will not be compelled to interact with them.

Earlier, we mentioned four aspects of language which the refugee child must master: pronunciation, structures, vocabulary, and style. It seems useful, at this point, to go into more detail as to what each of these aspects involves.

Learning to pronounce a new language involves, first, learning to hear it in terms of its own sound system (instead of the sound system of one's native language), and then learning to produce the sounds of the new system in such a way as to be understood.

The Vietnamese speaker, for example, will hear the *t* of *top* as a completely different sound from the *t* of *stop*; there is a difference in pronunciation between the two *t*'s, and in the Vietnamese language that difference is focussed on, and the two are heard as different sounds entirely. The Vietnamese speaker has to learn that in English this difference is ignored, and that English speakers react to the two *t*'s as though they were identical. Conversely, the Vietnamese speaker will not hear the difference between *th* and *t*, and so will hear *thank* and *tank* as the same word; the sound we spell as *th* does not exist in Vietnamese, and so he interprets it as the sound in Vietnamese phonetically the most similar to it, i.e. *t*. He has to learn to hear the difference between *th* and *t*, and to memorize which sound goes in which word, as well as learn how to pronounce the *th*.

Learning the structures of a language involves, basically, learning how to link words (and suffixes) together in sentences. There is much, much more to language than getting the proper vocabulary items and pronouncing them understandably. The following excerpt from a letter in the National Indochinese Clearinghouse files demonstrates this: "I'm is refugees from Vietnam please help me gives some books. . ."; the author intended to say "please help me by giving me some books", but we were able to figure this out only because he couldn't have meant anything else. Although all the nouns and verbs in this sentence are all right, the grammatical trappings which indicate the relationships among the words are either lacking or in the wrong place, and as a consequence the sentence doesn't say what the author means. In the absence of a firm knowledge of how words are grouped together to form sentences, the Vietnamese or Khmer or Lao speaker will arrange them in a way which seems natural to him, i.e. the way they are arranged in his native language. The result either will or will not communicate what he means, depending on how closely it happens to come to the English sentence we actually say. The Vietnamese or Khmer or Lao speaker must be shown, one by one, the sentence structures by which the various relationships among words are expressed, for example first the sentence pattern *This is a. . .*; and then perhaps the plural *These are. . .*; then the question forms *Is this a. . .?* and *Are these. . .?*; and so on.

It should be pointed out here that the language used in the third grade classroom is not structurally simpler than the language used in the seventh or eighth grade classroom; a comparison of textbooks will show that while the concepts and vocabulary increase in complexity, the language is pretty much the same. Compare, for example, the sentence

A resistance bridge employs a highly sensitive galvanometer as an indicating device, together with a calibrated variable-resistance standard and a voltage source in a suitable circuit arrangement.

with the sentence

Your library has a carefully chosen collection of books as its most important part, together with a selection of records and films in a special viewing room.

These sentences are structurally nearly identical; it's the vocabulary that makes the first so much more complex than the second.

Learning vocabulary involves at first learning the words for objects and actions in one's immediate environment, then branching out into more remote areas of interest. Specialists in the ESL field are agreed that learning vocabulary is best done in context: the child given a long list of words to memorize will never master them as well as the child who hears them used over and over, and who is required to use them himself in meaningful situations. The refugee child, by virtue of the fact that he is going to school in an English-speaking environment, will hear words used over and over, and will have to use them himself if he expects to communicate; his circumstances, therefore, will force him to learn vocabulary in the best possible way.

Learning the various styles of English will also be forced on him by his circumstances, assuming that care is taken to place him among peers he can identify and be friends with. We all use different styles of English in different social situations. A woman talks to her husband in one style ("Darling, I'm out of logs for the fire. . ."), to her children in another ("Jackie, if you don't get your muddy feet off that chair right now I'm gonna brain you!"), and to her boss in yet another ("I've read the proposals, and if it's all right with you I think we should schedule the workshop for the second week in October.") Children, also, use different styles on the playground, in the classroom, to their parents, and so on; the child who knows, say, only playground English will come across as brassy when he talks to his teachers, and the child who knows only English-teacher English will come across as stuffy and pedantic on the playground. The refugee child, if placed with his own age group, will quickly learn the different styles appropriate to his age and social situation by observing and imitating his peers.

A Manual for Indochinese Refugee Education 1976-1977. Prepared by the staff of The National Indochinese Clearinghouse, Center for Applied Linguistics, 1611 North Kent Street, Arlington, VA 1976

Directory of Bilingual Projects

CALIFORNIA

Berkeley
Contact person for Bilingual
  Programs:
Dr. Roberto Cruz, Director
BABEL/BASTA Consortium
2168 Shattuck Ave., 2nd floor
Berkeley, CA 94704
(415) 549-1820

Franklin School
1150 Virginia St.
Berkeley, CA 94702
Chinese, 4-6

Jefferson School
1400 Ada St.
Berkeley, CA 94702
Chinese, K-3

Lincoln School
225 11th St.
Oakland, CA 94606
Chinese, K-6
(See also Oakland)

Westmoor High School
131 Westmoor Ave.
Daly City, CA 94015
Filipino, 9-12
(See also Daly City)

Chula Vista
Chula Vista City School District
Title VII Bilingual Programs
84 East J Street
P.O. Box 907
Chula Vista, CA 92012
(714) 422-8341
Filipino, K-3

Daly City
Contact person for Title VII
  Filipino Bilingual Programs:
Ms. Nettie Herbert, Coord.
Jefferson Elementary School
  District
101 Lincoln Ave.
Daly City, CA 94015
Filipino, K-6

Christopher Columbus School
60 Christopher Ct.
Daly City, CA 94015
Filipino, K-6

Westmoor High School
Filipino, 9-12
Usin Pisingan, Teacher
(See Berkeley, BABEL/BASTA)

Contact person for Title VII
  Bilingual Programs:

Daly City (cont'd)
Ms. Shelley Brown, Coord.
Bayshore Elementary School
  District
Bayshore School
155 Oriente St.
Daly City, CA 94014
(415) 467-0442
Chinese, Filipino, Samoan, K-3

Ms. Betty Ng, Coord.
Robertson School
No. 1 Martin St.
Daly City, CA 94104
(415) 467-5443
Chinese, Filipino, Samoan, 4-8

El Monte
Mountain View School District
Title VII Bilingual Programs
2850 N. Mountain View Road
El Monte, CA 91732
(213) 448-9804
Filipino, 5-8

Long Beach
Hudson School
2335 Webster Avenue
Long Beach, CA 90810
(213) 426-0470
Filipino, 1-6
Stephen Dodge, Principal

Los Angeles
Contact person for Title VII
  Bilingual Programs:
Doris Wong, Program Adviser
Los Angeles Unified School
  District
1555 Norfolk St., Room 1
Los Angeles, CA 90033
(213) 223-3354, 3355;
  625-6185

Castelar School
850 Yale St.
Los Angeles, CA 90012
Chinese, K-6
Marilyn Choy, School Adviser

Hawaiian Avenue School
540 Hawaiian Ave.
Wilmington, CA 90744
Filipino, K-1

Wilton Place School
745 S. Wilton Place
Los Angeles, CA 90005
Korean, K-1

Berendo Jr. High School
1157 S. Berendo St.
Los Angeles, CA 90006
Korean, 7

Los Angeles (cont'd)

Nightingale Jr. High School
3311 N. Figueroa
Los Angeles, CA 90065
Chinese, 7

Virgil Jr. High School
152 N. Vermont Ave.
Los Angeles, CA 90004
Korean, 7

Mountain View

Mountain View High School
Title VII Program
650 Castro Street
Mountain View, CA 90404
(415) 967-5543
Filipino, 10-12
Ben Menor, Jr., Teacher

Oakland

Contact person for all
  Chinese Bilingual Programs:
Josephine Lee, Specialist
Oakland Public Schools
831 E. 14th St.
Oakland, CA 94606
(415) 836-2622,
ext. 626

Lincoln School
(See Berkeley, BABEL/BASTA)

McChesney Jr. High School
3748 13th Ave.
Oakland, CA 94610
Chinese, 7-9

Westlake Jr. High School
2629 Harrison St.
Oakland, CA 94615
Chinese, 7-9

Oakland High School
3233 Park Blvd.
Oakland, CA 94606
Chinese, 10-12

Oakland Technical High School
4351 Broadway
Oakland, CA 94611
Chinese, 10-12

Lincoln Children's Center
314 E. 10th St.
Oakland, CA 94606
(415) 465-4867
Chinese, Preschool
Susan Leong, Head Teacher

Contact person for Filipino
  Bilingual Programs:
Carmen Kirk, Project Dir.
831 E. 14th St.
Oakland, CA 94606
(415) 836-2622,
ext. 854

Oakland (cont'd)

Lincoln School
225 11th St.
Oakland, CA 94607
Filipino, K-4

Fruitvale Elementary School
3200 Boston
Oakland, CA 94606
Filipino, K-4

Pittsburg

Contact person for Title VII
  Filipino Bilingual Programs:
Ed Madrid, Project Manager
2000 Railroad Ave.
Pittsburg, CA 94565
(415) 432-4705, ext 62, 68

Pittsburg High School
250 School Street
Pittsburg, CA 94565
Filipino, 10-12
Pat A. Diokno, Counselor

Sacramento

Contact persons for Title VII
  Chinese and Japanese Bilin-
  gual Programs:
David Kan, Project Manager
Gladys Peng, Principal
Mandy Wong, Resource Teacher
Lois Asahara, Resource Teacher
William Land School
2020 12th St.
Sacramento, CA 95818
(916) 454-8278
Chinese, Japanese, K-6

C.K. McClatchy High School
3066 Freeport Blvd.
Sacramento, CA 95818
Chinese, 9-12

San Diego

Encanto Elementary School
822 65th St.
San Diego, CA 92114
(714) 263-7791
Filipino, K-6
Clifford Mendoza, Coord.

San Francisco

Contact person for Chinese Bilingual Programs:
Roger Tom, Curriculum and Inservice Coord.
San Francisco Unified School
  District
135 Van Ness Ave., Room 22
San Francisco, CA 94102
(415) 565-9255

San Francisco (cont'd)

Edison School
3531 22nd St.
San Francisco, CA 94114
Chinese, 4

Garfield School
420 Filbert St.
San Francisco, CA 94133
Chinese, K-3

Hancock School
940 Filbert St.
San Francisco, CA 94133
Chinese, 2-3

Jean Parker School
840 Broadway
San Francisco, CA 94133
Chinese, 2-3

Lafayette School
40 Vega St.
San Francisco, CA 94115
Chinese, 4-5

Sarah B. Cooper
2245 Jones St.
San Francisco, CA 94133
Chinese, 1-2

Starr King School
1215 Carolina St.
San Francisco, CA 94107
Chinese, 4-6

Sutro School
248 Funston Ave.
San Francisco, CA 94118
Chinese, 2-3

Twin Peaks School
445 Burnett St.
San Francisco, CA 94131
Chinese, K-3

Washington Irvin School
350 Broadway St.
San Francisco, CA 94133
Chinese, 4-6

Winfield Scott School
3630 Divisadero St.
San Francisco, CA 94123
Chinese, 4-6

Benjamin Franklin Jr. High School
1430 Scott St.
San Francisco, CA 94114
Chinese, 7-9

Galileo High School
1150 Francisco St.
San Francisco, CA 94109
Chinese, 10-12

Marina Jr. High School
3500 Fillmore St.
San Francisco, CA 94123
Chinese, 7-9

San Francisco (cont'd)

Mission High School
3758 18th St.
San Francisco, CA 94114
Chinese, 10-12

Commodore Stockton School
950 Clay St.
San Francisco, CA 94108
(415) 781-7898
Chinese, Prek-3
Anna Wong, Project Manager

Patrick Henry School
693 Vermont St.
San Francisco, CA 94107
Chinese, 4-6
(Anna Wong, see Commodore Stock-
   ton)

St. Mary's Day School
Clay and Stockton Streets
San Francisco, CA 94108
Chinese, 5
(Anna Wong, see Commodore
   Stockton)

Chinese Community Children's
   Center
979 Clay Street
San Francisco, CA 94133
(415) 986-2527
Ruth Yee, Director

Kai Ming Headstart
865 Jackson Street
San Francisco, CA 94133
(415) 982-4570
Marie Lee, Director

Wah Mei Bilingual and Bicultural School
25 Lake Street
San Francisco, CA 94118
(415) 387-1235
Margaret Yu, Teacher

Contact person for Title VII
   Korean Bilingual Programs:
Harry Bang, Project Manager
John Swett School
727 Golden Gate Ave.
San Francisco, CA 94102
(415) 863-6474
Korean, K-3

George Peabody School
250 7th Ave.
San Francisco, CA 94118
Korean, K-3

Contact person for Title VII
   Filipino Bilingual Programs:

Dr. Eliodoro Robles, Project
   Manager
John Swett School
727 Golden Gate Ave.
San Francisco, CA 94102
(415) 431-0260

San Francisco (cont'd)

Contact person for Filipino
  Bilingual Programs:
Ms. Ligaya Avenida, Resource
  Teacher
San Francisco Unified School
  District
135 San Francisco
San Francisco, CA 94102
(415) 565-9208, 9447

Alvarado School
625 Douglass St.
San Francisco, CA 94114
Filipino, 1-3

Bessie Carmichael School
55 Sherman St.
San Francisco, CA
Filipino, 4-6

Burnett School
1551 Newcomb Ave.
San Francisco, CA 94124
Filipino, 4-5

Clarendon School
500 Clarendon Ave.
San Francisco, CA 94131
Filipino, 4-5

McKinley School
126 Castro St.
San Francisco, CA 94114
Filipino, 1-3

Monroe School
171 Lisbon St.
San Francisco, CA 94112
Filipino, 4-6

Paul Revere Annex School
610 Tompkins Ave.
San Francisco, CA 94110
Filipino, K-1

Redding School
1421 Pine St.
San Francisco, CA 94115
Filipino, 4-6

Treasure Island School
13th and E Streets
U.S. Naval Station
Treasure Island, CA 94130
Filipino, K-1

Everett Jr. High School
450 Church St.
San Francisco, CA 94114
Filipino, 7-9

James Denman Jr. High School
241 Oneida Ave.
San Francisco, CA 94112
Filipino, 7-9

San Francisco (cont'd)

Mission High School
701 Frederick St.
San Francisco, CA 94117
Filipino, 10-12

Filipino Education Center
San Francisco Unified School
  District
390 4th Street
San Francisco, CA 94107
(415) 956-4240
Filipino, K-6
Ross Quema, Principal

Contact person for Japanese
  Bilingual Programs:
Tetsu Hojo, Project Manager
1541 12th Avenue
San Francisco, CA 94122
(415) 661-7860

Alvarado School
625 Douglass St.
San Francisco, CA 94114
(415) 826-2855
Japanese, K-6

Columbus School
1541 12th Avenue
San Francisco, CA 94122
Japanese, 4

Emerson School
625 Douglass Street
San Francisco, CA 94114
Japanese, K-3

Stockton
Contact persons for Bilingual
  Programs:
Manuel Montano, Director
Estela Pinga, Coord.
Steven Tom, Chinese Specialist
Stockton Unified School District
55 W. Flora Street
Stockton, CA 95202
(209) 466-3911, ext 294

Jackson School
324 E. Jackson St.
Stockton, CA 95206
Chinese, K-6
Filipino, 1-6

Taylor School
1101 Lever Blvd.
Stockton, CA 95206
Filipino, K-2

Marshall Jr. High School
1141 Lever Blvd.
Stockton, CA 95206
Chinese, 7-9
Filipino, 7-9

Stockton (cont'd)

Edison High School
1425 S. Center
Stockton, CA 95206
Chinese, 10-12
Filipino, 10-12

Franklin High School
300 N. Gertrude
Stockton, CA 95205
Chinese, 10-12

Stagg High School
1621 Brookside
Stockton, CA 95204
Chinese, 10-12

South El Monte

Valle Lindo School
Title VII Programs
1431 N. Central Ave.
South El Monte, CA 91733
(213) 442-2695
Chinese, 5-8
Filipino, 5-8

Visalia

Tulare County Department of
Education
Title VII Programs
202 County Civic Center
Visalia, CA 93277
(209) 732-5511
Filipino, K-6

DISTRICT OF COLUMBIA

Reno School
4820 Howard St., NW
Washington, D.C. 20202
(202) 245-2600
Chinese

FLORIDA

Jacksonville

Duval County School Board
Title VII Programs
1325 San Marco Blvd.
Jacksonville, FL 32207
Filipino, 1-6

HAWAII

Honolulu

Contact person for Title VII
Bilingual Programs:
Belen Ongteco, Administrator
Hawaii Bilingual Education Program
1750 Wist Place
Honolulu, HA 96822
(808) 946-7833
Filipino, K-6

ILLINOIS

Chicago

Contact persons for Asian Bilin-
gual Programs:
Eduardo Cadavid, Dir. of Special
Language and Bilingual Program
Frank Ventura, Title VII Admin-
istrator
Chicago Board of Education
228 North LaSalle, Room 1113
Chicago, IL 60601
(312) 641-4527

Bateman School
4214 N. Richmond St.
Chicago, IL 60616
Korean, K-8

Blaine School
1420 W. Grace St.
Chicago, IL 60613
Korean, K-8

Goudy School
5120 W. Winthrop
Chicago, IL 60640
Chinese, K-8

Haines School
247 W. 23rd Place
Chicago, IL 60640
Chinese, 1-8

Haugan School
4540 N. Hamlin Ave.
Chicago, IL 60625
Korean, K-8

Hibbard School
3244 W. Ainslie Ave.
Chicago, IL 60625
Korean, K-6

McCutcheon School
4865 N. Sheridan Rd.
Chicago, IL 60640
Korean, K-8

Peirce School
1423 W. Bryn Mawr Ave.
Chicago, IL 60660
Korean, K-8

Ray Harte School
5631 S. Kimbark Ave.
Chicago, IL 60637
Chinese, K-8
Filipino, K-8
Japanese, K-8

Senn High School
5900 North Greenwood Ave.
Chicago, IL 60660
Chinese, 9-12
Korean, 9-12

Chicago (cont'd)

Stewart School
4525 N. Kenmore Ave.
Chicago, IL 60640
Chinese, 1-5
Filipino, 1-5
Korean, 1-5

Voltaire School
4950 N. Avers Ave.
Chicago, IL 60625
Chinese, 1-3

Ward School
2701 S. Shields Ave.
Chicago, IL 60616
Chinese, 1-3

MARYLAND

Baltimore

Contact persons for Title VII
  Bilingual Programs:
Sylvia R. Brooks, Associate
Toby Rivkin, Resource Specialist
Baltimore City Public Schools
1401 E. Oliver St.
Baltimore, MD 21213
(301) 396-1557, 1558
Chinese, Korean, K-12

MASSACHUSETTS

Greater Boston

Contact person for Chinese Bilin-
  gual Programs:
Stephanie Fan
Boston City Schools
26 Court St.
Boston, MA 02118
(617) 261-3968
Chinese, Prek-12

Quincy School
90 Tyler St.
Boston, MA 02111
Chinese, Prek-6

Michaelangelo Middle School
70 Charter St.
Boston, MA 02113
Chinese, 7-9

Brighton High School
25 Warren Street
Brighton, MA 02135
Chinese, 10-12

Roxbury High School
35 Greenville
Roxbury, MA 02119
Chinese, 10-12

Theater Arts in Education
  Program
Boston City Schools
One City Hall Plaza

Greater Boston (cont'd)

Boston, MA 02201
(617) 722-4100, ext 497
Raffael DeGruttola, Dir.
Walter Chan, Artist/Choreographer
Chinese, 7-12

NEW YORK

Mt. Kisco

Bedford Central School District
Title VII Japanese Bilingual
  Programs
South Bedford Road
Mt. Kisco, NY 10506

New York City

Contact person for Chinese
  Bilingual Programs:
Jacob Wong, Project Dir.
Board of Education of the City
  of New York
Community School District #2
210 E. 33rd St.
New York, NY 10016

P.S. 1
8 Henry St.
New York, NY 10038

P.S. 2
112 Henry St.
New York, NY 10002

P.S. 23
70 Mulberry St.
New York, NY 10013

P.S. 42
71 Hester St.
New York, NY 10002

P.S. 65 (District 2)
New York, NY

P.S. 126
80 Catherine St.
New York, NY 10034

P.S. 130M
143 Baxter St.
New York, NY 10013

Seward Park High School
350 Grand St.
New York, NY 10002

OREGON

Portland

Contact persons for Asian Bilingual Programs:
Han Vo Qui, Director
Portland Public Schools
8020 N.E. Tillamock St., Rm. 301
Portland, OR 97213
(503) 255-9950

Portland (cont'd)

Eugenie Nashif, Coord.
Portland Public Schools
620 N. Fremont, Rm. 214
Portland, OR 97213
(503) 255-9950
Chinese, Japanese, Korean, K-12

PENNSYLVANIA

Philadelphia
Philadelphia City Schools
Title VII Chinese and Korean
   Bilingual Programs
21st and Parkwyn Ave.
Philadelphia, PA 19131

VIRGINIA

Arlington

Contact persons for Korean
   Bilingual Programs:
Ronald Saunders, Director
John Park, Resource Teacher

Arlington Public Schools
1426 N. Quincy St.
Arlington, VA 22207
(703) 558-2036
Korean, K-3

WASHINGTON

Seattle

Contact persons for Asian Bilingual Programs:
Nancy Chin, Coord.
Seattle Public Schools
815 Fourth Ave., N.
Seattle, WA 98109
(206) 587-6361

Janet Lu, Title VII Program Mgr.
Seattle Public Schools
Marshall Center
520 Ravenna Blvd., NE
Seattle, WA 98115
(206) 587-6434

Beacon Hill Elementary School
2025 14th Ave., So.
Seattle, WA 98144
Chinese, K-6

Brighton Elementary School
4425 S. Holly St.
Seattle, WA 98118
Filipino, K-6

Columbia Elementary School
4408 Delridge So.
Seattle, WA 98106
Korean, K-6

Seattle (cont'd)

Dearborn Elementary School
2820 S. Orcas
Seattle, WA 98108
Chinese, K-6

Gatzert Elementary School
615 12th Ave., So.
Seattle, WA 98144
Chinese, K-6

Kimball Elementary School
3200 23rd Ave., So.
Seattle, WA 98144
Chinese, K-6

Laurelhurst Elementary School
4530 46th Ave., NE
Seattle, WA 98105
Japanese, K-6

Lawton Elementary School
4017 26th Ave., W
Seattle, WA 98199
Filipino, K-6

Lowell Elementary School
1058 E. Mercer St.
Seattle, WA 98102
Korean, K-6

Sanislo Elementary School
1812 S. West Myrtle
Seattle, WA 98106
Korean, K-6

Van Asselt Elementary School
7201 Beacon Ave., S.
Seattle, WA 98108
Chinese, Samoan, K-6

Wing Luke Elementary School
3701 S. Kenyon
Seattle, WA 98118
Filipino, K-6

Hamilton Middle School
1610 N. 41st St.
Seattle, WA 98103
Korean, 5-8

So. Shore Middle School
8825 Rainier Ave., S.
Seattle, WA 98118
Samoan, 5-8

Marshall Curriculum and
   Instruction Center
520 Ravenna Blvd., NE
Seattle, WA 98115
Chinese

Boren Jr. High School
5950 Delridge Way,
SW
Seattle, WA 98106
Korean, 10-12

Seattle (cont'd)

Mercer Jr. High School
1600 Columbia
Seattle, WA 98108
Chinese, Filipino, 7-9

Sharples Jr. High School
3928 S. Graham St.
Seattle, WA 98118
Samoan, 7-9

Cleveland High School
5511 15th Ave., S.
Seattle, WA 98108
Chinese, 10-12

Franklin High School
3013 S. Mount Baker Blvd.
Seattle, WA 98136
Chinese, Filipino, 10-12

Sealth High School
2600 S. West Thistle St.
Seattle, WA 98126
Korean, 10-12

Tacoma

Contact person for Title VII
   Korean Bilingual Programs:
Richard Wiley
Basic Bilingual Program
Tacoma Public Schools
P.O. Box 1357
Tacoma, WA 98401
(206) 383-1811, ext. 473

"Directory of Bilingual Projects." Asian American
Bilingual Center, Berkeley Unified School District,
2168 Shattuck Avenue, Berkeley, CA 94704.

BILINGUAL RESOURCE CENTERS

EAST:

Connecticut
D.C.
Delaware
Kentucky
Maine
Maryland
Massachusetts
New Hampshire
New Jersey
New York
Pennsylvania
Rhode Island
Vermont
Virginia
West Virginia

Regional Cross-Cultural
   Training & Resource Ctr.
NYC Bd. of Ed.
Off. of Bilingual Ed.
110 Livingston St., Rm. 224
Brooklyn, NY 11201

(212) 858-5505

contact: Carmen Velkas, Dir.
          Vuong Gia Thuy

SOUTHWEST:

Arizona
Hawaii
New Mexico
Southern California
Southern Nevada

Inst. for Cultural Pluralism
San Diego State Univ.
San Diego, CA 92102

(714) 286-5193

contact: Reyes Mazon, Dir.
          Dr. Do Ba Khe
          Leonard Fierro
          Frances Lopez Beckers

MIDWEST:

Illinois
Indiana
Iowa
Kansas
Michigan
Minnesota
Missouri
Nebraska
North Dakota
Ohio
South Dakota
Wisconsin

Bilingual Ed. Service Ctr.
500 South Dwyer Ave.
Arlington Heights, IL 60005

(312) 255-9820

contact: Maria Swanson, Dir.
          Pat Guymont
          Guillermo DeHoogh

NORTH- & WEST:

Alaska
Colorado
Idaho
Montana
Northern California
Northern Nevada
Oregon
Utah
Washington
Wyoming
Trust Territories

Bay Area Bilingual Ed.
   League
1414 Walnut St.
Berkeley, CA 94709

(415) 644-6187

contact: Roberto Cruz, Dir.
          Joe Beard
          Pham Cao Duong

MID- & SOUTH:

Alabama
Arkansas
Florida
Georgia
Louisiana
Mississippi
North Carolina
Oklahoma
South Carolina
Tennessee
Texas

Nat'l Bilingual Resource Ctr.
P.O. Box 3410 USL
Lafayette, LA 70501

(318) 233-3850 x651

contact: Robt. Fontenot, Dir.
          Cal Ellis

NATIONAL INDOCHINESE CLEARINGHOUSE ● CENTER FOR APPLIED LINGUISTICS

Preschool Education Series:
1. English as a Second Language in Kindergarten: Orientation and Scheduling
2. English as a Second Language in Kindergarten: Teaching Pronunciation and Grammar
3. English as a Second Language in Kindergarten: Testing Young Children
4. English as a Second Language in Kindergarten: Language and Concept Development

Elementary Education Series:
1. On Keeping Lines of Communication with Indochinese Children Open
2. Classroom Instructions in Vietnamese/Inside the Classroom
3. Vietnamese History, Literature & Folklore
4. Classroom Instructions in Vietnamese/Outside the Classroom
5. Continuing English Studies During the Summer
6. Supplemental ESL Activities for Classroom Teachers

Intermediate/Secondary Education Series:
1. Vietnamese History, Literature & Folklore
2. Detailed Content of Vietnamese Secondary Curriculum
3. Continuing English Studies During the Summer

General Information Series:
1. Hints for Tutors
2. Testing English Language Proficiency
3. Education in Vietnam: Fundamental Principles and Curricula
4. Teaching English Pronunciation to Vietnamese
5. Textbooks and Classes for ESL
6. A Brief Look at the Vietnamese Language: Sounds & Spellings
7. Testing the Reading Ability of Cambodians
8. Academic Resources for Language & Culture
9. A Selected Bibliography of Dictionaries
10. Teaching English Pronunciation to Speakers of Black Tai (Tai Dam)
11. Teaching English Structures to the Vietnamese
12. Supplement to: "An Annotated Bibliography for Teaching English to Vietnamese"
13. Perspectives on a Cross-Cultural Problem: Getting to Know the Vietnamese

Adult Education Series:
1. Teaching English to Adult Refugees
2. Bibliography of Adult ESL Materials
3. Towards Methods of Learning English (In Viet./Cambodian/English)
4. ESL Reading Materials for Adults
5. Recreational Reading in Viet.
6. How to Teach Adult ESL: A Guide for Volunteers

Educational Administrator Series:
1. On Assimilating Vietnamese & Cambodian Students into U.S. Schools
2. Meeting the English Language Needs of Indochinese Students

Bilingual/Bicultural Education Series:
1. Information for Administrators & Teachers
2. A Selected, Annotated Bibliography on Bilingual/Bicultural Education
3. A Model for Bilingual Language Skill Building

Personnel Resources Directory Supplements:
Sept., 1975--A Personnel Resources Directory for the Education of Indochinese Refugees
October, 1975   -- Supplement #1
November, 1975   -- Supplement #2
November, 1975   -- Supplement #3
December, 1975   -- Supplement #4
May, 1976   -- Supplement #5
July, 1976   -- Supplement #6

Indochinese Refugee Alert Bulletins:
#1 August, 1975   #4 February, 1976
#2 September, 1975   #5 March/April, 1976
#3 October, 1975

"Indochinese Refugee Education Guides" and "Bilingual Resource Centers." National Indochinese Clearinghouse, Center for Applied Linguistics, 1611 North Kent Street, Arlington, VA 22209.

Part four:
Black

Black

FULFILLING THE LETTER AND SPIRIT OF THE LAW

Four years after the Supreme Court of the United States decision in *Brown* v. *Board of Education*,[1] the school bell summoned America to the spectacle of screaming parents and troops with bayonets at the ready, escorting nine black students to Central High School in Little Rock, Arkansas.

"I tried to see a friendly face," declared Elizabeth Eckford, one of the nine. "I looked into the face of an old woman and it seemed friendly, but when I looked at her again she spat on me." And then Elizabeth Eckford wept.

Her tears were but the prologue to a long drama of struggle that is not yet over. The Nation is still confronted with a basic question. That question has been reworded at various times since 1954, but it remains essentially the same: Are the Elizabeth Eckfords of this country to be denied equality of educational opportunity merely because many people oppose the remedies for constitutional violations and subvert their implementation? The Supreme Court answered this question in 1955 in *Brown II:* "the vitality of these constitutional principles cannot be allowed to yield simply because of disagreement with them."[2] Twenty-one years later, the implementing doctrine (*Brown II*) providing equal protection of the laws to minority children is under renewed and intense attack.

On July 10, 1776, the Declaration of Independence was published in the *Pennsylvania Gazette*. In that same issue, an advertisement also appeared offering a black slave for sale.[3] Thus our Nation came into existence 200 years ago with a serious flaw. The Constitution itself, as every student of history knows, bore the telltale marks in its first article, which apportioned representatives according to the free population and "three-fifths of all other Persons."

[1] 347 U.S. 483 (1954).
[2] Brown v. Board of Education, 349 U.S. 294, at 300 (1955).
[3] *Pennsylvania Gazette*, No. 2481, July 10, 1776, Philadelphia, Pa., p. 4.

For a short-lived period after the Civil War, the 13th, 14th, and 15th amendments protected the rights of black Americans. But the political compromise of 1877 effectively ended this era, and in 1896 the Supreme Court of the United States sanctioned the second-class status of blacks in the infamous *Plessy* v. *Ferguson* decision.[4]

By the early 1930s disparities in educational expenditures were evident in the South. In Randolph County, Georgia, $36.66 was expended annually for the education of each white child, while only 43 cents was spent on each black child.[5] Russell County, Alabama, spent $45.74 per white child each year and only $2.55 per black.[6] The values of educational facilities were similarly disproportionate. In Upson County, Georgia, for every $1.00 of the declared value of black schools, white schools were valued at $2,055.[7]

It was not until 1938 that the country began the long road to equality of educational opportunity. In that year, the Supreme Court embarked on a series of decisions attempting to enforce the "separate but equal" doctrine that led inexorably to the tardy rejection of that bankrupt maxim.

In *Missouri ex rel. Gaines* v. *Canada* (1938),[8] a black student sought entry to law school within his home State. The State in turn offered to pay his tuition at an out-of-State institution. The Court held this offer to be "a denial of the equality of legal right to the enjoyment of the privilege which the State has set up***the provision for the payment of tuition fees in another State does not remove the discrimination."[9]

In 1948 another black applicant asserted that she was entitled to a legal education at the University of Oklahoma Law School. The State contended that local law allowed for provision of a separate law school for blacks upon demand or notice and that the applicant had not sought such relief. In its decision in the case, *Sipuel* v. *University of Oklahoma*,[10] the Supreme Court recognized that the petitioner could not be expected to wait for construction of a law school before completing her education. The Court stated:

> The petitioner is entitled to secure legal education afforded by a State institution. To this time, it has been denied her although during the same period many white applicants have been afforded legal education by the State. The State must provide it for her in conformity with the equal protection clause of the Fourteenth Amendment and provide it as soon as it does for applicants of any other group.[11]

Oklahoma tried another tack with a black student admitted to a State university graduate school. Under a new law, the student was provided an education on a segregated basis. He sat in a section of the classroom surrounded by a rail with a sign reading "Reserved for Colored." He was assigned one desk in the library and

[4]163 U.S. 537 (1896).

[5]Charles S. Johnson, *Statistical Atlas of Southern Counties* (Chapel Hill: University of North Carolina, 1941), p. 107.

[6]Ibid., p. 52.

[7]Ibid., p. 111.

[8]305 U.S. 337 (1938).

[9]305 U.S. at 349. See *Argument: The Complete Oral Argument before the Supreme Court in Brown v. Board of Education of Topeka, 1952–55*, ed. Leon Friedman (New York: Chelsea House Publishers, 1969), pp. xiv–xvii for a summary of pre-*Brown* cases.

[10]332 U.S. 631 (1948).

[11]332 U.S. at 632–33.

prohibited from using any other, and was required to eat in the cafeteria at a different time from all other students.

This arrangement did not satisfy the Court. It ruled in *McLaurin* v. *Oklahoma State Regents* (1950)[12] that:

> [T]he State, in administering the facilities it affords for professional and graduate study, sits McLaurin apart from the other students. The result is that the appellant is handicapped in his pursuit of effective graduate instruction***. There is a vast difference—a Constitutional difference—between restrictions imposed by the State which prohibit the commingling of students, and the refusal of individuals to commingle where the State presents no such bar***.[13]

On the same day the Court decided in *Sweatt* v. *Painter*[14] that a new separate law school for blacks operated by the State of Texas could not, in reality, provide equal protection of the laws. In this case as well as in *McLaurin*, the Court emphasized the "intangibles" that make an educational institution equal: "Such qualities***include the reputation of the faculty, experience of the administration, position and influence of the alumni, standing in the community, traditions and prestige***."[15] The Court added that the new black law school excluded 85 percent of the population from which were drawn most of the lawyers, witnesses, jurors, judges, and other officials in the State that a black lawyer would eventually encounter. For this reason, the Court said, "We cannot conclude that the education offered petitioner is substantially equal to that which he would receive if admitted to the University of Texas Law School."[16]

With the handwriting on the wall, the South launched a crash program to build separate but "equal" schools for blacks. But it was too late then to prove *Plessy* v. *Ferguson* a possible answer to the requirements of the 14th amendment. Four years later the Court declared that the considerations enumerated in *Sweatt* and in *McLaurin* "apply with added force to children in grade and high schools." The verdict was in, and after *Brown* segregation was legally doomed. *Brown*, however, was not the end of segregation so much as the beginning of desegregation. The Court's work was not over—the question of implementation remained.

In this regard, the Court gave to the lower Federal courts the responsibility for dealing with specific plans and problems, so that plaintiffs would be admitted to public schools "on a racially nondiscriminatory basis with all deliberate speed."[17] "All deliberate speed" became the catchword that spawned massive resistance as the South deliberated but refused to desegregate. Ten years after *Brown*, only 1.2 percent of the nearly 3 million black students in the 11 Southern States attended school with white students.[18] The Court was forced to conclude in *Griffin* v. *County School Board of Prince Edward County* (1964, Virginia) that "The time for mere 'deliberate speed' has run out***."[19]

---

[12] 339 U.S. 637 (1950).
[13] 339 U.S. at 641.
[14] 339 U.S. 629 (1959).
[15] 339 U.S. at 634.
[16] Id.
[17] 349 U.S. 294 at 301 (1955).
[18] U.S., Commission on Civil Rights, *Twenty Years After Brown: Equality of Educational Opportunity* (1975), p. 46.
[19] 377 U.S. 218 at 234 (1964).

Prince Edward County had tried to solve the segregation problem by simply abolishing its public schools, but other school districts found less dramatic ways temporarily to circumvent the law. Chief among these was the "freedom of choice" plan that ostensibly permitted students to select the school they would attend. In practice, few chose to transfer. The Court took on this issue in *Green* v. *County School Board of New Kent County* (1968),[20] ruling that such plans were unacceptable where speedier and more effective means were available. In addition, the Court stressed, "The burden of a school board today is to come forward with a plan that promises realistically to work, and promises realistically to work now."[21] This urgency was reiterated the following year in *Alexander* v. *Holmes County Board of Education*,[22] where the Supreme Court ordered the court of appeals to "issue its decree and order, effective immediately*** "[23]

The techniques of desegregation became an issue again in *Swann* v. *Charlotte-Mecklenburg Board of Education* (1971),[24] which became known as the first "busing" case. Busing had been the way to more equitable educational opportunity for millions of schoolchildren across the country. Furthermore, children had been bused long distances for decades to perpetuate segregation. But when transportation for the purposes of desegregation was decreed, busing suddenly became a national issue. The Court held that a school desegregation plan was "to be judged by its effectiveness"[25] and that a plan might require student transportation as long as "the time or distance of travel is [not] so great as to either risk the health of the children or significantly impinge on the educational process."[26]

At this point, the Court had not ruled on the future of school systems in States where segregation had never been the law but where segregated schools existed nevertheless. In these States, such segregation was said to be *de facto* rather than *de jure*. This distinction appeared before the Court in the case of *Keyes* v. *School District No. 1, Denver, Colorado* (1973).[27] The Court declared that "***where no statutory dual system has ever existed, plaintiffs must prove that it was brought about or maintained by intentional State action."[28] This the plaintiffs had done, and the Court thus ordered that desegregation proceed. Its decision meant that countless northern school districts, guilty of such practices as gerrymandering school zones, setting up segregatory feeder systems, and assigning staff on a racially discriminatory basis, would be faced with correcting these violations of constitutional rights. But it also meant that plaintiffs would have to present convincing evidence of official action responsible for dual school systems on a case-by-case basis.

The consequences of massive resistance by the South need little repetition here. Schools were closed; State funds were cut off; com-

[20] 391 U.S. 430 (1968).
[21] 391 U.S. at 439.
[22] 396 U.S. 19 (1969).
[23] 396 U.S. at 20.
[24] 402 U.S. 1 (1971).
[25] 402 U.S. at 25.
[26] 402 U.S. at 30–31.
[27] 413 U.S. 189 (1973).
[28] 413 U.S. at 198.

pulsory attendance laws were suspended or repealed; private schools were opened with tuition paid for whites by public funds. Long dead constitutional doctrines were revived to buttress stalling tactics.

What has not been placed in proper perspective are the actions of school districts in the North and West. There official actions of school boards too frequently have obstructed, delayed, and denied the minority student equal protection of the laws. The actions of governmental bodies responsible for segregation have been ignored in the heated debate over remedies.

A clear example is the city of Boston. It would be totally misleading to examine the equity of the remedy ordered in the Boston case, *Morgan v. Hennigan* (1974),[29] without considering the findings of the court. Yet this is what many political leaders and media commentators have done. The judge in this case, W. Arthur Garrity, Jr., laid out the basis for his ruling in a meticulously documented opinion.

In the purchase and construction of new facilities, the judge found "The overwhelming effect***has been to increase racial segregation." In one situation, black children were bused involuntarily to a more distant school when seats were vacant at nearby white schools.[30] With regard to districting, Judge Garrity wrote:

> Year after year the defendants rejected proposals for redistricting carefully drawn with a view to lessening racial imbalance, while at all times displaying an awareness of the potential racial impact of their actions.[31]

One assistant superintendent testified at the trial of the case that he opposed redistricting in one instance "because he knew the attitude of the people in the area."[32] In another instance, the judge noted:

> [The district] configuration results in nearly the maximum possible amount of racial isolation***. Only small sections of the district lines coincide with natural boundaries***.[33]

In Boston, the judge noted, assignment to a particular high school is determined not by geography, but "by a combination of seat assignments, preferences and options collectively called feeder patterns."[34] Various elementary and intermediate schools feed into high schools at various grade levels depending on whether the high schools run from grade 9 to 12 or 10 to 12. The judge concluded that these feeder patterns "since***1966***have been manipulated with segregative effect."[35]

Open enrollment, similar to the freedom-of-choice plans so popular in the South, was another tool of the Boston School Committee. "Open enrollment as administered by the defendants," the judge said, "became a device for separating the races and contributed significantly to the establishment of a dual school system."[36] Black

[29] 379 F. Supp. 410 (D. Mass. 1974).
[30] Id. at 428.
[31] Id. at 433.
[32] Id. at 438.
[33] Id. at 435.
[34] Id. at 441.
[35] Id. at 442.
[36] Id. at 453.

parents sending their children to predominantly white schools were chasing a will-o'-the-wisp, since whites were free under the system to transfer elsewhere when integration appeared imminent.

The court found that in the 1971–72 school year when the student population in Boston schools was 96,000:

> Approximately one-third of Boston's students, a large majority of whom are in high school, use buses or other public transportation to travel to and from school. Approximately 3,000 elementary students are transported at city expense, most of whom attend schools over a mile away from their homes. In Charlestown some elementary students who live less than a mile from school are bused for safety reasons. Other elementary students are bused several miles, e.g., from the Dearborn district in Roxbury to the North End and East Boston; others from the South End to Brighton. The three examination high schools, sometimes called the "elite schools," were served in the school year 1971–72 by a combined total of 63 buses on 35 routes. Many other students travel between distant parts of the city.[37]

Faculty and staff were racially separated as well, despite the fact that their dispersal would not have required busing. The judge found that "Black teachers are segregated at black schools***. Black administrators are also segregated."[38] Black schools more frequently were assigned less experienced and less qualified teachers, and "the defendants have for years 'gone through the motions' of recruiting black teachers, but have never made a wholehearted effort to get results."[39]

The school committee offered standard defenses: that housing segregation led to the segregation found in the schools, and that their policy of maintaining neighborhood schools was constitutionally sound.[40] The plaintiffs pointed out that school district assignments themselves can affect housing patterns; that the school committee intentionally incorporated residential segregation into the school system; and that the committee policies were riddled with so many exceptions designed to increase segregation that its defenses need not be considered.[41]

The judge agreed, stating: "The defendents have, with awareness of the racial segregation of Boston's neighborhoods, deliberately incorporated that segregation into the school system."[42]

It is for all these reasons that school desegregation, implemented through student transportation, was ordered in Boston. The basis in law is really no different from that in *Brown*. The standard of proof has evolved, but the ruling is still based on the official actions of a government body, to wit: "***[T]he defendants have knowingly carried out a systematic program of segregation affecting all of the city's students, teachers, and school facilities and have intentionally brought about and maintained a dual school system."[43]

In 1966 an attempt in the House of Representatives to legitimize freedom-of-choice plans barely failed, by a vote of 127 to 136.[44] In

---

[37] Id. at 424.
[38] Id. at 459.
[39] Id. at 464.
[40] Id. at 469.
[41] Id. at 470.
[42] Id.
[43] Id. at 482.
[44] Michael Wise, "Congress, Busing, and Federal Law," *Civil Rights Digest*, vol. 5, no. 5, p. 30.

a press conference shortly after the issuance of the *Swann* decision in 1971, President Nixon indicated that the decision, which sanctioned the use of busing in remedying *de jure* segregation, was the law of the land and would be enforced by the executive branch. Soon thereafter, the administration reversed its position and announced it would not grant funds for court-ordered busing under the Emergency School Assistance Program and proposed that the Congress prohibit such funding in the future. [45]

In 1972 Congress wrangled over several antibusing amendments to pending legislation and President Nixon delivered a nationally televised address attacking "massive busing" and announced that he was sending legislation to the Congress designed to limit busing. [46] In 1974 President Gerald Ford stated at a press conference that he thought the law should be obeyed, but then went on to note that he had "consistently opposed forced busing to achieve racial balance as a solution to quality education." [47] More recently, the President has proposed legislation that would require the courts to limit the definition of illegal segregation and to limit the extent and duration of busing as a remedy. In addition, Attorney General Edward Levi has indicated that the Department of Justice may seek review by the Supreme Court of certain aspects of busing, although the issues he cited have already been considered and disposed of by the courts. [48]

The tragedy of these developments, and others discussed later in this report, is that they undermine the desegregation process in communities across the country. And despite the publicity given to violence in Pontiac, Boston, and Louisville, numerous communities have implemented the law peacefully. Although largely ignored by politicians and the national press, these communities represent in many ways the real story of desegregation today.

RECENT COMMISSION INITIATIVES

SCOPE AND METHODOLOGY

The Commission on Civil Rights in recent years has been increasingly concerned about the lack of accurate information and understanding on school desegregation. This problem, from the Commission's viewpoint, threatens further progress in school desegregation and other areas of civil rights as well. In November 1975 the Commission, therefore, announced a series of projects to provide the Nation with a national assessment of the school desegregation effort. [1] These projects included formal hearings, open meetings, case studies, and a national survey, the findings of which are incorporated into this report. Other sources of information for this report include: previous Commission studies on desegregation or other

---

[45] Ibid., p. 31.
[46] Ibid., pp. 31–33.
[47] *Press Documents*, Oct. 11, 1974.
[48] *New York Times*, May 30, 1976, p. 1.

---

[1] Statement on New School Desegregation by the U.S. Commission on Civil Rights, Nov. 11, 1975.

school-related considerations;[2] publications by organizations such as the Southern Regional Council;[3] and recent articles in periodicals, journals, and newspapers. These various sources provided data for analysis and also the views of key participants in the desegregation of school districts throughout the country. (See map 2.1.)

Map 2.1 **Public Hearing, Open Meeting and Case Study Sites**

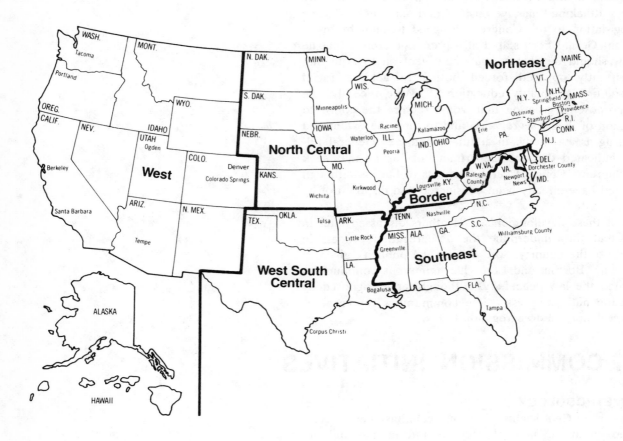

---

[2] These Commission reports include: *1961 Report*, vol. 2, *Education; Southern School Desegregation, 1966–67; Racial Isolation in the Public Schools* (1967); *Federal Enforcement of School Desegregation* (1969); *Your Child and Busing* (1972); *Five Communities: Their Search for Equal Education* (1972); *The Diminishing Barrier: A Report on School Desegregation in Nine Communities* (1972); *School Desegregation in Ten Communities* (1973); *Twenty Years After Brown: Equality of Educational Opportunity* (1975); and *The Federal Civil Rights Enforcement Effort–1974: To Ensure Equal Educational Opportunity* (1975).

Studies dealing with equal education problems among language-minority students include the 6-volume Mexican American Education Project: *Ethnic Isolation of Mexican Americans in the Public Schools of the Southwest* (1971); *The Unfinished Education* (1971); *The Excluded Student* (1972); *Mexican American Education in Texas: A Function of Wealth* (1972); *Teachers and Students* (1973); *Toward Quality Education for Mexican Americans* (1974); and a recent study, *A Better Chance to Learn: Bilingual-Bicultural Education* (1975).

The Commission has also explored developments in school desegregation in its quarterly journal, the *Civil Rights Digest*. The Summer 1973 issue, for example, was devoted entirely to school desegregation.

[3] See, for example, John Egerton, *School Desegregation: A Report Card from the South* (Atlanta: Southern Regional Council, 1976).

The school districts studied and surveyed during this research were selected in order to provide a broad cross-section of districts representing the entire spectrum of views and experiences concerning school desegregation. Those districts differ in many respects, such as the original impetus for desegregation, the nature of public reaction, the effectiveness of planning, the length of experience with desegregation, and the general success or ease with which desegregation has been implemented. However, these projects have enabled the Commission to draw conclusions about overall progress in desegregating the Nation's schools and to identify factors that contribute to effective desegregation.

Public Hearings

The Commission held public hearings on school desegregation in four major cities: Boston, June 16–20, 1975; Denver, February 17–19, 1976; Tampa, March 29–31, 1976; and Louisville, June 14–16, 1976.

Each of the four hearings was preceded by intensive staff investigation. A combined total of approximately 4,500 persons were interviewed for all four hearings. At least 100 persons were subpenaed and testified under oath at each hearing, including Federal, State, and local officials; representatives of business, law enforcement, religious, and other community groups, as well as higher education and the media; school officials and personnel, including school board members, administrators, and faculty; and parents and students. The witnesses included persons of diverse racial and ethnic groups, as well as persons with differing views toward desegregation. In addition to the 100 or so individuals scheduled to testify, there were between 10 and 15 unscheduled witnesses who testified at each hearing.

The hearings covered all aspects of desegregation, ranging from the history of the first desegregation efforts, through the manifold dynamics of the implementation process in the schools and the broader community, to retrospective evaluation of the actual effects of desegregation on the schools as a public institution and on students, teachers, and other individuals affected directly or indirectly. In particular, inquiry was directed toward specific reasons why desegregation had proceeded smoothly or had serious difficulties. Certain topics also received more attention at one hearing than at another. Thus the Boston and Louisville hearings focused in more detail on the role of the police during desegregation. The importance of bilingual education in desegregating school districts received much attention at the Denver and Tampa hearings.

Open Meetings

Four State Advisory Committees (SACs) to the Commission conducted four open meetings on school desegregation in 1976 in Berkeley, California, March 19–20; Minneapolis, Minnesota, April 22–24; Stamford, Connecticut, April 29; and Corpus Christi, Texas, May 4–5.[4]

Preparations for the meetings and the scope of testimony resem-

---

[4] The Commission has an Advisory Committee in each State and in the District of Columbia which reports on local civil rights issues and developments.

bled that of the public hearings. However, Advisory Committees do not have subpena power and testimony was not taken under oath. Approximately 50 persons spoke at each open meeting. Detailed evaluations and analyses of these meetings were prepared by the State Advisory Committees and the Commission's regional offices in Los Angeles, Chicago, New York, and San Antonio.

Case Studies

In February, March, and April 1976, 28 of the Commission's State Advisory Committees, with staff assistance from the eight regional offices, conducted 29 case studies of school desegregation. Four studies covered the four cities where Advisory Committee meetings were held. Table 2.1 shows the communities studied by State and Commission region.

These districts are of varying size and racial-ethnic composition. All had a student enrollment of at least 1,500, of which at least 5 percent were minority students. Some had desegregated voluntarily while others desegregated under Federal or State pressure or a court order. At least 10 percent of the students in each district were reassigned during desegregation, and transportation was included in all desegregation plans. The sample included both rural and urban districts with varying years of experience with desegregation. Some districts had desegregated with minimal difficulty and some had experienced considerable problems.

Commission staff and Advisory Committee members conducted personal interviews in each district with mayors, city council members, and law enforcement authorities; community leaders; school officials and personnel; parents and students; and media representatives. Standardized guides were used for both onsite and telephone interviews to elicit information about the individual's own role in desegregation, as well as his or her perceptions of events and the role played by others during desegregation. They also were designed to elicit personal judgments about the effectiveness of desegregation in their communities and the overall effect of desegregation on the schools and communities. In addition to these interviews, Advisory Committee members and regional staff collected data and reports pertinent to desegregation in each district. The Commission's regional offices analyzed and summarized the results of this research and submitted them to Washington for further evaluation.

National Survey

In late January 1976 the Commission mailed questionnaires to individuals in a random sample of approximately 1,300 school districts. These individuals included school superintendents, heads of local chambers of commerce, parent advisory councils, and local chapters of the National Association for the Advancement of Colored People (NAACP), and mayors or city managers. The districts included the 100 largest in the Nation, and approximately 47 percent of districts which had pupil enrollments of at least 1,500 and were at least 5 percent minority.

Information was sought on the stimulus for desegregation, the nature of the desegregation plan implemented, and the outcome of desegregation. The variables used for assessment were the perceived support for desegregation by community leaders and groups, the degree of disruption of the educational process during desegregation, and the perceived quality of education. The survey also sought to examine the withdrawal of whites from school systems in response to desegregation. Superintendents were asked about the activities of any multiracial or multiethnic committees, student suspension levels, and building improvements incident to desegregation. All those surveyed were asked about the extent and cost of pupil transportation, the role and attitudes of various community groups before and after desegregation, the quality of education, student retention and achievement, and interaction among pupils of different races or ethnic groups. Usable responses were received from about 76 percent of the superintendents and 20 percent of the community leaders. Some responses were obtained by telephone.

FOUR HEARINGS

Boston, Massachusetts

Massachusetts was the first State in the Nation to enact a school desegregation law, the Racial Imbalance Act of 1965.[5] Under the law, any school with a nonwhite enrollment of more than 50 percent was "imbalanced," and strong sanctions were available against any school district that failed to correct such imbalance. The act did not require integration of all-white schools; it prohibited involuntary, interdistrict transportation; and its compliance guidelines were vague, opening avenues for procrastination and evasion which the Boston School Committee used fully.

TABLE 2.1   Case Study Communities by State and Commission Region

Northeast Regional Office
Ossining, N.Y.
Providence, R.I.
Springfield, Mass.
Stamford, Conn.**

Mid-Atlantic Regional Office
Erie, Pa.
Newport News, Va.
Dorchester County, Md.
Raleigh County, W.Va.

Southern Regional Office
Nashville, Tenn.
Greenville, Miss.
Williamsburg County, S.C.

Central States Regional Office
Wichita, Kans.
Waterloo, Iowa
Kirkwood, Mo.

Mid-Western Regional Office
Racine, Wis.
Peoria, Ill.
Kalamazoo, Mich.
Minneapolis, Minn.**

Mountain States Regional Office
Ogden, Utah
Colorado Springs, Colo.
Tempe, Ariz.

Southwestern Regional Office
Bogalusa, La.
Tulsa, Okla.
Little Rock, Ark.
Corpus Christi, Tex.**

Western Regional Office
Portland, Ore.
Tacoma, Wash.
Santa Barbara, Calif.
Berkeley, Calif.**

** Indicates school district in which Advisory Committee open meetings were held.

---

[5]U.S., Commission Civil Rights, staff report, *School Desegregation in Boston* (June 1975), p. 63 (hereafter cited as *School Desegregation in Boston*). Mass. Gen. L. Ch. 71 §§37C and 37D

The city of Boston has a population of approximately 641,000 people, many of whom live in neighborhoods with strong ethnic identities. Its black population is approximately 17 percent of the total and its student population is 34 percent black and 6 percent Hispanic. In 1973, 85 percent of black public school students attended schools that were more than 50 percent minority; 54 percent attended schools that were 90 to 100 percent minority. [6]

The Boston School Committee, which formulates policy for city public schools, proved unrelenting in its opposition to school desegregation. For 8 years following passage of the Racial Imbalance Act, State education authorities were unsuccessful in their efforts to compel the Boston School Committee to desegregate at least a substantial portion of its schools. Several State agencies became involved, including the State department of education and the Massachusetts Commission Against Discrimination. Suits and countersuits were filed in State courts. By 1971, however, Boston's public schools were more segregated than ever. [7]

The Federal Government became involved for the first time in 1971 when the Department of Health, Education, and Welfare wrote to the Boston School Committee charging discrimination in certain educational programs. Two years later HEW threatened to cut off all Federal education funds to the city. [8]

In March 1972 the local chapter of the NAACP filed suit in Federal district court, alleging government discrimination in creating and maintaining a segregated public school system. In June 1974 the Federal district court in Boston rejected the school committee's defense that housing patterns were responsible for school segregation.

The court found that the school committee had unconstitutionally fostered and maintained a segregated public school system through policies which had been "knowingly" designed to that end. [9] As a result of these policies, the court found, racial segregation permeated schools "in all areas in the city, all grade levels, and all types of schools." [10] The court also observed that the school committee had thwarted school desegregation efforts of Massachusetts authorities, including the State supreme court, by "formalistic compliance followed by procrastination and evasion on technical grounds." [11]

The court ordered desegregation to begin in September 1974. The plan for desegregation involved two phases. Phase I, implemented in September 1974, used redistricting and pupil transportation to desegregate 80 of the city's approximately 200 schools. Phase II, implemented in September 1975, involved all remaining schools, except those in east Boston. Revision of attendance zones and grade structures, construction of new schools and the closing

[6] U.S., Department of Health, Education, and Welfare, Office for Civil Rights, Elementary and Secondary Public School Survey, Fall 1973.
[7] U.S., Commission on Civil Rights, *Desegregating the Boston Public Schools: A Crisis in Civic Responsibility* (August 1975) (hereafter cited as *Crisis in Civic Responsibility*), p. xvi.
[8] Ibid., p. xvii.
[9] Morgan v. Hennigan, 379 F. Supp. 410 (D. Mass. 1974).
[10] Id. at 424.
[11] Id. at 476–77.

of old ones, and a controlled transfer policy with limited exceptions were used to minimize further pupil transportation. [12]

Implementation of Phase I was accompanied by mob violence and boycotts in some areas of the city, the worst such incidents to occur during school desegregation in a northern city. In October 1974 Mayor Kevin White expressed concern about his ability to "maintain either the appearance or the reality of public safety" during desegregation in some parts of Boston, [13] but order was generally established.

In June 1975 the Commission on Civil Rights held a 5-day hearing in Boston and heard testimony from more than 100 subpenaed witnesses, including Federal, State, and local officials, community leaders, school staff, and students. From this testimony and research conducted in connection with the hearing, the Commission gained significant insight into the desegregation process in Boston.

The publicity surrounding opposition to desegregation in Boston overshadowed the fact that major problems occurred at only four of the schools desegregated in 1974. Violence was severe at only two, South Boston and Hyde Park High Schools. The desegregation process proceeded smoothly at the great majority of schools affected by Phase I, and the groundwork was laid for even more progress the following year. [14]

At the Jeremiah E. Burke High School in Roxbury, for example, many faculty and students viewed desegregation and the school year generally as a success. Burke teacher Joseph Day testified:

> ***the kids by October realized if they didn't do their work and weren't going to study, they were going to fail***. There was a lot of education, a lot of learning, a lot of teaching going on in the building, and the kids realized it. [15]

Burke student Jan Douglas told the Commission:

> At first***everybody was kind of scared because no one had really talked to each other to know where each other stood. Everybody was kind of walking around each other. And as the year progressed, we talked and we got to understanding, and we found a common ground***. That we had all come to Jerry [Burke] for one thing, and that was to get a quality education and that in doing so, we would do it together. [16]

The testimony of other witnesses, however, revealed that school desegregation in Boston was seriously hampered by virtually a total lack of public and private leadership. The city's elected officials refused to express support for the court order or for the goal of school desegregation. The school committee's position was one of determined, unrelenting opposition to desegregation. It had fought school desegregation from the beginning, and it refused any affirmative support for peaceful implementation of school desegregation.

The chairman of the Boston School Committee stated:

---

[12] *School Desegregation in Boston*, p. 77.

[13] *Boston Globe*, May 25, 1975, p. A–15, summarizing events of the previous year.

[14] *Crisis in Civic Responsibility*, p. v.

[15] U.S., Commission on Civil Rights, hearing, Boston, Mass., June 16–20, 1975, transcript, p. 283 (hereafter cited as Boston transcript).

[16] Boston transcript, p. 329.

***For my part, I will not go any further than doing what Judge Garrity directly orders me to do. And I will not end up as a salesman for a plan which I do not believe in.[17]

A member said:

It would appear that we have exhausted some of our legal remedies. I think we still have—at least on the implementation process—some appeals.
My instruction, and of course I am only one vote, is to appeal every word that comes out of Garrity's mouth.
So hopefully, somewhere along the line we can get some relief, because this order is just a destruction of the city***.[18]

The picture that emerged in 5 days of testimony was of an elected body so belligerent[19] and so derelict in its duties that the Commission recommended that the court consider suspending the committee's authority and placing the school system in receivership, a step that was partially taken by Judge Garrity in connection with Phase II of the court's desegregation order.

The records of other public officials—some of whom openly associated themselves with the "antibusing" organization, "Restore Our Alienated Rights" (ROAR)—were little better. City council members stongly opposed the court order,[20] and several State legislators from Boston introduced legislation to repeal the State's Racial Imbalance Act. The mayor's position on desegregation was equivocal, and on the national level, the lack of leadership extended to the White House. In October 1974 the President issued a public statement critical of the court order.

According to Thomas Atkins, president of the Boston NAACP,:

those kinds of hopes [that a desegregation order would be reversed] were fed by statementssuch as the one by the President when***he indicated disagreement with***the order of the Federal Court***.[21]

The posture of elected officials reinforced the belief of many individuals that desegregation, which had been successfully avoided for 10 years, would never come about. Rabbi Roland Gittelson said:

I'm very fearful that there will be increased tension and aggravation so long as the members of the Boston School Committee and many political leaders continue to make the whole desegregation problem a political football for their own political ambitions***.[22]

The absence of leadership involved all sectors of the city. Business leaders were generally passive, in part because of the mayor's position. Relatively few of the clergy provided strong moral leadership. Many social and community service agencies also adopted neutral positions toward school desegregation. South Boston com-

[17] Ibid., testimony of John McDonough, p. 1057.
[18] Ibid., testimony of John Kerrigan, p. 1057A.
[19] The testimony of one school committee member degenerated to the level of name-calling with respect to the Vice Chairman of the Commission. See testimony of John Kerrigan, Boston transcript. p. 1090.
[20] Ibid., testimony of Boston City Council members Louise Day Hicks, Gerald O'Leary, Lawrence Di Cara, and Albert O'Neil, pp. 1226–65.
[21] Boston transcript, p. 967.
[22] Ibid., p. 472.

munity groups, for example, neither assisted nor supported implementation of Phase I. This default at the community level, combined with the lack of guidance or leadership from city leaders, damaged the educational process in Boston.

Testimony made plain that the principal leadership for desegregation in Boston came from the U.S. district court. The court did not seek or arbitrarily seize that role. It was forced upon the court because, as Thomas Atkins, local NAACP leader, observed:

> The mayor [Kevin White] from time to time has refused to lead and has tried to hide. The Governor, this one [Michael Dukakis] and the last one, [Francis Sargent] from time to time has tried to say it's the mayor's problem, it's the judge's problem, it's anybody's problem; it's not my problem. [23]

Moreover, Judge W. Arthur Garrity, Jr., in his desegregation order was careful not to raise unreasonable administrative problems for the school system. Student transportation was held to a minimum, and the percentage of total enrollment transported increased by about 17 percentage points after desegregation. [24] Further, court-ordered bus rides were short, a fact that, in part, reflects the geographical compactness of Boston. [25]

Lack of leadership was also evident in the near total absence of effective planning for desegregation. Strong criticism was expressed of the "ill-defined low visibility policy" of the Boston Police Department and its lack of a "detailed master plan" for maintaining order during desegregation. [26] Black community leader Elma Lewis described the effect of this failure in South Boston:

> One of the most disenchanting experiences [our children] had was the day that they were set upon in South Boston High and the police expressed an inability to bring them out safely and they got out only by luck*** [27]

The situation became so dangerous that State police and Metropolitan District Commission police were called in to assist the Boston police.

Haphazard planning also typified the school administration's response to the court order. Desegregation training and guidelines for faculty were minimal. No effort was made to involve the communities affected by Phase I, nor was any effort made to promote student attendance. A sharp increase in the suspension rate of black students occurred. One data analyst found the great disparity between white and black suspension rates to be "systematically related to race." [28]

At the few schools where strong, conscientious administrators prepared effectively for desegregation, difficulties were minor. At Roslindale High School, for example, curriculum content was reviewed, and the social studies program was changed to deal with

---

[23] Ibid., pp. 967–68.
[24] *School Desegregation in Boston*, p. 100.
[25] Ibid., p. 98.
[26] James E. Fisk and Raymond T. Galvin, "Report on the Boston Police Department during the 1974–75 School Desegregation," report to the U.S. Commission on Civil Rights, June 30, 1975, p. 16.
[27] Boston transcript, p. 234.
[28] Affidavit of Paul V. Smith, educational data analyst, Children's Defense Fund of the Washington Research Project, Inc., filed in Morgan v Kerrigan, Civ. Action No. 72-911-G.

race relations and the background to school desegregation. An ethnic studies course was planned for Phase II.[29] Roslindale teachers also visited the 30 schools sending students to Roslindale under the desegregation plan.[30] Strong community support was another "key factor" contributing to relatively successful implementation of desegregation at Roslindale.[31]

Phase II of the desegregation effort provided a basis for improving the overall quality of education in Boston. A key feature of Phase II was the linking of various city schools with business and higher education institutions, labor organizations, and the arts. Local colleges and universities offered needed resources in the development of reading and communication skills, cross-cultural relations, mathematics and science, counseling, teacher training, preventive health care and health-related problems, social work, and many other areas.

As the court noted:

> The significance of this pairing effort is as a long-term commitment, a promise to the parents and students of Boston that these institutions, with their rich educational resources, are concerning themselves in a direct way with the quality of education in the public schools.[32]

Phase II also was designed to provide greater parental and community involvement in school affairs. A Citywide Coordinating Council, consisting of 42 citizens of varying opinions regarding desegregation, was assigned a monitoring, coordinating, and informational role in Boston school desegregation. The mayor's key aide for school desegregation, Peter Meade, expressed the hope that the council would fill the leadership "vacuum" in Boston.[33] Biracial parent and student councils at various schools were to serve as adjuncts to the council. Jim O'Sullivan, a South Boston parent who had served as a member of one biracial council, told the Commissioners: "if we could have half the success that the South Boston-Roxbury biracial council had, I think we will make great strides in getting quality education into the city of Boston this coming year."[34]

The Commissioners heard testimony concerning other problems in Boston's schools, such as absence of black faculty, administrators, custodial persons, and attendance officers,[35] and rundown conditions of some schools, such as South Boston High School. A 1940 graduate of South Boston High told the Commissioners he was "shocked and ashamed" at the "appalling condition" of the school as Phase I began.[36]

---

[29] Boston transcript, testimony of Donald Burgess, acting headmaster, Roslindale High School, p. 636–37.

[30] Ibid., testimony of Helen Moran, former headmistress, Roslindale High School, pp. 625–26.

[31] Ibid., Burgess testimony, pp. 634–35.

[32] Memorandum of Decision and Remedial Orders, Morgan v. Kerrigan, 401 F. Supp. 270 (D. Mass. 1975), *motion for stay denied*, 523 F.2d 917 (1975).

[33] Boston transcript, p. 94–95.

[34] Ibid., p. 709.

[35] Ibid., Atkins testimony, pp. 955–56.

[36] Ibid., O'Sullivan testimony, pp. 706–707. Mr. O'Sullivan noted the "filth, the paint peeling off the walls. The girls' gym hadn't been heated in 3 years***the ladies' room for the girl students hadn't had doors on them for 2 years."

It is clear, however, that some courageous leaders have resisted the prevailing winds of opposition. The black community provided many of these individuals. There have been instances of effective planning, notably by the deputy mayor with respect to public safety and neighborhood services, as well as by some individual school administrators. In addition, some police units, such as the State police, performed in a thoroughly professional and effective manner. Despite the failures described during 5 days of testimony, ample evidence was heard that desegregation had proceeded smoothly at the great majority of schools during Phase I, and that further progress in Phase II was likely, particularly if the school committee would begin to provide the positive and creative leadership the school system so badly needs.

Although a review of the 1975–76 school year indicates that the school committee and Mayor White have been criticized for failing to provide leadership to promote desegregation,[37] Phase II can be characterized as showing greater stabilization within the school system. A few minor incidents were reported in the spring of 1976, but conditions at previously troubled schools, such as Hyde Park High[38] and South Boston High,[39] reportedly had improved and tension had diminished. The Mayor's Committee on Violence[40] found that 150 out of 165 schools were "working well."[41]

School administrators expressed optimism over further progress under Phase II as a result of the refusal of the Attorney General of the United States to intervene in the appeal of Judge Garrity's Phase II order before the Supreme Court of the United States, and the Court's refusal to review four appeals of that order. They were pleased with increased involvement in the schools and improved administrative procedures in such areas as security.[42] Although a disproportionate number of black students continue to be suspended, the percentage has decreased.[43] The executive director of the Boston chapter of the NAACP observed that opposition to desegregation and student transportation had shifted to concern over the quality of education.[44]

Findings

From the Boston hearing and more current sources, several findings are evident concerning the desegregation process in Boston:

1. A virtual total lack of support for court desegregation orders

[37] Edward Redd, executive director, Boston NAACP, interview, Boston, Mass., July 14, 1976; and *Boston Globe*, July 1976, p. 82.

[38] Tom Marshall, field representative, Community Relations Service, U.S. Department of Justice, Region I, telephone interview, July 13, 1976.

[39] Martin Walsh, Regional Director, Community Relations Service, U.S. Department of Justice, Region I, telephone interview, July 13, 1976.

[40] Appointed Apr. 29, 1976, the 13-member committee met with senior city and State officials and community leaders and issued a report calling, among other things, for stronger leadership by the mayor, a uniform code of discipline for the school system, and a more "representative" Boston School Committee. Mayor's Committee on Violence, memorandum to Mayor Kevin White, June 23, 1976.

[41] Ibid.

[42] Marion Fahey, superintendent; Charles Leftwich, associate superintendent; Paul Kennedy, associate superintendent; Luis Perullo, director of evaluation; Francis X. Rich, acting director for reading; Jean Sullivan, Office of (Desegregation) Implementation, interviews, July 13 and 14, 1976.

[43] School Department Annual Report, p. 16.

[44] Edward Redd, interview, July 14, 1976.

by public and private leaders, especially the mayor, city council members, and those in business, reinforced the opposition view that desegregation would never come to pass.

2. President Ford's and Mayor White's equivocal public comments on the order of the Federal district court served to bolster opponents of school desegregation.

3. Because of the Boston School Committee's position of unyielding opposition to desegregation and its minimal compliance with the Federal district court order, the court was forced to implement its decision to desegregate through a series of detailed orders formulating educational policy and directing the administrative process.

4. Despite serious deficiencies in the planning and actions of the local police and Boston School Department and sensationalized reporting of violence in South Boston by the national media, the overwhelming majority of schools in Boston which desegregated did so without difficulty. Significantly, the local news media, visual as well as written, provided balanced coverage of Phase I.

Denver, Colorado

School desegregation in Denver has involved nearly two decades of organized community activity. As early as the late 1950s, individuals in the Park Hill section of the city organized to fight the growing segregation of neighborhood schools. [45]

Growing steadily since the 1950s, Denver is the major city of the Rocky Mountain region, with an economic base largely in professional services, trade, and public administration. It houses a considerable number of offices for agencies of the Federal Government.

The city's population is slightly over half a million, and 1975 estimates of the minority population indicate that more than 20 percent are Hispanic and about 12 percent are black. [46] Asian Americans and American Indians account for about 3 percent of the minority population. The student population of Denver's 122 public schools has a higher percentage of minorities than the general population; the students are roughly 50 percent white, 27 percent Hispanic, and 19 percent black. [47]

School District No. 1 and the city and county of Denver have the same geographical boundaries, but fiscally and politically, the school district is independent of the city. It is governed by a seven-member board of education elected for staggered 6-year terms. The membership and ideology of the board of education has been in constant flux since the mid-1960s when school desegregation became a serious issue in Denver.

Concern over segregation developed over a period of many years as the community witnessed the various techniques by which the school board and administration manipulated the distribution of students. Mobile classrooms were used to increase pupil capacity at black schools instead of assigning students to underutilized white schools. As the minority population increased and residential pat-

[45] Jessica Pearson and Jeff Pearson, "Litigation and Community Change: Desegregation of the Denver Public Schools," February 1976.
[46] U.S., Commission on Civil Rights, transcript of public hearings, Denver, Colo., Feb. 17–19, 1976, testimony of Minoru Yasui, Denver Commission on Community Relations, transcript, pp. 201–02 (hereafter cited as Denver transcript).
[47] Pearson and Pearson, "Litigation and Community Change," p. 1.

terns changed, attendance zones were changed and new schools were located in such a way as to contain blacks and continue the segregated education of black children. The exasperation of the community increased when the school board failed to respond to reports and recommendations submitted in 1962 and 1969 by the board's own citizens' committees assigned to study equality of educational opportunity. [48]

Community pressure for action reached a peak following the assassination of Dr. Martin Luther King on April 5, 1968. On the night of April 25, thousands of citizens attended a public school board meeting where Rachel Noel, the first black school board member, introduced a resolution instructing the school superintendent to submit an integration plan by the following September. The Noel resolution was passed at a subsequent meeting by a vote of 5 to 2. [49]

Three resolutions the following spring provided concrete measures to alleviate school segregation. However, a school board election was held shortly thereafter which brought two new antidesegregation candidates to the board, and the first action of the new board was to rescind these resolutions, bringing to an end 10 years of cumulative effort to desegregate the schools. [50]

On June 19, 1969, eight Denver schoolchildren and their parents filed suit, initiating nearly 6 years of litigation that would include two appeals to the United States Supreme Court. [51] In its first major desegregation decision outside the South, the Supreme Court ruled in June 1973 that the school board's segregative acts in one part of the city could require systemwide remedies. The Court also held that "Negroes and Hispanos in Denver suffer identical discrimination in treatment when compared with the treatment afforded Anglo students." [52] In April 1974 the Federal District Court for Colorado issued its final decree ordering desegregation of the Denver public school system. Both plaintiffs and defendants again appealed to the Supreme Court, and in January 1976 the Court declined to review the appeals. [53]

The U.S. Commission on Civil Rights held a 3-day hearing in Denver in February 1976 to examine closely all elements of the city's school desegregation efforts. More than 120 witnesses—Federal, State, and local officials; school administrators and staff; community leaders; parents and students—provided testimony on desegregation as they told the overall story.

Witnesses gave various opinions about expending so much time and money on lengthy court battles and appeals. Mrs. Noel told the Commission she considered the suit a necessity because "there was no real commitment***no real firm movement in the direction [of desegregation] until the suit was filed." [54] From a different perspec-

[48] Ibid., pp. 39–42.
[49] Ibid., p. 46.
[50] Ibid., p. 48.
[51] Keyes v. School District No. 1, 313 F. Supp. 61 and 313 F. Supp. 90 (D. Colo. 1970) aff'd in part, rev'd in part and remanded, 445 F.2d 990 (10th Cir. 1971), modified and remanded, 413 U.S. 189 (1973), 368 F. Supp. 207 (D. Colo. 1973), 380 F. Supp. 673 (D. Colo. 1974), aff'd in part, rev'd in part and remanded, 521 F. 2d 465 (10th Cir. 1975), cert. denied 46 L.Ed. 2d 657 (1976).
[52] 413 U.S. 189, 198 (1973).
[53] Keyes v. School District No. 1, 46 L.Ed. 2d 657.
[54] Denver transcript, p. 26.

tive, School Superintendent Louis Kishkunas saw the process as "a necessary exercise to achieve whatever success we may achieve here." He said he thought the school district had been unduly criticized for appealing the case so vigorously, but that the Supreme Court decision had removed all doubt about the issue.[55]

For successfully implementing "an unpopular court order," the superintendent credited the community for maturity and the staff for professionalism. He praised the school board for directing the use of "all available means at their disposal for an orderly and humane implementation of the orders of the district court so long as the order remains in effect."[56]

Other testimony, however, did not credit either the board or the school administration with more than minimal compliance, characterized by footdragging and inconsistent leadership. Several witnesses agreed with Katherine Schomp, a school board member whose assessment was that the board has been unable or slow to act on problems incident to desegregation and has contributed few ideas or programs to the educational improvement of schools.[57] She listed some specific criticisms:

> The practice of blaming every problem in the schools on the desegregation order ***A refusal to devote sufficient resources of personnel, time, and money to***deal positively and humanely with integration. A refusal to establish some kind of communication with the Community Education Council, thus failing to take advantage of a tremendous community resource.[58]

The Community Education Council was named frequently as the most significant source of leadership in implementation of the court order. The council, created by the district court, was composed of 40 community leaders. Its chairman, Maurice Mitchell, chancellor of the University of Denver and a former Commissioner of the U.S. Commission on Civil Rights, said:

> The judge created a committee of citizens, not policemen or lawyers to sit around and nitpick his decision endlessly, but a committee of citizens and asked them to tell him how to make the decree work better.[59]

The council played a key role in educating the community on the constitutional requirements of the desegregation order. Its members also worked within the schools, monitoring the process and keeping the court well apprised of the implementation of the order.

The superintendent opposed creation of the council and sought to reduce its monitoring role because he "didn't agree with the necessity of having such a commission or someone looking over our shoulder."[60] However, the council received consistent support from the court and was able to work well with school personnel, particularly at the principal level.

The positive leadership of principals who believed that integration

[55] Ibid., p. 542.
[56] Ibid., p. 533 (Board Resolution No. 1796, May 10, 1974).
[57] Ibid., p. 633 ff.
[58] Ibid., p. 635.
[59] Ibid., p. 86.
[60] Ibid., p. 543.

would work was also repeatedly credited for the overall smoothness of Denver's desegregation. Catherine Crandall, president of the Parents, Teachers, and Students Association, said:

> Schools that had good administrative leadership were able to correspond better with the teachers within the school building, who were then able to transmit their feelings to the students and parents*** They could [then] proceed on a much more harmonious basis***.[61]

Many witnesses told the Commission that widespread and continued involvement of citizens was the major reason for the absence of violence and hostility that desegregation decrees have met in other cities. Mentioned frequently as a highly successful example of citizen action was an organization called PLUS (People Let's Unite for Schools). This coalition of 49 organizations was created in April 1974 to promote the principles of obedience to the law, safety for all schoolchildren, and excellence of education in Denver.

Leaders of the religious community in Denver, through ecumenical efforts of the Council of Churches and individual participation in PLUS, also were an active moral force supporting peaceful school desegregation. Melvin Wheatly, Methodist Bishop of Denver, testified:

> We communicated with all of our clergy from the beginning of the plan***that our position [for the integration of schools] is unequivocal***part of the design that we interpret as God's will.[62]

Bishop George Evans of the Roman Catholic Archdiocese of Denver said that a directive was sent to Catholic parishes "alerting them***that Catholic schools are dedicated to the principles which are at the heart of democracy and in no way would be a haven for those trying to flee the law."[63]

The Denver Chamber of Commerce, the Denver Commission on Community Relations, and many public officials worked individually, with community groups, and with District Court Judge William Doyle urging "community support for the acceptance and good faith implementation of the court order."[64]   The mayor and police chief issued statements urging peaceful implementation of the school desegregation process.

Witnesses agreed that the media was cooperative, fair, balanced, and responsible in its coverage throughout the desegregation process.[65] Except for the efforts of individual faculty members, institutions of higher learning in the Denver area were criticized as indifferent to "the leadership role that they are both capable of***and have a responsibility" to exercise.[66]

The best assessment of the effects of desegregation was given by those whose lives are most affected, students, parents, and teachers. Several teachers testified that, in general, policies which have advanced school desegregation also have a beneficial effect on other

[61] Ibid., p. 658.
[62] Ibid., p. 120.
[63] Ibid., p. 122.
[64] Ibid., p. 301.
[65] Ibid., see, for example, testimony of Paul Blue, executive director, KRMA–TV, p. 749.
[66] Ibid., testimony of Richard E. Wylie, dean, School of Education, University of Colorado at Denver, p. 158.

aspects of the educational process, including academic achievement. Included were comments such as: "the desegregation process brought a new atmosphere***new enthusiasm for learning," "the level of parental involvement has improved," "attendance***attitude***has improved***school has come alive."[67]

Rex Jennings, president of the Chamber of Commerce, described the desegregation experience of his son, a high school student:

> ***academically***the process has had no [negative] influence***integration of that school has had a very meaningful influence upon his having a better understanding of human nature and gaining a new appreciation for people of minority races***.[68]

Radio executive Gene Amole said the experience for his daughter had been "an enrichment***a very positive aspect" of desegregation.[69] Another parent, Richard Nuechterlein, said it was a "positive experience for our family and for the neighborhood."[70]

Ted Conover, a high school senior, said that tension had existed the first few weeks after desegregation, but "in time everybody adjusted and settled down." He added:

> It's been a positive experience for me and***for the people who stuck it out and really tried to make something of the school***. Integration puts a lot of people through a lot of personal, family, and individual changes, but with the proper preparation and positive attitude***it can be a very worthwhile experience.[71]

Witnesses representing the Hispanic community testified that despite some real gains toward a desegregated system, they remained concerned about ethnic discrimination, cultural isolation, the failure to provide quality education for language-minority groups, and the lack of affirmative action for Hispanos. Chancellor Mitchell, chairman of the Community Education Council, agreed:

> ***the question of how they have been dealt with and how they have fared with this decree and how they should expect to be treated by the school district and by the citizens of this community [is] one***of the loose ends that has never really been tied up.[72]

The issue of bilingual-bicultural education received considerable attention at the hearing as it had in the *Keyes* litigation. Several witnesses testified that school officials have shown no enthusiasm for bilingual-bicultural programs although Hispanic students are the largest minority group in Denver's schools.

A school board member criticized those who refer to bilingual-bicultural education as a "problem" saying, "28 percent of our children are Hispano and have Hispano heritage***[this] should not be a problem but an advantage and something of which we should be taking advantage constantly in this school system."[73]

---

[67] Ibid., testimony of William Coker, p. 795; Kenneth Hailpern, p. 389; Carla de Herrera, p. 523.
[68] Ibid., p. 328.
[69] Ibid., p. 308.
[70] Ibid., p. 1065–66.
[71] Ibid., p. 1042.
[72] Ibid., p. 99.
[73] Ibid., testimony of Katherine Schomp, p. 635.

School officials contended that, in response to the demands from the Hispanic community, they have instituted various programs which meet the language and cultural needs of the children, and an expanded program is being developed for 10 more schools pursuant to Colorado's Bilingual and Bicultural Education Act of 1975.[74] Hispanic community leaders and educational experts, however, remain extremely critical of the system's "ineffective, fumbling, weak, and inadequate effort."[75] The records of the Community Education Council's bilingual-bicultural committee show "a steady stream of complaints about the lack of a viable program"[76] and positive suggestions offered by the council have not been put into effect.

More aggressive recruitment of Hispano teachers and real affirmative action at the classroom as well as the administrative level were mentioned repeatedly as major needs of Hispano students. According to Jim Esquibel, former president of the Congress of Hispano Educators, the Denver school system has failed for years to respond to this need.[77]

Minorities in Denver appear to look to the future with cautious optimism. They agree that constant vigilance and monitoring of the system are necessary, as Lt. Gov. George L. Brown suggested:

> I don't trust the system to do the things that are right***if they are not examined thoroughly and continually***they will easily fall back and adopt the practices and procedures of that portion of our community which doesn't believe in***equality of opportunity***.[78]

Many individuals agree, too, that continued progress rests, as it has throughout the desegregation process, with continued citizen involvement in the total educational process. Jean Emery, chairperson of the monitoring committee of the Community Education Council, said, "to have the community in the schools is hopefully a never-ending process."[79]

Findings

It is apparent from a summary of the preceding testimony that:

1. Leadership provided by a citizens' advisory council, established and supported by the court, and coordinated activity by a well-integrated coalition of community organizations helped school desegregation to proceed in a generally smooth and orderly fashion. Other groups which contributed to the successful implementation of desegregation include the religious community, the media, and principals at a number of schools.

2. Opposition to desegregation by the school superintendent and the school board slowed the desegregation process. The administration offered no new ideas or programs to achieve desegregation and in most instances refused to cooperate with the court-appointed citizens' advisory council.

---

[74] Colo. Rev. Stat. Ann. § 22–24–101 *et seq.* (Cum. Supp. 1975).
[75] Denver transcript, testimony of Maurice Mitchell, p. 97.
[76] Ibid., testimony of Francisco Rios, p. 503.
[77] Ibid., p. 969. (Less than 5 percent of the system's teachers are Hispano.)
[78] Ibid., p. 255.
[79] Ibid., p. 1013.

3. Throughout the desegregation process the local media, by and large, assumed a responsible posture toward desegregation. It refrained from sensationalizing school desegregation events; presented valuable information to the public; and reported in a fair, balanced, and responsible way.

4. Although the district established bilingual-bicultural programs for its large Mexican American school population, these programs have been inadequate. Advice from the Hispanic community and educational leaders appears to have been consistently ignored, few bilingual teachers have been hired, and adequate plans for the aggressive and affirmative recruitment of bilingual staff have not been developed.

Hillsborough County (Tampa), Florida

Situated halfway down the western coast of Florida on Tampa Bay, Hillsborough is one of two counties comprising the Tampa-St. Petersburg Standard Metropolitan Statistical Area, the second largest SMSA in Florida.[80] Possessing a high degree of industrialization compared to the rest of the State, Hillsborough County has rural and agricultural as well as urban and suburban characteristics. At the time of the 1970 census, the county had a population of 490,265, 13.6 percent of which was black and 10.1 percent of Spanish origin.[81] By 1975 the population had grown to an estimated 632,500 persons.[82] Tampa, the county's principal city, had a population of 277,748 in 1970 and an estimated 297,500 in 1975.[83] Blacks constituted 54,831 or 19.7 percent and Spanish-language persons numbered 40,349 or 14.5 percent of the total in 1970.[84]

Hillsborough County has one school system whose boundaries are the same as those of the county.[85] The Nation's 22d largest public school system, it has approximately 115,000 students attending 91 elementary schools, 26 junior highs, 11 senior highs, and 1 school for the educable mentally handicapped. Of these schools, 66 are within the city limits. Black students number 21,376 (18.1 percent) and Hispanic students number 5,662, constituting 4.9 percent of the total as of October 1975.[86]

The desegregation plan under which the Hillsborough County school system currently operates resulted from a suit filed by black parents in the U.S. District Court for the Middle District of Florida on December 12, 1958.[87] Specifically, the complaint alleged that 72 schools were limited to whites only and 18 schools were limited to blacks who were often required to travel up to 10 miles one way past closer white schools to attend a black school.[88] When the suit finally came to trial in 1961, the court found for the plaintiffs and

[80] U.S., Department of the Commerce, Bureau of the Census, *Statistical Abstract of the United States, 1974*, p. 906.
[81] U.S., Department of Commerce, Bureau of the Census, *1970 Census of Population, Characteristics of the Population*, Vol. I, Part 11, Florida, Section I, p. 11–163, 11–536 (hereafter cited as *1970 Census*).
[82] Hillsborough County, Planning Commission, Population and Housing Estimates: Apr. 1, 1970–Jan. 1, 1975, April 1975.
[83] *1970 Census*, p. 11–206 and *Hillsborough County Population Estimates*, p. 22.
[84] *1970 Census*, pp. 11–311, 11–341.
[85] Each of Florida's 67 counties has a school district.
[86] Hillsborough County, Elementary and Secondary Pupil Survey (1975).
[87] *Mannings v. Board of Public Instruction of Hillsborough County, Florida*, No. 3554 Civ. T (M.D. Fla. decided May 11, 1971).
[88] Id. at 4.

accepted a freedom-of-choice desegregation plan submitted by the Hillsborough School Board. This plan also contained a provision for year-by-year dissolution of separate attendance areas beginning with the first grade in the 1963–64 school year. [89]

In 1968 plaintiffs returned to court contending that the plan had failed to desegregate the schools. There ensued a series of court orders and proposed plans, concluding with a plan adopted in August 1969 that provided, among other things, for assignment of students in every school on the basis of geographic attendance areas beginning in the 1969–70 school year. [90]

Finding the plan deficient, the Court of Appeals for the Fifth Circuit ordered (1) utilization of a variety of desegregation techniques, including strict neighborhood assignment, pairing, and redrawing school zone lines; [91] and (2) retention of jurisdiction by the district court until it was clear that State-imposed segregation had been completely eradicated. Reopening the case by its own motion in May 1971 following the *Swann* v. *Charlotte-Mecklenburg* decision, the court ordered the school board to submit a plan tailored to specific terms. The resulting plan, which the court accepted and which remains in effect today, provided for desegregation of most of the county's 89 elementary schools by clustering, with the previously black schools becoming sixth grade centers. The 23 junior highs and 3 junior-senior high schools were desegregated by clustering and satellite zoning. The white senior high schools retained their 10–12 grade structure and the black senior high schools were converted to different grade levels. [92]

In 1972 and again in 1973, Commission staff visited Hillsborough County to observe and report on the desegregation process. [93] In March 1976 the Commission returned to Hillsborough to conduct a 3-day hearing at which witnesses testified about the school desegregation process. [94]

There was a consensus among witnesses that the comprehensive desegregation plan developed pursuant to the court order of May 11, 1971, was implemented smoothly. Hearing witnesses collectively cited numerous reasons for this, but two factors stood above all others. One was the broad range of community involvement sought by the school system in developing the plan. A 150-member Citizens Desegregation Committee was organized, consisting of a complete cross-section of people from all walks of life representing all geographical areas and ethnic, racial, and religious backgrounds. [95] Explaining the reasoning behind this policy of broad inclusion, school administrator E.L. Bing stated:

> It appeared to us that if we in Hillsborough County were to come up with a plan that was going to really be effective and accepted by the public and had assurances of some built-in chance of success in terms of implementation, then we really

---

[89] Id. at 8–9.

[90] Mannings v. Bd. of Public Instruction, 306 F. Supp. 497 (M.D. Fla. 1969).

[91] Mannings v. Bd. of Public Instruction, 427 F. 2d 874 (5th Cir. 1970). For definitions of these and other desegregation techniques, see "Restructuring of School Districts."

[92] Hillsborough County School Desegregation Plan, 1971.

[93] U.S., Commission on Civil Rights, *Five Communities: Their Search for Equal Education* (1972), and *School Desegregation in Ten Communities* (1973).

[94] U.S., Commission on Civil Rights, hearing, Tampa, Fla., Mar. 29–31, 1976 (hereafter cited as Tampa transcript).

[95] Tampa transcript, p. 38.

needed to put the problem back where the problem really existed, and that is with the people because the schools belong to the people.[96]

The second paramount factor was the positive role played by various leadership elements within the school system and in the community at large.

The Hillsborough County School Board set the tone for peaceful implementation by accepting the recommendations of the district court judge that the plan provide for an approximate 80–20, white-black ratio throughout the system. Although the school board could have appealed the subsequent court order, it chose not to do so but instead declared forcefully its unanimous position that the board would comply with the law. School Superintendent Raymond Shelton followed, taking a public position that his personal views or those of anyone else were unimportant. The issues, he said, were the education of children and obedience to the law.

Other individuals of the Tampa-Hillsborough community followed this lead. Several members of the Tampa Chamber of Commerce served on the School Desegregation Committee. One businessman testified that the maintenance of a good school system was of special importance to the community's commercial interests. The Tampa Chamber of Commerce, therefore, endorsed desegregation, strongly supported the school desegregation plans of the School Desegregation Committee, and was instrumental in selling and promoting the final plan to the community. In so doing, the chamber sought to neutralize the sensitive issue of busing and to avoid school disruptions that plagued some cities experiencing school desegregation.

By all accounts, the media—newspapers and television—also acted responsibly in reporting on desegregation of the county's schools. According to Joseph Mannion, director of news for WFLA–TV, the television station maintained a policy of providing information about the plan and its implementation in a noninflammatory manner. Paul Hogan, managing editor of the *Tampa Tribune*, said that the paper counseled the local community to accept the Federal court ruling and the inevitability of school desegregation and busing as a means toward this end. The newspaper editorialized:

> Parents, white and black, can help in the adjustment by not planting prejudice or fears in the minds of their children. Youngsters, left to themselves, generally have no problem in getting along together.[97]

Religious leaders and law enforcement administrators played lesser although essentially positive roles in the county's desegregation crisis. Acting independently of one another, most clerics urged their congregations to accept desegregation as in keeping with the Judeo-Christian tenet of the equality of people before God. Regarding collective action, however, one minister testified that religious organizations and associations had a role to play at the time of desegregation, but they did not become involved.

Representatives of the county and the city police departments

---

[96] Ibid., p. 39.
[97] *Tampa Tribune* editorial, July 7, 1971.

made contingency plans with school officials in preparation for implementation of the plan. Both police groups stressed the importance of opening and maintaining lines of communication with students and avoiding a show of force in resolving confrontations. Illustrating this point, Sheriff Malcolm Beard described a minor fracas at Plant High School at the time of plan implementation:

> I found that we were very acceptable to the kids. As a matter of fact, one young man***came off the bus. He was obviously a leader. He was a black kid. He was a football player. And he walked up to me and put his arm around me and I put my arm around him and he told me to go back to Tampa, that they were not going to have any trouble that day. So that is what I did and we didn't have any trouble. [98]

Elected county and city government officials testified that they avoided involvement in the desegregation controversy in the belief that this was a matter for the school board alone to address.

High school students testified that relations among Latin, black, and white students have improved generally since desegregation. A white youth stated:

> On the whole, when I was young the blacks tended to be looked down upon, especially in elementary school. In high school it seems to be different. There seems to be more cohesiveness among the young. [99]

A Latin youth indicated that most students now judge others by personality rather than by racial background:

> I remember in one case there was one white who wasn't really liked by his other white friends, but they***said, "Even though we don't like this guy, if he ever got in a fight with a black we would have to back him up." And I don't see this now. [100]

On the whole, junior and senior high school students seemed to feel that desegregation was working well. Most students either liked or did not mind the busing involved, and seemed to enjoy their schools. A black student leader indicated that the contributions of minority groups should be incorporated into the social studies curriculum.

By virtually any standard that might be applied, the Hillsborough County school desegregation plan of 1971 was implemented successfully. Picketing and boycotts were nonexistent, and the student disruptions that occurred were minor. Few whites chose to leave their assigned schools, perhaps due to the countywide nature of the plan, and the curricular improvements underway throughout the system prior to plan implementation. Of those who left, however, most reportedly have returned. School officials also testified that achievement test scores have improved, that greater numbers of minority students are seeking higher education and other kinds of postsecondary study, and that both black and white students have benefitted from interracial experiences.

There is evidence, however, that some problems persist in the county schools. One of these concerns voluntary participation of minorities in school affairs. School officials testified that despite the

[98]Tampa transcript, p. 177.
[99]Ibid., p. 559.
[100]Ibid., p. 564–65.

provision of buses for special activities, minority students, except athletes, generally have not participated in extracurricular activities. Similarly, minority parents reportedly have been reluctant to join PTAs and to participate in school programs. On the other hand, minority witnesses stated that while the black community continues to support desegregation, many are concerned about such problems as the disproportionate numbers of black students disciplined, and instances of racial and ethnic insensitivity and prejudice demonstrated by some white teachers.

School officials acknowledged that proportionately greater numbers of black students have been suspended, but they maintained that discipline has been administered fairly. One administrator suggested that the suspension rate for black students in Hillsborough County schools is roughly equivalent to the national suspension rate for black students. Upon request of the local NAACP chapter, however, the U.S. Department of Health, Education, and Welfare investigated the Hillsborough school system and found possible discrimination in disciplinary practices. One minority leader suggested that mandatory human relations training for all teachers could be one approach to solving the problems of black student suspensions and racial insensitivity displayed by some white teachers toward black students. School officials have rejected this approach, and although the absolute number of students suspended has been decreasing in recent years, suspensions of black students remain proportionately greater.

Witnesses from the minority community disapproved of the large percentage of black students transported for desegregation purposes and the related conversion of two black high schools to junior high schools. Generally, white students are bused 2 of their 12 school years in order to carry out the provisions of the plan; black students are bused 10 of their 12 years. Minority representatives testified that had Blake and Middleton been retained as high schools, the disproportionate transportation would have been less severe and those institutions would continue as sources of pride to the black community. School officials said that it had been their intention to retain both facilities as senior high schools. That course of action, however, was abandoned when it became clear that a satisfactory geographic zone with a stable enrollment probably could not be maintained. One school official indicated that whites' "fears" of sending "their kids to a school that was inherently inferior" also were a factor in the decision to convert those schools.[101] They also indicated that it was financially and logistically more feasible to convert the two black high schools and to disperse the minority population throughout the system than to adopt any other approach.[102]

The Hillsborough County school system has just begun to implement a bilingual-bicultural education program for its substantial number of students from non-English-speaking backgrounds. In March 1976 the school system completed a survey identifying 7,084 students from home environments in which English is not the dominant language. Although 28 different language groups were

---

[101] Ibid., p. 293.
[102] Ibid., pp. 292–93.

identified, the vast majority of these students are Spanish speaking. A second survey assessing the English language proficiency of these students is scheduled for completion by August 1976. Although there is a philosophical disagreement between the school administration and bilingual education program staff regarding the appropriate method for instructing non-English-speaking children, assistant superintendent Frank Farmer stated, "By 1976–77, we will have a complete bilingual program meeting the exact interpretation of the law." [103]

The Hillsborough County school system is not unlike numerous others across the Nation that have implemented desegregation plans. School officials, teachers, parents, students, and the community have made the adjustment quietly and without rancor. So smooth was their transition that they escaped the probing eyes of the national media. Like other school districts, however, Hillsborough has found that some problems remain to be resolved. A spokesperson for the school system alluded to the unfinished business as he differentiated between desegregation and integration:

> You know desegregation is a physical process of moving people and things. But integration is a long process of establishing attitudinal change***. In Hillsborough County we like to feel we are moving towards integration now. That is the point of having each youngster feel that this is his school and he is not imposing himself on anyone; he is welcome; he takes pride in the school; he knows when he leaves every morning that he's going to be treated fairly and impartially; he's going to get a chance to participate in all the activities. This is the process we are working on in this district now. [104]

Findings

The testimony as sumarized above reveals the following findings:

1. Once final judicial action was taken and the inevitability of desegregation became apparent, numerous leadership elements including school officials, business persons, the clergy, and law enforcement officials took forthright positions in Hillsborough in favor of obedience to the law and thus paved the way for peaceful desegregation.

2. The decision of the Hillsborough County school system to involve a broad cross-section of citizenry in the planning process facilitated the smooth implementation of desegregation in the Hillsborough-Tampa community.

3. Desegregation has had positive effects on the quality of education. Achievement test scores have improved and greater numbers of minority students are seeking higher education.

4. The minority communities of Hillsborough, while still supporting desegregation, are concerned that:

(a) black students are transported disproportionately,
(b) black students are suspended disproportionately,
(c) the needs of language-minority students are not being adequately addressed, and
(d) some teachers display racial insensitivity and bias.

---

[103] Ibid., p. 331.
[104] Ibid., p. 62.

5. Students have responded positively to desegregation. Relations among black, white, and Hispanic students have improved. Students are more highly motivated and the number of minority students seeking higher education has increased.

6. The news media of Hillsborough provided excellent coverage of the deliberations of the Citizens Desegregation Committee and kept the community informed as to all aspects of the desegregation plan. Most of the local media endorsed peaceful implementation of the plan and avoided sensationalism in reporting it.

Jefferson County (Louisville), Kentucky

Louisville and Jefferson County form a border community in a border State. The county covers 375 square miles and encompasses 76 cities, the largest of which is Louisville. Established in 1780 as a trading post, Louisville rests on the south bank of the busy Ohio River which separates it from the State of Indiana.

The metropolitan area has long been a major commercial and business center, producing everything from household appliances and rubber products to bourbon whiskey and baseball bats. Although it is also a financial and insurance center, Louisville's dependence on industry has made it a working person's town. General Electric Appliance Division is the largest single employer (20,000) followed by the Jeffboat Co. (16,000) and Ford Motor Co. (7,544).[105] In 1971, 84 unions were represented in the area by 219 locals.[106] More than 80 percent of the employees in manufacturing industries are organized.[107]

The county's population in 1975 was estimated at 733,220, of whom 327,500 reside in Louisville.[108] As is the case in many metropolitan areas, the vast majority of the area's 13.7 percent black population lives in the city, which is 23.8 percent black.[109] The Jefferson County public school system serves the entire metropolitan area and includes 121,763 students; 28,510, or 23.4 percent, are black.[110]

Prior to 1975, there were two school systems, one serving the city of Louisville, the other serving the surrounding county. Because the city's corporate limits extended beyond the Louisville school district lines, some 10,000 students who lived outside the school district but within the city limits, were in fact included in the Jefferson County school district,[111] but were permitted the choice of attending city schools, tuition paid by the county.[112]

The two systems merged in April 1975 when the Louisville system, as provided for by Kentucky law,[113] voted itself out of existence and was subsumed by the Jefferson County school system. Although merger had been discussed for 20 years, it was ultimately

[105] Louisville Area Chamber of Commerce, *Louisville Area Directory of Manufacturers*, 1975–76.
[106] Louisville Area Chamber of Commerce, *Louisville Fact File Manpower*, p. 10, undated.
[107] Ibid., p. 11.
[108] Louisville Area Chamber of Commerce, *Louisville Business Trends*, 1975.
[109] Percentages which were unavailable for 1975 are based on 1970 U.S. Bureau of the Census, *County and City Databook — 1972*.
[110] Jefferson County Board of Education, Number of Black and White Pupils and Percentage Black, Nov 17, 1975.
[111] Newburg Area Council, Inc., v. Board of Education, 489 F. 2d 925, 929 (6th Cir. 1973).
[112] Ky. Rev. Stat. Ann. §158.130.
[113] Ky. Rev. Stat. Ann. §160.041(1971).

necessitated by the failing financial condition of the city schools. [114]

The Jefferson County Board of Education now has 13 members. That number will fluctuate until 1978 when it will stabilize at 7 members elected from newly drawn districts. [115] There is considerable duplication of positions within the merged school administration. There are 35 positions titled "superintendent." The head of the new system is the former county superintendent, and the former city superintendent became one of three deputy superintendents (the other two are former county administrators). Administrative problems involved in merging the two different school systems are still being resolved. Sometimes described as educationally "progressive and urban oriented," the Louisville school system prior to merger had 45,000 students, 54 percent of whom were black. [116] Reflecting its not too distant rural past, Jefferson County's educational approach was described as "traditional." [117] The county had a relatively wealthy school system as a result of population growth from an influx of new businesses and families moving from the city. In 1950 county school enrollment was 16,000, [118] but at the time of merger the figure had soared to 90,000 students of whom only 4 percent were black. [119]

The two systems had one thing in common—both were unconstitutionally segregated, despite the fact that in 1956 both had formally abolished the dual school system that had been legally sanctioned in Kentucky. [120] Black students in Jefferson County had been assigned to a few majority-black schools that were underutilized, while nearby majority-white schools were operating with enrollments greater than capacity. [121] Portable classrooms and double shifts were used to accommodate the burgeoning numbers of white students. In Louisville a voluntary open enrollment policy operated to promote racial separateness; students simply transferred to schools where they would constitute the racial majority. More than one-third of the Louisville schools in 1973 were 90–100 percent black and another one-third were 90–100 percent white. [122]

Four months after merger, on July 17, 1975, the Jefferson County Board of Education was ordered to implement a desegregation plan by September 4, 1975. [123] This order climaxed 4 years of litigation initiated in 1971 when suit was filed against the Jefferson County Board of Education. [124] In 1972 a suit was filed against both the city

[114] At the time of the vote, however, it was clear that if a merger were not effected under State law, the Federal district court would have required merger pursuant to a sixth circuit ruling in December 1974 calling for interdistrict remedy. Newburg Area Council, Inc. v. Board of Education, 510 F.2d 1358 (6th Cir. 1974).
[115] Ky. Rev. Stat. Ann. §160.041(1971). A specific statutory provision insuring representation of Louisville constituencies on a merged board in the event the Louisville Board decided to cease operations was adopted by the State legislature in 1975.
[116] Louisville Public Schools, Department of Education and Research, 1974–75 Membership Report, p. 61.
[117] U.S., Commission on Civil Rights, hearing, Louisville, Ky., June 14–16, 1976, testimony of John Bell, Jefferson County Board of Education, p. 821–22 (hereafter cited as Louisville transcript).
[118] Marie T. Doyle, "The Public School Merger Issue in Jefferson County, Kentucky" (doctoral dissertation), University of Kentucky, 1974.
[119] Jefferson County Public Schools, 1974–75 Annual Statistical Report (January 1976), p. 24.
[120] Ky. Rev. Stat. Ann. §158.020.
[121] Newburg Area Council, Inc. v. Board of Education, 489 F.2d 925, 927–28 (6th Cir. 1973).
[122] Id., 489 F.2d at 930.
[123] Newburg Area Council, Inc. v. Gordon, 521 F.2d 578 (6th Cir. 1975).
[124] Complaint, Newburg Area Council, Inc. v. Board of Education, Civil Act. No. 7045, (W.D. Ky., filed Aug. 27, 1971).

and county boards of education seeking expansion of the Louisville district to include all areas within the city limits.[125] Subsequently, the NAACP intervened and sought desegregation and merger. From then on desegregation and merger became inseparable issues.

The case against both school boards was dismissed by the Federal district court, but in December 1973 the Sixth Circuit Court of Appeals reversed that decision.[126] With respect to merger, the circuit court held that upon a finding of unlawful segregation in neighboring school systems and a determination that only by means of a desegregation plan encompassing both school systems can the schools be desegregated, a district court has the power to devise a remedy which crosses school district lines. The circuit court noted that "school district lines have been disregarded in the past in conforming to State-enforced segregation."[127]

Although a desegregation plan that crossed city-county boundary lines was approved by the district court, merger and desegregation came to a halt after the Supreme Court's decision reversing the sixth circuit's order requiring interdistrict desegregation between Detroit and its suburbs in *Milliken* v. *Bradley*.[128] In December 1974, however, after reviewing the Louisville-Jefferson County case in light of the *Milliken* decision, the Sixth Circuit Court of Appeals reinstated its previous decision, ruling that the county is the basic educational unit of the State in Kentucky and the State law provides for merger.[129] Petitions for review to the Supreme Court to reverse this decision were denied in April 1975.[130] By this time merger was in process pursuant to State law.

The Louisville desegregation plan[131] stipulates that black student enrollment in elementary schools be no less than 12 percent and no more than 40 percent. At the junior and senior high levels, black enrollment is to range between 12.5 percent and 35 percent.

The primary means for implementing the plan is clustering schools that were previously predominantly white or black and transporting students within each cluster. Unlike most desegregation plans, which transport students according to geographic determinations, the Louisville plan determines which students are to be transported by the first letter of their last name. The plan calls for 84 percent of white students to be transported for 2 of their 12 school years and 16 percent to be transported for 1 year. In marked contrast, 66 percent of black students are to be transported for 8 years and 33 percent for 9 years. The plan also calls for reassignment of administrators and supportive staff, teachers, and classified personnel to reflect the systemwide racial composition of the staff.

The court order of July 1975 by no means marked the end of the struggle to desegregate the schools. The following August the merged school board sought a stay of implementation. Although the stay was denied, the school board appealed the plan and the case

[125] Complaint, Haycraft v. Board of Education, Civil Act No. 7291 (W.D. Ky., filed June 22, 1972).
[126] Newburg Area Council, Inc. v. Board of Education, 489 F.2d 925 (6th Cir. 1973).
[127] Id. at 932.
[128] Milliken v. Bradley, 418 U.S. 717 (1974).
[129] Newburg Area Council, Inc. v. Board of Education, 510 F.2d 1358, 1360 (6th Cir. 1974).
[130] Board of Education v. Newburg Area Council, Inc., 421 U.S. 931 (1975).
[131] Findings of Fact and Conclusions of Law, Newburg Area Council, Inc. v. Board of Education, Civil Act. Nos. 7045 and 7291, (W.D. Ky., July 30, 1975).

was argued before the circuit court in June 1976.[132] The county's chief executive officer, County Judge Todd Hollenbach, intervened at the district court level and joined in the appeal, arguing against the use of busing. His alternative plan was rejected by the district court after testimony that the plan would not eliminate the remaining vestiges of State-imposed segregation.[133]

Since the original court order to desegregate in July 1975, the school board has twice been permitted to extend the exemption of first graders from transportation. In December 1975 the court agreed to an interim exemption of first graders from the plan throughout the remainder of the school year,[134] and in March 1976 the school board proposed and the court approved extending the exemption through the 1976–77 school year, but ordered that first graders be transported as all other grades after that time.[135]

In March 1976 Commission staff went to Louisville to study the process of school desegregation. After 3 months of investigation, the Commission held a 3-day hearing June 14, 15, 16 in Louisville during which 117 witnesses were called to testify.

One of the most important facts to emerge from hearing testimony was that opposition to school desegregation existed only to a limited degree among the students. Student testimony highlighted the fact that the protests and occasional acts of violence staged by some groups had made it difficult for the students to settle down and accept the first year of desegregation in stride:

> The entire community was just sort of negative on the school system and it just drifted down and affected everyone.[136]

> We had a lot of trouble at the beginning of the school [year] because the parents would come out and protest in front of the school.[137]

> The worst thing that happened was our first football game was cancelled***because of demonstrations at Southern and Durrett. The only thing wrong at Thomas Jefferson was the things that happened around us***. Other than that our school year went really good.[138]

A student testified that significant changes occurred within the schools when community protests abated:

> I think after a lot of the protesting died down, [and] a lot of the media treatment of "the schools are being desegregated this year"***some of the antagonism just went away***. When it was possible for the students to start forgetting that they were being bused***they would forget about it***. I don't think there was hostility towards the end of the year.[139]

Although organizations were established as early as 1971 to prepare the community for desegregation, the lack of official chan-

[132] Newburg Area Council, Inc., v. Board of Education, Civil Act. Nos. 7045 and 7291 (W.D. Ky., appeal argued June 14, 1976, before three-judge panel, decision pending as of July 23, 1976).
[133] Memorandum Order and Opinion, Newburg Area Council, Inc. v. Board of Education (W.D. Ky., May 18, 1976).
[134] Order of Dec. 22, 1975, Newburg Area Council, Inc. v. Board of Education, C.A. Nos. 7045 and 7291 (W.D. Ky., Dec. 19, 1975).
[135] Order of Apr. 1, 1976, Newburg Area Council v. Board of Education, C.A. Nos. 7045 and 7291 (W.D. Ky., March 1976).
[136] Louisville transcript, testimony of Darrell Moore, Durrett High School, p. 27.
[137] Ibid., testimony of Wanda Hoosier, Iroquois High School, p. 30.
[138] Ibid., testimony of Mary Theresa McAnnally, Thomas Jefferson High School, p. 28.
[139] Ibid., testimony of Darrell Moore, Durrett High School, pp. 48–49.

nels for input from these groups resulted in their having little effect on the implementation process. Numerous witnesses testified that traditional community leaders—elected county and city officials, the clergy, business, organized labor, higher education—did little to urge the community to adhere to the court order or to promote acceptance of desegregation.

Suzie Post, women's coordinator for the Louisville and Jefferson County Human Relations Commission, testified that desegregation was ordered immediately prior to a general election and "every politician immediately jumped on an antibusing bandwagon***. I don't think there is any question in many of our minds that with some leadership from our elected officials, we could have gotten through this situation in a much more constructive, healthy way." [140]

The executive director of the Kentucky Commission on Human Rights, Galen Martin, testified that some individuals in leadership capacities thought that a neutral posture would be sufficient to ensure peaceful implementation. He said that many supported law and order but did "nothing in support of desegregation and ended up contributing to the confusion." [141]

Lois Cronholm, who chairs the Louisville-Jefferson County Human Relations Commission, said that she had been "markedly unsuccessful" in getting public leaders to express a commitment to the court order. [142] Most of them "did not really want to face the fact that it was going to happen," she said. [143] County Judge Hollenbach testified that although he and Louisville Mayor Harvey Sloane had appointed a Community Consensus Committee to prepare the community for desegregation, county funds provided to the committee in 1974 were not reallocated the year schools were desegregated. [144] He explained that time constraints had made it difficult for him and Mayor Sloane to continue meeting with the committee. [145]

Both the county judge and the mayor have proposed alternatives to the court order, and one witness said he thought this served to keep people from accepting the court order. [146] Judge Hollenbach's alternative desegregation plan is essentially a variation of voluntary open enrollment. [147] He said he believes that "the remedy applied by the Federal court was far excessive of what it should have been." [148] In testimony provided the U.S. Senate Committee on the Judiciary October 29, 1975, Mayor Sloane advocated "an alternative judicial approach for school desegregation." [149] During the Commission's hearing in Louisville, he explained that a "National Commission on Quality Education would relieve the responsibility from the judge in the district courts of making determinations as to desegregation." [150]

[140] Ibid., pp. 76–77.
[141] Ibid., p. 392.
[142] Ibid., p. 367.
[143] Ibid., p. 368.
[144] Ibid., p. 442–43.
[145] Ibid.
[146] Ibid., testimony of Galen Martin, executive director, Kentucky Commission on Human Rights, p. 392.
[147] Ibid., testimony of Todd Hollenbach, pp. 462–64, 474–75, 479–80.
[148] Ibid., p. 480.
[149] Louisville, Ky., Office of the Mayor, press release, testimony of Harvey I. Sloane, presented to the Committee on the Judiciary U.S. Senate, Oct. 29, 1975, p. 14.
[150] Louisville transcript, pp. 467–68.

Some witnesses said that the absence of leadership in support of the court order fueled the determination of those individuals bent on disruption. Lyman Johnson, president of the Louisville chapter of the NAACP stated: "When the mayor and the Governor and the county judge abdicated leadership responsibilities***that gives the violent prone elements in our community a chance to run wild."[151]

A major outbreak of violence occurred on the second day of school in the southwestern section of the county, in the vicinity of Valley High School. Injuries were suffered by 91 county policemen and State troopers, and county and State police officials estimated that the violence cost their departments over $1 million.[152] Hearing testimony leaves many unanswered questions as to why the violence was not contained.

The Louisville chief of police, Col. John Nevin, testified that on September 5, 250 to 300 officers trained in riot control were mobilized and waiting to assist county police if needed.[153] According to Police Chief Nevin, when the county police were unable to control demonstrations and requested city support, Judge Hollenbach refused to call for assistance from the city police.[154] Judge Hollenbach explained that he believed "the city needed [their police] resources to assure and preserve the peace in the city."[155]

Witnesses criticized the Chamber of Commerce for not taking a firm stand in support of peaceful desegregation, although the chamber did circulate a "Community Pledge" calling for peaceful desegregation which was published in the morning and evening papers August 1, 3, and September 3.[156] However, some businesses refused to sign as an expression of opposition to the court order.[157] Others refused to sign or withdrew their signatures in the face of adverse public reaction. Robinson Brown, president of the Chamber of Commerce, explained that the pledge was misunderstood because "antibusing groups***accused people of being probusing if they were not antibusing."[158]

There were many serious incidents of intimidation directed at businesses that refused to display antibusing posters. An official of a company that operates local variety stores stated that his refusal to place antibusing posters in his store windows led to attempts to burn down one of the stores. As a consequence, he said, the company decided to display antibusing signs,[159] and requested Chamber of Commerce support in the face of a proposed antibusing boycott of businesses. The chamber took no action. "This was a time when [the Chamber] should have stood up for the business people, and they did not," he said.[160]

A manager of one of the variety stores, who described himself as against busing because he believes it impractical, said that he was

---

[151] Ibid., p. 390.
[152] Ibid., testimony of Russell McDaniel, chief, Jefferson County Police, and Lt. Col. Leslie Pyles, commander, Kentucky State Police Department, pp. 421–22.
[153] Ibid., pp. 398–99, 418–19.
[154] Ibid., pp. 419–20, 428–29.
[155] Ibid., p. 453.
[156] Ibid., p. 190.
[157] Ibid., testimony of Roy H. Reubenstahl, vice president and general manager, A&P Foods, Inc., Louisville Division, p. 109.
[158] Ibid., p. 192.
[159] Ibid., testimony of Robert Kling, Kling Company, p. 172.
[160] Ibid., pp. 174–75.

harrassed after he refused to join the Ku Klux Klan and to display antibusing signs. He noted that persons who normally came into the store stopped coming, and others came specifically to harrass his sales people. Store windows were broken, he said, one the result of a shotgun blast. [161]

The failure of the business community to unite in support of peaceful desegregation was matched by the labor unions, united in their opposition to the desegregation plan. The management of General Electric refused to sign the community pledge calling for peaceful desegregation, [162] and approximately 95 percent of GE's employees were absent from work on September 4 and 5 in protest against the desegregation plan. [163] Despite the fact that the national policy of the American Federation of Labor, the Congress of Industrial Organizations, and the United Auto Workers was supportive of busing, members of local chapters formed an organization called United Labor Against Busing and participated in antibusing demonstrations. [164]

Some witnesses said the media treatment of desegregation was fair and informative, [165] and others were critical. One witness said he believes that the media in Louisville "is better than average as compared with many other cities," [166] and described the use of phrases such as "court ordered forced busing across racial lines to achieve balance" as unfortunate because they are misleading. [167] Another witness, citing an example of inflammatory media treatment, said that when the Supreme Court decided not to review the Boston desegregation case, a local television news program chose to use a picture of a school bus with the slogan, "Supreme Court Ignores Boston." [168]

Some witnesses cautioned that unless community organizations and elected officials take an affirmative stand in support of desegregation, the protests and disruptions that marred the opening of school in 1975 could be repeated in 1976. [169]

The absence of strong leadership among elected officials and community groups also prevailed in the Jefferson County Public School System. A school board member testified that he felt strongly that the board should have gone on record in support of "carrying out the judge's order***[but] there was no way this could have passed this board." [170] The school board was divided not only on the issue of desegregation but also on philosophies of education, apparently as a result of dissimilar experiences in the former city and county systems. Board divisiveness was communicated to the staff and consequently was destructive in terms of administrative functioning. [171]

[161] Ibid., testimony of James L. Watkins, manager, KIMECO Variety Store, Fairdale, pp. 177–78, 180.
[162] Ibid., testimony of Stanley Gault, vice president, Major Applicance Division, General Electric, p. 205.
[163] Ibid., p. 206.
[164] Ibid., testimony of John Harmon, president, UAW; Leonard Smith, executive secretary, AFL-CIO; John Shore, chairman, United Labor Against Busing, pp. 245-62.
[165] Ibid., testimony of Lyman Johnson, p. 387.
[166] Ibid., testimony of Galen Martin, p. 375.
[167] Ibid., p. 376.
[168] Ibid., testimony of Lois Cronholm, p. 379.
[169] Ibid., p. 395.
[170] Ibid., testimony of John Bell, p. 842.
[171] Ibid.

Joel Henning, a former school assistant superintendent who helped design the desegregation plan, identified four problem areas that he said threaten the integrity of the plan: a disproportionate number of black students are being suspended; hardship transfers, which allow students to be exempted from reassignment, have been granted to a greater extent to white students and thus have the effect of maintaining the former racial identity of the schools; enrollment in the Alternative School for students with serious disciplinary problems is disproportionately black, while enrollment in Youth Development Programs for students with less serious problems is disproportionately white; and the exemption of first graders from transportation changed the racial makeup of the schools specified by the court order. [172]

A black community leader said that the disciplinary code results in disproportionate numbers of black students being suspended and is an institutionalized means for pushing black students out of school. [173] She suggested that the school board find alternatives to suspending students. [174]

Several black community witnesses and Deputy Superintendent Milburn Maupin, the former Louisville school superintendent, expressed anger that a grant to study the suspension problem had been refused by the school administration. [175] Although another deputy superintendent explained that the grant was turned down because it was too heavily research oriented, [176] Mr. Maupin said he believed that "we ought to be jumping at any study on suspensions because little is known on how to solve the problem." [177]

A white student gave her views on student suspensions:

> The blacks are better known because they are caught so often. The whites aren't, because the whites seem to be able to get out of it. They always make up excuses. It is easier for a white to get out of class than a black because***[the teachers] think [black students] are lying to them, whereas they will believe [a white student] sooner. [178]

There are indications that some schools are beginning to face the suspension problem. Deputy Superintendent Maupin testified that a school principal had told him that: "I am convinced that whatever the reason I might have had, my posture on suspensions is just not effective, and I am changing that." [179]

Students in Louisville appear to be adjusting well to desegregation, and many student witnesses testified that desegregation is a positive experience:

> If I hadn't gone to Thomas Jefferson, I would really be a narrow-minded person, because before I went there I went to a private all-white school, and I had no idea what other people were like; I didn't want to associate with anybody except

[172] Ibid., testimony of Joel Henning, pp. 678–714.
[173] Ibid., testimony of Camellia Brown, chairperson, Louisville-Jefferson County Defense Project, p. 578.
[174] Ibid., p. 579.
[175] Ibid., p. 724.
[176] Ibid., testimony of J.C. Cantrell, p. 730.
[177] Ibid., p. 731.
[178] Ibid., testimony of Mary Theresa McAnnally, p. 40.
[179] Ibid., p. 722.

whites. But at Thomas Jefferson, I got to where color didn't matter to me. [180]

Testimony also indicates that students often took the initiative to help other students adjust to their new school. One student said:

We met the buses the first two or three days***and accompanied students to the classrooms and we introduced them to the teacher and other people around the schools***so they would feel more at home. [181]

The schools had different ways of easing tensions that resulted from community controversy about desegregation. The county school administration developed a human relations program to facilitate the desegregation process in the schools and in the community by promoting interaction among students and parents. The sponsor at Shawnee High School explained that the program was designed "to prepare our students to meet their anxieties***. So we began setting up discussion groups, small groups of students, and they began discussing any problems in the school." [182]

A student testified to the effectiveness of the program: "I think it is good because people got to express their feelings publicly instead of keeping everything locked up inside of them." [183]

In response to student and teacher concerns, one school provided a suggestion box to gather ideas for recommendations to the human relations committee. The same school developed a rumor control system to keep students informed of facts concerning any school incident. [184]

Despite the difficulty with which desegregation was implemented in the Jefferson County Public Schools and notwithstanding the problems that remain, education in the schools has carried on. A teacher characterized the school year in the following manner:

It has been a different year. It has not been a good year, it has not been a bad year. We consider ourselves at Smyrna very fortunate that things have gone as well as they have. We had a fairly good year. [185]

Community disruptions that caused tensions and anxiety among students and teachers in the first quarter of the 1975–76 school year have ceased. There appears to be a gradual realization that school desegregation is there to stay. A white parent explained:

At the beginning I was a little bit disappointed that [my son] was to be bused from his home school. But we decided, my husband and I, that if this was to be his life, then we would go right along with him. And he seemed to be happy, and he went to Central and he began to love Central. He said there was something there that he had not found any place else. [186]

Referring to the fact that black children are bused to a greater extent than white children, a black parent explained his rationale for accepting the court order:

[180] Ibid., testimony of Mary Theresa McAnnally, p. 29.
[181] Ibid., testimony of Gene Bolton, Fairdale High School, p. 517.
[182] Ibid., testimony of Paul Brown, p. 405.
[183] Ibid., testimony of Vicki Brewer, Shawnee High School, p. 525.
[184] Ibid., testimony of Fannie Gul, human relations coordinator, Valley High School, p. 509.
[185] Ibid., testimony of Martha Hedrick, teacher, Smyrna Elementary School, p. 114.
[186] Ibid., testimony of Gloria Fischer, president, Parent Teacher Association, Central High school, p. 602.

Black people have been unhappy so long, but we are used to it. The black community understood the dilemma of busing, how inconvenient it was and is for young children to be on the corner***to catch a bus***but we felt that it was worth the sacrifice***if that young child doesn't get on the bus to get an education, he may be on that corner the rest of his life.[187]

Findings

The above summary of testimony from the Louisville hearing contains the following findings:

1. Elected county officials abdicated their responsibility to maintain law and order and to take an affirmative stand in support of the desegregation order, and thus perpetuated the belief of opponents to desegregation that demonstrated opposition would yield results. The failure of County Judge Hollenbach to request city police assistance in the face of disruptions on September 5, 1975, in the southwestern section of the county resulted in extensive property damage and bodily injuries.

2. Although the Chamber of Commerce made some initial attempts to unify the business community in support of peaceful desegregation, it yielded to intimidation from dissident elements in the community. As a result, many businesses that would not have supported antibusing forces publicly did so in order to protect themselves and their property.

3. In spite of community disruption, the schools desegregated peacefully and with minimal difficulty. Well developed human relations programs in individual schools facilitated the desegregation process.

4. Students generally responded positively to desegregation. Any tension and anxiety that existed was generated by community controversy and opposition. When community opposition abated after the first quarter of the school year, students settled down and accepted the first year of desegregation as a normal school year.

5. The failure of the school board to commit itself to carrying out the court order has contributed to a trend towards resegregation. Hardship transfers granted to a greater degree to white students and the exemption of first graders from transportation have changed the racial makeup of the schools from that specified by the court order.

6. The failure of the school administration to examine the causes of disproportionate suspension rates for black students and a similar failure to evaluate assignment practices that place a disproportionate number of black students in the Alternative School have caused members of the black community to question the integrity of the school administration.

FOUR STATE ADVISORY COMMITTEE OPEN MEETINGS

Berkeley, California

Berkeley was one of the first northern school districts to desegregate voluntarily. Located within the metropolitan San Francisco bay area of northern California, the city has a population of 116,716.[188] Approximately 62.5 percent of the city's population is

---

[187] Ibid., testimony of Robert Cunningham, founder, Parents for Quality Education, p. 71.
[188] U.S., Department of Commerce, Bureau of the Census, *Characteristics of the Population*, part 6, *California*, table 6, p. 11.

Anglo, 23 percent black, 9 percent Asian American, and 5.5 percent of Spanish origin. [189]

In October 1975 the school district reported an enrollment estimated to be 45 percent white, 42 percent black, 7 percent Asian American, 3 percent Chicano, and 3 percent all other. [190] The ratio of minority to majority students has remained stable since desegregation was implemented 8 years ago. [191]

Efforts to desegregate the public schools began in 1957 when the local NAACP chapter proposed to the school board that a citizens' advisory committee be appointed to study the problems of segregation in Berkeley schools. [192] Such a committee was appointed. It sponsored numerous meetings with school personnel and community representatives and submitted a study of educational opportunities in the district. [193]

In 1963 the board voted to desegregate the junior high schools and to study methods for desegregating the elementary schools at a later date. [194] During the public meeting conducted by the Commission's California Advisory Committee in the spring of 1976, Judge Spurgeon Avakian, a former board member of the Berkeley school district, said of the board's decision:

> First of all was the conviction of the board that in our modern society, equal rights and equal opportunities are meaningless without equal education. Secondly, there was the belief that equal education is impossible in a segregated setting. And finally, there was a feeling on the part of the board that the community of Berkeley was ready to take a major step in trying to reduce some of the inequities which were prevalent in our society. [195]

Board and community representatives alike said that the strong leadership exerted by several superintendents and the school board plus community participation were critical elements in the successful implementation of desegregation plans in 1964 and 1968.

According to Judge Avakian, opposition to desegregation from all strata of the community took the form of attempts to delay desegregation. [196] Ultimately this opposition took the form of a recall election for members of the board who supported desegregation. The attempt to have these board members recalled failed. [197]

Although the recall election divided the community, Judge Avakian viewed the outcome as positive:

> ***[The outcome of the election] resulted in an overwhelming expression by the community of support for what had been done. The vote was something like 62 percent [against recall] to 38 percent [for recall]. And it meant that all of the people who were saying that this was a misguided decision***had to

---

[189] Ibid., table 23, p. 103, and, table 96, p. 679. The Anglo percentage was computed by subtracting the Spanish-origin population in table 96 from the white population in table 23.

[190] Berkeley Unified School District, Report of the Student Racial Census, Fall 1975 (mimeographed), p. 1.

[191] U.S. Commission on Civil Rights, California Advisory Committee open meeting, Berkeley, Calif., Mar. 19, 20, 1976, transcript , p. B–158. (hereafter cited as Berkeley transcript).

[192] Berkeley transcript, testimony of Judge Spurgeon Avakian, former school board member, p. A–13.

[193] Ibid., pp. A–13–15.

[194] Carol Sibley, *Never a Dull Moment* (Berkeley, Calif.: Documentation and Evaluation of Experimental Projects in Schools, 1972), p. 50.

[195] Berkeley transcript, p. A–8.

[196] Ibid., pp. A–18–19.

[197] Ibid., p. A–21.

accept the decision of the community***. It enabled the school system then to deal directly with the problems of implementing that decision without constantly having to deal with critics who were harping that this was not the will of the community. [198]

Elementary schools were desegregated in the fall of 1968, accompanied by faculty desegregation and extensive inservice training. The plan required all students to ride buses during some part of their elementary school years. The school administration, as well as parents, monitored the bus rides closely the first years and assured themselves that safety and convenience prevailed. "Really and truly," Carol Sibley, former president of the Berkeley School Board, told the California Advsiory Committee, "busing has not been much of an issue in Berkeley since we began it. We had very few complaints." [199]

There were also few if any complaints about racial violence in Berkeley schools during implementation of desegregation. The number of racial incidents was minimal and very few could be traced to desegregation. [200] Alan Young, a school counselor, testified that behavior which would normally be considered merely aggressive or even playful if it occurred between two students of the same race was interpreted by overreacting white parents as a racial incident if students of different races were involved. [201] Moreover, the California Advisory Committee heard testimony that since desegregation there has been minimal physical disruption in Berkeley's public schools. [202]

Desegregation has had positive effects on the quality of education. Dr. Arthur Dambacher, director of research and evaluation testified that achievement test scores of students within the different racial and ethnic groups had improved. [203] He also cited factors other than achievement scores that suggest positive results from desegregation in Berkeley:

> If we were to take a look at desegregation, the physical redistribution of youngsters***I feel that Berkeley gets a near perfect score***. If we're saying that white middle-class values and behavior patterns have been accepted by all of the minority groups***then we did not accomplish that because in my opinion it was not the objective that Berkeley set out to accomplish. If we instead mean by [integration] a greater awareness of the multicultural nature of our community, then yes, we've got a good score on that. [204]

Although desegregation has been generally successful, some complaints surfaced at the open meeting. Some black and white parents expressed concern that disparities continued to exist among the achievement levels of the different racial and ethnic groups. [205] Some minority parents criticized the placement of minorities in low tracks; others complained that white teachers had low expectations

---

[198] Ibid., pp. A–25–26.
[199] Ibid., p. A–43.
[200] Ibid., testimony of Alan Young, counselor, p. B–85.
[201] Ibid., pp. B–79–80.
[202] Ibid., testimony of Jimmy Harold, Jr., student body president, Berkeley High School, pp. A–123–24; testimony of Donna McKinney, parent, p. B–111; testimony of Judy Bingham, president, Berkeleyans for Academic Excellence, p. B–182.
[203] Ibid., pp. B–124–25.
[204] Ibid., p. B–123.
[205] Ibid., testimony of Judy Bingham, p. B–182.

of the capabilities of minority students. [206] Jesse Anthony, a music teacher in the district who is also active in the black community, said some classes are segregated:

> ***in music***you probably will find very few black students, and it's not because they are not terribly talented. It is because they are wiped out by the method of teaching, by the curriculum. [207]

Judy Bingham, a white parent, indicated that the school administration has not responded to student needs:

> I have never been of the belief that there was any reason why black students should not be given the sense that they must achieve, and I feel that the district has failed them in this regard. They failed the nonminority students as well because achievement has not been made a very big issue. [208]

Berkeley has hired minorities at administrative and staff levels within the school system. According to Gene Roh, president of the board of education: "[you] have to have minority representation from***one end of the district to the other, relative to classroom teachers, counselors, support service people and administrators***through members of the board." [209]

Dr. Laval Wilson, superintendent of Berkeley Unified School District, articulated the importance of minority hiring:

> ***the affirmative action aspect of any school district that is desegregated is very crucial because you need to have a variety of ethnic adult models [for] a variety of students***. Over a period of time we have found in our district*** the percentages of staff members, certificated and classified, have proportionately increased***. [210]

Although not without problems, Berkeley's experience with desegregation is a positive one. Judge Avakian summed it up:

> Berkeley***[went through]***the kind of thing every community is going to have to go through some time. And hopefully, some communities will learn from the Berkeley experience that it's not as traumatic as the critics proclaim it to be. [211]

Findings

The preceding summary of testimony provides the following findings:

1. Strong leadership exerted successively by several superintendents and the school board plus community participation were critical elements in the peaceful implementation of the desegregation plans of 1964 and 1968.

2. Achievement scores have improved for minority as well as majority students; however, disparities continue to exist among the different racial and ethnic groups.

3. The Berkeley school system hired a number of minorities, particularly for important administrative positions; however, minorities still remain underrepresented in the system's school staff.

---

[206] Ibid., testimony of Clementina Almaguer, coordinator, Chicano studies program, pp. A–172–73.
[207] Ibid., p. B–69.
[208] Ibid., p. B–69.
[209] Ibid., p. A–56.
[210] Ibid., p. B–149.
[211] Ibid., p. A–26.

Minneapolis, Minnesota

School desegregation in Minneapolis grew out of the combined activities of local citizens, the school board and administration, and the State board of education. The desegregation process began in 1967 when the Minneapolis Board of education, of its own volition and with the assistance of a committed superintendent, adopted human relations guidelines and established a voluntary transfer program permitting students to transfer within the school district.[212] In 1970 the State board of education issued desegregation guidelines setting a 30 percent ceiling for minority student enrollment in any school. In April 1971, 17 Minneapolis schools exceeded the ceiling and the State board ordered the school district to develop a desegregation plan.[213] Meanwhile, the local NAACP and members of a biracial group of citizens called the Committee for Integrated Education filed suit in Federal district court, charging the school district with *de jure* segregation of students and faculty.[214] On May 24, 1972, the court found the Minneapolis public schools segregated as a result of *de jure* practices, some of which are summarized as follows:

- siting and expanding schools in a manner that increased racial concentrations between schools
- use of portable classrooms at racially identifiable schools
- gerrymandering attendance zones at the senior high school level
- operating a transfer policy that had the effect of increasing existing racial isolation
- operating a policy of optional attendance zones that facilitated resegregation
- assigning minority teachers in a manner that perpetuated faculty segregation
- assigning less experienced and lower paid teachers to schools with the highest percentage of minority students[215]

Describing the deliberately discriminatory intent of the school board in the location, size, and construction of the Bethune Elementary School, the court stated, "It is hard to imagine how a school could be more clearly denominated a 'black school' unless the words themselves had been chiseled over the door."[216] The court also concluded, "These decisions as to size and location of schools have had the intended effect of increasing or at least maintaining segregation in the defendant's schools."[217]

The court ordered the implementation of a desegregation plan that the board had already developed and approved 1 month earlier. The plan called for new building construction, the institution of several educational alternatives in the curriculum, expansion of community schools, school pairing, clustered schools, initiation of the middle school concept, magnet-type programs in the central city to attract white students, and inservice human relations training for

[212] U.S. Commission on Civil Rights, Minnesota Advisory Committee, open meeting, Minneapolis, Minn., Apr. 22–24, 1976, transcript, pp. 18–27. (hereafter cited as Minneapolis transcript).
[213] Ibid., p. 19.
[214] Booker v. Special School District No. 1, Minneapolis, Minn., 351 F. Supp. 799 (D. Minn., 1972).
[215] Id. at 802–804.
[216] Id. at 803.
[217] Id. at 804.

faculty and staff.[218] The court set minority enrollment at each school at 35 percent and required progress reports every 6 months.[219] Under the 1972 plan, the court continues to require periodic adjustments to bring the enrollment of each school into compliance with the ordered ceiling. Currently, 7 percent of the city's 424,000 residents and 21 percent of the district's 55,000 public school students are minorities.[220]

Testimony before the Minnesota Advisory Committee indicated that after the Federal court issued its desegregation order, a number of organizations and institutions have played critical roles in the peaceful implementation of the plan. Dr. John B. Davis, Jr., superintendent of schools when Minneapolis desegregated in 1972, pointed out the commitments of the State board of education and the legislature, which had provided more than $4 million for a building program during desegregation, and the "remarkable" support of teacher leadership. The Federal court, Dr. Davis noted, "kept us***on our toes in terms of meeting what we said we wanted to do."[221]

Leadership was vital in smoothing the path of desegregation. Community leaders pointed out that the school board and school administration, though somewhat reluctant to initiate desegregation, later asserted a positive role during the process. According to Barbara Schwartz of the Committee for Integrated Education:

> I think Minneapolis was very fortunate to have the kind of school administration and school board we have. While there was reluctance and I think slow going in the beginning, I think it's without question that the great burden of providing leadership for desegregation rested with them***. The School Board was out among its constituents explaining [it] so that***desegregation [now] is an accepted notion.[222]

Curtis C. Chivers, who served as president of the local NAACP chapter during the early desegregation efforts, commented:

> I think what helped us greatly was the fact that we had an atmosphere of fairness in Minneapolis on the part of people who could have given us trouble, the business community and this type of thing. We had lines of communication being kept open; we had people on the school board you could talk with.[223]

According to John Warder, who served on the school board from 1964 to 1969, the business community not only supported desegregation, but also provided funds for new educational programs and human relations projects.[224] Dr. Davis noted the importance of outspoken clergymen.[225]

As the desegregation plan was implemented, the school district also undertook a recruitment program to hire minority teachers. According to Dr. Joyce Jackson, who served as assistant director of

[218]Minneapolis transcript, p. 398.
[219]Ibid., p. 26. The court recently stated that the enrollment of any particular minority group could not exceed 35 percent. The total of all minority groups could not exceed 42 percent in a particular school. Court Order of May 7, 1975, D. Minn. CA4–71–Civ 382.
[220]Minneapolis transcript, p. 18.
[221]Ibid., p. 421.
[222]Ibid., p. 69.
[223]Ibid., pp. 71–72.
[224]Ibid., p. 92.
[225]Ibid., p. 398.

personnel for the school district at that time, "the recruiting schedule was drastically changed in terms of the types of the schools where we went***We expanded to many colleges that were located in the South and colleges [that] had a large proportion of minority students." [226]

Desegregation under the court's jurisdiction has not been physically disruptive or violent. According to Dr. Robert Williams, associate superintendent for intergroup education, the plan was implemented, "to the surprise of many, without the violence and without the vandalism that is too often associated with school desegregation." [227] Dr. Davis said, "We had relatively few incidents of violence. While there were lamentable incidents, I do not think that they were tied in any way to the effort being made to desegregate the schools." [228] The desegregation effort did not go unopposed, however, and some residents and parents of Minneapolis schoolchildren voiced their negative opinions about desegregation. In one case, the pairing of Hale and Field Elementary Schools, a lawsuit opposing the action was filed by residents. [229] The lack of violence, according to Jean Cummings, the parent of four Minneapolis schoolchildren, did not indicate a lack of opposition. The lack of violence, she said, resulted from a "law-abiding citizenry who did not care to stand up and start throwing rocks at each other." [230]

Many opponents of desegregation reportedly considered removing their children from the public schools and enrolling them in either private or suburban schools. Lowry Johnson, principal at Field School (one of the first schools involved in pairing), noted that a number of residents said, "We're going to move, we're going to run" during the early stages of desegregation. But, Mr. Johnson said, "now I would be willing to say that those that ran are running back in." [231]

Gladys Anderson, principal of Nathan Hale School, agreed, "One of the persons who was most against the pairing of Hale and Field now has his child enrolled in Hale." [232]

The opposition to desegregation evident among some parents has not been apparent among the students directly affected by the action. Dr. Williams reported that tests of student attitudes have shown that "desegregation has been very positive in the eyes of the children." "So if we're waiting for the children to be segregationists, we'll be waiting a long time," he concluded; "Children are handling desegregation very well." [233]

Principals, teachers, administrators, and students reported that desegregation was taking place both in the classroom and in extracurricular activities. Mike O'Donnell, a teacher at Wilder School, said, "I definitely feel that there is more social interaction between

---

[226] Ibid., pp. 471–72.
[227] Ibid., p. 188.
[228] Ibid., p. 424.
[229] Ibid., pp. 392 and 411.
[230] Ibid., p. 963.
[231] Ibid., p. 564.
[232] Ibid., p. 566.
[233] Ibid., pp. 215 and 218.

all students and all races in our schools."[234] Richard Green, principal at North High School, observed:

> For some reason, either through desegregation or whatever, the 9th grade class which came to North for the first time last year saw***more pupils sharing, sitting in classrooms and lunchrooms at integrated lunch tables; it was much more prevalent among the 9th graders than it was amongst the 12th graders and the 11th graders.[235]

George Sell, a white student at Central High School, said,

> I feel that it has opened my mind in going to school with people from different backgrounds and that has probably more prepared me than sitting in an all-white school***If you put kids from a different race together without any influence from the parent, they're going to get along fine.[236]

During desegregation, student achievement levels reportedly rose in some schools. According to Geraldine Johnson, a teacher at Field Elementary School, math and reading scores of both majority and minority students rose.[237] Other teachers also noted that the quality of educational programs in the school system had improved.[238]

Commenting on the overall outcome of desegregation, Harry Davis, director (member) of the Minneapolis Board of Education, noted, "I think they [the students] are better educated, and integration and desegregation have improved the quality of education.[239]

Findings

The following findings were derived from the above statement on the Minneapolis open meeting:

1. Although the Board of Education had initiated a plan to desegregate Minneapolis schools through voluntary student transfer, the Federal district court found the school administration operated a *de jure*-segregated system because it had employed such segregatory practices as locating schools and gerrymandering attendance zones to increase segregation and assigning less experienced and lower-paid teachers to racially identifiable minority schools.

2. After the court order the school board and the school administration exerted strong positive leadership implementing the desegregation plan.

3. Although there was strong opposition to desegregation among some segments of the community, an acceptance of the law permitted desegregation to proceed with only a few disruptive incidents.

Stamford, Connecticut

Desegregation of Stamford public schools was carried out voluntarily and with little difficulty from 1962 to 1972. The board of education was committed to desegregation and the superintendent exerted his leadership and support. There was little opposition and busing was not a major issue.

---

[234] Ibid., p. 631.
[235] Ibid., p. 515.
[236] Ibid., p. 834.
[237] Ibid., p. 630.
[238] Ibid., testimony of Mike O'Donnell, teacher, Wilder School.
[239] Ibid., p. 330.

Located between wealthy suburban communities on the Long Island Sound, Stamford has a population of 108,798.[240] Approximately 83.2 percent of the population is white, 12.3 percent is black, and 3.8 percent is of Spanish origin; less than 1.0 percent are members of other racial and ethnic groups.[241] The city encompasses 40 square miles. Its northern section is predominantly white and affluent, and the low-income and minority population is concentrated in the southern section. In 1975, 19,118 students were enrolled in Stamford schools; approximately 31.4 percent were minorities.

Desegregation of the school system began with the opening of a second high school in 1961 and the redistricting of the two high schools in 1962. A common concern of both the community and the board of education was that the school system was becoming increasingly racially isolated. At the recommendation of a broadly-based citizen committee, the school board redistricted the high schools, changing the district line from east-west to north-south to ensure that students from both northern and southern sections of the city attended both high schools.

Subsequent steps to desegregate Stamford's public schools included closing predominantly black schools and opening new middle and elementary schools in an area readily accessible to both minority and majority communities. Although most black parents believed that desegregation would improve the quality of education in the schools, a small coalition of blacks and Hispanics disagreed and developed their own proposal, which stressed quality education and community control. The final elementary school plan, which went into effect in September 1972, was challenged in Federal district court on the grounds that it placed a disproportionate share of busing on the black community.[242] The court upheld the school board's plan.[243]

School officials, parents, and community and civic leaders generally agree that Stamford desegregated its schools with relative ease.[244] Although small groups of parents objected to specific school assignments, there was no significant opposition. Business and political leaders were not actively involved and considered desegregation a school board issue. Religious leaders supported desegregation but were not active. The media reported accurately on each phase of the plan.

Elementary school principal Michael D'Agostino said there was no general pattern of white flight. "We didn't see any swelling of the private schools after desegregation. I think some of the parents were apprehensive, but I think that apprehension diminished after the schools opened in September."[245] Dr. Robert Peebles, superintendent of schools, said, "I think there are isolated examples of students who have done this, but at the same time I think that's coun-

[240] U.S., Department of Commerce, Bureau of the Census, *Characteristics of the Population*, part 8, *Connecticut*, table 16, p. 36.
[241] Ibid., table 23, p. 53 and table 96, p. 311. The white percentage was computed by subtracting the Spanish-origin population in table 96 from the total white population in table 23.
[242] Moss v. Stamford Board of Educ. 350 F. Supp. 879 (D. Conn. 1972).
[243] Moss v. Stamford Board of Educ. 356 F. Supp. 675 (D. Conn. 1973).
[244] U.S., Commission on Civil Rights, Connecticut Advisory Committee open meeting, Stamford, Conn., Apr. 19, 1976, transcript (hereafter cited as Stamford transcript).
[245] Stamford transcript, p. 67.

tered by students that have chosen to leave private and parochial schools to come to our own schools***."[246]

Desegregation within the classroom remains a critical issue. Ability grouping, which is used to varying degrees at different age levels, frequently results in racial and ethnic isolation in academic classrooms at the middle and high school levels. Students, parents, and school staff differ in their views on ability grouping. Although parents support heterogeneous grouping with individualized instruction in the lower grades, they do not, in general, support heterogeneous grouping in basic skill courses in middle and high schools.

Students, particularly those in lower tracks, have a different view. One black student, describing the apathy of teachers in the lower grouping, said, "There isn't anybody to help you out***nobody down there to push you."[247]

Nevertheless, several persons expressed satisfaction with the desegregated school environment. One black high school student said:

> Now I feel that students should be integrated because most parents give their children, maybe unconsciously***an outline of people, like black people all take drugs and hang out in the streets and rob your house and everything***. You won't know about people until you mix with them. And I think school is really where people get together and people mix, and I'd rather go to an integrated school than an all-black school.[248]

A white parent, who chose to bus her children for 45 minutes to attend the predominantly black magnet school in the inner city, said:

> My daughter had been to an all-white nursery school and to a kindergarten where the black children were bused in and it made her think of them as being different***so when we heard about a public school in Stamford that had a type of educational program which we think is very, very good, we investigated that and since my daughter has been to that school I have seen her come around 100 percent. She never refers to race, ever. If she talks about the children in her classroom, she simply names them.[249]

Most school officials, parents, and students agreed that discipline was a continuing problem in the schools. A disproportionate percentage of students suspended—more than 60 percent in 1974—are black. Students and teachers differed about whether black and white students were treated equally in disciplinary procedures. One student put the problem in the following perspective:

> Basically a teacher doesn't want people to feel that they're treating the white kids better than the black kids and they overdo it to the point where they let the blacks get away with so much and the white kids get away with so little that it makes the white kids mad. But then you get a teacher who says, well, I'm not going to let these black kids get away with nothing on me***and it's just reverse and the black students get mad.[250]

Minority parents and students strongly criticized the lack of

[246] Ibid., p. 469.
[247] Ibid., p. 244.
[248] Ibid., p. 232.
[249] Ibid., p. 115.
[250] Ibid., p. 228.

adequate minority representation in the school system. This criticism appeared justified in light of the school system's employment profile. In 1975, 76 (5.7 percent) of the 1,338 total professional staff were black and 17 (1.3 percent) were of Spanish origin. In the spring of 1976 there were 20 social workers; only 3 (15 percent) were black and none was Hispanic. Of 14 psychologists, only one was black and none was Hispanic; of 56 special education teachers, none was black or Hispanic. Of 48 counselors, 3 or 6 percent were black and none was Hispanic. [251]

Although the percentage of black elementary students transported increased from 17 percent to 31 percent when the plan was implemented, allegations that minority students are bused in disproportionate numbers are not supported by the evidence. In 1975 the percentage of black students bused was approximately 5 percent above their representation in the elementary student body. For all grades, the percentage of black students bused was approximately equal to their representation.

School staff, parents, and community leaders generally believe that the quality of education has improved since desegregation. Many persons said they believed that the multiracial classroom provides a better education for Stamford's students.

Dr. Thomas Reardon, an assistant superintendent in the school system for many years, said: "I personally can say from observation and many other facts that the integration-desegregation program has improved the quality of education in Stamford significantly and contributed to the good racial relationship and harmony in the city itself." [252]

Findings

It is evident from the above Stamford open meeting that:

1. School officials, parents, community leaders, and civic leaders agree that Stamford had a relatively easy desegregation experience. This occurred even though small groups of parents were opposed, and business and political leaders generally did not take a stand on the issue.

2. Many students are reported to be satisfied with desegregation; however, ability grouping is tending to segregate racial and ethnic minorities by classroom at the middle and high school levels.

3. Student discipline is a continuing source of concern. A disproportionately high percentage of students suspended are blacks.

4. Minorities are poorly represented on the staffs of Stamford schools.

Corpus Christi, Texas

Desegregation in Corpus Christi, Texas, has grown from a neighborhood concern into a grueling legal battle between Mexican Americans and blacks and the predominantly Anglo school board.

Corpus Christi, located on the Gulf Coast, has a population of

---

[251] Margaret C. Toner, director of special pupil services, Stamford School Department, staff interview, Mar. 5, 1976.

[252] Ibid., p. 448.

204,525.[253] Approximately 41 percent of the city's population is
Mexican American, 5 percent is black, and 53 percent is Anglo.[254]
The Corpus Christi school district in December 1975 had a student
enrollment that was 57 percent Mexican American, 6 percent black,
and 37 percent Anglo.

Efforts to desegregate the public schools involve the landmark
case *Cisneros* v. *Corpus Christi Independent School District*.[255] On
July 22, 1968, Jose Cisneros and 25 other Mexican American and
black parents and students in the Corpus Christi Independent
School District filed suit in Federal district court alleging that local
school authorities had operated schools in a discriminatory fashion.
On June 4, 1970, a district court found that "Mexican American
students are an identifiable, ethnic-minority class sufficient to bring
them within the protection of *Brown*."[256] Further, the court found
that the Corpus Christi Independent School District had engaged in
the following acts of *de jure* segregation of Mexican American and
black students:

> ***administrative decisions by the school board in drawing
> boundaries, locating new schools, building new schools and
> renovating old schools in the predominantly Negro and Mex-
> ican parts of town, in providing an elastic and flexible subjec-
> tive transfer system***, by bussing [sic] some students, by
> providing optional transfer zones which resulted in Anglos
> being able to avoid Negro and Mexican-American schools, not
> allowing Mexican-Americans or Negroes the option of going to
> Anglo schools***by assigning Negro and Mexican-American
> teachers in disparate ratios to these segregated schools***.[257]

The court said that these acts were "calculated to, and did, maintain and promote a dual school system."[258]

After submission of plans by plaintiffs and defendants, the court
in 1971 issued an order to disestablish the dual school system.[259]
The student assignment plan required pairing of elementary schools
at two levels, a complete revision of high school attendance zones,
and further reassignment of pupils. The court found that the plan
would require transportation of approximately 15,000 students.[260]
Subsequent appeals have resulted in numerous plans being submitted to the court by the school district. These plans have varied,
but generally included such measures as pairing of schools, district
rezoning, and voluntary transfer programs.

Because of delays in the litigation only the voluntary transfer program was put into effect during the 1974–75 school year. When it
failed to meet the court's standard, Federal District Judge Owen
Cox called for an improved plan during the 1975–76 school year.

The major objective of the current plan is to satisfy court-ordered
ethnic ratios with a minimum of busing. A lottery system was
devised to determine which students would be bused when computer assignments failed to meet the court-imposed ratio. The system

[253] U.S. Department of Commerce, Bureau of the Census, *Characteristics of the Population*, part 45, *Texas*, table 16, p. 96.
[254] Ibid., table 23, p. 117 and table 96, p. 683. The Anglo percentage was computed by subtract-
ing the Spanish-origin population in table 96 from the total white population in table 23.
[255] 324 F. Supp. 599 (S.D. Texas, 1970).
[256] Ibid., p. 606.
[257] Ibid., pp. 617–19.
[258] Ibid., p. 620.
[259] Cisneros v. Corpus Christi Independent School District, 330 F. Supp. 1377 (S.D. Texas, 1971).
[260] Ibid., pp. 1393–96.

is rotational so that a different set of children is bused every year. About 5,000 students are bused by the school district; more than 2,300 or about 44 percent are transported for desegregation.

Throughout the entire legal proceedings up to the present, the school administration has opposed desegregation. Paul Montemayor, a Mexican American member of the United Steel Workers of America, in his remarks at the open meeting, described the frustrations of trying to work with the school board to improve equal educational opportunities for Mexican Americans and how the board's uncooperative stance led to the filing of the *Cisneros* suit. [261]

Madelin Olds, assistant professor at Del Mar Junior College in Corpus Christi, stated:

> While the***people in Corpus Christi want to obey the law, it***has not been clear to a number of people why the Corpus Christi schools are under Federal court order***. There has been no official acknowledgment by the Corpus Christi School Board of unconstitutional behavior, but evidence in the *Cisneros* case clearly shows and Federal courts have agreed that *de jure* segregation exists. [262]

Another witness, the Reverend Harold Branch, pastor of St. John's Baptist Church in Corpus Christi, said:

> [There] has not been a commitment on the part of our school administration that [desegregation] is good for us and***for our children, that this is the way to lead us out of***the ghettoized life***in Corpus Christi. [263]

The school administration's opposition has extended to Commission efforts to obtain information on overall desegregation progress in the district's schools. The superintendent refused to permit Commission staff to interview administrators or teachers. He also refused to testify or allow his staff to testify at the Advisory Committee's open meeting. As a result, the Commission held a hearing in Corpus Christi in August 1976.

Despite the negative position of Corpus Christi's educational leadership, there has been an almost total absence of violence or disorder during the district's limited desegregation efforts. [264] This is due, in large part, to the efforts of the business and religious community in Corpus Christi. The media has also played an important role in keeping the community informed. The local newspaper, the *Corpus Christi Caller-Times*, provided excellent coverage.

School administrators have cited white flight as an outcome of desegregation. Dr. Dwayne Bliss, assistant school superintendent, told the press that the normal attrition rate for the Corpus Christi school district is about 670. Since the July 1975 desegregation order, more than 1,600 students have not returned to school. Of this total, Dr. Bliss said, about 600 were Anglos. [265]

Since many Mexican American pupils in Corpus Christi schools have limited ability in English, there is a special need for bilingual-bicultural programs. Dr. Arturo Medina, professor at Texas A&I in Corpus Christi, told the Advisory Committee that school officials

[261] U.S., Commission on Civil Rights, Texas Advisory Committee open meeting, Corpus Christi, Tex., May 4–5, 1976 (hereafter cited as Corpus Christi transcript).
[262] Ibid., vol. I, p. 17.
[263] Ibid., vol. I, p. 39.
[264] *Corpus Christi Caller Times*, "Busing: First Year is Relatively Quiet," Dec. 21, 1975, p. 1–C.
[265] *Corpus Christi Caller Times*, "Junior High Shuffle Not Certain," Feb. 18, 1976, p. 1–B

often take the attitude that the goal of many bilingual programs in Texas is to eradicate the original home language. According to Dr. Medina, the poor academic performance of many Mexican American students can be attributed to the lack of good bilingual-bicultural programs. [266]

There is also a critical shortage of minorities in administrative and teaching positions. The school district historically has hired a disproportionately small number of Mexican Americans and blacks to fill professional positions on its administrative and teaching staffs. The district currently employs 3,923 full-time staff; 1,711 or about 44 percent are employed as teachers. Minorities are only about 30 percent of the faculty. Moreover, only six Mexican Americans and one black are employed in the top administrative positions. Out of a total of 56 principals, only 15 are identified as Mexican American or black. On the other hand, of the 810 service workers currently employed, 571 or 70 percent are minorities. Given the fact that Mexican Americans and blacks make up more than 63 percent of the current student enrollment in the district, there appears to be a severe disparity in the employment of minority staff. [267]

As a triethnic community, Corpus Christi provides a richly endowed setting for its students. A recalcitrant school administration and lack of strong leadership at the community level have severely restricted the benefits of desegregated education.

Findings

From the above statement on the Corpus Christi open meeting, the following findings are evident:

1. Although the Corpus Christi school administration is opposed to desegregation and 8 years of litigation were required before the school system was ordered to desegregate, violence and disruption have been almost totally absent since the limited desegregation process began.

2. A critical shortage of minority faculty exists in the schools. Although two-thirds of the district's enrollment is of minority background, minorities make up less than one-third of its teachers.

3. Despite the fact that more than half of Corpus Christi's student body is of Mexican American background and many are fluent only in Spanish, the system lacks a good bilingual-bicultural program to meet their educational needs.

SUMMARY OF DESEGREGATION EXPERIENCES—29 SELECTED SCHOOL DISTRICTS

Twenty-nine desegregating school districts were studied by the Commission's State Advisory Committees with assistance from regional Commission staff in order to discover patterns of the school desegregation process. These districts varied in locale, size, and minority representation. (See map 2.1 and table 2.2) Descriptions of 25 of the case studies follow. [268]

---

[266] Corpus Christi transcript, vol. III, p. 86.

[267] U.S., Equal Employment Opportunity Commission, Elementary-Secondary School Staff Information, EEO–5 Public School System–CCID, Oct. 1, 1975.

[268] Four of the case studies—Berkeley, California; Corpus Christi, Texas; Minneapolis, Minnesota; and Stamford, Connecticut—were also open meeting sites and were described in the previous section.

The 29 Case Study School Districts

Bogalusa, Louisiana, a rural southern town located on the State's eastern border, in 1975 had an estimated population of 17,415, about 33 percent black. The Bogalusa City School District in 1975 had a student population of 4,660, of which 1,771 or 38 percent was black. Of the 267 faculty members, 28 percent was black. In 1965 the school district began court-ordered desegregation under a freedom-of-choice plan which did not result in a significant degree of desegregation. Total desegregation was ordered in 1969.

Table 2.2 Summary of Characteristics of 25 School Districts**

	Year of Most Recent Desegregation	Population 1975	Percent Minority	School Enrollment	Percent Minority	Faculty 1975	Percent Minority
Bogalusa, La.	1969	17,415	33	4,660	38	267	28
Colorado Springs, Colo.	1970	175,000	15	34,201	17	1,953	7
Dorchester County, Md.	1971	29,405*	31	6,111	41	356	29
Erie, Pa.	1975	129,231*	7	17,462	19	1,109	5
Greenville, Miss.	1970	39,495*	53	10,048	70	535⁵	47
Kalamazoo, Mich.	1971	85,555*	12	14,551	24	817	10
Kirkwood, Mo.	1975	43,034²	5	6,792	11	409	9
Little Rock, Ark.	1975	132,483*	25	21,928	52	1,212	30
Nashville, Tenn. (Davidson County)	1971	448,000*	20	80,165	29	4,500	24
Newport News, Va.	1971	138,177*	28	30,268	37	1,318	36
Ogden, Utah	**1975**	73,283	4	15,665	20	605	4
Ossining, N.Y.	1974	47,000	³	5,136	24	300	11
Peoria, Ill.	1969	126,962	11	23,987	27	1,282	7
Portland, Ore.	1964¹	382,169	8	62,028	17	3,778	8
Providence, R.I.	1971	165,000	10⁴	20,680	25	1,256	8
Racine County, Wis.	1975	170,838	7	28,757	25	1,590⁶	8
Raleigh County, W.Va.	1973	70,080	10	17,338	10	843	9
Santa Barbara, Calif.	1972	75,000	19	4,850	48	366⁷	8
Springfield, Mass.	1974	163,905*	13	28,839	40	1,710	9
Tacoma, Wash.	1971	154,581*	10	32,671	19	1,612	10
Tempe, Ariz.	1973	62,907	14	13,482	20	671	12
Tulsa, Okla.	1971	330,350	14	64,207	22	3,179	14
Waterloo, Iowa	1973	75,563	9	16,312	16	938	13
Wichita, Kans.	1971	276,718	13	51,907	23	3,134	11
Williamsburg County, S.C.	1971	34,243	61	9,075	80	467	63

* 1970 Population

** For characteristics of Berkeley, Corpus Christi, Minneapolis, and Stamford, see section on open meetings.

¹ Portland had no specific desegregation plan, but desegregation activities began in 1964.

² Includes Kirkwood, Des Peres, Frontenac, and Glendale.

³ Minority population for the school district could not be determined as the Ossining Union Free School District No. 1 covers portions of several communities.

⁴ Figure is for blacks only. Another 10 percent of the population is Portuguese and Hispanic, sometimes classified as white.

⁵ Figures for 1974.

⁶ Figures for 1972.

⁷ Figures for 1974.

Colorado Springs, Colorado, on the eastern slope of the Rocky Mountains, is the State's second largest city. The estimated population in 1975 was 175,000, of which approximately 8.5 percent was Mexican American, 5.2 percent, black, and 1.3 percent, other minorities. Colorado Springs School District No. 11 for the 1975 school year had a student population of 34,201, with 3,330 Mexican Americans, 2,100 blacks, 379 Asian Americans, and 95 Native Americans. Of 1,953 faculty members, only 7 percent was minority. In 1970 the district voluntarily desegregated its high schools.

Dorchester County, Maryland, is a rural marshland area on the eastern shore. The county in 1970 had a total population of 29,405, 30.8 percent of which was black. In 1975 the school enrollment was 6,111, with 2,538 (41 percent) black students. Of 366 faculty members, 29 percent was black. In 1963 the Dorchester County School District initiated a freedom-of-choice plan which resulted in only token desegregation. In 1971 under pressure from the Department of Health, Education, and Welfare, the district implemented a comprehensive desegregation plan.

Erie, Pennsylvania, an industrial port city on Lake Erie, in 1970 had a population of 129,231 of which 6.8 percent was black. The

Erie City School District in 1975 had an enrollment of 17,462, with 3,234 (18.5 percent) black students. Erie employed 50 minority faculty members (4.5 percent) of a total of 1,109. The school district was initially required to desegregate in 1968 by the State department of education. A desegregation plan was ordered by the court and implemented in 1975.

Greenville, Mississippi, is a river port in the Mississippi Delta. In 1970, almost 53 percent of the 39,495 people living in Greenville were black. The Greenville Municipal Separate School District is a majority-black district enrolling 10,048 students in 1975. While 70 percent of the student body was black, only 46.7 percent of the faculty was black. In 1964 the school board voluntarily initiated a freedom-of-choice plan, the first such effort in Mississippi. In 1970 under court order, the district implemented a comprehensive plan for total desegregation.

Kalamazoo, Michigan, is an urban area of 85,555. While blacks are the largest minority group (8,534), there are 1,579 Latinos in Kalamazoo. In the fall of 1975 the Kalamazoo Public Schools had a student population of 14,551, of which 23 percent was black and 1.3 percent was of Spanish origin. Of 817 faculty members, 9.9 percent was minority. The district implemented court-ordered desegregation in 1971.

The **Kirkwood R-7 School District, Missouri**, is a surburban district of St. Louis, Missouri, serving the cities of Des Peres, Frontenac, Glendale, and Kirkwood and unincorporated areas in St. Louis County. The 1970 population of the district was approximately 43,034. Blacks constituted 5 percent of the population. The school district's student population for 1975 was 6,792, with a black enrollment of 756 or 11.1 percent. Almost 9 percent of the 409-member faculty was minority. Minimal efforts to desegregate the legally constituted dual school system were begun immediately after *Brown*. Under pressure from the Department of Health, Education, and Welfare, the Kirkwood R-7 district totally desegregated in 1975.

Little Rock, Arkansas, is the central city of a medium-sized metropolitan area. The 1970 population of the city was 132,483. There were 21,928 students attending public schools in the Little Rock School District in 1975. Blacks constituted about 52 percent of the student population. Black faculty members represented only 29.7 percent of the total faculty of 1,212. In 1957 Little Rock made national headlines as Federal troops escorted nine black children to enroll at Central High School when the school district was ordered to desegregate its public schools. In the following years a number of desegregation plans were implemented until 1975 when the district was totally desegregated.

Nashville, Tennessee, the State capital, is the urban and economic hub of the 36-county middle Tennessee area. Nashville and Davidson County have a consolidated government and a metropolitan school district known as the Metro Nashville-Davidson School District. In 1970 Davidson County had a total population of 448,000; approximately 19.9 percent was black. The 1975 student population was 80,165, with 23,372 (29 percent) blacks. Total faculty in 1975 numbered 4,500, with 1,092 (24.2 percent) blacks. The school district implemented court-ordered desegregation in 1971.

Newport News, Virginia, in the southeastern portion of the State on the James River, is an urban area with a total population in 1970 of 138,177 and a black population of 39,208 (28 percent.) The school population of the Newport News Public Schools in 1975 totaled 30,268, of which 37 percent was black. Minority faculty representation (36.3 percent) paralleled the minority student enrollment. Early efforts to desegregate in the late 1950s and in 1965 when the school district operated a freedom-of-choice plan did not eliminate the dual school system. After continued pressure from the Department of Health, Education, and Welfare resulting in a cutoff of Federal funds and a court order, the Newport News Public Schools implemented a comprehensive desegregation plan in 1971.

Ogden, Utah, is a medium-sized city with a population of 73,283. Minority students constituted 20 percent of the 1975 student population of 15,665. Mexican Americans are the largest minority group (1,850), Native Americans are second (639), and blacks, third (508). During the 1974–75 school year the district employed a total of 605 teachers; 96.2 percent of all teachers were white. Desegregation efforts began in 1970 in the Ogden City School District after the Department of Health, Education, and Welfare notified the district that it had a racially identifiable school in violation of Title VI of the Civil Rights Act of 1964. Final desegregation efforts were implemented in 1975.

Ossining Union Free School District No. 1, New York, serves the Village of Ossining, a portion of the Village of Briarcliff Manor, and portions of the Towns of Ossining, New Castle, and Yorktown. The population of this suburban area is approximately 47,000, and blacks and Puerto Ricans are the major minority groups. In the 1974–75 school year the district enrolled a total of 15,136 students of which blacks constituted 19 percent and Puerto Ricans, 5 percent. By contrast, the faculty of 300 had only 33 (11 percent) minority members. After notification from the State board of education in 1969, the district began consideration of its segregation problems and in 1974 implemented a desegregation plan.

Peoria, Illinois, is an urban area in the north-central portion of the State with a population of 126,962. Blacks totaled 14,492. The student enrollment in 1975 was 23,907, of which 26 percent was black, and less than 1 percent was other minorities. Other minorities totaled only 232. Of 1,282 faculty members, only 7.3 percent was minority. The Peoria Public School District No. 150 implemented a partial desegregation plan in 1969 which achieved a reduction in racial isolation. Since that time, shifts in housing patterns have caused resegregation.

Portland, Oregon, a port city of 382,619 on the Willamette River, has a minority population of 31,984, of which the majority (21,572) is black. Portland School District No. 1 had a student enrollment in 1975 of 62,028—12.5 percent black, 4.5 percent other minorities. Eight percent of a faculty totaling 3,778 was minority. Beginning in 1964 the district initiated a variety of programs in an effort to reduce racial isolation such as voluntary transfer, which evolved into a desegregation plan.

Providence, Rhode Island, is the capital of the State and its largest city. In 1975 an estimated 165,000 persons resided in Providence; 10 percent was black. The 1975 public school population was

20,680, of which 25 percent was black. In contrast, minorities made up less than 8 percent of the faculty. The Providence School District initiated a three-phase desegregation plan in 1967, which was completed in 1971.

Racine County, Wisconsin, located on the shores of Lake Michigan, had a 1970 population of 170,838, of which 6.6 percent was black. The Unified School District No. 1 of Racine County enrolled 28,757 students in 1975. The district has 25 percent minority population (5,739), mostly black (4,084) with 1,542 of Spanish origin. Only 134 of 1,590 (18.4 percent) faculty members were minority. Desegregation efforts began as early as 1961. In 1975 the current desegregation plan was implemented.

Raleigh County, West Virginia, is a rural, coal-mining district of 70,080 with 6,880 blacks. In 1975 Raleigh County Schools enrolled 17,338 students, of whom 10 percent was black. In comparison, 8.6 percent of the faculty was black. In 1956 the county initiated a voluntary transfer plan. In 1964 the district began consolidating its schools, and desegregation was completed in 1973 when, under pressure from the Department of Health, Education, and Welfare, a two-phase plan was implemented.

Santa Barbara, California, is a coastal city of 75,000 in the southern portion of the State. It has a minority population of 14,000, of which 12,570 are of Spanish origin, 1,500, black, and 600, Asian American. Of the 1975 public school enrollment, 48 percent was minority, compared to 8.4 percent of the faculty. As a result of State recommendations, the Santa Barbara School District developed a desegregation plan in 1972 to be implemented in three phases. To date only two schools have been involved. Phases two and three of the desegregation plan have not been implemented.

Springfield, Massachusetts, a city in the southwestern area of the State, had a 1970 population of 163,905, of which 13 percent was nonwhite.[269] In 1975 the school district's enrollment was 28,839, with 7,668 black and 3,844 Spanish-surnamed students (primarily Puerto Ricans.) While almost 40 percent of the students was minority, only 9.2 percent of the faculty was minority. In response to the 1965 Massachusetts Racial Imbalance Law, the district in 1966 began efforts to eliminate racial imbalance. In 1974 a final desegregation plan was implemented.

Tempe, Arizona, a suburb of Phoenix, is a small university city with a 1970 population of 62,907 persons. Of this total, approximately 14 percent were minorities—Mexican Americans (12 percent), blacks (1 percent), others (1 percent). In 1975 Tempe Elementary School District No. 3 enrolled 13,482 elementary children. Mexican American students accounted for 16 percent of the total, black students for 3 percent, and Native Americans for 0.5 percent. Of 671 faculty members, 11.7 percent was minority. In 1971 the Department of Health, Education, and Welfare notified the district that it had racially identifiable schools in violation of Title VI of the Civil Rights Act of 1964. In 1973 the district implemented a desegregation plan.

---

[269] Persons of Spanish origin were classified as white.

Tacoma, Washington, is a port city in the western portion of the State on Puget Sound. The city's 1970 population was 154,581 with 10,436 blacks, 2,248 Spanish-surnamed, 1,703 Native Americans, and 1,689 Asian Americans. Tacoma Public School District No. 10 enrolled 32,671 students in 1975, and 6,101 (18.6 percent) were minority. Only 9.7 percent of a faculty of 1,612 was minority. In 1966 the school district initiated a limited optional enrollment plan and in 1967, a more extensive open enrollment plan. Although there was no specific "desegregation plan," all schools were desegregated by 1971.

Tulsa, Oklahoma, a central city with a 1970 population of 330,350, is located in northeastern Oklahoma on the Arkansas River. Once known as the oil capital of the Nation, Tulsa has an 11 percent black population and a 3 percent Native American population. The Tulsa Independent School District had a 1975 student enrollment of 64,207, of which blacks and Native Americans, the largest minority groups, constituted 17.7 percent and 4.4 percent, respectively. Of 3,179 faculty members, 13.7 percent was black.[270] Tulsa's first desegregation efforts were made in 1955 when the district established new neighborhood attendance areas to eliminate the dual school system previously required by State law. After other efforts, Tulsa began implementation of a three-phase desegregation plan in 1971.

Waterloo, Iowa, population 75,563, is located in the northeast-central section of the State. Blacks, the only significant minority group, constitute 8 percent of the population. In 1975 the Waterloo School District enrolled 16,312 students, of which 8 percent was black. The faculty totaled 938, with 56 blacks (5.9 percent). The district began its first efforts to desegregate in 1968 with the initiation of an open enrollment program which was followed by limited redistricting. In 1973 a plan was implemented which completed the desegregation process.

Wichita, Kansas, located in the south-central part of the State on the Arkansas River, is a city of 276,718 persons, 9.8 percent of whom are black and 3.5 percent, of Spanish origin. The Wichita School District's 1975 population was 51,907. Blacks students numbered 9,530 and students of Spanish origin, 1,502, with 845 other minorities. Minorities made up 11.3 percent of a 3,134-member faculty. The district's first efforts to desegregate began in 1969 under pressure from the Department of Health, Education, and Welfare. In 1971 a comprehensive desegregation plan was implemented.

Williamsburg County, South Carolina, is a rural area with a total population of 34,243, most of whom (61 percent) are black. The student population for Williamsburg County Schools (9,075) is 80 percent black. The faculty of 467 is 63 percent black. Required to do so by the Department of Health, Education, and Welfare, the district desegregated in 1970 and 1971.

Experiences with School Desegregation

Analysis of the desegregation experiences of the 29 school districts is based upon information solicited from school systems and

---

[270] Native Americans were classified as white.

personal interviews with nearly 900 persons. The impressions and perceptions of school officials, teachers, students, and business, political, religious, and other community leaders in each school district have been analyzed and collated to provide a profile of each district's most recent school desegregation experience. (See table 2.3)

Table 2.3

Desegregation in 29 School Districts

School Districts	Leadership Support for Desegregation						Outcomes of Desegregation				
	Impetus for Desegregation	School Administration	School Board	Business	Religious	Political	Community Disruptions	Community Preparation	Staff Training	Curriculum Changes	Overall Progress *
Berkeley, Calif.	V	P	P	N	P	P	No	Yes	Yes	Yes	3
Bogalusa, La.	CO	C	C	C	P	NA	Yes	No	No	No	1
Colorado Springs, Colo.	V	P	P	N	N	N	No	Yes	Yes	Yes	3
Corpus Christi, Tex.	CO	C	C	N	P	C	No	Yes	Yes	No	1
Dorchester County, Md.	HEW	P	N	N	NA	NA	No	Yes	Yes	No	3
Erie, Pa.	CO	P	N	N	P	N	No	Yes	Yes	Yes	2
Greenville, Miss.	CO	P	P	P	P	P	No	Yes	Yes	Yes	3
Kalamazoo, Mich.	CO	P	C	P	P	N	No	Yes	NA	Yes	3
Kirkwood, Mo.	HEW	P	P	N	N	N	No	Yes	Yes	Yes	2
Little Rock, Ark.	CO	P	P	NA	P	C	No	Yes	Yes	Yes	2
Minneapolis, Minn.	CO	P	P	P	P	N	No	Yes	Yes	Yes	3
Nashville, Tenn.	CO	P	N	P	P	C	No	Yes	Yes	Yes	2
Newport News, Va.	CO	P	C	N	N	N	No	Yes	No	Yes	3
Ogden, Utah	HEW	P	NA	NA	NA	NA	No	Yes	Yes	Yes	3
Ossining, N.Y.	S	P	P	N	N	N	No	Yes	No	No	3
Peoria, Ill.	S	N	P	P	P	N	No	No	NA	Yes	1
Portland, Ore.	V	P	P	N	P	N	No	Yes	Yes	Yes	3
Providence, R.I.	V	P	N	N	P	P	Yes	Yes	Yes	Yes	2
Racine County, Wis.	V	P	P	P	P	N	No	Yes	Yes	Yes	3
Raleigh County, W.Va.	HEW	P	N	N	P	N	No	Yes	No	Yes	3
Santa Barbara, Calif.	V	P	P	N	N	N	No	Yes	Yes	Yes	2
Springfield, Mass.	S	P	N	N	P	N	No	Yes	Yes	Yes	3
Stamford, Conn.	V	P	P	N	N	N	No	Yes	Yes	Yes	3
Tacoma, Wash.	V	P	P	N	N	N	No	Yes	Yes	Yes	3
Tempe, Ariz.	HEW	P	P	N	N	N	No	Yes	Yes	Yes	3
Tulsa, Okla.	HEW/CO	P	N	P	P	NA	No	Yes	Yes	Yes	2
Waterloo, Iowa	V	P	P	N	P	P	No	Yes	Yes	No	3
Wichita, Kans.	HEW	P	N	P	N	N	No	Yes	Yes	No	2
Williamsburg County, S.C.	HEW	P	N	N	N	N	No	Yes	Yes	Yes	3

LEGEND:

V = Voluntary.
CO = Court Order.
HEW = Department of Health, Education, and Welfare.
S = State Department of Education.
* = The overall progress of desegregation was determined on the basis of the perceptions and impressions of persons interviewed in each community.
1 = Little Progress.

2 = Moderate Progress.
3 = Substantial Progress.
P = Actions or attitudes which created a positive atmosphere for desegregation, including public statements of support and initiation of activities to facilitate desegregation.
C = Actions or attitudes which created a negative atmosphere for desegregation, including public statements or actions opposing desegregation.
N = Noninvolvement.
NA = Determination could not be made from information gathered in the case study.

In rating school districts for the case study investigation, the following general criteria were used: (1) *Little Progress:* Any district which: (a) has undergone only token desegregation and where segregation remains a serious probem; (b) experienced serious problem in undergoing desegregation. (2) *Moderate Progress:* Any district which: (a) experienced minimal interracial violence in and around schools since 6 months after implementation of desegregation; (b) had no evidence of significant increases in dropouts or absenteeism; (c) is not currently involved in litigation concerning an inadequate plan to desegregate or refusal or failure to desegregate in accordance with a plan; (d) is considered by the National Association for the Advancement of Colored People, the Department of Health, Education, and Welfare, State human rights organizations, or other civil rights organizations, to have made moderate progress in desegregation. (3) *Substantial Progress:* Any district which meets the criteria for moderate progress and at least three of the following conditions: (a) minimal interracial violence during and since implementation of desegregation; (b) curriculum modifications that reflect mulitracial-multiethnic nature of the student body; (c) multiracial- multiethnic committee used to develop guidelines for discipline immediately before or since desegregation; (d) training provided teachers to prepare them for training in multiracial-multiethnic environment; (e) at least moderate integration of extracurricular acivities across racial-ethnic lines; (f) distribution of minority teachers within schools in approximately the same proportion as they are represented in the district as a whole; (g) little or no white flight as a result of desegregation. As a result, 18 districts were found to have made substantial progress, 8 moderate progress, and 3 little, if any, progress.

The Commission found that desegregation has been implemented smoothly without disruption in 27 of the communities. Of the 29 school districts analyzed, 9 were under court order; 11 desegregated under pressure from the Department of Health, Education, and Welfare or a State department of education; and 9 had voluntarily desegregated. The most frequent methods used to desegregate were reassignments and school closings. However, all districts used various combinations of reassignment, school closings, rezoning, pairing, grade structure reorganization, magnet schools, new construction, open enrollment, and clustering. [271]

School and Community Leadership

Active support and leadership from the school administration was found to be a factor in the desegregation process. In 26 of the 29 communities studied, the school administration supported desegregation and was instrumental in paving the way for the smooth implementation of desegregation in the community. Examples of positive superintendent actions include making public statements in support of desegregation, appointing human relations committees, and initiating activities and programs to facilitate the desegregation process.

School board support for desegregation is also important to effective implementation of desegregation. In more than half of the school districts, school boards supported desegregation. Advocacy from both the school administration and the school board was evident in 14 of the 29 communities.

Leadership from other community sources often made a valuable contribution to the desegregation process. In some communities various political, business, and religious leaders publicly supported school desegregation. In Greenville, Mississippi, for example, in the face of white opposition, the mayor, the chief of police, and members of the city council made public appeals for cooperation and calm during the desegregation process, and the business community mounted a campaign to sell desegregation to its opponents. Similarly, the business community in Nashville, Tennessee, advertised in support of peaceful desegregation. In Colorado Springs, Colorado, where community leaders did not actively support desegregation, a businessman said, "Desegregation has been as simple as changing to one-way streets—inconvenient but one of the least of our problems in this community."

Community Preparation

In 27 school districts special efforts were made to facilitate desegregation, including activities designed to inform the community on the progress of desegregation, to dispel rumors, to answer questions, to handle crises, and generally to smooth the way. In Tacoma, Washington, a summer counseling program made more than 1,500 home visits to provide parents and students an opportunity to consider options about new schools and voluntary transfers. In Newport News, Virginia, the superintendent established a hotline to respond to rumors and emphasized to school personnel the importance of accurately answering questions from parents and stu-

---

[271] For a definition of these and other desegregation techniques, see chap. III, sec., "Restructuring School Districts."

dents. Open houses, prior to opening day or during the first weeks of school, were held in Newport News, Virginia; Greenville, Mississippi; and Kirkwood, Missouri. Kirkwood developed a series of information sheets to inform and involve the community in the impending reorganization. Direct mail to parents explaining desegregation and soliciting cooperation was a project in Tempe, Arizona, and Greenville, Mississippi. Ice cream socials and orientation programs for incoming students were held in Racine, Wisconsin. Other districts mounted bumper sticker campaigns, promoted television discussion programs, and conducted speaker bureaus.

Quality of Education

School desegregation usually requires some revamping of a school system. Administrators often take this opportunity to make needed changes in curriculum, facilities, organization, and teaching methodology. Often the result is that the overall quality of education is improved.

In Kalamazoo, Michigan, the school administration began a systemwide revision of teaching methods to provide more individualized instruction and also developed an accountability model to measure student progress. In the Kirkwood R–7 School District, improvement of the educational program was one of the reasons given by the school administration for its reorganization which brought about desegregation. One of their endeavors was to initiate new teaching procedures. Team teaching was introduced in Santa Barbara and Greenville for a more individualized approach. In Ogden, Utah, the superintendent said, "Based on reading test scores there is evidence that our desegregation has had a noticeable [positive] effect on the quality of education."

Staff training is a vital aspect of a desegregation program when teachers are to be working with students of diverse cultures. Training was provided for teachers in 23 of the 29 districts studied. This training encompassed such factors as human relations, the diversity of a multicultural society, and retraining in academic areas. In Tempe, Arizona, 20 percent of the teachers received intensive training on the problems of minority students and the cultural differences among Anglo, Mexican American, and Yaqui Indian children. In Ogden, more than 80 percent of the faculty received intensive training in multicultural sensitivity and continue to receive training.

Twenty-three school systems made curriculum changes, which often included ethnic studies and bilingual education to meet the needs of a desegregated student body. In Tempe, however, the Mexican American and Yaqui Indian communities were critical of desegregation because bilingual-bicultural education was not provided for their children. In Providence, Rhode Island, a nongraded curriculum, innovative programs at two model schools, and a cross-cultural approach to social studies were introduced. The Erie, Pennsylvania, school district instituted minicourses to give students a greater variety of course offerings.

Bogalusa perhaps exemplifies the community where desegregation has not been successful because the administration failed to make an effort to succeed. School desegregation received no support from school administrators or from the white community. Very little effort was made to facilitate desegregation or prepare the community for acceptance of the plan. There were no curriculum changes. The white faculty was hostile and unprepared for the challenges of desegregation; black students have been the victims of continued classroom segregation. In the 7 years since desegregation, attitudes have not changed. There are still two teachers' unions, one white, one black; there are two proms, one white, one black; there is still classroom segregation. In Bogalusa, where the school and community failed to seize the initiative to prepare for a smooth transition, the quality of education offered all students has suffered.

Student Attitudes

In most of the 29 school districts, minority and white students are learning to live together harmoniously. Students in Nashville have said that the most important aspect of desegregation is that it brings a better understanding and appreciation of students of different races and backgrounds. Students in Raleigh County, West Virginia, and Williamsburg, South Carolina, expressed positive feelings about a desegregated education. They view it as an asset in a multiracial society. A white PTA president in Providence said, "The future looks good on the basis of the experience of a new generation which never attended anything but desegregated schools."

NATIONAL SURVEY

The objective of the national survey was to collect factual and attitudinal data on the recent desegregation experiences of a random sample of 1,292 school districts, 8.1 percent of the Nation's 16,032 districts, with nearly 70 percent of the Nation's minority students. These districts represent 47 percent of all school systems in the country which have enrollments of more than 1,500 students and are at least 5.0 percent minority. Usable responses were obtained from 993 school superintendents, or 77 percent of sampled school districts. [272]

Data from the questionnaires were merged with demographic data on the school districts which had been collected by the Office for Civil Rights of the Department of Health, Education, and Welfare. [273] Some of the following analyses deal only with information from Commission questionnaires, some with information from the Office for Civil Rights, and others with both sources.

Year of Desegregation

According to responses from superintendents, 612 or approximately two-thirds of the school districts have taken substantial steps to desegregate. Of these, 92 desegregated prior to 1966, but most (84 percent) have desegregated during the past decade, particularly

[272] Unusable responses to the superintendents' questionnaires were those which left 8 or more questions unanswered or did not indicate whether the district had taken steps to desegregate. Because of missing data on some questionnaires, the number of districts may vary from table to table. An attempt to sample opinion from others in the school districts yielded unreliably low levels of usable responses: only 23 percent of the heads of chambers of commerce, 35 percent of the NAACP chapter presidents, and 17 percent of the mayors or city managers produced usable questionnaires.

[273] Approximately 18 percent of the districts for which data are available in 1972 do not have comparable data for 1968. Those districts are not included in the analyses.

in the 4-year period 1968–71. (See table 2.4.) Of those that have desegregated, the courts were reported to be the most important impetus in 34 percent of the school districts; HEW, in 25 percent; and local pressures, in 41 percent. The courts and HEW played their most active roles during the period 1968–71, while over the last 4 years locally-initiated plans have assumed greater importance.

Desegregation by Region

Considerable variation exists among regions in the scope of desegregation efforts. Southern districts were most affected by desegregation, but desegregation occurred to a significant extent in other regions as well. As shown in table 2.5, only 5 percent of the 305 districts in the Southeast had not taken significant steps to desegregate. Approximately one-third of the districts in the Northeastern and North Central States, and 23 percent of those in the West, had taken significant steps to desegregate during the decade. Of the 196 incidents of desegregation achieved under court pressure, 141, or 72 percent, were in the southeastern region. (See map 2.2.) Despite recent publicity given court actions in Northern and Western States, the intervention of the courts has been concentrated in the Southern States; Commission data show that nearly half of those districts that desegregated were concentrated in Southern States.

Nature and Extent of Desegregation

To measure the extent to which desegregation was actually achieved within a school district, a previously developed index of segregation [274] was used to analyze changes over time. The data used to compute the index were provided by the Office for Civil Rights (HEW). The index ranges from zero (no segregation) to 1.0 (complete segregation). It measures the extent to which minority pupils are evenly distributed among the schools in a district. For instance, if the proportion of minority pupils is the same in every

Table 2.4 Districts that Desegregated, by Source of Intervention and Year of Greatest Desegregation

Time Period	Courts		HEW		State-Local		Total	
	No.	%	No.	%	No.	%	No.	%
1901–53	*	*	*	*	7	3	7	1
1954–65	13	6	18	12	53	21	84	13
1966–67	8	4	19	12	46	18	73	12
1968–69	53	26	42	28	34	13	129	21
1970–71	107	51	61	40	46	18	214	35
1972–73	12	6	5	3	38	15	55	9
1974–75	15	7	7	5	31	12	53	9
TOTAL	208	100	152	100	255	100	615	100

* None in Sample.

[274] See James S. Coleman, Sara D. Kelly, and John A. Moore, *Trends in School Segregation, 1968–73* (Washington, D.C.: The Urban Institute, 1975), p. 9.

school in the district, the index would be zero (no segregation). The more disparate the proportions of minority pupils are in the various schools, the higher the index will be; so that, if some schools have 100 percent minority enrollment and all the others have no minority enrollment, the index would be 1.0. If the index of segregation is below 0.20, the level of segregation may be described as relatively low. If the index of segregation is greater than 0.50, the degree of segregation in the district is substantial.

Table 2.5 Regional Distribution of Significant Steps to Desegregate School Districts, by Source of Intervention, for Districts Desegregated 1966–75

	Northeast		North Central		Border		Southeast		West S. Central		West		TOTAL	
	No.	%	No.	%	No.	%	No.	%	No.	%	No.	%	No.	%
Court-pressured	3	2	5	4	5	14	142	46	37	22	6	3	198	20
HEW-imposed	0	0	2	2	4	11	90	30	44	26	1	*	141	14
Locally-initiated	40	32	35	27	8	22	40	13	31	19	43	20	197	20
Significant steps prior to 1966	9	7	13	10	14	39	18	6	28	17	11	5	93	10
No significant steps	74	59	75	57	5	14	16	5	27	16	152	72	349	36
TOTAL	126	100	130	100	36	100	306	100	167	100	213	100	978	100

* Less than 0.5 percent

Map 2.2 **REGIONAL AREAS INCLUDED IN COMMISSION'S NATIONAL SURVEY**

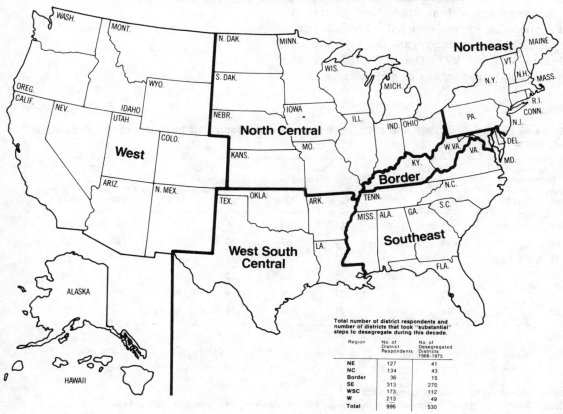

Total number of district respondents and number of districts that took "substantial" steps to desegregate during this decade.

Region	No. of District Respondents	No. of Desegregated Districts 1966-1975
NE	127	41
NC	134	43
Border	36	15
SE	313	270
WSC	173	112
W	213	49
Total	996	530

Table 2.6 shows the changes in the index of segregation from 1968 to 1972. In the 878 school districts for which complete data are available, the average index of segregation fell from 0.37 to 0.12 during the 4 years 1968 to 1972. For those districts that took substantial steps to desegregate, the average index reduced from 0.53 to 0.12. These sampled districts encompass 7,355,000 students. or 15 percent of the Nation's total student enrollment. Those 442 districts that experienced their major desegregation before 1966 or took no substantial steps to desegregate, according to the school superintendents, showed a reduction from 0.17 in 1968 to 0.11 in 1972. Of these districts, 30, or 7 percent, still had levels of segregation greater than 0.50 in 1972.

The changes were greatest in the Southern and Border States. According to school enrollment data provided by the Department of Health, Education, and Welfare, the index of segregation of the sampled school districts in the Southeastern States fell from 0.65 in 1968 to 0.09 in 1972. Among school districts desegregated during the decade, substantial reduction was also obtained in the North Central and Western States.

Nationwide, the reduction in the index of segregation was greatest in those districts where the impetus for desegregation came from the courts. Here the index dropped from 0.74 in 1968 to 0.15 in 1972. Districts subject to court order were those initially marked by a high degree of segregation. Thus, the imposition of court plans brought a fundamental change in the racial distribution of students within affected school systems between 1968 and 1972.

The remaining vestiges of public school segregation, according to 1972 data, appear to be concentrated in the school districts in larger cities; that is, those districts with an enrollment greater than 50,000. The index of segregation for the sampled school districts in these cities which reported steps to desegregate during the decade fell from 0.54 in 1968 to 0.27 in 1972. The index indicates that segregation in smaller cities and rural areas was greatly reduced.

Table 2.6 Average Index of Segregation, 1968 and 1972, by Region and by Source of Intervention, for School Districts Desegregated, 1966–75

Region	Court-Pressured 1968	1972	HEW-Imposed 1968	1972	Locally Initiated 1968	1972	Other District 1968	1972	Total 1968	1972
Northeast	.18	.07	*	*	.13	.09	.08	.07	.10	.08
North Central	.61	.35	.46	.23	.22	.17	.20	.21	.23	.20
Border	.27	.24	.46	.23	.07	.04	.12	.07	.17	.11
Southeast	.80	.12	.59	.07	.58	.10	.33	.06	.65	.09
West Southcentral	.76	.22	.52	.10	.39	.16	.19	.06	.45	.13
West	.39	.24	.58	.46	.21	.12	.15	.11	.17	.12
All Regions	.74	.15	.56	.08	.30	.12	.17	.11	.37	.12
Sample Size	173 Cases		137 Cases		184 Cases		384 Cases		878 Cases	

* None in Sample

1. Major source of intervention as perceived by school superintendents.
2. Districts that did not take "Substantial Steps" to desegregate during decade, or desegregated primarily before 1966.

White Withdrawal from Schools

There has been considerable controversy over the withdrawal of white children from the public schools as a response to school desegregation. By combining information from the Office for Civil Rights (HEW) on the proportion of white students in the school district and Commission survey data, it has been possible to examine the relationship between desegregation and the loss of whites from the public schools. Table 2.7 presents this data by showing the number of school districts desegregated over the decade,[275] the impetus for desegregation, the average percentage loss of white students, and the proportion of blacks enrolled in the district's schools. Between the years 1968 and 1972, the average percentage loss of white students from all 1,164 districts was 6 percentage points.

Very little variation is evident in the average reduction of proportion of white students between the districts that have desegregated and those that have not; or between those that have desegregated by court order, by HEW pressure, or by local initiative. These data, therefore, do not support the inference that there is a general relationship between desegregation and reduction in proportion of white students, or between desegregation by court order and such reductions. There was no significant difference between districts that desegregated under pressure from the courts and all districts in the sample.

The proportion of black students does appear to be related to the reduction in the percentage of white students. Between 1968 and 1972 districts which were greater than 40 percent black in 1968 experienced a reduction of 15 percentage points in the proportion of white students, a significantly greater loss than for districts with lower proportions of black enrollment. Among districts with equivalent proportions of minority enrollment, those that desegregated under pressure from the courts show no greater losses in white enrollment than other districts. Although these data do not exclude the possibility or even likelihood that many individual white families do withdraw their children from public schools when desegregation occurs or is expected to occur, those individual decisions are not of sufficient magnitude to create a pattern of specific association between desegregation and loss of white students.

Desegregation and Disruption

Superintendents of those school districts that desegregated during the last decade reported that the overwhelming majority (82 percent) desegregated without serious disruption.[276] Of the 96 respondents who indicated serious disruption, only 6 are outside Southern or Border States. Disruption was more likely to occur in those districts under court order than in those districts that took substantial steps without court order.

According to respondent superintendents in districts desegregated during the last decade, the extra assignment of police took place in

---

[275] Table 2.7 was also computed for those districts that desegregated during 1968–72 as well as 1968–70. The computations showed no significant departure from the figures presented in table 2.7 for those districts desegregated throughout the 10-year period.

[276] Serious disruption is defined as "serious disruptions of the educational process for a period greater than two weeks."

1 school district in every 15. Of the 34 districts in the sample that required extra assignment of police, 26 were in Southern and Border States. In only 10 districts did the additional police assignments exceed 2 months. In about half of the cases where police were assigned, the educational process was reported disrupted for a period exceeding 2 weeks.

Table 2.7 Number of Districts and Their Average Reduction in Proportion White 1968–72, by Source of Desegregation Intervention 1966–75, and by Proportion Black in 1968

Proportion Black Students in 1968		Court pressured	HEW pressured	Locally Initiated	Deseg. pre-1966	No Deseg.	No Response	All Districts
0–20% black	Average reduction	3%	3%	6%	3%	3%	3%	4%
	Number of districts	32	46	122	71	267	156	694
20–40% black	Average reduction	3%	1%	7%	+5%	5%	3%	3%
	Number of districts	52	58	42	9	15	72	248
40–100% black	Average reduction	14%	4%	25%	21%	28%	15%	15%
	Number of districts	89	32	20	4	15	55	215
All districts	Average reduction	9%	2%	8%	3%	5%	6%	6%
	Number of districts	173	136	184	84	297	283	1,157

Perceived Quality of Schools

School superintendents of the desegregated school districts reported positive attitudes toward schools and little change in the quality of education after desegregation. Among these superintendents, 75 percent saw no change in quality, 15 percent reported improvement, and only 10 percent reported deterioration. Seven percent described the quality of education as fair or poor, whereas 62 percent said it was good, and 31 percent considered it excellent.

Community Attitudes

During the years since the implementation of desegregation, superintendents reported a marked change in community attitudes toward school desegregation in most school districts. According to superintendents, while general opposition among white parents prevailed prior to desegregation, there is now widespread support. Of the desegregated districts, 20 percent of the superintendents reported that desegregation had the support of white parents and business leaders prior to implementation of desegregation. The support of these groups is now seen in over half of the districts. (See figures 2.1 and 2.2.) General support for desegregation by minority parents was reported in 79 percent of the desegregated districts.

Summary of Findings from Survey

The survey of school districts' experiences provides the following findings:

• *Extent of Desegregation*—Among school districts with enrollments in excess of 1,500 and 5 percent minority students, 54 percent took substantial steps to desegregate during the 1966–75 decade. The courts were described as the most important impetus for desegregation in 37 percent of the desegregated districts.

While desegregation was most concentrated in the South, substantial desegregation occurred in other parts of the country, affecting 33 percent of districts in the northeastern and north central regions.

• *Nature of Desegregation*—The districts that took substantial steps to desegregate showed major reductions in segregation, especially in those districts desegregated under court pressure. Courts were reported to act primarily when the degree of existing segregation was high.

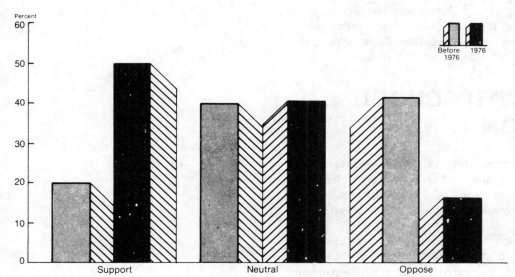

Figure 2.1—BUSINESS LEADERS: general response to school desegregation, just before desegregation and in 1976, in districts that desegregated 1966-75, as reported by school superintendents.

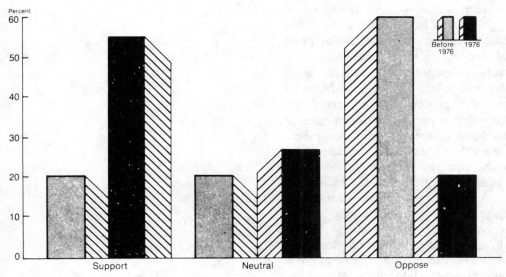

Figure 2.2—NONMINORITY PARENTS: general response to school desegregation, just before desegregation and in 1976, in districts that desegregated 1966-75, as reported by school superintendents.

• *Withdrawal of Whites*—While many school districts lost significant numbers of white students as shown by enrollment changes from 1968 to 1972, there are no significant differences between those districts that desegregate under pressure from the courts and HEW, and all districts in the country. The data do show that loss of white students is greater where black enrollments exceed 40 percent.

• *Disruption*—The overwhelming majority (82 percent) of school districts that desegregated are reported to have done so without serious disruption.

• *Community Acceptance*—A majority of school superintendents of the school districts desegregated during the last decade state that both white parents and minority parents generally support desegregation. Moreover, after desegregation there was a dramatic positive change in the attitudes of white parents.

EXPERIENCE WITH SCHOOL DESEGREGATION

The following section describes the various elements of the desegregation process, including the means by which it has been and is being brought about in hundreds of school districts, and the impact that it has on various important aspects of public education and community life generally.

Perhaps the most important ingredient in successful school desegregation is leadership, both at the community level and in the schools. The creation of one desegregated public school system involves substantial administrative and social change. The school board, school administrators, political leaders, police officials, religious and business groups, the media, and other public and private organizations can and must explain the law and insist that it will be enforced. They must also ensure that desegregation will be achieved through careful and thorough planning. The record shows that where such leadership exists, desegregation is more likely to be achieved with minimal difficulty. Where it is lacking, on the other hand, desegregation may be accompanied by confusion, anxiety, and perhaps disruption on the part of students or, more likely, parents.

As part of the planning for school desegregation, administrators should develop projects to involve and inform the community in all aspects of desegregation. Where such planning exists, school administrators have been able to develop support and acceptance of desegregation and bring the school and community into closer contact. In addition to examining the role of leadership in desegregation, this analysis also explores the changes often made in educational systems in order to make them serve the needs of all students. Desegregation usually involves a major review of the educational process. Such a review is certainly valuable in itself in that it leads to additional training of teachers and staff, revised curricula and textbooks, new instructional techniques, and improved physical conditions at many schools. In such ways, the quality of education is improved to benefit both white and minority children.

Another subject of concern to some is the technical or administrative feasibility of achieving desegregation. As the following section reveals, there are serious misconceptions about the role of pupil transportation in desegregation. The experiences of the school districts studied in connection with this report, however, make clear that the technical problems in achieving desegregation are far less formidable than previously believed.

Another subject examined here is faculty desegregation. In addition to the need to end the discrimination inherent in faculty segregation, minority administrators, faculty, and staff play a vital role in easing student adjustment to desegregation. Their understanding of the concerns of minority children is required at all levels of the educational structure, especially in view of the insensitivity which reduces the effectiveness of some white educators in desegregated schools. Such minority representation will strongly enhance the likelihood that school desegregation will be a positive experience for the entire community.

An examination of the school desegregation experiences of many school districts must also include a look at the extent of desegregation within schools and classrooms in ostensibly desegregated school systems. A problem common to many desegregated districts is resegregation within the classroom that may result from various student assignment practices. These practices and the need for and use of alternatives in many schools are described. Similarly, the techniques which many school districts have used to ensure uninterrupted opportunities for participation in desegregated extracurricular activities are illustrated.

Positive student attitudes clearly are important in assessing the success or failure of desegregation. The Commission has found in the past that desegregation often leads to more positive interracial attitudes and understanding among students. The Commission's latest research reaffirms the fact that students, particularly whites, continue to be more supportive of desegregation and busing than their parents.

Finally, the nature and scope of disciplinary problems in desegregated schools continues to be a subject about which there is much public misunderstanding. Many parents, minority and white, fear for their children's safety when threats or predictions of violence permeate the streets and schools prior to or during implementation of desegregation. In fact, there is far less racial conflict in desegregated schools than is commonly believed, and the scope of disruption in the schools, whatever its cause or nature, is often exaggerated. The problem of discrimination in disciplinary policy, however, is often acute, and this problem, not the myth of unrelieved turmoil and rampage, is the reality that must be dealt with for desegregation to be effective. As this discussion reveals, many school districts have provided human relations training for faculty and staff and have reviewed disciplinary codes and minority pupil suspension rates in order to ensure that student disciplinary policy is firm but fair.

Other factors also must be studied in assessing the national experience to date with school desegregation. For example, the increased degree of parental involvement in school affairs, as a direct result of the desegregation process, often helps to improve educational services in our public schools. Similarly, desegregation often leads to greater student involvement in such areas as a school's disciplinary policy and human relations programs.

The purpose of school desegregation is to provide equal educational opportunity for all students, a right guaranteed by the 14th amendment. While most Americans accept this human right in principle, many question whether school desegregation is necessary to achieve it. The evidence in such communities as Hillsborough County, Florida, Minneapolis, and Berkeley, for example, where desegregation has been in effect for some time, is that, contrary to the view that desegregation would be achieved at the expense of the white majority, desegregation has brought about changes which benefit everyone. Far from lowering the quality of education as some predict, desegregation has actually contributed to its improvement in many instances. Far from heightening racial tension and conflict, desegregation has contributed to improved interracial understanding and relations in most schools.

This report makes clear that although minority parents, teachers, and administrators frequently encounter obstacles to effective desegregation, even in ostensibly desegregated districts, the minority community remains the major impetus for desegregation. Most firmly believe that desegregation is indeed worth the effort, and they do not want to return to the segregated schools of the past. The Commission has found similar attitudes among many white parents, students, and educators in desegregated school districts.

School desegregation impacts at many different points in public education and community life. The experiences described here clearly indicate that, in the last analysis, whether that impact is generally beneficial or adverse depends in large measure upon the determination and the planning of school and community leaders. The Commission believes that the Nation's experience with school desegregation fully supports the conclusion of the principal at Little Rock's desegregated Central High School:

> ***we are moving in the right direction. The Constitution says it's right, and the quality of [our] democracy demands it***. There are frustrations and temporary setbacks***[but] we can have equity and quality. That's the goal, the principle. [1]

THE ROLE OF LEADERSHIP

The process of school desegregation is significantly affected by the support or opposition it receives from the local community's leadership. Across the Nation in the various school districts included in the Commission study, where officials and community leaders have given their support, the process of desegregating the schools has tended to go relatively smoothly. In these districts the community at large more readily accepted desegregation. Where civic leaders publicly oppose desegregation, however, they provide sanction to its opponents, who believe they have been given license to disobey the law and disrupt the community and its schools in protest.

As early as 1968 the Commission's study of school desegregation in Virginia found that effective desegregation had occurred where school officials had taken the position that Federal law must be

---

[1] John Egerton, *School Desegregation: A Report Card from the South* (Atlanta: Southern Regional Council, April 1976), p. 32.

obeyed and that desegregation could be accomplished.[2] More recently, the Commission has found further evidence to substantiate the importance of positive leadership in desegregation.

In its national survey, the Commission found that superintendents' responses in 532 school districts which had desegregated within the last 10 years showed that the level of opposition among local leaders just prior to implementation of desegregation was far greater in districts which reported serious disruptions of the educational process.[3] Of 411 districts where superintendents reported no serious disruptions on the issue of school desegregation, superintendents said:

- Business leaders were supportive or neutral in 65 percent.
- Political leaders were supportive or neutral in 67 percent.
- Religious leaders were supportive or neutral in 87 percent.

Of 95 districts which reported serious disruptions:

- Business leaders were supportive or neutral in 27 percent.
- Political leaders were supportive or in 30 percent.
- Religious leaders were supportive or neutral in 66 percent.

Superintendent and School Board

Affirmative leadership by school board members and superintendents is a critical factor for acceptance and peaceful implementation of desegregation. Individuals interviewed in 23 of 29 school districts in which case studies were conducted said that the superintendent's positive leadership had contributed to the smoothness with which desegregation was implemented. In 15 school districts, persons interviewed said the school board's support had a noticeable impact on the desegregation process. Support from superintendents and school boards included appointing human relations committees, making strong public statements in support of desegregation, and initiating activities or programs to facilitate desegregation.

According to school officials in Hillsborough County, the school board's decision not to appeal the 1971 court decision but to make every effort to comply was the first step toward successful desegregation.[4] In anticipation of the court order, the superintendent began developing a desegregation plan. The Hillsborough County School Board, recognizing the importance of involving the total community, set up a 156-member community desegregation task force. Businessmen, military personnel, students, parents, religious leaders, the media, as well as antibusing groups were represented on the task force. As a result, desegregation in Hillsborough County was implemented without violence or disruption.

In contrast, the Boston School Committee adamantly refused to take the affirmative steps necessary to desegregate Boston's public schools successfully. In a report on desegregation in Boston the Commission concluded that, "the effect of the Boston School Committee's statements, policy, and inaction was to foster within the

---

[2] U.S., Commission on Civil Rights, Virginia Advisory Committee, *The Federal Role in School Desegregation in Selected Virginia Districts* (1968), p. 5.

[3] It should be noted that there was opposition by leaders in districts which had no disruptions (e.g., in 35 percent of these districts, local business leaders were opposed to desegregation).

[4] U.S., Commission on Civil Rights, *School Desegregation in Ten Communities*) (1973), p. 20 (hereafter cited as *Ten Communities*).

community outright resistance to school desegregation."[5] The school superintendent also provided a minimum of guidance to the Boston school department.[6]

In Berkeley, Calfornia, which desegregated voluntarily in 1968, the board of education passed a resolution stating that desegregation was "absolutely their goal."[7] Asked what she considered the single most important factor in desegregation in Berkeley, a former school board member said, "I think it was the total community involvement under the leadership of both the board and the superintendent."[8]

Union Township, New Jersey, implemented an HEW-approved desegregation plan in 1969. Observers attribute its success to the school board's early unanimity, its ability to "stick to its guns," and the dedication and commitment of the superintendent of schools. Affirmative and determined leadership enabled the community to avoid most of the hysteria and blind resistance which troubled other school districts.[9] In Minneapolis, Minnesota, which desegregated in 1973, many residents believe that desegregation has been successful because of the consistent, positive approach taken by the school administration in informing and molding community support for the desegregation process.[10]

In Prince George's County, Maryland, which desegregated in the middle of the 1972–73 school year, the school board resisted to the very end, causing community polarization and dissension. In his final decree, Judge Frank Kaufman stated:

> ***the Prince George's County School Board has disregarded the mandates of the highest court of our land***the policy and practice apparently followed by a number of school board members of seeking at every stage and at every available moment, ever further delays, and of failing to exert affirmative leadership to effect required constitutional change, discourages further delay***.[11]

In Bogalusa, Louisiana, many school board members were opposed to any desegregation effort. Although the board directed the superintendent to develop a plan to comply with a court order, it made known its opposition and the fact that it was complying only because there was no alternative. A community representative cited the school board's attitude as most damaging to initial desegregation efforts because of its negative effect on the community.[12] In Greenville, Mississippi, on the other hand, leadership at all levels—school, community, business, and media—worked together to bring about desegregation in that community.[13]

In Charlotte-Mecklenburg, North Carolina, where court-ordered desegregation was implemented in 1970, the general view among

[5] U.S., Commission on Civil Rights, *Desegregating the Boston Schools: A Crisis in Civic Responsibility* (1975), p. viii (hereafter cited as *Crisis in Civic Responsibility*).
[6] Ibid., p. 66.
[7] Berkeley transcript, testimony of Carol Sibley, former school board member, p. A–47.
[8] Ibid., p. A–46.
[9] *Ten Communities*, p. 151.
[10] Minneapolis, Minn., Case Study, p. 25.
[11] U.S., Commission on Civil Rights, *A Long Day's Journey into Light: School Desegregation in Prince George's County* (1976), p. 343 (hereafter cited as *Long Day's Journey*); Vaughns v. Board of Education of Prince George's County, (355 F. Supp. 1038, 1063 (D. Md. 1972)).
[12] Bogalusa, La., Case Study, p. 24.
[13] Greenville, Miss., Case Study, pp. 6, 7.

those sympathetic to the plan is that the school board did not provide active support and there has been little support by leaders elsewhere in the city or county. To the extent the plan has worked, various individuals said, credit goes to the superintendent and his professional staff. In 1972 the Charlotte-Mecklenburg Community Relations Committee, after studying the causes of school disorders and community tensions, criticized the school board for its "interim" attitude and declared:

> ***our first and firmest attention should be turned from discontent with courts***to our schools and the way in which they educate our children. The Committee believes that leadership from the board of education and from others—elected and private civic leaders alike—will cause this community's parents to reaffirm their belief in good education. [14]

Pontiac, Michigan, desegregated in 1971–72 amidst turmoil and violence—10 school buses were bombed in the bus depot and buses carrying young children were attacked by mobs of adults. Community leaders in Pontiac criticized the board of education and top school administrators for their failure to exert affirmative leadership:

> The school board knew it was in the wrong, but refused to admit it, even after all court appeals had been exhausted; the board misled the public.

> The community would have been more cooperative if the superintendent had said, "We are desegregating because it is the right thing to do for the children." [15]

Political Leadership

Generally, local elected officials, other than school board members, have no direct authority over the public school system. However, their public response to a desegregation plan can have a positive or negative effect in a community where there is controversy. Where public officials actively support the desegregation process, the community generally directs its attention toward making the process work. Even where political leaders have actually opposed the specifics of a court order, the Commission has found that if they take a position of "obedience to the law," the result is a positive contribution to the desegregation process. This was true in a number of districts, including Springfield, Massachusetts; Newport News, Virginia; and Minneapolis, Minnesota.

Minoru Yasui, executive director of the Denver Commission on Community Relations, said:

> I think probably the greatest strength has been that in the City and County of Denver, both the administration and even those who oppose the specific court order have felt that obedience to the law is a very important and integral part of the community. I believe the city administration has always backed this kind of a stand, that if there is a law on the books, it should be obeyed by law-abiding citizens. [16]

Although no elected city officials in Denver made public statements in support of school desegregation, the mayor directed the

---

[14] *Ten Communities*, p. 109.
[15] Ibid., p. 66.
[16] Denver transcript, p. 197.

Denver Commission on Community Relations to "be involved in whatever was necessary to alleviate the tensions caused by school desegregation."[17]

In Boston the Commission found that public statements of the mayor during the school desegregation crisis confused the public and constituted a disservice to the rule of law.[18] Some of Mayor White's public statements included the following:

> We are all faced with the unpleasant task of implementing a court order.
>
> Compliance with law does not require acceptance of it; tolerance does not require endorsement of law.
>
> People who would boycott schools are asked to weigh the decision carefully, but it is their decision to make. Parents should attend open houses at schools before making final decision to send or not send students to school.[19]

Local and State politicans in Maryland as well as the district's Member of Congress made public statements on the anarchy and chaos that would accompany school desegregation in Prince George's County.[20] No leadership was exerted by most top county or State officials in behalf of compliance with the court order, and the community divided on the issue of desegregation.[21]

In contrast, officials in Tampa and Hillsborough County took a neutral position on school desegregation and credited the school board with the successful implementation of desegregation. Richard Greco, former mayor, said: "It was their responsibility. It was a tough problem. They got in there and did their job and I think that you would have to say that the city, the county, and everyone else was somewhat neutral***because it wasn't our realm of responsibility."[22] Local officials agreed that the political community refrained from making the desegregation issue a political football.

In Louisville the desegregation issue did become a political football. The Governor of Kentucky, the mayor of Louisville, and the Jefferson County judge testified against court-ordered desegregation during the Senate Judiciary Committee hearings prior to the 1975 election. In the wake of violence in Louisville, an editorial in *The State Journal* addressed the leadership problem:

> Both the Governor and Jefferson County Judge Todd Hollenbach, while strongly stating their intentions to restore order in the city, appeared determined to let everyone know how much they oppose court-ordered busing***if the Governor keeps saying how bad busing is, throwing a brick at a police car can be seen by emotion-laden minds as doing the Governor's business.[23]

The Jefferson County school system is about to enter its second year of desegregation. Asked if he has taken steps to bring the community together for better implementation of the court order, Coun-

---

[17] Ibid., p. 188.
[18] *Crisis in Civic Responsibility*, p. 29.
[19] Boston, Mass., Office of the Mayor, press release, Sept. 9, 1975.
[20] *Long Day's Journey*, p. 373.
[21] Ibid.
[22] Tampa transcript, p. 201.
[23] *The State Journal* (Frankfort, Ky.), Sept. 7, 1975, p. 4.

ty Judge Louis J. Hollenbach testified that he and Mayor Harvey Sloane have appeared before many groups to focus attention on alternatives to busing and have submitted these alternatives to the school board. The alternatives are not within the scope of the existing court order.[24] Thus, it appears that the chief executives of Louisville and Jefferson County will continue to undermine the letter and the spirit of the law with respect to school desegregation in the Louisville community.

Law Enforcement

Law enforcement agencies, as part of local government, often reflect the position of local officials. Consequently, if elected officials are committed to peaceful implementation of desegregation, law enforcement agencies respond accordingly.

Following the Denver court order in the spring of 1974, the police department began contingency planning for the possibility of violence or disorder. Police officials met with school officials to discuss potential problems during the remainder of the school year and in the fall. The chief of police testified:

> ***we felt that at one of our high schools we might have a problem***. We enabled the officers***to go to that school***to determine if there were any possibilities. We did have alert circumstances, not uniform cars, in the area, but available with helicopter surveillance***no problems came out.[25]

The Hillsborough County Sheriff's Department and the Tampa Police Department were involved in a workshop sponsored by the school administration to "let us in law enforcement know what the plan was to be." Sheriff Malcolm Beard said, "We were prepared for any problem that might arise***. We had no problems."[26] Both the sheriff and the chief of police said their departments maintained a very low profile although they were well prepared: "We had some areas where we thought***a problem might occur, and we had manpower there, but they were not conspicuous. They were not on the scene***but they were available."[27]

Law enforcement decisions made by Boston officials clearly influenced the course of events.[28] Although the police had prior information that resistance to desegregation would be massive in certain areas of the city, they neglected to provide adequate police presence in those areas. As a result, massive civil disorder occurred, leading the mayor to announce shortly after the opening of school that the city could not maintain public safety.

With tension at a peak and the potential for violence running high, Memphis schools opened in 1972–73 on a desegregated basis with no serious incidents or arrests.[29] This occurred despite opposition by the mayor and the city council and a national antibusing

---

[24] Louisville transcript, testimony of Jefferson County Judge Todd Hollenbach, pp. 474–76.
[25] Denver transcript, testimony of Art Dill, p. 191.
[26] Tampa transcript, p. 175.
[27] Ibid., p. 176.
[28] *Crisis in Civic Responsibility*, p. 29. See also, James F. Fisk and Raymond T. Galvin, "A Consultant Report on the Boston Police Department During the 1974–75 School Desegregation," draft report to the U.S. Commission on Civil Rights, June 30, 1975.
[29] John Egerton, *Promise of Progress, Memphis School Desegregation, 1972–1973* (Atlanta: Southern Regional Council, 1973).

rally in Memphis the weekend before school opened. The director of police made it clear that the police would enforce the court order:

> When the date for busing arrived, we wanted it done in a normal environment—no force, no strong-arm tactics, no sea of uniforms. We were totally mobilized and ready, but we were in the background, not in the schools or on the buses***. We were candid about what we would do, but we didn't want anybody but the school people involved in the actual movement of children. I know we've got some men with deep racial bias, but a real professional has to subordinate his personal feeling to his duty.[30]

Business, Religious, and Organizational Leadership

In many school districts affirmative leadership by members of business, religious, and social service organizations has contributed immeasurably to community acceptance of desegregation.

The Chamber of Commerce in Memphis made peaceful implementation of the court order its highest priority and helped form IMPACT—Involved Memphis Parents Assisting Children and Teachers. It also used its own public relations firm to enlist support. The executive director of the chamber said, "It had to be done. We don't want this town to go down the drain."[31] One community leader said of the leadership coalition of the chamber, the school system, the black community, and IMPACT:

> When a city's power structure makes up its mind to face up to an issue like desegregation, it can do it—and do it in an impressive and encouraging way. Even though officials of the local, State and Federal governments did all they could to stop busing, there were enough people here who wanted to do the right thing and they did it***and the result was a victory for Memphis.[32]

The Greater Tampa Chamber of Commerce endorsed desegregation of the schools. Its executive vice president said, "If the chamber endorses it***we represent about 4,000 business firms and individuals—I think it has a good bit to do with how the community responds."[33]

In Greenville, Mississippi, the business leadership reportedly raised $10,000 from private sources for a professional public relations firm to publicize school desegregation.[34]

On the other hand, the Louisville Chamber of Commerce has moved from a public position of support for the peaceful implementation of court-ordered desegregation to one of opposition to court-ordered busing.[35] The reversal, precipitated by community opposition and intimidation of small businesses by antibusing elements, fueled the discontent and disobedience.

There was considerable support for school desegregation from the Denver clergy. Ecumenical prayer services were held, and the

[30] Ibid., p. 13.
[31] Ibid., p. 8.
[32] Ibid., p. 23.
[33] Tampa transcript, testimony of W. Scott Christopher, pp. 72, 73.
[34] Greenville, Miss., Case Study, p. 6.
[35] Staff Investigation Summary, Louisville and Jefferson County, pp. 28–36.

Council of Churches and its Clergy Committee for Reconciliation spoke out in favor of peaceful implementation of the plan. Both the United Methodist Church and the Roman Catholic Church officially communicated their support for school desegregation to their clergy. [36] In addition, the Roman Catholic Church in Denver, as well as in Louisville, Tampa, Boston, and other communities, issued directives forbidding the use of Catholic schools as a haven for whites trying to avoid desegregation. [37]

A coalition of 49 Denver community organizations, PLUS (People Let's Unite for Schools), worked to involve the entire community in the desegregation process.

The Media

Media coverage of school desegregation has an enormous impact upon local and national opinions and perceptions. Consequently, many school districts have attempted to work closely with the news media. In Denver the court-appointed monitoring committee met with media executives to ask their cooperation in presenting the positive side of desegregation. A committee member said:

> ***I think that both of the newspapers have, in general, done a good job of this***. They have reported the facts, they have traced down rumors before putting them on the front page. [38]

Local newspapers in Memphis reportedly did a "superlative" job of covering school desegregation and took editorial positions favoring peaceful implementation of the court order. [39] Many people felt, however, that national coverage was misleading and had a negative effect on the city. [40] In Corpus Christi, Texas, the local media were strong advocates of desegregation, in particular, the *Corpus Christi Caller-Times* which won a Texas Associated Press Managing Editors' award. [41]

The Boston Community Media Council (BCMC), a biracial organization of print and broadcast news management personnel, made a constructive effort to plan the local media's role during Phase I of Boston's desegregation effort. [42] The council held training sessions:

> The briefings at times emphasized the obvious: the importance of checking out rumors and tips; the need to be inconspicuous and to stand back from any outbreaks to avoid the appearance of encouraging them. The television people weighed the use of film reports***to provide an overall sense of perspective***the newspaper people stressed the importance of avoiding code words or inflammatory descriptions ("cruel," "savage," or "brutal") in their copy. [43]

The *Boston Globe* was awarded the Pulitzer Prize in 1975 for its coverage of the school desegregation crisis. The local media later

[36] Denver transcript, testimony of Bishop Melvin Wheatly, United Methodist Church of Denver, p. 119–20, and Bishop George Evans, vicar of urban affairs, Roman Catholic Archdiocese of Denver, pp. 121–22.

[37] Ibid., p. 122.

[38] Denver transcript, testimony of Lorie Young, p. 740.

[39] Egerton, *Promise of Progress*, p. 11.

[40] Ibid., pp. 15–16.

[41] Corpus Christi, Tex., Case Study, p. 88.

[42] *Crisis in Civic Responsibility*, p. 200.

[43] Ibid., pp. 201–2.

abandoned the BCMC "plan" and each pursued an independent course of action. National media coverage, particularly of incidents of violence during the fall of 1974, engendered widespread feeling in Boston that reporting had been sensationalized and thereby distorted. [44]

According to community leaders in Dorchester County, Maryland, the media coverage of desegregation was negative and served to exacerbate the problems. In 1970 the superintendent, who was opposed to desegregation, wrote to the Department of Health, Education, and Welfare, criticizing *Dorchester News* stories as unethical. [45] The *Delta Democrat Times* in Greenville, Mississippi, was praised for keeping the community informed and for its positive response to desegregation. [46]

The media in Louisville was severely criticized by some community leaders. Dr. Lois Cronholm, director of the Louisville-Jefferson County Human Relations Commission, said:

> I think the news media produced a picture in this community that the great majority of the people, 90 percent or more***were opposed to busing. It became the expectation for most of our citizens to oppose busing because they really believed that not to oppose busing would have meant to have gone against what appeared to be the overwhelming moral current of opinion. From this standpoint I would criticize the news media. [47]

Galen Martin, director of the Kentucky Commission on Human Relations, testified that the media misled the community through its overuse of slogans and its "glamorization of the hate group leaders." He said:

> We have had more than 12 court orders for desegregation. But this is the first time***that the media have ever described it as court-ordered forced busing across racial lines to achieve balance***. [48]

There was also testimony that the media had failed in its responsibility to inform the public on the reasons for desegregation:

> [It] failed to tell white people about the brutality of segregation, how bad the schools were so that they see a little busing is better than the defects of segregation. [49]

Although the leading newspapers endorsed busing for desegregation and advocated peaceful implementation, a leading television station editorialized for a constitutional amendment or other alternatives to busing. The *Courier-Journal* printed an editorial on the responsibility of the media during desegregation:

> The most sensitive issue the news media in this community has had to handle in many, many years is that of school desegregation***.

[44] Ibid., pp. 202–3.
[45] Dorchester County, Md., Case Study, p. 19.
[46] Greenville, Miss., Case Study, p. 7, 15.
[47] Louisville transcript, testimony of Lois Cronholm, director, Louisville-Jefferson County Human Relations Commission, p. 375.
[48] Ibid., testimony of Galen Martin, director, Kentucky Commission on Human Relations, pp. 376–77.
[49] Ibid., p. 377.

On this issue we all bear an extra burden of accuracy—to publish or broadcast facts rather than unsubstantiated rumor. The way the community copes with integration this fall may well reflect the responsibility with which news organizations have kept people informed. Unreliable reporting damages the community***.[50]

The *Courier Journal* and WHAS-TV in Louisville won national Sigma Delta Chi awards for their coverage of desegregation.

In summary, where public and private leaders publicly supported the peaceful implementation of school desegregation, whether court-ordered or voluntary and irrespective of the mechanics used, the process tended to proceed smoothly and more effectively than in districts where such support was lacking. Affirmative leadership is crucial to the achievement of school desegregation in a community. Such leadership is most important in school districts where there is opposition because undisciplined opposition can lead to community disruption and violence. In periods immediately before and after implementation of desegregation, when apprehension is often widespread, local leaders must reassure the community that desegregation can and will be accomplished peacefully and successfully. Without commitment from the top, the task of desegregating is made more difficult.

PREPARATION OF THE COMMUNITY

Many school districts undertake a variety of activities to involve and educate the community, particularly parents, prior to school desegregation. The purpose is to engender acceptance and support for school desegregation and create an atmosphere of cooperation and comradeship between school and community.

Leadership for these activities may come from the school administration,[51] from community organizations,[52] or from principals of individual schools.[53] Often with the assistance of local parent teacher organizations, individual schools have been able to desegregate peacefully and smoothly, even when they are part of a school system otherwise marked by disruptions.[54]

A vital part of these activities is to keep the community thoroughly informed. A Greenville, Mississippi, school administrator reported that the school district had sponsored a television program explaining the desegregation plan so there would be "no surprises."[55] Information was notably absent in Phase I of the Boston school desegregation process.[56] This contributed to "confusion, duplication of effort, and inaction."[57]

Involving the Community

Community preparation has been handled in several ways and at different stages of the school desegregation process. In Hillsborough

---

[50] "The Burden of Responsibility," *Courier-Journal,* Aug. 6, 1975.

[51] See, for example, Minneapolis Case Study, p. 17; also, Tampa transcript, testimony of E.L. Bing, assistant superintendent for supportive services, Hillsborough County School District, p. 38.

[52] See, for example, testimony of Rev. Richard Kerr, chairman, People Let's Unite for Schools, Denver transcript, pp. 106–11.

[53] *Crisis in Civic Responsibility*, p. 80.

[54] Ibid., pp. 85–86.

[55] Greenville, Miss., Case Study, p. 13.

[56] *Crisis in Civic Responsibility*, Finding No. 13, p. 53.

[57] Ibid., Finding No. 21, p. 73.

County (Tampa), the school administration sought citizen involvement in the initial development of the plan:

> It was our feeling at that time since the schools belong to the people that the people should help resolve the problems. So it was part of the format or strategy for coming up with the plan to get some community involvement. [58]

Immediately following the 1971 court order, [59] school administrators organized a 156-member citizens' committee, the Hillsborough County Citizens Desegregation Committee, which included black and white leaders and opponents as well as advocates of school desegregation. This committee reviewed plans and options that had been developed by 20 school administrators and 5 lay persons under the direction of E.L. Bing, who is now assistant school superintendent for supportive services. All meetings of the committee were open, and newspaper and radio advertisements strongly urged the public to attend. [60] The press was present at all sessions and reported on all the proceedings. Broad involvement of the community and the media was cited by school administrators and private citizens as a major factor in the acceptance of school desegregation in Tampa. [61] Because a large segment of the community helped develop the plan, they had an investment in its outcome.

In other places, school administrations have not directly involved the community in the development of a plan, but have provided opportunities for participation at strategic points in the desegregation process and have sought to keep the community informed.

In Minneapolis, prior to desegregation, the board of education held several open meetings and a public hearing to explain its plan. After adoption, the board held nearly 100 meetings to provide further explanation. [62] By the time implementation began, the community had been assured that desegregation would be educationally beneficial. [63]

Community education was a basic component of the school desegregation plan developed in Kalamazoo, Michigan. Large public hearings were held for presentation of the plan and for citizen input. [64] The plan also included an information center staffed by community volunteers. [65]

Information and Rumor Control Centers

Information and rumor control centers have been established by numerous school systems in the process of desegregating. [66] Such centers generally begin operating a few months before school desegregation begins and continue for the first year or two of school desegregation. [67] Dependent mostly on the telephone, these centers have been effective tools for keeping the community informed and providing a readily accessible line of communication. Parents have

---

[58] Tampa transcript. Bing testimony. p. 38.
[59] Mannings v. Board of Public Instruction of Hillsborough County, Florida, 277 F.2d 370 (5th Cir. 1960).
[60] Tampa transcript. Bing testimony. p. 46.
[61] Prehearing interviews. Jan. 12, to Mar. 26, 1976. Commission files.
[62] Minneapolis, Minn., Case Study. p. 17.
[63] Ibid., p. 21.
[64] Kalamazoo, Mich., Case Study. p. 4.
[65] Ibid., p. 7.
[66] See, for example, *Long Day's Journey*, p. 354; Berkeley transcript, testimony of Ramona Maples, p. A-90.
[67] Harold Clark, general area director, Hillsborough County schools, interview in Tampa, Jan. 16, 1976.

been able to learn about curriculum changes, school hours, and bus routes and to clarify rumors. School administrators often use community volunteers, especially parents, to staff the centers. Private citizens have proved to be highly credible in relaying first-hand information to other citizens.[68]

In Tampa, rumors were investigated by human relations counselors in the schools and the results were reported back to callers.[69] Charles Vacher, former supervisor of the Tampa rumor control center, emphasized its importance:

> I think personally***that a desegregation process couldn't occur without it. You just have to sit and answer call after call from the concerned people***. I feel certain that it was a wonderful asset to Hillsborough County at that time.[70]

Mr. Vacher said that the center received 200 to 300 telephone calls a day from the preregistration period through the first few weeks of school.[71]

A similar center operated during the early stages of desegregation in Berkeley, California:

> ***[The] rumor clinic was to function for the community, to trace down every rumor that had to do with fears of desegregation***. [T]his rumor clinic was a catalyst to sort out the fears that had been openly expressed at many of the hearings that we had prior to adoption of the plan.[72]

In Boston, a black community organization, Freedom House Institute on Schools and Education, was "instrumental in setting up a [neighborhood] Rumor Control and Information Center, which was directly hooked into the Boston School Department and also to the Information Center located in City Hall."[73] Staffed by volunteers from various community agencies, the center was established because of rumors of violence and hostile receptions of black children at their "new" schools.[74]

Local School Activities

In addition to communitywide preparations, some school districts have provided parents with opportunities to become familiar with specific aspects of desegregation.[75] Parents were able to visit their child's "new" school,[76] experience a bus ride,[77] meet parents of transferring students,[78] and meet school personnel.[79] Other activities have included ice cream socials, picnics, coffee klatches, door-to-door home visits, and sensitivity sessions. Community organizations often give support and assistance to these endeavors.

---

[68] Fred Crawford, equal opportunity specialist, Community Relations Service, U.S. Department of Justice, interview in Tampa, Mar. 1, 1976.
[69] Tampa transcript, p. 399.
[70] Ibid., p. 400.
[71] Ibid., p. 399.
[72] Berkeley transcript, testimony of Ramona Maples, p. A–90.
[73] Boston transcript, testimony of Ellen Jackson, director, Freedom House Institute on Schools and Education, p. 212.
[74] Ibid., pp. 212–13.
[75] See, for example, U.S. Commission on Civil Rights, *The Diminishing Barrier: A Report on School Desegregation in Nine Communities* (1972), p. 46 (hereafter cited as *Diminishing Barrier*); Springfield, Mass., Case Study, p. 11.
[76] Ossining, N.Y., Case Study, p. 9.
[77] Berkeley, Calif., Case Study, p. 18.
[78] Denver transcript, testimony of Mary Ann McClain, p. 906.
[79] Ibid., testimony of Nancy Widmann, p. 961.

In Springfield, Massachusetts, the Bi-Racial Quality Integrated Education Committee helped with orientation programs at the "sending" and "receiving" schools. These programs generally consisted of building tours, explanation of curriculum, and discussion of parental concerns and questions.[80] In Louisville individual schools held orientation nights. Teachers were present to talk to parents and students about the curriculum and to allay fears and anxieties.[81] Nancy Jordan, a Denver parent, stressed the importance of this type of parent orientation: "For any other school district that plans to desegregate, I think this is absolutely crucial to get the parents together with the people who are going to be dealing with their children."[82]

Some school districts have responded to anxieties about desegregation by integrating parents into school operations. In Charlotte, North Carolina, the parent teacher association obtained Federal funds to hire a coordinator who solicited assistance from parents in tutorial positions.[83] By working in the schools, parents were able to see first hand that school desegregation was proceeding smoothly and their children were safe.[84] Parent volunteers in many school districts have continued to provide assistance during the school year in various paraprofessional and volunteer positions.[85]

A Boston parent, Jane Margulis, commented at the Commission hearing:

> ***I was born and brought up in Boston, but had very little to do with black people all my life; had always gone to segregated schools. And it was very frightening for me to think that I would be putting them on a bus and [sending them] to the black community which I knew nothing about***
>
> Well, I thought I had to make myself comfortable in order to make them feel comfortable about the change. The first thing I did was start working in my middle daughter's school*** [86]

Although Boston's central school administration did not provide leadership to prepare the community or parents for school desegregation, some individual school principals did involve their communities. They were able to win parents' acceptance and achieve integration in a way that made a significant contribution to the educational growth and development of their students.[87]

Leadership from Community Organizations

Although data collected by the Commission suggest that in most instances school superintendents and their staffs provided the strongest leadership in preparing communities for school desegregation, community organizations have also played positive roles in many school districts.[88] The Memphis Chamber of Commerce was instru-

[80] Springfield, Mass., Case Study, p. 11.

[81] Louisville transcript, testimony of Joseph McPherson, principal, Central High School, pp. 604–05.

[82] Denver transcript, p. 800.

[83] Title VII of the Education Amendments of 1972 provides funds for implementation of voluntary and court-ordered desegregation plans in schools. 20 U.S.C. §1601 et seq. (Supp. II 1972).

[84] Egerton, Report Card from the South, p. 18.

[85] Ten Communities, p. 163; Diminishing Barrier, p. 7.

[86] Boston transcript, pp. 251–52.

[87] Crisis in Civic Responsibility, p. vi.

[88] See, for example, Ossining, N.Y., Case Study, p. 13; Long Day's Journey, p. 336; Egerton, Promise of Progress, pp. 8–9.

mental in forming an organization, Involved Memphis Parents Assisting Children and Teachers (IMPACT), which sponsored a telephone rumor control system, newspaper and television advertisements supporting school desegregation, a speakers bureau, neighborhood meetings, and factsheets explaining the desegregation plan.[89] In Denver, two organizations, People Let's Unite for Schools (PLUS) and the Community Education Council (CEC), engaged in a variety of activities to involve and inform the community.[90] PLUS, a coalition of more than 40 organizations, operated a rumor control clinic; created a public education task force which developed a pamphlet explaining the court order[91] and the history of the case; established a speaker's bureau staffed by persons knowledgeable about the court order; and provided a forum for communication between parents, students, and teachers of the sending and receiving schools.[92]

Denver's Community Education Council, established by the court, consists of a cross-section of prominent citizens who coordinated the actions of a number of agencies involved in desegregation. The council also provided the community with factual information about the court order and served as a communication channel between the community and the schools. Council members continue to monitor implementation of the order.[93]

Ongoing Involvement

While the high level of communication established between the school and community during the early stages of desegregation tends to decrease after the school desegregation plan is implemented, many school districts continue to sponsor community-school activities throughout the first few years. Parent volunteers in some school districts have become a part of regular school operations, and local community organizations have continued to sponsor human relations activities.[94] Through such programs parental involvement in school districts often increased, bringing the home and the school in closer contact.

William Coker, a Denver parent, commented at the Commission's hearing:

> The level of parent involvement has certainly improved since integration***was implemented. It has tripled or quadrupled***resulting in, I think, a very excellent organization that, in my opinion, has done a tremendous job, not only in the Manual [High School] community, but extending as far as the southwest and southeast sections of the city.[95]

At the Tampa hearing, elementary school principal Dora Reeder also spoke of the increase in parent participation:

> ***before integration I had such a hard time getting PTA going and getting parent involvement***

> We do have more parent participation than we have ever had. Our teachers don't have to worry about the class parties and

[89]*Promise of Progress*, pp. 8–9.
[90]Denver transcript, testimony of Richard Kerr, p. 109; testimony of Maurice Mitchell, p. 71.
[91]Keyes v. School District No. 1, Denver, Colorado, 413 U.S. 189 (1973).
[92]Denver transcript, p. 109.
[93]Ibid., pp. 71-72.
[94]Ibid., p. 962. A parent organization in Denver, for example, sponsors monthly programs at individual schools which consist of a number of cultural exchange activities.
[95]Ibid., p. 795. Reference is made to The East and Manual Supporters (TEAMS), an active parent organization that assisted in the implementation of desegregation at those high schools.

all of the field trips and all the other things that parents get involved in***.[96]

Some school districts have more formal ongoing vehicles for community involvement which are often created by court orders. In
Louisville, a citizens' advisory committee was established by the
school administration to provide a forum for expression of
problems, concerns, and suggestions pertaining to school
desegregation.[97] However, the effectiveness of the committee has
been questioned by community leaders because it has no real
authority. A hearing witness stated that he felt an "essential ingredient" for such a committee was a "formal charge from the
Federal court" with specific responsibilities.[98] In Denver, as previously mentioned, the court-created Community Education Council
is responsible for continuous monitoring of the school desegregation
process. This results in regular observation of the school environment by community volunteers.[99] The Bi-Racial Advisory Committee to the Hillsborough County School Board also provides a line
of communication between the community and the school board.[100]
Although the responsibilities of these court-mandated committees
often have needed clarification,[101] they have provided the
"community" with an effective means of communication and helped
maintain community involvement in the ongoing school desegregation process.

With planning and ingenuity, school administrators have engendered community support and acceptance of school desegregation
and brought the community, home, and school in closer contact.

RESTRUCTURING OF SCHOOL DISTRICTS

An essential part of desegregation is the restructuring of school
districts, including changes in school attendance zones and grade
levels. This restructuring is accomplished in a number of ways
which include establishing satellite attendance areas, pairing and
clustering, grade-locking, establishing magnet schools, building new
schools, and closing schools.[102]

Restructuring often requires additional busing of students, but the
increase is substantially less than is popularly believed. Nationally,
slightly more than 50 percent of all school children are bused to
school, and of this percentage less than 7 percent are bused for the
purpose of school desegregation.[103] In fact, of the total number of

[96] Tampa transcript, pp. 656–57.

[97] Louisville transcript, testimony of Ernest C. Grayson, superintendent, Jefferson County Board
of Education, pp. 770–73.

[98] Ibid., testimony of Rev. Thomas Quigley, director, Louisville Area Interchurch Organization for
Service (LAIOS), p. 562.

[99] Denver transcript, p. 75.

[100] Tampa transcript, testimony of Stephen Sessums, former chairman of the Bi-Racial Advisory
Committee, p. 438. This committee, created by court order, serves in an advisory capacity in
three areas: the selection of school construction sites, the establishment of boundary lines, and
application for transfers from assigned schools.

[101] Ibid., testimony of Joanna Jones, member of the Bi-Racial Advisory Committee, p. 804.

[102] Satellite attendance zones are attendance areas that are geographically noncontiguous to the
school. Pairing or grouping of schools is achieved when attendance areas of two or more schools
are merged so that each serves different grade levels for a new larger attendance area. Clustering
is similar to the process of pairing but usually involves more schools. Grade-locking refers to the
establishment of one- or two-grade centers, for example, a school which serves only sixth graders
or sixth and seventh graders. A magnet school ranges from a full-time school with special
academic programs to a center with programs which supplement basic academic skills taught in
the regular classroom. In the South the black schools were frequently closed because of the inadequacy of the facilities.

[103] U.S., Department of Health, Education, and Welfare, National Institute of Education, Summary of Statistics on School Desegregation Issues, April 1976, pp. 1, 2.

children attending public school, only 3.6 percent are bused for school desegregation purposes. During the 1973–74 school year, $57 billion was spent for public education, and $1.858 billion of that total was spent for student transportation. Only $129 million of these transportation funds were used to achieve desegregation. [104]

Indeed, busing is not a new phenomenon in American education. As early as 1869, the State of Massachusetts enacted the first pupil transportation law. [105] Today 48 States provide student transportation, and 15 States provide it to private schools at public expense. [106] The use of pupil transportation was predicated upon providing educational opportunities not available at the neighborhood school, combined with a concern for safety. [107] While modern opponents of busing often cite safety as an argument against it, the data show that "students walking to school are three times more likely to be involved in an accident than those going to school by bus." [108]

On the average, 30 percent of the students in desegregated school districts, surveyed in the Commission's national study, were reassigned at the time of school desegregation. However, the average percentage of minority students bused increased 9 percent, from 47.1 percent to 55.9 percent. The average percentage of majority students bused increased from 50.0 percent to 53.2 percent, or about 3 percent. [109]

Analysis of the 29 case studies reveals that the number of students bused increased in 25, decreased in 1, and remained the same in 3. Furthermore, in 9 of the 25 districts, the increase was less than 12 percent and in none was the increase over 50 percent. [110] The burden of busing in 21 of the districts is disproportionately borne by minority students, in 3 by majority students, and in 5 is evenly balanced. [111] In addition, the percentage of the budget spent on busing increased less than 2 percent in the majority of the school districts and decreased in two. [112]

In Minneapolis, Minnesota, the school desegregation plan—which included wider attendance zones, clustering and pairing, and a pilot program of learning centers similar to magnet schools—balanced the proportion bused between minority and majority students. [113] The average bus ride before and after school desegregation was less than 20 minutes. [114] Roughly half of the district's 54,000 pupils are bused and of these 27,000, 11,000 are bused for desegregation purposes. [115] School desegregation in Ossining, New York, was accomplished by rezoning attendance areas and closing an elementary school in deteriorated condition. [116] The average bus ride remained

[104] The figure $129 million was compiled by multiplying the number of pupils bused for school desegregation purposes times the per pupil transportation cost. U.S. Department of Health, Education, and Welfare, National Center for Educational Statistics, 1973–74.
[105] Marian Wright Edelman, "Winson and Dovie Hudson's Dream," *Harvard Educational Review,* vol. 45, no. 4 (1975), p. 445.
[106] Ibid., pp. 444–445.
[107] Ibid., p. 445.
[108] U.S., Department of Health, Education, and Welfare, National Institute of Education, Statistics on Selected Desegregation Issues, April 1976, p. 2.
[109] Reassignment data were compiled from 491 school districts and busing data from approximately 250. U.S., Commission on Civil Rights, national survey data, 1976.
[110] The percentage increase ranged from 3.4 to 50. State Advisory Committee Case Study, Characteristic Profile Summary.
[111] Ibid.
[112] Data compiled from case study factsheets for each district.
[113] Minneapolis, Minn., Case Study, p. 11; Characteristic Profile, p. 213.
[114] Ibid., p. 14.
[115] Ibid., p. 15.
[116] Ossining, N.Y., Case Study, p. 5; Case Study Factsheet: Ossining, N.Y.

approximately 30 minutes and only an additional 6.6 percent of the students are bused.[117] There was an increase of only 1 percent of students bused in Erie, Pennsylvania, and the percentage of the budget used for busing remained the same, 2.3 percent.[118] The desegregation plan included closing three old school buildings, pairing, and rezoning attendance lines.[119] Similarly, in Ogden, Utah, school desegregation did not increase the number of students bused (less than 1 percent), or the percentage of the budget spent on busing (less than 1 percent).[120] The voluntary desegregation plan included consolidating five elementary schools into two new facilities and redrawing boundary lines for both elementary and junior high schools.[121]

In Hillsborough County, Florida, after numerous desegregation plans were used which included selective pairing and open enrollment, the school board adopted a plan which encompassed satellite attendance zones, clustering, and grade-locking.[122] Sixth and seventh grade centers were established in the formerly black schools, and white students at those grade levels are bused during the 2 years.[123] Black students are bused to formerly white schools for grades 1 through 5 and 8 through 12.[124] As a result of this desegregation plan, 125 new buses were purchased and the State provided approximately 60 percent of the operating budget for transportation.[125] Of 52,785 students transported the year following implementation of the plan, 38 percent were bused for school desegregation purposes.[126] A parent at the Tampa hearing responded to a question about her child being bused to school each day:

> I have no serious objection to it, personally. It has not caused a hardship in our family. Perhaps I would feel differently about it if what he got at the end of the line was not so good. But he does get a good deal at the end of the line.[127]

In most school districts, desegregation plans are developed for the purpose of providing equal educational opportunity for all students. Restructuring of schools and the busing involved are merely means to that end. It is not the busing, it is the education at the end of the ride that is important.

DESEGREGATED SCHOOLS AND QUALITY OF EDUCATION

Desegregation is the means through which children of all races and ethnic backgrounds are provided equal educational opportunity. Only in learning together as equals, sharing knowledge and experiences, can children hope to develop the cultural values which will prepare them to be fully contributing members of society. At the Commission's hearing in Louisville, a student explained:

---

[117] Ossining Case Study, p. 6.
[118] Erie, Pa., Case Study, p. 6.
[119] Ibid., p. 29.
[120] Case Study Factsheet: Ogden, Utah.
[121] Ogden, Utah, Case Study, pp. 6–7.
[122] U.S., Commission on Civil Rights, Staff Report, *Hillsborough County School Desegregation* (March 1976), pp. 105, 107, 108.
[123] Ibid.
[124] Ibid., pp. 110–12.
[125] Tampa transcript, testimony of Wayne Hull, assistant superintendent for business and research, Hillsborough County School District, pp. 359–60.
[126] Ibid., p. 361. The land area of Hillsborough County is approximately 1,040 square miles.
[127] Ibid., testimony of Janet M. Middlebrooks, PTA president, p. 654.

"[Desegregation] let us come together***to learn about things we would have to deal with in society***. A person's feelings are not in the textbook." [128]

The Supreme Court of the United States in the *Brown* decision addressed the intangible qualities that only desegregated schooling provides. Although *Brown* did not require improvements in curricular offerings, information available to the Commission indicates that many desegregating school districts in seeking to provide equal educational opportunity often simultaneously reevaluate their educational programs and services and as a result improve them. The superintendent of schools in Williamsburg County, South Carolina, explained:

> It would have been a mistake to have desegregated the schools without making other basic changes in the educational programs at the same time. We could see that many changes needed to take place***. It was a most opportune time to make changes. Desegregation was unavoidable; the law had to be complied with. We complied—and at the same time we turned our attention to***the individual child. [129]

The following section examines the changes in educational programs and services made by desegregated school districts. These include curriculum (multicultural and bilingual education, special programs, and magnet schools), preparation of the staff, and school facilities and supplies.

The Quality of Curriculum

Faced with the need to provide instruction to students of a variety of backgrounds, interests, and skills, many desegregated schools have begun to make the curriculum more responsive to a broad range of academic and emotional needs. The Commission heard testimony that teachers have become more sensitive to the kind of instruction that ensures student interest and academic success, [130] that teachers' expectations of minority students tend to increase, [131] that the academic performance of minority students generally improves, and that students are often more motivated and thus attend school more regularly. [132]

Educational research is inconclusive as to the effects of desegregation on achievement test scores of minority and majority students. [133] Research suggests, however, that improved achievement scores are more a function of the educational process than a function of the racial composition of the school. [134] The experience of Williamsburg, South Carolina, is an excellent example. The school system, with a majority black and low-income student enrollment, has dramatically improved achievement scores, reduced dropout rates, and increased the percentage of students seeking higher edu-

[128] Louisville transcript, testimony of Tuwana Roberts, p. 619.
[129] Egerton, *Report Card from the South*, p. 22.
[130] For example, see Denver transcript, testimony of Laura Hendee, vice principal, Merrill Junior High School, p. 412; Louisville transcript, testimony of Barbara Cummings, teacher, Crosby Middle School, p. 636.
[131] For example, see Denver transcript, testimony of Ramona McHenry, teacher, Merrill Junior High School, p. 401, and testimony of Teresa Torres, teacher, Baker Junior High School, p. 371.
[132] For example, see Tampa transcript, testimony of Ishmael Martinez, teacher, H.B. Plant High School, p. 547.
[133] See Nancy St. John, *School Desegregation Outcomes for Children* (New York: John Wiley & Sons, 1975), p. 36; Meyer Weinberg, "The Relationship Between School Desegregation and Academic Achievement: A Review of the Research," *Law and Contemporary Problems*, vol. 39, no. 2 (Spring 1975), pp. 242–43.
[134] Weinberg, "Relationship Between School Desegregation and Academic Achievement," p. 269.

cation after desegregation when changes were made in every area affecting the curriculum. The school system introduced an un-graded, individualized, sequential plan for the development of basic skills; added courses in black history and literature; maintained the number of minority teachers at a level proportionate to minority student enrollment; provided staff training in human relations; and took steps to ensure that disciplinary treatment is administered equitably. [135]

The Berkeley Unified School District provides another example. Achievement scores of both majority and minority students im-proved after desegregation. The director of research and evaluation attributed this to desegregation and the ensuing improvements in educational services and programs. [136]

A curriculum that reflects various cultural and racial backgrounds is essential to desegregated education. A school board member in Minneapolis stated:

> ***desegregation has a great effect on the quality of education. Because I think we are opening doors to our children today***speaking about my culture and background [which] they never knew about***they [learn] about all cultures***all major contributions***that one race or one individual na-tionality is not superior or inferior to another*** [137]

A school administrator in Berkeley agreed:

> ***the intent is to prepare youngsters to be effective members of society, and one of the kinds of skills that they can acquire in a desegregated system is a knowledge and an awareness of the differences that exist among youngsters and hopefully gain a respect for those differences and acceptance of them***. [138]

Many school districts have added ethnic studies and multicultural courses to the curriculum [139] and have begun using textbooks which reflect the contributions of all groups. For example, a teacher in Minneapolis stated, "I think***we have made a great amount of effort to make our material multiethnic and nonsexist." [140] Further-more, teachers on their own initiative have incorporated the cultures and histories of different racial and ethnic groups into their classroom presentations. [141]

Part of this general trend towards multicultural education is the increased use of bilingual-bicultural education, an indication that school districts are becoming more responsive to the needs of lan-guage-minority children. Boston offers programs for a variety of dif-ferent language groups, [142] Tampa for Spanish-speaking students, [143] and Louisville for Vietnamese-speaking students. [144] Denver, which

---

[135] Williamsburg, S.C., Case Study, and Egerton, *Report Card from the South*, pp. 21–24.

[136] Berkeley transcript, testimony of Arthur Dambacher, pp. B–124–28.

[137] Minneapolis transcript, testimony of W. Harry Davis, director, Minneapolis School Board, pp. 329, 330.

[138] Berkeley transcript, testimony of Arthur Dambacher, pp. B–139–140.

[139] Of the 29 districts investigated, 17 have instituted ethnic studies or multicultural programs.

[140] Minneapolis transcript, testimony of Mike O'Donnell, teacher, Wilder School, p. 620.

[141] Tampa transcript, testimony of Kenneth Otero, teacher, H.B. Plant Senior High School, p. 555.

[142] School systems in Massachusetts are required by the Transitional Bilingual Education Act of 1972 to provide bilingual instruction if the number of any one language group exceeds 20 stu-dents in each system. In Boston, 187 teachers are employed to teach children whose native lan-guages are Spanish, French, Chinese, Greek, Portuguese, and Italian. Boston School Department, Bilingual Programs, Boston Public Schools, Mar. 1, 1975. M.G.L.A. c. 71A, § 2.

[143] Tampa transcript, testimony of Norma Labato, coordinator, bilingual education, Hillsborough County Public Schools, pp. 917–34

[144] The Indochinese Migration Refugee Assistance Act of 1975, Public Law 94–23 *et seq.* (May 23, 1975), made this program available in January 1976.

has a large Mexican American student population, instituted bilingual-bicultural programs in 7 schools the first year of desegregation and extended them to 15 schools the following year.[145]

Although these programs have not necessarily been instituted as a part of the desegregation process, they are recognized by educators as prerequisite to providing equal educational opportunity for language-minority children.[146]

A school board member in Berkeley explained:

> I think that every school district in the country [with] non-English-speaking students has to establish some sort of bilingual program that will allow those students not to fall behind simply because of the lack of mastery of the language***. Simply desegregating wasn't enough, [the Chicano students] needed an opportunity in a bilingual-bicultural setting, not only allowing [them]***to appreciate and accept their culture and their way of life, but allowing others to***gain a respect for that kind of situation***.[147]

Bilingual-bicultural programs typically include both language-minority and English-speaking children. Language-minority children are given a real opportunity to learn since they are taught basic subject matter in the language they know best, and at the same time they acquire proficiency in English as a second language. Native English-speaking children in these programs are given an opportunity to learn another language and experience a different culture.[148]

Many desegregated schools offer students a wider choice of studies than was offered in segregated schools. School administrators attempt to ensure that courses offered in a student's former school are offered in the new school.[149] For example, in Tampa majority-black schools offered black history. Since desegregation, black history has been made available in all schools, to white as well as black students.[150] In Denver, instead of duplicating advanced academic and vocational courses that were offered in two high schools, East and Manual, a complex was formed. Although each school now has desegregated student bodies, students are encouraged to take courses in both schools.[151]

As a result of desegregation, school districts have implemented a variety of programs designed to improve basic skills such as reading and mathematics. These programs have benefitted both minority and majority children achieving below their potential. Many desegregated school districts have also attempted to identify gifted

[145] Denver transcript, testimony of Albert Aguayo, bilingual program supervisor, Denver Public Schools, pp. 774–75.

[146] U.S., Commission on Civil Rights, *A Better Chance to Learn: Bilingual-Bicultural Education* (1975) (hereafter cited as *Better Chance to Learn*).

[147] Berkeley transcript, testimony of Gene Roh, school board member, Berkeley Independent School District, p. A–71.

[148] *Better Chance to Learn*, pp. 29–30, 86–87.

[149] Denver transcript, testimony of Roscoe Davidson, associate superintendent, Denver Public Schools, p. 573.

[150] Tampa transcript, testimony of Frank Farmer, assistant superintendent, Hillsborough County Schools, p. 297.

[151] James D. Ward, principal, Manual High School, Denver, Colo., staff interview, Dec. 4, 1975.

students and provide programs that fully develop their talents and abilities. The availability of Federal money under the Emergency School Aid Act, established to provide financial assistance for special needs incident to the elimination of minority segregation,[152] has provided the impetus for many of these programs.

In planning for desegregation, the Prince George's County, Maryland, School District received Federal aid under ESAA to improve reading achievement and to identify gifted students from minority groups.[153] The school district provided a reading supervisor and staff of reading teachers for different geographical areas, and 20 "floating faculty" members were assigned to work with 20 elementary schools. A student tutorial service was expanded to include 20 junior high schools, 1,620 student tutors, and 4,860 children. Workshops were conducted over the summer to prepare reading teachers for elementary and secondary schools.[154]

Even where Federal funds are lacking, many individual schools in the process of desegregation have developed programs on their own initiative to help children achieving below their potential. The vice principal of Merrill Junior High School in Denver described their efforts:

> ***about 25 teachers came and received credit for [remedial reading training]***. We***started a core program for children who are not special education youngsters but have great problems with reading, with academics, with self-image***. Our very top teachers volunteered to teach***these youngsters***. This has helped a great deal.[155]

Magnet schools, which offer specialized curricula and teaching, are often used to attract students to desegregated schools.[156] School districts use magnet schools as testing grounds for innovative curricula and as a means for providing students alternative programs in truly integrated settings. These schools typically require specific racial percentages which may parallel racial composition districtwide or reflect equal distribution for each racial and ethnic group.

When an open enrollment policy in Louisville, Kentucky, was failing to desegregate schools, the Brown School, a magnet school which stipulated a 50 percent black and white enrollment, had long waiting lists.[157] The school offers a progressive curriculum and attracts white and black parents who want their children to experience learning in an open classroom and integrated environment.[158] Since the merger of the Jefferson County and Louisville school systems, two additional "alternative" magnet schools have been developed which also require 50 percent black and 50 percent white enrollment. Scheduled to open in the fall of

---

[152] The Emergency School Aid Act (ESAA) 20 U.S.C. §1601 *et seq.* (Supp. IV 1974) is designed to "encourage the voluntary elimination, reduction, or prevention of minority group isolation in elementary and secondary schools with substantial proportions of minority group students, and to aid school children in overcoming the educational disadvantages of minority group isolation." 20 U.S.C. §1601(G)(Supp. IV 1974).

[153] *Long Day's Journey*, p. 361.

[154] Ibid., p. 362.

[155] Denver transcript, testimony of Laura Hendee, vice principal, Merrill Junior High School, Denver Public Schools, pp. 404–05.

[156] Of the 29 case study districts, 10 established magnet schools. *SAC Case Study Analysis*, 1976.

[157] Nell Sweeney, Brown Instructional Center, Louisville, Ky., staff interview, July 9, 1976.

[158] Milburn Maupin, deputy superintendent, Federal Programs and Human Relations, Jefferson County Public Schools, staff interview, Mar. 1, 1976.

1976 and known as traditional schools because of the content and approach of the curriculum offered, they already have waiting lists.[159]

In Boston, Phase II of the desegregation order called for the creation of 22 magnet schools offering specialized and distinctive programs.[160] Institutions of higher learning, the business community, labor organizations, and creative arts groups have committed themselves to assist with the development of curricula for the magnet schools as well as other schools in the district. Businesses have been paired with specific schools to provide a more practical business orientation to academic programs, and labor organizations have begun developing occupational, vocational, technical, and trade programs.[161] The effectiveness of this liaison is yet to be determined since Phase II only began in the fall of 1975. However, the roles have been defined and program development is underway.[162]

The Tulsa, Oklahoma, school district reported that the greatest effect of desegregation was improvement of the curriculum.[163] The district established two magnet schools offering innovative curricula. Washington High School offers a variety of courses including: repertory theater, stage show ensemble, mass media, TV and film direction, business law, speed reading, Chinese I and II, building construction, elementary probability and statistics, music composition, electronics, and archaeology.[164] The curriculum at Carver Middle School is organized around courses in communication skills, mathematics, science, humanities, and exploratory activities. The school makes extensive use of community resources and conducts numerous field trips. In addition, the school day for students is divided into four periods of about 90 minutes duration to facilitate student-teacher interaction.[165]

Although magnet schools may provide broad educational opportunities for students, some education authorities have criticized their use as an "escape route for whites assigned to predominantly black schools." They have also been described as "a new type of dual structure with unequal educational opportunities" which drain resources from other schools in the system.[166] Magnet schools have a particularly deleterious effect when they are used as the only device for reassigning students in a desegregating district.

Preparation of the Staff

Desegregating school districts usually provide human relations training to ensure a positive learning environment and to help teachers understand children of different racial and ethnic backgrounds and socioeconomic levels. Of the 29 case study dis-

---

[159] J. C. Cantrell, assistant superintendent of instruction, Louisville, Ky., staff interview, July 9, 1976.

[160] Morgan v. Kerrigan, civil action, No. 72-911-g. Phase II Plan, pp. 11-42.

[161] Morgan v. Kerrigan, Draft Revisions of Masters' Report (Apr. 17, 1975), Phase II Plan, p. 50.

[162] U.S., Commission on Civil Rights, staff report, *School Desegregation in Boston* (1975) (hereafter cited as *School Desegregation in Boston*).

[163] Tulsa, Okla., Case Study, p. 59.

[164] Ibid., p. 60.

[165] Ibid.

[166] Gordon Foster, "Desegregating Urban Schools: A Review of Techniques," *Harvard Educational Review*, vol. 43, no. 1 (February 1973), p. 19.

tricts, 23 have provided inservice human relations training.[167] Such training involves identifying cultural differences among groups, preparing multicultural materials, and teaching methodology.

The Minneapolis school system provided human relations training for teachers to increase their effectiveness in educating children of different racial and ethnic backgrounds. A citywide network of faculty representatives from each school provided this training weekly during an early release period. Schools held all-day communications laboratories and the administration appointed two faculty members to obtain staff reactions to the desegregation plan. In addition, the administration held a series of workshops on institutional racism. Three years after desegregation, the school district continues to provide human relations training and racism workshops.[168]

The Berkeley school district launched a predesegregation and postdesegregation series of workshops and seminars to familiarize teachers and students with all elements of desegregation and to allow discussion of fears or problems. The school administration also required teachers to take a series of courses in human relations and multicultural education, for which they received credits towards eventual pay raises.[169]

In Denver the desegregation plan required 5 hours of inservice training per semester for every teacher. In response to subsequent complaints that training was ineffective and not all teachers attended, the court ordered that an accountability system be developed. Teachers are now required to report their views on effectiveness of the training.[170]

Human relations training provided in Louisville was based on "the ripple effect," meaning that a certain number of teachers from each school attended a training institute and returned to their individual schools to train other teachers.[171] For the most part it was ineffective. Some school administrators said that it was not effective because it was designed with the expectation that the school district had one full school year to prepare teachers before desegregation[172] A second reason for its lack of effectiveness was that it received minimal support and commitment from the central administration.[173] However, the few schools that were committed to the concept of human relations training held successful training workshops.[174]

---

[167] *SAC Case Study Analysis.* Title IV of the Civil Rights Act of 1964, Section 403, provides funds for such training. The Commissioner is authorized, upon application of a school board, to make grants to such board to pay, in whole or in part, the cost of: (1) giving to teachers and other school personnel inservice training in dealing with problems incident to desegregation, and (2) employing specialists to advise in problems incident to desegregation. For a review of Title IV see U.S., Commission on Civil Rights, *Title IV and School Desegregation, A Study of a Neglected Federal Program* (1973).

[168] Minneapolis, Minn., Case Study, pp. 15–16.

[169] Berkeley, Calif., Case Study, p. 13–14.

[170] Keyes v. School District No. 1, 413 U.S. 192 (1973) and Evie Dennis, community specialist, Denver, Colo., staff interview, Dec. 15, 1975.

[171] Robert Wynkoop, staff advisory specialist, Jefferson County Public Schools, interview, Mar. 3, 1976.

[172] Louisville transcript, testimony of Ernest Grayson, superintendent, Jefferson County Public Schools, p. 745.

[173] James Coleman, associate superintendent for community development, Jefferson County Public Schools, interview, March 3, 1976.

[174] Louisville transcript, testimony of Scott Horan, intergroup and community relations specialist; and Fannie Gul, human relations coordinator, pp. 502–13.

To implement broad changes in the curriculum successfully in a desegregated setting often requires new teaching techniques. As a direct result of desegregation, 18 of the 29 districts reviewed by the Commission developed and implemented new teaching methods to make the curriculum more responsive.[175] Many school districts attempted to individualize instruction by adding aides and other resource teachers and creating open classrooms to permit smaller groupings of students.

The principal of Crosby Middle School in Jefferson County, Kentucky, described instructional improvements made at his school:

> ***One part of our instructional program is***individualized instruction, which means that students work at their own pace. It means that each student can succeed at the level the student has achieved***. By using instructional packets, by subgrouping, we can facilitate***learning***for students who have different motivations.[176]

In Hillsborough County, Florida, one-grade schools were created for the sixth and seventh grades in which 120 students are heterogeneously grouped with one team leader and four teachers assigned to instruct all of them. At different times of the day, the students are divided into smaller groups for individualized instruction.[177]

After desegregation in Kalamazoo, Michigan, the concern for effective teaching brought about the development of a districtwide teacher accountability system. Extensive test data and other information on students are given to teachers in the form of student profiles so they can better tailor their instruction to the individual needs of students and at the same time be held accountable for the process.[178]

In general desegregation has a renewing effect on teachers. At Commission hearings and open meetings many teachers testified that desegregation has caused them to reevaluate their methods, techniques, and attitudes and develop new ways to communicate with children. One teacher said:

> We have, because of desegregation, thrown out***some of the practices that were detrimental to education***we have put in place of those, educational practices that are more beneficial for all students.[179]

School Facilities and Supplies

One of the most tangible and obvious effects of desegregation on the quality of education is the general upgrading of school buildings and facilities and the provision of adequate supplies. Information available to the Commission indicates that the reassignment of white students to previously minority schools has caused school administrators to correct the inadequate maintainance of buildings and grounds of minority schools that existed for years. Moreover, they

[175] SAC Case Study Analysis, 1976.
[176] Louisville transcript, testimony of W. Carlyle Maupin, p. 643.
[177] Tampa transcript, testimony of Frank Farmer, assistant superintendent of instruction, Hillsborough County Schools, p. 304; Dora L. Reeder, principal, and Arthur Fleming, teacher, Dunbar Elementary School, pp. 650–53.
[178] Kalamazoo, Mich., Case Study, pp. 12–13.
[179] Denver transcript, testimony of Ramona McHenry, teacher, Merrill Junior High School, p. 421.

have corrected the shortage of educational supplies, textbooks, and classroom furniture which generally existed in minority schools.

In Denver a black member of a school board advisory group testified that the school administration had different standards for minority and majority schools prior to desegregation. In addition to being older, black schools were inferior and unsafe. Ventilation was poor, roofs leaked, radiators were uncovered, bathroom facilities were limited, and gymnasiums often had cement floors. The schools were not provided air conditioning as most white schools were, and they were given mobile classrooms when the school became overcrowded. Predominantly black schools were generally short of textbooks, supplies, athletic equipment, and classroom furniture. [180]

In speaking about the inequality of supplies and textbooks between majority-black and majority-white schools, a black student at the Tampa hearing testified: "The books had no backs, half the pages were gone***and you had to share one book [with] three people." [181]

P. R. Wharton, assistant superintendent for administration, acknowledged that improvements had been made to a former minority school:

> I can think of one school where there was quite a bit to do about maintenance***I think it was run down. It was an elementary school, Carver School, and we went in there and did a great deal of maintenance prior to integrating that school, the summer prior to integration. [182]

The black principal of Manual High School, a previously all-black school in Denver, testified that before desegregation the school administration had generally ignored requests for supplies and improvements in facilities. [183] A parent of a Manual High School student testified:

> There have been drastic changes in the school since the implementation of the court order***. Manual began to***approach the equipment available in the other high schools***. My youngest son, who graduated in '75, had been Manual's athletic trainer for 3 years. He continually complained to me about the lack of basic equipment***.The equipment was below standard. The first time that Manual's tennis team had uniforms was when the kids from Washington and East and South [schools] came over and all of a sudden monies became available to provide equal equipment for black, white, Chicano students attending Manual, on a par with what the other schools had previously been used to. [184]

Similarly, in Berkeley a black parent testified that they had fought for years for remodeling of the cafeteria and lighting in the basement of the black school in her neighborhood, but they were ignored until the schools desegregated. [185]

MINORITY STAFF

Adequate minority representation on the school staff is critical to

---

[180] Ibid., testimony of Bettye Emmerson, pp. 676–79.
[181] Tampa transcript, testimony of Patricia Wingo, H. B. Plant High School, p. 562.
[182] Ibid., pp. 307–08.
[183] Denver transcript, testimony of James Ward, principal, Manual High School, p. 815.
[184] Ibid., testimony of William Coker, pp. 793–94.
[185] Berkeley transcript, testimony of Donna McKinney, pp. B–106–07.

integrated education. Just as student exposure to students of other races and ethnic groups helps develop racial understanding, tolerance, and appreciation, so also does the presence of a multiracial and multiethnic staff.

Minorities in positions of responsibility help dispel myths of racial inferiority and incompetence, provide positive role models for all students, help ease the adjustment of minority students and their parents as well as majority teachers, and help provide a multicultural curriculum.

Stereotypic ideas may be held by white and black students and staff. Day-to-day interaction with minorities as co-workers or as teachers and administrators can help eradicate such misconceptions. This point was stressed by Mogul Du Pree, an elementary school teacher in Tampa, who said: "I think that one of the things that has happened as a result of desegregation***[is that] the stereotyped idea that Negro teachers [are] inferior is rapidly disappearing."[186]

A Tampa school administrator said that some white parents request that their children be assigned to black teachers because they feel it is a vital educational opportunity.[187] A mother described her daughter's experience in this area:

> My child's favorite teacher in high school was her black Spanish teacher, and without desegregation, she never would have had this experience. I think it was a very rewarding experience for my child.[188]

Minority presence at all administrative and staff levels is necessary to reinforce positive images for both minority and majority students.[189] A community leader in Stamford stressed the need for minority staff:

> One other area that is constantly highlighted is the low minority representation throughout the school board's staff, especially the lack of black and Hispanic personnel. It is well known that students need to have that type imagery available***.[190] This point was also made by a principal at the Berkeley open meeting who said, "Oh, the kids definitely need role models. They need to have minority people, the majority kids need to have them, too."[191]

Moreover, the use of minority teachers in bilingual-bicultural education programs contributes to a child's self-concept through a positive reinforcement of his or her background and culture.[192] Self-concept is affected by interaction with teachers, and language-minority teachers are sometimes best able to communicate the encouragement and understanding needed by language-minority children.[193]

Additionally, minority staff can help ease the adjustment of

---

[186] Tampa transcript, p. 218.

[187] Thelma Shuman, interview, Tampa, Fla., Feb. 27, 1976.

[188] Tampa transcript, testimony of Katie Keene, p. 223.

[189] Nancy H. St. John, *School Desegregation: Outcomes for Children* (New York, N.Y.: Wiley, 1974), pp. 125–26.

[190] Stamford transcript, testimony of John Brown, director of Stamford's community action program, p. 161.

[191] Berkeley transcript, testimony of Beatrice Terreira, principal, Martin Luther King Junior High School, p. A–207.

[192] *Better Chance to Learn*, p. 39.

[193] Ibid.

minority students to school desegregation. In many instances, minority students are transferred from a school where they were the majority to a school where they are in the minority. In these instances, they are often reassured by the presence of minority staff members who are sensitive to their needs. A witness at the Boston hearing addressed this issue, saying, "Youngsters began to say that we don't feel comfortable unless we see some of ours there."[194]

A student, asked if there should be more minority teachers in his school, responded:

> Definitely so. Because black and Puerto Rican students feel that they can relate to somebody who is either black or Puerto Rican***because the majority of the teachers in the school are white***. They don't know what it's like, you know, to be living in a certain neighborhood.[195]

A study of school desegregation in Goldsboro, North Carolina, found that "black students were more likely to participate on a par with white students in open classrooms in desegregated schools where the teaching staff was balanced in leadership and competence between black and white teachers."[196]

The presence of minorities on the staff can help minority parents to become involved in school activities. Accustomed to relating to minority teachers at a segregated school, minority parents may find the desegregated environment threatening. This may be especially true for parents with limited proficiency in English. Carmen Castro, executive director of the Spanish International Center of Stamford, said:

> Parents [Hispanic] have no way of communicating to principals or teachers in other schools because they do not have interpreters. [There was the]***problem of the child having to interpret for the parent and interpret for the teacher, so that heaven knew what went on. The parent would never know what was going on.[197]

A teacher in Berkeley described how teachers of different races can gain understanding by sharing problems:

> [W]e [teachers] had meetings at least once a week where we sat around and tried to deal with each other and***work out problems that we were having***dealing with a multiethnic culture, ***[I]t was helpful to everyone***.[198]

As part of the desegregation process, many school districts introduce multicultural classes to the curriculum. Because most textbooks fail to treat the culture and historical contributions of minorities effectively, minority staff members are often the best source for knowledge in this area. Moreover, their presence gives credence to the school's effort to recognize and appreciate the contribution of all ethnic and racial groups. The contributions of black Americans to science and medicine may be taken more seriously if the nurse and the science department chairperson are black. Similarly, the

---

[194] Boston transcript, testimony of Paul Parks, secretary of education, Office of the Governor, p. 42.
[195] Stamford transcript, testimony of Michael Palmer, student, West Hill High School, pp. 222–23.
[196] Edgar G. Epps, "The Impact of School Desegregation on Aspirations, Self-Concepts, and Other Aspects of Personality," *Law and Contemporary Problems*, vol. 39, no. 2 (1975), p. 311.
[197] Stamford transcript, pp. 175–76.
[198] Berkeley transcript, testimony of Jesse Anthony, music teacher, pp. B–50–51.

role of Hispanos in American history may be more authentic to a student hearing it for the first time when Hispanos are in positions of responsibility. According to a recent study:

> Desegregation exposes minority pupils to cultural marginality and confusion as to their own identity, unless the staff is interracial, unless the curriculum recognizes the minority group culture, and unless there is opportunity for choice between assimilation and pluralism. [199]

The School Desegregation Experience

What happens to minority staff representation when school districts desegregate? Although no comprehensive statistics are available, analysis of the 29 case studies reveals that in 16 of the school districts, minority employment increased following school desegregation. In eight other school districts, minority employment remained the same, and a decrease was reported in two.

In some school districts increases have been reported solely for the teaching force; others have shown gains in administrative positions. For example, prior to desegregation in Providence, there were no black principals, assistant principals, or central administrative staff. [200] By 1975 there were three black principals and five blacks on the central administrative staff. Blacks in Memphis were successful in securing an act of legislature that restructured the school board to ensure the election of blacks. [201] By 1973 three blacks served on the nine-member board. [202]

In many instances an effective impetus for change was a court mandate. Some court orders have dealt only with the reassignment of teachers and called for minority teachers to be equally dispersed throughout the system; others have mandated specific ratios; i.e. the ratio of minority personnel should reflect the ratio of the city population or the minority student population.

Minority staff representation was addressed by the court orders in Boston, Denver, Tampa (Hillsborough County schools), and Louisville. In Tampa and Denver affirmative action plans have been in existence long enough to produce positive results. Only a few school districts have actively pursued affirmative hiring practices on a voluntary basis.

In many northern school districts there is underrepresentation of minorities in staff positions. With the advent of school desegregation, discriminatory hiring practices were often exposed and in some districts were directly addressed as part of the court order. The 1974 court order in Denver required the school administration to formulate an affirmative action plan to recruit and hire Hispanos and blacks. [203] As early as 1970 black and Hispanic organizations had pointed out the need for black and Hispanic personnel. [204] However, very little was accomplished in this area until the court mandate.

The judge subsequently indicated that the goal of the plan should

---

[199] St. John, *Outcomes for Children*, p. 108.
[200] Providence, R.I., Case Study, p. 18.
[201] Egerton, *Promise of Progress*, p. 7.
[202] Ibid.
[203] Keyes v. School District No. 1, 413 U.S. 192 (1973).
[204] Denver transcript, testimony of Bettye J. Emerson, p. 672; Letter to the President of the United States, Apr. 21, 1971, signed by representatives of 13 Denver-based Hispanic organizations (Commission files)

be to increase minority personnel hiring until the ratio mirrored that of Chicano and black students.

In 1975 the student population in Denver was 17.8 percent black and 24.1 percent Hispanic; the teaching force in 1975 was 10.6 percent black and 4.8 percent Hispanic. In compliance with the order, the Denver school system adopted an affirmative action plan in March 1975 which includes recruitment, employee development programs, and career counseling, and provides job advancement provisions at all staff levels. As of February 1976, blacks constituted 10.7 percent and Hispanics 6.1 percent of all teachers. In 1974 blacks accounted for 8.0 percent of all administrative personnel, and by 1976 their percentage had increased to 9.8 percent. Corresponding percentages for Hispanos were 4.7 and 6.1, respectively.[205]

In Boston inadequate representation of minorities on the school staff was also addressed directly by the court order.[206] While the student population during the 1972–73 school year was approximately 33 percent black, only 5.4 percent of the permanent teachers, 3.9 percent of the principals and headmasters, and 5.7 percent of the assistant principals and assistant headmasters were black.[207] The court required placement of black teachers in schools in accordance with the districtwide proportion of black teachers at that level of instruction. In addition, of 280 new permanent teachers, blacks and whites were to be hired on a one-to-one ratio until every qualified black applicant had been offered employment.[208] Three black recruiters were hired by the school committee to assist in this employment effort.[209]

A few school districts have instituted affirmative action programs voluntarily. As part of the desegregation process in Berkeley in 1968, the school administration adopted an affirmative action policy to "work as fast as possible to bring the number of minority teachers more in line with the number of minority students in the school district."[210] A former school board member described the recruitment efforts:

> ***[W]e instructed him [personnel director] to go out and search for minority teachers all across the country***. [H]e went on tour throughout the U.S. to try to find qualified teachers and workers in the clerical area who could be brought to Berkeley and interviewed for jobs because we felt we had to be aggressive about this.[211]

The Berkeley recruitment drive concentrated on predominantly black universities and colleges. Community and staff task forces served in an advisory capacity. Although the school system has not reached its goal, progress has been made. In 1968 blacks constituted 17 percent of the faculty, Asian Americans 4 percent, and

[205] Denver Superintendent's Report to the Honorable William E. Doyle, Judge, U.S. Court of Appeals, required by the April 17, 1974, Final Judgment and Decree, Civil Action No. C–1499, Court Order No. 19–1.
[206] Morgan v. Hennigan, 379 F. Supp. 410, 472 (D. Mass. 1974), aff'd sub nom. Morgan v. Kerrigan, 502 F.2d 58 (1st Cir. 1974) cert. denied 44L.W. 3713 (June 15, 1976).
[207] School Desegregation in Boston, p. 15.
[208] Ibid., appendix C. Qualified meant holding a Massachusetts certificate or appearing on the school department eligible list.
[209] Ibid.
[210] Berkeley transcript, testimony of Carol Sibley, p. A–44.
[211] Ibid.

Hispanos 2 percent; in 1975 the percentages had increased to 27 percent, 7 percent, and 4 percent, respectively. The system hired a black superintendent in 1974 and two of its three assistant superintendents are black. The student population in 1968 and in 1975 was approximately 45 percent black, 7 percent Asian American, and 3 percent Hispanic.[212] The Berkeley school system in the spring of 1976 was in the paradoxical situation of anticipating a layoff of approximately 120 teachers and because of a seniority stipulation, it was anticipated that 80 percent would be minority.

Under the segregated school system in the South, blacks were hired to staff and administer black schools at all levels.[213] However, as school systems were desegregated in the late 1960s, the number of black staff members decreased drastically. Black principals and department heads, as well as faculty members, were often demoted or fired.

In many instances, it was obvious discrimination since they were not given an opportunity to compete for the positions regardless of experience or education.[214] Other school districts, while using subtler forms of displacement, produced similar results—black teachers were often placed in classrooms out of their fields and then fired for incompetence; reassigned as co-teachers with domineering whites or as floating teachers without their own classrooms; or assigned to nonprofessional positions such as hall monitors.[215] Between 1954 and 1970 while the black student population in 17 Southern and Border States increased from 23 percent to 25 percent, the black teacher force decreased from 21 percent to 19 percent.[216]

In 1970 the Fifth Circuit Court of Appeals responded to the discriminatory treatment of minority educators in a consolidated opinion covering 11 southern school districts. In *Singleton* v. *Jackson Municipal Separate School District* the court stated that:

> Staff members who work directly with children and professional staff who work on the administrative level will be hired, assigned, promoted, paid, demoted, dismissed or otherwise treated without regard to race, color or national origin.
> ***[T]he district shall assign the staff***so that the ratio of Negro to white teachers in each school and the ratio of other staff in each, are substantially the same as each such ratio is to the teachers and other staff, respectively in the entire school system.[217]

Increasingly, court orders contain stipulations covering the employment and assignment of minority staff and often mandate specific minority staff ratios.

In Hillsborough County, the 1969 court order,[218] in addition to

---

[212] Berkeley, Calif., Case Study, pp. 2, 15.

[213] Walter Alexander Mercer, *Humanizing the Desegregated School* (New York: Vantage Press, 1973), p. 22.

[214] See for example, Arthur O. White, "Florida's State School Chief and Desegregation," *Integrated Education* (1974) p. 38.

[215] Mercer, *Humanizing the Desegregated School*, p. 22.

[216] Leon Hall, "School Desegregation: A (Hollow?) Victory," *Inequality in Education*, no. 17 (1974), p. 7.

[217] 419 F.2d 1211, at 1218 (5th Cir. 1970). Similar standards are used by HEW in determining Title VI and Emergency School Aid Act regulations, 40 Fed. Reg. 25171, June 12, 1975.

[218] Mannings v. Board of Public Instruction of Hillsborough county, Florida, No. 3554 Civ. T–K (M.D. Fla. May 11, 1971). This order contains a history of the case from its beginning in December 1958.

requiring faculty desegregation, mandated that faculty composition mirror the districtwide, black-white student ratio, which was approximately 18 percent black, 82 percent white. At that time black teachers constituted approximately 15 percent of the faculty. [219] In an effort to comply with the court order, the school administration launched a 4-year recruitment drive covering more than 20 predominantly black colleges and universities in 8 Southern States. [220] As a result of this drive, the number of black faculty members increased each succeeding year, from 732 in the 1969–70 school year to 915 in the fall of 1975. [221] While this is an increase of only one percentage point, it is a step in a positive direction, especially when contrasted with occurrences in other southern school districts. (For example, in Escambia County, Florida, between 1967 and 1970, 86 black teachers lost their jobs.) [222] Hillsborough County also recorded an increase in administrative positions. In 1969, blacks occupied 40 of 308 positions (13 percent), and in the fall of 1975, they held 60 of the 358 administrative positions (20 percent). Moreover, black teachers and administrators who leave the system are replaced with blacks. [223]

The Hillsborough County administration, as a result of Federal pressure, also plans to equalize employment opportunities for women. [224] Although women constitute 73 percent of the faculty, they hold none of the top administrative positions. [225] Additionally, of the 37 secondary principalships, only 3 are held by women. [226]

CLASSROOM DESEGREGATION

The constitutional and educational grounds for eliminating racially identifiable schools apply equally to classrooms. However, in desegregated school districts throughout the Nation, classes often are composed of students of one racial or ethnic group or vary considerably from the racial composition of the school. In the South, for example, statistics compiled by the Southern Regional Council show that two of every three school districts have one or more schools with racially identifiable classrooms. These districts include school systems in Alabama, Florida, Georgia, Mississippi, North Carolina, South Carolina, and Tennessee. [227] A study in 1973 reported that of 467 southern school districts, 35 percent of the high schools and 60 percent of the elementary schools had segregated classrooms. [228]

Ability Grouping

The most common cause of classroom segregation is the educational practice of ability grouping. With the exception of Mississippi, 7 out of 10 school districts surveyed (in the 7 States mentioned

---

[219] Data provided by the Office of Pupil Administrative Services. Report on Racial Breakdown of Pupils and Staff, submitted annually to the Honorable Bejamin Krentzman, U.S. District Court.
[220] Ibid.
[221] Ibid.
[222] *Diminishing Barrier*, p. 13.
[223] Rodney C. Colson, assistant superintendent, Hillsborough County Schools, staff interview, Feb. 12, 1976.
[224] Ibid.
[225] Egerton, *Report Card from the South*, p. 35.
[226] Ibid.
[227] Roger Mills and Miriam Bryan, *Testing—Grouping: The New Segregation in Southern Schools* (Atlanta, Ga.: Southern Regional Council, 1976), pp. 45–46. They have defined "racially identifiable classroom" as one in which the racial composition of the class varies more than 20 percent from the racial composition of the grade at the school.
[228] Winifred Green, "Separate and Unequal Again," *Inequality in Education*, July 1973, p. 15.

above) that have racially identifiable classrooms use ability grouping.[229]

In schools in Southwestern States where Mexican American students are less than 25 percent of the enrollment, they constitute 35 percent of the low ability group and 8 percent of the high ability group classes. In schools 25 to 50 percent Mexican American, they constitute 57 percent of the low group and 19 percent of the high group. In schools more than 50 percent Mexican American, more than three of every four students in the low groups are Mexican American, and only two of every five are Mexican American in the high groups.[230]

Research for the most part does not support ability grouping. While it is argued that grouping students according to their achievement levels ensures that academic needs are met, research findings are almost uniformly unfavorable with regard to its use in promoting scholastic achievement in low ability groups and are inconclusive in its use for high ability groups.[231]

Rather than providing an environment for meeting a variety of needs of individual students in each group, ability grouping assumes that students are equal in terms of needs and capabilities. Furthermore, teachers of low ability groups frequently are unprepared to teach these classes and generally have low expectations of their students. Course content may be watered down and stimulation from more academically prepared students is nonexistent.[232] A study by the National Education Association indicates that less than 5 percent of teachers at the elementary level and less than 2 percent at the secondary level want to teach low ability groups.[233] Students are thus denied the opportunity of academic challenge from both teachers and peers.

A Stamford teacher told the Commission, "Better teachers are rewarded the higher groups."[234] A student reported:

> Your teachers in the lower group[s]***they are put there just to make sure you don't do anything in class. You sit for a couple of hours and that's it***. The teachers in the lower class don't show any kind of interest.[235]

Students placed in low ability groups rarely perceive themselves as equal to nor are they considered equal by students in higher groups. This grouping tends to deflate the self-esteem of students in low groups and inflate the ego of those in high groups.[236] A student in Stamford explained:

> Well, the majority of the black students***when they realize***why all the blacks are in this class and***all the whites

[229] Mills and Bryan, *Testing—Grouping*, p. 46.

[230] U.S., Commission on Civil Rights, *Toward Quality Education For Mexican Americans* (1974), p. 23 (hereafter cited as *Toward Quality Education*).

[231] Warren G. Findley and Miriam M. Bryan, *Ability Grouping: 1970* (Athens, Ga.: University of Georgia, Center for Educational Improvement, 1970), p. 3. Also, see *Toward Quality Education*, p. 24. Gary Orfield, "How to Make Desegregation Work: The Adaptation of Schools to Their Newly-Integrated Student Bodies," *Law and Contemporary Problems*, vol. 39, (Spring 1975), pp. 327–28.

[232] *Toward Quality Education*, p. 25.

[233] National Education Association, "Ability Grouping: Teacher Opinion Poll," *NEA Journal*, vol. 57 (February 1968), p.

[234] Stamford transcript, testimony of Robert Kelley, p. 291.

[235] Stamford transcript, testimony of Michael Steadman, p. 213.

[236] Earl Ogletree and Velma E. Ujlaki, "The Effects of Ability Grouping on Inner City Children," *Illinois Schools Journal*, vol. 50 (1970), pp. 63–70. See also Leon J. Lefkowitz, "Ability Grouping: De Facto Segregation," *The Clearing House*, vol. 46, no. 5 (January 1972), pp. 293–97, and Findley and Bryan, *Ability Grouping: 1970*, pp. 31–38.

in that class***. Basically, it makes them feel like they are lower. And then that builds***to be a hatred of white people in general***.[237]

The courts have been fairly consistent in holding that pupil assignment by standardized achievement or IQ test scores is unconstitutional when the intended and actual result is the perpetuation of the dual system, whether segregation exists within the system as a whole,[238] within individual schools,[239] or within individual classrooms.[240]

In some districts school boards or school administrators have explicit policies prohibiting classes of any one race. The administration of Hillsborough County Public Schools sent directives to teachers and administrators stating that no one class should be more than 50 percent black.[241] At the Denver hearing, an associate superintendent testified that schools were directed to ensure that "classes not be allowed to reorganized on a segregated basis," and that schools were looking for "alternative ways of grouping youngsters and organizing classes and arranging for arrays of courses so that youngsters would not have to discontinue sequences they had already begun, but at the same time would not get involved in a tracking arrangement***that results in resegregation."[242] The Dorchester, Maryland, school district, in addition to eliminating tracking in the upper grade levels, screened all classes to avoid all-black or all-white classes.[243]

Some schools have abolished ability grouping in certain subjects. In Denver, for example, the principal of Smiley Junior High School said that teachers had discussed the problem of ability grouping and decided to abolish it first in social studies. Ability grouping for other subjects had been discussed, but no consensus was reached.[244]

Ability grouping traps those students in the low ability groups; they are rarely ever assigned to any other group.[245] Furthermore, some students are not only assigned a low ability group in one subject but "tracked" in the same level in all subjects regardless of strength or weakness. Ability grouping and tracking foreclose a student's chance for ever excelling.

Many schools replace ability grouping with new teaching approaches such as individualized instruction and team teaching, facilitated by the creation of open classrooms or learning centers. In open classrooms racial percentages are often stipulated. In the sixth and seventh grade centers of the Hillsborough County Public Schools, Florida, the minority percentage of each group was stipulated at 20 percent.[246]

---

[237] Stamford transcript, testimony of Michael Palmer, pp. 212–13.

[238] See, e.g. Lemon v. Bossier Parish School Board, 444 F.2d 1400 (5th Cir. 1971); United States v. Sunflower County School District, 430 F.2d 839, 841 (5th Cir.), cert. denied, 398 U.S. 951 (1970).

[239] See, e.g., Moses v. Washington Parish School Board, 456 F.2d 1285 (5th Cir.) cert. denied, 409 U.S. 1013 (1972).

[240] See, e.g., Acree v. County Board of Education, 458 F. 2d 486, 488, no. 3 (5th Cir.) cert. denied, 409 U.S. 1006 (1972).

[241] Tampa transcript, testimony of Raymond Shelton, superintendent, Hillsborough County Public Schools, p. 306.

[242] Denver transcript, testimony of Roscoe Davidson, associate superintendent for elementary education, Denver Public Schools, p. 574.

[243] Dorchester County, Md., Case study. pp. 23–24.

[244] Testimony of principal, Smiley Junior High School, Denver transcript, p. 433.

[245] *Toward Quality Education*, p. 21.

[246] Tampa transcript, testimony of Frank Farmer, assistant superintendent of instruction, p. 304.

Thus, although most data indicate that classroom segregation is a serious problem in desegregated districts, schools in the Commission's survey acknowledge the problem and said they are seeking ways to deal with it.

Assignment to "Special Education" Classes

Segregation also occurs in "special education" classes, such as those for children with problematic behavior or with learning disabilities in which minority students are often overrepresented. Minority students are often incorrectly assigned to such classes. IQ test scores, the basis for assignment to classes for the educable mentally retarded (EMR), have been found to be culturally biased and often reflect achievement or a child's ability to take tests rather than intelligence.[247] Moreover, white teachers and school administrators who recommend placement in EMR classes often are poor judges of minority student behavior or ability.[248]

A 1973 study of a California school district found that 91 percent of the black students and 60 percent of the Mexican American students placed in EMR classes on the basis of IQ tests had been incorrectly assigned.[249] In 1973 in Texas, the Commission found that Mexican American students were twice as likely to be placed in EMR classes as whites; the ratio of black students was 3 1/2 times greater.[250] The Office for Civil Rights of HEW in 1973 cited 14 districts in the Southwest in noncompliance with Title VI on the grounds of overinclusion of Mexican American students in special education classes.[251]

Testimony at the Tampa hearing indicates that black students are overrepresented in classes for the educable mentally handicapped (EMH). The dean of girls of a junior high school explained that although the basis for assignment is low IQ test scores, most of the black students who score low are "disruptive" rather than retarded and, thus, should not be placed in EMH classes. She said they score low because they have a history of absence from school and therefore test poorly.[252]

The Louisville-Jefferson County public school system has two programs for 700 disruptive students. One, called the Alternative School, is a self-contained school for students with "deviate behavior." It is 95 percent black. The other, the youth development program, consists of separate classrooms in 33 schools for students with less serious behavioral problems. Students in this program are 80 percent white.[253] School administrators explain that the alternative school was part of the majority-black Louisville school system and the youth development program was part of the majority-white

---

[247] EMR usually means mildly retarded, where a student is between two and three standard deviations below the norm; that is, having an IQ score between 50 and 70. Michael S. Sorgen, "Testing and Tracking in the Public Schools," *Hastings Law Journal*, vol. 24 (1972–73), pp. 1168 and Testimony of Mark Lohman, U.S., Senate, Hearings Before the Select Committee on Equal Educational Opportunity, 92d Cong., 1st Sess., p. 10170.

[248] *Toward Quality Education*, p. 29.

[249] Jane Mercer, *Labelling the Mentally Retarded* (Berkeley: University of California Press, 1973), p. 189.

[250] *Toward Quality Education*, p. 28.

[251] Ibid., pp. 59.

[252] Tampa transcript, testimony of Helen Wilds, pp. 617–22.

[253] Robert Wynkoop, staff advisory specialist for desegregation, Jefferson County Public Schools, interview, Mar. 3, 1976. See also Louisville transcript, testimony of Joel Henning, assistant superintendent for institutional organization, pp. 693–95, 702–03.

Jefferson County system prior to merger of the two districts in the fall of 1975. Most students, they said, were assigned prior to merger, but no attempt has been made to reevaluate and reassign students. Furthermore, the difference in criteria in assigning students to either program has not been clearly defined.[254]

In recognition of the discrimination involved, Federal courts have ruled against the use of IQ tests in assigning minority students to EMR classes.[255] In *Larry P.* v. *Riles*, the San Francisco Unified School restrained from placing black students in EMR classes "on the basis of criteria which place primary reliance on the results of IQ tests as they are currently administered, if the result of use of such criteria is racial imbalance in the composition of such classes."[256] In *Diana* v. *State Board of Education, California*,[257] plaintiffs successfully challenged the use of IQ tests in assigning Mexican American children to EMR classes on the grounds that low IQ test scores resulted from their unfamiliarity with the English language.

EXTRACURRICULAR ACTIVITIES

Participation in extracurricular activities helps students develop leadership skills, respect for the democratic process, competitiveness, and cooperation. It makes the school experience more meaningful and tends to enhance learning. In desegregated schools participation in extracurricular activities is crucial, since it develops feelings of belonging and a sense of pride in the new school. Furthermore, it contributes to producing a truly integrated school environment by providing students the opportunity to discover common interests and goals.

Participation in extracurricular activities by students of all races does not happen automatically when schools desegregate. School administrators and teachers facilitate participation by establishing policies governing participation, providing transportation, supporting and encouraging students to participate, publicizing events and activities, and by an unwillingness to accept anything but full participation. Since desegregation brings together an entirely new student body, activities, clubs, and sports that reflect the interests of all the students are planned. Many desegregated school districts have made some efforts to ensure the participation of all students, but these efforts usually are limited and generally have fallen short of what is required.

In Prince George's County, Maryland, school coaches were instructed to accept all transferring athletes as team members at the new school. Student government officers, yearbook and newspaper staffs, school band members, and cheerleaders from previous schools were to retain their positions and serve jointly with officers and members at their new schools.[258] Despite this policy, participation in extracurricular activities declined after desegregation because of limited activity buses, failure to duplicate special interest

[254] Louisville transcript, testimony of Joel Henning, pp. 694–95.
[255] For a discussion of court cases see "School Desegregation Litigation in the Seventies and the Use of Social Science Evidence: An Annotated Guide," *Law and Contemporary Problems*, vol. 39, no. 1 (Winter 1975), pp. 50–133.
[256] 343 F. Supp. 1306 (N.D. Cal. 1972).
[257] Civ. No. C–70–37 R.F.R. (N.D. Cal. June 18, 1973).
[258] *Long Day's Journey*, p. 354.

clubs, and lack of parental encouragement to participate in activities.[259]

Although most school districts report that they provide activity buses or bus tokens for public transportation, students testifying at Commission hearings often linked limited participation in extracurricular activities to transportation problems. A student from Brandon High School in Hillsborough County Public Schools said, "Most of [the black students] live too far away to get involved in activit[ies] at Brandon because of lack of transportation."[260] A student at Kennedy High School in Denver explained:

> Usually we have late gymnastics practice and it's hard for me to get home within a certain amount of time so I can still do my homework. That is the big problem at Kennedy, I think***it's transportation because I'm the only black coming from northeast Denver who is on the gymnastics team. They say that they can't get a bus for one student, so they give me these tickets to catch the city bus, but the city bus takes so much time***when I get home, I barely have time to study and then get a good night's rest. So it's really hard from the transportation part.[261]

In Louisville, a black student said:

> I was on the advisory council, but I never did make it to the meetings because I had no way to get out there. I called several times to tell them I had no transportation. I felt if they really wanted us on the advisory council and really wanted to hear what I had to say, they would have provided transportation.[262]

Schools sometimes compensate for inadequate transportation by providing activity periods during the regular school day. The principal of Dunbar Elementary School in Hillsborough County explained how the school surmounted the transportation problem:

> We have a club day which is every other Friday; it is from 1:30 to 2:30 and our students leave at 2:45. The clubs are sponsored by the teachers with varying talents and it is a delightful experience***we enjoy it.[263]

Similarly, in Little Rock, Arkansas, student activities such as student council meetings, drama, and art take place during the regular school hours to avoid transportation problems.[264]

Encouragement from teachers and administrators, though vital if minority students are to participate in extracurricular activities, is often lacking, and left alone, few students will choose to participate. Thelma Shuman, dean of girls of H.B. Plant High School, Hillsborough County, explained:

> It is hard for them to get into these extra activities because there is such a small number of them***they just feel [like] outsiders.
>
> ***If the total administration and teachers at the school would encourage the black students to become involved, help them to

[259] Ibid., p. 420.
[260] Tampa transcript, testimony of Debra Goldsmith, student, Brandon High School, p. 570.
[261] Denver transcript, testimony of Vernon Owens, p. 890.
[262] Louisville transcript, testimony of Tuwana Roberts, student, Central High School, p. 619.
[263] Tampa transcript, testimony of Dora Reeder, principal, Dunbar Elementary School, p. 662.
[264] Little Rock, Ark., Case Study, p. 45.

become involved, then I think it would help. But they just leave it up to the student***and they don't get involved. [265]

Publicizing activities is one way to encourage participation. A student from Brandon High School, Hillsborough, said:

[T]he whites tell their friends about it [extracurricular activities] and they tell their friendsblacks don't really get interested or know about the clubs***[There's a] lack of information. They just don't know about it. [266]

This student also said that encouragement is provided by black teachers but not white teachers. [267]

At Burke High School in Boston, white students hesitated to join sports teams that are predominantly black. According to Burke's coach, efforts to encourage white students to join the basketball team failed the first year, but continued encouragement yielded four times as many white students for the following year's team. He explained:

The [white] kids have become much more comfortable in the situation. The white kids are even causing trouble now, where they weren't at the beginning of the year, which is a—you don't want it, but it is a very natural thing. [268]

The Tulsa, Oklahoma, Independent School District faced the problem systemwide. School officials conducted workshops for the student council, cheerleaders, and pep club sponsors to explore the reason for lack of minority participation and to develop ways to encourage greater participation. [269] Some schools in Hillsborough County require the student council to be representative of both bused and nonbused students. Although this policy has been effective in ensuring minority participation on the student council, it has not been used for interest clubs. [270]

When schools have been successful in bringing about participation of all students in extracurricular activities, students of different racial and ethnic backgrounds are likely to view each other as equals. The dean of boys of a junior high school in Hillsborough County told the Commission:

We had a dance 2 weeks ago. It was formal, most of the boys appeared in tuxedos. The pupils elected a king and a queen from the ninth grade, and a prince and princess from the eighth grade. Our king is white; our queen is Cuban; our prince is black; our princess is Cuban. [271]

STUDENT ATTITUDES

Students, the major actors in the school desegregation process, consistently adjust to school desegregation in a positive manner.

Superintendents queried in the Commission's national survey said that a majority of students, both white and minority, supported desegregation in their districts. This was true of minority students in 72 percent of the districts and of white students in 62 percent.

[265] Tampa transcript, pp. 533–35.
[266] Ibid., testimony of Debra Goldsmith, student, Brandon High School, p. 571.
[267] Ibid.
[268] Boston transcript, testimony of Joseph Day, teacher and coach, p. 285.
[269] Tulsa, Okla., Case Study, p. 53.
[270] Tampa transcript, testimony of Thelma Shuman, p. 534.
[271] Tampa transcript, testimony of Ralph Fisher, dean of boys, Monroe Junior High School, pp. 600–01.

Furthermore, student support reportedly increased substantially after the desegregation plan was in operation. [272] In interviews and hearing testimony these feelings were generally expressed in very personal terms relating to individual experiences. One student in Denver said:

> When I first heard about going to Manual, I was ***in eighth grade***and I think I might have been really scared***except my mom had been working with Mr. Ward and a lot of the kids and teachers and she knew a lot about it.

> And I had a lot of support from the house, my mom and older friends who are going to Manual now, and they said, "Don't be scared of it, now it's really great." And I think so now. [273]

Positive attitudes have been expressed by students even in school districts marked by disruptions and chaos. In Pontiac, Michigan, where protests and violence characterized the beginning of school desegregation, parents and school personnel said that students, rather than the school board or central school administrators, had provided substantial leadership. [274] Students at one school formed an organization known as The Group "to show the positive side of integration." During the following school year, several thousand students throughout the system joined The Group in support of the motto "We Can Make it Work." [275]

In Boston, another district marked by violence, students testifying at the Commission's hearing emphasized the benefits of school desegregation. One student said:

> ***what really sort of made me mad about the whole school year was all the good things that happened at Jerry [Jeremiah E. Burke High School]***it was never brought out***[W]ithin the school it was brought out, but in the community, and the whole city of Boston, the media just kept [reporting] the bad things that were happening about desegregation in the schools. [276]

While busing is considered an inconvenience by some students, many students view it as a positive and often enjoyable experience. The Southern Regional Council found that students who are bused to school are more favorable toward busing than students who are not and that students in general are more positive about busing than adults. [277] A Tampa student concisely expressed his feelings about the bus ride, "It is all right with me because I like to ride." [278]

Another Tampa student testified that her mother drove her to school because the bus ride would necessitate arising at 4:45 a.m.:

> ***I would have to leave at a quarter to 6:00 if I wanted to ride the bus, therefore get up at a quarter to 5:00.

> This way, since I get a ride to school, I don't have to get up until 5:30, so I get extra sleep. [279]

[272] U.S., Commission on Civil Rights, national survey data, 1976. Data compiled from approximately 500 desegregated school districts.

[273] Denver transcript, testimony of Chris Sturgis, student, Manual High School, p. 820.

[274] *Ten Communities*, p. 67.

[275] Ibid.

[276] Boston transcript, testimony of Jan Douglas, student, Jeremiah E. Burke High School, p. 332.

[277] Egerton, *Report Card from the South*, p. 11.

[278] Tampa transcript, testimony of Craig Allen, student, Dowdell Junior High School, p. 774.

[279] Ibid., testimony of Aileen Miller, student, Greco Junior High School, p. 773.

A parent described her son's feelings about the bus ride: "He really rather enjoys the bus ride. On occasion I have offered to give him transportation home, and I have been reprimanded severely for that."[280]

Racial Attitudes

Student testimony received by the Commission indicated that although desegregation initially had been a frightening or difficult adjustment because of preconceived notions or prejudices, it subsequently proved to be a worthwhile experience and essential preparation for life. A white student in Stamford said:

> ***I happen to think that integration was the best thing that ever happened to me. I think it's really taught me to live with a lot of different people ***. [T]hrough six grades in school, I was with only whites, and only with people who were around me. And I was, of course, all of a sudden thrown into a completely different atmosphere. And the adjustment was tough. But I learned to deal with it***. So I think it's done me well and I happen to agree with it.[281]

A student in Minneapolis described his experience with school desegregation:

> ***I feel that it has opened my mind and going to school with people from different backgrounds***has probably far more prepared me than sitting in an all-white school and learning Greek and Latin and so-called classical education. I think that getting out and meeting people from different backgrounds has probably better prepared me than***spending all that time learning at an all-white school.[282]

A black student expressed his views:

> You won't know about people until you are mixed with them. And I think school is really where people get together and people mix, ***and I'd rather go to an integrated school than an all-black school.[283]

A student in Louisville said:

> If I hadn't gone to Thomas Jefferson, I would really be a narrow-minded person, because before I went there I went to a***private, all-white school, and I had no idea what other people were like, I couldn't care less
>
> I didn't want to associate with anybody except whites. But at Thomas Jefferson, I got to where color didn't matter to me***. I didn't care whether they were black or not, it was what type of person they were, and I couldn't understand why so many people were so bigoted or prejudiced.[284]

When student disruptions occur they are almost always of short duration and with time students quickly adjust to one another. Moreover, disturbances cited as racial incidents by the media or opponents of school desegregation most often are viewed differently by school personnel and students. Staff at several high schools in Tampa consistently cited overcrowding as the cause of school

[280] Ibid., testimony of Janet M. Middlebrooks, PTA president, p. 654.
[281] Stamford transcript, testimony of Bruce Spain, student, West Hill High school, pp. 229–230.
[282] Minneapolis transcript, testimony of George Sell, student, Minneapolis Central High School, p. 824.
[283] Stamford transcript, testimony of Michael Palmer, student, West High School, p. 232.
[284] Louisville transcript, testimony of Terry McAnnally, student, Thomas Jefferson High School, p. 29.

disturbances during the beginning stages of school desegregation, rather than racial confrontations. [285] Increasingly, disturbances are seen simply as conflicts between students rather than racial incidents. A student in Denver stated:

> It's not racial stuff—just fights. Two white kids, two black kids; maybe it's black and white. That doesn't make any difference, it's two kids that have to fight it out because of a disagreement. [286]

In Charlotte, North Carolina, black and white students held a press conference to request that the superintendent, school board, and media "leave them alone" and stop blowing minor incidents out of proportion. The students said they were getting along fine. [287]

Promoting Positive Racial Attitudes

Fostering positive student racial attitudes is one of the goals made possible by school desegregation. School districts have produced positive results by providing opportunities for students to meet and interact both before the beginning of school and during the school year. These activities range from picnics and ice cream socials to retreats and summer jobs helping to reorganize the school. Students in Hillsborough County schools were involved from the very beginning, with 30 students serving as members of the citizens' committee which helped draft the plan. [288] During the semester prior to school desegregation in Springfield, Massachusetts, orientation programs for parents and students were held at both sending and receiving schools. The program included a tour of the facilities, explanation of curricula, and question and answer sessions with the principal and faculty. [289]

Similarly, Denver students and staff from a number of receiving schools went to feeder schools to inform pupils about available courses and extracurricular activities and to reduce fears or anxieties. [290] A Denver organization sponsored a youth involvement program and brought students from various schools to YWCA facilities to swim and socialize prior to the beginning of the school year. [291] One Denver high school hired students over the summer to help prepare for school desegregation. [292] Students assisted in marking books, mimeographing, taking inventory, and working with teachers to plan student orientation activities and discuss potential problems. The principal expressed the philosophy behind establishing such programs.

> ***We felt that there had to be meetings where students could get together during that summer prior to the opening of school in the fall to see what they could do to alleviate some of the kinds of tensions and problems and negative feelings that both parents and students would have. [293]

In Minneapolis, black and white students, including proponents

---

[285] U.S., Commission on Civil Rights, prehearing interviews, Hillsborough County, Fla.
[286] Denver transcript, testimony of Chris Sturgis, student, Manual High School, pp. 826–27.
[287] Hall, "Hollow Victory," p. 12.
[288] Ten Communities, p. 18.
[289] Springfield, Mass., Case Study, p. 11.
[290] Denver transcript, testimony of LaRue Belcher, principal, Thomas Jefferson High School, p. 843; testimony of Bryan Tooley, student, Morey Junior High School, p. 468.
[291] Ibid., testimony of the Reverend Richard S. Kerr, director, People Let's Unite for Schools (PLUS), p. 111.
[292] Ibid., testimony of James Ward, principal, Manual High School, p. 792.
[293] Ibid., p. 791.

and opponents of school desegregation, participated in a retreat. Its purpose was to acquaint them with one another, discuss problems, and obtain suggestions and recommendations. [294] The Berkeley superintendent created a task force of students who met with him on a regular basis to discuss the expectations, fears, and differences between cultural groups. These students became advocates for desegregation in their respective schools. [295]

During the early stages of desegregation, schools used varied techniques to keep students informed, help them adjust, and promote intergroup contacts. A teacher in the Denver school system devoted some class time to an explanation of the school desegregation issue. A student testified to the importance of this class.

> He discussed the whole issue of***busing, how it came about and the constitutional issue; and it really helped me, because before that I didn't know about it.
> And this year, I know he's maybe touched on it a couple of times, and the students are aware. [296]

A teacher described her system of orienting students to their new environment:

> I made plans to make the children feel as comfortable as possible at the school, so I set up a buddy system***[T]he children who had been attending Moore School would be a buddy, paired with someone from the satellite area. And I felt like this would make them feel more at home. [297]

In many school districts, students are organized in human relations or biracial councils. Although known by various titles and with different organizational structures, the councils have generally been established to promote positive student relations and a positive school spirit. Student advisory committees in Tampa, consisting of an equal number of minority and majority students, were organized in all secondary schools. [298] The committees provided a forum for student interaction between the races and for developing appreciation of diverse backgrounds.

Similarly, in Austin, Texas, triethnic student human relations committees (black, white, and Mexican American) organized activities to foster positive attitudes toward desegregation. [299] Racially mixed student coordinating councils operate in the schools of Charlotte-Mecklenburg to promote student involvement. [300] In a Denver high school, black and white students who "had it together" were organized into the "Smiley Action Team." If a student encountered a problem of a racial nature, he or she would be "buddied" for a day or two with a member of the "Smiley Action Team," usually of the opposite race. [301]

In Bogalusa, Louisiana, orientation of students to school desegregation and human relations activities were notably absent. [302]

---

[294] Minneapolis transcript, testimony of George Sell, student, Minneapolis Central High School, p. 806.
[295] Berkeley transcript, testimony of Ramona Maples, associate director of research and evaluation, Berkeley School District, p. A–89.
[296] Denver transcript, testimony of Deborah Wheeler, student, Manual High School, p. 833.
[297] Ibid., testimony of Ruth C. Johns, teacher, Moore Elementary School, p. 966.
[298] Tampa transcript, testimony of Harold Clark, area general director, p. 393. Student advisory committees are established pursuant to ESAA regulations.
[299] Egerton, Report Card from the South, p. 40.
[300] Ten Communities, p. 107.
[301] Denver transcript, testimony of Harold Scott, principal, Smiley Junior High School, p. 436.
[302] Bogalusa, La., Case Study, p. 40.

Racial relations among students have been strained since the initial stages of school desegregation and remained the same in 1976.[303] In fact, school activities are kept to a minimum and each year two high school proms are held, one black and one white.[304]

School districts can contribute greatly to the promotion of positive student racial attitudes. By creating an environment that is not merely desegregated but truly integrated, much can be done to prepare students for life in a pluralistic society A Denver student, when asked what stood out as the most significant experience of her senior year, responded: "I think, to me, it was learning that the world wasn't made up of the Bear Valley that I had always known. Now it's not secluded and there is not such an ethnic idea about our little community."[305]

DISCIPLINE IN DESEGREGATED SCHOOLS

Minority parents in most desegregated school districts are seriously concerned that a higher proportion of minority youngsters are subject to disciplinary measures, primarily suspensions and expulsions, than white students. The disproportion is most evident in statistics on student suspensions. The Department of Health, Education, and Welfare reported the following facts based on an analysis of its 1973 school desegregation survey:

> ***minority students are being kept out of school as a disciplinary measure more frequently and for longer periods of time than nonminority students.
> ***the frequency of expulsions and suspensions of black, Spanish-surnamed, Asian American, and Native American-Indian students is nearly twice that of white students. The average length of a suspension is nearly a day more for a minority student than for a white student.[306]

The problem is of such magnitude that many studies have been conducted to determine its cause and consequences.[307]   Many school officials say that racially disproportionate suspensions do not mean racial discrimination, that "black overrepresentation among those suspended or expelled is simply incident to the fair administration of essential school rules designed to safeguard the integrity of the teaching and learning environment."[308] Minority students, on the other hand, often see racially disproportionate suspensions as a lack of fairness in the application of school rules and discipline. The disparity is of such a magnitude, however, as to make any nonracial explanation suspect in some quarters. The consequence of mass suspension and expulsion of minority students is that many of these

---

[303] Ibid., pp. 41, 43.
[304] Ibid., p. 43.
[305] Denver transcript, testimony of Cynthia McLelland, student, John F. Kennedy High School, p. 896.
[306] U.S., Department of Health, Education, and Welfare, Factsheet, Student Discipline, September 1975.
[307] See, for example, Southern Regional Council and Robert F. Kennedy Memorial, *The Student Pushout—Victim of Continued Resistance to Desegregation* (Atlanta: 1973) (hereafter cited as *The Student Pushout*); Children's Defense Fund, *School Suspensions: Are They Helping Children?* (Washington, D.C.: 1975) (hereafter cited as *School Suspensions*); Children's Defense Fund, *Children Out of School in America* (Washington, D.C.: 1974) (hereafter cited as *Children Out of School*).
[308] Mark G. Yodof, "Suspensions and Expulsion of Black Students from the Public Schools: Academic Capital Punishment and the Constitution," *Law and Contemporary Problems* (Spring 1975), no. 2, p. 379.

young people become disillusioned and drop out or, more accurately, are pushed out of school. [309]

In Hillsborough County, Florida, during 1970–71, the year prior to total desegregation, 4,805 students were suspended. During 1971–72, the first year of desegregation, 8,598 students were suspended. In 1973–74 the number increased to a peak of 10,149, almost 10 percent of the student population, and about half were minority students who were only 20 percent of the total school enrollment. [310] Hillsborough County school officials maintain that, although a disproportionate number of minority students are suspended, it is not due to discrimination but that a large proportion of black students are disobeying the rules. [311]

The black community, concerned for some time over the number of black student suspensions, filed a complaint with the Office for Civil Rights (OCR) of the Department of Health, Education, and Welfare charging discrimination in the administration of discipline. After an investigation, HEW notified the school district that its disciplinary policies had a discriminatory impact on minority students and it should develop an affirmative action plan to alleviate the problem. [312]

During the first 4 months of desegregation in Denver, 3,844 students were suspended, 2,748 of whom were minority students. Of the junior high school suspensions, 73 percent were minority students although they constituted only 45 percent of the junior high population. HEW's Office for Civil Rights had notified the Denver school superintendent of probable noncompliance with the Emergency School Aid Act regulation governing the administration of disciplinary sanctions [313] and recommended that they review and analyze incidents of suspension to determine what causes or procedures had led to the disproportionate suspension of minority students. OCR further suggested that alternatives be tried, using suspension only as a last resort, but warned against alternatives which segregate children and provide inferior services and education. In reference to the desegregation process, OCR stated that particular attention should be given to the transition pressure for children entering certain schools. [314]

Disproportionate discipline is evident even at the elementary level. A Denver elementary school teacher expressed his concern about the disparate treatment of minority children:

> I became very upset that every time I would walk into the office, the office would be full of blacks and Chicanos to be disciplined. It just didn't set right with me***why was it that

[309] *The Student Pushout*, pp. 12–16.

[310] Paul R. Wharton, assistant superintendent, Hillsborough County Public Schools, inter-office communication to secondary principals, on suspensions, Jan. 19, 1976, and Egerton, *Report Card from the South*, p. 36.

[311] Tampa transcript, testimony of Paul R. Wharton, assistant superintendent, Hillsborough County Schools, p.311.

[312] Egerton, *Report Card from the South*, p. 36.

[313] The Code of Federal Regulations, Title 45 (Public Welfare) *discrimination against children*, states that a school district is not eligible for assistance under the Emergency School Aid Act if it has a procedure which results in discrimination, including disciplinary sanctions which discriminate against minority-group children.

[314] Gilbert D. Roman, Director, Office for Civil Rights, HEW, letter to Louis J. Kishkunas, superintendent, Denver School District No. 1, July 13, 1975.

Chicanos and blacks were the only ones causing trouble in the school? Why were they always sitting on the bench?[315]

The suspension problem in the Jefferson County Public Schools in Louisville is a major concern of black leaders and parents.[316] In April 1976 the *Louisville Times* reported that some Jefferson County high schools were suspending black students at rates 7 to 15 times as high as the rate for white student suspensions, and that black suspensions were highest in newly desegregated schools that were part of the old, predominantly white, county school system. In schools formerly part of the Louisville city school system, the suspension rate for blacks was markedly lower. County principals maintain that the disparity is justified because they are having special discipline problems with black students who became used to lax discipline in the city schools they attended before desegregation.[317] The newspaper quoted several principals:

> Those kids just can't adjust to the fact that you don't leave class when you want to, you don't come to school when you want to.[318]

> ***those kids tend to talk back more, they tend to be louder, they tend to express themselves with less hesitation and reservation. They tend to fire back at you.[319]

Another white principal in a formerly predominantly white county school, who asked not to be named in the news article, was quoted as saying:

> I think there ought to be some alternative where a person is suspended as an in-school type of thing, but he doesn't go to a classroom. He goes to a rock pile and he's supervised by two Marine drill sergeants. He goes to the compound for six hours a day, and he works. He sweats.[320]

City principals deny that city schools are lax in requiring discipline and say that many of the problems are caused by insensitivity of county principals:

> Black kids have a different culture. They talk differently than white kids and some of the people in [the county] schools are not used to it. So, instead of trying to get used to it, the thing that they use to get the kids under control is *** suspension***[321]

In Berkeley, where disproportionately high suspension of black students also is an issue, Dr. Ramona Maples, associate director of research for the school district, offered this explanation: "Black children still do not know how to beat the system. They do not know the appropriate way to get through the system without getting

[315] Denver transcript, testimony of James E. Esquibel, p. 973.

[316] U.S., Commission on Civil Rights, prehearing interviews, Louisville, Ky.

[317] *Louisville Times*, Apr. 6, 1976, "Did Laxity in City High Schools Contribute to Suspensions," pp. A-1, A-8.

[318] Ibid. Arthur Draut, principal, Waggener High School with 61.8 suspensions for every 100 black students.

[319] Ibid. Dr. Irvin Rice, principal, West Point High School with 81.2 suspensions for every 100 black students.

[320] Ibid. Principal, name withheld by request.

[321] Ibid., Joseph McPherson, principal, Central High School, 13.6 suspensions for every 100 black students.

punished." Dr. Maples said that more black male children are disciplined than any other group. [322]

In Prince George's County almost 46 percent of the students suspended in the 3-month period following desegregation were black, although black students were only about 25 percent of the student population. [323] A white administrator for Prince George's County schools admitted that the racial attitudes of school personnel could contribute to the high number of black suspensions:

> I personally would expect that the suspension rate for whites and blacks would conform generally to the racial distribution of students in the system. If proportionately greater numbers of blacks are suspended than whites, I think we have a problem of discrimination. [324]

In Prince George's County, officials also cited inconsistency in the application of discipline. Black and white school personnel noted a general "inattentiveness" to the behavior of black students by many white teachers. One teacher stated that some white teachers say they are afraid of black students and allow them to cut class and roam the halls while compelling white students to follow the rules. This attitude, many felt, was "the most derogatory attitude possible" because it led black students to misbehave further. A black counselor said that "fear of black students" was a "copout" because "the plain and simple fact is that they [white teachers] don't care about these [black] children." [325]

Disciplinary policies which allow students to avoid suspension if their parents come to the school for a conference can result in lower suspension rates for white students. Minority parents often are unable to come to school for a teacher conference because they work or do not have transportation. A review of Richland County School District No. 1 in South Carolina revealed that, because of white parental conferences, white students receive fewer or shorter suspensions. [326] A black community leader in Tampa said:

> I submit that the reason more white students are disciplined within the school and kept there without having to be suspended or expelled is because more white parents are available for conference with the school administrators and to work out the problems on the spot or through a continuing basis. [327]

Discipline Codes

School desegregation frequently is followed by a toughening of disciplinary rules and regulations, often at the urging of white antidesegregation groups. Citizens for Community Schools, an antibusing group in Prince George's County, joined by some county teachers, shifted its attention from busing and desegregation to student conduct. The toughness of the system's disciplinary policies also became a key point of debate among candidates during the

[322] Berkeley transcript, p. A–99.
[323] *Long Day's Journey*, p. 388.
[324] Ibid., p. 390.
[325] Ibid., p. 401–2.
[326] William H. Thomas, Director, Office for Civil Rights (Region IV), HEW, letter to Dr. Brandon Sparkman, superintendent, Richland County School District No. 1, Aug. 14, 1975; also HEW internal report on Student Discipline Actions.
[327] Tampa transcript, testimony of Augusta Thomas, director, Tampa Urban League, p. 801.

1973 school board race.[328] In Louisville-Jefferson County with the implementation of desegregation, the teachers' union pushed for a strong disciplinary policy.[329]

Discipline or behavior codes are usually very general and most punishable offenses depend upon the subjective judgment of teachers, such as annoying classmates, lack of cooperation, rude and discourteous behavior, restlessness and inattentiveness, excessive talking, and mischief.[330]

Because individual principals usually have complete authority over discipline, all schools do not operate under the same behavior codes. Consequently, when desegregation reassigns students, they must often adjust to new rules and regulations. In Prince George's County schools, the Commission found:

> ***standards of discipline in individual schools varied widely throughout the county. The absence of a single, systemwide code of discipline caused the greatest adjustment problems for students who transferred from a relatively lenient school to a strict school. For these students the problem of adjusting was occasionally compounded by the fact that some schools reportedly failed to orient their new students adequately. As a result, some students learned the new rules the hard way***.[331]

Litigation and Civil Rights Complaints

Minority parents have begun to challenge the discriminatory aspects of the administration of discipline. In *Tillman* v. *Dade County School Board* the issue centered on fighting between black and white students.[332] Although evidence failed to prove whether blacks or whites had initiated the disruption, all but 6 of the 93 students initially suspended were black. With some suspensions lifted, 1 white student and 47 black students were suspended for 10 or more days. In this incident, school authorities had summoned the police, who separated black and white students who were fighting by pushing the white students off the campus while containing the blacks inside the school. The court accepted the defendants' position that police action had caused only black students to be easily identified and apprehended for misconduct.[333]

In contrast, a Federal court in Dallas, Texas, ruled that disciplinary policies were applied in a racially discriminatory manner following desegregation in that city's schools. Of 10,345 students suspended in 1971, 5,449 were black.[334] Asked to explain the high rate of black suspensions, the Dallas school superintendent testified that institutional racism and racism among individuals was the cause.[335]

Civil rights and parent groups also have filed complaints with HEW which, under Title VI of the Civil Rights Act of 1964 and the

[328] *Long Day's Journey*, p. 379.
[329] Remarks of Blanche Cooper, director of community development, Jefferson County Public Schools, at the National Conference on Desegregation Without Turmoil, May 19, 1976, Washington, D.C. Ms. Cooper was a panelist in a workshop, Influencing Student Disciplinary Procedures in a Desegregation Program.
[330] U.S., Department of Health, Education, and Welfare, Office for Civil Rights, internal files.
[331] *Long Day's Journey*, p. 397.
[332] See, 327 F. Supp. 930 (S.D. Fla. 1971); *Law and Contemporary Problems*, vol. 39, no. 2, p. 397.
[333] Ibid.
[334] *The Student Pushout*, p. 4. Roughly 9.1 percent of blacks, 6.4 percent of Chicanos, and 4.9 percent of Anglos were suspended. Note: Sources quoted refer to expulsions rather than suspensions which is an apparent error.
[335] *Law and Contemporary Problems*, vol. 39, no. 2, pp. 401–03; Hawkins v. Coleman, 376 F. Supp. 1330 (N.D. Tex. 1974).

Emergency School Aid Act, has a responsibility to ensure that school districts do not practice discrimination. In one such complaint filed against Richland County School District No. 1 (Columbia, South Carolina), HEW reviewed the district's student disciplinary practices, including statistical data and written policies and procedures. HEW also interviewed central staff, school personnel, and students at selected schools. The statistics showed a disproportionate suspension rate of minority students. The review found that the ratio of minority students suspended for subjective offenses was disproportionate to the ratio of whites suspended for similar offenses. It also found that administrators and teachers ("vestiges of the racially separate dual school system") had not been adequately prepared to deal with the problems of adjustment to a desegregated school environment. [336]

Minority students are more often suspended for "institutionally inappropriate behavior." [337] As one author said, "When a black student or parent refers to institutional racism***he is arguing***that the institution has an obligation to alter its rules to make them less arbitrary and more consistent with the behavior patterns among blacks." [338] On the other hand, the author notes, "When a white student or parent argues the need for discipline, he is implicitly sanctioning the system of institutional rules and maintaining that black children must learn to adapt to that system." [339]

Thus, basic differences in culture, lifestyle, and experiences in a white-dominated society and the reluctance of the system to accommodate these differences account, in part, for the high rate of suspension for minority students. In Hillsborough County a witness said:

> ***during [the human relations workshops]***there was no in-depth attention given to some***of the major problems***cultural awareness as to dress styles, language barriers, and the black psyche in general, by which I mean the way a student reacts to a verbal command of authority from a white teacher.
> I feel there was some insensitivity on the part of teachers because***there is a tendency of black people to view whites as the oppressor and the way in which you give a command to a student or order him to do something has a lot to do with his response. [340]

Efforts to Remedy the Problem

Individual schools have approached the problem of minority suspensions in a variety of ways. A principal in Richland County, South Carolina, does not believe in suspensions. Her technique for curbing suspensions includes working with classroom teachers to identify potential behavior problems, using the voluntary services of a local university's psychology department to test and interview these students, and, where necessary, working with community ser-

[336] William H. Thomas, Director, Office for Civil Rights (Region IV) HEW, letter to Brandon Sparkman, superintendent, Richland County School District No. 1, Aug. 14, 1975; also HEW internal report on Student Discipline Actions
[337] *Law and Contemporary Problems*, vol. 39, no. 2, p. 386.
[338] Ibid., p. 386.
[339] Ibid.
[340] Tampa transcript, testimony of Joanna Jones, Project Youth director, Tampa Urban League, and member of the biracial advisory committee, p. 788.

vice organizations to establish communication with the family. Where discipline is necessary, measures are used such as work details or special assignments with close teacher supervision. [341]

A Jefferson County, Kentucky, principal, whose school has the lowest suspension figures in the district for both black and white students, said he does not suspend students unless county school policy requires it. He noted that a youngster often has problems in a single class and, consequently, he will suspend the student only from that class. [342] A school in Berkeley has established a help center where students are counseled and can talk about their problems. Students involved in a fight for the first time are sent to the help center. If a second fight occurs, they are again sent to the center and their parents are told that a third referral will result in suspension. [343]

A Denver principal testified that her school uses overnight suspensions for students who repeatedly are involved in "some kind of minor infraction of school rules." According to the principal:

> In an attempt to involve the home and to let the parents know what we are saying and what we are doing and why we are doing it, we will suspend Tom Jones at the end of his schedule today, and say you cannot come back tomorrow morning until we talk with your parents. Please bring your parents back with you or contact us by phone, if they are working. So we have quite a number of***overnight suspensions. But the youngster is not missing school. [344]

While most administrators tend to deny categorically that racial discrimination is involved in the high suspension rates for minority students, few have studied the problems in their own districts. Where efforts have been made, it appears that school systems may not be able to evaluate themselves objectively. In both Hillsborough County, Florida, and Jefferson County, Kentucky, school administrators recognized the problem of disproportionate suspension rates of minority students. [345] But neither school district has made a thorough investigation of the issue.

In Jefferson County, the Federal judge ordered the school district to investigate disciplinary procedures, but the subsequent report, basically a survey of opinion on whether or not the disciplined student committed the offense, did not look at some of the core issues. [346] For example, no comparison was made of the types of offenses for which black and white students were suspended, or the length of time each was suspended. There was no analysis of the judgmental aspects of discipline or of teachers and schools with the most discipline referrals. The discipline codes were not analyzed for cultural bias.

The Office for Civil Rights of the Department of Health, Educa-

[341] U.S., Department of Health, Education, and Welfare, Office for Civil Rights, internal report on Student Discipline Actions.
[342] *Louisville Times*, Apr. 6, 1976, p. A–98.
[343] Berkeley transcript, testimony of Astor Mizuhara, principal of Franklin Intermediate, p. A–197–8.
[344] Denver transcript, testimony of LaRue Belcher, principal, Thomas Jefferson High School, p. 859.
[345] Tampa transcript, testimony of Richard Rodd, chairman, biracial advisory committee, p. 445.
[346] See, *A Report of Student Suspensions in Selected High Schools of Jefferson County Public Schools* to the Honorable James T. Gordon, Senior Judge, United States District Court, from E. C. Grayson, superintendent, Apr. 28, 1976.

tion, and Welfare has undertaken a program to determine compliance with civil rights statutes in school systems where there appear to be possible violations in the administration of student disciplinary actions. OCR has issued requirements for keeping records on student disciplinary procedures.[347] The kinds of records required by OCR will also be useful to a district doing a self-evaluation.

The complexity of the problem cannot be overlooked. School administrators must recognize that desegregation requires reevaluation of all school policies and procedures to ensure that they do not have a discriminatory effect on minority children. Discipline codes, the cultural standards on which they are based, and whether they are fair standards for all children must be examined. Similarly, teacher attitudes, the verbal and nonverbal signals they use to convey acceptance or disapproval, and how different groups of students receive such messages should be studied. Only when administrators and teachers become sensitive to the problem can effective solutions be found.

On the issue of discipline and its devastating effect on the education of both minority and poor children, a community leader in Louisville said: "There has to be a better way. Instead of trying to find an alternative to busing***our elected officials and***the school board [should] find alternatives to suspensions."[348]

SUMMARY AND CONCLUSIONS

At the end of what has been an exciting experience for the members of the Commission, there is one conclusion that stands out above all others: desegregation works. It is working in Hillsborough County, Florida; and Tacoma, Washington; Stamford, Connecticut; and Williamsburg County, South Carolina; Minneapolis and Denver, and in many other school districts where citizens feel that compliance with the law is in the best interests of their children and their communities. It is even working in the vast majority of schools in Boston and Louisville in spite of the determination of some citizens and their leaders to thwart its progress. The efforts of law-abiding citizens in these and other desegregating districts are not well-known, although they are more representative of the total desegregation experience than the more publicized resistance of opponents.

To be sure, none of these districts is without its problems; for some, the road ahead may be as difficult as the ground already covered. Beliefs and practices nurtured in decades of slavery and inequality do not die easily. But these communities have learned that through positive, forceful leadership and careful planning by a broad cross-section of the community, school desegregation can be implemented smoothly.

---

[347] U.S., Department of Health, Education and Welfare, Office for Civil Rights, Martin H. Gerry, Acting Director, Memorandum for Chief State School Officers, "Recordkeeping on Student Actions in School Districts," August 1975, rev. January 1976.
[348] Louisville transcript, testimony of Camellia Brown, chairperson, Louisville-Jefferson County Students Defense report, p. 578.

The support given by local leaders in implementing desegregation peacefully generally results in beneficial byproducts. School officials throughout the country have noted that institutional renewal frequently accompanies the desegregation process. The educational program is reviewed and revamped to include new instructional techniques and materials, to provide for the needs of language-minority students, to develop programs to assist gifted children and those achieving below their potential, and to promote racial and ethnic harmony among faculty and students. In addition, community race relations and the level of parental participation in school activities usually improve during the course of desegregation. Some school districts which have experienced desegregation for several years generally report that minority student achievement rises and that these students often exhibit greater motivation that ultimately leads to pursuit of higher education. Majority group students hold their own academically and they commonly report that experiences with minority students have dispelled long-held stereotypes.

While many school districts have implemented desegregation plans, numerous others remain segregated. Preliminary data for 1974 from the Office for Civil Rights of HEW reveal that in districts sampled each year from 1970 to 1974, 4 of every 10 black students and 3 of 10 Hispano students attended schools at least 90 percent minority. There were wide regional variations: those schools enrolled 23 percent of the black students in the South, 58 percent of black students in Border and Northeastern States, 62 percent in the Midwest, and 45 percent in the West. [1]

Segregation remains a problem, particularly in large districts. A recent analysis of school districts 20 to 40 percent black shows that large districts across the country tend to be more segregated than small ones. Virtually no blacks in very small districts (less than 2,000 students) were in schools where minorities represented more than 50 percent of the enrollment. On the other hand, in school districts with more than 100,000 students, 3 of every 5 black students in northern schools and 2 of every 5 black students in southern schools attended schools with an enrollment greater than 50 percent minority. Furthermore, 30 percent of the black students in these northern districts and 15 percent in the southern districts attended schools that were over 90 percent minority. [2] (See table 4.1)

On balance, however, this report makes it clear that substantial progress is being made in the desegregation of our schools. If the Nation is to build on this progress, there are certain "musts" that the Commission believes need to be kept in mind.

1. Leaders at the national, State, and local levels must accept the fact that desegregation of the Nation's schools is a constitutional imperative.

[1] *Congressional Record*, 94th Cong., 2d Sess., vol. 122, no. 95, June 18, 1976, p. 9938. The districts surveyed include approximately 92 percent of the Nation's black students and 74 percent of the Nation's Hispano students. Border States in the survey include the District of Columbia.
[2] The analysis was done by the Children's Defense Fund of data collected by the Office for Civil Rights, HEW. See Marian Wright Edelman, "Winson and Dovie Hudson's Dream," *Harvard Educational Review*, vol. 45, no. 4 (1975), p. 425.

Table 4.1
Black Enrollment in Schools 50 Percent or More Black in
Districts 20 to 40 Percent Black

Enrollment		Percent Black Enrollment of School Attended	
		Over 50%	Over 90%
Less than 2,000	South	0.0	0.0
	North	0.0	0.0
Greater than 100,000	South	40.3	15.0
	North	60.6	30.2

Source: Children's Defense Fund, reported in Marian Wright Edelman, "Winson and Dovie Hudson's Dream," *Harvard Educational Review*, vol. 45 (1975), p. 425.

The peaceful implementation of desegregation is not by chance. Luck plays no part in determining the degree of disruption that a desegregating school district experiences. One of the most important conclusions of this report is that the support of school officials and other local leaders strongly influences the outcomes of desegregation. The public generally follows the lead of officials who are responsible for school desegregation. Commitment and firm support from these officials encourage law-abiding citizens to make desegregation work. Under this type of leadership, even opponents of school desegregation conform to the standards of behavior exemplified by their leaders, thus ensuring tranquility and a peaceful learning environment for their children. Officials who are committed to desegregation and act decisively to ensure peaceful implementation are likely to be rewarded with a relatively smooth, peaceful transition.

Leaders who are committed to ensuring that desegregation works will solicit involvement of the community at various stages of the process, from planning through implementation and monitoring. When the community is involved in planning, it is committed to the outcome. During planning and implementation, for example, citizens may operate rumor control and information centers or work at their children's schools. Through a variety of actions, their frustrations and anxieties are channelled into productive activity; as they learn about the school desegregation plan, they are reassured, and, in turn, can inform and allay fears of the rest of the community. Disruptions are minimized.

Conversely, when school administrators and other public officials are opposed to school desegregation and attempt to appease opponents, the voices of resisters often are stronger than constitutional imperatives. Taking their cue from their leaders, citizens who would ordinarily comply are encouraged to resist. Supporters of desegregation are discouraged from taking a public stand. The result is turmoil and confusion and sometimes violence. The occurrence of disruption is basically a self-fulfilling prophecy. If local officials and leaders believe disruption will occur and do nothing to prevent it, it is much more likely to occur.

A peaceful transition from segregation to desegregation is not the end but only the beginning. Successful desegregation requires continued monitoring, evaluation, and periodic review and sometimes revision of the original plan. School officials and community people must deal with certain "second generation" problems that may jeopardize the goal of desegregation. These problems include classroom segregation, inequitable disciplinary procedures, low minority participation in extracurricular activities, lack of minority representation on administrative and teaching staffs, and the absence of multicultural, bilingual education for language-minority students.

These problems are not inherent in the school desegregation process. Where they do occur, they result from lack of foresight, planning, and evaluation on the part of school officials and the community. But where school officials act affirmatively to promote successful desegregation, these problems are less likely to result. This action should take place continuously once the desegregation plan is put into effect. Efforts to upgrade the curriculum and to hire minority staff, for example, must continue far beyond the original pupil assignment plan. When desegregation is seen in this way—as a process—school officials can continue to provide all students a better educational environment.

School officials and other local leaders are dependent on the tone set by leaders at the national level. This tone is determined not only by the statements officials make about the desirability of desegregation, but also by the support they give, or fail to give, to court decisions designed to implement the constitutional rights of children and young people. Under our system of government, in the absence of action by the executive or legislative branches, the courts when faced with the issue must determine what steps should be taken to ensure that the constitutional right to equal educational opportunity is provided. The Commission believes, for constitutional reasons, that efforts by either the executive or the legislative branches to curb the power of the courts, in the final analysis, will not prevail. However, such efforts to curb the courts in application of remedies undermine the desegregation process and jeopardize the rights of minority students. Furthermore, these attempts contribute to the position of some individuals that desegregation can be avoided.

This Commission, therefore, takes issue with the President and those Members of Congress who seek to curb the role of the courts. Title I of the President's recent submission of the School Desegregation Standards and Assistance Act of 1976 falls within this category. This title seeks both to narrow the definition of illegal segregation and to restrict the scope of remedies available to the courts.

2. The Federal Government must strengthen and expand programs designed to facilitate the school desegregation process.

For example, Congress should increase the funding and authority, under Title IV of the Civil Rights Act of 1964, of General Assistance Centers providing technical assistance and human relations training for desegregating school districts.[3] Additional funding should be made available under the Emergency School Aid Act of 1972 for curriculum development and teacher training in desegregating school systems.[4] Congress should provide funds to assist in the construction of new schools and additions to existing ones when such construction will maximize desegregation and lessen

[3] 42 U.S.C. §2000c (1970).
[4] 20 U.S.C. §1606.

the need to increase student transportation for desegregation. Also, Congress should rescind its prohibition against the use of Federal financial assistance for student transportation for desegregation.

3. There must be vigorous enforcement of laws which contribute to the development of desegregated communities.

The President and the Congress should make a concerted effort to provide the authority and resources necessary for facilitating metropolitan residential desegregation and thereby maximize school desegregation. Each State receiving Federal housing and community development grants should be required to establish a metropolitan agency with authority to plan and implement a program for metropolitan housing development, including provision of adequate, moderate- and low-income housing throughout the metropolitan area and various services to assist minority families to secure housing outside central cities. A special tax incentive should be granted to families who select housing in areas where residents are predominantly of another race or ethnic group. The Congress should strengthen the enforcement of Title VIII of the Civil Rights Act of 1968 by authorizing the Department of Housing and Urban Development to issue cease-and-desist orders to end discriminatory housing practices.

In addition, the Department of Housing and Urban Development should assign the highest priority to enforcement of fair housing laws, including an expanded Title VIII compliance review program. Such a program would require development of affirmative housing opportunities plans, providing for review and revision of local zoning ordinances, building codes, land use policies, real estate practices, and rental policies that prohibit or discourage housing opportunities for minorities.

4. A major investment of time and resources must be made in order to deal with misconceptions relative to desegregation.

Many of these misconceptions grow out of misunderstanding of what is constitutionally required. One of the most popular misconceptions is the view that segregation in the North and West arises from "natural causes" in contrast to the "separate" schools imposed by law in 17 Southern and Border States prior to 1954. The Supreme Court of the United States expressly spoke to such State-required separation, termed *de jure* in the *Brown* decision of 1954. In other sections of the country, however, segregation (often flourishing without mandatory or permissive statutes) was termed *de facto*, meaning that it arose without official action or acquiescence and therefore was not a constitutional violation.

It is incorrect to say, however, that in the absence of a State law requiring segregation, any existing segregation is *de facto*. Federal courts have ordered desegregation in northern and western jurisdictions only when faced with evidence showing that local or State school officials have deliberately used their powers to foster segregated schools, often despite State law to the contrary. It is this abuse of the State's authority, vested in local school boards or State education agencies, which is the essence of the difference between *de facto* and *de jure* segregation. It is the culpability of these officials in causing or intensifying segregation at the door of the State, and it is this "State action" which forms the basis for finding a constitutional violation. Such State action is not *de facto*, but is actually another form of *de jure* segregation, and thus, under current constitutional law, a proper matter for Federal judicial intervention. The desegregation of schools is necessary to eliminate the current effects of these unlawful acts of State or local officials who have used their powers to cause and maintain separation of children of different races or ethnic backgrounds in public schools. Some of the methods used by local or State school officials include:

1. Authorizing the construction of new schools in places where the resulting "neighborhood" attendance area will be predominantly uniracial despite the availability of other sites that would be available to students of different races.

2. Gerrymandering school attendance zones in a manner designed to maintain segregated schools by following racial shifts in population.

3. Changing the total enrollment of existing schools through the use of portable classrooms, permanent building additions, or double sessions in order to accommodate changes in the population of one race or ethnic group.

4. Utilizing racially-oriented feeder patterns instead of neutral geographic boundaries to determine the succession of schools a child will attend throughout that child's public school years.

The Supreme Court, in deciding its first northern school desegregation case, found that intentional actions of School District No. 1, Denver, Colorado, had resulted in segregation:

> ***respondent School Board alone, by use of various techniques such as manipulation of student attendance zones, school site selection and a neighborhood school policy, created or maintained racially or ethnically (or both racially and ethnically) segregated schools throughout the school district***.[5]

In Detroit, Michigan, a similar finding of *de jure* segregation was based upon unconstitutional practices of the Detroit school board. Although the Supreme Court overturned the interdistrict remedy ordered by the district court and affirmed by the appellate court, it affirmed the finding of *de jure* segregation and cited the following as illegal segregative practices:

> (1) creating and maintaining optional attendance zones within Detroit neighborhoods undergoing racial transition and between high attendance areas of opposite predominant racial compositions;
> (2) drawing school attendance zones along directional lines which had a segregative effect;
> (3) operating a school transportation program, designed to relieve overcrowding, in a manner that increased and perpetuated segregation; and
> (4) siting and constructing schools in a manner that tended to have segregative effect.[6]

As shown in Detroit, Denver, and other nonsouthern school districts, the claim that segregation arises from natural causes and is thus beyond the purview of the courts frequently fails to withstand close scrutiny.

Another misconception grows out of the constant use of the

---

[5] Keyes v. School District No. 1, Denver, Colorado, 413 U.S. 189, at 192 (1973).
[6] Milliken v. Bradley, 418 U.S. 717 (1974).

phrase, "forced busing to achieve racial balance." This has been used so often that few stop to consider its meaning.

Courts have not forced students to ride buses. Courts have required that boards of education reassign students to schools so as to eliminate dual education systems. Buses are a convenience made available to 3.6 percent of the students bused for desegregation just as they are a convenience to the approximately 47 percent of the students who use them for purposes other than desegregation.

Many Americans, if asked whether the courts require racial balance of schools in districts found to have practiced *de jure* segregation, would probably respond affirmatively. This perception, therefore, has become another of the misconceptions that preoccupies the public and draws attention from other more important issues.

The truth is that school districts, acting on their own initiative or under a voluntary plan, may determine that the racial composition of each school should mirror the racial composition of the system as a whole. Thus, they may devise and implement racial balance plans, but they are not required to do so. The Supreme Court in *Swann* v. *Charlotte-Mecklenburg Board of Education* addressed this issue, saying:

> School authorities are traditionally charged with broad power to formulate and implement educational policy and might well conclude, for example, that in order to prepare students to live in a pluralistic society each school should have a prescribed ratio of Negro to white students reflecting the proportion for the district as a whole. To do this as an educational policy is within the broad discretionary powers of school authorities.[7]

In providing a remedy for unlawful segregation, there is no constitutional or statutory requirement that all schools in a district be racially balanced. Courts may not and do not require racial balance in an imposed desegregation plan. When there has been a findng of *de jure* segregation, the constitutional requirement is that school districts eliminate the racial identity of schools in a dual school system. Should a school district fail to remedy illegal segregation, a Federal court may issue orders to abolish such duality. Speaking again for a unanimous Court, Chief Justice Warren Burger of the Supreme Court said:

> The constitutional command to desegregate schools does not mean that every school in every community must always reflect the racial composition of the school system as a whole***.[8]

What purpose was served by the use of racial ratios? The Court said:

> We see, therefore, that the use made of mathematical ratios was no more than a starting point in the process of shaping a remedy, rather than an inflexible requirement***. As we said in *Green*, a school authority's remedial plan or a district court's remedial decree is to be judged by its effectiveness. Awareness of the racial composition of the whole school system is likely to be a useful starting point in shaping a remedy to correct past constitutional violations.[9]

There is a mistaken belief that the courts have required

---

[7]402 U.S. 1, at 16 (1971).
[8]Id. at 24.
[9]Id. at 25.

desegregation as a means to obtain what some refer to as "quality" education. No court has made a connection between these two concerns. Courts have required school desegregation as a means of ensuring equality of educational opportunity. Equality of educational opportunity implies, moreover, that all children together will share—at the same time, and in the same place—whatever quality of education the State provides. Commission studies have shown, however, that most school district officials feel that the quality of education has not declined as a result of school desegregation and, in fact, many indicate it has improved for all students.

Another misconception relates to the widely-held belief that massive white flight results from school desegregation. The isolation of minority students in central city districts reflects the composition of the population in metropolitan areas. For at least three decades, whites have been leaving central cities for the suburbs. [10] A great many factors have contributed to this population shift: relocation of employment to suburban areas, the desire for more living space, higher incomes, as well as the unfounded fear of lowered property values as the minority population increases. Real estate speculators, playing on the fears of whites, have engaged in the practice of "blockbusting." [11] The role that desegregation of schools plays in the movement of whites to the suburbs is not clear. While certain school districts have experienced a significant decline in white enrollment, evidence does not support the widely-held belief that urban school desegregation causes massive white flight and the consequent resegregation of urban schools. [12] It does appear from the evidence, however, that policies and practices of Federal, State, and local officials, as well as those practices of the private sector, have contributed to that movement.

Regardless of the causes of white flight, it is not a constitutionally permissible argument for denying students equal protection of the laws. The courts have addressed this issue:

> "White flight" is one expression of resistance to integration, but the Supreme Court has held over and over that courts must not permit community hostility to intrude on the application of constitutional principles***. [D]issidents who threatened to leave the system may not be enticed to stay by the promise of an unconstitutional though palatable plan. [13]

The Supreme Court in *United States* v. *Scotland Neck City Board of Education* said:

> ***while [white flight] may be cause for deep concern to the [school board], it cannot***be accepted as a reason for achieving anything less than complete uprooting of the dual public school system. [14]

The Commission is disturbed that these public misconceptions

[10]Robert C. Weaver, "The Suburbanization of America," paper presented at the United States Commission on Civil Rights Consultation, "School Desegregation: The Courts and Suburban Migration," Washington, D.C., Dec. 8, 1975.
[11]By selling a house to one black family in a white neighborhood and convincing white residents that property values will subsequently plummet, these speculators buy houses inexpensively and sell families at inflated prices. U.S., Commission on Civil Rights, *Understanding Fair Housing* (1972), p. 14.
[12]Christine H. Rossell, "The Political and Social Impact of School Desegregation Policy: A Preliminary Report," paper presented at the 1975 Annual Meeting of the American Political Science Association, San Francisco, Calif., Sept. 2-5, 1975.
[13]Brunson v. Board of Trustees, 429 F.2d 820, at 827 (4th Cir. 1970).
[14]407 U. S. 484, at 491 (1972).

have gained such wide credibility. More serious is the increasing willingness of State and Federal officials to jeopardize the constitutional rights of minority children to equal educational opportunity.

It is clear that the story of the desegregation of the schools of our Nation is an unfinished story. It is also clear that in many respects it is an untold story. To date the story has been told primarily by focusing on sensational developments in some school districts where desegregation is underway. Very little has been written about those aspects of the story which involve a quiet acceptance of the constitutional imperative by thousands of citizens in many communities and their successes in implementing the truths imbedded in the Constitution.

The late Branch Rickey, when he was in the middle of the battle to open up professional baseball to blacks, urged those who were ready to give up "to never accept the negative until you have thoroughly explored the positive."

This report is designed to give the media, leaders in and out of public life, and citizens, generally, the opportunity to explore the positive and at the same time to recognize the nature of the problems that must be solved if desegregation is to succeed.

The Commission believes that a careful reading of the experiences of communities included in this report will convince the reader that we are moving forward as a Nation in our determination to make the Constitution a living reality in the lives of thousands of children and young people. We believe that such a reading will replace despair with hope for those individuals whose opportunities to achieve their highest possibilities depend on our willingness to do more than pay lipservice to the provisions of the Constitution.

After weighing all the evidence in this report, the Commission is convinced that those who are willing to make a serious commitment implementing the truths that are at stake in the controversy surrounding desegregation are meeting with success. Their success goes beyond simply providing for the physical proximity that children of different races and ethnicities enjoy in a desegregated school. In the past 10 years, desegregated schools have brought together more children of different races and ethnic groups than at any time in the history of the Nation. The opportunity they have, and others who come after them will have, to understand, know, and appreciate each other, provides the most important elements necessary to the success of 200 years of efforts to provide for each American the fact and not simply the promise of equality. We believe that these successes can be duplicated throughout the Nation.

We recognize that some will differ with the conclusions set forth in this report. We urge that these differences be identified after and not before examining the evidence. This report represents the most intensive effort to date to bring together relevant evidence. If the national debate on desegregation is based on this and other comparable evidence, as contrasted with hasty generalizations drawn from a few negative experiences, we have no doubt that the Nation will once again demonstrate its ability to deal in a constructive manner with a crisis growing out of the implementation of the Constitution of the United States.

Fulfilling the Letter and Spirit of the Law. A Report of the United States Commission on Civil Rights, Washington, D.C. 1976.

Testing Black Students: Implications for Assessing Inner-City Schools

LaMar P. Miller

INTRODUCTION

In recent years, one of the most controversial and complex issues affecting the education of Black children in America has been the role of educational and psychological testing. The controversy is viewed by many as a result of the long and ugly history of racism in the United States and its effect on the findings and interpretation of research. While it is beyond the scope of this discussion to trace the history of racism, we cannot overlook the fact that the issues related to testing are embedded in the historical framework of more than three hundred years of discrimination and subjugation of Black citizens as well as in the development of psychometrics.

Education, in general, and the related fields of psychology, sociology and mental health, in particular, clearly have been undergoing a painful reassessment of their roles in perpetuating racist attitudes and practices. The extent of such involvement has come as a shock to many professionals in the field who had assumed that their special training and dedication to humanistic values made them immune. This was a grave miscalculation, for it underestimated the deep traditional roots of racists thinking in the history of schools and other social service institutions concerned with human behavior and pointed to the ironic fact that researchers and educators were no more immune to racism than anyone else.

We might easily have predicted that the Civil Rights and Black Liberation movements would evoke reaction among social scientists in the form of scientific justification of racial inferiority. This position, in itself, was hardly a novel one. It had been advanced for years by strenuous critics of the equalitarina dogma. However, what was not anticipated was a growing body of Black professionals who would take the initiative by forming Black caucuses at professional meetings, by publishing in major journals, by raising serious issues at local, state and federal levels, by challenging researchers and other professionals to take a fresh look at long standing presuppositions, and by holding meetings to look at positive approaches to improving the education of Black children.

While the focus here is on the Testing of Black Students, it is obvious that similar problems exist for other minorities such as Mexican Americans, native Americans and Puerto Ricans. While Black students are, of course, not the only ones affected by the controversy over testing, they most assuredly represent the extreme views of the argument. As usual, in a period in which scientific controversy abounds, the issues become enmeshed in political and social philosophies. While it probably is not possible to resolve the current controversy in a single presentation, it is important to try to clarify matters so that what follows our efforts will lead to enlightenment and positive gains.

It does not seem unrealistic to try to put the issues into a context which identifies the views of various individuals. The controversy is viewed by many as the result of differences in the interpretation of research efforts concerned with the question of whether or not differences in IQ scores can be attributed to heredity or to environment. For others, the argument has centered on the nature of a variety of tests, including intelligence instruments, and how they are administered. And, still others are primarily concerned with the question of the purpose of tests and testing programs.

INTELLIGENCE, HEREDITY AND ENVIRONMENT

As I have already suggested, the intelligence, heredity and environment controversy is outmoded. At least once in every scientific generation, it restages itself in some form. During the past decade we have lived through a period in which the heredity, environment and intelligence argument has held center stage. As a result of an over emphasis on the issue by the general press, this controversy has tended to lead to more controversies rather than to enlightenment and an objective and scientific approach to gaining missing information. There are, of course, a range of positions which fall somewhere in between an extreme hereditarian who believes that an individual's characteristics are almost totally determined by his genetic structure, and the extreme environmentalist who holds that heredity plays a negligible part in the development of such traits as intelligence. The controversy in and of itself might not be so important if it were not for the profound affects on educational practice, and the tendency to obscure the need to achieve maximum intellectual competence for each individual in our society.

The most notable examples of the recent controversy over testing in the public interest began when Arthur Jensen reinstituted the intelligence, heredity, and environment controversy in 1969 with his article, "How Much Can We Boost IQ in Scholastic Achievement?"[1] Jensen asserted that the published studies justified the hypothesis that genetic factors are strongly implicated in the average group differences between Blacks and Whites found on intelligence testing. As a result of widespread publicity, the interpretation of his findings raised a storm of public opinion. Blacks were particularly incensed since his recommendations for education, if adopted, would guarantee inequality for Blacks. Hernstein followed Jensen in 1971 with an article in the *Atlantic Monthly*.[2] He held that not only was IQ inherited, but that better jobs which paid more money were held by persons of higher IQ

[1]Arthur Jensen, "How Much Can We Boost IQ and School Achievement?" *Harvard Educational Review*, XXXIX (Winter 1969), 1-123.
[2]R. Hernstein, "IQ," *Atlantic Monthly*, CCXXVIII (September 1971), 43-64.

and that, therefore, higher social status could be traced to genetic endowment. Hernstein suggested that if we were to equalize opportunities for all, the ultimate result would be meritocracy. There were other studies that influenced recommendations for public policy and education. For example, Armor contended that busing in six Northern cities did not raise academic achievement, and Jencks concluded that schools made little impact in closing the gap between rich and poor.[3] While the focus on these investigations may be different, their influence on education is similar. They seem to agree that schooling does not make a difference, although Jencks denied that this was his intention.

It is important to examine these findings in light of their effect on public education policy and, thus, the implications for the education of Black children in inner-city schools. Plotkin points out that no discussion of the testing of minority children can afford to neglect the political uses of research on Black intelligence.[4] Jensen's hypotheses that Whites inherit conceptual ability whereas Blacks are genetically capable of only rote associative learning provided a new basis for a segregated school system.[5] Jencks'[6] dismissal of schooling as irrelevant to the reduction of differences between black and white in achievement strongly suggested the inability of any educational reform to produce change, and Armor's condemnation of busing provided another scientific basis for separate schools.[7] The findings of these researchers generally have been discredited. The data are questionable, outdated, and manipulated statistically. Armor professed to find mandatory busing undesirable, although his data were derived from a voluntary busing program and the research was designed to answer far more specific questions than the overall effects of busing as a tool for desegregation. Similarly, the survey data from the Coleman report were used by Jencks although that research was severely criticized as deficient in several respects, including the use of inappropriate statistical techniques.[8] Jensen, also, used data known to be inconclusive for forty years because only flawed methodologies were available.[9]

The differences in interpretation of research efforts concerned with the heredity/environment controversy may not be the key issue. All of the investigations previously mentioned relied heavily on the assessment of Black children. Thus, the issue is the uncritical use of test scores to justify regressive public policy in the service of popular prejudices.

[3]David J. Armor, "The Evidence on Busing: Research Report," *The Public Interest*, XXVIII (Summer 1972), 90-126.

[4]Lawrence Plotkin, "Research, Education, and Public Policy," *The Testing of Black Students*, ed. LaMar Miller (Englewood Cliffs, N.J.: Prentice-Hall, 1974), pp. 67-75.

[5]Jensen, *op. cit.*

[6]Christopher Jencks *et al.*, *Inequality: A Reassessment of the Effect of Family and Schooling in America* (New York: Basic Books, 1972).

[7]Armour, *op. cit.*

[8]S. Bowles, and H. M. Levin, "The Determinants of Scholastic Achievement: An Appraisal of Some Recent Evidence," *Journal of Human Resources*, XXX (Winter, 1968), 3-24.

[9]G. E. McClearn, "The Inheritance of Behavior", in *Psychology in the Making*, ed. L. J. Postman. (New York: Knopf, 1962).

CRITICISMS OF TESTING PRACTICES

As I suggested earlier, there are those who believe that the central issue of the controversy over testing is the nature of tests and how they are administered. Let us turn now to specific criticisms leveled against tests and testing practices affecting minority group children. Williams is among those who raise questions about tests and testing programs.[10] He points out that for years psychologists have speculated that ability tests are biased in favor of white, native-born American children,—or the population on whom the tests were standardized. Yet, these tests continue to be administered to Black and other minority children who were not included in the original standardization sample. Some investigators believe that such practices violate the basic assumptions on which psychometric instruments are based, i.e., validity, reliability, and standardization.

Others complain that while the controversy continues regarding the unfairness of ability tests, the relationship of tests to the educational curriculum is often overlooked. More specifically, there is strong belief that tests are powerful instruments in shaping educational curricula and teacher expectations. Another argument stresses the point that since educational tests are used primarily to predict academic success and group children in school, the school becomes the main criterion by which the predicted validity of a test is established. Moreover, the reason educational and ability tests have been able to predict academic success so well is because of their similarity of content and structure. Another way of putting it is that test items are often representative samples of the context and structure of classroom materials. Incidentally, this agreement may hold true for all educational tests—IQ, achievement, and aptitude.

Another criticism of testing asserts that there are aptitudes in minority groups that are not tapped by the traditional test content. In other words, it is not that minority groups are deficient; rather they are different and their different aptitudes need to be recognized. The result is that tests are only predictive of success as the educational process now exists.

Flaugher has made a distinction among the various possible sources of test unfairness that exist within educational testing practices that is helpful in determining what constitutes test bias.[11] In general, sources of bias exist from the conception of the test to the utilization of test results. More specifically, the three major causes of unfairness in testing are described as content, program and interpretation.

The first, and by far the most commonly referred to, is that of test content. There is a widely held belief that the kinds of tests, or the questions asked within the tests, are biased against minority

---

[10]Robert L. Williams, "The Problem of Match and Mismatch", *The Testing of Black Students*, ed. LaMar Miller, *op. cit.*

[11]Ronald L. Flaugher, "Some Points of Confusion in Discussing the Testing of Black Students," *The Testing of Black Students*, ed. LaMar P. Miller, *op. cit.*

groups, causing them to perform poorly in ways that are not valid. Questions that one might ask about content include: are test items equally familiar to all test takers? do our tests give an optimal description of all test-takers? (For example, perhaps we should give more details than just the verbal and math scores.) are there particular items within a test which are unusually difficult for one minority group or another? Research is continuing on test content, but nothing dramatic has been found to-date.

Second, the test program itself may be conducted in such a way that the result is discriminatory. For example, the concern here is with program atmosphere such as, where the test is given, the treatment of the test-takers during the administration, and the effects of the examiners' race, sex and behavior on test performance. All of these have an impact on eventual test scores. Other aspects of the testing program that cause difficulty are the peripheral characteristics of the test itself, such as the clarity of the instructions.

Finally, we should also consider the use and interpretation of test scores as a cause of inaccuracy. A frequent use of test information, for example, is in the prediction of future performance such as success in college. In fact, most lay persons believe that tests are far more valid than they really are or can be. In any case, overinterpretation of test results is rampant, sometimes encouraged by test publishers and perpetuated by convenience. Underinterpretation, which can be just as serious, also occurs as when schools are no longer held accountable for student achievement.

There are two other major criticisms of testing practices that deserve special mention because they have had disastrous effects on Black children. The first has to do with the grouping of children in school. Since this is a practice that relies heavily on testing and one that is controversial, it is appropriate to place it in proper perspective.

In spite of the admission that homogeneous grouping by ability across the subjects of the school curriculum is impossible and in spite of conflicting evidence gathered over the years as to the benefits of ability grouping, such grouping is widely practiced in the nation's public schools. While grouping occurs in school districts of all sizes, it is especially characteristic of larger school systems; and while done at all grade levels, it is more common in the higher grades than in the lower grades. Although a relatively small proportion of schools rely on test scores alone for ability grouping, virtually all ability grouping plans depend on tests, aptitude and/or achievement, as an integral feature.

Ability grouping is widely approved by school administrators and teachers. Opinion polls show that an overwhelming number of teachers express preference for average, mixed, or superior classroom groups over classes of low ability, in which emotional disturbance and rebellious behavior, as well as poor achievement, are likely to abound.

The rationale for grouping children has been that by placing children in the same grade into classroom groups—often a high, middle, and a low group—they will learn more because it is more efficient to teach children with similar abilities. In pointing out the unsoundness of this rationale, it is important to remember the implications for Black children.

First, the problem is only partly ethnic, for it affects children in general. Also, Black children, like all children, differ so greatly that only about half the children in a grade will stand in the same third in reading and arithmetic on a well standardized test. Black children are not more alike, although some testing might make it appear so. Homogeneous grouping might work if only children were homogeneous, but they are not.

The second main point is far more crucial. Ability grouping fails to make good on its promise to produce better learning. It was tried extensively in the 1920's and 30's. It did not produce results in the 1950's when the increasing number of children from widely different home backgrounds seemed to revive its claims. All of the recent investigations seem to point to the fact that grouping often stresses a sense of failure in a consistent decline in morale and effort.

Findley-Bryan have summarized the present status of grouping.[12] First, homogeneous grouping on the basis of a unitary trait of general readiness for mastery of a graded curriculum is an impossibility. Intra-individual variation in abilities and subjects is too marked. Second, organization of instruction to produce homogeneous classes has had uneven effects on achievement. The worst effects have been on low-achieving groups, depriving them not only of self-respect, but of stimulation by higher-achieving peers and often of helpful teacher expectations. The effect is to deprive all children of heterogeneous experience, separating quite as sharply on socioeconomic as on ethnic lines. Third, heterogeneous grouping alone is not enough. Essential is a classroom atmosphere of natural peer helping (older-younger tutoring). Teacher leadership in setting moderately challenging goals adapted to the current competence of individuals plus support in believing mastery can be accomplished.

One of the most devastating effects of testing is the erroneous labeling of students as mentally retarded. From such labeling, and the role of the school in the process, there emerges in the literature a greater number of minority children identified as mentally retarded than one would expect. One of the most comprehensive studies in this area has been done by Mercer.[13] For over a period of eight years, she studied mental retardation in Riverside, California. The findings of her study strongly suggest that the crux of the problem is in the clinical perspective and in the kinds of instruments used to evaluate children. The first step in achieving the status of retardate in the public school is for the child to fail a

[12]Warren G. Findley and M. M. Bryan, *Ability Grouping, 1970: Status, Impact and Alternatives.* (Athens, Georgia: University of Georgia, Center for Educational Improvement, 1971).

[13]Jane R. Mercer, "Sociocultural Factors in Labeling Mental Retardates," *Peabody Journal of Education,* XLVIII (April, 1971), 188-203.

grade; that is, he achieves the status of a "retained student."

If, after being retained, a child still is not meeting the expectations of the class, the teacher is faced with the problem of deciding whether to give him a "social promotion," and thus keep him in the regular class, or to discuss the matter with the principal. If she takes the matter to the principal, the child moves to Stage 4 in the labeling process. He becomes an "academic problem." At this juncture, if the teacher and principal decide that he is a "reading problem," "speech problem," or "underachiever," the child may retain his status as a "normal student" in the regular classroom. However, if they decide that he is a "cause to be evaluated," he will then be sent to the school psychologist for diagnosis and move to Stage 5 in the labeling process.

There are several ways in which a child still may escape being labeled beyond Step 5 (steps 6-8) even if he is referred for psychological testing and evaluation. One way involves school psychologists, who do not have time to give individual intelligence tests to all children referred to them, but must decide which children to test. If a child is not tested, he cannot be labeled a retardate.

It is not possible in this discussion to explore all of the details or the ramifications of Mercer's work. However, one of the major conclusions is that the IQ tests now being used by psychologists are, to a large extent, Anglo-centric. Mercer's work is highly important. The use of her procedures of taking into account the socio-cultural characteristics of a child's background would eliminate the over-representation of Blacks and other minority children labeled as mentally retarded, thereby ending up in special education classes. Her work, incidentally, was done primarily with Mexican Americans and Blacks. It is clear from the research of Mercer and other investigators, that what happens to minority children in school depends to a large extent on the kinds of tests administered by the school. It is clear, also, that many of the decisions are based on value judgments made by a variety of individuals associated with the school, who may or may not have the best interest of minority children at heart. As noted earlier, moral presuppositions in educational evaluation is a frightening practice for it is often irrational and used to defend the status-quo.

TESTING PROGRAMS AND INTEGRATION

The third perspective considered to be important by many individuals is the purpose of tests and testing programs. Specifically, in assessing the performance of schools, there has been a change from the more traditional method of looking at schools in terms of the quality of school plant, facilities and the credentials of professional personnel, to a reliance on measuring performance of the children who attend the school. This change in thinking, over the past decade, was brought about by the National Assessment Program, the enactment of the Elementary and Secondary Education Act of 1965, the publication in 1966 of the Coleman Report,[14] and the Emergency School Aid Act in 1972. The legislations of 1967 and 1972 include requirements that school systems assess by objective means their effect on student achievement. One consequence of the Coleman Report was that State authorities became interested in using similar methods to assess schools in their own state educational programs. In the Fall of 1967, a survey conducted by the Educational Testing Service[15] established that there were 74 testing programs in 42 states (with 18 states offering two or more programs). And in the Fall of 1970 a new survey[16] was initiated to find out as much as possible about what the states were planning and doing with regard to educational assessment. The survey was conducted as a joint enterprise involving the Educational Commission of the States, Educational Testing Service, and the ERIC Clearinghouse on Tests, Measurement and Evaluation.

Dyer and Rosenthal suggest a number of emerging problems that, relevant to this discussion, are largely concerned with the strategies and tactics by which programs of assessment are to be brought into being and maintained.[17] Among these problems is the relation of assessment data to financial incentives, or, to put it another way, concern for the way in which test results will be used in allocating state funds to local school districts. A second problem has to do with the confidential nature of information supplied by teachers and others who may be involved in some aspect of the testing process. A new law, Public Law 93-380 under the General Education Provisions Act, protecting the Rights and Privacy of Parents and Students, was enacted in August of 1974. There are specific regulations regarding the rights and privacy of students with regard to student records. Basically, no federal funds are available to any institution which denies to students the right to "inspect and review any and all official records, files and data directly related to (themselves), including all material that is incorporated into each student's cumulative record folder." This material includes, but is not necessarily limited to, identifying data; academic work completed; level of achievement (grades, standardized achievement test scores); attendance data; scores on standardized intelligence, aptitude, and psychological tests; interest inventory results; health data; family background informationl teacher or counselor ratings and observations; and verified reports of serious or recurrent behavior patterns.

Although educational assessment, properly viewed, involves a good deal more than statewide testing programs, testing seems, nevertheless, to be looming larger and larger in the plans for

[14]J. S. Coleman, et al., Equality of Educational Opportunity, Washington, D.C.: U.S. Government Printing Office, 1966.

[15]Educational Testing Service, State Testing Programs: A Survey of Functions, Tests, Materials and Services (Princeton, N.J.: Educational Testing Service, 1968).

[16]Henry S. Dyer and Elsa Rosenthal, State Educational Assessment Program: An Overview. ERIC Clearinghouse on Tests, Measurement and Evaluation (Princeton, N.J.: Educational Testing Service, 1971).

[17]Henry S. Dyer, and Elsa Rosenthal. State Educational Assessment Program: An Overview, ERIC Clearinghouse on Tests, Measurement and Evaluation, E.T.S., Princeton, New Jersey, 1971.

assessment. In fact, many of the authorizations from legislatures are principally for the assessment of education by tests. There is, therefore, mounting legislative pressure for documenting the products of the educational process by statewide testing programs.

Regardless of the differences in perspectives, testing is far more complex and important than is realized by most individuals who must make crucial decisions affecting the education of children. Certainly, sociological and ideological differences regarding the function of assessment and the impact of testing on students against a background of a changing social and technological society are not understood clearly. Even more confusing to decision-makers is that a major premise of the American system of social morality—that everyone should have an equal opportunity—has already become a crucial issue insofar as testing is concerned, if one examines the continuing debate and litigation over the question of segregated schools.

The struggle to integrate public schools in the North is a perfect vehicle for the examination of the issue raised above. While de-jure segregation has been out-lawed, the Supreme Court has not yet clarified so called "de-facto" segregation. Since the landmark case of Brown vs Board of Education, we have accepted the notion that integrated education is a means of achieving equality. Recently, however, statistically oriented researchers have cast some doubt on conventional assumptions about the benefits of school integration. Since 1969, the courts have been jammed with cases arising from the desegregation orders made by Federal judges in all parts of the country. Integrationists insist that the law requires school desegregation under the 14th amendment wholly independent of social science data regarding its effect. And, so far, judges have upheld the principle that the requirement of desegregation and the law is independent of evidence about its effect.

Recently the courts have begun to hear social science evidence about the quality of achievement in schools. The Denver School Desegregation Case was an example.[18] The district court judge asked for evidence about the achievement of seventeen schools which he found to be segregated though not as a result of public policy. He ruled that the Denver board of education had a constitutional duty to equalize the educational opportunity offered by the White and Black schools. The court, largely following Coleman's findings, saw no effect on educational opportunity traceable to age of building or size of site, although it recognized that such factors may aggravate the aura of inferiority which surrounds the school. The court, however, recognized the validity both of achievement tests and teacher experience, following the findings of the Coleman Report.[19] The plaintiffs' experts had convinced the

---

[18]Keys v School District Number One, Denver, Colorado. 313. F. Suppl. 61, 313. F. Supp. 90 (1970) 445 F. 2ed 990 (10th Cir) (1971) cert. granted, 40 LW 3335, No. 71.507, 71-572, Oct. 12, 1972.

[19]Coleman, op. cit.

court that compensatory programs across the country had proved unworkable and wasteful; thus, the court held as a matter of fact that the only way to equalize the Denver schools was to integrate them.

While a number of judges have been disposed to accept, without hard evidence, that Black schools are significantly responsible for their pupils' lower levels of achievement, that proposition remains to be convincingly documented. It is true that the Coleman Report concluded that the socio-economic status, and, therefore, race of a pupil's classmate, is an important determinant of his academic achievement. A review of the Coleman data by Mosteller and Moynihan reaffirmed that conclusion.[20] The reliability of these studies, and the data upon which they are based, however, is a matter still hotly disputed among the experts. In other words, social scientists seem to be at odds in supporting a firm conclusion on the relation of racially imbalanced schools to the achievement disparities. The testing of Black and minority students, therefore, seems to be the key to the argument. As Herbst suggests, "if Northern school lawyers could prove that segregated schools actually cause their pupil-clients academic harm, their cause would be materially advanced."[21]

It should be noted that the Denver case was the first case involving racially imbalanced schools in the North to reach the court, eighteen years after *Brown vs Board of Education* ordered an end to racial segregation in public education. More important, as we have seen in Detroit, the Denver experience is not at all unique in the North. The struggle to integrate public schools has been and will continue to be like the corresponding battle in the South, one conducted largely in the Federal courts.

ESTABLISHING CRITERIA FOR TESTING PROGRAMS

The overall impression one gets from even a cursory examination of the situation in testing today is that the field is in a highly fluid state with new developments occurring daily. One is struck by the variety of ways in which testing is contaminated by political, social, and ideological questions relating to public policy as well as by emotional, often racist, attitudes which seem to color each new development. The reason for this is clear—science has been unable to yield any clear cut answers to questions of increasing complexity regarding testing. In the meantime, each year, numbers of Black children are denied equal access to quality education because of flaws in the testing apparatus of our schools. Yet, the research evidence which could provide us with the tools to redress the present situation, while provocative, is sketchy. The causes of the discrepancies are, as we have shown, often more ideological and political than technical. In short, and for all practi-

[20]Frederick Mosteller, and D. P. Moynihan (eds.), *On Equality of Educational Opportunity*, (New York: Vintage, 1971).
[21]Robert L. Herbst, "The Legal Struggle to Integrate Schools in the North", *The Annals of the American Academy of Political and Social Science, Blacks and the Law*, Vol. 407, May 1973, p. 61.

cal purposes, we have not been able to deal effectively with the many parameters of testing.

There appear to be, however, some encouraging trends in improving the present situation. The 1972 Human Relations Conference of the National Education Association called for a moratorium on school testing of minorities, and the California Assembly, in 1972, passed legislation which provides for a variety of measures designed to ameliorate testing abuse. This legislation includes provisions prohibiting the recording of entering test scores in cumulative records, bi-lingual testing and parental consent for retarded class placement. It also directed school districts to use a wider variety of instruments and resources to assess potential. Moreover, there are a number of class action suits in various parts of the country seeking to force school districts to cease and desist in the inaccurate testing of minority children. And, finally, new researchers and writers are attempting to develop new instruments and procedures such as locator and criterion tests and performance measures for classroom evaluation that will get us back into the mold of using scales to enable teachers to help children learn more effectively rather than of using them to curtail development.

While these trends are hopeful and will in all probability change the situation in the future, those who make decisions need to start asking some very basic questions about testing programs if reasonable criteria are to be established. The following questions are examples:

1. Is there an identifiable testing program in your school district? ("identifiable" meaning written)

2. What kinds of tests are administered in your schools with respect to type? (i.e., achievement, attitude, IQ)

3. What are the names of these tests?

4. Is your testing program aimed at diagnostic or prescriptive goals or aimed at achievement?

5. Who selects the tests in your program and on what basis are these tests selected? (i.e., from professional reviews, test publishers, school board, cost of tests or from recommendations from universities or Title I consultants)

6. Is the cost factor taken into consideration with respect to your testing program? (i.e., cost of having teachers and professionals score tests)

7. Who are the decision-makers with regard to your testing programs?

8. Who makes the decisions on childrens' progress in your schools?

9. Who provides the evidence for these decisions?

10. On the basis of what data is a child held back?

11. Is your testing program integrated with teaching, and, if so, how?

12. Are teachers inclined to use tests to help allocate their time and determine their range of options with respect to teaching techniques and procedures?

13. Are the tests used in your school district considered important by teachers, school board members, administrators, parents?

14. Are the questions included in these tests considered important by teachers, school board members, administrators, parents?

15. Are the deficiencies in children in contact areas such as classrooms determined by the results of some tests?

16. Are there specific ways in which you feel the tests you use are inappropriate for your students?

17. Are students in any grade levels in your school district grouped homogeneously? If so, at what grade levels is homogeneous grouping done?

18. On what basis are your students assigned to homogeneous grouping? (If on the basis of test scores, please name the tests.)

These are questions that must be squarely faced by educational leaders and planners who wish to fulfill their responsibilities for providing quality education in inner-city schools. Teachers, parents, community representatives, administrators, as well as researchers, professors, state and Federal officials are all a part of the system. It will not be enough simply to say, "let us do away with tests." As Doppelt and Bennet point out, "the rejection of measurement instruments which register the consequences of oppression is merely a modern version of killing the messenger who brings the bad news."[22] Since tests are merely mini-carbon copies of the educational system, the bad news is in the system, not in the victim.

SUMMARY

In sum, what seems to have evolved where schools are concerned and in the context of the social consequences of educational and psychological assessments, are three distinct reactions to the issues of testing: (1) Some educators, psychometricians and statisticians have reacted to the present dilemma in terms of the job they have been assigned to do, that is to screen and predict or measure achievement. (2) Others have taken the position that there are social ills to be remedied and tests as currently designed and used to contribute to the perpetuation of these social ills. And, (3) still others, Blacks in particular, have sparked a movement to get rid of biased tests in schools and research projects.

The primary purpose of this discussion was to review some of the specific issues that underlie the testing controversy. Serious questions have been raised regarding tests and testing programs. From the psychometric point of view the issues concern how test bias is defined and measured? How well tests predict and measure school achievement? And, what are the misuses of tests. There are also social and educational problems with which to be concerned. Should there be homogeneous grouping on the basis of testing

[22]J. E. Doppelt, and G. K. Bennett, "Testing Job Applicants from Disadvantaged Groups", *Psychological Corporation Test Bulletin*, 1967, No. 56, 1-5.

ability or anything else? What are the situational effects of testing? Are there latent functions of intelligence testing? Other questions which need our attention come under the heading of Research, Education and Public Policy. What kind of a position should educators take concerning the heredity-environment issue? What facts are available and do they add up to anything valuable to educational policy? If anyone of a variety of conclusions turned out to be supported by research, what effect should it have on education? Other questions include, can testing be dealt with apart from general educational policy? Is testing the place where reform should begin? What would be the effect of an immediate abandonment of testing either for all pupils or for Black pupils? Should tests be exclusively diagnostic, never evaluative? Finally, can there be a blueprint for educational testing programs of the future?

The examination of the issues surrounding testing has made it clear that the subject is not only complex and controversial, but highly important to those who are attempting to improve education for Black children. Clearly, it has become increasingly difficult to separate the issue of testing from the realities of a political situation which leaves Black children at the mercy of a unified White majority that is often antagonistic or indifferent to their educational welfare.[23] In any case, it is clear that we will succeed in clarifying the issues and in finding solutions when we deal effectively and efficiently with the technical problems as well as the issues related to our value system and when tests become a part of the solution rather than a part of the problem.

---

[23]For a detailed discussion of testing Black children, see: Miller, LaMar P., *The Testing of Black Students*, (Englewood Cliffs, N.J.: Prentice-Hall, Inc., 1974.)

"Testing Black Students: Implications for Assessing Inner-City Schools" by LaMar R. Miller. <u>The Journal of Negro Education,</u> Vol. XLIV, Summer 1975, No. 3. p. 406-20.

Enrollment

Persons not enrolled in school and not high school graduates as a percent of population group, by age and by race and sex: October 1967 to October 1975

Year and race and sex	Percent of population, not enrolled in school and not high school graduates				
	Total, 14 to 24 years old	14 and 15 years old	16 and 17 years old	18 and 19 years old	20 to 24 years old
1967					
Black male	23.9	3.5	11.7	30.6	42.6
Black female	21.9	4.0	14.6	22.0	36.1
White male	11.6	1.5	7.0	15.4	18.8
White female	13.1	1.4	9.4	16.3	19.0
1968					
Black male	20.8	1.4	10.1	23.8	39.7
Black female	22.3	3.0	14.2	24.8	35.9
White male	11.5	1.8	6.8	14.3	18.9
White female	12.4	2.0	7.6	14.6	18.5
1969					
Black male	20.8	1.8	10.2	31.5	34.7
Black female	21.3	2.3	11.5	23.1	35.7
White male	10.1	1.8	6.8	12.6	15.9
White female	12.0	1.8	8.8	14.2	17.3
1970					
Black male	23.0	2.0	13.3	36.4	35.3
Black female	21.5	2.8	12.4	26.6	33.5
White male	9.8	1.7	6.3	13.3	14.8
White female	11.7	1.8	8.4	14.8	16.3
1971					
Black male	20.2	2.3	9.4	26.0	34.2
Black female	17.7	1.0	9.2	22.5	28.2
White male	10.1	1.1	6.4	14.2	15.1
White female	12.0	1.5	8.6	13.8	16.7
1972					
Black male	17.8	2.4	9.4	27.1	27.2
Black female	17.2	2.7	7.6	21.0	27.3
White male	10.7	2.3	7.8	13.5	15.3
White female	11.9	2.5	9.6	13.2	16.6
1973					
Black male	17.6	3.1	10.6	27.7	24.9
Black female	18.9	3.1	10.0	23.0	29.0
White male	10.4	1.9	8.7	14.1	13.7
White female	11.3	2.8	9.2	15.2	14.2
1974					
Black male	16.3	3.9	8.3	26.9	23.6
Black female	18.1	2.1	12.6	20.2	27.7
White male	11.0	1.8	9.4	17.4	13.6
White female	11.0	1.9	9.1	13.9	14.5
1975					
Black male	18.1	2.4	9.7	27.7	27.9
Black female	18.9	2.8	10.7	23.4	28.4
White male	9.9	1.4	7.3	13.7	13.4
White female	11.0	1.9	9.6	15.6	13.6

SOURCE: U.S. Department of Commerce, Bureau of the Census, *School Enrollment --Social and Economic Characteristics of Students*, Series P-20, various years.

Population for School-Age Groups, by Race

The racial composition of the school-age population is also changing; minority groups will comprise 17.4 percent of the elementary school population in 1980, compared with 16.2 percent in 1975. In 1980, minorities will constitute 16.6 percent of the secondary and 15.2 percent of the young adult cohorts.

Elementary and Secondary

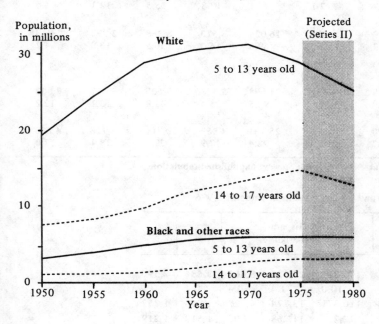

Postsecondary

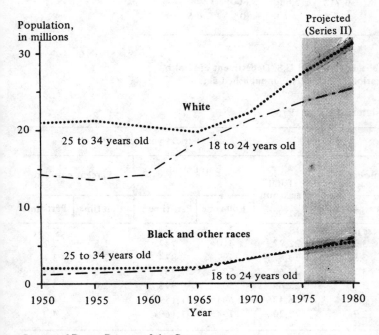

Source of Data: Bureau of the Census

Enrollment in education of persons 18 to 34 years old, by type of enrollment: 1970 and 1975

Age group and year	All persons	Enrolled					Not enrolled				
		Total enrolled	High school or below	College		Total	Not high school graduate	High school graduate	1 to 3 years college	4 or more years college
				Undergraduate	Graduate						
18 to 24 years old				(Numbers in thousands)							
1970											
Number.........	**20,633**	6,179	850	4,896	433	14,454	3,678	7,333	2,495	948
Percent	**100.0**	29.9	4.1	23.7	2.1	70.1	17.8	35.5	12.1	4.6
1975											
Number.........	**22,958**	6,932	919	5,559	454	16,026	3,673	8,388	2,992	973
Percent	**100.0**	30.2	4.0	24.2	2.0	69.8	16.0	36.5	13.0	4.2
25 to 34 years old											
1970											
Number.........	**22,973**	1,275	118	668	489	21,698	5,828	9,600	3,467	2,803
Percent	**100.0**	5.5	.5	2.9	2.1	94.5	25.4	41.8	15.1	12.2
1975											
Number.........	**27,201**	2,072	107	1,270	695	25,131	4,859	10,715	4,926	4,630
Percent	**100.0**	7.7	.4	4.7	2.6	92.4	17.9	39.4	18.1	17.0

SOURCE: U.S. Department of Commerce, Bureau of the Census, *Current Population Survey*, unpublished tabulations.

Racial composition of elementary and secondary teachers, 1974, and teacher education students, 1976

Student and staff status	Total	White	Black	Hispanic origin	Asian	Indian	Other
Staff in 1974							
Total.................	1,995,057	1,754,101	199,303	27,056	8,467	3,534	2,596
Percentage distribution	100.0	87.9	10.0	1.4	0.4	0.2	0.1
Elementary teachers..........	986,955	854,278	110,871	13,774	4,922	1,858	1,252
Secondary teachers	885,278	795,986	72,279	11,268	3,007	1,519	1,219
Other teachers..............	122,824	103,837	16,153	2,014	538	157	125
Teacher education students in 1976							
Total		1/366,900	30,715	7,600	3,600	1,900	–
Percentage distribution	100.0	89.3	7.5	1.8	0.9	0.5	

1/ Includes other.

SOURCES: Equal Employment Opportunity Commission, unpublished data, and U.S. Department of Health, Education, and Welfare, "National Survey of Preservice Preparation of Teachers," unpublished data.

College enrollment of persons 18 to 34 years old, by attendance status: 1970 to 1975

Year	18 to 24 years old					25 to 34 years old				
	Total age group	Enrollment		Percent enrolled		Total age group	Enrollment		Percent enrolled	
		Full-time	Part-time	Full-time	Part-time		Full-time	Part-time	Full-time	Part-time
				(Numbers in thousands)						
1970......	20,633	4,659	669	22.6	3.2	22,973	410	747	1.8	3.2
1971......	21,612	4,882	756	22.6	3.5	23,678	491	874	2.1	3.7
1972......	22,160	4,891	739	22.1	3.3	24,697	533	931	2.2	3.8
1973......	22,522	4,674	725	20.8	3.2	25,693	504	993	2.0	3.9
1974......	22,529	4,581	814	20.3	3.6	26,436	641	1,159	2.4	4.4
1975......	22,958	5,126	887	22.3	3.9	27,200	794	1,169	2.9	4.3

SOURCE: U.S. Department of Commerce, Bureau of the Census, *Current Population Survey*, unpublished tabulations.

In 1975, persons of Spanish origin were about 5 percent and Blacks about 11 percent of the U.S. population 4 years old or older. The percent of each ethnic group between 4 and 25 years old was higher for persons of Spanish origin than for any other ethnic group identified.

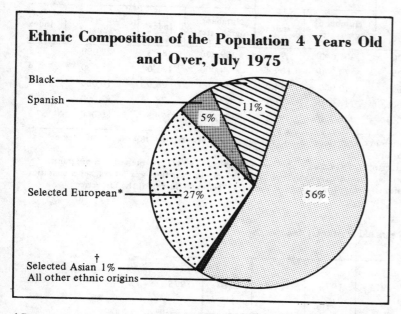

Ethnic Composition of the Population 4 Years Old and Over, July 1975

Black — 11%
Spanish — 5%
Selected European* — 27%
56%
Selected Asian† 1%
All other ethnic origins

*German, Italian, English, Scottish, Welsh, Irish, French, Polish, Russian, Greek, Portuguese

† Chinese, Japanese, Filipino, Korean

Source of Data: National Center for Education Statistics, July 1975 Survey of Languages

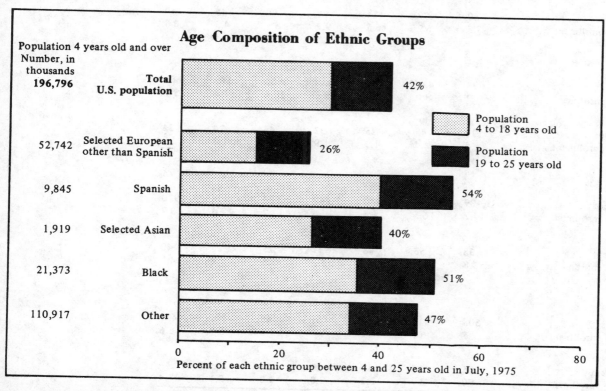

Age Composition of Ethnic Groups

Population 4 years old and over
Number, in thousands

196,796	Total U.S. population	42%
52,742	Selected European other than Spanish	26%
9,845	Spanish	54%
1,919	Selected Asian	40%
21,373	Black	51%
110,917	Other	47%

Population 4 to 18 years old

Population 19 to 25 years old

0   20   40   60   80
Percent of each ethnic group between 4 and 25 years old in July, 1975

Source of Data: National Center for Education Statistics, July 1975 Survey of Languages

Supply of beginning teachers, by selected area: 1972-73 to 1975-76

[Index: 1972-73 = 100]

Selected area, bachelor's degree	1972-73		1973-74		1974-75		1975-76	
	Number of graduates	Index	Number of graduates	Index	Number of graduates	Index	Number of graduates	Index
All bachelor.s	322,000	100	305,000	94.6	259,000	80.3	227,000	70.2
Special education [bachelor's]	21,000	100	23,000	109.9	24,000	111.0	25,000	117.4
Occupational/vocational [bachelor's]1/ . . .	15,000	100	13,000	84.0	12,000	78.0	10,000	65.3
General elementary [bachelor's]	121,000	100	116,000	96.2	94,000	78.2	87,000	71.7
General secondary [bachelor's]]	138,000	100	126,000	91.2	104,000	74.8	80,000	57.7

1/ This figure represents bachelor's degree recipients with certification in occupational/vocational education only and does not include nondegree teachers available for teaching in occupational/vocational education.

NOTE.– Figures for 1972-73 through 1974-75 are weighted national estimates based on a probability sample of 240 teacher preparation programs. Figures for 1975-1976 are weighted national estimates based on a probability sample of 3,600 persons in their final year of teacher preparation.

SOURCE: U.S. Department of Health, Education, and Welfare, National Center for Education Statisitcs, "National Survey of the Preservice Preparation of Teachers," unpublished data.

Enrollment in private elementary schools of persons 3 to 13 years old in primary families, by region and race: 1968 to 1975

Region and enrollment characteristic	1968	1970	1971	1972	1973	1974	1975
	(Numbers, in thousands)						
Northeast							
White							
Private enrollment	1,636	1,407	1,282	1,217	1,118	1,077	1,016
Percent of total enrollment	22.9	19.7	18.1	17.8	16.9	16.3	15.8
Black							
Private enrollment	60	72	74	97	90	45	40
Percent of total enrollment	5.5	6.2	6.5	9.2	8.4	4.5	3.8
Southeast							
White							
Private enrollment	393	420	437	433	503	568	606
Percent of total enrollment	7.2	8.0	8.5	8.5	10.4	11.4	12.6
Black							
Private enrollment	26	45	25	32	44	24	34
Percent of total enrollment	1.4	2.4	1.3	1.9	2.6	1.3	2.0
Central							
White							
Private enrollment	1,439	1,393	1,213	1,149	984	904	970
Percent of total enrollment	17.2	16.5	14.4	14.4	12.7	12.4	13.7
Black							
Private enrollment	33	55	48	37	29	25	40
Percent of total enrollment	3.8	5.8	5.1	4.3	3.5	2.9	4.5
West							
White							
Private enrollment	508	418	474	465	365	390	411
Percent of total enrollment	7.5	6.1	7.1	7.2	5.6	6.1	6.6
Black							
Private enrollment	25	25	15	20	26	35	49
Percent of total enrollment	4.0	3.9	2.2	3.0	4.0	5.1	7.4

SOURCE: U.S. Department of Commerce, Bureau of the Census, *Current Population Survey*, unpublished tabulations.

College Participation of Young Adults, by Region and Race

College participation rates for Blacks have risen in the Northeast and Central regions. They were about equal to those for Whites in 1975.

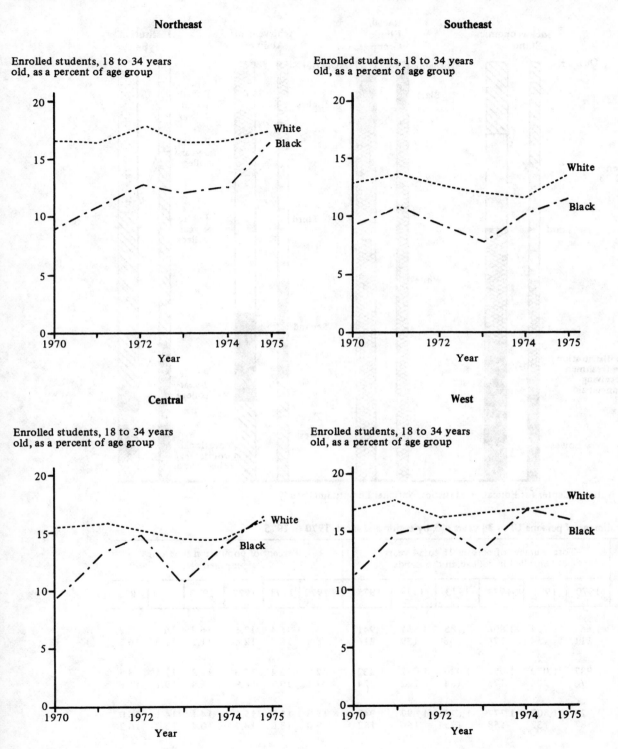

Source of Data: Bureau of the Census

Characteristics of Freshmen Receiving Federal Financial Aid

Recipients of Federal financial aid are more often persons from the lowest socioeconomic status group, non-Whites, high ability persons, and persons attending private 4-year institutions.

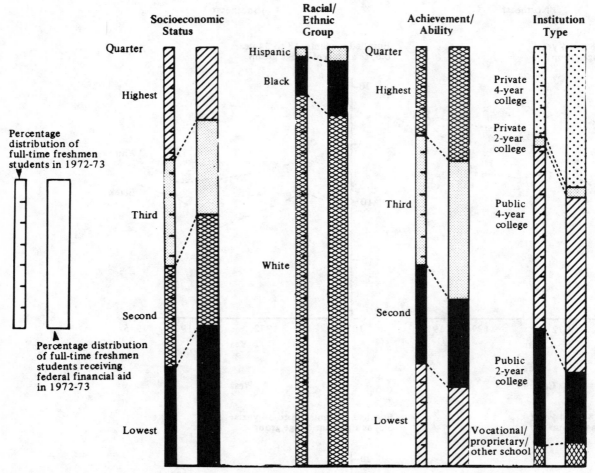

Source of Data: National Center for Education Statistics, National Longitudinal Study

Total college enrollment of persons 18 to 34 years old, by region and race: 1970 to 1975

	Total number of persons 18 to 34 years old enrolled in college, in thousands						Percent of population subgroup enrolled					
	1970	1971	1972	1973	1974	1975	1970	1971	1972	1973	1974	1975
Northeast												
White	1,664	1,734	1,896	1,788	1,841	1,941	16.5	16.4	17.6	16.4	16.5	17.2
Black	111	154	176	166	159	216	8.8	10.7	12.4	11.9	12.3	16.8
Southeast												
White	987	1,079	1,052	1,020	1,022	1,232	12.9	13.4	12.3	11.8	11.5	13.5
Black.	176	204	173	154	222	274	9.1	10.7	8.9	7.4	10.1	11.6
Central												
White	1,723	1,807	1,777	1,674	1,697	1,948	15.3	15.7	15.1	14.1	14.1	16.0
Black.	87	132	158	125	156	182	9.0	13.0	14.7	10.4	13.3	16.2
West												
White	1,564	1,678	1,623	1,725	1,771	1,867	16.8	17.5	16.2	16.4	16.8	17.1
Black.	76	102	131	116	144	146	11.2	14.8	15.4	13.2	16.6	16.0

SOURCE: U.S. Department of Commerce, Bureau of the Census, *Current Population Survey* , unpublished tabulations.

Enrollment in private elementary schools of persons 3 to 13 years old, by family income and region: October 1975

Region	Total enrolled	Enrollment, by family income (1967 dollar)					No report
		Less than $5,000	$5,000 to $7,499	$7,500 to $9,999	$10,000 to $14,999	$15,000 or more	
		(Numbers in thousands)					
Northeast							
Private enrollment	1,058	161	249	196	195	189	69
Percent of regional enrollment . . .	14.1	8.0	15.8	15.5	15.2	24.9	
Southeast							
Private enrollment	640	51	110	117	160	138	65
Percent of regional enrollment . . .	9.8	2.1	8.1	12.3	19.0	33.7	
Central							
Private enrollment	1029	95	207	229	288	138	73
Percent of regional enrollment . . .	12.8	5.6	11.0	14.2	18.5	20.4	
West							
Private enrollment	493	59	88	109	130	52	54
Percent of regional enrollment . . .	6.8	2.8	5.8	8.7	10.8	8.7	

NOTE.– Detail may not add to totals because of rounding.

SOURCE: U.S. Department of Commerce, Bureau of the Census, *Current Population Survey*, unpublished tabulations.

The Condition of Education. 1977 Edition. A Statistical Report on the Condition of Education in the United States. Volume 3, Part 1. By Mary A. Golladay. U.S. Department of Health, Education, and Welfare. Washington, D.C. 1977.

Part five:
Disadvantaged/white ethnic

Disadvantaged/white ethnic

Opportunity Program for the Disadvantages in Higher Education

Overview

In recent years several hundred thousand persons have enrolled in American institutions of higher education—persons who previously were denied access to college because of "limitations": socioeconomic status, ethnicity, poor elementary and secondary experience, and previous academic performance records. To accommodate these new students, many public and private institutions (in addition to those which historically have enrolled black students) have initiated special programs. The programs differ in practice and depth of commitment but all have responded to the demand to provide a successful post-secondary educational experience for a heterogeneous population of new students with needs and characteristics quite different from those of the American college student in the past.

This paper will describe current educational opportunity programs by considering: ways in which various institutions have responded to demands to serve disadvantaged populations and the difficulties encountered; selected studies and institutions in terms of their programs and the components that seem to indicate both progress and error; and the status of evaluation of these programs. The results of this survey suggest that, although numerous programs and practices encompassing various aspects of the higher education process (administration, curriculum, assessment, finance) have been initiated, as yet they have brought about little or no essential change in the overall process. Furthermore, despite the considerable amount of activity in collegiate compensatory education, there has been little systematic evaluative research. As noted elsewhere (Gordon 1972a), the best available data concerning educational attainment and college attendance by disadvantaged students are for Afro-Americans, who are the largest and most frequently studied disadvantaged population; underclass whites have not yet received much attention.

Historical Framework

One could preface the description of current practices by saying that American higher education has aspired to the democratic ideal of full equality in educational opportunity for every citizen, in part failing to attain this ideal, in part realizing it. The early colleges were contrived for the well-born; yet even prior to the Civil War, public pressure had brought about the founding of a number of colleges to educate the children on the lower strata. Most of these were created by state governments and most were supported by the Morrill Land Grant Act of 1862 (Cornell 1962). The City University of New York, founded in 1849 as the Free Academy, has been, since its inception, tuition-free (Irwin 1961). Although these institutions were created to increase access to higher education for all Americans, certain groups continued to be excluded. Women were first admitted on an equal basis with men at Oberlin College, which opened in 1833 (Irwin 1961). However, minority groups were shamefully underrepresented. Although institutions specifically for blacks were created (what is now Cheyney State College, Pa.; Lincoln University, Pa.; Wilberforce University, Ohio), usually by philanthropic or religious organizations, few higher educational opportunities existed for blacks in relation to their numbers (Pifer 1973). While total undergraduate enrollment was increasing steadily—from 232,000 in 1899 to 1,396,000 in 1939 (Cartter 1965)—the total number of blacks who received baccalaureate degrees during that same period increased only from 1,200 to 9,005, an insignificant figure indicative of limited access.

Aside from social/ethnic factors, inability to pay was the greatest limitation affecting higher educational access until the Second World War. The end of that war brought with it the Serviceman's Readjustment Act (the G.I. Bill) and a massive influx of new college students. Approximately three million persons were able to attend college under this provision. Between 1946 and 1948 roughly half of all American college students were receiving benefits as veterans (Armstrong 1939). The G.I. Bill was never intended to enable the poor to attend college, but rather to reward citizens for serving their country; still, to this day, the act remains a critical financial aid to a large number of disadvantaged students (veterans and their families).

By the 1950's a substantial number of Americans had attained access to postsecondary education. Those left out were those who had always been left out—the poor, and especially the minorities. In the case of Brown v. Board of Education, 1954, Justice Marshall declared that segregation "generates a feeling of inferiority as to . . . status in the community that may affect . . . hearts and minds in a way never likely to be undone . . . Separate educational facilities are inherently unequal" (quoted in Pifer 1973, p. 24). This decision heralded a renewal of hope—for minorities if not the poor in general—that the democratization of American education, implicitly including higher education, could more nearly approach a reality.

Significant events ensued. The post-sputnik national concern brought about the National Defense Education Act in 1958—the first instance of widely available federal loans for college that were awarded partly on the basis of need. The Kennedy and Johnson administrations' promises of equal opportunity, finding fulfillment in many areas, might be symbolized best in higher education by James Meredith's admission to the University of Mississippi, the last totally segregated institution of higher education. (Pifer 1973). During this period, when college students who had been active in civil rights work elsewhere began to look at conditions on their own campuses, a great many colleges and universities took steps to make a place for minorities and other historically underrepresented groups. This movement was aided substantially by measures taken by the federal government. The Civil Rights Act of 1964, under Title VI, required that for federal monies to be allocated, institutions of higher education must submit enrollment figures according to ethnic breakdown, which was indicative of efforts to diversify the student population. The Higher Education Act of 1965 incorporated a number of programs—Supplemental Opportunity Grants, College Work Study, Talent Search, Upward Bound—that were designed as direct or indirect help to disadvantaged/minority students.

Frequently, individual institutions took an elitist stance, seeking out minority students who would present the least risk to their standards (Gordon 1972a; Astin 1972; Wing and Wallach 1971; Thresher 1966; Gordon and Wilkerson 1966). However, other institutions took a more democratic approach. The City University of New York (CUNY), in many ways an exemplar for the entire country, began its SEEK (Search for Education, Elevation and Knowledge) program at several campuses as early as 1966 (New York State 1973; Dispenzieri 1969b). This program represented one of the first attempts (not including black colleges) to admit students without an academic screening process—the policy of taking students from where they are academically to quality higher education through a variety of culturally sensitive practices and services.

Then came the chaotic social climate of the mid 1960's, epitomized by the death of Martin Luther King in 1967 and the attendant public reaction, which forced colleges to respond quickly to disadvantaged populations (College Entrance Examination Board [CEEB] 1973; Astin 1972; Gordon 1972a). The well-publicized, violent campus incidents made clear to administrators the critical, immediate need for change in the higher education establishment. Although many institutions had initiated special programs for the disadvantaged by the end of the 1960's and had reformed their recruiting emphases accordingly, the national situation in 1970 showed much still had to be done (CEEB 1973; Astin 1972). For example, acccording to 1970 census data (U.S. Department of Commerce 1970), 21 percent of white persons ages 16 to 24 had completed at least two years of college and 9 percent had completed four; for blacks of this age span 9 percent had completed two years and 3 percent four. More revealing, approximately 62 percent of white persons 17 to 24 were enrolled in college in 1970 (evenly divided between upper and lower divisions); the figure for blacks enrolled in college is 34 percent; and for Spanish Americans 35 percent. However, of these latter two categories, twice as many students were in the lower divisions.

For equivalent representation to be evident in postsecondary enrollment statistics, places for approximately a half million additional persons from the minorities mentioned would have to be found (Crossland 1971). These figures do not include other minorities. Furthermore, they do not include the role of income in determining the concentration of whites in the survey. (See the Urban Ed, Inc. (1974) report for comprehensive enrollment data.)

The trend since these figures were generated shows increasing numbers of previously underrepresented populations seeking postsecondary education (CEEB 1973), while the 18 to 24 age group as a whole was increasing along with the percentage of high school graduates attending college. The CEEB report tabulates percentages of 18 to 24 year olds enrolled in college in 1970 by income level as follows: bottom quarter, 19.6 percent; second quarter, 33.1 percent; third quarter, 44.6 percent; top quarter, 59.9 percent. Nevertheless, the growth of financial aid entitlement programs, led by the Federal Basic Opportunity Grants program and more than 40 state grant programs, nearly all need-based (*Higher Education*, 1975), significantly increased opportunities for the disadvantaged in higher education.

The New Student

More and more institutions are admitting nontraditional students who bring to the campus characteristics very different from their traditional student counterparts. In terms of educational needs, the nontraditional student

> has not acquired the verbal, mathematical, and full range of cognitive skills required for collegiate level work. Generally, he is a student whose grades fall in the bottom half of his high school class, who has not earned a (college preparatory) diploma, and is assigned to a high school which has a poor record for student achievement or who has been tracked into a general, commercial or vocational high school program. . . . Such a student will generally rank low on such traditional measures of collegiate admissions as the SAT board scores, high school average class standing, or (state) examination (U.S. Department of Commerce 1970).

These "new" students come from a variety of ethnic groups and from subcultures within those groups; in some cases English is not their primary language. Almost inevitably they have been victimized by inferior school systems and, in addition to lacking academic skills, they are wary of formal school situations. They share a common poverty and concomitant feelings of impotence (McGrath 1966; Crossland 1971; Pifer 1973).

Federal, State and Institutional Responses

The New York State Regents have said, "We assume that persons of the various ethnic and racial groups in our society aspire to and are capable of obtaining all the various levels of educational achievement in approximately the same proportions. Such is not the case because social conditions have made the attainment of these various levels more difficult for some sectors of the population" (New York State Department of Education 1975, p. 10). One would think the amelioration of this inequitable situation should be one of this society's greatest concerns.

In some measure society has responded, but higher education's commitment to programs for disadvantaged students varies greatly. Astin (1972) describes a "pyramidical system . . . roughly composed of three groups: a few prestigious and wealthy institutions that, in fact, enroll only high achievers; a large number of 'middle' colleges that enroll a somewhat more diverse but still select student clientele; and a mass of small four-year colleges and public and private two-year colleges that enroll students whose achievement has been undistinguished (p. 3, 4). The validity of this model is supported by literature pertaining to the base of this pyramid—which certainly would include black colleges, community colleges, and nonselective four-year colleges.

Coleman (1966) reported the existence of two sets of colleges, one 98 percent black, the other 98 percent white. In the mid 1960's approximately 50 percent of black college students were enrolled in predominately black colleges (Gordon 1972a), an improvement (some would think, others would not) over approximately 66 percent in the 1950's (Jaffe 1968). The idea of the black college has been subject to controversy and its legality questioned (see Pifer 1973; Cheek 1972; Bowles 1971; Jaffe 1968; Jencks 1967 for differing views). The black college has been criticized harshly. An extremely negative view is presented by Jencks and Riesman (1967) who consider the black college far too narrowly focused (on teacher training and vocational training) and frequently dedicated to white middle-class values. Jaffe (1968) has criticized the quality of education at most black colleges. Others (Crossland, McGrath), while admitting weaknesses, view the black colleges more positively, sensing their value with better planning and greater financial support. An extremely positive view of the role of the black college is presented by Cheek (1972). He asserts that since equal opportunity in higher education has not become a reality, the burden of opportunity must be borne by the black college. The black college can be the vehicle through which blacks can gain dignity and self-respect as well as the professional means with which to share in the power structure of the country. In this way a greater number of blacks will be able to take a constructive part in a culturally pluralistic society and racism will be exposed.

Karabel (1973) reported that in 1973, one third of all students entering higher education entered through the doors of a community college (in California the figure is 80 percent). Further, he presents figures linking low socioeconomic status to enrollment in junior colleges. Twenty-nine percent of the respondents to the Gordon/Wilkerson (1966) survey that reported compensatory practices were two-year colleges. Controversy surrounds the idea of the junior or community college. Karabel deplores the tracking both into and within the junior college. The Center for Policy Research (1969) noted there are indications that some junior colleges may be more responsive to the affective needs of the disadvantaged student. Whatever its merit, the two-year college has been the subject of a considerable portion of the research in collegiate compensatory education (Baehr 1969; Karabel 1973; Losak 1971; Roueche 1968) and is a major force in higher education for the disadvantaged.

Finally, is is fairly well documented that disadvantaged students attend the least prestigious four-year colleges (Gordon 1972a; Kendrick 1965). Implications can be drawn from these statements regarding relationships between type and incidence of postsecondary enrollment and between socioeconomic status/ethnicity/prior educational experience and concomitant achievement level. These will become clearer upon closer examination of more specific practices in higher education in response to the need to serve diverse populations. Policy changes have occurred in three broad areas in the structure of higher education: admissions/recruitment, financial aid, and curriculum. The practical repsonses to the necessity for change in these areas will now be discussed along with the theoretical issues involved.

Admissions

During the 1950's much attention was given to the need for finding and developing America's human resources. There were some new developments in the area, notably the establishment of the National Merit Scholarship program in 1955 to select talented youth for scholarships to college. Many colleges organized their financial aid programs along similar lines, ability rather than need being the major criterion (Wing and Wallach 1971; Thresher 1966). The College Entrance Examination Board began its College Scholarship Service in 1954 to counter the rising competition that often resulted in students with promise but with very little need being awarded scholarships. This program has ensured that talented youth selected for CSS awards do in fact have real need for the funds.

By the end of that decade new issues were surfacing. Some scholars began to question previous academic performances as an appropriate, sole measure of social, entrepreneurial, and creative abilities (McClellan 1958). They also called for curricular revision of educational programs to allow a "student to realize his potential within the framework of his own culture" (Astin 1972, p. 24) rather than mere provision of supportive services to enable the disadvantaged, culturally diverse student population to manage traditional coursework (Eels 1953; Gordon 1972a). Recently the practice of searching only for talented, developed students has become unacceptable to minority groups (Lane 1969). They believe higher education has a responsibility to provide educational access and useful experience to all citizens who desire it (Astin 1972; McGrath 1966).

In some states with fairly progressive programs for minority and nontraditional students (for example New York, New Jersey, California and Ohio) significant inroads have been made in admissions practices, even at some of the more prestigious institutions (Pifer 1973; Higher Education 1975). However, provisions to accommodate previously unacceptable students usually relate to outside sources of funding and do not indicate substantive revision of admissions policies.

The sole use of traditional predictors of college success, high school achievement records and SAT scores, has been questioned (for example, by Gordon 1965; Kendrick 1965; Society 1964). These predictors have been studied by numerous researchers (see Gordon 1972a for discussion of the various studies) with general agreement that these measures, particularly past achievement, are not without accuracy in predicting standard success; however, this may work to the exclusion of the disadvantaged student population. These predictors "do not necessarily reveal a person's potential for being influenced by the college experience" (Astin 1972, p. 25). Furthermore, "we should not penalize students for their lack of preparation, but neither should we abolish all standards; to do so would be patronizing in that it would imply that the student is incapable" (Astin 1972, p. 25). But by using these predictors alone, we have penalized and excluded the poor and/or minority group members, which is antithetical to the ideal of equal opportunity (Rossmann 1975).

Some recent studies that investigated the value of biographical data for predicting college success have suggested using them in evaluating disadvantaged candidates. Nonintellective factors such as family background, income, motivation, and attitude toward education may also be useful, although the use of predictors of success in college may vary with different populations (Gordon 1970; Hills 1965; Willingham 1964; Brown 1964; Garcia 1958; Webb 1960; Rossmann 1975). On the other hand, if enough characteristics and their functions can be identified that differentiate students with respect to their academic needs and strengths, then appropriate kinds of college experiences can be prescribed for individual students. This would mark a change in approach from predictive selection to prescriptive development. Prescriptive development would entail finding that college with the potential to provide the best college experience for a given student. Clearly the criterion for the admission of a disadvantaged student should be his potential to complete a college program.

The use of differential admissions criteria for educationally disadvantaged students apparently is based on the belief that appropriate services (counseling, tutoring, remedial work) can bring the achievement level of these students to that of their regularly admitted counterparts (New York State [1973]). Although they may be educationally disadvantaged, nontraditional students often bring to the college a positive orientation, "street" sophistication, and motivation (Rossmann 1975). Colleges and universities can no longer be allowed to maintain a comfortably homogeneous student population.

Finance

Financial aid is the most critical factor in extending higher education to disadvantaged and minority groups. Progress cannot be made unless substantial amounts of money are available for the support of students in higher education and the programs that serve them. The majority of disadvantaged students are from families with annual incomes of less than $8,000. Their families cannot afford to contribute to the cost of college; in fact, it may be necessary for them to make sacrifices because they are losing the potential financial contribution of the student. Thus the student from a poverty background often has feelings of guilt, feelings that he or she is abandoning the family. In addition, such a student often cannot afford to participate in the social activities of the college environment and may suffer psychological difficulties as a result. These psychological factors may contribute to lack of success and persistence on the part of the student.

There are positive correlations between attendance and family income and between family income and ethnic group membership (New York State [1973]; CEEB 1973). Costs of education have risen in the past few years but financial aid to students and programs for the disadvantaged have not increased proportionately (CEEB 1973). To further compound the financial problems of poor/minority students, the prestigious institutions with the highest academic standards are those with the largest endowment and scholarship funds (Colvard 1974). Poor students are not likely to meet the admission standards of these institutions because of their inferior elementary and secondary experience, so they attend less selective schools. Because of this they receive little in the way of alumni or private foundation or endowment support, which tends to be concentrated in the more selective institutions.

Federal aid takes the following forms: public scholarships, grants, guaranteed loans, subsidized loans, contingent repayment plans, work-study programs, income tax relief, grants and favorable loans for buildings and equipment, and more general grants to institutions, including operation of low tuition schools by the government. The U.S. Office of Education presently administers five major programs for aiding students; Basic Educational Opportunity Grants, Supplemental Educational Opportunity Grants, College Work-Study Program, National Defense Student Loans, and Guaranteed Loans. Approximately 25 percent of the nation's postsecondary students have been receiving some form of federal assistance. The Serviceman's Readjustment Act and Social Security plan account for 60 percent of federal aid at private colleges, and 80 percent at public colleges in New York State (University of the State of New York 1974). Despite the existence of these programs, federal aid has not been adequately funded to meet the needs of students who require the most help.

Only the Basic and Supplemental Educational Opportunity Grants, the College Work-Study Program, and the National Defense Student Loan program endowments primarily serve needy students (CEEB 1973). Other federal grants (usually for research) are given to large universities rather than two- or four-year colleges, which enroll the greatest number of disadvantaged students. The amount of federal funds a student receives and the way in which the funds are packaged (the balance and mixture of grants, loans, etc.) affect college access, choice of institution, and even the quality of educational performance of the student.

There are several other problems that seem to be built into federal programs for financial aid. There are limits on the amount of aid that institutions can supply to individuals; colleges with a large number of disadvantaged students are in a particularly difficult position because of government matching funds requirements; loan funds are limited and low income students must compete with lower risk students for funds; and more funds are distributed to students in the more expensive institutions than to students in the less costly institutions. Although the federal government's efforts to make funds available to institutions and students in need have been great and consequential, adequate support for all students is lacking (CEEB 1973).

At present state aid is providing the most support for disadvantaged students. The type of aid varies from state to state. Some states distribute funds on the basis of need, some on the basis of ability, and some on a combination of these. Some of the best state programs are found in Massachusetts, Pennsylvania, Illinois, Michigan, California, Minnesota, New Jersey, New York, Connecticut, and Wisconsin (which makes special provisions for Indian American) (see *Higher Education in the States* (1975) and Boyd (1974) for comprehensive data).

Although recent federal legislation (Education Amendments of 1972) attempts to improve chances for disadvantaged populations to attain higher education, the problems of insufficient funds, inequitable distribution, and inefficient financial aid processes remain the most critical barriers to higher education for the disadvantaged.

Curriculum

No essential change in the overall college curriculum has occurred as a result of the addition of programs for the disadvantaged, although responsive practices have been introduced (Crossland 1971; Astin 1972; Gordon and Wilkerson 1966; Ruchkin 1972; Gordon 1970). There is a great deal of overlap among the various types of compensatory practices that have been implemented. The following discussion will focus on precollege preparatory programs, ethnic studies, remedial/developmental practices, counseling, tutoring, and study skills training.

Since high school graduation is a prerequisite for attendance at most colleges, precollege preparatory programs have been one of the most prevalent and successful innovations and it is well to begin a description of compensatory practices with them. Among them can be listed nationwide, federally funded programs such as Upward Bound and the Educational Talent Search program (Tinto 1973). Other programs have been sponsored by private foundations, for example College Bound and A Better Chance (ABC) (Gordon 1972a; Tinto 1973). Examples of noteworthy local programs should include SEEK and the College Discovery Program, both functions of CUNY (Tinto 1973; Dispenzieri 1969a and b); Dillard University's Prefreshman Program (Jennings 1967); the programs at Yale, Columbia, Rutgers, and Bronx Community College's Operation Second Chance. (These and many others are described in Gordon and Wilkerson (1966)).

Precollege preparatory programs typically involve recruitment from high schools, summer sessions on college campuses, and individual, intensive basic skills training. Evaluations of these programs are less than adequate and results are mixed, but generally these programs are considered successful, particularly in altering attitudes and fostering motivation.

Several programs have focused on recruiting and retaining disadvantaged students once they have been admitted. The Special Services Program, federally funded under the Higher Education Amendments of 1968, was directed toward this goal (Davis 1973). Some of the many colleges and universities that have made special efforts in this direction include Northeastern University in Boston, Morgan State University in Maryland, Knoxville College in Tennessee (Gordon and Wilkerson 1966), Michigan State University, New Mexico State University, Oklahoma State University, Stillwater (Tollefson 1973), University of Illinois at Urbana/Champaign (Aleamoni 1974), Boston University (Smith 1972), the State of Vermont institutions *(Carnegie Foundation,* 1973), and the Thirteen-College Curriculum Program in North Carolina, a cooperative effort between black colleges and the Institute for Services to Education (Gordon 1972a).

The critical question is what specifically are these institutions doing to help their new recruits? A general pattern of responses is evident. First, the addition of ethnic studies programs is probably the most fundamental curricular change employed by colleges and universities in their attempt to serve the disadvantaged, specially admitted students. The Willie and McCord (1972) survey of black students in white institutions found black students very much in favor of black studies as the most crucial part of their educational experience. And Oliver (1975) describes a statewide secondary/collegiate effort to develop an ethnic (black) studies program in Alabama. It should be noted that some scholars believe that ethnic studies are and should be of equal importance to traditional students. Some minority students share this view (the subjects in the Astin (1972) survey). Ethnic studies should be incorporated into the curriculum of all departments to give the most comprehensive view of the multicultural nature of our society to all students. The author doubts, however, that this view is shared by many administrators and faculty.

Another prevalent practice among compensatory programs is the inclusion of remedial or developmental coursework (this often overlaps with precollege program practices). At worst, these courses are offered on a noncredit basis, rather like a continuation of high school.

Understandably, this practice often demoralizes the new student (Gordon 1967; Gordon and Wilkerson 1966; Astin 1972; Roueche 1968). Some programs have begun to phase out this type of remedial course (Gordon 1967; Gordon and Wilkerson 1966). But at best, remedial courses have been characterized by innovative instructional techniques, such as a composite of classroom discussion, seminars, individual projects, field research, self-instructional or programmed materials, simulation, audio-visual instruction, study abroad, independent study, and interdisciplinary study. These are also some of the best techniques that have been used with the traditional student population. When compensatory, remedial courses are designed to meet the individual student where he is and build on his strengths, they facilitate his growth and transition into regular coursework.

Counseling, both vocational and personal, is characteristic of many of the programs for the disadvantaged. The literature that exists is not encouraging and quite equivocal. Astin (1972) cites several cases in which students either lost interest in the counseling facilities after a short time in the programs or expressed lack of interest from the outset. Rossmann, Astin et al. (1975) in their report of CUNY nontraditional students found that if students receive personal counseling there was a greater likelihood of attrition on their part. The Gordon (1972a) survey findings support Rossmann's in regard to the inefficiency of current counseling procedures for disadvantaged students. The Willie and McCord (1972) survey accounts show ambiguous findings regarding black students' attitudes toward black counselors. The author has observed negative attitudes toward counselors exhibited by nontraditional students, apparently the result of high school experiences, and suggests a change in approach from traditional techniques to "advocacy" for the disadvantaged student. It should be pointed out that findings indicative of failure of traditional counseling with disadvantaged students are not inconsistent with findings regarding counseling failure with regular students (Gordon 1969b).

Tutoring is an important feature of most programs for the disadvantaged. Research is more encouraging here, yet still conflicting and ambiguous. Astin (1972) and Rossmann (1975) found no evidence to support the value of tutoring. Other studies, however, have found evidence of its usefulness. Peer tutoring was reported a successful practice at Miami-Dade Junior College (Miami-Dade 1972), Northeast Missouri College, Kirksville (Wright 1971), and the Learning Center at the College of San Mateo (Wenrich 1971). Gordon (1972a) reported differing tutorial approaches and differing student reactions. Approaches included student tutors, paid tutors and faculty tutors, and students responded according to the tutor's personal characteristics and attitudes. For example, older peer tutors whose backgrounds were as disadvantaged as their tutees were effective in several of the responding institutions.

Study Skills Centers have also shown promise in the education of the disadvantaged (Gordon 1972a). These typically involve such features as seminars in note taking, preparing for exams, and assessing instructor styles and goals. Beitler and Martin (1971) reported a successful program in study skills training at the New York City Community College.

Outcomes

The literature on educational outcomes is sparse for those researchers interested in and concerned about the status of programs for the disadvantaged. Like preschool programs, collegiate compensatory programs have failed to document the design as well as the implementation. Also, systematic data collection and analysis have been infrequent (Tinto 1973; CEEB 1973). The appropriateness of success of compensatory programs cannot be determined from the enthusiasm with which they were begun or the speed with which the practices spread. The crucial question is what aspect of the program actually accounted for successes or failures? Often programs were born out of political expediency either because institutions felt political pressure or because money became available if they would institute compensatory programs (Tinto 1973; Rossman 1975). When outcomes failed to meet the expectations of administrators it was often forgotten that the lack of careful planning and clearly set goals have contributed more to failure than any lack of merit on the part of the educationally disadvantaged students. Staff for the compensatory programs were often quickly and therefore inappropriately chosen in the institutions' efforts to initiate special programs as rapidly as possible. As stated in the Gordon and Wilkerson (1966) study, little heed was paid to the compatibility of the intentions of special program staff and the intentions of the institution. Thus incongruence in goals often caused serious conflicts between administrators of the special programs and other university administrators. The program staff usually supported activist ideals not always espoused by the institution as a whole. Without tenure or other security, the incidence of staff turnover was quite high in special programs, which added another element of instability to these efforts (Astin 1972). In essence, the creators of compensatory programs neglected to address the issue of systematically changing the structure of the institution. The programs were often little more than political concessions, structural appendages without firm theoretical underpinnings, without well-thought-out practical foundations, and set apart from the main institutional process.

Funds necessary for effective program evaluation have yet to be appropriated for special programs. Agencies conducting evaluations from the outside sometimes evolve data quite different from that reported by the program participants. Most of the data are, in fact, narrative, self-reported descriptions. Self-evaluation is characterized by subjectivity in the absence of personnel trained in the methods of empirical evaluation.

Additionally, fears surrounding program evaluation have precluded or hindered sincere efforts in this direction. Program staff have felt threatened by evaluation because it seemed an indication of doubt regarding program effectiveness. In fact, evaluation at times preceded withdrawal of financial support or institutional backing. Institutional commitment to evaluation has been inconsistent and sometimes nonexistent. A primary reason is institutional unwillingness to deal with any inadequacies in these special programs, which would require extra expenditures for revisions or additional planning and valuable university manpower (Tinto 1973).

For evaluation of special programs to attain credence, criteria and procedures need careful planning. One of the most important areas to be examined is a program's ability to help a substantial number of its students complete the university's requirements for a degree. Prior to actual evaluation, a proper assessment of the items that are to be evaluated must be determined. These should include not only student performance but also program practices that may indicate effectiveness. The staff's interaction with students, the courses offered, the support services of counseling and tutoring all affect succcess with special students. Neither the program nor the institution should fear the discovery of lack of quality in their practices, for without feedback it becomes impossible to improve effectiveness or justify changes in procedures and practices to reach important goals.

To attain the sound evaluation necessary to determine and maintain program effectiveness, efforts must begin at the program level with stringent evaluation techniques and practices as part of the on-going program process. To meet these needs, graduate and professional schools need to research and develop programs for training persons in this field as researchers, evaluators, and practitioners. Properly trained personnel with a commitment to proper evaluation are extremely crucial for special program survival. The product of evaluation efforts will be a critical factor, since this information assists legislators and foundations who fund these programs and periodically judge their effectiveness.

Even though collegiate programs for the disadvantaged have not been evaluated properly or adequately, general statements regarding outcomes can be made and new questions can be raised. Generally, the performance of nontraditional students has been comparable to regularly enrolled students. Attrition rates have also been comparable, if not somewhat lower, for nontraditional students (see Gordon 1972a; Gordon and Wilkerson 1966; Astin 1972; Rossman 1975; Tinto 1973).

These findings must be qualified on several counts. Some institutions have made deliberate attempts to retain their nontraditional students, realizing that adjustment to college academic work is usually accomplished during the first two years of college. Universities have felt the need to help these students reduce their anxiety and alleviate their fears of failure and build an adequate social, psychological, and educational support system for subsequent years. Often nontraditional students' grade-point averages have been based on less than a full course load (Astin 1972; New York State 1973). However, the extent to which this condition has compromised the validity of comparison of averages is questionable given the multitude of variables affecting the averages of both groups. Also, some faculty have established less stringent standards of performance for non-standard students purely out of a patronizing attitude toward this clientele. Thus, the issue of achievement is confounded.

Perhaps one of the most important outcomes of collegiate compensatory programs is the evidence they give of postsecondary education's weakness in dealing with student diversities. The realization of the complexity of compensatory education has caused many educators to pause and reflect on how best to reverse the negative impacts of early educational and economic deprivation, social isolation, and ethnic discrimination. The problem is not simply pedagogical but involves family life and community life as well. As the breadth and complexity of the problem becomes clearer, so does the pedagogical issue and its interrelationship with these other factors. The pedagogical issue has to do with an awareness of the many ways learning takes place in diverse populations and the application of this awareness to follow optimum educational development on the part of students who have different backgrounds, opportunities, values, and patterns of intellectual and social functioning. Other considerations are the identification of academic standards and goals, and the influence of such factors as intervention by dedicated instructors and other students, as well as intangible factors such as the atmosphere of the university.

Compensatory education, in contrast to traditional higher education, has attempted to shift the responsibility for learning more toward the teacher than the student. In this context effective education is a product of the match between learner characteristics, the learning environment, and the learning tasks (Hunt 1961). More accurate measurement of academic success may be the key to making the basic educational process more meaningful for compensatory programs. There is emerging interest in the use of instruments to assess the learning process as well as the level of achievement. It is increasingly recognized that general approaches to remedial or tutorial help are less likely to be effective than those targeted at specific aspects of learning. However, an examination of existing instruments and strategies for assessing student achievement reveals that few are effective in elucidating process, and that most present special problems when used with minority groups (Samuda 1973).

There has been a tendency to separate affective development from cognitive development. For a young child the mastery of a skill can enhance his feelings of confidence and create positive expectations that will aid future learning. When this process is hindered, as it so often is with the disadvantaged student, special care must be taken to redesign educational programs from early education through college to compensate for this loss of confidence. At the elementary and secondary levels special care should be taken to ensure that teachers attend to children's affective needs, their individual learning style, and their learning strengths and weaknesses. At the college level, attention should be given to the development of any basic skill that has not been developed.

Many (Gordon, Astin, for example) believe that the university needs to redefine its role in society and its responsibility for the education of all its members, whether or not they fit the traditional college student model. Institutional nonresponsiveness to change not only affects the nontraditional student but all other students as well. In many cases it has been the compensatory program and its struggle for survival that has brought the problems, and some solutions, to the fore. For example, financial support is beginning to be seen as a necessity for the middle income student as well as the low income student in view of rising costs of higher education and the current economic situation in the U.S. In curriculum, innovations such as tutorials and study skills centers, originally designed for the poorly prepared special student, are now seen as valuable techniques from which many traditional students can benefit.

Traditional admissions policies have been questioned because of the special needs and demands of compensatory programs. The type of student that the special programs seek does not meet the usual admissions criteria. His poor high school preparation and low achievement scores eliminate him if regular admissions procedures are followed. However, this problem is not limited to minority students. Many other students are beginning to fall into this category, such as older persons and those returning to school for retraining. Thus there is a need for institutions to reexamine their admissions criteria. An alternative approach is the use of external degree programs such as the Urban League Street Academy in New York City (secondary level).

Little attention has been given to the overall appropriateness of contemporary education. Yet the emphasis on educational alternatives and compensatory education may require a basic change in institutions. Although it is easier to add extensions than to alter basic structures, clearly the best interests of disadvantaged students and compensatory education will be served when the quality of the mainstream programs and services of our schools is improved.

If higher education is to be democratized and made accessible to all segments of the population, the form and content of its offerings will have to be changed. There are several areas where change is needed. Unless postsecondary institutions are geographically accessible, many segments of the population will be left out (Crossland 1971). But physical access may not be as important as political considerations, since if the idea of equal access is not politically acceptable to the communities from which the students come, democratization will not take place. Higher education must have a change in image that is clearly articulated and reflects a desire to serve previously excluded clienteles.

Since wide differences exist in the characteristics and needs of diverse populations, the options available to students must be plentiful. They must range from traditional liberal arts and preprofessional programs to career orientations to open-ended and continuing education. The content of coursework will need to reflect the interests and values of people whose purposes significantly vary. The manner in which learning occurs or is available must include formal, informal, and incidental experiences. In other words, democratized higher education in a pluralistic society must include multipurpose institutions that provide variable routes by which continuting education can occur.

Conclusions

Given the confused state of compensatory education at the collegiate level and the equivocal status of evaluation efforts, what may be said that is useful to practitioners and policy makers in this field? Despite the fact that good evaluation studies in this area have been few and the findings contradictory, it does appear that some conclusions may be drawn.

1. Where programs have been implemented with full systems of student support services, special opportunity students showed equal or higher grade-point averages than regular students of comparable ability and showed equal or higher retention rates than regular students (New York State Department of Education 1975; Rossmann 1975; Baehr 1969; Bridge 1970; Christensen 1971; Losak and Burns 1971; Smith 1972).

2. Where programs with full systems of student support services have been implemented special opportunity students show increased

self-esteem and motivation (Maykovich 1970; Davis 1973; Gordon 1972a; Hunt and Hardt 1969).

3. Where special opportunity students are selected on the basis of previously demonstrated talent (good but not excellent high school academic average and/or moderately good college entrance exam scores), college completion rates exceed those of traditional college population and grade-point averages are comparable to those of traditional college populations (Clark and Plotkin 1963; Gordon and Wilkerson 1966).

4. If college completion is the criterion, high college admission test scores account for relatively little of the variance, since students completing college come in fairly equal numbers from the full range of scores (Astin 1969).

5. In programs for special opportunity students, where little systematic student support service is available or utilized, student achievement, retention rates, and graduation are low (Lavin and Jacobson 1973; Rosen 1973).

Although the state of the art is quite varied, some programs or program elements are emerging that show promise. Among these are:

1. Full systems of student support services that include:

● Financial aid, including necessary allowances for tuition, room and board, incidental expenses, and contributions to family support where necessary. The aid package may consist of Basic Opportunity Grant, loan, university grant, family contribution, and income from work

● Adjusted curriculum in which the special needs of the student are taken into account in planning course work

● Tutorial support

● Remediation where necessary, and

● Counseling and continuous social/psychological support (Gordon 1972a; New York State Department of Education 1975; Davis 1973; McDill 1969).

2. Many students, particularly special opportunity students, need to be protected from the impersonal atmosphere of the large university and provided with more intensive, small group, personal contact with faculty. A successful example has been described by Smith (1972). This program includes team teaching, core curriculum, extensive guidance counseling, and a highly student-centered orientation. The frequently reported success of tutorials (faculty and peer) is probably related to the personalization of the college learning experience. (See Miami-Dade 1972; Wright 1971; Wenrich 1971).

3. Traditional remedial courses seem relatively ineffective, but targeted remediation based on specific identified needs appears to be an effective approach. Such a program has been developed and implemented by John Monroe (Gordon 1972a) and includes, among other elements, special attention to 1,000-essential-words college vocabulary (without mastery of which students are known to fail), and to information processing skills in which the emphasis is placed on evaluating the differential quality of various kinds of information and information sources.

4. Student motivation, retention, and achievement can be enhanced through full service programs that also give attention to the sociopolitical life of students. A program rich in all these elements has been described by Lopate (Gordon 1972a) and has as principal features, in addition to standard elements, a strong student advocacy

stance and close, extensive ties to the third-world elements in the communities from which special opportunity students come.

5. Behavior modification or shaping—a method of altering attitudes and behaviors by means of positive and negative reinforcement —has been utilized with some success in promoting academic achievement and retention in college (Ruchkin 1972).

6. The introduction of course content that complements the nationalistic concerns of students has been widely utilized. Its direct impact on achievement has not been well documented, but its effect on student attitudes seems positive. For examples see Gordon (1972a) and Oliver (1975).

7. Since the test-taking behavior and study habits of many special opportunity students are weak, special attention to the development of these skills has been included in some programs. One of the early models for programs including these elements has been described by Froe (1966).

8. It is increasingly recognized that the problems of special opportunity students predate their admission to college. Several programs designed to prepare and aid adolescents in the transition from high school to college have been developed. Among these alternative schools, the best examples are the street academies (see Carpenter 1972). Other public school programs are described by Shaycroft (1967), Wessmann (1969 and 1973), Hawkridge (1968).

Opportunity Programs for the Disadvantaged in Higher Education. Edmund W. Gordon. ERIC/Higher Education Research Report No. 6. Published by the American Association for Higher Education, Washington, D.C. 1975.

Strategies and Approaches to Ethnic Studies Curriculum Development

Much of the interest and excitement around ethnic studies programs was stimulated by Title IX of the Elementary and Secondary Education Act, which established a national Ethnic Heritage Studies Program. Proposed in 1970 by Representative Roman Pucinski of Chicago, revised in 1971 by Senator Richard Schweiker of Pennsylvania, passed in 1972, funded in 1973 with an initial $2.5 million, it was finally implemented in 1974. In a dramatic display of interest, the U.S. Office of Education received nearly 9000 preliminary inquiries and 1000 completed applications on just a few weeks notice.

Early in 1972, between passage and appropriation of the Program, a section of the U.S. Office of Education investigated the status of ethnic studies throughout the country. Margaret Franck, of the Office of Special Concerns, contacted State Departments of Education and local school districts, gathering information on ethnic studies program legislation and implementation. This chapter grows out of the materials that came to Ms. Franck.

This paper will (1) offer different ways of looking at the broad and often misunderstood term, "ethnic studies," and (2) cite examples of the bibliographies, teachers' curriculum guides, supplements, manuals, student handbooks, and instructional materials on file in Washington, D.C., in late 1973. Too often such educational publications are limited to local use or just gather dust, while specialists and curriculum committees expend great effort, unaware of what has already been created.

WHAT GROUPS ARE "ETHNIC"?

School districts apply many meanings to the term "ethnic studies," and this confusion has lead to disjointed communication efforts. Some use the term as a substitute for Black Studies; others mean studies of traditional "out groups"—American Indians, Blacks, Puerto Ricans, Chicanos, and Orientals. Those that include white groups envision Catholics, Jews, and Eastern Europeans as ethnic groups open to study, while white Protestants are often just plain "Americans." Very few schools place everyone in an ethnic group, conceptualizing ethnic studies as dealing with any Americans who identify with groups on the basis of race, religion, national origin, and combinations of these factors.

Single Group Studies

What has been produced by the various school systems throughout the nation depends on their original conceptualization. By far most of the efforts take a mono-cultural or single group approach, that is, studies of a large minority not ostensibly integrated into the dominant social group. "Minority" is defined as a handicapped group, suffering from prejudice or discrimination that prevents them from participating and sharing fully in the American mainstream. The choice of minority depends on the geographic area. In Washington, D.C., the guide for teachers

452 : Disadvantaged/white ethnic

deals with Blacks; Texas' publication treats Mexican-Americans; and Maine focuses on Franco-Americans; while Browning, Montana, relates to a single Indian tribe, the Blackfoot.*

Some schools systems use the term "multiethnic" to define the study of two or more "outgroups" treated separately within the same course. Little or no attempt is made, as the term "multi-ethnic" suggests, to discuss similarities and differences among ethnic groups and approach the topic from a comparative perspective.

Examples of this extended single-group approach include the interesting and little known data found in units on Mexican-Americans and Indians in Riverton, Wyoming. Rochester, Minnesota, offers junior high schools Indian and Afro-American folklore and culture. Oklahoma has compiled primary sources on Black and Indian history suitable for senior high school youngsters. Clark County, Nevada, offers a factual narrative guide for teachers and students at all grade levels on Blacks, Indians, Chicanos and Orientals.

Rationale for the focus on usually non-white "out groups" is that European immigrants, while often victims of prejudice and discrimination, have the advantage of being white. Thus European groups are said to have achieved a high degree of assimilation, while nonwhites continue to experience blocks.

The advantages of a single group approach are that it deals thoroughly with a specific ethnic group that has historically been neglected and promotes pride among students of that background. But everyone outside the group is sometimes seen as a homogeneous mass, as one unified community, rather than plurally analyzed as clusters of subcommunities organized along ethnic or religio-ethnic lines.

In attempting to correct past distortions about the minority, single group materials tend to contradict almost automatically the conventional historical views on various topics. Since history has so often been written through the eyes of only some groups, this response often provides an important corrective. But it would be even more effective to teach the past as a matter of interpretive record, related to the "eye of the beholder," and only sometimes subject to "objective" empirical analysis.

Separate treatment of minorities from a mono-cultural focus risks becoming overly narrow and ethnocentric, too concerned with assigning blame. Good curriculum cannot afford either to be simplistic about the difficulties of a pluralistic society or, on the other hand, dishonest in its presentation of real responsibility for intergroup injustices. The progress that has been made need not be denied—in fact, it can engender hope in otherwise cynical young people—but neither can the long distance left to be traveled. Too cynical a view of minority life is neither totally honest nor fair to the existence of diversity within both minority and dominant groups.

Another single-group approach used by school systems examines groups outside the United States. Teaching cultural universals and/or developing an appreciation of the ethnic differences con-

---

* Names and addresses of school systems referred to in this chapter appear in the "Resources" section, p.74

cept is the rationale accompanying these units. For instance, Atlanta teaches about the Basques in Spain and the Kpelle in Africa. Salina, Kansas, has a teacher's factual guide to Black Africa. In Stockton, California, pupil workbooks illustrate economic life in Ileito, the Philippines, and Japanese paper folding.

Studies of life in other lands are not ethnic studies, they are "world culture" or "international studies." Non-U.S. content as a component of ethnic studies might include material on immigrant groups' histories before they came to America. It is advantageous to provide an international approach as used in Dade County, Florida, which offers its senior high students a comparative study of South African and Brazilian race relations. This type of comparative form is especially désirable when studying single American ethnic groups as it helps students to see racial, religious, and national origins problems as common to nations containing heterogeneous populations.

Bilingual Programs

Bilingual education programs are variations of the monocultural single group approach. Though early programs were targeted chiefly toward children of Spanish descent, many school systems are discovering similar needs among Chinese, Italians, Greeks, Filipinos, and others. Under a bilingual approach, traditional skill subjects such as arithmetic, social studies and literature are taught in two languages, or only in the child's native tongue. This approach differs from the Teaching of English as a Second Language (TESL) strategy, which teaches most material in English and helps non-English speaking children to master English.

There is a considerable and growing body of experience and literature on bilingual education. The purpose of noting it here is twofold: first, some educators still confuse "ethnic studies" with bilingualism; and secondly, many bilingual programs are introducing the idea of biculturalism as well. In Massachusetts numerous districts have bilingual-bicultural programs for Portuguese and other children, and New York City's bilingual programs emphasize cultural background and identity development.

Anti-Prejudice Curricula

To many curriculum designers, ethnic studies denotes human or intergroup relations and has as primary objective the lessening of prejudice. Guides and teaching supplements include myths of prejudice, bigotry, and discrimination and the evils of stereotyping. Notable is Georgia's *Changing Culture, Book Two,* that employs anthropological data on race and culture to enhance understanding and sympathetic attitudes toward those who are different. Monthly bulletins in Freeport, New York, contain human interest articles bearing such titles as "Irish and Italo-American Stereotyping" and "Slurs in Advertising Against Mexican Americans," prepared by the experimental Racial Ethnic Action Project.

The anti-prejudice approach to inter-ethnic relations is a crucial educational goal and should have the highest priority. But it may diminish its effectiveness by substituting moral indignation for cultural assessment of complex intergroup conflict and competition. Of course the grade level would determine the complexity of the presentation.

Too often, this kind of curriculum lends itself to what social researchers call the "influence of social desirability." Students know what are the "right" attitudes to express, making openness hard to come by and leaving ambivalence unexplored. Then, too, these programs often perpetuate the view that there are only two kinds of groups—a unified majority and left-out minorities. Such a view denies differences within the so-called majority, which students should also come to understand.

Finally, anti-prejudice programs sometimes become anti-difference courses, promoting concepts of universality which, though valid, do not leave room for positive group identity. Ideally, ethnic studies courses should help students understand that these two forces—unity and identity—can indeed coexist, but that it is difficult to work out such a balance. That would be the meaning of teaching about pluralism.

Multiethnic Studies

The cross-cultural, truly multiethnic concept of ethnic studies may be the most useful at this juncture of our nation's history. Milton Gordon, in his book, *Assimilation in American Life,* describes the American reality as one of "structural pluralism." Gordon points to "a considerable body of evidence which suggests that the various varieties of Americans . . . tend to remain within their own ethnic group for most of their primary group relationships." His view is of an America whose citizens after work are ethnically enclosed, compartmentalized by ethnic group in their marriage choices, dating patterns, friendship cliques, membership in social and charitable organizations, as well as religious life.[1]

If this is true, then multi-group approaches to ethnic studies should include the study of many groups on a comparative basis, investigating common problems and crucial differences. They should demonstrate such basic concepts as ethnicity, identity, discrimination, integration, assimilation, accommodation, amalgamation, acculturation, pluralism, marginality and others. This treatment includes the richness of cultural diversity, the role and contributions of both white and nonwhite cultural groups, and the expression of ethnicity in American life. Dade County, Florida; Rochester, New York; Greenwich, Connecticut; and Kaihua, Hawaii, come closest to this view. These programs are examined in detail in later sections.

WHAT DISCIPLINES ARE USED?

Whether an ethnic studies program is designed primarily around a single group, a bicultural concept, an anti-prejudice strategy or a comparative multiethnic perspective, there are many ways in which it can be organized. One question involves the social science and/or humanities disciplinary approach to the topic.

History

A majority of school systems appear to use an historical approach to ethnic data. This has the advantage of placing the group's experience in perspective, seeing the evolution of its culture, and explaining present conditions by relating to the past. As a discipline, history can be truly integrative and interdisciplinary, for it deals with politics, economics, anthropology, and sociology in a time dimension.

The historical approaches in most elementary and secondary curricula include a large "contributions" component, where accomplishments of various groups and individual ethnic heroes (not too many heroines) are related. By stressing contributions, curriculum writers hope to generate self pride among students studying their own ethnic groups, and to promote respect on the part of non-members taking the course.

Unfortunately, much ethnic studies material dwells too long on the past. Knowledge of the past is important, even crucial, but students, as members of the "now" generation, find the present intrinsically more interesting. To make history-based ethnic studies more vital, past must be connected to present. In some classrooms, family histories form the basis for ethnic group history, or even for a study of a city or state's past.

Local history can be meaningful, for what is close to the student is best understood. Some school districts have packaged regional historical information not found elsewhere. The Uintah (Utah) School District developed a Ute history book for high school students on the Uintah and Ouray Reservations. The District of Columbia provides its pupils with little known information about Blacks in the upper South in "Pioneers and Planters." The Corn State relates the story of "Kansas Negro Regiments" and "Black Coal Miners of Southeast Kansas." Laredo, Texas, focuses on "The Spanish and Mexican Influence in the Cultural Development of The Southwest." Jack Forbes of the Far West Laboratory for Educational Research and Development (California) calls his historical narrative about Indians "The Native American in California and Nevada."

This writer found two excellent publications dealing with an ethnic group on a national basis. Kentucky provides teachers with past-present connections about Blacks in its "Contributions of the Negro." Illinois has documentary and interpretive data that may be easily duplicated for high school students on "The Role and Contributions of American Negroes in the History of The United States and of Illinois." Blacks, neglected and negatively stereotyped for so long, are beginning to have their message heard, and a more realistic and positive approach to their history is being presented. The horrors of American racism and the Black drive for freedom, justice, and identity have tended to receive a major share of the attention in ethnic studies programs. Other groups are now legitimately calling for attention.

This need not mean a chunk of ethnic history for every group; indeed, schools would have a hard time teaching anything but history if they took such an approach. It does mean that multi-ethnic experiences be included in general history courses and texts, and that teachers become flexible and sensitive enough to offer assignments that relate students to their own ethnic backgrounds. For instance, teachers have begun to report on students' intense excitement at being assigned family and neighborhood history projects.

This type of program will enrich any history course and will not burden teachers and curriculum planners with the required ritual of prescribing a series of ethnic heroes, giving equal time regardless of historical accuracy. It would also prevent inter-ethnic comparisons of contributions and minimize the risk that an ethnic group will feel accepted and legitimate only to the extent that its forebears contained a high proportion of individuals whose achievements have been outstanding.

Psychology

The psychological dimension is often explored in the human relations approach, attempting to develop a youngster's sense of identity and build positive self concepts. The program content points out the beauty of ethnic diversity and the positive values in each ethnic culture.

One approach is to identify universal human psychological needs and then look at ethnic customs that meet these needs in different ways. Rochester, New York, calls its efforts in pluralist education "Project Beacon." They prepared a collection of readings and exercises employing a psychological approach entitled, "Reading to Improve the Self Concept." This teaching guide recommends stories from many ethnic experiences to illustrate character traits. For example, a story about Frederick Douglas tells how an individual sets personal goals that he strives to keep. The elementary-level guide provides teachers' plans to challenge children's creative talents particularly in written expression and in arts and crafts. By using biographies of many ethnic group members, this effort implicitly says that even though there are ethnic differences, there are also cultural universals.

Ethnic studies should deal with differences, but should not be so centered on the hyphen part as to lose sight of people's common aspirations for a better life. The psychological treatment is especially valid for elementary pupils struggling to develop identity and too unsophisticated to cope with inter-ethnic conflict. It offers the opportunity to develop the twin goals of ethnic studies—a better understanding of one's own group and a warmer feeling towards members of other groups.

Sociology and Economics

The socio-economic treatment is "present" centered. It deals with expressions of ethnicity in neighborhoods, organizational life, the business and occupational world, and politics. Materials produced for elementary and secondary school students too often tend to ignore this aspect. When ethnicity is mentioned in connection with economics it is generally on the basis of race. (One wonders if young Blacks are being helped or hindered by an emphasis only on their relative poverty. While successful models of Blacks who have achieved economic success should not be allowed to distort the economic deprivation of the group, the absence of those models also creates a problem.) The fact that other ethnic groups have a political-economic dimension— e.g., Italians in truck farming, Irish in certain unions, Jews in small business, Protestants in heavy industry—remains hidden.[2]

San Diego schools believe politics a fertile area for ethnic studies. This city produced "The Political Process in the Black Community," an anthology of clippings from Black-oriented magazines and newspapers ranging in content from Black Power, civil rights gains and profiles of Black politicians to problems within the Black community. San Diego's "Chicano Studies" is a collection of readings on political movements within the Mexican-American community. Similarly, any city's newspapers and magazines, both the general and the ethnic press, can serve as an "instant curriculum."

New York City's "Resource Bulletin in Ethnic Pluralism" includes reprints from popular newspapers and magazines dealing with ethnicity in general and with specific groups as they express themselves in neighborhoods, social institutions and politics. These accounts are more readable and interesting for high school students than textbooks, and they are the kinds of materials used by voting citizens to inform themselves on issues.

Dade County (Florida) has prepared "The People of Dade County," a curriculum guide for grades seven through nine. This effort focuses on interaction among Cubans, Blacks, Jews, and white Protestants. The publication examines "minorities: discriminated against, yet slowly entering the mainstream of American life." Such a formulation has important implications for the future of ethnic studies. Courses should include problems of ethnic group members in lower income brackets, but should not stress only negative aspects. Small victories and uneven advances require attention, both for the sake of honesty and to impart a sense of possibility rather than total cynicism.

Humanities

Examination of ethnic cultures and life styles is important for understanding America's pluralistic society. Folkfairs with their colorful historical costumes, exotic foods, and traditional music have opened children's eyes, noses, and ears to our nation of immigrants. More is needed, with additional subtleties injected into this approach.

It is patently incorrect to say no "melting" has occurred among early immigrants and their children. Most Americans, regardless of background, share a common core culture. Most third generation Americans cannot read or speak the "old country" language, nor are they likely to dress in traditional costumes. Religious customs are still followed but not in their most orthodox form.

Much of "American" culture is made up of contributions from many ethnic groups. For instance, American literature, since the founding of the Republic, has benefited from ethnic writers and is not solely "Yankee."[3] In the arts, many fine creators and performers blend their artistic and cultural universals with their particular ethnic communal background.

Subtle differences in mannerisms, lifestyle, world outlook, attitudes, values, and behavior remain after customs and costumes grow worn. Jews, for example, retain a respect and passion for formal education, Italians have strong attachments to "old neighborhoods," German-American young men gravitate towards careers in the hard sciences. Examined in books such as *The Decline of the WASP* by Peter Schrag, Glazer and Moynihan's *Beyond the Melting Pot,* Andrew Greeley's *Why Can't They Be Like Us?,* and Michael Novak's *The Rise of the Unmeltable Ethnics,* these subtle differences have yet to find their way into print for public school students.

A number of local programs have strong cultural and humanities components. Carnegie, Oklahoma, developed both a fifth grade and high school course on the history and culture of the Southern Plains Indians. Accompanying the texts are a descriptive guide and over 1200 slides depicting each tribe's "lifeways, legends, industries and subsistence techniques."

East Baton Rouge, Louisiana, explores local culture. Their resource guide, "The Cultural Heritage of East Baton Rouge," is designed for teacher use as part of the eighth grade social studies course. Dealing mainly with Franco-Americans, Blacks, and Indians, the guide stresses culture as meeting similar needs of all people and building the basic dignity of man. It employs such cultural factors as art, literature, and language, recognizing the importance of ethnic survival through those mechanisms.

Rochester, New York, has composed student booklets on a number of ethnic groups. These booklets contain a large cultural component of language, customs, games, songs, riddles, recipes, and folktales about Blacks, Indians, Puerto Ricans, Chinese, Japanese, Irish, Germans, Italians, Poles, and Jews. The student booklets are written on three levels: kindergarten and first grade; grades two and three; and grades four through six. The materials correlate with language arts, physical education, science and health, mathematics, and fine arts, as well as social studies, so that teachers may use portions during the entire school day.

The Rochester program is one of the few that includes white groups in ethnic studies and its treatment of Jews as a people, not merely a religious group, is rare. "The Jews are also a cultural group," states the introduction, "a people linked together by a common history, prayers, literature, customs and a feeling of oneness." Yiddish words comprise the language section since that tongue was most commonly used by emigrating Jews.

The question of dual loyalty, the old bone that so many still love to gnaw upon, is deftly handled through interethnic comparison: "American Jews watch the development of Israel with much interest. They give aid and have a strong loyalty to it, just as the Irish, Germans, Italians, and Polish people have a strong love for the land of their fathers. But like all Americans, the Jews will be loyal to America, their home."

One danger in emphasizing the old world culture of immigrant groups, as Rochester does, is that young people may become confused as to the true nature and character of ethnic groups today. Differences within a group need to be explained, including the various levels of practices in a given ethnic community and generational differences in the importance attached to culture.

Multi-Disciplinary

Educators seeking to introduce ethnic studies in elementary classrooms could start by supplying teachers with the Rochester material or the teachers' guide for Clark County (Las Vegas). This Nevada "Social Science Study Unit" contains an elementary school program model. Cross-cultural and cross disciplinary, it offers youngsters a positive self concept, insightful views of other groups, and a developmental social sciences program following traditional themes (i.e., this guide plugs in ethnicity to teach about the self, the home and parents, the immediate neighborhood, the larger community, the region, the state, and the nation). Material utilizes songs, games, biography, and other components. While it limits its definition of ethnicity as applied only to nonwhites, the ideas employed in the first three grades apply to all ethnic groups.

"Ethnic Studies, High School," the secondary Clark County guide, is also commendable. This cross disciplinary program aims at understanding the total experience of four ethnic groups (Blacks, Indians, Chicanos, and Orientals) through a study of histories, cultural contributions, and literature written by members of these groups. In portraying intra-group generational, class, and religious differences, it addresses everyday problems of real people and does not merely concentrate on heroes and cultural contributions.

The guide's method of dealing with the homelands of various immigrant minorities is worthy of imitation. The stress is on positive aspects of life in the motherlands, revealing those nations' histories and contributions, and avoiding the usual condescending textbook tone in discussing immigration and the conditions the immigrants "escaped" from.

One multi-disciplinary program, the Multi-Culture Institute, has several unique and exciting elements. Founded as a private school in San Francisco, it deliberately organized students in homogeneous ethnic classes for part of their day and in mixed groups at other times. The stress on various aspects of ethnicity— language, customs, history, local politics—is designed to foster appreciation of both one's own and other groups. From the original experiment, models have been developed for adaptation in different types of school settings and grade levels.

COURSE STRUCTURE AND TEACHING TECHNIQUES

Much work in education, in both research and practice, attempts to discern the best ways of introducing new subject matter. Levels, durations, and conceptual approaches to subject matter are constantly being refined, thus giving us terms like "New Math," "PSSC Physics," and, most recently, "New Social Studies." In the ethnic studies area, too, questions of structure and techniques need to be looked at in conjunction with issues of content and disciplinary viewpoint.

Separate or Integrative?

Basically, there are two approaches to teaching about ethnic pluralism: the separate course, in the form of a unit, elective, or mini-course; or the incorporative approach. A separate approach is based in a self-contained body of knowledge about one or more ethnic groups. An integrative strategy injects ethnic-related subject matter into established curricula.

A separate course in ethnic studies has several advantages. It provides a visibility for the field that is very important in legitimating it educationally. After so many ethnic experiences of absence and invisibility, there is some suspicion and skepticism over a curriculum that only allows for including ethnic dimensions and does not require it. Many ethnic studies activists argue against leaving the decision to include ethnic content in the overall curriculum to the individual teacher, pointing out that these very teachers have perpetuated the neglect that new ethnic studies courses are designed to remedy.

A separate course can cause political problems if it signals an overemphasis on one group or another, or if it suggests that a school is merely reacting to group pressure. If "ethnic studies" are separate, teachers in other courses may not feel the need for their classes to contain pluralistic content. Also, since many teachers are sensitive to charges of "educational fads," they may be more receptive toward an approach that does not require a restructuring of curriculum but rather calls for additional content in existing work.

Examples of separate curricula, mainly from the historical perspective, have been cited. Examples of incorporative approaches are coming to light. Acknowledging that textbooks tend to dominate the schools' curriculum, Ohio has supplementary materials integrating Black history into Tod and Curti's, *Rise of the American Nation.* Similarly, Peoria, Illinois, provides content on the Black experience to incorporate with Wade, Wilder and Wade's *A History of the United States.*

San Diego's "Role of The Mexican-American" demonstrates a practical method for incorporating Mexican-American experiences into history courses. The technique provides teachers with handouts that can be duplicated for students, including graphics and readings focusing on Mexican-American immigration for use as part of a larger immigration unit. In implementing ethnic studies, it is usually more effective to provide teachers with material for student use rather than presenting lesson plans and outlines that leave them the problem of finding suitable references for their classes.

A number of school systems seek to incorporate America's non-whites into existing American history courses, but Kentucky's curriculum guide goes further. Conventionally entitled, "Contributions of The Negro," it does outline content and activities that integrate Blacks into American history. But it also offers suggestions to incorporate *all* ethnic groups into economics, sociology, world culture, civics, geography, psychology, English, speech, journalism, foreign language, mathematics, science, music, art, industrial arts, home economics, and even health and physical education. The authors of this guide have a grasp of the many facets of ethnicity and of how ethnic solidarity, interests, and consciousness can be expressed in non-ethnic terms or through other institutionalized forms. Kentucky's efforts supply an excellent conceptual approach that can be adapted for white ethnic groups in the many areas of the school curriculum.

Duration of Courses

Mini-courses, micro-units, and short term electives are excellent ways for students to discover the pluralistic nature of our society. Yearlong studies may lead to weariness and diminished interest among youngsters. Although many different aspects of a subject can be dealt with in depth, students complain that they are studying "the same thing all the time." This writer's experience is that youngsters do best at "short distance running"—short courses in different areas. This adds an element of newness and a fresh start, thus student interest and motivation are recharged.

In these days of individualization and greater freedom for students, presenting many options in course design is probably wise. This means "chopping up" various aspects of the pluralistic experience into self-contained bodies of knowledge. A few lessons around a theme (e.g., immigrants at work) would constitute a micro-unit; more lessons around a larger theme (e.g., images of ethnic groups in 20th century literature would comprise a mini-course; and a course that takes a large fraction of the school year (e.g., multiethnicity in American cities) would make a short-term elective.

Dade County (Florida) has prepared outstanding curriculum guides on diverse facets of ethnic studies. These guides are geared to a school year divided into five parts (short distance running) so that one or more of these electives may be chosen by the student. The titles suggest a grasp of the dimensions of the field: "Black History and Culture" (grades 7-9), "Prejudice in America" (grades 7-12), "Minorities in American Society" (grades 7-12), "A Nation of Immigrants" (grades 10-12), "Race Relations Around The World" (grades 10-12), "The People of Dade County" (grades 7-9), "American Indian" (grades 7-9), and "Economics of Poverty" (grades 9-12).

Use of the "Inquiry" Method

Many of the materials referred to concentrate on the cognitive. They consist primarily of facts, data, knowledge, understandings, and concepts presented in a narrative expository form. The information received by the students includes generalizations, interpretations and reasoned conclusions developed by the authors and lends itself to learning by memorizing this pre-digested material.

In this sense, many ethnic studies materials remain out of tune with some recent thinking in teaching-learning theory. That thinking suggests that the best learning occurs when students actively engage in intellectual interaction with information to produce something beyond that information itself. True learning, according to this view, means finding out, seeing for oneself, discovering. The best teaching for such goals involves putting students into situations requiring them to develop these "finding out" intellectual skills. This type of teaching uses the inquiry method—the process of hypothesizing, testing hypotheses, and drawing conclusions.

Materials in the ethnic area have been developed around these methodological concepts. For instance, Georgia's State Department of Education collaborated with the Atlanta School System to publish two textbooks entitled, *Changing Culture.* Containing data on ethnic groups, particularly in the area of conflict, these books emphasize inquiry on the part of students. Young Georgians concern themselves with issues such as "Georgians versus Indians" and "What are the myths and realities of plantation life?" Thus, students can view history as a controversial record of the past. At the same time, they learn to see current conflicts in a framework where any one version of a debate needs critical evaluation.

Fact-oriented publications, such as the resource book on "Black History in Oklahoma" compiled by Oklahoma City Public Schools, could easily be utilized for inquiry teaching with a good teachers' guide. The Oklahoma book contains carefully selected, highly readable primary source documents related to the Black and Indian experiences, revealing little-known relationships between these two groups and their interactions with whites. Such a resource could be used to "show history" or, with supplementary teachers' suggestions, could generate discoveries about inter-minority conflicts applicable to contemporary as well as historical situations.

Educational research suggests that students become confused when working with masses of information not attached to conceptual handles. Concepts organize information, make facts more meaningful and generate critical questions. The more data provided for the development and understanding of concepts, the greater the likelihood that learners will internalize these concepts and apply them to new experiences outside of class. An up-to-date curriculum would provide inquiry experiences in which selected concepts are used repeatedly, each time with new data and increasing degrees of refinement.

School systems have produced individual learning packets employing conceptual-inquiry principles. These packets enable the learner to choose from a number of topics, dwell on certain aspects, and decide how deep he or she wishes to go. The guided program suggests audio-visual aids, books and periodicals, and other resources inside and outside the school to aid the student in accomplishing the chosen objectives. Providing structure and background to direct student learning, these packets are representative of the best works produced in the ethnic studies area.

The individual learning packets of Kaihua High School include the elements of diagnostic testing. Three booklets, "Immigration," "Minority Groups," and "Hawaii: A Case Study," demonstrate techniques to teach about ethnic groups' interaction. The approach to controversial historical situations is fair, many-sided and open-ended, and permits the reader to draw independent conclusions. Students are given a choice of activities with directed study questions. The exercises and activities are arranged under conceptual handles such as assimilation, cultural diffusion, competition, conflict, tolerance, and pluralism. The Teaching Manual differentiates assignments for the able, average, and less able students. It also contains a number of student handouts that plug into any unit dealing with pluralism or ethnic issues. There are readings from popular newspapers, magazines, and books, as well as guide sheets on how to make reports employing problem-solving techniques. The bibliographies include books and periodicals, audio-visual aids, and community resources.

A program in Greenwich, Connecticut, parallels Hawaii's in structure and content. Its "Minority Report" is used in grades 10-12, while its "Migration-Immigration" unit is designed for eighth graders. As in Hawaii, there are student packets and a teacher's handbook. Data are arranged around large concepts and suggested activities encourage high level thought processes. These individual learning packets can easily be utilized with either a whole class or part of a class. Teachers can be eclectic, plugging into certain lessons in the traditional curricula.

Attitudes and Feelings

In discussing ethnic studies content approaches, we have implicitly and explicitly suggested certain attitude outcomes as desirable or undesirable. To summarize them:

A balanced view of the activities and motivations of various groups should be understood, including their prejudices as well as their legitimate interests. Both the successes and the failures of democratic processes need to be accepted, as opposed to a view of America and its institutions as unredeemable. It may at times be difficult to counter youngsters' feelings of alienation and hopelessness, but it is important for students to develop a commitment to social change as well as understanding how difficult it can be to achieve.

Ethnic content should be honest about differences while emphasizing common problems, common humanity, and aspirations for a better life by all groups. This will help students understand that differences do not mean inferiority.

Problems, conflict, and competition need to be presented as part of the human condition, whose resolution is a task for the future. This will help prevent youngsters' polarizing around their own groups, and can minimize the hostility that might be generated by simplistic slogans focusing exclusively on oppression.

Emphasis should be on defining and achieving social justice, on conflict resolution, and on processes whereby we can live in a unified society without any group surrendering its uniqueness. Sophisticated lessons on the senior high school level may illustrate group interests and unmelted cultural aspects, yet help students recognize a common core culture.

These values and attitudes and others concerning family, neighborhood and political life, are not guaranteed results of ethnic studies programs. They can be anticipated, though, if attention is given to the affective domain of learning and teaching. So far, this attention is lacking and there are few connections between teaching theory in this field generally and the specific applications to ethnic studies.

"Affective" education relates to feelings, attitudes, interests and values. Lessons in this area need to be planned as carefully as those concerned with thinking, knowledge and understanding, i.e., the cognitive domain. The *raison d'etre* of ethnic studies lies in the affective domain, for such studies aim to help young people understand themselves and their heritage and develop an appreciation for their neighbors' similarities and differences.

The affective dimension, while recognized, is often under-programmed. Introductory comments in ethnic studies publications correctly state as among their objectives a "better self concept" and "building pride," and are designed to make students aware of cultural richness, the contributions of various groups and the multiethnic sources of American customs. This stress on immigrant and ethnic contributions might indeed have the effect of building pride; however it is necessary to consciously plan and evaluate this objective.[4]

An affective approach to ethnic studies offers the opportunity for value clarification. This teaching technique, familiar to many educators, involves a stress on the students looking at their own opinions without being told what is the "correct" position. Questionnaires are sometimes used to help raise issues which really have no formula answers; for instance, "Should student clubs be allowed to keep their membership to one ethnic group?" or "Should a highway that the whole city needs be allowed to split an ethnic neighborhood in half?"

Adding this value dimension to curriculum is difficult for many students and teachers alike, since stress is so often still placed on authority and answers. As yet, it is still too often neglected in designing ethnic curricula. Yet students make many decisions that have an ethnic dimension, such as choice of friends, mate, neighborhood, fraternal organizations, political parties, candidates, and positions on public issues. To make such decisions, young people must have a clear personal value system. A person's ethnic background, where many values originate, influences reactions to people and problems. If students understood the cultural base of value perceptions, perhaps they would think less in mutually exclusive moral absolutes and avoid overly rigid definitions of right and wrong.[5]

It is important that we learn to evaluate achievement in the affective domain. In Maine, a test has been developed to measure Indian and non-Indian children's attitudes toward Indians; Hawiii administers a social distance scale that indicates acceptance and rejection attitudes toward various ethnic groups. But we need better techniques to determine if programs meet their stated objectives of building better self images and lessening prejudice.

TEACHER TRAINING

An important key to effective (as well as good affective) ethnic studies is teacher training. Many teachers still have an oversimplified view of America as a melting pot. Their early experiences taught that America is a nation of individuals, not groups, and that the children of immigrants would shed their heritage and blend into the dominant American society. Indeed, many present-day teachers were taught that their own success would depend on their ability to "be American." Ethnic identification was implicitly looked down upon as a form of tribalism, an anomaly soon to wither away.

If teachers feel negative toward manifestations of ethnicity, and are uncomfortable with conflicts and differences, then the aims of ethnic studies programs will be unintentionally subverted, if they are implemented at all. Thus, the affective component is crucial in any program of teacher training, both to help teachers crystallize their own attitudes and values and to provide them with classroom model techniques.

Cognitive elements are also essential for the in-service or pre-service curriculum. Teachers need to understand the richness of American cultural diversity; the achievements of many ethnic individuals and groups; the multiethnic sources of American customs; inter-ethnic conflicts, past and present, how they arose and how they were resolved or left to fester; the recognition of cultural conflict as a reality of our history and its resolution as a necessity of our future.

An on-going teacher training program in ethnic studies should include readings in the field, guest lecturers, and techniques of examining ethnic communities. The local area can be a laboratory for research. In fact, each teacher-participant could prepare student material on an aspect of ethnic studies with accompanying lesson plans.

Teacher teams could gather information on the many aspects of ethnic community life to create a curriculum specific to the particular city or neighborhood.

A. Location of ethnic neighborhoods, demographic data

B. Ethnic fraternal organizations, their histories and activities

C. Ethnic churches and church-related organizations

D. Ethnic newspapers, foreign language and English

E. Self-help and mutual aid associations

F. Educational institutions and educational concerns

G. Work and occupational patterns and ethnic businesses

H. Politics—ethnic issues, leaders, party representation and preferences

I. Lifestyle—family life, roles of different family members, recreational activities, religious customs

A few school districts have developed material relating to teacher training. Ogden City (Utah), in conjunction with Weber State College, attempted to sensitize teachers to their own feelings about their identity, ethnicity and the ethnicity of others.

In New York City, the Office of Intergroup Education revised its Human Relations in-service training program from one based on a Black-white model to one that focused on New York's six major ethnic groups: Blacks, Puerto Ricans, Irish, Italians, Jews and Chinese. A film was made about each group, half historical and half a contemporary comment by an ethnic activist. A summary film, with excerpts from each ethnic interview, showed very dramatically how common themes were shared by all groups.

A manual for using the films, developed by the National Project on Ethnic America, contains cognitive and affective discussion questions keyed to the films and material related to various key concepts.

The Detroit school system has gone further than others in training a cadre of ethnic specialists. Working with Wayne State University, participants in training programs read learned journals and dissertations about groups in the area, visited ethnically-related places, and spoke with ethnic leaders and typical residents. A directory describing ethnic resources in the metropolitan area was compiled and a unique oral history project was begun, to provide valuable material on the immigrant experience through a store of taped data.

Introducing well-designed multiethnic training programs may sometimes be difficult, especially if teachers have already been exposed to models of intergroup education that stressed "correct" postures rather than a more open approach. A model that starts with the teachers' own ethnic backgrounds, feelings, and experiences—and accepts the ambivalence and confusion that surround them—seems to offer more possibilities for insight. Conceptual information also needs to find its way into training programs, including an updating as to our definitions and ideas about ethnicity and pluralism. As we have already suggested in discussing curriculum for students, analyses of ethnic power and interests have as much to do with "ethnic studies" as do history and cultural patterns. In many school systems, ethnicity acts as an organizing force for teachers, and a teacher training program might have a built-in case study if it looked at this phenomenon.

One way for a school system to begin the training process is to ask itself the general question, "How pluralistic is our school? How much do we program for diversity and group identity?" Many ongoing activities will probably be discovered and other ideas will be generated out of teachers' and students' own needs and experiences.

CONCLUSION

There are many ways school administrations, teachers, and curriculum developers interpret "ethnic studies." Most of the materials reviewed were extensions of traditional education methods. Yet, as the examples suggest, the area of ethnic studies offers many possibilities for innovation that go beyond adding textual content or new individual learning packets.

Ethnic studies are not only for ethnic groups. As we have said, there are many needs for sensitivity, self-understanding and a better grasp of the complexities of American reality among *all* children. Similar needs exist among teachers, who are once again asked to help alleviate some of society's problems through their classroom activities.

Publishers are beginning to shape materials more along truly multiethnic, pluralistic lines. One company, for instance (Education Design, Inc. of New York), has produced a multiethnic package using sound filmstrips and tape cassettes which cover 19 of America's major ethnic groups. Entitled, "Ethnic Studies: The Peoples of America," it combines concepts of ethnicity with history and culture, and adds a personal dimension through dramatizations of documents such as diaries and letters.

At the same time that this and other carefully thought-out materials are being produced, inevitably, a few are taking advantage of the new market and promoting what has been called "ethnic junk." Evaluating published work thus becomes a crucial task. A monograph developed by the Detroit-Wayne State group sets forth an approach to such evaluation.[6]

One purpose of this paper is to point to useful examples so that each school or system does not feel compelled to "reinvent the wheel." New materials will be developed out of the first round of Ethnic Heritage Studies Program grants. Much can come from students, their own parents and grandparents, and the popular press. Television programs and movies can be used to generate discussions of ethnicity, stereotypes, and prejudice.

In short, new curricula in ethnic studies, or adding an ethnic dimension to existing curricula, need not be difficult. Some ask if such effort is worthwhile. Of course it is, for it can result in humanizing school systems, sharpening perceptions of reality, broadening children's and teachers' sensitivities to themselves and others, and reducing suspicion and distrust. Done well, ethnic studies can help lead us toward a truly pluralistic America.

Footnotes

1. For a detailed look at one group affected by a combination of these forces, working class ethnic women, see Nancy Seifer, *Absent From the Majority: Working Class Women in America* (New York: National Project on Ethnic America, 1973).

2. See Andrew Greeley, *Why Can't They Be Like Us?* (New York: Institute of Human Relations Press, American Jewish Committee, 1969); Milton Gordon, *Ethnicity in American Life* (New York: Oxford University Press, 1964); and David Danzig, "The Social Framework of Ethnic Conflict in America," in Murray Friedman, ed., *Overcoming Middle Class Rage* (Philadelphia: Westminster Press, 1971).

3. Some examples of this ethnic influence are contained in Irving Levine and Judith Herman, "The Life of White Ethnics," *Dissent* (Winter 1972).

4. This and subsequent quotations are from Erik Erikson, *Identity: Youth and Crisis* (New York: W.W. Norton, 1968).

5. Kurt Lewin, *Resolving Social Conflicts* (New York: Harper and Row, 1948).

6. For a more detailed look at the psychological theories involving socialization and the relationship among ethnic group, family and individual development, see Joseph Giordano, *Ethnicity and Mental Health* (New York: National Project on Ethnic America, 1973).

The Schools and Group Identity. "Strategies and Approaches to Ethnic Studies Curriculum" by Judith Herman, Institute on Pluralism and Group Identity — American Jewish Committee, New York, NY. October 1974.

Title I Migrant Education Program

Nine out of 10 children of migrant farm workers never enter high school and only 1 out of 10 of those who do ever graduates.

The Nation has more than a million children whose parents follow the sun, picking fruits and vegetables in fields from Florida to Maine, Mississippi to Michigan, California to Washington State. They are born into some of the grimmest poverty in the country. They suffer from illnesses such as rickets, scurvy, pinworms, anemia, and malnutrition. They are isolated from the communities near their work. By 12 or 13 years of age they join their parents in the fields and spend the rest of their lives topping onions, pulling sugar beets, and snapping tomatoes from the vine.

Children of migrant workers seldom go past 4th or 5th grade, and since their families move so often--every few weeks at the peak of the harvest season--they are never in one school long enough to have a chance to really learn. Some never enter a classroom because they have to babysit for their younger brothers or sisters or, what is more often the case, they must work in the field because even their meager earnings are needed to help feed the family. To make matters worse, many of them can't speak English.

School records seldom move with the child; too many families stay only briefly in one place, moving on as a crop runs out or the weather hastens ripening. When the new school asks the child the name of the town and last school he attended, he knows only that he's come "from the potatoes" or "from the snap beans." State and city boundaries mean little to him or to his parents.

As a result, school officials seldom know the proper grades in which to place most migrant children. Furthermore, their health records are unknown. It may take several weeks of testing to place a child, and by that time the child is off to another school, another period in limbo, and, worse yet, another wasteful series of inoculations and eye tests.

There is never time to develop special education programs for migrant children. Besides, who really knows their needs? There is virtually no chance to get acquainted with them, to provide love and understanding; they are strangers in their schools.

In sum, the problems of the migrant child are many; the solutions difficult.

THE LAW MADE THE DIFFERENCE

The special educational needs of children of migratory agricultural workers were recognized by Congress in November 1966 when it amended title I of the Elementary and Secondary Education Act (ESEA). The amendment (Public Law 89-750) gave the U.S. Office of Education authority and funds to improve educational programs and offer supplementary services for these children.

Since its inauguration in fiscal year 1967, the title I migrant program has expanded to encompass all 50 States, Puerto Rico, Guam, American Samoa, the Virgin Islands, and the Trust Territory of the Pacific Islands. Today, it serves approximately 400,000 children at a cost of over $90 million.

The money goes to State departments of education, which, in turn, assess needs and then make allocations to local school districts·or other eligible applicants serving migrant children. Each year's allotment is based on a formula that takes into account the number of migrant children served in a State and per pupil expenditures.

Title I migrant programs concentrate on identifying and meeting the specific needs of migrant children. Continuity of instruction is a top priority with special focus on the individual educational problems of each child. And because you can't teach a hungry child, lunches, snacks—even breakfasts—are provided. Nutrition lessons are taught in the schools; health problems handled. If a child can't see properly, he is given eye glasses. If he has trouble hearing, the source of the trouble is sought and a remedy, if possible, provided. Health, nutrition, and psychological services figure high on the priority lists of title I migrant program directors. So, too, do cultural development and prevocational training and counseling.

Each year since the inception of the program funding for these educational services has increased—from approximately $10 million in fiscal year 1967 to $92 million in fiscal year 1975:

Fiscal Year	Allocations
1967	$ 9,737,847
1968	41,692,425
1969	45,556,074
1970	51,014,319
1971	57,608,680
1972	64,822,926
1973	72,772,187
1974	78,331,437
1975	91,953,160

The number of participating children has also increased—from 80,000 to the current 400,000. Yet an estimated 600,000 children remain unserved.

In 1974, Public Law 93-380 extended the migrant program to include children of migratory fishermen—those who move from place to place catching fish for commercial purposes and those working in the fish processing industry. How many children are involved, no one knows. The States are now making surveys. Calendar year 1975 is being devoted to recruiting the children of migrant fishermen and enrolling them in the program. These youngsters will receive the same special services as do the children of migrant agricultural workers.

In both instances, the children may participate in the program for 5 years after their families stop migrating. This is because they continue to need special educational services to assist them in becoming full-fledged members of their new communities. For many of them it will be their first opportunity to receive a full year of uninterrupted schooling.

THE COMPUTER FOLLOWS THE CHILD

P.L. 93-380 also authorizes the use of the Migrant Student Record Transfer System (MSRTS). The heart of the system is a central computer data bank (located in Little Rock, Arkansas) which can trace the whereabouts of each child as he migrates from one harvest to another. The MSRTS produces the official count of migrant children.

When the title I migrant education program was authorized by the Congress, no one really knew how many migrant children there were or even where they were. True, some did go to school, but they usually arrived at the door with no records and little recollection of where they had been. The MSRTS is significantly changing this.

It took 30 months for all the States to agree on what information should be included in the records of these children. There was the matter of privacy to be considered and the extent of the information needed. In the end, it was agreed that each record should contain the child's name, sex, birthday, and birthplace; his math and reading scores from the last four schools he attended; and coded information on health examinations and a variety of childhood diseases. A child's record can be supplied to school officials and health authorities within 4 to 24 hours after a request is made.

The MSRTS makes student placement easier and indicates where special help is needed. It eliminates multiple testing and physical examinations. It enables school officials to place the migrant child at the proper grade level in whatever school he enrolls within a day of his arrival.

And in at least one instance, it saved lives. In 1973 the MSRTS was used to find more than 200 children who were potential victims or carriers of typhoid fever. The network was called into play after more than 130 persons became ill with typhoid, apparently as the result of drinking contaminated water at a migrant labor camp in Homestead, Florida. By the time the outbreak was discovered, hundreds of people who had been exposed to the disease had left the area for work elsewhere. Thanks to the computer network, 232 children—and through them their families—were located within 48 hours. The data bank had traced the children to other parts of Florida and to Texas, Georgia, and Alabama.

EXAMPLES OF PROGRESS

Progress in migrant education has been significant since the enactment of the 1966 amendment to title I, ESEA. Federal funds have made it possible not only to give greater attention to the needs of migrant children but also to put into practice a variety of innovative, creative ideas. For example—

Florida.—One summer a cadre of 45 Florida teachers followed the eastern migrant stream for 6 weeks, visiting labor camps, schools, and work areas. As the field workers harvested the fruits and vegetables, the teachers harvested facts about their children.

So that others, too, could benefit from their experience, the Florida teaching cadre produced a film showing what it's like to be a child of the road. They developed and published teaching materials for use by others who work with migrant children. The sights and sounds of their travels became the basis for activity-centered programs for the migrant children who winter in Florida and attend school there.

California.--Each summer this State recruits some 200 young people with 1 or more years of college to work in the title I migrant program. Organized into a Mini-Corps, they assist in the classroom, initiate camp projects, and serve as liaison between the migrant community and the school. They also teach English to adults and serve as models for the younger children.

At the end of the summer the Mini-Corpsmen meet to evaluate their experiences. Almost invariably they say they have changed their attitudes about migrants, want to come back the following summer, and intend to devote their lives to teaching--especially to teaching the disadvantaged.

New Jersey.--It's a far cry from field work to employment in factories and offices. Recognizing this fact, the New Jersey Department of Education has set up a mobile industrial training unit for migrant youth. The unit consists of a trailer with a simulated office and an industrial assembly line. It operates 12 months of the year, serving five migrant education centers and 10 school districts throughout the State.

Here migrant young people are taught everything they need to know about getting and staying on a regular job. Training begins with the initial phone call inquiring about the job opening (few migrant children know how to use a phone) followed by an actual interview that is video taped and then critiqued. The youth is then hired, told how to operate a time clock, and told the importance of punctuality and dependability. Thereupon he or she starts on-the-job training, learning all the skills required for an assembly line or office job. At the end of the program, trainees receive their paychecks, plus instructions on how to open a bank account, pay their bills, budget, and systematically save.

The program takes 2 to 4 weeks with 24 students attending each day. So far it has helped an estimated 500 migrants successfully move from backbreaking field work to jobs offering increased income, prestige, and rapid advancement.

There are other stories of how the Federal migrant education program has given people the hope, the incentive, and the knowledge to get out of the migrant stream.

Maria M. is in her late teens. For almost as long as she can remember, she traveled each summer with her family from Puerto Rico to upstate New York. While her family worked on a fur farm, she participated in a title I ESEA migrant education program. When she was 16, Maria was trained as a classroom aide to work in the title I summer program. That fall she enrolled as a senior in the local high school and became its first migrant graduate. Maria is now enrolled in college in Puerto Rico. Her goal: to become a teacher.

The family of Julia G. also looks toward a brighter future--thanks to the migrant education program. Mrs. G., recently widowed at 46, has long realized that the only way to keep her 12 children from following in the occupational footsteps of their father is to help them get an education.

When she heard about the migrant education program in Billings, Montana, where the family helped harvest sugar beets each summer, she sent her children to school rather than to the fields. And she insisted they go each day, despite the serious loss in family income.

Mrs. G.'s eldest daughter has now graduated from college; her eldest son is married and going to college; another daughter is training to be a nurse. Mrs. G. herself has been attending night classes so that she may qualify for the General Education Development (GED) test. She goes to school after working all day in the fields because she, too, wants a high school diploma and the opportunity for a better, more rewarding future.

THE FUTURE IS NOW

But these are accomplishments of the past. What of the future?

The Office of Education is constantly seeking new and better ways to help migrant children and youth--in fact, to move them out of the fields and into more rewarding occupations.

A career education program is now being developed that will span kindergarten through 12th grade. It will give migrant children a picture of what occupations and professions lie beyond the vegetable fields and fruit orchards. It will introduce to them, grade by grade, the basic skills necessary to obtain meaningful, stable employment. It will show them which skills are needed for certain occupations and then help them gain these skills. Through guidance and counseling, migrant children will be able to arrive at realistic decisions about their future and will be more likely to achieve their occupational goals.

Also, if their parents should stop their migrations, these children will continue to be helped. In the years ahead, as more and more migrants leave the stream, title I's migrant education program will focus more and more on the 5-year child--the child who stays in one spot but still needs special help.

This change in focus is resulting in another shift in program emphasis. For years migrant children have filtered through rural schools. The new settling-in trend is now bringing migrants to our cities, and the urban school is becoming the new educational arena of the migrant child. So it is here that the title I migrant education program also must turn its attention.

But there are still hundreds of thousands of children who will continue to follow the sun as their parents harvest the crops--children who never stay in one State long enough to receive credit for their studies or to successfully complete any total course of study. For the highschooler, in particular, this has been a major problem. Now specific steps are being taken to remedy this situation. As a beginning, the Office of Education is analyzing and grouping courses offered in various States so that migrant children can receive proper course credit for classroom attendance wherever they are. The effort is expected to significantly alter the traditional credit system and permit the involvement of all States in providing a more realistic response to the special needs of the migrant child. However, which courses will constitute a diploma "core" and which schools will award the diploma are still under discussion.

All this will require considerable interstate cooperation. To benefit the migrant child, all States must work together, capitalizing upon the successes and failures of the others. The National Advisory Council on the Education of Disadvantaged Children firmly endorses interstate cooperation. In 1973 "cooperation" was designated as a top priority. Already schools are beginning to pool their expertise and to specialize in the education of teachers with skills and insights that permit them to identify effectively with migrant children.

"Title I Migrant Education Program." Education Briefing Paper. U.S. Department of Health, Education, and Welfare. Washington, D.C. May 1975.

Elementary and Secondary Education Act as Amended to Include Migrant Children

Purpose: Title I of the Elementary and Secondary Education Act was amended in November 1966, to include the children of migratory agricultural workers. In August 1974, the Act was further amended to include the children of migratory fishermen. Funds are provided to develop and implement special educational programs for these children.

Kinds of Programs: Title I migrant programs concentrate on identifying and meeting the specific needs of migrant children through remedial instruction; health, nutrition, and psychological services; cultural development; and prevocational training and counseling. Special attention in instructional programs is given to development of the language arts, including speaking, reading, and writing in both English and Spanish.

Scope: In fiscal year 1977, some $130 million in Title I funds are enabling 46 States and Puerto Rico to operate migrant education programs. Approximately 450,000 children will participate. This compares with an allottment of $97 million in 1976; $91 million in 1975; $78 million in 1974; $72 million in 1973; $65 million in 1972; $57 million in 1971; $51 million in 1970; $46 million in 1969; $42 million in 1968; and $10 million in 1967. The number of children participating has grown from 80,000 to the current 450,000. Approximately 70 percent of the children served are Mexican American, mostly from the Southwest.

Project Approval: Each State Department of Education submits its plan and cost estimate for migrant education programs to the Office of Education for approval. The State is then awarded a grant to support the administration and operation of the program. The amount allotted to each State is based on a formula which determines funding by the number of migrant children being served, as reported by the States to the Migrant Student Record Transfer System, headquartered in Little Rock, Arkansas.

Participation: A child is considered eligible to participate if he or she has moved with the family from one school district to another during the past year in order that a parent or other member of the immediate family might secure employment in agriculture, fishing, or related food processing activities. The child is considered eligible for up to five years after the parents have settled in one place.

Special Emphasis: A computerized Migrant Student Record Transfer System was developed in 1971. This system makes it possible to transmit academic and health data of a migrant child to any participating school district within 24 hours.

Legislation: Elementary and Secondary Education Act of 1965, P.L. 89-10; 1966 Amendments to ESEA, P.L. 89-750; 1967 Amendments to ESEA, P.L. 90-247; 1974 Amendments to ESEA, P.L. 93-380.

"Elementary and Secondary Education Act as Amended to Include Migrant Children." Office of Education, U.S. Department of Health, Education, and Welfare, Washington, D.C. October 1976.

New Directions for Federal Policy

If one accepts the two goals of "equality of opportunity" and "institutional health and diversity," then the policy question becomes: How does the Federal Government reconcile these goals in a coherent pattern for supporting American higher education?

In light of our discussion of the implications of current federal higher education financing, we submit that a more fruitful question be asked: Should and can the Federal Government support postsecondary education as an instrument of "equality of opportunity" and be a major guarantor of the "health and diversity" of American higher educational institutions? Depending on the answer to that question, different vehicles and different levels of federal funding are implied. The following recommendations are based upon the implications of current federal education policy and our corollary belief that although improved access, choice, and retention are goals worth pursuing, higher education should not and cannot effectively serve as the major vehicle for realizing greater social equality. In short, we base our recommendations on the interpretation that the Federal Government is attempting to accomplish too much and is not succeeding in its attempts. Taken together, these recommendations offer an alternative to current federal higher education policy. Before outlining our recommendations, it is appropriate to review the recommendations of several major commissions concerned with the federal role in postsecondary education and to explicate our guiding principles.

A Comparison of Two Major Reports

There have been many recent task force reports that have made recommendations concerning the role of the Federal Government in postsecondary education, as well as state and institutional roles, and outlined areas of future federal concern and initiative. These include: The Committee for Economic Development (1973), the National Commission on the Financing of Postsecondary Education (1973), the Carnegie Council for Policy Studies (1975), the Newman Reports (1971, 1973), in addition to a number of other reports that have been less widely circulated.

As a way of providing a context for our recommendations, it is useful to compare several reports that seem to most adequately reflect the direction of recent recommendations concerning the federal role, and which have already had, and are likely to have, considerable influence on federal policy. In our view, the Carnegie Commission Reports and the Newman Reports most satisfactorily meet this criteria. The Carnegie Commission on Higher Education has probably done more to influence higher education than any single group in this century. Indeed, three provisions of the 1972 Higher Education Amendments—the Basic Educational Opportunity Grants program, the cost-of-instruction supplements, and the Fund for the Improvement of Postsecondary Education—reflected the recommendations of the Commission. The Newman Reports, which are recommendations to the Secretary of the Department of Health, Education and Welfare, represent a logical extrapolation of current trends in federal higher education policy.

In this section, we shall neither summarize these reports nor outline them in great detail. Instead, we shall briefly concentrate on three major issues regarding the federal funding of postsecondary education: (1) To what extent should student aid programs be the major vehicle of federal funding? Should student aid, whether in the form of grants or loans, be portable so that students could bring their aid to the institution of their choice? Or should the aid be dispensed by institutions? (2) To what extent should institutional aid be an instrument of federal funding and in what forms? (3) To what extent should the private sector be assisted by the Federal Government?

Both reports agreed that because equality of opportunity was the major federal responsibility, student aid, chiefly in the form of grants to lower-income students, should be expanded. In *Quality and Equality: New Levels of Federal Responsibility,* the Carnegie Commission offered the following guidelines to achieve the overriding priority of the achievement of educational opportunity:

> The three interacting elements of the proposed federal aid program to remove financial barriers are all of great importance; financial aid to students, with a substantial component of grants for low-income students and a moderately expanded loan program primarily for middle-income students; cost-of-education supplements to institutions; and creation of new places to accommodate all qualified students (1970, p. 2).

In particular, the Carnegie Commission recommended full funding of the Basic Education Opportunity Grants. The Newman Report, with its almost complete attention to student aid as the major vehicle of federal funding, is even more forceful in its recommendations for increased federal funding for students.

Both reports recommend that student aid, including grants and loans, should be portable in the sense that students would receive their support independently of the institutions they chose to attend. Portable student aid would widen student choice of institutions and would motivate institutions to respond more directly to students. The 1971 Newman Report emphatically recommended portability of student aid: "Providing funding through grants accompanying students (portable grants) has the advantage of encouraging a sense of competition and willingness to change as society changes" (U.S. Office of Education 1971, p. 74).

Neither the Carnegie Commission nor the Newman Reports recommended direct institutional support for postsecondary education. Both groups recommended that federal grants to institutions be directly related to student grants. To encourage colleges to foster equality of educational opportunity, the Carnegie Commission recommended "that the federal government grant cost-of-education supplements to colleges and universities based on the number and levels of students holding federal grants enrolled in the institutions" (1970, p. 6). The first Newman Report recommended more broadly that "both the state and federal governments provide funds to institutions (both public and private) in the form of grants that accompany certain categories of students" (1971, p. 74). The Newman Reports did not consider other types of institutional aid except for recommending categorical grants for innovative programs. Meanwhile, the Carnegie Commission recommended that the only other funds awarded institutions should be for construction and special purpose grants, such as aid for developing institutions. Federal categorical aid, which was previously the major instrument of federal support, received little support relative to institutional aid directly tied to student grants. Direct federal support for educational expenses, which was recommended by many groups in the late 1960's, is not even a major issue in these and other major reports.

The Carnegie Commission and the Newman Task Forces both acknowledged the educational contributions of private institutions and expressed concern about the future of private higher education. In our view, both groups overlooked the importance to higher education of the private sector. The Carnegie Commission, however, recommended state aid to private institutions in the form of capitation grants to students attending private schools. The Newman Reports only recommended that needy students attending private institutions should receive additional grants to help defray high tuition costs. Neither the Carnegie Commission nor the Newman Task Force suggested that private higher education may require major federal as well as state support. For example, neither recommended direct federal sponsorship of programs or matching grants to states.

In summary, these recommendations include several major themes for the proposed federal role:

• Student aid programs should be expanded as the major vehicle for the federal funding of postsecondary education. Student aid, especially in the form of grants to low-income students and loans to low- and middle-income students, is the preferred method of directly achieving universal acccess and indirectly supporting postsecondary education. In effect, the Federal Government should finance higher education through students or, more colloquially, through a "market model."

• Student aid should be portable in the sense that students should receive support independent of the institutions they choose to attend.

• The majority of federal institutional aid should be through grants tied directly to student grants. The remainder of federal institutional aid should include only carefully designated categorical aid programs, such as those to encourage research and innovation. The Federal Government should not provide for general institutional support for colleges and universities.

• The governmental responsibility for private higher education rests largely with the states. Federal support should not go beyond additional grants to help defray the higher costs of private education.

These recommendations are largely incremental, emphasizing a direction in which the Government is already moving. The recommendations of the Carnegie Council, in particular, probably hastened these overall trends. Yet even though these two groups and the previously mentioned policy-recommending bodies broadly support the direction of current federal policy, we propose a set of recommendations that offers modified goals for federal policy and alternative mechanisms of federal funding. Stated below are the principles that have guided our own policy recommendations.

Guiding Principles

Our recommendations are based on two major principles:

• Basic support and responsibility for higher education should remain with the states and private individuals. It is, however, in the national interest to provide strong and consistent federal support for postsecondary education.

• The two major priorities for federal funding in higher education should be the maintenance of a healthy and diverse structure of postsecondary education, and the realization of the goal of universal access.

The rationale for the first principle will be elaborated in the discussion of the second. The rationale for the second principle deserves immediate attention.

Like many Americans, we share the belief that equality of opportunity is a national goal that should be encouraged and realized throughout American life. It follows that postsecondary education, as a major social institution, should be made available to all citizens who wish to participate, allowing them to enjoy the fruits of further education. The goal of universal access, as public policy, represents a federal commitment to the achievement of that goal. But universal access, both for many new participants in postsecondary education and for many public policy-makers, has nearly become synonymous with greater social equality; that is, rather than access being viewed simply as a means of ensuring educational opportunity, it is seen as the most realistic way to provide for greater social equality in American society. It has been argued earlier that the current federal emphasis on access implicitly suggests that access is not simply an attempt to realize equal opportunity within postsecondary education, but also to realize equality of opportunity in the larger society.

For both empirical and normative reasons, we submit that federal higher education policy should not be built around the "broad" conception of equality of opportunity. On the one hand, access to higher education is no longer a guarantee of greater social equality. It was documented that the highly unstable relationship between a college education and the job market had undermined earlier relationships between education and work. Thus, if current patterns continue as projected, federal student aid programs, no matter how generously funded, are unlikely to have the previously expected impact in terms of leading to greater social equality. From all indications, the Federal Government simply cannot appreciably affect the "broad" conception of equality of opportunity by merely providing access to postsecondary education.

On the other hand, it is our normative belief that education alone should not be the vehicle for the redistribution of income and occupational status in American society. The argument of many proponents of federal student aid programs is that education, in light of the unwillingness of the citizenry to change the distribution of wealth and opportunity through the tax structure, is the only remaining instrument to realize the achievement of equality of opportunity in the larger society. While we are personally supportive of those values, it is our conviction that the related issues of equality of opportunity and the redistribution of wealth are ultimately political questions. They should be confronted in the political system and should not become the cornerstone of a federal policy that is ostensibly directed toward the more limited goal of equality of educational opportunity.

In short, we submit that federal higher education policy cannot, and should not, both provide access to postsecondary education and (either implicitly or explicitly) characterize participation in higher education as the means of upward social mobility. The narrower goal of insuring access is the more legitimate and realizable undertaking for the Federal Government. Thus for us the central problem is one of combining the goals "universal access" and "institutional health and diversity" into a broad pattern of federal funding.

Recommendation I: Increasing Federal Support

Federal expenditures for higher education have risen steadily in current dollars, although there was a decline in constant dollars between 1973-1974 and 1974-1975. Our rationale for increasing federal assistance to postsecondary education is the following:

• Increasing federal assistance is necessary to help preserve the institutional health and diversity of postsecondary education; without continuing high levels of support, the social benefits of postsecondary education can no longer be fully enjoyed by participating individuals and American society at large. Although the main responsibility for funding institutions should continue to rest with the states, it is apparent that the majority of states will not provide sufficient assistance to insure the survival of many institutions. Lyman Glenny, for example, has argued that future state governments will allocate a decreasing proportion of their budgets to higher education: ". . . with the exception of a few states, the proportion of the state budget going to higher education will be no greater in 1980 than it is now—whether there are boom times or bad, Republicans or Democrats in office" (1973, p. 1). Without federal support, many private institutions will simply cease to exist.

• Increasing federal assistance is necessary to achieve the goal of universal access. Current federal support, in the form of student grants and loans, has only begun to move the nation toward the achievement of universal access. Without increasing federal assistance, it is doubtful that many persons historically denied access will have substantial educational opportunity.

• The federal tax structure is a more equitable base of funding than the state and local structures. The progressive income tax now appropriates the greatest portion of the income tax advantage resulting from education to federal, rather than state and local, tax revenues.

In short, we submit that a considerable increase in funding from the federal tax system is socially desirable and economically sound. This is consistent with our belief that a substantial social benefit accrues from investment in higher education at both public and private institutions.

Recommendation I Expanded: The Federal Government's share of total public financial support of postsecondary education should be gradually increased from its present 44.4 percent in 1974-1975 to 50 percent by the early 1980's (Carnegie Council . . . 1975, p. 14).

Due primarily to the financial crisis in American postsecondary education and the slow progress toward the achievement of universal access, the Federal Government must increase its overall level of support. This recommendation closely parallels a recent recommendation of the Carnegie Council on Policy Studies (1975, p. 14).

This recommendation is in the same direction as the Carnegie Commission and the Newman Reports, as well as most of the other commission and groups proposing recommendations for the federal role. In our view, the critical decisions concern the major forms of federal support for defined national goals. Accordingly, the following recommendation suggests a new direction for the Federal Government that differs markedly from the recommendations of the other groups.

Recommendation II: Institutional Grants for Instructional Purposes As the Major Vehicle of Federal Support

As discussed in the first chapter, direct federal institutional support for higher education, especially in the form of categorical grants and grants for special purposes, was in large measure responsible for the rapid growth of postsecondary education in the last decade. But in the late 1960's, it was clear that the decade of financial prosperity in American higher education would not be repeated. Even though enrollments were increasing, educational costs were rising rapidly. To deal with this situation, attention turned to the possibility of institutional grants for educational expenses from the Federal Government. The American Council on Education (*The Federal Investment in Higher Education*, 1967; *Federal Programs for Higher Education*, 1969), the Association of American Colleges (*Federal Institutional Grants for Instructional Purposes*, 1968), and The Association of American Universities (*The Federal Financing of Higher Education*, 1968) went on record in favor of institutional grants.

According to Howard Bowen:

> The proposal for institutional grants was based on three tacit assumptions. One was that expenditures would continue to rise rapidly because of growing enrollments and rising costs. Another was that, though federal categorical aid was desirable, it did little to meet the basic operating costs of institutions and unrestricted funds were needed as well. The third assumption was that a steady rise of tuitions would be on principle socially harmful (Bowen 1974, p. 4).

The Carnegie Commission gave considerable attention to federal institutional aid (Wolk 1968: *Institutional Aid: Federal Support to Colleges and Universities*, 1972; *Quality and Equality: New Levels of Federal Responsibility for Higher Education*, 1968) and a number of formulas were devised that could be used to distribute institutional aid. But following the passage of the 1972 Amendments, and the authorization and expansion of the overall student assistance program to help realize equality of opportunity, emphasis on the issue of direct funding to institutions declined. The Federal Government had adopted a new course of action, and even proponents of institutional aid conceded that there was little they could do. Based on the implications of the current federal funding of postsecondary education, we submit that current federal funding policies should be revamped to include support for direct educational expenses in the form of federal institutional grants. Our rationale is as follows:

• Additional operating funds beyond traditional sources of support are essential to maintain quality of instruction and more immediately to insure that quality institutions experiencing financial difficulty survive. Despite soaring tuition fees, large increases in philanthropy, and major efforts by the states, the health and diversity of our postsecondary enterprise has steadily deteriorated. Although the majority of states now indirectly support private higher education, these monies are insufficient to maintain the vigor of the private sector. Without federal support, the well-being of private higher education in particular is threatened.

• General institutional support is needed to counter-balance existing federal institutional aid programs. Federal funds now go only to certain types of institutions for certain types of programs, and many institutions are bypassed altogether. Other institutions only receive minor categorical aid for carefully designated purposes, the exception being institutions involved in the Aid for Developing Institution's program.

• Institutional grants are necessary because federal student aid programs, which were designed to simultaneously provide equal educational opportunity and to assist postsecondary institutions in meeting their educational expenses, have failed to accomplish the latter goal. Despite the compelling logic of student aid, few institutions have financially benefited from enrolling disadvantaged students. Because of rising costs and declining enrollments, the attraction of new students with federal monies has not always had the intended effect. This is especially true in the private sector, where the financial gains attributable to new students has been minimal at best.

• Institutional grants are also necessary because federal student aid programs differentially favor institutions. Only colleges with relatively high enrollments of disadvantaged students can enjoy the marginal institutional benefits of federal funding via students.

In summary, we believe that federal institutional grants must be authorized and funded if the health and diversity of postsecondary education is to be maintained. Additional funding for institutional grants might come in part from the federal monies previously earmarked for veteran's benefits. Due to recent Congressional action, these benefits will require substantially less federal funding in the future.

Institutional grants will be defined as grants made directly to institutions for general support of the educational program. On the basis of our rationale, we offer the following recommendations for federal institutional grant programs.

Recommendation II Expanded: A substantial portion of federal support should be through the mechanism of direct institutional grants to postsecondary institutions. Institutional grants in roughly equal proportions should take the form of cost-of-education supplements and direct institutional grants.

Title IV of the 1972 Education Amendments had provisions for cost-of-education supplements for colleges and universities. First recommended by the Carnegie Commission on Higher Education (1970, p. 21), this legislation authorized that the Federal Government grant cost-of-education supplements to postsecondary institutions based on the numbers and levels of students holding federal grants enrolled in the institutions.

We recommend that the cost-of-education supplements be funded as rapidly as possible for the following reasons. Most important, this plan will assist colleges in meeting the increased educational costs associated with educating disadvantaged students. Second, student aid does little to solve, and perhaps aggravates, the financial problems of institutions; therefore cost-of-education allowances would provide a step in this direction.

Third, these supplements would especially help the financially troubled private sector, at least under current student assistance programs. Private higher education is in a less competitive position overall than is public higher education primarily because of the large tuition gap between the two sectors. Recent federal student aid programs (BEOG and SSIG) were expected to disproportionately aid private institutions. Leslie and Fife (1974, p. 667) have found that when enough student assistance is available, grant recipients generally choose to attend private institutions. Thus under current student assistance programs, accompanying cost-of-education allowances will contribute to the financial strength of the private sector.

The Carnegie Commission, in *The Federal Role in Postsecondary Education,* recommends that "funds should be provided for the cost-of-education supplements adopted under the Education Amendments of 1972, with annual appropriations rising to about $800 million in constant 1974 dollars by 1979-1980" (1975, p. 51). While we support the thrust of the Commission's recommendation in this area, we are less persuaded that cost-of-education allowances, no matter how generously funded, will, in a fair and equitable manner, make a significant contribution to the health of both the public and private sectors. Our reason for this position is that the manner in which federal student aid programs are targeted will result in an inequitable distribution of student aid funds and thus of cost-of-education allowances. That is, cost-of-education allowances following students based upon particular student-aid criteria will have the effect of allowing those students to help determine the fate of many of the nation's colleges and universities. An artificial "market model," based upon continually changing patterns and levels of support, will determine which institutions are to receive the greatest federal funding. Thus, on the one hand, we view cost-of-education grants as a sensible method of providing federal aid to help institutions meet the rising educational costs of disadvantaged students and, at least in the short run, a good vehicle for aiding the private sector. On the other hand, given the vagaries of student aid funding and the dangers of a "market model," it is an inadequate method of federal funding to help provide stability for both public and private higher education, especially over the long run.

Accordingly, we recommend that a substantial amount of federal institutional aid be funnelled through direct institutional grants in order to enlist the Federal Government as a partner in meeting future increases in the educational costs of colleges and universities. A number of specific formulas were introduced into the debate on institutional grants in the late 1960's. Howard Bowen (1968, pp. 18-21) offered a plan in one of the first monographs sponsored by the Carnegie Commission on Higher Education. In the past few years, and especially following the 1972 Amendments, there have been few alternative formulas introduced. Given this lacuna, we recommend the enactment of new legislation that would provide general institutional support on the following broad principles:

• All nationally and regionally accredited institutions should be eligible for institutional grants.

• All federal institutional grants should be based (in large measure) on a formula related to full-time equivalent (FTE) enrollment, both at the undergraduate and graduate levels.

• There should be a factor in the formula for institutional grants that takes into account the variance of instructional costs according to the level of instruction.

• The formula should take "quality" into account as a way of rewarding existing quality and of encouraging other institutions to strive for excellence.

We believe that institutional grants for educational expenses should complement cost-of-education allowances. By themselves, these supplements will allow institutions to meet the costs associated with educating the new student clientele. Institutional grants, for reasons cited earlier, will provide an equitable and broad base in support of the overall health and diversity of American postsecondary education.

To the extent that the states are unable to ensure the health and diversity of American postsecondary education, we believe that it is incumbent upon those persons and organizations concerned with American education to reevaluate the notion of direct institutional aid. Since the initial funding of the Education Amendments of 1972, there has been little evidence of support from the higher education community for direct institutional aid due to the high priority given to student aid. Another major explanation for this is that some view the current political climate as less than conducive to recommendations that, in effect, broaden the base of federal responsibility. Others fear that federal funds may simply replace funds raised from non-federal sources.

Political realities notwithstanding, we believe that the future vitality of our postsecondary education system is at stake. Furthermore, the history of federal funding illustrates that we can build safeguards to assure that federal funds are not used to replace other financial sources. To cite one example, federal funding for the support of land-grant colleges has greatly stimulated both state and private support of institutions founded under the Morrill Act. The federal emphasis on supporting postsecondary education chiefly through disadvantaged students must be challenged. For reasons cited in the rationale, the issue of institutional aid must be re-examined.

Recommendation III: Student Assistance to Promote Universal Access

In the late 1960's, there was a widespread sentiment in Congress that a major goal of federal programs should be to encourage needy and low-income students to attend college. The 1969 Rivlin report (*Toward a Long-Range Plan for Federal Financial Support for Higher Education: A Report to the President,* 1969) argued that federal aid should increasingly take the form of grants and loans to low-income students, with institutional aid in the form of added cost-of-education allowances to assist those institutions accepting needy students. The 1972 Education Amendment marked the authorization of the Congressional decision that federal support for higher education would henceforth come primarily through grants to students rather than through institutional aid for special purposes deemed in the national interest.

In light of our second recommendation, we believe that the overall trend of funding postsecondary education chiefly through student grants and loans be reexamined. Yet, it is also our belief that student aid funding should be continued. Our rationale is the following:

• Because college attendance is closely related to background variables, such as parental education and income-level, only direct federal funding of disadvantaged students will move the nation closer to the achievement of universal access.

• Because the Federal Government, unlike state government, is supported on a generally progressive tax structure, it is the most appropriate level of government to sponsor universal access through student aid programs.

• Because there are many individual nonpecuniary benefits of participation in postsecondary education—such as improved interpersonal relations, greater political participation, and better mental health (Withey 1972)—disadvantaged students must be assured the fruits of further education.

• Federal funding through student aid programs, however, should not be construed as a federal commitment to education as the vehicle though which greater social equality in the larger society can and should be achieved. Far too many disadvantaged have attended and currently are attending college on the premise that attendance will lead to greater social mobility. While the Federal Government has not explicitly funded student aid programs on this assumption, this premise has subtly underpinned the recent federal emphasis on student aid assistance. We believe that student aid programs should be funded solely for the purpose of equalizing educational opportunity, so that persons previously denied access can also enjoy the benefits of postsecondary education.

Recommendation III Expanded: Direct institutional support for postsecondary education should be complemented by student aid programs for disadvantaged students, especially the BEOG, SSIG, and CWS programs.

In general, we submit that student aid programs should be funded on the following broad principles:

• All persons disproportionately denied access to postsecondary education because of income level and educational background, regardless or race, ethnic background, sex, and age should be the main recipients of federal student aid programs.

• Private as well as public institutions should indirectly be assisted.

• Student aid programs should not serve as the only major mechanism for the funding of postsecondary education.

There are a number of existing federal student aid programs that meet this criteria. In our view, three in particular are the most promising of the student aid programs, although modifications in their features and changes in the level of funding are necessary.

The Basic Educational Opportunity Grants (BEOG) program is, we believe, a preferred federal strategy because these grants are allocated solely on the basis of need. However, there are several problems with the existing BEOG program. First, the eligibility conditions are too restrictive. For example, very little BEOG aid can be received by a student from a family of four with an income above $9,000. Second, the provision requiring that grants may not exceed 50 percent of the students' cost of attendance does not go far enough toward ensuring equality of educational opportunity. Third, the funds appropriated for the BEOG program have been inadequate. In 1975-1976, for example, only $715 million has been appropriated. Based on these limitations, we recommend that the eligibility conditions of

BEOG be liberalized, the program be restructured to cover all noninstructional costs, and that federal appropriatons for BEOG be substantially increased. These recommendations, though less specific, closely parallel the recommendations concerning BEOG in the recent publication of the Carnegie Council on Policy Studies in Higher Education (1975, p. 29).

We also urge adequate funding of the State Student Incentive Grant (SSIG) program. The primary reason for this recommendation is that we believe that state governments as well as the Federal Government should provide financial aid to both private and public institutions. In many cases, it is not perceived to be in a state's economic interest to fund private institutions, often because many of the students are from out of state and/or the existing public institutions are suffering from a combination of rising costs and enrollment losses and require strong support. SSIG grants would further encourage the states, many of which already have effective student aid programs, to continue supporting students at all institutions, and at increasingly higher levels. Federal funds currently made available under the SSIG program have encouraged 41 states to adopt scholarship programs. Although there have been problems of inequity in the allocation of funds for the College Work Study (CWS) program, we also believe that it has proven to be a successful form of both student aid and institutional support.

Finally, we are not suggesting that other federal student aid programs, especially the Supplementary Educational Opportunity Grants Program (SSEOG) and National Direct Student Loan Program (NDSL), be left unfunded. However, we do believe that the remaining federal student grant and loan programs should be reexamined and perhaps eliminated in a move toward previous recommendations for institutional aid.

Although student aid has been recommended as a vehicle for the federal support of universal access, we have recommended moving away from student aid as the only major vehicle of funding postsecondary education. Our reasons relate to the preferred goals of federal policy and the most appropriate means of achieving them.

In stating our guiding principles, it was made clear that the goal of institutional health and diversity should be equal in importance to universal access. While federal student assistance has brought federal monies to postsecondary institutions, it is our position, for reasons elaborated upon earlier, that institutional grants are a better means of federal support to maintain a healthy postsecondary enterprise. To the extent that these two goals are of equal importance, institutional grants should complement, rather than be replaced by, student aid programs for disadvantaged students.

A widely held point of view is that student aid is the logical federal vehicle both for promoting access and encouraging institutional health. Accordingly, a much publicized government strategy is the stimulation of competition among institutions. The Basic Educational Opportunity Grant program and the phasing-out of institutional aid have ostensibly been the vehicle through which the government encourages institutions to compete for students, thereby insuring the "survival-of-the fittest." This "market model" is in our view a poor method of insuring a healthy and vigorous public and private sector of higher education. Larry Leslie, a critic of the market model philosophy, offers a viewpoint similar to our own:

> Total or near total funding of higher education through student vouchers may represent good economics but it represents poor "higher education" . . . Other social functions may be cast aside when a social institution is placed on a market system. Nevertheless, the temptation does exist to turn higher education completely upside down and shake it, so severe is present disillusionment with the system (1973, p. 16).

Federal student assistance programs have especially failed to meet the resource needs of private higher education. Without direct federal aid, many private and public institutions may find it impossible to continue if left to the vagaries of the marketplace.

Conclusion

We support current federal policy to the extent that the best allocation of resources to postsecondary education and the best use of resources by the system will result from a policy of stabilized public support for higher education. Moreover, we support current federal funding of a variety of student aid programs as a way of moving toward the achievement of universal access. At the same time, we do not believe that student aid programs should be funded on the premise that a college degree is a medium of social mobility for disadvantaged students. As discussed earlier, it is our belief that the Federal Government should not and cannot effectively fund student aid programs as a way of realizing greater social equality in American society. Put differently, student aid programs should be funded solely as a tool through which disadvantaged students can continue their education. We are optimistic that the existing student aid programs, with modifications and additional federal funding, will help to insure that every student capable of benefiting from higher education will have the opportunity and incentive to continue her or his education. At the same time, we recognize that even with the current emphasis on student aid, progress toward the achievement of universal access has been gradual and uneven.

We have also recommended a major shift in the federal role by advocating federal support in the form of cost-of-education allowances and institutional grants for direct educational expenses. The latter proposal is contrary to current federal policy, the recommendations of most of the major commissions, and the widely-shared sentiment against increasing federal funding of postsecondary institutions. Heretofore, federal funding for institutions has taken the form of categorical grants and grants for special purposes. While we are not opposed to traditional forms of institutional funding, we believe that without direct federal support, the health and diversity of postsecondary education is at issue, especially that of private higher education. Student aid programs, no matter how amply funded, are inequitable and are an ineffective method of preserving the financial integrity of postsecondary education.

Therefore, a different direction in federal policy is recommended. Federal policy should be altered to reflect a major commitment to the health and diversity of public and private higher education in America. This is not a recommendation to place renewed emphasis on the old indirect forms of institutional aid. The intent is to consider the possibilities of cost-of-education allowances and institutional grants for general educational support as ways of federal support for the goals of universal access and institutional health and diversity. Although gradual progress toward universal access may occur, strict reliance on student aid programs implies a standard of achievement that may lead only to disillusionment among those institutions that survived and may have become increasingly homogeneous. A vigorous and diverse system of postsecondary education requires more direct federal support.

Our intent in this monograph has been to review federal higher education policy, discuss the implications of that policy, and offer a broad set of recommendations concerning federal support, with a focus on the undergraduate level. To the extent that we have addressed the central issues regarding the federal role, in part by questioning trends in recent federal policy, we hope to stimulate a more imaginative and thoughtful dialog concerning the purposes of federal higher education policy and the most effective means of their implementation.

* This material has not been excerpted in its entirety.

The Implications of Federal Education Policy. Clifton Conrad and Joseph Cosand. ERIC/Higher Education Research Report, No. 1. Published by the American Association for Higher Education, Washington, D.C. 1976.

Part six:
Hispanic

Hispanic

PERSONS OF SPANISH ORIGIN IN THE UNITED STATES: MARCH 1976

This report presents advance data on selected social, economic, and demographic characteristics of persons of Spanish origin in the United States; the data were collected in the March 1976 Current Population Survey. The tables in this report present data for some or all of the subcategories of persons of Spanish origin, that is, persons of Mexican, Puerto Rican, Cuban, Central or South American, and other Spanish origin. A more detailed report on the characteristics of these persons is forthcoming.

There were about 11 million persons of Spanish origin in the United States in March 1976, with an estimated 6.6 million of them reporting Mexican origin and 1.8 million reporting Puerto Rican origin. The total number of persons of Cuban origin was estimated at about 700,000, and persons of Central or South American origin at 800,000. Also, an additional 1.3 million persons reported they were of some other Spanish origin.

Inasmuch as the estimates in this report are based on a sample survey, they are subject to sampling error. The sampling error is mainly a measure of the variations that occur by chance because a sample rather than a complete census enumeration is used to survey the population. Thus, because of sampling error, the estimate of the number of persons of Spanish origin presented in this report determines an interval of confidence. For example, if a complete census instead of a sample survey had been taken in March 1976, there are 68 chances out of 100 (one standard error) that the census would show a total number of persons of Spanish origin within the range of 10.8 to 11.4 million persons (table 1), and 95 chances out of 100 (two standard errors) that the census total would be between 10.5 and 11.7 million persons.

In this report all statements of comparison between estimates are statistically significant at the two standard error level—this means that there are 95 chances out of 100 (19 out of 20) that a difference specified in the text indicates a true difference in the population.

According to the March 1976 CPS there were 2.5 million families of Spanish origin in the United States. Most of these families were living in metropolitan areas with the majority residing in the central cities of these areas; thus,

about 2.1 million families of Spanish origin—84 percent of all Spanish origin families—were living in metropolitan areas. Moreover, there was marked residential preference among the categories of Spanish origin families. For instance, families of Mexican origin, the majority of whom lived in the Southwest of the United States particularly in the States of Arizona, California, Colorado, New Mexico, and Texas, were more partial to residence outside of metropolitan areas than were families of Puerto Rican origin. About 23 percent of all Mexican families in the United States lived in a nonmetropolitan area compared to only 3 percent of all Puerto Rican families (table 2).

The Spanish origin population is a young population relative to the overall population; for example, the median age of persons of Spanish origin in March 1976 was 20.9 years compared to a median of 28.9 years for the overall population. Furthermore, about 13 percent of all persons of Spanish origin were under 5 years of age, but only about 7 percent of the total United States population was under 5 years of age (table 3).

The March 1976 survey indicated that the proportion of single men of Spanish origin is higher than the proportion of single women of Spanish origin—this may be because men, in general, usually marry at a later age than women. Furthermore, women of Spanish origin were much more likely to be divorced or widowed than were men of Spanish origin; one reason for this is that men are more likely to remarry than women (table 4).

The overall population was ahead of the Spanish origin population in educational attainment. About 64 percent of all persons 25 years old and over were high school graduates; 39 percent of Spanish origin persons 25 years old and over had achieved that level of education. Furthermore, although only about 4 percent of all persons 25 years old and over in the United States had completed less than 5 years of school, about 19 percent of all persons of Spanish origin had completed less than 5 years of school.

Differences in educational level were also apparent among categories of Spanish origin persons. For example, the Mexican origin category had the highest proportion with less than 5 years of school completed; in contrast, a

Figure 1. Number of Persons of Spanish Origin by Type of Spanish Origin: March 1976

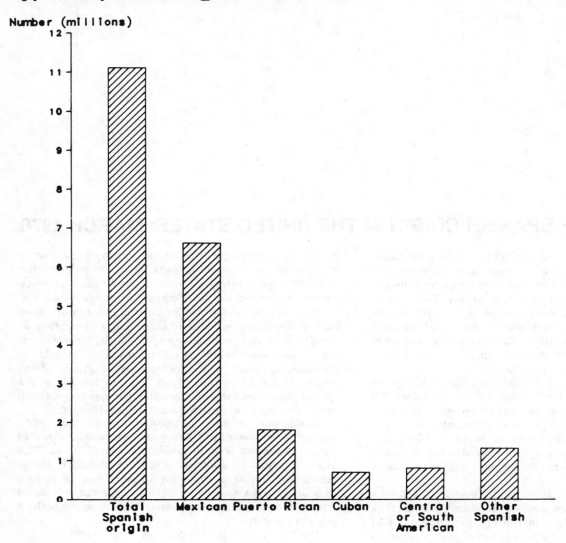

Number (millions)

greater proportion of Cuban origin persons, 52 percent, had completed 4 years of high school or more than had Mexican or Puerto Rican origin persons, 33 percent and 30 percent, respectively (table 5).

The labor force participation rate (the percent of the civilian noninstitutional population 16 years old and over that is in the labor force) was 77 percent for Spanish origin men. The rate varied, however, between men of certain Spanish origin groups; for example, Puerto Rican men had a lower labor force participation rate (67 percent) than did men of Mexican origin (79 percent).

Approximately 43 percent of Spanish origin women 16 years old and over were in the labor force as of March 1976, and, like Puerto Rican men relative to Mexican men, Puerto Rican women had a lower labor force participation rate—31 percent—than did women of Mexican origin, 44 percent.

In March 1976, there were substantially more employed Spanish origin men than employed Spanish origin women; about 2.2 million men of Spanish origin were employed compared to about 1.3 million Spanish origin women. The unemployment rate for men of Spanish origin at 11 percent, however, was not statistically significant from that of Spanish origin women, 13 percent.

Among all employed Spanish origin men, the most prevalent occupation was that of operative, including transportation. But among selected categories of Spanish origin men, occupational differences occurred; for example: a substantially greater proportion of Mexican origin men were employed as farm workers—8 percent— than were Puerto Rican men—3 percent—or men of other Spanish origin combined, 1 percent (tables 6 and 7).

In 1975, median income[1] of men of Spanish origin was $6,800, about double the median income of Spanish origin women, at $3,200. Although only 37 percent of Spanish origin men had income of less than $5,000 in 1975, about

71 percent of women of Spanish origin had income of less than $5,000 (table 8).

The median income in 1975 of all families in the United States was considerably higher, at $13,700, than the median income of families with the head of Spanish origin, at $9,600. Moreover, differences in family income also

Information in this report on persons of Spanish origin was obtained from response to the following question:

What is your origin or descent?

01 German	10 Mexican-American
02 Italian	11 Chicano
03 Irish	12 Mexican
04 French	13 Mexicano
05 Polish	14 Puerto Rican
06 Russian	15 Cuban
07 English	16 Central or South American
08 Scottish	17 Other Spanish
09 Welsh	20 Negro

21 Black
OR
30 Another group not listed

FORM CPS-597
(1-3-74)

U.S. DEPARTMENT OF COMMERCE
SOCIAL AND ECONOMIC STATISTICS ADMIN.
BUREAU OF THE CENSUS
ORIGIN FLASHCARD
CURRENT POPULATION SURVEY

---

existed between types of Spanish origin families. For example, the median income of families with the head of Mexican origin was higher than that for families with the head of Puerto Rican origin, and families of other Spanish origin combined had a substantially higher income than either Mexican or Puerto Rican origin families (table 9).

About 630 thousand families with the head of Spanish origin, one of every four Spanish-headed families, were below the low-income level in 1975. However, there were differences in the proportions of low-income families of Spanish origin by type of Spanish origin: although only one of every six families of Cuban origin were of low-income status in 1975, one of every four families of Mexican origin, and one of every three families of Puerto Rican origin were below the low-income level in that year (table 10).

Persons of Spanish origin were persons who reported themselves as Mexican-American, Chicano, Mexican, Mexicano, Puerto Rican, Cuban, Central or South American, or other Spanish origin. Persons who reported themselves specifically as Mexican-American, Chicano, Mexican, or Mexicano were consolidated into the one category, Mexican.

The numbers in this report are in thousands and were rounded to the nearest thousand without being adjusted to group totals; hence, the sum of the parts may not exactly equal the total shown. Also, because of rounding, the figures may differ slightly from table to table, and individual percentages may not always add to 100 percent.

[1] In processing the data collected in the March 1976 Current Population Survey, the Bureau of the Census utilized a new computer processing system designed to take maximum advantage of the Bureau's expanded computer capabilities. The revised system also incorporates many improvements in the procedures used to process the data. For a detailed discussion of these improvements regarding the processing of income data see the report: U.S. Bureau of the Census, **Current Population Reports**, Series P-60, No. 103, "Money Income and Poverty Status of Families and Persons in the United States: 1975 and 1974 Revisions," (Advance Report) U.S. Government Printing Office, Washington, D.C., 1976.

Table 1. POPULATION OF SPANISH ORIGIN BY TYPE OF SPANISH ORIGIN FOR THE UNITED STATES: MARCH 1976

(Numbers in thousands)

| Type of Spanish origin | Number | Percent | Confidence interval[1] (One standard error) | |
			Number	Percent
Total, Spanish origin................	11,117	100.0	10,811 to 11,423	(X)
Mexican...........................	6,590	59.3	6,352 to 6,828	57.9 to 60.7
Puerto Rican.....................	1,753	15.8	1,629 to 1,877	14.8 to 16.8
Cuban............................	687	6.2	609 to 765	5.5 to 6.9
Central or South American........	752	6.8	670 to 834	6.1 to 7.5
Other Spanish....................	1,335	12.0	1,226 to 1,444	11.1 to 12.9

X Not applicable.

[1]Estimates in this table (as well as in the rest of this report) are based on sample data and hence are subject to sampling error. If a census were conducted, the chances are about 68 out of 100 that the census result would be contained in the one-standard error interval given in this table.

Figure 2. Spanish Origin Population by Age and Type of Spanish Origin, for the United States: March 1976

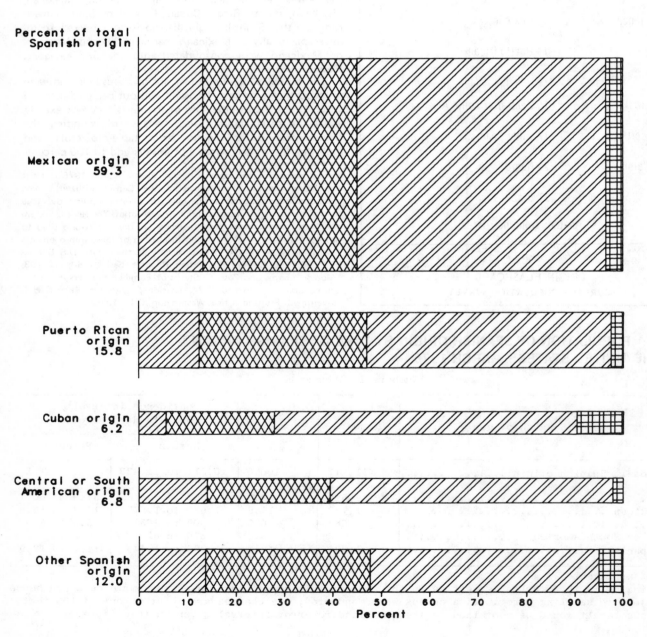

Figure 3. Metropolitan—Nonmetropolitan Residence of Families With Head of Spanish Origin by Type of Spanish Origin of the Head: March 1976

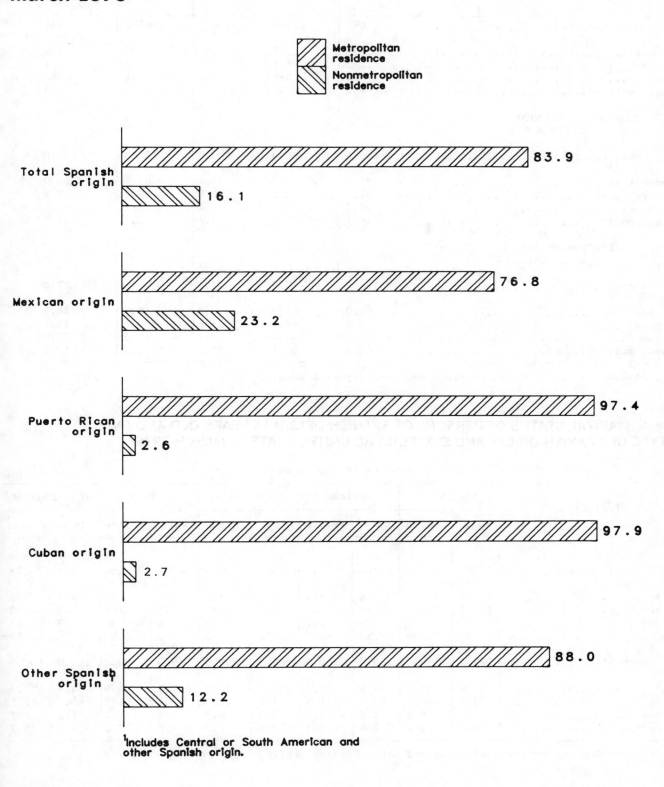

¹Includes Central or South American and other Spanish origin.

Table 2. RESIDENCE OF FAMILIES WITH HEAD OF SPANISH ORIGIN BY TYPE OF SPANISH ORIGIN OF THE HEAD, FOR THE UNITED STATES: MARCH 1976

(Numbers in thousands)

Residence	Total, Spanish origin	Mexican origin	Puerto Rican origin	Cuban origin	Other Spanish origin[1]
Total families...................	2,499	1,442	436	187	434
Metropolitan..........................	2,096	1,107	424	183	382
Central cities.....................	1,292	621	357	92	221
Balance...........................	804	486	67	91	161
Nonmetropolitan......................	403	335	11	5	53
PERCENT BY METROPOLITAN RESIDENCE					
Total families..................	100.0	100.0	100.0	100.0	100.0
Metropolitan..........................	83.9	76.8	97.4	97.9	88.0
Central cities.....................	51.7	43.1	82.0	49.2	50.9
Balance...........................	32.2	33.7	15.4	48.7	37.1
Nonmetropolitan......................	16.1	23.2	2.6	2.7	12.2
PERCENT BY TYPE OF SPANISH ORIGIN					
Total families..................	100.0	57.7	17.4	7.5	17.4
Metropolitan..........................	100.0	52.8	20.2	8.7	18.2
Central cities.....................	100.0	48.1	27.6	7.1	17.1
Balance...........................	100.0	60.4	8.3	11.3	20.0
Nonmetropolitan......................	100.0	83.1	2.7	1.2	13.2

[1] Includes Central or South American and other Spanish origin.

Table 4. MARITAL STATUS OF PERSONS OF SPANISH ORIGIN 14 YEARS OLD AND OVER BY TYPE OF SPANISH ORIGIN AND SEX, FOR THE UNITED STATES: MARCH 1976

(Numbers in thousands)

Marital status	Total		Mexican		Puerto Rican		Cuban		Other Spanish[1]	
	Male	Female	Male	Female	Male	Female	Male	Female	Male	Female
Total persons, 14 years and over.......	3,415	3,777	2,067	2,147	502	599	251	302	596	728
Single......................	1,197	1,006	714	574	198	152	79	81	206	199
Married.....................	2,065	2,293	1,259	1,321	287	376	157	165	362	430
Widowed.....................	55	242	36	131	4	28	6	33	9	49
Divorced....................	99	236	58	121	13	43	10	22	19	49
Percent.............	100.0	100.0	100.0	100.0	100.0	100.0	100.0	100.0	100.0	100.0
Single......................	35.0	26.6	34.5	26.7	39.5	25.3	31.4	26.8	34.6	27.3
Married.....................	60.5	60.7	60.9	61.5	57.1	62.7	62.6	54.7	60.7	59.1
Widowed.....................	1.6	6.4	1.8	6.1	0.8	4.7	2.2	11.1	1.5	6.7
Divorced....................	2.9	6.3	2.8	5.7	2.6	7.3	3.8	7.4	3.2	6.7

[1] Includes Central or South American and other Spanish origin.

Table 3. TOTAL AND SPANISH ORIGIN POPULATION BY AGE AND TYPE OF SPANISH ORIGIN, FOR THE UNITED STATES: MARCH 1976

Age	Total population	Spanish origin					
		Total	Mexican	Puerto Rican	Cuban	Central or South American	Other Spanish
Total.........(thousands)..	211,140	11,117	6,590	1,753	687	752	1,335
Percent..............	100.0	100.0	100.0	100.0	100.0	100.0	100.0
Under 5 years..............	7.4	12.8	13.3	12.5	5.6	14.1	13.7
5 to 9 years...............	8.2	12.5	12.8	13.4	6.0	11.0	14.1
10 to 17 years.............	15.3	19.0	19.0	21.2	16.4	14.4	19.9
18 to 20 years.............	5.7	6.1	6.4	6.0	5.5	3.7	5.8
21 to 24 years.............	7.0	6.8	7.5	6.7	5.5	5.6	5.7
25 to 34 years.............	14.8	14.7	14.9	14.4	8.0	23.1	12.6
35 to 44 years.............	10.8	11.4	10.5	12.3	16.6	15.5	9.4
45 to 54 years.............	11.1	8.1	7.8	6.6	16.9	6.8	7.5
55 to 64 years.............	9.4	4.9	4.3	4.5	10.0	3.7	6.3
65 years and over..........	10.3	3.8	3.5	2.5	9.6	2.1	4.9
18 years and over..........	69.0	55.7	54.9	53.0	72.0	60.6	52.2
21 years and over..........	63.3	49.6	48.4	46.9	66.5	56.9	46.4
Median age........(years)..	28.9	20.9	20.3	19.6	36.8	25.5	19.1

Table 5. PERCENT OF TOTAL AND SPANISH ORIGIN POPULATION 25 YEARS OLD AND OVER BY TYPE OF SPANISH ORIGIN, YEARS OF SCHOOL COMPLETED, AND AGE, FOR THE UNITED STATES: MARCH 1976

Years of school completed and age	Total population	Spanish origin				
		Total	Mexican	Puerto Rican	Cuban	Other Spanish[1]
PERCENT OF PERSONS WHO COMPLETED LESS THAN 5 YEARS OF SCHOOL						
Total, 25 years and over..	3.8	18.7	24.2	18.7	9.5	7.0
25 to 29 years.................	0.8	5.3	6.0	9.4	(B)	1.6
30 to 34 years.................	0.8	8.4	12.0	4.9	(B)	3.2
35 to 44 years.................	2.1	14.8	19.7	16.1	5.2	4.5
45 to 64 years.................	3.8	26.3	34.7	27.4	11.8	9.9
65 years and over..............	10.2	51.1	67.5	(B)	(B)	26.8
PERCENT OF PERSONS WHO COMPLETED 4 YEARS OF HIGH SCHOOL OR MORE						
Total, 25 years and over..	64.1	39.2	32.5	29.8	51.5	60.3
25 to 29 years.................	84.7	58.1	53.7	48.7	(B)	73.4
30 to 34 years.................	80.3	50.2	43.0	38.3	(B)	76.4
35 to 44 years.................	72.5	40.3	32.2	27.5	60.1	65.4
45 to 64 years.................	59.8	28.3	20.5	17.9	45.3	47.7
65 years and over..............	36.8	13.8	4.4	(B)	(B)	28.0

- Represents zero or rounds to zero.   B Base less than 75,000
[1]Includes Central or South American and other Spanish origin.

Table 6. BROAD OCCUPATION GROUP OF EMPLOYED PERSONS OF SPANISH ORIGIN 16 YEARS OLD AND OVER BY SEX AND TYPE OF SPANISH ORIGIN: MARCH 1976

Broad occupation group	Total, Spanish origin	Mexican	Puerto Rican	Cuban	Other Spanish origin[1]
MALE					
Total, employed persons...(thousands)..	2,160	1,358	259	160	384
Percent.........................	100.0	100.0	100.0	100.0	100.0
White-collar workers...................	23.8	18.2	22.1	34.2	40.4
Blue-collar workers....................	57.4	62.5	51.2	47.2	47.7
Service workers........................	13.1	10.9	24.0	18.6	11.5
Farm workers...........................	5.7	8.4	2.7	-	0.8
FEMALE					
Total, employed persons...(thousands)..	1,325	753	148	122	303
Percent.........................	100.0	100.0	100.0	100.0	100.0
White-collar workers...................	46.4	44.0	42.9	45.8	54.5
Blue-collar workers....................	29.9	27.1	38.9	45.9	26.4
Service workers........................	22.1	26.3	18.2	8.3	19.1
Farm workers...........................	1.5	2.6	-	-	0.3

- Represents zero or rounds to zero.
[1]Includes Central or South American and other Spanish origin.

Table 9. INCOME IN 1975 OF ALL FAMILIES AND OF FAMILIES WITH HEAD OF SPANISH ORIGIN, FOR THE UNITED STATES: MARCH 1976

Family income	Total families	Families with head of Spanish origin				
		Total	Mexican origin	Puerto Rican origin	Cuban origin	Other Spanish origin[1]
Total families........(thousands).	56,245	2,499	1,442	436	187	434
Percent.....................	100.0	100.0	100.0	100.0	100.0	100.0
Less than $4,000...................	8.0	15.5	15.8	20.1	14.0	10.4
$4,000 to $6,999.....................	12.4	19.8	19.2	27.8	13.6	17.1
$7,000 to $9,999.....................	12.8	17.0	17.6	18.1	11.4	16.6
$10,000 to $14,999....................	22.3	22.6	22.2	20.4	26.5	24.9
$15,000 to $19,999....................	18.7	14.2	15.1	7.2	17.6	16.6
$20,000 to $24,999....................	11.6	5.8	5.4	3.6	9.7	7.8
$25,000 or more.....................	14.1	4.9	4.5	2.8	7.1	7.6
Median income....................	$13,719	$9,551	$9,546	$7,291	$11,772	$11,067

[1]Includes Central or South American and other Spanish origin.

Table 7. EMPLOYMENT STATUS AND MAJOR OCCUPATION GROUP OF THE SPANISH ORIGIN POPULATION 16 YEARS OLD AND OVER BY SEX AND TYPE OF SPANISH ORIGIN, FOR THE UNITED STATES: MARCH 1976

Employment status and occupation	Male				Female			
	Total, Spanish origin	Mexican origin	Puerto Rican origin	Other Spanish origin[1]	Total, Spanish origin	Mexican origin	Puerto Rican origin	Other Spanish origin[1]
Persons, 16 years old and over.................(thousands)..	3,150	1,912	453	786	3,530	1,995	561	974
In civilian labor force.....(thousands)..	2,420	1,517	301	602	1,516	876	171	468
Percent in labor force................	76.8	79.4	66.5	76.6	42.9	43.9	30.5	48.0
Percent unemployed....................	10.7	10.5	14.3	9.5	12.5	14.0	14.0	9.4
Employed..................(thousands)..	2,160	1,358	259	544	1,325	753	148	425
Percent................................	100.0	100.0	100.0	100.0	100.0	100.0	100.0	100.0
Professional, technical, and kindred workers....................................	7.7	5.5	6.1	13.6	7.8	6.0	8.1	10.8
Managers and administrators, except farm.	6.7	5.6	5.9	9.9	3.1	3.2	0.5	3.8
Sales workers............................	3.0	2.1	3.8	4.8	4.8	4.8	4.5	4.7
Clerical and kindred workers.............	6.4	4.9	6.3	10.3	30.8	30.1	29.7	32.2
Craft and kindred workers................	19.4	19.1	15.0	22.1	2.7	3.0	2.7	1.9
Operatives, including transport..........	26.5	29.0	27.6	19.5	25.8	22.3	34.5	28.9
Laborers, excluding farm.................	11.6	14.3	8.5	6.1	1.5	1.7	1.8	0.9
Farmers and farm managers................	0.4	0.6	-	0.2	0.1	0.1	-	-
Farm laborers and supervisors............	5.3	7.8	2.7	0.4	1.5	2.5	-	0.2
Service workers, except private household	13.1	10.9	24.0	13.6	17.3	20.8	16.0	11.5
Private household workers................	-	-	-	-	4.8	5.5	2.1	4.7

- Represents zero or rounds to zero.
[1] Includes Cuban, Central or South American, and other Spanish origin.

Table 8. INCOME IN 1975 OF PERSONS OF SPANISH ORIGIN 14 YEARS OLD AND OVER BY TYPE OF SPANISH ORIGIN AND SEX, FOR THE UNITED STATES: MARCH 1976

Type of Spanish origin and sex	Median income	Percent with income below $5,000	Percent with income of $25,000 or more
MALE			
Total, Spanish origin.............	$6,777	36.6	1.5
Mexican.................................	6,450	39.0	1.2
Puerto Rican............................	6,687	34.9	0.8
Other Spanish origin[1].................	7,508	31.5	3.0
FEMALE			
Total, Spanish origin.............	3,202	70.6	-
Mexican.................................	2,750	75.2	0.1
Puerto Rican............................	3,837	68.6	-
Other Spanish origin[1].................	3,736	63.1	-

- Represents zero or rounds to zero.
[1] Includes Cuban, Central or South American, and other Spanish origin.

Table 10. LOW-INCOME STATUS IN 1975 OF ALL FAMILIES AND FAMILIES WITH HEAD OF SPANISH ORIGIN BY TYPE OF SPANISH ORIGIN, FOR THE UNITED STATES: MARCH 1976

(Numbers in thousands)

Origin	Total population	Below the low-income level	
		Number	Percent
Total families......................	56,245	5,450	9.7
Families with head of Spanish origin.......	2,499	627	25.1
Mexican....................................	1,442	381	26.4
Puerto Rican..............................	436	146	33.5
Cuban.....................................	187	32	17.1
Central or South American.................	181	33	18.2
Other Spanish.............................	253	35	13.8
Families with head not of Spanish origin...	53,745	4,823	9.0

U.S. Bureau of the Census, Current Population Reports, Series P-20, No. 302, "Persons of Spanish Origin in the United States: March 1976." U.S. Government Printing Office, Washington, D.C. 1976.

PERSONS OF SPANISH ORIGIN IN THE UNITED STATES: MARCH 1975

YEARS OF SCHOOL COMPLETED BY PERSONS OF SPANISH ORIGIN 14 YEARS OLD AND OVER BY AGE, SEX, AND TYPE OF SPANISH ORIGIN, FOR THE UNITED STATES: MARCH 1975

Age, sex, and type of Spanish origin	Total (thousands)	Percent	Years of school completed							Median school years completed
			Elementary school			High school		College		
			0 to 4 years	5 to 7 years	8 years	1 to 3 years	4 years	1 to 3 years	4 years or more	
MALE										
Total Spanish origin, 14 years and over......................	3,520	100.0	12.6	16.8	11.7	23.2	20.5	9.4	5.8	10.1
14 to 19 years.........................	797	100.0	1.4	19.4	20.1	48.4	9.2	1.5	-	9.5
20 to 24 years.........................	465	100.0	4.7	11.2	5.6	18.5	36.8	19.8	3.4	12.2
25 years and over......................	2,258	100.0	18.2	17.1	10.0	15.3	21.1	10.0	8.3	9.9
25 to 34 years......................	740	100.0	9.3	13.6	9.3	17.4	25.9	15.5	8.8	12.0
25 to 29 years....................	440	100.0	9.0	15.9	7.3	16.8	25.9	15.0	10.0	12.0
30 to 34 years....................	300	100.0	9.9	10.3	12.3	18.3	26.0	16.3	7.0	11.8
35 to 44 years......................	629	100.0	15.7	18.9	8.6	15.3	21.5	9.5	10.5	10.3
45 to 64 years......................	700	100.0	23.3	18.4	11.1	14.9	19.3	6.4	6.6	8.7
65 years and over....................	189	100.0	41.5	19.0	13.2	9.0	7.9	3.2	5.8	6.3
Mexican origin, 14 years and over.........................	2,115	100.0	15.9	19.4	11.2	23.0	18.9	7.7	3.8	9.4
14 to 19 years.........................	481	100.0	2.1	21.4	20.0	47.4	8.5	0.6	-	9.4
20 to 24 years.........................	318	100.0	5.0	14.5	5.7	18.9	37.1	16.7	2.2	12.1
25 years and over......................	1,317	100.0	23.7	19.9	9.2	15.2	18.2	8.1	5.6	8.6
25 to 34 years......................	463	100.0	11.9	17.1	8.9	17.3	23.1	13.8	8.0	11.1
25 to 29 years....................	297	100.0	11.2	19.9	6.4	16.8	22.6	13.1	10.1	11.2
30 to 34 years....................	166	100.0	13.6	12.0	13.3	18.1	24.1	15.1	3.6	10.8
35 to 44 years......................	359	100.0	21.5	21.2	9.2	13.9	19.8	7.5	7.0	8.7
45 to 64 years......................	388	100.0	30.2	22.4	9.3	15.5	15.5	4.4	3.1	7.6
65 years and over....................	107	100.0	58.8	18.7	10.3	9.3	2.8	-	0.9	3.4
Puerto Rican origin, 14 years and over......................	463	100.0	11.2	15.3	18.1	28.9	16.6	7.1	2.8	9.5
14 to 19 years.........................	122	100.0	0.8	18.9	24.6	47.5	7.4	1.6	-	9.3
20 to 24 years.........................	53	(B)	(B)	(B)	(B)	(B)	(B)	(B)	(B)	(B)
25 years and over......................	288	100.0	16.7	16.3	16.3	21.5	17.7	7.6	4.2	9.1
25 to 34 years......................	105	100.0	8.6	12.4	16.2	28.6	21.0	8.6	3.8	10.3
25 to 29 years....................	55	(B)	(B)	(B)	(B)	(B)	(B)	(B)	(B)	(B)
30 to 34 years....................	50	(B)	(B)	(B)	(B)	(B)	(B)	(B)	(B)	(B)
35 to 44 years......................	97	100.0	13.4	19.6	11.3	24.7	17.5	7.2	6.2	9.7
45 to 64 years......................	77	100.0	31.2	16.9	24.7	9.1	11.7	6.5	1.3	8.0
65 years and over....................	9	(B)	(B)	(B)	(B)	(B)	(B)	(B)	(B)	(B)
Other Spanish origin, 14 years and over[1]......................	942	100.0	5.6	11.8	10.0	20.8	26.0	14.1	11.7	12.0
14 to 19 years.........................	194	100.0	0.5	14.9	17.5	51.5	11.9	3.6	-	9.9
20 to 24 years.........................	95	100.0	3.2	5.3	2.1	12.6	37.9	30.5	8.4	12.7
25 years and over......................	653	100.0	7.5	11.8	8.9	13.0	28.5	14.9	15.6	12.3
25 to 34 years......................	172	100.0	2.9	5.2	6.4	10.5	36.6	24.4	14.0	12.6
25 to 29 years....................	87	100.0	-	5.7	3.4	12.6	42.5	24.1	11.5	12.6
30 to 34 years....................	85	100.0	5.9	4.7	9.4	8.2	30.6	24.7	15.3	12.7
35 to 44 years......................	173	100.0	5.2	13.9	5.8	12.7	27.2	15.0	20.2	12.4
45 to 64 years......................	235	100.0	9.4	11.9	10.2	15.7	28.1	9.8	14.5	12.0
65 years and over....................	73	(B)	(B)	(B)	(B)	(B)	(B)	(B)	(B)	(B)
FEMALE										
Total Spanish origin, 14 years and over......................	3,744	100.0	13.2	16.8	11.8	22.6	24.5	7.7	3.4	10.0
14 to 19 years.........................	714	100.0	1.1	15.3	20.6	47.9	13.3	1.8	-	9.8
20 to 24 years.........................	526	100.0	3.2	9.7	5.3	23.2	38.6	17.3	2.9	12.2
25 years and over......................	2,504	100.0	18.8	18.7	10.6	15.3	24.7	7.4	4.6	9.3
25 to 34 years......................	824	100.0	7.5	17.2	8.7	18.9	32.4	9.8	5.5	11.6
25 to 29 years....................	438	100.0	6.3	15.3	7.3	18.7	35.6	9.4	7.3	12.0
30 to 34 years....................	386	100.0	8.9	19.2	10.1	19.2	28.8	10.4	3.4	10.8
35 to 44 years......................	671	100.0	16.0	18.2	9.2	16.8	25.8	8.3	5.7	10.1
45 to 64 years......................	791	100.0	24.4	20.0	13.7	12.8	20.0	5.4	3.7	8.4
65 years and over....................	218	100.0	49.4	21.1	11.0	5.5	9.2	2.8	0.9	5.0
Mexican origin, 14 years and over.........................	2,133	100.0	17.0	18.4	11.3	22.4	22.6	6.7	1.7	9.4
14 to 19 years.........................	447	100.0	1.6	15.9	20.8	44.7	15.4	1.6	-	9.7
20 to 24 years.........................	337	100.0	3.9	12.5	5.6	24.6	35.3	15.7	2.1	12.0
25 years and over......................	1,350	100.0	25.4	20.7	9.7	14.4	21.6	6.1	2.2	8.4
25 to 34 years......................	463	100.0	9.3	19.7	9.9	16.8	30.9	9.7	3.9	10.9
25 to 29 years....................	257	100.0	8.3	19.5	8.9	17.1	32.7	8.9	4.7	11.3
30 to 34 years....................	206	100.0	10.4	19.9	11.2	17.0	28.6	10.2	2.4	10.5
35 to 44 years......................	360	100.0	22.7	21.9	8.9	15.8	22.5	6.4	1.7	8.5
45 to 64 years......................	410	100.0	33.7	21.2	11.2	13.2	15.6	3.7	1.2	7.2
65 years and over....................	117	100.0	68.4	17.9	6.0	4.3	4.3	-	-	2.6

See footnotes at end of table.

YEARS OF SCHOOL COMPLETED BY PERSONS OF SPANISH ORIGIN 14 YEARS OLD AND OVER BY AGE, SEX, AND TYPE OF SPANISH ORIGIN, FOR THE UNITED STATES: MARCH 1975—Continued

Age, sex, and type of Spanish origin	Total (thousands)	Percent	Years of school completed							Median school years completed
			Elementary school			High school		College		
			0 to 4 years	5 to 7 years	8 years	1 to 3 years	4 years	1 to 3 years	4 years or more	
FEMALE--Continued										
Puerto Rican origin, 14 years and over...	590	100.0	12.9	18.1	14.4	26.8	20.0	4.7	3.1	9.5
14 to 19 years...	115	100.0	-	19.1	19.1	48.7	10.4	2.6	-	9.7
20 to 24 years...	73	(B)	(B)	(B)	(B)	(B)	(B)	(B)	(B)	(B)
25 years and over...	402	100.0	17.9	19.7	13.9	20.4	20.1	4.0	4.0	8.8
25 to 34 years...	161	100.0	9.9	21.1	9.9	26.7	22.4	5.6	4.3	10.0
25 to 29 years...	82	100.0	6.1	17.1	7.3	30.5	24.4	8.5	6.1	10.9
30 to 34 years...	80	100.0	13.8	25.0	12.5	22.5	21.3	2.5	2.5	8.9
35 to 44 years...	117	100.0	13.7	19.7	11.1	21.4	26.5	1.7	6.0	9.7
45 to 64 years...	108	100.0	29.6	16.7	24.1	11.1	12.0	4.6	1.9	8.1
65 years and over...	16	(B)	(B)	(B)	(B)	(B)	(B)	(B)	(B)	(B)
Other Spanish origin, 14 years and over[1]...	1,021	100.0	5.6	12.7	11.1	20.6	31.0	11.8	7.3	12.0
14 to 19 years...	153	100.0	1.3	10.5	20.9	56.2	8.5	2.6	-	9.9
20 to 24 years...	116	100.0	-	2.6	1.7	15.5	50.9	24.1	5.2	12.5
25 years and over...	753	100.0	7.4	14.7	10.4	14.1	32.5	11.7	9.2	12.1
25 to 34 years...	200	100.0	2.0	8.5	5.0	17.0	44.0	13.5	10.5	12.4
25 to 29 years...	99	100.0	2.0	3.0	3.0	13.1	53.5	10.1	15.2	12.5
30 to 34 years...	100	100.0	2.0	13.0	6.0	21.0	35.0	17.0	5.0	12.2
35 to 44 years...	195	100.0	4.6	10.3	8.7	15.9	31.8	15.9	12.8	12.3
45 to 64 years...	273	100.0	8.4	19.8	12.8	12.8	29.7	8.8	8.1	11.1
65 years and over...	85	100.0	22.4	24.7	20.0	7.1	17.6	5.9	2.4	8.1

- Represents zero or rounds to zero.
B Base less than 75,000.
[1]Includes Cuban, Central or South American, and other Spanish origin.

INCOME IN 1974 OF FAMILIES WITH HEAD OF SPANISH AND MEXICAN ORIGIN 25 YEARS OLD AND OVER BY YEARS OF SCHOOL COMPLETED OF THE HEAD, FOR THE UNITED STATES: MARCH 1975

Income and type of Spanish origin	Total	Years of school completed of the head									Median school years completed
		Elementary school			High school			College			
		Total	Less than 8 years	8 years	Total	1 to 3 years	4 years	Total	1 to 3 years	4 years or more	
SPANISH ORIGIN											
Families with head 25 years old and over...(thousands)..	2,213	1,023	796	228	822	366	456	368	203	164	9.7
Percent...	100.0	100.0	100.0	100.0	100.0	100.0	100.0	100.0	100.0	100.0	(X)
Under $2,000...	3.1	4.2	3.6	6.4	2.3	2.6	2.1	1.7	1.2	2.4	(B)
$2,000 to $2,999...	4.1	6.8	7.1	5.8	2.3	3.3	1.4	0.8	0.8	1.0	6.5
$3,000 to $3,999...	6.5	9.2	9.8	7.1	5.2	7.1	3.7	1.6	2.0	1.0	7.3
$4,000 to $4,999...	6.6	8.6	9.7	4.6	6.1	8.2	4.4	2.0	2.4	1.4	7.5
$5,000 to $6,999...	12.2	17.0	17.2	16.4	10.2	12.8	8.0	3.3	5.2	1.0	7.9
$7,000 to $7,999...	5.9	6.7	6.8	6.3	6.0	6.7	5.4	3.4	5.4	1.0	8.8
$8,000 to $9,999...	12.2	13.4	12.8	15.3	12.0	12.4	11.8	9.4	10.0	8.6	9.0
$10,000 to $14,999...	24.6	21.3	21.2	21.8	27.1	24.0	29.5	27.7	32.7	21.6	10.8
$15,000 to $24,999...	19.7	10.6	9.7	14.0	24.3	19.6	28.1	34.4	31.8	37.6	12.3
$25,000 and over...	5.3	2.1	2.1	2.4	4.6	3.3	5.7	15.6	8.5	24.4	13.0
Median income...	$9,920	$7,624	$7,373	$8,427	$11,023	$9,492	$12,120	$15,020	$13,691	$18,211	(X)
MEXICAN ORIGIN											
Families with head 25 years old and over...(thousands)..	1,239	660	542	118	425	191	234	154	95	59	8.7
Percent...	100.0	100.0	100.0	100.0	100.0	100.0	100.0	100.0	100.0	(B)	(X)
Under $2,000...	3.2	4.2	3.9	5.6	2.2	1.7	2.7	1.6	1.9	(B)	(B)
$2,000 to $2,999...	4.0	6.3	6.6	5.1	1.5	2.5	0.6	1.0	0.8	(B)	(B)
$3,000 to $3,999...	6.3	8.7	9.0	7.5	4.5	5.6	3.7	0.6	-	(B)	6.3
$4,000 to $4,999...	5.6	7.5	8.3	4.1	4.6	6.3	3.2	0.6	0.9	(B)	(B)
$5,000 to $6,999...	12.3	16.3	16.3	16.6	10.8	10.8	7.4	4.2	6.9	(B)	6.9
$7,000 to $7,999...	5.5	6.3	6.5	5.4	4.9	6.2	3.9	3.8	6.1	(B)	(B)
$8,000 to $9,999...	13.2	14.9	14.2	18.3	11.8	13.0	10.8	9.1	9.0	(B)	8.2
$10,000 to $14,999...	27.4	22.4	22.8	19.9	31.7	29.7	33.5	37.1	42.5	(B)	10.2
$15,000 to $24,999...	18.3	11.0	10.4	14.0	25.1	20.9	28.5	30.6	27.0	(B)	12.0
$25,000 and over...	4.3	2.3	2.0	3.3	4.6	3.4	5.7	11.4	4.9	(B)	(B)
Median income...	$9,982	$8,071	$7,909	$8,599	$11,623	$10,565	$12,533	$13,999	$13,069	(B)	(X)

- Represents zero or rounds to zero.
B Base less than 75,000.
X Not applicable.

INCOME IN 1974 OF PERSONS OF SPANISH AND MEXICAN ORIGIN 25 YEARS OLD AND OVER BY SEX AND NUMBER OF SCHOOL YEARS COMPLETED, FOR THE UNITED STATES: MARCH 1975

Income, type of Spanish origin, and sex	Total	Years of school completed									Median school years completed
		Elementary school			High school			College			
		Total	Less than 8 years	8 years	Total	1 to 3 years	4 years	Total	1 to 3 years	4 years or more	
SPANISH ORIGIN											
Male											
Number of persons.......(thousands)..	2,258	1,021	795	226	823	346	477	414	226	188	9.9
Number of persons with income................(thousands)..	2,236	1,010	785	225	814	341	473	412	225	187	9.9
Percent.....................	100.0	100.0	100.0	100.0	100.0	100.0	100.0	100.0	100.0	100.0	(X)
$1 to $999 or loss...................	2.3	3.0	2.7	3.8	1.5	1.0	1.9	2.2	2.7	1.8	(B)
$1,000 to $1,999....................	5.4	8.4	8.8	7.0	3.0	5.1	1.5	2.3	3.8	0.6	6.9
$2,000 to $2,999....................	6.2	9.9	10.2	8.8	3.4	4.0	3.1	2.3	1.2	3.5	6.9
$3,000 to $3,999....................	7.1	9.2	9.3	8.7	5.8	6.8	5.0	4.5	3.9	5.1	8.3
$4,000 to $4,999....................	6.5	9.7	10.8	5.7	4.5	5.9	3.4	2.6	3.4	1.7	7.0
$5,000 to $6,999....................	15.8	20.7	21.9	16.5	13.8	15.5	12.6	8.0	7.8	8.2	8.1
$7,000 to $7,999....................	8.3	8.4	8.4	8.1	9.2	10.4	8.4	6.1	7.2	4.7	9.7
$8,000 to $9,999....................	14.0	13.2	12.4	16.3	16.2	16.8	15.7	11.8	16.2	6.5	10.2
$10,000 to $14,999..................	23.5	14.3	12.8	19.5	31.2	27.3	34.0	30.7	34.3	26.4	12.2
$15,000 to $24,999..................	9.2	2.7	1.9	5.4	10.2	6.2	13.1	23.3	17.4	30.4	12.9
$25,000 and over....................	1.9	0.7	0.8	-	1.1	0.9	1.3	6.2	2.1	11.2	(B)
Median income of persons with income.	$7,826	$5,869	$5,679	$6,906	$9,073	$8,143	$9,788	$11,665	$10,549	$13,399	(X)
Female											
Number of persons.......(thousands)..	2,504	1,205	939	265	1,000	382	618	300	185	114	9.4
Number of persons with income................(thousands)..	1,666	781	619	162	661	252	409	224	134	90	9.6
Percent.....................	100.0	100.0	100.0	100.0	100.0	100.0	100.0	100.0	100.0	100.0	(X)
$1 to $999 or loss...................	12.3	14.9	16.0	10.7	10.8	12.0	9.9	8.3	10.5	5.2	8.2
$1,000 to $1,999....................	16.4	23.3	23.7	21.6	10.6	12.9	9.1	9.8	8.1	12.2	7.5
$2,000 to $2,999....................	14.4	18.6	18.5	18.9	10.5	12.2	9.5	10.9	10.4	11.4	8.2
$3,000 to $3,999....................	12.3	13.4	13.2	14.0	12.6	14.6	11.3	7.9	9.0	6.4	8.9
$4,000 to $4,999....................	12.1	11.4	10.9	13.5	14.8	17.7	13.0	6.6	6.8	6.3	9.8
$5,000 to $6,999....................	16.2	13.6	13.2	15.3	18.5	16.3	19.8	18.2	24.5	9.0	11.1
$7,000 to $7,999....................	5.0	2.0	1.9	2.4	7.7	4.5	9.7	7.6	8.5	6.4	12.4
$8,000 to $9,999....................	6.2	1.8	1.7	2.0	8.2	5.6	9.8	16.1	14.0	19.2	12.6
$10,000 to $14,999..................	4.1	0.7	0.6	1.1	5.8	3.2	7.4	10.7	6.0	17.7	(B)
$15,000 to $24,999..................	0.8	0.3	0.3	0.6	0.5	0.7	0.4	3.5	1.7	6.3	(B)
$25,000 and over....................	0.1	-	-	-	0.1	0.3	-	0.4	0.6	-	(B)
Median income of persons with income.	$3,559	$2,646	$2,556	$2,945	$4,378	$3,881	$4,774	$5,818	$5,534	$6,893	(X)
MEXICAN ORIGIN											
Male											
Number of persons.......(thousands)..	1,317	695	574	121	440	200	240	181	107	74	8.7
Number of persons with income................(thousands)..	1,305	589	569	120	436	197	239	181	106	74	8.7
Percent.....................	100.0	100.0	100.0	100.0	100.0	100.0	100.0	100.0	100.0	(B)	(X)
$1 to $999 or loss...................	2.5	3.1	3.2	2.5	1.7	1.7	1.7	2.4	2.4	(B)	(B)
$1,000 to $1,999....................	5.4	8.5	9.1	6.1	1.7	2.9	0.8	2.8	4.6	(B)	(B)
$2,000 to $2,999....................	6.7	9.9	9.8	10.5	2.9	4.8	1.3	3.0	2.6	(B)	6.3
$3,000 to $3,999....................	7.4	9.7	9.3	11.2	5.2	1.7	5.5	4.0	4.3	(B)	7.3
$4,000 to $4,999....................	7.5	10.2	11.0	6.3	5.4	6.7	4.3	2.5	2.6	(B)	6.5
$5,000 to $6,999....................	16.8	20.6	22.0	14.0	13.9	16.4	12.0	9.4	9.6	(B)	7.0
$7,000 to $7,999....................	7.1	7.3	7.5	6.3	7.5	7.2	7.8	5.4	5.4	(B)	8.5
$8,000 to $9,999....................	13.6	13.2	12.1	18.0	15.4	17.7	13.6	11.2	14.6	(B)	8.9
$10,000 to $14,999..................	23.7	14.5	13.5	19.2	33.8	29.7	37.2	34.2	38.1	(B)	11.8
$15,000 to $24,999..................	8.2	2.6	1.9	6.0	11.8	7.7	15.2	20.9	15.7	(B)	12.6
$25,000 and over....................	1.1	0.5	0.6	-	0.6	0.5	0.8	4.3	-	(B)	(B)
Median income of persons with income.	$7,520	$5,783	$5,659	$6,907	$9,513	$8,630	$10,424	$11,375	$10,494	(B)	(X)
Female											
Number of persons.......(thousands)..	1,350	752	621	131	487	195	292	111	82	29	8.4
Number of persons with income................(thousands)..	854	463	389	74	309	112	196	83	58	25	8.5
Percent.....................	100.0	100.0	100.0	(B)	100.0	100.0	100.0	100.0	(B)	(B)	(X)
$1 to $999 or loss...................	15.5	19.1	20.6	(B)	11.0	12.8	9.9	12.3	(B)	(B)	6.6
$1,000 to $1,999....................	17.6	23.2	23.9	(B)	10.9	13.7	9.2	11.4	(B)	(B)	6.5
$2,000 to $2,999....................	15.1	18.8	18.9	(B)	11.8	11.6	12.0	6.1	(B)	(B)	7.1
$3,000 to $3,999....................	13.0	13.4	12.7	(B)	13.5	14.5	13.0	9.1	(B)	(B)	8.5
$4,000 to $4,999....................	10.2	9.6	8.6	(B)	12.8	12.8	12.8	4.0	(B)	(B)	8.9
$5,000 to $6,999....................	15.2	11.2	10.6	(B)	18.3	18.1	18.3	25.9	(B)	(B)	11.0
$7,000 to $7,999....................	4.7	2.2	2.2	(B)	8.2	5.0	10.0	5.0	(B)	(B)	(B)
$8,000 to $9,999....................	5.5	1.7	1.6	(B)	7.9	6.1	8.9	18.4	(B)	(B)	(B)
$10,000 to $14,999..................	2.7	0.3	0.4	(B)	5.4	4.5	5.9	5.9	(B)	(B)	(B)
$15,000 to $24,999..................	0.5	0.3	0.4	(B)	0.3	0.7	-	1.9	(B)	(B)	(B)
$25,000 and over....................	-	-	-	(B)	-	-	-	-	(B)	(B)	(B)
Median income of persons with income.	$3,135	$2,437	$2,283	(B)	$4,212	$3,808	$4,456	$5,655	(B)	(B)	(X)

- Represents zero or rounds to zero.
B Base less than 75,000.
X Not applicable.

EMPLOYED MALES OF SPANISH AND MEXICAN ORIGIN 25 TO 64 YEARS OLD BY INCOME IN 1974, BROAD OCCUPATION GROUP, AND NUMBER OF SCHOOL YEARS COMPLETED, FOR THE UNITED STATES: MARCH 1975

| Occupation, income, and type of Spanish origin | Total population (thousands) | Percent distribution by years of school completed | | | | | | | | Median school years completed |
| | | Total | Elementary school | | | High school | | College | | |
			0 to 4 years	5 to 7 years	8 years	1 to 3 years	4 years	1 to 3 years	4 years or more	
SPANISH ORIGIN										
Total employed.............	1,684	100.0	13.8	17.0	8.8	15.0	23.8	11.4	10.1	11.1
Under $3,000....................	114	100.0	28.7	25.4	11.3	8.6	13.1	7.0	5.9	7.5
$3,000 to $5,999................	302	100.0	26.8	23.9	10.2	12.3	16.9	5.5	4.4	7.9
$6,000 to $9,999................	570	100.0	14.7	20.7	9.4	18.3	22.8	9.3	4.8	9.8
$10,000 to $14,999.............	466	100.0	6.6	11.3	8.7	17.4	30.5	15.4	10.1	12.2
$15,000 and over...............	232	100.0	1.8	6.5	4.8	8.9	26.8	18.2	33.0	13.2
White-collar workers.......	478	100.0	1.7	6.8	3.6	9.0	25.7	21.4	31.9	13.5
Under $6,000....................	66	(B)	(B)	(B)	(B)	(B)	(B)	(B)	(B)	(B)
$6,000 and over.................	413	100.0	1.2	5.8	4.1	8.2	25.7	22.0	32.9	13.7
Blue-collar workers........	920	100.0	15.3	21.2	10.7	18.4	25.0	7.8	1.6	9.4
Under $6,000....................	226	100.0	28.3	26.5	11.1	13.7	15.5	4.0	0.9	7.4
$6,000 and over.................	696	100.0	11.1	19.5	10.5	19.8	28.0	9.1	2.0	10.3
Service workers............	197	100.0	18.2	16.7	13.6	18.7	21.7	9.0	2.0	9.2
Under $6,000....................	68	(B)	(B)	(B)	(B)	(B)	(B)	(B)	(B)	(B)
$6,000 and over.................	130	100.0	14.6	13.1	11.5	23.8	23.1	10.0	3.8	10.4
Farm workers...............	88	100.0	53.8	29.5	7.4	4.5	4.8	-	-	4.7
Under $6,000....................	58	(B)	(B)	(B)	(B)	(B)	(B)	(B)	(B)	(B)
$6,000 and over.................	29	(B)	(B)	(B)	(B)	(B)	(B)	(B)	(B)	(B)
MEXICAN ORIGIN										
Total employed.............	990	100.0	19.5	20.4	8.6	14.9	20.0	9.3	7.2	9.3
Under $3,000....................	80	100.0	37.8	30.9	10.1	6.2	3.8	6.8	4.5	6.2
$3,000 to $5,999................	199	100.0	35.4	23.1	10.4	11.2	12.4	4.1	3.4	6.9
$6,000 to $9,999................	328	100.0	19.6	25.5	8.9	16.8	17.9	7.3	3.9	8.5
$10,000 to $14,999.............	271	100.0	9.6	14.1	7.4	18.8	28.1	14.3	7.6	12.0
$15,000 and over...............	113	100.0	2.2	8.3	6.4	12.6	31.7	14.1	24.8	12.6
White-collar workers.......	235	100.0	2.3	10.0	3.7	11.7	24.4	19.8	28.1	12.9
Under $6,000....................	36	(B)	(B)	(B)	(B)	(B)	(B)	(B)	(B)	(B)
$6,000 and over.................	199	100.0	2.5	9.5	4.0	11.1	24.1	20.6	28.1	12.9
Blue-collar workers........	587	100.0	20.2	24.0	10.6	17.2	21.5	6.0	0.5	8.6
Under $6,000....................	151	100.0	35.8	29.1	11.9	11.3	9.9	4.0	-	6.5
$6,000 and over.................	436	100.0	14.9	22.2	10.1	19.5	25.5	6.9	0.9	9.4
Service workers............	88	100.0	26.8	15.3	9.1	19.1	15.3	11.6	2.7	8.9
Under $6,000....................	38	(B)	(B)	(B)	(B)	(B)	(B)	(B)	(B)	(B)
$6,000 and over.................	50	(B)	(B)	(B)	(B)	(B)	(B)	(B)	(B)	(B)
Farm workers...............	80	100.0	57.6	30.0	8.2	3.1	1.1	-	-	4.3
Under $6,000....................	54	(B)	(B)	(B)	(B)	(B)	(B)	(B)	(B)	(B)
$6,000 and over.................	26	(B)	(B)	(B)	(B)	(B)	(B)	(B)	(B)	(B)

- Represents zero or rounds to zero.
B Base less than 75,000.

U.S. Bureau of the Census, Current Population Reports, P-20, No. 290, "Persons of Spanish Origin in the United States: March 1975." U.S. Government Printing Office, Washington, D.C. 1976.

FOR THE CHILDREN: IMPROVING EDUCATION FOR MEXICAN AMERICANS

Parent. Teacher. Child. Each gives and receives from the educational experience. A parent watches a child grow, question, and learn. A teacher with skill imparts knowledge to her class. A youngster in the classroom accepts and responds to words, books, instructions, and attitudes. It is a universal exchange, unless obstacles are placed in the way, unless the two-way street of learning—the giving and the taking—is blocked by school-made barriers that damage the student's spirit and deaden the mind.

For many of the 1.6 million Mexican American students in the Southwest, such barriers are painfully real and seemingly unavoidable. And too often, too many of these young people give up and drop out.

The statistics are shocking. Each year tens of thousands of Mexican Americans end their schooling prematurely. Four out of every 10 Chicano students do not graduate from high school. In comparison, 9 out of every 10 Anglo students do finish high school. These are people, not numbers—people who are branded as failures early in life at something that society values highly.

But are the children the failures? Or has the educational system failed them?

Mexican American parents and many educational experts believe it is the schools that have set up the pattern leading to failure, leaving only the luckiest and most adaptable to survive. They are alarmed that generally Mexican American children do less well than their Anglo classmates in school and score lower on reading and other achievement tests.

The U.S. Commission on Civil Rights, after a 5-year study of schools in the Southwest, found "a systematic failure of the educational process, which not only ignores the educational needs of Chicano students, but suppresses their culture and stifles their hopes and ambitions."

The Commission's Mexican American Education Study was the most comprehensive of its type ever conducted. It documented with facts and figures what Chicanos long have known—that Mexican Americans are being denied equal educational opportunity in the schools.

The complex process of school failure starts when the child enters the first grade.

From the beginning, many Mexican American school children are made to feel that they have some things that are not wanted—the wrong language, an accent, a different lifestyle and culture. They know they lack some things that *are* wanted—the right language, the right background, a Dick and Jane house, and Pilgrim ancestors.

About half of the Chicanos starting school do not have a working knowledge of English. People in this situation, such as Elena López, perhaps face the toughest time in school systems that make no provisions for non-English-speaking youngsters. For them it is sink or swim.

Yet speaking English doesn't remove all the barriers.

Even for those Chicano students whose families have lived in the Southwest for generations and who speak English as well as Anglos, the school-made barriers are great. They also find that they are often overlooked in class, are advised by counselors to take auto shop instead of college prep courses "because they might find them too difficult," or have to listen in history class about the settling of the Southwest by courageous Texans and stalwart Easterners.

These students and those like Elena López all know that something is wrong.

Listen to them.

"Where I come from everybody speaks Spanish and that's all you know, Spanish," says a 16-year-old Texas student. "And when you are 6 years old, all of a sudden they put you in this Anglo school and it's English right away, but nobody knows how to speak English. Then they try to counteract this by forbidding you to speak Spanish. 'Spanish is bad, Spanish is bad.' When I was little I had the idea Spanish was a dirty language and I felt kind of rotten."

A Tucson teenager recalls that in elementary school "The houses in the Dick and Jane readers didn't look anything like mine. I wondered if there was something wrong with my house. And often, the things teachers discussed had no meaning in my life, but I tried to pretend they did. Teachers were always talking about getting a good breakfast—orange juice, cereal, milk, bacon, and eggs. But these foods didn't mean anything to me. Our family had tortillas with beans and cheese or chorizo."

A young Chicano in a Texas school says, "I remember phrases from my history book such as 'Santa Anna knew that he was dealing with a superior class of men.' It is phrases like that that stay in your head until it gets to your subconscious. 'A superior class of men.' What am I—inferior or something?"

"When I was going to elementary school in Anglo middle-class West Los Angeles, there were only seven or eight Mexican Americans in the whole school," says Rachel, 21, a university student. "I spoke English, but they laughed and ridiculed me for my pronunciation of church, chair, ship. They laughed when I brought burritos for lunch, so I quit doing that. I was very uptight about what I did. I wanted to fit in.

"Then I went to live in the East Side barrio and found that many of the teachers didn't expect students there to do anything. It used to upset me to hear a teacher say, 'If I were in another school, I'd be expected to teach such and such, but not here.' The teacher was telling us in so many words that we weren't as good as students in other parts of the city.

"When I was in high school, I told my counselor I wanted to go to college, but she said, 'Don't try to achieve that. It's not for you. Instead, why don't you try secretarial studies?'

"So I took secretarial studies, but still I wanted to go to college. I went to junior college for 2 years to try it. And then I went on to Cal. State L.A. I'll graduate this year."

Roberto, a 20-year-old university student, says he can't forget that in his last year at a South Texas high school, "We wanted a Mexican American club on campus and Mexican American teachers, counselors, and books on Chicanos. But we ran into all kinds of trouble. We tried but couldn't get anywhere with the principal, so we went to the district office. They told us to come back 'mañana' and later a bunch of us got arrested. They said we were 'parading without a permit.' Eventually they did hire one Chicano counselor, but things were pretty much the same. We were labeled 'rabble rousers' and 'Communists.' I can't understand it. Why do they want to destroy our language and culture?"

These young Chicano students are frustrated and angry to find that their education is not a challenge, but a battle with the odds stacked against them. It is not enough to ask anymore why Chicano students don't learn. But what should be asked is why teachers do not teach and why schools do not care.

WHAT TEACHERS EXPECT

San Jose was hot and muggy that day. In one of the largest high schools in the city, an Anglo teacher, in her mid-forties and smartly dressed, walked slowly down the hall to her next class. She seemed surprised and a bit flattered to be greeted by a visitor at the classroom door who wanted to sit in on her history class, which was filled with mostly male Chicano students.

The teacher agreed, but turned to the visitor apologetically and said, "Don't expect very much from these students. This is my slow class."

Asked for an explanation, she replied quietly, "We consider these students low achievers. You should really visit one of my high ability classes."

It would be nice if every classroom were filled with eager young minds, just as it would be nice if every teacher who walks into a classroom were filled with excitement and zeal for teaching. It would also be nice if teachers greeting a class of Chicano children would expect them to be as interested, studious, and ambitious as a class of Anglo students. But too often they do not.

One teacher who works in a predominantly Mexican American school expressed it this way: "I am a good teacher, I think. If I had a normal bunch of kids, I could teach. But this certainly is not a normal bunch of kids."

The heart of the educational experience, the give-and-take between teacher and student, can be damaged seriously when a student senses that the teacher is displeased or disinterested in his or her work.

It is not difficult, then, to understand why Chicano students become discouraged. A Civil Rights Commission study showed that teachers gave praise or encouragement to Anglo students 36 percent more often than to Mexican Americans. They directed questions to Anglos 21 percent more frequently than to Chicanos and accepted and used the ideas and responses of Anglo students 40 percent more often than those of Chicanos.

The study found that Mexican American students receive less overall attention than Anglos from teachers and, not surprisingly, that Chicanos participate less in class. The total picture that emerged from the survey was that Mexican American students often are ignored in the classroom.

Commission staff members observed these examples of educational neglect:

In a San Antonio schoolroom one Chicano sat in the back and volunteered several answers. At one point the teacher did not even acknowledge his answer. At another time he volunteered an answer which was perfectly suitable. Yet the teacher stated: "Well yes, uh huh, but can anyone else put it in different terms?" The teacher then called on an Anglo boy who gave the same basic response with very little rephrasing. The teacher then beamed and exclaimed: "Yes, that's it exactly."

In a Phoenix classroom, several Chicanos kept raising their hands eagerly at every question. Mrs. G. repeatedly looked over their heads and called on some of the same Anglo students over and over. In some cases, she called on the Chicanos only because the Anglos were not raising their hands. After a while, the Mexican Americans stopped raising their hands.

Any progressive program in Southwestern schools aimed at opening the door to better education for Mexican American students will have to look to its teachers. They hold the key.

"You're doing a report on Mexican American education?" a teacher at predominantly Chicano Lincoln High School in Los Angeles asked. "Well, don't blame the poor teachers. We have enough problems."

Blaming the teachers is not the issue. Training them properly is.

Training programs that erase erroneous ideas about Mexican Americans, teach Spanish, present an accurate picture of Chicano family life, and reveal the rich Mexican American heritage will do much to remove the "cultural handicaps" of teachers and student teachers and help them respond better to Chicano children.

But this training is not being provided.

Few colleges and universities require any ethnic studies or Spanish courses as part of their teacher training programs.

Even the required education courses make little mention of situations and cases that might affect the teaching of Mexican Americans and other minority group students. One teacher remembers that "The only discussion of minorities in our college education classes was in a very general way when professors would point out that 'the problems of hunger and housing have to be solved before we can teach these low-income people anything.' "

And, finally, since most student teachers do their practice teaching in schools where the majority of the students are Anglos, they are basically unprepared when assigned to schools with heavy Chicano enrollments.

Only one Southwestern State, California, has officially recognized the need for this type of preparation. Under recently enacted legislation known as the Ryan Act, student teachers must have some teaching experience with minority children before they can receive their State certification. This law will go into effect in the 1974–75 school year. It is a hopeful sign for the future, but it comes too late for those teachers who already deal with thousands of Chicano students daily.

Linda, 26, is in her third year teaching in a predominantly Chicano school in central Los Angeles. She says that she had no special training in college for teaching Mexican Americans and other ethnic groups even though her college was located in a Mexican American area.

"I just wasn't prepared to teach Mexican Americans," she said. "I took Spanish on my own because I figured I probably would have Chicano children in my classes at some time. It helped me out because I have had many students who didn't speak English."

Linda was told this year that her first graders would be "slow learners" judged by their work in kindergarten. "But I've held them to high standards and they do excellent work," she said, beaming.

"My neighbor is also a teacher in this school but she criticizes her students, calling them 'my monsters.' If she doesn't have any respect for them, I don't know how she expects them to learn."

Linda added that she stills feels there are "gaps in my knowledge about Mexican Americans. I would like to know more about my students' culture and homelife."

She described a telling incident with one of her 6-year-old students. "They were drawing pictures and I asked them to draw one showing the people in their family. I noticed Carlos had about 12 figures in his picture. I laughed at first and told him, 'No just draw your family.' He told me, 'This is my family.' He then pointed out favorite cousins, his grandparents, aunts and uncles whom he was close to. They were all 'his family.' He taught me something.'

Linda is one of many teachers who could

benefit from some practical programs on teaching minority students. Effective "in-service" training courses for experienced teachers can open their minds to various aspects of Chicano values and culture, giving them higher expectations and new respect for Mexican American children.

A change in teacher attitudes was demonstrated in one training course when teachers were asked about the statement, "There is an absence of educational tradition in Mexican American families." At the beginning of the course almost all teachers agreed with the statement. Following discussions with parents, interviews, and research on the subject, the teachers at the end of the course reversed their opinions and disagreed with the statement. They had found through personal contact with the parents that there was a traditional emphasis on education in Chicano families. Attitudes had been changed. Minds had been opened.

Programs that provide training in Spanish and courses that deal with Chicano culture and history are just as vital for counselors as for teachers. The Commission found, however, that none of the Southwestern States has established requirements for cross-cultural courses that would help counselors in their work with Chicano youngsters. As is the case with teachers, few counselor trainees have an opportunity to work with Chicano students.

Understanding breeds sensitivity, but lack of awareness encourages stereotyped thinking. There are thousands of examples of Chicano students who have been shunted off to vocational courses because counselors have not thought of them as "smart enough to go on to college."

Rita is only one case.

"I want to attend college and become a teacher, but I've been taking business courses because of my counselor," says Rita, a California high school student. "He kept telling me that I didn't know anything. I think he thought he was doing it for my own good, but he could have looked into the matter a little more and tried to help. My grades are good. I could pass those college prep classes just as well as anybody else."

Advising Rita, who had the potential and the interest to be a teacher, to seek another career disregards not only the student's ambitions but the critical need for Chicano teachers in the Southwest.

In the last several years, waves of protest by students and parents in Southwestern schools have focused on the lack of Mexican American teachers. Although Chicanos have begun to fill a few school positions, the Commission estimated that in 1972 less than 5 percent of the 350,000 teachers in the Southwest were Mexican American.

Plainly, Rita is needed.

Chicano teachers and counselors can smoothly bridge the gap between home and school for Chicano children. A Mexican American teacher is more likely to have an understanding of the language and cultural needs of Mexican American children. Chicano students also would find it easier to identify with a Mexican American teacher, which would strengthen the bonds of communication and the students' desire to learn.

If more students like Rita are encouraged to become teachers, instead of being advised against it, Chicano teachers will be not a rarity but a reality in the Southwest.

But Mexican Americans need training and experience in teaching minority group children as much as non-Chicano teachers and student teachers.

A Chicano teacher in San Diego explained, "It was a traumatic experience when I was assigned to teach at a Mexican American school. My college training had given me no skills in dealing with my own ethnic group. In college, professors implied that the language of Mexican Americans was a handicap. It took me some time to see the real situation. At first it never dawned on me to look at the linguistic and cultural richness of the Chicano children."

Opening avenues of understanding can make a difference.

Teachers and counselors who are informed and not misinformed, who encourage and not discourage, can influence Chicano children to learn, to achieve, and to excel.

When teachers have high expectations for every student, a classroom can be a place where all children, including the culturally different, can be considered a "normal bunch."

WHAT SCHOOLS ARE DOING

There are varying opinions among principals and school officials about what, if anything, should be done to give Mexican Americans an even break at education.

Some believe no problem exists. "We treat all our students alike," one Arizona principal said. "They are all the same to us."

Others recognize that Chicanos as a group do not perform as well as Anglo students. But they place the blame on the students or their parents. Thus, principals who responded to a Commission question about the high Chicano dropout rate commented:

"It's primarily an economic problem. Kids quit school in order to work."

"They are handicapped by the lack of importance given to education by their parents."

"It is not the fault of the school. I have never seen a school that discriminates against Latins."

"I think it is a social problem rather than an educational one."

A third group of educators admits candidly that the shortcomings of the schools are causing Mexican American students to drop out. Typical reasons were:

"Schools have pushed kids out because they have not offered the right programs."

"Here in Texas, I attribute it to our educational procedures. We have not adequately met the needs of Mexican American students."

"Our curriculums are not meaningful to Mexican Americans. No attempt is made to teach early Southwestern history. The Mexican American child feels he has no place in our society."

"There is a need for Chicano teachers and counselors."

"The schools create conflict in the students. In the past we tried to 'Anglocize' them. That was a mistake. I feel that the damage is done in the early years."

The opinions of principals and school officials are in, but they don't mean very much if you are 9 years old and can't read, or if you are 16 and just want to drop out and forget school.

Relevant school programs to insure better education for Chicano children are badly needed, but those in existence are few and far between.

Some schools are trying. They are taking a new look at the subjects they teach, adding courses on Chicano heritage, trying to recruit more Chicano teachers and counselors, putting more Mexican American aides in the classroom, and attempting to start bilingual programs.

But most schools are doing nothing—or, worse yet, continuing practices that practically condemn Chicano children to failure. One of the worst of these is ability grouping.

Grouping of students according to their abilities is done by schools "in the best interests of students," so they won't have to compete with children who are "out of their league." But this backfires.

In practice, ability grouping separates students from their friends and creates in them a false sense of their worth. Students in lower groups tend to feel and behave like failures, while those in upper groups may think of themselves as superior.

A review of grouping practices in schools throughout the Southwest shows that Chicanos are much more likely to be found in low ability groups than in high ability groups.

A Mexican American mother in a New Mexico town said, "My son told me one day that he was in the 'dummies' group at school. I didn't know what he was talking about until the teacher told me he was in a low ability group in his class."

Much like a prisoner, the Chicano child frequently is confined to a low achievement group, often from grade to grade, without reevaluation of his true ability.

Placement into a low ability class usually is based on the recommendations of teachers or counselors or on results of an intelligence (IQ) test. Both methods can shortchange Mexican American students.

Teachers and counselors who easily "track" Chicanos into slow groups quickly deny that they do so because they believe Mexican Americans are intellectually inferior. Of course not. They try to be more reasonable. Chicano children are "culturally deprived" or "emotionally immature," they say.

And then there are those educators who feel that bright Mexican American students shouldn't be in "honors" or high ability classes because they "might not be comfortable."

In other cases, the IQ test—that neat, precise package of questions, black on white—can spell failure for Mexican Americans. The test is supposed to measure a child's intelligence. But, since the test is designed for middle-class Anglo students, Chicanos are placed at a disadvantage. It becomes a test of language ability.

"Many Mexican Americans score low because they haven't mastered English," says Dr. Steve G. Moreno of California State University, San Diego, an authority on IQ testing.

The unfairness of IQ tests is widely acknowledged by educators, as evidenced by these statements made by principals to the Commission:

"IQ testing is not a true evaluation of a child's intellect. It is an outdated measure and should be declared obsolete."

"IQ tests are really language tests. Many Chicanos don't know the names of items on tests. They find it difficult to follow the instructions in English."

"IQ tests should not be used—not even for Anglos."

Some schools and school districts have discontinued IQ testing, especially in the early grades, at the urging of parents and committed educators. Yet, the testing continues at many Southwestern schools, affecting the lives of thousands of children.

Mexican American parents, students, and educational reformers are turning increasing attention to the school curriculum, the basic plan for a child's schooling that includes courses, textbooks, and teaching methods.

It is in the daily classroom routine that the Chicano student's language is suppressed and his culture and heritage are ignored or distorted Many schools still stress "don't speak Spanish" as the cure-all to the "language problem." Only about 4 percent of the elementary schools and about 7 percent of the secondary schools offer courses in Mexican American history. Chicano home experiences and interests are not considered as having anything to do with the curriculum.

Mexican Americans dream of using the school's curriculum to open up the two-way street of learning, to give Chicano culture a place in all subjects from reading to history and to make Spanish not a stumbling block but a stepping stone to better use of English.

Bilingual-bicultural education is considered by many persons to be the best vehicle to make this dream a reality. But it is being approached cautiously. Where given a chance, however, bilingual-bicultural education is showing that Mexican American students can learn, and learn well, with dignity and purpose. A look at an effective bilingual classroom best illustrates that.

SE HABLA INGLES Y ESPAÑOL

A Mexican American third grader in a bilingual classroom in Los Angeles is reading. to her classmates from the book, *Harriet the Spy*.

"Thank you, that was very good," the teacher says. "Now would you read from this one?"

"Había una vez un gusanito que vivía . . ." the student begins. It is immediately evident that the pupil is equally at ease in reading either English or Spanish. She reads effectively, with understanding, emphasis, and feeling.

The bilingual reading exercise at this school is a dramatic event because as recently as 5 years ago it was against the law to use Spanish as the language of instruction in California, as well as in some other Southwestern States. Now, bilingual-bicultural programs especially developed for Mexican Americans are a reality in a few selected schools and classrooms.

The results are encouraging. To a classroom observer, the students appear self-assured, enthusiastic, and involved. One pupil may ask a classmate a question in Spanish and receive an answer in English, or vice versa. It is all very natural—as natural as the students' home and neighborhood surroundings where varying degrees of bilingualism are a way of life.

In the last several years, this use of both English and Spanish in teaching has come to the classrooms of a small number of schools in the Southwest—a number much too small, its supporters believe. Across the Nation, a scattering of other minority group members also are beginning to reap the rewards of bilingual education. In addition to programs for Spanish speakers, federally-funded bilingual projects are in operation in 18 languages for such groups as Chinese Americans in California, Native Americans on reservations, French Americans in Louisiana, and Portuguese Americans in Rhode Island.

Bilingual education is not new. Various bilingual methods have been used throughout the world for many years. Some forms of bilingual education existed in the United States up to World War I, when they virtually disappeared from the public schools.

Then in the early 1960's bilingual education was revived. Mexican Americans had been pushing for some form of bilingual education for years before, but the first modern day English-Spanish program was started in Florida for Cuban immigrants after the Cuban revolution. This increased the interest in bilingual programs throughout the country. In late 1967, an important step was taken when Congress passed Title VII of the Elementary and Secondary Education Act. Title VII, also known as the Bilingual Education Act, provides Federal money for bilingual programs in many schools throughout the country.

The first bilingual programs for Mexican Americans were started in Texas, and scattered programs now exist in all five Southwestern States. For the fortunate few who are in true bilingual-bicultural classrooms, the experience is exciting and enriching.

One such bilingual program is at Bridge Street Elementary School in the predominantly Chicano area of East Los Angeles. The program there is in its fourth year and going strong.

The drab concrete exterior of the Bridge Street School building contrasts sharply with the bright, warm faces inside the classrooms. Along the walls on bulletin boards of the bilingual classes are posters reminding you that "A" stands for águila (eagle) as well as apple. An exhibit of heroes includes not only Washington and Lincoln but also Mexican patriots Juarez and Hidalgo and U.S. leaders of all ethnic groups. One child's display reports the "News of the Day" in English and another summarizes "Las Noticias del Día" in Spanish.

A sense of commitment to bilingual education comes through in conversations with the school's teachers, principal Luis Salcido, and Title VII bilingual coordinator Marta Acosta. For years Mrs. Acosta felt frustrated by not being permitted to use Spanish in teaching Mexican Americans. Now she supervises bilingual-bicultural instruction at Bridge in kindergarten through fourth grade. With pride, Mrs. Acosta invites visitors to view the bilingual classes.

In one kindergarten, teacher Rita Cázares is about to begin her "magic circle" session. She and 10 pupils are clustered in a circle on the floor. Behind them, hanging on a string, is a rainbow of colorful student drawings.

"Today we are going to talk about what makes us feel very happy," Mrs. Cázares begins. "Hoy vamos hablar de algo que nos hace sentir muy feliz. . . . Who wants to be first?"

"I like to watch TV," Jenny says.
"Yo quiero un carro de carreras," Alfonso chimes in.

"I like swings," Sandra adds.

In turn, the students continue to volunteer answers. Which language they use is not important. Their expressions of thoughts and ideas are what matter. The goal is to develop the students' positive image of themselves. Pupils readily take part because they are talking about their ideas and feelings.

"The children's experiences are the curriculum," says Mrs. Acosta. "Use of their own language allows them to express themselves— their thoughts, wishes, and feelings."

Every few minutes, Mrs. Cázares has the children review what the others have said, encouraging them to listen carefully and aiding their awareness of others. Each student uses his own language and hears a second language in a meaningful situation . . . a method that allows the pupil to increase his bilingual skills.

Down the hall, third grade teacher Arturo Selva is dictating a letter in English to a dozen pupils. Earlier he had dictated a similar letter in Spanish to them.

In another part of this classroom, a Mexican American parent who serves as a teacher's aide gives individual attention in English reading to a pigtailed girl who speaks only Spanish at home. Other students, meanwhile, work by themselves, reading from English skills workbooks.

Then teacher Selva ends the group sessions and goes to the blackboard. He writes out the Spanish sentence "Adonde vas" and asks for a volunteer to punctuate it. Fifteen boys and girls raise their hands and wave them with enthusiasm saying, "I know, I know."

Selva calls on a girl of Japanese background who correctly places question marks at the beginning and end of the sentence and an accent on the "o".

Turning to the class, Selva asks, "¿Estan de acuerdo?" "Do you agree?" He then compares the accentuation of the Spanish "¿Adónde vas?" with the English "Where are you going?" Selva uses both languages to stress points, reinforce ideas, and introduce new concepts.

The bilingual technique continues throughout the day. Selva teaches all subject areas—including mathematics, history, and science—in both English and Spanish. Use of the two languages follows no hard and fast plan but develops naturally as teacher and students see fit. And more than that, the teacher increases student understanding and interest by drawing from experiences of two cultures to explain his points.

"We use examples and descriptions that will be familiar to the students," Selva says. "If I'm talking to my students about what one-half means, I give them a tortilla, have them cut it into two equal pieces and give a half to a classmate. Then they all understand what one-half means.

"Many of the hangups some students had about themselves have been erased," Selva says. "Last year we had a tough time convincing one boy that it was all right to speak Spanish. He thought there was something wrong with it. Now he's comfortable using it and is well on his way to becoming perfectly bilingual."

The majority of third graders in Selva's class are already reading considerably above the fourth grade level. Selva is confident that by the sixth grade, when the students' bilingual training is due to end, almost all will be reading above the sixth grade level in both English and Spanish.

Five of his students—four of them Mexican Americans—out of a class of 26 have been tested as "gifted" (IQ above 132). One girl moved into Selva's bilingual classroom and scored a below-average 33 on her September math test. In the State testing several months later, she came up with a near-perfect 58 out of 60.

"I'm able to establish a good relationship with the students because I speak their language and I know their culture," Selva explains. "I've lived in East L.A. most of my life and I am familiar with the community and the people. This facilitates my teaching and our community involvement.

"What these children need is a composite picture of themselves, not a jigsaw puzzle with parts missing. What bilingual-bicultural education does is to allow a child to say: 'I have a culture that is as beautiful as any other. Different is not wrong. I can speak two languages. Perhaps I can learn to speak three, four, five. I am proud of my heritage. I know I live differently. Isn't that nice?' "

Educators involved in Title VII programs consider community support important. People from the community serve on advisory boards that select bilingual teachers and make decisions on courses. Neighborhood adults are also used as aides and classroom volunteers. Many schools invite parents to workshops where teachers show how bilingual programs work.

When the Bridge Street School bilingual program was getting started, some parents were worried. One parent, María Ybarra, now a teacher's aide at Bridge, explains: "When I first learned about bilingual education for our children, I was against it because I felt that Mexican Americans had to learn English to do well in this society. But now that I have worked in this program and understand bilingual education, I see I was wrong. Our children are speaking better English and better Spanish than if they were in a regular English-only class. Estoy encantada. [I am delighted]."

Other parents quickly saw the benefits of bilingual instruction. One Mexican American mother drives her son in from another section of the city so that he can have a bilingual education. Having grown up in an Anglo neighborhood, the boy did not speak Spanish. Now he is gaining fluency and confidence in Spanish.

Yumi, a Japanese American girl in Selva's class, is driven to school by her parents, who live outside the school's boundaries. With district permission, the parents bring her to this school because they like the teacher and believe in the value of a bilingual program.

In the overall picture of the Los Angeles schools and all the schools serving Chicanos in the Southwest, Bridge Street School is a glowing asset. It is important to point out, however, that the bilingual program at Bridge school is but one type of bilingual education used in American schools. Some bilingual programs, for example, set up specific parts of the day for speaking either English or Spanish instead of using the "concurrent" method; that is, the switching back and forth between two languages as is done at Bridge school. Others use varying combinations of these approaches. Although there is considerable disagreement as to which type of bilingual program to use, there is general agreement on the value of the bilingual approach.

The new bilingual-bicultural program at Bridge Street School and at a few other schools is encouraging. But thousands of other students are still caught up in the unresponsive programs of most schools. For example, the Los Angeles Unified School District is the second largest in the Nation and has the largest number of Chicano students. During 1973–74, this district included approximately 90,000 Mexican American students in elementary schools. However, Title VII bilingual programs included only about 1,850 students, or 2 percent. A small number of other Chicano students attended local- and State-funded bilingual programs.

In the Southwest as a whole, Title VII bilingual

programs enroll about 4 percent of the 1.6 million Mexican American students. During the 1972–73 school year, 123 projects for Mexican Americans were funded, with about 70,000 students participating.

State funding for bilingual education has been limited and slow in coming. Of the five Southwestern States, only Texas starting in the 1974–75 school year will require bilingual education for Spanish speaking children. In contrast, Massachusetts, which has a much smaller Spanish speaking population than any of the Southwestern States, in 1972 became the first State to require bilingual programs for non-English-speaking children.

More Federal and State funds and more bilingual teachers will be needed before bilingual education can reach a significant number of Chicanos. So, for most Mexican Americans, bilingual education is a distant hope. But for Leticia Prieto, a third grader at the Bridge Street School, bilingualism is here and she knows its value. She wrote the following with the rich excitement and imagination of an 8-year-old:

"How It Feels To Be Bilingual"

One day I was walking down the street suddenly I thought if I could go to the beach. So I went. Then I saw a castle. Then I went inside the castle I saw a giant crying. Then I said, What happened?

The giant said I want to speak bilingual. Well that's simple I'll teach you. The giant said, When do we start? I said Right now. So we went on until the night. The giant said, si means yes. I said now you know how to speak bilingual. The giant said, I love to speak bilingual so much.

The next day I told my mother how it feels to speak bilingual. Well it feels good. It feels like I speak all kinds of languages.

CONCLUSION: ¡SI SE PUEDE!

When change is needed, the educational system is better known for caution than for quick action.

As early as 1940 George I. Sánchez, a noted scholar and educator, described the deficiencies of Southwestern schools in relating to Mexican American students. In 1971, a year before his death, Dr. Sánchez looked back at the Mexican American movement for educational reform and concluded:

> While I have seen some changes and improvements in this long-standing dismal picture, I cannot . . . take any satisfaction in those developments. The picture is a shameful and embarrassing one.

Time moves on. But relatively few school improvements occur for the largest minority group in the Southwest. While educators and officials have debated why Juanito can't read, generations of Mexican Americans have been doomed to school failure. Forty percent of Chicano students drop out of schools, but most school districts continue business as usual.

Today, for the most part, the language and culture of Mexican Americans are still excluded from the classroom, and the Chicano heritage is omitted in textbooks and course work. Teachers and counselors, most of whom are Anglo, are not trained to work effectively with Mexican American children. Schools put larger numbers of Chicano children in low ability classes instead of starting effective learning programs. Reforms are overdue.·

Mexican American parents are ready to help, but schools must show more initiative in getting their assistance and in using it, especially in the making of school policy. If the system is not ready to listen, Chicanos will have to take their cases to their elected officials—or, in some instances, to the courts. Encouragement for such action has been provided by the January 1974 unanimous Supreme Court decision in a San Francisco case involving Chinese American students. The court ruled that a school system receiving Federal funds violates the law when it fails to meet the needs of non-English-speaking children.

What Chicano students want is a fair break— an equal chance to get a quality education. But they also want to feel proud of who they are. America is a land enriched by different ethnic groups, and Mexican Americans do not believe they should have to give up their identity to enjoy success in school.

The U.S. Commission on Civil Rights, in the final report of its Mexican American Education Study, made many recommendations to improve the quality of education offered to Chicanos. These recommendations in brief, stress that:

- The language and culture of Mexican Americans should be a basic part of the educational process.

- Mexican Americans should be fully represented in educational decisionmaking at all levels.

- Federal, State, and local governments should provide sufficient funds to reach these goals.

Whether these recommendations are followed or ignored depends on people in the educational system—superintendents, principals, teachers. It also depends on State and Federal government agencies that are involved in these programs and provide policy guidelines.

The Mexican American community has taken up a slogan that spurs forward its movement for equality in American life: ¡Sí Se Puede!—It can be done! It can be done, but will it be done for the Chicano child? That is a question to which American society must provide a positive response.

Para Los Ninos—For the Children: Improving Education for Mexican Americans. Clearinghouse Publication 47, U.S. commission on Civil Rights, Washington, D.C. October 1974.

PUERTO RICANS IN THE CONTINENTAL UNITED STATES: *AN UNCERTAIN FUTURE*

Introduction

One of every twenty persons in the United States today is a Hispanic American.

Mexican Americans are the largest single Hispanic group, with 6.7 million persons.

Next largest is the Puerto Rican community. Nearly 1.7 million persons of Puerto Rican birth or parentage live on the United States mainland. If we add to this the 3.1 million residents of the island Commonwealth of Puerto Rico, we find that the number of U.S. citizens of Puerto Rican birth or descent is fast approaching the 5 million mark (see Table 1).[1]

This report focuses upon the U.S. mainland Puerto Rican population, which achieved significant size after the Second World War and whose incidence of poverty and unemployment is more severe than that of virtually any ethnic group in the United States.[2]

Puerto Ricans share the major concerns and problems of all their fellow Americans, particularly those who reside in urban areas, and specifically those whose language, culture, and/or skin color has caused them to be victims of discrimination.

However, the facts contained in this report (even, indeed, the very existence of this report) confirm that Puerto Ricans comprise a distinct ethnic group, with concerns and priorities that frequently differ from those of other minorities, even other Spanish heritage groups. (It is often overlooked, for example, that although Puerto Ricans, Cubans, Mexicans, and Dominicans share a common linguistic and cultural heritage, differences among them are as distinct as those among Americans, Australians, British, and other English-speaking peoples.)

Puerto Ricans represent less than 1 percent of the continental United States population. But in New York City, 10 percent of the residents (and 23 percent of the school children) are Puerto Rican.[3] Just across the Hudson River, in Hoboken, almost one-fourth of the population is Puerto Rican.[4] Major cities such as Chicago, Philadelphia, Cleveland, Newark, Hartford, and Boston also have large Puerto Rican communities.[5] In short, the quality of life achieved by Puerto Ricans is inextricably linked with the quality of life in many of America's key urban centers.

During the 1960s—the period of the "War on Poverty"—an unprecedented number of laws and special programs were enacted, whose aim was to improve the socioeconomic position of this nation's impoverished minorities. The facts, as documented in this report, show that Puerto Ricans have benefited very little from these programs and, that in some respects, their lot has deteriorated.

Not long ago, Representative Herman Badillo (the only mainland Puerto Rican who has won an elected seat in Congress) reminisced about his first few weeks in public office:

> I came to Washington brimming with ideas; I knew all about the problems that afflicted my people, and I had made up a lengthy list of proposed laws that would remedy the situation. Then, to my surprise, I slowly came to find out that most of the necessary laws were already on the books. Trouble is, they weren't being implemented![6]

This report will also document cases of specific government laws and

Table 1

Total U.S. Population and Persons of Spanish Origin

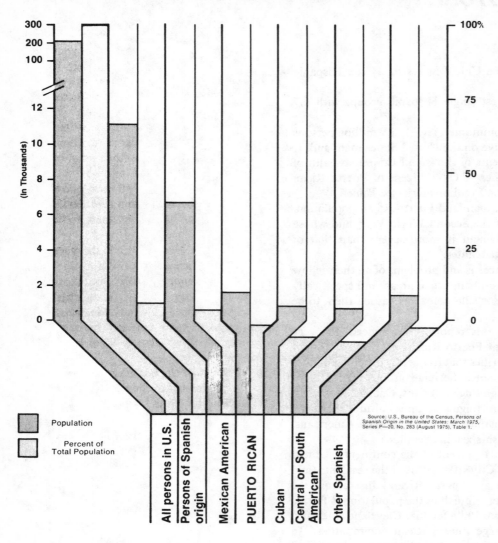

Source: U.S., Bureau of the Census, *Persons of Spanish Origin in the United States: March 1975*, Series P—20, No. 283 (August 1975), Table 1.

programs that are designed to assist Puerto Ricans and other minority groups, yet have fallen far short of their mandated goals.

With the exception of statistical surveys by the U.S. Bureau of the Census, this is the first report by a Federal Government agency that focuses upon the entire population of mainland Puerto Ricans. The purpose of this report is to:

1. Provide policymakers and the general public with greater insight into the unique history of mainland Puerto Ricans and the continuing grave difficulties that afflict a large sector of the community;

2. Provide useful source material for further research; and

3. Recommend government action to address the special needs of mainland Puerto Ricans.

A tangential purpose of this report is to dispel the generally poor images of Puerto Ricans residing in the continental United States, for example, the image of young Puerto Ricans as gang members.

Any study that focuses upon the problems of an entire ethnic group faces a dilemma:

●If severe problems are left unmentioned, or if their importance is minimized, the likelihood of their solution is greatly reduced.

●On the other hand, an exclusive focus upon problems can, perhaps, tend to create or reinforce prejudiced attitudes in the minds of uninformed readers.

For example, the mere act of stating (without any qualification) that mainland Puerto Ricans are poorer, have less education, and are more dependent upon welfare than the national average can create a distorted image—an image of an entire people who are uniformly poor, uneducated, and welfare-prone.

Therefore, this survey of legitimate problems must be tempered by facts that place the problems in a realistic perspective:

●It should be remembered that, while compared with the majority white population a disproportionate number of Puerto Ricans live in poverty, most do not, and a substantial number have entered the middle class. (One

Table 4

Growth of Puerto Rican Population on the U.S. Mainland

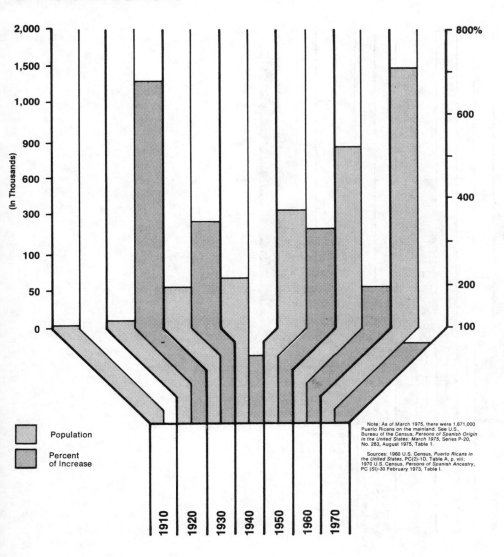

Note: As of March 1975, there were 1,671,000 Puerto Ricans on the mainland. See U.S. Bureau of the Census, *Persons of Spanish Origin in the United States: March 1975*, Series P-20, No. 283, August 1975, Table 1.

Sources: 1960 U.S. Census, *Puerto Ricans in the United States*, PC(2)-1D, Table A, p. viii; 1970 U.S. Census, *Persons of Spanish Ancestry*, PC (SI)-30 February 1973, Table I.

Population

Percent of Increase

1910 1920 1930 1940 1950 1960 1970

hundred and four thousand Puerto Rican workers earned $10,000 or more in 1974; about 25,000 earned in excess of $15,000; about 5,000 had earnings of $25,000 or more. However, while about 33 percent of mainland Puerto Ricans were living below the low-income level, the percentage of all Americans living in poverty was less than 12 percent.)[7]

●It should be remembered that, while the educational level of mainland Puerto Ricans is far below the national average, thousands are of high school and university graduates. (As of 1975, there were 198,000 high school graduates.[8] There were also more than 12,500 college graduates, and more than 17,000 enrolled college students.[9])

●It should be remembered that, while a disproportionate number of Puerto Rican adults are engaged in menial, low-paying work, thousands have rewarding jobs that require great skill. (In 1975, more than 42,000 Puerto Ricans held professional, technical, or managerial jobs.[10])

Table 6

Dispersion of Puerto Ricans Among New York City Boroughs

(expressed in terms of percent of Puerto Rican population)

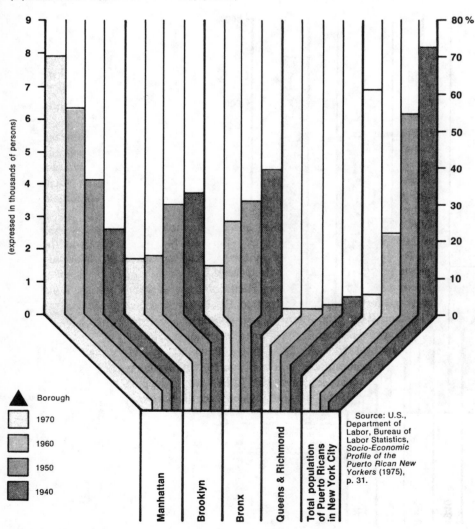

(expressed in thousands of persons)

Borough
1970
1960
1950
1940

Manhattan

Brooklyn

Bronx

Queens & Richmond

Total population of Puerto Ricans in New York City

Source: U.S., Department of Labor, Bureau of Labor Statistics, *Socio-Economic Profile of the Puerto Rican New Yorkers* (1975), p. 31.

●It should be remembered that, while the percentage of Puerto Ricans on welfare is higher than the national average for all Americans, three-fourths of the Puerto Rican families on the mainland are wholly self-sufficient and receive not one cent of welfare or other Federal aid.[11]

The purpose of stating these facts is to demonstrate that in the face of hostility, prejudice, and government neglect, many Puerto Ricans have successfully made the transition from their native land to the United States.

But the facts also have their gloomier side. As one recent study reported:

> ... Puerto Ricans continue to inherit the slums abandoned by other groups....As the cost of living skyrockets, poverty-level wages continue to shrink; the educational problem continues to degenerate; capital resources are still unavailable because of prejudice, discrimination and unequal opportunity....[12]

Table 7

Population Trends of Puerto Ricans on the U.S. Mainland, by Region, State, and City, 1950, 1960, 1970

	1950	1960	1970
United States			
Total	301,375	892,513	1,391,463
Northeast	264,530	740,813	1,126,410
New York	252,515	642,622	878,980
New York City	245,880	612,574	817,712
Buffalo	–	2,176	6,090
Rochester	–	1,990	5,916
New Jersey	5,640	55,351	136,937
Newark	545	9,698	27,663
Jersey City	655	7,427	16,325
Paterson	–	5,123	12,036
Hoboken	–	5,313	10,047
Passaic	–	–	6,853
Pennsylvania	3,560	21,206	44,947
Philadelphia	1,910	14,424	26,948
Connecticut	1,305	15,247	38,493
Bridgeport	590	5,840	10,048
Hartford	–	–	8,631
Massachusetts	1,175	5,217	24,561
Boston	–	995	7,335
Regional Balance	335	1,170	2,492
North Central	10,675	67,833	135,813
Illinois	3,570	36,081	88,244
Chicago	2,555	32,371	79,582
Ohio	2,115	13,940	21,147
Cleveland	–	4,116	8,104
Lorain	–	3,799	6,031
Indiana	1,800	7,218	9,457
Gary	–	2,946	5,228
Regional Balance	3,190	10,594	16,965
South	13,480	45,876	69,742
Florida	4,040	19,535	29,588
Miami	–	6,547	6,835
Regional Balance	9,440	26,341	40,154
West	12,690	38,030	59,498
California	10,295	28,108	46,955
Los Angeles	–	6,424	10,116
San Francisco	–	–	5,037
Regional Balance	2,395	9,922	12,543

Note: "Regional Balance" represents the balance of the Puerto Rican population in the respective regions.

Source: U.S. Census reports for 1950, 1960, and 1970.

Even more recently, an observer summed up the status of the large Puerto Rican community in New York City, exclaiming:

> People would not believe what is happening to Puerto Ricans in the city.... We need to be treated like a devastated nation—requiring a domestic Point Four program....[13]

A dismayingly high percentage of Puerto Ricans are still trapped in poverty. As of March 1975, while 11.6 percent of all Americans were below the low-income level, this was the case for 32.6 percent of mainland Puerto Ricans (compared with 24 percent of Mexican Americans and 14.3 percent of Cuban Americans).[14]

At the same time, while the median income for all U.S. families was $12,836 per year, Puerto Rican families earned only $7,629 (compared with $9,498 for Mexican American families and $11,410 for Cuban American and "Other Spanish" families).[15]

While only 3.3 percent of all U.S. adults had completed less than 5 years of school, this was the case for 17.4 percent of mainland Puerto Rican adults.[16]

While more than 62 percent of all U.S. adults were high school graduates, only 28.7 percent of Puerto Rican adults had finished high school (compared with 51 percent of Cuban American and 31 percent of Mexican American adults).[17]

As these figures demonstrate, the mainland Puerto Rican community is not only far below the U.S. average in key socioeconomic areas, but also below other major Hispanic groups. The challenge now is to focus upon the neediest members of the Puerto Rican community. Specific, highly selective action must be taken to help these U.S. citizens achieve equal access to economic and education opportunities.

Notes to Introduction

1. Since the passage of legislation in March 1917, all Puerto Ricans are citizens of the United States. Jones Act, 39 Stat. 951 (1917), as amended, 48 U.S.C. §731 et seq. (1970).

2. It is not Commission policy to compare one racial or ethnic group with another. Normally, socioeconomic comparisons are made with the average figures for the total U.S. population. However, since there are often great differences even among different groups of Hispanic origin, it was felt that such comparisons would better illustrate the specific situation of mainland Puerto Ricans.

3. Kal Wagenheim, *A Survey of Puerto Ricans on the U.S. Mainland in the 1970s* (New York: Praeger, 1975), Table 44, p. 104.

4. Ibid., Table 68, p. 125.

5. Ibid., Table 6, p. 74.

6. Luncheon address at conference of book publishers and editors, Plaza Hotel, New York City, Oct. 24, 1974.

7. U.S., Bureau of the Census, *Persons of Spanish Origin: March 1975* (Advance Report), Table 7, p. 8 (hereafter cited as *Persons of Spanish Origin* (month/year)).

8. Ibid., Tables 2 and 4.

9. U.S., Bureau of the Census, 1970 Census of Population, *Puerto Ricans in the United States,* Table 4, p. 34 (hereafter cited as *Puerto Ricans in the United States*).

10. *Persons of Spanish Origin* (March 1975), Table 5, p. 7.

11. *Puerto Ricans in the United States,* Table 9, p. 89.

12. Puerto Rican Forum, *A Study of Poverty Conditions in the New York Puerto Rican Community* (1970), p. iv.

13.   Edward Gonzales, Puerto Rican Manpower and Leadership Training Center, Cornell University, interview in New York City, N.Y., Sept. 12, 1974.

14.   *Persons of Spanish Origin* (March 1975), Table 8, p. 8.

15.   Ibid., Table 6, p. 7.

16.   Ibid., Table 4, p. 6.

17.   Ibid.

Table 11

Population by Age, March 1975

	Total U.S. Pop.	Mexican American	Puerto Rican	Cuban
Total (thousands)	209,572	6,690	1,671	743
Percent	100.00	100.0	100.0	100.0
Under 5 years	7.7	13.7	13.0	4.6
5 to 9 years	8.3	12.5	13.0	6.5
10 to 17 years	15.7	19.5	20.7	16.7
18 to 20 years	5.7	6.6	6.2	4.0
21 to 24 years	6.9	7.8	5.8	5.4
25 to 34 years	14.4	13.8	15.9	9.3
35 to 44 years	10.8	10.7	12.8	15.6
45 to 54 years	11.3	8.1	7.0	18.6
55 to 64 years	9.3	3.8	4.1	10.7
65 years and over	10.1	3.3	1.5	8.6
18 years and over	68.3	54.3	53.3	72.2
21 years and over	62.6	47.7	47.1	68.2
Median age (years)	28.6	19.8	19.4	37.3

Source: U.S., Bureau of the Census, *Persons of Spanish Origin in the United States: March 1975*, Series P-20, No. 283, August 1975, Table 2.

Table 12

Reporting Ability to Read and Write English, Total U.S. Population, Mainland Puerto Ricans, and All Persons of Spanish Origin, 1969

	Total U.S. Pop.	Puerto Ricans	Total Spanish Origin
Percent, age 10 and over	95.0	69.4	80.2
age 10 to 24	96.8	80.6	91.1
age 25 and over	94.2	59.7	71.9
Percent males, age 10 and over	95.3	72.9	82.8
males, age 10 to 24	96.7	82.3	91.7
males, age 25 and over	94.6	65.1	75.9
Percent females, age 10 and over	94.8	66.1	77.9
females, age 10 to 24	96.9	79.1	90.6
females, age 25 and over	93.9	55.6	68.1

Source: U.S., Bureau of the Census, *Persons of Spanish Origin in the United States, November 1969*, Series P-20, No. 213, February 1971, Table 17.

Puerto Ricans and Job Training Programs: In 1970 only 18,600 Puerto Ricans in New York City had completed some type of job training program, contrasted with a total of 300,000 Puerto Ricans in need of training. Half had studied in high school, trade school, or junior college; another 1,200 had received training in the Armed Forces. Only 900 had been served by the Neighborhood Youth Corps, and only 200 had received training in MDTA programs.[93]

Nationwide figures for fiscal year 1973 showed a similarly dismal picture. Of the 119,600 persons enrolled in MDTA training programs, only 1,794 were Puerto Rican.[94]

Such figures dramatize the failure of Federal job training programs to serve Puerto Ricans adequately, and indicate that, at present levels of funding, only a miniscule portion of the needy population will be served in the future.

A Chicago study found that persons of Spanish origin were "underrepresented as program participants, particularly in skill training programs." Training funds were used to provide English as a Second Language (ESL) only as an "isolated, individual" program. Because of inadequate funds, programs were offering "short-duration, semi-skilled occupational training, while higher-skill, longer-duration training in higher-demand occupations is...crucially needed."[95]

Table 14

Relative Growth of Island-born and U.S.-born Puerto Rican Populations on the U.S. Mainland

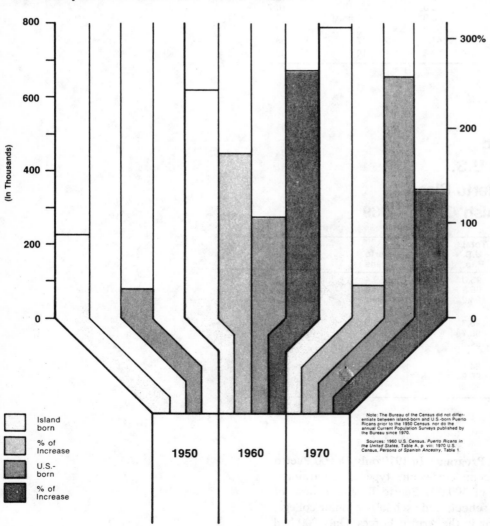

Island born

% of Increase

U.S.-born

% of Increase

1950   1960   1970

Note: The Bureau of the Census did not differentiate between island-born and U.S.-born Puerto Ricans prior to the 1950 Census, nor do the annual Current Population Surveys published by the Bureau since 1970.

Sources: 1960 U.S. Census, Puerto Ricans in the United States, Table A, p. viii; 1970 U.S. Census, Persons of Spanish Ancestry, Table 1.

Table 13

Family Characteristics of Total U.S. Population, Mainland Puerto Ricans, Mexican Americans, 1972

	Total U.S. Population	Puerto Ricans	Mexican Americans
Families (in thousands)	53,296	363	1,100
Percent with own children under age 18	55.2	75.8	77.0
Average number of own children under age 18 per family	1.22	1.97	2.11
Percent families with:			
1 own child	18.9	19.2	19.8
2 own children	17.6	22.7	21.3
3 own children	10.2	13.9	12.5
4 own children	4.9	10.1	10.7
5 own children	2.1	4.8	6.9
6 or more own children	1.6	5.0	5.9
Percent families headed by a woman (one-parent families)	11.6	28.9	14.1

Source: U.S., Bureau of the Census, *Persons of Spanish Origin, March 1972*, Series P-20, No. 238, July 1972.

Table 20

Median Family Income

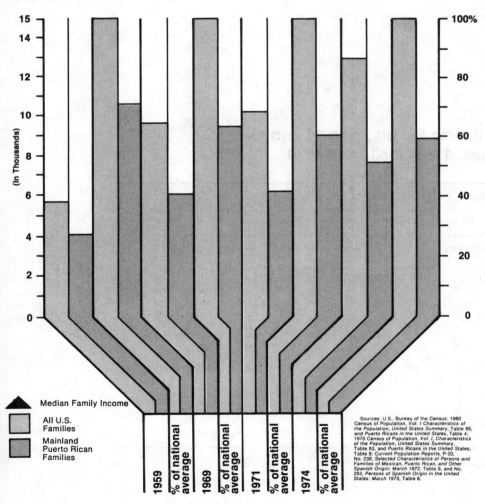

Median Family Income

All U.S. Families

Mainland Puerto Rican Families

Sources: U.S., Bureau of the Census: 1960 Census of Population, *Vol. I Characteristics of the Population, United States Summary*, Table 95, and *Puerto Ricans in the United States*, Table 4; 1970 Census of Population, *Vol. I, Characteristics of the Population, United States Summary*, Table 83, and *Puerto Ricans in the United States*, Table 9; Current Population Reports, P-20, No. 238, *Selected Characteristics of Persons and Families of Mexican, Puerto Rican, and Other Spanish Origin: March 1972*, Table 9, and No. 283, *Persons of Spanish Origin in the United States: March 1975*, Table 6.

Table 22

Sources of Family Income
Puerto Rican and Total Population: United States, 1970

Number and Percent of Families by Sources of Income, and Average (Mean) at Each Level, 1970[1]	Puerto Ricans		Total Population	
Wages or Salaries	254,133	77.8	44,134,271	86.2
Average	$7,479	—	$10,170	—
Nonfarm self-employment income	11,369	3.5	5,460,817	10.7
Average	$6,490	—	$8,186	—
Farm self-employment income	553	0.2	2,369,558	4.6
Average	$3,897	—	$3,462	—
Social Security income	26,282	8.1	10,070,743	19.7
Average	$1,490	—	$1,626	—
Public assistance or public welfare income	79,863	24.5	2,719,074	5.3
Average	$2,366	—	$1,298	—
Other Income	34,636	10.6	17,945,700	35.1
Average	$1,607	—	$2,097	—

[1] Percentages do not add to 100.0 because certain families receive more than one type of income.

Source: U.S., Bureau of the Census.

Table 24

Occupations of Employed Puerto Ricans, Age 14 and Over, by Sex, for the United States, 1950, 1960, and 1970

	1950				1960				1970			
	Male		Female		Male		Female		Male		Female	
Occupations	Number	Percent[1]	Number	Percent[1]	Number	Percent[1]	Number	Percent[1]	Number	Percent[1]	Number	Percent[1]
Total Employed	63,895	100.0	38,930	100.0	181,991	100.0	85,068	100.0	263,735	100.0	123,659	100.0
Professional and Technical	3,355	5.3	1,320	3.4	5,307	2.9	3,384	4.0	12,277	4.7	8,926	7.2
Managers and Administrators	3,450	5.4	465	1.2	6,134	3.4	1,044	1.2	10,970	4.2	1,989	1.6
Clerical	6,160	9.6	4,280	11.0	14,268	7.8	11,824	13.9	27,956	10.6	36,688	29.7
Sales	—	—	—	—	5,261	2.9	2,409	2.8	11,234	4.3	5,477	4.4
Skilled Crafts and Supervisory	7,125	11.2	665	1.7	20,647	11.3	1,650	1.9	41,281	15.7	3,002	2.4
Operatives	21,115	33.0	28,225	72.5	75,299	41.4	56,524	66.4	88,451	33.5	49,038	39.7
Services, Nondomestic	16,040	25.1	2,530	6.5	33,215	18.3	6,186	7.3	46,244	17.5	15,453	12.5
Domestic Service	105	0.2	905	2.3	123	0.1	998	1.2	234	0.1	1,271	1.0
Nonfarm Laborers	4,670	7.3	385	1.0	15,882	8.7	799	0.9	21,201	8.0	1,370	1.1
Farmers and Farm Workers	1,875	2.9	155	0.4	5,855	3.2	250	0.3	3,887	1.5	445	0.4

[1] Percentages do not always add to exactly 100.0 due to rounding.

Source: U.S. Census reports of 1950, 1960, and 1970.

Table 25

Employment by Industry of Employed Puerto Ricans Age 14 and Over, Compared with Total Population: United States, 1960 and 1970[1]

Industry	1960 Puerto Ricans Number	1960 Puerto Ricans Percent	1960 Total Pop. Percent	1970 Puerto Ricans Number	1970 Puerto Ricans Percent	1970 Total Pop. Percent
Total Employed	270,103	100.0	100.0	387,394	100.0	100.0
Agriculture, Forestry, Fishery and Mining	6,974	2.6	8.1	6,048	1.6	4.6
Construction	5,884	2.2	6.2	9,401	2.4	5.8
Manufacturing—Total	(148,236)	(54.9)	(28.2)	(159,993)	(41.3)	(26.0)
Durables	62,880	23.3	15.9	76,697	19.8	15.4
Nondurables	85,356	31.6	12.3	83,296	21.5	10.6
Transportation, Communications and other utilities	11,636	4.3	7.2	23,834	6.2	6.8
Wholesale and Retail Trade	42,327	15.7	19.0	69,968	18.1	20.1
Finance, Insurance and Real Estate	8,195	3.0	4.3	23,639	6.1	5.0
Business and Repair Services	6,074	2.2	2.6	14,860	3.8	3.1
Personal Services	16,575	6.1	6.2	18,115	4.7	4.5
Entertainment and Recreation	1,667	0.6	0.8	2,967	0.8	0.3
Professional Services	16,530	6.1	12.4	44,632	11.5	17.6
Public Administration	6,005	2.2	5.0	13,937	3.6	5.6

1 Excludes persons for whom industry was not reported; due to rounding of decimals, percentages do not always add exactly to 100.0 percent.

Source: U.S., Bureau of the Census.

The study noted that constraints on Hispanic participation included:

> The lack of parity for Latins, and programs designed specifically for the Spanish-speaking; credibility between outreach and the final programs has widened; decrease in strong training facilities to provide vocational and educational components; little or no concern on the part of local administrators to provide satellite centers for training within barrios; Spanish-speaking now are forced into black centers where they are in the minority and feel unwelcome and cannot relate; little representation on advisory councils and boards by Spanish-speaking representatives and leaders.[96]

Another analysis of job training policies and programs found that:

> Too often [programs] have failed to recognize and deal with the uniqueness of the needs of the Spanish-speaking people. The decisionmakers often do not know enough about the language and cultural characteristics of the people to develop viable and effective programs. The fact that Hispanos speak a foreign language and have different backgrounds is regarded as being their own problem, and the need to establish programs built upon serving people from different cultures is not always recognized....As a result, while the basic idea of training and education for the disadvantaged may be sound, the policy for implementation has built-in deficiencies. There must be an urgent, full-scale effort to develop sufficient numbers of skilled Spanish-speaking policy makers and managers and place them at all levels of the delivery system if manpower programs are to serve the Spanish-speaking effectively.[97]

Probably the most frequent complaint of Puerto Ricans about training programs concerns language. In the February 1972 Commission hearing in New York, Representative Herman Badillo (D.-N.Y.) criticized the lack of bilingual training:

> It doesn't make any sense to be spending a lot of money on poverty programs or model cities programs in order to train people when we do not appropriate funds for training people in Spanish because it is more important, in fact, that training be in Spanish for adults who can't speak English, or those that just came from Puerto Rico. They are the ones who desperately need employment and we should have training programs in Spanish so that the adult Puerto Rican community can begin to participate....[98]

In Bridgeport, Connecticut, an aide of the mayor said that he was "not pleased with any manpower program" for the Spanish-speaking. "English is the hump they never get over," and as a result, the "Spanish-speaking are underserved in most programs."[99]

A New York job training specialist believed that the programs were not reaching those who need them most because the programs "are geared to those most able to profit from them. People have to be trained to be trainable."[100]

Some applicants were unable to pass the tests required for entry to training programs. In Chicago, applicants had to pass a Stanford Achievement Test before entry into the CEP program. The CEP program offered on-the-job training opportunities for unskilled Hispanics, many of whom could not read English beyond the fourth grade level. A CEP administrator in Chicago criticized the test as not being job related, as "culturally biased" in favor of "middle-Americans," and generally "irrelevant and immaterial."[101] The problem was reportedly compounded by the fact that the test was administered by English speakers.

The lack of data on Puerto Ricans also limits the effectiveness of training programs for them. An official of the Bureau of Labor Statistics said that a major barrier to an evaluation of the situation was the lack of current information on significant labor force characteristics. He noted:

> There is no group that addresses itself to developing a body of background information on the economic status of the Puerto Rican in the labor market on a continuing basis, and that is almost pitiful. I suspect that you don't have half the awareness of the problems of the Puerto Ricans in New York that you do have, for example, for the other groups, simply because of the lack of availability of data that calls continuous attention to it.[102]

The now defunct U.S. Cabinet Committee on Opportunities for Spanish-Speaking People also noted that data were "fragmented, scattered, hard to obtain, and frequently non-existent....There is no repository of hard data upon which to conduct further analysis that will lead to the development, improvement or betterment of programs for the Spanish-speaking."[103]

At a conference held by the National Commission for Manpower Policy in January 1976 on employment problems of low income groups, one issue of concern was inadequate statistical information on particular groups to determine manpower services. The conference report noted:

> This deficiency is particularly important when such data is used to estimate the numbers and characteristics of minority group members, particularly those who are Spanish speaking or are of Spanish heritage.[104]

The allocation of Federal funds under CETA is based upon available data. Eighty percent of Title I funds are distributed to States and eligible prime sponsors within States according to a formula based on:

(1) the allotment for job training in the previous fiscal year;

(2) the relative number of unemployed; and

(3) the relative number of adults in low-income families.

Accurate figures for the number of Puerto Rican unemployed and poor are thus vitally important in determining CETA allocations. Yet such data are, in many cities, little better than guesses. Dr. Fred Romero, Special Assistant to the Undersecretary for Rural Affairs, Department of Labor, notes that the data reporting systems for CETA "should be better established later in 1976," and thus information about minority participation may not yet be accurate. According to Dr. Romero, data for Puerto Ricans will not be broken out, so Puerto Rican participation in CETA will be difficult to measure.[105]

Most of the complaints against pre-CETA job training programs were supported by a 1971 study which found that:

(1) the proportion of Spanish-origin enrollees in training programs was lower than that for other disadvantaged groups; and

(2) those training programs with the lowest rates of Spanish-origin participation (MDTA Institutional, OJT, NAB/JOBS,[106] and Job Corps) were the major activities in terms of dollars, number of trainees, and opportunities for upgrading skills.[107]

The study noted that monolingual persons and the severely educationally disadvantaged were screened out; that programs were not tailored to unique language and cultural needs; and that few persons of Spanish origin were involved in program planning and administration. Limited budgets permitted only small-scale experiments that reached relatively few participants and the selection of only a handful of sites to serve persons of Spanish origin.

The study faulted all branches of the Federal Government for failing to "enunciate the principle of parity, or fair share, in targeting manpower services on disadvantaged racial and ethnic minorities, with the result that program administrators have left out the Spanish-speaking." It also criticized the Labor Department for "preoccupation with guidelines" and "lack of clear direction to Regional Offices, the Employment Service, and manpower administrators generally."[108]

The Assistant Secretary for Manpower (Employment and Training), Department of Labor, later claimed that the study resulted in an additional $7 million being set aside by the Employment and Training Administration (ETA) to help assure equity for Hispanics in the programs. The money, he said:

> ...was earmarked for such key items as increased language training and hiring 40 Spanish-speaking staffers in 40 cities to work on the local and state manpower planning councils (CAMPS). The latter action involved the Spanish-speaking in mainline planning of manpower programs at the grassroots levels....The Manpower Administration [recently renamed Employment and Training Administration] also directed the State Employment Service to hire more Spanish speaking individuals and subcontractors to carry out the expanded WIN program....More technical assistance was ordered for Spanish-speaking organizations seeking manpower funds at the local level.[109]

On the other hand, another Labor Department official commented that followup on the report's recommendations was minimal. "Nothing much happened," he said, except for "a few, scattered activities" undertaken largely in response to 1972 election year pressures. The study group "had a hell of a time getting the study "reviewed" in the first place. An "action plan" was announced, but "never did get implemented."[110]

Puerto Ricans and the Comprehensive Employment and Training Act (CETA): Many Puerto Ricans with experience in job training programs indicate that the new CETA program offers some promise, at least on paper. They point to Title I, which stipulates that State and local prime sponsors must provide employment and training services, including the development of job opportunities, to those most in need of them, including low-income persons and "persons of limited English speaking ability." In addition, Title III authorizes the Department of Labor to undertake separate special projects, such as the teaching of occupational language skills in the primary language of persons with limited proficiency in English and the development of new employment opportunities.

According to one Labor Department Official of Spanish origin: "Everything the Spanish speaking have been asking for is provided in the act."[111]

The key question to some, however, is whether or not the relationship between the local prime sponsor and Puerto Rican community groups still in their political infancy will permit sufficient Puerto Rican participation in program planning and administration.[112]

An official in New York City complained that Puerto Ricans were still not getting their fair share because they lack "political clout."[113] It was feared that CETA could "face off Puerto Ricans against blacks" for available resources in many cities.[114] After reviewing several CETA applications, a Labor Department official told Commission staff that it was clear Hispanic community organizations were having a minimal effect on local governments.[115]

The Department of Labor rejected this Commission's recommendation that members of each minority group be represented on CETA planning councils in approximately the same proportions they comprise of the service population. Nor did the Department accept the recommendation that special programs under Title I be developed when persons of limited English-speaking ability constitute 5 percent of the unemployed, underemployed, and poverty level population. A similar suggestion concerning public employment projects under Title II was also turned down.[116]

Concern has also been voiced about funding under the CETA formula. According to several administrators, the formula based on the previous year's pre-CETA employment and training allocation would perpetuate previous shortcomings of such funds in several cities. Moreover, the formula based on the number of unemployed would not include those who have stopped looking for work, a substantial number of whom may be Puerto Rican. And, the formula based on low-income adults would cheat big cities with large concentrations of minorities, a disproportionate number of whom were not counted in the decennial census.

Job training administrators in Boston and Chicago feared that the CETA funding formula would result in a decrease in monies for the nation's large cities in the long run.[117] "All big cities are in the same boat," said a Chicago official, who projected a gradual decline from $32 million to $20 million for Chicago CETA programs.[118] Boston's job training director feared that "big cities will get murdered" by the funding formula, and those most hurt will be persons of Spanish origin in the inner cities.[119]

Both job training administrators stated that CETA money would be disproportionately allotted to suburbs and middle size towns. Thus, Newton, a wealthy "bedroom community" in Massachusetts, would enjoy a 400 percent increase in funds, in contrast to the gradual decreases in funds for large cities where most of the severely disadvantaged reside.[120]

Under CETA, local governments would be hard pressed to show quick results. If job training programs were to face cost-benefit analysis, said a New York official, the client of Spanish origin would be most affected.[121] CETA deals primarily with the "employables" to get fast results, according to another observer, and thus would not reach the "neediest of the needy" for whom more time and efforts would naturally be required.[122]

Thus, despite the attractive CETA design, Puerto Ricans and some job training administrators voice deep fear that the basic barriers which minimized Puerto Rican opportunities under OEO and Department of Labor training programs will continue to deny them the same vitally needed opportunities under CETA.

The results of the first year of CETA confirm some of these fears. A study prepared for the National Academy of Sciences on the first-year implementation of CETA indicates that, as a result of the economic recession and allowing more suburbs to be prime sponsors, the trend is toward a broader client group that includes older workers and the recently unemployed. Prime sponsors are placing more emphasis on work experience and less on classroom learning and on-the-job training. The more adversely affected by CETA appear to be those most in need in the cities.[123]

Statistics from ETA indicate that CETA enrollees are older, better educated, and less disadvantaged, and that Spanish-speaking participation has declined. During fiscal year 1975, Spanish-speaking participation in CETA was 12 percent under Title I, 16 percent under Title II, and 12.9 percent under Title VI. Through the third quarter of that fiscal year, Spanish-speaking participation in these three Titles was 13.7 percent, 8.5 percent, and 9.7 percent, respectively. Under pre-CETA categorical programs, Spanish-speaking participation was higher (no separate data are available on Puerto Ricans): 15 percent in fiscal year 1974.[124]

In an interview, Dr. Fred Romero indicated that CETA may well be serving greater numbers of Spanish Americans, but that their relative share of resources may be less than before. CETA data, according to Dr. Romero, may not be very accurate. The Department, he said, is trying to get a "better handle" on the problems of the Spanish speaking and that "they [DOL] know that they don't have good information" on the manpower needs of this group.[125]

A study of the impact of CETA revealed that less than 5 percent of the manpower services received by the Spanish speaking was for English as a Second Language (ESL).[126] Dr. Romero noted that the resources for the ESL program under CETA are "woefully inadequate." Funds for these services are given to the prime sponsors for use at their discretion, he said, but the Department does not know how such funds are being allocated.

Dr. Romero said that persons of Spanish origin generally believe that the resources for CETA are inadequate. But, for the most part, those not involved in the administration of CETA programs were more critical. CETA seems to be serving the Spanish speaking where they reside in large numbers, he said, but small Spanish-speaking communities appear to be ignored in some large cities.[127]

Data on the implementation of CETA are mixed. Some areas have been more successful than others in administering the programs. In Middlesex, New Jersey, Spanish-speaking members of the manpower advisory council thought that the planned number of their group to be served was too low for the area. Recently, a contract was negotiated with a Puerto Rican organization for prevocational training that would raise the number of enrollments.[128] In Newark, New Jersey, community pressure and commitments by elected officials have increased Hispanic (mainly Puerto Rican) participation on advisory councils and manpower planning staffs. Spanish-speaking staff of CETA subcontractors, however, are still underrepresented.[129]

Job Corps: Job Corps, a program aimed as assisting disadvantaged youth, continues under Title IV of CETA. A Job Corps director once observed that, "Many people believe the Job Corps is a second chance for Spanish speaking youth, but that's not true. It's a first chance. And the hardest thing about running this center is knowing that, for some, the chance may be coming too late."[130]

When Job Corps was initially set up, no programs were established for the Spanish speaking, many centers were ill-equipped to deal with persons of Spanish origin, and there were few Spanish-speaking staff. In 1971 only 7.5 percent of the staff (including those in Puerto Rico) spoke Spanish, while 11.7 percent of all Job Corps trainees were of Spanish origin.[131]

Between 1970 and 1972, however, there were some changes in Job Corps: four national centers were redirected to serve the Spanish speaking; three centers were set up in or near barrios, a program to serve Puerto Rican youth in New York City was established, and new guidelines for bilingual instruction and cultural awareness were developed.[132]

Currently, 60 Job Corps centers are in operation. According to statistics from ETA, there were 45,799 new Job Corps enrollees during fiscal year 1975. Spanish-speaking groups were 11.5 percent of the new enrollees; Puerto Ricans enrollees (412) were only 0.9 percent of the total.[133]

Given the need for such job training within the Puerto Rican communities and in light of the severe economic recession, Puerto Rican enrollment in the program would appear to be very low.

According to ETA, Job Corps has sought to be more responsive to new demands and has emphasized, in addition to other activities, "provision of increased opportunities for youth with limited English speaking ability."[134]

Under CETA, manpower services have been expanded to marginal areas where the Spanish speaking were never before represented, but for many in the inner city, opportunities in Job Corps may very well decrease and be unavailable to those most in need of job training.

Puerto Ricans and the United States Employment Service (USES): Established by the Wagner-Peyser Act of 1933,[135] the United States Employment Service (USES) has been the "operational centerpiece" of the Federal Government's job training system.[136] USES is federally-funded and part of the Employment and Training Administration. Its 2,400 local offices provide testing, counseling, referral to training, job development, job placement, and followup services.

The employment service has been criticized on the grounds that it is "employer oriented" and discriminatory. The Urban Coalition has charged that USES:

> ...mirrors the attitudes of employers in the community. The ES should provide a model of vigilance and aggressiveness toward affirmative action for equal employment opportunity. Instead, it is frequently a passive accessory to discriminatory employment practices; it is widely viewed in that light by the minority community.
>
> The staff of the state employment agencies are hired pursuant to state civil service laws, or in some states, according to state patronage systems. Repeatedly and consistently, evaluation of

the state agencies conducted by the Department of Labor has shown that the staffs do not include enough minorities, or a sufficient number of people experienced in dealing with the disadvantaged who can effectively carry out the "employability development" programs.[137]

According to a former Assistant Secretary of Labor:

> The Wagner-Peyser Act...assumes that the Employment Service must provide services to all, to whoever asks for them. Strictly interpreted, this could mean that there should not be a concentration of effort on the disadvantaged. In the sixties, particularly, we rejected that interpretation; nevertheless, it was, and remains, one of the reasons why it has been so difficult to redirect the effort of the Employment Service.[138]

In Boston as well the charge has been made that the employment service, in this case the Massachusetts State Department of Employment Security (DES), was "employeroriented when it should have been "employee-oriented." It did not, therefore, serve the disadvantaged. The city's job training director claimed that since DES funding is based upon the number of people it places, it prefers to work with the "cream" of the employed, and mainly aids veterans and the marginally employed.[139]

According to a Hispanic community organization leader in Boston, no Puerto Rican is in a decisionmaking position at the State department of employment service and there is no Puerto Rican employment counselor.[140]

Puerto Ricans complain that the USES has few Puerto Rican staff, even in cities of considerable Puerto Rican population. In New York and New Jersey, USES services for minority workers are a "crime," according to the regional job training director. He noted that the USES staff had grown by 25 percent in New York and 40 percent in New Jersey, but the increase included relatively few minority workers since the USES claimed that it could not find "qualified people."[141] In Chicago, the number of staff persons of Spanish origin has reportedly increased, but it is still small.[142]

Staff at New York's Puerto Rican Community Development Project (PRCDP) said that the employment service continually referred clients to their office because of insufficient Spanish-speaking staff.

PRCDP had only a few training programs, all of which operated without stipends for trainees. The ES, on the other hand, had access to the full range of job training programs. PRCDP was not authorized under existing legislation to certify their clients as being disadvantaged for the purpose of establishing eligibility for placement in NAB/JOBS contract training slots. Puerto Ricans must be certified either by the New York ES or by the city Manpower Career Development Agency (MCDA), coordinator of all city job training programs. Neither of those units were satisfactory to Puerto Ricans, who believed that MCDA deliberately excluded them.[143]

The program director of an Hispanic neighborhood employment center in Chicago complained that the Illinois State Employment Service "does not come here to look for people. No Federal or other organization comes to this office, [which is] visited by 4,500 Puerto Ricans in one month."[144]

Another serious aspect of this communication gap between the ES and the Hispanic neighborhood employment office is that the Chicago Civil Service Commission does not provide the ES with job announcements. The personnel director of the Chicago commission stated, "We don't expect minorities to come to us through the State Employment Service. Only a small percentage of people are placed through the ES."[145]

It was pointed out by job training officials that the lack of birth certificates, Social Security cards, or proper identification often hurts Puerto Rican job applicants. New York City is "credential happy," according to one official. "I don't care whether you can do the job. If you haven't got that piece of paper, they are going to hold it against you."[146]

For all of these reasons, Puerto Ricans appear to utilize employment service offices far less than would be expected, given their high unemployment rates and comparatively greater lack of skills. The Department of Labor has observed that "use of the State Employment Service by the Spanish-speaking was greater than their representation in the population, but less than their presence among the poor."[147] To many Puerto Ricans, the USES along with the Government's job training programs are simply examples of governmental neglect and exclusion of Puerto Ricans. The Lawyers' Committee for Civil Rights under Law concluded that:

> The experience of dealing with this insensitive [ES] bureaucracy in many States has generated mistrust, hostility, and discouragement among the disadvantaged and resulted in more individuals dropping out of the labor force, thereby contributing to the very problem the manpower programs were designed to solve.[148]

Notes

93. *Employment Profiles,* 1972, Table 32a, p. 178.

94. 1974 *Manpower Report of the President,* Table F-6, p. 363.

95. Chicago Alliance of Businessmen, Task Force on Latin American Manpower Development, *Public and Private Manpower and Educational Programs Serving Latin Americans in Chicago Cook County* (1973), pp. 6, 24.

96. Ibid., p. 28.

97. Henry Ramirez, "American's Spanish-Speaking: A Profile," *Manpower* magazine, September 1972, p. 34.

98. *New York Hearing,* p. 19.

99. Tom Corso, Human Resources Director, Office of Mayor, Bridgeport, Conn., telephone interview June 5, 1974.

100. Edward Gonzales, Puerto Rican Manpower and Leadership Training Center, Cornell University, interview in New York City, N.Y., Sept. 12, 1974 (hereafter cited as Gonzales Interview).

101. Cesar Rivera, Urban Progress Center, interview in Chicago, Ill., Sept. 17, 1974 (hereafter cited as Rivera Interview).

102. Herbert Bienstock, Regional Director, Bureau of Labor Statistics, New York, in *Employment Problems of the Puerto Ricans,* pp. 37, 61.

103. Cabinet Committee on Opportunities for Spanish-Speaking People, Task Force on Manpower, *Working Paper on Manpower Policies and Programs Affecting Spanish-Speaking Americans* (Feb. 23, 1971), p. 7 (hereafter cited as *Working Paper on Manpower Policies*).

104. *Problems of Low Income Groups,* p. 3.

105. Dr. Fred Romero, Special Assistant to the Undersecretary for Rural Affairs, Department of Labor, telephone interview with Commission staff, July 28, 1976 (hereafter cited as Romero Interview, July 28, 1976).

106. National Alliance of Businessmen/Job Opportunities in the Business Sectors (NAB/JOBS) linked the National Alliance of Businessmen with the Federal Government to

establish a program for the hardcore unemployed, giving them on-the-job training after they were hired but before they were put to work.

107.   Thompson, Lewin, and Associates, *Strengthening Manpower Programs for Spanish Speaking Americans,* Report of the Department of Labor Study Group on Manpower Needs of Spanish-Speaking Americans (Nov. 10, 1971), pp. 5 – 6.

108.   Ibid., p. 7.

109.   Lovell, *Manpower* magazine, September 1972, p. 6.

110.   Dr. Fred Romero, Regional Director, Department of Labor, telephone interview, Denver, Colo., Oct. 23, 1974 (hereafter cited as Romero Interview, Oct. 23, 1974). Dr. Romero is now Special Assistant to the Undersecretary for Rural Affairs in the Department of Labor.

111.   Romero, *The Spanish Speaking and CETA,* p. 21.

112.   See New Jersey Advisory Committee (SAC) to the U.S. Commission on Civil Rights, *Hispanic Participation in Manpower Programs in Newark, New Jersey* (July 1976) for an analysis of CETA programs in Newark.

113.   Cuiros Interview.

114.   Gonzales Interview.

115.   Romero Interview, Oct. 23, 1974.

116.   John A. Buggs, Staff Director, U.S. Commission on Civil Rights, letter to Pierce A. Quinlan, Acting Associate Manpower Administrator for the Office of Manpower Development Programs, Department of Labor, May 2, 1974.

117.   Under the formula 50 percent of funds provided are based on the previous year's fund allotment, 37 1/2 percent on the current number unemployed, and 12 1/2 percent on the number of low-income persons.

118.   Bernstein Interview.

119.   Duggan Interview.

120.   Ibid.

121.   Erazo Interview.

122.   Nicholas Avitabile, Action for Boston Community Development (ABCD), interview Sept. 19, 1974.

123.   National Academy of Sciences, National Research Council, *The Comprehensive Employment and Training Act: Impact on People, Places, and Projects, An Interim Report* (Washington, D.C., 1976), pp. 130, 138 – 9. A staff report prepared under a grant from the Ford Foundation.

124.   U.S., Department of Labor, Employment and Training Administration, *Employment and Training Report of the President* (1976), p. 100 (hereafter cited as 1976 *Employment and Training Report).* See also *Continuous Longitudinal Manpower Survey, Report No. 1, Characteristics of CETA Participants Enrolled During Third Quarter of FY 1975* (January 1976), pp. 3–23 – 3–25. Report MEL 76–02, Contract No. 23–24–75–07, prepared for the Employment and Training Administration by Westat, Inc., Rockville, Md.

125.   Romero Interview, July 28, 1976.

126.   SER/Jobs for Progress Inc., *The Impact of the First Year Implementation of CETA on the Spanish Speaking* (November 1975). Results of a survey conducted by Services, Employment, Redevelopment (SER), a self-help organization for the Spanish speaking, under a grant from the Ford Foundation. Although this report deals mainly with Mexican Americans, the data and findings are useful in assessing CETA and Hispanic participation in the programs in general.

127.   Romero Interview, July 28, 1976.

128.   National Academy of Sciences, National Research Council, *Transition to Decentralized Manpower Programs, Eight Area Studies, An Interim Report* (Washington, D.C., 1976), p. 39.

129.   See the New Jersey SAC report on Hispanic participation in Newark, N.J., manpower programs.

130.   El Paso Center Director, David Carrasco, as quoted in "The Job Corps Learns Spanish," *Manpower* magazine, September 1972, p. 14.

131.   Ibid., p. 7.

132.   Ibid.

133.   1976 *Employment and Training Report*, p. 109.

134.   Ibid.

135.   29 U.S.C. §§ 49 *et seq.* (1970).

136.   The USES is a component of the Bureau of Employment Security (BES), part of the Labor Department's Employment and Training Administration.

137.   Lawyer's Committee for Civil Rights Under Law and the National Urban Coalition, *Falling Down on the Job: The United States Employment Service and the Disadvantaged* (June 1971), p. 127 (hereafter cited as *Falling Down on the Job*).

138.   Ruttenberg, *Manpower Challenge of the 1970's*, pp. 44 – 45.

139.   Duggan Interview.

140.   Carmen Pola, Cardinal Cushing Center for the Spanish-Speaking, interview in Boston, Mass., Sept. 20, 1974.

141.   Aponte Interview.

142.   Miriam Cruz, Special Assistant, Office of the Mayor, interview, Chicago, Ill., Sept. 17, 1974.

143.   Petra Arroyo, Acting Manpower Director, PRCDP, interview in New York City, N.Y., Sept. 13, 1974.

144.   Rivera Interview.

145.   Dr. Charles A. Pounion, Personnel Director, Civil Service Commission, interview in Chicago, Ill., Sept. 17, 1974.

146.   Gomez in *Employment Problems of Puerto Ricans*, p. 87.

147.   *Manpower* magazine, September 1972, p. 35.

148.   *Falling Down on the Job*, p. 133.

The Crisis in Education

Data in the previous chapter showed that mainland Puerto Ricans have lower incomes than whites, blacks, and other Hispanic minorities in the United States. The same relationship is evident in terms of education. The typical white American adult has graduated from high school and has had a taste of college; the typical black has completed 9.8 years of school; and the typical mainland Puerto Rican has completed only 8.7 years.[1]

Recent census figures (1975) also show clear differences in education among major Hispanic groups (Puerto Ricans, Mexican Americans, and Cubans), with Puerto Ricans generally at the lowest rung of the ladder. There is a sharp difference, for example, between the educational picture for Cubans and Puerto Ricans. As for Mexican Americans, while they are less likely than Puerto Ricans to have completed 5 years of school, they are more likely to have graduated from high school. In the younger age brackets (25 to 29 years) Puerto Ricans have made notable progress in education, but still lag behind other groups. (See Tables 27 and 28.)

SCHOOL ENROLLMENT AND DROPOUT RATES

Between 1960 and 1970 the dropout rate for school-age Puerto Ricans fell, particularly for young adults. But a severe dropout problem persists.

During the elementary school years (age 5 to 13), the staying power of Puerto Rican children is quite comparable to the national average: 72 percent of all youngsters age 5 to 6, and 97 percent of those age 7 to 13, are enrolled in school.

The dropout problem becomes evident in the age 14 to 17 group. Nationwide, 93 percent of all youngsters in this age group remain in school, compared with 85 percent of Puerto Rican youngsters.

The difference grows more acute in the age 18 to 24 group. Nationwide, while 37 percent of young males remain in school, only 18 percent of the Puerto Rican males are still enrolled (the figures are comparable for women). In other words, young adult Puerto Ricans are only half as likely to be in school as their peers. (See Table 29.)

Table 27

Percent of Persons (25 Years Old and Over) Who Have Completed Less Than 5 Years of School

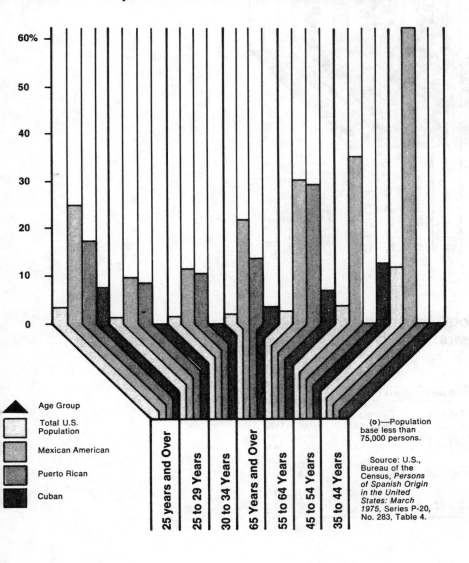

Age Group
Total U.S. Population
Mexican American
Puerto Rican
Cuban

25 years and Over
25 to 29 Years
30 to 34 Years
65 Years and Over
55 to 64 Years
45 to 54 Years
35 to 44 Years

(o)—Population base less than 75,000 persons.

Source: U.S., Bureau of the Census, *Persons of Spanish Origin in the United States: March 1975*, Series P-20, No. 283, Table 4.

Table 28

Percent of Persons (25 Years Old and Over) Who Have Completed 4 Years of High School or More, March 1975

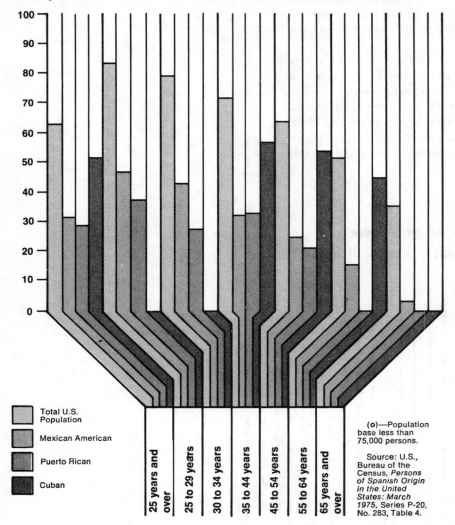

Total U.S. Population

Mexican American

Puerto Rican

Cuban

25 years and over

25 to 29 years

30 to 34 years

35 to 44 years

45 to 54 years

55 to 64 years

65 years and over

(o)—Population base less than 75,000 persons.

Source: U.S., Bureau of the Census, *Persons of Spanish Origin in the United States: March 1975*, Series P-20, No. 283, Table 4.

Table 29

School Enrollment of the Total U.S. and Puerto Rican Populations Age 5 to 34 Years: United States— 1960 and 1970

(by percent)

| | | | Puerto Rican Residents of the U.S. | | | | | |
| | Total in U.S. | | Total | | Born in Puerto Rico | | Born in U.S. | |
Age	1960	1970	1960	1970	1960	1970	1960	1970
5 and 6 years old	63.8	72.4	66.4	72.4	64.7	67.5	67.0	73.7
7 to 13 years old	97.5	97.3	94.9	94.9	94.2	93.2	95.7	95.6
14 to 17 years old:								
Male	87.8	93.2	75.8	85.5	73.7	78.5	83.5	90.7
Female	87.1	92.7	72.5	83.7	69.5	75.8	84.9	90.0
18 to 24 years old:								
Male	27.8	37.5	10.9	18.4	9.5	13.3	21.4	32.6
Female	18.4	27.2	8.4	14.3	7.6	10.3	13.6	26.3
25 to 34 years old	4.6	6.3	3.3	2.5	3.1	1.9	5.5	6.8

Source: 1960 Census, *Puerto Ricans in the United States;* 1970 Census, *Puerto Ricans in the United States.*

In a study conducted in Chicago, the dropout rate for Puerto Ricans in grammar and high school was 71.2 percent. The study indicated that 12.5 percent dropped out in grammar school, while 58.7 percent dropped out in high school.[2]

Students drop out of school for a variety of reasons. While some drop out because they cannot keep up academically, this is by no means the sole reason. Of the 30 percent of U.S. high school students who drop out each year, one-third are in their senior year and have already completed most of the required courses. Most dropouts are bored, find the school unresponsive to their cultural backgrounds, or feel compelled to obtain a job.[3]

By examining several aspects of the Puerto Rican youngster's experience in school, the multiple reasons for dropping out become clear.

LANGUAGE AND CULTURE

More than 30 percent of the 437,000 Puerto Rican students enrolled in mainland schools are born in Puerto Rico. Each year thousands of children transfer from schools in Puerto Rico to those on the mainland. (See Table 30 for student transfers between Puerto Rico and New York City.) Spanish is the mother tongue of a major segment of the Puerto Rican school-age population (and is the language used most often in the home, even for those students born on the mainland).

In New York City in 1970, of 362,000 Puerto Ricans under age 18, nearly one-fourth (80,370) had been born in Puerto Rico. About one-fourth (nearly 80,000) of the Puerto Rican and other Hispanic students in New York City's public schools speak poor or hesitant English.[4] Birthplace is, obviously, a major determinant of ability to speak English.

It is also clear that birthplace, language ability, and dropping out are closely intertwined. Great disparities exist in the dropout rates of island-born and U.S.-born Puerto Rican youngsters. Those born on the mainland tend to enroll earlier in school and tend to drop out less frequently.

About 47 percent of all mainland Puerto Ricans age 3 to 34 are enrolled in school. But this overall average is misleading: 67 percent of the mainland-born Puerto Ricans in that age group are enrolled, compared with only 28 percent of those born in Puerto Rico. The disparity is very pronounced in the age 18 to 24 group. Among males of this age group, for example, 33 percent of the U.S.-born were still in school, compared with only 13 percent of the island-born. Among males age 16 to 21, about 12,000 of the U.S.-born are not enrolled in school, compared with 32,000 island-born youngsters. (See Table 31.)

These figures indicate that the dropout rate is more severe among Puerto Rican youngsters born on the island than among those youngsters of Puerto Rican parentage born on the mainland. Island-born youngsters are more likely to have problems communicating in English, more likely to be unemployed or underemployed, and more likely to be doomed to a life of poverty.

While the education problems of mainland Puerto Ricans are certainly not limited to the island-born, this group is more adversely affected by inadequate schooling. Language is often the key factor that makes them different from other Puerto Rican students, many of whom may sit in the same classroom, or may even be siblings. The fact that these language-handicapped students achieve less and drop out more is compelling evidence that the schools' response to the problem has been inadequate.

One Puerto Rican parent expressed his dismay at the lack of special instruction for his children:

...They are practically wasting their time because they are not learning anything. First of all, they don't understand the language. What good does it do to sit there in front of the teacher and just look at her face? It is wasting their time. They don't learn anything because they don't understand what she is saying.[5]

ACHIEVEMENT LEVELS

In a sample taken by the New York City Board of Education, schools with heavy Puerto Rican enrollment had much lower reading averages than predominantly black or white schools. At every level sampled, Puerto Rican students were behind the other two groups in reading.[6]

In 1972 two-thirds of the elementary schools in New York City that contained 85 percent or more students reading below grade level had a student population which was more than 50 percent Puerto Rican.[7]

In Chicago, 1970 – 71 test scores in reading and mathematics indicated a much lower achievement rate for Puerto Rican students than the citywide median. The lag increased with each succeeding grade.[8]

TESTING

The use of standardized achievement tests contributes to the failure of public schools to teach Puerto Rican students. IQ and achievement test scores often are used as guides in assigning students to ability groups and to classes for the educable mentally retarded (EMR).

Since most tests are given in English, many children are programmed for failure. In Philadelphia, a school official acknowledged that psychological tests are often given only in English and that they form the basis for assessing the mental and emotional states of Puerto Rican students.[9]

Commenting on this point, a Philadelphia psychologist said:

In my clinic, the average underestimation of IQ for a Puerto Rican kid is 20 points. We go through this again and again. When we test in Spanish, there's a 20 point leap immediately—20 points higher than when he's tested in English.[10]

Table 31

School Enrollment of Mainland Puerto Ricans, by Birthplace, 1970

	Mainland Puerto Ricans	Born in Puerto Rico	Born in U.S. Mainland
Total enrolled, age 3-34	437,863	134,501	303,362
Nursery School	5,439	928	4,511
Kindergarten	29,112	5,747	23,365
Elementary (Grades 1-8)	294,785	81,006	213,779
High School (Grades 9-12)	90,822	37,279	53,543
College	17,705	9,541	8,164
Percent enrolled, age 3-34	46.8	27.7	67.4
3 and 4 yrs. old	10.6	11.4	10.4
5 and 6 yrs. old	72.4	67.5	73.7
7 to 13 yrs. old	94.9	93.2	95.6
14 to 17 yrs. old:			
Male	85.5	78.5	90.7
Female	83.7	75.8	90.0
18 to 24 yrs. old:			
Male	18.4	13.3	32.6
Female	14.3	10.3	26.3
25 to 34 yrs. old	2.5	1.9	6.8
Male 16 to 21 yrs. old	81,056	49,387	31,669

Source: U. S., Bureau of the Census, *Puerto Ricans in the United States*, PC(2)-1E, June 1973, Table 4.

Table 30

Transfers of Public School Students Between Puerto Rico and New York City

School Year	Came from Puerto Rico	Moved to Puerto Rico	Net Migration to New York[1]
1954-55	9,496	3,662	5,834
1955-56	11,727	3,934	7,793
1956-57	12,905	5,020	7,885
1957-58	11,505	5,557	5,948
1958-59	10,737	6,491	4,246
1959-60	10,315	7,806	2,509
1960-61	9,414	7,688	1,726
1961-62	8,777	8,428	349
1962-63	7,942	8,508	−566
1963-64	8,245	7,849	396
1964-65	8,496	8,179	317
1965-66	9,232	7,986	1,246
1966-67	11,191	8,193	2,998
1967-68	13,706	8,696	5,010
1968-69	14,840	10,095	4,745
1969-70	12,586	12,254	332
1970-71	11,466	12,752	−1,286
1971-72	8,482	14,079	−5,597
1972-73	8,445	13,434	−4,989
1973-74	9,892	10,771	−879
10-year totals,			
1954-1963	101,063	64,943	36,120
1964-73	108,336	106,439	1,897
5-year totals,			
1969-1973	50,871	63,290	−12,419

[1] A minus sign (−) denotes net return migration from New York City to Puerto Rico.

Source: Joyce Garnes, Bureau of Attendance, New York City Board of Education, memorandum dated Oct. 6, 1975.

Some school systems have attempted to overcome the language gap by translating standard IQ tests into Spanish, but these tests are often designed for Mexican American children. (Although Spanish is common to both Mexico and Puerto Rico, there are many colloquialisms peculiar to each area.) A few school systems have experimented with tests developed in Puerto Rico, but testing continues to be a major linguistic and cultural barrier for many Puerto Rican students.

STUDENT ASSIGNMENT PRACTICES

School systems frequently place underachieving students in low-ability groups, or in classes for the educable mentally retarded, or retain them in grade. Recent arrivals from Puerto Rico are often assigned to lower grades. The rationale for such practices is that students will benefit from special instruction in low-level classes, but the correlation between such placement and improved academic performance is dubious. In fact, the lower level of curriculum and the absence of stimulation from higher-achieving students may be negative factors that further retard the student.[11] If anything, the stigma attached to being labeled a "slow learner" can result in a loss of self-esteem and reinforce the student's sense of failure.[12] Rather than progress out of EMR classes or low-ability groups, students tend to remain there, be assigned vocational (rather than college-bound) curricula, or drop out altogether.[13]

A former president of the New York City Board of Education has testified:

Historically, in New York City we have had two school systems, one school system for those youngsters who are expected to achieve, and one for the youngsters who were not expected to achieve, and don't achieve. And most of the minority group youngsters are in that second school system, and the system is pretty much set up to see to it that they don't succeed. And I think that's why they drop out of schools.[14]

The Office for Civil Rights (OCR) of the U.S. Department of Health, Education, and Welfare (HEW) has investigated ability-grouping practices in several school districts that have large Puerto Rican student populations. In East Chicago, Indiana, for example, these practices resulted in racially identifiable "tracks": students appeared to be assigned arbitrarily to a group with no apparent pedagogical justification. The school district was required by HEW to develop new assignment policies.[15] The Philadelphia school system has reported that its practice of using achievement tests as the basis for placing students in "tracking systems" has resulted in a disproportionate number of black and Puerto Rican students in low ability groups.[16]

Placement in educable mentally retarded classes is also largely determined by a child's score on a standardized IQ test given in English or upon subjective teacher evaluation. In New York City, almost 30 percent of the students in special classes for children with retarded mental development have Hispanic backgrounds. It has been suggested that faulty analysis of test results (by psychologists who do not speak the same language as the children) is responsible.[17]

The Office for Civil Rights has documented that the school district in Perth Amboy, New Jersey, assigned language-minority students to EMR classes on the basis of criteria that essentially measured English language skills, even though it appeared that the majority of the Hispanic students had difficulty with the English language. OCR also found that some regular classroom teachers were more inclined to refer Puerto Rican children to the department of special services for EMR placement than Anglo children "because they do not know how to deal with the behavioral problems of these children."[18]

The New York State Commissioner of Education has reported that non-English-speaking children are sometimes placed in classes for slow learners or EMR classes without sufficient justification. Some students were judged to be mentally retarded because they were quiet in class.[19]

These types of practices result in a high number of "over-age" Puerto Rican students in the schools. In New England, it has been reported that 25 percent of the Hispanic children have been held back at least three grades in school and that 50 percent have been held back at least two grades. Only 12 percent were found to be in the correct grade for their age group.[20] A field survey in Boston found that nearly 75 percent of the Hispanic high school students were in classes behind students of their own age.[21]

The problem is particularly acute among transfer students from Puerto Rico. A witness at the Massachusetts Advisory Committee's open meeting testified:

> They came from Puerto Rico, they're in the 10th, 11th, or senior year of high school, and they're 17, 18, 19 years old.... They came to Boston and they placed them in the 6th and 7th grades. You're wondering why they dropped out. A person who does not feel his identity is lost right there.... Here's a kid trying to learn and he automatically gets an inferiority complex and quits.[22]

PROGRAMS FOR LANGUAGE-MINORITY CHILDREN

During the 1960s two types of approaches emerged to overcome the linguistic barriers of language-minority children.[23] One approach, English as a Second Language (ESL), teaches students to communicate in English as quickly as possible. The programs provide instruction and practice in listening, speaking, reading, and writing English. Students are taken from their regular classrooms for 30 to 40 minutes per day for this special help, but otherwise remain in their regular classes for content matter instruction.

By themselves, ESL programs are very limited since they use only English to teach literacy and communication rather than the student's native language to transmit concepts and skills (which might facilitate the learning of English). ESL students inevitably fall behind in the regular classroom, where content courses are being taught.[24]

The second approach, slowly growing in acceptance, is bilingual-bicultural education. A program of bilingual education is:

> (4)(A)...a program of instruction, designed for children of limited English-speaking ability in elementary or secondary schools, in which, with respect to the years of study to which such program is applicable—
>
> (i)there is instruction given in, and study of, English and, to the extent necessary to allow a child to progress through the educational system, the native language of the children of limited English-speaking ability, and such instruction is given with appreciation for the cultural heritage of such children, and with respect to elementary school instruction, such instruction shall, to the extent necessary, be in all courses or subjects of study which will allow a child to progress effectively through the educational system....[25]

This attempt at a total approach includes the teaching of English as a second language, development of literacy in the mother tongue, and the uninterrupted learning of subject areas. It is based on the principle that learning should continue in the mother tongue rather than be postponed until a new language has been acquired. Teaching a child to read first in the language that he or she speaks makes it easier to read and write in a second language, since the basic skills are transferable from one language to another. The inclusion of curriculum materials on the student's culture and background experience also heightens interest in the subject matter.[26]

Hernan LaFontaine, a Puerto Rican educator and the executive administrator of the Office of Bilingual Education for the New York City Board of Education, has noted:

> Our definition of cultural pluralism must include the concept that our language and our culture will be given equal status to that of the majority population. It is not enough simply to say that we should be given the opportunity to share in the positive benefits of modern American life. Instead, we must insist that this sharing will not be accomplished at the sacrifice of all those traits which make us what we are as Puerto Ricans.[27]

PERSONNEL

School personnel have profound influence over the success or failure of students. Not only do they make decisions to promote or retain students in school programs, but also their attitudes and expectations often are reflected in student performance.[28] When they perceive low expectations on the part of teachers, for example, students tend to do less well on tests.[29]

In its investigation into Mexican American education, the Commission found that Anglo teachers tended to favor Anglo children over Mexican Americans in their praise, encouragement, attention, and approval. Predictably, it was also found that Mexican American students participated in class less than Anglo students.[30] No similar study of Puerto Rican students has been carried out, but it is reasonable to assume that the results would be the same.

The impact that teachers and administrators have on the learning environment for students underscores the need for school personnel who reflect the background of students and thus are more likely to relate positively to them. As the Educational Policies Commission noted:

> Despite their better judgment, people of another background often feel that disadvantaged children are by nature perverse, vulgar, or lazy. Children sense quickly the attitudes of school people toward them, and they retaliate against condescension or intolerance with hostility, absenteeism, and failure.[31]

The Office for Civil Rights recognized the influence of school personnel on equal educational opportunities in its memorandum of January 1971, "Nondiscrimination in Elementary and Secondary School Staff Practices." School superintendents were informed that discrimination in hiring, promotion, demotion, dismissal, or other treatment of faculty or staff serving students had a direct adverse effect on equal educational services for students and was therefore prohibited by Title VI of the Civil Rights Act of 1964. Since that year, OCR has required school districts to submit affirmative action plans in cases where minority faculty is underrepresented.

Despite the importance of having Puerto Rican teachers and administrators in districts with large numbers of Puerto Rican students, none of the districts surveyed by the Commission had an adequate representation.[32] Few school systems gather data on the number of Puerto Rican students and teachers, nor is such data now required by the Federal Government. The data that are collected usually refer to "Spanish surnamed" students or teachers, which includes other Hispanic Americans. Table 32 reflects the percentage of students and teachers of Spanish origin in several cities with large concentrations of Puerto Ricans.

New York City has the single largest concentration of Puerto Rican students in its public schools. In fiscal year 1974, nearly 300,000 Hispanic children were enrolled in the public schools, including 256,000 Puerto Rican students. Hispanics accounted for 27.0 percent of total school enrollment (23.1 percent Puerto Rican and 3.9 percent other Hispanic).

Table 32

Spanish-Surnamed Students and Teachers in Selected Cities: 1972

City	% Spanish-Surnamed Students	% Spanish-Surnamed Teachers
New York	26.6	2.2
Philadelphia	3.4	0.0
Bridgeport	21.2	1.9
Hartford	21.5	3.7
New Haven	9.8	1.6
Boston	5.3	0.7
Springfield	7.7	1.3
Camden	16.8	1.8
Elizabeth	19.9	3.9
Hoboken	56.8	3.3
Passaic	31.5	1.4
Paterson	22.1	2.1
Perth Amboy	49.2	4.6
Union City	64.6	7.1
Rochester	5.6	1.4
Chicago	11.1	1.2

Source: U.S., Department of Health, Education, and Welfare, Office for Civil Rights, *Directory of Public Elementary and Secondary Schools in Selected Districts: Enrollment and Staff by Racial/Ethnic Group*, Fall 1972.

(See Table 33.) Despite the fact that more than one-fourth of the student body was Hispanic, only 2.5 percent of the total number of school teachers were of Spanish origin. Only 1,391 of the 56,168 teachers in New York City had Spanish surnames. This figure is considerably larger than the 0.8 percent share 5 years previous, but the disparity between the percentage of teachers and students remained enormous (see Table 34).[33]

One study has estimated that at least 13,700 more teachers of Spanish origin would need to be hired to approach equitable representation in the New York City public schools. This would be nearly 10 times the number in 1973.[34]

The situation is no better in other major cities where Puerto Ricans live. In Chicago (1972), there were 27,946 Puerto Rican students, but only 91 Puerto Rican teachers in the entire system. Of 1,706 administrative and supervisory personnel, only 17 were Puerto Rican. No statistics were available for the number of Puerto Rican counselors.[35]

Table 33

Puerto Ricans and Other Spanish-Surnamed-Students in New York City Public Schools: 1973-74

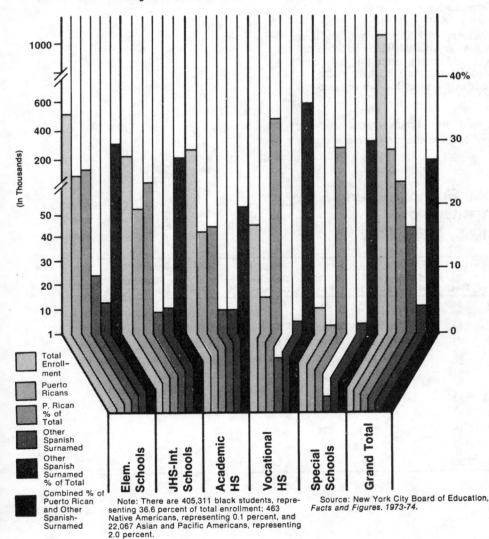

Total Enrollment

Puerto Ricans

P. Rican % of Total

Other Spanish Surnamed

Other Spanish Surnamed % of Total

Combined % of Puerto Rican and Other Spanish-Surnamed

Elem. Schools

JHS-Int. Schools

Academic HS

Vocational HS

Special Schools

Grand Total

Note: There are 405,311 black students, representing 36.6 percent of total enrollment; 463 Native Americans, representing 0.1 percent, and 22,067 Asian and Pacific Americans, representing 2.0 percent.

Source: New York City Board of Education, *Facts and Figures, 1973-74.*

In Boston (1972), only 5 of the city's 4,729 teachers were Puerto Rican, and not one guidance counselor could speak Spanish. In Springfield, Massachusetts, there were only 5 Puerto Rican and 5 other Hispanic teachers for 1,485 Puerto Rican students.[36] In Philadelphia, less than 1 percent of the teachers were Puerto Rican; only 2 of 532 guidance counselors were Puerto Rican, about 1 for every 4,750 Puerto Rican students.[37] In Bridgeport, Connecticut (1971), the board of education employed only 10 Puerto Rican teachers for nearly 4,000 Puerto Rican students. None of the 23 full-time counselors was Puerto Rican. A plan to recruit more teachers of Spanish origin was vetoed by the school board.[38]

COUNSELING

Many Puerto Rican students perceive their non-Hispanic teachers and counselors as indifferent or insensitive. One student in Connecticut testified:

> I feel that the teachers don't care about the students....A Spanish-speaking student comes into the room, immediately that person is considered dumb without even being given a chance.[39]

A Puerto Rican student in Camden, New Jersey, echoed the belief that counselors are insensitive to Puerto Rican students:

> The attitude that a lot of counselors had with a lot of friends of mine, because a lot of the individuals that graduated with me from high school are now shooting drugs and doing time in jail [is] to generalize and tell me that my people are dumb, that we make good dishwashers. We can't manipulate our minds, but we're good with our hands, and we are docile....[40]

Another Puerto Rican student told the Pennsylvania Advisory Committee of her efforts to be admitted to an academic course and of the

Table 34

Staff of New York City Public School System, Including number and percentage of Spanish-Surnamed Staff, 1968, 1972, 1973

Job Category	Total	Fall 1968 Spanish Surnamed	%	Total	Fall 1972 Spanish Surnamed	%	Total	Fall 1973 Spanish Surnamed	%	Total	Fall 1974 Spanish Surnamed	%
Principals	893	1	0.1	940	20	2.1	962	31	3.2	981	39	4.0
Assistant principals	1,841	6	.3	2,600	40	1.5	2,645	38	1.4	2,705	48	1.8
Teachers	54,908	522	1.0	55,242	1,158	2.1	56,168	1,391	2.5	55,415	170	3.1
Other professional staff	6,080	156	2.6	–	–	–	–	–	–	–	–	–
Other instructional staff	–	–	–	4,110	220	5.4	4,038	232	5.7	4,120	227	5.5
Full-time Clerical office staff	–	–	–	3,465	165	4.8	898	26	2.9	–	–	–
Part-time professional staff	–	–	–	2,217	37	1.7	2,371	46	1.9	–	–	–

Note: In spring 1975 the New York City Board of Education began laying off thousands of teachers and other staff. Statistical information reflecting the current situation in New York City is not yet available.

Source: New York City Board of Education, Division of Teacher Personnel.

repeated warnings of guidance counselors that "I should not aim too high because I would probably be disappointed at the end result."[41]

Few Puerto Rican students are encouraged by high school counselors or teachers to think about college. The president of Hostos Community College in Bronx, New York, cited several instances in which counselors told Puerto Rican high school students that they were not "college material." One girl, who, according to this official, eventually completed her junior and senior years in 1 year at Queens College, allegedly had been removed from a college preparatory curriculum in high school and put into a secretarial course.[42] A counselor at Temple University (Philadelphia) said, "A lot of Puerto Rican kids don't think of college. They're not exposed to the right counselors in high school. They're in the wrong programs: most are in nonacademic courses."[43]

PARENT AND COMMUNITY INVOLVEMENT

Families exercise great influence on student attitudes toward education. By working in concert with parents, schools maximize chances that students will effectively participate in public education.[44]

In their open meetings, the Commission's State Advisory Committees heard testimony that Puerto Rican parents and community leaders were frequently excluded from participation in school matters. In Massachusetts, it was found that "poor communication, if any, exists between the local school districts and the Puerto Rican community."[45] A major reason was difficulty with the English language. Often, parents could not communicate with authorities because of this language barrier; school notices generally were in English.

In Illinois, a parent representative on a Title I advisory council said that meetings were sometimes imcomprehensible to her. The council's agenda and related information were always prepared in English.[46]

In Bridgeport, Connecticut, 89 percent of the Puerto Rican parents surveyed said that they had difficulty in communicating in English, but only 20 percent received written notices in Spanish.[47]

Puerto Rican parents have been frustrated in attempts to join councils and organizations representing the school community. They often do not participate in PTA organizations, whose meetings are conducted in English.[48] Community involvement in advisory councils to Federal programs, such as those under Titles I and VII of the Elementary and Secondary Education Act, has also been limited, despite the requirement that communities be involved in decisionmaking. Although Puerto Ricans were about 5 percent of the student enrollment in Boston, the Title I advisory council of 66 members and 42 alternates had no Puerto Rican representatives.[49]

In Chicago, most of the six Hispanic members of the citywide advisory council were employees of the school system. This would appear to create some difficulty over their ability to function as impartial advisers to school programs.[50]

DECENTRALIZATION

Because advisory groups have been unable to influence unresponsive school districts, Puerto Rican and other minority communities have in recent years demanded decentralization and community control of schools which serve their children. For Puerto Ricans, this demand has been most vehement in New York City.

In the wake of the 1968 teachers' strike in New York City, the State passed a decentralization law.[51] It established the central board of education; created the position of chancellor to replace the superintendent of schools; and established a system of 32 elected community school boards. Decisionmaking was split between the central board and the community boards, with the central board retaining much of the final authority.[52]

Community boards are comprised of, and elected by, parents who have resided in the district 1 year, are U.S. citizens, over 21 years of age, and are registered voters. Within their attendance zones, the boards have jurisdiction over elementary through eighth grade education. They appoint a community superintendent; oversee instruction of students;[53] assign, promote, and dismiss principals and teachers; prepare operating budgets; and apply for State and Federal grants.[54]

The central board determines district boundaries and conducts elections of local school board members. All high schools and special schools are centrally controlled.

The central board, the chancellor, and the board of examiners[55] have residual powers over the local districts as follows: First, local boards are limited in that personnel decisions and policies may not conflict with any collective bargaining agreement; such agreements are negotiated by the central board. Second, teachers and supervisors are selected (under a civil service system) from among those passing competitive or qualifying examinations administered by the board of examiners. Third, the central board determines minimum educational and experience requirements for teachers and supervisory personnel.[56] And, fourth, regulations concerning staff dismissals and cutbacks due to budget reductions and declining enrollments continue to be promulgated by the central board.

Decentralization is intended to open the way to greater parental involvement in operating the schools. But in New York City problems remain unsolved. For example, the central board is responsible for supplying technical aid to community boards in the preparation of project proposals to the Federal and New York State governments, but the board has been lax in this duty.[57] Problems are most acute in the design of proposals for Title I and State urban education financing and in applications for education projects under other Federal programs. In 1972, for example, community boards were given only 2 days notice to submit Title I proposals. Title VII proposals were prepared by local boards without any consultation with staff of the central board.

The benefits to date of decentralization appear mixed as far as Puerto Ricans are concerned. Recent modest increases in Puerto Rican teachers and administrators in New York City may be partially due to decentralization, but parental involvement in important school decisions remains limited.

THE GOVERNMENT'S ROLE IN THE EDUCATION OF PUERTO RICAN PUBLIC SCHOOL STUDENTS

The Federal Government has traditionally provided leadership to equalize educational opportunity for students from minority groups. Federal attention was first focused on the issue of school desegregation when several States and local school boards resisted implementation of desegregation laws. The Federal role was later extended to meet the special needs of language-minority students and to enforce laws that provide them with equal access to education.

State governments have also increasingly concerned themselves with development of special programs for disadvantaged and language-minority students.

Federal Special Aid Programs: The Elementary and Secondary Education Act (ESEA) of 1965 was the first comprehensive legislation designed to support programs for low-income students with special educational needs.[58] The act contains eight titles, three of which—Titles I, VII, and VIII—can fund programs for language-minority students.

Title I provides the bulk of ESEA funding. In fiscal year 1974, school districts received $1.6 billion to support compensatory education for low-income students. Funds are disbursed to States according to the numbers of low-income students and may be utilized for a variety of purposes, including early childhood education, reading, mathematics, ESL, and bilingual programs.

Title I has enormous potential for meeting the needs of language-minority students. In fiscal year 1971, Congress appropriated $1.8 billion under Title I, of which New York State received $192 million. Although about 23 percent of New York City's students were Puerto Rican, only $4 million (3.2 percent) of the $125 million allocated to the city went to Title I programs serving them. A total of $673,213 was spent on bilingual programs. In 1972 funding for bilingual programs increased to more than $3 million, while $503,322 was allocated for ESL programs. Approximately 14,400 students benefited from Title I language programs, the majority of whom were Hispanic.

Title I funds were also utilized to recruit and train teachers of Spanish origin. The program recruits native Spanish-speaking graduate and undergraduate students and trains them for teaching in New York schools. Nearly half of the Puerto Rican teachers now in the public school system are products of the program. Title I funds also help underwrite programs to motivate pupils who have dropped out of school.[59]

Title VII, also known as the Bilingual Education Act, funds demonstration projects to meet the special needs of low-income children who speak limited English.[60] Unlike Title I, the program could not meet the needs of all or even most needy children because of its limited funding. In fiscal year 1971, for example, proposals for Title VII funds submitted by local districts in New York City alone totaled $70 million, yet the appropriation of funds for the entire nation was only $25 million. New York State received slightly more than $1 million.[61]

Most of the projects funded by the U.S. Office of Education served Mexican American children in California and Texas. In 1971 New York received $1.2 million, California received $17.3 million, and Texas received $12.5 million.[62]

Increased Federal funding is needed for curriculum development, nationwide teacher training programs, and research into evaluation measures for bilingual education.[63] A combination of these activities and techniques, along with experience gained in demonstration programs, could increase the nation's capacity to provide quality education for all children.

Title VIII provides funds to local educational agencies for developing school dropout prevention programs. Since language difficulties are a major cause of dropouts among Puerto Ricans, Title VIII can be used to support language programs. Like Title VII, Title VIII projects are designed for demonstration purposes and support must later be assumed by the local school district. Schools qualifying for Title VIII aid may be located in urban or rural areas, must have a high percentage of low-income children, and must have a high proportion (35 percent or more) of children who do not complete their elementary or secondary education.

Funding for Title VIII has never exceeded $10 million nationwide, and thus has had little impact on the dropout problem among Puerto Ricans. Only 19 school districts had received Title VIII grants by 1972. In New York State, where the majority of mainland Puerto Ricans live, only one district, Fredonia, had received a Title VII grant.[64]

Since 1972 funds have been available for bilingual education under the Emergency School Aid Act (ESAA), a program designed to help school districts in implementing desegregation plans. In addition to a fiscal year 1974 appropriation of more than $236 million, ESAA provides $9 million as a set-aside for bilingual education programs; 47 programs have been so funded. Most were in Texas. New York received the second largest amount of bilingual set-aside funds.[65]

State Governments: School districts receive most of their financial support from their State governments. State agencies set academic standards and credential requirements, and influence policy and practice at all levels in local districts. States have fought to protect their jurisdiction over local education and therefore have major responsibility for ensuring equal educational opportunity for language-minority students. Several States have passed legislation, authorized funds, or issued policy regulations that address the needs of language-minority students.

In Massachusetts the 1971 Transitional Bilingual Education Act has involved the State and local school districts in a comprehensive program. The bill mandates that transitional bilingual education programs be implemented in each district with 20 or more children of limited English-speaking ability in one language classification.[66] It provides for supplemental financial aid to help school districts meet the extra costs of such programs.[67]

In Illinois bilingual education is supported almost exclusively by State funds. State funds for bilingual education in the 1972 – 73 school year totaled approximately $2.4 million. Public Law 78 – 727, which became effective in September 1973, mandates bilingual education by July 1, 1976, in attendance zones having 20 or more students whose first language is other than English.[68] However, Illinois school districts are making little progress to prepare for bilingual education. Efforts to recruit bilingual personnel still have not been fully undertaken. The Chicago board of education has no affirmative action plan with goals and timetables for hiring Hispanic teachers.[69]

In New Jersey, an office for Hispanic affairs in the division of curriculum and instruction at the State department of education assists in allocating State resources more effectively to meet the needs of students of Spanish origin.[70] In January 1975 the State legislature passed a compulsory bilingual education bill that requires school districts with 20 or more children of limited English-speaking ability to provide bilingual education programs.

Ironically, New York State, home of the great majority of mainland Puerto Rican students, has no law mandating bilingual education. Its "English only" law has been amended to permit 3-year programs of bilingual instruction in the public schools.[71]

In lieu of a legislative mandate for bilingual education, the Board of Regents of the University of the State of New York stated that they "believe it is the duty of the school to provide programs which capitalize on the strengths of the non-English-speaking child and his family."[72] Less commitment to the needs of language-minority children is inherently discriminatory, according to the board.

The regents directed increased use of Title I ESEA and State Urban Education funds for bilingual education and ESL programs, and defined the responsibility of local school districts in New York State as follows:

In any case, where there are approximately 10 or more children of limited English-speaking ability who speak the same language and are of approximately the same age and level of educational attainment, every effort should be made to develop a bilingual rather than second language program.[73]

The New York State Department of Education has also established an office of bilingual education to oversee programs for non-English-speaking children. Under the auspices of that office, according to the regents, the State will actively press for adherence to the guidelines established in the May 25 memorandum of the Office for Civil Rights, HEW.[74]

In Pennsylvania, the State secretary of education directed school districts to provide bilingual education in every district having 20 or more non-English-speaking students in a language category.[75] New guidelines stipulate that basic State subsidy money must be used by the districts to teach children in their dominant language:

> ...every school district with 20 or more students whose dominant language is not English...will have to use its basic per pupil instructional subsidy plus its Title I per pupil allocation plus whatever other categorical funds are available to educate its Puerto Rican students. This means basic instruction—not just supplementary help.[76]

Moreover, the Pennsylvania education department says it will use its authority to force school districts, through the threat of fund cutoffs, to provide Puerto Rican children with an adequate education.

Although several States have demonstrated concern over the quality of education received by Puerto Rican students, school districts have claimed that they lack funds to implement new programs. Additional funds are needed to extend these programs to thousands of Puerto Rican students.[77]

School districts currently receive millions of dollars each year to educate children in their attendance zones. Per-pupil expenditures are virtually wasted on Puerto Rican and other language-minority children unless they can be redirected for compensatory language training and other special programs.

States could require, as a necessary first step, that local districts survey the language dominance of students; the achievement test scores of language-minority students; placement of language-minority students in low-ability groups or educable mentally retarded classes; and dropout rates for language-minority students. Based on such data, schools and districts could prepare operating budgets and requests for special State and Federal funds. States could also evaluate district budgets to monitor the extent to which a good faith effort is being made.

THE COURTS AND LANGUAGE-MINORITY CHILDREN

The continued unresponsiveness of school districts to the needs of language-minority students has stimulated court action. In *Lau* v. *Nichols* the Supreme Court of the United States ratified HEW guidelines contained in the May 25, 1970, memorandum known as the "May 25th Memorandum." The Court decided that:

> Basic English skills are at the very core of what these public schools teach. Imposition of a requirement that before a child can effectively participate in the educational program, he must already have acquired those basic skills is to make a mockery of public education. We know that those who do not understand English are certain to find their classroom

experiences wholly incomprehensible and in no way meaningful.[78]

The decision in *Lau* v. *Nichols* found that a monolingual educational policy does violate HEW guidelines. The Court did not rule on whether the private plaintiffs had a constitutional right to bilingual education. While finding the school district to be in noncompliance with Title VI of the 1964 Civil Rights Act, the Court explicitly declined to state what an appropriate remedy for such a violation may be. As of September 1976, Federal district court in San Francisco was reviewing a master plan for bilingual-bicultural education submitted by the school district.[79]

Aspira of New York, Inc. v. *Board of Education of the City of New York*[80] was the first major case concerning equal educational opportunity for Puerto Rican children.[81] Puerto Rican students and their parents, ASPIRA of New York, Inc., and ASPIRA of America, Inc.[82] brought action against the Board of Education of New York City individually and on behalf of a class comprising an estimated 182,000 Spanish-speaking students in New York City public schools.

The suit alleged that the school system had failed either to teach Spanish-speaking children in a language that they understood, or to provide them with the English language skills needed to progress effectively in school. Plaintiffs charged they were faced with unequal treatment based on language, and thus were denied equal educational opportunity as compared with English-speaking students.

After the *Lau* decision, plaintiffs moved for a summary judgment. The court, in ruling on the motion, asked both parties to submit plans which, in their view, satisfied the mandate of *Lau* as applied to Puerto Rican and other Spanish-speaking students in New York City's public schools.[83]

Negotiations followed the submission of these plans. With the approval of the court, the parties entered into a consent decree on August 29, 1974,[84] which provided that:

1. The board of education would identify and classify those students whose English language deficiency prevents them from effectively participating in the learning process, and who can effectively participate in Spanish.

2. By September 1975, the defendants were to provide all the children described above with: (a) a program to develop their ability to speak, understand, read, and write English; (b) instruction in Spanish, in such substantive courses as mathematics, science, and social studies; (c) a program to reinforce and develop the child's use of Spanish, including a component to introduce reading comprehension in Spanish to those children entering the school system, where an assessment of reading readiness in English indicates the need for such development. In addition to, but not at the expense of, the three central elements of the required program, entitled students were to spend maximum class time with other children to avoid isolation from their peers.

3. By the beginning of the second semester of the 1974--75 school year, the defendants were to provide all elements of the program to all children within the defined class at pilot schools designated by the chancellor. By September 1975 the program was to encompass all children within the defined class.

4. The board of education was to promulgate minimum educational standards to ensure that the program would be furnished to all children within the defined class, and ensure that the program would be provided in each of the community school districts. (On July 21, 1975, after lengthy negotiations, the minimum educational standards were issued by the chancellor.)

5. The defendants were obligated to use their maximum feasible efforts to obtain and expend the funds required to implement the program. If there are insufficient funds to implement the program, defendants were to notify plaintiffs' lawyers. (As of March 1976, they had not yet notified the Puerto Rican Legal Defense and Education Fund, Inc. that there were insufficient funds or insufficient staff.[85])

In addition to these stipulations, the consent decree included agreements regarding the use, development, and dissemination of appropriate materials and tests, and the recruitment, training, or retraining of adequate staff.

The decree also set specific timetables for completing each task. The defendants were required to consult with plaintiffs concerning the development and implementation of all items in the consent decree. The court retained jurisdiction to hear and settle disputes concerning the adequate implementation of the decree.

Implementing the Decree: The chancellor for the city school district of New York is ultimately responsible for implementing the consent decree.[86] He has set up a project management team to monitor the progress of the program and to coordinate the different divisions of the board of education.[87]

The decree required that an improved system of student identification and eligibility for the program was to be developed. A complete battery of tests was designed in the fall of 1974. This is commonly referred to as the L.A.B. (Language Assessment Battery). The board of education agreed to use the results of that test to place children in those special classes provided for by the consent decree. The L.A.B. was administered in the spring of 1975 (the only previous test was an assessment of oral language skills in English).[88]

Not until September 1975 were procedures established to monitor adherence to the standards and to the decree.

The minimum educational standards included:

1) English language instruction;
2) Subject area instruction in the pupil's dominant language;
3) Reinforcement and development of the child's use of Spanish, including development of reading and writing skills;
4) Opportunity for spending maximum time with other pupils in order to avoid isolation and segregation from peers without diluting or abrogating the above mentioned three elements.

Forty schools (including elementary, junior high, and senior high schools) were designated as "pilot schools" to serve as models and training centers in preparation for full implementation in September 1975. Their selection was based on whether or not the schools were already implementing one or more phases of the program.[89]

An evaluation of the pilot schools was undertaken by the Community Service Society of New York.[90]

The chancellor has emphasized that, for the most part, basic city tax levy funds (rather than State or Federal funds) would be utilized to implement the consent decree. The district also receives $11 million in supplementary tax levy funds, and an increased amount is being requested by the board to help implement the decree.[91]

The city school district also receives funds from State and Federal sources, and is exploring the possibility of using some of these funds to implement the decree.

On July 11, 1975, Judge Frankel settled another dispute generated by this lawsuit, ruling that parents of Hispanic students found entitled to the program could withdraw their children. Appended to the court's memorandum and order were the forms of notice to school administrators and letters to Hispanic parents which established the opting-out procedures. As described by the court, the form letters and notice were intended to "permit opting-out while refraining from encouraging it." The form letters and notice were agreed to by counsel for the plaintiffs only after negotiations, and even then outstanding differences had to be finally resolved by the court.[92]

On September 9, 1975, the court ordered the defendants to provide certain information essential to determining the degree of compliance with the program. As of that month, there appeared to be sufficient numbers of adequately trained persons available to implement one aspect of the decree, the hiring of trained personnel. But certain schools had not yet hired staff to implement the program. On December 22, 1975, plaintiffs' lawyers moved to hold the chancellor and members of the board of education in civil contempt for failing to fully implement the decree.[93]

In his response to this report, Chancellor Anker stated that "The larger part of the effort briefly described here had taken place before the Consent Decree was signed in August of 1974. Although it is true that the impact of the decree had obviously accelerated many of these activities we certainly feel that recognition should be given to our willingness to address a major educational problem in an innovative and responsible manner."

This view conflicts considerably with that of Federal District Judge Frankel, who heard the case and approved the consent decree. In an opinion granting attorney's fees to the plaintiffs, Judge Frankel said:

> Nevertheless, however positive we may wish to be and whatever the naivete of judges, the defendants must surely recall the long and sometimes bitter times before the era of good feelings set in. This is not a subject the court desires to dwell upon now or, if possible, ever. It should be sufficient to remind everyone, without detailed documentation, that even though 18 or 20 months of struggle and a motion for summary judgment led to negotiations for a consent decree, there were bargaining sessions when the court was driven to speak as more than a "mere moderator," [citations omitted]...occasions when the Board was chided for what seemed tardy and grudging concessions, and a penultimate stage at which the Board's adversary passion led to blatant infringement of first amendment rights. To the very end, it must be said, steady and energetic pressure by plaintiffs' attorneys was required so that pertinent information and responsive proposals would be forthcoming on a reasonably prompt and orderly schedule. (Aspira of New York, Inc. v. Board of Education of the City of New York, 65 F.R.D. 541,544 (S.D. N.Y. 1975)).

Although the consent decree has not yet been fully implemented, it is viewed as a vital step in achieving equal educational opportunity for Puerto Rican students in New York City's public schools, and a basis for protecting the rights of other non-English-speaking children in the city.[94]

PUERTO RICANS AND HIGHER EDUCATION

An estimated 25,000 mainland Puerto Ricans were enrolled as full-time college undergraduates in 1972.[95] This figure reflects vigorous growth in recent years. In New York City, for example, 1970 census data showed that there were only 3,500 Puerto Rican college graduates (compared with 2,500 in 1960). That year, only 1 percent of the Puerto Rican adults in New York City were college graduates, compared with 4 percent of black adults and 13 percent of white adults.

The City University of New York (CUNY) had 5,425 Puerto Rican undergraduates in 1969. By 1974 CUNY had 16,352 Puerto Rican undergraduates. This is not only a substantial leap in numerical terms, but also a sign of growing Puerto Rican participation in higher education. In 1969 Puerto Ricans at CUNY represented 4.0 percent of total enrollment; by 1974, they were 7.4 percent of the undergradutes. (See Table 35.)

In 1974 Puerto Ricans and other Hispanics (defined as Spanish-surnamed Americans) represented 13.4 percent of the first-time freshmen in the CUNY system, compared with 6.0 percent 5 years previous. (See Table 36.) Further growth of Puerto Rican college enrollment is an immediate possibility since in the 1974 – 75 school year Puerto Ricans represented 16.1 percent of all students in New York City's academic high schools (the pathway to college), and other Hispanics represented another 4.9 percent. (See Table 37.)

While there is reason for optimism, the growth trend rests on shaky foundations. Much of the increased enrollment is due to the "open enrollment" policy of the CUNY system and fluctuating levels of federally-funded financial aid and support services. The New York City fiscal crisis has profoundly affected CUNY. On June 1, 1976, Chancellor Robert Kibbee closed CUNY for 2 weeks owing to lack of funds. On June 12, the Board of Higher Education, under intense pressure from State and city officials, voted to charge tuition for the first time. The cost is $775 a year for freshman and sophomores and $925 for upperclass students. As part of the $27 million State aid package, $3 million was authorized for the educational needs of Spanish-speaking students in Hostos Community College.[96]

Figures are not yet available to ascertain how many Puerto Ricans students are dropping out due to academic or financial problems. Nor are figures available to show how many Puerto Ricans are actually graduating from college, in comparison with previous years.

In the absence of this data, the only reliable source that offers means of comparison is the limited information supplied by the 1970 census. These data show that, although more Puerto Ricans are going to college, they are much less likely to attend college than are high school graduates from

Table 35

Ethnic Composition of CUNY Undergraduates by Numbers and Percentages: Fall 1969-1974

Group	1960	1970	1971	1972	1973	1974
White	77.4% (104,974)	74.0% (117,566)	71.8% (129,232)	64.0% (125,804)	58.2% (121,887)	55.7% (123,079)
Black	14.8 (20,072)	16.9 (26,850)	19.5 (35,098)	22.4 (44,031)	25.8 (54,033)	25.6 (56,568)
Puerto Rican	4.0 (5,425)	4.8 (7,626)	5.9 (10,619)	6.9 (13,563)	7.5 (15,707)	7.4 (16,352)
Other Spanish-Surnamed American[1]	N/A	N/A	N/A	1.8 (3,538)	2.3 (4,817)	3.0 (6,629)
American Indian	0.4 (543)	0.2 (318)	0.3 (540)	0.3 (590)	0.3 (628)	0.4 (884)
Oriental	2.0 (2,713)	2.1 (3,336)	2.0 (3,600)	2.1 (4,128)	2.2 (4,607)	2.6 (5,745)
Other	1.4 (1,899)	2.0 (3,177)	0.5 (900)	2.5 (4,914)	3.7 (7,749)	5.3 (11,711)
Total	100.0% (135,626)	100.0% (158,873)	100.0% (179,989)	100.0% (196,568)	100.0% (209,428)	100.0% (220,968)

[1] The ethnic category "Other Spanish-Surnamed American" was not required by HEW until 1972.
Source: City University of New York.

Table 36

Ethnic Composition of Matriculated First-time Freshman by Numbers and Percentages, Fall 1969-1974

Group	NEW YORK STATE						Estimated 1974 New York City U.S. Graduates
	1969	1970	1971	1972	1973	1974	
Black	13.9% (2,815)	17.3% (6,144)	21.3% (8,370)	21.8% (8,340)	26.9% (10,221)	28.8% (12,087)	22.2% (15,595)
Puerto Rican & Spanish-Surnamed American[1]	6.0 (1,215)	7.8 (2,769)	8.7 (3,332)	11.8 (4,514)	14.1 (5,358)	13.4 (5,624)	14.8 (10,396)
Other[2]	80.1 (16,223)	74.9 (26,598)	70.0 (27,509)	66.4 (25,402)	59.0 (22,419)	57.8 (24,259)	63.0 (44,255)
Total	100.0% (20,253)	100.0% (35,511)	100.0% (39,211)	100.0% (38,256)	100.0% (37,998)	100.0% (41,970)	100.0% (70,246)

[1] Figures were derived by applying the ethnic distribution of New York City public and nonpublic 12th graders to the actual numbers of New York City graduates of public and nonpublic high schools.

[2] Includes whites, Asian Americans, Native Americans, and others.

Source: New York State Education Department, Information Center on Education.

Table 37

Total, Puerto Rican and Spanish-Surnamed Student Enrollment in New York City Public Schools, 1974-75.

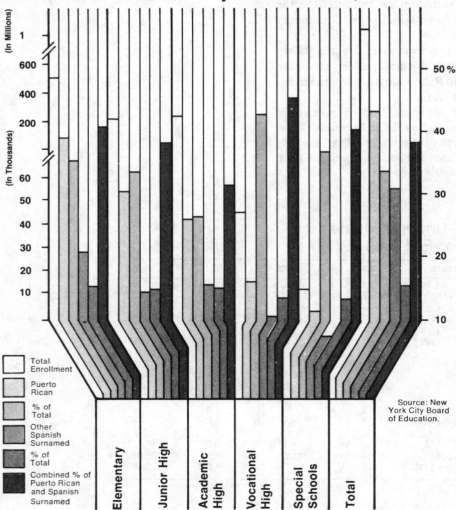

Total Enrollment

Puerto Rican

% of Total

Other Spanish Surnamed

% of Total

Combined % of Puerto Rican and Spanish Surnamed

Elementary

Junior High

Academic High

Vocational High

Special Schools

Total

Source: New York City Board of Education.

other racial or ethnic groups. In 1970, 45 percent of college-age youths in the U.S. were reported to be engaged in higher education, compared with 15 to 20 percent of blacks, and only 5 percent of Puerto Ricans.[97]

Among college freshmen there has been a smaller percentage of Puerto Ricans than of blacks, Mexican Americans, Asian Americans, or Native Americans. Between 1971 and 1973, the percentage of black freshmen dropped from 8.6 to 7.6 percent, and of Puerto Rican freshmen from 0.6 to 0.4 percent.[98] At the other end of the academic spectrum, Puerto Ricans constituted only 0.01 percent of all minority group doctoral degree recipients in 1973. (Of 2,884 minority group recipients that year, only 37 were Puerto Rican, with 2 from Puerto Rico.)[99]

The limited data available, and results from Commission field research in New York, Philadelphia, Newark, and Chicago, suggest the following composite of the mainland Puerto Rican college student: The student is more likely to be male than female and from a low-income family.[100] He is the first in his family to go to college and is somewhat older than the average student, as he may have worked or completed military service prior to entering college.

He is likely to be a first-year student at a relatively low-cost, 2-year or community college, or at a college or university with open enrollment policies. He commutes to class in an Eastern metropolitan area or in Chicago. He is receiving financial aid, probably from a variety of sources. He is majoring in the social sciences, perhaps education, Spanish, or social work, rather than the physical sciences. He is severely handicapped by earlier educational deficiencies, particularly in communication skills.

The following profile of Puerto Rican college students was offered in 1970:

> This new population in higher education comes to the university with some very special problems and concerns. They are all concerned with the fact that they are the survivors...of an educational system which has succeeded in eliminating 50 percent of their group before they completed school. They are all concerned about the extent of racism in our society.
>
> In a group with a varied racial background, sometimes white, black or, more commonly, some shade in between, they struggle with racial identity and its consequences. They are also concerned with the future status of Puerto Rico and the questions of the time—whether "Puerto Rico is a slave colony of the United States," or "A Showcase for Democracy."
>
> They enter college in a period of general disaffection with the university, its purpose and role in our society. They make increasing demands for courses and programs in the field of Puerto Rican studies and at the same time are anxious that their education pay off in a job which will break the bonds of poverty.[101]

The Puerto Rican student is unlikely to complete his or her education in the normal 2– or 4-year period, but will drop out for a semester or more and return later. Even over the long run, the student has less than a 50 – 50 chance of graduating. If a Puerto Rican manages to survive the high dropout rate in high school, he or she then must face the steep cost of college and the difficulty of securing financial aid.[102]

Not all Puerto Rican students have access to the open enrollment City University of New York system. Even at CUNY, the cost of fees and related expenses has risen dramatically. Going to a private college is prohibitive for the majority of Puerto Rican students. (Average yearly costs for various types of colleges are shown in Table 38.)

Table 38

Average Total Expenses for Resident and Commuter Students at Postsecondary Institutions 1975-76

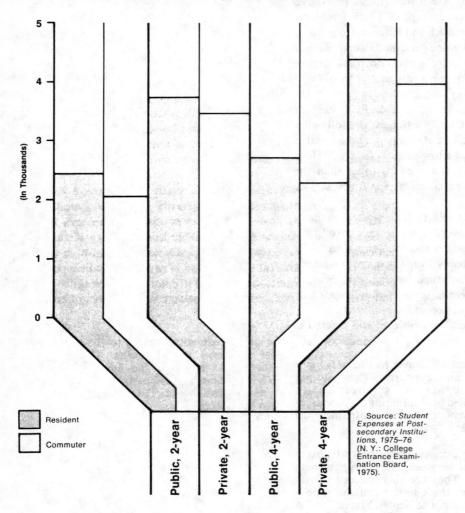

Source: *Student Expenses at Post-secondary Institutions, 1975–76* (N. Y.: College Entrance Examination Board, 1975).

Given the impoverished circumstances of the mainland Puerto Rican community, college costs can be met by very few Puerto Rican families, since median family income for mainland Puerto Ricans in 1974 was only $6,779. Tuition alone at Ivy League schools, which averages than $3,800 per year, is more than half the annual income of most Puerto Rican families. For the 1975 – 76 school year, fees are $387.50 per semester at Hostos Community College (part of New York's CUNY system), $11 per credit hour at Loop Community College (part of the City College of Chicago), $21 per credit hour at Essex County Community College in Newark, and $242 per semester at Philadelphia Community College. But not all needy students have access to such low-cost institutions.

Shortage of Colleges in the Cities: A shortage of colleges in large cities reduces the opportunities for Puerto Ricans and other low-income students, who can only afford to attend if they live at home.

In 1970 the Carnegie Commission found:

> ...a major deficit in two types of institutions— community colleges and comprehensive colleges in metropolitan areas, especially those

with a population over 500,000. The inner cities, in particular, are not well served. Higher education has not adequately reflected the urbanization of America. Deficits in North Jersey and the eastern side of Chicago are illustrative.[103]

Puerto Rican populations are largest in the Northeastern States and in the Chicago area, both of which were net exporters of college students in 1970. The Carnegie Commission called for 175 to 235 new community colleges in the United States by 1980, 80 to 125 of them to be located in metropolitan areas.[104] It also called for 85 to 105 new comprehensive colleges by 1980, with 60 to 70 of them in large metropolitan areas.

Another study found that nearly three-fifths of the nation's total population does not live near (within 45 minutes drive, one-way) a "free access" college, and that metropolitan residents are only somewhat better served by such colleges than those living in rural areas.[105]

All of these factors have shaped Puerto Rican perceptions about educational opportunities beyond high school. They have combined to reinforce each other, from one generation to the next, so that to the Puerto Rican junior or senior in high school, college is likely to be an alien or remote institution.

Despite this prevailing noncollege orientation, however, many low-income Puerto Rican parents will "sacrifice tremendously" to obtain for their children the highest possible degree of education. They have learned that social and economic mobility depends heavily upon academic credentials. The Puerto Rican student who graduates from high school tends to be very "hardy" and "fiercely determined to enter the mainstream of American society."[106]

Financial Barriers: While financial aid for college students is more plentiful than it was 10 years ago, Puerto Rican applicants and their parents still must shoulder a heavy share of the cost. In Illinois, for example, after Federal and State financial sources have been used, the remaining unmet need for students of Spanish origin averages $1,097, a very high percentage of family income.[107] In New Jersey, the comparable figure is $337.[108]

Several sources complain that student aid funds allocated to colleges have remained the same, or have been cut, despite enrollment increases. Only about one-third of the 55,000 students who need Federal aid at CUNY are expected to receive it in fiscal year 1976.[109]

The "red tape" involved in getting or renewing aid is often a greater problem than the availability of aid. At Hostos Community College in the Bronx, New York, staff said that "No one knows" when aid might be stopped or cut back, and, partly because some aid programs are so new, "You can't get any straight information on them."[110]

Lack of Information: Since so few mainland Puerto Ricans have attended college, important information concerning applications, forms, required statements, curricula, special programs, financial aid, and so forth may not be available from relatives or friends.

College counseling staffs are usually limited, and few have Puerto Rican or other Hispanic counselors. The City College of New York (CCNY) has only one Puerto Rican or Spanish-speaking counselor and one Puerto Rican financial aid counselor for about 1,350 Puerto Rican students.[111] Puerto Rican students frequently complain of the lack of counseling aid, both in high school and in college. It is felt, for example, that more Hispanic counselors are needed at CUNY to reinforce the "self-image" of Puerto Rican students there. Some Puerto Ricans feel that non-Hispanic counselors tend to be more rigid and "go by the book," when more sympathetic and imaginative advice is needed.[112]

A faculty member at the University of Illinois Chicago Circle campus charges that counseling there is "poisonous." He asserts that counseling helped Puerto Ricans to survive "by teaching them tricks, pacifying them, and showing them easy courses." That is one reason, he said, why nearly three-fourths of Puerto Ricans drop out of college, leaving only a miniscule number of graduates.[113]

Puerto Ricans also lack adequate counseling with reference to graduate school opportunities. Furthermore, many counselors are unable to appreciate the "overwhelming" health and financial crises and "intense" emotional problems that face many Puerto Rican students.[114] One observer stated that counseling for Puerto Ricans in college was superior to that which they received in high school: In high school they were told not to attend college.[115]

Admission Standards and Examinations: Largely because of the poor quality of education received in city schools and the failure of educational system to meet their needs, Puerto Ricans frequently graduate from high school with low grade point averages. They also tend to score lower on college entrance examinations, such as the Scholastic Aptitude Test (SAT).

In 1965 the estimated median achievement test score (nonverbal, reading, math, and general information) for 12th grade Puerto Rican students was 43.1 compared with 52 for white students.[116] An official at the Educational Testing Service(ETS) which designs most college entrance tests, feels that the lack of college experience among most minority group families probably explains their lower SAT scores.[117]   Thus, the "B" grade average or high SAT scores required by many colleges are beyond the reach of the typical Puerto Rican high school graduate.

At Essex County Community College in Newark, New Jersey, an estimated 85 percent of the Puerto Rican students require ESL (English as a Second Language) training.[118]

At Northeastern Illinois University, 90 percent of all Hispanic students (including Puerto Ricans) need language assistance, according to a counselor. "Most of the Latin American students here are products of the Chicago school system. Their difficulties are not always one of language, but of inadequate preparation and indifferent educational techniques," he said.[119]

A New York educator said that many Puerto Ricans (as well as other students) continue to graduate from high school ill-equipped for college work.[120] Since Puerto Rican students often are not encouraged to follow a college preparatory program, they may not be as adept at preparing for tests or writing term papers as their white counterparts. A college may have to teach them not only subject matter, but also how to write a term paper.[121]

Tutoring and Remedial Services: Few tutors are available to assist Puerto Rican students who have difficulty with college-level work. A teacher at Essex County Community College in Newark, commenting upon teacher overload, noted that he teaches seven courses and so has no time for counseling or tutoring. Many Puerto Ricans "still cannot function" after 2 years because programs of assistance at the college are so limited and ineffective, he said.[122]

Many of the remedial courses designed to upgrade essential skills reportedly fail to achieve their purpose. At Temple University, Puerto Ricans "were thrown into a remedial English course along with other non-English-speaking minority students," and few profited, according to one observer. "They needed a Spanish-speaking teacher."[123]

Speaking of support services at the college level, a Rutgers official said that, "Kids are brought in like cattle" and then "dumped." Students tend to drift and have to counsel each other.[124]

Student Alienation: Largely because of inadequate support services, low-income students often feel like "intruders" in a traditionally white, middle-class environment.[125] Having managed to ride into college on "the coattails" of black students, Puerto Rican students are often "an anonymous entity" in affirmative action programs.[126] Receiving little attention from college staff, sometimes living away from home for the first time, noting the absence of Puerto Rican administrators, faculty, and even clerical staff, many are often "lost in the shuffle." Finding the college atmosphere "cold" and "rigid," the temptation to drop out looms large.[127]

For these reasons, Puerto Rican students at most colleges and universities have formed student unions. Unlike the traditional student union, which is primarily involved in planning dances and social events, Puerto Rican groups often perform administrative functions such as student recruiting and tend to devote themselves to key issues concerning their education. These issues include: demands for more Puerto Rican administrators, faculty, and admissions and recruitment staff; increased or continued funding for support programs for Puerto Ricans; support for or creation of Puerto Rican studies programs or departments; greater recruitment efforts aimed at Puerto Rican students in the surrounding community; the alleged channeling of Puerto Rican students into certain curricula and departments; and the steady rise in tuition costs.

Many Puerto Rican students and faculty members perceive themselves on the defensive, as objects of discrimination, fearing that the broadened access to higher education in recent years is now narrowing, and that minority programs face extinction. These views have provoked demonstrations by Puerto Rican students at City College in New York,[128] Yale,[129] the University of Illinois Chicago Circle Campus,[130] and Macalester College in Minnesota.[131] Tension and unrest over feared cutbacks in minority programs and staffs exist at other schools, such as Temple, Lehman College in New York City, and Rutgers' Livingston College.[132]

Many Puerto Rican students assume that, unless they relentlessly press college administrators, they will be neglected. A common sentiment is that the administration "distrusts the legitimacy of Puerto Rican needs and will only respond to pressure."[133] Whatever small gains have been achieved are done by the students themselves with Puerto Rican staff support. Thus, a decision to dismiss an English teacher considered especially effective in developing the writing skills of Latino students at Northeastern Illinois University was rescinded after Latino protests.[134] Macalester College announced it would not terminate its Puerto Rican program after Puerto Rican and other minority students seized an administration building to protest budget cuts in the school's minority program.[135]

The perspective from which some Puerto Rican students view college administrators and policies is shaped, at least in part, by what one faculty member termed an "anti-colonial" attitude and a strong need among many Puerto Rican youth to maintain their cultural and linguistic identity.[136] They are bitter that their language is considered detrimental and a "handicap" in college; they resist what they perceive to be the destruction of their individuality in what they see as the "melting pot" approach to higher education. They want desperately to develop skills that will enable them to live useful, rewarding lives, but they want to do so without having their values and heritage ridiculed or denied.

GOVERNMENT'S ROLE IN EDUCATION OF PUERTO RICAN UNIVERSITY STUDENTS

Federal expenditures for university student aid rose from $941 million in 1966 to an estimated $5 billion in 1972. About $3.9 billion of this amount was used to pay tuition and fees, with the remainder applied to cover living costs.[137]

The Education Amendments of 1972 extended many of the existing Federal aid programs. The amendments added a new program of basic student grants for every high school graduate who wants to continue his or her education but lacks the resources to do so, and encouraged establishment of new planning structures at the State level to improve all forms of planning for postsecondary education.[138]

Federal financial aid for college students consists of grants, loans, and work-study funds. Most of the grant and scholarship aid given up to 1973 was provided by the Veterans Administration (VA) and the Social Security Administration (SSA).

The largest Federal student aid program was the G.I. Bill, which allows up to 36 months of full-time schooling or on-the-job training for eligible veterans and military personnel. Expenditures for the program by the VA were nearly $1.8 billion in fiscal year 1972. In the same fiscal year, the Social Security Administration provided $475.3 million in benefits to 432,863 students who were children of retired, disabled, or deceased social security beneficiaries.[139]

The principal student grant program administered by the U.S. Office of Education in fiscal year 1972 was the Education Opportunity Grant (EOG) program. Federal funds of up to $1,000 were granted to college students with "exceptional financial need." Colleges administer the program, which has varying definitions of need. The college must match each grant with other Federal or non-Federal aid. EOG grants of $210.3 million were obligated in fiscal year 1972 to participating institutions.[140]

The Basic Education Opportunity Grant (BEOG) program, created in 1972, allows low-income students even greater access to higher education. Administered by the Office of Education, BOG provides direct grants that help qualified undergraduates finance their postsecondary education.

BEOG differs from EOG in that it is an entitlement program with a standard definition of need. Both full- and part-time students are eligible for up to 5 years of study.

In fiscal year 1975, BEOG provided a maximum of $1,050 each to about 700,000 first- and second-year students.[141] When fully funded, it is to provide annual grants of up to $1,400 (minus expected family contribution) but not more than one-half the total cost of college attendance. The Carnegie Commission has estimated that 500,000 to 1 million additional students "might be induced to attend college if BOG were fully funded."[142]

The two principal Federal loan programs are the National Direct Student Loan program (NDSL, formerly the National Defense Student Loan Program) and the Guaranteed Student Loan program, authorized by the Higher Education Act of 1965.

State Aid: In fiscal year 1973, the 50 States spent an estimated $348 million for undergraduate student aid in the form of scholarships and grants, plus a substantial sum for guaranteed and direct loans, tuition waivers and reductions, and various restricted grants to special categories of students.[143] Despite recent increases in such aid, State spending for these programs accounts for no more than 4 or 5 percent of total measurable State and local support for postsecondary education.[144] Six States—California, Illinois, New Jersey, New York, Ohio, and Pennsylvania—account for 78 percent of the total student-aid financing and 67 percent of the student recipients. Most State programs cover only tuition, or tuition and mandatory fees, but a few now provide aid primarily for disadvantaged students from low-income families and/or with marginal records of achievement.

One such program is the Educational Opportunity Fund (EOF), which aided 13,000 students (including 1,050 Puerto Ricans) at public and independent institutions in New Jersey and other States in fiscal year 1974.[145]

Under EOF in New Jersey, State funds go directly to students via grants and to institutions to maintain supportive services (tutoring, developmental courses, counseling, diagnostic testing, and full-time summer programs). Three-fourths of EOF students are from families earning less than $6,000 per year.[146] The average family income of the EOF student is $4,464, compared to $11,082 for the average New Jersey family. The average EOF grant is $817. This covers half the cost of attending a community college, and less than a third of the cost of attending a State college or Rutgers University.

Lack of data on Puerto Rican participation in both Federal and State student aid programs prevents efforts to ensure that they are in fact receiving their fair share. Some Puerto Rican educators believe that a disproportionately large share of that aid goes to Mexican American students west of the Mississippi River.[147]

Many Puerto Ricans believe that much student aid is not based on financial need. This has been confirmed in at least one study by the College Entrance Examination Board:

> A cherished myth of educators and the general public is that student financial aid today is primarily based on relative need. However, when the source and application of all aid funds (including the G.I. Bill, Social Security, athletic grants, and scholarships from restricted funds) are considered, the greater amount of student aid appears to be beyond institutional control and is commonly awarded on the basis of criteria other than need....[148]

Similarly, the Carnegie Commission pointed out that:

> Because many students from upper-income families attend institutions with tuition charges that are far below costs (true in the case of many private colleges and universities, as well as public institutions), these educational subsidies are not distributed as effectively as might be the case if minimizing the financial barrier to attendance were the primary goal. For example, of the total monetary outlays on higher education, students and their families on the average contribute about 37 percent of the total ($8.1 billion out of $22 billion in 1970–71).[149]

Special Admissions and Support Programs: A number of new policies and programs that focus on the needs of low-income, disadvantaged students have been established in recent years. These have permitted access to college for a significant number of Puerto Rican students.

The introduction of open admissions at the City University of New York in 1970 played a major role in increasing Puerto Rican college attendance in the system. Under this policy, admission to a college within the CUNY system was guaranteed to all New York City high school graduates. Puerto Rican undergraduate enrollment at CUNY increased from 5,425 (4 percent of total enrollment) in 1969 to 15,707 (7.5 percent) in 1973.

Other schools have also instituted open admission programs. The Temple Opportunity Program (TOP) at Temple University, *Proyecto Pa'lante* at Northeastern Illinois University, and the Equal Education Opportunity (EEO) program at Macalester College, among others, offer (to a limited number of Puerto Rican and other low-income, minority students) admission based only on indications of potential and motivation. These programs provide counseling and academic tutoring services, and help students put together financial aid packages.

One of the oldest special programs for low-income students is the College Discovery Program (CDP), created at CUNY in 1964. Its purpose was to:

> demonstrate that students who were then being excluded from college because of the existing admissions criteria could, with the proper supportive services, attain a college degree. From the beginning, it was understood that students fail not only because they are underprepared but also because they are economically disadvantaged. For this reason, stipends for books, fees and personal expenses were made available to the student as was intensive counseling, remediation and tutoring.[150]

Since 1964 CDP has expanded its enrollment from 231 students at two community colleges to well over 4,000 students in eight programs at seven community colleges. Thirty percent of CDP enrollment is Puerto Rican.[151]

Special Services for Disadvantaged Students (SSDS)[152], a Federal program created in 1965, offers remedial and other supportive services to disadvantaged students with academic potential who need such services to commence or continue higher education. Grants are made on the basis of proposals submitted by eligible applicants on a competitive basis. In 1973 – 74, Puerto Ricans numbered 3,945 of participants in SSDS. This was 5.3 percent of all participants, compared to 5 percent of participants in 1972 – 73 and 4 percent in 1971 – 72.[153]

Open admissions and special academic support programs for low-income minority students are so new that it is difficult to evaluate their effectiveness. A study at CUNY, however, found that the university has not become the "revolving door" which some had expected with the advent of open admissions, and that attrition rates under open admissions were, overall, about the same as the national average.[154]

EOF students in New Jersey "continually perform at a respectable level of achievement, and although they come to college with lower SAT scores than their regularly admitted counterparts, they quickly close the gap."[155]

As the result of help provided by *Proyecto Pa'lante* at Northeastern Illinois University, the *Proyecto* director expects as many as 60 percent of Latino students to graduate.[156]

Notes

1.   According to the 1970 U.S. census, among persons aged 25 years and above, whites had a median of 12.1 school years completed, blacks had 9.8 school years, and mainland Puerto Ricans had 8.7 school years.

2.   Isidro Lucas, "Puerto Rican Dropouts in Chicago: Numbers and Motivations" (Manuscript, 1971), p. 23. Research conducted under grant no. OEG-5-70–0037(509) for the Office of Education, U.S. Department of Health, Education, and Welfare.

3.   Daniel Schreiber, ed., *The School Dropout* (Washington, D.C.: National Education Association, January 1964), pp.3, 18–19.

4.   City of New York, Board of Education, *Community School Profiles, 1973–74.* According to a study undertaken for the Board of Education of the City of New York, in May 1974 there were more than 65,000 Hispanic school children with severe or moderate difficulty in English comprehension. Of this number, more than 47,000 were Puerto Rican children. The study concluded that "English language disability among pupils of Hispanic origin is substantial, encompassing about a third of Puerto Rican pupils...." See Donald Treiman, Thomas Di Prete, and Kermit Terrell, "Preliminary Report on a Survey of Educational Services for Hispanic Pupils with English Language Difficulty, Conducted in the New York City Schools, May 1974" (Center for Policy Research, mimeograph, July 1, 1974), Table 1 and p. 16.

5.   Testimony of Antonio Candido Martinez in *Hearing Before the United States Commission on Civil Rights*, Hearing Held in New York, N.Y., Feb. 14 – 15, 1972, p. 43 (hereafter cited as *New York Hearing*).

6.   Data are from the *Metropolitan Reading Achievement Test* (April 1968), Table H, which contains city and borough average reading scores for 2nd, 5th, and 8th grades.

7.   Bureau of Educational Research, Board of Education of the City of New York, "Ranking of Schools by Reading Achievement," attachment to *amicus curiae* brief for the Puerto Rican Legal Defense and Education Fund in Lau v. Nichols, 414 U.S. 563 (1974).

8.   Illinois Advisory Committee (SAC) to the U.S. Commission on Civil Rights, *Bilingual/Bicultural Education---a Privilege or a Right?* (May 1974), p. 42. (hereafter cited as *Illinois Sac Report*).

9.   See testimony of Dr. Marechal-Neal Young, Associate Superintendent for Special Education, in Pennsylvania Advisory Committee (SAC) to the U.S. Commission on Civil Rights, *Transcript of Open Meeting*, June 7, 1972, vol. II, pp. 433 – 57 (hereafter cited as Pennsylvania SAC, *Transcript of Open Meeting*).

10.   Testimony of Braulio Montalvo, Psychologist, Philadelphia Child Guidance Clinic, in Pennsylvania SAC, *Transcript of Open Meeting*, pp. 415 – 16.

11.   Warren G. Findley and Miriam M. Bryan, *Ability Grouping: 1970 – Status, Impact, and Alternatives (University of Georgia)*, p. 25.

12.   David N. Aspy, "Groping or Grouping for Teachability," *Contemporary Education* , Vol. 41, No. 6. May 1970, pp. 306 – 10.

13.   U.S., Commission on Civil Rights, *Toward Quality Education for Mexican Americans*, Report VI: Mexican American Education Study (February 1974), pp. 25, 31.

14.   Testimony of Joseph Monserrat in *New York Hearing*, pp. 122 – 23.

15.   John R. Hodgdon, Regional Civil Rights Director, OCR/HEW, Region V, letter to Dr. Robert Krajewski, Superintendent, East Chicago Public Schools, June 9, 1972 (hereafter cited as Hodgdon Letter).

16.   Pennsylvania Advisory Committee, *In Search of a Better Life---The Education and Housing Problems of Puerto Ricans in Philadelphia* (1974), pp. 23 – 6 (hereafter cited as *Pennsylvania SAC Report*).

17.   "Children With English Language Difficulties," *The Fleischman Commission Report*, Part III, Vol. II, reprinted from the Fleischman Commission, *A Report of the New York State Commission on the Cost, Quality and Finance of Elementary and Secondary Schools*, 3 Vols (1972), p. 8.

18.   Westry G. Horne, Chief, Elementary and Secondary Education Branch, Region II, memorandum to Dr. Lloyd Henderson, Director, Education Division, Office for Civil Rights, Apr. 30, 1973.

19.   Testimony of Ewald B. Nyquist, President, University of the State of New York and Commissioner of Education, in *New York Hearing*, p. 519.

20.   New England Regional Council, *Overview of the Problems Encountered by New England's Spanish-Speaking Population*, (July 7, 1970), pp. 14 – 15.

21.   Adriana Gianturco and Norman Aronin, *Boston's Spanish Speaking Community*: *Findings of a Field Survey* (Boston, Prudential Insurance Co., 1971), p. 45. Prepared under a grant from the U.S. Department of Labor.

22.   Massachusetts Advisory Committee to the U.S. Commission on Civil Rights, *Issues of Concern to Puerto Ricans in Boston and Springfield* (February 1972), p. 9.

23.   "Language-minority" children speak a non-English native language and belong to an identifiable minority group of generally low socioeconomic status.

24.   Nancy Modiano, "National or Mother Language in Beginning Reading: A Comparative Study," *Research in the Teaching of English* (1968). For a thorough discussion of the ESL approach, see Mary Finocchiaro, *Teaching English as a Second Language in Elementary and Secondary Schools* (New York, 1969) and Harold B. Allen, ed., *Teaching English as a Second Language* (New York, 1965).

25.   20 U.S.C. §880(b)-1(4)(A) (Supp. IV 1974).

26.   For a detailed discussion of the bilingual education approach, see Muriel Saville and Rudolph Troike, *A Handbook of Bilingual Education* (Washington, D. C., 1971) and Theodore Anderson and Mildred Boyer, *Bilingual Schooling in the United States*, Vols. I and II (Austin, Texas, January 1970).

27.   Hernan LaFontaine, "Bilingual Education for Puerto Ricans: Si o No?" in *Introduction to Bilingual Education*, Bilingual-Bicultural Educational Series, ed. Luis Ortega (Anaya Las Americas: New York, 1975) (unpaged).

28.   Ray C. Rist, "Student Social Class and Teacher Expectations: The Self-Fulfilling Prophecy in Ghetto Education," *Challenging the Myths: The Schools, The Blacks, and The Poor* (Cambridge, Mass.: Harvard Educational Review, 1971), p. 70. See also, Clarence Senior, "Newcomers, Strangers, and Schools," in Schreiber, *The School Dropout.*

29.   Ronald J. Samuda, "Racial Discrimination through Mental Testing: A Social Critic's Point of View", *IRCD* (Information Retrieval Center on the Disadvantaged) *Bulletin*, May 1973.

30.   U.S., Commission on Civil Rights, Report V: Mexican American Education Study, *Teachers and Students* (March 1973), p. 43.

31.   National Education Association and American Association of School Administrators, Educational Policies Commission, *Education and the Disadvantaged American,* p. 19, as cited by Clarence Senior in Schreiber, *The School Dropout*, p. 112.

32.   Cities investigated by the Commission and its State Advisory Committees included Boston, Mass.; Chicago, Ill.; New York, N.Y.; Bridgeport, Conn.; Springfield, Mass.; and Philadelphia, Pa.

33.   According to a recent *New York Times* article, Hispanics (Puerto Ricans and other Spanish origin groups) comprised 27.7 percent of the 1974 student population in the New York City public school system (grade and high school) while Hispanic teachers were 3.1 percent of all teachers in the school system. "Laid-Off Teachers Tell About Broken Careers," *New York Times*, June 24, 1976, p. 36M.

34.   "Statistical Projection of Need for Spanish-Speaking Teachers: 50 States and 18 Leading Cities," paper presented by Samuel B. Ethridge, Director, Teacher Rights, National Education Association, before the National Bilingual Institute, Albuquerque, N.M., Nov. 30, 1973.

35.   *Illinois SAC Report*, pp. 7, 13, and 15.

36.   *Massachusetts SAC Report*, pp. 9 and 95.

37.   *Pennsylvania SAC Report*, pp. 5 and 8.

38.   Connecticut Advisory Committee to the U.S. Commission on Civil Rights, *El Boricua: The Puerto Rican Community in Bridgeport and New Haven* (January 1973), p. 22.

39.   Ibid., p. 19.

40.   New Jersey Advisory Committee to the U. S. Commission on Civil Rights, *Transcript of Open Meeting*, Camden, N.J., July 12, 1971, p. 125.

41.   Testimony of Lydia Corcino in Pennsylvania SAC, *Transcript of Open Meeting*, p. 570.

42.   Candido de Leon, President, Hostos Community College, interview in New York City, N.Y., Nov. 22, 1974 (hereafter cited as De Leon Interview).

43.   Mike Fucili, Counselor, Temple Opportunity Program, Temple University, interview in Philadelphia, Pa., Dec. 3, 1974. For additional comments on the negative role of some

guidance counselors in the Philadelphia public school system, see the *Pennsylvania SAC Report*, pp. 11 – 13.

44.   John H. Niemeyer, "Home-School Interaction in Relation to Learning in the Elementary School," in *The School Dropout*, p. 122.

45.   *Massachusetts SAC Report*, p. 16.

46.   *Illinois SAC Report*, p. 53.

47.   Sylvia Ortega, "Some Needs of the Spanish-Speaking Child in Bridgeport, Connecticut" (West Hartford, Conn.: University of Hartford, 1970), cited in Perry Alan Zeikel, *An Evaluation of the Effectiveness of Selected Experimental Bilingual Education Programs* (1972), p. 29.

48.   *Illinois SAC Report*, p. 17.

49.   *Massachusetts SAC Report*, p. 17.

50.   *Illinois SAC Report*, p. 52.

51.   N.Y. Education Law §2590.

52.   For a discussion of the Decentralization Law of 1969, see U.S., Commission on Civil Rights, *Public Education for Puerto Rican Children in New York City*, Staff Report, printed as Exhibit 5 in *New York Hearing*, pp. 305 – 319 (hereafter cited as *Staff Report: Education*).

53.   This includes selection of textbooks and other educational materials, provided that materials have been approved by the chancellor.

54.   *Staff Report: Education*, in *New York Hearing*, p. 317.

55.   The Board of Examiners is the body which qualifies all candidates for positions in the New York City school system.

56.   N.Y. Education Law §§2590-e,g,j (McKinney 1970).

57. The Board of Education of the City of New York states: "Since September 1972 there has been an Office of Bilingual Education at the Central Board which has responsibility for providing such technical assistance." Irving Anker, Chancellor of the Board of Education of the City of New York, letter to John A. Buggs, Staff Director, U.S. Commission on Civil Rights, June 18, 1976, p. 4. It appears likely that the office of bilingual education was created in response to the criticisms such as those voiced at the Commission's hearing in New York City in February 1972.

58.   20 U.S.C. §236 *et seq.* (1970).

59.   *Staff Report: Education* in *New York Hearing*, p. 377 – 380.

60.   20 U.S.C. §800 (b) *et seq.* (Supp. IV 1974).

61.   *Staff Report: Education* in *New York Hearing*, p. 379. According to Hernan LaFontaine, executive administrator of the Office of Bilingual Education, New York City Board of Education, $4 million were received by the city for Title VII programs for the school year 1973 – 74. See Hernan LaFontaine, "Introduction to Bilingual Education," in *Urban, Social, and Educational Issues*, eds. Dr. L. Golubchick and Dr. B. Persky (Kendall Hunt: Dubuque, Iowa, 1974), p. 26.

62.   *Staff Report: Education*, pp. 380, 382.

63.   See Statement of the U.S. Commission on Civil Rights on Bilingual Bicultural Education before the General Education Subcommittee of the House Education and Labor Committee, Apr. 17, 1974. The Commission strongly supported the extension and expansion of Title VII, with increased appropriations for research, teacher training, and curriculum development. The Commission supported similar measures before the Senate Committee on Labor and Public Welfare, Oct. 31, 1973.

64.   *Staff Report: Education* in *New York Hearing*, p. 383 – 384.

65.   Larry Kaseman, staff member, Bureau of Equal Educational Opportunities, U.S. Office of Education, HEW, interview in Washington, D.C., July 8, 1974.

66.   In these programs, national origin minority children are grouped in transitional classrooms away from the regular classes in a school. This separation can last up to 3 years.

67.   The Commonwealth of Massachusetts General Laws, Chapter 71A. 1971.

68.   *Illinois SAC Report*, p. 64.

69.   Ibid., p. 66.

70.   Diego Castellanos, *Perspective, The Hispanic Experience in New Jersey Schools*, New Jersey State Department of Education, (January 1972), p. 8.

71.   However, "The New York State law actually permits six years of bilingual instruction if the local school administrators apply for approval of three years beyond the initial three year period." Irving Anker, Chancellor of the Board of Education of the City of New York, letter to John A. Buggs, Staff Director, U.S. Commission on Civil Rights, June 18, 1976.

72.   "Bilingual Education, A Statement of Policy and Proposed Action by the Regents of the University of the State of New York" (1972), p. 10. The Regents of the University of the State of New York is the policymaking body for the State educational system.

73.   Ibid., p. 7.

74.   Ibid., p. 11.

75.   School Administrator's Memorandum 491 of Mar. 10, 1972, cited in *Pennsylvania SAC Report*, p. 21.

76.   Ibid., p. 22.

77.   Statement of Ewald B. Nyquist, President, University of the State of New York and Commissioner of Education in *New York Hearing*, p. 521. In Chicago, more than 60 percent of the 40,800 students who spoke Spanish as a first language received no special English language assistance. Only 4,000 received any form of bilingual-bicultural instruction. Another 12,000 are estimated to be enrolled in ESL programs. (*Illinois SAC Report*, pp. 46 – 47).

78.   414 U.S. 563, 566 (1974).

79.   Paul Berdue, attorney, San Francisco Neighborhood Legal Aid Foundation, Chinatown office, telephone interview, Sept. 3, 1976.

80.   Aspira of New York, Inc. v. Board of Education of the City of New York, 72, Civ. 4002 (S.D. N.Y., Sept. 20, 1972).

81.   This chapter was submitted to the Board of Education of the City of New York for review and comment prior to publication. See letter from Chancellor Anker to John A. Buggs, Staff Director, U.S. Commission on Civil Rights, June 18, 1976.

82.   ASPIRA of America, founded in New York City in 1961, is an educational nonprofit organization which provides counseling and leadership development programs for Puerto Rican youth. Funded by Federal and State governments and by various private foundations and corporations, ASPIRA has affiliates in New Jersey, Pennsylvania, New York, Illinois, and Puerto Rico.

83.   A motion to dismiss the complaint had been filed by defendants on November 15, 1972. On January 23, 1973, the court denied that motion in all respects, and the defendants filed an answer to the complaint on February 9, 1973. After lengthy pretrial discovery, plaintiffs in February 1974 moved for summary judgment, asking the court to render a decision on whether a violation of law existed, without a trial of disputed facts. The defendants opposed summary judgment, stating that adequate supportive services were being provided to plaintiffs. Plaintiffs argued that, in actuality, there were students not receiving services. (See "History of Bilingual Suit," Aspira of New York, Inc., pp. 1 – 3.)

84.   Consent Decree at 2, Aspira v. Board of Education, 72 Civ. 4002 (Aug. 29, 1974). By consenting to the entry of the decree, plaintiffs did not waive any rights they have under the 14th amendment, and defendants did not admit to having committed any violations.

85.   Richard J. Hiller, staff attorney, Puerto Rican Legal Defense and Education Fund, Inc., interview in New York, N.Y., Mar. 3, 1976 (hereafter cited as Hiller Interview).

86.   Dr. Murray Hart, Superintendent, Board of Education of the City of New York, interview in New York City, N.Y., Dec. 11, 1974 (hereafter cited as Hart Interview).

87. Dr. Michael Costelloe, Director, Project Management Team, Office of the Chancellor, Board of Education of the City of New York, interview, Dec. 11, 1974 (hereinafter cited as Costelloe Interview).

88. The L.A.B. has been the subject of some dispute between the parties, and was eventually brought before the court for consideration. See 394 F. Supp. 1161 (S.D.N.Y. 1975). The court ruled that the English L.A.B. was to be administered to all Hispanic students. Those who fell within the bottom 20th percentile were to be given the Spanish L.A.B. Those who scored better in Spanish than in English were members of the class, and were entitled to the program.

89. Marco Hernandez, Assistant Director, Office of Bilingual Education, Board of Education for the City of New York, interview, Dec. 10, 1974 (hereafter cited as Hernandez Interview).

90. Community Service Society of New York, *Report on Bilingual Education: A Study of Programs for Pupils With English-Language Difficulty in New York City* (June 1974).

91. In addition to its basic per capita allowance from tax levy funds, the district receives supplementary tax levy funds, for funding special programs. The basic tax levy funds are city funds allocated to the school districts on a formula basis. They amount to the per capita allocations which are disbursed to the districts.

92. Hiller Interview.

93. Ibid. The Board of Education commented that "in fairness it should be made clear that the Board of Education is more than 90% in compliance with the Consent Decree. This is a remarkable achievement considering the fact that more than 60,000 eligible children had to be identified, tested, and programmed." See letter from Chancellor Anker to John A. Buggs, Staff Director, U.S. Commission on Civil Rights, June 18, 1976.

94. Victor Marrero, Chairman of the Board, and Herbert Teitelbaum, Legal Director, Puerto Rican Legal Defense and Education Fund, Inc., Press Release, Aug. 29, 1974, p. 2.

95. This figure was reached by estimating the percentage of Puerto Ricans included in the Spanish-surnamed total enrollment in several States for fall 1972 (from HEW's Racial and Ethnic Enrollment Report). The percentages of total Puerto Rican student enrollment (85 percent in New York and Connecticut, 90 percent in New Jersey, 45 percent in Illinois) were based on estimates by HEW, Aspira, and various higher education officials in the different States.

96. See *New York Times*, June 13, 1976.

97. Hearings before the Select Committee on Equal Educational Opportunity for the U.S. Senate, 91st Congress, Part 8, *Equal Opportunity for Puerto Rican Children* (November 1970), p. 3796.

98. American Council on Education, *The American Freshman: National Norms*, reports for fall 1972 and 1973 (Washington, D.C.).

99. National Academy of Sciences, Commission on Human Resources, *Summary Report 1973: Doctorate Recipients from United States Universities* (Washington, D.C., May 1974), p. 4.

100. Of 337 students placed in college by ASPIRA of Illinois in 1972–73, half came from families receiving public assistance, and the remainder from families earning less than $7,000. ASPIRA of America *Annual Report*, 1972–73 (New York), p. 23.

101. Statement of Louis Nunez, ASPIRA of America, in Senate Hearings on *Equal Education Opportunity for Puerto Rican Children*, p. 3796.

102. Elizbeth W. Suchar, Stephen H. Ivens, and Edmund C. Jacobson, *Student Expenses at Postsecondary Institutions, 1975–76* (New York: College Entrance Examination Board, 1975), p. 41.

103. The Carnegie Commission on Higher Education recommended that 29 to 41 new community colleges and 19 to 26 comprehensive colleges be established in the major cities of the eight States with largest Puerto Rican population: New York, New Jersey, Pennsylvania, Massachusetts, Illinois, Connecticut, California, and Florida. See *New Students and New Places: Policies for the Future Growth and Development of American Higher Education* (New York: McGraw Hill, 1971), pp. 142–44.

104. "Free access" higher education is defined to include "low cost, admission of 'the majority' of high school graduates, and an absence of geographical and psychological

barriers." (College Entrance Examination Board, *Barriers to Higher Education* (New York, 1971), p. 11.

105.   De Leon Interview.

106.   Isidro Lucas, Chicago Regional Office, Department of Health, Education, and Welfare, interview, Nov. 19, 1974 (hereafter cited as Lucas Interview).

107.   Illinois State Scholarship Commission (1974).

108.   New Jersey Department of Higher Education, *The Educational Opportunity Fund, Fourth Annual Report*, 1973 – 74 (Trenton, N.J.).

109.   Pat O' Reilly, Office of Student Financial Aid, CUNY, New York City, telephone interview, Jan. 14, 1975.

110.   De Leon Interview.

111.   Yolanda Sanchez, Office of the President, City College of New York, telephone interview, Jan. 10, 1975 (hereafter cited as Sanchez Interview).

112.   Frank Negron, Director of Affirmative Action Program, CUNY, interview in New York City, N.Y., Nov. 26, 1974.

113.   James Blout, Geography Department, telephone interview, Nov. 20, 1974.

114.   De Leon Interview, and Estella McDonnell, Aspira of New Jersey, interview , Nov. 26, 1974.

115.   Aleda Santana, counselor, City College "Seek" Program, New York City, telephone interview, Jan. 16, 1975.

116.   U.S., Department of Health, Education and Welfare, *Digest of Educational Statistics*, 1971, p. 137.

117.   Bob Smith, ETS, Princeton, N.J., telephone interview, Dec. 12, 1974.

118.   Jerry Lieberman, Department of Behavioral Science, Essex County Community College, interview in Newark, N.J., Nov.26, 1974 (hereafter cited as Lieberman Interview).

119.   Maximino Torres, Proyecto Pa'lante Director, Northeastern Illinois University, Chicago, interview, Nov. 19, 1974 (hereafter cited as Torres Interview).

120.   Carmen Puigdollers, Puerto Rican Studies Department, Lehman College, New York City, interview, Jan. 13, 1974 (hereafter cited as Puigdollers Interview).

121.   Samuel Betances, Political Science Department, Northeastern Illinois University, interview in Chicago, Ill., Nov. 19,1974 (hereafter cited as Betances interview).

122.   Lieberman Interview.

123.   Russell Daniel, former director, Student Resource Center, Temple University, interview in Philadelphia, Pa., Dec. 3, 1974.

124.   Maria Blake, Department of Community Education, Newark-Rutgers University, N.J., interview, Nov. 26, 1974.

125.   De Leon and Betances Interviews.

126.   Manuel del Valle, Puerto Rican Legal Defense and Education Fund, interview in New York City. N.Y., Nov. 22, 1974.

127.   Elaine Girod, Office of Admissions, Temple University, Philadelphia, Pa., interview, Dec. 3, 1974 (hereafter cited as Girod Interview).

128.   Puerto Rican students seized the college's administration building in the spring of 1973.

129.   "Puerto Rican Students Claim Yale Hiring Bias," *New Haven Register*, Mar. 28, 1974, p. 60; "Puerto Ricans Stage Protests Against Institutional Racism," Yale *Daily News*, Apr. 3, 1974, p. 1.

130.   Latin Community Advisory Board, "Circle Campus vs. the Latin Community of

Chicago," (mimeograph, October 1973), cited in Samuel Betances, "Puerto Ricans and Mexican Americans in Higher Education," *The Rican: Journal of Contemporary Puerto Rican Thought*, May 1974, p. 27.

131.   "Students Protesting Cut in Minority Program Occupy Macalester Building," *Minneapolis Tribune*, Sept. 14, 1974, p. B – 8; "Minorities Occupy 77 Mac; Compromise Reached on Budget Cuts," *Macalester Today* (October 1974), p. 2.

132.   Girod, Puigdollers, and Nieves Interviews.

133.   Torres Interview.

134.   Northeastern Illinois University, *Print*, Oct. 21, 1974.

135.   Macalester College, *Macalester Today*, October 1974; Micheal O' Reilly, Puerto Rican Program, Macalester College, letter to James Corey, U.S. Commission on Civil Rights, Dec. 11, 1974.

136.   Maria Calanes, Spanish Department, Temple University, Philadelphia, Pa., interview, Dec. 6, 1974.

137.   National Commission on the Financing of Postsecondary Education, *Financing Postsecondary Education in the United States* (December 1973), p. 114. (hereafter cited as *Financing Postsecondary Education*).

138.   20 U.S.C. § 1070c (Supp. IV 1974).

139.   *Financing Postsecondary Education*, p. 115.

140.   Ibid., p. 116.

141.   Data from the Bureau of Postsecondary Education, HEW.

142.   Carnegie Commission on Higher Education, *Higher Education: Who Pays? Who Benefits? Who Should Pay?* (New York: McGraw, 1973), p. 41 (hereafter cited as *Higher Education: Who Pays?*).

143.   *Financing Postsecondary Education*, p. 95.

144.   Ibid., p. 96.

145.   New Jersey, *The Educational Opportunity Fund, Fourth Annual Report*, 1973–74, pp. 1 and 8.

146.   Ibid., Table 2.

147.   Girod and Fucili Interviews.

148.   College Entrance Examination Board, *New Approaches to Student Financial Aid: Report of the Panel on Financial Need Analysis* (New York, 1971), p. 9.

149.   *Higher Education: Who Pays?* p. 41.

150.   CUNY, College Discovery Program Fact Sheet (February 1974).

151.   Ibid.

152.   20 U.S.C. § 1070d (Supp. IV 1974).

153.   U.S., Department of Health, Education, and Welfare, Bureau of Postsecondary Education, Division of Special Services for Disadvantaged Students.

154.   David E. Lavin and Barbara Jacobson, *Open Admissions at the City University of New York: A Description of Academic Outcomes After Three Semesters* (April 1973).

155.   New Jersey, *The Educational Opportunity Fund, Fourth Annual Report* 1973 – 74, p. 8.

156.   Torres Interview.

Findings and Recommendations

1.   *Based on such key indices as income, education, unemployment, and incidence of poverty, Puerto Ricans on the United States mainland are a severely disadvantaged minority group.*

RECOMMENDATION No. 1:

The Federal Government should officially recognize that Puerto Ricans are a minority group whose problems require specific forms of aid. Therefore, the President should assign the Director of the Domestic Council to coordinate interagency research, planning, and action to improve the effectiveness of Federal and federally-assisted programs designed to aid Puerto Ricans.

a. The Director should oversee implementation of the recommendations made in this report and others to be developed in the course of a special review.

b. Liaison should be established on a systematic basis among the Domestic Council, the Office of Management and Budget (OMB), and personal representatives of the Governors of States with cities having an estimated Puerto Rican population of 5 percent or more (hereafter referred to as "target States"), as well as the mayors of those cities (hereafter referred to as "target cities").

2.   *One obstacle to the effective implementation of government action to aid Puerto Ricans is the lack of reliable, continuous socioeconomic data. The paucity and lack of uniformity of available data makes it difficult to focus adequately on key problem areas, and to measure progress in the solution or alleviation of problems. The scarcity of comparable data makes it difficult, if not impossible, to measure the cost effectiveness of government expenditures designed to improve the living standards of Puerto Ricans.*

RECOMMENDATION No. 2:

The Federal Government should obtain, and make available, current, reliable data on the mainland Puerto Rican population.

a. The Bureau of the Census should substantially revise its methods of collecting data on Puerto Ricans by:

(1)   Collecting such data in all census forms, rather than limiting such data collection to a 5 percent sample;

(2)   Standardizing the definition of "Puerto Rican" by using the most inclusive one available, which is "Puerto Rican origin";

(3)   Identifying and eliminating factors that resulted in the 1970 census undercount (see the Commission's *Counting the Forgotten: The 1970 Census Count of Persons of Spanish-Speaking Background in the United States*, April 1974);

(4)   Conducting periodic, special population surveys in target States and cities to update socioeconomic data on Puerto Ricans.

b. The Bureau of Labor Statistics (BLS) should improve its data collection on Puerto Rican employment conditions by:

(1)   undertaking studies in target cities, similar to those conducted by the BLS Middle Atlantic regional office in poverty areas of New York City (these are cited in the Bibliography);

(2)   rectifying inadequacies by such means as those proposed in the Middle Atlantic regional BLS office report, *A Program for Developing Social and Economic Data on the Population of New York City and Area from the Current Population Survey and Other Sources.*

c. Accurate, current data on the education problems of Puerto Ricans should be collected by Federal, State, and local government agencies:

(1)   The Office for Civil Rights (OCR) of the Department of Health, Education, and Welfare (HEW) should collect separate data on Puerto Rican students, faculty, and staff at all educational levels through all reporting forms submitted by school districts;

(2)   State education agencies should also require submission of data on Puerto Rican dropout rates and rates of inclusion in low-ability groups and classes for the educable mentally retarded. These data should be compared with operating budgets and requests by local districts for additional funding;

(3)   The U.S. Office of Education (OE), the Veterans Administration, the Social Security Administration, and State education agencies should collect data on Puerto Rican participation in all student financial aid programs.

(4)   Boards of education in target cities should collect and publish data that show a racial-ethnic breakdown of students in their schools.

d. The Office of Management and Budget, which has oversight responsibilities for Federal statistical procedures, should develop and enforce a Federal policy for the uniform collection and use of racial-ethnic data in Federal and federally-assisted programs to determine if such programs reach intended beneficiaries on an equitable basis. Such a data collection system should provide for the collection of data on Puerto Ricans, who should be enumerated on the basis of self-identification. (Other recommendations related to this proposal were included in the Commission's report, *To Know or Not to Know: Collection and Use of Racial and Ethnic Data in Federal Assistance Programs* (February 1973) and should also be implemented by OMB.)

3.   *The poor, deteriorating position of Puerto Ricans in terms of jobs and income is due to a combination of factors: Many Puerto Ricans of working age are limited, by lack of skills and inability to communicate in English, to jobs in light manufacturing, an industry that is in a state of decline in the areas where they live; others who seek, and are qualified for, jobs in more rewarding types of work are victims of discrimination, both on an individual and institutional basis, and in both the private and public sectors. Federal efforts to improve job opportunities (such as employment training programs) have reached relatively few Puerto Ricans, largely due to lack of adequate funding and the lack of bilingual instruction services. Federal enforcement of civil rights laws has been hampered by inadequate guidelines, insufficient compliance monitoring, and lack of interagency coordination.*

RECOMMENDATION No. 3:

The Federal Government should intensify its efforts to improve employment opportunities for Puerto Ricans:

a. Congress should increase Federal appropriations for employment training under the Comprehensive Employment and Training Act (CETA).

b. The Department of Labor's Employment and Training Administration should promptly establish guidelines for Title III bilingual training programs. The Employment and Training Administration should:

(1)   Ensure that, in addition to the standardized skill training, a language component is available in job training programs in target cities;

(2)   Institute an affirmative action program at United States

Employment Service offices in target cities to increase Puerto Rican and other Spanish-origin staff to a level comparable to the percentages of Puerto Ricans served by the USES offices;

(3) Identify those training programs in target cities that have low Puerto Rican participation or completion rates and determine how they can recruit and graduate more Puerto Rican workers.

c. The Civil Service Commission should promptly eliminate discriminatory barriers to Puerto Ricans who seek public employment by:

(1) Reviewing, together with the Equal Employment Opportunity Commission (EEOC), the Equal Employment Opportunity Coordinating Council (EEOCC), and independent experts on validation of selection standards, all Federal selection procedures that have an adverse impact on Puerto Ricans and other Hispanic minorities. The purpose would be to determine whether the standards applied for hiring, placement, and promotion are job related and free of cultural bias. For example, the PACE and other civil service examinations should be immediately validated according to EEOC guidelines for employment selection procedures;

(2) Requiring State and local governments that participate in the Federal Intergovernmental Personnel Program to follow the employee selection standards developed by EEOC;

(3) Adopting rules that permit State and local governments participating in the Federal Intergovernmental Personnel Program to make race, ethnicity, and sex a criterion of selection when hiring or promoting, if qualified, individuals in accordance with affirmative action plans that are designed to eliminate underutilization of Puerto Ricans, other minorities, and women;

(4) Examining the degree of Puerto Rican participation in the Federal "Upward Mobility" program;

(5) Collecting separate data on Puerto Ricans in all its reporting programs in target States and cities.

d. The Equal Employment Opportunity Commission should be more aggressive in its efforts to encourage State and local government "affirmative action" hiring of Puerto Ricans by:

(1) Collecting separate data on Puerto Ricans in all reporting forms submitted by employers and unions;

(2) Holding public hearings in major target cities to investigate barriers that cause low Puerto Rican participation in State and local civil service employment;

(3) Assigning the Office of Voluntary Programs to work with State and local governments to eliminate such barriers; and

(4) Filing Commissioner charges in those target States or cities where recruitment and employment of Puerto Ricans is clearly inadequate.

4. *The median educational level for Puerto Ricans on the United States mainland is lower than that of the general population and other minorities except Native Americans. Linguistic and cultural barriers, as well as discrimination, contribute to a high dropout rate of Puerto Ricans from public schools and colleges. The lack of adequate bilingual-bicultural personnel and curriculum materials has been a major factor in generally poor academic achievement by Puerto Rican students. There is discrimination against Puerto Ricans in various school districts by teachers, counselors, and other school personnel. Poor communication between schools and parents of Puerto Rican children tends to exclude parents from important school activities. Few school districts collect and*

make available data on Puerto Rican student enrollment, dropout rates, or teaching and administrative personnel. Federal and State Governments have been deficient in ensuring equal educational opportunity for Puerto Rican students.

RECOMMENDATION No. 4:

a. Bilingual-bicultural instruction should be provided in all school districts with significant enrollments of Puerto Rican or other language-minority children. Target States which do not have bilingual education statutes should adopt compulsory bilingual-bicultural education laws and should adequately fund such programs. These States should develop program standards and monitoring mechanisms to enforce the standards.

b. Prior to approving operating budgets for school districts, or for supplemental Federal or State grants, State education agencies should determine the extent to which per-pupil operating costs are meeting the needs of Puerto Rican and other language-minority students.

c. OCR, in its annual school surveys, should direct States to ensure that school districts utilize operating funds, as well as special program funds, to meet the needs of Puerto Rican and other language-minority students.

d. Congress should substantially increase funding of Title VII of the Elementary and Secondary Education Act (ESEA) to support bilingual teacher training, curriculum development, and evaluation instrument development. Funds appropriated under other legislation, such as the Emergency School Aid Act (ESAA), which have been earmarked as a set-aside for bilingual education, should also be increased.

e. HEW should develop guidelines that clearly identify the responsibilities of federally-aided school districts, State education agencies, and nonpublic schools, under Title VI of the Civil Rights Act of 1964. HEW should also:

    (1)   Increase its compliance reviews of school districts and college campuses with significant Puerto Rican enrollments and/or with significant nearby Puerto Rican populations;

    (2)   Include in its reviews of school districts an analysis of the extent to which Puerto Ricans attend segregated or ethnically isolated schools;

    (3)   Implement all the recommendations in the Commission's report, *The Federal Civil Rights Enforcement Effort—1974,* Vol. III, *To Ensure Equal Educational Opportunity,* January 1975.

f. The National Institute of Education (NIE) should provide research for the development of curriculum materials and evaluation instruments for Puerto Rican and other language-minority students. Also, OE and target States should utilize the resources of higher education institutions in target cities to improve teacher training and counseling in school districts that have substantial Puerto Rican enrollment.

g. Local school districts in target cities should develop affirmative action plans to strike a more equitable balance between levels of Puerto Rican student enrollment and the numbers of Puerto Rican faculty.

h. Schools should consult with Spanish-origin psychologists and staff prior to placing Puerto Rican students in classes for the educable mentally retarded. Ability grouping should be utilized only in cases where it is the sole means of providing special, individualized attention.

i. School districts should ensure that Puerto Ricans parents are involved in school activities, including teacher selection and textbook selection and review. All school notices should be provided in Spanish for Puerto Rican and other Spanish origin parents.

j. To minimize financial barriers to higher education, Congress should:

(1)   appropriate full funding for State Student Incentive matching grants;

(2)   provide full funding for the Basic Education Opportunity Grant (BEOG) program in fiscal year 1978;

(3)   increase the BEOG maximum award, consistent with recent increases in student expenses; and

(4)   raise the ceiling on awards to actual costs, at least for lower division students.

k. The Office of Education should seek increased Federal cost-of-instruction aid for higher education institutions.

1. The States should provide better access to college for Puerto Rican and other minority students by:

(1)   graduating tuition rates at 4-year institutions, with lower rates for lower division students;

(2)   providing direct aid to private colleges and universities to permit reduced tuition costs;

(3)   seeking to maintain a policy of low, or no, tuition at 2-year community colleges; and

(4)   supplementing Federal aid with increased financial aid for low-income students.

5.   *Although the level of net migration from Puerto Rico to the U.S. mainland has decreased in recent years (the net trend during the past few years has been one of return migration to Puerto Rico) thousands of newcomers from Puerto Rico settle on the mainland each year. These newcomers suffer particularly acute problems of linguistic and cultural adjustment, which result in lower income and higher unemployment in comparison with Puerto Ricans who are long-term residents of the mainland, or mainland-born persons of Puerto Rican origin.*

RECOMMENDATION No. 5:

The Director of the Domestic Council should create an advisory body that includes top-level representation from the Government of Puerto Rico and target States and cities on the mainland. This advisory body should be consulted on such important matters as:

a. Improved monitoring of migration between Puerto Rico and the U.S. mainland;

b. Improved processing and translation of school, employment, and other records, such as professional degrees and certificates earned in Puerto Rico, and improved mechanisms to grant equivalency credits for school and professional experience; and

c. The establishment of federally-funded information centers in target cities that would be staffed by bilingual personnel who can assist Puerto Ricans in adjusting to their new environment by offering information, direct social services, and referrals to existing services.

* This material has not been excerpted in its entirety.

Puerto Ricans in the Continental United States: An Uncertain Future. A Report of the United States Commission on Civil Rights, Washington, D.C. October 1976.

POCHO SPANISH: The Case for a "Third" Language in the Classroom

By Enrique Lopez

During the past few years, interest in bilingual education for Chicano and other Hispanic youngsters has grown throughout the U.S. Substantial funds have been allocated for federal and state programs in schools and day-care centers heavily attended by several hundred thousand Spanish-surnamed children, and such expenditures will hopefully increase in the next decade.

Unfortunately (though understandably, given the urgency of the problem), many of these bilingual programs have been hastily conceived and launched without sufficient thought having been given to defining the issue in all of its dimensions. Hence, some bilingual projects have, predictably, fallen far short of expectations. Just as predictably, some of the failures have assumed the aspect of self-fulfilling prophecies for certain Anglo cynics who are anxious to believe that "these damned Chicanos can't do anything right."

At the same time, there have been a number of successful projects which provide clues as to how more viable programs may be structured, such as the programs directed by Dr. José Cardenas for the Edgewater district of San Antonio, Texas, and the bilingual classes at the Coral Way School in Miami, Florida. However, it is imperative that additional homework be done in advance to maximize the possibilities for future success. That homework would involve conducting in-depth research, evaluation and experimental pilot programs which could provide basic data and methodologies for bilingual education in *early childhood*.

"Home" Languages

Whether or not a bilingual program is used primarily as a means of preserving Hispanic culture and language or simply as a communication strategy, in order to be effective the "home" language of Chicano children must be taken into account. Indeed, the home language must be given status — that is, become an *acceptable* part of their general social environment — so that children will not feel ashamed, but will be proud of themselves and of their parents. When deprived of their home language, such children become linguistic orphans in a hostile, alien atmosphere.

Children who are unable but required to communicate in English lose confidence in themselves and begin to "feel dumb" and intellectually defenseless. Denied the rewards and reinforcement all children need to progress, they start to "drop out" on the very first day at school or day-care center. The gap between them and their English-speaking peers begins to widen at this early stage, getting wider day-by-day and year-by-year, until they finally give up. Note: this dropping-out among Chicanos is so pervasive that their drop-out rate exceeds that of Black ghetto youngsters. Recent statistics show that the average educational achievement for Anglos is 12 years of schooling, for Blacks 9.2 years, and for Chicanos and Puerto Ricans less than 8 years, with Chicanos in Texas averaging 7 years of schooling. *And those gaps are widening.*

Regrettably, certain educators, having accepted the above premises, go on to assume that most Spanish-surnamed youngsters come from homes where *conventional* Spanish is spoken — and their programs are based upon that misconception. Rather than being truly bilingual (conversant in both Spanish and English), or monolingual in conventional Spanish, most Chicanos are actually *schizolingual*. They speak an amalgam of Spanish and English that results from borrowing words back and forth between the two languages. Obviously, the variations are multiple and complex, both philologically and syntactically. Some experts refer to this "third language" as Spanglish, *pocho* or *caló*. For convenience sake, we shall use *pocho* hereafter, uneasily aware of the fact that it is a pejorative term to some of my fellow Chicanos. (In Mexico a *pocho* was originally defined as *un pinche mexicano que tiene pretenciones de ser un gringo sonofabitch:* (A bastard Mexican who has pretensions of being a gringo sonofabitch.)

Research Is Needed

The *barrio* language actually spoken by the child must be initially identified before one can structure a bilingual program based upon that particular idiom. If the home language is conventional Spanish, it is probably advisable to use conventional Spanish as part of the bilingual instruction; but if the home language is really *pocho*, conventional Spanish could be almost as alien to the child as English. For many preschool children, *pocho* is the sole medium of verbal expression. It is, therefore, their principal learning tool and is indispensable to their continuing intellectual development.

We would propose that research and evaluation programs be designed to produce verifiable information on the following basic questions:

(A) What language is actually spoken in the homes of Spanish-surnamed children, from two to ten years of age, who are in day-care centers or elementary schools? Is it (1) conventional English of a particular locale — Texas dialect, for example; (2) conventional Spanish as it is widely spoken in Mexico; (3) Southwest Spanish as it is spoken in New Mexico or northern Colorado or (4) *pocho* Spanish, an amalgam of Spanish and English. Regarding the latter, is the variation spoken (a) *total pocho*, in which there is a constant switch from Spanish to English and vice versa (Example: This *pinche* professor *siempre* explains *los* details *de todo* like we're *unos* dumb *batos* from *los meros* sticks); (b) *moderate pocho*, in

which occasional phrases are spoken in Spanish (Example: I'm getting tired of these damned politicians *siempre fregando y promiseando* during election year); or (c) *minimal pocho*, in which Spanish phrases are used only intermittently to stress a particular point. (One should note that in all variants of *pocho*, there is frequent hispanization of English words or anglization of Spanish words. In speaking *pocho*, certain elements of the Spanish language seem less susceptible to being borrowed than others, i.e., verbs are less easily transformed than nouns. Example: On loan to Spanish, the English verb "batting" becomes *bateado*; "puncturing" becomes *ponchando*. But the loan word for the noun "tire" is *talla* — *llanta* in conventional Spanish and "market" becomes *marketa* — conventionally, *mercado*.)

(B) Regarding language patterns, what variations exist between Chicanos from different socio-economic levels within or outside of the *barrio*? Do the patterns vary according to geographic proximity to Mexico, i.e., do Texas Chicanos speak less *pocho* than California Chicanos?

(C) What if anything, do the grammatical and structural differences between English and Spanish say about the cultural perspective of Chicanos? Example: Speakers of Spanish frequently use what I choose to call the "exculpatory reflexive," as in: *Se me hizo tarde* — It got late for me. Thus, the apersonal "it" takes the weight rather than the personal "I," as in "I was late." Does this grammatical difference in emphasis express and reinforce a lack of punctuality (a negative trait from the Anglo point of view), or does it merely reflect an ethos that conceptualizes time differently? To explain the nature of this question further, I would note that in the United States "time is money." That concept underlies the Anglo American's high regard for punctuality. Spanish cultures, and many others as well, subscribe to concepts of time that derive largely from non-materialistic sources. Considerations in this area are extremely important because too many teachers are insensitive to the existence of cultural norms and standards other than Anglo ones. They must learn not only that such standards exist, but that they are not inferior and/or dysfunctional — they are merely different.

(D) Do certain linguistic differences between Spanish and English influence the learning processes of preschool children who are being taught the two languages simultaneously?

Having made a quantitative and qualitative analysis of the home language of Chicanos in various sections of the U.S., we can then address ourselves to developing more sophisticated teaching strategies at the day-care center and elementary school levels.

"Poncho Spanish: The Case for a 'Third' Language in the Classroom" by Enrique Lopez. Council on Interracial Books for Children, 1841 Broadway, New York, NY 10023

National Spanish-speaking organizations

American G.I. Forum of the United States
Founded: 1948
Membership: 20,000; 500 chapters
An organization primarily of Mexican-American Veterans and their families.
Purpose: Develop leadership for participation in community, civic, and political affairs; understanding among people; preserve democracy; promote religious and political freedom; and strive for social and economic equality for all citizens.
Address: 621 Gabaldon Rd., N.W., Albuquerque, NM 87104
Publications: G.I. Forum Bulletin, monthly.
Convention: Annual

American G.I. Forum Auxiliary
Founded: 1948
Membership: 6000
An organization of Forum members' wives and female relatives plus other married Mexican American women over 21 years of age.
Purpose: To promote equality for Mexican-Americans and to assist local chapters of the Forum.
Address: 621 Gabaldon Rd., N.W., Albuquerque, NM 87104
Convention: Annual

League of United Latin American Citizens (LULAC)
Founded: 1929
Membership: 120,000
A civic oriented organization.
Purpose: Civic minded persons, primarily of Latin American extraction for the progress and advancement of Latin Americans. Involvement in education and community development projects.
Address: 2218 S. Birch St., Santa Ana, CA 92707
Publications: LULAC News, monthly
Convention: Annual

IMAGE:
Founded: 1973
Membership: 42 chapters
Purpose: A national organization concerned with broadening employment opportunities for Spanish-speaking Americans, in Federal, State and local government. Has chapters in major U.S. cities. Of recent origin but fast growing.
Address: 112 North Central, Phoenix, AZ 85003 (602) 261-3882
Convention: Annual

National Education Task Force De La Raza
Founded: 1970
Membership: 350
An organization primarily of Mexican-American educators and community leaders.
Purpose: Organized to work for the improvement of educational opportunities for the Mexican American student. Has provided leadership desparately needed by people of Mexican descent in the field of education.
Address: College of Education-University of New Mexico, Albuquerque, NM 87131
(505) 277-2231

SER/Jobs for Progress, Inc.
Founded: 1964
Membership: 20 chapters in 6 states
Sponsored by G.I. Forum and LULAC
Purpose: To plan and execute manpower and related services focusing on disadvantaged Spanish speaking Americans so that through education and training they can overcome obstacles that have denied them employment, economic opportunity and self-sufficiency.
Address: 9841 Airport Blvd., Los Angeles, CA 90045 (213) 649-1511
Publications: "SER", a program folder.

National Puerto Rican Forum, Inc.
Founded: 1957
Chapters: Northeast, Midwest, and Puerto Rico
Purpose: To develop effective leadership in Puerto Ricans in the continental United States, through educational institutions, city, state, and Federal agencies and other entities concerned with solutions of America's minority groups. Conducts training in language, human relations, urban affairs, assistance to communities, housing and redevelopment.
Address: 214 Mercer Street, New York, NY 10012 (212) 533-0100

ASPIRA of America
Founded: 1961
A principal organization serving the New York - New England Area.
Objectives: To develop leadership and capability among Puerto Rican youth by encouraging them to pursue their education beyond that offered by the public school system and to provide remedial education to prepare them for advanced study in colleges and universities.
Address: 245 5th, New York, NY 10016 (212) 638-6054

National Association for Puerto Rican Civil Rights (NAPCR)
Founded: 1963
Membership: 20,000
Individual members and some 100 organizations representing Puerto Ricans in the continental United States. Concerned with civil rights problems in legislative, labor, policy, legal, housing, and education matters, especially in New York City.
Address: 175 E. 116th St., New York, NY 10029 (212) 348-3973

Cuban Municipalities in Exile
Founded: 1964
Cuban refugees living in the U.S. organized according to provinces of origin.

Objectives: To promote the values of their cultural heritage; promote democracy and combat Communism; extend aid to newly arrived refugees. Provide information on educational opportunities for Cubans.
Address: 1460 West Flager St., Miami, FL 33134 (305) 634-9174
Publications: La Nacion
Meetings: Monthly

Raza Association of Spanish Surnamed Americans (RASSA)
Founded: 1968
Membership: 1. sustaining; 2. subscription; 3. organizational
A lobbying organization covering 17 states to promote legislative action beneficial to Spanish surnamed Americans.
Address: 400 1st N.W., Suite 706, Washington, DC 20001
Publications: The Lobbyist
Conventions: Yearly

Chicano Press Association (CPA)
Founded: 1968
Membership: 50
Chicano Publications
Purpose: A confederation of newspapers dedicated to promotion of the movement of self determination and unity among Chicanos. Condemns exploitation and oppression. Seeks to build a society where human dignity, justice and brotherhood prevail
Address: P.O. Box 31004, Los Angeles, CA 90031 (213) 261-0128

Mexican American Legal Defense and Educational Fund (MALDEF)
Founded: 1968   Staff: 15
Funded mainly by the Ford Foundation.
Purpose: To protect by legal action the constitutional rights of all Mexican Americans; to help educate young Mexican American lawyers so that they can join in the areas of civil rights litigation, combatting de facto school

segregation, upgrading education, eliminating job discrimination, participation in juries, fair public accommodations, voting rights, municipal services, consumer protection, and welfare-social rights.
Address: 145 9th St., San Francisco, CA 94103 (415) 626-6196

Spanish-Speaking Women's Organizations*

National Chicana Institute
P.O. Box 336
Tempe, AZ 85281

National Chicana Foundation
507 East Ellington Dr.
Montebello, CA 90604

National Chicana Welfare Rights
P.O. Box 33286
Los Angeles, CA 90033

National Institute for Chicana Women
1718 P. Street, N.W. #206
Washington, DC 20036

National Conference of Puerto Rican Women
3502 Taylor Street
Chevy Chase, MD 20015

*Extent of information on these organizations

National Spanish Speaking Organizations, Office for Spanish Speaking Programs, U.S. Office of Education. Excerpted from U.S. Civil Service Commission, "A Guidebook for Coordinators." Washington, D.C. September 1975.

Part seven:
Women

Women

A STATISTICAL PORTRAIT OF WOMEN IN THE UNITED STATES
POPULATION GROWTH AND COMPOSITION

The female population of the United States on July 1, 1975 is estimated at 109,377,000. This figure is about 5.6 million larger than the number of men and represents 51.3 percent of the total population of 213,137,000 (table 1-1). Since 1910 the female population has grown faster in each decade than the male population. The sex ratio (number of males per 100 females) has declined steadily from 106.2 in 1910 to 94.9 in 1975. At the turn of the century, men constituted 51.1 percent of the total U.S. population; in 1950, for the first time in any decennial census, women outnumbered men.

Growth. In the 20th century the largest rate of population increase for both sexes during a decade was recorded between 1900 and 1910, mainly as a result of the large volume of net immigration. The smallest percent increase occurred between 1930 and 1940, a decade when birth rates were low and net immigration was very small. Between 1970 and 1975, the female population increased by 4.9 percent, or at an average annual rate of 0.9 percent, a rate very similar to the average annual growth rate of 0.8 percent registered during the 1930's.

Age composition. As a consequence of fluctuations in fertility and declines in mortality, the age distribution of the female population has been changing substantially. The median age of the population may be used as a general indicator of change in the age distribution. The female figure rose from 22.4 years in 1900 to 30.5 in 1950. Thus, within a period of five decades, the median age of the female population increased by 8 years, or by over 1½ years per decade. This increase resulted from declines in fertility during most of the period; declines in death rates and net immigration retarded the rise to a small extent. During the 1960's the trend toward an older population was temporarily interrupted, with a decline of 1 year in the median age of the female population. Between 1970 and 1975, however, the median age again increased by more than one-half year, to 30 years.

The proportion of the female population below age 15 increased rapidly from the latter part of the 1940's to 1960 reflecting the higher birth rates during the "baby boom" years than earlier (table 1-2). As a result of the decline in fertility over the past 15 years, however, children have become a steadily decreasing proportion of the population. The numbers of young women 15 to 24 years of age have been similarly affected by fluctuating fertility rates. The decline in the proportions in this age group between 1940 and 1960 reflects earlier declines in fertility, inasmuch as women in this age group were born before the onset of the post-World War II wave of higher fertility. By 1975, however, this age group had increased to approximately 18 percent of the female population from its 13 percent in 1960.

Because of the much lower fertility in the 20-year period from 1925 to 1945 than in the pre-1925 years, the proportion of women in the younger adult working ages (those 25 to 44 years old) declined about 7 percentage points between 1950 and 1970. Since 1970, however, this segment has increased slightly as the enlarged "baby boom" cohorts have begun to replace the smaller cohorts. In 1975 one-fourth of the female population was in this age group. The proportion of women in the older working ages (45 to 64 years old) rose from 13.3 percent in 1900 to 20.2 percent in 1950. Since 1950 women in this age range have remained a relatively constant proportion of the female population—roughly one-fifth.

Women aged 65 years old and over have constituted a larger share of the female population in every successive decade since 1900. By 1975, 12 percent of the female population was in this age group; the corresponding proportion in 1900 was 4 percent. This uninterrupted increase during the 20th century in the proportion of the population in this age category has resulted largely from generally declining fertility rates, although declines in death rates may have contributed to the increase in small part.

Sex ratios. The sex composition of the resident population of the United States may be viewed as determined by four factors: (1) sex ratios at birth, (2) differences between the sexes in age-specific death rates, (3) differences between the sexes in net immigration, and (4) the balance of the sexes in other net movements overseas (e.g., movement to outlying areas, movement of Armed Forces personnel, and Federal civilian employees outside the United States). For example, the dramatic increase between 1970 and 1975 in the sex ratio of the resident population at ages 15 to 24 years resulted primarily from military personnel returning from overseas. The proportions of females and males as a whole and in various age groups, as shown by census statistics (table 1-3), are also affected by net coverage errors and age reporting errors in census data.

Although the sex ratio (number of males per 100 females) at birth is a little above 105, this small preponderance of males at the start of life is reduced, first, by the higher infant mortality of males and, then, by the higher death rates of males at other ages. With advancing age, the sex ratio decreases more and more rapidly.

Moreover, there have been dramatic declines in sex ratios over time. The most marked change over the past 75 years occurred in the age group 65 years and over, which fell by almost one-third, from 102.1 in 1900 to 69.3 in 1975. This decline is largely the result of the widening gap between female and male mortality rates for this age group. The number of survivors of the heavy immigration that occurred during the first quarter of this century, when male immigrants were more numerous than female immigrants, has dwindled. The "mortality" factor has in fact produced an increase in the proportion of women among persons surviving to successively older ages. Approximately 53 percent of all women 65 years and over in March 1975 were widowed, and this fact has profound implications for social and economic policy.

Population projections. Projections regarding the course of future population change depend on the assumptions made with respect to future fertility, mortality, and net immigration. The alternative projections of the female population of the United States from 1975 to the year 2000 presented here vary on the basis of the assumed levels of fertility. For the three series of projections featured, the assumed fertility levels all yield

substantial increases in the female population to the year 2000 (table 1-4). Series I projections assume that women who enter the childbearing ages in future years will have an average of 2.7 births per woman; Series II and Series III assume averages of 2.1 and 1.7 births, respectively. All projection series use the same assumptions for mortality and net immigration. The projections assume only slight reductions in death rates and hence only slight rises in survival rates in future years; net immigration is assumed to be 400,000 per year. Over the 25-year period, the female population is projected to grow by 17.1 million for the low projection (Series III) and by more than twice that much, 37.5 million, for the high projection (Series I).

All three projection series indicate that women will continue to outnumber men throughout the next quarter of the century, and that the gap between the number of women and the number of men will continue to increase. The excess of women over men is projected to range between 6.2 million and 6.5 million by 1985 and between 6.9 million and 7.9 million by 2000.

Some perspective on the future age structure of the female population is given in table 1-5. In projection Series II and Series III, the proportion of females below age 15 would drop from one-fourth in 1975 to roughly one-fifth in both 1985 and 2000. Under the high fertility assumption of Series I, the proportion of female children would stabilize at approximately one-fourth of the total female population for the last quarter-century.

The future numbers of women 15 to 44 years old are significant, particularly in connection with the growth of the population, for these are the women in the childbearing ages. Because of differences in the future course of the fertility rates which underlie the alternative projections, the rate of change in the number of women 15 to 24 years old varies substantially among the three series of projections. Between 1975 and 2000, the numbers of such women would increase 13 percent under Series I and decrease 18 percent under Series III. The proportion of women at ages 25 to 44 is expected to rise only slightly according to all three series. Although

Table 1-1. Population of the United States by Age and Sex: 1900 to 1975

(Numbers in thousands. Resident population as of July 1 for 1975 and as of April 1 for other years)

Sex and year	All ages	Under 15 years	15 to 24 years	25 to 44 years	45 to 64 years	65 years and over	Median age
WOMEN							
1975	109,377	26,284	19,902	27,248	22,715	13,228	30.0
1970	104,300	28,395	17,890	24,547	21,818	11,650	29.3
1960	90,992	27,428	12,114	23,965	18,428	9,056	30.3
1950	76,139	19,964	11,232	23,112	15,349	6,482	30.5
1940	65,815	16,321	12,095	20,042	12,739	4,619	29.0
1930	[1]60,807	17,875	11,357	17,959	10,262	3,311	26.2
1920	[1]51,935	16,685	9,529	15,286	7,927	2,452	24.7
1910	[1]44,727	14,626	9,029	12,784	6,268	1,965	23.5
1900	[1]37,243	12,951	7,529	10,221	4,940	1,526	22.4
MEN							
1975	103,760	27,365	20,102	26,294	20,829	9,172	27.6
1970	98,912	29,505	17,551	23,449	19,992	8,416	26.8
1960	88,331	28,358	11,906	22,935	17,629	7,503	28.7
1950	75,187	20,708	10,989	22,302	15,375	5,813	29.9
1940	66,350	16,803	11,938	19,778	13,413	4,418	29.0
1930	[1]62,395	18,333	11,150	18,316	11,211	3,333	26.7
1920	[1]54,086	17,034	9,231	16,090	9,151	2,488	25.8
1910	[1]47,501	14,942	9,136	14,131	7,189	1,989	24.6
1900	[1]38,969	13,220	7,402	11,168	5,480	1,558	23.3

[1]Includes persons with age not reported, not shown separately.
Source: U.S. Department of Commerce, Bureau of the Census, 1970 Census of Population, Vol. I, Part 1(B), and Current Population Reports, Series P-25, No. 614.

the overall proportion of women 15 to 44 years old is expected to remain relatively unchanged between 1975 and 2000, the number of women in these ages is expected to rise in this period by 16 percent. This increase would more than counterbalance the decline in the average number of births per woman assumed in Series III, the series with subreplacement fertility, assuring a sufficient number of births to produce some population growth.

The proportions of women in the age groups 45 to 64 and 65 and over are expected to increase somewhat by the year 2000. Moreover, there will be a 40-percent increase between 1975 and 2000 in the number of women over 65 years old because of past rises in the numbers of births and past reductions in age-specific death rates. Regardless of which projection series is employed, the median age of the female population is expected to increase between 1975 and 2000. Under the low fertility assumption (Series III), the median age would increase by approximately 8.2 years; under the high fertility assumption (Series I), the median age would rise by 3.1 years.

Table 1-2. Percent Distribution of the Population by Age and Sex: 1900 to 1975

(Resident population as of July 1 for 1975 and as of April 1 for other years)

Sex and year	All ages	Under 15 years	15 to 24 years	25 to 44 years	45 to 64 years	65 years and over
WOMEN						
1975	100.0	24.0	18.2	24.9	20.8	12.1
1970	100.0	27.2	17.2	23.5	20.9	11.2
1960	100.0	30.1	13.3	26.3	20.3	10.0
1950	100.0	26.2	14.8	30.4	20.2	8.5
1940	100.0	24.8	18.4	30.5	19.4	7.0
1930	[1]100.0	29.4	18.7	29.5	16.9	5.4
1920	[1]100.0	32.1	18.3	29.4	15.3	4.7
1910	[1]100.0	32.7	20.2	28.6	14.0	4.4
1900	[1]100.0	34.8	20.2	27.4	13.3	4.1
MEN						
1975	100.0	26.4	19.4	25.3	20.1	8.8
1970	100.0	29.8	17.7	23.7	20.2	8.5
1960	100.0	32.1	13.5	26.0	20.0	8.5
1950	100.0	27.5	14.6	29.7	20.4	7.7
1940	100.0	25.3	18.0	29.8	20.2	6.7
1930	[1]100.0	29.4	17.9	29.4	18.0	5.3
1920	[1]100.0	31.5	17.1	29.7	16.9	4.6
1910	[1]100.0	31.5	19.2	29.7	15.1	4.2
1900	[1]100.0	33.9	19.0	28.7	14.1	4.0

[1]Includes persons with age not reported, not shown separately.
Source: Same as table 1-1.

Table 1-3. Sex Ratios of the Population by Age: 1900 to 1975

(Resident population as of July 1 for 1975 and as of April 1 for other years)

Year	All ages	Under 5 years	5 to 14 years	15 to 24 years	25 to 44 years	45 to 64 years	65 years and over
1975	94.9	104.4	104.0	101.0	96.5	91.7	69.3
1970	94.8	104.0	103.9	98.1	95.5	91.6	72.2
1960	97.1	103.4	103.4	98.3	95.7	95.7	82.9
1950	98.7	103.9	103.6	97.8	96.5	100.2	89.7
1940	100.8	103.2	102.8	98.7	98.7	105.3	95.6
1930	102.6	103.0	102.4	98.2	102.0	109.2	100.7
1920	104.1	102.5	101.9	96.9	105.3	115.4	101.5
1910	106.2	102.5	102.0	101.2	110.5	114.7	101.2
1900	104.6	102.1	102.0	98.3	109.3	110.9	102.1

Note: Number of males per 100 females.
Source: Same as table 1-1.

Table 1-5. Projections of the Percent Distribution of the Population by Age and Sex: 1975 to 2000

(As of July 1. Total population including Armed Forces overseas)

Sex and age	1975 (estimate)	1985			2000		
		Series I	Series II	Series III	Series I	Series II	Series III
Women, all ages	100.0	100.0	100.0	100.0	100.0	100.0	100.0
Under 5 years	7.1	9.5	8.0	6.9	8.2	6.6	5.5
5 to 14 years	16.9	14.6	13.9	13.2	17.0	14.5	12.6
15 to 24 years	18.2	15.4	15.8	16.2	15.4	14.2	12.9
25 to 44 years	24.9	29.1	30.0	30.7	26.2	28.5	30.4
45 to 64 years	20.8	18.5	19.0	19.4	20.6	22.5	24.0
65 years and over	12.1	12.9	13.3	13.6	12.6	13.7	14.7
Men, all ages	100.0	100.0	100.0	100.0	100.0	100.0	100.0
Under 5 years	7.8	10.5	8.9	7.6	9.0	7.4	6.2
5 to 14 years	18.5	16.1	15.3	14.6	18.7	16.2	14.1
15 to 24 years	19.5	16.5	17.1	17.5	16.6	15.5	14.2
25 to 44 years	25.4	29.9	30.9	31.7	26.7	29.3	31.5
45 to 64 years	20.0	17.9	18.4	18.9	20.2	22.2	23.9
65 years and over	8.8	9.1	9.4	9.6	8.6	9.4	10.2

Source: Same as table 1-4.

Table 1-4. **Projections of the Population of the United States by Age and Sex: 1975 to 2000**

(Numbers in thousands. As of July 1. Total population including Armed Forces overseas)

Sex and age	1975 (estimate)	1985			2000		
		Series I	Series II	Series III	Series I	Series II	Series III
Women, all ages...............	109,393	123,714	120,201	117,415	146,935	134,973	126,481
Under 5 years.....................	7,777	11,727	9,652	8,050	12,011	8,948	6,963
5 to 14 years.....................	18,507	18,100	16,661	15,477	24,954	19,597	15,899
15 to 24 years....................	19,913		19,046		22,570	19,122	16,376
25 to 44 years....................	27,251		36,030			[1]38,428	
45 to 64 years....................	22,715		22,836			30,319	
65 years and over................	13,228		15,975			18,558	
Median age..................years..	30.0	31.4	32.3	33.0	33.1	36.2	38.2
Men, all ages.................	104,239	117,560	113,866	110,940	140,072	127,521	118,617
Under 5 years.....................	8,119	12,315	10,132	8,448	12,643	9,416	7,325
5 to 14 years.....................	19,246	18,956	17,445	16,203	26,246	20,602	16,706
15 to 24 years....................	20,357		19,450		23,305	19,721	16,869
25 to 44 years....................	26,508		35,146			[1]37,380	
45 to 64 years....................	20,836		21,007			28,360	
65 years and over................	9,172		10,684			12,041	
Median age..................years..	27.6	28.9	29.8	30.6	29.7	33.3	35.7

[1]The base date for the projections was July 1, 1974; thus projections for age 25 differ slightly for Series I, Series II, and Series III.

Source: U.S. Department of Commerce, Bureau of the Census, Current Population Reports, Series P-25, Nos. 541 and 614.

EDUCATION

Although women have made strides toward achieving educational parity with men, equality has not been reached. The educational distribution of persons 25 to 29 years old shows this clearly (table 6-1). Since most persons of these ages have recently completed their schooling, their educational attainment can be used as an indicator of current trends. Among persons 25 to 29 years of age in 1950, there were only 66 women who had completed at least 4 years of college for every 100 men who had done so. The corresponding ratio in 1975 was 77 female college graduates for every 100 comparable males. Thus, while the proportion completing 4 or more years of college has risen more rapidly for young women than for young men, a higher proportion of men than women in both 1950 and 1975 had completed this much schooling.

A similar picture is shown by changes in college enrollment of women and men from 1950 to 1974 (table 6-2). While the enrollment rates of women have risen more rapidly than those of men since 1950, there are still fewer women than men attending college in 1974. However, those women who were attending college have been moving into traditionally "male" majors in increasing numbers. Table 6-3, which shows the percent female for the major fields of study of college students in 1966, 1972, and 1974, indicates a trend toward increasing proportions of women in most majors. This increase reflects, in part, the fact that a higher proportion of all college students were women in 1974 than was the case in 1966. Moreover, women still constitute a very small proportion of students enrolled in some of the traditional "male" majors. For example, the per-

centage of engineering majors who were women rose from 2 percent in 1966 to 7 percent in 1974. The comparable figures for agriculture and forestry were 3 percent in 1966 and 14 percent in 1974. Female college students in 1974 remain a large proportion of traditional female majors, such as education (73 percent), English or journalism (59 percent), and health or medical professions (64 percent).

The proportion of college-age women (18 to 24) enrolled in school was significantly higher in 1974 than in 1960. In 1960, 30 percent of the females 18 to 19 years old were enrolled in school; the enrollment ratio increased to 42 percent in 1970 and has since remained at approximately that level. Between 1960 and 1974 enrollment rates increased by 13 percentage points for 20-and-21-year-olds and by 8 percentage points for 22-to-24-year-olds.

These increases in college attendance by women are being reflected in the proportion of bachelor's and higher degrees awarded to women. In the academic year 1949-50, about one-fourth of all bachelor's and higher degrees were awarded to women, but only 10 percent of all doctorates given in that year went to females. By 1972 women earned 41 percent of all degrees at or above the B.A. level and 16 percent of all doctorates.

None of the indicators of educational achievement examined here—attainment, enrollment, field of study, or degrees awarded—show that women have reached the same levels as men. But in most areas the educational gap between the sexes has narrowed since 1950.

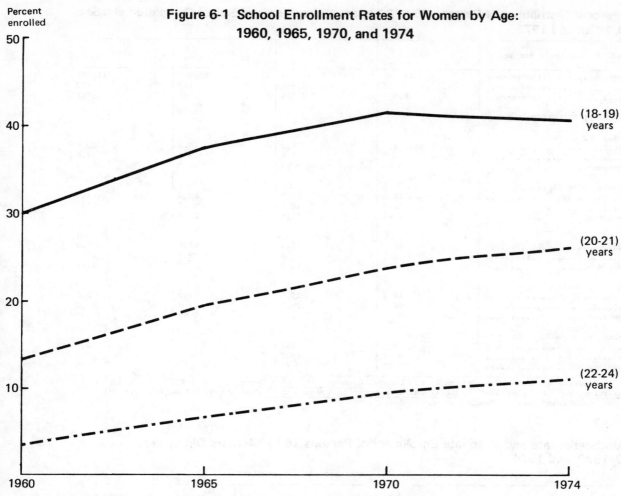

Percent enrolled

Figure 6-1 School Enrollment Rates for Women by Age: 1960, 1965, 1970, and 1974

(18-19) years

(20-21) years

(22-24) years

Source: U. S. Department of Commerce, Bureau of the Census Current Population Reports, Series P-20, Nos. 110, 162, 222 and 286.

Table 6-4. Bachelor's and Higher Degrees Conferred in Institutions of Higher Education by Level of Degree and Sex: Selected Years, 1950 to 1972

Level of degree and sex	1971-72	1969-70	1959-60	1949-50	Change, 1950 to 1972	
					Number	Percent
All levels, bachelor's and higher.	1,215,680	1,065,391	476,704	496,661	+719,019	+144.8
Women...............................	496,727	429,703	162,942	120,796	+375,931	+311.2
Men.................................	718,953	635,688	313,762	375,865	+343,088	+91.3
Ratio: women/men....................	0.69	0.68	0.52	0.32	(X)	(X)
Bachelor's and first professional.	930,684	827,234	392,440	432,058	+498,626	+115.4
Women...............................	389,371	343,060	138,377	103,217	+286,154	+277.2
Men.................................	541,313	484,174	254,063	328,841	+212,472	+64.6
Ratio: women/men....................	0.72	0.71	0.54	0.31	(X)	(X)
Master's...........................	251,633	208,291	74,435	58,183	+193,450	+332.5
Women...............................	102,083	82,667	23,537	16,963	+85,120	+501.8
Men.................................	149,550	125,624	50,898	41,220	+108,330	+262.8
Ratio: women/men....................	0.68	0.66	0.46	0.41	(X)	(X)
Doctorate..........................	33,363	29,866	9,829	6,420	+26,943	+419.7
Women...............................	5,273	3,976	1,028	616	+4,657	+756.0
Men.................................	28,090	25,890	8,801	5,804	+22,286	+384.0
Ratio: women/men....................	0.19	0.15	0.12	0.11	(X)	(X)

X Not applicable.

Source: Department of Health, Education, and Welfare, National Center for Education Statistics, Digest of Educational Statistics, 1974 and unpublished data.

Table 6-1. Percent Distribution of Persons 25 to 29 Years Old by Years of School Completed and Sex: 1950, 1960, 1970, and 1975

Years of school completed and sex	1975	1970	1960	1950
Total persons.........thousands..	16,395	13,394	10,876	11,921
Women.......................thousands..	8,347	6,824	5,537	6,169
Men........................thousands..	8,048	6,569	5,339	5,751
PERCENT DISTRIBUTION				
Elementary: 8 years or less				
Women...................................	5.4	8.3	15.5	23.2
Men......................................	6.0	9.6	19.7	27.6
Ratio: women/men......................	0.94	0.90	0.82	0.90
Some high school: 9 to 11 years				
Women...................................	12.8	18.2	23.0	21.9
Men......................................	9.5	16.2	20.7	21.9
Ratio: women/men......................	1.41	1.16	1.15	1.07
High school: 12 years				
Women...................................	45.7	45.3	42.6	39.4
Men......................................	37.2	38.2	32.2	29.8
Ratio: women/men......................	1.28	1.23	1.37	1.42
Some college: 1 to 3 years				
Women...................................	17.3	15.0	11.2	9.6
Men......................................	22.2	16.7	13.0	11.0
Ratio: women/men......................	0.81	0.93	0.89	0.93
College: 4 years or more				
Women...................................	18.7	13.2	7.8	5.9
Men......................................	25.1	19.3	14.4	9.6
Ratio: women/men......................	0.77	0.71	0.56	0.66

Source: U.S. Department of Commerce, Bureau of the Census, Current Population Reports, Series P-20, No. 207; 1960 Census of Population, Vol. II, Part 5(B), "Educational Attainment"; 1950 Census of Population, Volume IV, Part 5(B), "Education"; and unpublished Current Population Survey data.

Table 6-2. Undergraduate and Graduate Enrollment of Persons 16 to 34 Years Old by Sex: 1950, 1960, 1970, and 1974

(Numbers in thousands. Civilian noninstitutional population)

College enrollment and sex	1974	1970	1960	1950[1]	Percent change: earliest year to 1974
TOTAL PERSONS 16 TO 34 YEARS					
Women...................................	32,542	28,754	22,342	18,259	+78.2
Men......................................	30,641	26,100	20,216	16,915	+81.1
Total Persons Enrolled in College					
Women...................................	3,898	3,013	1,231	701	+456.1
Percent enrolled....................	12.0	10.5	5.5	3.8	(X)
Men......................................	4,924	4,401	2,339	1,474	+234.1
Percent enrolled....................	16.1	16.9	11.6	8.7	(X)
Ratio: women/men......................	0.79	0.68	0.53	0.48	(X)
Enrolled College, 1 to 4 Years					
Women...................................	3,306	2,647	(NA)	(NA)	+24.9
Percent enrolled....................	10.2	9.2	(NA)	(NA)	(X)
Men......................................	4,025	3,627	(NA)	(NA)	+11.0
Percent enrolled....................	13.1	13.9	(NA)	(NA)	(X)
Ratio: women/men......................	0.82	0.73	(NA)	(NA)	(X)
Enrolled College, 5 Years or More					
Women...................................	593	366	(NA)	(NA)	+62.0
Percent enrolled....................	1.8	1.3	(NA)	(NA)	(X)
Men......................................	897	774	(NA)	(NA)	+15.9
Percent enrolled....................	2.9	3.0	(NA)	(NA)	(X)
Ratio: women/men......................	0.66	0.47	(NA)	(NA)	(X)

NA Not available.   X Not applicable.   [1]Data are for persons 14 to 29 years old.

Source: U.S. Department of Commerce, Bureau of the Census, Current Population Reports, Series P-20, Nos. 278, 222, 110, and 34.

Table 6-3. **Percent Female by Major Field of Study for College Students 14 to 34 Years: October 1966, 1972, and 1974**

(Civilian noninstitutional population)

Major field of study	Percent female		
	1974	1972	1966
Total enrolled.........................	44.2	41.6	38.2
Agriculture/forestry..........................	13.5	11.3	2.6
Biological sciences..........................	41.0	36.6	([1])
Business or commerce.........................	31.7	23.2	23.0
Education.......................................	72.6	72.3	67.9
Engineering.....................................	6.8	2.0	1.9
English or journalism.........................	59.1	51.5	50.9
Other humanities.............................	48.0	47.3	
Health or medical profession..................	64.2	56.5	[2]44.5
Law..	23.2	17.7	(NA)
Mathematics or statistics.....................	44.6	34.3	36.5
Physical sciences.............................	26.9	27.4	11.1
Social sciences...............................	44.4	47.5	37.6
Vocational-technical studies..................	25.4	(NA)	(NA)
Computer science..............................	20.0	(NA)	(NA)
Other..	41.0	39.7	27.4
None and not reported.........................	44.7	41.9	41.9

NA Not available.
[1]Included in health or medical profession.
[2]Includes biological sciences.

Source: U.S. Department of Commerce, Bureau of the Census, Current Population Reports, Series P-20, No. 260 and unpublished data.

LABOR FORCE PARTICIPATION

The dramatic increase in women's labor force participation during recent years has been one of the strongest indications of the changing social and economic roles of women. Between 1950 and 1974, the number of women workers nearly doubled while the number of men in the labor force increased by only about one-fourth. Accordingly, the ratio of women per 100 men in the labor force has risen from 41 in 1950 to 63 in 1974. Increases in labor force participation have been evident for women of all ages under 65, but the size and timing of the growth have varied by age. For older women of working age, those 45 to 64 years old, the proportion in the work force rose dramatically between 1950 and 1960; this development was possibly a carry-over effect of work experience gained by this group of women during World War II. In the 1960's, however, the increases leveled off somewhat, and during the last few years the labor force rates for this age group have remained more nearly stable or even declined. During the 1960's and early 1970's, younger women began entering the labor force in increasing numbers. The labor force rates for 20-to-24-year-olds increased from 46 percent in 1960 to 63 percent in 1974, and the rates of women 25 to 34 years old rose from 36 percent to 52 percent during the same period. So pronounced have been the increases in labor force participation among women that the labor force rates for all age groups between 16 and 54 years in 1974 exceeded the rate for the most active age group (20 to 24 years old) in 1950.

Projections of the size of the labor force by sex and age indicate that by 1990 there may be about 43.7 million women in the labor force, a 22-percent increase over the number in 1974 (table 7-8). Primarily because of changes in the age distribution of the population, the largest increases in the female labor force are expected for women between the ages of 25 and 44 years. Smaller increases are projected for older women, and the number of working women 16 to 24 years old is expected to decline somewhat. These projections assume no drastic changes in the propensity of women to seek work, and any substantial change in the labor force participation rates would alter the size of the labor force from that projected.

One important factor related to labor force participation is the level of educational attainment. Increases in years of schooling, especially graduation from high school and from college, and associated gains in earnings potential are normally associated with greater work force activity. As seen in the previous section, the proportions of young women completing high school and completing college have grown over the past 25 years. At the same time, the labor force participation rates of women who were at least high school graduates have risen (table 7-3). For example, about half of the women college graduates were in the labor force in 1952, but nearly two-thirds were working in 1975. Therefore, the absolute increase in the number of women workers reflected both the rise in educational attainment and the increased labor force participation among women with higher attainment levels.

Historically, marital status and the presence and age of children have affected labor force participation. Single (never married) women have higher rates of labor force activity than other women, and these rates have been fairly close to the rates of single men (table 7-4). However, the participation rates for married women with a husband present have risen sharply between 1950 and 1975. In 1950 only about one-fourth of the married women were in the work force, but in 1975 the rate of labor force participation reached 44 percent. Although the labor force rates for women of other marital status also rose during this period, the increases were not so large. Therefore, the differential in labor force participation between married women and other women has lessened.

Among married women the presence of preschool-age children generally reduces the level of labor force activity (table 7-5). In 1975, 37 percent of the women with children under 6 years of age were in the labor force, but the labor force rates of women whose children were all of school age and women with no children under 18 were 52 percent and 44 percent, respectively. Although the presence of preschool-age children does affect participation rates, there has been considerable growth over the past 25 years in the labor force activity of this group. The labor force rate for women with children under 6 years was only about 12 percent in 1950, but in 1975 this rate had tripled to about 37 percent. Furthermore, in 1975 the participation rate for women with children under 3 years was about 33 percent, approximately double the 1960 rate for this group. Thus, the roles of wife and mother are seemingly

becoming more compatible with work in the marketplace for greater numbers of women.

One often cited reason for the growth in women's labor force participation is the expansion in the service sector of the economy (see chapter 8). This growth in the service industries has resulted in more part-time jobs and has, therefore, created employment opportunities for women who otherwise may not have entered the work force. In the 1950 Census of Population, there were slightly more male than female part-time workers (3.9 million vs. 3.0 million), but in the 1960 and 1970 censuses, there were more women than men working part time (8.9 million vs. 7.2 million in 1970). Certainly, the availability of part-time work is an important factor for many women, especially those with young children, in reaching the decision about whether or not to work.

The unemployment rate for adult women (20 years old and over) has historically been higher than that for adult men (table 7-7). Women normally have more frequent periods of withdrawal from the labor force and subsequent reentry, which contributes to higher unemployment. Also, tenure or years of experience are usually lower for women than for men, and this increases the likelihood of layoff or job loss.

Table 7-1. Size of Labor Force by Age and Sex: 1950, 1960, 1970, and 1974

(Noninstitutional population. Numbers in thousands)

Sex and age	Number in labor force				Change, 1950 to 1974	
	1974	1970	1960	1950	Number	Percent
TOTAL, 16 YEARS AND OVER						
Women	35,892	31,560	23,272	18,412	+17,480	+94.9
Men	57,349	54,343	48,870	45,446	+11,903	+26.2
Ratio: women/men	0.63	0.58	0.48	0.41	(X)	(X)
16 to 19 Years						
Women	4,005	3,250	2,062	1,714	+2,291	+133.7
Men	5,189	4,395	3,184	2,821	+2,368	+83.9
Ratio: women/men	0.77	0.74	0.65	0.61	(X)	(X)
20 to 24 Years						
Women	5,867	4,893	2,590	2,681	+3,186	+118.8
Men	8,105	7,378	5,089	5,224	+2,880	+55.1
Ratio: women/men	0.72	0.66	0.51	0.51	(X)	(X)
25 to 34 Years						
Women	7,826	5,704	4,140	4,101	+3,725	+90.8
Men	13,993	11,974	10,930	11,044	+2,949	+26.7
Ratio: women/men	0.56	0.48	0.38	0.37	(X)	(X)
35 to 44 Years						
Women	6,354	5,971	5,308	4,166	+2,188	+52.5
Men	10,614	10,818	11,340	9,952	+662	+6.7
Ratio: women/men	0.60	0.55	0.47	0.42	(X)	(X)
45 to 54 Years						
Women	6,687	6,533	5,280	3,328	+3,359	+100.9
Men	10,491	10,487	9,634	8,152	+2,339	+28.7
Ratio: women/men	0.64	0.62	0.55	0.41	(X)	(X)
55 to 64 Years						
Women	4,158	4,153	2,986	1,839	+2,319	+126.1
Men	7,032	7,127	6,405	5,800	+1,232	+21.2
Ratio: women/men	0.59	0.58	0.47	0.32	(X)	(X)
65 Years and Over						
Women	996	1,056	907	584	+412	70.5
Men	1,925	2,164	2,287	2,453	-528	-21.5
Ratio: women/men	0.52	0.49	0.40	0.24	(X)	(X)

X Not applicable.
Source: U.S. Department of Labor, Manpower Administration, 1975 Manpower Report of the President.

Table 7-3. **Labor Force Participation Rates by Years of School Completed for Persons 18 Years Old and Over:**
1952, 1959, 1970, and 1975

(Civilian noninstitutional population 18 years old and over)

Sex and years of school completed	Labor force participation rates				Percent change, 1952 to 1975
	1975	1970	1959[1]	1952[1]	
NOT HIGH SCHOOL GRADUATE					
Women	31.6	33.0	31.6	31.2	+1.3
Men	65.2	72.6	81.2	85.3	-23.6
Ratio: women/men[2]	0.48	0.45	0.39	0.37	(X)
HIGH SCHOOL GRADUATE-NO COLLEGE					
Women	52.5	50.3	42.8	40.7	+29.0
Men	87.6	90.1	92.7	93.1	-5.9
Ratio: women/men[2]	0.60	0.56	0.46	0.44	(X)
1 TO 3 YEARS OF COLLEGE					
Women	53.5	48.6	40.5	37.5	+42.7
Men	81.3	80.6	83.4	85.6	-5.0
Ratio: women/men[2]	0.66	0.60	0.49	0.44	(X)
4 OR MORE YEARS OF COLLEGE					
Women	64.1	59.7	53.3	50.2	+27.7
Men	90.4	90.2	92.8	88.0	+2.7
Ratio: women/men[2]	0.71	0.66	0.57	0.57	(X)

X Not applicable.
[1] Data exclude persons who did not report years of school completed.
[2] Ratios of labor force participation rates.

Source: U.S. Department of Commerce, Bureau of the Census, Current Population Reports, Series P-50, No. 49 and unpublished data, and U.S. Department of Labor, Bureau of Labor Statistics, Special Labor Force Reports, Nos. 125 and 1.

Table 7-5. **Labor Force Participation Rates for Ever-Married Women by Presence and Age of Children:**
1950, 1960, 1970, and 1975

(Civilian noninstitutional population 16 years and over in 1975 and 1970, 14 years and over in 1960 and 1950)

Presence and age of children	Labor force participation rates				Percent change, earliest year to 1975
	1975	1970	1960	1950	
Married women, husband present	44.4	40.8	30.5	23.8	+86.6
No children under 18	43.9	42.2	34.7	30.3	+44.9
With children under 18	44.8	39.7	27.6	18.4	+143.5
Children 6 to 17 only	52.3	49.2	39.0	28.3	+84.8
Children under 6	36.6	30.3	18.6	11.9	+207.7
Children 3 to 5, none under 3	41.9	37.0	25.1	(NA)	+66.9
Children under 3	32.7	25.8	15.3	(NA)	+113.7
Other ever-married women[1]	40.7	39.1	40.0	37.8	+7.7
No children under 18	33.2	33.4	35.7	33.7	-1.5
With children under 18	62.4	60.6	55.5	54.9	+13.7
Children 6 to 17 only	67.2	67.3	66.2	63.6	+5.7
Children under 6	55.0	50.7	39.8	41.4	+32.9
Children 3 to 5, none under 3	59.4	58.8	51.7	(NA)	+14.9
Children under 3	49.7	43.6	32.4	(NA)	+53.4

NA Not available.
[1] Includes widowed, divorced, and married, husband absent.

Source: Same as table 7-4.

Table 7-6. Number of Part-Time Workers by Age and Sex: 1950, 1960, and 1970

(Numbers in thousands)

Sex and age	1970	1960	1950	Percent change, 1950 to 1970
PART-TIME WORKERS[1]				
Total, 14 Years Old and Over				
Women..	8,866	5,657	3,007	+194.8
Men..	7,175	5,157	3,853	+86.2
Ratio: women/men.............................	1.24	1.10	0.78	(X)
14 to 19 Years Old				
Women..	1,494	823	371	+302.7
Men..	2,207	1,463	724	+204.8
Ratio: women/men.............................	0.68	0.56	0.51	(X)
20 Years Old and Over				
Women..	7,372	4,835	2,636	+179.7
Men..	4,968	3,695	3,129	+58.8
Ratio: women/men.............................	1.48	1.31	0.84	(X)

X Not applicable.
[1]Persons working 1 to 34 hours during the census reference week.

Source: U.S. Department of Commerce, Bureau of the Census, 1970 Census of Population, Vol. II, Part 6(A), "Employment Status and Work Experience;" 1960 Census of Population, Vol. II, Part 6(A), "Employment Status and Work Experience;" and 1950 Census of Population, Vol. II, Part 1(A), "Employment and Personal Characteristics."

Table 7-7. Number Unemployed and Unemployment Rates by Age and Sex: 1950, 1960, 1970, and 1974

(Numbers in thousands)

Sex and age	1974	1970	1960	1950
Number Unemployed				
Total, 16 years old and over				
Women..	2,408	1,853	1,366	1,049
Men..	2,668	2,235	2,486	2,239
Ratio: women/men.............................	0.90	0.83	0.55	0.47
16 to 19 years old				
Women..	660	506	286	195
Men..	750	599	425	318
Ratio: women/men.............................	0.88	0.84	0.67	0.61
20 years old and over				
Women..	1,747	1,346	1,078	854
Men..	1,919	1,636	2,058	1,922
Ratio: women/men.............................	0.91	0.82	0.52	0.44
PERCENT DISTRIBUTION				
Unemployment Rate				
Total, 16 years old and over				
Women..	6.7	5.9	5.9	5.7
Men..	4.8	4.4	5.4	5.1
Ratio: women/men[1].........................	1.40	1.34	1.09	1.12
16 to 19 years old				
Women..	16.5	15.6	13.9	11.4
Men..	15.6	15.0	15.3	12.7
Ratio: women/men[1].........................	1.06	1.04	0.91	0.90
20 years old and over				
Women..	5.5	4.8	5.1	5.1
Men..	3.8	3.5	4.7	4.7
Ratio: women/men[1].........................	1.45	1.37	1.09	1.09

[1]Ratios of unemployment rates.
Source: U.S. Department of Commerce, Bureau of the Census, Current Population Reports, Series P-50, No. 31 and U.S. Department of Labor, Bureau of Labor Statistics, Special Labor Force Reports, Nos. 178, 129, and 14.

Table 7-8. **Projected Size of Labor Force by Age and Sex: 1980, 1985, and 1990**

Sex and age	Number in labor force (thousands)				Change, 1974 to 1990	
	1974 (actual)	1980	1985	1990	Number	Percent
TOTAL, 16 YEARS AND OVER						
Women.........................	35,892	39,219	41,699	43,699	+7,807	+21.8
Men...........................	57,349	62,590	66,017	68,907	+11,558	+20.2
16 to 19 Years						
Women.........................	4,005	3,669	3,203	3,188	-817	-20.4
Men...........................	5,189	4,668	3,962	3,901	-1,288	-24.8
20 to 24 Years						
Women.........................	5,867	6,592	6,523	5,826	-41	-0.7
Men...........................	8,105	8,852	8,496	7,404	-701	-8.6
25 to 34 Years						
Women.........................	7,826	9,256	10,339	10,678	+2,852	+36.4
Men...........................	13,993	17,523	19,400	19,853	+5,860	+41.9
35 to 44 Years						
Women.........................	6,354	6,869	8,560	10,219	+3,865	+60.8
Men...........................	10,614	11,851	14,617	17,398	+6,784	+63.9
45 to 54 Years						
Women.........................	6,687	6,537	6,542	7,364	+677	+10.1
Men...........................	10,491	9,908	9,744	10,909	+418	+4.0
55 to 64 Years						
Women.........................	4,158	5,057	5,213	5,003	+845	+20.3
Men...........................	7,032	7,730	7,716	7,307	+275	+3.9
65 Years and Over						
Women.........................	996	1,239	1,319	1,391	+395	+39.7
Men...........................	1,925	2,058	2,082	2,135	+210	+10.9

Source: U.S. Department of Labor, Bureau of Labor Statistics, Special Labor Force Report No. 156.

OCCUPATION AND INDUSTRY

Occupation. Although the employment of women increased substantially (about 38 percent) between 1960 and 1970, women remained fairly concentrated in a few major occupation groups. In both 1960 and 1970, over half of employed women were working in clerical, operative, or service positions. In fact, a higher proportion of employed women were clerical or service workers in 1970 than in 1960 (48 percent to 43 percent). The employment growth in these two areas was primarily in traditionally female occupations (e.g., secretaries, stenographers, and typists, and health service workers) but was not entirely restricted to such areas. The number of women mail carriers and bartenders, for example, did increase during the period.

Between 1960 and 1970, both men and women had strong employment gains among professional, technical, and kindred workers. In both years, however, the vast majority of women professionals were employed in normally lower-paying occupations—health workers, except practitioners (mostly registered nurses), and elementary and secondary school teachers—whereas men's employment was distributed more evenly among the various professional and technical occupations. In 1970 about 30 percent of the men professional and technical workers were employed in the relatively high-paying fields of engineering, law, and medicine; only about 2 percent of women professionals were in these occupations.

The number of women managers and administrators increased about 22 percent from 1960 to 1970, but there were still approximately five times as many men as women in managerial positions in 1970. Occupation groups with even smaller proportions of women workers include the craft, transport equipment operative, and laborer groups. For each of these, there was very little change between 1960 and 1970 in the ratio of employed women to employed men. However, among transport equipment operatives, there was a substantial increase in women bus drivers during this period. The emergence of many women school bus drivers probably was the principal reason for this growth. Finally, the number of women and men employed as private household workers or in farm occupations decreased from 1960 to 1970.

Educational attainment is a major factor in determining the types of occupations available to persons, but there are variations in the occupational distribution of women and men with similar education (table 8-2).

Nearly three-fourths (71 percent) of employed women between 25 and 64 years of age in March 1974 who had completed 4 years or more of college were professional and technical workers; this is a higher proportion than that for male college graduates. However, about 14 percent of female college graduates in the same age group were working in clerical jobs and only about 7 percent in managerial positions. Among male college graduates, over one-fourth were working as managers and administrators. The dominant occupation group for women with 4 years of high school (with no college) was clerical workers; service occupations ranked second. For men high school graduates, the blue-collar craft and operative occupations were the most important areas of employment, but there was still a relatively strong representation in managerial jobs. Women with less than 4 years of high school were concentrated primarily in service occupations and to a lesser degree in operative jobs; the majority of men of this educational level were working in craft and operative positions.

Among married couples in which both the husband and wife were employed in 1970, there were differences in the occupational distribution of wives according to the husband's occupation. The vast majority of wives of white-collar workers were also working in white-collar occupations. Women whose husbands worked in professional and technical occupations were more likely than other wives to be professional or technical workers. Wives of blue-collar workers were somewhat more evenly distributed among sales and clerical, blue-collar, and service occupations.

Industry. The expansion of service industries in the United States is often cited as one of the most important factors in the growth of the female work force. More than one-third (39 percent) of employed women in 1970 were working in the service industries, with the largest proportion (about 28 percent) in professional and related services; e.g., in positions at schools, hospitals, and welfare agencies. Approximately 2.3 million women worked in the personal service industry, but less than 1 million working women were in business, repair, or entertainment and recreation services. Other industries employing large numbers of women were wholesale and retail trade and manufacturing. Also, about half of the jobs in finance, insurance, and real estate and nearly one-third of the jobs in public administration were held by women.

There was some change from 1950 to 1970 in the pattern of employment by industry for women. In terms of the ratio of women to men in an industry, women strongly increased their representation in wholesale and retail trade; finance, insurance, and real estate; and most service industries. Relatively smaller gains were made in other industries. As was true in 1950 and 1960, the only major industrial groups employing more women than men in 1970 were personal services and professional and related services.

Table 8-2. Years of School Completed By Employed Persons 25 to 64 Years Old by Major Occupation Group and Sex: March 1974

Major occupation	Years of school completed									
	Elementary, 8 years or less		High school, 1 to 3 years		High school, 4 years		College, 1 to 3 years		College, 4 years or more	
	Male	Female	Male	Female	Male	Female	Male	Female	Male	Female
Total employed..........thousands..	6,280	2,630	5,823	3,640	14,368	10,908	5,531	3,187	7,778	5,549
Percent......................	100.0	100.0	100.0	100.0	100.0	100.0	100.0	100.0	100.0	100.0
Professional, technical, and kindred workers...................	0.9	1.0	1.9	1.6	6.3	7.0	17.1	22.5	54.1	71.4
Managers and administrators, except farm......................	5.5	2.9	8.8	5.2	15.5	6.3	24.2	7.7	26.3	6.8
Sales workers......................	1.3	3.7	3.4	7.4	5.9	7.8	10.6	5.0	8.3	3.0
Clerical and kindred workers.......	2.9	6.5	4.6	19.0	8.3	45.4	10.0	46.8	3.1	13.5
Craft and kindred workers..........	25.4	2.7	31.8	3.0	29.4	1.9	18.7	1.2	3.9	0.5
Operatives, including transport....	29.7	35.1	28.7	27.9	19.3	11.5	8.9	4.4	1.1	1.3
Laborers, except farm.............	13.4	1.4	8.3	1.5	4.2	0.7	2.2	0.7	0.4	-
Farm workers......................	10.4	4.0	4.2	1.3	3.8	1.3	1.9	0.7	1.2	0.4
Service workers...................	10.6	42.9	8.5	33.0	7.3	18.1	6.4	11.0	1.6	3.1

- Represents zero.

Source: U.S. Department of Commerce, Bureau of the Census, Current Population Reports, Series P-20, No. 274.

Table 8-1. Occupation of Employed Persons 14 Years and Over by Sex: 1960 and 1970

(Numbers in thousands)

Occupation	1970			1960			Change, 1960 to 1970	
	Women	Men	Women/men ratio	Women	Men	Women/men ratio	Women	Men
Total employed[1]................	29,170	48,139	0.61	21,172	43,467	0.49	+7,998	+4,672
Professional, technical, and kindred workers.........................	4,314	6,517	0.66	2,683	4,303	0.62	+1,631	+2,214
Engineers....................	20	1,188	0.02	7	853	0.01	+13	+335
Lawyers and judges...............	13	259	0.05	7	210	0.04	+6	+49
Life and physical scientists.......	27	176	0.15	13	143	0.09	+14	+33
Physicians, dentists, and other related practitioners............	46	493	0.09	27	435	0.06	+19	+58
Health workers, ex. practitioners..	1,073	132	8.13	729	67	10.88	+344	+65
Teachers, college and university...	138	348	0.40	46	147	0.31	+92	+201
Teachers, except college and university.....................	1,929	817	2.36	1,293	487	2.66	+636	+330
Engineering and science technicians.....................	88	716	0.12	54	543	0.10	+34	+173
Managers and administrators, ex. farm.	1,014	5,126	0.20	829	4,797	0.17	+185	+329
Bank officers and financial managers.........................	55	225	0.22	2	22	0.09	+53	+233
Sales managers and dept. heads, retail trade.....................	49	157	0.31	26	86	0.30	+23	+71
Managers and administrators, n.e.c.[2]......................	489	3,216	0.15	533	3,678	0.14	-44	-462
Salaried.........................	345	2,457	0.14	311	2,137	0.15	+34	+320
Self-employed...................	143	759	0.19	223	1,541	0.14	-80	-782
Sales workers.....................	2,000	3,268	0.61	1,652	2,986	0.55	+348	+282
Real estate agents and brokers.....	84	179	0.47	46	147	0.31	+38	+32
Sales workers and sales clerks, retail trade.....................	1,542	1,213	1.27	1,378	1,176	1.17	+164	+37
Clerical and kindred workers.........	9,582	3,452	2.78	6,204	2,922	2.12	+3,378	+530
Bookkeepers......................	1,259	277	4.55	774	154	5.03	+485	+123
Mail carriers, post office.........	20	233	0.09	4	189	0.02	+16	+44
Secretaries, stenographers and typists........................	3,684	130	28.34	2,179	80	27.23	+1,505	+50
Stock clerks and storekeepers......	103	351	0.29	56	310	0.18	+47	+41
Telephone operators...............	385	23	16.74	342	15	22.80	+43	+8
Craft and kindred workers...........	495	9,502	0.05	277	8,668	0.03	+218	+834
Blue collar worker supervisors, n.e.c.[2].......................	128	1,463	0.09	78	1,084	0.07	+50	+379
Construction craft workers.........	45	2,498	0.02	17	2,322	0.01	+28	+176
Decorators and window dressers.....	40	30	1.33	24	27	0.89	+16	+3
Mechanics and repairers...........	49	2,399	0.02	18	2,118	0.01	+31	+281
Operatives, except transport.........	3,720	6,096	0.61	3,135	5,687	0.55	+585	+409
Assemblers.......................	455	490	0.93	289	416	0.69	+166	+74
Precision machine operatives.....	37	374	0.10	19	247	0.08	+18	+127
Sewers and stitchers..............	814	55	14.80	719	46	15.63	+95	+9
Transport equipment operatives.......	122	2,644	0.05	38	2,488	0.02	+84	+156
Bus drivers......................	66	170	0.39	18	163	0.11	+48	+7
Laborers, except farm...............	269	2,945	0.09	173	3,149	0.05	+96	-204
Freight, stock, and material handlers...........................	145	1,010	0.14	87	712	0.12	+58	+298
Farmers and farm managers...........	62	1,281	0.05	118	2,389	0.05	-56	-1,108
Farm laborers and supervisors........	141	783	0.18	248	1,239	0.20	-107	-456
Farm laborers, wage workers........	99	681	0.15	123	1,053	0.12	-24	-372
Farm laborers, unpaid family wkrs..	39	68	0.57	125	156	0.80	-86	-88
Service workers.....................	4,424	3,640	1.22	2,963	2,791	1.06	+1,461	+849
Bartenders.......................	39	150	0.26	19	153	0.12	+20	-3
Health service workers............	1,045	140	7.46	587	120	4.89	+458	+20
Personal service workers..........	776	393	1.97	481	424	1.13	+295	-31
Protective service workers........	58	895	0.06	26	674	0.04	+32	+221
Private household workers............	1,052	37	28.43	1,657	61	27.16	-605	-24

[1]Includes employed persons with occupation not reported.
[2]Not elsewhere classified.

Note: Because some occupations are not included in this table, subgroups may not add to total for major occupational categories.

Source: U.S. Department of Commerce, Bureau of the Census, 1970 Census of Population, Vol. I, Part 1(D).

Table 8-3. **Industry of Employed Persons 14 Years Old and Over by Sex: 1950, 1960, and 1970**

(Numbers in thousands)

Industry	1970			1960			1950		
	Women	Men	Women/men ratio	Women	Men	Women/men ratio	Women	Men	Women/men ratio
Total employed[1]................	29,170	48,139	0.61	21,172	43,467	0.49	15,773	40,662	0.39
Agriculture, forestry, and fisheries...	289	2,411	0.12	418	3,932	0.11	593	6,441	0.09
Mining.............................	48	556	0.09	32	622	0.05	23	908	0.03
Construction.......................	253	3,966	0.06	154	3,662	0.04	99	3,359	0.03
Manufacturing......................	5,321	13,568	0.39	4,401	13,112	0.34	3,648	11,026	0.33
Durable goods...................	2,349	8,775	0.27	1,728	8,105	0.21	1,218	6,515	0.19
Metal industries.............	333	2,065	0.16	267	1,986	0.13	216	1,783	0.12
Machinery, except electrical.....	331	1,662	0.20	214	1,354	0.16	168	1,085	0.15
Elect. mach., equip. and supplies..	728	1,179	0.62	509	981	0.52	290	572	0.51
Transportation equipment...........	285	1,855	0.15	221	1,598	0.14	155	1,189	0.13
Nondurable goods................	2,963	4,793	0.62	2,673	5,008	0.53	2,394	4,429	0.54
Food and kindred workers...........	363	1,031	0.35	430	1,393	0.31	327	1,172	0.28
Textile mill products...........	446	521	0.86	418	536	0.78	527	702	0.75
Apparel and other fabricated textile products......................	947	274	3.46	866	294	2.95	757	310	2.44
Chemical and allied products.......	222	766	0.29	165	699	0.24	126	512	0.25
Not specified manufacturing industries......................	44	89	0.49	21	39	0.54	36	82	0.44
Transportation, communications, and other public utilities...........	1,056	3,850	0.27	771	3,687	0.21	699	3,751	0.19
Transportation.....................	405	2,428	0.17	236	2,518	0.09	195	2,759	0.07
Communication......................	521	554	0.94	425	395	1.08	408	303	1.35
Utilities and sanitary services......	129	868	0.15	110	775	0.14	96	690	0.14
Wholesale and retail trade.............	5,928	8,685	0.68	4,395	7,398	0.59	3,562	6,954	0.51
Wholesale trade.....................	694	2,295	0.30	451	1,762	0.26	380	1,584	0.24
Retail trade........................	5,234	6,390	0.82	3,944	5,636	0.70	3,181	5,371	0.59
General merchandise stores........	1,436	663	2.17	1,085	507	2.14	647	384	1.68
Food stores.......................	744	1,206	0.62	567	1,123	0.50	482	1,184	0.41
Eating and drinking places........	1,393	983	1.42	1,060	742	1.43	867	824	1.05
Finance, insurance, and real estate....	1,814	1,838	0.99	1,230	1,465	0.84	782	1,138	0.69
Banking and credit agencies...........	795	500	1.59	497	371	1.34	260	271	0.96
Insurance............................	644	689	0.93	487	590	0.83	335	427	0.78
Real estate..........................	283	471	0.60	199	400	0.50	161	376	0.43
Business services.....................	520	780	0.67	282	476	0.59	118	241	0.49
Repair services.......................	107	846	0.13	57	792	0.07	44	906	0.05
Personal services.....................	2,341	953	2.46	2,777	1,085	2.56	2,301	1,164	1.98
Private households....................	1,082	122	8.87	1,729	188	9.20	1,395	206	6.77
Hotels and motels....................	323	247	1.31	258	245	1.05	256	271	0.95
Laundering, cleaning, and other garment services....................	326	212	1.54	355	266	1.33	371	324	1.15
Beauty and barber shops..............	440	209	2.11	282	214	1.32	183	201	0.91
Entertainment and recreation services..	209	381	0.55	157	346	0.45	127	367	0.35
Professional and related services......	8,048	4,732	1.70	4,629	3,066	1.51	2,789	2,040	1.37
Health services......................	3,174	1,085	2.93	1,822	790	2.31	1,079	592	1.82
Hospitals.........................	2,077	619	3.36	1,247	421	2.96	708	281	2.52
Health, except hospitals...........	1,098	467	2.35	575	369	1.56	371	311	1.19
Educational services.................	3,843	2,298	1.67	2,136	1,242	1.72	1,328	751	1.77
Welfare services....................	236	109	2.17	104	58	1.79	159	243	0.65
Public administration.................	1,229	2,827	0.43	846	2,240	0.38	658	1,856	0.35
Postal services......................	144	576	0.25	68	483	0.14	53	403	0.13
Federal public administration........	546	983	0.56	444	813	0.55	345	683	0.51
State public administration..........	202	336	0.60	126	235	0.54	101	166	0.61
Local public administration..........	336	932	0.36	208	709	0.29	160	605	0.26

[1]Includes persons with industry not reported.

Note: Because some industries are not included in this table, subgroups do not always add to major industrial divisions.

Source: U.S. Department of Commerce, Bureau of the Census, 1970 Census of Population, Vol. I, Part 1(D) and Technical Paper 18, Changes Between 1950 and 1960 Occupation and Industry Classifications.

WORK EXPERIENCE

Further evidence of women's increasing attachment to the labor force is seen in the data on annual work experience. About 43 million women, over half of the women 16 years old and over, worked at some time during 1974. This represented an 84 percent increase over the number of women with work experience in 1950. The number of women working 50 to 52 weeks at full-time jobs grew even more dramatically during the period; in 1950 there were only about 29 women for every 100 men working year round full time, but in 1974 this ratio had risen to 47 women per 100 men.

As was true for labor force participation rates, the largest increases in annual work experience occurred between 1950 and 1960 for older women (45 to 64 years old) and since 1960 for the younger age groups (20 to 34 years old). Also, the relative increase in the proportion with work experience during the year has been stronger for married women with husband present than for never-married women. For other women, the percent with annual work experience actually declined slightly between 1950 and 1974, probably because of an increasing number of elderly widowed women within this group.

Although the number of women with work experience has increased, the median number of years that employed women have worked in their current jobs has not shown a consistent pattern of change (table 9-4). There was evidence of an increase in the median years on the job between 1951 (2.2 years) and 1963 (3.0 years), but there was no increase between 1963 and 1973. This may be partially explained by the influx of women workers in recent years since new labor force entrants obviously deflate the figures on median years on the job. Only for the oldest age group, 55 to 64 years old, has there been a steady increase in the median number of years in the current job. Also, it is noteworthy that for persons 45 to 54 years old, the period during a

career when earnings normally reach a peak, the median years on current job for women has consistently been only about half that for men.

Variations in the lifetime work experience of women according to educational attainment can be seen from data based on the 1967 Longitudinal Survey of Work Experience.[1] One of the studies resulting from this survey shows that about 21 percent of women 30 to 44 years old with at least 1 year of college had worked for 6 months or more in every year since leaving school.[2] The comparable proportion for women with less than 4 years of high school was only 8 percent. Further, 30-to-44-year-old women college graduates had worked, on the average, for two-thirds of the years since completing school, but women high school graduates of the same age worked for only about half the years since completing their education.

---

[1] 1967 National Longitudinal Survey of Work Experience is conducted by the Bureau of the Census, under contract with the Employment and Training Administration (then Manpower Administration), U.S. Department of Labor. Dr. Herbert Parnes of the Ohio State University is the director of the National Longitudinal Surveys. There are four separate survey panels: men 14 to 24 years old and 45 to 54 years old (both begun in 1966), women 30-44 years old (begun in 1967) and women 14-24 years old (begun in 1968).

[2] Larry E. Suter and Herman P. Miller, "Income Differences Between Men and Career Women," **The American Journal of Sociology,** Vol. 78, No. 4, January 1973.

Table 9-1. **Annual Work Experience by Sex: 1950, 1960, 1970, and 1974**

(Numbers in thousands. Civilian noninstitutional population 16 years and over in 1974 and 1970, 14 years and over in 1950 and 1960)

Work experience and sex	1974	1970	1960	1950	Percent change, 1950 to 1974
NUMBER WORKED DURING YEAR					
Women...........................	42,841	38,704	30,585	23,350	+83.5
Men.............................	58,908	54,919	50,033	45,526	+29.4
Ratio: women/men................	0.73	0.70	0.61	0.51	(X)
Percent Worked During Year[1]					
Women...........................	53.9	52.5	46.9	41.1	+31.1
Men.............................	83.0	84.1	84.5	86.8	-4.4
Ratio: women/men[2].............	0.65	0.62	0.56	0.47	(X)
NUMBER WORKED 50 TO 52 WEEKS AT FULL-TIME JOBS					
Women...........................	18,311	15,738	11,299	8,592	+113.1
Men.............................	39,211	36,295	31,966	29,783	+31.7
Ratio: women/men	0.47	0.43	0.35	0.29	(X)
Percent Of Workers Who Worked 50 To 52 Weeks At Full-Time Jobs[3]					
Women...........................	42.7	40.7	36.9	36.8	+16.0
Men.............................	66.6	66.1	63.9	65.4	+1.8
Ratio: women/men[2].............	0.64	0.62	0.58	0.56	(X)

X Not applicable.
[1] Percents based on all persons.
[2] Ratios of percents.
[3] Percents based on persons who worked during the year.

Source: U.S. Department of Commerce, Bureau of the Census, Current Population Reports, Series P-50, No. 35, and unpublished data and U.S. Department of Labor, Bureau of Labor Statistics, Special Labor Force Reports, Nos. 141 and 19.

598 : Women

Table 9-4. **Median Years in Current Job for the Employed by Sex and Selected Age Groups: 1951, 1963, and 1973**

(Civilian noninstitutional population)

Sex and age	Median years in current job		
	1973	1963	1951
TOTAL EMPLOYED[1]			
Women	2.8	3.0	2.2
Men	4.6	5.7	3.9
Ratio: women/men	0.61	0.53	0.56
20 to 24 years			
Women	1.2	1.1	1.4
Men	1.2	1.0	1.2
Ratio: women/men	1.00	1.10	1.17
25 to 34 years			
Women	2.2	2.0	1.8
Men	3.2	3.5	2.8
Ratio: women/men	0.69	0.57	0.64
35 to 44 years			
Women	3.6	3.6	3.1
Men	6.7	7.6	4.5
Ratio: women/men	0.54	0.47	0.69
45 to 54 years			
Women	5.9	6.1	4.0
Men	11.5	11.4	7.6
Ratio: women/men	0.51	0.54	0.53
55 to 64 years			
Women	8.8	7.8	4.5
Men	14.5	14.7	9.3
Ratio: women/men	0.61	0.53	0.48

[1]Persons 16 years old and over in 1973, persons 14 years old and over in 1963 and 1951.

Source: U.S. Department of Commerce, Bureau of the Census, Current Population Reports, Series P-50, No. 36 and U.S. Department of Labor, Bureau of Labor Statistics, Special Labor Force Reports, Nos. 172 and 36.

Table 9-5. **Lifetime Work Experience of Women 30 to 44 Years Old by Years of School Completed: 1967**

(Numbers in thousands. Restricted to women with income in 1966)

Years of school completed	Total (thousands)	Percent of adult life worked[1]					
		Total	100	75 to 99	50 to 74	1 to 49	Never worked
Total women, 30 to 44	8,802	100.0	12.3	19.3	19.6	42.8	6.0
Less than 4 years high school	3,140	100.0	8.2	16.8	19.5	45.6	9.9
4 years high school	4,006	100.0	12.1	19.8	20.3	43.3	4.4
1 or more years college	1,656	100.0	20.8	22.6	18.1	36.0	2.5

[1]Number of years since leaving school in which woman worked at least 6 months as a proportion of the total years elapsed since leaving school.

Source: Larry E. Suter "Occupation, Employment and Lifetime Work Experience of Women" paper presented at the August 1975 meeting of the American Sociological Association. Data were collected by the Bureau of the Census in the 1967 National Longitudinal Survey of Work Experience.

Table 9-6. **Average Proportion of Years Worked Since Leaving School for Women 30 to 44 Years Old by Marital Status and Years of School Completed: 1967**

Years of school completed	Total	Never married	Ever married, no children	Ever married, with children
Total women, 30 to 44	52.7	90.3	79.0	46.6
Less than 4 years high school	47.4	89.3	68.9	43.5
4 years high school	53.4	87.1	81.3	47.5
1 to 3 years college	55.6	91.9	88.0	46.7
4 or more years college	66.8	95.0	88.2	56.3

Note: Number of years since leaving school in which woman worked at least 6 months as a proportion of the total years elapsed since leaving school.

Source: Same as 9-5.

INCOME AND POVERTY STATUS

Income and Earnings of Persons. Although women have made gains toward equality with men in education, labor force participation, and in some occupational fields, differences between the income of women and men workers remain substantial. In 1974 the median income of women year-round full-time workers was about 57 percent of the median for comparable men. The number of women income recipients working year round full time increased relative to men between 1960 and 1974, from a ratio of 32 women per 100 men in 1960 to 46 women per 100 men in 1974. However, during this period the female/male income ratio for year-round full-time workers did not improve.

Part of this differential between women and men is attributable to differences in such factors as educational attainment, occupational distribution, industry of employment, and work experience. In both 1970 and 1974, however, the median income of women college graduates aged 25 and over who worked year round full time was only about 60 percent of the comparable male median income. In fact, women college graduates had incomes that were, on the average, lower than men with only a high school education. A study of male and female earnings differentials, based on Current Population Survey data and Social Security Administration records, found that in 1972 the relative return in earnings for completing 4 years of college was significantly less for women than for men. However, as the level of education increased to 5 or more years of college, the difference in the "pay-off" for education narrowed considerably.[1]

There is some variation in female/male earnings ratios for different major occupation groups, but for most groups women year-round full-time workers earned only about 55 to 60 percent as much as men in 1974. The only occupation group with a relatively large number of women workers and an earnings ratio above 0.60 was professional, technical, and kindred workers. Of course, some of the earnings difference between women and men in the same occupation group results from variations in the specific occupations held (see chapter 8). Data from a National Science Foundation study of scientists and engineers indicate that women in scientific and engineering fields have basic annual salary rates (excluding bonuses, commissions, etc.) ranging from about 72 percent to about 88 percent of men's salaries (table 10-5). The fields of science or engineering do not refer specifically to occupations but, instead, reflect

groupings defined on the basis of education, employment, and self-identification of field.

Differences between the earnings of women and men working in the same industry group are affected by differences in the occupational mix of women and men within the industry, but the industry differentials are noteworthy in their own right. Personal services, the industry with the largest proportion of workers who were women, had one of the lowest female/male earnings ratios in 1974 (0.49); but professional and related services, in which the majority of workers are women, had a female/male earnings ratio of 0.60. Both in transportation, communication, and other public utilities and in business and repair services, industries with relatively small numbers of women workers, women's median earnings were approximately two-thirds as high as men's.

The above comparisons have been restricted to persons who worked at full-time jobs for the entire year (50 to 52 weeks). However, over half of the women and over one-fourth of the men with earnings in 1974 worked at part-time jobs or worked fewer than 40 weeks at full-time jobs. The earnings for women working at part-time jobs were much closer to their male counterparts (ratio of 0.90) than was true for year-round full-time workers. Also, women working at full-time jobs for less than 40 weeks during the year had earnings equal or nearly equal with those of comparable men. Thus, the relative returns for working year round full time do not seem to be as great for women as for men. In a study of female/male earnings ratios based on the 1960 and 1970 Censuses of Population, it was estimated that this earnings ratio, adjusted for age, education, weeks worked, and hours worked, did not change from 1959 to 1969. In both years, women's actual earnings were only slightly more than half as high as they would have been if women's returns for these factors (weeks worked, age, etc.) had equalled the returns realized by men.[2]

A factor which is critical in assessing differences between the earnings of women and men is the extent of lifetime work experience. Data available from a longitudinal study of women 30 to 44 years old in 1967[3] provide some insight into the effects of differences in lifetime work experience (table 10-8). For example, women year-round full-time workers who had worked at least 6 months of every year since leaving school had a median wage or salary income in 1967 about three-fourths that of men. The median wage or salary income for comparable women who had worked in only half of the years since leaving school was only about half that of men. The effect of varying amounts of work experience differed according to education. The wages of women high school graduates with continuous work experience were more equivalent to those of male high school graduates than were the wages of female college graduates to those of male college graduates. Although discontinuous work experience does explain some of the differential between the wages earned by women and men, studies have shown that adjusting for such dif-

---

[1] Joyce A. Stevens and Roger A. Herriot, "Current Earnings Differentials of Men and Women: Some Explanatory Regression Analyses," paper presented at the August 1975 meetings of the American Statistical Association.

[2] John McNeil and Douglas Sater, "Recent Changes in Female to Male Earnings Ratios", paper presented at the April 1975 meetings of the Population Association of America.

[3] 1967 National Longitudinal Survey of Work Experience, conducted by the Bureau of the Census, under contract with the Employment and Training Administration (then Manpower Administration), U.S. Department of Labor.

ferences still leaves much to be explained. For example, a study based on the 1967 longitudinal study of women indicated that even after adjusting for differences in occupational status, education, and lifetime work experience, the wages of women were estimated to be only about 62 percent as high as those of men.[4] Also, results from a study based on Census Bureau and Social Security Administration records corroborate the finding that women do not receive the same returns from continuous work experience as do men.[5] Obviously, some variables that were not covered in these studies account for the residual differences between the income levels of women and men.

Family income and poverty status. The contribution of the wife's income to the total income of husband-wife families has become somewhat more important in recent years. In 1960, working wives contributed, on the average, about 20 percent of their families' total income; in 1974 their earnings accounted for approximately 27 percent of the total family income (table 10-10). Also, in 1974 husband-wife families in which the wife was in the paid labor force had a median income about 36 percent higher than husband-wife families with nonworking wives (table 10-9). The wife's contribution was relatively greater in young families (with husband under 25 years old) than in older families. Furthermore, the percent of family income accounted for by the wife's earnings was related to the extent of her work experience during the year (table 10-10).

The median income of families headed by women is much lower than that of husband-wife families or other families headed by men (table 10-9). This is partially because husband-wife families more often have a greater number of persons contributing to the family's total income and partially because men in general have higher incomes than women. In 1974 the median income of families with female heads was substantially lower than the median for husband-wife families in which the wife was not in the paid labor force and for male-headed families with no wife present.

The number of families with female heads has grown substantially over the past quarter-century for a variety of reasons, as mentioned in previous chapters. At the same time, the income of female-headed families has not increased as greatly as the income of male-headed families. In 1950 families with female heads had a median income which equalled about 56 percent of the median for male-headed families; in 1974 this had dropped to about 47 percent. Although the percent of all families with female heads below the poverty level declined from about 42 percent in 1960 to about 33 percent in both 1970 and 1974, the number of female-headed families in poverty increased between 1970 and 1974. For families with male heads, both the number and percent below the poverty level declined between 1960 and 1970 as well as between 1970 and 1974. In 1960 there were about 31 female-headed families for every 100 male-headed families below the poverty level, while in 1974 there were 85 female-headed families for every 100 male-headed families. Also, the growth in the number of families with female heads below the poverty level occurred exclusively among families with children under 18 years old. Thus, the number of children in female-headed families below the poverty level increased by approximately one-third between 1960 and 1974, and in 1974 the majority of children in poverty were in families headed by women.

[4] Larry E. Suter and Herman P. Miller, op. cit...
[5] Joyce A. Stevens and Roger A. Herriot, op. cit..

Table 10-2. Median Income of Year-Round Full-Time Civilian Workers 25 Years Old and Over With Income by Educational Attainment and Sex: 1970 and 1974

(Medians in current dollars. Age as of March of the following year)

Educational attainment and sex	Median income		Ratio: women/men	
	1974	1970	1974	1970
WOMEN				
Total, 25 years and over	$7,370	$5,616	0.58	0.59
Elementary: Less than 8 years	5,022	3,798	0.63	0.63
8 years	5,606	4,181	0.57	0.55
High school: 1 to 3 years	5,919	4,655	0.53	0.55
4 years	7,150	5,580	0.57	0.58
College: 1 to 3 years	8,072	6,604	0.59	0.59
4 years or more	10,357	8,719	0.60	0.63
MEN				
Total, 25 years and over	$12,786	$9,521	(X)	(X)
Elementary: Less than 8 years	7,912	6,043	(X)	(X)
8 years	9,891	7,535	(X)	(X)
High school: 1 to 3 years	11,225	8,514	(X)	(X)
4 years	12,642	9,567	(X)	(X)
College: 1 to 3 years	13,718	11,183	(X)	(X)
4 years or more	17,188	13,871	(X)	(X)

X Not applicable.

Source: U.S. Department of Commerce, Bureau of the Census, Current Population Reports, Series P-60, Nos. 99 and 80.

Table 10-3. **Median Earnings of Year-Round Full-Time Civilian Workers 14 Years Old and Over With Earnings by Sex: 1960 to 1974**

(Medians in current dollars)

Year	Median earnings		
	Women	Men	Ratio: women/men
1974............................	$6,772	$11,835	0.57
1973............................	6,335	11,186	0.57
1972............................	5,903	10,202	0.58
1971............................	5,593	9,399	0.60
1970............................	5,323	8,966	0.59
1969............................	4,977	8,455	0.59
1968............................	4,457	7,664	0.58
1967............................	4,134	7,174	0.58
1966............................	3,946	6,856	0.58
1965............................	3,828	6,388	0.60
1964............................	3,669	6,203	0.59
1963............................	3,525	5,980	0.59
1962............................	3,412	5,754	0.59
1961............................	3,315	5,595	0.59
1960............................	3,257	5,368	0.61

Source: U.S. Department of Commerce, Bureau of the Census, Current Population Reports, Series P-60, Nos. 99, 93, 90, 85, 80, 75, 66, 60, 53, 51, 47, 43, 41, 39, and 37.

Table 10-8. **Median Wage or Salary Income in 1966 for Persons 30 to 44 Years Old by Sex, Lifetime Work Experience of Women, and Years of School Completed: 1967**

Subject	Men	Women with work experience				
		Total	Percent of adult life worked[1]			
			100 percent	75 to 99	50 to 74	Less than 50 percent
Total with income.....thousands..	15,781	8,337	1,059	1,636	1,632	4,010
Median...........................	$7,221	$2,743	$5,281	$3,950	$3,132	$1,583
Ratio: women/men.................	(X)	0.38	0.73	0.55	0.43	0.22
Year-round full-time workers...........	$7,529	$4,363	$5,618	$4,727	$4,155	$3,655
Ratio: women/men.....................	(X)	0.58	0.75	0.63	0.55	0.49
Less than 4 years high school..........	$5,660	$2,227	$3,132	$2,915	$2,680	$1,533
Ratio: women/men.....................	(X)	0.39	0.55	0.52	0.47	0.27
4 years high school....................	$7,362	$2,982	$5,511	$3,962	$3,231	$1,726
Ratio: women/men.....................	(X)	0.41	0.75	0.54	0.44	0.23
1 to 3 years college...................	$8,310	$3,135	$5,608	$4,128	$3,421	$1,467
Ratio: women/men.....................	(X)	0.38	0.67	0.50	0.41	0.18
4 or more years college................	$10,726	$5,450	$6,862	$6,085	$5,240	$2,399
Ratio: women/men.....................	(X)	0.51	0.64	0.57	0.49	0.22

X Not applicable.

[1]Number of years since leaving school in which person worked at least 6 months as a proportion of the total years elapsed since leaving school.

Source: Larry E. Suter and Herman P. Miller, "Income Differences Between Men and Career Women," The American Journal of Sociology, Vol. 78, No. 4, January 1973. Data were collected by the Bureau of the Census in the 1967 National Longitudinal Survey of Work Experience.

Table 10-9. Median Income of Families by Type of Family: 1950, 1960, 1970, and 1974

(Medians in current dollars. Families as of March of the following year)

Type of family	1974	1970	1960	1950
Families With Female Heads				
Number.....................thousands..	7,242	5,950	4,609	4,040
Median family income..................	$6,413	$5,093	$2,968	$1,922
Families With Male Heads				
Number.....................thousands..	48,470	45,998	40,826	35,782
Median family income..................	$13,788	$10,480	$5,857	$3,435
Husband-Wife Families				
Number.....................thousands..	46,971	44,739	39,624	34,556
Median family income..................	$13,847	$10,516	$5,873	$3,446
Wife in Paid Labor Force				
Number.....................thousands..	20,273	17,568	12,007	(NA)
Median family income..................	$16,461	$12,276	$6,900	(NA)
Wife Not in Paid Labor Force				
Number.....................thousands..	26,698	27,172	27,617	(NA)
Median family income..................	$12,082	$9,304	$5,520	(NA)
Other Families With Male Heads				
Number.....................thousands..	1,499	1,258	1,202	1,226
Median family income..................	$11,737	$9,012	$4,860	$3,115
RATIOS OF MEDIAN FAMILY INCOME				
Families with female heads/families with male heads......................	0.47	0.49	0.51	0.56
Wife in paid labor force/ wife not in paid labor force......................	1.36	1.32	1.25	(NA)

NA Not available.

Source: U.S. Department of Commerce, Bureau of the Census, Current Population Reports, Series P-60, Nos. 99, 80, 37, and 9.

Table 10-10. Contribution of Wife's Earnings to Total Family Income For Husband-Wife Families by Selected Characteristics: 1960, 1970, and 1974

(Civilian noninstitutional population)

Characteristic	Median percent of family income accounted for by wife's earnings		
	1974	1970	1960
Total wives with work experience.....................	26.5	26.7	20.2
AGE OF HUSBAND			
Under 25 years........................	30.0	30.2	25.6
25 years and over.....................	26.1	26.3	19.8
WORK EXPERIENCE OF WIFE			
Worked 50 to 52 weeks full time........	38.0	38.6	38.1
Worked 27 to 49 weeks full time........	29.1	29.7	31.7
Worked 1 to 26 weeks full time or 1 to 52 weeks part time..............	12.1	11.9	6.2

Note: Data for each year shown were collected in March of the following year. For 1974 and 1970, data include only families in which the wife had paid work experience; for 1960 the data include wives with unpaid work experience.

Source: U.S. Department of Labor, Bureau of Labor Statistics, Special Labor Force Reports, Nos. 173, 130, and 13.

Table 10-12. Family Status of Persons Below the Poverty Level by Sex: 1960, 1970, and 1974

(Numbers in thousands. Persons as of March of following year)

Family status	Number below poverty level			Percent change, 1960 to 1974
	1974[1]	1970	1960	
Persons in families with female head...........................	8,563	7,620	7,247	+18.2
Head.......................................	2,351	1,934	1,955	+20.3
Related children under 18..............	5,387	4,828	4,095	+31.6
Other family members...................	825	858	1,197	-31.1
Female unrelated individuals, 14 years and over.............................	3,212	3,592	3,416	-6.0
Persons in families with male head...........................	10,877	12,879	27,678	-60.7
Head.......................................	2,757	3,280	6,288	-56.2
Related children under 18..............	4,809	5,665	13,193	-63.5
Other family members...................	3,310	3,934	8,197	-59.6
Male unrelated individuals, 14 years and over.............................	1,607	1,431	1,510	+6.4
Women/Men ratios of number below poverty level[2]				
Persons in families....................	0.79	0.59	0.26	(X)
Head...................................	0.85	0.59	0.31	(X)
Related children under 18............	1.12	0.85	0.31	(X)
Other family members.................	0.25	0.22	0.15	(X)
Unrelated individuals, 14 years and over..................................	2.00	2.51	2.26	(X)

[1] Data not strictly comparable with earlier years because based on 1970 census population controls.
[2] Ratios of persons in families with female head to persons in families with male head and female unrelated individuals to male unrelated individuals.

Source: U.S. Department of Commerce, Bureau of the Census, Current Population Reports, Series P-60, Nos. 99 and 81.

BLACK WOMEN

In a study on the status of women, it is important to specifically examine changes in the status of black women since their progress sometimes presents a picture different from that for women in general. In this chapter emphasis is placed on the time span since the mid-1960's, when the passage of Civil Rights legislation began to have a significant impact on the status of black women.

Black women have made important strides in many aspects of life. Their health and education have improved, and gains have been made in entering white-collar occupations and in achieving incomes more nearly equal those of white women. Yet much remains to be achieved for, in most instances, black women still lag behind white women. Black women are more likely to be unemployed, to be overrepresented in low-paying jobs, to be increasingly assuming the role of family head with children to support, and to account for a larger proportion of the poor.

In March 1974 there were 12.5 million black females in the United States, an increase of 4.7 million since 1950. The black female population is characteristically younger than the white female population, and despite improvements in health status, black women continue to have a lower life expectancy than white women. The black woman is nearly six times as likely to die as a result of homicide as is the white woman, about four and a half times as likely to die from tuberculosis, and more than twice as likely to die from diabetes mellitus or cirrhosis of the liver, but less likely to die from suicide.

Although the proportion of black women living in the South declined from about 68 percent in 1950 to about 53 percent in both 1970 and 1974, black women are still more concentrated in the South than are white women. Also, black women continue to be overrepresented among the female residents in central cities of metropolitan areas and underrepresented in the suburbs.

Most women, both black and white, have been married at some time, but the proportion remaining single has been increasing especially rapidly for black women. Among ever-married women, only about 54 percent of blacks were living with their husbands in 1975, a substantial decline from the 1950 level of 64 percent. Corresponding to this decline has been an increase in the percentages of black women separated and divorced and in the percent of black families headed by women.

In 1974, black women still had higher rates of children ever born than white women. However, in recent years black women, on the average, have given birth to fewer children than in the past and expect to have fewer children in the future. Among the younger women (18 to 24 years old in 1974) the lifetime birth expectations of black women are the same as those for white women (2.2 children per woman).

Education is one area where black women have made major advancements. Since the mid-1960's, there has been a sharp increase in the number enrolled at the college level. In 1964 slightly more than 100,000 black women under 35 years old were attending college, compared with 392,000 in 1974. Enrollment in college among white women also has expanded over the same period; however, the growth has not been as pronounced as that for black women. Increased school enrollment and higher retention rates among black teenagers have resulted in rising educational attainment. By 1975 the proportion of black women 25 to 29 years old who were high school graduates (including those going on to college) reached 70 percent, a substantial increase over the 39 percent who were high school graduates in 1960. Yet, in 1975 an educational gap still remained between black women and white women, as 83 percent of the white women of this age group had completed high school.

For more than two decades the labor force participation rate for black women has been higher than that for white women. This pattern continued to hold true in 1974 although the labor force rate of white women has been rapidly approaching that of black women. In 1974, 49 percent of black women were in the civilian labor force, compared with 45 percent of white women. In every age group, except 16 to 19 and 20 to 24, black women were more likely than their white counterparts to be in the labor force. Also, a somewhat larger proportion of black women than white women who worked during 1974 worked year round full time.

The presence of young children in the family affects the work status of black women to a lesser extent than white women. In 1975, 51 percent of married black women with children under 6 years old were in the labor force, compared with 35 percent of white women.

Unemployment has been traditionally more prevalent among black women than white women. In 1974, the unemployment rate for black women averaged about 11 percent as compared with 6 percent for white women. The unemployment situation among black teenage girls is particularly significant.

There have been substantial changes since 1965 in the occupations of employed black women. The proportion of black women working in white-collar jobs increased from 24 percent in 1965 to 42 percent in 1974, whereas the percent employed in the normally low-paying private household worker positions declined from 30 percent to 11 percent.

By 1974 the median earnings of black women who worked year round full time was approaching income parity with their white counterparts. The median earnings ratio of black to white women rose from 75 percent in 1967 to 92 percent in 1974.

In 1974 there were 1.0 million female-headed black families and 1.3 million female-headed white families below the poverty level. Families with female heads have accounted for an increasing proportion of all black families in poverty so that by 1974 the proportion was about 67 percent. For white families the proportion was 37 percent.

A smaller proportion of black women than white women register and vote in Congressional and Presidential elections. Registration rates for black women in 1974 were at the lowest level reported for any of the last five general elections. In 1974, about 57 percent of black women registered to vote; for the previous four elections (1966 to 1972), the levels ranged from 61 to 66 percent.

Note: In this chapter, the term "black" is used although some of the data are for "black and other races." Blacks constitute about 90 percent of this group.

Table 13-9. Children Ever Born Per Woman by Marital Status and Age: 1965, 1970, and 1974

Marital status and age	Black			White		
	1974	1970	1965	1974	1970	1965
TOTAL WOMEN[1]						
Total, 15 to 44 years.........	1.6	2.0	2.1	1.4	1.6	1.7
15 to 19 years.....................	0.1	0.1	0.2	0.1	-	-
20 to 24 years.....................	0.7	0.9	1.2	0.6	0.7	0.9
25 to 29 years.....................	1.6	2.0	2.6	1.4	1.7	2.1
30 to 34 years.....................	2.5	3.0	3.4	2.3	2.6	2.7
35 to 39 years.....................	3.5	3.5	3.5	2.8	2.9	2.8
40 to 44 years.....................	3.5	3.5	3.1	3.0	2.9	2.7
WOMEN EVER MARRIED						
Total, 15 to 44 years.........	2.7	3.0	3.1	2.1	2.3	2.4
15 to 19 years.....................	0.9	1.0	(B)	0.5	0.6	0.6
20 to 24 years.....................	1.3	1.6	1.8	0.9	1.0	1.3
25 to 29 years.....................	2.1	2.5	3.0	1.6	1.9	2.3
30 to 34 years.....................	3.0	3.4	3.9	2.4	2.7	2.8
35 to 39 years.....................	3.8	3.8	3.8	2.9	3.1	2.9
40 to 44 years.....................	3.8	3.8	3.4	3.2	3.0	2.8

- Rounds to zero.
B Base too small for rate to be shown.
[1] Includes single (never married) women, not shown separately.

Source: U.S. Department of Commerce, Bureau of the Census, Current Population Reports, Series P-23, No. 54.

Table 13-10. School Enrollment of Women 14 to 34 Years Old: 1964, 1970, and 1974

(Numbers in thousands)

Year and race	Enrolled below college level		Enrolled in college	
	Number	Percent	Number	Percent
1974				
Total, 14 to 34 years[1]	7,851	21.4	3,901	10.6
Black	1,146	25.2	392	8.6
White	6,589	20.9	3,413	10.8
1970				
Total, 14 to 34 years[1]	7,531	23.0	3,013	9.2
Black	1,024	26.1	269	6.9
White	6,429	22.6	2,693	9.5
1964				
Total, 14 to 34 years[1]	6,510	23.6	1,755	6.4
Black	788	25.2	114	3.6
White	5,628	23.4	1,617	6.7
PERCENT CHANGE 1964 TO 1974				
Total, 14 to 34 years[1]	20.6	(X)	122.3	(X)
Black	45.4	(X)	243.9	(X)
White	17.1	(X)	111.1	(X)

X Not applicable.
[1] Includes other races, not shown separately.

Source: U.S. Department of Commerce, Bureau of the Census, Current Population Reports, Series P-20, Nos. 148, 222, and 278.

Table 13-11. Percent Distribution of Women 25 to 29 Years Old by Years of School Completed: 1960, 1965, 1970, and 1975

Education	1975	1970	1965	1960
Total, 25 to 29 years..(thousands)[1]	8,345	6,854	5,677	5,537
Black women	935	751	651	581
White women	7,238	6,013	4,962	4,840
ELEMENTARY: 8 YEARS OR LESS				
Black women	6.8	9.7	19.2	27.7
White women	5.2	6.1	8.9	13.5
Ratio: black to white	0.17	0.20	0.28	0.25
SOME HIGH SCHOOL: 9 TO 11 YEARS				
Black women	23.1	32.5	30.7	33.6
White women	11.7	17.5	18.3	21.8
Ratio: black to white	0.26	0.23	0.22	0.19
HIGH SCHOOL: 12 YEARS				
Black women	44.2	39.1	35.8	26.0
White women	46.2	49.0	51.0	44.9
Ratio: black to white	0.12	0.10	0.09	0.07
SOME COLLEGE: 1 TO 3 YEARS				
Black women	15.8	10.8	7.8	7.7
White women	17.6	14.1	12.1	11.7
Ratio: black to white	0.12	0.10	0.09	0.08
COLLEGE: 4 YEARS OR MORE				
Black women	10.1	8.0	6.8	5.0
White women	19.4	13.3	9.8	8.1
Ratio: black to white	0.07	0.08	0.09	0.07

[1] Includes other races, not shown separately.

Source: 1960 Census of Population, Vol. I, Part 1(D) and unpublished 1-in-1,000 Sample data; Current Population Reports, Series P-20, Nos. 158 and 207; and unpublished Current Population Survey data.

Table 13-13. **Annual Work Experience of Women by Full- and Part-Time Job Status: Selected Years, 1950 to 1974**

(Civilian noninstitutional population)

Extent of employment	1974	1970	1965	1960	1950
BLACK AND OTHER RACES					
Percent					
With work experience[1].................	55	58	56	58	58
Worked year round full time[2]..........	45	42	35	31	25
Worked part time[2].....................	27	30	32	37	31
WHITE					
Percent					
With work experience[1].................	54	52	47	46	39
Worked year round full time[2]..........	42	41	39	38	39
Worked part time[2].....................	33	33	31	32	26
RATIO: BLACK AND OTHER RACES/WHITE[3]					
With work experience...................	1.02	1.12	1.19	1.26	1.49
Worked year round full time...........	1.07	1.02	0.90	0.82	0.64
Worked part time.......................	0.82	0.91	1.03	1.16	1.19

[1]Percents based on all persons.
[2]Percents based on persons who worked during the year.
[3]Ratio of percents.

Note: The figures for 1970 and 1974 are for the population 16 years old and over. The figures prior to 1970 are for the population 14 years old and over.

Source: U.S. Department of Commerce, Bureau of the Census, Current Population Reports, Series P-50, No. 31 and Series P-23, No. 54 and U.S. Department of Labor, Bureau of Labor Statistics, Special Labor Force Reports, Nos. 19, 76, and 141.

Table 13-14. **Unemployment Rates of Women by Age: Selected Years, 1950 to 1974**

Year	Total, 16 years and over	16 and 17 years	18 and 19 years	20 years and over
BLACK AND OTHER RACES				
1974.........................	10.7	36.2	33.7	8.4
1970.........................	9.3	36.9	32.9	6.9
1965.........................	9.2	37.8	27.8	7.4
1960.........................	9.4	25.7	24.5	8.3
1950.........................	8.4	17.6	14.1	(NA)
WHITE				
1974.........................	6.1	16.4	13.0	5.0
1970.........................	5.4	15.3	11.9	4.4
1965.........................	5.0	15.0	13.4	4.0
1960.........................	5.3	14.5	11.5	4.6
1950.........................	5.3	13.8	9.4	(NA)
RATIO: BLACK AND OTHER RACES/WHITE				
1974.........................	1.75	2.21	2.59	1.68
1970.........................	1.72	2.41	2.76	1.57
1965.........................	1.84	2.52	2.07	1.85
1960.........................	1.77	1.77	2.13	1.80
1950.........................	1.58	1.28	1.50	(NA)

NA Not available.

Source: U.S. Department of Labor, Manpower Administration, 1975 Manpower Report of the President.

Table 13-16. Employed Women by Occupation: 1965, 1970, and 1974

Occupation	1974 Black and other races	1974 White	1970 Black and other races	1970 White	1965 Black and other races	1965 White
Total number employed.....thousands..	4,136	29,281	3,642	26,025	3,147	21,601
Percent...............................	100.0	100.0	100.0	100.0	100.0	100.0
White-collar workers......................	41.8	64.4	36.0	63.9	23.9	61.8
Professional and technical workers.......	11.7	15.4	10.8	15.0	8.5	13.9
Managers and administrators, except farm.	2.4	5.3	1.9	4.8	1.6	4.9
Sales workers.............................	2.7	7.4	2.5	7.7	2.0	8.3
Clerical workers..........................	24.9	36.4	20.8	36.4	11.8	34.7
Blue-collar workers.......................	19.8	14.9	19.2	15.7	15.9	16.8
Craft and kindred workers................	1.4	1.6	0.8	1.2	0.7	1.1
Operatives, except transport.............	16.8	11.8	17.6	14.1	14.5	15.3
Transport equipment operatives...........	0.4	0.5	0.7	0.4	0.7	0.4
Nonfarm laborers.........................	1.2	1.0				
Farm workers...............................	1.1	1.5	1.7	1.8	5.3	2.7
Service workers...........................	37.3	19.2	43.1	18.7	54.8	18.6
Private household........................	11.3	2.5	17.5	3.4	30.1	4.5
Other....................................	26.1	16.7	25.6	15.3	24.7	14.1

Note: Beginning with 1971, occupational employment data are not strictly comparable with statistics for 1970 and earlier years as a result of changes in the occupational classification system for the 1970 Census of Population that were introduced in January 1971, and the addition of a question to the CPS in December 1971 relating to major activities and duties. For an explanation of these changes, see Bureau of the Census, Technical Paper No. 26.

Source: U.S. Department of Commerce, Bureau of the Census, Current Population Reports, Series P-23, No. 48 and U S. Department of Labor, Bureau of Labor Statistics, Employment and Earnings, Vol. 21, No. 7.

Table 13-17. Median Income of Women With Income and Median Earnings of Women With Earnings: 1967 to 1974

(Medians in current dollars)

Year	Total women Black	Total women White	Total women Ratio: black to white	Year-round full-time workers Black	Year-round full-time workers White	Year-round full-time workers Ratio: black to white
MEDIAN INCOME						
1974....................................	$2,806	$3,114	0.90	$6,371	$7,021	0.91
1973....................................	2,548	2,823	0.90	5,595	6,598	0.85
1972....................................	2,444	2,616	0.93	5,280	6,172	0.86
1971....................................	2,145	2,448	0.88	5,092	5,767	0.88
1970....................................	2,063	2,266	0.91	4,536	5,536	0.82
1969....................................	1,840	2,182	0.84	4,126	5,182	0.80
1967[r].................................	1,453	1,855	0.78	3,185	4,307	0.74
MEDIAN EARNINGS						
1974....................................	$3,368	$3,628	0.93	$6,258	$6,823	0.92
1973....................................	3,030	3,299	0.92	5,487	6,434	0.85
1972....................................	3,042	3,190	0.95	5,147	5,998	0.86
1971....................................	2,376	3,064	0.78	5,014	5,651	0.89
1970....................................	2,344	2,800	0.84	4,447	5,412	0.82
1969....................................	1,991	2,683	0.74	4,009	5,078	0.79
1967[r].................................	1,623	2,449	0.66	3,178	4,265	0.75

[r]Revised, based on processing corrections.

Note: A year-round full-time worker is one who worked primarily at full-time civilian jobs (35 hours or more per week) for 50 weeks or more during the year.

Source: U.S. Department of Commerce, Bureau of the Census, Current Population Reports, Series P-60, Nos. 75, 80, 85, 90, 91, and 99 and unpublished Current Population Survey data.

SPANISH WOMEN

The preceding chapters of this report have focused on the changing status of women over time, but because data on the Spanish origin population are available only for recent years, the assessment of the status of Spanish origin women is restricted to 1974.

Women of Spanish origin are, on the average, younger than women in the overall population; in 1974 the median age of Spanish origin women was 20.9 years old compared with a median age of 29.6 years old for all women. One of every two women of Spanish origin was under 21 years old, but only about 36 percent of all women in the population were in that age category. Although there were differences among the median ages of women in the subcategories of Spanish origin (e.g., Mexican, Puerto Rican, etc.), the median age of women in each Spanish origin subcategory (table 14-1) was lower than the median age of all women in the population.

The proportion single (never married) among Spanish women was greater than for all women in the population, but the proportion divorced among Spanish women was about the same as for all women. However, a larger proportion of Puerto Rican origin women were either divorced or married with spouse absent than were women in the other subcategories of Spanish origin.

The majority of Spanish origin families headed by women lived in metropolitan areas in 1974, mostly residing in the central cities of these areas, but the proportion varied according to type of Spanish origin; for example, only about one of every two families headed by women of Mexican origin lived in a central city in 1974, but about 86 percent of families headed by a woman of Puerto Rican origin lived in a central city. In contrast, one of every four female-headed families of Mexican origin lived in a nonmetropolitan area in 1974.

Female-headed Spanish families tended to be larger, on the average, than female-headed families in the overall population. About 45 percent of all families headed by a woman had only two persons in the family, compared with one of every three for corresponding Spanish origin families.

In 1974 women of Spanish origin were at a lower educational attainment level than were all women in the Nation, but younger women of Spanish origin were closing the gap in educational attainment. About 28 percent of Spanish origin women 45 to 54 years old had completed high school, but about 50 percent of Spanish origin women 25 to 29 years old had done so.

The unemployment rate for Spanish origin women was higher than the rate for all women in 1974; about 10 percent of Spanish women 16 years old and over in the civilian labor force were unemployed compared with 6 percent of all women in the civilian labor force. Labor force participation rates differed by type of Spanish origin. Although 40 percent of Mexican women, and 50 percent of women of other Spanish origin were in the civilian labor force, only one-third of Puerto Rican women were in the civilian labor force in 1974.

A larger proportion of employed Spanish women were working in blue-collar jobs than were employed women in the overall population. About one-third of the employed women of Spanish origin had a blue-collar occupation in 1974, yet only 16 percent of all employed women in the Nation were blue-collar workers (e.g., craft and kindred workers, operatives, and nonfarm laborers). By contrast, a lower proportion of employed Spanish women, as compared to all employed women, were working in professional and technical jobs; about 6 percent of Spanish women were in professional occupations in 1974 compared with 16 percent for all employed women. Puerto Rican women were less prone to be working in a service occupation than were other employed Spanish origin women; although approximately one of every four to five employed Mexican origin women or women of other Spanish origin were doing service-type work in 1974, only 1 of every 10 Puerto Rican origin women were employed in a service occupation.

Median income of Spanish origin women in 1973, at $2,700, was not significantly different from that of all women, $2,800. But there was a difference in median income by type of Spanish origin: women of Mexican origin had a lower median income ($2,300) than women of Puerto Rican origin ($3,600) and women of other Spanish origin ($3,100).

Earnings of professional women of Spanish origin were not, on the average, significantly different from earnings of professional women in the overall population. Also the median earnings of Spanish women employed as service workers (except private household workers) were not significantly different than the median earnings of all women in the population similarly employed.

There was some evidence that Spanish women earning wages or salaries in 1973 (by working) in private industry had lower median earnings, $2,800, than all women wage and salary workers in private industry. Also, Spanish women earning wages or salaries in government had substantially lower median earnings, $3,400, than the median for all women earning wages or salaries in government employment, $5,300.

A significant proportion of female-headed Spanish origin families were below the poverty level in 1974. About one-half of the families headed by women of Spanish origin were below the poverty level in 1974; by contrast, one-third of the female-headed families in the Nation were below the poverty level.

Table 14-1. All Women and Women of Spanish Origin by Age and Type of Spanish Origin: March 1974

(Noninstitutional population)

Age	Total women	Women of Spanish origin			
		Total	Mexican	Puerto Rican	Other[1]
Total women..........thousands..	107,077	5,510	3,196	830	1,483
Percent.......................	100.0	100.0	100.0	100.0	100.0
Under 5 years.......................	7.5	12.7	13.6	12.4	11.0
5 to 13 years.......................	15.6	22.4	23.2	24.2	19.8
14 and 15 years.....................	3.9	4.5	4.5	5.1	4.2
16 to 19 years.....................	7.5	8.7	9.2	7.4	8.2
20 to 24 years.....................	8.6	8.7	9.0	8.7	7.9
25 to 34 years.....................	13.8	14.5	13.4	17.9	15.0
35 to 44 years.....................	10.8	11.5	11.4	11.1	12.1
45 to 54 years.....................	11.4	8.1	7.9	7.1	9.2
55 to 64 years.....................	9.5	5.0	4.3	4.1	6.9
65 years and over..................	11.3	3.8	3.5	1.9	5.7
18 years and over..................	69.1	55.9	53.8	54.9	60.8
21 years and over..................	63.6	49.9	47.6	48.9	55.4
Median age....................years..	29.6	20.9	19.7	20.4	24.3
Sex ratio[2].....................	94.2	95.9	102.0	86.4	88.3

[1]Includes Cuban, Central or South American, and other Spanish origin.
[2]Number of males per 100 females.

Source: U.S. Department of Commerce, Bureau of the Census, Current Population Reports, Series P-20, No. 280.

Table 14-4. Selected Characteristics of All Female-Headed Families and Families With Female Head of Spanish Origin by Type of Spanish Origin: March 1974

Characteristic	Total	Spanish origin			
		Total	Mexican	Puerto Rican	Other[1]
Total persons in female-headed families............thousands..	21,823	1,557	790	473	294
All female-headed families............thousands..	6,804	411	196	127	88
Percent.......................	100.0	100.0	100.0	100.0	100.0
2 persons............................	44.9	30.4	26.0	28.3	42.0
3 persons............................	24.4	25.1	25.0	25.2	26.1
4 persons............................	13.9	18.2	19.4	20.5	12.5
5 persons............................	8.2	12.4	14.3	11.0	10.2
6 persons............................	4.1	6.6	7.7	6.3	3.4
7 persons or more....................	4.4	7.3	7.7	8.7	4.5
Mean number of persons................	3.21	3.79	4.03	3.72	3.34
Mean number of members:					
Under 18 years.......................	1.46	2.20	2.37	2.37	1.56
18 to 64 years.......................	1.48	1.49	1.55	1.31	1.63
65 years and over....................	0.27	0.10	0.11	0.04	0.16
Mean number of own children under 18 years................................	1.27	1.95	1.98	2.25	1.44
Own children under 6 years...........	0.31	0.56	0.55	0.73	0.34
Own children under 3 years...........	0.12	0.22	0.26	0.27	0.08

[1]Includes Cuban, Central or South American, and other Spanish origin.

Source: U.S. Department of Commerce, Bureau of the Census, Current Population Reports, Series P-20, No. 280.

Table 14-5. **Percent of All Women and Women of Spanish Origin 25 Years Old and Over by Type of Spanish Origin, Years of School Completed, and Age: March 1974**

(Noninstitutional population)

Years of school completed and age	Total women	Women of Spanish origin			
		Total	Mexican	Puerto Rican	Other[1]
PERCENT COMPLETED LESS THAN 5 YEARS OF SCHOOL					
Total women 25 years and over....	4.1	19.5	25.8	19.8	8.3
25 to 29 years.........................	1.0	9.6	11.9	9.2	4.7
30 to 34 years.........................	0.9	7.4	10.1	(B)	1.7
35 to 44 years.........................	1.8	16.7	22.4	19.1	3.4
45 to 54 years.........................	2.8	23.0	30.2	(B)	8.1
55 to 64 years.........................	4.6	29.4	40.8	(B)	11.7
65 years and over.....................	10.8	49.1	64.0	(B)	25.9
PERCENT COMPLETED 4 YEARS OF HIGH SCHOOL OR MORE					
Total women, 25 years and over...	60.9	34.9	27.7	28.9	50.5
25 to 29 years.........................	80.8	50.1	44.2	40.4	72.0
30 to 34 years.........................	77.1	47.5	41.9	(B)	60.0
35 to 44 years.........................	70.4	37.5	30.0	26.9	58.1
45 to 54 years.........................	63.7	28.2	18.4	(B)	51.5
55 to 64 years.........................	51.6	16.1	9.1	(B)	25.2
65 years and over.....................	34.5	12.1	4.8	(B)	22.4
PERCENT COMPLETED 4 YEARS OF COLLEGE OR MORE					
Total women, 25 years and over...	10.1	4.0	1.5	3.1	8.7

B Base less than 75,000.

[1] Includes Cuban, Central or South American, and other Spanish origin.

Source: U.S. Department of Commerce, Bureau of the Census, Current Population Reports, Series P-20, No. 280 and unpublished data.

Table 14-6. **Employment Status of All Women and Women of Spanish Origin 16 Years Old and Over by Marital Status and Type of Spanish Origin: March 1974**

(Noninstitutional population. Numbers in thousands)

Type of Spanish origin and employment status	Total	Marital status				
		Single	Married		Divorced	Widowed
			Spouse present	Spouse absent		
All women, 16 years and over.......	78,131	14,389	47,324	2,975	3,629	9,814
Percent in civilian labor force..	45.2	57.2	43.0	55.2	72.9	24.8
Percent unemployed..............	6.0	9.1	4.7	10.3	4.8	4.7
Total Spanish origin women, 16 years and over...................................	3,325	718	1,979	254	155	220
Percent in civilian labor force......	42.1	52.7	39.7	36.6	62.2	21.3
Percent unemployed...................	9.8	14.6	8.0	12.9	4.2	(B)
Mexican origin women, 16 years and over..	1,877	417	1,155	116	75	115
Percent in civilian labor force......	40.3	51.5	36.3	44.5	61.2	22.2
Percent unemployed...................	9.8	13.5	8.1	(B)	(B)	(B)
Puerto Rican origin women, 16 years and over...................................	483	90	253	83	30	28
Percent in civilian labor force......	33.7	35.5	36.1	18.5	(B)	(B)
Percent unemployed...................	9.8	(B)	7.7	(B)	(B)	(B)
Other Spanish origin women, 16 years and over[1]...................................	965	212	571	55	50	77
Percent in civilian labor force......	49.7	62.3	48.0	(B)	(B)	22.1
Percent unemployed...................	9.8	13.6	7.7	(B)	(B)	(B)

B Base less than 75,000.

[1] Includes Cuban, Central or South American, and other Spanish origin.

Source: U.S. Department of Commerce, Bureau of the Census, Current Population Survey, unpublished data.

Table 14-7. Employment Status and Major Occupation Group of All Women and Women of Spanish Origin 16 Years Old and Over by Type of Spanish Origin: March 1974

(Noninstitutional population)

Employment status and occupation	Total women	Women of Spanish origin			
		Total	Mexican	Puerto Rican	Other[1]
Total women, 16 years and over..................thousands..	78,108	3,325	1,877	483	965
In civilian labor force.thousands..	35,321	1,400	757	163	480
Percent unemployed.............	6.0	9.8	9.7	9.8	9.9
Employed.............thousands..	33,200	1,262	683	147	433
Percent......................	100.0	100.0	100.0	100.0	100.0
White-collar workers.................	62.0	41.2	37.6	42.1	46.0
Professional, technical, and kindred workers.....................	15.5	6.0	4.5	8.8	7.6
Managers and administrators, except farm............................	4.9	2.9	1.6	4.8	4.2
Sales workers......................	6.7	4.0	4.0	2.0	4.4
Clerical and kindred workers.........	34.9	28.3	27.5	26.5	29.8
Blue-collar workers.....................	15.5	33.4	32.1	44.3	32.2
Craft and kindred workers............	1.7	2.1	1.6	4.8	2.1
Operatives, including transport......	12.9	30.2	29.3	38.1	28.9
Laborers, excluding farm.............	0.9	1.1	1.2	1.4	1.2
Farm workers..........................	1.3	2.6	4.2	2.0	0.2
Farmers and farm managers...........	0.3	–	–	–	–
Farm laborers and supervisors........	1.0	2.6	4.2	2.0	0.2
Service workers.......................	21.2	22.9	26.1	10.9	21.7

– Represents zero or rounds to zero.
[1] Includes Cuban, Central or South American, and other Spanish origin.

Source: U.S. Department of Commerce, Bureau of the Census, Current Population Reports, Series P-20, No. 280.

Table 14-8. Income in 1973 of All Women and Women of Spanish Origin 14 Years Old and Over by Type of Spanish Origin: March 1974

(Noninstitutional population)

Income	Total women	Women of Spanish origin			
		Total	Mexican	Puerto Rican	Other[1]
Total women, 14 years and over....................thousands..	82,244	3,575	2,022	526	1,027
Total women with income...thousands..	57,029	2,154	1,177	295	681
Percent...........................	100.0	100.0	100.0	100.0	100.0
$1 to $999 or loss.........................	21.0	21.0	25.4	10.5	17.9
$1,000 to $1,999.........................	17.7	18.0	19.0	13.2	18.4
$2,000 to $2,999.........................	13.4	15.9	17.7	15.6	13.1
$3,000 to $3,999.........................	10.1	12.1	11.5	18.3	10.3
$4,000 to $4,999.........................	8.4	10.3	9.1	13.6	11.2
$5,000 to $6,999.........................	12.8	12.9	10.6	18.3	14.5
$7,000 to $7,999.........................	4.5	3.3	2.8	3.1	4.4
$8,000 to $9,999.........................	5.8	3.8	2.2	4.7	6.2
$10,000 to $14,999.........................	4.8	2.1	1.5	2.7	2.9
$15,000 to $24,999.........................	1.1	0.4	0.1	0.3	1.0
$25,000 and over.........................	0.2	0.1	0.1	–	0.1
Median income of women with income.........	$2,796	$2,652	$2,270	$3,593	$3,067

– Represents zero or rounds to zero.
[1] Includes Cuban, Central or South American, and other Spanish origin.

Source: U.S. Department of Commerce, Bureau of the Census, Current Population Reports, Series P-20, No. 280.

Table 14-9. **Median Earnings in 1973 of All Women and Women of Spanish Origin 14 Years Old and Over With Earnings by Occupation of Longest Job in 1973 and Class of Worker of Longest Job in 1973: March 1974**

(Civilian noninstitutional population)

Occupation and class of worker	All women	Women of Spanish origin
OCCUPATION		
Total, with earnings......................	$3,268	$2,815
Professional, technical, and kindred workers...	6,909	5,745
Managers and administrators, except farm.......	5,669	(B)
Sales workers...............................	1,646	1,215
Clerical and kindred workers....................	4,392	3,802
Craft and kindred workers.......................	4,327	(B)
Operatives, including transport.................	3,605	3,484
Laborers, excluding farm........................	2,018	(B)
Farmers and farm managers.......................	1,396	(B)
Farm laborers and supervisors...................	439	768
Service workers, except private household......	1,824	2,050
Private household workers.......................	436	815
CLASS OF WORKER		
Private wage or salary workers.................	3,050	2,760
Government wage or salary workers..............	5,284	3,370
Self-employed workers..........................	1,433	(B)
Unpaid family workers..........................	560	(B)

B Base less than 75,000.

Source: U.S. Department of Commerce, Bureau of the Census, Current Population Reports, Series P-60, No. 97 and Series P-20, No. 280.

Table 14-10. **Poverty Status in 1973 of Families With Female Heads and Female Unrelated Individuals by Age for All Women and Women of Spanish Origin: March 1974**

(Noninstitutional population. Numbers in thousands)

Age	Total			Spanish origin		
	Total	Below poverty level		Total	Below poverty level	
		Number	Percent		Number	Percent
Female family heads............	6,804	2,193	32.2	411	211	51.4
Under 25 years......................	606	391	64.5	46	33	(B)
25 to 34 years......................	1,485	706	47.6	106	72	68.0
35 to 44 years......................	1,419	493	34.8	107	57	53.4
45 to 54 years......................	1,256	261	20.7	73	28	(B)
55 to 64 years......................	902	150	16.7	52	14	(B)
65 years and over..................	1,136	191	16.8	25	6	(B)
Female unrelated individuals...	10,719	3,179	29.7	214	89	41.6
Under 35 years......................	2,404	657	27.3	82	31	38.4
35 to 54 years......................	1,538	351	22.8	39	13	(B)
55 years and over..................	6,777	2,166	32.0	92	45	48.9

B Base less than 75,000.

Source: U.S. Department of Commerce, Bureau of the Census, Current Population Reports, Series P-60, No. 98 and unpublished data.

* This material has not been excerpted in its entirety.

U.S. Bureau of the Census, Current Population Reports, Series P-23, No. 58. "A Statistical Portrait of Women in the U.S." U.S. Government Printing Office, Washington, D.C. April 1976.

Why Women Work

Despite unfavorable economic conditions in the first quarter of 1975, an average of nearly 37 million women were in the labor force (working or looking for work) during the year. Of this number, almost 33.6 million were actually employed. During the decade 1965 to 1975, some 14 million additional jobs were developed in new or expanding industries. These new jobs have provided employment opportunities for more than 9 million women and nearly 5 million men.

Women work for the same reasons men do--most importantly, to provide for the welfare of themselves, their families, or others. This was true of most of the 8.5 million women workers who were never married. Nearly all of the 6.9 million women workers who were widowed, divorced, or separated from their husbands--particularly the women who were raising children--were working for compelling economic reasons. In addition, the 3.1 million married women workers whose husbands had incomes below $5,000 in 1974 almost certainly worked because of economic need. Finally, about 2.2 million women would be added if we take into account those women whose husbands had incomes between $5,000 and $7,000.1/ Forty-three percent of women workers had husbands whose incomes were $7,000 or more.

Among the 4.7 million women of minority races who were workers in March 1975, slightly more than half (54 percent) were never married, widowed, divorced, or separated from their husbands; about one-tenth (11 percent) were wives whose husbands had 1974 incomes below $5,000. In fact, only 1 out of 4 minority women workers was a wife whose husband had an income of $7,000 or more.

The marital status of women workers in March 1975 was as follows:

Marital status	All women		Women of minority races	
	Number	Percent distribution	Number	Percent distribution
Total	36,507,000	100.0	4,695,000	100.0
Never married	8,464,000	23.3	1,130,000	24.1
Married (husband present)	21,111,000	57.8	2,161,000	46.0
Husband's 1974 income:				
Below $3,000	1,500,000	4.1	251,000	5.3
$3,000 - $4,999	1,633,000	4.5	251,000	5.3
$5,000 - $6,999	2,178,000	6.0	355,000	7.6
$7,000 - $9,999	4,194,000	11.5	514,000	10.9
$10,000 and over	11,601,000	31.8	799,000	17.0
Other marital status	6,932,000	19.0	1,403,000	29.9
Married (husband absent)	1,606,000	4.4	604,000	12.9
Widowed	2,453,000	6.7	357,000	7.6
Divorced	2,873,000	7.9	442,000	9.4

1/ The Bureau of Labor Statistics estimate for a low standard of living for an urban family of four was $9,838 in autumn 1975. This estimate is for a family consisting of an employed husband aged 38, a wife not employed outside the home, an 8-year-old girl, and a 13-year-old boy.

Women heads of families.--Of the 55.7 million families in March 1975, 7.2 million were headed by women. About 3.9 million, or 54 percent, of the women family heads were in the labor force, and nearly two-thirds of these women workers were the only earners in their families. About 1 out of 10 women workers was head of a family. Among the 2.0 million minority women heading families in March 1975, about half were workers. More than 1 out of 5 women workers of minority races headed a family.

Nearly one-third of the families headed by women had incomes below the poverty level in 1974.2/ This was true for more than half of all minority families headed by women. For those families headed by women who worked during 1974, however, about 1 out of 5 (2 out of 5 minority families) had an income below the poverty level. Among families headed by women who worked the year round at full time jobs, 8 percent (15 percent of minority families) were poor in 1974.

Mothers with husbands present.--Of the 21.1 million married women (husband present) who were in the labor force in March 1975, 11.4 million had children under 18 years of age. About 2.2 million of these mothers were working to supplement the low incomes of their husbands. Included were 517,000 mothers whose husbands had 1974 incomes below $3,000; 651,000 whose husbands had incomes between $3,000 and $5,000; and 1 million whose husbands had incomes between $5,000 and $7,000.

Among the 1.4 million minority women who were working wives and mothers in March 1975, about 500,000 had husbands whose 1974 incomes were below $7,000. Of these mothers, 105,000 had husbands with incomes below $3,000; 149,000 had husbands with incomes from $3,000 to $5,000; and 229,000 had husbands with incomes between $5,000 and $7,000.

Wives whose husbands are unemployed or unable to work.--In the 46.1 million husband-wife families, there were 2.3 million husbands (some 315,000 minority husbands) who were unemployed in March 1975, although they were in the labor force and actively looking for work; 7.9 million husbands (nearly 736,000 minority husbands) were not in the labor force. Some 1.2 million wives of unemployed husbands and 1.7 million wives whose husbands were not in the labor force were working or seeking work. Many of these women were the sole support of their families.

Women whose husbands are employed in low-wage occupations.--In March 1975 there were 562,000 married working women whose husbands were farm workers; another 728,000 had husbands who were nonfarm laborers; and 1.1 million had husbands employed in service occupations. The median

---

2/ The low-income or poverty level is based on the Social Security Administration's poverty thresholds, adjusted annually in accordance with the Department of Labor's Consumer Price Index. Classified as poor in 1974 were those nonfarm households where total money income was less than $2,495 for an unrelated individual; $3,211 for a couple; and $5,038 for a family of four. (The poverty level for farm families is set at 85 percent of the corresponding level for nonfarm families.)

wage or salary income of men in these occupations was low in 1974--$2,940 for farm laborers and supervisors; $2,368 for farmers and farm managers; $5,406 for nonfarm laborers; and $5,695 for service workers (except private household).

Note.--Figures are from the U.S. Department of Commerce, Bureau of the Census, and U.S. Department of Labor, Bureau of Labor Statistics.

Data for minority races refer to all races other than white. Negroes constitute about 90 percent of persons other than white in the United States. Spanish-origin persons are generally included in the white population--about 93 percent of the Spanish-origin population is white.

Why Women Work. U.S. Department of Labor, Employment Standards Administration Women's Bureau, Washington, D.C. July 1976 (revised).

Mature Women Workers: A Profile

INTRODUCTION

In 1975 nearly one-third of all women workers were 45 years of age or over. The labor force participation rate of mature women 1/ has risen dramatically since 1950, although the rate has stabilized somewhat since the late 1960's. This is in marked contrast to the rate of their male counterparts, which has persistently declined.

Increases in labor force activity have been particularly pronounced for married women. Women who drop out of the labor force when they marry or start a family have increasingly sought to return to work when the youngest child begins school or when family responsibilities have lessened.

Mature married women, however, are still less likely to be working than mature women who are widowed, divorced, or separated, because they encounter many obstacles in the job market as they seek to enter or reenter the labor force. They often find employers unwilling to credit their previous work experience or their activities during the period they were out of the labor force as evidence of future potential. Consequently, with rusty or outmoded job skills, little or no recent experience, inadequate counseling, or a lack of job contacts, they frequently must settle for low-skilled and low-paying jobs which require little or no specialized training, and which afford limited opportunity for upward mobility.

These entry or reentry difficulties are reflected in mature women's occupational status and earnings, in the incidence of poverty, and in the duration of their unemployment. On the other hand, once mature women obtain jobs, they have a lower incidence of unemployment than younger women.

LABOR FORCE STATUS

In 1975, 12 million mature women--more than one-third of all mature women--had jobs or were looking for work. Fifty-six percent of these women workers were within the 45- to 54-year age group.

As expected, mature women's labor force participation decreases with age, with a sharp decline among those in the retirement years of 65 and over. In 1975 the labor force participation rate of women aged 45 to 49 was 56 percent; for those 50 to 54 it was 53 percent. The rate for women 65 and over was 8 percent, although 15 percent of the women 65 to 69 were in the work force.

1/ In this publication the term "mature women" generally refers to women 45 years of age and over. However, where recent data are not available for this specific age group, other age classifications are used. For example, the data on occupations are for women 35 years of age and over, and the data on unrelated women living alone are for those 55 and over.

Table 1.--Labor Force Status of Women 16 Years of Age and Over and 45 and Over, Annual Averages, 1975

(Numbers in thousands)

Age	Total civilian population	Civilian labor force			Unemployed		Not in labor force
		Number	Partici-pation rate	Employed	Number	Rate	
16 years and over	79,886	36,998	46.3	33,553	3,445	9.3	42,868
16 to 44 years	44,807	25,055	55.9	22,272	2,782	11.1	19,752
45 years and over	35,060	11,943	34.1	11,280	661	5.5	23,117
45 to 54 years	12,207	6,666	54.6	6,272	393	5.9	5,541
45 to 49 years	6,028	3,371	55.9	3,168	203	6.0	2,657
50 to 54 years	6,179	3,295	53.3	3,104	190	5.8	2,884
55 to 64 years	10,347	4,244	41.0	4,028	216	5.1	6,103
55 to 59 years	5,466	2,618	47.9	2,488	131	5.0	2,848
60 to 64 years	4,881	1,626	33.3	1,540	85	5.2	3,255
65 years and over	12,506	1,033	8.3	980	52	5.1	11,473
65 to 69 years	4,420	640	14.5	603	38	5.9	3,780
70 years and over	8,085	392	4.8	378	15	3.7	7,693

Note: The sums of component numbers may not add exactly to subtotals or totals due to rounding.

Source: U.S. Department of Labor, Bureau of Labor Statistics: Employment and Earnings, January 1976.

More than 660,000 mature women workers--or 5.5 percent of all mature women in the labor force--were unemployed in 1975. This is substantially lower than the 11.1-percent unemployment rate registered for women 16 to 44 years of age. However, when older women are out of work they can anticipate a longer period of unemployment than younger women; the average duration of unemployment for women aged 16 to 44 was 11.4 weeks, but for mature women (45 and over) it was 17.7 weeks. Also, among unemployed women, a much larger proportion of those aged 45 and over (39 percent) than of those 16 to 44 (25 percent) were unemployed 15 weeks or more.

There were 509,000 additional mature women on involuntary part-time work schedules. Although they were classified as employed, they had accepted part-time work only because they were unable to find full-time jobs.

EDUCATION

Women workers aged 45 to 54 had attained a median of 12.4 years of schooling in March 1974, equaling the attainment of working men of similar ages. Those women aged 55 to 64 and 65 and over had somewhat lower educational attainments--12.3 and 11.1 years, respectively--yet both of these medians were higher than the corresponsing figures for men.

Table 2.--Duration of Unemployment Among Women Workers,
by Age, Annual Averages, 1975

Age	Number (in thousands)	Average (mean) duration in weeks	Percent of all unemployed	
			Less than 5 weeks	15 weeks or more
16 years and over	3,445	12.6	41.7	27.8
16 to 44 years	2,782	11.4	43.7	25.2
16 to 19 years	795	8.6	50.5	16.0
20 to 24 years	769	11.2	44.3	24.9
25 to 34 years	773	13.0	39.6	31.0
35 to 44 years	445	14.1	37.8	32.1
45 years and over	662	17.7	32.9	38.5
45 to 54 years	394	16.4	33.6	36.4
55 to 64 years	216	18.1	34.2	39.6
65 years and over	52	25.1	22.8	50.3

Note: The sums of component numbers may not add exactly to subtotals or totals due to rounding.

Source: U.S. Department of Labor, Bureau of Labor Statistics: Employment and Earnings, January 1976.

Table 3.--Median Years of School Completed by Mature Women and Men, by Age and Labor Force Status, March 1974

Age	Women		Men	
	In labor force	Not in labor force	In labor force	Not in labor force
45 to 54 years	12.4	12.2	12.4	10.3
55 to 64 years	12.3	11.4	12.1	9.6
65 years and over	11.1	8.9	10.7	8.7

Source: U.S. Department of Labor, Bureau of Labor Statistics: Special Labor Force Report No. 175.

Labor force attachment of mature women is positively associated with educational attainment. Among white women aged 45 to 54 who did not graduate from high school, less than half (45 percent) were in the work force, while nearly three-fifths (59 percent) of those with diplomas were workers. The impact of a high school diploma was even greater among minority women.2/   Only 48 percent of the 45- to 54-year-old minority women nongraduates, but 67 percent of the graduates, were in the labor force.

Table 4.--Labor Force Participation Rates of Mature Women, by Age, Race, and Years of School Completed, March 1974

Years of school completed	Age		
	45 to 54 years	55 to 64 years	65 years and over
All Women			
Total	54.5	42.0	8.2
Elementary:			
Less than 5 years 1/	29.8	26.1	4.1
5 to 7 years	43.2	34.5	6.0
8 years	46.1	34.4	6.9
High school:			
1 to 3 years	48.7	37.6	10.2
4 years	58.0	46.3	9.9
College:			
1 to 3 years	58.4	50.0	11.5
4 years	63.0	54.1	9.7
5 years or more	80.8	64.9	14.7
White Women			
Total	54.3	41.5	8.1
Less than 4 years of high school 1/	45.1	34.0	6.6
Elementary: 8 years or less	42.2	31.8	5.4
High school: 1 to 3 years	47.7	37.2	10.3
4 years of high school or more	58.9	47.9	10.6
High school: 4 years	57.5	45.5	9.9
College: 1 or more years	62.4	52.9	11.7
Minority Women			
Total	55.8	46.5	9.5
Less than 4 years of high school 1/	48.4	40.3	9.8
Elementary: 8 years or less	43.6	39.7	10.0
High school: 1 to 3 years	54.1	41.7	8.9
4 years of high school or more	67.4	63.8	7.0
High school: 4 years	64.2	62.9	9.6
College: 1 or more years	75.7	65.3	(2/)

1/ Includes persons reporting no years of school completed.
2/ Percent not shown where base is less than 75,000.

Source: U.S. Department of Labor, Bureau of Labor Statistics: Special Labor Force Report No. 175.

2/ Minority women includes black women and other women not counted as white. Spanish-origin women are usually included in the white population--93 percent of the Spanish-origin population is white.

Mature Women Workers: A Profile. U.S. Department of Labor, Women's Bureau, Washington, D.C. 1976.

Socialization and the Educational System

This section reviews research on two broad and related topics: (a) the impact of the socialization process whereby boys and girls learn the sex-role stereotypes of our culture, and (b) the impact of the formal educational system, which contains structural elements that reinforce sex-role stereotypes. It also considers some of the changes currently under way in both the socialization process and the educational system and the possible effects of these changes on the lives of women and men.

Both socialization and formal education are sorting mechanisms that have worked to channel males and females into different categories. More specifically, females get sorted out of the formal educational system; at each successive level, their proportion decreases. Slightly more girls than boys complete high school, but fewer enroll in college. More women drop out during the college years, though a slightly larger proportion complete the baccalaureate within four years after college entry. Women are much less likely than men to enter graduate or professional schools and, once enrolled, more likely to drop out before completing an advanced degree. Thus, at every step, female talent is lost, despite the consistently higher grade averages of women. Indisputably, there are forces at work against women to prevent them from realizing their full intellectual potential.

The discussion is divided into: (1) preschool socialization, (2) early socialization—the elementary school, (3) adolescent socialization—the secondary school, (4) college, (5) graduate and professional training, and (6) the mass media as "educational supplements."

Preschool Socialization

The field of infant and child development has been widely examined in the last 50 years, but most pioneer investigators either ignored sex differences in behavior or assumed any observed differences are biologically determined. More recently, it has come to be acknowledged that most of these behavioral differences are learned and that preschool socialization is extremely important in fixing sex stereotypes as well as in general personality development (Froschl, 1973; Howe, 1971; Lipman-Blumen, 1972; Maccoby and Jacklin, 1974). Some authorities, particularly those with psychoanalytic backgrounds, have tended to emphasize the necessity of socializing the child to his or her "appropriate" sex role. But the women's movement—and the more general cultural trend toward acceptance of a wide range of life styles and rejection of the concept of adjustment to social norms as the key to mental health—emphasizes personhood, leaving individuals free to choose their own options.

To what extent is this possible? An answer requires that we identify those differences, if any, between the sexes—in perception, cognition, emotional responsiveness—that are attributable to biological factors, and that we must know much more about how sex stereotypes are "taught" to the child. Some of the questions involved here will be considered in the discussion of parenting. Other problems requiring investigation are: Do parents typically talk to and fondle girl infants and boy infants differently? How important in sex-linked behavior is the presence of the mother and the father? What role do siblings or other children play? To what extent do children's early toys determine their sex-role perceptions and later behavior? The study of infants and young children is notoriously difficult because so many variables must necessarily go uncontrolled; human beings cannot be isolated for long periods of time in experimental laboratories as rhesus monkeys can. Perhaps the only feasible method is to compare large numbers of children in different family situations: the mother at home and the father at work, or the mother and father working and sharing equally in child-rearing. Cross-cultural studies would be valuable as well. For instance, many people want to solve the problem of sex stereotyping by putting babies in nurseries and raising them communally, but this solution may be overhasty. There is some evidence that the communal system of child care may produce different personality characteristics. More studies of child care in China, Israel, and Russia are needed to see how children raised in infant centers develop, as compared with those raised in the family (Bettelheim, 1969; Boocock, 1973; Spiro, 1958). If government policy encourages the establishment of child care centers, what are the best arrangements for such centers? What are the advantages and disadvantages of the collective versus home care? What does each plan offer to the woman who does or does not want to work? We must recognize that currently the mother is the key to preschool socialization, so the whole question is inextricably entwined with the issue of whether, when, and where mothers work.

Early Socialization—The Elementary School

The pervasiveness of sex stereotyping in elementary schools has been solidly documented. For instance, analyses of the stories in readers commonly used in the classroom show that the protagonists tend to be male; that when girls appear as characters they are portrayed as timid, helpless, dependent upon the boys; that mothers are depicted only in the role of homemakers; and that occupations are sex-stereotyped, with police*men*, fire*men*, and male doctors featured but females limited to the roles of nurses and teachers. Moreover, classes and activities are often segregated by sex. Indeed, the authority structure of the school itself reinforces the stereotypes, since 85 percent of all elementary teachers are women, and 79 percent of all elementary principals are men. A number of groups (e.g., The Feminist Press, SUNY/Old Westbury, New York; KNOW, Inc., Pittsburgh; the Resource Center on Sex Roles in Education, National Education Association, Washington, D.C.) are attempting to correct some of these deficiencies by providing bibliographies and lists of materials that are free of sex stereotypes, and by urging teachers to create their own sex-free instructional aids. A central agency to gather data on sex-free curricula and materials, to function as a clearinghouse, and to carry out general research is needed. What materials do and do not work? When sex-free readers and other materials are not available or are too expensive, what methods can the teacher use to make children aware of the sex stereotypes in older material?

Some authorities have suggested that it is not enough to leave children free to choose their own activities and playthings, since by the time they enter kindergarten the damage is done: boys have learned to shun "girl" activities, and vice versa. Therefore, some kind of teacher intervention is necessary to direct children away from stereotyped behavior and open their eyes to new options. Only substantive findings, however, will prove the validity of such interventions and indicate the curricular content and teaching methods most effective in counteracting stereotypic thinking and in encouraging children of both sexes to learn and develop. (See Eliasberg, n.d.; Frisof, 1969; Mattfeld and Van Aken, 1965; Moberg and Froschl, 1973; Weitzman et al., 1972.)

Pronounced differences in the achievement patterns of males and females do not usually emerge until adolescence; one exception is reading ability. Studies in the United States (and the Philippines) show that girls outrank boys in reading achievement during the early years. To what extent is this superiority attributable to their earlier maturation rate, and to what extent to factors in the classroom environment? Does the difference arise because women teachers are the models in countries where girls show higher reading skills?

Critics of the American educational system indict women teachers for feminizing the boys but overlook the damage done to the girls (Levy, 1973). By rewarding girls—with high grades or words of praise—for being "good" pupils (i.e., docile, quiet), teachers reinforce the notion that girls should be passive and conforming. Boys, even though they may be reprimanded more frequently for their boisterousness, may ultimately benefit simply because they get more attention from the teacher. In the long run, however, both boys and girls suffer from being pressured into roles often hard to fulfill. Girls are made to feel ashamed for behaving in an "unladylike" manner, boys for expressing emotions (Olds, 1973).

Much of what has been written about the deficiencies of the woman elementary school teacher—her attitudes, her behavior, her differential treatment of boys and girls—is conjectural and may itself reflect stereotypic thinking. Extensive surveys of the attitudes and opinions of elementary school teachers would shed some light on the truth of such assertions. But even more crucial are studies of actual behavior. Do teachers discipline and reward boys and girls differently? Are larger numbers of male elementary school teachers the answer to such problems? Fragmentary evidence suggests that it is not the sex but the style of the teacher that counts. Systematic data, based on objective observation in the classroom, are badly needed to discover what constitutes effective and ineffective teaching. In particular, we need studies of teachers other than white females. The University of Missouri (Columbia) study reported in Adams and Biddle (1970) constitutes one example of how studies of teaching might be carried out.

Feminist groups have devoted considerable energy to consciousness-raising among teachers: making them more aware of their part in perpetuating sex stereotypes, encouraging them to develop new materials and try new techniques. But so far such efforts have been somewhat random and haphazard; moreover, many teachers—set in their ways, perhaps, and unsympathetic to the women's movement—may well resist new and seemingly radical ideas. It is imperative, then, to explore ways of incorporating these ideas into present teacher training programs. The curricula in schools and departments of education may require thorough revision to accomplish this aim.

Adolescent Socialization—The Secondary School

Current research indicates that most junior high school girls still have a traditional orientation. Moreover, at adolescence, girls typically become pre-occupied with their own attractiveness and their popularity with boys. It is in this period that sex differences in abilities emerge: Girls draw ahead of boys in both high-level and low-level verbal skills, and boys draw ahead in visual-spatial and in mathematical skills (Maccoby and Jacklin, 1974). Girls tend to suppress their intelligence, however, and may even register drops in IQ.

Estelle Ramey (Georgetown University Medical School) notes that even among gifted children (a group that comprises a larger proportion of girls than boys), girls tend to fall behind at this point. One contributing factor may be that resources for the gifted are more often channeled to boys than to girls. Are there other differences in the treatment of gifted boys and girls? Is the boy who shows unusual artistic ability given the direction and training he needs? Is the girl who demonstrates superior ability in such male-dominated areas as mathematics and the sciences encouraged and counseled into appropriate courses? Or is there a tendency to encourage only sex-appropriate talent?

Making the "hard" sciences absorbing to young people—boys as well as girls—presents a special challenge to the educator. If more women are to become natural scientists, they must be attracted into the field early, since training in mathematics, chemistry, physics, and biology is sequential and difficult to make up later (Mattfeld and Van Aken, 1965; Theodore, 1971; Sells, 1973; White, 1970). Indeed, efforts to stimulate interest in the sciences should probably begin at the elementary school level and may require interventions in the early socialization process to prevent girls from being "turned off" to what they may perceive as a male preserve. Adeline Naiman (Education Development Center, Boston) suggests that educators in elementary science need to be urged (and trained) to address scientific education to everyone. Using a film-based program in the schools that permits study of children's responses to parts of the film directed at certain decision points in career development, Naiman concludes that junior high school students are very reactionary even after they have taken a model elementary science program. Creative and innovative potential seems to diminish at puberty, and this decrease is particularly apparent among girls. Some members of the Association of Women in Science (AWIS) are encouraging younger women scientists to lecture in high schools, on the grounds that they may provide particularly effective role models because they are closer in age to the girls in the audience.

More generally, children should be exposed to science as something familiar and possible. For instance, guided tours through such scientific establishments as the Massachusetts Institute of Technology and other laboratories and scientific centers might arouse their interest. Such programs need coordination and funding; in addition, studies of their long-term impact should be undertaken.

Many of the patterns of sex discrimination already noted in elementary schools extend into junior and senior high schools. For instance, textbooks emphasize the achievements of men to the exclusion of women, although some efforts at revision are under way. One particular deficiency that needs remedy involves the treatment of minority women in secondary school textbooks. For example, although some slight progress has been made in describing the role that black men have played in American history, the role of black women has been virtually ignored (Miller, 1973). Lists of books about black women are available, and these books should be included in secondary school curricula. The culture of other minority groups, and the contributions of women in these groups, should be covered as well.

Sex-segregated classes and activities also continue into secondary school; the most obvious examples are the channeling of girls into home economics and secretarial courses and of boys into technical and industrial courses (McCune, 1974). This kind of discrimination is particularly insidious in that it locks many young women (particularly those who do not aspire to college) into the lowest-paying kinds of jobs. Under recent federal legislation, more funds now go into vocational and career training at the high school level, and many innovative and promising programs are under way. But most of them are directed at boys only. Girls continue to be shuttled into classes like "Teen-Age Boutique." Research is needed to document the extent to which sex segregation in vocational and technical education still exists, despite laws that forbid it. The next step is to consider how to assure that the law is enforced and training programs are desegrated.

Sally Hillsman Baker (1974) has some interesting findings about the process whereby racism and racial tracking continue in vocational schools. Her work might provide a model for work on sex tracking as a product of unconscious discrimination on the part of counselors and teachers—the institutionalized racism or sexism which perpetuates inequity long after formal regulations abolish it.

The vocational and educational counseling available to high school students often serves not to open up options but to reinforce sex stereotypes. The vocational interest inventories frequently used in counseling have come under much criticism from feminists. For instance, Gloria Leon (Rugters University), after analyzing the "male" and "female" forms of the Strong Vocational Interest Blank, concludes that the activities and occupations listed on the male form are much more numerous and varied than those on the female form and that girls are forced to respond to items that place them in the derived status of wife. For instance, they are asked whether they would prefer to be married to a rancher or a corporation president (Boring, 1973). Inventories should permit girls a wider range of choices (Cole, 1972).

In addition, high school counselors may themselves manifest sex bias that in turn influences the counseling interaction. The problems of reeducating guidance counselors resemble the problems already mentioned in connection with teachers. Sporadic efforts at consciousness-raising may not be sufficient; the better solution might be to reform training programs.

Even when adolescent girls have high aspirations and expectations, they may encounter opposition in both overt and subtle forms. For instance, research has shown that high school boys think that girls should not aim too high in their career plans. Any study of socialization, therefore, should take into account the attitudes of the peer group and the pressures it exerts on the individual. The possibilities of coeducational counseling might be explored.

In addition, the effect of what Harry Stack Sullivan (1953) has called "significant others" on the lives of adolescent boys and girls should be studied. Parents, other relatives, teachers, counselors, and other authority figures all play a part in the development of attitudes and career motivations among young people. Case studies that focus on key figures and crucial points in the young person's career decision should help to explain the developmental process and to suggest effective interventions.

One final question that must be addressed in considering any reform in the socialization of young people is the reaction of the parents. How will they respond to efforts to break down sex stereotypes? Will they favor this opening up of options to boys and girls? Will they draw back in alarm? What kinds of opposition can feminist-oriented teachers expect? Research is needed to describe and analyze various parental responses and to suggest ways of winning parental support.

College

The proportion of women among first-time, full-time freshmen has risen steadily in recent years, from 43 percent in 1968 to 48 percent in 1974. But considerable talent is still being lost, particularly among academically able women at lower socioeconomic levels who are often not motivated or encouraged to attend college (Astin et al., 1974; Creager et al., 1968; Cross, 1974). Many institutions (other than the open-door community colleges) still apply stricter admission standards to women than to men. One example of such bias is giving heavier weight to scores on tests of academic ability (where men do better than women) than to high school grades (where women do better than men). In 1974, women tended to be concentrated more heavily at private two-year colleges (whereas men were over-represented at the far more numerous public two-year colleges), at public, Protestant, and Roman Catholic four-year colleges (but not at private nonsectarian colleges), at universities of low selectivity, and at predominantly black colleges. We need studies that will indicate the reasons for this institutional distribution of women and trace its implications.

In recent years, the proportion of young women who, at college entry, aspire to male-dominated professional fields (engineering, law, and medicine) and to professional degrees has increased steadily. For instance, in 1968, only 0.6 percent of entering freshman women said they planned to become lawyers; in 1974, the figure was 2.3 percent. The percentages of women who plan to major in physical and biological science, however, have registered only slight increases. Elementary and secondary school teaching have lost female aspirants, whereas nursing and other non-M.D. health professions (e.g., therapy, dietetics, optometry, veterinary medicine) have gained; but these changes over time probably reflect the changing job market more than anything else. Nonetheless, it would be helpful to identify some of the factors related to changes in initial aspirations and plans among women. It is suggestive that these same entering freshman women have become less traditional in their attitudes on women's issues. For example, in 1970, over one-third agreed with the statement that "the activities of married women are best confined to the home and family"; by 1972, the ratio had dropped to one in four, and in 1974, only one in five female freshmen (but two in five male freshmen) endorsed the statement. Moreover, 95 out of 100 women in the most recent freshman class felt that women should get the same salary and opportunities for advancement as men in comparable positions. In short, some of the basic tenets of the women's movement seem to have been adopted by college women. (See American Council on Education, 1970, 1972.)

But what happens to women once they are in college? They are more likely to drop out than men (even though they generally make better college grades), but the factors associated with attrition are difficult to specify. Getting married and becoming pregnant account for some of the female dropouts but by no means all (Astin, 1972; Bayer, 1969; Patterson and Sells, 1973). More research is needed to explain their higher attrition rates.

It is known that, in the past, women undergraduates have depended more on their parents for financial support, whereas men have depended more on earnings from employment and savings; men were more likely to take loans, and women slightly more likely to get scholarships and grants. Recently, the federal government has put a much greater emphasis on loan programs than on grants (except to students from very low-income families), and many institutions no longer have funds for scholarship support to their students. Have these shifts in student aid affected women? Are larger proportions now dropping out—or failing to enroll in college at all—because women are more hesitant than men to incur indebtedness?

Despite their higher attrition rates, women are more likely than men to complete the bachelor's degree within four years after college entry. What accounts for this sex difference in persistence rates? Since men are more likely to take outside jobs to support themselves in college, it may be that they take reduced course loads and thus do not complete the degree requirements in the four-year span.

It would be instructive to see how women do in various kinds of innovative programs that allow flexible scheduling, self-pacing, acceleration, and time out from college for a semester or so (Carnegie Commission on Higher Education, 1973). Are they less apt to drop out permanently in any of these circumstances? Do they attain the baccalaureate more rapidly? What kinds of progress do they make in programs of independent study? Comparisons of women in different kinds of innovative programs and of men and women in the same kinds of innovative programs would be helpful.

That more women, at college entry, are naming male-dominated fields as their career choice does not necessarily mean that the proportion of women doctors, lawyers, and engineers will increase dramatically in the near future. Astin and Panos (1969), in a study of 1961 freshmen followed up in 1965, report that during the college years, women who had initially named a masculine career choice were likely to switch to a more feminine field (especially teaching or paraprofessional health careers) and unlikely to be recruited into a masculine career choice. In other words, college women may be subjected to pressures that force them into more "appropriate" fields. Such a change is discouraging; one would hope that the college experience frees women from sex-stereotyped career choices. On the other hand, the situation may have changed in more recent years, a possibility supported by indirect evidence: Astin and Panos found not only that women had lower degree aspirations than men at the time of college entry but also that women tended to lower their degree aspirations during the college years. In a more recent study, however, Bayer et al. (1973), reporting on a 1971 followup of 1967 freshmen, found that degree aspirations tended to rise over the college years, and that this increase was particularly marked among women. Studies are needed that will trace undergraduate patterns of stability in, defection from, and recruitment to various career choices.

Although there is much anecdotal material on the structural barriers that impede college women—e.g., inadequate counseling, negative attitudes on the part of college professors, a male-oriented curriculum—little empirical evidence exists about causal relations between characteristics of the college environment and a student's progress, plans, and eventual career choice. Indeed, many studies of college effects conclude that student "input" (i.e., the characteristics that students bring with them to college) accounts for most of the differences in the "output" of different colleges and that the college itself may have very little impact (Astin, 1968b; Feldman and Newcomb, 1969). Perhaps researchers should look at the differential effects for each sex separately.

In addition, the college effects that have been identified require careful interpretation to discover just how and why a particular kind of institution influences particular outcomes. For instance, attendance at a university increases a student's chances of dropping out, decreases aspirations for the Ph.D., and increases aspirations for a professional degree; attendance at a liberal arts college has the opposite pattern of effects. The sharp contrast may in part be attributable to the lack of contact between students and professors and the impersonality and coldness that characterize universities, as opposed to the warmer and friendlier atmosphere of the liberal arts college (Astin and Panos, 1969; Astin, 1968). Attending a college with a cohesive atmosphere (e.g., where the typical student has many close friends) has a positive effect on persistence and increases the student's interest in a career as a physical scientist. We need to identify other elements of college life that have a favorable impact on women tudents. More particularly, we need to know what conditions and interventions will encourage women to go into male-dominated fields of study and remain in those fields. Some institutions have undertaken active programs to recruit women into science and engineering. Lynne Brown (Purdue University) has established a program of counseling and of exposure to role models designed to keep women in science programs. A similar program for women engineering students has also proved successful. Organizations of women students within particular disciplines (e.g., an extracurricular "club" for women undergraduates in engineering) may contribute to a cohesive and supportive atmosphere; special discussion sections for women only have also been suggested (Carnegie Commission on Higher Education, 1973). Other kinds of support systems should be developed, and their success evaluated.

Many single-sex institutions have recently closed down or turned coeducational. For instance, the number of Catholic women's colleges has been sharply reduced, and several of the elite women's colleges now admit men. Many observers lament the passing of women's colleges, pointing out that these institutions produced large proportions of women who went on to outstanding professional achievement. Tidball (1973) attributes this relation to the high proportion of women faculty who serve as role models to their students. Others have suggested, however, that the superior academic ability of the women who attend these elite institutions accounts for their high production of outstanding women. More systematic research is needed to determine to what extent these somewhat opposing interpretations hold true.

Women's colleges can be studied in terms of other issues as well. What problems (in women's colleges and coeducational institutions) are involved when male professors teach women students? Are there sex-related differences in faculty attitudes toward students? If such differences can be demonstrated, how can they be managed so that student development is maximized?

What happens at the single-sex college turned coeducational? Yale, for instance, recently opened its doors to women, some of whom have described their experiences in that strongly masculine atmosphere (Lever and Schwartz, 1971; Jelly, 1974; Getman, 1974; Deinhardt, 1974). It would be instructive to examine changes in student status and achievement patterns at these colleges. The differential rate at which men and women contribute to classroom discussion provides one example for comparative study: Do the patterns differ according to the sex composition of the class? What kind of teacher behavior encourages female participation?

Another area for investigation is the comparative Ph.D. productivity of various colleges (i.e., the proportion of their graduates who go on to earn the doctorate). Historical and comparative studies of different undergraduate institutions might reveal why some are successful at channeling their women students into graduate study in the sciences (Campbell, 1971; Rossi, 1971), while others are not.

A final topic for research in connection with women in college is women's studies, a field which in the last five years or so has proliferated on the nation's campuses and even at some high schools (Robinson, 1973). A number of groups (e.g., The Feminist Press, KNOW, Inc.) have issued publications that list and describe various courses, programs, and available materials. Do these courses help raise women's aspirations? Do they help free women of sexual stereotypes? What is their effect on male students? Several rather controversial points arise in connection with women's studies. Should they be taught as separate courses or within existing disciplines? Should they take an activist or an academic stance? Can excluding or restricting participation by men, both as teachers and students, be justified? Cynthia Fuchs Epstein (CUNY, Queens College) and others have argued that if women's studies are separatist, activist, and limited to women only, they will inevitably be regarded as "second-class" disciplines. Studies that compare the effects of women's studies courses that vary along these dimensions might help to resolve these questions.

Graduate and Professional Training

In 1970, women constituted 37 percent of the resident graduate student population and 10 percent of the medical and law student population. Women outnumber men in master's programs; and for the many women enrolled in library science, social work, and education, the master's will probably be the terminal degree. Most authorities agree that the women admitted to graduate or professional schools are a highly select group, more able, on the average, than their male counterparts. Despite their superiority, however, they encounter difficulties in pursuing advanced training.

Discriminatory practices in graduate and professional school admissions are exemplified by the quotas for women that medical and law schools have had in the past. Such quotas are now illegal (Dunkle and Sandler, 1974) and in the last few years, the enrollment of women in first professional degree programs has risen, particularly in law schools. Thelma Z. Lavine (1974) suggests that many of these women may not have a deep commitment to the field of law and will probably drop out before completing the degree. Longitudinal studies of the characteristics of women entering law schools, and of their degree completion rates, would prove or disprove this contention. What is attracting so many women to the profession of law? What are their expectations and career aspriations?

The attrition rate of women in advanced training—and particularly in doctoral programs—is high, and some of the reasons why are obvious. Many 20-to-24-year-old women get married and start families, and marriage and family often demand much more of women than of men graduate students. Even those women who do not have children spend considerable time and energy at household tasks. Compounding this problem, women are less likely to be enrolled in the physical sciences (where the normal time span for doctorate completion is 7.3 years) than in the social sciences and humanities (where the normal time span is 11.7 years). It requires a high degree of persistence and commitment to stay in a program for that length of time, as evidenced by the generally higher attrition rates (among men as well as women) in these fields. (See Carnegie Commission on Higher Education, 1973; Patterson and Sells, 1973; Roby, 1973.) Medical training too is a lengthy process, although some medical schools are now experimenting with accelerated programs. Can similar programs be initiated in graduate schools without "cheapening" the degree? Are there ways of encouraging graduate students—both male and female—to complete the dissertation promptly, without the agonizing delays that too often characterize that final stage of doctoral work? Are more graduate students now leaving graduate study for financial reasons since the federal government has cut back sharply on funds for gradaute fellowships and for research and development? Do women suffer from these cutbacks more than men?

The woman graduate student is hampered also by the negative attitudes she encounters. Many professors and male graduate students believe that women are not as deeply committed to their discipline as men and that money spent on their training (especially in such costly fields as medical education and graduate science education) is wasted since they will never make use of it. (All the evidence indicates that this contention is false; the labor force participation of the woman doctorate is impressively high; see Astin, 1969.) In short, men may refuse to take women graduate students seriously and may even be contemptuous of them for not playing the traditional woman's role. Such attitudes can result in demoralization, emotional stress, dissatisfaction with graduate study, and a loss of motivation to remain in graduate school. Moreover, faculty availability has been found to be directly related to satisfaction and performance in graduate school, and women graduate students typically have fewer contacts with professors than do male graduate students (Feldman, 1974; Holmstrom and Holmstrom, 1974). We need studies to identify other psychological barriers that confront women graduate students. Ways of overcoming these barriers—such as more informal contacts with professors and with women in the field who can serve as role models—should be explored and evaluated. The effectiveness of campus child care centers in relieving some of the burdens imposed on married women graduate students should also be examined.

The Mass Media as "Educational Supplements"

The existence of sex-role stereotypes in the mass media, especially television, has been thoroughly documented (Bem and Bem, 1970; Clark and Esposito, 1971; Courtney and Lockeritz, 1971; Vogel et al., n.d., Weitzman et al., 1972). These stereotypes reinforce the lessons learned first in the home and later in the classroom.

Further studies are needed to determine just how the sex stereotypes purveyed by the mass media affect the self-image and behavior pattern of various age groups (Gardner, 1970). How do boys and girls, men and women, react to the image of the woman (as seductress or as housewife) presented in television commercials? How are one's views of others, one's motivations and occupational goals, one's level of achievement affected by stereotyped presentations on television, in magazines, in films? (See Kinzer, 1973; Komisar, 1971; Lefkowitz, 1972; Ray, 1972; Rosen, 1973.) Recent collections of quantitative data (Cantor, 1973; NOW, 1973) may prove useful in answering these questions.

The impact of stereotypes in the media cannot be ascertained without careful consideration of what the stereotypes include and how they are affected by changing times (Flora, 1971). Moreover, we must know more about categories of male and female behavior as they actually occur in society; such a study might demonstrate wide variations within each sex and thus support the view that the presentation of the sexes in the media is inaccurate.

In addition, cross-cultural studies would be useful. For instance, fragmentary evidence suggests that adolescent children in Denmark are less influenced by sex-role stereotypes than are children in the United States; some ascribe this difference to the lack of television in Denmark.

Research on such topics leads to larger issues: To what extent are stereotypes reversible or modifiable? If they can be reinforced by the media, can they be broken down in the same way? Some television stations are now allotting time to serious and thoughtful women's programs, and some companies (e.g., Santa Fe Railroad) are sponsoring commercials that emphasize their employment of women in what were previously men's jobs. Have these changes reduced the audience's sex stereotypes and sex-biases?

Affirmative Action Issues

Over the last decade, federal legislation to promote equal employment opportunities for women has gradually evolved to cover more job settings and more types of workers; at the same time, it has moved from the negative concept of nondiscrimination to the positive doctrine of affirmative action, requiring that a federal contractor take definite steps to hire formerly excluded groups, including women. This requirement has caused much concern among employers. Perhaps one of the most visible groups affected is colleges and universities. Their concern is exacerbated by the tight financial squeeze on higher education. (See Carnegie Commission on Higher Education, 1973; Eastwood, 1972; Sandler, 1973a, 1973b; Weitzman, 1973.) Some academic administrators may not understand the responsibility and legal necessity for complying with the various government regulations and guidelines. They may be confused, for instance, about goals as opposed to quotas in hiring (Rumbarger, 1974). To study noncompliance or poor compliance, one might formulate categories of informal resistance to—and even subversion of—federal orders and analyze systematically the various institutional responses to the requirements (Goodwin, 1973). It might also be instructive to compare the differential success of affirmative action in academia and in the world of business/industry.

One difficulty that arises is how to conduct a job analysis that will make clear the extent to which women and minorities are underemployed (as well as identify other employment conditions, including salary levels, that may indicate discriminatory practices) without violating confidentiality of records. Examination of cases where such an analysis has been carried out successfully would help in the delineation of appropriate guidelines and procedures (Fleming, 1974).

Another difficulty involves present procedures for redress of inequities. In most cases the person complainig of inequities must directly confront those against whom the complaint is made. This procedure may cause embarrassment and lead to later punitive retaliation. Research might explore alternative procedures for managing such situations—procedures that would violate neither fair play nor due process requirements.

In evaluating the efficacy of an affirmative action plan, the question of how to ascertain what standards should be included is paramount. To introduce women into management or academic administration positions, for example, the often intuitive judgments by which managerial "material" is usually selected must be understood (Ginzberg and Yohalem, 1973). How can these judgments be made explicit?

The present situation is sometimes divisive in that it may often create frictions among groups that should be working together toward mutual goals (most notably, women and racial/ethnic minorities) and may encourage playing out adversary relations between employers and employees in the courtroom. Accusations of "reverse discrimination" (that is, discrimination against white males) are widespread. But these oratorical conflicts merely obscure the issues and postpone efforts to promote equality (Sandler, 1975).

Moreover, existing affirmative action legislation is viewed by some as punitive—threatening termination of federal contracts and the withholding of funds. Federal contract support has become so commonplace that many people do not see this continued support as sufficient reward for "good-faith efforts." Learning theory tells us that positive reinforcement is much more effective in producing desirable behavior than negative reinforcement. Therefore, more research is needed on positive ways of encouraging institutions to develop programs, as well as direct encouragement of women to enter and remain in the labor force. For instance, the federal government might allow deductions for educational and child-care costs, thus showing support for women who return to school or join the paid labor force if they wish. Corporations might be willing to fund a study of such "carrot" legislation (Laws, n.d.a.).

Any research undertaken should stress the benefits for all—not just for one segment of the population—that derive from greater equality in employment. Indeed, it may be difficult to get funding for research that is not aimed at helping everyone. But some issues will be of greater concern to women than others, and researchers should be encouraged to pursue these topics. A scholarship or fellowship program to encourage women to carry out research on projects of high priority would be helpful.

Another way in which research on incentives to affirmative action might be undertaken is through the study of successful integration programs, particularly of cases where women have been integrated "naturally." Hennig's study of female business executives (1971) and Epstein's study of women lawyers (forthcoming) may provide models for further investigation of what makes some affirmative action efforts succeed and others fail.

Pools of the Eligible. Under present HEW requirements, departments within colleges and universities must define available pools of eligible women and minorities. The completeness of such studies varies, depending on the commitment of a particular discipline or department and on the availability of such data. One direction that research might take, then, is the examination of ways in which pools of eligible job candidates are constructed (Apter, 1974; Astin, 1974; Graham, 1970; Ross, 1974). Such studies should examine not only formal procedures but also informal patterns of behavior (and informal pressures to sidestep guidelines).

Faculty wives are an underutilized resource in many college communities. Faculty women might undertake surveys, outside of university jurisdiction, of this pool of highly qualified women. Not only would such surveys offer systematic data on underutilizaion, but also they would be of direct practical value to well-intentioned administrators.

Part-Time Appointments and Tenure. Women are more likely than men to have part-time faculty appointments. However, they are usually penalized for this status, being less likely than men to advance through the ranks to tenure positions. Now a movement is underway to regularize extended part-time employment so that these faculty members will receive the rewards and benefits of regular faculty. Sheila Tobias has conceptualized the principles around which part-time tenure has been argued, but so far little documentation or case law on the subject exists. A related development is to treat maternity leave like any other short-time disability and to allow both male and female faculty members equal access to leave for child rearing, should they so desire. (See Carnegie Commission on Higher Education, 1974; Tobias and Rumbarger, 1974; Truax, 1974.) Data collected now will indicate the potentialities of such work arrangements. How many part-time positions actually exist? How many allow for tenure? How rapidly are part-time tenure positions developing around the country? Evidence exists that such arrangements are differently managed at public than at private universities; what are these differences?

Some argue that part-time tenure will result in a loss of full-time faculty positions and suggest that some system of guaranteed employment be initiated instead. Such a system would protect, for example, the teacher who has served for 19 years as a part-time math teacher and who is dropped from the college faculty with the advent of hard times. What are the implications for women of such a system over part-time tenure?

As nepotism regulations have generally been eliminated on the grounds that they discriminate against women (chiefly faculty wives), many institutions are making joint husband-wife appointments, with each partner working on a part-time basis. In-depth studies of such tandem teaching teams might be illuminating for what they tell us not only about work arrangements but also about family arrangements.

Retirement and Pension Benefits. Under many retirement plans (including TIAA-CREF, which covers many employees in educational institutions), women, on retirement, are paid smaller monthly benefits than are men, the argument being that since women have a longer life expectancy, the "average woman" will receive as much (or more) than the "average man" over the total retirement period. The fairness of this assumption has been challenged by such groups as the Association of American University Professors. Indeed, the Equal Employment Opportunity Commission guidelines of March 31, 1972, would seem to forbid differential payments based on sex. Opponents of the present system point out that an established principle in antidiscrimination suits is that no particular woman should be treated as the "average woman" (and no man as the "average man") since the two sexes overlap with respect to mortality rates; and that the present system in effect forces retired faculty women into a much lower standard of living than retired faculty men. It is interesting to note that many industrial and state teachers retirement plans now distribute equal benefits. Further research may be needed to assess the full implications of equal retirement benefits. In addition, statistics on male and female mortality rates may need reassessing to determine whether working women have been adequately counted into the actuarial tables in current use. Studies might also be made to evaluate the best way to change insurance and pension systems to a unisex actuarial basis.

A Survey of Research Concerns on Women's Issues. By Arlene Kaplan Daniels. Project on the Status and Education of Women, Association of American Colleges, Washington, D.C. May 1975.

What You Should Know About Women [1]

Labor Force Participation Rates, Age 16–64, 1975 [2]

(Percentage of the Population in or Seeking Paid Employment)

White men	86.8	White women	53.3
Black men	76.8	Black women	53.9

Percentage of Workers Full-Time, Age 16 and Over, 1975 [3]

White men	91.8	White women	74.9
Minority men	91.5	Minority women	81.7

Median Earnings Year Round, Full-Time Workers, Age 14 and Over, 1974 [4]

White men	$12,104	White women	$6,823
Black men	8,524	Black women	6,258

Weekly Earnings, Full-Time Workers, May 1974 [5]

White men	$209	White women	$125
Minority men	160	Minority women	117

Unemployment Rates, 1975 [6]

(Percentage of persons in the labor force who are unemployed)

White men	7.2	White women	8.6
Black men	14.7	Black women	14.8
Teenage white men	18.3	Teenage white women	17.4
Teenage black men	38.1	Teenage black women	41.0

Occupations of Employed Men and Women by Race, 1974 [7]

	White		Minority	
	Men	Women	Men	Women
Total employed—				
thousands	47,340	29,280	5,179	4,136
Percent	100	100	100	100
Professional & technical	15	15	9	12
Managers & administrators	15	5	5	2
Sales workers	6	7	2	3
Clerical workers	6	36	7	25
Blue-collar workers	46	15	57	20
Service workers	7	19	15	37
Farm workers	5	2	4	1

Why Women Work [8]

In 1973

23 percent were single;

19 percent widowed, divorced, or separated; and

29 percent had husbands earning less than $10,000.

Working Mothers and Their Children, March 1974 [9]

43 percent of all married women (husbands present) were working.

46 percent of all women with children under 18 were working.

63 percent of all working mothers have children between 6–17 years.

19 percent of all working mothers have children under 3 years.

62 percent of mothers without husbands were working.

6.8 million families, 12 percent of all families, were headed by women in 1974 (between 1970 and 1974, the number increased by over 1 million).

Children of Working Mothers, March 1974 [10]

5.1 million women in the labor force in March of 1974 had children under 6 years of age.

---

[1] Comparable figures are not available for Spanish origin, Asian-American, and American Indian women. Sections on each of these groups follow using available data.

Where available, data for black women and men are included in the first sections. In some cases, only figures for all minorities are available and are used, (blacks constitute 89 percent of minorities).

[2] U.S. Department of Labor, Employment and Earnings, Jan. 1976, table 1 and unpublished data.

[3] Ibid., table 1 and 5.

[4] U.S. Department of Commerce, Bureau of the Census, "Money Income in 1974 of Families and Persons in the United States," Current Population Reports, Series P–60, No. 101, Jan. 1976, table 67.

[5] Department of Labor, Women's Bureau, Handbook on Women Workers, 1975, table 51.

[6] U.S. Department of Labor, Employment and Earnings, Jan. 1976, table 1 and unpublished data.

---

[7] U.S. Department of Commerce, Bureau of the Census, "The Social and Economic Status of the Black Population in the United States," 1974, Special Studies, Series P–23, No. 54, tables 48, 49.

[8] Department of Labor, Women's Bureau, Handbook on Women Workers, 1975, chart L.

[9] Department of Labor, Women's Bureau, Handbook on Women Workers, 1975, pp. 3, 20, 25, 26.

[10] Ibid., pp. 4, 30, 35.

26.8 million children had working mothers.

6.1 million children with working mothers were under the age of 6.

4.6 million children had working mothers who were heads of households.

913,000 of the 4.6 million children whose working mothers were heads of households were under 6 years of age.

The estimated number of day care slots in 1972 was 1 million.

Women in Unions[11]

5.7 million women were in unions, including 1.2 million professional and State employee association members (1972).

1 out of 6 women in the labor force were in collective bargaining unions and associations in 1974, 1 out of 8 in unions alone.

7 percent of membership on the governing boards of unions and associations in 1973 were women.

Alimony and Child Support[12]

Only 14 percent of divorced or separated women are awarded alimony. Only 46 percent of these collect it regularly.

Only 44 percent of divorced mothers are awarded child support, and only 45 percent of those collect it regularly.

Birth, Marriage, and Divorce[13]

In 1975 the estimated total fertility rate was 1,800 children per 1,000 women or 1.8 children per woman over her lifetime. In 1970 the rate was 2,480, a drop of 27 percent.

Divorces hit a record high in 1975, exceeding 1 million for the first time in U.S. history, representing a 6 percent increase over 1974.

Marriages declined to the lowest point since 1969, representing a 4 percent drop from 1974.

The divorce rate per 1,000 population was:

4.8 in 1975
3.5 in 1970
2.2 in 1960

The marriage rate per 1,000 population was:

10.0 in 1975
11.0 in 1972
10.6 in 1970

Elementary and Secondary Education[14]

67.4 percent of all teachers were women, but women held only 15 percent of all principalships (1970)

- At the elementary level, 20 percent of the principals were women (1976);
- At the secondary level—3 percent were women (1970).

Higher Education[15]

25 percent of public college and university faculties were women (1975).

10 percent of full professors were women (1975).

In 1975–76 the average college and university salary for women was $14,252.

In 1975–76 the average college and university salary for men was $17,312.

Of the over 2,500 accredited institutions of higher education, only 148 identify a woman as the chief executive officer.

Students

In the fall of 1973, 43 percent of all college students under 35 years of age were women.

In 1973, 326,000 black women were enrolled in college, nearly 3 times the number in 1964.[16]

The percentage of women in 1st-year law school classes for the fall of 1974 was 23.7 percent, up from 20.2 percent in 1972 and 15.7 percent in 1971. In medical schools 22.2 percent of the entering class were women, up from 19.7 percent in 1973 and 11.1 percent in 1970.[17]

New Careers[18]

One out of six (16.9 percent) entering college freshmen women in 1975 planned a career in

[11] Department of Labor, Women's Bureau, *Handbook on Women Workers, 1975*, pp. 76 and 78.

[12] Market Opinion Research, Detroit, Mich. Study done for IWY Commission in 1975.

[13] U.S. Department of Commerce, Bureau of the Census, "Population Profile of the United States: 1975," Current Population Reports, Series P–20, no. 292, Mar. 1976, pp. 1, 3, 9.

[14] Education Commission of the States, *Equal Rights for Women in Education*, Rep. No. 77, Denver, Col., Jan. 1976, p. 25.

[15] *Chronicle of Higher Education*, Feb. 9, 1976, p. 5 and *Comment*, Fall 1975, p. 3.

[16] Department of Labor, Women's Bureau, *Handbook on Women Workers, 1975*, p. 5.

[17] *Women's Movement in the U.S., 1960–1975, Government Role in the Women's Movement*, IWY #8, Rev. June 1975.

[18] *Memo*, American Association of State Colleges and Universities, vol. 16, no. 2, Jan. 15, 1976.

business, engineering, law, or medicine; only 5.9 percent said this in 1966. Twice as many women (16.6 percent in 1975 up from 9.1 percent in 1971) plan on postgraduate work.

Stock Holders [19]

Market value of shares held in all public corporations, 1975:

Men	157,083 billion	56.9%
Women	118,820 billion	43.1%

ASIAN-AMERICAN WOMEN [20]

Employment 1970

Some 2 million Asian-Americans lived in the United States in 1973. Roughly one-half were women; however, recent immigration is predominately female. Accurate figures are not available in 1976. Over 50 percent of all Asian women 16 years and older were in the labor force in 1970. Of the married Asian women, almost 50 percent were also in the labor force. Figures on unemployment for women indicate a lower than national average.

Occupations 1970

	Women (%)	Men (%)
Professional, technical, managerial	24	32
Sales and clerical workers, administration	38	14
Service workers, farm managers	21	30
Operatives, craftsmen, laborers	17	25

Income 1970

Some 60 percent of all Asian-American women 16 years and older earned under $4,000, somewhat lower than the national average in 1970. About 5 percent of all Asian-American women earned over $10,000 in 1970, somewhat higher than the national average for women.

Education 1970

Of the Asian-Americans, 16-years-old and over in 1970, the percentage of those who have completed 4 years of college or more was:

	Women	Men
Japanese	11	19
Chinese	17	25
Filipino	27	15

AMERICAN INDIAN WOMEN [21]

Employment 1970

There were 827,000 American Indians and Alaskan Natives, constituting .4 percent of the total population; 50.1 percent were women.

One-half the rural Indian population and 40 percent of the urban Indian population were under 18 years of age.

Of the American Indian women, 16 years and over, 35 percent were in the labor force; 63 percent of the men.

Unemployment 1970

The unemployment rate for American Indian women was 10.2 percent.

The unemployment rate for American Indian men was 11.6 percent.

Occupations—Urban

	Women (%)	Men (%)
Professional, technical	14	17
Clerical and sales	34	10
Operatives	19	26
Craftsmen		23
Services	34	24

(Other patterns for occupations for American Indians not available.)

Income 1970

The median income of females 16 years and over was $1,697.

The median income of males 16 years and older was $3,509.

Education 1970

Only 1.2 percent of rural American Indian women have had 4 years of college; only 1.5 percent of rural American Indian men. Only 3.8 percent of urban American Indian women have had 4 years of college education; only 5.6 percent of urban American Indian men.

[19] New York Stock Exchange Census of Shareowners 1975, midyear, (Public Companies).

[20] *A Study of Selected Socio-Economic Characteristics of Ethnic Minorities Based on the 1970 Census*, vol. II: Asian Americans, Office of Special Concerns, Department of Health, Education, and Welfare, no. (OS) 75–121, pp. 84, 86, 87, 105.

[21] A Study of Selected Socio-Economic Characteristics of Ethnic Minorities Based on the 1970 Census, Vol. III, *American Indians*, Office of Special Concerns, Department of Health, Education, and Welfare, No. (OS) 75–122, pp. i, 25, 40, 49, 53.

SPANISH ORIGIN WOMEN

Employment 1974 [22.]

In 1974, 5.5 million women were of Spanish-origin in the United States. Of those 16 years of age and over, 42.1 percent were in the labor force in March 1974, (or 1.4 million women).

Unemployment 1975 [22]

The unemployment rate of Spanish-origin women 20 years of age was 11.2 percent; 9.2 percent was the unemployment rate of Spanish-origin men over 20 years of age. The unemployment rate for teenage men and women of Spanish-origin (16–19) was 26.1 percent (third quarter 1975).

Occupations 1974 [23]

	Women (%)	Men (%)
Professional, technical	6.0	6.7
Managers, administrators	2.9	7.3
Sales workers	4.0	3.0
Clerical workers	28.3	7.0
Craft workers	2.1	17.6
Operatives, including transport	30.2	27.0
Farm workers	2.6	7.4
Service workers	22.9	12.0

* This material has not been excerpted in its entirety.

"...To Form A More Perfect Union..." A Report of the National Commission on the Observance of International Women's Year, Washington, D.C. 1976.

Income 1975 [24]

The median income of women 14 years or older of Spanish-origin was $3,072; $6,507 was the median income for males of Spanish-origin 14 years or older.

Working Mothers [25]

Of working mothers of Spanish-origin, 43.5 percent had children 6–17 years of age (1970); 28.4 percent had children under 6 (1970).

Education [26]

Of the women of Spanish-origin, 4 percent were enrolled in college in October 1973; 5.6 percent of the men of Spanish-origin were enrolled in college in October 1973.

[22] U.S. Department of Labor, Women's Bureau, 1976, *Women of Spanish Origin in the United States*, pp. 2, 8, 9.
[23] *Ibid.*, table 7.
[24] U.S. Department of Commerce, Bureau of the Census, "Persons of Spanish Origin in the United States, March 1975," Series P–20, no. 283, Aug. 1975, table 7.
[25] *Women of Spanish Origin in the United States*, U.S. Department of Labor, Women's Bureau, 1976.
[26] U.S. Department of Commerce, Bureau of the Census; "Social and Economic Characteristics of Students" CPR p. 20, no. 272, table 1.

How to Combat Sexism in Textbooks

BY JUDITH KRAM

The techniques described in the article below can of course also be used in the fight against racism in all child-oriented materials. — Editors.

Boys are clever, resourceful, industrious, independent and strong; girls are altruistic, emotional, fearful, weak and incompetent. This is the lesson children learn from their elementary school readers.

Quite a few individuals and organizations have carried out content analyses of textbooks, and their findings have led to the same conclusion: Textbooks are tracking children into narrowly defined sex roles, which are demeaning to girls and detrimental to both girls and boys.

The first step in seeking to eliminate sex-role stereotyping from instructional materials is to research the material currently in use in order to arm oneself with specific examples. The next step is to publicize these findings.

USE THE MEDIA

The media is a useful tool for communicating the problem and for recruiting support. *Send letters to the editor.* These columns constitute free publicity for your efforts and reach a wide and diverse audience. Keep your local newspapers, radio and television stations informed of your efforts to combat sexually biased instructional material. In addition to dealing with the media directly, contact businesses and urge them to sponsor a program on the subject.

Concerned individuals and organizations should pressure legislatures — state and federal — and Boards of Education to prohibit the use of stereotypical sex-role material in the public schools. Write letters to these agencies. A letter from a group carries more weight than one from an individual. Even if there are only two of you,

it pays to establish yourselves as a group and have stationery printed. Write to your senators, congresspeople and the chairperson of the State Board of Education. For local grievances, write the chairperson of your local school committee. If you do not receive a response, write to the Commissioner of Education. Make some investigatory calls — it is important to address your initial complaint to the appropriate party to save time and to avoid alienating potential supporters.

At present, at least three states — California, Iowa and New Jersey — have passed legislation against sex-biased school materials and the Boards of Education of Colorado, Maryland, New Jersey, South Dakota and West Virginia have passed or proposed resolutions.

You are apt to meet resistance from people who contend that such legislation and resolutions abridge the First Amendment guarantee of freedom of speech. However, Holly Knox, director of PEER (Project on Equal Education Rights), a new project of the NOW Legal Defense and Education Fund, points out that "state and local school officials already routinely review and select textbooks." Feminists are only asking that these officials incorporate measures to avoid the adoption of sex-biased materials.

Strong legislation would enable feminists to take school systems to court. Under Title IX of the Education Amendments of 1972, the Kalamazoo Committee to Study Sex Discrimination in the Public Schools filed a complaint against the Kalamazoo School System for its purchase of a $68,000 Houghton Mifflin reading series which the Committee claims discriminates against women. [This case has not yet been decided. For information, contact Ms. Jo Jacobs, Chairperson, Commission to Study Sex Bias in Kalamazoo Public Schools, 732 Garland St., Kalamazoo, Mich. 49008. — *Editors.*]

While lobbying for legislation, you should also meet with the textbook selection officials. At the state level, this may mean contacting a textbook selection committee or a division of curriculum planning/instructional materials. Within an individual system, a coordinator of elementary education or individual teachers may be responsible for textbook selection. It is important to let the proper officials know you are concerned and want to meet with them.

School systems — state or local — can also exert pressure. They can refuse to buy material which does not meet established guidelines for portrayal of the sexes. Official letters from the school system should be sent to every textbook publishing company informing them of the decision not to purchase material that fails to meet specific criteria; a copy of the guidelines should be included. The system may choose to develop its own guidelines or may adopt those already compiled by a publishing house, State Department of Education, or feminist group.

Write to textbook publishing companies about their materials. Address the editor of the textbook division and send a carbon copy to the company president; *Literary Market Place* — available in most libraries — will give you the exact person to write. Criticize sexist material, giving specific examples and offering alternatives wherever possible. Also, remember to commend companies for their good material.

CHANGE IS EXPENSIVE

It must be noted that the problem of eliminating sex-role stereotypes from textbooks involves economics — the cost of publishing a single textbook is extremely high. While textbook publishing houses are concerned about the problem of sex bias, they can rarely afford to make more than cosmetic changes in their present publications. Many companies have committed themselves to eliminating sex bias from future publications; however, it takes *at least* two years for the writing, production and printing of a textbook. Then it must be approved by adoption committees and ordered, usually one year in advance of its usage, by teachers or school systems. According to an education kit developed by the Women's Equity Action League, "It takes half a million dollars to launch a new series and five years to get that series from writer to child."

Because textbooks are so expensive to produce, the current trend away from their use is a significant development. Many elementary schools have replaced traditional reading programs with individualized ones. Paperback readers are replacing such notorious textbooks as the Dick and Jane series. For several years now, feminists have been writing children's books which can be used in these individualized reading programs. (Feminist presses have been established to facilitate the publication of books of this kind.)

These same books can be used outside of the classroom to supplement a child's classroom reading material. Speak to both the school and local librarians. Encourage them (1) to purchase storybooks from available lists of non-sexist books; (2) to provide biographies of famous women, particularly those who excelled in traditionally male roles like Elizabeth Blackwell, the first female doctor, and those who worked for women's rights like Susan B. Anthony and the Pankhursts; (3) to purchase women's magazines such as *Ms.* and *Womansport*.

A need exists for new material on women, integrated material and easily accessible bibliographies and samples of non-sexist curricula. The latter would be of particular use to teachers who are concerned about sex-role stereotyping but who for lack of time, commitment or resources are unable to do their own research.

For those interested in developing bibliographies, the following is suggested:

1. Decide on the subject area and reading level for investigation. Choose a narrow focus, e.g., fifth grade history or fifth grade math, and combine bibliographies at the end if so desired.
2. Decide what type of instructional material to investigate, e.g., integrated textbooks, or supplementary material.
3. Familiarize yourself with the field

before investigating available material in order to clearly define beforehand what an acceptable text should include. (In an area, such as history, most people are unfamiliar with women's contributions and therefore, are unaware of what constitutes accurate and adequate material.)

4. Remember: Written authorization is required for each piece of copyrighted material to be included in any document intended for publication, unless it is an excerpt of less than 300 words used for illustrative purposes.

In the absence of adequate material, teachers must acquire compensatory skills. In Kalamazoo, the Committee to Study Sex Discrimination in the Public Schools pasted annotations and supplements into the present material while awaiting the outcome of their complaint. *Stop Sex Role Stereotypes in Elementary Education,* by Martha Cohen for ConnPIRG (Public Interest Research Group), contains an excellent section on teacher training as well as methods for using deficient material. This is just one of many in-service training manuals.

Ethel Sadowsky, Chairwoman of the Education Task Force of the Massachusetts Governor's Commission on the Status of Women, suggests using such slide tapes as "Dick and Jane as Victims" by Women on Words and Images and "The Hidden Curriculum," studies of elementary textbooks by a group of Seattle women, to help teachers become aware of what is harmful and inhibiting in the instructional material they are using.

Finally, contact the women's organizations in your area. Keep them informed of your plans; you may be able to work together.

RESOURCES

1. *Stop Sex Role Stereotypes in Elementary Education.* Available free of charge from ConnPIRG, Box 1517, Hartford, Conn.

2. Education kit for K-12 available for $1.25 from Women's Equity Action League, 538 National Press Building, Washington, D.C. 20036.

3. *You Won't Do* by Jennifer S. Macleod and Sandra T. Silverman. Includes annotated source list called "Sexism in Textbooks: 150+ Studies and Remedies."

Available from KNOW, Inc., P.O. Box 86031, Pittsburgh, Pa. 15221. $2.25 (fourth class); $3.00 (air mail).

4. *Dick and Jane as Victims: Sex-Role Stereotyping in Children's Readers.* Developed by Women on Words and Images, 1972. Contact: Phyllis Alroy, P.O. Box 2163, Princeton, N.J. 08540.

5. For information on legislation, contact: Holly Knox, PEER, 522 Connecticut Avenue, N.W., Washington, D.C. 20036.

6. For a list of bibliographies and catalogs of non-sexist children's literature and bibliographies on sexism and related publications, write to Massachusetts Governor's Commission on the Status cf Women, Room 2108, 100 Cambridge St., Boston, Mass. 02202.

7. "A Resource for Eliminating Sex-Role Stereotyping in Textbooks:" bibliographies of readers, biographies, integrated textbooks, supplementary material and literature on sexism in children's books. Also textbook guidelines developed by publishing houses, state departments of education, professional and feminist organizations. Legislation and instructional material. *Available for consulting only* in office of Massachusetts Governor's Commission on the Status of Women, Room 2108, 100 Cambridge Street, Boston, Mass. 02202.

ABOUT THE AUTHOR

JUDITH KRAM was a volunteer with the Massachusetts' Governor's Commission on the Status of Women in connection with her undergraduate studies at Cornell University. She is currently studying at Hebrew University in Jerusalem.

"How to Combat Sexism in Textbooks." by Judith Kram. Sexism in Texts. Published by the Council on Interracial Books for Children, 1841 Broadway, New York, NY 10023.

D is for Dictionary   S is for Stereotyping

By Barbara A. Schram

Being aware of the sex and race role stereotyping that is rampant in children's story books and text books, I find myself carefully "checking out" each new book before I give it to a child. I'm always surprised and delighted when I find one that is a rare exception to the usual vicious pattern. I was not prepared, however, for the magnitude of stereotyping I uncovered when "checking out" children's dictionaries. While story books are, after all only fabrications of someone's imagination, dictionaries, so I thought, were filled with *facts,* objective *truths.*

After carefully reading through the eight dictionaries listed at the end of this article, ranging from those intended for preschoolers to those suggested for junior high use, I discovered that words can be defined in such a way that what might seem like *facts* and *truth* are really the *opinion* and *bias* of the editors. I also found an article describing a large-sample, computerized study conducted by lexicographers of a major publishing company—Alma Graham's "The Making of a Non-Sexist Dictionary." *Ms.* magazine, December, 1973 (see also the *Bulletin,* Vol. 5, No. 3). It reached the same conclusions as did my less rigorous research using all the children's dictionaries on the shelf of a midtown Manhattan public library.

I examined these dictionaries primarily to see how sexist they were. I did not concentrate on their racism, but it must be said that the dictionaries are, in general, racist by omission if not be commission.

For example, Black and other Third World people are rarely included in the illustrations, especially in the older books. When minorities *are* shown, they serve mainly as "props" for "exotic" dress—for parkas (Eskimos), saris (Indian women), burnooses (Arabs), and the like. The two most recent dictionaries—the Xerox Intermediate Dictionary (1973) and the American Heritage School Dictionary (1972)—have of course begun to make an effort to include minorities in all types of illustrations—but there is still a long way to go.

I would also add that, in not focusing on the racism in dictionaries, I did not seek to document the value structure built into the use of the words "white" and "black." I did not count the number of positive synonyms or connotations associated with "black." However, a quick look at the words paired with white—pure, innocent, etc.—and those matched with black—evil, gloomy, etc.—will reveal to the most casual reader why Ossie Davis has said, in another context: "The English language is my enemy."

These are my findings from two solid days of reading children's dictionaries, days filled with eyestrain, boredom and outrage.

1. *Editors of dictionaries, especially of those written for very young children, are uncreative copycats* (I shudder to use the word plagiarists).

While the definition of a word—*hit,* for example—cannot vary dramatically from one dictionary to the next, there is no reason why the sentence used to help children place the word in its logical context can not vary a lot. Yet, in three picture dictionaries, I read:

John *hit* the ball.

Tom will *hit* the ball with his tennis racket.

The boy will *hit* the ball with his bat.

When they put the word *strong* into a sentence, I read:

The *strong* man lifts the weights.

The man is *strong.* He can lift heavy weights.

A *strong* man can lift heavy things.

These and countless other such "stimulating" sentences—obviously paraphrased from one book to the next—lead me to believe that new picture dictionaries are written with scissors and Scotch tape. Thus, whatever inanities and biases exist in one dictionary are mirrored and thus perpetuated in each subsequent "new" book or "revised" edition. Lining up each of the books' entries for several different words led me inevitably to my next conclusion.

2. *In dictionaries, just as in the rest of the world of children's books, females (and of course Third World people as well) are virtually invisible. This holds true for most of the dictionaries I read, but the picture dictionaries are the worst offenders.*

In their dull simplicity and their underestimation of the intelligence of children, the dictionaries almost always use a pronoun or person's name in each sentence. Thus it is always *John, Tom* or the *boys* who hit the ball. Rarely do they risk using a sentence as complex and sexually neutral as, perhaps, "The ball hit the side of the house and broke a window." They also rarely use collective pronouns—the children, the club, friends, the class, or they, us or we. But when they do use words less clearly descriptive of the sex of the actors—for example, "The children are going on a hike."—they quickly dispel any possibility that "children" might include girls by providing a picture of five little boys and their male leader. So, through the use of highly specific words and pictures the dictionaries used by the youngest—and most impressionable—children are the most effective at rendering females invisible.

Of all the picture dictionaries on the market (and on library and preschool classroom shelves) Richard Scarry's *Best Word Book Ever* is probably the most blatant example of this phenomenon of erasing most of 51 per cent of the population. Since Scarry's sales have exceeded the million mark (he has made the *New York Times* Index of the ten best-selling children's books), I assume he is also erasing about 500,000 of his young readers.

By using marvelously humorous animals to help define words, he does avoid the insidious racism of most of the other books which consistently show Anglo- Saxon looking people and use Anglo-Saxon names. But he does make it very possible for us to tell which animals are male and which are female. The few females that do turn up in his pages are clearly labeled with aprons, ribbons and skirts. They are found in the following numbers in these sections:

At the Playground	32 boys	11 girls
Using Tools	10 boys	0 girls
Toys	14 boys	2 girls
Boats and Ships	13 boys	0 girls
Making Music	24 boys	2 girls
Making Things Grow	4 boys	0 girls
At the Airport	11 boys	1 girl

And on and on and on. Others might come up with slightly different counts since some animals have no clothes or are very small. I won't quibble since the ratios are still very dramatic. The lexicographer's computer found that "overall the ratio in schoolbooks of *he* to *she, him* to *her* was almost 4 to 1." Scarry usually does much worse than that.

The Best World Book Ever can certainly leave its young readers wondering just what little girls and women do. Well, in *When You Grow Up* Scarry shows us that females can be secretaries, singers, teachers, dancers, librarians and mommies: in *Health,* he shows us a nurse and a dental hygienist. So girls can have jobs, but they don't do much playing, planting, making things, or going places. In *Things We Do,* while 32 male animals are pursuing a whole host of life-sustaining activities (riding bikes, driving cars, planting and selling food), the two females on the pages are used to illustrate the activities "sitting" and "watching."

While the picture dictionaries are blatantly sexist, the more sophisticated ones for older readers show a similar myopia. In reading the definition of "professional," I was shocked to find the helpful sentence. "A lawyer or a doctor is a professional man." Obviously, the remote possibility that a lawyer or a doctor might be a professional *women* never crossed the editor's mind. Yet the sentence would have read well and been sexually neutral by the simple omission of the last word in the sentence.

The dictionaries for older children also show few illustrations of females. If they're illustrating how one plays an accordian or uses a compass, if they're showing the position of the alimentary canal in the human body or a facial expression, most pictures show male figures— unless the task or object in unequivocally or stereotypically linked with women like an item of clothing or a domestic, especially childcaring, activity.

This leads us to our third, not very surprising, conclusion.

3.   *When female pronouns, names or pictures are used, they help define or illustrate the most intransitive, passive verbs and the most negative or subordinate nouns and objectives.*

*The Golden Dictionary,** a best-selling classic like *The Best Word Book Ever,* helped me quickly identify this pattern. I needed only to look at its first page, where I found:

Able: John is *able* to touch his toes.
          Ann is *not able* to touch her toes.
At: John is *at* the top of the ladder.
          Ethel is *at* the bottom (actually on the ground, ac-
          cording to the illustration).
Asleep: Jenny is *asleep.*
Awake: Bob is *awake*

Lest I too quickly generalize, however, I decided to systematically explore the active-male, passive-female bias I suspected existed in all the books. I listed several often-used verbs, nouns and adjectives and then looked them up in the dictionaries. Here is a sampling of what I found (in some instances the word was not used in a sentence or was not sex-linked). The active verbs were always linked to males.

Lead: The *man leads* the horse.
          I will *lead* my pony through the door, (picture of
          a *boy*)
          He *leads* the horses to water.

In the few instances in which active verbs were linked to a female pronoun, they were often used in the most passive, trival or negative way. For example:

          Tom swims in the water.
          James swan to the other side of the pool.
          Most *boys* like to *swim.*
          He *swam* the river.

---

* I used the 1944 edition of this book. Although a more recent one has been issued, the library did not own it. So a young child going to the shelf would have been exposed to this sex-role stereotyping just as I was. Although publishers like to remind critics that revisions have been done, it is important to remember that libraries and schools do not often have the budgets to throw out and replace books. Thus the most blatantly racist and sexist books remain for the use of children long after many school officials and parents have been made aware of their corrosive impact on youngsters.

But *"Her* eyes were *swimming* with tears." While *Father was fixing* broken toys, *"Mother fixed* 6:00 as dinner hour" and *"Regina fixed* her collar."

>*He* always takes the *lead* when we plan to do something.
>*Bob* wanted to *lead.*
>*He* plays the *lead* in the school play.

Fix: Patsy broke her doll. *Father fixed* it.
>I broke my toy. *Daddy* will *fix* it. (picture of a girl).
>The man *fixed* the post into the ground.
>See *father fix* the tree.
>*Jim fixed* the tent stakes firmly in the ground.

More passive verbs were represented by collective pronouns, animals or females.

Sit: I sit in a chair. (picture of both a boy and a girl).
>The *dog,* Chips, can *sit* up and ask for food.
>The *woman sat* the little boy down hard.

Lay: Ruth lay her doll in the cradle
>See *mother lay* the baby on the bed.
>*Ma laid* the baby in the cradle.
>*She lay* down when she was tired.

While the *boys were hitting* the ball with a bat or racket, "the *girls hit* upon a good name for their club." While *he threw* himself at his opponent, *"she threw* a cape over her shoulders."

When I looked up definitions of nouns and adjectives, I found those with great social prestige were almost uniformly male. For example,

Brave: Jim was *brave* in the dentist's chair.
>*Firemen* are *brave.*
>The *soldiers braved* much danger.
>*He braved* the king's anger.
>The *soldier* was *brave.*
>The *men braved* the blizzard.

Wise: My *father* is a *wise* man.
>The three *wise men* came from the east to honor the baby Jesus.
>The *man* is very *wise.*
>*Wise men.*
>A *wise* state*man.*

Those words with less social prestige were associated with animals or females or were not sex-linked.

Afraid: The *cat* is *afraid* of the dog.
>The *cat* is *afraid* to jump.
>*Alice* is *afraid* of snakes.
>*Cat* is *afraid* of the dog.
>*Jane* is *afraid* of spiders.

Wrong: Mrs. Brown is doing her child a *wrong by* spoiling him.
>*Mary* spelled three words *wrong.*
>Tom *rarely* does the *wrong* thing.
>*He's not wrong.*

Purple is the *wrong* color for *her.*
They *wronged her* by telling lies.

Mixed-up: The children *mix* their *mother up* when they ask her to do so many things at once. She doesn't know what she is doing.

4.   *While the stereotyping in children's dictionaries is pervasive, there are some hopeful signs of publishers' awareness of the issues.*

Of the eight books I reviewed, the *Xerox Intermediate Dictionary* (published in 1973) and the *The American Heritage School Dictionary* (published in 1972) appear to be substantial improvements over their outdated but still much-in-use predecessors. Though it looks quite modern and liberated at first glance, the *Xerox Dictionary* is still probably not worth buying. On closer reading I found it cautious and non-committal to a fault. While it avoids negatively stereotyping women in many definitions, it also rarely positively affirms female strength, nor, for that matter, does it affirm male warmth and vulnerability. I found little evidence that it has taken note of the civil rights movement or other recent political or social developments. It simply screens out blatantly stereotyped allusions by avoiding sex linking and continues to repeat worn-out male-oriented phrases.

The American Heritage Dictionary, while still skewed in the direction of male and Anglo-Saxon dominance, does confront stereotyping in several instances. It not only avoids perpetuating stereotypes but deliberately overthrows several. For example, while the very inadequate *Webster's New World Dictionary for Young Readers* (supposedly revised in 1971) defines:

Prostitute: *"A person who does immoral things for* money, especially a woman who offers herself to men for money."

and *Xerox* avoids the issue by not listing the word, the *American Heritage* defines:

Prostitute: "Someone who debases himself or his abilities for money or an unworthy motive. Someone who performs sexual acts for pay."

Clearly, thought was given to the latter definition; it more adequately mirrors reality, and explains the term. *The American Heritage* declares itself to be the first dictionary to list and define the title Ms. (although it doesn't feel ready to confirm how to pronounce it). Although it is the only dictionary I read that listed NAACP, it did not, regrettably, do more than explain what the initials stood for. It mentions student anti-war protests in one of its definitions and offers a very dignified description of the suffragist Amelia Bloomer, who is often not credited with the seriousness of purpose she deserves. In providing phrases for the word proud, it quite appropriately uses the phrase "Black pride."

In its choice of illustration, *The American Heritage Dictionary* has made an obvious effort to include more females and in some instances it shows Third World youngsters. A photograph of two Black girls illustrates the game of "leap frog," while an Asian girl shows us how to play the "triangle."

The comparison of these two shiny new books leads me to my final conclusion.

5. *Since you can't tell how stereotyped a dictionary is by its sales totals, fancy cover or date of revision, you must check out for yourself each dictionary you find on the school, library or bookstore shelf.*

It's a good idea to develop a few tests to "check out" a dictionary. First you might list five active and five passive words, five negative and five positive ones, and see how the book defines them both in words and pictures. Then look up traditionally stereotyped words like gossip, tattle, tease, leader, cheerleader, courage, and determination to see how they are handled. Check out your favorite sport or hobby and see who is defined or shown pursuing it. See how often they use man and mankind rather than people or humans. Flip through the illustrations and see who is shown using the compass and who is shown using the typewriter.

When you find a dictionary that lists the term cavepeople and shows a sketch of Neanderthal woman, uses George Washington in a sentence to show the word "slave holder" in context, shows a female demonstrating how a microscope is used, and routinely avoids he, his and him by using plural nouns and pronouns, buy a copy for yourself and pass the news on to several teachers and librarians.

Dictionaries Consulted

Best Word Book Ever, Richard Scarry, Golden Press, N.Y., 1964.

Golden Dictionary, Ellen Wales Walpole, Golden Press, N.Y., 1944.

The American Heritage School Dictionary, American Heritage and Houghton Mifflin, N.Y., 1972.

The Picture Dictionary, Garnette Walters and S.A. Courtis, Grosset & Dunlap, N.Y., 1939, 1945, 1948, 1958.

The Rainbow Dictionary, Wendell Wright, ed., World Publishing, Ohio, 1947, 1959.

Thorndike Barnhart Dictionary, Doubleday, Garden City, N.Y., 1969.

Webster's New World Dictionary for Young Readers, David Guralnik, ed., World Publishing, N.Y., 1971 and 1961, 1966.

Xerox Intermediate Dictionary, William Morris, ed., Grosset & Dunlap, N.Y., 1973.

ABOUT THE AUTHOR

BARBARA A. SCHRAM is co-ordinator of the Human Services Program in the School of Education, Northeastern University, and a consultant to Bank Street College of Education's Day Care Unit. She has worked as a community organizer for welfare rights and community participation in schools and is active in several feminist groups.

"D is for dictionary S is for Stereotyping" By Barbara A. Schram. Council on Interracial Books for Children, 1841 Broadway, New York, NY 10023.

Federal Laws Prohibiting Sex Discrimination and How To Use Them

Equal Pay Act of 1963, as amended

Effective Date

Generally, for nonprofessional employees—June 1964; for executive, administrative, professional and outside sales employees—July 1972; for most Federal, state and local government employees—May 1974.

Prohibited Acts

Any discrimination[1] in wages (including overtime, sick and vacation pay) and fringe benefits (including health and life insurance, pension and other retirement benefits,[2] profit sharing and bonus plans, credit union benefits) which is based on sex.

Who is Covered?

Generally, if your employer must pay you according to the minimum wage law, the employer is also covered by the Act.[3]

Exemptions From Coverage/Exclusions

Some.[4] See below for listing of exemptions.

Are Labor Organizations Covered?

Yes, a labor organization is forbidden from causing or attempting to cause the employer to discriminate against employees on the basis of sex.

Who Enforces the Provisions?

The Department of Labor's Wage and Hour Division enforces the Act as it applies to private and state and local government employees. By a special agreement, the Division also enforces the law for employees of the Library of Congress, the U.S. Postal Service, the Postal Rate Commission, and the T.V.A. The U.S. Civil Service Commission enforces the Act as it applies to other employees of the Federal government.

How Quickly Does the Agency Act?

The Division does not have a serious backlog of complaints and the Division generally begins its investigation about 90 days after you file.[5]

Procedures in Enforcing the Provisions

You may engage private counsel and file suit immediately[6] or you may choose to have the Division handle your complaint. If the Division concludes that there has been discrimination, it has, in 90 percent of its complaints, obtained back pay and/or wage increases from the employer voluntarily. If voluntary compliance fails, the Division can file suit in court on your behalf.[7]

Remedies and/or Sanctions

In suits filed by the aggrieved employee, the court may grant up to 2 years of back pay (3 years for cases of willful discrimination); a sum equal to the back pay award as compensatory damages or interest; attorney's fees; and wage increases. In suits filed by the Division, the court may grant the back pay, compensatory damages, or interest on the back pay and wage increases. Additionally, the Division may obtain an injunction against future violations.

Affirmative Action Requirements

None.

Time Limit for Filing Complaint

Suits for nonwillful discrimination must be filed within 2 years of the time the discriminatory act occurred, or within 3 years for willful discrimination. If your employer continues to violate the Act, your suit will always be filed on time. The statute of limitations limits the time period for which you receive back pay to 2 years from the time of filing in cases of nonwillful discrimination and 3 for willful discrimination.

How is a Complaint Made?

By telephone or letter or in person to the office of the Wage and Hour Division. No special form is required.

Who Can Make a Complaint?

Aggrieved employees or anyone acting on their behalf and organizations acting on their own behalf or others'.

Can Complaints of a Pattern or Practice of Discrimination be Made as Well as Individual Complaints?

Yes.

Notification of Complaints

Complaint procedure is very informal. The Division may or may not inform the employer that a complaint has been filed.

Are Investigations Made Without Complaints on File?

Yes, the Division conducts thousands of routine investigations each year.

Is Harassment Forbidden?

Employers are forbidden from discriminating against or discharging any employee because of a complaint filed or any assistance provided during the enforcement process.[8]

Confidentiality of Names

The Division does not reveal the name of the complainant except for instances when the Division files a suit in court on behalf of the complaining party.

Recordkeeping Requirements and Government Access

Employers are required to keep specific records to which the government has access.

For more information, contact:

Wage and Hour Division
Employment Standards Administration
Department of Labor
Washington, D.C. 20210

or

A Division office near you. Check the white pages of your phone book under "United States Government," Labor Department.

Notes

1. Wage systems which result in unequal pay rates but are based on a merit system, a seniority system, a system that measures earnings by the quality or quantity of production or any other factor than sex are not covered by the Act. (However, each of these systems must be applied equally to men and women.)

2. Employers are permitted to maintain fringe benefits policies which have a differential effect on persons because of their sex, if equal contributions are made for both groups.

3. You should call the Department of Labor's Wage and Hour Division before you decide you are not covered by the Act. If you are not covered, it is possible you might be covered by another Federal statute or a state statute.

4. Exempted from coverage are:

Military personnel of federal government. State and local elected public officials, their staffs, and appointed public officials with policymaking responsibility.

Some employees of small retail or service businesses.

Employees of stores with yearly gross sales of less than $225,000 which are part of a chain or conglomerate (exempt until 1977).

Employees of seasonal recreational centers.

Some fishing and agricultural workers.

Employees of local newspapers with a circulation of less than 4,000.

Newspaper delivery employees.

Switchboard operators of telephone companies that have less than 750 stations.

Domestic workers who work less than a total of 8 hours a week or who earn less than $50 during a 3-month period.

Babysitters and companions to elderly or sick persons who are employed on an occasional or sporadic basis.

5. Although the Act does not reach as many forms of sex discrimination as Title VII, the comparative speed with which your complaint may be handled, can make the Act a more useful way to proceed, especially if your complaint alleges discrimination in wages only.

6. Under the Act the court may award attorney's fees to the successful complainant.

7. If the Division handles your complaint and you agreed for the Division to obtain a particular sum of money from your employer, you cannot bring a court suit on the same claim if the Division succeeds in collecting that sum. Similarly, you may not sue on the same claim in court, if the Division files a suit on your behalf and the court decides the case.

8. If the employer does discriminate against the complainant, the Division is empowered to file suit against the employer for harassment of the employee. However, it is not settled whether an individual may sue on her own behalf.

Title VII of the Civil Rights Act of 1964, as amended

Effective Date

July 1965, for nonprofessional and professional workers in private sector.

March 1972, for employees of state and local governments and educational institutions.

Prohibited Acts

Any discrimination based on sex in hiring, firing, promotion, wages, classification, employment referrals, or assignment, extending or assigning the use of facilities, training, apprenticeships, fringe benefits, including medical, maternity benefits, life insurance, pension and retirement programs, and any other conditions or privileges of employment.

Who is Covered?

Employers of 15 or more employees, including public and private employees, public and private employment agencies, labor organizations, labor-management apprenticeship committees, state and local governments and educational institutions.

Exemptions From Coverage/Exclusions

The Federal Government, the government of the District of Columbia, Indian tribes, and bona fide private membership clubs are not covered by Title VII, although Title VII obliges the Federal government to undertake an affirmative equal employment opportunity program. Sex-based classification is permitted in the very narrow and limited circumstances where it can be shown to a bona fide occupational qualification (BFOQ).

Are Labor Organizations Covered?

Yes, labor organizations which operate a hiring hall or office, or have 15 or more members are covered by Title VII.

Who Enforces the Provisions?

Equal Employment Opportunity Commission (EEOC).

How Quickly Does the Agency Act?

The average time required for resolution is 30 months.

Procedures in Enforcing the Provisions

When your complaint is received at an EEOC district office, you will be interviewed to verify the contents and asked if you are willing to proceed with your complaint. If there is a qualified state or local fair employment agency, EEOC will refer your complaint to them.[1] Because of EEOC's enormous backlog of cases and problems in processing, some time may elapse before investigation begins. EEOC will attempt to conciliate and if that fails, it may file and prosecute a law suit.[2] You may obtain private counsel and request a "right to sue" letter, rather than rely on EEOC for investigation and enforcement.[3]

Remedies and/or Sanctions

Among the remedies available are reinstatement, hiring, promotion, back pay,[4] increased fringe benefits, and orders enjoining future discrimination. Attorney's fees may be given to the prevailing party.

Affirmative Action Requirements

Affirmative action may be part of a conciliation agreement worked out by EEOC, or it may be ordered by a Federal court.

Time Limit for Filing Complaint

180 days.

How is a Complaint Made?

By a sworn complaint form which you may obtain from EEOC.

Who Can Make a Complaint?

Complaints may be filed by an individual, a class of individuals, a third party on behalf of others or a commissioner of EEOC.

Can Complaints of a Pattern or Practice of Discrimination be Made as Well as Individual Complaints?

Yes.

Notification of Complaints

The employer is notified of the complaint filed against it 10 days after the EEOC district office receives the complaint.

Are Investigations Made Without Complaints on File?

No, a complaint must be filed with EEOC before it may conduct investigations.

Is Harassment Forbidden?

Employers are forbidden from discriminating against or discharging any employee because of a complaint filed or any assistance provided during the enforcement process.

Confidentiality of Names

The complainant's name is revealed to the party charged with discrimination when the investigation is made. EEOC cannot make public any information about complaints filed with it.

Recordkeeping Requirements and Government Access

EEOC prescribes the recordkeeping requirements for those subject to Title VII. Reports are filed with EEOC.

For more information, contact:

Equal Employment Opportunity Commission
2401 E Street, NW.
Washington, D.C. 20506
or
A regional EEOC office.

Notes

1. EEOC must defer complaints to state and local fair employment agencies which operate under laws comparable to Title VII in scope, and have powers comparable to EEOC's. These agencies are given 60 days to resolve the complaint and if they fail to do so, it is returned to EEOC.

2. Suits against state and local governments can be filed only by the Department of Justice, or individuals.

3. You may request a "right to sue" letter from the EEOC as soon as you file your complaint, or if EEOC must defer to a qualified state or local fair employment agency, at the end of the 60-day deferral period. You must file suit within 90 days after receipt of a "right to sue" letter or notification by EEOC of the conclusion of its proceedings.

4. Backpay is limited to a period beginning 2 years prior to the filing of a complaint with EEOC.

Executive Order 11246, as amended by Executive Order 11375

Effective Date

October 1968.

Prohibited Acts

Discrimination in employment including wages, hiring, promotion, and benefits.[1]

Who is Covered?

Employers and institutions which have contracts[2] with the Federal government in excess of $10,000, and their subcontractors. (All divisions or branches of the contractor are covered.)[3] Applicants for Federal assistance must include prohibitions against discrimination in construction contracts for work performed on Federally assisted programs.

Exemptions From Coverage/Exclusions

Some.[4]

Are Labor Organizations Covered?

The contractor's agreement with a union cannot conflict with the nondiscrimination and affirmative action requirements.[5]

Who Enforces the Provisions?

The Department of Labor's Office of Federal Contract Compliance Programs (OFCCP) has overall responsibility. OFCCP has designated 11 Federal agencies as compliance agencies, and they are responsible for enforcing the Order.[6]

How Quickly Does the Agency Act?

The answer depends upon the compliance agency responsible for enforcement. However, many of the compliance agencies have experienced long delays in processing complaints, and you may wish to pursue your complaint under other statutes as well.

Procedures in Enforcing the Provisions

Complaints may be filed with OFCCP or with the compliance agency. The agency should review it within 60 to 90 days.[7] The compliance agency notifies OFCCP if no discrimination is found.[8] If a finding of discrimination is made, the agency should issue a notice to the contractor requiring it to show why sanction proceedings should not begin. In practice, the compliance agency first tries to negotiate with the contractor to cure the violations.[9]

Remedies and/or Sanctions

The Secretary or the contracting Federal agency may cancel, terminate, or suspend any contract or part of it, and the contractor may be barred from future Federal contracts.[9]

Affirmative Action Requirements

These include the hiring, training, and promotion of women. A contractor with 50 or more employees and a contract of $50,000 or more is required to develop a written plan with goals and timetables for increasing the number of women employed.

Time Limit for Filing Complaint

180 days.

How is a Complaint Made?

By a letter to the OFCCP or the compliance agency directly. No special form is required.

Who Can Make a Complaint?

Any person or organization acting on their own behalf or on behalf of any aggrieved individuals.

Can Complaints of a Pattern or Practice of Discrimination be Made as Well as Individual Complaints?

Yes, OFCCP usually processes class action complaints, those alleging a pattern or practice of discrimination. Individual complaints of discrimination are referred to the Equal Employment Opportunity Commission (EEOC).[10]

Notification of Complaints

There is no uniform time period for notifying the contractor of the complaint filed.

Are Investigations Made Without Complaints on File?

Yes, compliance agencies are required to conduct compliance reviews before contracts over $1 million are awarded. Compliance agencies may conduct periodic compliance reviews of all contractors.

Is Harassment Forbidden?

Contractors are forbidden from discriminating against or discharging any applicant or employee because of a complaint filed or any assistance provided during the enforcement process.

Confidentiality of Names

No pledge of confidentiality is made by OFCCP or any of the compliance agencies.

Recordkeeping Requirements and Government Access

The Order requires contractors to gather and keep certain kinds of information which will aid the compliance agencies in their reviews.

For more information, contact:

Office of Federal Contract Compliance Programs
Employment Standards Administration
Department of Labor
Washington, D.C. 20210
or
The regional office of the Labor Department.

Notes

1. Present guidelines do not require contractors to provide same benefits for maternity as are provided for other temporary disabilities. Contractors are permitted to maintain fringe benefit policies which have a differential effect on persons because of their sex, so long as the contractor makes equal contributions for both groups.

2. The term "contract" is given a broad meaning and covers many Federal government contracts nominally entitled "grants" which involve a benefit to the Federal government. The term "assistance" includes grants, loans, insurance, or guarantees.

3. Guidelines exempt divisions or agencies of state and local governments which do not specifically participate in work under the Federal contract.

4. The Secretary of Labor may exempt a contractor and certain classes of contracts from the nondiscrimination provisions of the Order.

5. If a union interferes with the nondiscrimination requirements, the Secretary of Labor may report the interference to the EEOC for further proceedings.

6. Generally, the compliance agencies are assigned their enforcement responsibilities in specified areas or industries and not on the basis of which Federal agency signed the contract.

7. However, many reviews have taken longer.

8. If no discrimination is found, you will be notified and informed of your right to appeal the finding of OFCCP. If OFCCP decides no discrimination has occurred, the question of whether you may obtain judicial (court) review of the decision remains unclear.

9. Fund cut-offs have rarely been applied and the Order has not been very effective in curtailing discrimination. OFCCP has recently taken the position that backpay be awarded, but it has not developed a standard for determining the amount due a class of women.

10. You should file your complaint with EEOC at the same time you file with OFCCP. If your complaint is referred to EEOC after the 180-day period for filing has passed, some courts have decided that it is barred by the statute of limitations, even though it was filed with OFCCP in time.

ECOA amendments may change information contained in this section.

Title IX of the Education Amendments of 1972, as amended

Effective Date

July 1973, for admissions provisions.
July 1972, for all other provisions.

Prohibited Acts

Generally,[1] Title IX and the implementing regulations prohibit discrimination based on sex including admissions, financial aid, rules governing behavior, access to courses and training programs, extracurricular activities, other educational programs and employment discrimination including wages, recruitment, hiring, job classification, and most fringe benefits. Regulations provide that recipients must treat pregnancy, childbirth, and termination of pregnancy the same as any other temporary disability.

Who is Covered?

All educational institutions which receive Federal money including preschools, elementary, secondary and vocational schools, colleges and universities, and noneducational institutions which receive Federal money for educational programs.

Exemptions From Coverage/Exclusions

Girl and boy scouts, the YWCA and YMCA, certain single-sex youth services, and social fraternities and sororities. Religious institutions are exempt to the extent the nondiscrimination provisions conflict with religious doctrine. Military schools are exempt if their primary purpose is to train individuals for the military services of the United States or Merchant Marine. Certain institutions are exempt from the admissions provisions.

Are Labor Organizations Covered?

No, however, the agreement may not contain provisions inconsistent with Title IX.

Who Enforces the Provisions?

The Office for Civil Rights (OCR) of the Department of Health, Education, and Welfare.

How Quickly Does the Agency Act?

There is a substantial backlog of complaints on file; lengthy delays are common.

Procedures in Enforcing the Provisions

Title IX regulations require institutions to establish internal grievance procedures which may be used by the complainant if she wishes. The regional office conducts an investigation to determine if violations have occurred.[2] OCR will then try to secure voluntary compliance. If that fails, OCR may begin administrative procedures to suspend or terminate Federal financial assistance, or it may refer the matter to the Justice Department with a recommendation that court proceedings begin.

Remedies and/or Sanctions

Remedies for employment discrimination include reinstatement, backpay, promotion, tenure and equalization of most benefits. For discrimination against students, remedies include equal access to training programs, equalization of rules governing behavior, equal admissions and financial aid criteria, and other remedies. Sanctions that may be applied include the suspension or termination of Federal financial assistance.

Affirmative Action Requirements

If discrimination is found to have occurred, affirmative action may be required.

Time Limit for Filing Complaint

180 days.

How is a Complaint Made?

By letter to OCR. No special form is required.

Who Can Make a Complaint?

Any person or organization acting on their own behalf or another's.

Can Complaints of a Pattern or Practice of Discrimination be Made as Well as Individual Complaints?

Yes, however, most individual complaints of employment discrimination will be referred to other Federal agencies having jurisdiction.

Notification of Complaints

There is no set time period for notification; however, OCR will inform an institution shortly before investigation begins.

Are Investigations Made Without Complaints on File?

Yes, OCR can conduct periodic reviews in absence of complaints.

Is Harassment Forbidden?

Institutions are forbidden from discriminating against or discharging any person because of a complaint filed or any assistance provided during the enforcement process.

Confidentiality of Names

At present, no pledge of confidentiality can be made.

Recordkeeping Requirements and Government Access

Covered institutions are required to keep specific records.

For more information, contact:

Office for Civil Rights
Department of Health, Education, and Welfare
Washington, D.C. 20201
or
A regional office near you.

Notes

1. Title IX's requirement of nondiscrimination in admissions does not apply to private undergraduate schools, nonvocational elementary and secondary schools and public undergraduate institutions which have continuously admitted members of one sex since their beginning; Title IX regulations do not forbid an institution from awarding single-sex scholarships according to the terms of a will or bequest or trust, if the overall effect of financial aid is not discriminatory; Title IX regulations require physical education classes be coed except for contact sports, and classes based on ability, and permit single-sex teams when selection is based on competitive skill and for contact sports.

2. OCR is using the procedural regulations applicable to Title VI of the Civil Rights Act of

1964 pending adoption of consolidated procedural regulations.

Title VII and Title VIII of the Public Health Service Act, as amended

Effective Date

November 1971.

Prohibited Acts

As a condition of receiving Federal financial support, institutions may not discriminate on the basis of sex: in admissions; in participation in any research or training program; against employees who work directly with applicants to or students in the program;[1] in providing financial aid[2] or any other benefit. Regulations provide that institutions must treat pregnancy, childbirth, and termination of pregnancy the same as any other temporary disability.

Who is Covered?

Schools of medicine, dentistry, osteopathy, pharmacy, optometry, podiatry, veterinary medicine, public health, nursing, allied health professions, affiliated hospitals and undergraduate institutions which provide health training programs which receive Federal financial support[3] under the Titles.

Exemptions From Coverage/Exclusions

Some.[4]

Are Labor Organizations Covered?

No, but the terms of a collective bargaining agreement applicable to employees covered by Titles VII and VIII may not discriminate on the basis of sex. Therefore, institutions may not be a party to discriminatory agreements.

Who Enforces the Provisions?

The Office for Civil Rights (OCR) of the Department of Health, Education, and Welfare.

How Quickly Does the Agency Act?

There is a significant backlog of complaints and long delays frequently characterize enforcement efforts.

Procedures in Enforcing the Provisions

Complaints which allege individual discrimination are usually referred to the Department of Labor and then to EEOC, since most institutions covered by the Act are also covered by Executive Order 11246. Student complaints and complaints which allege discrimination against a class, a pattern or practice, are sent to the HEW regional office for investigation. OCR will attempt conciliation with the institution, and if that fails, may begin sanction proceedings.[5]

Remedies and/or Sanctions

Remedies for employment discrimination include reinstatement, backpay, promotion, tenure, and equalization of most benefits. For discrimination against students, remedies include equal access to training programs, equal admissions and financial aid criteria. Sanctions that may be applied include the suspension or termination of Federal financial assistance.

Affirmative Action Requirements

If OCR finds an institution has discriminated, it may require such action from the institution.

Time Limit for Filing Complaint

180 days.

How is a Complaint Made?

By letter addressed to OCR. No special forms are required.

Who Can Make a Complaint?

Any person or organization acting on their own behalf or that of any aggrieved person.

Can Complaints of a Pattern or Practice of Discrimination be Made as Well as Individual Complaints?

Yes. Most individual employment complaints will be referred to the Department of Labor and then to EEOC for processing. You should file with EEOC at the same time you file with OCR.

Notification of Complaints

No procedure has been established for informing an institution of complaints filed against it.

Are Investigations Made Without Complaints on File?

Yes, OCR is empowered to conduct periodic compliance reviews.

Is Harassment Forbidden?

Institutions are forbidden from discriminating against or discharging any person because of a complaint filed or any assistance provided during the enforcement process.

Confidentiality of Names

At present, no pledge of confidentiality can be made.

Recordkeeping Requirements and Government Access

Institutions are required to keep certain information which assists OCR in making its determinations under the Act.

For more information, contact:

Office for Civil Rights
Department of HEW
Washington, D.C. 20201
                    or
A regional office near you.

Notes

1. The institution is prohibited from discriminating against such employees in recruitment, hiring, promotion, layoffs, firing, wages, job assignment, leaves of absence for pregnancy or childcare, fringe benefits, and other conditions and privileges of employment.
2. Institutions may administer scholarships, fellowships and other forms of financial assistance according to the terms of the will or bequest requiring the award be given to members of one sex only, so long as the overall effect of these does not discriminate on the basis of sex.
3. Federal support includes grants, contracts, a loan guarantee or interest subsidy payment.
4. Title VII of PHSA was amended in 1974 to exclude from the sex discrimination provisions any medical school in the process of changing its

admission of women only to admission of both sexes, if the school is changing its admission policy in accordance with a plan approved by the Secretary of HEW.
5. OCR is using the procedural regulations applicable to Title VI of the Civil Rights Act of 1964 until it issues final consolidated regulations. Administrative enforcement is more likely to result in the delay of new funding to the institution than termination of funding.

Title VIII of the Civil Rights Act of 1968, as amended

Effective Date

August 22, 1974.

Prohibited Acts

To refuse to sell or rent or negotiate the sale or rental of housing; to discriminate in the terms, conditions, privileges, services or facilities related to the sale or rental of housing because of sex; to advertise in a manner that indicates discrimination based on sex; to falsely represent the nonavailability of housing because of the applicant's sex; to discriminate in lending or otherwise because of the applicant's sex; and to discriminate in membership in real estate broker's organizations and similar services because of sex.[1]

Who is Covered?

Multifamily dwellings of five units or more or those containing four or fewer units if the owner does not reside in one unit; single-family houses not owned by private individuals or those owned by private individuals who own more than three such houses; and single-family houses owned by private individuals who in any 2-year period sell more than one in which the owner was not the most recent resident. These kinds of housing are covered whether federally assisted or not.

Exemptions From Coverage/Exclusions

Some.[2]

Are Labor Organizations Covered?

Yes, if involved in real estate transactions described above.

Who Enforces the Provisions?

The Office of the Assistant Secretary for Equal Opportunity of the Department of Housing and Urban Development (HUD).

How Quickly Does the Agency Act?

There is a backlog of complaints in some regions and delays may be encountered.

Procedures in Enforcing the Provisions

HUD must refer complaints to state or local agencies which operate under laws providing rights and remedies substantially equivalent to Title VIII. HUD may reactivate the complaint if proceedings are not instituted within 30 days or other later action is not taken. For these and complaints not requiring referral, HUD decides whether to resolve the complaint. If HUD decides not to, the complainant must be notified of the right to file suit within 30 days.[3] If HUD decides to resolve the complaint, it will use informal methods of conciliation and persuasion to end the discriminatory practice. If voluntary compliance is unsuccessful, the aggrieved individual shall be informed of the right to file suit.

Remedies and/or Sanctions

Administrative enforcement can result in securing the housing or dwelling for complainant, affirmative action requirements, and/or money damages. Judicial remedies include all of the above, and injunctive relief and punitive damages.

Affirmative Action Requirements

An affirmative nondiscrimination policy may be part of a conciliation agreement with HUD.

Time Limit for Filing Complaint

180 days. Civil suits must be filed within 30 days after the complainant receives notice from HUD that it will not resolve the complaint or that conciliation efforts are being terminated.

How is a Complaint Made?

Either by a sworn complaint form or a sworn statement which provides sufficient information. Complaints may be telephoned to HUD by calling a toll free number:
800–424-8590.

Who Can Make a Complaint?

Any person who has been injured by a discriminatory practice or believes she is about to be injured, or any organization acting on behalf of the aggrieved person.

Can Complaints of a Pattern or Practice of Discrimination be Made as Well as Individual Complaints?

Yes.

Notification of Complaints

The party named in the complaint will be notified after HUD decides that it will resolve the complaint.

Are Investigations Made Without Complaints on File?

No.

Is Harassment Forbidden?

Yes.

Confidentiality of Names

No pledge of confidentiality can be made.

Recordkeeping Requirements and Government Access

No, but the power to issue subpoenas and use interrogatories is available for administrative enforcement.

For more information, contact:

Assistant Secretary for Equal Opportunity
Department of Housing and Urban
 Development
Washington, D.C. 20410
                    or
A regional office near you.

Notes

1. Section 109 of the Housing and Community Development Act of 1974 provides that no

person shall be excluded from participation in, be denied the benefits of or be subjected to discrimination under any program or activity funded wholly or partially with funds provided under Title I of the Act because of their sex, race, color, or national origin. Title I covers most community development plans such as urban renewal, model cities, public facilities, water and sewerage programs, open space programs, and historic restorations. Employment in any of these programs as well as the receipt of any services or benefits must be non-discriminatory. Compliance activities include conciliation efforts, civil action by the Attorney General, and the suspension or termination of funding. To determine if a particular community development plan is covered by the Act, you may contact any of HUD's 39 area offices, listed under "United States Government" in the white pages of the phone book, or write to the Assistant Secretary for Community Planning and Development, Department of HUD; Washington, D.C. 20410.

2. Single-family houses owned by a private individual who owns less than three houses are not covered if a broker is not used, discriminatory advertising is not used and no more than one house in which the owner was not the most recent resident is sold during any 2-year period; rental of rooms or units in owner-occupied multi-unit dwellings for two to four families; religious organizations in giving preference to members if the dwellings are not operated for commercial purposes; and private clubs in giving preference to members in "lodging" which is not operated for commercial purposes and is an incident of their primary purpose.

3. Title VIII permits suits to be filed by aggrieved individuals in federal district courts unless the individual has a judicial remedy under a state or local law which is substantially equivalent to Title VIII.

ECOA amendments may change information contained in this section.

Equal Credit Opportunity Act of 1974 (Amendments to the Act will probably become law early in 1976)

Effective Date

October 28, 1975.[1]

Prohibited Acts

Creditors are prohibited from discriminating against any applicant on the basis of sex or marital status in any aspect of a credit transaction.[2] Discrimination is defined by regulations as treating an applicant less favorably than another.[3]

Who is Covered?

Those who regularly extend credit to individuals, including banks, finance companies, department stores, credit card issuers, and government agencies such as the Small Business Administration. All types of credit are covered by the Act, including credit for business, consumer goods, home financing and education.

Exemptions From Coverage/Exclusions

None; however, creditors in credit transactions other than consumer credit must only comply with portions of the regulations.

Are Labor Organizations Covered?

Yes, if they regularly extend credit to individuals.

Who Enforces the Provisions?

Compliance with the Act is enforced by private litigation and Federal agencies. Section 704 of the Act (P.L. 93–495) designates particular areas of responsibility for each agency.[4] The Federal Trade Commission is given enforcement power for areas not specifically designated, including retail credit and small loan companies.

How Quickly Does the Agency Act?

Private suits may be brought under the Act. The enforcing agencies generally do not obtain relief for individuals. Instead the agency will try to make the creditor's policy conform with the Act. There is no uniform procedure which determines when the agencies may begin their enforcement process.

Procedures in Enforcing the Provisions

The enforcement process involves two separate procedures. Aggrieved individuals may file suit in any federal district court without utilizing or exhausting the administrative process. Individuals may also notify the particular agency charged with enforcement. The agency may investigate according to its own procedures.

Remedies and/or Sanctions

Aggrieved individuals may obtain money damages in civil suits. An amount equal to the actual damages suffered may be recovered by an individual or class of individuals. Punitive damages not exceeding $10,000 are available in individual actions, in class actions they may not exceed the lesser of $100,000 or 1 percent of the creditor's net worth. Injunctive relief is available as are attorney's fees and costs if the action is successful. Enforcing agencies may exercise any authority conferred by law including cease and desist powers and levying fines.

Affirmative Action Requirements

None.

Time Limit for Filing Complaint

One year.

How is a Complaint Made?

No uniform procedure has been established by the enforcing agencies. Civil suits may be filed in any Federal district court.

Who Can Make a Complaint?

Any person or organization acting on their own behalf or others' may notify the enforcing agency. Individuals and organizations acting on their own behalf and others' may file suit.

Can Complaints of a Pattern or Practice of Discrimination be Made as Well as Individual Complaints?

Yes.

Notification of Complaints

No uniform procedure has been established by the enforcing agencies for notifying creditors of complaints received.

Are Investigations Made Without Complaints on File?

Yes, enforcing agencies may do so in carrying out responsibilities delegated by other statutes.

Is Harassment Forbidden?

At present, there is no specific provision concerning harassment.

Confidentiality of Names

No uniform procedure has been established; however, agencies will generally try to keep a complainant's name confidential, if so requested.

Recordkeeping Requirements and Government Access

Consumer creditors must keep application forms and other written information used in evaluation and an applicant's statement alleging discrimination for 15 months after final action is taken on the application.[5] Other statutes require creditors to keep information which may assist in determining if discrimination has occurred.

For more information, contact:

Board of Governors
Federal Reserve System
Washington, D.C. 20051

Notes

1. Some specific regulations to enforce the Act do not take effect until 1976.
2. Sex discrimination in home financing is also prohibited by the Fair Housing Act of 1968, as amended.
3. Among the specific acts prohibited by regulations are the discounting of the income of an applicant or spouse on the basis of sex or marital status; a credit "scoring" system used for evaluation of applicants which assigns a value to one sex or marital status; requesting information about birth control or childbearing capability; and requiring a change in the terms of an existing account, or reapplication or termination on the basis of a change of name or marital status of a person who is contractually liable on an account without evidence that the applicant is unable or unwilling to pay.
4. The Board of Governors of the Federal Reserve Board issues regulations to enforce the Act. However, each of the enforcement agencies may establish rules concerning enforcement procedure.
5. If the creditor is notified that its actions are

under review by an enforcement agency or a court, it must retain the information until final disposition of the case, or until notified.

ECOA amendments may change information contained in this section.

Revenue Sharing (State and Local Fiscal Assistance Act)

Effective Date

October 1972.

Prohibited Acts

Any department or division of government or any program or activity funded in whole or part by general revenue sharing money may not discriminate on the basis of sex. The Act reaches a wide variety of activities including the denial of services or benefits, employment discrimination, and the establishment of different criteria for eligibility or admission to various programs. Regulations provide that recipients must treat pregnancy, childbirth, and termination of pregnancy the same as any other temporary disability.

Who is Covered?

All general governments receiving general revenue sharing money, including state governments and the District of Columbia, local governments, Indian tribes and Alaskan native villages and "secondary recipients" (nonprofit and private groups and other government units receiving revenue sharing funds directly from the recipient). Over 38,000 state and local entities are covered.

Exemptions From Coverage/Exclusions

None.

Are Labor Organizations Covered?

No; however, the terms of an agreement applicable to covered employees may not discriminate on the basis of sex.

Who Enforces the Provisions?

The Compliance Division of the Office of Revenue Sharing (ORS), Department of Treasury.

How Quickly Does the Agency Act?

There is no set time within which ORS will act.

Procedures in Enforcing the Provisions

ORS initially acknowledges receipt of your complaint and notifies local and state officials of its receipt. ORS may conduct its own investigation and will seek voluntary compliance. If that fails, ORS may begin administrative proceedings that can result in the withholding of all future revenue sharing payments and the recovery of sums spent, or the matter may be referred to the Department of Justice with a recommendation that civil action be instituted.

Remedies and/or Sanctions

If employment discrimination has occurred, ORS will seek whatever remedies are appropriate, including backpay, promotion, and reinstatement. If discrimination has occurred in the denial of benefits to a group, ORS will seek the provision of such services. ORS may recover money spent in violation of the statute and/or may withhold future payments until satisfactory compliance is achieved.

Affirmative Action Requirements

Yes, it may be required if ORS finds discrimination has occurred. In the absence of a finding of discrimination, regulations "encourage" recipients to correct any imbalance in services or facilities to a group, to overcome the effects of past discrimination.

Time Limit for Filing Complaint

None.

How is a Complaint Made?

By letter to ORS. No specific form is required.

Who Can Make a Complaint?

Any person or organization acting on their own behalf or another's.

Can Complaints of a Pattern or Practice of Discrimination be Made as Well as Individual Complaints?

Yes.

Notification of Complaints

ORS will notify state and/or local officials, if it believes violations have occurred.

Are Investigations Made Without Complaints on File?

Yes, the Act permits periodic reviews in the absence of complaints.

Is Harassment Forbidden?

Yes, regulations forbid any discrimination or intimidation of any person because of a complaint filed or any assistance provided during the enforcement process.

Confidentiality of Names

No pledge of confidentiality is made; however, ORS policy is to not reveal the complainant's name without permission.

Recordkeeping Requirements and Government Access

Recipient governments must maintain certain records which assist ORS in determining if violations have occurred.

For more information, contact:

Compliance Manager
Office of Revenue Sharing
Department of Treasury
2401 E Street, NW.
Washington, D.C. 20004

This list of Federal laws and regulations has been compiled by Denise Brender Leary, Women's Equity Action League, under contract with the National Commission on the Observance of International Women's Year, March 1976.

"...To Form A More Perfect Union..." A Report of the National Commission on the Observance of International Women's Year, Washington, D.C. 1976.

A GUIDE TO FEDERAL LAWS AND REGULATIONS PROHIBITING SEX DISCRIMINATION

APPENDIX IV HEW TITLE IX
REGULATIONS

PART 86—NONDISCRIMINATION ON THE BASIS OF SEX IN EDUCATION PROGRAMS AND ACTIVITIES RECEIVING OR BENEFITING FROM FEDERAL FINANCIAL ASSISTANCE

Subpart A—Introduction
Sec.
86.1   Purpose and effective date.
86.2   Definitions.
86.3   Remedial and affirmative action and self-evaluation.
86.4   Assurance required.
86.5   Transfers of property.
86.6   Effect of other requirements.
86.7   Effect of employment opportunities.
86.8   Designation of responsible employee and adoption of grievance procedures.
86.9   Dissemination of policy.

Subpart B—Coverage
86.11   Application.
86.12   Educational institutions controlled by religious organizations.
86.13   Military and merchant marine educational institutions.
86.14   Membership practices of certain organizations.
86.15   Admissions.
86.16   Educational institutions eligible to submit transition plans.
86.17   Transition plans.
86.18–86.20   [Reserved].

Subpart C—Discrimination on the Basis of Sex in Admission and Recruitment Prohibited
86.21   Admission.
86.22   Preference in admission.
86.23   Recruitment.
86.24–86.30   [Reserved].

Subpart D—Discrimination on the Basis of Sex in Education Programs and Activities Prohibited
86.31   Education programs and activities.
86.32   Housing.
86.33   Comparable facilities.
86.34   Access to course offerings.
86.35   Access to schools operated by L.E.A.s.
86.36   Counseling and use of appraisal and counseling materials.
86.37   Financial assistance.
86.38   Employment assistance to students.
86.39   Health and insurance benefits and services.
86.40   Marital or parental status.
86.41   Athletics.
86.42   Textbooks and curricular material.
86.43–86.50   [Reserved].

Subpart E—Discrimination on the Basis of Sex in Employment in Education Programs and Activities Prohibited
86.51   Employment.
86.52   Employment criteria.
Sec.
86.53   Recruitment.
86.54   Compensation.
86.55   Job classification and structure.
86.56   Fringe benefits.
86.57   Marital or parental status.
86.58   Effect of State or local law or other requirements.
86.59   Advertising.
86.60   Pre-employment inquiries.

86.61   Sex as bona-fide occupational qualification.
86.62–86.70   [Reserved].

Subpart F—Procedures
86.71   Interim procedures.
    SOURCE: 40 FR 24128, June 4, 1975, unless otherwise noted.

Subpart A—Introduction
§ 86.1   **Purpose and effective date.**

The purpose of this part is to effectuate title IX of the Education Amendments of 1972, as amended by Pub. L. 93–568, 88 Stat. 1855 (except sections 904 and 906 of those Amendments) which is designed to eliminate (with certain exceptions) discrimination on the basis of sex in any education program or activity receiving Federal financial assistance, whether or not such program or activity is offered or sponsored by an educational institution as defined in this part. This part is also intended to effectuate section 844 of the Education Amendments of 1974, Pub. L. 93–380, 88 Stat. 484. The effective date of this part shall be July 21, 1975.

(Secs. 901, 902, Education Amendments of 1972, 86 Stat. 373, 374; 20 U.S.C. 1681, 1682, as amended by Pub. L. 93–568, 88 Stat. 1855, and Sec. 844, Education Amendments of 1974, 88 Stat. 484, Pub. L. 93–380)

§ 86.2   **Definitions.**

As used in this part, the term—
(a) *"Title IX"* means title IX of the Education Amendments of 1972, Pub. L. 92–318, as amended by section 3 of Pub. L. 93–568, 88 Stat. 1855, except sections 904 and 906 thereof; 20 U.S.C. 1681, 1682, 1683, 1685, 1686.
(b) *"Department"* means the Department of Health, Education, and Welfare.
(c) *"Secretary"* means the Secretary of Health, Education, and Welfare.
(d) *"Director"* means the Director of the Office for Civil Rights of the Department.
(e) *"Reviewing Authority"* means that component of the Department delegated authority by the Secretary to appoint, and to review the decisions of, administrative law judges in cases arising under this part.
(f) *"Administrative law judge"* means a person appointed by the reviewing authority to preside over a hearing held under this part.
(g) *"Federal financial assistance"* means any of the following, when authorized or extended under a law administered by the Department:
(1) A grant or loan of Federal financial assistance, including funds made available for:
(i) The acquisition, construction, renovation, restoration, or repair of a

building or facility or any portion thereof; and
(ii) Scholarships, loans, grants, wages or other funds extended to any entity for payment to or on behalf of students admitted to that entity, or extended directly to such students for payment to that entity.

(2) A grant of Federal real or personal property or any interest therein, including surplus property, and the proceeds of the sale or transfer of such property, if the Federal share of the fair market value of the property is not, upon such sale or transfer, properly accounted for to the Federal Government.

(3) Provision of the services of Federal personnel.

(4) Sale or lease of Federal property or any interest therein at nominal consideration, or at consideration reduced for the purpose of assisting the recipient or in recognition of public interest to be served thereby, or permission to use Federal property or any interest therein without consideration.

(5) Any other contract, agreement, or arrangement which has as one of its purposes the provision of assistance to any education program or activity, except a contract of insurance or guaranty.

(h) *"Recipient"* means any State or political subdivision thereof, or any instrumentality of a State or political subdivision thereof, any public or private agency, institution, or organization, or other entity, or any person, to whom Federal financial assistance is extended directly or through another recipient and which operates an education program or activity which receives or benefits from such assistance, including any subunit, successor, assignee, or transferee thereof.

(i) *"Applicant"* means one who submits an application, request, or plan required to be approved by a Department official, or by a recipient, as a condition to becoming a recipient.

(j) *"Educational institution"* means a local educational agency (L.E.A.) as defined by section 801(f) of the Elementary and Secondary Education Act of 1965 (20 U.S.C. 881), a preschool, a private elementary or secondary school, or an applicant or recipient of the type defined by paragraph (k), (l), (m), or (n) of this section.

(k) *"Institution of graduate higher education"* means an institution which:

(1) Offers academic study beyond the bachelor of arts or bachelor of science degree, whether or not leading to a certificate of any higher degree in the liberal arts and sciences; or

(2) Awards any degree in a professional field beyond the first professional degree (regardless of whether the first professional degree in such field is

awarded by an institution of undergraduate higher education or professional education) ; or

(3) Awards no degree and offers no further academic study, but operates ordinarily for the purpose of facilitating research by persons who have received the highest graduate degree in any field of study.

(l) *"Institution of undergraduate higher education"* means:

(1) An institution offering at least two but less than four years of college level study beyond the high school level, leading to a diploma or an associate degree, or wholly or principally creditable toward a baccalaureate degree; or

(2) An institution offering academic study leading to a baccalaureate degree; or

(3) An agency or body which certifies credentials or offers degrees, but which may or may not offer academic study.

(m) *"Institution of professional education"* means an institution (except any institution of undergraduate higher education) which offers a program of academic study that leads to a first professional degree in a field for which there is a national specialized accrediting agency recognized by the United States Commissioner of Education.

(n) *"Institution of vocational education"* means a school or institution (except an institution of professional or graduate or undergraduate higher education) which has as its primary purpose preparation of students to pursue a technical, skilled, or semiskilled occupation or trade, or to pursue study in a technical field, whether or not the school or institution offers certificates, diplomas, or degrees and whether or not it offers fulltime study.

(o) *"Administratively separate unit"* means a school, department or college of an educational institution (other than a local educational agency) admission to which is independent of admission to any other component of such institution.

(p) *"Admission"* means selection for part-time, full-time, special, associate, transfer, exchange, or any other enrollment, membership, or matriculation in or at an education program or activity operated by a recipient.

(q) *"Student"* means a person who has gained admission.

(r) *"Transition plan"* means a plan subject to the approval of the United States Commissioner of Education pursuant to section 901(a)(2) of the Education Amendments of 1972, under which an educational institution operates in making the transition from being an educational institution which admits only students of one sex to being one which admits students of both sexes without discrimination.

(Secs. 901, 902, Education Amendments of 1972, 86 Stat. 373, 374; 20 U.S.C. 1681, 1682)

§ 86.3 Remedial and affirmative action and self-evaluation.

(a) *Remedial action.* If the Director finds that a recipient has discriminated against persons on the basis of sex in an education program or activity, such recipient shall take such remedial action as the Director deems necessary to overcome the effects of such discrimination.

(b) *Affirmative action.* In the absence of a finding of discrimination on the basis of sex in an education program or activity, a recipient may take affirmative action to overcome the effects of conditions which resulted in limited participation therein by persons of a particular sex. Nothing herein shall be interpreted to alter any affirmative action obligations which a recipient may have under Executive Order 11246.

(c) *Self-evaluation.* Each recipient education institution shall, within one year of the effective date of this part:

(i) Evaluate, in terms of the requirements of this part, its current policies and practices and the effects thereof concerning admission of students, treatment of students, and employment of both academic and non-academic personnel working in connection with the recipient's education program or activity;

(ii) Modify any of these policies and practices which do not or may not meet the requirements of this part; and

(iii) Take appropriate remedial steps to eliminate the effects of any discrimination which resulted or may have resulted from adherence to these policies and practices.

(d) *Availability of self-evaluation and related materials.* Recipients shall maintain on file for at least three years following completion of the evaluation required under paragraph (c) of this section, and shall provide to the Director upon request, a description of any modifications made pursuant to paragraph (c)(ii) of this section and of any remedial steps taken pursuant to paragraph (c)(iii) of this section.

(Secs. 901, 902, Education Amendments of 1972, 86 Stat. 373, 374; 20 U.S.C. 1681, 1682) |40 FR 21428, June 4, 1975; 40 FR 39506, Aug. 28, 1975]

§ 86.4 Assurance required.

(a) *General.* Every application for Federal financial assistance for any education program or activity shall as condition of its approval contain or be accompanied by an assurance from the applicant or recipient, satisfactory to the Director, that each education program or activity operated by the applicant or recipient and to which this part applies will be operated in compliance with this part. An assurance of compliance with this part shall not be satisfactory to the Director if the applicant or recipient to whom such assurance applies fails to commit itself to take whatever remedial action is necessary in accordance with § 86.3(a) to eliminate existing discrimination on the basis of sex or to eliminate the effects of past discrimination whether occurring prior or subsequent to the submission to the Director of such assurance.

(b) *Duration of obligation.* (1) In the case of Federal financial assistance extended to provide real property or structures thereon, such assurance shall obligate the recipient or, in the case of a subsequent transfer, the transferee, for the period during which the real property or structures are used to provide an education program or activity.

(2) In the case of Federal financial assistance extended to provide personal property, such assurance shall obligate the recipient for the period during which it retains ownership or possession of the property.

(3) In all other cases such assurance shall obligate the recipient for the period during which Federal financial assistance is extended.

(c) *Form.* The Director will specify the form of the assurances required by paragraph (a) of this section and the extent to which such assurances will be required of the applicant's or recipient's subgrantees, contractors, subcontractors, transferees, or successors in interest.

(Secs. 901, 902, Education Amendments of 1972, 86 Stat. 373, 374; 20 U.S.C. 1681, 1682)

§ 86.5 Transfers of property.

If a recipient sells or otherwise transfers property financed in whole or in part with Federal financial assistance to a transferee which operates any education program or activity, and the Federal share of the fair market value of the property is not upon such sale or transfer properly accounted for to the Federal Government both the transferor and the transferee shall be deemed to be recipients, subject to the provisions of Subpart B of this part.

(Secs. 901, 902, Education Amendments of 1972, 86 Stat. 373, 374; 20 U.S.C. 1681, 1682)

§ 86.6 Effect of other requirements.

(a) *Effect of other Federal provisions.* The obligations imposed by this part are independent of, and do not alter, obligations not to discriminate on the basis of sex imposed by Executive Order 11246, as amended; sections 799A and 845 of the Public Health Service Act (42 U.S.C. 295h-9 and 298b-2) ; Title VII of the Civil Rights Act of 1964 (42 U.S.C. 2000e et seq.) ; the Equal Pay Act (29 U.S.C. 206 and 206(d)) ; and any other Act of Congress or Federal regulation.

(Secs. 901, 902, 905, Education Amendments of 1972, 86 Stat. 373, 374, 375; 20 U.S.C. 1681, 1682, 1685)

(b) *Effect of State or local law or other requirements.* The obligation to comply with this part is not obviated or alleviated by any State or local law or other requirement which would render any applicant or student ineligible, or limit the eligibility of any applicant or student, on the basis of sex, to practice any occupation or profession.

(c) *Effect of rules or regulations of private organizations.* The obligation to comply with this part is not obviated or alleviated by any rule or regulation of any organization, club, athletic or other league, or association which would render any applicant or student ineligible to participate or limit the eligibility of any applicant or student, on the basis of sex, in any education program or activity operated by a recipient and which receives or benefits from Federal financial assistance.

(Secs. 901, 902, Education Amendments of 1972, 86 Stat. 373, 374; 20 U.S.C. 1681, 1682)

§ 86.7 Effect of employment opportunities.

The obligation to comply with this

part is not obviated or alleviated because employment opportunities in any occupation or profession are or may be more limited for members of one sex than for members of the other sex.

(Secs. 901, 902, Education Amendments of 1972, 86 Stat. 373, 374; 20 U.S.C. 1681, 1682)

§ 86.8 Designation of responsible employee and adoption of grievance procedures.

(a) *Designation of responsible employee.* Each recipient shall designate at least one employee to coordinate its efforts to comply with and carry out its responsibilities under this part, including any investigation of any complaint communicated to such recipient alleging its noncompliance with this part or alleging any actions which would be prohibited by this part. The recipient shall notify all its students and employees of the name, office address and telephone number of the employee or employees appointed pursuant to this paragraph.

(b) *Complaint procedure of recipient.* A recipient shall adopt and publish grievance procedures providing for prompt and equitable resolution of student and employee complaints alleging any action which would be prohibited by this part.

(Secs. 901, 902, Education Amendments of 1972, 86 Stat. 373, 374; 20 U.S.C. 1681, 1682)

§ 86.9 Dissemination of policy.

(a) *Notification of policy.* (1) Each recipient shall implement specific and continuing steps to notify applicants for admission and employment, students and parents of elementary and secondary school students, employees, sources of referral of applicants for admission and employment, and all unions or professional organizations holding collective bargaining or professional agreements with the recipient, that it does not discriminate on the basis of sex in the educational programs or activities which it operates, and that is required by title IX and this part not to discriminate in such a manner. Such notification shall contain such information, and be made in such manner, as the Director finds necessary to apprise such persons of the protections against discrimination assured them by title IX and this part, but shall state at least that the requirement not to discriminate in education programs and activities extends to employment therein, and to admission thereto unless Subpart C does not apply to the recipient, and that inquiries concerning the application of title IX and this part to such recipient may be referred to the employee designated pursuant to § 86.8, or to the Director.

(2) Each recipient shall make the initial notification required by paragraph (a) (1) of this section within 90 days of the effective date of this part or of the date this part first applies to such recipient, whichever comes later, which notification shall include publication in: (i) Local newspapers; (ii) newspapers and magazines operated by such recipient or by student, alumnae, or alumni groups for or in connection with such recipient; and (iii) memoranda or other written communications distributed to every student and employee of such recipient.

(b) *Publications.* (1) Each recipient shall prominently include a statement of the policy described in paragraph (a) of this section in each announcement, bulletin, catalog, or application form which it makes available to any person of a type described in paragraph (a) of this section, or which is otherwise used in connection with the recruitment of students or employees.

(2) A recipient shall not use or distribute a publication of the type described in this paragraph which suggests, by text or illustration, that such recipient treats applicants, students, or employees differently on the basis of sex except as such treatment is permitted by this part.

(c) *Distribution.* Each recipient shall distribute without discrimination on the basis of sex each publication described in paragraph (b) of this section, and shall apprise each of its admission and employment recruitment representatives of the policy of nondiscrimination described in paragraph (a) of this section, and require such representatives to adhere to such policy.

(Secs. 901, 902, Education Amendments of 1972, 86 Stat. 373, 374; 20 U.S.C. 1681, 1682)

Subpart B—Coverage

§ 86.11 Application.

Except as provided in this subpart, this Part 86 applies to every recipient and to each education program or activity operated by such recipient which receives or benefits from Federal financial assistance.

§ 86.12 Educational institutions controlled by religious organizations.

(a) *Application.* This part does not apply to an educational institution which is controlled by a religious organization to the extent application of this part would not be consistent with the religious tenets of such organization.

(b) *Exemption.* An educational institution which wishes to claim the exemption set forth in paragraph (a) of this section, shall do so by submitting in writing to the Director a statement by the highest ranking official of the institution, identifying the provisions of this part which conflict with a specific tenet of the religious organization.

(Secs. 901, 902, Education Amendments of 1972, 86 Stat. 373, 374; 20 U.S.C. 1681, 1682)

§ 86.13 Military and merchant marine educational institutions.

This part does not apply to an educational institution whose primary purpose is the training of individuals for a military service of the United States or for the merchant marine.

(Secs. 901, 902, Education Amendments of 1972, 86 Stat. 373, 374; 20 U.S.C. 1681, 1682)

§ 86.14 Membership practices of certain organizations.

(a) *Social fraternities and sororities.* This part does not apply to the membership practices of social fraternities and sororities which are exempt from taxation under section 501(a) of the Internal Revenue Code of 1954, the active membership of which consists primarily of students in attendance at institutions of higher education.

(b) *YMCA, YWCA, Girl Scouts, Boy Scouts and Camp Fire Girls.* This part does not apply to the membership practices of the Young Men's Christian Association, the Young Women's Christian Association, the Girl Scouts, the Boy Scouts and Camp Fire Girls.

(c) *Voluntary youth service organizations.* This part does not apply to the membership practices of voluntary youth service organizations which are exempt from taxation under section 501(a) of the Internal Revenue Code of 1954 and the membership of which has been traditionally limited to members of one sex and principally to persons of less than nineteen years of age.

(Secs. 901, 902, Education Amendments of 1972, 86 Stat. 373, 374; 20 U.S.C. 1681, 1682; Sec. 3(a) of P.L. 93–568, 88 Stat. 1862 amending Sec. 901)

§ 86.15 Admissions.

(a) Admissions to educational institutions prior to June 24, 1973, are not covered by this part.

(b) *Administratively separate units.* For the purposes only of this section, §§ 86.16 and 86.17, and Subpart C, each administratively separate unit shall be deemed to be an educational institution.

(c) *Application of Subpart C.* Except as provided in paragraphs (d) and (e) of this section, Subpart C applies to each recipient. A recipient to which Subpart C applies shall not discriminate on the basis of sex in admission or recruitment in violation of that subpart.

(d) *Educational institutions.* Except as provided in paragraph (e) of this section as to recipients which are educational institutions, Subpart C applies only to institutions of vocational education, professional education, graduate higher education, and public institutions of undergraduate higher education.

(e) *Public institutions of undergraduate higher education.* Subpart C does not apply to any public institution of undergraduate higher education which traditionally and continually from its establishment has had a policy of admitting only students of one sex.

(Secs. 901, 902, Education Amendments of 1972, 86 Stat. 373, 374; 20 U.S.C. 1681, 1682)

[40 FR 21428, June 4, 1975; 40 FR 39506, Aug. 28, 1975]

§ 86.16 Educational institutions eligible to submit transition plans.

(a) *Application.* This section applies to each educational institution to which Subpart C applies which:

(1) Admitted only students of one sex as regular students as of June 23, 1972; or

(2) Admitted only students of one sex as regular students as of June 23, 1965, but thereafter admitted as regular students, students of the sex not admitted prior to June 23, 1965.

(b) *Provision for transition plans.* An educational institution to which this section applies shall not discriminate on the basis of sex in admission or recruitment in violation of Subpart C unless it is carrying out a transition plan approved by the United States Commissioner of Education as described in § 86.17, which plan provides for the elimination of such discrimination by the earliest practicable date but in no event later than June 23, 1979.

(Secs. 901, 902, Education Amendments of 1972, 86 Stat. 373, 374; 20 U.S.C. 1681, 1682)

§ 86.17 Transition plans.

(a) *Submission of plans.* An institution to which § 86.16 applies and which is composed of more than one administratively separate unit may submit either a single transition plan applicable to all such units, or a separate transition plan applicable to each such unit.

(b) *Content of plans.* In order to be approved by the United States Commissioner of Education, a transition plan shall:

(1) State the name, address, and Federal Interagency Committee on Education (FICE) Code of the educational institution submitting such plan, the administratively separate units to which the plan is applicable, and the name, address, and telephone number of the person to whom questions concerning the plan may be addressed. The person who submits the plan shall be the chief administrator or president of the institution, or another individual legally authorized to bind the institution to all actions set forth in the plan.

(2) State whether the educational institution or administratively separate unit admits students of both sexes, as regular students and, if so, when it began to do so.

(3) Identify and describe with respect to the educational institution or administratively separate unit any obstacles to admitting students without discrimination on the basis of sex.

(4) Describe in detail the steps necessary to eliminate as soon as practicable each obstacle so identified and indicate the schedule for taking these steps and the individual directly responsible for their implementation.

(5) Include estimates of the number of students, by sex, expected to apply for, be admitted to, and enter each class during the period covered by the plan.

(c) *Nondiscrimination.* No policy or practice of a recipient to which § 86.16 applies shall result in treatment of applicants to or students of such recipient in violation of Subpart C unless such treatment is necessitated by an obstacle identified in paragraph (b)(3) of this section and a schedule for eliminating that obstacle has been provided as required by paragraph (b)(4) of this section.

(d) *Effects of past exclusion.* To overcome the effects of past exclusion of students on the basis of sex, each educational institution to which § 86.16 applies shall include in its transition plan, and shall implement, specific steps designed to encourage individuals of the previously excluded sex to apply for admission to such institution. Such steps shall include instituting recruitment programs which emphasize the institution's commitment to enrolling students of the sex previously excluded.

(Secs. 901, 902, Education Amendments of 1972, 86 Stat. 373, 374; 20 U.S.C. 1681, 1682)
[40 FR 21428, June 4, 1975; 40 FR 39506, Aug. 28, 1975]

§ 86.18–86.20 [Reserved]

Subpart C—Discrimination on the Basis of Sex in Admission and Recruitment Prohibited

§ 86.21 Admission.

(a) *General.* No person shall, on the basis of sex, be denied admission, or be subjected to discrimination in admission, by any recipient to which this subpart applies, except as provided in §§ 86.16 and 86.17.

(b) *Specific prohibitions.* (1) In determining whether a person satisfies any policy or criterion for admission, or in making any offer of admission, a recipient to which this Subpart applies shall not:

(i) Give preference to one person over another on the basis of sex, by ranking applicants separately on such basis, or otherwise;

(ii) Apply numerical limitations upon the number or proportion of persons of either sex who may be admitted; or

(iii) Otherwise treat one individual differently from another on the basis of sex.

(2) A recipient shall not administer or operate any test or other criterion for admission which has a disproportionately adverse effect on persons on the basis of sex unless the use of such test or criterion is shown to predict validly success in the education program or activity in question and alternative tests or criteria which do not have such a disproportionately adverse effect are shown to be unavailable.

(c) *Prohibitions relating to marital or parental status.* In determining whether a person satisfies any policy or criterion for admission, or in making any offer of admission, a recipient to which this subpart applies:

(1) Shall not apply any rule concerning the actual or potential parental, family, or marital status of a student or applicant which treats persons differently on the basis of sex;

(2) Shall not discriminate against or exclude any person on the basis of pregnancy, childbirth, termination of pregnancy, or recovery therefrom, or establish or follow any rule or practice which so discriminates or excludes;

(3) Shall treat disabilities related to pregnancy, childbirth, termination of pregnancy, or recovery therefrom in the same manner and under the same policies as any other temporary disability or physical condition; and

(4) Shall not make pre-admission inquiry as to the marital status of an applicant for admission, including whether such applicant is "Miss" or "Mrs." A recipient may make pre-admission inquiry as to the sex of an applicant for admission, but only if such inquiry is made equally of such applicants of both sexes and if the results of such inquiry are not used in connection with discrimination prohibited by this part.

(Secs. 901, 902, Education Amendments of 1972, 86 Stat. 373, 374; 20 U.S.C. 1681, 1682)

§ 86.22 Preference in admission.

A recipient to which this subpart applies shall not give preference to applicants for admission, on the basis of attendance at any educational institution or other school or entity which admits as students or predominantly members of one sex, if the giving of such preference has the effect of discriminating on the basis of sex in violation of this subpart.

(Secs. 901, 902, Education Amendments of 1972, 86 Stat. 373, 374; 20 U.S.C. 1681, 1682)

§ 86.23 Recruitment.

(a) *Nondiscriminatory recruitment.* A recipient to which this subpart applies shall not discriminate on the basis of sex in the recruitment and admission of students. A recipient may be required to undertake additional recruitment efforts for one sex as remedial action pursuant to § 86.3(a), and may choose to undertake such efforts as affirmative action pursuant to § 86.3(b).

(b) *Recruitment at certain institutions.* A recipient to which this subpart applies shall not recruit primarily or exclusively at educational institutions, schools or entities which admit as students only or predominantly members of one sex, if such actions have the effect of discriminating on the basis of sex in violation of this subpart.

(Secs. 901, 902, Education Amendments of 1972, 86 Stat. 373, 374; 20 U.S.C. 1681, 1682)

§§ 86.24–86.30 [Reserved]

Subpart D—Discrimination on the Basis of Sex in Education Programs and Activities Prohibited

§ 86.31 Education programs and activities.

(a) *General.* Except as provided elsewhere in this part, no person shall, on the basis of sex, be excluded from participation in, be denied the benefits of, or be subjected to discrimination under any academic, extracurricular, research, occupational training, or other education program or activity operated by a recipient which receives or benefits from Federal financial assistance. This subpart does not apply to actions of a recipient in connection with admission of its students to an education program or activity of (1) a recipient to which Subpart C does not apply, or (2) an entity, not a recipient, to which Subpart C would not apply if the entity were a recipient.

(b) *Specific prohibitions.* Except as provided in this subpart, in providing any aid, benefit, or service to a student, a recipient shall not, on the basis of sex:

(1) Treat one person differently from another in determining whether such person satisfies any requirement or condition for the provision of such aid, benefit, or service;

(2) Provide different aid, benefits, or services or provide aid, benefits, or services in a different manner;

(3) Deny any person any such aid, benefit, or service;

(4) Subject any person to separate or different rules of behavior, sanctions, or other treatment;

(5) Discriminate against any person in the application of any rules of appearance;

(6) Apply any rule concerning the domicile or residence of a student or applicant, including eligibility for in-state fees and tuition;

(7) Aid or perpetuate discrimination

against any person by providing significant assistance to any agency, organization, or person which discriminates on the basis of sex in providing any aid, benefit or service to students or employees;

(8) Otherwise limit any person in the enjoyment of any right, privilege, advantage, or opportunity.

(c) *Assistance administered by a recipient educational institution to study at a foreign institution.* A recipient educational institution may administer or assist in the administration of scholarships, fellowships, or other awards established by foreign or domestic wills, trusts, or similar legal instruments, or by acts of foreign governments and restricted to members of one sex, which are designed to provide opportunities to study abroad, and which are awarded to students who are already matriculating at or who are graduates of the recipient institution; *Provided,* a recipient educational institution which administers or assists in the administration of such scholarships, fellowship, or other awards which are restricted to members of one sex provides, or otherwise makes available reasonable opportunities for similar studies for members of the other sex. Such opportunities may be derived from either domestic or foreign sources.

(d) *Programs not operated by recipient.* (1) This paragraph applies to any recipient which requires participation by any applicant, student, or employee in any education program or activity not operated wholly by such recipient, or which facilitates, permits, or considers such participation as part of or equivalent to an education program or activity operated by such recipient, including participation in educational consortia and cooperative employment and student-teaching assignments.

(2) Such recipient:

(i) Shall develop and implement a procedure designed to assure itself that the operator or sponsor of such other education program or activtiy takes no action affecting any applicant, student, or employee of such recipient which this part would prohibit such recipient from taking; and

(ii) Shall not facilitate, require, permit, or consider such participation if such action occurs.

(Secs. 901, 902, Education Amendments of 1972, 86 Stat. 373, 374; 20 U.S.C. 1681, 1682)

§ 86.32 Housing.

(a) *Generally.* A recipient shall not, on the basis of sex, apply different rules or regulations, impose different fees or requirements, or offer different services or benefits related to housing, except as provided in this section (including housing provided only to married students).

(b) *Housing provided by recipient.* (1) A recipient may provide separate housing on the basis of sex.

(2) Housing provided by a recipient to students of one sex, when compared to that provided to students of the other sex, shall be as a whole:

(i) Proportionate in quantity to the number of students of that sex applying for such housing; and

(ii) Comparable in quality and cost to the student.

(c) *Other housing.* (1) A recipient shall not, on the basis of sex, administer different policies or practices concerning occupancy by its students of housing other than provided by such recipient.

(2) A recipient which, through solicitation, listing, approval of housing, or otherwise, assists any agency, organization, or person in making housing available to any of its students, shall take such reasonable action as may be necessary to assure itself that such housing as is provided to students of one sex, when compared to that provided to students of the other sex, is as a whole: (i) Proportionate in quantity and (ii) comparable in quality and cost to the student. A recipient may render such assistance to any agency, organization, or person which provides all or part of such housing to students only of one sex.

(Secs. 901, 902, 907, Education Amendments of 1972, 86 Stat. 373, 374, 375; 20 U.S.C. 1681, 1682, 1686)

§ 86.33 Comparable facilities.

A recipient may provide separate toilet, locker room, and shower facilities on the basis of sex, but such facilities provided for students of one sex shall be comparable to such facilities provided for students of the other sex.

(Secs. 901, 902, Education Amendments of 1972, 86 Stat. 373, 374)

§ 86.34 Access to course offerings.

A recipient shall not provide any course or otherwise carry out any of its education program or activity separately on the basis of sex, or require or refuse participation therein by any of its students on such basis, including health, physical education, industrial, business, vocational, technical, home economics, music, and adult education courses.

(a) With respect to classes and activities in physical education at the elementary school level, the recipient shall comply fully with this section as expeditiously as possible but in no event later than one year from the effective date of this regulation. With respect to physical education classes and activities at the secondary and post-secondary levels, the recipient shall comply fully with this section as expeditiously as possible but in no event later than three years from the effective date of this regulation

(b) This section does not prohibit grouping of students in physical education classes and activities by ability as assessed by objective standards of individual performance developed and applied without regard to sex.

(c) This section does not prohibit separation of students by sex within physical education classes or activities during participation in wrestling, boxing, rugby, ice hockey, football, basketball and other sports the purpose or major activity of which involves bodily contact.

(d) Where use of a single standard of measuring skill or progress in a physical education class has an adverse effect on members of one sex, the recipient shall use appropriate standards which do not have such effect.

(e) Portions of classes in elementary and secondary schools which deal exclusively with human sexuality may be conducted in separate sessions for boys and girls.

(f) Recipients may make requirements based on vocal range or quality which may result in a chorus or choruses of one or predominantly one sex.

(Secs. 901, 902, Education Amendments of 1972, 86 Stat. 373, 374; 20 U.S.C. 1681, 1682)

§ 86.35 Access to schools operated by L.E.A.s.

A recipient which is a local educational agency shall not, on the basis of sex, exclude any person from admission to:

(a) Any institution of vocational education operated by such recipient; or

(b) Any other school or educational unit operated by such recipient, unless such recipient otherwise makes available to such person, pursuant to the same policies and criteria of admission, courses, services, and facilities comparable to each course, service, and facility offered in or through such schools.

(Sections 901, 902, Education Amendments of 1972, 86 Stat. 373, 374; 20 U.S.C. 1681, 1682)

§ 86.36 Counseling and use of appraisal and counseling materials.

(a) *Counseling.* A recipient shall not discriminate against any person on the basis of sex in the counseling or guidance of students or applicants for admission.

(b) *Use of appraisal and counseling materials.* A recipient which uses testing or other materials for appraising or counseling students shall not use different materials for students on the basis of their sex or use materials which permit or require different treatment of students on such basis unless such different materials cover the same occupations and interest areas and the use of such different materials is shown to be essential to eliminate sex bias. Recipients shall develop and use internal procedures for ensuring that such materials do not discriminate on the basis of sex. Where the use of a counseling test or other instrument results in a substantially disproportionate number of members of one sex in any particular course of study or classification, the recipient shall take such action as is necessary to assure itself that such disproportion is not the result of discrimination in the instrument or its application.

(c) *Disproportion in classes.* Where a recipient finds that a particular class contains a substantially disproportionate number of individuals of one sex, the recipient shall take such action as is necessary to assure itself that such disproportion is not the result of discrimination on the basis of sex in counseling or appraisal materials or by counselors.

§ 86.37 Financial assistance.

(a) *General.* Except as provided in paragraphs (b) and (c) of this section, in providing financial assistance to any of its students, a recipient shall not: (1) On the basis of sex, provide different amount or types of such assistance, limit eligibility for such assistance which is of any particular type or source, apply different criteria, or otherwise discriminate; (2) through solicitation, listing, approval, provision of facilities or other services, assist any foundation, trust, agency, organization, or person which provides assistance to any of such recipient's students in a manner which discriminates on the basis of sex; or (3) apply any rule or assist in application of any rule concerning eligibility for such assistance which treats persons of one sex differently from persons of the other sex with regard to marital or parental status.

(b) *Financial aid established by certain legal instruments.* (1) A recipient may administer or assist in the administration of scholarships, fellowships, or other forms of financial assistance established pursuant to domestic or foreign wills, trusts, bequests, or similar legal instruments or by acts of a foreign government which requires that awards be made to members of a particular sex specified therein; *Provided,* that the overall effect of the award of such sex-restricted scholarships, fellowships, and other forms of financial assistance does not discriminate on the basis of sex.

(2) To ensure nondiscriminatory awards of assistance as required in subparagraph (b) (1) of this section, recipients shall develop and use procedures under which:

(i) Students are selected for award of financial assistance on the basis of nondiscriminatory criteria and not on the basis of availability of funds restricted to members of a particular sex;

(ii) An appropriate sex-restricted scholarship, fellowship, or other form of financial assistance is allocated to each student selected under subparagraph (b) (2) (i) of this paragraph; and

(iii) No student is denied the award for which he or she was selected under paragraph (b) (2) (i) of this section because of the absence of a scholarship, fellowship, or other form of financial assistance designated for a member of that student's sex.

(c) *Athletic scholarships.* (1) To the extent that a recipient awards athletic scholarships or grants-in-aid, it must provide reasonable opportunities for such awards for members of each sex in proportion to the number of students of each sex participating in interscholastic or intercollegiate athletics.

(2) Separate athletic scholarships or grants-in-aid for members of each sex may be provided as part of separate athletic teams for members of each sex to the extent consistent with this paragraph and § 86.41.

(Secs. 901, 902, Education Amendments of 1972, 86 Stat. 373, 374; 20 U.S.C. 1681, 1682; and Sec. 844, Education Amendments of 1974, Pub. L. 93–380, 88 Stat. 484)

[40 FR 21428, June 4, 1975; 40 FR 39506, Aug. 28, 1975]

§ 86.38 Employment assistance to students.

(a) *Assistance by recipient in making available outside employment.* A recipient which assists any agency, organization or person in making employment available to any of its students:

(1) Shall assure itself that such employment is made available without discrimination on the basis of sex; and

(2) Shall not render such services to any agency, organization, or person which discriminates on the basis of sex in its employment practices.

(b) *Employment of students by recipients.* A recipient which employs any of its students shall not do so in a manner which violates Subpart E of this part.

(Secs. 901, 902, Education Amendments of 1972, 86 Stat. 373, 374; 20 U.S.C. 1681, 1682)

§ 86.39 Health and insurance benefits and services.

In providing a medical, hospital, accident, or life insurance benefit, service, policy, or plan to any of its students, a recipient shall not discriminate on the basis of sex, or provide such benefit, service, policy, or plan in a manner which would violate Subpart E of this part if it were provided to employees of the recipient. This section shall not prohibit a recipient from providing any benefit or service which may be used by a different proportion of students of one sex than of the other, including family planning services. However, any recipient which provides full coverage health service shall provide gynecological care.

(Secs. 901, 902, Education Amendments of 1972, 86 Stat. 373, 374; 20 U.S.C. 1681, 1682)

§ 86.40 Marital or parental status.

(a) *Status generally.* A recipient shall not apply any rule concerning a student's actual or potential parental, family, or marital status which treats students differently on the basis of sex.

(b) *Pregnancy and related conditions.* (1) A recipient shall not discriminate against any student, or exclude any student from its education program or activity, including any class or extracurricular activity, on the basis of such student's pregnancy, childbirth, false pregnancy, termination of pregnancy or recovery therefrom, unless the student requests voluntarily to participate in a separate portion of the program or activity of the recipient.

(2) A recipient may require such a student to obtain the certification of a physician that the student is physically and emotionally able to continue participation in the normal education program or activity so long as such a certification is required of all students for other physical or emotional conditions requiring the attention of a physician.

(3) A recipient which operates a portion of its education program or activity separately for pregnant students, admittance to which is completely voluntary on the part of the student as provided in paragraph (b) (1) of this section shall ensure that the instructional program in the separate program is comparable to that offered to non-pregnant students.

(4) A recipient shall treat pregnancy, childbirth, false pregnancy, termination of pregnancy and recovery therefrom in the same manner and under the same policies as any other temporary disability with respect to any medical or hospital benefit, service, plan or policy which such recipient administers, operates, offers, or participates in with respect to students admitted to the recipient's educational program or activity.

(5) In the case of a recipient which does not maintain a leave policy for its students, or in the case of a student who does not otherwise qualify for leave under such a policy, a recipient shall treat pregnancy, childbirth, false pregnancy, termination of pregnancy and recovery therefrom as a justification for a leave of absence for so long a period of time as is deemed medically necessary by the student's physician, at the conclusion of which the student shall be reinstated to the status which she held when the leave began.

(Secs. 901, 902, Education Amendments of 1972, 86 Stat. 373, 374; 20 U.S.C. 1681, 1682)

§ 86.41 Athletics.

(a) *General.* No person shall, on the basis of sex, be excluded from participation in, be denied the benefits of, be treated differently from another person or otherwise be discriminated against in any interscholastic, intercollegiate, club or intramural athletics offered by a recipient, and no recipient shall provide any such athletics separately on such basis.

(b) *Separate teams.* Notwithstanding the requirements of paragraph (a) of this section, a recipient may operate or sponsor separate teams for members of each sex where selection for such teams is based upon competitive skill or the activity involved is a contact sport. However, where a recipient operates or sponsors a team in a particular sport for members of one sex but operates or sponsors no such team for members of the other sex, and athletic opportunities for members of that sex have previously been limited, members of the excluded sex must be allowed to try-out for the team offered unless the sport involved is a contact sport. For the purposes of this part, contact sports include boxing, wrestling, rugby, ice hockey, football, basketball and other sports the purpose of major activity of which involves bodily contact.

(c) *Equal opportunity.* A recipient which operates or sponsors interscholastic, intercollegiate, club or intramural athletics shall provide equal athletic opportunity for members of both sexes. In determining whether equal opportunities are available the Director will consider, among other factors:

(1) Whether the selection of sports and levels of competition effectively accommodate the interests and abilities of members of both sexes;

(2) The provision of equipment and supplies;

(3) Scheduling of games and practice time;

(4) Travel and per diem allowance;

(5) Opportunity to receive coaching and academic tutoring;

(6) Assignment and compensation of coaches and tutors;

(7) Provision of locker rooms, practice and competitive facilities;

(8) Provision of medical and training facilities and services;

(9) Provision of housing and dining facilities and services;

(10) Publicity.

Unequal aggregate expenditures for members of each sex or unequal expenditures for male and female teams if a recipient operates or sponsors separate teams will not constitute noncompliance with this section, but the Director may consider the failure to provide necessary funds for teams for one sex in assessing equality of opportunity for members of each sex.

(d) *Adjustment period.* A recipient which operates or sponsors interscholastic, intercollegiate, club or intramural athletics at the elementary school level shall comply fully with this section as expeditiously as possible but in no event later than one year from the effective date of this regulation. A recipient which operates or sponsors interscholastic, intercollegiate, club or intramural athletics at the secondary or post-secondary school level shall comply fully with this section as expeditiously as possible but in no event later than three years from the effective date of this regulation.

(Secs. 901, 902, Education Amendments of 1972, 86 Stat. 373, 374; 20 U.S.C. 1681, 1682; and Sec. 844, Education Amendments of 1974, Pub. L. 93-380, 88 Stat. 484)

[40 FR 21428, June 4, 1975; 40 FR 39506, Aug. 28, 1975]

§ 86.42 Textbooks and curricular material.

Nothing in this regulation shall be interpreted as requiring or prohibiting or abridging in any way the use of particular textbooks or curricular materials.

(Secs. 901, 902, Education Amendments of 1972, 86 Stat. 373, 374; 20 U.S.C. 1681, 1682)

§ 86.43—86.50 [Reserved]

Subpart E—Discrimination on the Basis of Sex in Employment in Education Programs and Activities Prohibited

§ 86.51 Employment.

(a) *General.* (1) No person shall, on the basis of sex, be excluded from participation in, be denied the benefits of, or be subjected to discrimination in employment, or recruitment, consideration, or selection therefor, whether full-time or part-time, under any education program or activity operated by a recipient which receives or benefits from Federal financial assistance.

(2) A recipient shall make all employment decisions in any education program or activity operated by such recipient in a nondiscriminatory manner and shall not limit, segregate, or classify applicants or employees in any way which could adversely affect any applicant's or employee's employment opportunities or status because of sex.

(3) A recipient shall not enter into any contractual or other relationship which directly or indirectly has the effect of subjecting employees or students to discrimination prohibited by this Subpart, including relationships with employment and referral agencies, with labor unions, and with organizations providing or administering fringe benefits to employees of the recipient.

(4) A recipient shall not grant preferences to applicants for employment on the basis of attendance at any educational institution or entity which admits as students only or predominantly members of one sex, if the giving of such preferences has the effect of discriminating on the basis of sex in violation of this part.

(b) *Application.* The provisions of this subpart apply to:

(1) Recruitment, advertising, and the process of application for employment;

(2) Hiring, upgrading, promotion, consideration for and award of tenure, demotion, transfer, layoff, termination, application of nepotism policies, right of return from layoff, and rehiring;

(3) Rates of pay or any other form of compensation, and changes in compensation;

(4) Job assignments, classifications and structure, including position descriptions, lines of progression, and seniority lists;

(5) The terms of any collective bargaining agreement;

(6) Granting and return from leaves of absence, leave for pregnancy, childbirth, false pregnancy, termination of pregnancy, leave for persons of either sex to care for children or dependents, or any other leave;

(7) Fringe benefits available by virtue of employment, whether or not administered by the recipient;

(8) Selection and financial support for training, including apprenticeship, professional meetings, conferences, and other related activities, selection for tuition assistance, selection for sabbaticals and leaves of absence to pursue training;

(9) Employer-sponsored activities, including social or recreational programs; and

(10) Any other term, condition, or privilege of employment.

(Secs. 901, 902, Education Amendments of 1972, 86 Stat. 373, 374; 20 U.S.C. 1681, 1682)

§ 86.52 Employment criteria.

A recipient shall not administer or operate any test or other criterion for any employment opportunity which has a disproportionately adverse effect on persons on the basis of sex unless:

(a) Use of such test or other criterion is shown to predict validly successful performance in the position in question; and

(b) Alternative tests or criteria for such purpose, which do not have such disproportionately adverse effect, are shown to be unavailable.

(Secs. 901, 902, Education Amendments of 1972, 86 Stat. 373, 374; 20 U.S.C. 1681, 1682)

§ 86.53 Recruitment.

(a) *Nondiscriminatory recruitment and hiring.* A recipient shall not discriminate on the basis of sex in the recruitment and hiring of employees. Where a recipient has been found to be presently discriminating on the basis of sex in the recruitment or hiring of employees, or has been found to have in the past so discriminated, the recipient shall recruit members of the sex so discriminated against so as to overcome the effects of such past or present discrimination.

(b) *Recruitment patterns.* A recipient shall not recruit primarily or exclusively at entities which furnish as applicants only or predominantly members of one sex if such actions have the effect of discriminating on the basis of sex in violation of this subpart.

(Secs. 901, 902, Education Amendments of 1972, 86 Stat. 373, 374; 20 U.S.C. 1681, 1682)

§ 86.54 Compensation.

A recipient shall not make or enforce any policy or practice which, on the basis of sex:

(a) Makes distinctions in rates of pay or other compensation;

(b) Results in the payment of wages to employees of one sex at a rate less than that paid to employees of the opposite sex for equal work on jobs the performance of which requires equal skill, effort, and responsibility, and which are performed under similar working conditions.

(Secs. 901, 902, Education Amendments of 1972, 86 Stat. 373, 374; 20 U.S.C. 1681, 1682)

§ 86.55 Job classification and structure.

A recipient shall not:

(a) Classify a job as being for males or for females;

(b) Maintain or establish separate lines of progression, seniority lists, career ladders, or tenure systems based on sex; or

(c) Maintain or establish separate lines of progression, seniority systems, career ladders, or tenure systems for similar jobs, position descriptions, or job requirements which classify persons on the basis of sex, unless sex is a bona-fide occupational qualification for the positions in question as set forth in § 86.61.

(Secs. 901, 902, Education Amendments of 1972, 86 Stat. 373, 374; 20 U.S.C. 1681, 1682)

[40 FR 21428, June 4, 1975; 40 FR 39506, Aug. 28, 1975]

§ 86.56 Fringe benefits.

(a) *"Fringe benefits" defined.* For purposes of this part, "fringe benefits" means: Any medical, hospital, accident, life insurance or retirement benefit, service, policy or plan, any profit-sharing or bonus plan, leave, and any other benefit or service of employment not subject to the provision of § 86.54.

(b) *Prohibitions.* A recipient shall not:

(1) Discriminate on the basis of sex with regard to making fringe benefits available to employees or make fringe benefits available to spouses, families, or dependents of employees differently upon the basis of the employee's sex;

(2) Administer, operate, offer, or participate in a fringe benefit plan which does not provide either for equal periodic benefits for members of each sex, or for equal conrtibutions to the plan by such recipient for members of each sex; or

(3) Administer, operate, offer, or participate in a pension or retirement plan which establishes different optional or compulsory retirement ages based on sex or which otherwise discriminates in benefits on the basis of sex.

(Secs. 901, 902, Education Amendments of 1972, 86 Stat. 373, 374; 20 U.S.C. 1681, 1682)

§ 86.57 Marital or parental status.

(a) *General.* A recipient shall not apply any policy or take any employment action:

(1) Concerning the potential marital, parental, or family status of an employee or applicant for employment which treats persons differently on the basis of sex; or

(2) Which is based upon whether an employee or applicant for employment is the head of household or principal wage earner in such employee's or applicant's family unit.

(b) *Pregnancy.* A recipient shall not discriminate against or exclude from employment any employee or applicant for employment on the basis of pregnancy, childbirth, false pregnancy, termination of pregnancy, or recovery therefrom.

(c) *Pregnancy as a temporary disability.* A recipient shall treat pregnancy, childbirth, false pregnancy, termination of pregnancy, and recovery therefrom and any temporary disability resulting therefrom as any other temporary disability for all job related purposes, including commencement, duration and extensions of leave, payment of disability income, accrual of seniority and any other benefit or service, and reinstatement, and under any fringe benefit offered to employees by virtue of employment.

(d) *Pregnancy leave.* In the case of a recipient which does not maintain a leave policy for its employees, or in the case of an employee with insufficient leave or accrued employment time to qualify for leave under such a policy, a recipient shall treat pregnancy, childbirth, false pregnancy, termination of pregnancy and recovery therefrom as a justification for a leave of absence without pay for a reasonable period of time, at the conclusion of which the employee shall be reinstated to the status which she held when the leave began or to a comparable position, without decrease in rate of compensation or loss of promotional opportunities, or any other right or privilege of employment.

(Secs. 901, 902, Education Amendments of 1972, 86 Stat. 373, 374; 20 U.S.C. 1681, 1682)

§ 86.58 Effect of State or local law or other requirements.

(a) *Prohibitory requirements.* The obligation to comply with this subpart is not obviated or alleviated by the existence of any State or local law or other requirement which imposes prohibitions or limits upon employment of members of one sex which are not imposed upon members of the other sex.

(b) *Benefits.* A recipient which provides any compensation, service, or benefit to members of one sex pursuant to a State or local law or other requirement shall provide the same compensation, service, or benefit to members of the other sex.

(Secs. 901, 902, Education Amendments of 1972, 86 Stat. 373, 374; 20 U.S.C. 1681, 1682)

§ 86.59 Advertising.

A recipient shall not in any advertising related to employment indicate preference, limitation, specification, or discrimination based on sex unless sex is a *bona-fide* occupational qualification for the particular job in question.

(Secs. 901, 902, Education Amendments of 1972, 86 Stat. 373, 374; 20 U.S.C. 1681, 1682)

§ 86.60 Pre-employment inquiries.

(a) *Marital status.* A recipient shall not make pre-employment inquiry as to the marital status of an applicant for employment, including whether such applicant is "Miss or Mrs."

(b) *Sex.* A recipient may make pre-employment inquiry as to the sex of an applicant for employment, but only if such inquiry is made equally of such applicants of both sexes and if the results of such inquiry are not used in connection with discrimination prohibited by this part.

(Secs. 901, 902, Education Amendments of 1972, 86 Stat. 373, 374; 20 U.S.C. 1681, 1682)

§ 86.61 Sex as a bona-fide occupational qualification.

A recipient may take action otherwise prohibited by this subpart provided it is shown that sex is a bona-fide occupational qualification for that action, such that consideration of sex with regard to such action is essential to successful operation of the employment function concerned. A recipient shall not take action pursuant to this section which is based upon alleged comparative employment characteristics or stereotyped characterizations of one or the other sex, or upon preference based on sex of the recipient, employees, students, or other persons, but nothing contained in this section shall prevent a recipient from considering an employee's sex in relation to employment in a locker room or toilet facility used only by members of one sex.

(Secs. 901, 902, Education Amendments of 1972, 86 Stat. 373, 374; 20 U.S.C. 1681, 1682)

§§ 86.62—86.70 [Reserved]

Subpart F—Procedures [Interim]

§ 86.71 Interim procedures.

For the purposes of implementing this part during the period between its effective date and the final issuance by the Department of a consolidated procedural regulation applicable to title IX and other civil rights authorities administered by the Department, the procedural provisions applicable to title VI of the Civil Rights Act of 1964 are hereby adopted and incorporated herein by reference. These procedures may be found at 45 CFR 80-6—80-11 and 45 CFR Part 81.

A Guide to Federal Laws and Regulations Prohibiting Sex Discrimination. U.S. Commission on Civil Rights, Washington, D.C. Clearinghouse Publication No. 46. July 1976 (revised).

WOMEN'S STUDIES PROGRAMS

Most of the programs listed below are interdisciplinary, i.e., they combine courses in literature, language or culture with work in sociology, anthropology, economics, political science, history, philosophy, psychology, biology and related fields. Some programs offer minors (denoted by *), others award the B.A. (denoted by **) or A.A. degree (denoted by ***), still others offer the M.A. (denoted by +). Three programs offer the Ph.D. (denoted by †). Programs listed without a specific label offer a roster of elective courses. Where no chairperson is listed, either the program is still in the process of organization or it has chosen to function through a committee, rather than a single individual. Write to the individual programs for more specific information, bulletins, catalogs and course lists.

*Alabama, U of, University 35486—Women's Studies (101 Manly), Elizabeth A. Meese, Coord: Program offers a minor.

Alverno C, 3401 S 39 St, Milwaukee, WI 53215—Research Center on Women.

Antioch C, Yellow Springs, OH 45387—Women's Studies.

Arizona S U, Tempe 85281—Ad Hoc Chartering Committee of Women's Studies.

*Arizona, U of, Tucson 85721—Women's Studies, Myra Dinnerstein, Dir: Program offers an interdisciplinary minor.

Barnard C, New York, N Y 10027—The Women's Center, Jane Gould, Dir.

Bennett C, Greensboro, N C 27401—Women's Studies, Dorinda Trader, Coord.

Boston U, Boston, MA 02215—Women's Studies, Debi Croes, Coord.

**Brooklyn C, CUNY, Brooklyn, N Y 11210—Women's Studies (2157 Boylan Hall), Renate Bridenthal, Pamella Farley, Frederica Wachsberger, Coords: Program offers the B.A. degree through a "dual major."

Cabrillo C, Aptos, CA 95003—Women's Studies, Claire Delano, Coord.

California S C. Bakersfield 93309—Women's Studies, Jane Lester Watts, Coord.

California S C/Sonoma, Rohnert Park 94928—Women's Studies, Ruth Mahoney, Coord.

*California S U, Chico 95296—Women's Studies, Gayle Kimball, Coord: Program offers a minor.

*California S U, Fresno 93740—Women's Studies, Kathryn H. Brooks, Coord: Program offers a minor.

*California S U, 25800 Hillary Rd., Hayward 94542—Women's Studies, Marilyn Blawie, Coord: Program offers a minor.

*California S U, Long Beach 90840—Women's Studies, Betty Edmunden and Sharon Sievers, Coords: Program offers a minor.

California S U, 5151 State College Dr, Los Angeles 90032—Women's Studies.

California S U, Northridge 91324—Women's Studies.

*California S U, Sacramento 95819—Women's Studies Committee: Program offers a minor.

California, U of, Berkeley 94720—Campus Women's Forum (201 Sproul Hall), Betty Jones, Coord.

**California, U of, Davis 95616—Women's Studies: Program
    offers a major.

California, U of, Irvine 92664—Women's Studies Committee.

**California, U of, Los Angeles 90024—Women's Studies
    (2907 Math Sciences), Peg Strobel, Dir: Program offers
    the B.A. degree through specialization in women's studies.

California, U of, Santa Cruz 95064—Women's Studies Com-
    mittee, Madeline Hummel, Coord.

† ————————— History of Consciousness, Feminist Sub-
    group, May Diaz, Faculty Sponsor: Program offers an
    interdisciplinary Ph.D. in feminist studies.

+Cambridge Goddard Graduate School for Social Change,
    5 Upland Rd, Cambridge, MA 02140—Feminist Studies:
    Program offers the M.A. degree.

Cincinnati, U of, Cincinnati, OH 45221—Women's Studies,
    Dana V. Hiller, Dir.

City C, The, CUNY, New York, N Y 10031—Women's Studies,
    Barbara Bellow Watson, Dir.

**Colorado, U of, Boulder 80309—Women Studies, Carol Pearson,
    Dir: Program offers the B.A. degree as individually struc-
    tured major.

*Colorado Women's C, Montview Blvd and Quebec, Denver
    80220—Women's Studies, Kathleen O'Connor Blumhagen,
    Advisor: Program offers the equivalent of a minor.

Connecticut, U of, Storrs 06268—Women's Studies, Joan
    Geetter, Dir.

Cornell U, Ithaca, N Y 14850—Women's Studies, Jennie
    Farley, Dir.

Delaware, U of, Newark 19711—Women's Studies Inter-
    disciplinary Program, Joyce J. Walstedt, Dir.

**Diablo Valley C, Pleasant Hill, CA 94523—Women's Studies,
    Janet W. McAfee, Coord: Program offers the A.A. degree.

**Douglass C, Rutgers U, New Brunswick, N J 08903—Women's
    Studies, Elaine Showalter, Coord: Program offers a certi-
    ficate minor and the B.A. degree through Individual Majors
    option.

Edmonds C C, Lynwood, WA 98036—Women's Programs,
    Ruth McCormick, Coord.

*Eastern Michigan U, Ypsilanti 48197—Women's Studies,
    Margaret Rossiter, Bette White, Coords: Program offers
    a minor.

Five Colleges (Amherst C, Hampshire C, Mount Holyoke C,
    Smith C, and the U of Massachusetts)—Women's Studies
    Committee (c/o Jackie Pritzen, Five Colleges Coordinators
    Office, Amherst College, Amherst, MA 01002), Vicki
    Spelman, Coord.

*Florida International U, Tamiami Campus, Tamiami Trail,
    Miami 33199—Institute for Women, Charlotte Tatro, Dir.

*Florida S U, Tallahassee 32306—Women's Studies, Jean
    Hales, Coord: Program offers a minor.

**Foothill C, Los Altos Hills, CA 94022—Women's Studies,
    Nayan McNeill, Coord: Program offers the A.A. degree.

+George Washington U, Washington D C 20052—Women's
    Studies (2031 F St N W), Elaine Reuben, Dir: Program
    offers the M.A. degree.

**Goddard C, Plainfield, VT 05667—Feminist Studies, Sally
    Binford, Marilyn Webb, Coords: Program offers the B.A.
    degree.

+ ————————— The M.A. degree in women's studies may be
    pursued as part of Goddard's nonresident graduate program.

Golden Gate U, 536 Mission St, San Francisco, CA 94105—
Career Counseling Center for Women, Char Hamada, Coord.

**+Governors S U, Park Forest South, IL 60466—Women's
Studies, Harriet Gross, Coord: Program offers the B.A.
and M.A. degrees.

Green River C C, Auburn, WA 98002—Women's Studies.

Hampshire C, Amherst, MA 01002—Feminist Studies, Debbie
Curtis, Coord.

**Hawaii, U of, Honolulu 96822—Women's Studies (252 Spalding
Hall), Marilyn Harman, Coord: Program offers the B.A.
degree through a "major equivalent" in women's studies
in the Liberal Studies Program.

**Henderson S U, Arkadelphia, AR 71923—Women's Studies,
Juanita Sandford, Coord: Program offers the B.A. degree
through a double major in sociology and women's studies.

**Hobart and William Smith Colleges, Geneva, N Y 14456—
Women's Studies, Janet M. Wedel, Coord: Program offers
an "individual major" in women's studies.

Humboldt S U, Arcata, CA 95521—Women's Studies, Janice
Erskine, Coord.

* **Hunter C, CUNY, New York, N Y 10021—Committee on
Women's Studies, Sarah B. Pomeroy, Contact: Program
offers a minor in the social science division and the B.A.
degree through a "collateral major."

**Illinois, U of, Champaign 61820—Women's Studies, Bette
Adelman, Acting Coord: Program offers the B.A. degree
through the Individual Plans of Study program in the
College of Liberal Arts and Sciences.

* **Indiana U, Bloomington 47401—Women's Studies (Memorial
Hall East M 39), Ellen Dwyer, Dir: Program offers a minor
and the B.A. degree through the Independent Learning
Program.

Indiana U—Purdue U, Ft Wayne 46805—Women's Studies,
Marthe Rosenfeld (Indiana U), Cathryn Adamsky (Purdue
U), Coords.

**Jersey City S C, Jersey City, N J 07305—Women's Studies,
Elizabeth Diggs, Coord: Program offers the B.A. degree.

**Kansas, U of, Lawrence 66045—Women's Studies, Janet
Sharistanian, Coord: Program offers a "special major"
leading to the B.A. or B.G.S. degree.

**Kentucky, U of, Lexington 40506—Women's Studies Com-
mittee (658 S Limestone), Christine Havice, Coord:
Program offers Topical Major in women's studies.

Laney C, Oakland, CA 94606—Women's Studies Committee,
Laura B. Stenson, Coord.

* Long Island U, C W Post Ctr, Greenvale, N Y 11548—
Women's Studies, Alice Scourby, Coord: Program offers
a minor.

*Loretto Heights C, 3001 S Federal Blvd, Denver, CO 80236—
Research Center on Woman, Women's Studies, Brenda
Miller, Coord: Program offers a minor.

Los Angeles Harbor C, 1111 Figueroa Pl, Wilmington, CA
90744—Women's Studies, Marilyn Brock, Coord.

Louisville, U of, Louisville, KY 40208—Women's Studies
Committee, Sydney Schultze, Dir.

Lower Columbia C, Longview, WA 98632—Women's Studies,
Gisela E. Taber, Coord.

Maryland, U of, College Park 20742—Women's Studies,
Berenice Carroll, Acting Dir.

Marymount C, Tarrytown, N Y 10591—Women's Studies,
Ellen Silber, Chairperson.

* * *Massachusetts, U of, Amherst 01002—Women's Studies
- (508 Goodell), Catherine Portuges, Coord: Program offers
a certificate minor and the B.A. degree through "individual
concentration."

*Massachusetts, U of, Boston 02125—Women's Studies, Ann
Froines, Coord: Program offers a minor.

*Metropolitan S C, Denver, CO 80204—Women's Studies,
Barbara Blansett, Coord: Program offers a minor.

**Michigan, U of, Ann Arbor 48104—Women's Studies (L.S. &
A. Bldg.), Louise Tilly, Coord: Program offers the B.A.
degree.

**Mills C, Oakland, CA 94613—Women's Studies: Program offers
the B.A. degree.

**Minnesota, U of, Minneapolis 55455—Women's Studies (492
Ford Hall), Toni McNaron, Coord: Program offers the B.A.
degree.

**Mundelein C, 6363 N Sheridan Rd, Chicago, IL 60626—
Women's Studies (Continuing Education), Marianne Littau,
Dir: Program offers the B.A. and B.S. degree.

Nassau C C, Garden City, N Y 11530—Women's Studies.

Nebraska, U of, Lincoln 68508—Committee on Women's
Studies, Sarah L. Hoagland, Chairperson.

Nevada, U of, Reno 89507—Women's Faculty Caucus, Ann
Ronald, Chairperson.

+†——————— - Women's Studies in Education, The School of
Education: Program will offer the M.A. and Ph.D. degrees
as of fall 1976.

**New Mexico, U of, Albuquerque 87131—Women's Studies,
Gail Baker, Coord: Program offers a concentration in
women's studies through the Bachelor of University Studies.

* **New Rochelle, C of, New Rochelle, N Y 10801—Women's
Studies, Sr. Kristen Wenzel, Dir: Program offers a minor
and the B.A. degree in women's studies.

*New York, S U of, Albany 12222—Women's Studies (1400
Washington Ave), Joan Schulz, Dir: Program offers a
second field.

†New York, S U of, Binghamton 13901—History of Women,
Roxane Witke, Coord: Program offers a Ph.D. concentration in women's history.

**——————— - University Committee for Women's Studies,
Evelyn Rosenthal, Gail Bundy, Diane Hamlin, Coords:
B.A. degree in women's studies may be earned through the
Innovational Projects Board.

New York, S U of, Buffalo 14214—Women's Studies College
(108 Winspear Ave), Ann Williams, Kathleen McDermott,
Coords.

**+——————— - American Studies, Concentration in Women's
Studies, Elizabeth Kennedy, Coord: Program offers the
B.A. and M.A. degrees.

New York, S U of, Stony Brook 11794—Women's Studies,
Ellice Gonzales, Coord.

**New York, S U C, Brockport 14420—Women's Studies Board,
Vera King Farris, Coord: Program offers the B.A. degree.

New York, S U C, Fredonia 14063—Women's Studies Committee, Laura Strumingher, Coord.

*New York, S U C, New Paltz 12561—Women's Studies, Jane
Lee Yare, Coord: Program offers a minor.

**New York, S U C, Old Westbury 11568—American Studies,
Concentration in Women's Studies, Florence Howe, Naomi
Rosenthal, Coords: Program offers the B.A. degree.

New York, S U C, Oneonta 13820—Women's Studies, Helen
    Baldo, Contact.
**New York, S U C, Plattsburgh 12901—Women's Studies,
    Charles C. Herod, Coord: Program offers the B. A. degree
    through General Studies.
North Seattle C C, 9600 College Way N, Seattle, WA 98103—
    Women's Center (Rm 2254-A).
**+Northeastern Illinois U, Chicago 60625—Women's Studies,
    Blanche Hersh, Coord: Program offers the B.A. degree
    through the Center for Program Development or the
    University Without Walls. The M.A. degree with a con-
    centration in women's studies may be earned in the
    social sciences.

Northwestern U, Evanston, IL 60201—The Program on Women
    (619 Emerson St), Arlene Kaplan Daniels, Chairperson.
*Northern Colorado, U of, Greeley 80631—Women's Studies,
    Marcia Willcoxon, Coord: Program offers a minor.
Ohio S U, Columbus 43210—Office of Women's Studies (250
    Welding Engineering, 190 West 19 Ave), Pam Unger,
    Acting Dir.
Oregon S U, Corvallis 97331—Women's Studies, Jeanne Dost,
    Dir.
*Oregon, U of, Eugene 97403—Women's Studies, Patricia Pond,
    Chairperson: Program offers an undergraduate certificate.
**Pennsylvania, U of, Philadelphia 19174—Women's Studies
    (106 Logan Hall), Elsa Greene, Coord: Program offers the
    B.A. degree.
Pittsburgh, U of, Pittsburgh, PA 15260—Women's Studies,
    Mary Louise Briscoe, Coord.
Portland S U, Portland, OR 97207—Women's Studies, Nancy
    Porter, Coord.
Puget Sound, U of, Tacoma, WA 98416—Women's Studies,
    Ann Neel, Coord.
Queens C, CUNY, Flushing, N Y 11367—Women's Studies
    Committee, Wendy Martin, Coord.

Ramapo C, Mahwah, N J 07430—Women's Studies (School of
    Human Environment), Lynne Farrow, Coord.

Regis C, 235 Wellesley St, Weston, MA 02193—Women's
    Studies, Mary Bryan, Sr. Catherine Meade, Co-dirs.
**Richmond C, CUNY, Staten Island, N Y 10301—Women's
    Studies, Bertha Harris, Coord: Program offers the B.A.
    degree.
**Roger Williams C and University Without Walls, 24 DeBaum
    Ave, Suffern, N Y 10901—Women's Studies, Lynne Farrow,
    Coord: Program offers a dual B.A. from Roger Williams C
    (Rhode Island) and University Without Walls (Ohio).
*Rutgers U, Newark, N J 07102—Women's Studies (Newark C
    of Arts and Sciences), Virginia Tiger, Dir: Program offers
    a minor.
***Saddleback C C, 2800 Marguerite Pkwy, Mission Viejo, CA
    92675—Women's Studies, Anna L. McFarlin, Dir: Pro-
    gram offers the A.A. degree.
*St. Cloud S U, St. Cloud, MN 56301—Women's Studies,
    Eleanor E. Simpson, Coord: Program offers a minor.
*San Diego S U, San Diego, CA 92182—Women's Studies,
    Marilyn Boxer, Chairperson: Program will offer a minor
    as of fall 1976.
San Francisco, City C of, 50 Phelan Ave, San Francisco, CA
    94112—Women's Studies, M. Aron, Coord.
**+San Francisco S U, San Francisco, CA 94132—Women's

Studies Committee, Nancy McDermid, Coord: Program offers the B.A. degree and the M.A. as a special major.

Sangamon S U, Springfield, IL 62708—Women's Studies, Judith L. Everson, Coord.

*+San Jose S U, San Jose, CA 95192—Women's Studies, Sybil Weir, Coord: Program offers a minor and the M.A. degree in social science with an emphasis in women's studies.

***Santa Ana C, Santa Ana, CA 92706—Women's Studies, Joanne McKim, Coord: Program offers the A.A. degree.

+Sarah Lawrence C, Bronxville, N Y 10708—Women's History Program, Alice Kessler-Harris, Dir: Program offers the M.A. degree in women's history.

Seattle C C, 1718 Broadway, Seattle, WA 98122—Women's Studies.

Sierra C, 5000 Rocklin Rd, Rocklin, CA 95677—Women's Studies, Arthur Peterson, Coord.

*South Carolina, U of, Columbia 29208—Women's Studies Institute, Constance Ashton Myers, Coord: Program offers a minor.

**South Florida, U of, Tampa 33620—Women's Studies (College of Social and Behavioral Sciences), Juanita Williams, Dir: Program offers an area of concentration in an interdisciplinary major.

Southern California, U of, Los Angeles 90007—Women's Studies (Von Kleinsmid Center), Beverly P. Kivel, Coord.

*Southern Illinois U, Edwardsville 62025—Women's Studies, Sheila Ruth, Dir: Program offers a minor.

Southern Methodist U, Dallas, TX 75275—Women's Studies, Victoria Jacoby, Coord.

Stanford U, Stanford, CA 94305—Center for Research on Women, Cynthia L. Davis, Coord.

Staten Island C C, CUNY, 715 Ocean Terr, Staten Island, N Y 10301—Women's Studies, Jo Gillikin, Coord.

Stephens C, Columbia, MO 65201—Women's Studies, Betty Littleton, Elizabeth Barnes, Co-dirs.

Stockton S C, Pomona, N J 08240—Women's Studies, Suzanne Levin, Dir.

Tacoma C C, 5900 S 12 St, Tacoma, WA 98465—Women's Studies.

Texas, U of, Arlington 76010— Women's Center Jeanne Ford, Dir.

Texas, U of, Austin 78712—Women's Studies.

Towson S C, Towson, MD 21204—Women's Studies, Jan Wilkotz, Elaine Hedges, Coords.

*Trenton S C, Trenton, N J 08625—Women's Studies, Cecile Hanley, Coord: Program offers a minor.

**Utah, U of, Salt Lake City 84112—Women's Resource Center, Shauna Adix, Dir: Program offers the B.A. degree.

Vassar C, Poughkeepsie, N Y 12601—Women's Studies, Teresa Vilardi, Coord.

Virginia, U of, Charlottesville 22903—Women's Studies, Suzette Henke, Coord.

**Washington, U of, Seattle 98195—Women Studies, Sue Ellen Jacobs, Dir: Program offers the B.A. degree in General Studies with a concentration in women studies.

Washington U, St Louis, MO 63130—Women's Studies.

Wayne County C C, 4612 Woodward, Detroit, MI 48201—Women's Studies, Marilyn Becker, Miriam Frank, Helen Howe, Coords.

Wayne S U, Detroit, MI 48202—Women's Studies.

Weber S C, Ogden, UT 84403—Women's Activities, Sue
Stevenson, Coord.

+Webster C, 470 E Lockwood, St Louis, MO 63119—Women's
Studies, Carol L. McCart, Coord: Program offers the M.A.
degree through the Master of Arts - Independent Program.

Wesleyan U, Middletown, CT 06457—Women's Studies,
Sheila Tobias, Coord.

*Western Washington S C, Bellingham 98225—Women's Studies,
Meredith Cary, Coord: Program offers a minor.

**Wichita S U, Wichita, KS 67208—Women's Studies, Dorothy
Walters, Coord: Program offers the B.A. degree and some
work on the graduate level.

Wilson C, Chambersburg, PA 17201—Women's Studies,
Eleanor Bustin Mattes, Coord.

*Wisconsin, U of, Oshkosh 54901—Women's Studies, Virginia
Cox, Coord: Program offers a minor.

Wisconsin, U of, Milwaukee 53201—Office of Women's Studies
(Bolton 211), Rachel I. Skalitzky, Dir.

Wisconsin, U of, Superior 54880—Women's Programs, Delores
Harms, Coord.

Wittenberg U, Springfield, OH 45501—Wittenberg Women's
Program, Patricia O'Connor, Dir.

PROGRAM DEVELOPMENT
TRENDS IN DEVELOPING WOMEN'S STUDIES PROGRAMS

	Programs	Degree-Granting/ Minors	Percentage Degree-Granting/ Minors
December 1970[1]	2	0	0
December 1971[2]	15	5	33.0
Summer 1973[3]	75	20	26.5
December 1974[4]	112	40	35.7
December 1975[5]	152	90	59.2

TRENDS IN DEGREE-GRANTING AND MINOR-GRANTING WOMEN'S STUDIES PROGRAMS

	Minor	A.A.	B.A.	M.A.	Ph.D.	Totals
December 1970[1]	0	0	0	0	0	0
December 1971[2]	0	0	4	1	0	5
Summer 1973[3]	4	1	10	5	0	20
December 1974[4]	13	2	19	5	1	40
December 1975[5]	31	6	39	11	3	90

[1] See Florence Howe and Carol Ahlum, "Women's Studies and Social Change," in *Academic Women on the Move*, eds. Alice S. Rossi and Ann Calderwood (Russell Sage, 1973).

[2] *Ibid.*

[3] See *Women's Studies Newsletter*, Vol. I, No. 4, Summer 1973.

[4] See *Who's Who and Where in Women's Studies*, eds. Tamar Berkowitz, Jean Mangi, and Jane Williamson (The Feminist Press, 1974).

[5] See *Women's Studies Newsletter*, Vol. IV, No. 1, Winter 1975. It is important to note that the Clearinghouse on Women's Studies did not repeat in 1974 the widespread survey it administered in 1974 in order to produce *Who's Who and Where in Women's Studies*. Thus, the 1975 figures may not include *all* new programs.

"Women's Studies Programs." Clearinghouse on Women's Studies, an Education Project of the Feminist Press, SUNY/College at Old Westbury, Old Westbury, NY.

WOMEN'S ORGANIZATIONS

Federal government

AGENCY FOR INTERNATIONAL DEVELOPMENT
Department of State
Washington, D.C. 20523

COMMISSION ON CIVIL RIGHTS
1121 Vermont Avenue, NW
Washington, D.C. 20425

EMPLOYMENT STANDARDS ADMINISTRATION
Women's Bureau
Washington, D.C. 20523

EQUAL EMPLOYMENT OPPORTUNITY COMMISSION
2401 E Street, NW
Washington, D.C. 20506

INTERDEPARTMENTAL COMMITTEE ON THE
STATUS OF WOMEN
New Department of Labor Building
Washington, D.C. 20210

OFFICE OF EDUCATION
Department of Health, Education and
Welfare
400 Maryland Avenue, SW
Washington, D.C. 20202

For State listings contact State
offices of education

Non-governmental organizations

AMERICAN ASSOCIATION OF UNIVERSITY
WOMEN
2401 Virginia Avenue, NW
Washington, D.C. 20037

ASSOCIATION FOR INTERCOLLEGIATE
ATHLETICS FOR WOMEN
1201 16th Street, NW
Washington, D.C. 20036

ASSOCIATION FOR WOMEN IN MATHEMATICS
Department of Mathematics
Wellesley College
Wellesley, MA 02181

ASSOCIATION FOR WOMEN IN PSYCHOLOGY
Women's Studies
University of Delaware
Newark, DE 19711

ASSOCIATION FOR WOMEN IN SCIENCE
1346 Connecticut Avenue, NW
Room 1122
Washington, D.C. 20036

CLEARINGHOUSE ON WOMEN'S STUDIES
P.O. Box 334
Old Westbury, NY 11568

COMMISSION ON THE STATUS OF WOMEN IN
ADULT EDUCATION
1331 H Street, NW, No. 608
Washington, D.C. 20005

COUNCIL ON INTERRACIAL BOOKS FOR
CHILDREN
Racism & Sexism Resource Center
1841 Broadway St.
New York, NY 10023

INTERCOLLEGIATE ASSOCIATION FOR
WOMEN STUDENTS
2401 Virginia Avenue, NW
Box 2
Washington, D.C. 20037

NATIONAL ASSOCIATION FOR PHYSICAL
EDUCATION OF COLLEGE WOMEN
University of Massachusetts
Amherst, MA 01002

NATIONAL ASSOCIATION OF COLLEGE
WOMEN
1501 11th Street, NW
Washington, D.C. 20001

NATIONAL COUNCIL OF ADMINISTRATIVE
WOMEN IN EDUCATION
1815 Ft. Myer Drive, N.
Arlington, VA 22209

THE NATIONAL FOUNDATION FOR THE IMPROVE-
MENT OF EDUCATION
1201 16th Street, NW
Room 804E
Washington, D.C. 20036

NATIONAL ORGANIZATION FOR WOMEN
5 S. Wabash St.
Suite 1615
Chicago, IL 60603

NATIONAL VOCATIONAL GUIDANCE ASSOCIATION
1607 New Hampshire Avenue, NW
Washington, D.C. 20009

NATIONAL WOMEN'S EDUCATION FUND
1532 16th Street, NW
Washington, D.C. 20036

NATIONAL WOMEN'S STUDIES ASSOCIATION
C/O Sybil Weir
Women's Studies
San Jose State University
San Jose, CA 95192

PROJECT ON THE STATUS AND EDUCATION
   OF WOMEN
C/O Association of American Colleges
1818 R Street, NW
Washington, D.C. 20009

WIDER OPPORTUNITIES FOR WOMEN
1649 K Street, NW
Washington, D.C. 20006

WOMEN ON WORDS AND IMAGES (WOWI)
P.O. Box 2163
Princeton, NJ 08540

WOMEN TODAY
National Press Building
Washington, D.C. 20004

WOMEN'S ACTION ALLIANCE
370 Lexington Avenue
New York, NY 10017

WOMEN'S CAUCUS
c/o National Education Association
1201 16th Street, NW
Washington, D.C. 20036

WOMEN'S COLLEGE COALITION
Suite 303, 1700 K Street, NW
Washington, D.C. 20006

WOMEN'S EDUCATIONAL AND INDUSTRIAL
   UNION
356 Boylston Street
Boston, MA 02116

*Compiled by in-house staff.

WOMEN'S NATIONAL BOOK ASSOCIATION
Chatham College
Woodland Road
Pittsburgh, PA 15232

Non-sexist publishers

ALL OF US, INC.
176 Broad Street
Monmouth, OR 97361

BOOKLEGGER PRESS
555 29th Street
San Francisco, CA 94131

CHANGE FOR CHILDREN
2588 Mission Street, Rm. 226
San Francisco, CA 94110

THE FEMINIST PRESS
Box 334
Old Westbury, NY 11568

JOYFUL WORLD PRESS
468 Belvedere Street
San Francisco, CA 94117

KNOW INC.
P.O. Box 86031
Pittsburgh, PA 15221

LOLLIPOP POWER, INC.
P.O. Box 1171
Chapel Hill, NC 27514

NEW SEED PRESS
P.O. Box 3017
Stanford, CA 94305

WOMEN'S PRESS COLLECTIVE
5251 Broadway
Oakland, CA 94618

Catalyst's National Network of Local Resource Centers for Women

Catalyst is a national nonprofit organization that helps women choose, launch and advance their careers. It works with women (three main constituencies: the undergraduate woman, the upwardly mobile woman, the "returning woman"), counselors, educators, employers, professional organizations, government and media.

Catalyst provides career information and self-guidance materials...Interprets the needs of the marketplace to a national network of advisors to women, and offers services to help these professionals guide women effectively...Helps employed women respond to opportunities for upward mobility...Assists employers with the recruitment, assimilation and advancement of women who are seeking administrative, managerial, professional or technical positions...Disseminates and interprets research findings to those whose work requires an understanding of the changing status of women.

Services, publications and programs include:

. Educational and career counseling, job referral and placement services for women by referral to 150 local Resource Centers in Catalyst's National Network.

. 40 self-guidance, educational and career opportunity booklets for women entering or re-entering the workforce.

。 13 self-guidance and career option booklets for undergraduate women.

. Resume preparation manual and kit - a self-help individual or group program - for women.

。 Specialized library and information service which answers telephoned and written inquiries regarding women and careers.

. Topical occasional papers and bibliographies.

. Resume Screening Service for employers sending job specifications for their current openings.

. Corporate Board Service to assist interested corporations in finding distinguished and qualified women to serve on their Boards of Directors.

Catalyst is continually developing and expanding its outreach activities.

Alabama

University of Alabama
Birmingham

Arizona

University of Arizona
Tucson

California

Advocates for Women, Inc.
San Francisco

American River College
Sacramento

California State University
Sacramento

Career Planning Center
Los Angeles

The Claremont Colleges
Claremont

Creative Resources for Women
San Diego

Crossroads: Institute for
Career Development
Berkeley

Cypress College
Cypress

Foothill College
Los Altos Hills

Mills College
Oakland

New Ways to Work
Palo Alto

Resource Center for Women
Palo Alto

San Francisco State University
San Francisco

San Jose State University
San Jose

The Center for the
Transitional Person
Tarzana

University of California
Berkeley

University of California
Extension
Irvine

Woman's Place, Inc.
Los Angeles

Woman's Way
San Anselmo

Colorado

Boulder County
Women's Resource Center
Boulder

Colorado Springs Center
Colorado Springs

Connecticut

Connecticut College
New London

Information and
Counseling Service for Women
New Haven

Young Women's
Christian Association
Stamford

Delaware

McElroy & Doban, Inc.
Wilmington

District of Columbia

George Washington University
Washington

Florida

Stetson University
DeLand

Valencia Community College
Orlando

Georgia

Kennesaw Junior College
Marietta

Illinois

Affirmative Action Consultants
Wheeling

Applied Potential
Highland Park

Flexible Careers
Chicago

Moraine Valley Community
College
Palos Hills

Oakton Community College
Morton Grove

Sangamon State University
Springfield

Southern Illinois University
Edwardsville

University of Illinois
Champaign

Y.W.C.A.
Champaign

Women's Inc.
Hinsdale

Indiana

Indiana University
Bloomington

Indiana University
Indianapolis

Purdue University
Fort Wayne

St. Mary's College
Notre Dame

Women Alive! Inc.
Hammond

Iowa

Drake University
Des Moines

University of Iowa
Iowa City

Women's Work
Davenport

Kansas

University of Kansas
Lawrence

Maryland

Baltimore New Directions
for Women
Baltimore

College of Notre Dame
Baltimore

Women In Touch, Inc.
Bethesda

Massachusetts

Civic Center and
Clearing House Inc.
Boston

Massasoit Community College
Brockton

Middlesex Community College
Bedford

New Environments for
Women Associates
Lexington

Resource Center for
Educational Opportunities
Hingham

Smith College
Northampton

Why Not? Program
Worcester

Women's Educational &

Industrial Union
Boston

Michigan

Every Woman's Place
Muskegon

Macomb County Community
College
Mt. Clemens

Michigan Technological
University
Houghton

Montcalm Community College
Sidney

C.S. Mott Community College
Flint

Northern Michigan University
Marquette

Oakland University
Rochester

Western Michigan University
Kalamazoo

Women's Resource Center
Grand Rapids

Minnesota

Hamline University
St. Paul

Southwest State University
Marshall

University of Minnesota
Minneapolis

Missouri

University of Missouri
Kansas City

University of Missouri
St. Louis

Washington University
St. Louis

New Jersey

Adult Service Center
Towaco

Bergen Community College
Hackensack

Caldwell College
Caldwell

Douglass College
New Brunswick

Drew University
Madison

Fairleigh Dickinson University
Madison

Jersey City State College
Jersey City

Jewish Vocational Service
East Orange

Kean College of New Jersey
Union

Montclair State College
Upper Montclair

Reach, Inc.
Convent Station

Rutgers University
Newark

The Professional Roster
Princeton

New York

Academic Advisory Center
for Adults
Rye

Barbra Holt Associates, Inc.
New York

Barnard College
New York

Career Services for Women,

Inc.
Port Washington

Communiversity
New York

County Counseling Center
Yonkers

Hofstra University
Hempstead

Hunter College
New York

Janice LaRouche Associates,
Inc.
New York

Kingsborough Community
College
Brooklyn

Marymount College
Tarrytown

Mercy College
Dobbs Ferry

More for Women, Inc.
New York

New School for
Social Research
New York

Pace University
Pleasantville

Pace University
New York

Orange County Community
College
Middletown

Personnel Sciences Center
New York

Regional Learning Service of
Central N.Y.
Syracuse

Ruth Shapiro Associates
New York

State University of New York
Buffalo

State University of New York
Stony Brook

Syracuse University/
University College
Syracuse

Wonderwomen Employment,
Inc.
Buffalo

North Carolina

Duke University
Durham

Meredith College
Raleigh

Salem College
Winston-Salem

Ohio

Center for Continued Learning
Bowling Green

Cleveland Jewish Vocational
Service
University Heights

Cuyahoga Community College
Cleveland

University of Akron
Akron

Oklahoma

Women's Resource Center, Inc.
Norman

Pennsylvania

Bryn Mawr College
Bryn Mawr

Cedar Crest College
Allentown

Institute of Awareness
Philadelphia

Job Advisory Service
Pittsburgh

Options for Women
Philadelphia

Swarthmore College
Swarthmore

Temple University
Philadelphia

University of Pennsylvania
Philadelphia

Villa Maria College
Erie

Wilson College
Chambersburg

South Carolina

Converse College
Spartanburg

Tennessee

Scarritt College
Nashville

Women's Services of Knoxville,
Inc.
Knoxville

Texas

Foster and Wood Associates
Dallas

The University of Texas
Austin

Vocational Guidance Service,
Inc.
Houston

Women for Change Center
Dallas

Virginia

Hollins College
Hollins College

Mary Baldwin College
Staunton

Psychological Consultants, Inc.
Richmond

Virginia Commonwealth
University
Richmond

Washington

Individual Development Center,
Inc.
Seattle

University of Washington
Seattle

Women's Resource Center
Richland

West Virginia

West Virginia University
Morgantown

Wyoming

University of Wyoming
Laramie

"Catalyst's National Network of Local Resource Centers for Women."
Catalyst, 14 East 60th Street, New York, NY.

Part eight:
Indexes

Subject index

Geographic index